Library of Congress Cataloging-in-Publication Data

Chase, Oscar G.

Civil litigation in New York / Oscar G. Chase, Robert A. Barker. — 5th ed.

   p. cm.

Includes index.

ISBN 0-8205-7072-9 (hard cover)

1. Civil procedure — New York (State) — Cases. I. Barker, Robert A., 1931- II. Title.

KFN5995.A7C48 2007

347.747'05 — dc22   2007013867

Editorial Offices
744 Broad Street, Newark, NJ 07102 (973) 820-2000
201 Mission St., San Francisco, CA 94105-1831 (415) 908-3200
701 East Water Street, Charlottesville, VA 22902-7587 (804) 972-7600
www.lexis.com

(Pub.0497)

CIVIL LITIGATION IN NEW YORK

Fifth Edition

OSCAR G. CHASE
Russell D. Niles Professor of Law
New York University School of Law

ROBERT A. BARKER
Professor Emeritus of Law
Albany Law School of Union University

DEDICATION

To Jane
O.G.C.

To Ellen,
my wife
R.A.B

PREFACE TO THE FIFTH EDITION

We are very pleased to present the fifth edition of Civil Litigation in New York. We are gratified by the warm reception the casebook continues to receive from students and professors throughout New York and beyond. Our goal continues to be the provision of a book that is readable, as reasonably thorough as space permits, and as thought-provoking as the many interesting issues raised by modern litigation allow. We have maintained the basic structure of the book that has well-served students and teachers in the more than twenty years since the appearance of the first edition. You will find that important new cases have been added and statutory changes noted, but we have avoided change for change's sake and have thus retained the cases that make up the "canon" of our subject.

We are grateful to Alan Lawn, NYU School of Law, Class of 2008, for his helpful research assistance. From Albany Law School, Donna Parent has been of inestimable help. We again thank our fellow teachers of New York Practice throughout New York and beyond for their ongoing support and friendly suggestions.

Professor Chase acknowledges with thanks the financial support provided by the Filomen D'Agostino and Max E. Greenberg Research Fund of the New York University School of Law.

O.G.C.
R.A.B
December, 2006

PREFACE TO THE FOURTH EDITION

It is gratifying to present the fourth edition of our casebook. This new edition is necessitated by the law's many changes since the third edition appeared, by the continuing use of Civil Litigation in New York as the primary teaching vehicle for contemporary courses on New York civil practice, and by the importance of the subject matter. Reflected in the fourth edition are legislative and case-law changes to the "commencement by filing" system, the statute of limitations, and disclosure, among others.

We are grateful to Leah M. Chan, Seth R. Gassman, and Joseph J. Welch, all of NYU School of Law, for their helpful research assistance. From Albany Law School, Donna Parent has again been of inestimable help.

Above all, we thank our fellow teachers of New York Practice throughout the State, and beyond, for their ongoing support and friendly suggestions.

O.G.C.
R.A.B
June, 2002

PREFACE TO THE THIRD EDITION

The wide acceptance of the second edition has been a source of satisfaction to each of us. We are pleased to have played a role in introducing many law students to the intricacies of civil litigation rules in New York State. We continue to believe that New York's litigation system is worthy of careful study, even by students who have already completed a basic civil procedure course. They will find much in this volume that goes beyond the basic principles to which the first-year course has exposed them, as well as an introduction to the many points at which New York departs from the Federal Rules of Civil Procedure.

A third edition is necessary because of the many changes in practice that have occurred during the six years that have passed since the completion of the second edition. We have done our utmost to insure a reliable incorporation of them into the current volume. We invite all users of this volume-students as well as professors-to alert us to any errors or suggestions for improvement.

Our thanks to the following student research assistants, all of whom provided invaluable assistance: From NYU School of Law, Adam Cantor, Beth Graddy, Scott Pasternack, David Schiff, and Sandy Yu. From Albany Law School, Donna Parent has been of inestimable help.

O.G.C.
R.A.B
October, 1996

PREFACE TO THE SECOND EDITION

Our aim in preparing this book has been to give the student the materials necessary to achieve a sophisticated understanding of litigation in the New York court system, emphasizing practice in the Supreme Court. The second edition of Civil Litigation in New York retains the transactional approach used in the first. The organization of the chapters follows, to the extent feasible, the usual development of an action as experienced by counsel. While this approach gives the student a way of fitting each piece into a cognizable whole, it should not suggest invariability. In our own teaching we ask our students to confront the choices available to the parties at each stage and to analyze the reasons for choosing one path over another.

We have again interspersed litigation problems throughout the book designed to encourage the student to read the surrounding material carefully. Often, discussion of a problem will highlight ambiguity in doctrine which purports to be straightforward. Evaluation of competing approaches should call for reference to underlying policy and value assumptions. The student (and teacher) will then be encouraged to think about the values that a procedural system can and should serve.

Reflecting the many legal developments in the past six years, as well as our own ambition to improve the book, the second edition includes much new material. The chapter on personal jurisdiction has been particularly affected by the close attention the Supreme Court of the United States has paid to the area. We found that these cases worked best when folded into the subdivisions of personal jurisdiction doctrine, rather than as a separate treatment of constitutional issues. We have broadened the scope of the book as well, most notably by the addition of new chapters on appeals and enforcement of judgments.

As with the preparation of any casebook, we faced many difficult decisions of inclusion and exclusion. We hope we have struck the right balance between preservation and dynamism.

Professor Chase acknowledges with thanks the financial support provided by the Filomen D'Agostino and Max E. Greenberg Research Fund of the New York University School of Law.

O.G.C.
R.A.B
January, 1990

PREFACE

This book grew out of my experience as a teacher of New York Practice at New York University School of Law and at Brooklyn Law School. Its authorship is in some sense shared by the many students who, through our classroom discussions, helped me develop my thinking about the subject and how to teach it. Similarly, my fellow proceduralists on the faculties of both of those institutions were a frequent source of stimulation and encouragement. I must single out Professors Margaret A. Berger, Sheila L. Birnbaum, Samuel Estriecher, Richard T. Farrell, Stephen Gillers, Andreas F. Lowenfeld, Burt Neuborne, Linda J. Silberman and the late David H. Schwartz. I am especially grateful to Professor Michael A. Schwind, who read and commented on portions of the manuscript.

I would also like to thank those who, as student research assistants, worked hard to help keep errors to a minimum: Derick P. Berlage, Charles A. Bryant, Mark Fant, Sally Frank, James Kleinbaum, Patrick W. Kocian, Lola E. Langner, Alan S. Trust, and Judi Scott.

I am grateful, too, to Phyliss Goldberg and Brenda Thompson for their indispensable clerical assistance.

Finally, I gratefully acknowledge the generous financial support provided by the New York University Law Center Foundation; it was extraordinarily important in making this project possible.

Oscar G. Chase
July, 1983

INTRODUCTION

A. About This Book: A Memo to the Student

Civil litigation in New York is complex and demanding. It calls on such advocacy skills as oral argument, brief writing and cross-examination, but even more does it demand familiarity with the "law" of litigation. The purpose of this book is to help you learn that law in the context in which an advocate must apply it. We hope that you will not only become familiar with the rules of New York practice but that you will develop a sense of how they can be creatively applied. To that end we have included in each chapter litigation problems which are designed to help you put the law into a practical perspective. The problems are based on realistic situations (sometimes on actual cases) and therefore raise the sorts of difficult issues which can arise in the course of any action. Usually you will find that we have presented the problem prior to the material which bears on it. This will hopefully make the material less abstract and more involving. Many of the problems do not have a single answer which is correct in an absolute sense. As with most legal issues there are various possible solutions, each with its own supporting arguments. Please approach them in that spirit.

In keeping with its purposes, the book is organized roughly along the path litigation normally takes, starting with the rules governing the choice of forum. Since there is no route which all lawsuits must follow, and since there are some rules of litigation (*e.g.*, those governing motion practice) which are relevant to several stages of a lawsuit, you should not take the linear organization we have adopted as exemplifying all lawsuits or as an approach you would always follow in practice. Use it, rather, to gain and keep a general sense of litigation as a process with a beginning, middle and clearly defined goal.

The variety of paths litigation can take brings us to another point about the study of it. The flexibility of modern civil procedure, including that of New York, allows and therefore requires the lawyer to make frequent tactical choices. Should one make a particular motion? Obtain a provisional remedy? Seek discovery? If so, what kind? How should the pleading be drafted? It is our view that an effective advocate knows what the ethical choices are in every situation and does his or her best to pick the alternative which will maximize the client's chances of success. Thus, as you read the cases and problems which follow, we urge you to think about and evaluate the choices that the litigants made.

The management of the litigation system in pursuit of success is not the only challenge to the student or attorney. Equally fulfilling, if not more so, is participation in the ongoing effort to reform and improve the system. This book goes to press during a period of widespread criticism of civil litigation as a method of resolving disputes. How the system can and should be changed in response to its critics is therefore a particularly timely issue now; there is no

doubt that the search for improvement will continue during the professional lifetime of today's student. Thus, these materials frequently encourage you to step
back from the process and ask "How can we make this better?"

B. Sources of New York's Law of Civil Procedure

The Civil Practice Law and Rules, the "CPLR," is the primary focus of this
book, as it is the primary source of the law of civil litigation in New York.
Adopted in 1962, effective September 1, 1963 (*see* CPLR 10005), it was the
product of over five years of study by distinguished academicians and lawyers.[1]

CPLR 101 states that the CPLR governs the procedure in "civil judicial proceedings in all courts of the state and before all judges, except where the procedure is regulated by inconsistent statute." As we shall see momentarily, there
are several statutes which are either inconsistent with the CPLR or at least supplementary to it. Note first that the CPLR, like every rule of procedure, must
of course accord with the federal and state constitutions. The United States
Constitution is relevant primarily because of the "Due Process" clause of the
Fourteenth Amendment, prohibiting the taking of life, liberty, or property,
without the due process of law . . . . " The basic requisite of due process, "a meaningful opportunity to be heard,"[2] remains a lively ingredient in the discussion
of concepts as varied as provisional remedies[3] and jurisdiction.[4]

The Constitution of the State of New York has its own due process clause, in
Article 1, § 6, which in language and substance generally tracks that of the federal constitution but which stands as an independent guardian of procedural
fairness.[5] In other provisions the state constitution regulates civil practice in
some detail. It has on most points been amplified by statute or rule, but remains
supreme in case of conflict with them. The right to jury trial, as well as its
waiver, and jury composition are covered in Article I, § 2. The Judiciary Article
(Article VI) establishes a "unified court system,"[6] defines the subject matter
jurisdiction of the various courts which it creates or authorizes to be created,[7]

---

[1] The principal drafts were the work of the Advisory Committee on Practice and Procedure,
which was appointed for this purpose in 1956 and which submitted its final report in January, 1961.
The legislative history is reviewed in the Sixth Report Of The Senate Finance Committee On The
Proposed Revision Of The Civil Practice Act And Rules (1962), reprinted in part at 1962 N.Y. Ses-
sion Laws, p. 3333. *See also* Weinstein, *Proposed Revision of New York Civil Practice*, 60 Colum. L.
Rev. 50 (1960).

[2] *Boddie v. Connecticut*, 401 U.S. 371, 377, 91 S. Ct. 780, 785 (1971).

[3] *Carey v. Sugar*, 425 U.S. 73, 96 S. Ct. 1208 (1976).

[4] *Shaffer v. Heitner*, 433 U.S. 186, 97 S. Ct. 2569 (1977).

[5] *See Sharrock v. Del Buick-Cadillac, Inc.*, 45 N.Y.2d 152, 408 N.Y.S.2d 39, 379 N.E.2d 1169
(1978), *infra* (holds "state action" present for the purposes of the state due process clause even if
lacking for the purposes of federal due process).

[6] N.Y. Const. Article VI, § 1.

[7] *See* Chapter 3, *infra*.

and provides for judicial appointments and discipline, and for administrative supervision of the court system.[8]

The statute of most general applicability which supplements the CPLR is the Judiciary Law. It details the jurisdiction of some of the courts created by, or authorized to be created by, the Constitution.[9] Here, too, are set forth some of the powers and duties, administrative and otherwise, of the judges of the various courts[10] as well as other court officers,[11] including attorneys.[12] Also important from the point of view of the student of civil practice is Article 2, General Provisions Relating to Courts and Judges, which includes matters of procedural detail not found in the CPLR.[13]

The CPLR is the general code of procedure for two of the major trial courts of the state: the Supreme Court (which is the court of general jurisdiction) and the County Courts. Individualized codes of procedure have been developed for all other courts and are set forth in the Court of Claims Act, Family Court Act, Surrogate's Court Procedure Act, Uniform District Court Act, Uniform City Court Act, Uniform Justice Court Act, and New York City Civil Court Act. These court acts are, however, coordinated with the CPLR to some extent. Thus, the Family Court Act provides that the CPLR is applicable "to the extent . . . appropriate" whenever the former does not cover the point in question.[14]

The Surrogate's Court Procedure Act makes the CPLR "and other laws applicable to practice" relevant in the Surrogate's Courts except where "other procedure is provided by this act."[15] The New York City Civil Court Act, the Uniform District Court Act, the Uniform Justice Court Act, and the Uniform City Court Act contain identical provisions, which read as follows:

> The CPLR and other provisions of law relating to practice and procedure in the supreme court, notwithstanding reference by name or classification therein to any other court, shall apply in this court as far as the same can be made applicable and are not in conflict with this act.[16]

The major factor that determines whether any CPLR provision applies in an action pending in a court that has its own practice act is whether and in what

---

[8] N.Y. Const., Art. VI, § 28.

[9] *E.g.,* Jud. L. § 190 (County Court Jurisdiction).

[10] *See* Jud. L. § 2-b, enumerating the general powers of all courts of record. *See also id.,* § 147-a, describing the general power of supreme court justices.

[11] *See* Jud. L. Article 8, dealing with court clerks.

[12] *See generally* Jud. L. Article 15.

[13] *E.g.,* Jud. L. § 4 (court sessions to be public, subject to enumerated exceptions); Jud. L. § 28 (court not to amend transcripts in relation to objections without consent of party making the objection); *see also* Jud. L. art. 19. (contempt powers and procedures).

[14] Family Ct. Act § 165.

[15] Surr. Ct. Pr. Act § 102.

[16] Section 2102 of each act.

manner the court act covers the particular aspect of procedure in question. If the act specifically covers the subject, its provisions govern.[17] When there is doubt whether the CPLR or another act governs a point, the broad scope of CPLR 101 has been relied upon in resolving ambiguity in favor of the CPLR.[18]

The CPLR incorporates both law and rules of civil practice in a single integrated document. Each provision of the law is designated a "section" or "rule." Sections have always been alterable only by the legislature. The rules were formerly amendable by the Judicial Conference subject to legislative veto[19] but may, as of this writing, be amended only by the legislature itself.[20] Sections and rules are interspersed, with the provisions numbered in the order in which they appear regardless of their status as section or rule.[21]

Students and practitioners must also be aware of another set of rules relevant to practice in New York: the Uniform Rules for the New York State Trial Courts. These rules, which were promulgated by the Chief Administrator of the Courts in 1986, supplement the CPLR and provide additional detail regulating the conduct of litigation. They should not be confused with the "rules" in the CPLR itself. They are codified in Title 22 of the Official Compilation of Codes, Rules and Regulations of the State of New York ("NYCRR"), and are posted at www.courts.state.ny.us/ucsrules.html. These rules are uniform in the sense that they provide a common set of rules for each court (e.g., the Supreme Court), which apply in every county or city in which that court sits. There are, however, different uniform rules for each of the courts of inferior jurisdiction, and each appellate court has its own rules. Therefore, you must be careful to consult the appropriate rules in 22 NYCRR whenever you practice in a court which is new to you. Moreover, Parts 125-136 of 22 NYCRR set forth some general rules and apply throughout the state. In the readings that follow we direct your attention to them as they become relevant.

The Judicial Conference, acting pursuant to CPLR 107, adopted an Appendix of Official Forms which became effective September 1, 1968.[22]

---

[17] Id.

[18] *Santiago v. Johnson*, 61 Misc. 2d 746, 305 N.Y.S.2d 717 (Civ. Ct. 1969) (disbursements taxed in accordance with CPLR provision).

[19] The Judicial Conference enjoyed this power pursuant to N.Y. Const., Art. 6, § 30 and Judiciary Law § 229, but this power was removed by constitutional and statutory amendments, *see* N.Y. Const., Art. 6, § 30, as amended, Nov. 8, 1977; L. 1978 Ch. 156, § 6.

[20] N.Y. Const. Art. 6 § 30. This power may be delegated by the legislature to a court or to the Chief Administrator of the Courts, *id.*, but no such delegation is currently in force.

[21] In citing a provision, an attorney need not indicate whether it is a rule or a section. CPLR 101. It has been held, however, that a rule must yield to a section in case of conflict, CPLR 102; *Foley v. Roche*, 68 A.D.2d 558, 418 N.Y.S.2d 588 (1st Dep't 1979).

[22] CPLR 107 initially empowered the Judicial Conference of the State of New York to "adopt, amend and rescind an appendix of forms." Effective May 30, 1974, such power was transferred to the state administrator. *See* L. 1974, Ch. 615, § 12.

Among the papers they include are pleadings, summonses, and motion papers. Because CPLR 107 provides that papers promulgated under it "shall be sufficient," they should not be rejected by any court subject to the CPLR when used appropriately.[23] Unofficial commentary to the forms has also been provided by the Judicial Conference. Although use of the forms is not mandatory, they are intended to "exemplify the simplicity and brevity of statement which the CPLR contemplates."[24]

C. Bibliography

We who practice in New York are fortunate to have available several helpful works. The preeminent multi-volume treatise is Weinstein, Korn and Miller, New York Civil Practice (Rev. ed. 2006). Also a multi-volume work is Carmody-Wait 2d Cyclopedia of New York Practice. Useful single volume texts are David D. Siegel, New York Practice (4th ed. 2005); and Oscar G. Chase, Weinstein, Korn and Miller, CPLR Manual (Rev. ed. 2006); and David L. Ferstendig, New York Civil Litigation (2005).

Annotated editions of the CPLR are published in 7B McKinney's Consolidated Laws (which also has practice commentaries that are updated regularly) and in 4 New York Consolidated Laws Service.

The best sources of the legislative history of the CPLR are the Final Report of the Advisory Committee on Practice and Procedure (1961), the four preliminary reports of the Advisory Committee on Practice and Procedure (1957-1961) and the Sixth Report of the Senate Finance Committee on the Proposed Revision of the Civil Practice Act and Rules (1962). Legislative history of some of the amendments to the CPLR is found in the various annual reports of the Advisory Committee on Civil Practice to the Chief Administrator of the Courts of the State of New York and in annual reports to the legislature of the Law Revision Commission.

Statistics, calendar conditions, and other information about the court system are published each year in the annual reports of the Chief Administrator of the Courts. A website on which this material and other information about the courts, including official forms, court rules, and guidance for attorneys, may be found is www.courts.state.ny.us.

Developments in New York's law of civil procedure are discussed in the annual survey of New York law of the Syracuse Law Review and in the monthly publication, Siegel's Practice Review, written by Professor David D. Siegel.

As to more specialized works, the jurisdiction of the Court of Appeals is surveyed in Arthur Karger, The Powers of the New York Court of Appeals (2005).

---

[23] *Pritzer v. Falk,* 58 Misc. 2d 989, 297 N.Y.S.2d 622 (Sup. Ct. 1969) (official form used as a model of sufficiency).

[24] Introductory Statement, Appendix of Official Forms.

Two other useful monographs on appeals are The Practioner's Handbook For Appeals to the Court of Appeals of the State of New York (2d ed. 1991) and The Practitioner's Handbook For Appeals to the Appellate Divisions of the State of New York (1979), both of which were published by the New York State Bar Association.

TABLE OF CONTENTS

Part Two: TIMELINESS OF THE LITIGATION

**Chapter 7: The Statutes of Limitations and Related
                 Concepts** 267

End MPS

Part Five: RESOLVING THE LITIGATION

Chapter 16: Accelerated Judgment

Part One
SELECTING THE LITIGATION FORUM

Chapter 1

JURISDICTION OVER THE DEFENDANT: IS NEW YORK THE RIGHT FORUM?

§ 1.01 INTRODUCTION

Begin with the assumption that the plaintiff has decided to start legal proceedings. The next likely step for lawyer and client is to choose a forum. It need not be a judicial forum; an administrative proceeding may be an option or, in certain cases, a requirement. Arbitration is another possibility. But even if they have decided to go to court, they must make further choices. Should the case be brought in the federal system or in a state court? If the latter, which state? What court within the chosen state? This chapter responds to the question, "Which state?" More specifically, it deals with whether New York is a permissible choice as a matter of law.

Before we look at the relevant legal doctrine, it may be useful to think about how to decide whether a particular forum would be a good one, bearing in mind that, when presented with alternatives, the good litigator will make the choice which maximizes his client's interests. When the plaintiff's lawyer is a New York practitioner, a forum in New York is a likely choice. As one federal judge observed:

> Every lawyer is at an advantage when he practices his art in his own area. He is familiar with the local rules, customs and practices, opposing counsel, courts and clerks. He can remain in close contact with his office and staff; necessary resource persons are available at all times. His knowledge of local practice and procedure will be of inestimable value at trial. A lawyer is at a disadvantage, on the other hand, if he is forced to bring or defend a suit in an inconvenient locale.*

But New York need not always be the choice, even for a local attorney. Why not? It is surely relevant that the substantive law applied in an action may depend on which state's court is deciding the choice of law issue. It has been suggested, for example, that the choice of law decisions of the New York courts have been said to favor New York residents. *O'Connor v. Lee-Hy Paving Corp.*, 579 F.2d 194, 205 (2d Cir.), *cert. denied*, 439 U.S. 1034 (1978). What other factors are there?

---

* Charles L. Brieant & Shira A. Scheindlin, *Venue in the Second Circuit: A Topic Whose Time has Come, A Review of Civil and Criminal Venue Cases, 1970-76*, 43 Bklyn. L. Rev. 841 (1977). An informative tactical analysis of the choice of forum problem is found in S. Speiser, Lawsuit at 30-34 (1980).

Reprinted by permission of Bklyn. L. Rev. and author, © 1977.

Let's turn to the doctrine which tells us whether New York is available as a forum.

§ 1.02 GENERAL PRINCIPLES

Jurisdiction concerns the power of the courts to affect legal interests. Obtaining jurisdiction is essential, since any court action taken in its absence is subject to nullification directly in the action or, collaterally, in another action in or outside of New York State. Exercise of judicial power by the state through its courts requires the satisfaction of requirements which fall under two broad heads: (1) subject matter jurisdiction (to be considered in the third chapter) and (2) jurisdiction over the defendant. Even if these requirements are met, the courts can decline to exercise jurisdiction if "in the interest of substantial justice the action should be heard in another forum." CPLR 327.

Jurisdiction over the defendant has two requirements: a jurisdictional "basis" and proper notice of the commencement of the action. Notice is provided by proper service of the summons, a matter considered in Chapter 5. Basis may be defined as a relationship between the defendant and the state which is sufficient to justify the exercise of the state's judicial power over the defendant's interests. To pass muster the relationship must be substantial enough to satisfy the due process clauses of the federal and state constitutions, which mandate that it not be unfair to the defendant — considering "the relationship among the defendant, the forum and the litigation"* — to exercise the state's power. It must also be shown that the state has, by statute, authorized its courts to exercise power over the defendant. Article 3 of the CPLR is the primary source of such authority for the New York Supreme Court. (The jurisdictional reach of the inferior courts is briefly treated in Chapter 3.)

Jurisdictional basis can be usefully divided into two categories, "general" and "specific" jurisdiction. If the defendant is "present" within the state when the summons is served, the court acquires what is sometimes called "general jurisdiction." This means that the court can entertain a cause of action regardless of whether it arises out of the defendant's activities in the state. Jurisdiction over a defendant who is not present in the state when the summons is served is limited to claims arising from the defendant's contacts, ties or relations with the state. This is sometimes called "specific" jurisdiction. For further discussion of these concepts, see Arthur T. von Mehren and Donald T. Trautman, *Jurisdiction to Adjudicate: A Suggested Analysis*, 79 Harv. L. Rev. 1121 (1966); Mary Twitchell, *The Myth of General Jurisdiction*, 101 Harv. L. Rev. 610 (1988).

Jurisdictional basis was, traditionally, separated into two additional categories, one of which gave power over the defendant's person and the other

---

* Shaffer v. Heitner, 433 U.S. 186, 204, 97 S. Ct. 2569, 2580 (1977).

power only over his property. As the U.S. Supreme Court described this traditional dichotomy in *Shaffer v. Heitner:**

> If a court's jurisdiction is based on its authority over the defendant's person, the action and judgment are denominated "in personam" and can impose a personal obligation on the defendant in favor of the plaintiff. If jurisdiction is based on the court's power over property within its territory, the action is called "in rem" or "quasi in rem." The effect of a judgment in such a case is limited to the property that supports jurisdiction and does not impose a personal liability on the property owner, since he is not before the court.

The impact of *Shaffer* on New York's exercise of jurisdiction over property will be discussed in more detail in § 1.07 of this chapter. Before reaching it, we will look at the other bases on which personal jurisdiction has been exercised in the light of modern constitutional principles. These are:

- Presence (including the fictional presence of corporations)
- Domicile
- Consent
- Contacts or "long arm"
- Property in the state
- Family relationships

§ 1.03 PRESENCE — REAL AND FICTIONAL

[A] Presence of Natural Persons

It has long been the rule in New York and throughout the United States that the state may exercise jurisdiction over a person present in that state at the time the summons is served, *e.g., Pennoyer v. Neff*, 95 U.S. 714 (1877), even if the presence was fleeting. CPLR 301 preserves this rule.

In connection with the following problem, consider whether the traditional doctrine is applicable, consistent with the modern principles relied upon in *Burnham v. Superior Court of California*, which follows. Consider, too, whether the exceptions to the presence doctrine described in the accompanying cases would affect the resolution of the problem.

---

* *Id.* at 199, 97 S. Ct. at 2577.

PROBLEM A

Bob is President of Acme, Inc., a California corporation which has no New York contacts. One of its customers, P & P, a Massachusetts partnership, claimed that goods it purchased from Acme were defective and has refused to pay the contract price. Paul, a general partner in P & P, wrote to Bob asking him to meet them at a New York City hotel to try to resolve the dispute. After two hours of fruitless negotiations, Tim, Paul's lawyer, handed Bob two summonses in a breach of contract action brought in Supreme Court, New York County. The defendants named in the summons were Bob personally and Acme, Inc.

Does the court have jurisdiction over Bob?

BURNHAM v. SUPERIOR COURT OF CALIFORNIA
United States Supreme Court
495 U.S. 604, 110 S. Ct. 2105, 109 L. Ed. 2d 631 (1990)

JUSTICE SCALIA announced the judgment of the Court and delivered an opinion in which THE CHIEF JUSTICE and JUSTICE KENNEDY join, and in which JUSTICE WHITE joins with respect to Parts I, II-A, II-B, and II-C.

The question presented is whether the Due Process Clause of the Fourteenth Amendment denies California courts jurisdiction over a nonresident, who was personally served with process while temporarily in that State, in a suit unrelated to his activities in the State.

I

Petitioner Dennis Burnham married Francie Burnham in 1976 in West Virginia. In 1977 the couple moved to New Jersey, where their two children were born. In July 1987 the Burnhams decided to separate. They agreed that Mrs. Burnham, who intended to move to California, would take custody of the children. Shortly before Mrs. Burnham departed for California that same month, she and petitioner agreed that she would file for divorce on grounds of "irreconcilable differences."

In October 1987, petitioner filed for divorce in New Jersey state court on grounds of "desertion." Petitioner did not, however, obtain an issuance of summons against his wife and did not attempt to serve her with process. Mrs. Burnham, after unsuccessfully demanding that petitioner adhere to their prior agreement to submit to an "irreconcilable differences" divorce, brought suit for divorce in California state court in early January 1988.

In late January, petitioner visited southern California on business, after which he went north to visit his children in the San Francisco Bay area, where his wife resided. He took the older child to San Francisco for the weekend. Upon returning the child to Mrs. Burnham's home on January 24, 1988, petitioner was served with a California court summons and a copy of Mrs. Burn-ham's divorce petition. He then returned to New Jersey.

Later that year, petitioner made a special appearance in the California Superior Court, moving to quash the service of process on the ground that the court lacked personal jurisdiction over him because his only contacts with California were a few short visits to the State for the purposes of conducting business and visiting his children.

II

A

To determine whether the assertion of personal jurisdiction is consistent with due process, we have long relied on the principles traditionally followed by American courts in marking out the territorial limits of each State's authority. That criterion was first announced in *Pennoyer v. Neff, supra*, in which we stated that due process "mean[s] a course of legal proceedings according to those rules and principles which have been established in our systems of jurisprudence for the protection and enforcement of private rights," *id.*, at 733, including the "well-established principles of public law respecting the jurisdiction of an independent State over persons and property," *id.*, at 722. In what has become the classic expression of the criterion, we said in *International Shoe Co. v. Washington*, 326 U.S. 310 (1945), that a state court's assertion of personal jurisdiction satisfies the Due Process Clause if it does not violate "traditional notions of fair play and substantial justice." *Id.*, at 316.

Since *International Shoe*, we have only been called upon to decide whether these "traditional notions" permit States to exercise jurisdiction over absent defendants in a manner that deviates from the rules of jurisdiction applied in the 19th century. We have held such deviations permissible, but only with respect to suits arising out of the absent defendant's contacts with the State. . . . *See, e.g., Helicopteros Nacionales de Colombia v. Hall*, 466 U.S. 408, 414 (1984). The question we must decide today is whether due process requires a similar connection between the litigation and the defendant's contacts with the State in cases where the defendant is physically present in the State at the time process is served upon him.

Among the most firmly established principles of personal jurisdiction in American tradition is that the courts of a State have jurisdiction over nonresidents who are physically present in the State. The view developed early that each State had the power to hale before its courts any individual who could be found within its borders, and that once having acquired jurisdiction over such a person by properly serving him with process, the State could retain jurisdiction to enter judgment against him, no matter how fleeting his visit. *See, e.g., Potter v. Allin*, 2 Root 63, 67 (Conn. 1793); *Barrell v. Benjamin*, 15 Mass. 354 (1819). That view had antecedents in English common-law practice, which sometimes allowed "transitory" actions, arising out of events outside the country, to be maintained against seemingly nonresident defendants who were present in England. *See, e.g., Mostyn v. Fabrigas*, 98 Eng. Rep. 1021 (K.B. 1774); *Cartwright v. Pettus*, 22 Eng. Rep. 916 (Ch. 1675). Justice Story believed the principle, which he traced to Roman origins, to be firmly grounded in English tradition: "[B]y the common law[,] personal actions, being transitory, may be brought in any place, where the party defendant may be found," for "every nation may . . . rightfully exercise jurisdiction over all persons within its domains." J. Story, Commentaries on the Conflict of Laws at 554, 543 (1846). *See also id.*, at 530-538; *Picquet v. Swan, supra*, at 611-612 (Story, J.) ("Where a party is within a territory, he may justly be subjected to its process, and bound personally by the judgment pronounced, on such process, against him").

Recent scholarship has suggested that English tradition was not as clear as Story thought, *see* Hazard, *A General Theory of State-Court Jurisdiction*, 1965 S. Ct. Rev. 241, 253-260; Ehrenzweig, *The Transient Rule of Personal Jurisdiction: The "Power" Myth and Forum Conveniens*, 65 Yale L.J. 289 (1956). Accurate or not, however, judging by the evidence of contemporaneous or near-contemporaneous decisions, one must conclude that Story's understanding was shared by American courts at the crucial time for present purposes: 1868, when the Fourteenth Amendment was adopted.

. . . .

Most States, moreover, had statutes or common-law rules that exempted from service of process individuals who were brought into the forum by force or fraud . . . or who were there as a party or witness in unrelated judicial proceedings. . . . These exceptions obviously rested upon the premise that service of process conferred jurisdiction. . . . Particularly striking is the fact that, as far as we have been able to determine, not one American case from the period (or, for that matter, not one American case until 1978) held, or even suggested, that in-state personal service on an individual was insufficient to confer personal jurisdiction.[3]

Commentators were also seemingly unanimous on the rule. . . .

This American jurisdictional practice is, moreover, not merely old; it is continuing. It remains the practice of, not only a substantial number of the States, but as far as we are aware all the States and the Federal Government — if one disregards (as one must for this purpose) the few opinions since 1978 that have erroneously said, on grounds similar to those that petitioner presses here, that this Court's due process decisions render the practice unconstitutional. . . . We do not know of a single state or federal statute, or a single judicial decision rest-

---

[3] Given this striking fact, and the unanimity of both cases and commentators in supporting the in-state service rule, one can only marvel at Justice Brennan's assertion that the rule "was rather weakly implanted in American jurisprudence," *post*, at 633-634, and "did not receive wide currency until well after our decision in *Pennoyer v. Neff*" *post*, at 635. I have cited pre-*Pennoyer* cases clearly supporting the rule from no less than nine States, ranging from Mississippi to Colorado to New Hampshire, and two highly respected pre-*Pennoyer* commentators. . . .

ing upon state law, that has abandoned in-state service as a basis of jurisdiction. Many recent cases reaffirm it. . . .

C

Despite this formidable body of precedent, petitioner contends, in reliance on our decisions applying the *International Shoe* standard, that in the absence of "continuous and systematic" contacts with the forum, a nonresident defendant can be subjected to judgment only as to matters that arise out of or relate to his contacts with the forum. This argument rests on a thorough misunderstanding of our cases.

The view of most courts in the 19th century was that a court simply could not exercise in personam jurisdiction over a nonresident who had not been personally served with process in the forum. *See, e.g., Pennoyer v. Neff.* . . .

Later years, however, saw the weakening of the *Pennoyer* rule. In the late 19th and early 20th centuries, changes in the technology of transportation and communication, and the tremendous growth of interstate business activity, led to an "inevitable relaxation of the strict limits on state jurisdiction" over nonresident individuals and corporations. *Hanson v. Denckla,* 357 U.S. 235, 260 (1958) (Black, J., dissenting). . . . Our opinion in *International Shoe* . . . made explicit the underlying basis of these decisions: Due process does not necessarily require the States to adhere to the unbending territorial limits on jurisdiction set forth in *Pennoyer*. The validity of assertion of jurisdiction over a nonconsenting defendant who is not present in the forum depends upon whether "the quality and nature of [his] activity" in relation to the forum, 326 U.S., at 319, renders such jurisdiction consistent with "traditional notions of fair play and substantial justice." *Id.*, at 316 (citation omitted). Subsequent cases have derived from the *International Shoe* standard the general rule that a State may dispense with in-forum personal service on nonresident defendants in suits arising out of their activities in the State. . . . As *International Shoe* suggests, the defendant's litigation-related "minimum contacts" may take the place of physical presence as the basis for jurisdiction . . . .

Nothing in *International Shoe* or the cases that have followed it, however, offers support for the very different proposition petitioner seeks to establish today: that a defendant's presence in the forum is not only unnecessary to validate novel, nontraditional assertions of jurisdiction, but is itself no longer sufficient to establish jurisdiction. That proposition is unfaithful to both elementary logic and the foundations of our due process jurisprudence. The distinction between what is needed to support novel procedures and what is needed to sustain traditional ones is fundamental, as we observed over a century ago. The short of the matter is that jurisdiction based on physical presence alone constitutes due process because it is one of the continuing traditions of our legal system that define the due process standard of "traditional notions of fair play and substantial justice." That standard was developed by analogy to "physical presence," and it would be perverse to say it could now be turned against that touchstone of jurisdiction.

D

Petitioner's strongest argument, though we ultimately reject it, relies upon our decision in *Shaffer v. Heitner*, 433 U.S. 186 (1977). In that case, a Delaware court hearing a shareholder's derivative suit against a corporation's directors secured jurisdiction quasi in rem by sequestering the out-of-state defendants' stock in the company, the situs of which was Delaware under Delaware law. Reasoning that Delaware's sequestration procedure was simply a mechanism to compel the absent defendants to appear in a suit to determine their personal rights and obligations, we concluded that the normal rules we had developed under *International Shoe* for jurisdiction over suits against absent defendants should apply — viz., Delaware could not hear the suit because the defendants' sole contact with the State (ownership of property there) was unrelated to the lawsuit. 433 U.S., at 213-215.

It goes too far to say, as petitioner contends, that *Shaffer* compels the conclusion that a State lacks jurisdiction over an individual unless the litigation arises out of his activities in the State. *Shaffer*, like *International Shoe*, involved jurisdiction over an absent defendant, and it stands for nothing more than the proposition that when the "minimum contact" that is a substitute for physical presence consists of property ownership it must, like other minimum contacts, be related to the litigation. Petitioner wrenches out of its context our statement in *Shaffer* that "all assertions of state-court jurisdiction must be evaluated according to the standards set forth in *International Shoe* and its progeny," 433 U.S., at 212. When read together with the two sentences that preceded it, the meaning of this statement becomes clear:

> "The fiction that an assertion of jurisdiction over property is anything but an assertion of jurisdiction over the owner of the property supports an ancient form without substantial modern justification. Its continued acceptance would serve only to allow state-court jurisdiction that is fundamentally unfair to the defendant.

> "We *therefore conclude* that all assertions of state-court jurisdiction must be evaluated according to the standards set forth in *International Shoe* and its progeny." *Id.* (emphasis added).

Shaffer was saying, in other words, not that all bases for the assertion of in personam jurisdiction (including, presumably, in-state service) must be treated alike and subjected to the "minimum contacts" analysis of *International Shoe*; but rather that quasi in rem jurisdiction, that fictional "ancient form," and in personam jurisdiction, are really one and the same and must be treated alike — leading to the conclusion that quasi in rem jurisdiction, i.e., that form of in personam jurisdiction based upon a "property ownership" contact and by definition unaccompanied by personal, in-state service, must satisfy the litigation-relatedness requirement of *International Shoe*. The logic of *Shaffer*'s holding — which places all suits against absent nonresidents on the same constitutional footing, regardless of whether a separate Latin label is attached to one particular basis of contact — does not compel the conclusion that physically present defendants must be treated identically to absent ones.

. . . .

It is fair to say, however, that while our holding today does not contradict *Shaffer*, our basic approach to the due process question is different. We have conducted no independent inquiry into the desirability or fairness of the prevailing in-state service rule, leaving that judgment to the legislatures that are free to amend it; for our purposes, its validation is its pedigree, as the phrase "traditional notions of fair play and substantial justice" makes clear. *Shaffer* did conduct such an independent inquiry, asserting that "'traditional notions of fair play and substantial justice' can be as readily offended by the perpetuation of ancient forms that are no longer justified as by the adoption of new procedures that are inconsistent with the basic values of our constitutional heritage." 433 U.S., at 212. Perhaps that assertion can be sustained when the "perpetuation of ancient forms" is engaged in by only a very small minority of the States.[4]

Where, however, as in the present case, a jurisdictional principle is both firmly approved by tradition and still favored, it is impossible to imagine what standard we could appeal to for the judgment that it is "no longer justified." While in no way receding from or casting doubt upon the holding of *Shaffer* or any other case, we reaffirm today our time-honored approach, *see, e.g., Ownbey v. Morgan*, 256 U.S. 94, 110-112 (1921); *Hurtado v. California*, 110 U.S., at 528-529; *Murray's Lessee v. Hoboken Land & Improvement Co.*, 59 U.S. 272, 276-277 (1856). For new procedures, hitherto unknown, the Due Process Clause requires analysis to determine whether "traditional notions of fair play and substantial justice" have been offended. *International Shoe*, 326 U.S., at 316. But a doctrine of personal jurisdiction that dates back to the adoption of the Fourteenth Amendment and is still generally observed unquestionably meets that standard.

III

A few words in response to JUSTICE BRENNAN's opinion concurring in the judgment: It insists that we apply "contemporary notions of due process" to determine the constitutionality of California's assertion of jurisdiction. *Post*, at 632. But our analysis today comports with that prescription, at least if we give it the only sense allowed by our precedents. The "contemporary notions of due process" applicable to personal jurisdiction are the enduring "traditional notions of fair play and substantial justice" established as the test by *International Shoe*. By its very language, that test is satisfied if a state court adheres to jurisdictional rules that are generally applied and have always been applied in the United States.

---

[4] *Shaffer* may have involved a unique state procedure in one respect: JUSTICE STEVENS noted that Delaware was the only State that treated the place of incorporation as the situs of corporate stock when both owner and custodian were elsewhere. *See* 433 U.S., at 218 (opinion concurring in judgment).

But the concurrence's proposed standard of "contemporary notions of due process" requires more: It measures state-court jurisdiction not only against traditional doctrines in this country, including current state-court practice, but also against each Justice's subjective assessment of what is fair and just. Authority for that seductive standard is not to be found in any of our personal jurisdiction cases. It is, indeed, an outright break with the test of "traditional notions of fair play and substantial justice," which would have to be reformulated "our notions of fair play and substantial justice."

The subjectivity, and hence inadequacy, of this approach becomes apparent when the concurrence tries to explain why the assertion of jurisdiction in the present case meets its standard of continuing-American-tradition-plus-innate fairness. JUSTICE BRENNAN lists the "benefits" Mr. Burnham derived from the State of California — the fact that, during the few days he was there, "[h]is health and safety [were] guaranteed by the State's police, fire, and emergency medical services; he [was] free to travel on the State's roads and waterways; he likely enjoy[ed] the fruits of the State's economy." *Post*, at 637-638. Three days' worth of these benefits strike us as powerfully inadequate to establish, as an abstract matter, that it is "fair" for California to decree the ownership of all Mr. Burnham's worldly goods acquired during the 10 years of his marriage, and the custody over his children. We daresay a contractual exchange swapping those benefits for that power would not survive the "unconscionability" provision of the Uniform Commercial Code. Even less persuasive are the other "fairness" factors alluded to by JUSTICE BRENNAN. It would create "an asymmetry," we are told, if Burnham were permitted (as he is) to appear in California courts as a plaintiff, but were not compelled to appear in California courts as defendant; and travel being as easy as it is nowadays, and modern procedural devices being so convenient, it is no great hardship to appear in California courts. *Post*, at 638-639. The problem with these assertions is that they justify the exercise of jurisdiction over everyone, whether or not he ever comes to California. The only "fairness" elements setting Mr. Burnham apart from the rest of the world are the three days' "benefits" referred to above — and even those, do not set him apart from many other people who have enjoyed three days in the Golden State (savoring the fruits of its economy, the availability of its roads and police services) but who were fortunate enough not to be served with process while they were there and thus are not (simply by reason of that savoring) subject to the general jurisdiction of California's courts. *See, e.g., Helicopteros Nacionales de Colombia v. Hall,* 466 U.S., at 414-416. In other words, even if one agreed with JUSTICE BRENNAN's conception of an equitable bargain, the "benefits" we have been discussing would explain why it is "fair" to assert general jurisdiction over Burnham-returned-to-New-Jersey-after-service only at the expense of proving that it is also "fair" to assert general jurisdiction over Burnham-returned-to-New-Jersey-without-service — which we know does not conform with "contemporary notions of due process."

There is, we must acknowledge, one factor mentioned by JUSTICE BRENNAN that both relates distinctively to the assertion of jurisdiction on the basis of personal in-state service and is fully persuasive — namely, the fact that a defendant voluntarily present in a particular State has a "reasonable expectation[n]" that he is subject to suit there. *Post*, at 637. By formulating it as a "reasonable expectation," JUSTICE BRENNAN makes that seem like a "fairness" factor; but in reality, of course, it is just tradition masquerading as "fairness." The only reason for charging Mr. Burnham with the reasonable expectation of being subject to suit is that the States of the Union assert adjudicatory jurisdiction over the person, and have always asserted adjudicatory jurisdiction over the person, by serving him with process during his temporary physical presence in their territory. That continuing tradition, which anyone entering California should have known about, renders it "fair" for Mr. Burnham, who voluntarily entered California, to be sued there for divorce — at least "fair" in the limited sense that he has no one but himself to blame. JUSTICE BRENNAN's long journey is a circular one, leaving him, at the end of the day, in complete reliance upon the very factor he sought to avoid: The existence of a continuing tradition is not enough, fairness also must be considered; fairness exists here because there is a continuing tradition.

While JUSTICE BRENNAN's concurrence is unwilling to confess that the Justices of this Court can possibly be bound by a continuing American tradition that a particular procedure is fair, neither is it willing to embrace the logical consequences of that refusal — or even to be clear about what consequences (logical or otherwise) it does embrace. JUSTICE BRENNAN says that "[f]or these reasons [*i.e.*, because of the reasonableness factors enumerated above], as a rule the exercise of personal jurisdiction over a defendant based on his voluntary presence in the forum will satisfy the requirements of due process." *Post*, at 639. The use of the word "rule" conveys the reassuring feeling that he is establishing a principle of law one can rely upon — but of course he is not. Since JUSTICE BRENNAN's only criterion of constitutionality is "fairness," the phrase "as a rule" represents nothing more than his estimation that, usually, all the elements of "fairness" he discusses in the present case will exist. But what if they do not? Suppose, for example, that a defendant in Mr. Burnham's situation enjoys not three days' worth of California's "benefits," but 15 minutes' worth. Or suppose we remove one of those "benefits" — "enjoy[ment of] the fruits of the State's economy — by positing that Mr. Burnham had not come to California on business, but only to visit his children. Or suppose that Mr. Burnham were demonstrably so impecunious as to be unable to take advantage of the modern means of transportation and communication that JUSTICE BRENNAN finds so relevant. Or suppose, finally, that the California courts lacked the "variety of procedural devices," *post*, at 639, that JUSTICE BRENNAN says can reduce the burden upon out-of-state litigants. One may also make additional suppositions, relating not to the absence of the factors that JUSTICE BRENNAN discusses, but to the presence of additional factors bearing upon the ultimate criterion of "fairness." What if, for example, Mr. Burnham were visiting a sick child? Or a dying child? *Cf. Kulko v. Superior Court of California, City and County of San Francisco*, 436 U.S. 84, 93 (1978) (finding the exercise of long-arm jurisdiction over an absent parent unreasonable because it would "discourage parents from entering into reasonable visitation agreements"). Since, so far as one can tell, JUSTICE BRENNAN's approval of applying the in-state service rule in the present case rests on the presence of all the factors he lists, and on the absence of any others, every different case will present a different litigable issue. Thus, despite the fact that he manages to work the word "rule" into his formulation, JUSTICE BRENNAN's approach does not establish a rule of law at all, but only a "totality of the circumstances" test, guaranteeing what traditional territorial rules of jurisdiction were designed precisely to avoid: uncertainty and litigation over the preliminary issue of the forum's competence. It may be that those evils, necessarily accompanying a freestanding "reasonableness" inquiry, must be accepted at the margins, when we evaluate nontraditional forms of jurisdiction newly adopted by the States, *see, e.g., Asahi Metal Industry Co. v. Superior Court of California, Solano County*, 480 U.S. 102, 115 (1987). But that is no reason for injecting them into the core of our American practice, exposing to such a "reasonableness" inquiry the ground of jurisdiction that has hitherto been considered the very baseline of reasonableness, physical presence.

The difference between us and JUSTICE BRENNAN has nothing to do with whether "further progress [is] to be made" in the "evolution of our legal system." *Post*, at 631, n. 3. It has to do with whether changes are to be adopted as progressive by the American people or decreed as progressive by the Justices of this Court. Nothing we say today prevents individual States from limiting or entirely abandoning the in-state-service basis of jurisdiction. . . . The question is whether, armed with no authority other than individual Justices' perceptions of fairness that conflict with both past and current practice, this Court can compel the States to make such a change on the ground that "due process" requires it. We hold that it cannot.

Because the Due Process Clause does not prohibit the California courts from exercising jurisdiction over petitioner based on the fact of in-state service of process, the judgment is Affirmed.

JUSTICE WHITE, concurring in part and concurring in the judgment.

I join Parts, I, II-A, II-B, and II-C of JUSTICE SCALIA's opinion and concur in the judgment of affirmance. The rule allowing jurisdiction to be obtained over a nonresident by personal service in the forum State, without more, has been and is so widely accepted throughout this country that I could not possibly strike it down, either on its face or as applied in this case, on the ground that it denies due process of law guaranteed by the Fourteenth Amendment. Although the Court has the authority under the Amendment to examine even traditionally accepted procedures and declare them invalid, *e.g., Shaffer v. Heitner*, 433 U.S. 186 (1977), there has been no showing here or elsewhere that as a general proposition the rule is so arbitrary and lacking in common sense in so many instances that it should be held violative of due process in every case. Furthermore, until such a showing is made, which would be difficult indeed, claims in individual cases that the rule would operate unfairly as applied to the particular nonresident involved need not be entertained. At least this would be the case where presence in the forum State is intentional, which would almost always be the fact. Otherwise, there would be endless, fact-specific litigation in the trial and appellate courts, including this one. Here, personal service in California, without more, is enough, and I agree that the judgment should be affirmed.

JUSTICE BRENNAN, with whom JUSTICE MARSHALL, JUSTICE BLACKMUN, and JUSTICE O'CONNOR join, concurring in the judgment.

I agree with JUSTICE SCALIA that the Due Process Clause of the Fourteenth Amendment generally permits a state court to exercise jurisdiction over a defendant if he is served with process while voluntarily present in the forum State.[1] I do not perceive the need, however, to decide that a jurisdictional rule that "has been immemorially the actual law of the land," *ante*, at 619, *quoting Hurtado v. California*, 110 U.S. 516, 528 (1884), automatically comports with due process simply by virtue of its "pedigree."

Although I agree that history is an important factor in establishing whether a jurisdictional rule satisfies due process requirements, I cannot agree that it is the only factor such that all traditional rules of jurisdiction are, *ipso facto*, forever constitutional. Unlike JUSTICE SCALIA, I would undertake an "independent inquiry into the . . . fairness of the prevailing in-state service rule." *Ante*, at 621. I therefore concur only in the judgment.

I believe that the approach adopted by JUSTICE SCALIA's opinion today — reliance solely on historical pedigree — is foreclosed by our decisions in *International Shoe Co. v. Washington*, 326 U.S. 310 (1945), and *Shaffer v. Heitner*, 433 U.S. 186 (1977). In *International Shoe*, we held that a state court's assertion of personal jurisdiction does not violate the Due Process Clause if it is consistent with "traditional notions of fair play and substantial justice." 326 U.S., at 316, *quoting Milliken v. Meyer*, 311 U.S. 457, 463 (1940). In *Shaffer*, we stated that "*all assertions* of state-court jurisdiction must be evaluated according to the standards set forth in *International Shoe* and its progeny." 433 U.S., at 212 (emphasis added). The critical insight of *Shaffer* is that all rules of jurisdiction, even ancient ones, must satisfy contemporary notions of due process. . . .

While our holding in *Shaffer* may have been limited to quasi in rem jurisdiction, our mode of analysis was not. Indeed, that we were willing in *Shaffer* to examine anew the appropriateness of the quasi in rem rule — until that time dutifully accepted by American courts for at least a century — demonstrates that we did not believe that the "pedigree" of a jurisdictional practice was dispositive in deciding whether it was consistent with due process. We later characterized *Shaffer* as "abandon[ing] the outworn rule of *Harris v. Balk*, 198 U.S. 215 (1905), that the interest of a creditor in a debt could be extinguished or other-

---

[1] I use the term "transient jurisdiction" to refer to jurisdiction premised solely on the fact that a person is served with process while physically present in the forum State.

wise affected by any State having transitory jurisdiction over the debtor." *World-Wide Volkswagen Corp. v. Woodson*, 444 U.S. 286, 296 (1980); *see also Rush v. Savchuk*, 444 U.S. 320, 325-326 (1980). If we could discard an "ancient form without substantial modern justification" in *Shaffer, supra*, at 212, we can do so again. . . .

II

Tradition, though alone not dispositive, is of course relevant to the question whether the rule of transient jurisdiction is consistent with due process.[7] Tradition is salient not in the sense that practices of the past are automatically reasonable today; indeed, under such a standard, the legitimacy of transient jurisdiction would be called into question because the rule's historical "pedigree" is a matter of intense debate. The rule was a stranger to the common law . . . and was rather weakly implanted in American jurisprudence "at the crucial time for present purposes: 1868, when the Fourteenth Amendment was adopted." *Ante*, at 611. For much of the 19th century, American courts did not uniformly recognize the concept of transient jurisdiction,[9] and it appears that the transient rule did not receive wide currency until well after our decision in *Pennoyer v. Neff*, 95 U.S. 714 (1878).

Rather, I find the historical background relevant because, however murky the jurisprudential origins of transient jurisdiction, the fact that American courts have announced the rule for perhaps a century (first in dicta, more recently in holdings) provides a defendant voluntarily present in a particular State today "clear notice that [he] is subject to suit" in the forum. *World-Wide Volkswagen Corp. v. Woodson*, 444 U.S., at 297. Regardless of whether Justice Story's account of the rule's genesis is mythical, our common understanding now, fortified by a century of judicial practice, is that jurisdiction is often a function of geography. The transient rule is consistent with reasonable expectations and is entitled to a strong presumption that it comports with due process. . . . Thus, proposed revisions to the Restatement (Second) of Conflict of Laws § 28, p. 39 (1986), provide that "[a] state has power to exercise judicial jurisdiction over an individual who is present within its territory unless the individual's relationship

---

[7] I do not propose that the "contemporary notions of due process" to be applied are no more than "each Justice's subjective assessment of what is fair and just." *Ante*, at 623. Rather, the inquiry is guided by our decisions beginning with *International Shoe Co. v. Washington*, 326 U.S. 310 (1945), and the specific factors that we have developed to ascertain whether a jurisdictional rule comports with "traditional notions of fair play and substantial justice." *See, e.g., Asahi Metal Industry Co. v. Superior Court of California, Solano County*, 480 U.S. 102, 113 (1987) (noting "several factors," including "the burden on the defendant, the interests of the forum State, and the plaintiff's interest in obtaining relief"). This analysis may not be "mechanical or quantitative," *International Shoe*, 326 U.S., at 319, but neither is it "freestanding," *ante*, at 626, or dependent on personal whim. Our experience with this approach demonstrates that it is well within our competence to employ.

[9] . . . It is possible to distinguish these cases narrowly on their facts, as JUSTICE SCALIA demonstrates. . . [*See* SCALIA opinion at n. 3 — Eds.] But such an approach would mistake the trees for the forest. The truth is that the transient rule as we now conceive it had no clear counterpart at common law. . . .

to the state is so attenuated as to make the exercise of such jurisdiction unreasonable."[11]

By visiting the forum State, a transient defendant actually "avail[s]" himself, *Burger King, supra,* at 476, of significant benefits provided by the State. His health and safety are guaranteed by the State's police, fire, and emergency medical services; he is free to travel on the State's roads and waterways; he likely enjoys the fruits of the State's economy as well. Moreover, the Privileges and Immunities Clause of Article IV prevents a state government from discriminating against a transient defendant by denying him the protections of its law or the right of access to its courts.

The potential burdens on a transient defendant are slight. Finally, any burdens that do arise can be ameliorated by a variety of procedural devices.[13] For these reasons, as a rule the exercise of personal jurisdiction over a defendant based on his voluntary presence in the forum will satisfy the requirements of due process.[14] *See* n. 11, *supra.*

---

[11] As the Restatement suggests, there may be cases in which a defendant's involuntary or unknowing presence in a State does not support the exercise of personal jurisdiction over him. The facts of the instant case do not require us to determine the outer limits of the transient jurisdiction rule.

[13] For example, in the federal system, a transient defendant can avoid protracted litigation of a spurious suit through a motion to dismiss for failure to state a claim or through a motion for summary judgment. Fed. Rules Civ. Proc. 12(b)(6) and 56. He can use relatively inexpensive methods of discovery, such as oral deposition by telephone (Rule 30(b)(7)), deposition upon written questions (Rule 31), interrogatories (Rule 33), and requests for admission (Rule 36), while enjoying protection from harassment (Rule 26(c)), and possibly obtaining costs and attorney's fees for some of the work involved (Rules 37(a)(4), (b)-(d)). Moreover, a change of venue may be possible. 28 U.S.C. § 1404. In state court, many of the same procedural protections are available, as is the doctrine of forum non conveniens, under which the suit may be dismissed. *See generally* Abrams, *Power, Convenience, and the Elimination of Personal Jurisdiction in the Federal Courts,* 58 Ind. L.J. 1, 23-25 (1982).

[14] JUSTICE SCALIA's opinion maintains that, viewing transient jurisdiction as a contractual bargain, the rule is "unconscionabl[e]," *ante,* at 623, according to contemporary conceptions of fairness. But the opinion simultaneously insists that because of its historical "pedigree," the rule is "the very baseline of reasonableness." *Ante,* at 627. Thus is revealed JUSTICE SCALIA's belief that tradition alone is completely dispositive and that no showing of unfairness can ever serve to invalidate a traditional jurisdictional practice. I disagree both with this belief and with JUSTICE SCALIA's assessment of the fairness of the transient jurisdiction bargain.

I note, moreover, that the dual conclusions of JUSTICE SCALIA's opinion create a singularly unattractive result. JUSTICE SCALIA suggests that when and if a jurisdictional rule becomes substantively unfair or even "unconscionable," this Court is powerless to alter it. Instead, he is willing to rely on individual States to limit or abandon bases of jurisdiction that have become obsolete. *See ante,* at 627, and n. 5. This reliance is misplaced, for States have little incentive to limit rules such as transient jurisdiction that make it easier for their own citizens to sue out-of-state defendants. That States are more likely to expand their jurisdiction is illustrated by the adoption by many States of long-arm statutes extending the reach of personal jurisdiction to the limits established by the Federal Constitution. . . . Out-of-staters do not vote in state elections or have a voice in state government. We should not assume, therefore, that States will be motivated by "notions of fairness" to curb jurisdictional rules like the one at issue here. The reasoning of JUSTICE SCALIA's opinion today is strikingly oblivious to the raison d'etre of various constitutional doctrines designed to protect out-of-staters, such as the Art. IV privileges and Immunities Clause and the Commerce Clause.

In this case, it is undisputed that petitioner was served with process while voluntarily and knowingly in the State of California. I therefore concur in the judgment.

NOTES

(1) An extreme example of the exercise of general jurisdiction based on the temporary presence of the defendant is *Grace v. MacArthur*, 170 F. Supp. 442 (E.D. Ark. 1959), in which the defendant was served while in an airplane over Arkansas airspace. Would this be constitutionally valid today?

(2) The implications of *Burnham* are discussed in *The Future of Personal Jurisdiction: A Symposium on* Burnham v. Superior Court, 22 Rutgers L.J. 559 (1991).

(3) An individual may also be subject to jurisdiction because of a fictional presence in New York resulting from activities conducted here on that person's behalf. See *Laufer v. Ostrow*, *infra*, and the notes following it.

HAMMETT v. HAMMETT
Appellate Division, First Department
74 A.D.2d 540, 424 N.Y.S.2d 913 (1980)

MEMORANDUM DECISION.

Order, Family Court, New York County, entered August 27, 1979, denying respondent-appellant's motion to dismiss the petition on the ground of improper service (CPLR 3211[a][8]) is affirmed with costs.

As stated by our dissenting colleagues, petitioner wife and respondent husband are attorneys who, until their separation in March 1979, lived in Philadelphia following their 1973 marriage. After the separation, petitioner moved into a Greenwich Village apartment and respondent remained in Philadelphia. Petitioner claims that the Greenwich Village apartment was used by herself and respondent as an alternate residence throughout their marriage, but respondent claims it was used mostly by petitioner as a place to stay when engaged in her New York law practice. The question presented is whether the affidavits concerning the service on respondent of a summons and support petition, effected at petitioner's Greenwich Village apartment on May 12, 1979, require a hearing to determine whether such service must be vacated.

The general rule is that when a nonresident defendant (or respondent) has been enticed into the jurisdiction by fraud and deceit for the purpose of obtaining service upon him, the service thereby effectuated will be vacated. . . . It is equally well established that if the defendant is not lured into the jurisdiction, but is here of his own free will, the service will not be invalidated merely because it was accomplished through the use of deception. *Gumperz v. Hofmann*, 245 App.Div. 622, 283 N.Y.S.2d 823, *aff'd* 271 N.Y. 544, 2 N.E.2d 687. While the affidavits presented below raise a factual issue whether petitioner used deception to effectuate service, no real issue is raised whether respondent was voluntarily in New York at the time of service, thereby rendering the deception issue academic.

Petitioner's affidavit in opposition to respondent's motion to vacate service relates the substance of a telephone conversation on May 11, 1979 during which petitioner attempted to persuade respondent to end his love affair with a Mrs. Palmer and to effect a reconciliation. Petitioner alleges respondent said "that he was coming into New York this very weekend with Mrs. Palmer and that he would be staying in a hotel in Manhattan but would like very much to meet with me quickly. *I did not, and I emphasize, did not request him to come into the City.*" [emphasis in original]

Respondent's reply affidavit states: "I absolutely did not say that I was coming into New York that very weekend with Mrs. Palmer, nor did I say that I would be staying in a hotel in Manhattan."

Significantly, respondent's carefully worded denial does not in fact put in issue the petitioner's main allegation that respondent intended to come to New York that weekend and told petitioner he intended to do so. Whether respondent's affidavit is deemed a negative pregnant with an admission that he was voluntarily in New York at the time in question (*see* 3 Weinstein-Korn-Miller, N.Y.Civ.Prac., ¶ 3018.07) or whether his affidavit simply fails to place in issue the determinative facts, the result is the same; petitioner's statement that she did not request respondent to come into the city is uncontroverted, and therefore the motion was properly denied. As Mr. Justice Steuer stated in *Freybergh v. Geliebter*, 16 Misc.2d 621 at p. 622, 184 N.Y.S.2d 902 at p. 903: "In no decided case has a defendant who suggested of his own volition that he come into the jurisdiction been successful on this type of motion."

We find it pertinent that respondent acknowledged that during the course of the marriage he spent one weekend per month at the Greenwich Village apartment and on the date of service respondent arrived with an empty suitcase to remove his remaining clothing from the apartment. It is also a fair inference from his affidavits that he came up to New York from time to time during the week on business and social occasions. We need not determine here whether the *Gumperz v. Hofmann* principle is applicable to a nonresident who comes to New York on a regular basis but who on the occasion of the disputed service was induced to enter the jurisdiction by deceptive means. We note only that the aforesaid circumstances lend additional weight to the conclusion here reached from the respondent's failure to dispute that he had come to New York that weekend for personal reasons.

All concur, except FEIN, J.P., and MARKEWICH, J., who dissent in a memorandum by MARKEWICH, J., as follows:

MARKEWICH, JUSTICE, dissenting.

The parties are both attorneys who, until their separation in 1979, had lived in Philadelphia following their 1973 marriage. Indeed, their joint tax returns were filed from there. They also maintained a Manhattan apartment, used from time to time for business visits here, the expense of which constituted a tax deduction. After their separation, petitioner-respondent wife moved into the New York apartment. According to respondent-appellant husband, she telephoned him in Philadelphia to come to the apartment here to discuss a problem. He consented, specifying a Sunday, to which she countered that only the day before would be convenient. He arrived at the apartment as requested and, when his wife opened the door in response to his ring, he was served by a male with Family Court process. The foregoing summarizes respondent-appellant's factual presentation to Family Court on his motion to dismiss for invalid service of process. The wife's claim is that the husband is a dual resident of both states, that there was no need to lure him here because he was here often to service corporate clients, and that, indeed, he used the Manhattan apartment to further romantic adventures, although somewhat incongruously she uses as evidence on this score the matchbook of a hotel claimed by her to have been the scene of assignation.

Two alternative issues of fact are presented: was he a Manhattan resident as to whom the alleged "luring" was irrelevant, or was he brought here on a false representation (Weinstein-Korn-Miller, New York Civil Practice, section 308.10)? The picture is that of a classic traverse, requiring in accordance with ancient New York Law, a hearing as to both described issues. The very recitals in the majority writing emphasize that there is a basic question of fact in this traverse which may not be decided on papers alone. . . .

NOTES

(1) *See also Waljohn Waterstop, Inc. v. Webster*, 37 Misc. 2d 96, 97, 232 N.Y.S.2d 665, 666-67 (Sup. Ct. 1962), in which service was held valid when it was made on a non-resident defendant in New York at the end of a series of negotiations which had fallen through. Defendant unsuccessfully objected to the exercise of jurisdiction on the ground that the negotiations were a sham, set up to entice him into New York. Rejecting this defense, the court said:

> Notwithstanding plaintiff may have intended, in the event negotiations were not successful, to take advantage of defendant's presence in New York to serve process upon him, such intent alone would be insufficient to support defendant's claim of being enticed into this jurisdiction by fraud and deceit. Additionally, the affidavit in opposition to the motion alleges that "the defendant had been told that the plaintiff would sue him if an agreement could not be reached." Defendant has not denied this statement was made.

Compare Olean Street Ry. Co. v. Fairmount Constr. Co., 55 App. Div. 292, 67 N.Y.S. 165 (4th Dep't 1900) (finding that no jurisdiction was obtained when defendant's president was served while in New York for negotiations at plaintiff's suggestion; service was made soon after the negotiation started).

Some federal district courts have applied a per se rule under which a defendant who is in the jurisdiction for settlement negotiations at the behest of the plaintiff is immune from service. For example, one opinion states, "The better rule is a flat prohibition on service unless the plaintiff *warns* the defendant before he enters the jurisdiction that he may subject himself to process, or else when settlement talks fail the plaintiff must give the defendant *an opportunity to leave the jurisdiction* before service is made." *K Mart Corp. v. Gen-Star Industries Co.*, 110 F.R.D. 310, 313 (E.D. Mich. 1986) (emphasis in original). The court articulates a desire to eliminate investigation into the sequence of events and the parties' motives. Moreover, the rule affords both sides the opportunity to participate with good faith in settlement negotiations while simultaneously distancing the court from the stench of possible chicanery. Is the federal rule preferable to New York's?

(2) What advice should you give a client who has been asked to go to another state in order to discuss a conflict with a potential adversary? *Patino v. Patino*, 283 App. Div. 630, 129 N.Y.S.2d 333 (1st Dep't), *appeal dismissed*, 307 N.Y. 910 (1954), held that a non-resident voluntarily in New York pursuant to a litigation "armistice" with his estranged wife could not properly be served until the period agreed to had ended.

MERIGONE v. SEABOARD CAPITAL CORP.
Supreme Court, Nassau County
85 Misc. 2d 965, 381 N.Y.S.2d 749 (1976)

BERTRAM HARNETT, JUSTICE.

Time and again we are reminded that a lawsuit is not a game. It is a serious enterprise, where the social end of justice preponderates. Yet we do have procedural rules which may serve proper purposes in the doing of justice. How to separate the game from the juridical purpose?

Here we have an action on a $15,000 promissory note payable on demand after December 30, 1966. . . .

Shwidock's primary defense is that the Court lacks personal jurisdiction because his summons was improperly served upon him.

The summons was served on Shwidock personally on April 4, 1973 when he was a resident of New Jersey. The summons was served while he was in New York voluntarily attending a traverse hearing in a previous action based on this same note. That action was dismissed as to Shwidock as a result of the hearing because of previous defective service.

qu he

Under most general circumstances, New York exempts from service of civil process a non-resident party or witness who comes to the state voluntarily to attend court. This rule allows non-residents to participate in New York trials without fear that they are subjecting themselves to other lawsuits here. It is calculated "to encourage voluntary attendance upon courts and to expedite the administration of justice." *Netograph Manufacturing Co. v. Scrugham*, 197 N.Y. 377, 380, 90 N.E. 962, 963.

However, this cloak of immunity does not cover Bernard Shwidock in this case. . . . An out-of-stater who is otherwise readily amenable to service does not need this rule to encourage his in-state appearance, and so he cannot claim its protection. . . .

In this case, Shwidock could have been served anywhere, and the Court would have obtained jurisdiction over him pursuant to CPLR 302(a)(1). New York's long arm statute gives jurisdiction over nondomiciliaries for actions arising out of business they transact here. . . . The transaction in question was totally New York contacted. Under CPLR 302(a)(1), this suit could have been commenced by appropriate service anywhere.

Since Shwidock was as exposed to this summons while at home in New Jersey as he was coming to court in New York, no purpose would be served by granting him immunity for the trip. . . . In fact, to rule otherwise would give us the absurd result that on this particular day, Shwidock could be served anywhere in the world except inside New York.

Moreover, Shwidock claims to have been employed in New York City and physically present in New York State every business day. It would be patently unjust to suggest that a man who came to New York almost daily should have special immunity on the particular day that he happened to be coming here for court instead of work. . . . No sensible purpose would be served by invoking such a special judicial rule of immunity. . . .

    . . . .

NOTES

(1) The immunity from service accorded litigants voluntarily in New York to attend litigation extends to plaintiffs as well as to defendants and witnesses, *see Chauvin v. Dayon*, 14 A.D.2d 146, 217 N.Y.S.2d 795 (3d Dep't 1961), and cases cited. But, under CPLR 303, the commencement of an action in New York serves as a jurisdictional basis for any action brought subsequently against the plaintiff by anyone who is a party to the first action. Moreover, any defendant in the first action may assert a counterclaim against the plaintiff simply by including it in the answer and serving it on the plaintiff's attorney. CPLR 2103(b); 3012(a). Can you think of any situation in which a plaintiff might wish to use the immunity rule as a shield?

(2) Service of a summons is invalid if made on a Sunday. This is true regardless of the defendant's religious beliefs. *See* Gen. Bus. Law § 11. *But see* Jud. Law § 5, which allows Sunday service by court order in a few unusual situations. Service on a sabbatarian on Saturday is likewise void (as well as being a misdemeanor) but only if done with malice. *See* Gen. Bus. Law § 13.

[B] Presence of Partnerships and Unincorporated Associations

PROBLEM B

Suppose that at the meeting described in Problem A, it was Bob who handed Paul a summons. It named Acme, Inc. as the plaintiff and, as defendants, each of the following: Paul, P & P (the partnership) and Peter (another general partner who resides in Massachusetts but who was not present at the negotiations). Has jurisdiction been acquired over any of the defendants?

FIRST AMERICAN CORP. v. PRICE WATERHOUSE LLP
United States Court of Appeals, Second Circuit
154 F.3d 16 (1998)

JACOBS, J.

This appeal . . . reviews orders of the United States District Court for the Southern District of New York enforcing a non-party witness subpoena against a United Kingdom accounting partnership, and finding the firm in contempt for failure to comply.

In the several years leading up to the collapse of the Bank of Commerce and Credit International ("BCCI"), Price Waterhouse United Kingdom Firm ("PW-UK") was its worldwide auditor. In accordance with its normal practice, PW-UK was assisted in these audits by Price Waterhouse partnerships in other countries . . . . Two companies alleged to have been acquired surreptitiously by BCCI - First American Corporation and First American Bankshares ("First American") — commenced an action relating to the BCCI debacle in the United States District Court for the District of Columbia . . . . In aid of discovery in its District of Columbia action, First American sought a subpoena pursuant to Fed. R. Civ. P. 45 from the United States District Court for the Southern District of New York, directing, inter alia, that PW-UK produce what PW-UK represents to be a great quantity of documents. Judge Sweet [the Federal District judge] concluded that jurisdiction over PW-UK is well-founded because that partnership "does business" in New York, within the meaning of N.Y. C.P.L.R. 301, through the affiliated partnership of PW-US.

On appeal, PW-UK argues that (1) PW-UK is not "doing business" in New York, because PW-US is not its agent, is a distinct entity, and lacks power to bind PW-UK; [and] (2) the exercise of personal jurisdiction over PW-UK violates due process . . . .

. . . .

In September 1996, First American served a subpoena for documents on "Price Waterhouse," which was defined to include Price Waterhouse (U.K.) . . . . Only PW-US responded to the subpoena . . . .

In August 1997, First American served three copies of a new document subpoena seeking production of documents from "Price Waterhouse, the worldwide accounting firm." Again, that term was expressly defined to include PW-UK. One copy was served in New York on the Manhattan office of PW-US. The other two were addressed to "Price Waterhouse c/o Clive D.J. Newton," and served on Mr. Newton, a PW-UK partner who had been seconded to PW-US, worked out of the Manhattan office of PW-US, and was living in Connecticut. Mr. Newton was served with one copy at his home in Connecticut and the other at the PW-US office in New York. Once again, the only response was by PW-US, which refused to produce any documents of the so-called "worldwide accounting firm," or the constituent parts identified in the subpoena definitions.

. . . .

First American filed a Petition to Compel in the district court on September 29, 1997. On December 17, 1997, Judge Sweet found that PW-UK's coordinated activities with and through PW-US in New York were sufficient to sustain jurisdiction. The court found that the subpoena served upon Newton in Connecticut did not confer jurisdiction upon a court in New York, and indicated that in any event due process would not be satisfied even if the subpoena had been served upon Newton in New York . . . .

On January 7, 1998, PW-US and PW-UK moved for reconsideration. The district court made additional findings that PW-UK was doing business in New York at the jurisdictionally significant time (that is, at the time the subpoena was served, *cf. Darby v. Compagnie National Air France*, 735 F. Supp. 555, 560 (S.D.N.Y. 1990) (finding relevant time for jurisdictional purposes to be when complaint is filed)), and again ordered PW-UK to produce the requested documents.

On April 3, 1998, Judge Sweet found that PW-UK was in contempt of court for its failure to comply with the subpoena, and ordered it to pay $1,000 per day as a sanction, but (upon the parties' stipulation) stayed the sanction pending appeal.

We affirmed on June 23, 1998, with opinion to follow, and now explain our reasons.

A

The district court focused the personal jurisdiction inquiry on whether PW-UK, acting through the affiliated partnership of PW-US, "does business" in New York within the meaning of N.Y. C.P.L.R. 301. This is a vexed question, which turns in part on the complex, possibly unique, and sharply disputed issue of how the Price Waterhouse accounting firms around the world relate to each other. We do not reach that question, because we see a more straightforward avenue to the exercise of personal jurisdiction over PW-UK. Section 310(a) of the C.P.L.R. provides that:

"Personal service upon persons conducting a business as a partnership may be made by personally serving the summons upon any one of them." N.Y. C.P.L.R. 310(a) (McKinney Supp. 1997-98).

One commentator has pointed out the absence of any additional requirement that a partnership be doing business in New York, and attributes that omission to the fact that a partnership (unlike a corporation) has no separate existence. Joseph M. McLaughlin, N.Y. C.P.L.R. 310, Practice Commentaries, at 371 (McKinney 1990). Section 310 thus telescopes service and personal jurisdiction into a single inquiry. If valid service is effected on one partner within the state, personal jurisdiction over the partnership is achieved. *See Cooper v. Lubell*, 1987 U.S. Dist. LEXIS 6242, No. 83 Civ. 2506, at 2 (S.D.N.Y. July 13, 1987) (noting that service upon a partner confers personal jurisdiction over the partnership and each partner served).

There is no dispute that Mr. Newton was a partner in PW-UK in August 1997. And the undisputed June 11, 1998 affidavit shows that Mr. Newton was served by hand in New York at that time. These facts suffice to confer personal jurisdiction over PW-UK.

PW-UK argues that New York law provides for jurisdiction over a partnership by service on a partner only in the partner's state of residence; because Mr. Newton was a Connecticut resident (although concededly working in New York on a daily basis), PW-UK argues that service upon him in either state cannot subject PW-UK to personal jurisdiction in New York. However, the cases cited by PW-UK, *ITC Entertainment, Ltd. v. Nelson Film Partners*, 714 F.2d 217, 222 n.5 (2d Cir. 1983) and *Bulkley v. O'Donnell*, 148 Misc. 186, 187, 265 N.Y.S. 495, 496 (Sup. Ct. Albany Cty.), *aff'd*, 240 A.D. 929, 267 N.Y.S. 983 (3d Dep't 1933), address the residency of a partner (and thus the residency of the partnership) for purposes of C.P.L.R. 308 — a section which presumes an independent basis of jurisdiction and merely concerns the giving of notice to a defendant — and not where or how a partnership can be served under C.P.L.R. 310. Moreover, C.P.L.R. 308 provides that sufficient notice is supplied by service upon an individual within New York . . . . Under the circumstances, we do not think PW-UK can reasonably contend that it was oblivious to the fact that it was a target of the subpoena.

B

The district court focused on the subpoena that was served on Mr. Newton in Connecticut, while we focus on the subpoena served on him in New York. We respectfully disagree with the district court's observation that even if service had been accomplished in New York, such service would not comport with due process, because maintenance of the suit would offend "traditional notions of fair play and substantial justice." *International Shoe Co. v. Washington*, 326 U.S. 310, 316, 66 S. Ct. 154, 158, 90 L. Ed. 95 (1945) (internal quotation marks and citations omitted).

We are satisfied that in light of *Burnham v. Superior Court*, 495 U.S. 604, 110 S. Ct. 2105, 109 L. Ed. 2d 631 (1990), the assertion of personal jurisdiction over PW-UK based upon service pursuant to C.P.L.R. 310 satisfies due process. In *Burnham*, the Supreme Court rejected a due process challenge to the assertion of personal jurisdiction over a New Jersey resident who was temporarily in California in connection with activities unrelated to the suit. *Id.* . . .

PW-UK argues that *Burnham* should be distinguished on the grounds that PW-UK is a non-U.S. citizen and is a non-party to the underlying suit. We see no reason for such per se distinctions. PW-UK is a non-party, but it is unclear which way that should cut; a person who is subjected to liability by service of process far from home may have better cause to complain of an outrage to fair play than one similarly situated who is merely called upon to supply documents or testimony. Further, although a non-party, PW-UK's position as auditor gave it unique access to documents that may be critical in unraveling a bank fraud of unprecedented scale and, perhaps, a correspondingly unique responsibility. At the risk of sounding naive, we think PW-UK could be expected to feel a professional commitment to clearing up the financial frauds that were committed by PW-UK's client and that presumably escaped PW-UK's scrutiny.

. . . .

PW-UK thus fails to distinguish *Burnham*; indeed, Burnham had less reason to expect suit in California than PW-UK had to expect that Newton's presence would subject it to suit in New York. Burnham was briefly in California, mixing pleasure with a business mission unrelated to the subject of the summons. Mr. Newton was in New York working on a prolonged assignment for an affiliated partnership, having been seconded to do so by the PW-UK partnership of which he is a member. And the U.S. affiliate for which Mr. Newton was working had audited BCCI's U.S. subsidiaries (a class to which First American allegedly belonged, although its ownership had been concealed) to assist PW-UK in the preparation of consolidated financial statements.

The rule that service upon a partner in New York subjects a partnership to personal jurisdiction is a venerable one. PW-UK knew, or should have known, that by seconding one of its partners to the New York office of an affiliate, PW-UK was risking exposure to personal jurisdiction in New York. *See Burnham*, 495 U.S. at 635, 110 S. Ct. at 2124 (historical pedigree of transient jurisdiction provides a defendant voluntarily present in a particular state with "'clear notice that he is subject to suit' in the forum") (quoting *World-Wide Volkswagen Corp. v. Woodson*, 444 U.S. 286, 297, 100 S. Ct. 559, 567, 62 L. Ed. 2d 490 (1980)) (alterations omitted). Under the circumstances, due process is not offended by the enforcement of the Rule 45 subpoena against PW-UK.

. . . .

The district court's orders are affirmed.

NOTES

(1) In answering Problem B, consider CPLR 1501, 1502 and 5201(b) in addition to the principal case and CPLR 310. As to Peter, the "absent" partner, see *Levin v. Total Hockey Associates*, 64 A.D.2d 622, 406 N.Y.S.2d 554 (2d Dep't 1978) (individually owned property of general partners who were not parties to the action against the partnership could not be reached; partnership assets distinguished).

(2) The principal case demonstrates that jurisdiction can be acquired over a partnership when a partner is served in New York, even if the partner is not a resident or domiciliary. *See also Equitable Trust Co. v. Halim*, 133 Misc. 678, 234 N.Y.S. 37 (Sup. Ct. 1929), in which the partner served was only temporarily in New York and the partnership was doing business in India, yet the court upheld jurisdiction. At odds with this New York rule is the position of the Restatement (Second) of Conflict of Laws § 40, comment (b) (1971), which would not allow the mere presence of a partner to serve as a basis for jurisdiction over the partnership.

(3) CPLR 310 was amended in 1991 to add subdivisions (b)-(e), which allow methods of serving partnerships in addition to serving one of the partners personally. CPLR 310(a) still allows the summons to be served personally on any partner but, as amended in 1991, no longer requires the service to be made "within the state." How could jurisdiction be obtained if service is made without the state?

(4) CPLR 310-a (added in 1999), specifies the methods of serving a limited partnership. Note that it does not authorize service on a limited partner. *See also* Partnership Law § 115 (only general partners are proper parties to an action by or against a partnership).

(5) Domestic limited partnerships and foreign limited partnerships that are authorized to do business in New York are subject to personal jurisdiction in New York pursuant to the Revised Limited Partnership Act. Section 121-104 of the Act requires all such limited partnerships to designate the Secretary of State of New York as their agent for the service of process. Service may also be made on such partnerships by "delivering a copy [of the legal process] personally to any managing or general agent or general partner of the limited part-

nership in this state, or the registered agent of the limited partnership in this state . . . ." *Id.*, § 121-109(a). These methods of service are not exclusive. *See id.*, § 121-109(e).

(6) An action may be commenced against an unincorporated association in accordance with Gen. Ass'ns Law § 13, which provides:

> An action or special proceeding may be maintained, against the president or treasurer of such an association, to recover any property, or upon any cause of action, for or upon which the plaintiff may maintain such an action or special proceeding, against all the associates, by reason of their interest or ownership, or claim of ownership therein, either jointly or in common, or their liability therefore, either jointly or severally. Any partnership, or other company of persons, which has a president or treasurer, is deemed an association within the meaning of this section.
>
> The service of summons, subpoena or other legal process of any court upon the president, vice president, treasurer, assistant treasurer, secretary, assistant secretary, or business agent, in his capacity as such, shall constitute service upon a labor organization. Such service shall be made on such individuals in the manner provided by law for the service of a summons on a natural person.

An unincorporated association is, under traditional New York jurisdictional doctrine, "present" in the state if one of the officers upon whom service can be made pursuant to Gen. Ass'ns Law § 13 is found within the state. As one court said: "There is no requirement in section 13 that the individuals sued in their representative capacities must be residents of this State or that the association which they represent must be doing business in this State." *Gross v. Cross*, 28 Misc. 2d 375, 377, 211 N.Y.S.2d 279, 281 (Sup. Ct. 1961).

(7) In 1994, the legislature authorized the formation of a new form for business and professional service organizations by enacting the "Limited Liability Company Law" as Chapter 34 of the Consolidated Laws. A domestic limited liability company is defined as "an unincorporated organization of one or more persons having limited liability for the contractual obligations and other liabilities of the business . . . other than a partnership or trust, formed and existing under this chapter [chapter 34 of the consolidated laws] and the laws of the state." Limited Liability Company Law § 102(m).

Service of process on limited liability companies is provided for in Limited Liability Company Law § 303. It creates a jurisdictional basis over domestic limited liability companies and foreign limited liability companies that are authorized to do business in New York and provides for proper methods of service.

[C] Presence of Corporations

One does not have to believe that corporations are to blame for society's problems, or think ill of the persons who (in the popular but overstated expression) "run them," to be concerned about corporate accountability. Public focus is justified, if only by the increasing importance of corporations in our lives. More and more, it is they, and perhaps an increasingly concentrated group of them, who produce, pollute, distribute, invest, swindle, and farm. And to whom else do we look to plumb — and market — the mysteries of the human cell? In this setting, the success of the law as a social instrument — deterring, rehabilitating, securing effective compensation for victims, educating citizens between right and wrong — turns upon its capacity to deal with the corporation as a basic unit of communal activity.[*]

Christopher D. Stone, *The Place of Enterprise Liability in the Control of Corporate Conduct*, 90 Yale L.J. 1 (1980) (footnotes omitted).

One method of making corporations accountable for their behavior is to subject them to civil liability when they behave unlawfully. But civil liability is dependent first of all on a basis for the exercise of jurisdiction over the defendant. A corporate defendant may be subject to jurisdiction under any of several doctrines. If it is a "domestic" corporation, *i.e.*, has been incorporated in this state, then it has appointed the Secretary of State as its agent for the service of process pursuant to § 304(b) of the Bus. Corp. Law ("B.C.L.") (the mechanics of which are treated in Chapter 5 *infra*) and there need be no further search for a jurisdictional basis[**].

A "foreign" (*i.e.*, other than domestic) corporation that has obtained authorization to do business here will also necessarily have designated the Secretary of State as its agent for the service of process. *See* B.C.L. § 304(b). This designation has been held to be the equivalent of consent to the exercise of general jurisdiction. *Augsbury v. Petrokey*, 97 A.D.2d 173, 470 N.Y.S.2d 787 (3d Dep't 1983); *accord Laumann Mfg. Corp. v. Casting USA*, 913 F. Supp. 712 (E.D.N.Y. 1996). Some recent decisions, however, have questioned this view, holding that under the federal Due Process Clause, designations of this kind are not sufficient to justify the exercise of jurisdiction over the corporation in the absence of other contacts with the state. *Metropolitan Life Insurance Company v. Robertson-Ceco Corp.*, 84 F.3d 560 (2d Cir. 1996) (Vermont did not have jurisdiction over a foreign corporation that had registered to do business there); *Wenche*

---

[*] Reprinted by permission of the Yale L.J. Company, Fred B. Rothman & Company, and the author, © 1980.

[**] Bus. Corp. Law § 102(4) defines "domestic corporation" as "a corporation for profit formed under this chapter, or existing on its effective date. . . ." Similar service of process provisions apply to authorized foreign corporations which were not formed for profit. *See* Not-For-Profit Corporation Law § 306. *C.f.*, CPLR 105(h), defining "domestic" and "foreign" corporations for the purposes of the CPLR.

Siemer v. Learjet Acquisition Corp., 966 F.2d 179 (5th Cir. 1992) (same result under Texas registration statute); *Cognitronics Imaging Sys. v. Recognition Research Inc.*, 83 F. Supp. 2d 689 (E.D. Va. 2000) (listing cases on both sides of the issue); *see* discussion in Vincent Alexander, *"Doing Business" Jurisdiction: Some Unresolved Issues*, N.Y.L.J., Mar. 29, 2001, p. 3.

Still more difficult problems arise when the plaintiff seeks to sue a foreign corporation which has not obtained authorization or has not otherwise consented to be sued in New York. Two very different doctrines may provide a jurisdictional basis in such case. One, which we mention here but put aside for the moment, depends on a showing that the plaintiff's claim arises out of a particular corporate contact with the state. This is "specific" or "long arm" jurisdiction and is covered by CPLR 302. The second doctrine, treated in the following pages, is that of corporate presence, which yields "general" jurisdiction: If the corporation is, as a matter of law, present in New York, then it may be sued here on any claim, whether or not the claim is related to the particular activity which constitutes the corporate presence. But what does it mean to be "present"? Problem C presents one version of the question.

PROBLEM C

International Conglomerate, Inc. (ICI) is a Japanese corporation which manufactures robots for household use and sells them throughout the world. It has no office in the United States but its employees make occasional visits to California, where they consult with California Conglomerates, Inc. (CalCon), a wholly owned subsidiary of ICI. CalCon purchases products from ICI and then sells them to local retailers. In charge of wholesale selling for CalCon in New York is Susan, who has the title "Eastern Sales Chief." She is not a CalCon employee but rather is a sales agent for a variety of manufacturers. She works on a commission basis and has her own sales staff working for her. All sales prices are set by CalCon, although Susan can reduce prices if she absorbs the cost out of her own commissions. As CalCon usually has a large inventory, it ships to New York purchasers within 10 days of receiving a purchase order from Susan. Last year CalCon sold several million dollars worth of products through Susan's efforts.

Fred, a lifelong New York resident, was injured in Boston by a moody ICI robot which had been sold to CalCon by ICI and then to a Boston emporium. May Fred properly commence an action against CalCon in New York? Against ICI?

TAUZA v. SUSQUEHANNA COAL CO.
Court of Appeals
220 N.Y. 259, 115 N.E. 915 (1917)

CARDOZO, J.

The plaintiff, a resident of this state, has brought suit against the Susque-hanna Coal Company, a Pennsylvania corporation. The defendant's principal office is in Philadelphia; but it has a branch office in New York, which is in charge of one Peterson. Peterson's duties are described by the defendant as those of a sales agent. He has eight salesmen under him, who are subject to his orders. A suite of offices is maintained in the Equitable Building in the city of New York, and there the sales agent and his subordinates make their head-quarters. The sign on the door is "Susquehanna Coal Company, Walter Peter-son, sales agent." The offices contain eleven desks and other suitable equipment. In addition to the salesmen there are other employees, presumably stenogra-phers and clerks. The salesmen meet daily and receive instructions from their superior. All sales in New York are subject, however, to confirmation by the home office in Philadelphia. The duty of Peterson and his subordinates is to pro-cure orders which are not binding until approved. All payments are made by cus-tomers to the treasurer in Philadelphia; the salesmen are without authority to receive or indorse checks. A bank account in the name of the company is kept in New York, and is subject to Peterson's control, but the payments made from it are for the salaries of employees, and for petty cash disbursements inciden-tal to the maintenance of the office. The defendant's coal yards are in Pennsyl-vania, and from there its shipments are made. They are made in response to orders transmitted from customers in New York. They are made, not on isolated occasions, but as part of an established course of business. In brief, the defen-dant maintains an office in this state under the direction of a sales agent, with eight salesmen, and with clerical assistants, and through these agencies sys-tematically and regularly solicits and obtains orders which result in continuous shipments from Pennsylvania to New York.

To do these things is to do business within this state in such a sense and in such a degree as to subject the corporation doing them to the jurisdiction of our courts. The decision of the Supreme Court in *International Harvester Co. v. Kentucky* (234 U.S. 579) is precisely applicable. There sales agents in Kentucky solicited orders subject to approval of a general agent in the home state. They did this, not casually and occasionally, but systematically and regularly. Unlike the defendant's salesmen, they did not have an office to give to their activities a fixed and local habitation. The finding was that travelers negotiating sales were not to have any headquarters or place of business in that state, though they were permitted to reside there (234 U.S. at p. 584). Yet because their activ-ities were systematic and regular, the corporation was held to have been brought within Kentucky, and, therefore, to be subject to the process of the Kentucky courts. "Here," said the court (p. 585), "was a continuous course of business in the solicitation of orders which were sent to another State and in response to which the machines of the Harvester Company were delivered within the State of Kentucky. This was a course of business, not a single transaction." That case goes farther than we need to go to sustain the service here. It distinguishes *Green v. Chicago, B. & Q. Ry. Co.* (205 U.S. 530) where an agent in Pennsylvania solicited orders for railroad tickets which were sold, delivered and used in Illinois. The orders did not result in a continuous course of shipments from Illinois to Pennsylvania. The activities of the ticket agent in Pennsylvania brought nothing into that state. In the case at bar, as in the *International Harvester* case, there has been a steady course of shipments from one state into the other. The business done in New York may be interstate business, but business it surely is.

. . . We are to say, not whether the business is such that the corporation may be prevented from being here, but whether its business is such that it is here. If in fact it is here, if it is here, not occasionally or casually, but with a fair measure of permanence and continuity, then, whether its business is interstate or local, it is within the jurisdiction of our courts. . . .

Unless a foreign corporation is engaged in business within the state, it is not brought within the state by the presence of its agents. But there is no precise test of the nature or extent of the business that must be done. All that is requisite is that enough be done to enable us to say that the corporation is here. . . .

We hold, then, that the defendant corporation is engaged in business within this state. We hold further that the jurisdiction does not fail because the cause of action sued upon has no relation in its origin to the business here transacted. . . . The essential thing is that the corporation shall have come into the state. When once it is here, it may be served; and the validity of the service is independent of the origin of the cause of action. It is not necessary to show that express authority to accept service was given to the defendant's agent. His appointment to act as agent within the state carried with it implied authority to exercise the powers which under our laws attach to his position. . . . The corporation is here; it is here in the person of an agent of its own selection; and service upon him is service upon his principal.

. . . .

NOTES

(1) A classic statement of the issues raised by the corporate presence doctrine is found in *International Shoe Co. v. Washington*, 326 U.S. 310, 66 S. Ct. 154 (1945):

> Since the corporate personality is a fiction . . . it is clear that unlike an individual its "presence" without, as well as within, the state of its origin can be manifested only by activities carried on in its behalf by those who are authorized to act for it. . . . For the terms "present" or "presence"

are used merely to symbolize those activities of the corporation's agent within the state which courts will deem to be sufficient to satisfy the demands of due process. L. Hand, J. in *Hutchinson v. Chase & Gilbert*, 45 F.2d 139, 141. Those demands may be met by such contacts of the corporation with the state of the forum as make it reasonable, in the context of our federal system of government, to require the corporation to defend the particular suit which is brought there. An "estimate of the inconveniences" which would result to the corporation from a trial away from its "home" or principal business is rendered in this connection. . . .

(2) The principal case finds it significant that the activities of the defendant's New York agent resulted in a flow of goods from Pennsylvania (the defendant's home state) to New York. Was that fact critical to the decision? Would it be critical today?

BRYANT v. FINNISH NATIONAL AIRLINE
Court of Appeals
15 N.Y.2d 426, 260 N.Y.S.2d 625, 208 N.E.2d 439 (1965)

CHIEF JUDGE DESMOND.

. . . Plaintiff is a resident of New York. The complaint in this suit alleges that at an airport in Paris plaintiff, an employee of Trans World Airlines, was injured through the negligence of defendant Finnish National Airline when she was struck by a baggage cart blown against her by an excessive blast of air produced by one of defendant's aircraft which was moving across the airfield to a parking spot. The question is whether within the statute and cases defendant was "doing business" in New York State so as to subject it to personal jurisdiction here. . . .

The Appellate Division . . . summarized the facts: "The defendant is a foreign corporation organized under the laws of Finland, with its principal operating base, its head executive and administrative offices located in Helsinki, Finland, and is not registered in the United States. None of its stockholders, directors or officers are citizens or residents of the United States and defendant has not qualified to do business in the State of New York. All of Finnair's flights begin and end outside of the United States. It operates no aircraft within the United States and . . . the office in New York does not sell tickets even for its own flights and receives no payment of fares for defendant's flights at its New York office. Defendant maintains a one and a half-room office at 10 East 40th Street, New York, staffed with three full-time and four part-time employees, none of whom is an officer or director of defendant. Its principal function is to receive from international air carriers or travel agencies reservations for travel on Finnair in Europe which it transmits to defendant's space control office in Europe. Upon occasion the New York office will transmit information concerning a reservation from the international air carrier or travel agency to defendant's space control office in Europe and relay the confirmation or reply, when received, to such airline or agency. The New York office does some information and publicity work for defendant, and places a certain amount of advertising regarding Finnair's European services in connection with its publicity work. None of the New York office employees has authority to bind the defendant and contracts in connection with such office activities must be sent to the office in Helsinki for approval. Finnair maintains a bank account in which . . . the average balance is less than $2,000 and out of which is paid the salaries of the employees, the rent and normal operating expenses of the New York office . . . ."

The majority opinion [of the Appellate Division] discussed a number of decisions and elicited from them the rule that a foreign corporation in order to be subject to jurisdiction must transact, with a fair measure of continuity and regularity, a reasonable amount of business within this state . . . .

Miller v. Surf Props. (4 N.Y.2d 475, *supra*) was a suit against a Florida hotel and plaintiff's effort was to get service on it by delivering a summons to a member of a New York City partnership which represented in New York City a number of out-of-State hotels including defendant's and which by telephone listing and otherwise held itself out to be the New York office of defendant. The activities of the agency included taking reservations for rooms in the hotel which reservations were subject to acceptance by the hotel. We tried to make it clear in the *Miller* opinion that solicitation of prospective customers and the reception and transmission of hotel reservations did not constitute doing business. However, it must be kept in mind that the person attempted to be served in *Miller* was not an employee of the defendant but an independent travel agency representing defendant in New York City. . . .

. . . .

. . . The test for "doing business" is and should be a simple pragmatic one, which leads us to the conclusion that defendant should be held to be suable in New York. The New York office is one of many directly maintained by defendant in various parts of the world, it has a lease on a New York office, it employs several people and it has a bank account here, it does public relations and publicity work for defendant here including maintaining contacts with other airlines and travel agencies and, while it does not make reservations or sell tickets, it transmits requests for space to defendant in Europe and helps to generate business. These things should be enough.

. . . .

NOTES

(1) What is the "simple pragmatic test" under which the Court of Appeals determined that the defendant was "doing business" in New York and therefore present here for jurisdictional purposes?

(2) To the degree that the principal case does establish a simple pragmatic test, it rests on the defendant's maintenance of an office in the state continuously staffed by its employees. It is clear after *Bryant* that such presence will be enough. At the other extreme, it is also clear that periodic visits to the state by corporate employees or officers engaged in corporate business do not amount to presence. See, for example, the *Helicopteros* case reprinted in § 1.03[C] *infra*; *Fontanetta v. American Board of Internal Medicine*, 421 F.2d 355 (2d Cir. 1970) (Iowa corporation which periodically administered medical board exams in New York held not "doing business" in New York); *compare Erving v. Virginia Squires Basketball Club*, 349 F. Supp. 709 (E.D.N.Y. 1972), *aff'd*, 468 F.2d 1064 (2d Cir. 1972) (regular visits for games by professional basketball team which belonged to a league with headquarters in New York amounted to doing business in New York).

(3) It is emphatically clear that jurisdiction is not acquired over a foreign corporation simply because the summons is served on its president or other officer while in the state. *See Dollar Co. v. Canadian Car & Foundry Co.*, 220 N.Y. 270, 115 N.E. 711 (1917). As far as jurisdictional *basis* is concerned, the "presence" of a corporation does not follow its officers about, notwithstanding that *notice* for jurisdictional purposes may be given to the corporation by serving an officer. CPLR 311.

(4) In the preceding two cases (*Tauza* and *Bryant*), the defendant foreign corporation maintained a staffed office in the state. Is this a *sine qua non* of "presence"?

(5) The most difficult "doing business" cases which arise in current litigation are those in which the foreign defendant has major interests in New York which are served by a nominally independent but related entity, such as a subsidiary. The cases that follow are illustrative. Consider both the state law definition of the "doing business" test and the constitutional issues raised in the *Helicopteros* case, *infra*.

DELAGI v. VOLKSWAGENWERK AG OF WOLFSBURG, GERMANY
Court of Appeals
29 N.Y.2d 426, 328 N.Y.S.2d 653, 278 N.E.2d 895 (1972)

JASEN, J.

This action, based on negligence and breach of warranty, comes to us in the pleadings stage for a determination as to whether jurisdiction was validly acquired over the defendant, Volkswagenwerk AG of Wolfsburg, Germany, a German corporation, hereinafter referred to as VWAG.

The plaintiff in his complaint alleges that, in 1965, he purchased a Volkswagen automobile from an authorized Volkswagen dealer in Germany. While operating said vehicle in Germany, plaintiff claims that "the front wheel suspension and its appurtenant parts broke and collapsed, causing the front wheels to cave in and the motor vehicle to run out of control and hit a bridge abutment with such force as to cause [him] serious injuries."

Upon his return to the United States, plaintiff brought suit in New York against VWAG, alleging that "the defendant transacted sufficient of its business within the State of New York to subject itself to the jurisdiction of the courts of this State." Service of process was made on the defendant, pursuant to CPLR 313, in Germany.

The following facts are not in dispute. Defendant, VWAG, a German corporation, manufactures and sells, in Germany, Volkswagen automobiles and parts. VWAG has never qualified to do business in New York and has no office or place of business here. VWAG exports its automobiles into the United States through Volkswagen of America, Inc. (VWoA), a New Jersey corporation, which is a wholly owned subsidiary of VWAG[1] and the exclusive American importer of Volkswagen automobiles. Likewise, VWoA has never qualified to do business in New York and has no office or place of business here. After these cars arrive in the United States at various ports, none of which are in New York, they are resold to 14 wholesale distributors franchised by VWoA. These distributors take title to the vehicles at the delivery point and, in turn, reship the cars to local independent franchised dealers. In New York State, the franchised wholesale distributor is World-Wide Volkswagen Corp. (World-Wide). The entire capital stock of World-Wide and its New York franchised dealers is owned by United States investors unrelated to either VWoA or VWAG.

Plaintiff does not claim that his cause of action arose from the German corporation's direct transaction of any business in New York in order to bring the defendant within the jurisdiction of our courts pursuant to CPLR 302 (subd. [a], par. 1), but argues that jurisdiction was properly acquired over the defendant VWAG because it is "engaged in a systematic and regular course of business" in New York which subjects it to our jurisdiction pursuant to CPLR 301.

Our most recent pronouncement in this area of the law, *Frummer v. Hilton Hotels Int.* . . . , reiterated the rule that a foreign corporation is amenable to suit in our courts if it is engaged in such a continuous and systematic course of "doing business" in New York as to warrant a finding of its "presence" in this jurisdiction. *Frummer* held that Hilton (U.K.) was "doing business" in New York in the "traditional sense" because of services performed — specifically publicity work and the making of final room reservations — by the Hilton Reservation Service as agent for Hilton (U.K.). The affiliate relationship exist-

---

[1] The relationship between VWAG and VWoA is governed by a written agreement, designated "Exclusive Importer Agreement," which states in pertinent part:

Exclusive Importer [VWoA] will transact all business pursuant to this Agreement on its own behalf and for its own account; it has no power or authority whatsoever to act as agent or otherwise for or on account or on behalf of VW [VWAG].

ing between the Reservation Service and Hilton (U.K.)[2] was significant only as it gave rise to an inference of an agency relationship. This "valid inference" may not, however, extend the actual scope of the agency.[3] "The 'presence' of Hilton (U.K.) in New York," Chief Judge Fuld wrote, "for purposes of jurisdiction, is established by the activities conducted here on its behalf by its agent, the Hilton Reservation Service, and the fact that the two are commonly owned is significant only because it gives rise to a valid inference as to the broad scope of the agency in the absence of an express agency agreement such as the one which existed in the *Berner* case (3 N Y 2d 1003, *supra*) . . . ."

In the case before us, however, the undisputed facts do not give rise to a valid inference of agency. Concededly, World-Wide is an independently owned corporation, in no way directly related to VWAG, and related to VWoA only by way of a "Distributor Agreement." Under this agreement, World-Wide purchases Volkswagen automobiles and parts outright from VWoA, takes possession at dock in Newark, New Jersey, and resells same to local Volkswagen dealers in its franchise area of New York, New Jersey and Connecticut. Where, as here, there exists truly separate corporate entities, not commonly owned, a valid inference of agency cannot be sustained.

One point remains — whether jurisdiction was properly acquired over VWAG by reason of the "control" the foreign corporation exerts over World-Wide and the franchise dealers in the State. Specifically, plaintiff asserts that VWAG maintains a rigid control over World-Wide and its dealers by requiring: (1) sale by each dealer of a minimum number of automobiles upon penalty of forfeiture of their dealer franchise; (2) uniform design for dealer service departments; (3) service personnel to be trained in Germany; (4) uniform purchase and sales prices; and (5) prior approval of prospective dealers. In substance, plaintiff asserts that such control by the defendant manufacturer over its representatives in the State constitutes "doing business" sufficient to warrant the inference of "presence."

Aside from the fact that these assertions are seriously disputed by the foreign corporation, this court has never held a foreign corporation present on the basis of control, unless there was in existence at least a parent-subsidiary relationship. (*Taca Int. Airlines, S. A. v. Rolls Royce of England*, 15 N Y 2d 97; *Public Administrator of County of N. Y. v. Royal Bank of Canada*, 19 N Y 2d 127.) The control over the subsidiary's activities, we held, must be so complete that the subsidiary is, in fact, merely a department of the parent. (*See Public Administrator of County of N. Y. v. Royal Bank of Canada*, *supra*.) Even if World-Wide were a subsidiary of VWAG, which it is not, the alleged control activities of

---

[2] Hilton (U.K.) was a wholly owned subsidiary of Hilton Hotels Int., Inc., a Delaware corporation, which was, in turn, a wholly owned subsidiary of Hilton Hotels Corporation, also a Delaware corporation. Hilton Hotels International and Hilton Hotels Corporation jointly owned the Hilton Credit Corp., a Delaware corporation, one branch of which was the Hilton Reservation Service.

[3] The Reservation Service represented, in addition to Hilton Hotels, 50 unaffiliated hotels.

VWAG would not be sufficient to make World-Wide a mere department of VWAG. . . .

Nor does advertising in New York media by VWoA permit a different result. Even if these activities by VWoA were to be found attributable to VWAG, they still would constitute no more than "mere solicitation". *(Miller v. Surf Props.,* 4 N Y 2d 475.)

The court's attention has been directed to *Gelfand v. Tanner Motor Tours* (385 F 2d 116), where the plaintiffs, New York residents, were injured in the course of defendants' package tours to the Grand Canyon. The only contact of defendant corporations to New York State was membership in a nonprofit corporation organized under Maryland law which, in turn, generated publicity and contracted with a New York travel agent who "Until informed . . . that space was no longer available . . . confirmed reservations, except group reservations, without obtaining Las Vegas' approval . . . ." The nature of the agency relationship was clear in *Gelfand,* since the New York agent was authorized to make final reservations, rather than merely confirming availabilities, and the additional factor was present that the purchase of the tour tickets took place in New York. We would only add that mere sales of a manufacturer's product in New York, however substantial, have never made the foreign corporation manufacturer amenable to suit in this jurisdiction. Thus, we conclude that VWAG was not "doing business" in New York in the traditional sense and, therefore, our courts did not acquire personal jurisdiction over the foreign corporation.

NOTES

(1) The principal case should be compared with *Crose v. Volkswagenwerk, AG,* 88 Wash. 2d 50, 558 P.2d 764 (1977), in which VWAG was held to be "doing business" in Washington through a contractual relationship identical to that described above.

(2) In *Frummer v. Hilton Hotels International, Inc.,* 19 N.Y.2d 533, 539, 281 N.Y.S.2d 41, 45, 227 N.E.2d 851, 854 (1967), *cert. denied,* 389 U.S. 923 (1967), discussed in the preceding case, the Court of Appeals said:

> We are not unmindful that litigation in a foreign jurisdiction is a burdensome inconvenience for any company. However, it is part of the price which may properly be demanded of those who extensively engage in international trade. When their activities abroad, either directly or through an agent, become as widespread and energetic as the activities in New York conducted by Hilton (U.K.), they receive considerable benefits from such foreign business and may not be heard to complain about the burdens.

The *Frummer* reasoning was relied upon in *Wiwa v. Royal Dutch Petroleum Company,* 226 F.3d 88 (2d Cir. 2000), *cert. denied,* 149 L. Ed. 2d 345, 121 S. Ct.

1402 (2001). The court held that a Nigerian national suing two international oil companies under the Alien Tort Claims Act in New York could maintain jurisdiction over the oil companies because an agency relationship existed between the companies and representatives in New York. The court specifically stated that the agent must go beyond solicitation and must be performing a service that is sufficiently important such that the corporation would perform the service itself if no such agent existed.

Note that the "quid pro quo" approach to jurisdiction can lead to results very different from Judge Hand's suggested focus on an "estimate of the inconveniences" to the foreign corporation. Perhaps the conflicting results in *Frummer*, on one hand, and *Delagi*, on the other, are due to their respective adoptions of a different one of these approaches to the underlying issue. Which approach is better? The quid pro quo concept is appealing in almost a Biblical sense of fairness. But it may be inconvenient for a corporation to defend a New York action even though it earns a great deal of money from products sold here if, for example, it cannot effectively participate in the litigation because it has no responsible officials nearby. To the degree that this handicap leads to skewing of litigation results, even New Yorkers may be disserved. Erroneous civil judgments entail costs because they reduce the law's effectiveness in promoting desired social policy. See *The Costs of Error in Civil Cases, in* Richard A. Posner, Economic Analysis of Law 602-04 (5th ed. 1998). Also, the cost of regularly litigating in an inconvenient forum will no doubt soon be passed on to consumers, including New Yorkers. Does this justify depriving a plaintiff of a New York court when the issue is a close one?

(3) The *Helicopteros* case, *infra*, § 1.03[C], found that due process concerns prevented the exercise of general jurisdiction based on the facts presented. Under the *Helicopteros* analysis, are the results in *Frummer v. Hilton Hotels, Inc.*, or *Gelfand v. Tanner Motor Tours* constitutional? Is the result in *DeLagi* constitutionally compelled?

(4) It has been held that even if a defendant has contacts with a state that are "continuous and systematic" enough to meet the corporate "presence" test, the Due Process Clause prohibits the exercise of jurisdiction over the particular case if it would be unreasonable to hear it in the forum state. *Metropolitan Life Insurance Co. v. Robertson-Ceco Corp.*, 84 F.3d 560 (2d Cir. 1996) (action brought in Vermont was dismissed despite defendant's contacts, which included authorization to do business in Vermont; neither plaintiff nor defendant were incorporated in Vermont or had their principal place of business there, and the cause of action did not arise in Vermont). The concept of "reasonableness" as a limit on the exercise of jurisdiction is relied upon and discussed in *Asahi Metal Industry Co. Ltd. v. Superior Court of California, infra.*

LAUFER v. OSTROW
Court of Appeals
55 N.Y.2d 305, 449 N.Y.S.2d 456, 434 N.E.2d 692 (1982)

MEYER, J.

. . . .

I

Defendant Mt. Olive Corporation is a New Jersey corporation the sole business of which is acting as sales agent for Pem-Kay Furniture Company, a North Carolina manufacturer. Ira Ostrow is president and chief salesman of Mt. Olive and a principal in Pem-Kay. Mt. Olive is not licensed to do business in New York and maintains no office, telephone or bank account in New York. Plaintiff Laufer, a New York resident, was hired by Ostrow to act as one of several sales representatives for Mt. Olive on a commission basis and was paid for his services by that corporation. The relationship continued for several years, during which plaintiff solicited the business of purchasers both within and outside New York, and serviced the accounts he obtained by following up on the order, attending to complaints, delivering swatches and sales materials, and running clinics for the personnel of the purchasers. Though he was not required by Mt. Olive to do so and was not reimbursed for the expense of doing so, plaintiff maintained an office in his home. Representatives other than plaintiff also solicited and serviced New York accounts as well as accounts outside New York. Ostrow on at least 8 to 10 occasions per year called on New York accounts with plaintiff, as he did also with the other representatives.

Sales orders obtained by Mt. Olive in 1978 approximated $2,000,000 from such New York accounts as Macy's, Saks Furniture, W&J Sloane and Gertz. All sales were approved by Mt. Olive in New Jersey and forwarded by Mt. Olive to Pem-Kay to be filled. The furniture purchased was shipped by Pem-Kay directly to the purchaser, which made payment either to Pem-Kay or its factors in North Carolina.

Plaintiff's relationship with Mt. Olive having terminated in 1979 by mutual consent, plaintiff brought an action in New York seeking to recover commissions due, for conversion of moneys due and owing plaintiff and for an accounting. Defendants moved to dismiss pursuant to CPLR 3211 (subd [a], par 8) . . . .

We conclude that the corporate defendant was amenable to jurisdiction because it was doing business in New York, but that the individual defendant, who performed no act in New York for himself, as distinct from the corporation, is not.

II

. . . .

Solicitation of business alone will not justify a finding of corporate presence in New York with respect to a foreign manufacturer or purveyor of services (*Miller v. Surf Props.*, 4 N.Y.2d 475, 480), but when there are activities of substance in addition to solicitation there is presence and, therefore, jurisdiction (*Bryant v. Finnish Nat. Airline*, 15 N.Y.2d 426, 432, *supra* [office, office staff and bank account in New York]; *Elish v. St. Louis Southwestern Ry. Co.*, 305 N.Y. 267, 270 [office, officers, financial transactions and directors meetings in New York]; *see, also, Miller v. Surf Props.*, 4 N.Y.2d 475, 481, *supra*; *Aquascutum of London v. S.S. American Champion*, 426 F.2d 205, 211; *Dunn v. Southern Charter*, 506 F. Supp. 564, 567). Mt. Olive argues from *Miller v. Surf Props. (supra)*, and *Delagi v. Volkswagenwerk AG of Wolfsburg, Germany* (29 N.Y.2d 426, *supra*) that as a matter of law it cannot be found present in New York, its activity here, no matter what the volume of sales concluded, being no more than solicitation. Those cases afford it no protection, however, for they hold simply that a foreign supplier of goods or services for whom an independent agency solicits orders from New York purchasers is not present in New York and may not be sued here, however substantial in amount the resulting orders. In the context of the present case the rules of those cases would, as Trial Term noted, protect Pem-Kay Furniture Company, the North Carolina manufacturer, from suit in New York on the basis of Mt. Olive's activity here, unless it could be shown additionally that Pem-Kay exercised parent-subsidiary control over Mt. Olive (*Delagi v. Volkswagenwerk AG, supra*, at p. 432).

At issue here, however, is not jurisdiction over the foreign supplier but over Mt. Olive, the soliciting agency. A corporation, the business of which is limited to the soliciting of orders and servicing of purchasers' accounts, engages directly in its corporate activity when, by persons in its employ and present in New York, it solicits and services New York accounts on a continuous basis. . . .

Solicitation and servicing by a foreign corporate sales agency of New York accounts through sales representatives present in New York, if systematic and continuous, is enough to subject the sales agency corporation to New York jurisdiction. The volume of business thus generated, while not determinative, may have relevance. As noted above, Trial Term found that Mt. Olive's activities in New York, were "systematic, regular and continuous" and that finding, having been affirmed by the Appellate Division, is beyond our review unless there is no support for it in the record. That it is adequately supported cannot be doubted. Mt. Olive employed three sales representatives, each of whom were assigned accounts not only in New York but throughout the country. They not only solicited sales in New York, but ran clinics for the customers, followed up on complaints or difficulties, delivered swatches and sales materials. Moreover, Ostrow, Mt. Olive's president, worked with the sales representatives in calling on New York accounts, making 8 to 10 such calls in a year with plaintiff alone. Such activity is purposeful and continuing rather than casual and limited in time (*compare Reiner & Co. v. Schwartz*, 41 N.Y.2d 648, *with McKee Elec. Co. v. Rauland-Borg Corp.*, 20 N.Y.2d 377). Such sustained and systematic activity in New York by Mt. Olive is sufficient to subject it to suit by one of the salesmen engaged in the solicitation and servicing without regard to the volume of business done, but the volume of Mt. Olive's New York sales is relevant as to whether there is any unfairness or unreasonableness in allowing the action to be brought against it in New York. That volume being at the rate of $2,000,000 a year, it is evident that there is no unfairness in so doing.

Nor is there any problem in that jurisdiction is predicated in part upon plaintiff's activities or in that the commissions for which he sues involve both New York and out of New York sales. Though a plaintiff may not for purposes of CPLR 302 jurisdiction rely solely upon his own activity in New York (*Haar v. Armendaris Corp.*, 31 N.Y.2d 1040, *rev'g on the dissent below* 40 A.D.2d 769; *Parke-Bernet Galleries v. Franklyn*, 26 N.Y.2d 13, 19, n 2), there are here substantial activities by Ostrow and sales representatives other than plaintiff to sustain jurisdiction. We need not, therefore, consider whether the rule against basing jurisdiction on plaintiff's activities alone applies in CPLR 301 cases as well (*compare Del Bello v. Japanese Steak House*, 43 A.D.2d 455, *with Traub v. Robertson-American Corp.*, 82 Misc.2d 222, 228).

As concerns the fact that not all of the commissions sought arise out of New York sales, we held in *Tauza v. Susquehanna Coal Co.* (220 N.Y. 259, 268, *supra*) that jurisdiction predicated upon corporate presence "does not fail because the cause of action sued upon has no relation in its origin to the business here transacted" and the Supreme Court has made several similar rulings (*Perkins v. Benguet Min. Co.*, 342 U.S. 437, 446; *International Shoe Co. v. Washington*, 326 U.S. 310, 318, *supra; accord* Restatement, Conflict of Laws 2d, § 47, subd [2], and Comment e).

III

Insofar as that order held defendant Ostrow individually to be subject to New York jurisdiction, however, it was erroneous. We may assume, without deciding, that an individual who is in fact doing business so as to be present within the State is subject to jurisdiction (*see Abkco Inds. v. Lennon*, 52 A.D.2d 435, *affg on this point* 85 Misc.2d 465; Restatement, Conflict of Laws, 2d, § 35, subd [3], and Comment e; Siegel, New York Practice, § 84, McLaughlin, Supplementary Practice Commentaries, McKinney's Cons Laws of NY, Book 7B CPLR 301-500 [1981-1982 Supp], pp 8-9; 1 Weinstein-Korn-Miller, NY Civ Prac, par 301.15). Here, however, although the complaint alleges that Ostrow "is and was . . . doing business in the State of New York," there was no evidence at the trial to establish that Ostrow as an individual engaged in any activity whatsoever in New York. Ostrow testified without contradiction that in hiring plaintiff, as well as in calling upon accounts in New York with plaintiff, he acted on behalf of Mt. Olive rather than himself. Although a corporation can act only through an employee or agent, the employee or agent being a live rather than a fictional being can act on behalf of himself or his employer or principal. He does not subject himself, individually, to the CPLR 301 jurisdiction of our courts, however, unless he is doing business in our state individually. Nor does the claimed conversion cause of action furnish any basis for CPLR 302 jurisdiction over Ostrow individually (*Fanits Foods v. Standard Importing Co.*, 49 N.Y.2d 317, 326-327).

. . . .

NOTES

(1) Does the *Laufer* case apply or change the legal standard of the "doing business" test as described in *DeLagi*? What is now the relevance of the in-state agent's power to bind the out-of-state principal?

(2) What about non-corporate persons? If they are "doing business" in New York are they subject to jurisdiction even if they do not physically enter the state but rather conduct business through employees? In *ABKCO Indus., Inc. v. Lennon*, 85 Misc. 2d 465, 377 N.Y.S.2d 362 (Sup. Ct. 1975), *modified on other grounds*, 52 A.D.2d 435, 384 N.Y.S.2d 781 (1st Dep't 1976), a person named Richard Starkey (a.k.a. Ringo Starr) was held subject to New York jurisdiction on this theory. This result accords with the position of the Restatement (Second) of Conflict of Laws § 35 (1971). But isn't the impact of a judgment against an individual very different from one against a corporation? Does this argue for a result different from that reached in *ABKCO*? The question is open, as the principal case states. The Second Department has rejected such jurisdiction. *Nilsa B.B. v. Clyde Blackwell H.*, 84 A.D.2d 295, 445 N.Y.S.2d 579 (2d Dep't 1981).

(3) Should the presence of substantial corporate assets in New York lead one to conclude that the corporation is "present" in the state? Given New York's role in world capital markets, the question is not a trivial one. The next case provides some guidance.

LANDOIL RESOURCES CORP. v.
ALEXANDER & ALEXANDER SERVICES, INC.
Court of Appeals
77 N.Y.2d 28, 565 N.E.2d 488, 563 N.Y.S.2d 739 (1990)

SIMONS, J.

Plaintiff Landoil Resources Corporation, a Philippine construction company, instituted this action against defendants Alexander & Alexander Services, Inc., et al. (Alexander), a group of United States corporations engaged in the insurance brokerage business. It sought to recover damages allegedly sustained as a result of defendants' wrongful acts in acquiring two policies of political risk insurance to cover plaintiff's foreign projects. Alexander had secured the insurance from Lloyd's of London. Accordingly, it asserted third-party claims for indemnification and contribution against Lloyd's Syndicate 317, a group of insurance underwriters who conduct their underwriting business at Lloyd's.

The matter comes to us from the United States Court of Appeals for the Second Circuit, which certified the question of whether Syndicate 317 is "doing business" in New York and therefore subject to personal jurisdiction under CPLR 301 (see, 22 NYCRR 500.17). We accepted the certified question and now answer it in the negative.

I

Before addressing the question, it is important to understand how Lloyd's of London conducts its business.

The Corporation of Lloyd's is a nonprofit corporation created by a Special Act of Parliament in 1871. It does no underwriting, but instead provides services to members who perform underwriting in their individual capacities. The individual members transact their business in groups called syndicates, managed by agents who in turn employ an active underwriter to handle the business for the syndicate. The managing agent keeps the syndicate's books while the active underwriter accepts or rejects the risks submitted for underwriting, collects premiums, pays losses and disburses all funds. All the syndicates conduct their business at the market place known as Lloyd's of London located at One Lime Street, London, England.

Lloyd's policies can only be obtained by registered Lloyd's brokers who have been appointed either by the prospective insured or by the insured's non-Lloyd's broker. In placing policies, a registered Lloyd's broker prepares a "slip" which states the details of the insurance required and then offers the risk to the active underwriters. Any underwriter who wishes to underwrite all or a portion of the risk indicates this on the slip. Once the entire risk has been subscribed, the Lloyd's broker informs its principal that the insurance has been effected. A policy is prepared by Lloyd's Policy Signing Office, a department of the Corporation of Lloyd's, and the transaction is consummated.

Landoil's policies were obtained in this manner. In 1982 and 1983 it requested Alexander to acquire political risk insurance policies covering its operations in the Middle East and Africa. Since Alexander was not a registered Lloyd's broker, the policies had to be negotiated in London between an appointed Lloyd's broker and certain Lloyd's underwriters. Alexander secured the insurance from a group of Lloyd's underwriters, including Syndicate 317.

Subsequently, disputes arose between Landoil and the various underwriters, including Syndicate 317, over the coverage of certain losses. The claims were settled following arbitration proceedings in London to which Alexander was not a party. Landoil then instituted this action against Alexander in the United States District Court to recover the balance of its loss. Alexander filed a third-party complaint for indemnification and contribution against Syndicate 317 and other Lloyd's underwriters alleged to have subscribed to Landoil's policies and Syndicate 317 responded by filing the motion to dismiss the third-party complaint for lack of personal jurisdiction. The District Court denied the motion to dismiss, holding that Syndicate 317 was "doing business" in New York within the meaning of CPLR 301 (*Landoil Resources Corp. v Alexander & Alexander*, 720 F Supp 26).

The court rested its decision on the existence of a fund held in trust at Citibank in New York City by the Corporation of Lloyd's. The fund, known as the American Trust Fund (Fund), was originally established in 1940 to provide security to United States policyholders during World War II, when England was under siege by Germany. It consists of United States dollar premiums collected worldwide by Lloyd's brokers and subsequently transferred through Lloyd's accounting system in London to Citibank in New York. The Fund is used to pay American claims underwritten by Lloyd's. It also serves as security for New York insureds pursuant to New York Insurance Department regulations which provide that a New York broker or insurance company cannot place New York risks with an unauthorized alien or foreign insurer unless it has ascertained that such insurer maintains a trust fund at a New York bank, in an amount specified by regulation, as security for the insured (*see*, 11 NYCRR 27.5[a][1][ii]; *see also*, 125.4[c]). Thus, the Fund enables New York brokers and insurance companies to submit risks to Lloyd's underwriting syndicates which are not authorized to write insurance in New York. The Lloyd's underwriters do not directly deposit or withdraw any moneys from the Fund, but a portion of United States dollar premiums attributable to risks underwritten by groups such as Syndicate 317, including some derived from New York insureds and risks, are part of its assets. The Fund is administered by the Finance & Market Services Group (FMSG), one of Lloyd's administrative departments and, as of December 31, 1988, it had $9.4 billion dollars on deposit at Citibank.

From these facts, the District Court concluded that FMSG "is performing a service in New York" on behalf of Syndicate 317, by administering — from London — the Lloyd's American Trust Fund. . . . Syndicate 317 appealed to the Second Circuit Court of Appeals and that court certified the question to us. We conclude that Syndicate 317 is not subject to in personam jurisdiction in New York State.

II

A foreign corporation is amenable to suit in New York courts under CPLR 301 if it has engaged in such a continuous and systematic course of "doing business" here that a finding of its "presence" in this jurisdiction is warranted . . . . That test is not satisfied by the evidence in the record before us.

Alexander's submission focuses on three general areas.

A

First, Alexander contends that Syndicate 317 is doing business in New York because it underwrites policies for New York insureds and risks. Such activity standing alone, however, will not support jurisdiction. In *Delagi v Volkswagenwerk AG* (29 NY2d 426, 433, *supra*), we held that "mere sales of a manufacturer's product in New York, however substantial, have never made the foreign corporation manufacturer amenable to suit in this jurisdiction."

Delagi involved a German automobile manufacturing corporation which sold its vehicles to a New Jersey importing corporation, a wholly owned subsidiary, which in turn sold them to a corporate wholesale distributor in New York owned by American investors. We concluded that the manufacturer, which was not qualified to do business in this State and did not have an office or place of business here, was not subject to jurisdiction because it had not engaged in a systematic and regular course of business in New York (*Delagi v Volkswagenwerk AG*, 29 NY2d 426, *supra*).

Similarly, the sale of insurance policies in New York, which are underwritten by a group of unauthorized foreign underwriters, does not, without more, support a finding that the underwriters are engaging in a systematic and regular course of business in New York (*cf., Bryant v Finnish Natl. Airline*, 15 NY2d 267, 270, *supra* [office, staff and bank account in New York constituted doing business]; *Tauza v Susquehanna Coal Co.*, 220 NY 259, *supra* [office and direct and continuous sales and shipment of goods into New York constituted doing business]). Syndicate 317 does not have an office in New York, it does not solicit business in New York, it has no real or personal property in New York and it does not maintain a bank account in New York. Rather, it conducts its business in London and considers risks brought to it there by registered Lloyd's brokers. A New York broker may seek to place insurance with Syndicate 317, through a Lloyd's broker, but Syndicate 317 does not directly or purposefully solicit, sell or promote its underwriting activity in New York.

B

Alexander next contends that Syndicate 317 has sufficient interest in the Lloyd's American Trust Fund to warrant a finding of its "presence" in New York. It notes that a portion of United States dollar premiums, including income derived from the underwriting of New York risks by Syndicate 317, is deposited in the trust fund and that without it or a similar type of fund, New York brokers and insurance companies could not conduct business with the Syndicate. Syndicate 317's indirect interest in that Fund does not provide a basis for CPLR 301 jurisdiction, however.[2]

---

[2] This is not to say that the Fund can never serve as a predicate for exercising jurisdiction over a Lloyd's syndicate. The Fund might, in an appropriate case, serve as a predicate for exercising jurisdiction based on quasi in rem or long-arm principles. Contrary to the third-party plaintiffs' contention, however, this Court's analysis in *Banco Ambrosiano v Artoc Bank & Trust* (62 NY2d 65), which was based on quasi in rem principles, is not equally applicable to "doing business" cases. In *Banco*, we held that the relationship between the defendant, the litigation and the State was suf-

Syndicate 317 does not "maintain an account" at Citibank in the usual sense. Funds cannot be withdrawn from or deposited into the account by Syndicate 317 and it is not administered by Syndicate 317 or the underwriters, but rather by FMSG, an administrative branch of the Corporation of Lloyd's. But even if it is assumed that Syndicate 317 does "maintain" the account, because a portion of the income derived from the underwriting of New York risks by Syndicate 317 is on deposit there, that alone does not establish that Lloyd's underwriters do business in New York on a continuous and systematic basis (*see, Nemetsky v Banque de Developpement,* 48 NY2d 962 [involving a correspondent banking relationship]; *see also, Bank of Am. v Whitney Bank,* 261 U.S. 171). . . .

C

Finally, Alexander maintains that FMSG is an agent of Syndicate 317 and that its activities in administering the New York account are sufficient to confer jurisdiction over Syndicate 317 under the ruling in *Laufer v Ostrow* (55 NY2d 305, *supra*) and other agency cases (*see, e.g., Gelfand v Tanner Motor Tours,* 385 F2d 116; *Frummer v Hilton Hotels Intl.,* 19 NY2d 533, *supra*). Assuming that FMSG is an agent of Syndicate 317 because of its administrative activities, more than an agency relationship is needed to support in personam jurisdiction. FMSG is not physically present in New York, it does not solicit business for the Lloyd's underwriters in New York and it performs all of its administrative functions relating to the Fund from London. It cannot be said to be performing acts in New York on a systematic and continuous basis or for the benefit of Syndicate 317 (*cf., Laufer v Ostrow, supra; Frummer v Hilton Hotels Intl., supra*).

The plaintiff in this case is a Philippine corporation which was insured by a British insurer for risks in foreign countries. The dispute in the third-party action is between an American broker, not the insured, and the British insurer. Personal jurisdiction in New York between the two must necessarily rest upon the existence of the Citibank account but to hold in favor of Alexander on that basis would subject any foreign insurer to suit in New York merely because of the existence of a security fund, whether the insurer had sold insurance here or not. The facts presented do not support a finding of "doing business" under the New York statute. Accordingly, the certified question should be answered in the negative.

---

ficient to make it fair that defendant be compelled to defend in New York. In distinguishing cases where the maintenance of a bank account in New York was found not to be sufficient to sustain jurisdiction, we stated that the *Banco* case did not involve property coincidentally located within the State's borders which formed the only relevant link to defendant; rather, defendant's account with the New York bank was closely related to plaintiff's claim making quasi in rem jurisdiction proper under the facts of that case. Here, the Trust Fund does not relate in any way to the direct cause of action or to the third-party complaint.

NOTES

(1) While the *Landoil* court rejects a claim of presence jurisdiction based on the substantial corporate assets in the state, it does not hold those assets irrelevant to all jurisdictional issues. In this respect, the court's footnote 2 is intriguing. Keep it in mind when thinking about jurisdiction based on property attachments.

At least one court has held that the maintenance of a bank account in New York is sufficient to subject an entity to general jurisdiction. *Georgia-Pacific Corp. v. Multimark's International, LTD*, 265 A.D.2d 109, 706 N.Y.S.2d 82 (1st Dep't 2000). The defendant foreign corporation used the account for the receipt of substantially all of its income and to pay most of its business expenses.

Incidentally, what form of business entity was Lloyd's Syndicate 317, the defendant whose jurisdictional objection was considered in *Landoil*? Is this issue relevant to the holding?

(2) Refer again to Problem C in § 1.03[C], *supra*. Assume that a court would hold CalCon (the California corporation) present in New York by applying the "doing business" test. What conclusions would follow as to ICI, the Japanese parent corporation?

New York's approach to finding jurisdiction against a corporation when its parent or its subsidiary is present here is helpfully discussed in *Volkswagenwerk, AG v. Beech Aircraft Corp.*, 751 F.2d 117 (2d Cir. 1984). As that court said:

> New York courts regard one factor as essential to the assertion of jurisdiction over a foreign related corporation and three others as important. The essential factor is common ownership. . . . The second factor is financial dependency of the subsidiary on the parent corporation. . . . The third factor is the degree to which the parent corporation interferes in the selection and assignment of the subsidiary's executive personnel and fails to observe corporate formalities. . . . The fourth factor is the degree of control over the marketing and operational policies of the subsidiary exercised by the parent.

The *Beech* court then weighed the various factors and found that the parent corporation was present in New York because of its relationship with its New York subsidiary.

(3) Note the degree of factual detail required to decide the jurisdictional issue in these interlocking entity cases. How would the plaintiff obtain knowledge of these facts?

(4) For a thorough analysis of the problem of interlocking corporations, see Lea Brilmayer & Kathleen Paisley, *Personal Jurisdiction and Substantive Legal Relations: Corporations, Conspiracies, and Agency*, 74 Cal. L. Rev. 1 (1986).

(5) The presence doctrine is, of course, subject to the limits of fundamental fair play imposed by the Due Process Clause. After you read the next case, consider whether New York has observed the limits discussed and applied there. Would those limits affect your answer to Problem C?

HELICOPTEROS NACIONALES DE COLOMBIA, S.A. v. HALL
United States Supreme Court
466 U.S. 408, 104 S. Ct. 1868, 80 L. Ed. 2d 404 (1984)

[Hall and his co-plaintiffs were the representatives of the estates of four Americans who were killed in a helicopter crash in Peru. All of the crash victims were employees of Consorcio/WSH, a multinational enterprise headquartered in Houston, Texas, which was constructing an oil pipeline in Peru. The helicopter was owned by defendant Helicopteros Nacionales de Colombia, S.A. (Helicol), a Colombian corporation with its principal place of business in Bogota. The question before the court was whether jurisdiction could be exercised over Helicol in Texas. — Eds.]

JUSTICE BLACKMUN delivered the opinion of the Court.

We granted certiorari in this case to decide whether the Supreme Court of Texas correctly ruled that the contacts of a foreign corporation with the State of Texas were sufficient to allow a Texas state court to assert jurisdiction over the corporation in a cause of action not arising out of or related to the corporation's activities within the State.

I

. . . .

Consorcio/WSH needed helicopters to move personnel, materials, and equipment into and out of the construction area. In 1974, upon request of Consorcio/WSH, the chief executive officer of Helicol, Francisco Restrepo, flew to the United States and conferred in Houston with representatives of the three joint ventures. At that meeting, there was a discussion of prices, availability, working conditions, fuel, supplies, and housing. Restrepo represented that Helicol could have the first helicopter on the job in 15 days. The Consorcio/WSH representatives decided to accept the contract proposed by Restrepo. Helicol began performing before the agreement was formally signed in Peru on November 11, 1974. The contract was written in Spanish on official government stationery and provided that the residence of all the parties would be Lima, Peru. It further stated that controversies arising out of the contract would be submitted to the jurisdiction of Peruvian courts. In addition, it provided that Consorcio/WSH would make payments to Helicol's account with the Bank of America in New York City.

Aside from the negotiation session in Houston between Restrepo and the representatives of Consorcio/WSH, Helicol had other contacts with Texas. During the years 1970-1977, it purchased helicopters (approximately 80% of its fleet), spare parts, and accessories for more than $4,000,000 from Bell Helicopter Company in Fort Worth. In that period, Helicol sent prospective pilots to Fort Worth for training and to ferry the aircraft to South America. It also sent management and maintenance personnel to visit Bell Helicopter in Fort Worth during the same period in order to receive "plant familiarization" and for technical consultation. Helicol received into its New York City and Panama City, Fla., bank accounts over $5,000,000 in payments from Consorcio/WSH drawn upon First City National Bank of Houston.

Beyond the foregoing, there have been no other business contacts between Helicol and the State of Texas. Helicol never has been authorized to do business in Texas and never has had an agent for the service of process within the State. It never has performed helicopter operations in Texas or sold any product that reached Texas, never solicited business in Texas, never signed any contract in Texas, never had any employee based there, and never recruited an employee in Texas. In addition, Helicol never has owned real or personal property in Texas and never has maintained an office or establishment there. Helicol has maintained no records in Texas and has no shareholders in that State. None of the respondents or their decedents were domiciled in Texas,[5] but all of the decedents were hired in Houston by Consorcio/WSH to work on the Petro Peru pipeline project.

. . . .

II

. . . .

Even when the cause of action does not arise out of or relate to the foreign corporation's activities in the forum State,[9] due process is not offended by a State's subjecting the corporation to its in personam jurisdiction when there are sufficient contacts between the State and the foreign corporation. *Perkins v. Benguet Consolidated Mining Co.*, 342 U.S. 437, 72 S. Ct. 413, 96 L. Ed. 485 (1952). In *Perkins*, the Court addressed a situation in which state courts had asserted general jurisdiction over a defendant foreign corporation. During the Japanese

---

[5] . . . We mention respondents' lack of contacts merely to show that nothing in the nature of the relationship between respondents and Helicol could possibly enhance Helicol's contacts with Texas. The harm suffered by respondents did not occur in Texas. Nor is it alleged that any negligence on the part of Helicol took place in Texas.

[9] When a State exercises personal jurisdiction over a defendant in a suit not arising out of or related to the defendant's contacts with the forum, the State has been said to be exercising "general jurisdiction" over the defendant. *See* Brilmayer, *How Contacts Count: Due Process Limitations on State Court Jurisdiction*, 1980 S. Ct. Rev. 77, 80-81; von Mehren & Trautman, [*Jurisdiction to Adjudicate: A Suggested Analysis*], 79 Harv. L. Rev., at 1136-1144 [1966].

occupation of the Philippine Islands, the president and general manager of a Philippine mining corporation maintained an office in Ohio from which he conducted activities on behalf of the company. He kept company files and held directors' meetings in the office, carried on correspondence relating to the business, distributed salary checks drawn on two active Ohio bank accounts, engaged an Ohio bank to act as transfer agent, and supervised policies dealing with the rehabilitation of the corporation's properties in the Philippines. In short, the foreign corporation, through its president, "ha[d] been carrying on in Ohio a continuous and systematic, but limited, part of its general business," and the exercise of general jurisdiction over the Philippine corporation by an Ohio court was "reasonable and just." 342 U.S., at 438, 445, 72 S. Ct., at 414, 418.

All parties to the present case concede that respondents' claims against Helicol did not "arise out of," and are not related to, Helicol's activities within Texas.[10]

The dissent suggests that we have erred in drawing no distinction between controversies that "relate to" a defendant's contacts with a forum and those that "arise out of" such contacts. This criticism is somewhat puzzling, for the dissent goes on to urge that, for purposes of determining the constitutional validity of an assertion of specific jurisdiction, there really should be no distinction between the two.

We do not address the validity or consequences of such a distinction because the issue has not been presented in this case. Respondents have made no argument that their cause of action either arose out of or is related to Helicol's contacts with the State of Texas. Absent any briefing on the issue, we decline to reach the questions (1) whether the terms "arising out of" and "related to" describe different connections between a cause of action and a defendant's contacts with a forum, and (2) what sort of tie between a cause of action and a defendant's contacts with a forum is necessary to a determination that either connection exists. Nor do we reach the question whether, if the two types of relationship differ, a forum's exercise of personal jurisdiction in a situation where the cause of action "relates to," but does not "arise out of," the defendant's contacts with the forum should be analyzed as an assertion of specific jurisdiction. We thus must explore the nature of Helicol's contacts with the State of Texas to determine whether they constitute the kind of continuous and systematic general business contacts the Court found to exist in *Perkins*. We hold that they do not.

It is undisputed that Helicol does not have a place of business in Texas and never has been licensed to do business in the State. Basically, Helicol's contacts with Texas consisted of sending its chief executive officer to Houston for a contract-negotiation session; accepting into its New York bank account checks

---

[10] *See* Brief for Respondents 14; Tr. of Oral Arg. 26-27, 30-31. Because the parties have not argued any relationship between the cause of action and Helicol's contacts with the State of Texas, we, contrary to the dissent's implication, assert no "view" with respect to that issue.

drawn on a Houston bank; purchasing helicopters, equipment, and training services from Bell Helicopter for substantial sums; and sending personnel to Bell's facilities in Fort Worth for training.

The one trip to Houston by Helicol's chief executive officer for the purpose of negotiating the transportation-services contract with Consorcio/WSH cannot be described or regarded as a contact of a "continuous and systematic" nature, as *Perkins* described it, *see also International Shoe Co. v. Washington*, 326 U.S., at 320, 66 S. Ct., at 160, and thus cannot support an assertion of in personam jurisdiction over Helicol by a Texas court. Similarly, Helicol's acceptance from Consorcio/WSH of checks drawn on a Texas bank is of negligible significance for purposes of determining whether Helicol had sufficient contacts in Texas. There is no indication that Helicol ever requested that the checks be drawn on a Texas bank or that there was any negotiation between Helicol and Consorcio/WSH with respect to the location or identity of the bank on which checks would be drawn. Common sense and everyday experience suggest that, absent unusual circumstances, the bank on which a check is drawn is generally of little consequence to the payee and is a matter left to the discretion of the drawer. Such unilateral activity of another party or a third person is not an appropriate consideration when determining whether a defendant has sufficient contacts with a forum State to justify an assertion of jurisdiction. . . .

The Texas Supreme Court focused on the purchases and the related training trips in finding contacts sufficient to support an assertion of jurisdiction. We do not agree with that assessment, for the Court's opinion in *Rosenberg Bros. & Co. v. Curtis Brown Co.*, 260 U.S. 516, 43 S. Ct. 170, 67 L. Ed. 372 (1923) (Brandeis, J., for a unanimous tribunal), makes clear that purchases and related trips, standing alone, are not a sufficient basis for a State's assertion of jurisdiction.

The defendant in *Rosenberg* was a small retailer in Tulsa, Okla., who dealt in men's clothing and furnishings. It never had applied for a license to do business in New York, nor had it at any time authorized suit to be brought against it there. It never had an established place of business in New York and never regularly carried on business in that State. Its only connection with New York was that it purchased from New York wholesalers a large portion of the merchandise sold in its Tulsa store. The purchases sometimes were made by correspondence and sometimes through visits to New York by an officer of the defendant. The Court concluded: "Visits on such business, even if occurring at regular intervals, would not warrant the inference that the corporation was present within the jurisdiction of [New York]." *Id.*, at 518, 43 S. Ct., at 171.

This Court in *International Shoe* acknowledged and did not repudiate its holding in *Rosenberg*. See 326 U.S., at 318, 66 S. Ct., at 159. In accordance with *Rosenberg*, we hold that mere purchases, even if occurring at regular intervals, are not enough to warrant a State's assertion of in personam jurisdiction over a nonresident corporation in a cause of action not related to those purchase transactions. Nor can we conclude that the fact that Helicol sent personnel into Texas for training in connection with the purchase of helicopters and equipment in that State in any way enhanced the nature of Helicol's contacts with Texas. The training was a part of the package of goods and services purchased by Helicol from Bell Helicopter. The brief presence of Helicol employees in Texas for the purpose of attending the training sessions is no more a significant contact than were the trips to New York made by the buyer for the retail store in *Rosenberg*. . . .

III

We hold that Helicol's contacts with the State of Texas were insufficient to satisfy the requirements of the Due Process Clause of the Fourteenth Amendment.

Justice Brennan, dissenting.

Decisions applying the Due Process Clause of the Fourteenth Amendment to determine whether a State may constitutionally assert in personam jurisdiction over a particular defendant for a particular cause of action most often turn on a weighing of facts. To a large extent, today's decision follows the usual pattern. . . .

What is troubling about the Court's opinion, however, are the implications that might be drawn from the way in which the Court approaches the constitutional issue it addresses. First, the Court limits its discussion to an assertion of general jurisdiction of the Texas courts because, in its view, the underlying cause of action does "not aris[e] out of or relat[e] to the corporation's activities within the State." . . . [B]y refusing to consider any distinction between controversies that "relate to" a defendant's contacts with the forum and causes of action that "arise out of" such contacts, the Court may be placing severe limitations on the type and amount of contacts that will satisfy the constitutional minimum. . . .

By asserting that the present case does not implicate the specific jurisdiction of the Texas courts, the Court necessarily removes its decision from the reality of the actual facts presented for our consideration. Moreover, the Court refuses to consider any distinction between contacts that are "related to" the underlying cause of action and contacts that "give rise" to the underlying cause of action. In my view, however, there is a substantial difference between these two standards for asserting specific jurisdiction. Thus, although I agree that the respondents' cause of action did not formally "arise out of" specific activities initiated by Helicol in the State of Texas, I believe that the wrongful death claim filed by the respondents is significantly related to the undisputed contacts between Helicol and the forum. . . .

. . . It is eminently fair and reasonable, in my view, to subject a defendant to suit in a forum with which it has significant contacts directly related to the underlying cause of action. Because Helicol's contacts with the State of Texas meet this standard, I would affirm the judgment of the Supreme Court of Texas.

NOTES

(1) The principal case is discussed in Mary Twitchell, *The Myth of General Jurisdiction*, 101 Harv. L. Rev. 610, 639-43 (1988).

(2) Under the traditional "doing business" test, it is irrelevant that the cause of action is totally unrelated to the defendant's activities in the state. But some courts have held (as Justice Brennan argued in his dissent in *Helicopteros*) that where the "doing business" issue is a close one, the existence of a relationship between the cause of action and the activities of the defendant's agent in New York will buttress the argument in favor of jurisdiction. The same approach was taken in *Bulova Watch Co. v. K. Hattori & Co.*, 508 F. Supp. 1322 (E.D.N.Y. 1981) (Japanese parent held present in New York through wholly owned subsidiary for purposes of competitor's action alleging that in setting up the subsidiary the defendant had raided plaintiff's personnel). Does the majority opinion in *Helicopteros* put this line of reasoning to rest?

§ 1.04 DOMICILE

Pursuant to CPLR 313, a domiciliary of New York is subject to in personam jurisdiction on any claim, regardless of where the claim arose and regardless of where the defendant is served. Domicile has been distinguished from residence in that "[a] person may have two places of residence, as in the city and country, but only one domicile." *Rawstone v. Maguire*, 265 N.Y. 204, 208, 192 N.E. 294, 295 (1934). According to Holmes, "[w]hat the law means by domicile is the one technically pre-eminent headquarters, which . . . every person is compelled to have in order that by aid of it certain rights and duties . . . may be determined." *Bergner & Engel Brewing Co. v. Dreyfus*, 172 Mass. 154, 157, 51 N.E. 531, 532 (1898). More recently, the Court of Appeals has said, "Establishment of a domicile in a State generally requires a physical presence in the State and an intention to make the State a permanent home. . . . The term residence, on the other hand, has been employed by Legislatures for a variety of purposes, often with a meaning which is different from that of domicile." *Antone v. General Motors Corp.*, 64 N.Y.2d 20, 28, 484 N.Y.S.2d 514, 516, 473 N.E.2d 742 (1984).

The constitutionality of domicile as a jurisdictional basis was upheld in *Milliken v. Meyer*, 311 U.S. 457, 61 S. Ct. 339 (1940).

It has been held that the maintenance of a residence in New York is itself sufficient to serve as a jurisdictional basis for an action against a non-domiciliary. *Bourbon v. Bourbon*, 259 A.D.2d 720, 687 N.Y.S.2d 426 (2d Dep't 1999) (the defendant, a domiciliary of France, was a New York resident and thus subject to jurisdiction).

It is ordinarily the domicile of the defendant which is relevant to jurisdiction over him, but in actions affecting matrimonial status, the domicile of the plaintiff alone can be sufficient for the court to assert jurisdiction over the status of the marriage. *See Carr v. Carr*, §1.08, *infra*.

§ 1.05 CONSENT

A person or entity may consent to be sued in New York even if not otherwise subject to the state's jurisdiction. The consent of which we speak here is given in advance of any litigation. It should be distinguished from the related concept of an appearance, covered in Chapter 6, which also involves a kind of consent to the exercise of jurisdiction. But in an appearance, the consent is expressed after the action has begun simply by failing to assert the affirmative defense that jurisdiction over the defendant is lacking.

CPLR 318 provides one of the formal mechanism by which consent may be effected. It allows appointment of an agent in New York who may be served with a summons as the representative of the principal. The appointment under CPLR 318 is rather cumbersome because it requires the filing of a copy of the appointment in a county clerk's office. Agents for service may also be designated in a writing which does not comply with CPLR 318; such designations have been held effective. *Fashion Page, Ltd. v. Zurich Ins. Co.*, 50 N.Y.2d 265, 272, 428 N.Y.S.2d 890, 893, 406 N.E.2d 747 (1980).

A person may agree to be subject to suit in New York without necessarily appointing an agent to be served here. An agreement which includes a consent by one or both of the parties to be sued in a given state (often called a "forum selection clause") is presumptively valid and enforceable. The following case illustrates an expansive application of this principle.

BOSS v. AMERICAN EXPRESS
FINANCIAL ADVISORS, INC.
Court of Appeals
6 N.Y.3d 242, 811 N.Y.S.2d 620, 844 N.E.2d 1142 (2006)

G.B. SMITH, J.

The issue here is whether a forum selection clause requiring that any action be brought in Minnesota courts should be enforced. We agree with the Appellate Division that the forum selection clause is valid and affirm its order dismissing the action.

Facts

The three plaintiffs in this action, all of whom resided in the Syracuse, New York area, sue on behalf of themselves and the putative class action members who are similarly situated (*see* CPLR 901). At issue is whether the "expense allowance" paid by each advisor for the maintenance of office space and overhead expenses was a violation of the laws of New York State and requires that the matter be heard in New York State courts.

The plaintiffs were all first-year financial advisors at the time that they signed their contracts with IDS Life Insurance Co. (IDS). Plaintiffs earned $2,000 per month and were required to pay $900 per month for expense allowances. These allowances covered all overhead expenses such as building rent and maintenance, office support staff, and office supplies, among other expenses.

In December 2002, plaintiffs filed suit in Supreme Court, New York County alleging a violation of Labor Law § 193 and 12 NYCRR 195.1. [These laws limit the authority of employers to make deductions from employees' wages, provide additional punishment for employers who breach agreements to provide employee benefits or wage supplements, and limit permitted wage deductions to at most 10 percent. — Eds.] American Express Financial Advisors, Inc. (AEFA) and IDS filed joint motions to dismiss based, in part, upon inconvenient forum, a defense founded on documentary evidence, and a failure to state a cause of action (CPLR 327, 3211[a][1], [7]).

. . . .

[Supreme Court granted the defendants' motions on the grounds that the forum selection clause in the parties' employment contract required Minnesota jurisdiction, and that the plaintiffs weren't denied their day in court, despite the apparent running of the Minnesota statute of limitations. The court decided that the statute of limitations is not the "sort of grave difficulty and inconvenience" that justifies the application of New York law. The Appellate Division affirmed, stating: "[The plaintiffs] have not been deprived of a forum. Rather, they are time-barred from proceeding in the agreed-upon forum. The fact that New York provides a longer statute of limitations does not avail plaintiffs where they specifically agreed to proceed under Minnesota law." — Eds.]

Discussion

Plaintiffs argue first that the forum selection clause is permissive but not mandatory. It reads as follows:

> "This Agreement is a Minnesota contract, governed by Minnesota law. All of the payments you make to IDS Life are payable in Hennepin County, Minnesota. You expressly waive any privileges contrary to this provision. You agree to the jurisdiction of [the] State of Minnesota courts for determining any controversy in connection with this Agreement."

The contractual language here provides unambiguously that any disputes are to be decided in the courts of Minnesota and that Minnesota law should govern. The parties thus waived any privilege to have their claims heard elsewhere.

Plaintiffs also argue that the wage deductions were in contravention of Labor Law § 193(1), § 198-c, and 12 NYCRR 195.1, and unreasonable, unjust and contrary to the public policy concerns of New York. Plaintiffs argue that New York State law forbids deductions of more than 10% from an employee's wages (*see* 12 NYCRR 195.1). As a result of these provisions of New York law, plaintiffs argue that defendants should not be able to enforce the forum selection clause.

Plaintiff's argument, however, is misdirected. The issue they raise is really one of choice of law, not choice of forum; it is the choice of law clause that, according to plaintiffs, may not be enforced. They say, in substance, that, since plaintiffs worked in New York, New York law must govern the deductions from their wages, even though the contract contains a Minnesota choice of law clause.

We express no opinion on the merits of plaintiffs' argument. It could and should have been made to a court in Minnesota — the forum the parties chose by contract. If New York's interest in applying its own law to this transaction is as powerful as plaintiffs contend, we cannot assume that Minnesota courts would ignore it, any more than we would ignore the interests or policies of the State of Minnesota where they were implicated. In short, objections to a choice of law clause are not a warrant for failure to enforce a choice of forum clause.

"Forum selection clauses are enforced because they provide certainty and predictability in the resolution of disputes" (*see Brooke Group v. JCH Syndicate 488*, 87 N.Y.2d 530, 534, 640 N.Y.S.2d 479, 663 N.E.2d 635 [1996]). The Supreme Court noted that all of the proceedings regarding the contract and the employment training took place in Minnesota. Further, defendants, incorporated in Delaware, had their principal places of business in Minnesota. All paychecks were generated from the Minnesota office. There does not appear to be a reason why IDS or AEFA would contemplate coming into New York for litigation. Here it is clear from the setup of the agreement that plaintiffs' reasonable expectations were that all litigation would take place in Minnesota, not New York.

Accordingly, the order of the Appellate Division should be affirmed, with costs.

NOTES

(1) In *Carnival Cruise Lines, Inc. v. Shute*, 490 U.S. 585, 111 S. Ct. 1522, 113 L. Ed. 2d 622 (1991), the Supreme Court upheld the constitutionality of personal jurisdiction based on a forum selection clause printed in boilerplate on the back of a cruise ticket. Despite the clause's stipulation of Florida as the forum, respondents had attempted to bring suit in their home state of Washington for injuries sustained while cruising off the coast of Mexico. The Court rejected respondents' argument that the clause was invalid because it was not the product of negotiation, stating: "Common sense dictates that a ticket of this kind will be a form contract the terms of which are not subject to negotiation, and that an individual purchasing the ticket will not have bargaining parity with the cruise line." The Court also noted a few reasons why a forum selection clause

would be particularly beneficial in this context: a forum selection clause enables a cruise line, a carrier of passengers from various locales, to avoid multi-forum litigation; a forum selection clause obviates costly confusion about where suits must be brought and defended; and these savings should result in lower fares for passengers. In response to the argument that respondents are physically and financially unable to litigate in the stipulated forum, the Court found that Florida is neither a "remote alien forum," nor is Washington transactionally appropriate. For these reasons, and because respondents did not claim lack of notice of the clause, the Court held that respondents did not meet the high standard for setting aside the clause on grounds of inconvenience. Finally, the Court proclaimed: "It bears emphasis that forum-selection clauses contained in form passage contracts are subject to judicial scrutiny for fundamental fairness." That said, the Court found no evidence of abuse or bad faith on the part of petitioner. Two Justices dissented, observing that passengers are effectively forced to accept the forum selection clause, given that they cannot readily read it until they have received their tickets, which cannot be refunded.

Carnival Cruise should be read with *Stewart Organization, Inc. v. Ricoh Corp.*, 487 U.S. 22, 108 S. Ct. 2239, 101 L. Ed. 2d 22 (1988), holding that in a diversity case which has been brought in or removed to federal court, federal law governs a motion to transfer venue pursuant to 28 U.S.C. § 1404. The motion is addressed to the discretion of the federal district judge. A forum selection clause should be a significant but not necessarily determinative factor in exercising that discretion, said the Supreme Court. A useful treatment of these cases is provided in Walter W. Heiser, *Forum Selection Clauses in State Courts: Limitations on Enforcement After* Stewart *and* Carnival Cruise, 45 Fla. L. Rev. 361 (1993), and Walter W. Heiser, *Forum Selection Clauses in Federal Courts: Limitations on Enforcement After* Stewart *and* Carnival Cruise, 45 Fla. L. Rev. 554 (1993).

Dean Borchers, who is critical of *Carnival Cruise*, would limit the use of forum selection clauses in contracts below a specified monetary value. *See* Patrick J. Borchers, *Forum Selection Agreements in the Federal Courts After* Carnival Cruise: *A Proposal for Congressional Reform*, 67 Wash. L. Rev. 55 (1992).

(2) In *Brooke Group Ltd. v. JCH Syndicate 488*, 87 N.Y.2d 530, 640 N.Y.S.2d 479, 663 N.E.2d 665 (1996), cited in the principal case, the Court held that a clause in which the defendant agreed that it would, "at the request of the [plaintiff] submit to the jurisdiction of a Court of competent jurisdiction within the United States" was a "service of suit" clause, not a "forum selection" clause and that the clause was therefore merely permissive, not mandatory. Thus, it was held that the defendant could properly move to dismiss the New York action on forum non conveniens grounds. Is *Brooke Group* overruled by the principal case?

(3) New York state courts have held that a service of suit or forum selection clause will not be enforced if unconscionable. In *Paragon Homes, Inc. v. Carter*,

56 Misc. 2d 463, 288 N.Y.S.2d 817 (Sup. Ct.), *aff'd*, 30 A.D.2d 1052, 295 N.Y.S.2d 606 (2d Dep't 1968), the plaintiff, an assignee of a Maine corporation in the home improvement business, sought to rely on a consent clause in the assignor's contract with defendant consumer, a Massachusetts resident. The latter had consented to submit to the jurisdiction of New York Supreme Court, Nassau County. The court held jurisdiction lacking on the grounds of unconscionability, indicating that the clause was inserted to harass the defendant. Would the result have been different if the assignor had been a New York corporation? *Cf. National Equipment Rental, Ltd. v. Szukhent*, 375 U.S. 311, 84 S. Ct. 411 (1964).

(4) A forum selection clause may be unenforceable if it is part of a contract that itself would not be enforced because it was procured by fraud. *De Sola Group, Inc. v. Coors Brewing Co.*, 199 A.D.2d 141, 605 N.Y.S.2d 83 (1st Dep't 1993) (alternate ground). *Compare Rokeby-Johnson v. Kentucky Agricultural Energy Corp.*, 108 A.D.2d 336, 489 N.Y.S.2d 69 (1st Dep't 1985) (stating that the validity of the clause is not in issue unless the party challenging it alleges that the clause itself was induced by fraud).

(5) Sometimes parties to a contract will include a clause providing that the law of a particular forum will apply. While consent to be sued in the jurisdiction whose law is chosen is not necessarily implicit in such a clause, *Pal Pools, Inc. v. Billiot Bros., Inc.*, 57 A.D.2d 891, 394 N.Y.S.2d 280 (2d Dep't 1977), the clause may be a factor in deciding whether litigation in the chosen forum is permissible for due process purposes.

(6) You should gather from this brief discussion that problems of forum choice and choice of law must be considered by an attorney well in advance of litigation, indeed, whenever involved in the preparation of agreements to which one or more parties are non-residents.

§ 1.06 JURISDICTION BASED ON SPECIFIC CONTACTS WITH THE STATE

We have seen that under traditional and still lively principles, a defendant present or domiciled in the state is subject to jurisdiction regardless of whether the cause of action itself has any relationship to the state, *i.e.*, "general" jurisdiction. Jurisdiction may be available in other cases under CPLR 302, subject to constitutional restraints. So-called "specific" or "long arm" jurisdiction is distinguished from jurisdiction based on presence (including "doing business") or domicile, in that it is limited to cases in which the cause of action arises from the New York contacts of the defendant. *See* CPLR 302.

The constitutional limits on the states' power to exercise long arm jurisdiction have been addressed in a number of Supreme Court decisions in recent years. In this chapter, the leading decisions will be presented in the context in which they are most relevant, even though they do not deal directly with the New York statute under consideration.

[A] Transacting Business in New York: CPLR 302(a)(1)

PROBLEM D

Mantua is an Italian investor who occasionally trades on exchanges in Europe. Enticed by an advertisement in an international publication ("The White Meat That Will Earn You Green"), he allegedly ordered 8,000 pork bellies on the New York market by telephone and e-mail to Rhoan, Loads, a New York brokerage house. After a precipitous subsequent drop in the price, he denied placing the order and refused to pay. Rhoan, Loads now sues for the price, causing a summons to be served on Mantua in Italy. Is there jurisdiction under CPLR 302(a)(1)? Can jurisdiction be exercised constitutionally?

BURGER KING CORP. v. RUDZEWICZ
United States Supreme Court
471 U. S. 462, 105 S. Ct. 2174, 85 L. Ed. 2d 528 (1985)

JUSTICE BRENNAN delivered the opinion of the Court.

The State of Florida's long-arm statute extends jurisdiction to "[a]ny person, whether or not a citizen or resident of this state," who, inter alia, "[b]reach[es] a contract in this state by failing to perform acts required by the contract to be performed in this state," so long as the cause of action arises from the alleged contractual breach. Fla.Stat. § 48.193(1)(g) (Supp.1984). The United States District Court for the Southern District of Florida, sitting in diversity, relied on this provision in exercising personal jurisdiction over a Michigan resident who allegedly had breached a franchise agreement with a Florida corporation by failing to make required payments in Florida. The question presented is whether this exercise of long-arm jurisdiction offended "traditional conception[s] of fair play and substantial justice" embodied in the Due Process Clause of the Fourteenth Amendment. *International Shoe Co. v. Washington*, 326 U.S. 310, 320, 66 S.Ct. 154, 160, 90 L.Ed. 95 (1945).

I

. . . .

B

Burger King commenced the instant action in the United States District Court for the Southern District of Florida in May 1981, invoking that court's diversity jurisdiction pursuant to 28 U.S.C. § 1332(a) and its original jurisdiction over federal trademark disputes pursuant to § 1338(a). Burger King alleged that Rudzewicz and MacShara had breached their franchise obligations "within [the jurisdiction of] this district court" by failing to make the required payments "at plaintiff's place of business in Miami, Dade County, Florida" . . . .

After a 3-day bench trial, the court concluded that it had "jurisdiction over the subject matter and the parties to the cause." App. 159. Finding that Rudzewicz and MacShara had breached their franchise agreements with Burger King and had infringed Burger King's trademarks and service marks, the court entered judgment against them, jointly and severally for $228,875 in contract damages. The court also ordered them "to immediately close Burger King Restaurant Number 775 from continued operation or to immediately give the keys and possession of said restaurant to Burger King Corporation," *id.*, at 163. . . .

[On appeal, the Court of Appeals for the Eleventh Circuit reversed the judgment, concluding that the District Court could not properly exercise personal jurisdiction over Rudzewicz. — Eds.]

II

A

The Due Process Clause protects an individual's liberty interest in not being subject to the binding judgments of a forum with which he has established no meaningful "contacts, ties, or relations." *International Shoe Co. v. Washington*, 326 U.S., at 319, 66 S.Ct., at 160. By requiring that individuals have "fair warning that a particular activity may subject [them] to the jurisdiction of a foreign sovereign," *Shaffer v. Heitner*, 433 U.S. 186, 218, 97 S.Ct. 2569, 2587, 53 L.Ed.2d 683 (1977) (STEVENS, J., concurring in judgment), the Due Process Clause "gives a degree of predictability to the legal system that allows potential defendants to structure their primary conduct with some minimum assurance as to where that conduct will and will not render them liable to suit," *World-Wide Volkswagen Corp. v. Woodson*, 444 U.S. 286, 297, 100 S.Ct. 559, 567, 62 L.Ed.2d 490 (1980).

Where a forum seeks to assert specific jurisdiction over an out-of-state defendant who has not consented to suit there, this "fair warning" requirement is satisfied if the defendant has "purposefully directed" his activities at residents of the forum . . . and the litigation results from alleged injuries that "arise out of or relate to" those activities. . . . Thus "[t]he forum State does not exceed its powers under the Due Process Clause if it asserts personal jurisdiction over a corporation that delivers its products into the stream of commerce with the expectation that they will be purchased by consumers in the forum State" and those products subsequently injure forum consumers. *World-Wide Volkswagen Corp. v. Woodson, supra*, 444 U.S., at 297-298, 100 S.Ct., at 567-568. Similarly, a publisher who distributes magazines in a distant State may fairly be held accountable in that forum for damages resulting there from an allegedly defamatory story. *Keeton v. Hustler Magazine, Inc., supra; see also Calder v. Jones*, 104 S.Ct. 1482, 79 L.Ed.2d 804 (1984) (suit against author and editor). And with respect to interstate contractual obligations, we have emphasized that parties who "reach out beyond one state and create continuing relationships and obligations with citizens of another state" are subject to regulation and sanctions in the other State for the consequences of their activities. *Travelers Health Assn. v. Virginia*, 339 U.S. 643, 647, 70 S.Ct. 927, 929, 94 L.Ed. 1154 (1950). . . .

We have noted several reasons why a forum legitimately may exercise personal jurisdiction over a nonresident who "purposefully directs" his activities toward forum residents. A State generally has a "manifest interest" in providing its residents with a convenient forum for redressing injuries inflicted by out-of-state actors. *Id.*, at 223, 78 S.Ct., at 201; *see also Calder v. Jones, supra.* Moreover, where individuals "purposefully derive benefit" from their interstate activities, *Kulko v. California Superior Court*, 436 U.S. 84, 96, 98 S.Ct. 1690, 1699, 56 L. Ed.2d 132 (1978), it may well be unfair to allow them to escape having to account in other States for consequences that arise proximately from such activities; the Due Process Clause may not readily be wielded as a territorial shield to avoid interstate obligations that have been voluntarily assumed. And because "modern transportation and communications have made it much less burdensome for a party sued to defend himself in a State where he engages in economic activity," it usually will not be unfair to subject him to the burdens of litigating in another forum for disputes relating to such activity. *McGee v. International Life Insurance Co., supra*, 355 U.S., at 223, 78 S.Ct., at 201.

Notwithstanding these considerations, the constitutional touchstone remains whether the defendant purposefully established "minimum contacts" in the forum State. *International Shoe Co. v. Washington, supra*, 326 U.S., at 316, 66 S.Ct., at 158. Although it has been argued that foreseeability of causing injury in another State should be sufficient to establish such contacts there when policy considerations so require, the Court has consistently held that this kind of foreseeability is not a "sufficient benchmark" for exercising personal jurisdiction. *World-Wide Volkswagen Corp. v. Woodson*, 444 U.S., at 295, 100 S.Ct., at 566. Instead, "the foreseeability that is critical to due process analysis . . . is that the defendant's conduct and connection with the forum State are such that he should reasonably anticipate being haled into court there." *Id.*, at 297, 100 S.Ct., at 567. In defining when it is that a potential defendant should "reasonably anticipate" out-of-state litigation, the Court frequently has drawn from the reasoning of *Hanson v. Denckla*, 357 U.S. 235, 253, 78 S.Ct. 1228, 1239-1240, 2 L.Ed.2d 1283 (1958):

> The unilateral activity of those who claim some relationship with a nonresident defendant cannot satisfy the requirement of contact with the forum State. The application of that rule will vary with the quality and nature of the defendant's activity, but it is essential in each case that there be some act by which the defendant purposefully avails itself of the privilege of conducting activities within the forum State, thus invoking the benefits and protections of its laws.

This "purposeful availment" requirement ensures that a defendant will not be haled into a jurisdiction solely as a result of "random," "fortuitous," or "attenuated" contacts . . . or of the "unilateral activity of another party or a third person,". . . . Jurisdiction is proper, however, where the contacts proximately result from actions by the defendant himself that create a "substantial connection" with the forum State.

Jurisdiction in these circumstances may not be avoided merely because the defendant did not physically enter the forum State. Although territorial presence frequently will enhance a potential defendant's affiliation with a State and reinforce the reasonable foreseeability of suit there, it is an inescapable fact of modern commercial life that a substantial amount of business is transacted solely by mail and wire communications across state lines, thus obviating the need for physical presence within a State in which business is conducted.

Once it has been decided that a defendant purposefully established minimum contacts within the forum State, these contacts may be considered in light of other factors to determine whether the assertion of personal jurisdiction would comport with "fair play and substantial justice." *International Shoe Co. v. Washington*, 326 U.S., at 320, 66 S.Ct., at 160. Thus courts in "appropriate case[s]" may evaluate "the burden on the defendant," "the forum State's interest in adjudicating the dispute," "the plaintiff's interest in obtaining convenient and effective relief," "the interstate judicial system's interest in obtaining the most efficient resolution of controversies," and the "shared interest of the several States in furthering fundamental substantive social policies." *World-Wide Volkswagen Corp. v. Woodson*, *supra*, 444 U.S., at 292, 100 S.Ct., at 564. These considerations sometimes serve to establish the reasonableness of jurisdiction upon a lesser showing of minimum contacts than would otherwise be required. *See, e.g., Keeton v. Hustler Magazine, Inc.*, *supra, Calder v. Jones, supra, McGee v. International Life Insurance Co., supra.* On the other hand, where a defendant who purposefully has directed his activities at forum residents seeks to defeat jurisdiction, he must present a compelling case that the presence of some other considerations would render jurisdiction unreasonable. Most such considerations usually may be accommodated through means short of finding jurisdiction unconstitutional. For example, the potential clash of the forum's law with the "fundamental substantive social policies" of another State may be accommodated through application of the forum's choice-of-law rules. Similarly, a defendant claiming substantial inconvenience may seek a change of venue.

Nevertheless, minimum requirements inherent in the concept of "fair play and substantial justice" may defeat the reasonableness of jurisdiction even if the defendant has purposefully engaged in forum activities. *World-Wide Volkswagen Corp. v. Woodson*, 444 U.S., at 292, 100 S.Ct., at 564; *see also* Restatement (Second) of Conflict of Laws §§ 36-37 (1971). As we previously have noted, jurisdictional rules may not be employed in such a way as to make litigation "so gravely difficult and inconvenient" that a party unfairly is at a "severe disadvantage" in comparison to his opponent. . . .

B

(1)

Applying these principles to the case at hand, we believe there is substantial record evidence supporting the District Court's conclusion that the assertion of personal jurisdiction over Rudzewicz in Florida for the alleged breach of his franchise agreement did not offend due process. At the outset, we note a continued division among lower courts respecting whether and to what extent a contract can constitute a "contact" for purposes of due process analysis.

If the question is whether an individual's contract with an out-of-state party alone can automatically establish sufficient minimum contacts in the other party's home forum, we believe the answer clearly is that it cannot. The Court long ago rejected the notion that personal jurisdiction might turn on "mechanical" tests, *International Shoe Co. v. Washington*, 326 U.S., at 319, 66 S.Ct., at 159, or on "conceptualistic . . . theories of the place of contracting or of performance," *Hoopeston Canning Co. v. Cullen, supra*, 318 U.S., at 316, 63 S.Ct., at 604. Instead, we have emphasized the need for a "highly realistic" approach that recognizes that a "contract" is "ordinarily but an intermediate step serving to tie up prior business negotiations with future consequences which themselves are the real object of the business transaction." *Id.*, at 316-317, 63 S.Ct., at 604-605. It is these factors — prior negotiations and contemplated future consequences, along with the terms of the contract and the parties' actual course of dealing — that must be evaluated in determining whether the defendant purposefully established minimum contacts within the forum.

In this case, no physical ties to Florida can be attributed to Rudzewicz other than [his partner] MacShara's brief training course in Miami. Rudzewicz did not maintain offices in Florida and, for all that appears from the record, has never even visited there. Yet this franchise dispute grew directly out of "a contract which had a *substantial* connection with that State." *McGee v. International Life Insurance Co.*, 355 U.S., at 223, 78 S.Ct., at 201 (emphasis added). Eschewing the option of operating an independent local enterprise, Rudzewicz deliberately "reach[ed] out beyond" Michigan and negotiated with a Florida corporation for the purchase of a long-term franchise and the manifold benefits that would derive from affiliation with a nationwide organization. *Travelers Health Assn. v. Virginia*, 339 U.S., at 647, 70 S.Ct., at 929. Upon approval, he entered into a carefully structured 20-year relationship that envisioned continuing and wide-reaching contacts with Burger King in Florida. In light of Rudzewicz's voluntary acceptance of the long-term and exacting regulation of his business from Burger King's Miami headquarters, the "quality and nature" of his relationship to the company in Florida can in no sense be viewed as "random," "fortuitous," or "attenuated." . . . Rudzewicz's refusal to make the contractually required payments in Miami, and his continued use of Burger King's trademarks and confidential business information after his termination, caused foreseeable injuries to the corporation in Florida. For these reasons it was, at the very least, presumptively reasonable for Rudzewicz to be called to account there for such injuries.

The Court of Appeals concluded, however, that . . . Rudzewicz had no "reason to anticipate a Burger King suit outside of Michigan." 724 F.2d, at 1511. *See also post* (STEVENS, J., dissenting). This reasoning overlooks substantial record evidence indicating that Rudzewicz most certainly knew that he was affiliating himself with an enterprise based primarily in Florida. The contract documents themselves emphasize that Burger King's operations are conducted and supervised from the Miami headquarters, that all relevant notices and payments must be sent there, and that the agreements were made in and enforced from Miami. . . . Throughout these disputes, the Miami headquarters and the Michigan franchisees carried on a continuous course of direct communications by mail and by telephone, and it was the Miami headquarters that made the key negotiating decisions out of which the instant litigation arose.

Moreover, we believe the Court of Appeals gave insufficient weight to provisions in the various franchise documents providing that all disputes would be governed by Florida law. . . . The Court in *Hanson* and subsequent cases has emphasized that choice-of-law analysis — which focuses on all elements of a transaction, and not simply on the defendant's conduct — is distinct from minimum-contacts jurisdictional analysis — which focuses at the threshold solely on the defendant's purposeful connection to the forum. Nothing in our cases, however, suggests that a choice-of-law provision should be ignored in considering whether a defendant has "purposefully invoked the benefits and protections of a State's laws" for jurisdictional purposes. Although such a provision standing alone would be insufficient to confer jurisdiction, we believe that, when combined with the 20-year interdependent relationship Rudzewicz established with Burger King's Miami headquarters, it reinforced his deliberate affiliation with the forum State and the reasonable foreseeability of possible litigation there. . . .

(2)

Nor has Rudzewicz pointed to other factors that can be said persuasively to outweigh the considerations discussed above and to establish the unconstitutionality of Florida's assertion of jurisdiction. We cannot conclude that Florida had no "legitimate interest in holding [Rudzewicz] answerable on a claim related to" the contacts he had established in that State. . . .

The Court of Appeals also concluded, however, that the parties' dealings involved "a characteristic disparity of bargaining power" and "elements of surprise," and that Rudzewicz "lacked fair notice" of the potential for litigation in Florida because the contractual provisions suggesting to the contrary were merely "boilerplate declarations in a lengthy printed contract." . . . To the contrary, Rudzewicz was represented by counsel throughout these complex transactions and, as Judge Johnson observed in dissent below, was himself an experienced accountant "who for five months conducted negotiations with

Burger King over the terms of the franchise and lease agreements, and who obligated himself personally to contracts requiring over time payments that exceeded $1 million." 724 F.2d, at 1514. Rudzewicz was able to secure a modest reduction in rent and other concessions from Miami headquarters; moreover, to the extent that Burger King's terms were inflexible, Rudzewicz presumably decided that the advantages of affiliating with a national organization provided sufficient commercial benefits as to offset the detriments.

III

Notwithstanding these considerations, the Court of Appeals apparently believed that it was necessary to reject jurisdiction in this case as a prophylactic measure, reasoning that an affirmance of the District Court's judgment would result in the exercise of jurisdiction over "out-of-state consumers to collect payments due on modest personal purchases" and would "sow the seeds of default judgments against franchisees owing smaller debts." 724 F.2d, at 1511. We share the Court of Appeals' broader concerns and therefore reject any talismanic jurisdictional formulas; "the facts of each case must [always] be weighed" in determining whether personal jurisdiction would comport with "fair play and substantial justice." *Kulko v. California Superior Court*, 436 U.S., at 92, 98 S.Ct., at 1696-1697.

For the reasons set forth above, however, these dangers are not present in the instant case. Because Rudzewicz established a substantial and continuing relationship with Burger King's Miami headquarters, received fair notice from the contract documents and the course of dealing that he might be subject to suit in Florida, and has failed to demonstrate how jurisdiction in that forum would otherwise be fundamentally unfair, we conclude that the District Court's exercise of jurisdiction pursuant to Florida Stat. § 48.193(1)(g) (Supp. 1984) did not offend due process.

. . . .

NOTES

(1) The Court sets forth a two step approach to the constitutionality of an exercise of long arm jurisdiction. First, the forum court must determine whether the defendant has purposefully established minimum contacts with the state such that it would be reasonable to anticipate being sued there. If not, there is no jurisdiction. If yes, the court should then examine the contacts in the light of other factors to determine whether the exercise of jurisdiction would comport with "fair play and substantial justice." Note that if the first of the preceding two issues is resolved against the defendant, the burden shifts to him to present a compelling case that other factors make it unreasonable to exercise jurisdiction.

(2) Relevant literature includes Martin B. Louis, *Jurisdiction Over Those Who Breach Their Contracts: The Lessons of* Burger King, 72 N.C. L. Rev. 55 (1993); William J. Knudsen, Keeton, Calder, Helicopteros *and* Burger King — International Shoe*'s Most Recent Progeny*, 39 U. Miami L. Rev. 809 (1985); David A. Sonenshein, *The Error of a Balancing Approach to Due Process Jurisdiction Over the Person*, 59 Temp. L.Q. 47 (1986).

DEUTSCHE BANK SECURITIES, INC. v. MONTANA BOARD OF INVESTORS
Court of Appeals
7 N.Y.3d 65, 818 N.Y.S.2d 164, 850 N.E.2d 1140 (2006)

CHIEF JUDGE KAYE.

This appeal concerns a March 25, 2002 bond transaction between plaintiff Deutsche Bank Securities, Inc. (DBSI) and defendant Montana Board of Investments (MBOI). DBSI, a Delaware Corporation with its headquarters in New York, is (among other things) engaged in trading securities for its own account and for clients. MBOI is a Montana state agency charged with managing an investment program for public funds, the public retirement system and state compensation insurance fund assets. In the 13 months prior to the transaction at issue here, DBSI and MBOI had engaged in approximately eight other bond transactions with a face value totaling over $100 million. These transactions were principally negotiated between Stephen Williams, a director in the Global Market Sales Division of DBSI in New York, and Robert Bugni, Senior Investment Officer-Fixed Income with MBOI in Montana.

On the morning of March 25, 2002, from New York City, Williams contacted Bugni to ask if MBOI was interested in swapping its Pennzoil-Quaker State Company 2009 bonds for DBSI's Toys R Us bonds, or selling the Pennzoil bonds to DBSI for a stated price. Williams communicated with Bugni electronically through the Bloomberg Messaging System, an instant messaging service provided to Bloomberg subscribers. Bugni responded that MBOI was not interested in the swap proposal. Williams countered that the Pennzoil bid looked good but Bugni replied that the bonds "will get a lot tighter" (increase in price) and MBOI wanted to hold onto them. Williams ended the exchange with a simple "THX" (thanks).

Approximately ten minutes later, Bugni, knowing that Williams was in New York, sent him a new instant message asking whether the price originally quoted by Williams applied only to the swap, or if it would be the same for a cash purchase. Bugni indicated that MBOI had $15 million of Pennzoil bonds it might be interested in selling. Williams replied that DBSI would like to purchase $5 million of the bonds outright and could probably "trade the balance with one phone call." Bugni countered with a request that Williams investigate whether all $15 million could be sold at the price he quoted. After a DBSI colleague contacted some of his clients and found that DBSI had a sufficient market for all $15 million, Williams replied to Bugni that DBSI would purchase all $15 million at his quoted price, with a settlement date of March 28, 2002. Bugni agreed, and Williams sent a trade ticket and confirmation of the deal.

Hours after the parties concluded their agreement, on the evening of March 25, 2002, Shell Oil publicly announced that it had agreed to acquire Pennzoil-Quaker State Company, an announcement that would potentially increase the value of the bonds. The following day, MBOI advised DBSI that it was breaking the trade because it believed the buyer had inside information and the trade was "unethical & probably illegal." As a result of MBOI's cancellation, DBSI purchased the Pennzoil bonds elsewhere, paying an additional $1.6 million.

DBSI then commenced this action in Supreme Court, New York County, alleging breach of contract, and MBOI answered. After limited discovery, DBSI sought summary judgment as to liability as well as dismissal of MBOI's affirmative defenses. MBOI cross-moved for dismissal of the action based on its affirmative defenses of lack of personal jurisdiction, sovereign immunity, and comity. Supreme Court granted MBOI's cross-motion to dismiss the complaint for lack of personal jurisdiction and denied DBSI's motion for partial summary judgment. The Appellate Division in a comprehensive opinion unanimously reversed, dismissing MBOI's affirmative defenses and granting DBSI's motion for partial summary judgment as to liability.[1] We now affirm.

Discussion

. . . .

Personal Jurisdiction

New York's long-arm statute provides that "a court may exercise personal jurisdiction over any non-domiciliary . . . who in person or through an agent . . . transacts any business within the state or contracts anywhere to supply goods or services in the state" (CPLR 302[a][1]). By this "single act statute", . . . proof of one transaction in New York is sufficient to invoke jurisdiction, even though the defendant never enters New York, so long as the defendant's activities here were purposeful and there is a substantial relationship between the transaction and the claim asserted" (*Kreutter v McFadden Oil Corp.*, 71 NY2d 460, 467 [1988]).

As we noted in *Kreutter*, the growth of national markets for commercial trade, as well as technological advances in communication, enable a party to transact enormous volumes of business within a state without physically entering it. Thus, we held that "[s]o long as a party avails itself of the benefits of the forum, has sufficient minimum contacts with it, and should reasonably expect to defend its actions there, due process is not offended if that party is sub-

---

[1] The Appellate Division granted MBOI leave to appeal, certifying to us the following "Was the order of this Court, which reversed the order of Supreme Court, properly made?"

jected to jurisdiction even if not 'present' in that State" (*id.* at 466). We have in the past recognized 302(a)(1) long-arm jurisdiction over commercial actors and investors using electronic and telephonic means to project themselves into New York to conduct business transactions (*see e.g. Parke-Bernet Galleries, Inc. v Franklyn*, 26 NY2d 13 [1970]; *Ehrlich-Bober & Co., Inc. v University of Houston*, 49 NY2d 574 [1980]), and we do so again here.

MBOI should reasonably have expected to defend its actions in New York. As distinct from an out-of-state individual investor making a telephone call to a stockbroker in New York (*see L.F. Rothschild, Unterberg, Towbin v McTamney*, 59 NY2d 651 [1983]), MBOI is a sophisticated institutional trader that entered New York to transact business here by knowingly initiating and pursuing a negotiation with a DBSI employee in New York that culminated in the sale of $15 million in bonds. Negotiating substantial transactions such as this one was a major aspect of MBOI's mission — "part of its principal reason for being" (21 AD3d 90, 95 [2005]). Further, over the preceding 13 months, MBOI had engaged in approximately eight other bond transactions with DBSI's employee in New York, availing itself of the benefits of conducting business here, and thus had sufficient contacts with New York to authorize our courts to exercise jurisdiction over its person.[2] As Professor Siegel has observed, where a defendant "deals directly with the broker's New York office by phone or mail [or email] in a number of transactions instead of dealing with the broker at the broker's local office outside New York, long arm jurisdiction may be upheld" (Siegel, NY Prac § 86, at 152 [4th ed]).

In short, when the requirements of due process are met, as they are here, a sophisticated institutional trader knowingly entering our state — whether electronically or otherwise — to negotiate and conclude a substantial transaction is within the embrace of the New York long-arm statute.

. . . .

[The Court found MBOI's sovereign immunity claim to be without merit and rejected MBOI's comity claim. The Court also affirmed the grant of partial summary judgment for DBSI and found that the Appellate Division did not abuse its discretion in denying MBOI's request for additional discovery. — Eds.]

NOTES

(1) The principal case should be compared with *George Reiner & Co. v. Schwartz*, 41 N.Y.2d 648, 394 N.Y.S.2d 844, 363 N.E.2d 551 (1977), which emphasizes the physical presence of the defendant in the state as a factor in determining whether the defendant has transacted "any business within the

---

[2] Although we do not consider whether MBOI is "doing business" in New York such that it was "present" here (*see* CPLR 301), we note that, in the year preceding the transaction at issue, MBOI purchased approximately $471 million worth of securities directly from the New York offices of various entities in the securities industry.

state" for the purposes of CPLR 302(a)(1). George Reiner & Co., a New York corporation, sued Schwartz, a former employee who worked as a sales representative in his home state of Massachusetts, for allegedly drawing commissions in excess of the terms of his employment contract. The court upheld jurisdiction over Schwartz on the grounds that, at the request and expense of the plaintiff, he had traveled to the plaintiff's headquarters in New York, where he was interviewed, hired, and given a memorandum stipulating the terms of his employment. The Court wrote:

> [H]ere we have the "clearest sort of case" in which our courts would have 302 jurisdiction. Here, Schwartz was physically present in New York at the time the contract, establishing a continuing relationship between the parties, was negotiated and made and, the contract, made in New York, was the transaction out of which the cause of action arose. Additionally, we note that by such holding we have not overstepped constitutional bounds, for the acts upon which we rely, the defendant's coming into New York purposefully seeking employment, his interview and his entering into an agreement with a New York employer which contemplated and resulted in a continuing relationship between them, certainly are of the nature and quality to be deemed sufficient to render him liable to suit here. There can be no question that, by his acts, defendant has purposefully availed himself of the privilege of conducting activities in our jurisdiction, thus invoking the benefits and protection of our laws [citation omitted].

(2) The principal case illustrates that physical presence in New York is not necessary for a defendant to be subject to personal jurisdiction under CPLR 302(a)(1). The Court of Appeals reached this conclusion in prior cases: In *Parke-Bernet Galleries v. Franklyn*, cited in the principal case, the Court found presence through an "open" telephone line that allowed participation at an auction. However, in *M. Katz & Son Billiard Products, Inc. v. G. Correale & Sons, Inc.*, 26 A.D.2d 52, 270 N.Y.S.2d 672 (1st Dep't), *aff'd*, 20 N.Y.2d 903, 285 N.Y.S.2d 871, 232 N.E.2d 864 (1966), defendant, a New Jersey corporation, was held not to have transacted business when its employee ordered goods from the New York plaintiff by a phone call from New Jersey to New York.

(3) Problem D raises the problem of electronic transactions in the context of a securities purchase by an individual. Does *Deutsche Bank* help solve this problem? Prior to *Deutsche Bank*, the court in *L.F. Rothschild, Unterberg, Towbin v. McTamney*, 89 A.2d 540, 452 N.Y.S.2d 630 (1st Dep't 1982), *aff'd*, 59 N.Y.2d 651, 463 N.Y.S.2d 197 (1983), reached an opposite result, rejecting a claim of jurisdiction over a Pennsylvania defendant whose "several" telephone conversations with the New York broker had resulted in a single purchase order. On the other hand, the Appellate Division had held that a New York stock broker could properly rely on CPLR 302(a)(1) to assert a claim against an Alabama customer who had placed all his orders (some twenty-five transactions over four months) by phone and mail, never coming to New York himself, *L.F.*

Rothschild, Unterberg, Towbin v. Thompson, 78 A.D.2d 795, 433 N.Y.S.2d 6 (1st Dep't 1980).

(4) In *Ehrlich-Bober & Co. v. University of Houston*, 49 N.Y.2d 574, 427 N.Y.S.2d 604, 404 N.E.2d 726 (1980), the court upheld 302(a)(1) jurisdiction based on phone calls that were part of a series of similar securities transactions, some of which had been made when the defendant's representative came to the plaintiff's New York office. The court advanced an economic rationale for extending long arm jurisdiction in commercial cases:

> New York's recognized interest in maintaining and fostering its undisputed status as the preeminent commercial and financial nerve center of the Nation and the world naturally embraces a very strong policy of assuring ready access to a forum for redress of injuries arising out of transactions spawned here. Indeed, access to a convenient forum which dispassionately administers a known, stable, and commercially sophisticated body of law may be considered as much an attraction to conducting business in New York as its unique financial and communications resources.

(5) The issue of whether a defendant has transacted business for the purposes of CPLR 302(a)(1) without physically entering the state (personally or through an agent) has also bedeviled the courts in cases that do not involve the securities industry. Cases involving professional services are common. For example, a consensus is emerging under which out-of-state attorneys who perform legal services in New York for non-residents will be held subject to jurisdiction under CPLR 302(a)(1). *See Liberatore v. Calvino*, 293 A.D.2d 217, 221, 742 N.Y.S.2d 291, 293 (1st Dep't 2002), and cases cited. In *Liberatore*, jurisdiction was upheld over a Rhode Island lawyer sued for legal malpractice in New York in a suit brought by a Rhode Island resident who alleged the negligent prosecution of plaintiff's underlying New York personal injury action which arose out of a New York accident. The lawyer, who had referred the case to a New York attorney after preliminary investigation from Rhode Island,

> projected himself into the state to perform services by contracting with plaintiff to legally represent her here for . . . her New York personal injury claim . . . in accordance with New York law. He transacted business in New York by purposefully pursuing redress for plaintiff over a three-year period. . . . He engaged in numerous written and telephonic communications with New York. . . . In rendering his services, he availed himself of the benefits and protections offered by various New York statutes. . . . The totality of the circumstances . . . makes it unquestionably fair and just that he be subject to New York jurisdiction for the legal malpractice claim resulting from his negligence in providing such services.

That said, there are still limits to the exercise of 302(a)(1) jurisdiction. The detailed opinion in *O'Brien v. Hackensack Univ. Med. Ctr.*, 305 A.D.2d 199, 760

N.Y.S.2d 425 (1st Dep't 2003), exemplifies that the jurisdictional inquiry has been intensely fact-specific. Reversing the lower court, the Appellate Division held in this medical malpractice action brought by a New York resident, that jurisdiction could not be obtained over a New Jersey medical center even though it allegedly solicited and treated patients from New York, including plaintiff. There were insufficient contacts to justify jurisdiction under CPLR 302(a)(1). Nor was CPLR 302(a)(3) applicable because the injury took place where the alleged act of malpractice was committed.

Similarly, in *Concrete Pipe & Products Corp. v. Modern Building Materials, Inc.*, 213 A.D.2d 1023, 624 N.Y.S.2d 496 (4th Dep't 1995), the court found jurisdiction lacking over a Florida defendant who had allegedly breached a lease agreement that was negotiated and consummated through telephone, fax and mail communications. The court said: "It is well established that a foreign defendant whose only contact with New York is the purchase of goods by telephone or mail from a New York plaintiff is not subject to long-arm jurisdiction. . . ." 624 N.Y.S.2d at 497.

See also Libra Global Technology Services v. Telemedia International, LTD., 279 A.D.2d 326, 719 N.Y.S.2d 53 (1st Dep't 2001) (a 45-minute video conference for contract negotiations was insufficient for jurisdiction); *Granat v. Bochner*, 268 A.D.2d 365, 702 N.Y.S.2d 262 (1st Dep't 2000) (faxes and phone calls do not amount to transacting business in New York under the long-arm statute).

One of the authors of this book has argued for a bright line test: "If one telephone call is really significant in the transaction of a piece of business in New York there should be jurisdiction over a cause of action arising from that call. When the defendant picks up the phone, directs a call into New York and makes a deal, he or she is clearly engaging in purposeful activity in New York just as certainly as if he or she came bodily into the state, struck a deal and left the same day." Robert A. Barker, *Phone Calls and Long-Arm Jurisdiction*, N.Y.L.J., March 15, 1993, p. 3. Do you agree? What are the implications of this bright line rule for email and web transactions? What if a California sender of an email is not sure where the recipient is, but suspects that the message will be read in New York? Did the Court of Appeals in *Deutsche Bank* adopt Prof. Barker's approach?

(6) Not all modern cases applying CPLR 302(a)(1) have turned on the nature and frequency of electronic communications. For example, *Indosuez Int'l Fin. B.V. v. Nat'l Reserve Bank*, 98 N.Y.2d 238, 746 N.Y.S.2d 631, 774 N.E.2d 696 (2002), was an action by a Dutch corporation against a Russian bank, that alleged a default on a series of option contracts. Long arm jurisdiction was found by virtue of the following facts: The defendant maintained a New York bank account, the agreement provided that payments were to be made through that account, and some payments had in fact been so made. Alternatively, jurisdiction was proper because some of the documents contained a clause designating New York as the forum and the court found that the parties intended the forum selection clause to apply to all of the agreements.

PROBLEM E

Mr. Windswept runs a wilderness touring business in Wyoming. Each year, he visits New York City to give a promotional slide show and sign up customers. Ms. Climber, who attended the show and then bought a place on the tour, was injured while on a trek in the Wyoming hills. Do the New York courts have jurisdiction over Windswept if he is served personally in Wyoming with a summons commencing an action to redress Climber's injuries?

JOHNSON v. WARD
Court of Appeals
4 N.Y.3d 516, 797 N.Y.S.2d 33, 829 N.E.2d 1201 (2005)

GRAFFEO, J.

In this case, we are asked whether long-arm jurisdiction exists over a non-resident holding a New York driver's license and car registration for a tort claim arising from an out-of-state motor vehicle accident. We conclude that personal jurisdiction does not lie under CPLR 302(a)(1) because there is an insufficient nexus between plaintiffs' personal injury action and any New York transactions.

On October 12, 1997, plaintiffs Roger Johnson and Monique White allegedly sustained injuries when their vehicle was struck from behind by a car driven by defendant Daniel Ward. Although the accident occurred in New Jersey, all three individuals were New York residents. At that time, defendant possessed a New York driver's license and had registered his vehicle in New York. In December 1997, defendant moved to New Jersey and in 1998 he surrendered his New York license in favor of a New Jersey license.

After these events, plaintiffs commenced this negligence action against defendant in Supreme Court, New York County, in October 2000. Defendant moved to dismiss the complaint for lack of personal jurisdiction pursuant to CPLR 3211(a)(8). Supreme Court granted the motion and dismissed the complaint, finding no basis for long-arm jurisdiction. Upon reargument, the court adhered to its original determination.

The Appellate Division, with one Justice dissenting, reversed and reinstated the complaint. The majority reasoned that defendant's New York license and vehicle registration satisfied the "transacting business" requirement of CPLR 302(a)(1) and that a substantial nexus existed between the cause of action and defendant's New York activities inasmuch as plaintiffs' claim "arose over the operation by a driver licensed in New York of a vehicle registered in New York" (6 A.D.3d 286, 287, 775 N.Y.S.2d 297 [1st Dept 2004]). In contrast, the dissent determined that defendant's possession of a New York license and vehicle registration did not constitute a transaction of business within the meaning of CPLR 302(a)(1) because the statute contemplates only commercial or financial activities. Alternatively, the dissent concluded that the New York license and vehicle registration were not "in any way related to this out-of-state accident so as to create the necessary nexus to invoke long-arm jurisdiction" (*id.* at 292). The Appellate Division granted leave to this Court, certifying the following question: "Was the order of this Court, which reversed the order of the Supreme Court, properly made?" We answer in the negative and therefore reverse.

CPLR 302 provides in part:

"(a) Acts which are the basis of jurisdiction. As to a cause of action arising from any of the acts enumerated in this section, a court may exercise personal jurisdiction over any non-domiciliary . . . who in person or through an agent:

"1. transacts any business within the state or contracts anywhere to supply goods or services in the state."

As relevant in this case, long-arm jurisdiction over a nondomiciliary exists where (i) a defendant transacted business within the state and (ii) the cause of action arose from that transaction of business. If either prong of the statute is not met, jurisdiction cannot be conferred under CPLR 302(a)(1).

We have recognized that a "substantial relationship" must be established between a defendant's transactions in New York and a plaintiff's cause of action in order to satisfy the nexus requirement of the statute (*Kreutter v. McFadden Oil Corp.*, 71 N.Y.2d 460, 467, 522 N.E.2d 40, 527 N.Y.S.2d 195 [1988]). Consequently, we have upheld long-arm jurisdiction over a nondomiciliary where the claim had the requisite nexus to an in-state transaction (*see e.g. George Reiner & Co. v. Schwartz*, 41 N.Y.2d 648, 653, 363 N.E.2d 551, 394 N.Y.S.2d 844 [1977] [concluding there was jurisdiction over a Massachusetts resident for breach of an employment contract entered into in New York]; *Singer v. Walker*, 15 N.Y.2d 443, 467, 209 N.E.2d 68, 261 N.Y.S.2d 8 [1965] [sustaining jurisdiction because plaintiff's personal injury claim resulting from the use of a defective hammer arose from "the purposeful activities engaged in by [defendant] in this State in connection with the sale of its products in the New York market"], *cert denied sub nom. Estwing Mfg. Co. v. Singer*, 382 U.S. 905, 15 L. Ed. 2d 158, 86 S. Ct. 241 [1965]). On the other hand, we have ruled that jurisdiction is not justified where the relationship between the claim and transaction is too attenuated (*see e.g. Talbot v. Johnson Newspaper Corp.*, 71 N.Y.2d 827, 829, 522 N.E.2d 1027, 527 N.Y.S.2d 729 [1988] [holding that the nexus between a coach's defamation action and a former student's pursuit of a college degree in New York was insufficient to support jurisdiction]).

Here, we conclude that plaintiffs have failed to establish a sufficient nexus between the purported transactions of business in New York and the negligence claim.* Plaintiffs' cause of action arose out of defendant's allegedly neg-

---

* In light of this determination, it is unnecessary for us to decide whether defendant's possession of a New York driver's license and vehicle registration qualifies as a transaction of "business" within the meaning of CPLR 302(a)(1).

ligent driving in New Jersey, not from the issuance of a New York driver's license or vehicle registration. The relationship between the negligence claim and defendant's possession of a New York license and registration at the time of the accident is too insubstantial to warrant a New York court's exercise of personal jurisdiction over defendant. The negligent driver could have had a license from any state, or no license — that defendant had a New York license and registration is merely coincidental. As such, plaintiffs cannot rely on CPLR 302(a)(1) to establish long-arm jurisdiction based on the facts of this case.

Accordingly, the order of the Appellate Division should be reversed, with costs, defendant's motion to dismiss the complaint granted and the certified question answered in the negative.

NOTE

Deciding whether a claim for personal injury "arises from" a transaction of business in New York is difficult when the injury occurs outside the state but was preceded by related activities in New York. As in the principal case, the requisite "substantial relationship" between the New York transaction and the cause of action was found lacking in *Talbot v. Johnson Newspaper Corp.*, 71 N.Y.2d 827, 527 N.Y.S.2d 729, 522 N.E.2d 1027 (1988). Plaintiff Talbot, a coach at St. Lawrence University in New York brought a defamation action against Patricia MacLaren, a graduate of the college, and her father, both of whom were California residents. Talbot claimed that they had defamed him by telling the trustees and a student newspaper in 1984 that Patricia had seen Talbot drunk at a fraternity party in 1982 while she was a student. The Court held that her attendance at the university was a purposeful activity in New York, but the alleged defamation, "years after the termination of that relationship" did not have the nexus to the New York activities required by CPLR 302(a)(1). *See also Gelfand v. Tanner Motor Tours, Ltd.*, 339 F.2d 317 (2d Cir. 1964), in which the plaintiffs sought to recover for personal injuries sustained in a bus crash occurring on a trip between Las Vegas and the Grand Canyon. The Second Circuit refused to sustain jurisdiction under CPLR 302, even if the sale of tickets to plaintiffs in New York could be held to constitute the transaction of business by the defendant, because the cause of action in tort did not arise from that sale:

> The alleged negligence of defendants, the subsequent injury to plaintiffs, and every relevant occurrence connecting these two events, all took place three thousand miles from Long Island, New York. It cannot even be said that the duty of due care owed by defendants to plaintiff arose in New York, for that duty did not finally arise until plaintiffs boarded defendants' bus in Las Vegas.

Id. at 321-22.

Compare *Lebel v. Tello*, 272 A.D.2d 103, 707 N.Y.S.2d 426 (1st Dep't 2000), which involved an airplane crash in New Mexico. The court held that New York had jurisdiction over the injured passenger's action against the defendant pilot (a California resident) pursuant to CPLR 302(a)(1) because there was "a clearly articulable nexus between the accident and the transactions in New York." The airplane had been purchased by the defendant in New York, the defendant had spent the three days in New York prior to the flight getting flying instructions from the plaintiff (a New York resident), and had hired the plaintiff to continue the instruction on the cross-country flight that ended in the accident.[*]

Try to apply the "arising from" test to Problem E.

[B] Contracting to Supply Goods and Services in New York: CPLR 302(a)(1)

The second clause of CPLR 302(a)(1) allows jurisdiction over a cause of action arising from a contract to supply goods or services in New York, regardless of where the contract was made. It was added in 1979 (L. 1979, ch. 252). Prior to the amendment, it had been held that the shipment of goods into New York by a non-resident who neither came into the state nor had a sales agent in the state was not a "transaction of business" in New York which would sustain the exercise of jurisdiction. *Kramer v. Vogl*, 17 N.Y.2d 27, 267 N.Y.S.2d 900, 215 N.E.2d 159 (1966).

PARADISE PRODUCTS CORP. v. ALL-MARK EQUIPMENT CO., INC.
Appellate Division, Second Department
138 A.D.2d 470, 526 N.Y.S.2d 119 (1988)

. . . .

The plaintiff, a New York corporation, contacted Carmel, a New Jersey corporation, by telephone seeking to purchase a 500-gallon copper kettle. Carmel indicated that it did not have such a kettle but offered to attempt to locate one. Carmel contacted Allmark, also a New Jersey corporation, which had a 500-gallon kettle in its yard in New Jersey. After learning from Carmel, again by telephone, that a kettle had been found, two of the plaintiff's representatives traveled to New Jersey and met with Carmel's president. Together they traveled to Allmark's New Jersey yard and examined the kettle. The plaintiff agreed to purchase the kettle, but wanted to avoid paying a $150 delivery charge. Accordingly, the plaintiff arranged to have the kettle picked up rather than delivered. It was later found to contain pinholes which rendered it useless for the plaintiff's business.

---

[*] Jurisdiction was sustained under a "doing business" approach.

The due process standards that govern the determination of whether a non-resident defendant is amenable to suit under the forum State's long-arm statute have as their guidepost the fundamental notion that the defendant have certain "minimum contacts with it such that the maintenance of the suit does not offend 'traditional notions of fair play and substantial justice'" (*International Shoe Co. v Washington*, 326 US 310, 316). The plaintiff, in essence, argues that regardless of who picked up the kettle, Allmark contracted to supply it in New York and as such should be amenable to suit in this State (*see* CPLR 302[a][1]). The plaintiff argues that since Allmark knew the kettle would eventually be delivered to New York, the fact that it did not actually ship it is irrelevant. We conclude to the contrary.

Knowledge that a product may be destined for a particular forum is insufficient, in the context of this case, to sustain jurisdiction. Here, title to the property passed in New Jersey. The plaintiff agreed to assume responsibility for shipping the product to New York. In *Cooperstein v Pan-Oceanic Mar.* (124 AD2d 632, 633, *lv denied* 69 NY2d 611), involving a loan transaction, this court noted that the defendant did not contract to supply goods or services within New York where it made a loan to the New York plaintiff and sent the proceeds to Florida, because "while the loan was made to a New York resident, the proceeds were not supplied within New York, even though Mutual [the defendant] knew that some of the proceeds might find their way to this State" (*see also*, 1 Weinstein-Korn-Miller, NY Civ Prac ¶ 302.11a).

The instant sale, being the only purported contact with the State of New York, cannot support the exercise of jurisdiction by the courts of this state. It cannot be said that Allmark's conduct and connections with New York are such that it should reasonably have anticipated being haled into court here (*see, World-Wide Volkswagen Corp. v Woodson*, 444 US 286). Nor can it be said that Allmark purposefully availed itself of the privilege of conducting activities here. . . .

. . . .

NOTES

(1) Why does the court find a lack of jurisdiction? Would the result be different if the defendant entered into a series of contracts, each of which contemplated that a New York buyer would pick up the goods in New Jersey? Should the result be different? Compare *Drake America Corp. v. Speakman Co.*, 144 A.D.2d 529, 534 N.Y.S.2d 679 (2d Dep't 1988), in which the same court that decided the principal case found jurisdiction over the defendant foreign corporation in a breach of contract action on these facts: Defendant had agreed to sell plumbing equipment to plaintiff, an exporting company with New York facilities, exclusively for resale abroad. The contract provided for delivery to the plaintiff "f.o.b. Wilmington, Delaware," but provided for a discount to plaintiff for large shipments "consigned to freight forwarders or warehouse facilities in the Met-

ropolitan New York City area." The latter clause, said the court, showed that the defendant contracted to supply goods in New York within the meaning of CPLR 302(a)(1).

(2) The "contracts to supply goods" clause of CPLR 302(a)(1) has been held to support jurisdiction in a personal injury action by a consumer against a non-resident manufacturer which shipped the product to a New York retailer, even though the plaintiff had purchased the item from the retailer, not the defendant. *Tonns v. Speigel's*, 90 A.D.2d 548, 455 N.Y.S.2d 125 (2d Dep't 1982). The court also found jurisdiction under CPLR 302(a)(3), discussed in the next sub-section. Compare *Etra v. Matta*, 61 N.Y.2d 455, 474 N.Y.S.2d 687, 463 N.E.2d 3 (1984), refusing to find jurisdiction over a Massachusetts physician who provided a small quantity of prescriptive drugs to a New York patient. The statute, said the Court, "was not meant . . . to cover a transaction of this nature."

(3) The Second Department, construing CPLR 302(a)(1) with concern for constitutional limits (prior to the Supreme Court's decision in *Burger King, supra*), held that a promissory note payable in New York was not a contract to supply goods or services in the state. *American Recreation Group, Inc. v. Woznicki*, 87 A.D.2d 600, 448 N.Y.S.2d 51 (2d Dep't 1982). On the other hand, a federal district court found jurisdiction over a non-resident who was a guarantor of a contract to construct a restaurant in New York. An important factor was that the contract required the guarantor to actually complete the performance of the contract if the guaranteed party failed to do so. *Culp and Evans v. White*, 524 F. Supp. 81 (W.D.N.Y. 1981).

(4) Many states go further than New York in exercising jurisdiction over non-residents who deal with their own citizens. For example, Fla. Stat. § 48.193(1)(g) allows jurisdiction over one who "breach[es] a contract in this state by failing to perform acts required by the contract to be performed in this state." Florida courts rely on this section to find jurisdiction over a non-resident whose only breach was the failure to pay money due under a contract with a Floridian. *See Burger King v. Rudzewicz, supra*.

[C] Tortious Act Within the State: CPLR 302(a)(2); Veh. & Traf. Law § 253

CPLR 302(a)(2) applies when a cause of action arises from the commission of a "tortious act within the state" (except for defamation). In the leading opinion interpreting this section, the Court of Appeals construed it narrowly. The case, *Feathers v. McLucas*, 15 N.Y.2d 443, 261 N.Y.S.2d 8 (1965), involved a negligently manufactured truck trailer tank which exploded in New York, injuring the plaintiff. The tank had been manufactured in Kansas, so any negligence took place there, though there was no tort until the injury. The Court of Appeals asserted:

If, in fact, the Legislature . . . had intended to confer jurisdiction on the strength of injurious forum consequences alone, without regard to the locus of the commission of the tortious act itself, it would presumably have used language appropriate to reflect such a design. . . . In sharp contrast, the Legislature chose to adopt language which, in so many words, demands that the "tortious act" be one committed by the defendant, "in person or through an agent," within this State.

Id. at 461-62, 261 N.Y.S.2d at 22.

Subsequently, the legislature added CPLR 302(a)(3) to deal with cases such as *Feathers*. Subsection (a)(2) remains in CPLR 302 but is useful only if the tortious conduct occurs in New York.

To some extent CPLR 302 overlaps Vehicle and Traffic Law [V.T.L.] § 253, which subjects non-resident motorists to jurisdiction in actions arising from accidents in this state. Both statutes provide similar bases for jurisdiction, but each provides for a different method of service, as we shall see in Chapter 5. As to jurisdictional basis, V.T.L. § 253(1) provides:

1. The use or operation by a non-resident of a vehicle in this state, or the use or operation in this state of a vehicle in the business of a non-resident, or the use or operation in this state of a vehicle owned by a non-resident if so used or operated with his permission, express or implied, shall be deemed equivalent to an appointment by such non-resident of the secretary of state to be his true and lawful attorney upon whom may be served the summons in any action against him, growing out of any accident or collision in which such non-resident may be involved while using or operating such vehicle in this state or in which such vehicle may be involved while being used or operated in this state in the business of such non-resident or with the permission, express or implied, of such non-resident owner; and such use or operation shall be deemed a signification of his agreement that any such summons against him which is so served shall be of the same legal force and validity as if served on him personally within the state and within the territorial jurisdiction of the court from which the summons issues, and that such appointment of the secretary of state shall be irrevocable and binding upon his executor or administrator. . . .

V.T.L. § 254 makes the basis and service provision of § 253 applicable to a New York "resident who departs from the state subsequent to the accident or collision and remains absent therefrom for thirty days continuously . . . ."

[D] Tortious Act Without the State Causing Injury Within It: CPLR 302(a)(3)

LaMARCA v. PAK-MOR MANUFACTURING CO.
Court of Appeals
95 N.Y.2d 210, 735 N.E.2d 883, 713 N.Y.S.2d 304 (2000)

ROSENBLATT, J.

The case before us involves a challenge to New York's long-arm jurisdiction. Plaintiff, a Town of Niagara employee, sued defendant Pak-Mor Manufacturing Company, a Texas corporation, alleging that he was injured when he fell from a sanitation truck equipped with a defective Pak-Mor loading device. In his complaint against Pak-Mor, plaintiff alleged negligence, breach of warranty, failure to warn and strict products liability. Pak-Mor moved to dismiss for lack of personal jurisdiction. Supreme Court granted the motion and the Appellate Division affirmed. For reasons that follow, we conclude that the exercise of long-arm jurisdiction over Pak-Mor is compatible with both CPLR 302 and due process. Accordingly, we reverse.

Pak-Mor is a Texas corporation that manufactures garbage hauling equipment. It has a manufacturing facility in Virginia. The company has no property, offices, telephone numbers or employees in this State. It does, however, maintain a New York distributor, Truckmobile Equipment Corp., and a district representative. In the year of the accident, Pak-Mor's total sales revenue was $18,245,292.00, $514,490.00 of which was derived from New York. The company advertised in nationally published trade magazines using a logo that read "Sanitation for the Nation." It also offered warranties and provided troubleshooting advice to the ultimate purchasers of its equipment.

Pak-Mor sold the rear-loading device that was alleged to have caused plaintiff's injuries to its New York distributor, which in turn sold it to the Town of Niagara. Its "invoice and final inspection sheet" indicates that the rear loader was destined for Niagara, New York. The document also lists a "New York Light Bar" under the heading "Additional or Special Information." Pak-Mor installed the device on the truck at its Virginia facility, where its distributor picked up the truck in Virginia and delivered it to the Town of Niagara. Several months later, plaintiff was injured when he fell off the back of the truck while standing on the riding platform of the rear-loader.

To determine whether a non-domiciliary may be sued in New York, we first determine whether our long-arm statute (CPLR 302) confers jurisdiction over it in light of its contacts with this State. If the defendant's relationship with New York falls within the terms of CPLR 302, we determine whether the exercise of jurisdiction comports with due process.

New York's Long-Arm Statute CPLR 302(a) provides:

"As to a cause of action arising from any of the acts enumerated in this section, a court may exercise personal jurisdiction over any non-domiciliary who:

"3. commits a tortious act without the state causing injury to person or property within the state, except as to a cause of action for defamation of character arising from the act, if he

. . . .

"(ii) expects or should reasonably expect the act to have consequences in the state and derives substantial revenue from interstate commerce or international commerce" (CPLR 302[a][3][ii]).

The conferral of jurisdiction under this provision rests on five elements. First, that defendant committed a tortious act outside the State; second, that the cause of action arises from that act; third, that the act caused injury to a person or property within the State; fourth, that defendant expected or should reasonably have expected the act to have consequences in the State; and fifth, that defendant derived substantial revenue from interstate or international commerce. No one disputes the first three elements. Plaintiff has alleged that his cause of action arises from defendant's tortious acts outside the State, which caused him injury in Niagara, New York. The fourth element — contemplating "in-State consequences" — is met when "the nonresident tortfeasor expects, or has reason to expect, that his or her tortious activity in another State will have *direct* consequences in New York" (*Ingraham v Carroll,* 90 N.Y.2d 592, 598, 665 N.Y.S.2d 10, 687 N.E.2d 1293 [emphasis added]). The element "is intended to ensure some link between a defendant and New York State to make it reasonable to require a defendant to come to New York to answer for tortious conduct committed elsewhere" (*Ingraham,* 90 N.Y.2d at 598, *supra*). Moreover, the defendant need not foresee the specific event that produced the alleged injury. The defendant need only reasonably foresee that any defect in its product would have direct consequences within the State (*see,* 12th Ann Report of NY Jud Conf, at 343-344; *see generally,* Siegel, New York Practice 88, at 151 [3d ed]).

Pak-Mor's invoice, including its reference to a "New York Light Bar," shows that it knew the rear-loader was destined for use in New York. Clearly, Pak-Mor had reason to expect that any defects would have direct consequences in this State.

The fifth element — defendant's deriving substantial revenue from interstate or international commerce — is designed to narrow "the long-arm reach to preclude the exercise of jurisdiction over nondomiciliaries who might cause direct, foreseeable injury within the State but 'whose business operations are of a local character'" (*Ingraham,* 90 N.Y.2d at 599 [quoting the 12th Ann Report of NY Jud Conf, at 342-343], *supra*). Therefore, in *Ingraham,* we held that a physician who practiced only in Vermont and earned his entire revenue from his local medical services did not derive "substantial interstate revenue" as contemplated by CPLR 302(a)(3)(ii).

By contrast, Pak-Mor's business can hardly be characterized as "local." A Texas corporation with a manufacturing facility in Virginia is inherently engaged in interstate commerce. Moreover, the company had a New York distributor and a district representative. Its national advertising and New York sales figures alone show that the company derives substantial revenue from interstate commerce.

In short, we have no difficulty in concluding that CPLR 302(a)(3)(ii) was satisfied in this case. Pak-Mor derived substantial revenue from interstate commerce and the circumstances surrounding its sale of the subject rear-loader gave it reason to expect that its acts in connection with the manufacture of the rear-loader would have consequences in this State. Because CPLR 302(a)(3)(ii) did not authorize jurisdiction over the defendant in *Ingraham* (*supra*), we had no need to consider Federal due process. Here, we do.

Due Process: "Minimum Contacts" and "Fair Play and Substantial Justice"

Under the Due Process Clause, the standards of "minimum contacts" and "fair play and substantial justice" are implicated in the decisional law governing personal jurisdiction. We therefore discuss both.

Due process is not satisfied unless a non-domiciliary has "minimum contacts" with the forum State. The test has come to rest on whether a defendant's "conduct and connection with the forum state" are such that it "should reasonably anticipate being haled into court there" (*World-Wide Volkswagen Corp.*, 444 U.S. 286, 297, 62 L. Ed. 2d 490, 100 S. Ct. 559; *see also, Kulko v California Superior Ct.*, 436 U.S. 84, 97-98, 56 L. Ed. 2d 132, 98 S. Ct. 1690). A non-domiciliary tortfeasor has "minimum contacts" with the forum State — and may thus reasonably foresee the prospect of defending a suit there — if it "'purposefully avails itself of the privilege of conducting activities within the forum State'" (*see, World-Wide Volkswagen Corp.*, 444 U.S. at 297 [quoting *Hanson v Denckla*, 357 U.S. 235, 253, 2 L. Ed. 2d 1283, 78 S. Ct. 1228], *supra; see also, Burger King Corp. v Rudzewicz*, 471 U.S. 462, 475, 85 L. Ed. 2d 528, 105 S. Ct. 2174).

The United States Supreme Court's decision in *World-Wide Volkswagen* (444 U.S. 286, 62 L. Ed. 2d 490, 100 S. Ct. 559, *supra*) illustrates the application of this standard. There, a New York automobile retail dealer sold a car to plaintiffs, a family in New York (444 U.S. at 288, *supra*). While driving through Oklahoma on the way to Arizona, plaintiffs had an accident and sued the dealer (and its wholesaler) in Oklahoma (444 U.S. at 288, *supra*). Jurisdiction failed because the New York defendants could not reasonably foresee being sued in Oklahoma based on "the fortuitous circumstance that a single Audi automobile, sold in New York to New York residents, happened to suffer an accident while passing through Oklahoma" (444 U.S. at 295, *supra*). The Supreme Court, however, distinguished cases in which manufacturers purposefully direct their products into the forum state:

"if the sale of a product of a manufacturer or distributor is not simply an isolated occurrence, but arises from the efforts of the manufacturer or distributor *to serve directly or indirectly*, the market for its product in other States, it is not unreasonable to subject it to suit in one of those States if its allegedly defective merchandise has there been the source of injury to its owner or to others" (444 U.S. at 297 [emphasis added], *supra*).

Pak-Mor argues that it had no contacts or purposeful affiliation with New York, asserting that "it did not direct activities at New York residents" and that it "performed manufacturing in Virginia for customers who paid, received title and accepted delivery in Virginia." This may be true, but it is far from dispositive. Unlike the defendant in *World-Wide Volkswagen Corp.*, Pak-Mor itself forged the ties with New York. It took purposeful action, motivated by the entirely understandable wish to sell its products here. This contrasts with cases in which the defendant's connection with the forum State resulted from decisions made by others, as in *World-Wide Volkswagen Corp.*, where the plaintiff customer chose to drive to the forum State (444 U.S. at 288, 295, *supra*) or where, in a child support case, the plaintiff former spouse chose to settle in the forum State (*see, Kulko v California Superior Ct.*, 436 U.S. at 86-87, *supra*). In all, Pak-Mor had every reason to foresee that its self-initiated contact with New York raised the prospect of defending this suit.

Minimum contacts alone do not satisfy due process. The prospect of defending a suit in the forum State must also comport with traditional notions of "'fair play and substantial justice'" (*Burger King v Rudzewicz*, 471 U.S. at 476 [quoting *International Shoe Co.*, 326 U.S. at 316, *supra*], *supra*). This is in essence another way of asking what is reasonable. Indeed, a defendant "who purposefully has directed [its] activities at forum residents must present a compelling case that the presence of some other considerations would render jurisdiction unreasonable" (*Burger King*, 471 U.S. at 477, *supra*).

In *Asahi Metal Indus. v Superior Ct.*, 480 U.S. 102, 94 L. Ed. 2d 92, 107 S. Ct. 1026, the Supreme Court articulated the test:

"A court must consider the burden on the defendant, the interests of the forum State, and the plaintiff's interest in obtaining relief. It must also weigh in its determination 'the interstate judicial system's interest in obtaining the most efficient resolution of controversies; and the shared interest of the several States in furthering fundamental and substantive social policies'" (480 U.S. at 113 [quoting *World-Wide Volkswagen*, 444 U.S. at 292], *supra*).

In *Asahi*, Cheng Shin, a Taiwanese tire tube manufacturer defending a California product liability action, attempted to implead Asahi, a Japanese tube valve manufacturer that had installed valves on Cheng Shin's tubes in Japan (480 U.S. at 106, *supra*). Asahi allegedly knew that Cheng Shin distributed its tubes around the world, but resisted personal jurisdiction on the ground that it had performed all of its work in Japan with no reasonable expectation of being sued in California (480 U.S. at 107, *supra*). The Supreme Court concluded that subjecting Asahi to jurisdiction in California would be unreasonable.

Pak-Mor is no Asahi. Its posture toward New York is considerably different from Asahi's posture toward California. Asahi was a Japanese corporation doing business with a Taiwanese tire tube manufacturer, whereas Pak-Mor is a Texas corporation that maintains a manufacturing facility in Virginia and used a New York distributor. The burden on Pak-Mor is not great. Unlike Asahi, Pak-Mor is a United States corporation fully familiar with this country's legal system. Moreover, New York has an interest in providing a convenient forum for LaMarca, a New York resident who was injured in New York and may be entitled to relief under New York law. In *Asahi*, the main action had been settled and all that remained was Cheng Shin's indemnification claim against Asahi (480 U.S. at 114, *supra*). Finally, it would be orderly to allow plaintiff to sue all named defendants in New York. A single action would promote the interstate judicial system's shared interests in obtaining the most efficient resolution of the controversy.

Fair play involves a set of corresponding rights and obligations. When a company of Pak-Mor's size and scope profits from sales to New Yorkers, it is not at all unfair to render it judicially answerable for its actions in this State. Considering that Pak-Mor's long business arm extended to New York, it seems only fair to extend correspondingly the reach of New York's jurisdictional long-arm. In all, we conclude that asserting jurisdiction over Pak-Mor in New York would not offend traditional notions of fair play and substantial justice.

NOTES

(1) One important difference between the principal case and *Asahi*, cited and discussed in the principal case, is that in *Asahi*, the injured individual plaintiff had settled, so there was no longer a California resident involved in the case. Suppose the New York plaintiff had settled his claims against Pak-Mor and Truckmobile, the New York distributor, and that the only remaining dispute was between the two defendants over the degree of liability of each. Suppose further that Pak-Mor renewed its motion to dismiss. How should the jurisdictional issue be resolved?

(2) Compare with the principal case, *Martinez v. American Standard*, 91 A.D.2d 652, 457 N.Y.S.2d 97 (2d Dep't 1982), *aff'd*, 60 N.Y.2d 873, 470 N.Y.S.2d 367, 458 N.E.2d 826 (1983). Plaintiff's decedent suffered injuries resulting in death due to a faulty air conditioner. Plaintiff sued the ultimate manufacturer, American Standard, and the maker of a compressor in the air conditioner, Tecumseh Products Co. Tecumseh impleaded Vitreous State Products, a Rhode Island corporation which, on Tecumseh's orders, had shipped terminal pins for the compressor to Tecumseh's midwestern plant. Vitreous contested the asser-

tion of personal jurisdiction in New York. Its motion to dismiss was granted by the Appellate Division, which held that the showing required by CPLR 302(a)(3)(ii), that Vitreous have foreseen consequences in New York of its sale, was not made. The court also held that in the absence such showing, jurisdiction could not be exercised consistent with the Fourteenth Amendment.

(3) As to substantiality of revenue under CPLR 302(a)(3), compare *Chunky Corp. v. Blumenthal Bros. Chocolate Co.*, 299 F. Supp. 110 (S.D.N.Y. 1969) (four per cent of total sales revenue not substantial), with *Allen v. Canadian Gen. Electric Co.*, 65 A.D.2d 39, 410 N.Y.S.2d 707 (3d Dep't 1978), *aff'd*, 50 N.Y.2d 935, 431 N.Y.S.2d 526 (1980) (one per cent of nine million dollar annual income held substantial).

(4) These "substantial revenue" cases implicitly raise the question of how the plaintiff learns about and documents the defendant's financial situation. Once the action has been commenced, plaintiff may use normal discovery devices to obtain information relevant to any jurisdictional defenses which may be interposed. The court, apparently using its "jurisdiction to determine if it has jurisdiction," has power to require the defendant to comply with discovery demands even while he asserts that the court lacks any power over him. *See Peterson v. Spartan Industries, Inc.*, 33 N.Y.2d 463, 354 N.Y.S.2d 905, 310 N.E.2d 513 (1974); *Ins. Corp. of Ireland, Ltd. v. Compagnie des Bauxites de Guinee*, 456 U.S. 694, 102 S. Ct. 2099 (1982). What other steps could a plaintiff take to learn these facts? One possibility is illustrated by *Prentice v. Demag Material Handling, Ltd.*, 80 A.D.2d 741, 437 N.Y.S.2d 173 (4th Dep't 1981), which upheld the use of a recent Dun & Bradstreet report to determine the extent of defendant's interstate commerce.

(5) As the next case shows, CPLR 302(a)(3)(ii) is not limited to personal injury cases.

SYBRON CORP. v. WETZEL
Court of Appeals
46 N.Y.2d 197, 413 N.Y.S.2d 127, 385 N.E.2d 1055 (1978)

CHIEF JUDGE BREITEL.

Plaintiff Sybron, among other things a manufacturer and reliner of glass-lined vessels used in processing corrosive chemicals, sues its former employee, Wetzel, and a competitor corporation, De Dietrich, to enjoin the employment of Wetzel by De Dietrich and to prevent Wetzel from divulging alleged trade secrets. . . . At issue is whether, for purposes of CPLR 302(a)(3), a nondomiciliary competitor causes injury in New York when it hires a former employee of a corporation engaged in manufacture in this State allegedly to obtain protected trade secrets.

. . . .

Wetzel had been employed in New York by the Pfaudler Company, a division of plaintiff Sybron, and one of three competitors in the United States engaged in the design, manufacture, and sale of glass-lined chemical processing vessels . . . . In 1974, however, at age 55, Wetzel took early retirement on reduced pension and moved to Florida.

In early 1977, defendant De Dietrich (USA), an American subsidiary of the French De Dietrich & Cie, advertised the installation in Union, New Jersey, of a new furnace for reglassing reactors and tanks. As a principal competitor of Sybron, De Dietrich has reglassed some 4,500 of Sybron's "Pfaudler" vessels in its French plants, and intends for its New Jersey plant to reglass Sybron equipment.

This action was started after Sybron learned that De Dietrich's American manager of manufacturing, a former chief ceramist at the Pfaudler division for whom Wetzel worked for many years, approached Wetzel in Florida and asked him to supervise the New Jersey facility. Evidently, only one other person, also a former Pfaudler employee, was interviewed for the position.

. . . .

As noted, the admitted and controverted facts give rise to the probable inference that there is a conscious plan to engage in unfair competition and misappropriation of trade secrets. That should be enough to justify application of CPLR 302 (subd [a], par 3). If a tort must already have been committed for jurisdiction to be available under the statute, then that section would never be usable by a plaintiff seeking anticipatory injunctive relief. Such a result is unacceptable.

The more difficult question is whether the out-of-State acts ascribed to De Dietrich will result in injury in New York . . . . CPLR 302 (subd [a], par 3), as noted, was added after the *Feathers* case (15 NY2d 443, *supra*) to fill a statutory gap. Some contend, therefore, that it was not motivated with commercial torts in mind where the locus of injury is not as readily identifiable as it is in torts causing physical harm (*see, e.g., Chemical Bank v World Hockey Assn.*, 403 F Supp 1374, 1379). And, indeed, in the legislative history of the 1966 addition there is no discussion of commercial cases. . . .

It is equally significant, however, that nowhere in the pertinent studies or reports were commercial torts excluded. Most important, save for the exclusion of causes of action for defamation (a specific exclusion of a nonphysical harm), the statute, drafted by sophisticated experts, does not limit the kinds of tortious acts covered to personal injury, property damage, or other noncommercial torts. Under such circumstances the statute should be read with the breadth it easily carries, and the unqualified legislative enactment respected.

It has been said that remote injuries located in New York solely because of domicile or incorporation here do not satisfy CPLR 302 (subd [a], par 3). . . . Plaintiff's case does not rest on so narrow a foundation nor does its case depend on whether unfair competition injures it in every State in which it does business. It is, however, critical that it is New York where plaintiff manufactures and relines glass-lined equipment and the alleged trade secrets were acquired, and the economic injury plaintiff seeks to avert stems from the threatened loss of important New York customers.

It also need not be decided whether the loss of a small New York account would suffice. From the hearing testimony it may be inferred that, should plaintiff's alleged trade secrets be disclosed, business from New York sales could suffer significantly. It was shown, for instance, that De Dietrich sales persons have actively solicited Sybron's Rochester neighbor, the multinational Eastman Kodak Company, a major customer of Sybron. In fact, by September, 1977, Kodak ordered from De Dietrich two 500-gallon reactors.

American Eutectic Welding Alloys Sales Co. v Dytron Alloys Corp. (439 F2d 428, 432-35, *supra* [Feinberg, J.]) supports the analysis. It is true that no injury within New York was found in the *American Eutectic* case, but in rejecting jurisdiction the court stressed that the only customers wrongfully solicited by defendants were located outside New York. . . .

That the extraterritorial conduct of De Dietrich produces injury in New York does not, however, end the matter. The drafters of paragraph 3 sought to insure its constitutionality by further requiring that the nonresident either have reason to foresee that its actions will produce forum consequences or have enough other "contacts" with the State so as to make the exercise of personal jurisdiction reasonable (Twelfth Ann Report of NY Judicial Conference, 1967, pp 342-343).

It is not disputed that De Dietrich derives substantial revenue from interstate or international commerce. What is questioned is whether the New Jersey based De Dietrich should expect the hiring of Wetzel from Florida to have consequences in New York. Given that Sybron manufactures the equipment in New York, that Wetzel worked at Sybron in New York for 34 years, and that Sybron customers in New York are being pursued, it is reasonable that De Dietrich fores[aw] New York as the place injury will occur. Thus, the requirements of clause ii of paragraph 3 are also met, and De Dietrich should be subject to the personal jurisdiction of the court.

. . . .

WACHTLER, C.J., dissenting.

. . . .

In this case there is no legitimate reason for recognizing the plaintiff's claim that De Dietrich's hiring of Wetzel should be considered an actionable wrong. The plaintiff does not seek damages and indeed the majority notes that any injury is "still anticipated." Characterizing this defendant's conduct as tortious is only necessary to avoid the restrictions of the longarm statute which would otherwise deny the courts of this State jurisdiction to grant the plaintiff the injunctive relief it actually seeks.

By reaching out to find jurisdiction in this case the majority has created a cause of action which can only serve to further inhibit the movement of skilled workers from one employer to another. In fact, in many instances it may result in their becoming virtual serfs of their former employers. . . .

NOTE

When the defendant's out-of-state tortious conduct causes economic but not physical injury, locating the place of injury is difficult, as the principal case indicates. *Fantis Foods, Inc. v. Standard Importing*, 49 N.Y.2d 317, 425 N.Y.S.2d 783, 402 N.E.2d 122 (1980), held that the locus of of injury stemming from the conversion of goods belonging to a New Yorker was at the place of the conversion, not New York. *Compare Hargrave v. Oki Nursery, Inc.*, 636 F.2d 897 (2d Cir. 1980) (fraud against New Yorker by a Californian held to cause injury in New York pursuant to CPLR 302(a)(3) because the plaintiff made a payment from New York).

[E] Ownership of Property Within the State: CPLR 302(a)(4)

TEBEDO v. NYE
Supreme Court, Onondaga County
45 Misc. 2d 222, 256 N.Y.S.2d 235 (1965)

RICHARD D. SIMONS, J.

Defendants McLaughlin move pursuant to Civil Practice Law and Rules § 3211(a)8 to dismiss the complaint in the above entitled action on the sole ground that the Court lacks personal jurisdiction over them. They are residents of the State of Florida and were served personally in that State in accordance with Civil Practice Law and Rules § 313.

Plaintiff seeks to obtain conveyance of a thirty foot strip of land adjacent to his property, or in the alternative, damages by reason of improvements made thereon by him in reliance upon promises by the defendants that the property would be conveyed to plaintiff. Plaintiff has paid the consideration for the realty. Defendants Nye sold the property to the movants, however, without conveying to plaintiff and it is alleged that the movants accepted the conveyance with the understanding and agreement that they would convey by separate deed to the plaintiff the strip in dispute. Likewise, when the movants sold the premises and moved to Florida, plaintiff alleges it was understood and agreed that the strip would be conveyed. They failed to do so.

The movants sold the property to the defendants Barrows in 1959. They presently own no real estate in the State of New York. Obviously, they cannot convey title to the property and relief against them would be limited to damages if the plaintiff should succeed.

. . . .

Civil Practice Law and Rules § 302(a)3 [now (4)] grants in personam jurisdiction when the cause of action arises out of the fact of ownership, use or possession of New York realty.

The fact that defendants no longer have an interest in the realty and no longer live in this State is immaterial, as is the nature of the remedy sought. Jurisdiction is grounded on the relationship existing between the defendant and the realty out of which the cause of action arose at the time the cause of action arose. *Cf. Hempstead Medical Arts Co. v. Willie*, New York Law Journal, December 9, 1963, page 18, col. 6, Sup. Ct., 1963.

The power to convey real estate is an incident of ownership. The wrongful failure to do so gives rise to a cause of action.

. . . .

Defendant's motion denied.

NOTES

(1) If specific performance to convey land is available as a matter of substantive law, plaintiff can avoid the sticky problem of enforcing an equity decree against a non-resident by obtaining an order directing the appropriate clerk to transfer title to the property. CPLR 5107; *Garfein v. McInnis*, 248 N.Y. 261, 162 N.E. 73 (1928).

(2) Jurisdiction acquired under CPLR 302(a)(4) should not, of course, be confused with jurisdiction in rem, although it can in many cases obviate the need to rely on in rem principles.

[F] The Challenge of Internet-Based Jurisdiction

CITIGROUP, INC. v. CITY HOLDING CO.
Eastern District of New York
97 F. Supp. 2d 549 (2000)

SWEET, J.

. . . .

[Citigroup, owner of various "CITI" trademarks and the associated "Blue Wave" symbol, sued City Holding Company and City National Bank of West Virginia for trademark infringement, alleging that the defendants' websites displayed confusingly similar marks. The defendants move, among other things, to dismiss for lack of personal jurisdiction. — Eds.]

The Parties

Plaintiff Citigroup is a Delaware corporation with its principal office in New York, New York.

Defendant City Holding is a West Virginia corporation with its principal office in Cross Lanes, West Virginia.

Defendant City National is a wholly-owned subsidiary of City Holding and is a West Virginia corporation with its principal office in Charleston, West Virginia.

. . . .

Discussion

. . . .

IV. Personal Jurisdiction

. . . .

   A. Specific Jurisdiction

. . . .

      1. Jurisdiction Under CPLR § 302(a)(1)

      a. City National

The transacting business prong of Section 302(a) confers jurisdiction over "a defendant who purposefully avails itself of the privilege of conducting activities within New York, thus invoking the benefits and protections of its laws," where the cause of action arises out of the subject matter of the business transacted. See, e.g., Viacom Intern., Inc. v. Melvin Simon Productions, 774 F. Supp. 858, 862 (S.D.N.Y. 1991). New York courts look to the totality of circumstances to determine whether the defendant has engaged in some purposeful activity in New York in connection with the matter in controversy. See Longines-Wittnauer

Watch Co. v. Barnes & Reinecke, Inc., 15 N.Y.2d 443, 209 N.E.2d 68, 75, 261 N.Y.S.2d 8 (N.Y. 1965).

A single transaction of business is sufficient to give rise to jurisdiction under CPLR § 302(a)(1), even where the defendant never enters the state, if the claim arises out of the transaction. See Pilates, 891 F. Supp. at 179; Kreutter v. McFadden Oil Co., 71 N.Y.2d 460, 522 N.E.2d 40, 43, 527 N.Y.S.2d 195 (N.Y. 1988); see also Parke-Bernet Galleries, Inc. v. Franklyn, 26 N.Y.2d 13, 256 N.E.2d 506, 308 N.Y.S.2d 337 (N.Y. 1970).

In the instant case much, although not all, of the activity engaged in by City National which goes towards a specific jurisdiction analysis occurred via the internet. This raises the question of what type of internet activity may be deemed as supporting the exercise of personal jurisdiction over a defendant, and where such transactions should be viewed as having occurred.

It has long been observed that technological advances affecting the nature of commerce require the doctrine of personal jurisdiction to adapt and evolve along with those advances. See Hanson v. Denckla, 357 U.S. 235, 250-52, 2 L. Ed. 2d 1283, 78 S. Ct. 1228 (1958) ("As technological progress has increased the flow of commerce between States, the need for jurisdiction has undergone a similar increase.") With the advent of the internet, the courts have been confronted with a new set of challenges in this regard. The guiding principle which has emerged from the case law is that whether the exercise of personal jurisdiction is permissible is "'directly proportionate to the nature and quality of commercial activity that an entity conducts over the internet,'" K.C.P.L., Inc. v. Nash, No. 98 Civ. 3773, 1998 U.S. Dist. LEXIS 18464, at *5 (S.D.N.Y. 1998) (citing Zippo Mfg. Co. v. Zippo Dot Com, 952 F. Supp. 1119, 1124-25 (W.D. Pa. 1997). This principle applies to an analysis under CPLR § 302(a)(1). See K.C.P.L., 1998 U.S. Dist. LEXIS 18464, at *4-*5.

More precisely, the courts have identified a spectrum of cases involving a defendant's use of the internet. At one end are cases where the defendant makes information available on what is essentially a "passive" web site. This use of the internet has been analogized to an advertisement in a nationally-available magazine or newspaper, and does not without more justify the exercise of jurisdiction over the defendant. See K.C.P.L., 1998 U.S. Dist. LEXIS 18464, at *4-*5; Hearst Corp. v. Goldberger, No. 96 Civ. 3620, 1997 U.S. Dist. LEXIS 2065, at *10 (S.D.N.Y. Feb. 26, 1997); see also Zippo, 952 F. Supp. at 1123. At the other end of the spectrum are cases in which the defendant clearly does business over the internet, such as where it knowingly and repeatedly transmits computer files to customers in other states. See CompuServe, Inc. v. Patterson, 89 F.3d 1257 (6th Cir. 1996). Finally, occupying the middle ground are cases in which the defendant maintains an interactive web site which permits the exchange of information between users in another state and the defendant, which depending on the level and nature of the exchange may be a basis for jurisdiction. See American Home Care Fed. Inc. v. Paragon Scientific Corp., 27 F. Supp. 2d 109, 113 (D. Conn. 1998); Zippo, 952 F. Supp. at 1124.

City National maintains two web sites pertaining to its mortgage origination business, <www.citylending.com> (the "City Lending site") and <www.city-mortgageservices.com> (the "City Mortgage site"). The City Lending site involves more than the passive posting of information about City Lending's loan products and services. Customers in New York may apply for loans on-line as well as print out an application for submission by facsimile, they may click on a "hyper link" to "chat" on-line with a City Lending representative, and they may e-mail City Lending with home loan questions and receive a response from an "online representative . . . in less than an hour."

At the very least, the interactivity of the City Lending site brings this case within the middle category of internet commercial activity.[8] Moreover, the interaction is both significant and unqualifiedly commercial in nature and thus rises to the level of transacting business required under CPLR § 302(a)(1). See K.C.P.L., 1998 U.S. Dist. LEXIS 18464, at *6; Zippo, 952 F. Supp. at 1124; see also American Network, Inc. v. Access America/Connect Atlanta, Inc., 975 F. Supp. 494, 498-99 (S.D.N.Y. 1997). The cause of action arises from this transaction of business because it is "precisely the bona fides of these products and services that [Citigroup] challenges." Pilates, 891 F. Supp. at 179. The Court concludes that City National's activity over the internet confers personal jurisdiction under CPLR § 302(a)(1).

Even if City National's internet activity were not enough, jurisdiction under CPLR § 302(a)(1) is further bolstered by other activities. City National has engaged in direct mail solicitation of New York business. See Pilates, 891 F. Supp. at 179. City National has also used New York companies to record mortgages on behalf of City Mortgage Services to perfect the liens on real property located in New York which secure the loan contracts. Thus, there is no question that Citigroup has met its burden to show a basis for jurisdiction under this provision of the CPLR.

b. City Holding

Under CPLR § 302(a)(1), a defendant who has contracted anywhere to supply goods or services within New York is subject to personal jurisdiction here. A licensor/owner of intellectual property rights which are exploited by licensees within this state may be subject to personal jurisdiction under this provision in a trademark infringement suit involving the licensed property. See Firma Melodiya v. ZYX Music GmbH, No. 94 Civ. 6798, 1995 U.S. Dist. LEXIS 795, at *3 (S.D.N.Y. Jan. 25, 1995); Pony Int'l, Inc. v. Genfoot Am., Inc., No. 82 Civ. 65171, 1983 U.S. Dist. LEXIS 15161, at *2-*3 (S.D.N.Y. July 27, 1983). CPLR § 302(a)(1) is satisfied where the licensee of intellectual property uses the licensed material in commerce in New York pursuant to the license agreement, since the licensor is thereby deemed to have contracted to supply services in the

---

[8] It is not clear that the transaction can actually be consummated on line, a scenario which brings this case out of the middle category and into the category of a business that clearly does business over the internet in New York. See National Football League, 2000 U.S. Dist. LEXIS 3929, at *1.

state. See, e.g., Lipton v. Nature Co., 781 F. Supp. 1032, 1035 (S.D.N.Y. 1992); Greenky v. Irving Music, Inc., No.80 Civ. 2776, 1981 U.S. Dist. LEXIS 13432, at *1-*2 (S.D.N.Y. July 13, 1981). This principle applies even where the license agreement did not specifically contemplate use of the intellectual property in New York, so long as such use was foreseeable. See Firma Melodiya, 1995 U.S. Dist. LEXIS 795, at *3.

City Holding contends that even if City National is subject to personal jurisdiction in New York, City Holding is not. In support of this contention, City Holding points out that it is a West Virginia corporation that is not registered to do business in New York, that it has no real estate, officers, directors, employees, or bank accounts here, and that it has not earned any income here.

City Holding's attempt to distance itself from the use of the CITY marks in this state is unavailing. City Holding is the owner and licensor of the CITY marks, of which all but the CITY HOLDING COMPANY mark itself are used by City Holding's wholly-owned subsidiaries. At least one of these subsidiaries, City National, has used CITY marks within New York to solicit and engage in business activity with New York residents with respect to mortgage loans and services. City Holding is also the named plaintiff in the West Virginia action, in which it seeks a declaratory judgment pertaining to the entire family of CITY marks. The September 28 letter concerning the City Financial mark was sent on behalf of City Holding, not City Financial. Thus, City Holding cannot separate itself from the use of the CITY marks by its subsidiaries, or say that such use was unforeseeable, and there is jurisdiction under CPLR § 302(a)(1).

2. Jurisdiction Under CPLR § 302(a)(2)

There is an alternative basis for personal jurisdiction over City National pursuant to CPLR § 302(a)(2), which confers jurisdiction over a defendant who commits a tortious act within the state where the cause of action arises from that act. This is an action arising out of and challenging alleged trademark infringement and dilution activity. Trademark infringement occurs where the attempted passing off of an infringing mark occurs. See Pilates, 891 F. Supp. at 180; Exovir, Inc. v. Mandel, M.D., No. 94 Civ. 3546, 1995 U.S. Dist. LEXIS 9677, at *3 (S.D.N.Y. July 21, 1995). Moreover, there is no minimum threshold of activity required so long as the cause of action arises out of the allegedly infringing activity in New York. "Offering one copy of an infringing work for sale in New York . . . constitutes commission of a tortious act within the state sufficient to imbue [the] Court with personal jurisdiction over the infringers." Editorial Musical Latino Americana, S.A. v. Mar Int'l Records, Inc., 829 F. Supp. 62, 64 (S.D.N.Y. 1993); see also Dave Guardala Mouthpieces, Inc. v. Sugal Mouthpieces, Inc., 779 F. Supp. 335, 337-38 (S.D.N.Y. 1991).

City National sent direct mailings to New York residents directed at soliciting their business and displaying the allegedly infringing marks. The attempt to pass off these marks, which is allegedly tortious conduct, occurred within New York because that is where the marks were received and viewed by the direct mailing recipients. This activity provides a basis for exercising personal jurisdiction over City National for purposes of a suit challenging the use of those very marks. See Pilates, 891 F. Supp. at 180.

The import of the City National web sites displaying allegedly infringing mark, is more complicated. The mere existence of these web sites does not confer jurisdiction under CPLR § 302(a)(2). Although it is in the very nature of the internet that the allegedly infringing marks contained in these web sites can be viewed anywhere, this does not mean that the infringement occurred everywhere. Instead, courts have held that in the case of web sites displaying infringing marks the tort is deemed to be committed where the web site is created and/or maintained. See . . . American Network, 975 F. Supp. at 497; see also Hearst, 1997 U.S. Dist. LEXIS 2065, at *10. This rule may seem incongruous when juxtaposed with the rule applicable to ordinary infringing goods, which is that "the wrong takes place not where the deceptive labels are affixed to the goods or where the goods are wrapped in the misleading packages, but where the passing off occurs." German Educational Television Network, Ltd. v. Oregon Public Broadcasting Co., 569 F. Supp. 1529, 1532 (S.D.N.Y. 1983). A rationale for the difference may be that literal application of the "where viewed" rule would result in jurisdiction anywhere in the world in every infringement case involving a web site.

There is no evidence that the City Lending and City Mortgage web sites were created in New York or are maintained on New York servers. Thus, the mere display of the CITY marks on these web sites cannot be deemed a tort committed within this State.

However, as with the analysis under CPLR § 302(a)(1), the significance of the web sites shifts to the extent that there is interaction between City National and New York residents. It was noted above that the City Lending site offers the possibility of an on-line "chat" with City National representatives. To the extent that such chats involve the transmission of messages that contain allegedly infringing marks to New York residents, City National should be deemed to have attempted to pass off the mark within New York rather than outside it. See Zippo, 952 F. Supp. at 1127 (defendant who transmitted messages bearing infringing mark to residents of another state committed trademark infringement in recipient state). This type of internet activity further supports jurisdiction under CPLR § 302(a)(2).

3. Jurisdiction Under CPLR § 302(a)(3)

a. City National

Finally, there is yet a third basis for exercising specific jurisdiction, i.e., pursuant to CPLR § 302(a)(3). This provision confers jurisdiction over a defendant where the cause of action arises out of a tort committed outside of New York but the tort causes harm within New York, the defendant expected or should reasonably have expected the act to have consequences in the state, and the defendant derives substantial revenue from interstate or international commerce. See

CPLR § 302(a)(3).

As explained above, the mere creation and maintenance of web sites bearing infringing marks does not constitute a tort in any state where the sites can be viewed. Thus, to the extent that the web sites at issue are simply capable of being viewed in New York, without more, any tortious activity must be deemed to have occurred outside of New York.[9] The question then becomes whether the other requirements of CPLR § 302(a)(3) are satisfied.

Injury within the state includes harm to a business in the New York market in the form of lost sales or customers. See American Network, Inc. v. Access America/Connect Atlanta, 975 F. Supp. 494, 497 (S.D.N.Y. 1997) (citations omitted). This rule is satisfied by Citigroup's claim that its actual and potential customers in New York are confused or deceived when they view and interact with the City National web sites. See id.; National Football League, 2000 U.S. Dist. LEXIS 3929, at *2.

Furthermore, it was reasonably foreseeable that publication of web sites with the offending marks would have consequences in New York. See American Network, 975 F. Supp. at 497; National Football League, 2000 U.S. Dist. LEXIS 3929, at *2. Finally, there is little doubt that City National derives substantial revenue from interstate commerce. Commerce involving banking institutions constitutes interstate commerce, especially where as here the institution is insured by the Federal Deposit Insurance Corporation. See, e.g., United States v. Trammell, 133 F.3d 1343, 1353 (10th Cir. 1998); Securities & Exch. Comm'n v. S&P Nat'l Corp., 265 F. Supp. 993, 995 (S.D.N.Y. 1966), modified on other grounds, 360 F.2d 741 (2d Cir. 1966). Moreover, City Mortgage solicits home, equity, and mortgage loans on behalf of City National throughout the United States, and City Mortgage has over 80,000 accounts nationwide and services nearly $2 billion in loans. Also City National has branches and or employees located in West Virginia, Ohio, and California. In conclusion, jurisdiction over City National pursuant to CPLR § 302(a)(3) is proper.

b. City Holding

As the licensor of the CITY marks, City Holding is also subject to jurisdiction under CPLR § 302(a)(3). Entering into a licensing agreement outside of New York for an infringing mark constitutes a tort committed outside of New York. The alleged injury occurred within the State, however, due to use of the mark by City Holding's licensee, City Mortgage, in direct mailings and via the internet. See Firma Melodiya, 882 F. Supp. at 1311-12; Pony Int'l, 1983 U.S. Dist. LEXIS 15161, at *1.

There is little doubt that it was foreseeable to City Holding that use of CITY marks by its wholly-owned subsidiary would have consequences in New York. City Holding's Annual Report states that "City Holding and its affiliates have

---

[9] This conclusion only applies to City National's internet activity. Its direct mailing activities are subject to a different analysis, as explained earlier.

become leaders in the mortgage obligation business in West Virginia and throughout the country." In addition, City Holding and City National have several officers and directors in common. City Holding cannot disclaim knowledge of City National's use of CITY marks within New York. Finally, City Holding and its subsidiaries derive significant income from interstate commerce. Therefore, personal jurisdiction over City Holding under CPLR § 302(a)(3) is proper.

4. Due Process

The exercise of personal jurisdiction under a state long-arm statute comports with constitutional due process only if the defendant has "certain minimum contacts with [the forum] such that the maintenance of the suit does not offend traditional notions of fair play and substantial justice." International Shoe, 326 U.S. at 316 (citation and internal quotation marks omitted); World-Wide Volkswagen Corp. v. Woodson, 444 U.S. 286, 292, 62 L. Ed. 2d 490, 100 S. Ct. 559 (1980); Chew v. Dietrich, 143 F.3d 24, 28 (2d Cir. 1998). The Court has considered the factors relevant to this inquiry and finds that the assertion of personal jurisdiction over the individual defendants would not offend the standards of due process. See Metropolitan Life Ins. Co. v. Robertson-Ceco Corp., 84 F.3d 560, 567-69 (2d Cir. 1996).

B. General Jurisdiction Under CPLR § 301

Although it is unnecessary to determine whether there is general jurisdiction over City National and City Holding because the Court has found that there is specific jurisdiction, a brief discussion of this issue is warranted.

CPLR § 301 states that a New York court "may exercise jurisdiction over persons, property, or status as might have been exercised heretofore." The statute incorporates all grounds of jurisdiction previously recognized at common law. See Penny v. United Fruit Co., 869 F. Supp. 122, 125 (E.D.N.Y. 1994). Pursuant to CPLR § 301, a foreign corporation will be subject to personal jurisdiction in New York if it is present or "doing business" in the state. A corporation's activity rises to the level of "doing business" only when it is engaged in "such a continuous and systematic course of activity that it can be deemed present in the state of New York." Klinghoffer v. S.N.C. Achille Lauro, 937 F.2d 44, 50-51 (2d Cir. 1991) (quoting Laufer v. Ostrow, 55 N.Y.2d 305, 434 N.E.2d 692, 694, 449 N.Y.S.2d 456 (N.Y. 1982) (citations omitted)); see Mareno v. Rowe, 910 F.2d 1043, 1046 (2d Cir. 1990); Frummer v. Hilton Hotels Int'l, Inc., 19 N.Y.2d 533, 227 N.E.2d 851, 853, 281 N.Y.S.2d 41 (N.Y. 1967).

A foreign corporation may be subjected to the jurisdiction of New York even without any physical presence here if the corporation conducts, or purposefully directs, business "'not occasionally or casually, but with a fair measure of permanence and continuity.'" Landoil Resources Corp. v. Alexander & Alexander Servs., 77 N.Y.2d 28, 565 N.E.2d 488, 490, 563 N.Y.S.2d 739 (N.Y. 1990) (quoting Tauza v. Susquehanna Coal Co., 220 N.Y. 259, 267, 115 N.E. 915, 917 (N.Y. 1917)). The test, a "simple pragmatic one," Bryant v. Finnish Nat. Airline, 15 N.Y.2d 426, 208 N.E.2d 439, 441, 260 N.Y.S.2d 625 (N.Y. 1965), is necessarily fact sensitive. See Landoil Resources Corp. v. Alexander & Alexander Servs., 918 F.2d 1039, 1043 (2d Cir. 1990); Stark Carpet Corp. v. M-Geough Robinson, Inc., 481 F. Supp. 499, 504 (S.D.N.Y. 1980).

"In assessing jurisdiction under this pragmatic standard, New York courts have generally focused on the following indicia of jurisdiction: the existence of an office in New York; the solicitation of business in New York; the presence of bank accounts or other property in New York; and the presence of employees or agents in New York." Landoil, 918 F.2d at 1043; see Hoffritz, 763 F.2d at 58. However, "solicitation of business alone will not justify a finding of corporate presence in New York with respect to a foreign manufacturer or purveyor of services." Laufer, 449 N.Y.S.2d at 459; see Frummer, 227 N.E.2d at 853. Yet, under the "solicitation plus" test, if the solicitation "is substantial and continuous, and defendant engages in other activities of substance in the state, then personal jurisdiction may properly be found to exist." Landoil, 918 F.2d at 1043-44; see Beacon, 715 F.2d at 763; Aquascutum of London, Inc. v. S.S. American Champion, 426 F.2d 205, 211 (2d Cir. 1970).

Citigroup avers that this Court has general jurisdiction over City National and City Holding under the "solicitation plus" test. As explained below, Citigroup has demonstrated substantial and continuous solicitation activity by City National of business in New York. The Court declines to resolve whether Citigroup has demonstrated sufficient "plus" factors but observes that it is unlikely that the Court would conclude Citigroup has done so.

1. Solicitation Activity

As described above, City National conducts a nationwide mortgage origination business through its City Mortgage and City Lending Divisions. City National solicits business for its lending products and services in New York through advertising circulars mailed directly to New York residents and through its web sites. The direct mail circulars display the allegedly infringing CITY marks and promote the lending products and services offered by City National. They also include a toll-free number, the location of the City Lending web site, and the statement that City National is a "Licensed Mortgage Banker, NYS Banking Department." The City Lending web site provides comprehensive information about City Lending's loan products and services, allows customers in New York to apply for loans on-line or print out an application for submission by facsimile, and offers the opportunity to "chat" on-line with a City National representative. Prospective customers may also e-mail City Lending with home loan questions and are promised a response from an "online representative . . . in less than an hour." The City Mortgage site advertises City National's loan servicing products and invites prospective customers to call or e-mail regarding those products.

2. Plus Factors

Solicitation must be accompanied by other "activities of substance" in order for there to be general jurisdiction over the defendant. Landoil, 918 F.2d at

1043-44. The first difficulty with Citigroup's argument in this regard is that much of it is speculative. Thus, Citigroup offers the predictions of an experienced real estate attorney as to ways in which City National's lending business would likely require it to conduct activities other than solicitation within New York, such as conducting title searches, commencing foreclosure proceedings, and taking title to property in New York as a result of any foreclosures. These predictions, however, are not in themselves evidence that such activities actually occur.

There is evidence that the loans issued by City National are secured by mortgages on New York property which are recorded in New York. This activity involves the use of New York companies to record the liens on behalf of City Mortgage. The cases cited by Citigroup as support for the proposition that this activity rises to the level of sufficient "plus" factors, however, involved more substantial activity. See Stursburg & Veith v. Eckler Indus., Inc., No. 95 Civ. 5147, 1995 U.S. Dist. LEXIS 18228, at *4 (S.D.N.Y. Dec. 8, 1995); Bicicletas Windsor S.A. v. Bicycle Corp. of Am., 783 F. Supp. 781, 784-85 (S.D.N.Y. 1992); Laufer, 55 N.Y.2d at 310-12. Nor does it appear that City National exercises the requisite degree of control for there to be jurisdiction over City National by virtue of its relationship to these New York companies. See Landoil, 918 F.2d at 1046; Ball v. Matallurgie Hoboken-Overpelt, S.A., No. 87 Civ. 191, 1989 U.S. Dist. LEXIS 9107, at *9-*10 (N.D.N.Y. July 31, 1989).

Finally, as discussed above, City National's contact with New York residents via the internet does go beyond solicitation and provides a basis for exercising specific jurisdiction. Whether it satisfies the requirements for general jurisdiction, however, is another question. This is a particularly underdeveloped area of the law. Most courts considering the significance of internet activity for the exercise of personal jurisdiction have done so in the context of a specific, rather than general, jurisdictional analysis. In this case, the Court is not convinced that the activities herein satisfy the "solicitation plus" test for general jurisdiction. Nor do the cases cited by Citigroup assist much in this regard, as one concerns specific jurisdiction, see Zippo, 952 F. Supp. 1119, while the other concerns a general jurisdiction statute that, unlike § CPLR 301, reaches to the full extent of the constitutional due process test, see Mieczkowski v. Masco Corp., 997 F. Supp. 782, 784 (E.D. Tex. 1998).

On the facts of this case, the Court would be hesitant to conclude that CPLR § 301 is satisfied. Moreover, given the finding of specific jurisdiction, it is unnecessary to resolve this question or to venture into the essentially uncharted waters of the significance of the defendant's internet activity for a general jurisdiction analysis, and the Court declines to do so.

NOTES

(1) In contrast to the principal case, the court in *Hearst Corp. v. Goldberger,* 1997 U.S. Dist. LEXIS 2065 (S.D.N.Y. 1997), declined to find internet-based jurisdiction. The plaintiff, publisher of *Esquire* magazine, sued the out-of-state defendant for trademark infringement via his website "Esqwire.com." At the time of the suit, the website had yet to even offer to sell any products or services. In rejecting jurisdiction under CPLR 302(a)(1), the court analogized the website to an advertisement in a national magazine, which hardly constitutes a transaction of business in New York. In rejecting jurisdiction under 302(a)(2), the court noted that because the defendant had not sold or offered to sell any products in New York, trademark infringement could not have occurred in-state. Furthermore, 302(a)(2) jurisdiction almost always requires the defendant's physical presence in the forum state. Finally, the court rejected 302(a)(3) jurisdiction on the grounds that the defendant had not solicited any business in, nor derived any revenue from, New York (or elsewhere) via the website.

(2) A tortious act may be committed in New York through the internet, as in *National Football League v. Miller*, 2000 U.S. Dist. LEXIS 3929 (S.D.N.Y. 2000), a trademark infringement action in which the defendant operated a website that used the NFL mark and provided football related information and links to gambling pages. The website generated substantial revenue from advertisements and was regularly visited by people in New York. The court found jurisdiction under 302(a)(3)(ii), since it was "likely that his site would ultimately appear on thousands of computer screens in New York," even though the website did not specifically target New York. *See also Roberts-Gordon v. Superior Radiant*, 85 F. Supp. 2d 202 (S.D.N.Y. 2000), where the defendant put metatags featuring trademarks of the plaintiff on his website. Thus, people using a search engine to look for Roberts-Gordon were instead directed to the defendant's website. The court found this action diverting viewers from a New York website met the "expects or should reasonably expect the act to have consequences in the state" requirement of foreseeability. In *Telebyte, Inc. v. Kendaco, Inc.*, 105 F. Supp. 2d 131 (E.D.N.Y. 2000), the defendant's motion to dismiss for lack of personal jurisdiction was granted because the court determined that the tort was committed in the state where the website was created and maintained.

§ 1.07 JURISDICTION BASED ON PROPERTY WITHIN THE STATE: CPLR 301; CPLR 314

Introductory Note

Courts have traditionally had power to adjudicate rights to real or personal property located within their respective states even if they had no in personam jurisdiction over the owner of the property. This power is codified in CPLR 301 and, more particularly, in CPLR 314(2) and (3). Jurisdiction over property has been categorized as falling into three distinct types. The Supreme Court in *Shaffer v. Heitner*, 433 U.S. 186, 199 n.17 (1977), *infra*, quoted the following formulation:

> A judgment in rem affects the interests of all persons in designated property. A judgment quasi in rem affects the interests of particular persons in designated property. The latter is of two types. In one the plaintiff is seeking to secure a pre-existing claim in the subject property and to extinguish or establish the nonexistence of similar interests of particular persons. In the other the plaintiff seeks to apply what he concedes to be the property of the defendant to the satisfaction of a claim against him. Restatement, Judgments, 5-9.

These concepts are elucidated in this passage from James, Hazard & Leubsdorf, Civil Procedure 58-59 (4th ed. 1992):[*]

> *In rem,* against-all-the-world: The action concerns disputed claims to particular property (for example, a tract of land or a bank account), is accompanied by an appropriate form of notice . . . addressed to all persons who may have claims to the property, and has the effect of determining the interests of all persons who might have claims to it.

> *Quasi in rem,* against-specific-persons: The action concerns the claims to particular property of specifically named persons who are made parties to the proceeding, and has the effect of determining the interests of those persons but not others. [For example, a mortgage foreclosure proceeding against a non-resident mortgagor who has mortgaged land in the forum state and defaulted on required payments.]

> *Quasi in rem,* attachment: The action concerns a claim that does *not* relate to the property. Through attachment or sequestration, property concededly owned by defendant is seized at the beginning of the action and held with a view to giving it to the plaintiff if his claim against the defendant is sustained on its merits. For example, plaintiff may attach a bank account of the defendant in the state where the bank is located, plead a claim for tort or contract or whatever, and, if judgment is for plaintiff on the claim, then obtain an order directing the bank to pay the account (up to the amount of the judgment) to the plaintiff. [Footnotes omitted.]

Some New York cases and commentators have adopted a different formulation. Professor Siegel, for example, uses the term "strictly in rem" for the concept of jurisdiction to bind all potential claimants to property, the term "in rem" to designate jurisdiction against specific persons' interests in property, and the term "quasi in rem" to designate jurisdiction based on attachment. David D. Siegel, New York Practice 179-80 (4th ed. 2005).

---

[*] Reprinted with permission of Little Brown and Company, © 1977.

Common to all forms of property-based jurisdiction is that the power it gives the court is limited to the in-state property which is at issue or which has been attached. *Schwinger v. Hickok*, 53 N.Y. 280 (1873).

The traditional approach to jurisdiction based on the presence of property was profoundly shaken by *Shaffer v. Heitner*, 433 U.S. 186, 97 S. Ct. 2569 (1977).

SHAFFER v. HEITNER
United States Supreme Court
433 U.S. 186, 97 S. Ct. 2569, 53 L. Ed. 2d 683 (1977)

MR. JUSTICE MARSHALL delivered the opinion of the Court.

I

Appellee Heitner, a nonresident of Delaware, is the owner of one share of stock in the Greyhound Corp., a business incorporated under the laws of Delaware with its principal place of business in Phoenix, Ariz. On May 22, 1974, he filed a shareholder's derivative suit in the Court of Chancery for New Castle County, Del., in which he named as defendants Greyhound, its wholly owned subsidiary Greyhound Lines, Inc.,[1] and 28 present or former officers or directors of one or both of the corporations. In essence, Heitner alleged that the individual defendants had violated their duties to Greyhound by causing it and its subsidiary to engage in actions that resulted in the corporations being held liable for substantial damages in a private antitrust suit and a large fine in a criminal contempt action. The activities which led to these penalties took place in Oregon.

Simultaneously with his complaint, Heitner filed a motion for an order of sequestration of the Delaware property of the individual defendants pursuant to Del. Code Ann., Tit. 10, § 366 (1975). This motion was accompanied by a supporting affidavit of counsel which stated that the individual defendants were nonresidents of Delaware. The affidavit identified the property to be sequestered as [common stock issued by Greyhound to the defendants]. . . . The requested sequestration order was signed the day the motion was filed. Pursuant to that order, the sequestrator "seized" approximately 82,000 shares of Greyhound common stock belonging to 19 of the defendants, and options belonging to another 2 defendants. These seizures were accomplished by placing "stop transfer" orders or their equivalents on the books of the Greyhound Corp. So far as the record shows, none of the certificates representing the seized property was physically present in Delaware. The stock was considered to be in Delaware, and so subject to seizure, by virtue of Del. Code Ann., Tit. 8, § 169 (1975), which makes Delaware the situs of ownership of all stock in Delaware corporations.

---

[1] Greyhound Lines, Inc., is incorporated in California and has its principal place of business in Phoenix, Ariz.

. . . The 21 defendants whose property was seized (hereafter referred to as appellants) responded by entering a special appearance for the purpose of moving to quash service of process and to vacate the sequestration order. They . . . asserted that under the rule of *International Shoe Co. v. Washington*, 326 U. S. 310 (1945), they did not have sufficient contacts with Delaware to sustain the jurisdiction of that State's courts.

. . . .

II

The Delaware courts rejected appellants' jurisdictional challenge by noting that this suit was brought as a quasi in rem proceeding. Since quasi in rem jurisdiction is traditionally based on attachment or seizure of property present in the jurisdiction, not on contacts between the defendant and the State, the courts considered appellants' claimed lack of contacts with Delaware to be unimportant. This categorical analysis assumes the continued soundness of the conceptual structure founded on the century-old case of *Pennoyer v. Neff*, 95 U.S. 714 (1878).

From our perspective, the importance of *Pennoyer* is not its result, but the fact that its principles and corollaries derived from them became the basic elements of the constitutional doctrine governing state-court jurisdiction. *See, e.g.*, Hazard, *A General Theory of State-Court Jurisdiction*, 1965 Sup. Ct. Rev. 241 (hereafter Hazard). As we have noted, under *Pennoyer* state authority to adjudicate was based on the jurisdiction's power over either persons or property. This fundamental concept is embodied in the very vocabulary which we use to describe judgments. If a court's jurisdiction is based on its authority over the defendant's person, the action and judgment are denominated "in personam" and can impose a personal obligation on the defendant in favor of the plaintiff. If jurisdiction is based on the court's power over property within its territory, the action is called "in rem" or "quasi in rem." The effect of a judgment in such a case is limited to the property that supports jurisdiction and does not impose a personal liability on the property owner, since he is not before the court.[17] In *Pennoyer*'s terms, the owner is affected only "indirectly" by an in rem judgment adverse to his interest in the property subject to the court's disposition.

By concluding that "[t]he authority of every tribunal is necessarily restricted by the territorial limits of the State in which it is established," 95 U.S., at 720,

---

[17] "A judgment in rem affects the interests of all persons in designated property. A judgment quasi in rem affects the interests of particular persons in designated property. The latter is of two types. In one the plaintiff is seeking to secure a pre-existing claim in the subject property and to extinguish or establish the nonexistence of similar interests of particular persons. In the other the plaintiff seeks to apply what he concedes to be the property of the defendant to the satisfaction of a claim against him. Restatement, Judgments, 5-9." *Hanson v. Denckla*, 357 U.S. 235, 246 n. 12 (1958).

As did the Court in *Hanson*, we will for convenience generally use the term "in rem" in place of "in rem and quasi in rem."

Pennoyer sharply limited the availability of in personam jurisdiction over defendants not resident in the forum State. If a nonresident defendant could not be found in a State, he could not be sued there. On the other hand, since the State in which property was located was considered to have exclusive sovereignty over that property, in rem actions could proceed regardless of the owner's location. . . .

The *Pennoyer* rules generally favored nonresident defendants by making them harder to sue. This advantage was reduced, however, by the ability of a resident plaintiff to satisfy a claim against a nonresident defendant by bringing into court any property of the defendant located in the plaintiff's State. *See, e.g.*, Zammit, *Quasi-In-Rem Jurisdiction: Outmoded and Unconstitutional?*, 49 St. John's L. Rev. 668, 670 (1975). For example, in the well-known case of *Harris v. Balk*, 198 U.S. 215 (1905), Epstein, a resident of Maryland, had a claim against Balk, a resident of North Carolina. Harris, another North Carolina resident, owed money to Balk. When Harris happened to visit Maryland, Epstein garnished his debt to Balk. Harris did not contest the debt to Balk and paid it to Epstein's North Carolina attorney. When Balk later sued Harris in North Carolina, this Court held that the Full Faith and Credit Clause, U.S. Const., Art. IV, § 1, required that Harris' payment to Epstein be treated as a discharge of his debt to Balk. This Court reasoned that the debt Harris owed Balk was an intangible form of property belonging to Balk, and that the location of that property traveled with the debtor. By obtaining personal jurisdiction over Harris, Epstein had "arrested" his debt to Balk, 198 U.S., at 223, and brought it into the Maryland court. Under the structure established by *Pennoyer*, Epstein was then entitled to proceed against that debt to vindicate his claim against Balk, even though Balk himself was not subject to the jurisdiction of a Maryland tribunal. . . . [The Court here traced the development of the modern law of jurisdiction. — Eds.]

. . . .

Thus, the relationship among the defendant, the forum, and the litigation, rather than the mutually exclusive sovereignty of the States on which the rules of *Pennoyer* rest, became the central concern of the inquiry into personal jurisdiction. The immediate effect of this departure from *Pennoyer*'s conceptual apparatus was to increase the ability of the state courts to obtain personal jurisdiction over nonresident defendants. . . .

It is clear, therefore, that the law of state-court jurisdiction no longer stands securely on the foundation established in *Pennoyer*. We think that the time is ripe to consider whether the standard of fairness and substantial justice set forth in *International Shoe* should be held to govern actions in rem as well as in personam.

III

The case for applying to jurisdiction in rem the same test of "fair play and substantial justice" as governs assertions of jurisdiction in personam is simple and straightforward. It is premised on recognition that "[t]he phrase, 'judicial jurisdiction over a thing,' is a customary elliptical way of referring to jurisdiction over the interests of persons in a thing." Restatement (Second) of Conflict of Laws § 56, Introductory Note (1971) (hereafter Restatement). This recognition leads to the conclusion that in order to justify an exercise of jurisdiction in rem, the basis for jurisdiction must be sufficient to justify exercising "jurisdiction over the interests of persons in a thing." The standard for determining whether an exercise of jurisdiction over the interests of persons is consistent with the Due Process Clause is the minimum-contacts standard elucidated in *International Shoe.*

This argument, of course, does not ignore the fact that the presence of property in a State may bear on the existence of jurisdiction by providing contacts among the forum State, the defendant, and the litigation. For example, when claims to the property itself are the source of the underlying controversy between the plaintiff and the defendant,[24] it would be unusual for the State where the property is located not to have jurisdiction. In such cases, the defendant's claim to property located in the State would normally . . . indicate that he expected to benefit from the State's protection of his interest. The State's strong interests in assuring the marketability of property within its borders and in providing a procedure for peaceful resolution of disputes about the possession of that property would also support jurisdiction, as would the likelihood that important records and witnesses will be found in the State. The presence of property may also favor jurisdiction in cases, such as suits for injury suffered on the land of an absentee owner, where the defendant's ownership of the property is conceded but the cause of action is otherwise related to rights and duties growing out of that ownership.

It appears, therefore, that jurisdiction over many types of actions which now are or might be brought in rem would not be affected by a holding that any assertion of state-court jurisdiction must satisfy the *International Shoe* standard.[30] For the type of quasi in rem action typified by *Harris v. Balk,* and the present case, however, accepting the proposed analysis would result in significant change. These are cases where the property which now serves as the basis for state-court jurisdiction is completely unrelated to the plaintiff's cause of action. Thus, although the presence of the defendant's property in a State might suggest the existence of other ties among the defendant, the State, and the litigation, the presence of the property alone would not support the State's jurisdiction. If those other ties did not exist, cases over which the State is now thought to have jurisdiction could not be brought in that forum. . . .

---

[24] This category includes true in rem actions and the first type of quasi in rem proceedings. *See* n. 17, *supra.*

[30] *Cf.* Smit, *The Enduring Utility of In Rem Rules: A Lasting Legacy of Pennoyer v. Neff,* 43 Brooklyn L. Rev. 600 (1977). We do not suggest that jurisdictional doctrines other than those discussed in text, such as the particularized rules governing adjudications of status, are inconsistent with the standard of fairness. . . .

The primary rationale for treating the presence of property as a sufficient basis for jurisdiction to adjudicate claims over which the State would not have jurisdiction if *International Shoe* applied is that a wrongdoer should not be able to avoid payment of his obligations by the expedient of removing his assets to a place where he is not subject to an in personam suit . . . .

This justification, however, does not explain why jurisdiction should be recognized without regard to whether the property is present in the State because of an effort to avoid the owner's obligations. Nor does it support jurisdiction to adjudicate the underlying claim. At most, it suggests that a State in which property is located should have jurisdiction to attach that property, by use of proper procedures, as security for a judgment being sought in a forum where the litigation can be maintained consistently with *International Shoe*. . . . Moreover, we know of nothing to justify the assumption that a debtor can avoid paying his obligations by removing his property to a State in which his creditor cannot obtain personal jurisdiction over him. The Full Faith and Credit Clause, after all, makes the valid in personam judgment of one State enforceable in all other States.

It might also be suggested that allowing in rem jurisdiction avoids the uncertainty inherent in the *International Shoe* standard and assures a plaintiff of a forum. . . . We believe, however, that the fairness standard of *International Shoe* can be easily applied in the vast majority of cases. Moreover, when the existence of jurisdiction in a particular forum under *International Shoe* is unclear, the cost of simplifying the litigation by avoiding the jurisdictional question may be the sacrifice of "fair play and substantial justice." That cost is too high.

We are left, then, to consider the significance of the long history of jurisdiction based solely on the presence of property in a State. Although the theory that territorial power is both essential to and sufficient for jurisdiction has been undermined, we have never held that the presence of property in a State does not automatically confer jurisdiction over the owner's interest in that property. This history must be considered as supporting the proposition that jurisdiction based solely on the presence of property satisfies the demands of due process, *cf. Ownbey v. Morgan*, 256 U.S. 94, 111 (1921), but it is not decisive. "[T]raditional notions of fair play and substantial justice" can be as readily offended by the perpetuation of ancient forms that are no longer justified as by the adoption of new procedures that are inconsistent with the basic values of our constitutional heritage. . . . The fiction that an assertion of jurisdiction over property is anything but an assertion of jurisdiction over the owner of the property supports an ancient form without substantial modern justification. Its continued acceptance would serve only to allow state-court jurisdiction that is fundamentally unfair to the defendant.

We therefore conclude that all assertions of state-court jurisdiction must be evaluated according to the standards set forth in *International Shoe* and its progeny.

IV

The Delaware courts based their assertion of jurisdiction in this case solely on the statutory presence of appellants' property in Delaware. Yet that property is not the subject matter of this litigation, nor is the underlying cause of action related to the property. Appellants' holdings in Greyhound do not, therefore, provide contacts with Delaware sufficient to support the jurisdiction of that State's courts over appellants. If it exists, that jurisdiction must have some other foundation. . . .

Appellee suggests that by accepting positions as officers or directors of a Delaware corporation, appellants performed the acts required by *Hanson v. Denckla*. He notes that Delaware law provides substantial benefits to corporate officers and directors, and that these benefits were at least in part the incentive for appellants to assume their positions. It is, he says, "only fair and just" to require appellants, in return for these benefits, to respond in the State of Delaware when they are accused of misusing their power. Brief for Appellee 15.

But . . . this line of reasoning establishes only that it is appropriate for Delaware law to govern the obligations of appellants to Greyhound and its stockholders. It does not demonstrate that appellants have "purposefully avail[ed themselves] of the privilege of conducting activities within the forum State," *Hanson v. Denckla, supra*, at 253, in a way that would justify bringing them before a Delaware tribunal. Appellants have simply had nothing to do with the State of Delaware. Moreover, appellants had no reason to expect to be haled before a Delaware court. Delaware, unlike some States, has not enacted a statute that treats acceptance of a directorship as consent to jurisdiction in the State. And "[i]t strains reason . . . to suggest that anyone buying securities in a corporation formed in Delaware 'impliedly consents' to subject himself to Delaware's . . . jurisdiction on any cause of action." . . . Appellants, who were not required to acquire interests in Greyhound in order to hold their positions, did not by acquiring those interests surrender their right to be brought to judgment only in States with which they had "minimum contacts."

The Due Process Clause

> "does not contemplate that a state may make binding a judgment . . . against an individual or corporate defendant with which the state has no contacts, ties, or relations." *International Shoe Co. v. Washington*, 326 U. S., at 319.

Delaware's assertion of jurisdiction over appellants in this case is inconsistent with that constitutional limitation on state power. The judgment of the Delaware Supreme Court must, therefore, be reversed.

It is so ordered.

Mr. Justice Powell, concurring.

I agree that the principles of *International Shoe Co. v. Washington*, 326 U.S. 310 (1945), should be extended to govern assertions of in rem as well as in personam jurisdiction in a state court. . . .

I would explicitly reserve judgment, however, on whether the ownership of some forms of property whose situs is indisputably and permanently located within a State may, without more, provide the contacts necessary to subject a defendant to jurisdiction within the State to the extent of the value of the property. In the case of real property, in particular, preservation of the common-law concept of quasi in rem jurisdiction arguably would avoid the uncertainty of the general *International Shoe* standard without significant cost to "'traditional notions of fair play and substantial justice.'" *Id.*, at 316, *quoting Milliken v. Meyer*, 311 U. S. 457, 463 (1940).

Subject to the foregoing reservation, I join the opinion of the Court.

[Justice Stevens, in a separate concurrence, agreed with Justice Powell that the opinion should not be read to "invalidate quasi in rem jurisdiction where real estate is involved [or] as invalidating other long-accepted methods of acquiring jurisdiction . . . ."]

. . . .

NOTES

(1) An analysis of *Shaffer*, with special attention given to New York law, is found in *Symposium on* Shaffer v. Heitner, 45 Brook. L. Rev. 493 (1978). *See generally,* Linda Silberman, Shaffer v. Heitner: *The End of an Era*, 53 N.Y.U. L. Rev. 33 (1978).

(2) Quasi in rem jurisdiction pursuant to CPLR 314(2), which applies when the plaintiff seeks to exclude the defendant from an interest in specific property found within the state, apparently survives. In *McCasland v. McCasland*, 68 N.Y.2d 748, 506 N.Y.S.2d 329, 497 N.E.2d 696 (1986), it was held that service was properly made under CPLR 314(2) in Florida on the defendant husband (a resident of Florida) in an action to determine the plaintiff wife's interest in certain New York corporations owned by the husband.

(3) The apotheosis of quasi in rem jurisdiction by attachment had been reached in *Seider v. Roth*, 17 N.Y.2d 111, 269 N.Y.S.2d 99 (1966). That case held that jurisdiction could be acquired over a non-resident defendant in an action arising from an out-of-state auto accident by the stratagem of attaching the defendant's interest in a liability insurance policy, a fictional debt found within the state because the "debtor," the insurer, was present in New York by virtue of doing business in the state. Jurisdiction was limited to the amount of the insurance. Although the New York courts (in addition to those of a few

other states) continued to adhere to the *Seider* doctrine notwithstanding *Shaffer v. Heitner*, the Supreme Court ultimately held that *Seider* could not survive in the modern jurisdictional era. *Rush v. Savchuk*, 444 U.S. 320, 100 S. Ct. 571, 62 L. Ed. 2d 145 (1980). In *Rush*, in which the Minnesota version of the *Seider* doctrine was at issue, the Supreme Court said:

> We held in *Shaffer* that the mere presence of property in a State does not establish a sufficient relationship between the owner of the property and the State to support the exercise of jurisdiction over an unrelated cause of action. The ownership of property in the State is a contact between the defendant and the forum, and it may suggest the presence of other ties. . . . Jurisdiction is lacking, however, unless there are sufficient contacts to satisfy the fairness standard of *International Shoe*.

> Here, the fact that the defendant's insurer does business in the forum State suggests no further contacts between the defendant and the forum, and the record supplies no evidence of any. State Farm's decision to do business in Minnesota was completely adventitious as far as Rush was concerned. He had no control over that decision, and it is unlikely that he would have expected that by buying insurance in Indiana he had subjected himself to suit in any State to which a potential future plaintiff might decide to move. In short, it cannot be said that the defendant engaged in any purposeful activity related to the forum that would make the exercise of jurisdiction fair, just, or reasonable, . . . merely because his insurer does business there.

> Nor are there significant contacts between the litigation and the forum. The Minnesota Supreme Court was of the view that the insurance policy was so important to the litigation that it provided contacts sufficient to satisfy due process. The insurance policy is not the subject matter of the case, however, nor is it related to the operative facts of the negligence action. The contractual arrangements between the defendant and the insurer pertain only to the conduct, not the substance of the litigation, and accordingly do not affect the court's jurisdiction unless they demonstrate ties between the defendant and the forum.

> In fact, the fictitious presence of the insurer's obligation in Minnesota does not, without more, provide a basis for concluding that there is any contact in the *International Shoe* sense between Minnesota and the insured. . . . 433 U.S. at 329-330. . . .

(4) When *Rush v. Savchuk* was decided, there were cases pending which, if *Rush* were applied to them, would be dismissed. In many such cases, moreover, the statute of limitations would bar re-commencement of the action in the state of the defendant's residence. Nonetheless, in *Gager v. White*, 53 N.Y.2d 475, 483, 442 N.Y.S.2d 463, 466, 425 N.E.2d 851, 853 (1981), the Court of Appeals applied the general rule that "a change in decisional law usually will be applied retrospectively to all cases still in the normal litigating process" and held that

any pending cases in which the jurisdictional defense was properly asserted must be dismissed. A similar approach was taken by the Second Circuit: *Rush* was held to require dismissal of a pending case even though the statute of limitations had run in New Jersey, the only other possible forum, in *Holzsager v. Valley Hospital*, 646 F.2d 792 (2d Cir. 1981).

(5) Many cases that traditionally would have required jurisdiction in rem as a basis would today also find jurisdictional support in CPLR 302(a)(4). Consider the mortgage foreclosure action against the non-resident: Even if the defendant had never come into the state to execute or negotiate the mortgage, CPLR 302(a)(4) would apply. What advantage does it offer that CPLR 314(2) does not? (The relationship between long-arm jurisdiction and in rem jurisdiction is discussed in the Recommendation of the Law Revision Commission to the 1978 Legislature, 1978 McKinney's Session Laws of New York 1641, 1648-1650.)

Does CPLR 302(a)(4) help Alice, the plaintiff in the following problem? Does CPLR 314(2) or (3)?

PROBLEM F

(a) Stephen, a California domiciliary who operates a vintage automobile dealership in San Francisco, loaned his prize possession, a Dusenberg, to a museum in New York for an exhibition dealing with the industrial arts. Stephen has no other New York contacts. While the car was on display there, Alice, Stephen's former business partner and now a New York domiciliary, brought an action in the Supreme Court, New York County, to obtain possession of it, claiming that he had conveyed it to her. Does the court have jurisdiction?

(b) Would the court have jurisdiction if Alice first attached the auto and alleged that Stephen owed her money under an agreement executed in California when the partnership was dissolved?

BANCO AMBROSIANO, S.P.A. v. ARTOC BANK & TRUST LTD.
Court of Appeals
62 N.Y.2d 65, 476 N.Y.S.2d 64, 464 N.E.2d 432 (1984)

WACHTLER, J.

Plaintiff commenced this action by the attachment of approximately $8 million, representing the balance of defendant's account with its New York correspondent bank. Defendant's appeal, taken pursuant to leave granted by the Appellate Division, focuses primarily on the question of whether this attempted assertion of quasi-in-rem jurisdiction over defendant's property is consistent with due process.

Plaintiff Banco Ambrosiano (Ambrosiano) is an Italian banking corporation, the principal office of which is in Milan. Prior to being placed in liquidation, Ambrosiano was involved in the international banking business and, in this connection, maintained a representative office in New York City. Defendant Artoc Bank and Trust Limited (Artoc), also a banking corporation, is organized under the laws of Nassau, Bahamas, and regularly engages in international transactions. Many of these transactions involve the borrowing and lending of United States dollars, which requires that the transfers be handled through a United States bank. For this purpose, Artoc utilizes an account with its New York correspondent bank, Brown Brothers Harriman and Co. (Brown Brothers). Neither Ambrosiano nor Artoc is authorized to engage in the banking business in this State.

Ambrosiano brought this action to recover $15 million which it allegedly loaned to Artoc, and which has not been repaid. Three transactions, each involving $5 million, were entered into by the parties. The memoranda drawn by Artoc indicate that Ambrosiano was to deposit these sums in Artoc's account with Brown Brothers, and that repayment was to be made to Ambrosiano's account with its New York correspondent bank. Artoc contends, in its defense, that the purpose of the transaction was to reloan the funds to Ambrosiano's controlled subsidiary in Peru and that it was understood that Artoc was to repay these sums only if and when the ultimate recipient repaid them.

With respect to the jurisdictional issue, it appears that all negotiations concerning this agreement were made outside of New York and all communications took place among the Bahamas, Italy, and Peru. The only connection with New York is that the funds were deposited to a New York bank account, were to be repaid to another New York bank account, and apparently were transferred to a New York account on behalf of the ultimate recipient. Artoc argues that the sole reason New York banks were utilized is that the transaction was to be in United States dollars and therefore had to be handled through such clearing accounts. In any event, it is clear that Artoc's sole contact with this State was its maintenance of the correspondent bank account with Brown Brothers.

Ambrosiano commenced this action by obtaining an ex parte restraining order, enjoining Brown Brothers from transferring the funds in Artoc's account. Ambrosiano's motion to confirm the attachment was granted over Artoc's challenge to the exercise of jurisdiction over its property. Special Term, noting that Ambrosiano conceded the lack of in personam jurisdiction, found that the property bore a reasonable relationship to the cause of action and that this relationship was sufficient to form the basis for quasi-in-rem jurisdiction. The Appellate Division unanimously affirmed.

Prior to the Supreme Court's expansion of the recognized bases for extraterritorial jurisdiction over a nondomiciliary, those who wished to sue in this State often resorted to the doctrine of quasi-in-rem jurisdiction to force a nondomiciliary defendant to litigate a claim in a forum where the defendant happened to own property. The conceptual basis for the State's power to adjudicate the claim was defendant's property, which was brought before the court by virtue of its seizure or attachment. Any resulting judgment was viewed as a judgment against the property only.

With the holding in *International Shoe Co. v. Washington* (326 U.S. 310), the approach to jurisdictional analysis was greatly altered. . . .

The long-arm jurisdiction legitimized by the *International Shoe* court was implemented in this State by statute. When the CPLR took effect in 1963, it contained two relevant sections. CPLR 301 preserves all previously existing jurisdictional bases, providing that the courts "may exercise such jurisdiction over persons, property, or status as might have been exercised heretofore." The long-arm statute, CPLR 302, provides that when a cause of action arises out of certain activities either occurring within the State or having an impact within the State, jurisdiction may be exercised over a nondomiciliary. Importantly, in setting forth certain categories of bases for long-arm jurisdiction, CPLR 302 does not go as far as is constitutionally permissible. Thus, a situation can occur in which the necessary contacts to satisfy due process are present, but in personam jurisdiction will not be obtained in this State because the statute does not authorize it (Siegel, N.Y. Prac., § 84, p. 95; Note, *Minimum Contacts and Jurisdictional Theory in New York: The Effect of Shaffer v. Heitner*, 42 Alb. L. Rev. 294, 306).

Even with the adoption of the long-arm statute, quasi-in-rem jurisdiction, which had been carried forward by virtue of CPLR 301, remained a viable method for subjecting a nondomiciliary to suit in this State. The use of this doctrine was drastically limited, however, by the Supreme Court's decision in *Shaffer v. Heitner* (433 U.S. 186). There, the court held that the minimum contacts analysis set forth in *International Shoe* is applicable to actions involving quasi-in-rem as well as in personam jurisdiction (*id.*, at p. 207). Thus, when the property serving as the jurisdictional basis has no relationship to the cause of action and there are no other ties among the defendant, the forum and the litigation, quasi-in-rem jurisdiction will be lacking (*id.*, at pp. 208-209).

Although it may appear, at first blush, that the usefulness of quasi-in-rem jurisdiction has been eliminated by *Shaffer*, inasmuch as the minimum contacts necessary to support it will also generally provide in personam jurisdiction, that is not the case, at least in New York. As noted above CPLR 302 does not provide for in personam jurisdiction in every case in which due process would permit it. Thus, a "gap" exists in which the necessary minimum contacts, including the presence of defendant's property within the State, are present, but personal jurisdiction is not authorized by CPLR 302. It is appropriate, in such a case, to fill that gap utilizing quasi-in-rem principles (Siegel, N.Y. Prac., § 104, p. 124; Note, *Minimum Contacts and Jurisdictional Theory in New York: The Effect of Shaffer v. Heitner*, 42 Alb. L. Rev. 294, 306).

Whether quasi-in-rem jurisdiction exists in a given case involves an inquiry into the presence or absence of the constitutionally mandated minimum contacts . . . .

Turning to the facts of the present case, we hold that the relationship between the defendant Artoc, the litigation and this State is sufficient to make it fair that Artoc be compelled to defend here. Artoc stresses that its only contact with New York is the maintenance of its correspondent bank account and urges that the mere presence of this property is insufficient to sustain jurisdiction. What Artoc appears to overlook is the quality of this contact and its significance in the context of this litigation. This is not a case in which property is coincidentally located within the State's borders and forms the only relevant link to defendant; rather, Artoc's account with Brown Brothers is closely related to plaintiff's claim. It is the very account through which Artoc effectuated the transaction at issue, directing Ambrosiano to pay funds to the account and presumably directing Brown Brothers to transfer the funds out of this account to their ultimate recipient. Nor is this transaction an isolated one, for it appears that Artoc utilizes this account regularly to accomplish its international banking business, communicating with Brown Brothers for disbursements of funds on its behalf and directing others to deposit funds there. Finally, with respect to performance of the agreement which forms the basis for Ambrosiano's claim, Artoc not only directed that the funds be deposited in its New York account, but it also agreed to repay these amounts (according to Artoc, only if Ambrosiano's Peruvian subsidiary repaid them) to Ambrosiano's New York account. These factors — the relationship between the cause of action and the property, the activities to be performed in New York under the parties' agreement, and Artoc's other ties with New York — combine to render the exercise of quasi-in-rem jurisdiction appropriate in this case. The dictates of due process are not offended by requiring Artoc to defend this claim in New York, as it has maintained a significant connection with the State and undertaken purposeful activity here (*see Sterling Nat. Bank & Trust Co. v. Fidelity Mtge. Investors*, 510 F.2d 870 [2d Cir.] [finding personal jurisdiction on somewhat similar facts]; *Federal Deposit Ins. Corp. v. Interbanca-Banca Per Finanziamenti a Medio Termine*, 405 F. Supp. 1118 [SDNY] [same]).

NOTES

(1) In addition to the principal case, other decisions of state and federal courts in New York authorize jurisdiction based on attachment after *Shaffer v. Heitner, supra. See, e.g., Intermeat, Inc. v. American Poultry, Inc.*, 575 F.2d 1017 (2d Cir. 1978) (plaintiff obtained jurisdiction by attaching a debt owed to defendant by a third party which was a New York corporation; the court held that the defendant, which had in the past sold large quantities of meat in New York, had sufficient contacts with New York to satisfy the Fourteenth Amendment and that it was therefore not improper to invoke CPLR 314 as a statutory

source of jurisdiction); *Majique Fashions, Ltd. v. Warwick & Co.*, 67 A.D.2d 321, 414 N.Y.S.2d 916 (1st Dep't 1979) (defendant Korean corporation had a checking account at a New York bank, which plaintiff attached; the court justified jurisdiction because defendant had allegedly breached an agreement to inspect goods in Korea for the New York plaintiff and thus defendant's omission had foreseeable consequences in New York); *ACLI International, Inc. v. E.D. & F. Man, Ltd.*, 76 A.D.2d 635, 430 N.Y.S.2d 858 (2d Dep't 1980) (attachment of defendant's assets upheld due to defendant's maintenance of a commodity trading account in New York and defendant's agreement to arbitration in New York, which entails similar expected costs to a lawsuit); *Desert Palace, Inc. v. Rozenbaum*, 192 A.D.2d 340, 595 N.Y.S.2d 768 (1st Dep't 1993) (attachment of defendant debtor's New York bank account upheld because defendant had used the account as a reference to obtain credit from plaintiff and had issued drafts for repayment against the account, which were subsequently dishonored); *Feder v. Turkish Airlines*, 441 F. Supp. 1273 (S.D.N.Y. 1977) (attachment of defendant's New York bank account in case arising from an air crash in Turkey; court relied on defendant's voluntary opening of the New York account to further its own business interests). Other possibly valid uses of attachment jurisdiction are discussed in Richard T. Farrell, *Civil Practice, 1977 Survey of N.Y. Law*, 29 Syracuse L. Rev. 449, 456-59 (1978).

The principal case and its teaching is criticized in Michael B. Mushlin, *The New Quasi In Rem Jurisdiction: New York's Revival of a Doctrine Whose Time Has Passed*, 55 Brook. L. Rev. 1059 (1990). *See also* Richard W. Bourne, *The Demise of Foreign Attachment*, 21 Creighton L. Rev. 141 (1987); Oscar G. Chase, *Quasi in Rem Jurisdiction in Social Context: Some Thoughts on a New Statute*, 45 Brook. L. Rev. 617 (1979).

(2) To the degree that property-based jurisdiction survives in the post-*Shaffer* era, it still depends on finding the defendant's property in the jurisdiction. This is simple in the case of tangibles. Intangibles are another matter. Note, in this connection, that CPLR 6202 makes debts as well as property attachable. When is a debt "in" New York? *See, e.g., Intermeat, Inc. v. American Poultry Inc.*, *supra. See generally* Andreas F. Lowenfeld, *In Search of the Intangible: A Comment on* Shaffer v. Heitner, 53 N.Y.U. L. Rev. 102 (1978). Some aspects of the problem are treated in Chapter 12, *infra* in connection with attachment itself.

(3) An exemption from attachment or other seizure in New York is provided to "any work of fine art" while it is on exhibit in a museum or other non-profit institution and when en route to or from such exhibition pursuant to N.Y. Arts and Cultural Affairs Law § 12.03. *People v. Museum of Modern Art*, 93 N.Y.2d 729, 697 N.Y.S.2d 538, 719 N.E.2d 897 (1999), which involved a grand jury investigation into the ownership of two paintings on loan to the Museum of Modern Art in New York, held that the protection of art from seizure applied to criminal proceedings and quashed a subpoena the District Attorney served on the Museum.

§ 1.08 MATRIMONIAL LITIGATION

PROBLEM G

Tom and Sally met while both were students at a North Carolina college. (He was a North Carolinian; she a New Yorker.) Shortly after graduation, they moved to New York, got married and took an apartment near her parents. One year later, the firm for which Tom worked asked him to transfer to Chicago, which he did. Sally found a new job and moved to Chicago also. Six months after the move, a child was born to them. Unfortunately, marital discord developed around the same time, and ten months after the child's birth, Sally returned to New York and shared her parents' home. Two months thereafter, she decided to seek a divorce. She will also seek child support, a property award and permanent custody of the child. If Sally seeks your opinion as to whether she should commence an action in New York or Illinois, what is your response?

In preparing a response consider CPLR 302(b), CPLR 314(1), CPLR 105(p) and N.Y. Domestic Relations Law § 230 in addition to the following material.[*]

CARR v. CARR
Court of Appeals
46 N.Y.2d 270, 413 N.Y.S.2d 305, 385 N.E.2d 1234 (1978)

COOKE, J.

We hold that, in the absence of "minimum contacts," New York courts have no jurisdiction over the nonresident second wife of a deceased husband, where the first wife seeks to obtain a declaration as to the validity of the first marriage.

Plaintiff Ann Carr, a resident of New York, alleges that she married decedent Paul Carr in Nevada on November 16, 1956. The couple lived in a number of marital abodes in various countries incidental to Paul's tenure with the United States Foreign Service. In 1965 Ann, citing the harsh treatment she received at the hands of her husband, departed the marital residence in Honduras and returned to the United States, ultimately settling in New York. Some two years

---

[*] N.Y. Domestic Relations Law § 230 imposes a residency requirement as an element of an action for divorce. A divorce action may be maintained only if, inter alia, one of the parties has been a resident of the state for at least a year and the parties were married in the state, or the cause of action for divorce arose in the state, or one party has resided in the state for two years. This requirement does not affect the in personam or subject matter jurisdiction of the court, however. *Lacks v. Lacks*, 41 N.Y.2d 71, 390 N.Y.S.2d 875, 359 N.E.2d 384 (1976). It has been held that the residency requirement is satisfied if a party is a New York domiciliary, even if not a current resident. *Esser v. Esser*, 277 A.D.2d 926, 716 N.Y.S.2d 257 (4th Dep't 2000); *Wittich v. Wittich*, 210 A.D.2d 138, 620 N.Y.S.2d 351 (1st Dep't 1994).

after Ann's departure, Paul obtained an ex parte Honduran divorce on the ground of abandonment.

Defendant Barbara Carr has resided in California continuously since 1962. She claims that she and Paul Carr were joined in matrimony in Nevada on December 3, 1974. During the relevant time frame, Barbara had no contacts with New York State. When Paul died in 1975, Barbara applied for survivor benefits furnished by the Foreign Service Retirement and Disability System. Learning of this, plaintiff Ann Carr commenced this action to invalidate the Honduran divorce and to declare her the lawful surviving spouse of Paul. Of course, this controversy is between Ann and Barbara, and any adjudication of their respective rights will be effectual only if Barbara is bound by the judgment.

. . . .

Status adjudications enjoy a rather unique place in our jurisprudence. Long ago the notion developed that a divorce proceeding is an action in rem (2 Bishop, Marriage and Divorce [4th ed], § 164), with the marital status of the parties being fictitiously deemed an intangible res (*Geary v Geary*, 272 N.Y. 390, 399). While the analytical value of the in rem label has been questioned (*see, e.g., Williams v North Carolina*, 317 U.S. 287, 297), status adjudications nonetheless possess a different quality than that of the typical in personam action (*see, e.g., Estin v Estin*, 334 U.S. 541, 546-549). However ultimately classified, the principles of divorce jurisdiction are of ancient origin but enduring validity.[1] There is apparently no disagreement as to the nature of these general principles.

A basic maxim in this area, not to be disputed at this late date, is that divorce jurisdiction may be exercised only when at least one of the parties to the marriage is domiciled in the State. So fundamental is the domicile requirement that it is a constitutional prerequisite to the recognition of a divorce decree under the full faith and credit clause (U.S. Const., art. IV, § 1; *see, e.g., Sosna v. Iowa*, 419 U.S. 393, 407.) This is not to say, of course, that in personam jurisdiction would be an insufficient predicate for a status adjudication in all circumstances (*cf. Whealton v. Whealton*, 67 Cal. 2d 656). But surely the alteration of a party's status in the absence of both recognized forms of jurisdiction would amount to a gross injustice.

That is precisely the situation here.[2] Defendant Carr is not a New York domiciliary, and the other party to the marriage, Paul Carr, is deceased. Nor does Ann

---

[1] There is little doubt but that the classical concepts of divorce jurisdiction survive the recent decision in *Shaffer v. Heitner* (433 U.S. 186). As the Supreme Court stated "[w]e do not suggest that jurisdictional doctrines other than those discussed in text, such as the particularized rules governing adjudications of status, are inconsistent with the standard of fairness" (*Shaffer v. Heitner, supra*, at p. 208, n. 30).

[2] We recognize, of course, that the present case is not a traditional status suit. Typically, a status action would be one seeking to terminate or to declare void an existing marriage. In such a case, there is no doubt at the commencement of the action that a marriage exists to serve as the juris-

Carr's status as a domiciliary of this State provide any basis for asserting jurisdiction over Barbara. The fiction of the marital res, with the consequence that it provides the predicate for in rem jurisdiction, however useful and appropriate it may be during the joint lives of the husband and wife, ceases to have any vitality or legal substance after the death of either husband or wife. Thereafter, save possibly in some unusual case, the only issues to be litigated are those concerning property rights. Any determination described as relating to the marital status of the parties can no longer have any meaning with respect to the interpersonal relations of the parties to the marriage, but can only serve as an intermediate step en route to some adjudication of property rights. It is precisely for such an objective that a declaration is sought in this action as to the invalidity of the Honduran divorce obtained by Paul from Ann. No case is brought to our attention, however, in which the marital res has been recognized, following the death of one of the parties to the marriage, as sufficient to provide a jurisdictional basis for an in rem adjudication binding on third parties over whom the forum court has no in personam jurisdiction.

Plainly, the absence of any contact between defendant and New York is an obstacle to the exercise of personal jurisdiction. If defendant had even a minimal relationship with the State, there is little doubt that jurisdiction in this declaratory judgment action could be sustained (*see, e.g., International Shoe Co. v Washington*, 326 U.S. 310, 316). As the record reveals, however, Barbara Carr has engaged in no activity in New York, and certainly has not "purposefully derive[d] benefit[s] from any activities relating to" the State of New York (*Kulko v Superior Ct. of Cal.* . . . .) To uphold in personam jurisdiction in such a case would be to ignore the restraints, however limited they may be in this modern era, imposed by the due process clause.

Accordingly, the order of the Appellate Division should be reversed, without costs, and the action should be dismissed.

CHIEF JUDGE BREITEL and WACHTLER, J. (dissenting).

We dissent and vote to affirm on the opinion of Mr. Justice James D. Hopkins at the Appellate Division . . . .

True, the marital res may be a legal fiction, but neither in fiction nor in reality does the marriage relationship terminate, for all purposes, at the death of one spouse. Important legal rights accrue to a spouse, as a spouse, even after death. The intestate share statute and the right of election provide obvious examples. The majority's analysis would presumably prevent even a woman

---

dictional res. Here, by contrast, since plaintiff seeks a determination as to the validity of the marital res, the existence of the jurisdictional predicate is the very question to be resolved by the litigation (*cf. New York Life Ins. Co. v Dunlevy*, 241 U.S. 518). It may be argued, therefore, that declaratory judgment actions such as the instant one may not be maintained absent personal jurisdiction of the defendant (*see Gray-Lewis v Gray-Lewis*, 5 A.D.2d 238, 241-242 [Valente, J., concurring]). In view of our disposition of the appeal, however, this problem need not be addressed at the present time.

married in New York and a life-long resident from seeking in New York a declaration, for estate purposes, that her husband's out-of-State divorce was invalid, all on the theory that the marital res expired at the husband's death. The result is unrealistic and unacceptable, however "consistent" it may purport to be with a mechanical logic.

NOTES

(1) Simply because New York has jurisdiction to adjudicate the status of the marriage does not mean that it can affect other rights of the parties. Yet, the break-up of a marriage can involve disputes beyond the marital status itself. CPLR 302(b) attempts to fill part of the gap. It covers the case in which the defendant is no longer a resident or domiciliary but the plaintiff is, provided that there has been one of several specified contacts between the parties and the state. Too expansive a reading of this paragraph could lead to a violation of the defendant's due process right to be heard in a fair forum. Relevant restraints are discussed in *Kulko*, the next case.

(2) The *Kulko* opinion is also useful because of its description of the Revised Uniform Reciprocal Enforcement of Support Act of 1968 and New York's Uniform Support of Dependents Law. See notes 13 and 14 of the opinion and related text.

KULKO v. SUPERIOR COURT OF CALIFORNIA
United States Supreme Court
436 U.S. 84, 98 S. Ct. 1690, 56 L. Ed. 2d (1978)

MR. JUSTICE MARSHALL delivered the opinion of the Court.

The issue before us is whether, in this action for child support, the California state courts may exercise in personam jurisdiction over a nonresident, non-domiciliary parent of minor children domiciled within the State. For reasons set forth below, we hold that the exercise of such jurisdiction would violate the Due Process Clause of the Fourteenth Amendment.

I

Appellant Ezra Kulko married appellee Sharon Kulko Horn in 1959, during appellant's three-day stopover in California en route from a military base in Texas to a tour of duty in Korea. At the time of this marriage, both parties were domiciled in and residents of New York State. Immediately following the marriage, Sharon Kulko returned to New York, as did appellant after his tour of duty. Their first child, Darwin, was born to the Kulkos in New York in 1961, and a year later their second child, Ilsa, was born, also in New York. The Kulkos and their two children resided together as a family in New York City continuously until March 1972, when the Kulkos separated.

Following the separation, Sharon Kulko moved to San Francisco, California. A written separation agreement was drawn up in New York; in September 1972, Sharon Kulko flew to New York City in order to sign this agreement. The agreement provided, inter alia, that the children would remain with their father during the school year but would spend their Christmas, Easter, and summer vacations with their mother. While Sharon Kulko waived any claim for her own support or maintenance, Ezra Kulko agreed to pay his wife $3,000 per year in child support for the periods when the children were in her care, custody, and control. Immediately after execution of the separation agreement, Sharon Kulko flew to Haiti and procured a divorce there; the divorce decree incorporated the terms of the agreement. She then returned to California, where she remarried and took the name Horn.

The children resided with appellant during the school year and with their mother on vacations, as provided by the separation agreement, until December 1973. [The children then moved to California, apparently with their father's permission. — Eds.]

Less than one month after Darwin's arrival in California, appellee Horn commenced this action against appellant in the California Superior Court. She sought to establish the Haitian divorce decree as a California judgment; to modify the judgment so as to award her full custody of the children; and to increase appellant's child-support obligations. Appellant appeared specially and moved to quash service of the summons on the ground that he was not a resident of California and lacked sufficient "minimum contacts" with the State under *International Shoe Co. v. Washington*, 326 U.S. 310, 316 (1945), to warrant the State's assertion of personal jurisdiction over him.

[The California Supreme Court held that that state had jurisdiction over Kulko.]

. . . .

A

In reaching its result, the California Supreme Court did not rely on appellant's glancing presence in the State 13 years before the events that led to this controversy, nor could it have. Appellant has been in California on only two occasions, once in 1959 for a three-day military stopover on his way to Korea, and again in 1960 for a 24-hour stopover on his return from Korean service. To hold such temporary visits to a State a basis for the assertion of in personam jurisdiction over unrelated actions arising in the future would make a mockery of the limitations on state jurisdiction imposed by the Fourteenth Amendment. Nor did the California court rely on the fact that appellant was actually married in California on one of his two brief visits. We agree that where two New York domiciliaries, for reasons of convenience, marry in the State of California and thereafter spend their entire married life in New York, the fact of their California marriage by itself cannot support a California court's exercise of jurisdiction over a spouse who remains a New York resident in an action relating to child support.

Finally, in holding that personal jurisdiction existed, the court below carefully disclaimed reliance on the fact that appellant had agreed at the time of separation to allow his children to live with their mother three months a year and that he had sent them to California each year pursuant to this agreement. As was noted below, 19 Cal. 3d, at 523-524, 564 P.2d, at 357, to find personal jurisdiction in a State on this basis, merely because the mother was residing there, would discourage parents from entering into reasonable visitation agreements. Moreover, it could arbitrarily subject one parent to suit in any State of the Union where the other parent chose to spend time while having custody of their offspring pursuant to a separation agreement. As we have emphasized:

> The unilateral activity of those who claim some relationship with a nonresident defendant cannot satisfy the requirement of contact with the forum State. . . . [I]t is essential in each case that there be some act by which the defendant purposefully avails [him]self of the privilege of conducting activities within the forum State. . . .

Hanson v. Denckla, supra, 357 U.S., at 253.

The "purposeful act" that the California Supreme Court believed did warrant the exercise of personal jurisdiction over appellant in California was his "actively and fully consent[ing] to Ilsa living in California for the school year . . . and . . . sen[ding] her to California for that purpose." 19 Cal. 3d, at 524, 564 P.2d, at 358. We cannot accept the proposition that appellant's acquiescence in Ilsa's desire to live with her mother conferred jurisdiction over appellant in the California courts in this action. A father who agrees, in the interests of family harmony and his children's preferences, to allow them to spend more time in California than was required under a separation agreement can hardly be said to have "purposefully availed himself" of the "benefits and protections" of California's laws. *See Shaffer v. Heitner*, 433 U.S., at 216.

B

The circumstances in this case clearly render "unreasonable" California's assertion of personal jurisdiction. There is no claim that appellant has visited physical injury on either property or persons within the State of California. *Compare Hess v. Pawloski*, 274 U.S. 352 (1927). The cause of action herein asserted arises, not from the defendant's commercial transactions in interstate commerce, but rather from his personal, domestic relations. . . .

. . . It is appellant who has remained in the State of the marital domicile, whereas it is appellee who has moved across the continent. Appellant has at all times resided in New York State, and, until the separation and appellee's move to California, his entire family resided there as well. As noted above, appellant did no more than acquiesce in the stated preference of one of his children to live with her mother in California. This single act is surely not one that a reasonable parent would expect to result in the substantial financial burden and personal strain of litigating a child-support suit in a forum 3,000 miles away . . . .

III

. . . [A]ppellee argues that California has substantial interests in protecting the welfare of its minor residents and in promoting to the fullest extent possible a healthy and supportive family environment in which the children of the State are to be raised. These interests are unquestionably important. But while the presence of the children and one parent in California arguably might favor application of California law in a lawsuit in New York, the fact that California may be the "'center of gravity'" for choice-of-law purposes does not mean that California has personal jurisdiction over the defendant. . . . And California has not attempted to assert any particularized interest in trying such cases in its courts by, *e.g.*, enacting a special jurisdictional statute.

California's legitimate interest in ensuring the support of children resident in California without unduly disrupting the children's lives, moreover, is already being served by the State's participation in the Revised Uniform Reciprocal Enforcement of Support Act of 1968. This statute provides a mechanism for communication between court systems in different States, in order to facilitate the procurement and enforcement of child-support decrees where the dependent children reside in a State that cannot obtain personal jurisdiction over the defendant. California's version of the Act essentially permits a California resident claiming support from a nonresident to file a petition in California and have its merits adjudicated in the State of the alleged obligor's residence, without either party's having to leave his or her own State. Cal. Civ. Proc. Code Ann. § 1650 *et seq.* (1972 and Supp. 1978).[13] New York State is a signatory to a similar Act.[14] Thus, not only may plaintiff-appellee here vindicate her claimed right to additional child support from her former husband in a New York court,

---

[13] In addition to California, 24 other States are signatories to this Act. 9 Uniform Laws Ann. 473 (Supp. 1978). Under the Act, an "obligee" may file a petition in a court of his or her State (the "initiating court") to obtain support. 9 Uniform Laws Ann. §§ 11, 14 (1973). If the court "finds that the [petition] sets forth facts from which it may be determined that the obligor owes a duty of support and that a court of the responding state may obtain jurisdiction of the obligor or his property," it may send a copy of the petition to the "responding state." § 14. This has the effect of requesting the responding State "to obtain jurisdiction over the obligor." § 18(b). If jurisdiction is obtained, then a hearing is set in a court in the responding State at which the obligor may, if he chooses, contest the claim. The claim may be litigated in that court, with deposition testimony submitted through the initiating court by the initiating spouse or other party. § 20. If the responding state court finds that the obligor owes a duty of support pursuant to the laws of the State where he or she was present during the time when support was sought, § 7, judgment for the petitioner is entered. § 24. If the money is collected from the spouse in the responding State, it is then sent to the court in the initiating State for distribution to the initiating party. § 28.

[14] [The Court refers to N.Y. Dom. Rel. Law § 30 *et seq.* (McKinney 1977) (Uniform Support of Dependents Law). This statute was repealed in 1997 and replaced by the Uniform Interstate Family Support Act, N.Y. C.L.S. Family Ct. Act § 580-201 (2000), which also permits reciprocity between states, *see id.*, §§ 580-202 to 580-206. — Eds.]

but also the uniform Acts will facilitate both her prosecution of a claim for additional support and collection of any support payments found to be owed by appellant.

NOTES

(1) Even prior to *Kulko*, some New York courts had read restrictively that clause of CPLR 302(b) which allows jurisdiction when the "state was the matrimonial domicile of the parties before their separation." It was held to apply only when the state was the place where the parties "when last together made their home," *Lieb v. Lieb*, 53 A.D.2d 67, 71, 385 N.Y.S.2d 569, 571 (2d Dep't 1976). The court there dismissed an action for want of jurisdiction on these facts: The parties were married in New York in 1943. In 1957 they moved to Virginia where they stayed until 1969, when the plaintiff was allegedly abandoned. Plaintiff returned to New York and two years later commenced her action for support. By then the defendant was living in France. *But see Levy v. Levy*, 185 A.D.2d 15, 592 N.Y.S.2d 480 (3d Dep't 1993), finding jurisdiction over a non-resident spouse because of a prior marital domicile in New York, even though the couple had changed their domicile to California approximately ten years prior to the commencement of the action.

(2) Jurisdiction over non-residents for support of dependents is available under several New York statutes. CPLR 302(b) applies, inter alia, when "the claim for support . . . accrued under the laws of this state." When does a person's claim for support from a spouse or parent accrue? Under Family Court Act § 412, a married person is chargeable with the support of his or her spouse. Does this answer the question?

Section 413 of the Family Court Act provides that parents are responsible for the support of their children. The Uniform Interstate Family Support Act (adopted in New York in 1997) specifies a number of jurisdictional bases for child support proceedings, including that "the individual resided with the child in this state," or "the child resides in this state as a result of the acts or directives of the individual," or "the individual engaged in sexual intercourse in this state and the child may have been conceived by that act of interocurse," or "there is any other basis consistent with the constitutions of the this state and the United States for the exercise of personal jurisdiction." *See* Family Court Act § 580-201.

(3) Congressional concern with the continuing problem of low rates of compliance with child support orders led to the enactment of the Full Faith and Credit to Support Orders Act of 1994, P.L. 103-383, 108 Stat 4063. It adds section 1738B, "Full faith and credit for child support orders" to Title 28 of the U.S. Code. This law requires state courts to enforce a child support order made by another state if it was made "consistently" with 28 U.S.C. § 1738B: The issuing state must have had jurisdiction over the subject matter and over the parties, and proper notice must have been provided. A child support order made by a

state meeting these criteria may not be modified by another state unless the issuing state is no longer the residence of the child or of a contestant, and a new state has jurisdiction, or unless the parties consent in writing to a new state's exercise of jurisdiction, 28 U.S.C. § 1738B(e).

NOTE ON CHILD CUSTODY JURISDICTION

Neither CPLR 302(b) nor CPLR 314(1) deal with child custody issues. Traditionally, jurisdiction over defendants in custody disputes was dependent on either the child's presence in the state or personal jurisdiction over the parent. The traditional approach sometimes led to the problem of parental "child snatching" when parents involved in a custody battle were in different states. If the mother, for example, obtained an order of custody in state A, the father might take the child to state B and seek a different ruling from a court there. Because circumstances affecting the child's welfare might change, res judicata does not apply to custody determinations, and neither state was required to enforce the custody award of the other. In 1977, however, New York enacted the Uniform Child Custody Jurisdiction Act (the "UCCJA") as Article 5-A of the Domestic Relations Law. The purpose of the UCCJA was "to give stability to child custody decrees, minimize jurisdictional competition between sister States, [and] promote co-operation and communication between the courts of different States, all to the end of resolving custody disputes in the best interest of the child . . . ." *Vanneck v. Vanneck*, 49 N.Y.2d 602, 608, 427 N.Y.S.2d 735, 738, 404 N.E.2d 1273 (1980). A revised and improved version of the UCCJA, the Uniform Child Custody Jurisdiction and Enforcement Act (the "UCCJEA") was adopted in 2001 as a new Article 5-A. *See* Dom. Relations Law §§ 75-78 (2001).

The UCCJEA establishes a standard for determining in the first instance whether the necessary predicate for jurisdiction exists. Custody may be determined in New York if it is the child's "home state," or was the child's home state within six months before the commencement of the proceeding and the child is absent from the state but a parent or person acting as a parent continues to live in the state. *See* Domestic Relations Law § 76(1)(a). New York may also exercise jurisdiction under other narrowly prescribed circumstances, such as when a court of another state has determined that New York would be a more appropriate forum for the proceeding, or no other state has jurisdiction. § 76(1)(b). The child's "home state" is defined as "the state in which the child lived with a parent or a person acting as parent for at least six consecutive months immediately before the commencement of a child custody proceeding." § 75-a(7). Pointedly, the "physical presence of, or personal jurisdiction over, a party or child is not necessary or sufficient to make a child custody determination." § 76(3). In general, a court which has made a child custody determination consistent with the UCCJEA has "exclusive, continuing jurisdiction" until neither the child or a parent has a "significant connection" with the state. § 76-a. New York's courts are required to enforce the custody determinations of the courts of other states that had jurisdiction to make the award. § 77-b. Thus, there is no longer an incentive for the parent who lost custody to try to relitigate the issue in another state.

Congress also became concerned with the child snatching problem and enacted the Parental Kidnapping Prevention Act (the "PKPA") of 1980 (P.L. 96-611) which, *inter alia,* added § 1738A to Title 28 of the United States Code. This law requires the states to enforce child custody decisions made by courts of other states so long as the determination to be enforced was made in a state which (1) had jurisdiction under its own laws and (2) was a state in which one of several other conditions was met. The 2001 revision of N.Y. Domestic Relations Law Article 5-A and adoption of the UCCJEA, described above, brought New York's law into substantial conformity with the Federal PKPA. Courts have held that both the state and federal laws apply to subject matter as well as personal jurisdiction. As a result, their requirements are non-waivable. *See, e.g., Gomez v. Gomez,* 86 A.D.2d 594, 446 N.Y.S.2d 130 (2d Dep't), *aff'd,* 56 N.Y.2d 746, 452 N.Y.S.2d 13 (1982).

To the extent that there is any difference between the federal and state laws, the federal must govern. In *Mott v. Patricia Ann R.,* 91 N.Y.2d 856, 691 N.E.2d 623, 668 N.Y.S.2d 551 (1997), the New York Court of Appeals held that, while the version of the Domestic Relations Law then in effect would have allowed New York to exercise personal jurisdiction over the instant custody dispute, the PKPA preempted the UCCJA and New York was required to defer to and enforce a prior Florida decision that met the PKPA standards. On the same day, however, the Court of Appeals decided another matter dealing with the same family at issue in *Mott.* In *In re Sayeh R.,* 693 N.E.2d 724, 91 N.Y.2d 306, 670 N.Y.S.2d 377 (1997), the Court held that a child protective proceeding is distinct from a custody proceeding and, hence, not a "custody determination" that would fall under the PKPA or New York's UCCJA. Thus, in a proceeding brought by a government official to protect a child, a New York court was free to override the Florida court's determination.

Problems arise if two states issue conflicting child custody orders. The Supreme Court has held that a contestant may not bring a federal action under the PKPA to compel compliance with one of two conflicting state custody decrees. Ultimate review of a state decision alleged to conflict with the PKPA, the Court noted, remains available in the Supreme Court itself, by appeal from a state court. *Thompson v. Thompson,* 484 U.S. 174, 108 S. Ct. 513 (1988).

In furtherance of the purposes of the PKPA and the UCCJEA, the Court of Appeals in *Vernon v. Vernon,* 800 N.E.2d 1085, 100 N.Y.2d 960, 768 N.Y.S.2d 719 (2003), upheld subject matter jurisdiction over a child custody dispute, although the child had left New York several years earlier with her mother, the appellant. New York had jurisdiction according to the original divorce settlement agreement, and the court found that the PKPA did not bar continuing jurisdiction. The court rejected appellant's claim that the PKPA's "home State" requirement applies equally to initial and continuing custody determinations. In addition to its textual analysis, the court wrote: "According to the mother, a state that has made an initial custody dispute loses subject matter jurisdiction over the case once another state has become the child's 'home State,' which occurs in six months. . . . Such interpretation would essentially encourage 'unilateral removal of children undertaken to obtain [favorable] custody and visitation' . . . — the very antithesis of the statutory purpose." 100 N.Y.2d at 971, 800 N.E.2d at 1091, 768 N.Y.S.2d at 725. The court proceeded to consider the PKPA's requirement that state law authorize continuing jurisdiction. New York's version of the UCCJA, the relevant statute in effect at the time, gave the state jurisdiction when the child and at least one contestant have a significant connection with the state and when the state is the location of substantial evidence regarding the child's care. The court determined that both of these requirements were met. Although the child had lived in three states since leaving New York, she retained a significant connection with the state because she spent the first year of her life there, because she regularly visited her father and other relatives, and because New York courts had been making decisions about her best interests for years. The court also found that substantial evidence of her care was in New York, notably the testimony and report of a forensic psychologist who had worked on the case since 1992.

By the same token, New York defers to the continuing jurisdiction of courts in other states. In *Stocker v. Sheehan*, 13 A.D.3d 1, 786 N.Y.S.2d 126 (1st Dep't 2004), the Appellate Division found that New York lacked subject matter jurisdiction to determine an issue of custody and visitation originally decided in Rhode Island, because Rhode Island maintained continuing jurisdiction in the matter as long as the father remained a Rhode Island resident.

As of this writing, all fifty states, the District of Columbia, and the U.S. Virgin Islands have adopted some version of the UCCJEA. *See* 9:1 Uniform Laws Annotated 20-21 (Supp. 1994).

The United States is a signatory to the Hague Convention on the Civil Aspects of International Child Abduction (1980), a treaty that requires signatory nations to return children to their country of habitual residence and to cooperate in enforcing visitation rights. *See* 19 International Legal Materials 1501 (Nov. 1980); 88 Dep't of State Bull. No. 2136 at 76 (July 1988). Legislative implementation is at 42 U.S.C. § 11,601 *et seq.* Orders made by the court of foreign nations pursuant to the Hague Convention are enforceable in New York's courts. *See* Domestic Relations Law, § 77-a. *See generally* Linda Silberman, *The Hague Child Abduction Convention Turns Twenty: Gender Politics and Other Issues*, 33 N.Y.U. J. Int'l Law and Politics 221 (2000).

Chapter 2
JUDICIAL DISCRETION
TO DECLINE JURISDICTION

INTRODUCTORY NOTE

to get dismissed 327

CPLR 327 authorizes the courts to "stay or dismiss the action in whole or in part on any conditions that may be just" if it finds that "in the interest of substantial justice" the action should be heard in another forum. This is a codification of the common law doctrine of forum non conveniens. This doctrine (like those of venue, personal jurisdiction and subject matter jurisdiction) thus governs the place the action will be heard. The following case, *Martin v. Mieth*, helps one to understand the distinction between venue and forum non conveniens. How does the latter relate to the jurisdictional doctrines? On this score, it is of interest that a court may not invoke CPLR 327 to stay or dismiss an action unless a party seeks such relief by motion — the court may not raise the matter on its own. *VSL Corp. v. Dunes Hotels and Casinos, Inc.*, 70 N.Y.2d 948, 524 N.Y.S.2d 671, 519 N.E.2d 617 (1988).

The standards governing the application of CPLR 327 are vague. Subdivision (a) provides that a party's residence or domicile in the state "shall not preclude" stay or dismissal, but otherwise leaves undefined the "substantial justice" which should govern the outcome of any motions made under that section. CPLR 327(b), treated in *Credit Francais Int'l, S.A. v. Sociedad Financiera de Comercio, C.A., infra*, does prohibit the application of forum non conveniens to actions relating to certain contracts in which the parties have agreed that New York will be the proper forum for litigation. In general, however, the law of forum non conveniens is judge-made.

For a critical survey of the development of the doctrine, see Allan R. Stein, *Forum Non Conveniens and the Redundancy of Court Access Doctrine*, 133 U. Pa. L. Rev. 781 (1985).

MARTIN v. MIETH
Court of Appeals
35 N.Y.2d 414, 362 N.Y.S.2d 853, 321 N.E.2d 777 (1974)

WACHTLER, J.

On December 20, 1970 the plaintiff, Lisa Martin, was a passenger in an automobile owned and operated by the defendant, Erna Mieth. Both were, and still are, residents of Toronto, Canada. They were traveling on Route 60 in Chautauqua County when for reasons unexplained the vehicle left the public road-way, overturned and came to a halt on the front lawn of one William Penhollow. The plaintiff sustained serious injuries including multiple fractures of the cervical spine and was rushed from the scene to the Buffalo General Hospital.

Shortly thereafter, the plaintiff commenced this personal injury action in the Supreme Court, New York County. Jurisdiction over the defendant was duly obtained pursuant to the nonresident motorist statute (Vehicle and Traffic Law, § 253). The defendant contending that there was no substantial nexus between the action and this State, moved for an order dismissing the complaint on the ground of forum non conveniens. (CPLR 3211, subd. [a], par. 2.) In opposition to that motion plaintiff's counsel submitted an affidavit which asserted: that the accident occurred in New York and had been investigated by the New York State Police and that the plaintiff had been treated in a New York hospital and, therefore, the police and hospital records were within the State and subject to subpoena by New York courts. Additionally, the affidavit asserted that the investigating officer and the treating physicians, as well as Mr. Penhollow, who was listed in the police report as a witness and characterized by the plaintiff as an "important New York witness," would not be subject to subpoena in Canada.

Special Term relying on the factors enumerated in the affidavit of plaintiff's counsel, denied the motion to dismiss.

Subsequently, the defendant moved for a change of venue from New York County to Chautauqua County. Defendant's supporting affidavit argued that since the investigating officer, and the treating physicians and Mr. Penhollow lived in or near Chautauqua County the convenience of witnesses and the interests of justice would best be served by changing the place of trial to Chautauqua County.

In opposition to the change of venue motion plaintiff's counsel submitted an affidavit substantially contradicting the one which he had submitted in connection with the previous motion. To establish that venue was properly laid, plaintiff's counsel asserted, "Nevertheless, the plaintiff will show that in fact, the necessity for these 'witnesses' to testify is completely illusory." The affidavit went on to claim that Mr. Penhollow did not see the accident and that all Mr. Penhollow did was to call the State Police who arrived afterwards. "Accordingly, except for the fortuitous circumstance that the defendant's automobile ended up on Mr. Penhollow's front lawn, there is nothing that Mr. Penhollow knows that can be material to the trial of this action." The records and testimony of the State Police were also discounted by plaintiff's counsel in this affidavit as not probative of any material fact. "All that Mr. Penhollow and Trooper Blumen can do is to confirm the fact that the defendant's motor vehicle ended up in Mr. Penhollow's front lawn which is not an issue." The necessity of the testimony of the treating physicians was similarly deprecated in the affidavit. Since the plaintiff was subsequently hospitalized in Toronto and was presently under the care of Toronto physicians "there is no need to require the testimony of any Buffalo physicians who treated her at the Buffalo General Hospital."

Since no witnesses were necessary Special Term denied the venue motion.

The defendant appealed both the order denying the forum non conveniens motion and the order denying the venue motion. A majority at the Appellate Division affirmed both orders upon a memorandum which concluded that Special Term had not abused its discretion in denying the relief requested. The dissenting Justices, focusing on the plaintiff's conflicting affidavits, noted that "[i]t would be hard to visualize a more unabashed instance of forum shopping."

This appeal is before our court by leave of the Appellate Division on a certified question of law (CPLR 5713). We interpret the certified question as applying to the Appellate Division's affirmance of the denial of the forum non conveniens motion. In so doing we consider the entire record which was before the Appellate Division, including the inconsistent and contradictory affidavits of plaintiff's counsel. Thus, the question raised is whether or not the motion to dismiss on the ground of forum non conveniens should have been denied as a matter of law.

We believe that the certified question should be answered in the negative. Forum non conveniens is an equitable doctrine whereby a court in its discretion may decline to exercise jurisdiction over a transitory cause of action upon considerations of justice, fairness and convenience. (*Silver v. Great Amer. Ins. Co.*, 29 N Y 2d 356; . . . .) By traditional standards, the mere occurrence of an accident within our borders might suffice to insure a New York forum. . . . However, these rigid standards have been superseded by more flexible analysis. . . . Thus, in *Silver*, to counterbalance the expansion of long-arm jurisdiction, we relaxed the principle requiring New York courts to accept jurisdiction when one of the parties was a resident. . . . A parity of reasoning dictates that forum non conveniens be available even though the accident occurs in this State.

Since the touchstone of forum non conveniens is flexibility, our courts need not entertain causes of action lacking a substantial nexus with New York. . . . When the plaintiff's two affidavits are considered jointly it becomes apparent that the latter contradicts the former and negatives all connections with New York except the adventitious circumstance that the accident occurred here. That happenstance alone does not constitute a substantial nexus so as to mandate the retention of jurisdiction and, on the facts that are not self-contradicted, there would be no rational basis for a discretionary retention of jurisdiction.

Accordingly, the order of the Appellate Division, insofar as appealed from, affirming the denial of defendant's motion to dismiss on the ground of forum non conveniens, should be reversed and the complaint dismissed, on condition that within 10 days from the date hereof defendant stipulates to accept service of process in Canada and to appear in an action to be commenced in Canada for the same relief demanded in the complaint herein and that in any such action commenced in Canada she will not plead the Statute of Limitations as a defense, but will waive the same. In the event of defendant's failure to comply with the foregoing conditions, the order should be affirmed.

Q - need a substantial nexus? - who's burden

NOTES

(1) The principal case illustrates the breadth of the forum non conveniens doctrine inasmuch that the court holds that an action arising out of an accident in New York did not bear a "substantial nexus" to the state. Ordinarily, an action arising from an accident in New York will be held to have a substantial nexus to the state, even if the parties are non-residents. *E.g.*, *Brodherson v. Ponte & Sons*, 209 A.D.2d 276, 618 N.Y.S.2d 350 (1st Dep't 1994). Can a substantial nexus be found if the accident occurred outside the state? In *Nevander v. Deyo*, 111 A.D.2d 548, 489 N.Y.S.2d 420 (3d Dep't 1985), the action grew out of a two car accident in Quebec in which plaintiff's intestate, a New York resident, was killed. Plaintiff sued the owner (also a New Yorker) of the car in which the deceased was killed and the Firestone Tire and Rubber Company, alleging that negligent driving, negligent maintenance and defective tires had caused the accident. The defendants moved to dismiss on inconvenient forum grounds, pointing out that the driver of the other car was a Canadian not subject to the jurisdiction in New York and that the witnesses and all the hospital records were in Quebec. The Appellate Division affirmed a denial of the motion, stating that:

> [P]laintiff has established a substantial nexus with New York, *i.e.*, two of the parties reside in New York and the other does business throughout the State; some of the tortious conduct complained of took place in New York; and the trip planned (*sic*), began and was to conclude in New York. Moreover, plaintiff chose New York as the forum and there exists a presumption that New York residents are entitled to use its judicial system, a presumption which defendants have not overcome.

See also Elson v. Defren, 279 A.D.2d 361, 719 N.Y.S.2d 246 (1st Dep't 2001) (forum non conveniens dismissal denied; although the action grew out of an auto accident in Idaho, all of the individual parties were New York residents and had received extensive medical treatment in New York).

(2) The presumption in favor of New York plaintiffs is often, but not always, determinative. Thus, the Court of Appeals affirmed a dismissal of an auto accident case in *Belachew v. Michael*, 59 N.Y.2d 1004, 466 N.Y.S.2d 954, 453 N.E.2d 1243 (1983), even though the plaintiffs and one of the defendants were New Yorkers. The accident had occurred in Pennsylvania, potential third party defendants were Pennsylvanians not subject to New York jurisdiction and related litigation had been brought in Pennsylvania.

PROBLEM A

Recall *Bryant v. Finnish National Airline*, § 1.03[C], *supra*. Plaintiff was a New York resident who was injured at an airport in Paris due to the alleged negligent operation of one of the defendant's airplanes. Defendant, a Finnish corporation, was held subject to New York jurisdiction because it was "present" by virtue of its maintenance of a promotional office in New York City. What result if the defendant moved to dismiss on the grounds of forum non conveniens?

BEWERS v. AMERICAN HOME PRODUCTS CORP.
Appellate Division, First Department
99 A.D.2d 949, 472 N.Y.S.2d 637 (1984),
aff'd, 64 N.Y.2d 630, 485 N.Y.S.2d 39, 474 N.E.2d 247 (1984)

. . . .

The plaintiffs, all of whom are residents of the United Kingdom, make claim for personal injuries and loss of consortium arising from the ingestion by the female plaintiffs of oral contraceptives known as Ovran and Ovranette. These products, which are available by prescription only, allegedly caused the female plaintiffs to suffer severe and permanently disabling thromboemoblic strokes during March and April of 1977. The complaints, which seek to recover compensatory and punitive damages, sound in negligence, breach of warranty, strict liability in tort and fraud, as well as the aforementioned loss of consortium.

Defendant American Home Products Inc. ("AHP") is a Delaware Corporation with its principal place of business in New York. Defendant Wyeth Laboratories Division of American Home Products is not a discrete legal entity but is a part of AHP. The other defendant-appellant, Wyeth Laboratories Inc., is a wholly-owned subsidiary of AHP, and is a New York corporation with its principal place of business in Pennsylvania. AHP holds the appropriate licenses to the pharmaceuticals which plaintiffs allege caused their injuries.

Defendants sought dismissal of plaintiffs' actions on the grounds of forum non conveniens, claiming that the injuries allegedly suffered by plaintiffs all occurred in the United Kingdom, that the drugs complained of were prescribed, purchased and ingested in England. Moreover, argue defendants, the pharmaceuticals were manufactured, tested, labelled, marketed and distributed in the United Kingdom by or on behalf of an English company, John Wyeth and Brother, Ltd., which holds a subsidiary license from AHP. Thus, the defendants contend, New York is an inconvenient forum and the matter should be litigated in the United Kingdom.

Plaintiffs assert that defendants, while in New York decided and undertook to promote, market, sell and distribute the drugs complained of throughout the United Kingdom, without the proper warning as to the side effects of the drugs they knew to be dangerous. Thus, contend plaintiffs, the actionable wrong occurred in New York and not in the United Kingdom. [Plaintiffs also argued that no forum other than New York was reasonably available to them because the United Kingdom does not recognize strict liability in tort and a loss of the New York forum would therefore result in the forfeiture of their strongest substantive claim. They asserted that dismissal would also deprive them of certain procedural advantages, such as the right to a jury trial and the use of extensive American style pretrial discovery. Moreover, in an English court, the plaintiffs would be liable for defendants' legal fees if the defendants won the case. — Eds.]

Special Term concluded, in a thoughtful opinion, that defendants' motion should be denied for reasons of justice, fairness and convenience. We disagree. It seems quite clear that the United Kingdom would have the greater interest in determining whether pharmarceuticals which were licensed, manufactured, marketed and distributed therein were appropriately tested and labelled in that country. Such a determination should be made pursuant to that country's own regulatory scheme and in accordance with its laws. "It would, in the circumstances [of these cases] constitute an unnecessary burden on our courts to be compelled to apply foreign law, as the case demands in our courts." (*Crown Cork & Seal Co., Inc. v. Rheem Manufacturing Co., Inc., et al.*, 64 A.D.2d 545, 406 N.Y.S.2d 849). Nor do we perceive any unfairness to the plaintiffs in requiring that they prosecute these actions in the United Kingdom. Indeed, it clearly appears that all of the facts and circumstances surrounding these lawsuits, except for the alleged decision by the defendants, allegedly made in New York, to market the drugs in the United Kingdom without adequate warnings respecting known dangerous side effects, occurred in the United Kingdom. The vast majority of witnesses and documentation regarding the testing, labelling and marketing of these drugs in the United Kingdom are in England, as well as the witnesses and documentary evidence respecting the medical treatment of plaintiffs. Thus not only would continued prosecution of these cases here unduly burden our courts, it would not serve the convenience of the parties. (*Silver v. Great American Insurance Co.*, 23 N.Y.2d 356, 328 N.Y.S.2d 398, 278 N.E.2d 619.)

Although not in any way critical to our decision, we note that cases brought in the Federal courts in New York and Pennsylvania and in the state courts of Pennsylvania, New Jersey, Illinois and California, by similarly situated plaintiffs were also dismissed by those courts pursuant to the forum non conveniens doctrine and principles of international comity.

Order, Supreme Court, New York County, . . . entered December 7, 1982, which denied defendants' motion to dismiss the action pursuant to CPLR Rule 327 on grounds of forum non conveniens, is unanimously reversed, on the law, the facts and in the exercise of discretion in the interest of justice, without costs, and defendants' motion to dismiss is granted, on the condition that within 90 days of service of the order entered hereon, defendants-appellants stipulate: (1) to waive objection to suit being brought in the United Kingdom for the relief sought in the complaints herein and to waive objection to the jurisdiction of the courts of the United Kingdom in this matter; (2) to accept the service of process in the United Kingdom; (3) to waive objection to compulsory process requiring the appearances of witnesses and production of documents and to make the same available at their own expense; (4) to consent to full faith and credit for any judgment obtained against them in the United Kingdom and to consent to pay the same; and (5) to waive any defense of limitation of time, whether statutory or otherwise, provided, however, that the suit in the United Kingdom be commenced within 90 days from the date of service of the defendants' stipulation upon counsel for the plaintiffs. In the event of defendants' failure to comply with the foregoing conditions, the order of Supreme Court is affirmed without costs.

NOTES

(1) Is it the function of New York courts to protect the world's population from alleged misdeeds of corporations incorporated or doing business in New York? Is that role more appropriately served by the courts of the victim's homeland? Or should it be shared by both nation's courts? What are the likely economic effects of the rule adopted by the court? On corporations deciding where to locate? On the New York bar?

(2) In *Piper Aircraft Co. v. Reyno*, 454 U.S. 235, 102 S. Ct. 252 (1982), the U.S. Supreme Court held that the federal courts should not refuse to apply the forum non conveniens doctrine solely because the alternate forum would apply substantive law less favorable to plaintiff's claim. A poignant case applying the forum non conveniens doctrine is *In re Union Carbide Plant Disaster*, 809 F.2d 195 (2d Cir.), *cert. denied*, 108 S. Ct. 199 (1987), which affirmed the dismissal of an action brought by the victims of the Bhopal disaster of 1984 against the Union Carbide Corporation, a corporation headquartered in New York. The latter was the parent of the Indian corporation that owned and operated the plant from which poisonous fumes escaped that killed and injured thousands of people. Forum non conveniens was held appropriate because the plaintiffs were not residents or citizens of the United States; the accident occurred in India; the negligence, if any, apparently occurred in India (although this was a matter in dispute); the witnesses and records were located predominantly in India and the Indian courts were well equipped to handle the litigation.

(3) Following the decision in *Bewers* (the principal case), plaintiffs were, of course, free to bring an action in the United Kingdom. What of a plaintiff who has no forum but New York in which to sue? May dismissal be granted on inconvenient forum grounds nonetheless? See *Varkonyi v. S.A. Empresa de Viacao A.R.G. (VARIG)*, 22 N.Y.2d 333, 292 N.Y.S.2d 670, 239 N.E.2d 542 (1968), which grew out of an air crash in Lima, Peru. No plaintiffs were residents of New York. The defendants were the airline (a Brazilian corporation doing business in New York), its New York subsidiary, and Boeing, the plane's manufacturer, which was a Delaware corporation doing business in New York. Reversing a forum non conveniens dismissal, the Court of Appeals noted the "special circumstances" that there was no forum other than New York in which suit could be brought against both the airline and the manufacturer and that the proof relating to those defendants was inseparably connected. What public safety issues are at issue here?

(4) No "special circumstance" rule saved the plaintiffs in *Islamic Republic of Iran v. Pahlavi*, 62 N.Y.2d 474, 478 N.Y.S.2d 597, 467 N.E.2d 245 (1984), *cert. denied*, 469 U.S. 1108, 105 S. Ct. 783 (1985):

> Plaintiff, the Islamic Republic of Iran, brings this action against Iran's former ruler, Shah Mohammed Reza Pahlavi, and his wife, Empress Farah Diba Pahlavi. It alleges in its complaint that defendants accepted bribes and misappropriated, embezzled or converted 35 billion dollars in Iranian funds in breach of their fiduciary duty to the Iranian people and it seeks to recover those funds and 20 billion dollars in exemplary damages. It asks the court to impress a constructive trust on defendants' assets located throughout the world, for an accounting of all moneys and property received by the defendants from the government of Iran, and for other incidental relief.

> The action was commenced in November, 1979 by substituted service on the Shah made at New York Hospital where he was undergoing cancer therapy. . . . Thereafter, defendants moved to dismiss the complaint alleging that . . . the complaint should be dismissed on grounds of forum non conveniens. . . .

> Plaintiff contends that the availability of an alternative forum is not merely an additional factor for the court to consider but constitutes an absolute precondition to dismissal on conveniens grounds. . . .

> Without doubt, the availability of another suitable forum is a most important factor to be considered in ruling on a motion to dismiss but we have never held that it was a prerequisite for applying the conveniens doctrine. . . . Indeed, plaintiff's counsel conceded on oral argument that ideally the action should be maintained in Iran but contended that New York was the better forum. If the action cannot be maintained in Iran, however, under laws which result in judgments cognizable in the United States or other foreign jurisdictions where the Shah's assets may be found, then that failure must be charged to plaintiff. It is, after all, the government in power, not a hapless national, victimized by its country's policies.

(5) Is it likely that the courts of New York would entertain actions based on the defalcations of other deposed rulers, such as former President Marcos of the Philippines or former President for Life of Haiti Duvalier? What facts might the plaintiffs in such actions attempt to show in an effort to distinguish the principal case? In *Republic of the Philippines v. Marcos*, 806 F.2d 344, 361 (2d Cir. 1986), the Second Circuit upheld the refusal of a federal district court to dismiss an action on forum non conveniens grounds. The plaintiff Republic alleged that the defendant had used money stolen from it to purchase real property in New York. In upholding the decision below, the court noted that (unlike the situation in Islamic Republic of Iran) the action concerned only specific property located in New York and that the underlying dispute would be tried in the Philippines.

Similarly, an action brought by the Republic of Haiti to recover funds allegedly stolen by Jean-Claude Duvalier and held in his name by the Irving Trust Company in New York survived various motions to dismiss in the Supreme Court, New York County. The Appellate Division later granted summary judgment to the plaintiffs. *See Republic of Haiti v. Duvalier*, 211 A.D.2d 379, 626 N.Y.S.2d 472 (1st Dep't 1995).

Also of interest is *Wiwa v. Royal Dutch Petroleum Company*, 226 F.3d 88 (2d Cir. 2000), *cert. denied*, 149 L. Ed. 2d 345, 121 S. Ct. 1402 (2001). The Second Circuit overturned a forum non conveniens motion granted in the District Court because the lower court failed to take into account both the plaintiff-resident's interest and the interest of the United States in adjudicating claims of human rights abuses.

(6) Apart from forum non conveniens, a New York court which has jurisdiction over the defendant may decide to decline its exercise under the doctrine of comity, which involves deferring to the interest some other forum has in deciding the matter. For a discussion of comity in relation to a sister state's claim of sovereign immunity, see *Ehrlich-Bober & Co. v. University of Houston*, 49 N.Y.2d 574, 427 N.Y.S.2d 604, 404 N.E.2d 726 (1980).

(7) As the next case shows, the forum non conveniens doctrine is also relevant to corporate litigation.

HART v. GENERAL MOTORS CORP.
Appellate Division, First Department
129 A.D.2d 179, 517 N.Y.S.2d 490 (1987)

SULLIVAN, J.

In October 1984, General Motors (GM), a Delaware corporation with its principal place of business in Michigan, acquired 100% of the voting securities of Electronic Data Systems Corp. (EDS), a highly successful computer services firm, at a cost of some $2,500,000,000. Under the terms of the acquisition, . . . H. Ross Perot, the then chairman of EDS . . . became GM's largest individual shareholder in the process. Perot remained as chairman of EDS and was also named a director of GM.

Problems began to develop between EDS and GM almost immediately, and Perot became an increasingly vocal critic of GM. As the end of 1986 approached, Perot's differences with GM's board of directors had intensified to the point that they decided to buy him out. Accordingly, GM's directors and Perot negotiated an agreement whereby GM, for a total price of approximately $750,000,000, the purported equivalent of approximately $61.90 per share and related note, would purchase Perot's Class E stock and corresponding contingent notes and those of three of his associates in return for, inter alia, Perot's resignation as a GM director and chairman of EDS and his agreement not to criticize GM publicly or repurchase its stock or otherwise seek to exercise control over GM for the next five years. If Perot were to voice any public criticism of GM or its management, he could be penalized up to $7,500,000. On November 30, 1986, approval of the transaction was recommended by a special review committee of GM's board of directors, which, itself, on the following day, gave its unanimous approval. [The board meeting was meeting held in New York. — Eds.] The transaction was consummated that same day.

On December 5, 1986, plaintiff, a Texas resident who had become a holder of several hundred thousand shares of GM Class E stock and related notes in 1984 in exchange for his stock holdings in EDS, purporting to act derivately on behalf of GM and as a class representative of all its Class E stockholders, commenced this action against GM, its directors and Perot, challenging the board's December 1, 1986 decision authorizing the purchase transaction. Alleging breach of fiduciary duty and waste, plaintiff claims that GM's purchase of Perot's stock and notes, as well as Perot's resignations from both GM and EDS, damaged GM, EDS and GM's Class E stockholders. In essence, plaintiff contends that the payment of $750,000,000 incorporated a premium amounting to hundreds of millions of dollars over the fair market value of the surrendered stock and notes, and that the premium was paid to induce Perot to remove himself from his corporate offices and directorship of GM. In effect, plaintiff alleges a sale of corporate office for personal gain. In the only cause of action asserted against Perot, plaintiff seeks rescission of the transaction. Plaintiff did not, however, prior to the commencement of this action, make a demand on GM's board of directors that it cause GM to pursue the claim. In conclusory terms, he alleges that such a demand would have been futile.

On December 4, 1986, the day before the commencement of this action, two similar derivative actions were filed in the Delaware Chancery Court by other GM shareholders, and four additional State court actions were instituted in Delaware between December 5, 1986 and February 4, 1987. On April 13, 1987, during the pendency of this appeal, the Delaware Chancery Court dismissed one of the December 4th actions on the ground that the plaintiffs had failed to make a prelitigation demand on the board of directors, or to plead with particularity facts which, if proved, would excuse such demand. We note that the complaint there apparently contained allegations substantially more particularized than those pleaded here as to the futility of a prelitigation demand.

A total of nine additional actions have been filed in Federal courts in five different States. . . . These nine actions, four of which currently name Perot as a defendant, were referred to the Judicial Panel on Multi-district Litigation, which consolidated them and transferred the eight actions pending in districts other than the District of Delaware to the Delaware court "to prevent duplication of discovery and avoid inconsistent pretrial rulings (especially with respect to class and derivative action issues)."

After the defendants had moved in the Delaware State court actions to dismiss due to the plaintiffs' failure to make a demand on GM's board of directors, the GM defendants moved, at the court's direction, to dismiss this action on two independent grounds: plaintiff's failure to make a demand on GM's board of directors — the precise issue already before the Delaware Chancery Court — and forum non conveniens, or, alternatively, on the latter ground only, for a stay of the action. Perot also moved to dismiss or to stay the New York proceedings. The motions were denied in all respects, and this appeal followed. We reverse and dismiss the complaint on the ground of forum non conveniens.

The nature of the challenged transaction itself, as well as the equitable relief sought, militates against separate determinations by courts in different jurisdictions. One of the abiding principles of the law of corporations is that the issue of corporate governance, including the threshold demand issue, is governed by the law of the State in which the corporation is chartered, in this case, Delaware. . . .

In this regard, the motion court erred in concluding that the December 1st transaction "falls within that category of corporate acts where the liability of a director can be decided by different local law rules in different states." The validity of the GM/Perot transaction cannot be decided on a State-by-State basis. In this case, for example, plaintiff asks the court to order "the return to GM of the payments made to Mr. Perot and the return to him of his Class E shares and the contingent notes." Plaintiff also seeks Perot's reinstatement as a director of GM and EDS. Most of the other 15 pending derivative actions also seek rescission. The confusion which would be created by a New York judgment granting rescission nullifying the December 1st transaction and reinstating Perot as a director and the denial of such relief in Delaware is self-evident. "Uniform treatment of directors, officers and shareholders," the Restatement notes, "is an important objective which can only be attained by having the rights and liabilities of those persons with respect to the corporation governed by a single law." (Restatement [Second] of Conflict of Laws § 302, comment e, at 309.)

The motion court's reasoning that "[b]y choosing to do business in every state GM has subjected itself to public policy as embodied in the laws of those states," an argument that has some merit, ignores the risk that every State might seek to judge the same board of directors' decision under different public policy standards, and completely disregards, as well, the need for uniform application of one body of law to corporations and their directors on issues involving the regulation of a corporation's internal affairs. . . .

Moreover, contrary to the motion court's finding, GM's incorporation in Delaware cannot be dismissed as merely "fortuitous." In incorporating in a particular State, shareholders, for their own particular reasons, determine the body of law that will govern the internal affairs of the corporation and the conduct of their directors. Delaware is obviously a State in which, for various reasons, many businesses choose to incorporate. The corporation and its shareholders rightfully expect that the laws under which they have chosen to do business will be applied. For choice of law purposes, the decision of shareholders to incorporate under the law of one jurisdiction is no different from designating the law governing a business trust, which, prima facie (*Greenspun v Lindley, supra*, 36 NY2d, at 477), determines the applicable law.

Furthermore, contrary to the motion court's finding, it is Delaware, not New York, which has an interest superior to that of all other States in deciding issues concerning directors' conduct of the internal affairs of corporations chartered under Delaware law. . . .

Given Delaware's paramount interest in determining whether a Delaware corporation properly purchased securities from a group of its shareholders, including one of its directors, the pendency of virtually identical actions in that jurisdiction and the need for uniformity in the application of the pertinent law to this controversy, the court erred in denying the motion to dismiss on the ground of forum non conveniens.

We are aware, of course, that the "internal affairs" rule is, by current legal standards, only one aspect under the general principles of forum non conveniens. (*Koster v Lumbermens Mut. Co.*, 330 US 518, 527; *Broida v Bancroft*, 103 AD2d 88, 91; Restatement [Second] of Conflict of Laws § 84, comment d, at 252.) Among the relevant considerations in forum non conveniens applications are "the burden on the New York courts, the potential hardship to the defendant, and the unavailability of an alternative forum in which plaintiff may bring suit." (*Islamic Republic of Iran v. Pahlavi, supra*, 62 NY2d, at 479.) Each of these factors suggests dismissal here, rather than a stay, in deference to the pending Delaware actions in which plaintiff may seek to intervene or any action that he may be advised to institute there. Since derivative actions challenging the same transaction on behalf of the same corporation are being litigated in Delaware, the courts of this State should not be burdened with unnecessarily expending their resources on a duplicative action governed by Delaware law. Furthermore, this action subjects GM and its 20 individual directors to the expense of litigating the same claims in separate forums, as well as exposing them to the possibility of inconsistent judgments as to the ownership of GM's Class E stock and the composition of its board of directors. Plaintiff's counsel has openly admitted that he believes the outcome in New York may well differ from that in Delaware.

Finally, plaintiff has another readily available forum in which to pursue his claim. "Without doubt, the availability of another suitable forum is a most important factor to be considered in ruling on a motion to dismiss" (*Islamic Republic of Iran v. Pahlavi, supra*, 62 NY2d, at 481). Dismissal of his claim here in favor of the duplicative actions pending in Delaware in which he may intervene or any proceeding he may be disposed to bring there will not impose any undue hardship on plaintiff, a man of substantial resources. Indeed, this court has directed dismissal pursuant to the forum non conveniens doctrine even where a duplicative litigation was not already pending in a foreign court. . . .

NOTES

(1) Would the result have been different if the plaintiff had been a New York resident instead of a Texan? *See Bader & Bader v. Ford*, 66 A.D.2d 642, 414 N.Y.S.2d 132 (1st Dep't 1979). Plaintiff, a New York resident and a Ford stockholder, brought a stockholders' derivative action on behalf of the Ford Motor Company. The complaint made various allegations of wrongful conduct, breach of fiduciary duty and waste of corporate assets by the individual defendants, officers and directors of Ford Motor Company. The Appellate Division, reversing the Supreme Court, held that the action should have been dismissed:

> The lower court, in balancing the competing considerations, took cognizance of plaintiffs' residence within the State, a relevant although no longer a controlling factor. . . . In a stockholder's derivative action, however, the real party in interest is the corporation. The plaintiff in such action appears as nominal representative of the corporate defendant. It is appropriate, therefore, to consider plaintiff in relation to the group of stockholders whom he seeks to represent. . . . Therefore, the fact that plaintiffs reside within the State is not controlling. Other stockholders of a multi-state corporation such as Ford Motor Company, could lay similar if not equal claim to maintenance of the suit in their home jurisdiction.

> Ford Motor Company is a Delaware corporation, with its principal headquarters in Michigan. All of the material events pertaining to each of the ten causes of action alleged in the complaint took place in Michigan, Indonesia and the Philippines. The decisions and actions of the Board of Directors complained of herein resulted from meetings held at the corporate headquarters in Michigan. . . . Moreover, most if not all of the documents and witnesses relevant to the action are located in that State. Most of the individual defendants reside without the State, have not been served with process and are apparently not amenable to appropriate service here. All of the individual directors, however, are alleged to be subject to the jurisdiction of the courts of Michigan by reason of their status as officers and/or directors of the corporation (M.C.L.A. § 600.705[6], under which an officer or director of a corporation with its principal place of business in Michigan is subject to limited long arm jurisdiction). . . .

> Accordingly, . . . defendants' motion to dismiss the third amended complaint on the ground of forum non conveniens, is granted on condition that defendants . . . stipulate that they will accept service of process in and submit to the jurisdiction of the courts of the State of Michigan. . . .

Why did the court in *Bader & Bader v. Ford, supra,* order that the defendants agree to accept jurisdiction over them by the courts of Michigan? In the principal case, the same court expressed a strong view that the proper forum for shareholder derivative suits is the state of incorporation. Can the cases be reconciled?

(2) Not all stockholders' derivative actions brought on behalf of foreign corporations are dismissed on forum non conveniens grounds. In *Broida v. Bancroft*, 103 A.D.2d 88, 478 N.Y.S.2d 333 (2d Dep't 1984), the Second Department allowed the action to go forward even though it concerned the internal affairs of a Delaware corporation. The court stressed the facts that the plaintiffs were New York residents and that the defendant had its principal place of business in New York.

CREDIT FRANCAIS INTERNATIONAL, S.A. v. SOCIEDAD FINANCIERA DE COMERCIO, C.A.
Supreme Court, New York County
128 Misc. 2d 564, 490 N.Y.S.2d 670 (1985)

GREENFIELD, JUSTICE:

Plaintiff Credit Francais International, S.A. is a French banking corporation headquartered in Paris which was part of an international consortium of nine banks which loaned $25,000,000 to defendant Sociedad Financiera De Comercio, C.A., a Venezuelan financial institution, pursuant to a written Deposit Agreement entered into on November 24, 1980. Plaintiff bank deposited $3,000,000 of the total pursuant to the Agreement terms. The Agreement provided for repayment of principal and interest in six semi-annual installments. The Marine Midland Bank, which is headquartered in New York City, was designated as the Agent for the participating banks. It was to receive the payments made by the defendant, to be applied pro rata to the accounts of the participating banks. Defendant made the requisite payments in February and August of 1982, reducing the principal amount owed to the plaintiff to $2,000,000. However, in February and March, 1983, the Government of Venezuela, in attempting to cope with its problem of foreign debt, adopted certain currency control regulations restricting the use of dollars and calling on all Venezuelan financial institutions to restructure their debt payments, and to suspend all payments of principal until 1986. Thus, while defendant continued to pay interest on the loan, it has made no payments on account of principal in 1983 and 1984.

Plaintiff contends that the failure of defendant to make the payments required constitutes a clear breach of the Deposit Agreement, and sues for the principal balance owing. Plaintiff has attached sums allegedly owing to the defendant, and this attachment was confirmed by decision and order of Mr. Justice Alvin Klein dated July 5, 1984. Plaintiff now moves for partial summary judgment on the first cause of action in its amended complaint for breach of the Agreement. The defendant has cross-moved to dismiss on the grounds of forum non conveniens, and alternatively, for summary judgment on the ground that the Venezuelan decrees prohibiting repayment should be respected and accorded comity, and that plaintiff is not a proper party to bring suit individually under the terms of the Deposit Agreement.

FORUM NON CONVENIENS

Before dealing with any of the other procedural or substantive issues which are raised on this motion, the court of necessity must determine the threshold issue of whether New York is the appropriate forum for resolution of the dispute, or whether it should be handled elsewhere, since neither plaintiff nor defendant is a New York resident and the critical question of law allegedly involves the interpretation and application of Venezuelan currency decrees. Defendant points out that the suit is brought by a French bank headquartered in Paris against a Venezuelan financial institution with offices in Caracas. Neither plaintiff nor defendant maintains any offices in New York. Defendant professes concern about a possible New York judgment ordering repayment of a Venezuelan debt which is prohibited by the decrees of the Venezuelan Government. . . .

It is clear that the residence of the parties is no longer the controlling consideration in determining whether or not New York courts are an appropriate forum under CPLR § 327. . . .

In this case, the lending banks which made up the consortium, other than plaintiff, a French bank, are located in England, Panama, Texas, Minnesota, the Netherlands Antilles and three in the Bahamas. The Marine Midland Bank of New York was designated as Agent, and Marine Midland Ltd. of London is designated by the Agreement as the Manager. It is alleged, however, that the underlying agreement was negotiated in New York, that the text of the Deposit Agreement was drafted in New York, that payments under the Agreement were to be made to Marine Midland in New York and that meetings between the parties to the Agreement were held in New York.

Given the multi-national character of the Agreement, the parties obviously anticipated that situations could arise where disputes might be litigated in any one of a number of jurisdictions, with widely varying results. Therefore, the parties provided that the Agreement was to be governed and interpreted in accordance with the laws of the State of New York, the place of payment and they further provided what is known as a "forum-selection clause" pursuant to which defendant

> . . . irrevocably consents that any legal action or proceeding against it or any of its property arising under or relating to this Agreement . . . may be brought in any court of the State of New York or any federal court of the United States of America located in the City and State of New York, or in the appropriate courts in Caracas, Venezuela as the Agent, the Manager or any Depositor may elect. . . .

Defendant appointed an agent headquartered in New York City to receive service of process in its behalf, and agreed to submit to and accept the jurisdiction of the New York courts.

Defendant further explicitly and irrevocably waived "any objection which it may now or hereafter have to the laying of the venue of any suit, action or proceeding arising out of or relating to this Agreement . . ." and further explicitly waived "any claim that the State of New York is not a convenient forum for any such suit, action or proceeding." It further waived any right that it had to insist on any action in connection with the Agreement being brought before a Venezuelan court. Lastly, it waived any right to assert a defense of sovereign immunity with respect to its obligations.

> When all the parties to an agreement have designated a particular jurisdiction as the forum for the resolution of their disputes, such a forum-selection clause "is prima facie valid and should be enforced . . . unless unreasonable under the circumstances." *M-S Bremen v. Zapata Off-Shore Co.*, 407 U.S. 1, 10, 92 S. Ct. 1907, 1913, 32 L. Ed.2d 513 (1972). . . .

. . . .

The State of New York has explicitly provided for the enforceability of a Choice-of-Forum Clause [L.1984, c. 421, § 1]. That statute, effective July 1, 1984, applies retroactively to contracts entered into earlier, where the action or proceeding has commenced after the effective date. It added a new Title 14 to the General Obligations Law. Section 5-1401 thereof provides that:

> The parties to any contract, agreement or undertaking . . . relating to any obligation arising out of a transaction covering in the aggregate not less than Two Hundred and Fifty Thousand Dollars . . . may agree that the law of this State shall govern their rights and duties in whole or in part whether or not such contract, agreement or undertaking bears a reasonable relation to this state.

Section 5-1402 deals with forum selection. It provides that:

> 1. Notwithstanding any act which limits or affects the right of a person to maintain an action or proceeding, including, but not limited to, paragraph (b) of section thirteen hundred fourteen of the business corporation law . . . any person may maintain an action or proceeding against a foreign corporation, non-resident, or foreign state where the action or proceeding arises out of or relates to any contract, agreement or undertaking for which a choice of New York law has been made in whole or in part . . . relating to any obligation arising out of a transaction covering in the aggregate, not less than one million dollars, and which contains a provision or provisions whereby such foreign corporation or non-resident agrees to submit to the jurisdiction of the courts of this state.

2. Nothing contained in this section shall be construed to affect the enforcement of any provision respecting choice of forum in any other contract, agreement or undertaking.

. . . .

CPLR 327, which spells out the power of the court to dismiss an action for forum non conveniens, has been amended by this enactment. A new subdivision (b) now provides:

(b) Notwithstanding the provisions of subdivision (a) of this rule, the court shall not stay or dismiss any action on the ground of inconvenient forum, where the action arises out of or relates to a contract, agreement or undertaking to which section 5-1402 of the general obligations law applies, and the parties to the contract have agreed that the law of this state shall govern their rights and duties in whole or in part.

New York, as the center of international trade and finance, has expressly recognized, as a service to the business community, that its courts will be hospitable to the resolution of all substantial contractual disputes in which the parties have agreed beforehand that our neutrality and expertise should govern their relationships. Just as the dollar has become the international standard for monetary transactions, so may parties agree that New York law is the standard for international disputes. *See* Note, 59 St. John's Law Review 413-419 (Winter 1985).

. . . .

The matter could hardly be clearer. . . . The Agent designated to act on behalf of the lenders is a New York bank. The place of payment is at its office in New York. It is the New York Agent who has the responsibility of distributing all payments to each of the participating banks. New York law is expressly declared to be governing. Thus, it cannot be said that the controversy in question is devoid of any nexus with New York even in the absence of the explicit consent to jurisdiction. . . .

STANDING TO SUE

[The court concluded that the plaintiff had no standing to sue without the other banks which were part of the consortium. — Eds.]

NOTES

327(b) —can't remove

(1) Subdivision (b) of CPLR 327 was added in 1984. "Ostensibly, the purpose of the amendment to Rule 327 [and related changes to the General Obligations Law] is to enhance the status of New York as a leading commercial and financial center. Proponents of the amendment urged that by removing the possibility that courts will refuse to entertain qualifying actions, parties will be encouraged to choose New York as the governing law and forum. It is argued

that the result will be extensive economic benefits, particularly within the New York financial community." *Survey of New York Practice*, 59 St. John's L. Rev. 411, 415-16 (1985) (citations omitted).

Do you see a conflict between these amendments and the result in cases like *Bewers v. American Home Products Corp., supra*, and *Islamic Republic of Iran v. Pahlavi, supra*?

(2) CPLR 327(b) is binding in any action brought in a New York State court. If the action is removed to federal court (or was commenced there initially), federal law applies, and CPLR 327(b) will not prevent the court from exercising its discretion to transfer the action to another district pursuant to 28 U.S.C. § 1404(a). *Stewart Organization, Inc. v. Ricoh Corp.*, 487 U.S. 22, 108 S. Ct. 2239, 101 L. Ed. 2d 22 (1988).

(3) Forum selection clauses will generally be enforced to defeat a forum non conveniens motion even if CPLR 327(b) does not apply. *See, e.g., Arthur Young & Co. v. Leong*, 53 A.D.2d 515, 383 N.Y.S.2d 618 (1st Dep't 1976). *But see 3H Enterprises v. Bennett*, 276 A.D.2d 965, 715 N.Y.S.2d 90 (2000) (upholding a forum non conveniens dismissal despite a forum selection clause designating New York as the exclusive forum because enforcing the provision would be unreasonable; there was no substantial nexus to New York and the defendants were elderly Floridians for whom travel would be difficult).

(4) So-called "service of suit" clauses are distinguished from forum selection clauses. These clauses typically obligate one party to submit to the jurisdiction of a particular court, but do not say that the action "shall" or "must" be brought in that court. For this reason, the Court of Appeals has held, a "service of suit" clause is but one factor that a court should take into consideration in deciding a forum non conveniens motion. *Brooke Group Ltd. v. JCH Syndicate*, 488, 87 N.Y.2d 530, 640 N.Y.S.2d 479, 663 N.E.2d 665 (1996) (the lower courts did not abuse their discretion in granting a motion to dismiss on the grounds that New York was an inconvenient forum, notwithstanding that the contract obligated the defendant to "submit to the jurisdiction of a Court of competent jurisdiction within the United States").

Chapter 3

CHOOSING THE PROPER
FORUM WITHIN THE STATE —
SUBJECT MATTER JURISDICTION

§ 3.01 INTRODUCTORY NOTE

Once one is satisfied that jurisdiction can be obtained over the person or property of the defendant in New York, the attorney choosing a forum must decide which courts of the state, if any, have jurisdiction over the subject matter of the action. Since the state has nine types of trial level courts (*see* chart in § 3.04[L][3], *infra*), this is often not an easy task. Before looking at specific subject matter jurisdiction limits, it might be well to refresh your understanding of the underlying concept.

§ 3.02 THE CONCEPT OF SUBJECT MATTER
JURISDICTION

The Court of Appeals has stated that subject matter jurisdiction "embraces the competence of a court to entertain a particular kind of litigation." *Gager v. White*, 53 N.Y.2d 475, 485 n.2, 442 N.Y.S.2d 463, 466 n.2, 425 N.E. 2d 851, 854 n.2 (1981). *See also Fry v. Village of Tarrytown*, 89 N.Y.2d 714, 718, 658 N.Y.S.2d 205, 680 N.E.2d 578 (1997) ("The question of subject matter jurisdiction is a question of judicial power: whether the court has the power, conferred by the Constitution or statute, to entertain the case before it."). This description, while useful shorthand, masks the considerable difficulty courts have had on occasion in distinguishing subject matter jurisdiction from in personam jurisdiction and, as the next case illustrates, from the merits themselves. Yet as the following case also indicates, it is important to know whether a limit on a court's power goes to subject matter jurisdiction because its lack presents a non-waivable defense.

LACKS v. LACKS
Court of Appeals
41 N.Y.2d 71, 390 N.Y.S.2d 875, 359 N.E.2d 384 (1976)

CHIEF JUDGE BREITEL.

Defendant wife in a protracted litigation, one of several between the parties, by post judgment motion sought to set aside the final judgment of divorce against her on the ground that the court never had subject matter jurisdiction

141

(CPLR 5015, subd [a], par 4). Plaintiff husband started the action, originally only for a separation, in August, 1965. After an appeal and two trials the husband obtained the judgment of divorce in 1970. The Appellate Division affirmed that judgment in 1972, and both that court and this denied leave to appeal to the Court of Appeals. Special Term, in 1975, granted the wife's motion to set aside the judgment, but the Appellate Division modified the order by denying the motion and reinstating the final judgment of divorce. Defendant wife appeals.

In the post-judgment motion, by a newly retained lawyer, made four years after the final judgment and almost two years after appeal had been exhausted, the wife argued that the Supreme Court had been without subject matter jurisdiction. There had been failure, she contended, to satisfy the durational residence requirement by the husband in order for him to obtain a divorce under the State's liberal divorce laws enacted while the action was pending. Her theory is that the Supreme Court's jurisdiction in matrimonial actions for separation and divorce is exclusively statutory and absent the basic facts upon which to ground such actions the court is without subject matter jurisdiction, which, she argues, may never be cured, waived, or overcome. The issue is, therefore, whether, as the wife argues, the residence requirements in matrimonial actions, often described as jurisdictional, involve a kind of subject matter jurisdiction without which a court is powerless to render a valid judgment.

The order of the Appellate Division should be affirmed. Just as one of the statutory grounds in section 170 of the Domestic Relations Law must exist to obtain a divorce, the existence of at least one of the connections with the State set forth in section 230 of the same law is equally essential. The requirements of section 230, however, go only to the substance of the divorce cause of action, not to the competence of the court to adjudicate the cause. Hence, a divorce judgment granted in the absence of one of the specified connections with the State, even if erroneously determined as a matter of law or fact, is not subject to vacatur under CPLR 5015 (subd [a], par 4). . . .

. . . .

The confusion, if there be confusion, starts with a line of decisions dating back to the last century and continuing into the present in which this court has said with less than perfect meticulousness that "jurisdiction" of New York courts in matrimonial cases is limited to the powers conferred by statute. . . . Jurisdiction is a word of elastic, diverse, and disparate meanings (*see Nuernberger v. State*, 41 NY2d 111).

A statement that a court lacks "jurisdiction" to decide a case may, in reality, mean that elements of a cause of action are absent (*see, e.g., McNamara v. Allstate Ins. Co.*, 3 AD2d 295, 299). Similarly, questions of mootness and standing of parties may be characterized as raising questions of subject matter jurisdiction (. . .). But these are not the kinds of judicial infirmities to which CPLR 5015 (subd. [a], par. 4) is addressed. That provision is designed to preserve objections so fundamental to the power of adjudication of a court that they survive even a final judgment or order (*see, generally*, 5 Weinstein-Korn-Miller, NY Civ. Prac., par. 5015.10).

In *Thrasher v. United States Liab. Ins. Co.* (19 NY2d 159, 166), this court, in discussing subject matter jurisdiction, drew a clear distinction between a court's competence to entertain an action and its power to render a judgment on the merits. . . . Absence of competence to entertain an action deprives the court of "subject matter jurisdiction"; absence of power to reach the merits does not.

The implications of this distinction are serious. It is blackletter law that a judgment rendered without subject matter jurisdiction is void, and that the defect may be raised at any time and may not be waived (*see* 21 CJS, Courts, §§ 108-110, 116). Thus stated, the rule is grossly oversimple. The problem requires better analysis, and one long overdue (*see, e.g.*, Dobbs, *Validation of Void Judgments: Bootstrap Principle*, 53 Va L Rev 1003, 1241). Nevertheless, the breadth with which the rule is often stated indicates the importance traditionally attached to so-called subject matter jurisdiction, really competence of courts, and the grave consequences, including denial of res judicata effect to judgments, which may result from a lack of true subject matter jurisdiction or competence. Beyond the confusion engendered by a misapplication of the terminology and concept of subject matter jurisdiction, there is more created by the locution that in this State the courts' power in matrimonial actions is exclusively statutory. Yet in counterpoint, it has often been said: "the Supreme Court is a court of original, unlimited and unqualified jurisdiction" and "competent to entertain all causes of action unless its jurisdiction has been specifically proscribed" (*Kagen v. Kagen*, 21 NY2d 532, 537). . . .

Against the State Constitution's broad grant of jurisdiction to the Supreme Court, defendant offers the language of section 230 of the Domestic Relations Law. It provides merely that "[a]n action . . . for divorce or separation may be maintained only when" the residence requirements are met. Not even the catchall word "jurisdiction" appears in the statute, much less an explicit limitation on the court's competence to entertain the action. In no way do these limitations on the cause of action circumscribe the power of the court in the sense of competence to adjudicate causes in the matrimonial categories. That a court has no "right" to adjudicate erroneously is no circumscription of its power to decide, rightly or wrongly.

The case law is similarly unavailing to the wife. None of the cases in this court which have rather broadly stated that, absent statutory authorization, the Supreme Court has no "jurisdiction" over matrimonial actions, has dealt with a party seeking to vacate a final judgment after direct appeals had been exhausted. Instead, in some the court was dealing with the initial appeal of the trial court's determination on the "jurisdictional" issue. . . . In others, the jurisdictional pronouncements were general relevant observations not decisive of any issue. . . . Hence, although some of these were not matrimonial actions as now defined in CPLR 105 (subd [o]), each case is explained on the basis that, absent statutory authority, no matrimonial cause of action exists and absent the essential elements prescribed it may not prevail.

The court has never before considered the unlikely question, until this case, whether the judicial error on an essential element of the cause of action was so fundamental as to permit vacatur of a final judgment, collaterally or after final judgment beyond ordinary appellate review. Had that ever been the problem unlikely until this case, perhaps the need for a less elastic and encompassing term than the word "jurisdiction" would have been apparent.

Moreover, even if defendant's dubious interpretations of prior case law be accepted, this court has held that the 1962 revised article VI of the State Constitution expanded the Supreme Court's jurisdiction to include "any proceeding not recognized at common law" (*Kagen v. Kagen*, 21 NY2d 532, 536-537, *supra*; *Matter of Seitz v. Drogheo*, 21 NY2d 181, 185-186, *supra*). Matrimonial actions were not known to the common-law courts, but were instead a creation of the ecclesiastical courts (*Langerman v. Langerman*, 303 NY 465, 469-470, *supra*). It would appear, therefore, that by virtue of the constitutional amendment, the Supreme Court is now vested constitutionally with "subject matter jurisdiction" in matrimonial cases, assuming that such an assertion is necessary to give the Supreme Court a competence in matrimonial causes equal to that in common law or equity causes.

Hence, any error of law or fact which might have been committed in the divorce action did not deprive the court of jurisdiction to adjudicate the case, CPLR 5015 (subd [a], par 4) is inapplicable, and Special Term erroneously vacated the final judgment.

In sum, the overly stated principle that lack of subject matter jurisdiction makes a final judgment absolutely void is not applicable to cases which, upon analysis, do not involve jurisdiction, but merely substantive elements of a cause for relief. To do so would be to undermine significantly the doctrine of res judicata, and to eliminate the certainty and finality in the law and in litigation which the doctrine is designed to protect.

. . . .

Accordingly, the order of the Appellate Division should be affirmed, without costs.

NOTE

What of the distinction (not dealt with in the preceding case) between subject matter jurisdiction and jurisdiction over the person or property of the defendant? The important practical distinction between the two is that the defense of a lack of jurisdiction over the defendant's person or property is waived if the defendant fails to raise it in timely fashion, CPLR 3211(e), whereas a defect of subject matter jurisdiction is not waivable. But this does not help you tell whether a particular limit on jurisdiction falls into one category or the other. Is the following helpful? "A rough but useful test for distinguishing between the two broad categories of jurisdiction is that a question is one of personal jurisdiction if it would be obviated by timely service of valid process in some specified geographic area, and is otherwise one of subject-matter jurisdiction." Note, *Filling the Void: Judicial Power and Jurisdictional Attacks on Judgments*, 87 Yale L.J. 164, n. 1 (1977). Or does that test beg the question?

In *Fry v. Village of Tarrytown*, 89 N.Y.2d 714, 718-719, 658 N.Y.S.2d 205, 680 N.E.2d 578 (1997), the Court held that a mistake in the papers the plaintiff had filed to commence the proceeding did not result in a defect of subject matter jurisdiction. As the Court explained:

> A review of the statutory language and the structure of the filing system, considered in light of its purpose and historical antecedent, compels the conclusion that respondents waived their objection to the defective filing. Turning first to the statutory language, it is significant that none of the provisions of the filing statute purport to limit or condition Supreme Court's "competence" to entertain particular categories of actions (*see,* CPLR 203, 304, 306-a, 306-b). "Not even the catchall word 'jurisdiction' appears in the statute, much less an explicit limitation on the court's competence to entertain the action" (Lacks v Lacks, 41 NY2d 71, 75).

> Aside from the absence of an express statutory limitation on the courts' subject matter jurisdiction, the purpose and the structure of the filing requirements likewise do not evince an implicit limitation on subject matter jurisdiction. . . .

§ 3.03 GENERAL LIMITS ON NEW YORK'S SUBJECT MATTER JURISDICTION

Some limits on subject matter jurisdiction apply to every court in New York. The most notable general source of such limits is federal law, insofar as it vests exclusive jurisdiction over certain matters to the federal courts. Examples include actions arising under federal statutes relating to patents and copyrights. *See* 28 U.S.C. § 1338. The Securities Litigation Uniform Standard Act of 1998 ("SLUSA," Pub. L. No. 105-353, 112 Stat. 3227) gives federal courts exclusive jurisdiction over many securities fraud class actions. If a covered class action is filed in state court, it "shall be removed" to federal court. A case will not be removed, however, if the action deals mainly with corporate governance issues under the state law in the state in which the corporation is incorporated. Moreover, state pension funds and similar entities can bring suit in state court. *See* Elizabeth S. Strong, *How the Courts and Congress are Changing Securities Litigation*, N.Y.L.J., Mar. 4, 1999, p.1, col. 2.

A second general limit is found in a state law, Business Corporation Law § 1314, described and set forth in the next case.

CALZATURIFICIO GIUSEPPE GARBUIO S.A.S. v. DARTMOUTH OUTDOOR SPORTS, INC.

United States District Court, Southern District of New York
435 F. Supp. 1209 (1977)

MacMahon, District Judge.

This is a diversity action for damages of $72,854.24, brought by an Italian partnership manufacturing ski boots against a New Hampshire corporation, for goods sold and delivered under a distributorship contract. Defendant is a foreign corporation not subject to *in personam* jurisdiction in New York. Plaintiff, therefore, attempted to establish jurisdiction quasi-in rem by attaching certain escrow monies held in New York by Beconta, Inc., a corporation which succeeded defendant as plaintiff's United States distributor. The monies represent sums payable by Beconta to defendant under the parties' agreement terminating defendant's distributorship.

We conclude that the attachment must be vacated, even if it is otherwise proper and valid, because the action is barred by New York Business Corporation Law § 1314(b) (McKinney Supp. 1977), a statute which must be applied by a federal court sitting in diversity. . . .

Section 1314(b) bars suit in New York by a non-New Yorker, or by a foreign corporation, against a foreign corporation, except in specified circumstances.[1] It is apparent that the instant case fits none of the enumerated categories in which suit between foreigners would be permitted. The action lacks any requisite nexus to New York. New York was neither the place of the making, nor the contemplated performance of the contract upon which suit is based,[2] § 1314(b);

---

[1] Section 1314(b) provides:

Except as otherwise provided in this article, an action or special proceeding against a foreign corporation may be maintained by another foreign corporation of any type or kind or by a nonresident in the following cases only:

   (1) Where it is brought to recover damages for the breach of a contract made or to be performed within this state, or relating to property situated within this state at the time of the making of the contract.

   (2) Where the subject matter of the litigation is situated within this state.

   (3) Where the cause of action arose within this state, except where the object of the action or special proceeding is to affect the title of real property situated outside this state.

   (4) Where, in any case not included in the preceding subparagraphs, a non-domiciliary would be subject to the personal jurisdiction of the courts of this state under section 302 of the civil practice law and rules.

   (5) Where the defendant is a foreign corporation doing business or authorized to do business in this state.

[2] Plaintiff admits in its moving papers and affidavits that the agreements between the parties were actually executed in Italy and Massachusetts, respectively.

nor did the cause of action arise here,[3] § 1314(b)(3); nor is defendant doing business here, § 1314(b)(5).[4]

Plaintiff contends, however, that a choice of law clause in the subject contract operates to bring the case within § 1314(b)(1). The clause provides: "This agreement shall be deemed to have been made in, and shall be construed under, the laws of the State of New York." We believe, however, that the clause does not bring the case within § 1314(b)(1). The provision that the contract "shall be construed under" New York law is a mere choice of substantive law. It does not bring the case within § 1314, for the statute does not confer subject matter jurisdiction merely because New York substantive law applies.

The provision that the contract "shall be deemed to have been made in" New York presents a more difficult question. Clearly, jurisdiction would be conferred by § 1314(b)(1) if the contract were actually "made" in New York. The question to be answered, therefore, is whether a contract in fact made outside New York can by agreement of the parties become one "made" here for purposes of § 1314.

Counsel do not cite and our own research has not revealed any New York decision directly in point. However, in *Fidan v. Austral American Trading Corp.*, 8 Misc.2d 598, 168 N.Y.S.2d 27 (Sup.Ct.1957), a contractual provision similar in effect to the one at issue here was held ineffective to confer subject matter jurisdiction under § 1314. There, non-New Yorkers agreed that "only the New York courts shall have jurisdiction over" the subject contract which was in fact made outside New York. 168 N.Y.S.2d at 29. Nevertheless, the court dismissed the action under a predecessor to § 1314, holding that it lacked jurisdiction over the subject matter. That the defendant had agreed to suit in New York was held insufficient to confer jurisdiction, "[f]or, if this were permitted, it would render Section 225 ineffective." *Id.* at 31. . . .

While we would not be *Erie*-bound by this decision of a lower New York court, even if it were directly in point, . . . we believe that *Fidan* suggests the proper resolution of the question now before us. Were we to give effect to the deemed made in New York provision, we would allow the parties by agreement to bring within the statute, and hence within our jurisdiction, a contract claim which would not otherwise be cognizable in this court. Yet, it is fundamental that subject matter jurisdiction cannot be conferred by agreement of the parties. This principle, we believe, is sufficient to dispose of plaintiff's contentions based on the agreement. . . .

---

[3] In its moving papers, plaintiff does not allege that acts constituting a breach occurred in New York. Nor does it allege the occurrence here of any other event which could possibly support a conclusion that the cause of action arose here.

[4] If it were, this very motion seeking attachment for quasi-in rem jurisdiction would have been superfluous. *Cf.* N.Y. CPLR § 301 (McKinney 1972) ("doing business" as basis for in personam jurisdiction).

We note further that our decision has the added virtue of preventing the parties from unilaterally avoiding New York's sovereign policy, expressed in § 1314(b), "against lending its courts to the resolution of disputes between non-resident parties. . . ." *Simonson v. International Bank*, 14 N.Y.2d 281, 285, 251 N.Y.S.2d 433, 435, 200 N.E.2d 427, 429 (1964). Accordingly, we conclude that the contract was not made in New York and that this case therefore does not fall within § 1314(b)(3).

Since this is an action between an Italian partnership and a foreign corporation, and fits within no subdivision of § 1314(b), we lack subject matter jurisdiction. Plaintiff's motion for an order approving the attachment is therefore denied, the attachment is vacated, and the action is dismissed without prejudice to the bringing of another action in a proper forum. Defendant's motion seeking to dismiss or transfer the action on the ground of improper venue or forum non conveniens is denied as moot. In view of our disposition vacating the attachment on statutory grounds, we need not address the question whether our assumption of jurisdiction in these circumstances would comport with due process. . . .

So ordered.

NOTES

(1) In the principal case, it was not alleged that defendant was subject to in personam jurisdiction. Can you think of any cases in which personal jurisdiction could be obtained over a defendant sued by a foreign corporation in which B.C.L. § 1314(b) would nonetheless bar the action? In this regard consider carefully the list of exceptions in B.C.L. § 1314(b)(1)-(5).

As to sub-paragraph (5), note that there is authority, albeit somewhat dated, that the mere fact that defendant is "doing business" in New York does not suffice to yield subject matter jurisdiction unless "special circumstances" are shown, such as the lack of any other reasonable forum. *Yesuvida v. Pennsylvania R.R. Co.*, 200 Misc. 815, 111 N.Y.S.2d 417 (Sup. Ct. 1951). Is there any place for such an approach, given the modern use of forum non conveniens?

(2) B.C.L. § 1314(a) provides:

An action or special proceeding against a foreign corporation may be maintained by a resident of this state or by a domestic corporation of any type or kind for any cause of action.

Does this mean that the doctrine of forum non conveniens is not available when a New York resident sues a domestic corporation?

(3) A limit on a plaintiff's choice of forum which does not go to subject matter jurisdiction but which can conveniently be treated in this chapter is found in B.C.L. § 1312(a), which provides:

A foreign corporation doing business in this state without authority shall not maintain any action or special proceeding in this state, unless and until such corporation has been authorized to do business in this state and it has paid to the state all fees and taxes imposed under the tax law or any related statute, as defined in section eighteen hundred of such law, as well as penalties and interest charges related thereto, accrued against the corporation. This prohibition shall apply to any successor in interest of such foreign corporation.

Violation of this statute may lead to dismissal on a motion under CPLR 3211(a)(3).

The meaning of the phrase "doing business" in B.C.L. § 1312 is not clear. Some cases have held that to meet this test, more must be shown than would be necessary under CPLR 301 for purposes of obtaining personal jurisdiction over the defendant. *E.g., Netherlands Ship Mortgage Corp. v. Madias*, 717 F.2d 731 (2d Cir. 1983). *See also Paper Mfrs. Co. v. Ris Paper Co.*, 86 Misc. 2d 95, 381 N.Y.S.2d 959 (Civ. Ct. 1976), and cases cited. But this view is not uniform. It is clear that the intra-state business of the corporation must be substantial before the state can require it to obtain authority as a condition of using state courts. Otherwise, the state offends the Commerce Clause of the federal Constitution. *Allenberg Cotton Co. v. Pittman*, 419 U.S. 20, 95 S. Ct. 260 (1974).

The federal courts will also apply B.C.L. § 1312 to cases before them by virtue of diversity jurisdiction. *Netherlands Ship Mortgage Corp. v. Madias*, 717 F.2d 731 (2d Cir. 1983). *See also Woods v. Interstate Realty Co.*, 337 U.S. 535, 69 S. Ct. 1235 (1949) (applying a Mississippi statute similar to New York's B.C.L. § 1312). When the claim at issue is governed by federal law, however, B.C.L. § 1312 cannot be used to bar a foreign corporation from using the federal courts, even in a diversity case. *Grand Bahama Petroleum Co., Ltd. v. Asiatic Petroleum Corp.*, 550 F.2d 1320 (2d Cir. 1977).

§ 3.04 SUBJECT MATTER JURISDICTION OF THE VARIOUS COURTS

PROBLEM A

Ellen, a resident of Nassau County, wishes to commence a breach of contract action against Joan, by which she seeks to recover $6,500 in damages. Joan lives in Queens County but works in Mineola in Nassau County, to which she commutes each day. In what courts may Ellen sue Joan?

[A] Supreme Court

KAGEN v. KAGEN
Court of Appeals
21 N.Y.2d 532, 289 N.Y.S.2d 195, 236 N.E.2d 475 (1968)

BURKE, J.

This appeal requires us to determine the effect of the 1962 amendment to section 7 of article VI of the State Constitution upon the general original jurisdiction of the Supreme Court.

In August 1962, Anita and Theodore Kagen entered into a separation agreement which was thereafter incorporated in a Mexican divorce decree. Under one of its provisions, defendant was paying his wife $60 a week for the support and maintenance of their two children. Plaintiff infants, by their parent and natural guardian, Anita Reisner, and Anita Reisner individually commenced the present action in September, 1965. Their complaint sets forth four causes of action, three of which are involved herein. Specifically, plaintiffs seek a declaratory judgment establishing the right of the infants to (1) annual support payments of $7,500 for each infant; (2) an annual vacation fund of $1,000 apiece; and (3) an annual educational fund of $2,000 each.

Defendant moved to dismiss this portion of the complaint. In granting this motion on the ground that the Supreme Court was without subject-matter jurisdiction, the court said: "There is no statute, relevant to this case, providing for award of support and maintenance for children other than section 240 of the Domestic Relations Law and article 4 of the Family Court Act. Section 240 of the Domestic Relations Law is self-limiting to [specifically enumerated actions] and therefore is not applicable to this action. Support proceedings pursuant to article 4 . . . are within the 'exclusive original jurisdiction' of the Family Court (Family Ct. Act, § 115, subd. [a], par. [ii]; § 411)." (48 Misc 2d 856, 857.)

The Appellate Division reversed.

Prior to the 1962 amendment to the Constitution, that document provided in part: "The supreme court is continued with general jurisdiction in law and equity" (N Y Const., art. VI, § 1). Under this provision, it was well settled that the Supreme Court lacked jurisdiction to order support and maintenance for the children of a dissolved marriage except as an incident to a proper matrimonial action. Thus, in *Langerman v. Langerman* (303 N Y 465), it was held that an action such as the present one — commenced solely for the support and maintenance of the children — was not within the jurisdiction of the Supreme Court. "The relief sought may be granted only as an incident to a marital action." (*Id.*, p. 471.)

. . . .

Under the new amendment, the Supreme Court is endowed with general original jurisdiction in law and equity. (N.Y.Const., art. VI, § 7, subd. a.) Furthermore, "If the legislature shall create new classes of actions and proceedings, the supreme court shall have jurisdiction over such classes of actions and proceedings," even though the Legislature confer other courts with jurisdiction over these same actions and proceedings. (N. Y. Const., art. VI, § 7, subd. c.)

Prior to this amendment, we had held that, whenever the Legislature created a cause of action unknown at common law, jurisdiction to entertain this action vested in the Supreme Court unless this jurisdiction was specifically proscribed. (*Thrasher v. United States Liab. Ins. Co.*, 19 N Y 2d 159, 166.)

Undoubtedly, an argument can be advanced that the words "new classes of actions and proceedings" were intended to refer only to "classes of actions and proceedings" not recognized prior to the effective date of this amendment, merely obliging the Legislature to confer at least concurrent jurisdiction on the Supreme Court each time a new class of action or proceeding was subsequently created — thus unaffecting the jurisdiction of the Supreme Court as it theretofore existed. This same end could have been attained without the aid of a constitutional amendment. (*Thrasher v. United States Liab. Ins. Co., supra.*)

An alternative construction, which we have adopted, giving the amendment greater significance, is that it was intended to increase the jurisdiction of the Supreme Court even as to "classes of actions and proceedings" recognized at the time of the amendment's adoption. This reading of the amendment removed all limitations previously imposed upon the court's jurisdiction. In our recent decision, *Matter of Seitz v. Drogheo* (21 N Y 2d 181, 185-186), we determined that the right to commence any proceeding not recognized at common law should be considered a new action or proceeding for jurisdictional purposes under section 7 of article VI of the Constitution. In this way, we are merely adhering to one of our earliest rules of construction, *i.e.*, that the Supreme Court is a court of original, unlimited and unqualified jurisdiction. . . .

With reference to this particular action, section 461 (subd. [b], par. [ii]) of the Family Court Act empowers that court to entertain applications for the modification of prior support orders on the basis of a change of circumstances. While a comparable procedure existed in the New York City Domestic Relations Court Act (§ 137) and the Children's Court Act (§ 33) prior to the adoption of this amended Constitution, such relief was unknown at common law. (*Langerman v. Langerman, supra.*) Thus, this action is encompassed within the "new classes of actions and proceedings" of which the Supreme Court is given jurisdiction in article VI (§ 7, subd. c) of the amended Constitution.

As noted earlier, the Supreme Court, in dismissing these causes of action, relied upon section 411 of the Family Court Act which purports to confer *exclusive original jurisdiction* upon the Family Court for all proceedings commenced under article 4 of that act. This position is supported by a provision in the Constitution providing that this particular action be maintained in the Family

Court. (N Y Const., art. VI, § 13, subd. b.) Neither provision, however, requires that this action be dismissed. With reference to section 411, it is sufficient to note that this section also applied to the action in *Seitz (supra)* wherein we held that concurrent jurisdiction existed between the Supreme Court and the Family Court. Also, while subdivision b of section 13 of article VI provides that this action be brought in the Family Court, subdivision d of the same section states that "The provisions of this section shall in no way limit or impair the jurisdiction of the supreme court as set forth in section seven of this article." Thus, this section can only be construed as evidencing an intent that the jurisdiction of the Supreme Court, as provided for under any other provision of the Constitution, should be unaffected by this grant of jurisdiction to the Family Court.

Our decision that the jurisdiction of the Supreme Court has been expanded by the amendment to the Constitution in no way signals a contraction of the jurisdiction of specialized courts such as the Family Court. In matters such as this, plaintiffs are at liberty to commence their proceeding in the Family Court. If, instead, they should choose the Supreme Court for purposes of litigation, that court is empowered to "transfer any action or proceeding, except one over which it shall have exclusive jurisdiction . . . to any other court having jurisdiction of the subject matter" (N Y Const., art. VI, § 19, subd. a), or to retain jurisdiction over such an action. . . . In such instances, the Supreme Court must exercise its discretion as to whether it would be appropriate to transfer a particular matter to a court of concurrent jurisdiction, possessing unique, specialized capabilities and expertise. In many cases, obviously, this would be the better practice.

Conversely, our decision in this case may not be read as affecting the exclusive jurisdiction of the Court of Claims over claims against the State. Over a half century ago this court held that the Supreme Court lacked jurisdiction of claims against the State not because of the nature of the matter litigated but solely because of the immunity of the State from suit . . .; and in light of these holdings it would be improper, indeed, to construe this amendment to the Constitution as affecting the Court of Claims' jurisdiction.

Accordingly, the order appealed from should be affirmed, without costs, and the question certified should be answered in the affirmative.

JASEN, J. (dissenting).

Indisputably, the Supreme Court possessed no subject-matter jurisdiction over the instant type of support action prior to the 1962 amendment to section 7 of article VI of the State Constitution. (*Langerman v. Langerman*, 303 N Y 465.) A comparable procedure existed in the New York City Domestic Relations Court Act (§ 137) and the Children's Court Act (§ 33) prior to the adoption of the amended Constitution. The case at bar clearly, therefore, cannot be considered a "new class of action or proceeding" unknown prior to the 1962 constitutional amendment.

The general jurisdiction of the Supreme Court historically included its common-law jurisdiction plus all causes of action created subsequently *except* where the Legislature *specifically proscribed* its jurisdiction. (N.Y. Const., art. VI; *Thrasher v. United States Liab. Ins. Co.*, 19 N Y 2d 159, 166.) The Legislature specifically proscribed the subject-matter jurisdiction of the Supreme Court over the type of support action involved in the instant case prior to the 1962 amendment of article VI by conferring exclusive jurisdiction upon the Domestic Relations and Children's Courts.

The new amendment provides, "If the legislature *shall create new* classes of actions and proceedings, the supreme court shall have jurisdiction over such classes of actions and proceedings." (N.Y. Const., art. VI, § 7, subd. c; emphasis supplied.) The clear and unequivocal meaning of this amendment is to abolish the power of the Legislature to proscribe the jurisdiction of the Supreme Court concerning classes of actions and proceedings created subsequent to the effective date of the amendment. The exclusive jurisdiction possessed by specialized courts prior to the amendment is unaffected. We recently construed this language for the first time in *Matter of Seitz v. Drogheo* (21 N Y 2d 181), an action to enforce the support provisions of a Mexican divorce decree. Prior to the amendment of section 466 of the Family Court Act . . ., the courts of this State were without jurisdiction to enforce or modify the provisions of a foreign matrimonial decree under the facts in *Seitz*. . . . In *Seitz*, we found that the Legislature necessarily vested the Supreme Court with concurrent jurisdiction because article VI (§ 7, subd. c) does not allow the vesting of exclusive jurisdiction of a new class of action or proceeding in the Family Court. *Seitz* is unquestionably correct law because jurisdiction over the class of action involved in that case was conferred upon the courts of this State for the first time in 1965 (L. 1965, ch. 355) subsequent to the effective date of the amendment to section 7 of article VI.

This construction of the effect of the 1962 amendment is confirmed by the fact that article VI (§ 13, subd. a) established the Family Court and subdivision b of section 13 provided that the proceeding involved in the case at bar be *originated* in the Family Court in the manner to be provided by the Legislature. It should be noted that article VI (§ 13, subd. b) does not limit or impair the jurisdiction of the Supreme Court because the Supreme Court has never had jurisdiction over this type of action. . . . Section 411 of the Family Court Act, implementing the constitutional amendment, confers exclusive jurisdiction over the instant proceeding upon the Family Court.

The Report of the Joint Legislative Committee on Court Reorganization (McKinney's 1962 Session Laws, pp. 3428-3447) reveals that the Family Court Act represents a carefully considered legislative policy judgment of the best method of dealing with the sensitive problems of family life. The Joint Legislative Committee acknowledged in its report that the proposed Family Court would be controversial because it faced sensitive and delicate areas of life about which reasonable men may differ. However, the structure and powers of the Family Court are properly within the authority of the Legislature, and the Legislature has clearly and unequivocally spoken.

The majority's strained construction of the amendment to section 7 of article VI of the State Constitution abolishes the exclusive jurisdiction of the Family Court. The majority, in effect, has construed the words "shall create new classes of actions and proceedings" in section 7 of article VI to mean "all classes of actions and proceedings *whenever created*." (Emphasis supplied.) This construction ignores the plain wording of section 7 of article VI, renders the words "shall create new" meaningless, and frustrates clear legislative intent. Worse, this construction includes within the Supreme Court's general original jurisdiction all non-common-law actions and proceedings which the Legislature conferred exclusively upon other courts prior to the amendment of section 7 of article VI. Presumably, this decision abolishes the exclusive jurisdiction of all specialized courts. Thus this decision spawns the very evil of forum shopping which the Legislature sought to avoid by conferring exclusive jurisdiction upon specialized courts possessing unique capabilities and expertise.

The Legislature possessed the power to increase the general jurisdiction of the Supreme Court to include the instant type case prior to the new amendment. Perhaps some litigants prefer the familiar procedures of the Supreme Court to the more informal proceedings of the Family Court. However, this is clearly a legislative decision requiring policy judgments. The Legislature chose not to strip the Family Court of its exclusive jurisdiction. Recognition of the exclusive jurisdiction of the Family Court is now compelled by article VI (§ 13, subd. b) of the amended Constitution.

NOTES

(1) Consider the tactical aspects of the *Kagen* case: Why did the attorneys for the plaintiffs pursue their choice of forum in the teeth of the jurisdictional difficulties they encountered?

(2) The "unlimited" subject matter jurisdiction of the Supreme Court is subject to the limitation (mentioned in *Kagen* case) under which claims for damages against the state and its subdivisions must be brought in the Court of Claims. An exception to this exception has been made for damage claims arising under the state Human Rights Law. These may be brought in the Supreme Court even if the state is a defendant. *Koerner v. State*, 62 N.Y.2d 442, 478 N.Y.S.2d 584, 467 N.E.2d 232 (1984).

(3) A further limitation on the jurisdiction of the Supreme Court results when authority has been vested in an administrative agency. In reading the next case, consider whether the constitutional rule, so robust in *Kagen*, was given due weight.

SOHN v. CALDERON
Court of Appeals
78 N.Y.2d 755, 587 N.E.2d 807, 579 N.Y.S.2d 940 (1991)

TITONE, J.

In this action and proceeding, the Supreme Court, New York County, granted plaintiff landlord judgment declaring that he is entitled under the New York City Rent and Eviction Regulations and the Rent Stabilization Code to demolish his building, to evict his rent-control tenants and to refrain from offering renewal leases to his rent-stabilization tenants. The primary question presented by this appeal is whether the Supreme Court had concurrent authority to entertain the dispute in light of the various sections of the Regulations and the Code that specifically provide for the resolution of such disputes, at least in the first instance, by the Division of Housing and Community Renewal (DHCR), the administrative agency charged with implementing those statutes. We hold that DHCR had exclusive original jurisdiction in this situation and, accordingly, that plaintiff's complaint and petition should have been dismissed.

This landlord-tenant dispute has its origins in a three-alarm fire that occurred on March 8, 1986 in a 39-unit apartment building located at 306-310 West 51st Street in Manhattan. Most of the apartment units in the building, which was severely damaged in the fire, are subject to either rent-control or rent-stabilization laws.

As a result of the fire damage, the New York City Department of Housing Preservation and Development (HPD) issued notices that the building contained violations of the Housing Maintenance Code. Additionally, the tenants, who had lived in the building from 8 to 45 years, brought an action in Civil Court to compel plaintiff, the building's owner, to make the repairs necessary to render their units habitable.

In response, plaintiff commenced an action in Supreme Court against the tenants and HPD for a declaration that under the applicable rent-control and rent-stabilization regulations he was entitled either to demolish the building or to remove the housing accommodations from the market because the cost to render them safely habitable was equal to or exceeded the building's assessed value (*see,* Administrative Code of City of New York § 26-408[b][3], [4], [5][a]; 9 NYCRR 2204.8[a][1]; 2524.5[a][2]). In addition, plaintiff sought a declaration that he was entitled to be issued "certificates of eviction," which the law requires as a condition precedent to an owner's regaining possession of rent-controlled premises in these circumstances (*see,* Administrative Code § 26-408[a]). Finally, plaintiff sought permanent injunctive relief precluding HPD and the tenants from pursuing their efforts to force him to correct outstanding violations through administrative or Civil Court proceedings. [The Supreme Court denied the defendants' motion to dismiss for lack of subject matter jurisdiction, conducted a trial, and awarded judgment for the plaintiff. — Eds.]

. . . .

Where a section 26-408 (b) eviction is sought, the landlord must apply for and obtain a "certificate of eviction," which "the city rent agency [now the DHCR] shall issue . . . in accordance with its rules and regulations," Administrative Code of the City of New York §26-408(b). . . . When the specific ground for eviction is the owner's "good faith" intention to demolish the building, a certificate cannot be issued unless "[the] agency determines" that the new building will contain a greater number of apartment units than the demolished building, "[the] agency determines that the issuance of such certificate is not inconsistent with the purpose" of the rent control laws and the owner complies with the agency's regulations regarding relocating tenants . . . (*id.*, §26-408(b)(4)(a)-(d)). The Sound Housing Law adopted in 1974 (L 1974, ch. 1022) also requires a landlord seeking to withdraw a rent-controlled unit from the marketplace to satisfy the agency that "there is no reasonable possibility that the landlord can make a net annual return of (8½%)" (*id.*, 26-408(b)(5)(a)), and the landlord must obtain "prior written approval" by the agency if an existing tenant is to be evicted (*id.*, 26-408(j)(1)).

The Rent Stabilization Code contains analogous rules requiring determinations by DHCR before a landlord may withdraw the protected apartment units from the market and demolish the building (9 NYCRR 2524.5(a)(2)). Finally, both the New York City rent control law and the Rent Stabilization Code give DHCR the responsibility of adjudicating claimed violations of the rules prohibiting landlords from harassing tenants to induce them to leave their apartments (Administrative Code 26-413(b)(2); 26-412(d); 26-516(c); *see also,* 9 NYCRR 2526.2(c)(2); *id.,* part 2206). The harassment question is one that must also be considered by HPD, under the Special Clinton District Provisions of the City Zoning Resolution (NY City Zoning Resolution 96-109, 96-110).

It is clear beyond question that the Legislature intended disputes over a landlord's right to demolish a regulated building to be adjudicated by the DHCR and, to a lesser extent, HPD. The question presented here, which in this instance is dispositive, is whether by virtue of its constitutional role as a court of general original jurisdiction, the Supreme Court has authority to adjudicate such disputes.

Article VI, § 7 of the NY Constitution establishes the Supreme Court as a court of "general original jurisdiction in law and equity" (NY Const, art VI, § 7 [a]). Under this grant of authority, the Supreme Court "is competent to entertain all causes of action unless its jurisdiction has been specifically proscribed" (*Thrasher v United States Liab. Ins. Co.,* 19 NY2d 159, 166), and to that extent its powers are "unlimited and unqualified" (*Kagen v Kagen,* 21 NY2d 532, 537).

However, as all parties agree, rent-control and rent-stabilization disputes are a modern legislatively created category not encompassed within the traditional categories of actions at law and equity referred to in section 7(a) of article VI of the NY Constitution (*see generally, Langerman v Langerman,* 303 NY

465). Thus, the Supreme Court's authority in this case depends on the reach of section 7(b) of article VI, which provides: "If the legislature shall create new classes of actions and proceedings, the supreme court shall have jurisdiction over such classes of actions and proceedings," even though "the legislature may provide that another court or courts shall also have jurisdiction and that actions and proceedings of such classes may be originated in such other court or courts."

It has been held that the "new class of actions and proceedings" to which article VI, § 7(b) specifically refers are those which were unknown at common law and therefore would otherwise be outside the general jurisdiction continued and preserved by section 7(a) (*Matter of Seitz v Drogheo*, 21 NY2d 181; *Kagen v Kagen*, 21 NY2d 532, 536-537, *supra*). However, it has never been suggested that every claim or dispute arising under a legislatively created scheme may be brought to the Supreme Court for original adjudication. To the contrary, in *Loretto v Teleprompter Manhattan CATV Corp.* (58 NY2d 143, 152-153), this Court observed that concurrent original jurisdiction is not necessarily conferred on the Supreme Court when the Legislature provides for the adjudication of regulatory disputes by an administrative agency within the executive branch, as distinguished from a court within the judicial branch. Indeed, we stated in *Loretto* that there is nothing in article VI, § 7(b) or the relevant case law "to suggest that administrative agencies cannot be given a first instance adjudicatory function, subject to judicial review" (58 NY2d, at 153, *supra; cf., Flacke v Onondaga Landfill Sys.*, 69 NY2d 355, 362-363 [Supreme Court does not have jurisdiction concurrent with that of Department of Environmental Conservation with respect to agency's legislative licensing and regulatory functions]).

Accordingly, the constitutionally protected jurisdiction of the Supreme Court does not prohibit the Legislature from conferring exclusive original jurisdiction upon an agency in connection with the administration of a statutory regulatory program. In situations where the Legislature has made that choice, the Supreme Court's power is limited to article 78 review, except where the applicability or constitutionality of the regulatory statute, or other like questions, are in issue. . . .

The only issues raised by plaintiff's complaint were his satisfaction of the regulatory conditions for obtaining certificates of eviction and demolishing a structure containing protected apartment units. The earlier described provisions of the rent-control and rent-stabilization laws demonstrate that the Legislature intended DHCR and HPD to be the exclusive initial arbiters of whether an owner has, in fact, met these regulatory conditions. . . .

Since concurrent Supreme Court jurisdiction was not contemplated in this situation and the Constitution does not require it (*see, Loretto v Teleprompter Manhattan CATV Corp.*, 58 NY2d 143, 152-153, *supra*), Supreme Court erred in entertaining plaintiff's claims on the merits. Furthermore, Supreme Court's consideration of the delays that purportedly typify the administrative adjudicative process was inappropriate, since that factor, to the extent it might ever be relevant at all, would apply only in the application of the doctrine of "primary jurisdiction." That doctrine, which represents an effort to "co-ordinate the relationship between courts and administrative agencies," generally enjoins courts having concurrent jurisdiction to refrain from adjudicating disputes within an administrative agency's authority, particularly where the agency's specialized experience and technical expertise is involved (*Capital Tel. Co. v Pattersonville Tel. Co.*, 56 NY2d 11, 22). While the rule is certainly not without exceptions, no such exception is possible where, as here, the agency's original jurisdiction is exclusive (*see, Flacke v Onondaga Landfill Sys., supra*, at 362).

For all of the foregoing reasons, the Supreme Court should not have entertained plaintiff's action for declaratory and related relief in connection with his efforts to demolish the building. . . . Rather than adjudicating the controversy, the Supreme Court should have dismissed the complaint for lack of subject matter jurisdiction. . . .

NOTES

(1) The jurisdiction of the Supreme Court is, of course, also subject to those limits which apply to all courts of the state (discussed previously in § 3.03). Further, the Court of Appeals held (in a rather surprising decision) that, by virtue of CPLR 506(b), the Supreme Court has no subject matter jurisdiction to hear a proceeding against a Supreme Court Justice or judge of a county court. Only the Appellate Division has jurisdiction. *Nolan v. Lungen*, 61 N.Y.2d 788, 473 N.Y.S.2d 388, 461 N.E.2d 874 (1984).

(2) Although it has jurisdiction to entertain actions regardless of the amount of the claim, the Supreme Court will seek to avoid hearing actions in which the damages sought are so low that a court of inferior jurisdiction (such as the Civil Court of the City of New York) may entertain them. The court enforces this policy through its removal powers which are discussed in § 3.05, *infra*. Additionally, CPLR 8102, by denying costs, punishes the plaintiff who recovers a judgment in the Supreme Court which is below a stated monetary amount.

(3) The Supreme Court sits in each county. The proper county in which to sue is a question of venue, not jurisdiction.

[B] The County Court

J. A. MENNELLA FOODS CORP. v. NEPTUNE'S NUGGETS, INC.
County Court, Suffolk County
74 Misc. 2d 839, 346 N.Y.S.2d 43 (1973)

FRANK L. GATES, JR. JUDGE.

Motion by defendants to vacate the default judgment entered by the Clerk of this court on August 2, 1972 in the amount of $11,327.90 exclusive of interest and costs.

The complaint herein contains two causes of action:

1. Waste allegedly committed by defendant Neptune Nuggets, to property at Bay Shore, Suffolk County, New York occupied by said defendant under a lease from plaintiff, itself a lessee thereof. This cause of action alleges damages in the amount of $5,061.

2. Rent from January 1, 1972 up to the date of the judgment.

Said complaint also alleged that defendant Neptune Nuggets, Inc. consolidated with defendant Matlaw's Food Products, Inc. on December 1, 1971 and continued to operate as "Matlaw's Food Products, Inc." with principal offices at West Haven, Connecticut.

A default judgment was entered by the Clerk of Suffolk County on August 2, 1972 in the total amount of $11,836.82 consisting of: "amount claimed in complaint" $11,327.90, $453.12 interest and $55.80 costs and disbursements.

. . . .

. . . [D]efendants question the jurisdiction of this court over this action, alleging that defendants were not doing business in this county at the commencement of the action and upon the further ground that the judgment was in excess of the $10,000 monetary jurisdiction of this court.

Plaintiff contends, in effect, that this action arises out of acts committed by defendants in this county and as a result thereof this court has jurisdiction under CPLR 302 (the "long-arm statute").

The question arises, however, whether CPLR 302 takes precedence over section 190-a of the Judiciary Law . . ., which defines the residential requirements as to domestic and foreign corporations for the purpose of determining jurisdiction of this court under section 190 of the Judiciary Law.

Said section 190-a now reads as follows: "For the purpose of determining jurisdiction under section one hundred ninety, a domestic corporation or joint-stock association is deemed a resident of a county in which its principal place

of business is established by or pursuant to a statute or by its articles of association, or in which its principal place of business or any part of its plant,
shops, factories or offices is actually located . . . and a foreign corporation is to
be deemed a resident of a county if it maintains any plant, store, office, warehouse or other facility for doing business within such county."

At the commencement of this action, defendants had no place of business in
this county and were not doing business in this county. This court would therefore have no jurisdiction of this action unless the "long-arm statute," CPLR
302 is applicable herein.

This question appears to be one of first instance, research by this court having failed to disclose any precedent.

In the analogous situation of a nonresident motorist involved in an accident
in this State, subdivision 2 of section 253 of the Vehicle and Traffic Law permits
service of process arising out of such accident upon the nonresident motorist by
mailing the summons to the Secretary of State at Albany, New York. However,
the majority of the cases hold that county courts are prevented from exercising
jurisdiction over such nonresident motorists by the limitations contained in
section 190 of the Judiciary Law. (*Bonk v. Hodgkins*, 68 Misc 2d 148.)

This court finds that CPLR 302 is not applicable to actions brought in county
courts of this State and this court has no jurisdiction of this action. (Judiciary
Law, § 190, subd. 5; § 190-a.)

. . .

Finally, defendants contend that the entry of judgment in an amount in
excess of $10,000 violated the monetary jurisdictional limit of this court as
contained in subdivision 5 of section 190 of the Judiciary Law. [The monetary
limit of the County Court was subsequently raised to $25,000. — Eds.]

The pertinent portion of said statute sets forth the monetary jurisdiction of
this court as follows: "and wherein in any such action the *complaint* demands
judgment for a sum of money only not exceeding ten thousand dollars exclusive of
interest and costs" (emphasis added; *see, also*, N.Y. Const., art. VI, § 11, par. a).

Plaintiff argues that said limit of $10,000 applies to each cause of action
thereby allowing a complaint containing two causes of action, as in the instant
case, to demand judgment for $20,000.

This contention is without merit since it is contrary to the express language
of the statute.

The complaint herein demands damages of $5,061 on the first cause of action
and does not specify the amount demanded on the second cause of action.

In a court of limited jurisdiction, however, the complaint must contain a
statement of necessary jurisdictional facts. (*Wachtel v. Diamond State Eng.
Corp.*, 215 App. Div. 15.)

This court finds that:

1. The complaint herein fails to set forth facts showing jurisdiction of this court over this action.

2. That this court does not have jurisdiction over the defendants.

3. That the judgment herein was improperly entered by the Clerk of this court and was therefore void.

The motion to vacate said judgment is granted and the complaint herein is dismissed without prejudice to the commencement of a new action in the proper forum.

NOTES

(1) In the principal case the concern with the defendant's residence arises from Judiciary Law § 190, which defines County Court jurisdiction:

> The jurisdiction of each county court . . . extends to the following actions and special proceedings, in addition to the jurisdiction, power and authority conferred upon a county court in a particular case by special statutory provision:
>
> [§190(1) deals with actions affecting real property and subdivision (2) with actions to enforce a judgment. Neither subdivision has a residency requirement.]
>
> 3. An action for any other cause, where the defendant, or if there are two or more defendants, where all of them, at the time of the commencement of the action, reside in the county, or where a defendant has an office for the transaction of business within the county and the cause of action arose therein, or where the defendant is a foreign corporation that is doing business within the county and the cause of action arose therein and where the complaint in such action demands judgment for a sum of money only not exceeding twenty-five thousand dollars, or to recover one or more chattels the aggregate value of which does not exceed twenty-five thousand dollars with or without damages for the taking or detention thereof.

What is the nature of the jurisdictional limitation keyed to residence as found in Judiciary Law § 190(3)? Does it concern subject matter or in personam jurisdiction? The requirement has been held waivable by the defendant. *Haas v. Scholl*, 68 Misc. 2d 197, 325 N.Y.S.2d 844 (Sup. Ct. 1971).

(2) The holding in the principal case that the monetary limit on County Court jurisdiction applies to the entire complaint rather than to each cause of action was endorsed in *Mandel v. Kent*, 70 A.D.2d 903, 417 N.Y.S.2d 306 (2d Dep't 1979), but is not always followed, *see Benson v. Cohoes School Bd.*, 98 Misc. 2d

110, 413 N.Y.S.2d 600 (County Ct. 1979) (jurisdictional amount is not exceeded, so long as each separate and distinct claim in the complaint does not exceed the monetary limit). Which rule is better?

In other courts in which jurisdiction is limited to a stated amount, it is quite clear that the complaint as a whole may demand recovery in excess of that amount, so long as each separate claim does not exceed it. *See* N.Y.C. Civil Ct. Act § 211 and other uniform court acts.

(3) There is no monetary limit on the jurisdiction of the County Court over counterclaims. The court also has jurisdiction over certain real property actions and over some incompetency proceedings. Judiciary Law § 190(1), (4).

(4) There is a County Court in each county outside the City of New York. Within the City, the analogous civil court is the New York City Civil Court.

[C] The Civil Court of the City of New York

The Civil Court, which sits in each borough, has jurisdiction over any cause of action at law where the amount sought to be recovered does not exceed $25,000, exclusive of interest and costs.[1] There is no requirement that either of the parties reside in the city.

The court does not have general equity jurisdiction but has been given some specific grants of equitable authority. For example, the court has jurisdiction over actions for rescission or reformation of contracts if the amount in controversy is $25,000 or less.[2] The Civil Court also has power over some kinds of actions relating to real property located in New York City, subject to a general limit of $25,000.[3] For example, the court may entertain an action to foreclose a mortgage when the mortgage lien does not exceed $25,000 in value at the time the action is commenced.[4] The most important aspect of the court's power over real property, as measured by the number of cases commenced, is its jurisdiction over eviction proceedings and other landlord-tenant disputes.[5] A special branch of the court, the Housing Part (which sits in all boroughs), has been established to handle these cases.[6]

One problem which has arisen from the court's limited equity jurisdiction concerns the court's lack of power to grant equitable relief to stay an eviction of a commercial tenant alleged to be in violation of its lease. In order to get a stay and thus have time to cure the violation, the tenant must obtain an injunction

---

[1] N.Y.C. Civ. Ct. Act § 202.

[2] N.Y.C. Civ. Ct. Act § 213.

[3] *See* the list in N.Y.C. Civ. Ct. Act § 203.

[4] N.Y.C. Civ. Ct. Act § 203(b).

[5] N.Y.C. Civ. Ct. Act § 204.

[6] N.Y.C. Civ. Ct. Act § 110.

in an independent proceeding brought in the Supreme Court. These are commonly referred to as "Yellowstone" injunctions, after a seminal case. *First National Stores v. Yellowstone Shopping Center*, 21 N.Y.2d 630, 290 N.Y.S.2d 721, 237 N.E.2d 868 (1968). *See* discussion in *Post v. 120 East End Avenue Corp.*, 62 N.Y.2d 19, 475 N.Y.S.2d 821, 464 N.E.2d 125 (1984), and in § 12.05, *infra.*

In addition to having jurisdiction over any counterclaim over which the court would have jurisdiction if sued upon separately, the Civil Court has jurisdiction over any counterclaim for money only, regardless of the amount.[7] The court also has a small claims part which hears claims not exceeding $5,000.[8]

Process of the court must ordinarily be served and executed within the City of New York, but the New York City Civil Court Act provides for service outside the city or state in situations analogous to those governed by the long-arm statute, CPLR 302.[9] Appeals from the New York City Civil Court are taken to the Appellate Term of the Supreme Court.[10] Procedure is governed by the New York City Civil Court Act.

[D] District Courts

The Uniform District Court Act is currently of limited application, for district courts have been established only in Nassau County and in part of Suffolk County. Under section 16 of the Judiciary Article of the Constitution, any county outside New York City may, with the approval of its voters, establish a district court for all or a part of the county.

The basic maximum jurisdictional limit is $15,000, but there is no limit on monetary counterclaims.[11] Process may be served in the county in which the court sits and beyond if defined contacts between the defendant and the county are present.[12] Jurisdiction of appeals from the District Courts of Nassau and Suffolk Counties lies in the Appellate Term of the Second Department.[13]

---

[7] N.Y.C. Civ. Ct. Act § 208, but see § 208(d) restricting counterclaims which may be asserted in actions commenced in the housing part.

[8] N.Y.C. Civ. Ct. Act §§ 207, 1801. For procedure in Small Claims Part, see *id.* at §§ 1801-1810.

[9] N.Y.C. Civ. Ct. Act §§ 404. N.Y.C. Civ. Ct. Act § 408 provides that when an action is pending in Civil Court, statewide service is permitted to bring in an additional party if such service would be permissible in an action pending in Supreme Court. It also permits service outside the city when the defendant is a city resident and domiciliary of the state.

[10] N.Y.C. Civil Ct. Act § 1701.

[11] Uniform Dist. Ct. Act §§ 202, 211.

[12] Uniform Dist. Ct. Act §§ 403-404.

[13] 22 NYCRR § 730.1(e)(2).

[E] City Courts

Article 6, § 17 of the state constitution provides for the existence of courts for "towns, villages and cities outside the city of New York." Practice in these courts is governed by the Uniform City Court Act (UCCA).[14]

The monetary jurisdiction of most of the City Courts is $15,000.[15] The UCCA includes other provisions affecting subject matter jurisdiction, e.g., UCCA § 208(b), allowing unlimited counterclaims for money only, and UCCA § 211, permitting the total amount of aggregated claims to exceed otherwise applicable limits. Service of process is generally limited to the county in which the court is located, but under some circumstances, may be served in an adjoining county.[16] Appeals are taken to the County Court, except in the Second Department. There, appeals go to the Appellate Term.[17]

[F] Village, Town and Justice Courts

In many townships and in a few cities are justice courts and town, village and city courts whose jurisdiction is limited to actions at law for breach of contract or negligence where the damages claimed are not in excess of $3,000, actions to recover chattels not exceeding a like value and eviction proceedings.[18] Jurisdiction over counterclaims is limited to $3,000, and any amount claimed in excess is deemed waived.[19] Pursuant to the Uniform Justice Court Act, procedure in these courts is virtually identical to that in the various City and District Courts. Process must generally be served within the county.[20] Appeals are taken to the County Court or, where authorized, to an Appellate Term.[21]

[G] Small Claims and Commercial Claims

The Civil Court of the City of New York, the District Courts, the City Courts and the Justice courts are authorized to maintain special "parts" or sessions known as Small Claims Courts. These parts use informal procedures so that attorneys are not needed. The monetary limit on small claims, $5,000, is found

---

[14] UCCA § 2300.

[15] See UCCA § 202, as amended by Ch. 397, Laws of 1988, §§ 4-5.

[16] UCCA §§ 403-404.

[17] UCCA § 1701. For the jurisdiction of the Appellate Term in the Second Department, see 22 NYCRR § 730.1.

[18] Uniform Justice Ct. Act § 201. Some local variation is permitted. Id.

[19] Id., § 208.

[20] Id., § 403.

[21] Id., § 1701.

in § 1801 of the relevant court acts. A useful description of small claims practice is found in Siegel, New York Practice 1005-19 (4th ed. 2005).

A related institution is the commercial claims parts, which were introduced into New York law by Ch. 653 of the Laws of 1987. This statute mandates the creation of special parts for the hearing of "commercial claims" in the New York City Civil Court, the District Courts and the City Courts.[21]

A "commercial claim" is a claim for money only which does not exceed $5,000, when the claimant is a corporation, partnership or association.[22]

Commercial claims parts use informal rules of procedure similar to those used in the small claims parts. The commercial claims parts are essentially small claims courts for local businesses.

[H] Family Courts

The Family Courts have original statewide jurisdiction over proceedings involving support, paternity, custody, adoption, family offenses, juvenile delinquents, persons in need of supervision and other juvenile matters.[23] There is one in each county. Curiously, they have no jurisdiction over divorce or separation proceedings, which must be heard in the Supreme Court. Language in the Family Court Act purporting to vest exclusive jurisdiction over some matters in Family Court[24] should not be relied upon. In *Kagen v. Kagen, supra,* the Court of Appeals held that the broad grant of jurisdiction to the Supreme Court in Article 6, § 7 of the Constitution overrode any apparent limitations on Supreme Court jurisdiction in the Family Court Act. With few exceptions, however, the Supreme Court will not entertain cases over which Family Court also has jurisdiction. Appeals from Family Court are heard by the Appellate Division.[25] Family Court process may be served statewide and beyond when the CPLR or the Family Court Act permits.[26]

---

[21] *See* New York City Civil Court Act Article 18-A; Ch. 653, L. 1987.

[22] To use the commercial claims parts of the New York City Civil Court the claimant must have its principal office in New York City and the defendant must either reside in the City or have an office for the transaction of business there or have regular employment in the City. N.Y.C. Civil Court Act § 1801-A.

[23] N.Y. Const. Art. 6, § 13; Family Ct. Act § 115. Family Ct. Act § 641 provides that the Surrogate's Court and Family Court may exercise concurrent jurisdiction over adoption proceedings.

[24] *E.g.,* Family Ct. Act § 115, *cf.* Family Ct. Act § 114.

[25] Family Ct. Act § 1111.

[26] N.Y. Const. Art. 6, § 1(c); Family Ct. Act § 165. *See also* Uniform Child Custody Jurisdiction Act, Dom. Rel. Law § 75-a to § 75-z.

[I] Surrogate's Courts

This court's jurisdiction pertains to matters relating to the affairs of decedents, their estates, infants and incompetents.[27] It will also exercise jurisdiction over a broad range of disputes if they impact on estate litigation already before the court.[28]

Each county has a Surrogate's Court, though in some counties the Judge of the County Court is also the Surrogate. The court enjoys some long-arm jurisdiction.[29] Appeals are heard in the Appellate Division.[30]

[J] Court of Claims

The Court of Claims has exclusive jurisdiction over a broad list of claims against the state, including those sounding in tort and contract.[31] Claims against some, but not all, public authorities must be brought in the Court of Claims. The question turns in each case on the relationship between the given body and the state.[32]

Another problem arises when an action is brought against an employee of the state who committed the actionable wrong during the course of his duties. The action must be brought in the Court of Claims notwithstanding that the individual is the named defendant if the state is the real party in interest. The Court of Appeals discussed the issue in *Morell v. Balasubramanian*:[33]

> A suit against a State officer will be held to be one which is really asserted against the State when it arises from actions or determinations of the officer made in his or her official role and involves rights asserted, not against the officer individually, but solely against the State. Thus, an action for damages against the director of the State Lottery Division stemming from a disputed termination of claimant's licensee agreement, was, in actuality, an action against the State; it could, therefore, be brought only in the Court of Claims. . . . Where, however, the suit against the State agent or officer is in tort for damages arising from the breach of duty owed individually by such agent or officer directly to the injured party, the State is not the real party in interest — even though

---

[27] N.Y. Const. Art. 6, § 12; Surr. Ct. Proc. Act §§ 201, 1750; Fam. Ct. Act § 641.

[28] *In re Estate of Piccione*, 57 N.Y.2d 278, 456 N.Y.S.2d 669 (1982) (eviction proceeding); *Matter of Rothko*, 69 Misc. 2d 752, 330 N.Y.S.2d 915 (Surr. Ct.), *aff'd*, 40 A.D.2d 1083, 338 N.Y.S.2d 855 (1st Dep't 1972) (action to rescind contracts to sell paintings by the deceased).

[29] Surr. Ct. Proc. Act § 210.

[30] *Id.*, § 2701; CPLR 5701.

[31] N.Y. Const. Art. 6 § 9; Court of Claims Act §§ 8, 9.

[32] *E.g.*, *Easley v. N.Y.S. Thruway Auth.*, 1 N.Y.2d 374, 153 N.Y.S.2d 28, 135 N.E.2d 572 (1956).

[33] 70 N.Y.2d 297, 300, 520 N.Y.S.2d 530, 531-32, 514 N.E.2d 1101, 1102-03 (1987).

it could be held secondarily liable for the tortious acts under respondeat superior. Thus, an action arising out of a traffic accident against a hospital operating a State ambulance service was not one against the state as real party in interest.

Procedure, which is governed by the Court of Claims Act, is in some respects markedly different from that provided in the CPLR. Appeals are to the Appellate Division in the department in which the claim arose.[34]

[K] Courts on the Judiciary

A number of different procedures and tribunals are provided for the removal, retirement and disciplining of judges in sections 22 to 24 of Article 6 of the New York Constitution. The most important tribunal for trying judges is the Commission on Judicial Conduct, which consists of eleven members appointed variously by legislative leaders, the Governor, and the Chief Judge of the Court of Appeals.[35] Decisions of the Commission are subject to review by the Court of Appeals.

[L] Appellate Courts

[1] Court of Appeals

The Court of Appeals — the state court of last resort — has only appellate judicial jurisdiction.[36]

In addition, it has the power to make rules regulating the admission of attorneys and to appoint the state board of examiners.[37] With but few exceptions it hears appeals only from the Appellate Division. Its jurisdiction is described in Chapter 21, *infra*. The Court has an official website that is a very rich source of information, www.courts.state.ny.us/ctapps. It includes recent decisions, the Court's docket, biographies of the judges, and webcasts of the oral arguments of selected cases.

[2] Appellate Division of the Supreme Court

The Appellate Division, though technically a branch of the Supreme Court, a court of statewide jurisdiction, acts through four judicial departments, each covering a separate geographical area. Its members are appointed from among

---

[34] Ct. Cl. Act § 24.

[35] N.Y. Const. Art. 6, § 22.

[36] N.Y. Const. Art. 6, § 3.

[37] Judiciary Law §§ 53, 56.

Supreme Court Justices by the Governor for five-year terms. While basically a court of appellate jurisdiction, with jurisdiction over appeals from the Supreme Court, the Appellate Terms and County Courts, it has some original jurisdiction as well.[38] Its jurisdiction is described in § 11.04 and Chapter 21, *infra*.

[3] Appellate Term of the Supreme Court

The Appellate Division in each department is authorized by the Constitution to establish an Appellate Term staffed by Justices of the Supreme Court to hear appeals from the Civil Court of the City of New York, City Courts outside the City of New York, District Courts and County Courts.[39] Only the First and Second Departments have exercised their powers to establish an Appellate Term.[40]

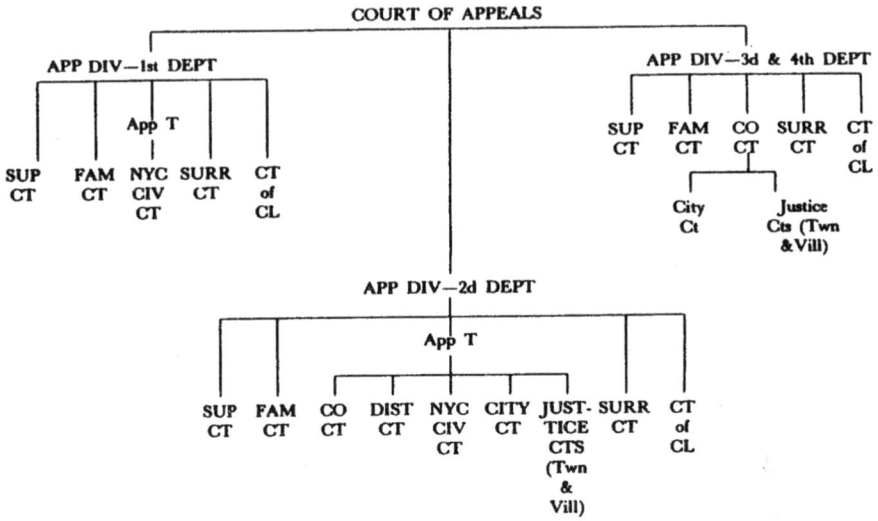

NEW YORK COURTS OF CIVIL JURISDICTION

---

[38] *See, e.g.*, CPLR 506(b) (Article 78 proceeding against certain judges); CPLR 3222(b) (action on submitted facts); CPLR 7002(b) (habeas corpus); CPLR 9401 (admission of attorneys).

[39] N.Y. Const. Art. 6, § 8.

[40] 22 NYCRR §§ 640.1 *et seq*; § 730.1.

NOTE

The existence of the many trial courts described in this chapter, each with its own peculiarities of jurisdiction, is confusing to the public, not to mention law students and even the bar. (A description of each of New York State's courts as well as their location is available at the official web site, www.courts.state.ny.us. This site also post reports, news releases and the decisions of some of the courts.) Errors inevitably caused by this confusion lead to extra cost and delay for litigants, if not more serious injustice. Further, overlap and duplication of functions in the courts is probably inefficient. One obvious solution, the merger of several of these courts into more comprehensive tribunals, has been proposed by Judith Kaye, Chief Judge of the Court of Appeals for the State of New York, and Jonathan Lippman, the Chief Administrative Judge of New York. They have posted their proposal at www.courts.state.ny.us/reform.html. In essence, it would create two tiers: One would be a supreme court of general jurisdiction (including cases now brought before the Supreme Court, the surrogate's courts, the family courts, the county courts, and the Court of Claims) and the second would be a "district court" to hear minor civil and criminal cases. Judge Lippman has argued that merger will have a two-pronged benefit for the state court system. First, it will reduce the cost of litigation and create a more efficient judiciary. This will further attract businesses to New York, creating economic and social stability. Second, merging the present court system will assist minorities, women and children in establishing a voice as a greater proportion of a more meaningful judiciary. *See* N.Y.L.J., May 6, 1998, pp. 25-26.

Opponents of court merger argue that specialized courts are more, not less, efficient because of the expertise of the judges and administrators who serve on them; that the unification would be prohibitively expensive because of the need to increase the salaries of now inferior court judges who would effectively be promoted by the reorganization; and that the prestige of the present Supreme Court would suffer if merged with other courts, making it more difficult to attract the best quality lawyers to serve. Political considerations have been relevant to this debate, as any court reorganization would shift appointive powers from one group to another. According to Professor Johnstone, "the existing structure is so archaic and the arguments for retaining it so weak that major reform seems probable within the next decade." Quintin Johnstone, *New York State Courts: Their Structure, Administration and Reform Possibilities,* 43 N.Y. L. Sch. L. Rev. 915, 972 (1999). *See generally* Fox, *Legislators Hear Pros, Cons of Court Merger*, 178 N.Y.L.J. 62, Sept. 28, 1977, at 1, col. 4; Barbanel, *Simplifying New York's Complex Court System*, New York Times, Mar. 13, 1982 at 28. An informative analysis of court unification efforts throughout the United States is provided by Larry Berkson, et al., *Organizing the State Courts: Is Structural Consolidation Justified?*, 45 Brook. L. Rev. 1 (1978). The merits of court specialization receive sophisticated attention in Rochelle C. Dreyfuss, *Forums of the Future: The Role of Specialized Courts in Resolving Business*

Disputes, 61 Brook. L. Rev. 1 (1995), and Jeffrey W. Stempel, *Two Cheers for Specialization*, 61 Brook. L. Rev. 67 (1995).

§ 3.05 REMOVAL WITHIN THE STATE COURT SYSTEM

What happens when a litigant confronted with the confusing panoply of courts just described makes the wrong choice? A court lacking subject matter jurisdiction may, of course, dismiss the action. An alternative, permitted by Article 6 of the State Constitution and CPLR 325 is the transfer or "removal" of certain cases from one court to another. These rules are also intended to afford the courts power to protect their dockets from cases which should properly be in inferior courts. Rules allowing removal of an action or proceeding from one court to another should not be confused with other rules allowing a change of venue. The latter, discussed in Chapter 4, concern transfer from one locale to another, *e.g.*, from Supreme Court, Queens County to Supreme Court, Duchess County, rather than from one court to another.

OFFNER v. ROTHSCHILD
Supreme Court, Kings County
87 Misc. 2d 565, 386 N.Y.S.2d 188 (1976)

MEMORANDUM

CHARLES R. RUBIN, JUSTICE.

. . . .

From many months of presiding in the trial term calendar part of this court, it appears to me that this case is just one of many which should not have been brought in this court in the first instance, and which should properly be in the Civil Court of the City of New York. However, it has come to the court's attention that the current practice of transferring cases from this court to the Civil Court results in a pattern of preference to those cases brought in an improper forum over those cases properly brought, without any penalty to the plaintiffs in the former. In the interests of the proper administration of the calendars of this court this practice must cease. Judicial efficiency is a goal which should be striven for and attained by both the courts and practicing bar.

Although the instant case is just an example of this type of abuse, a brief summary of the circumstances here involved will assist the bar in more fully understanding the problem which confronts the court.

This action arises from a fall on a sidewalk on August 12, 1974 in Brooklyn, New York.

The medical reports submitted by plaintiff indicate that she fell forward on her hands and struck her forehead. Dr. Lloyd G. Bayme, the treating physician, diagnosed the injuries as follows: cerebral concussion; contusion of the right forehead with periorbital hematoma; contusion and abrasion of right hand; contusion and abrasion of left hand; severe sprain of right wrist.

Neither doctor found any disability or permanent injury as a result of the accident. The medical expenses claimed are $35 for Dr. Bayme's consultation, $90 for six office visits, $40 for x-rays, $20 for Dr. Freilich's examination, plus $65 for new eyeglasses, for a total of $250. Plaintiff was a housewife and no loss of earnings is claimed.

The examining physician for one of the defendants reported that on November 14, 1974, there were no scars and that plaintiff "has made an excellent recovery from the alleged injuries."

It is obvious that any damages that may have been suffered by plaintiff can be compensated for well within the monetary limits of the Civil Court, to wit, $10,000 [now $25,000. — Eds]. The complaint herein demands damages of $100,000.

In light of these circumstances the court requested that plaintiff consent, pursuant to CPLR 325(c), to a removal to Civil Court with a reduction in amount of damages sought to the monetary limit of that court. This request was refused.

The practice of this court has been in such instances to order a removal to Civil Court pursuant to subdivision (d) of CPLR 325. . . . However, subdivision (d) provides that an action removed pursuant to that portion of the law retains limitation as to monetary jurisdiction of the court in which the action was originally commenced.

This court is aware of the fact that since the advent of no fault automobile insurance, with its threshold requirement for the institution of lawsuits (Insurance Law 670 *et seq.*), as well as efficient disposition of cases, the calendars in the Civil Court, Kings County are not backlogged and that a trial may be had within a short period of time after filing of a note of issue. On the other hand, this court has become burdened with numerous newly popular types of actions such as products liability and medical malpractice, often involving large amounts of damage, as well as the normal equity and criminal jurisdictions reserved to this court, to such an extent that litigants often wait years before their cases are reached for trial.

Thus, by transferring a case to the Civil Court with an ad damnum clause above the monetary limitation of that court, a preference is created whereby a plaintiff who should have brought suit in Civil Court in the first instance, receives a trial far in advance of plaintiffs who properly commenced their actions in Supreme Court, with no difference in limitation of the monetary amount sought.

It is the opinion of this court that it is within the power of the Supreme Court under its constitutional jurisdiction to remedy this situation.

Article 6, section 19(a) of the New York State Constitution provides:

> The supreme court may transfer any action or proceeding, except one over which it shall have exclusive jurisdiction which does not depend upon the monetary amount sought, to any other court having jurisdiction of the subject matter within the judicial department provided that such other court has jurisdiction over the classes of persons named as parties.

It thus appears that this court is authorized by its inherent constitutional powers to make transfers to the Civil Court with the monetary limits of the Civil Court to apply. . . .

Accordingly, in the exercise of its inherent constitutional powers this court transfers this action to the Civil Court of the City of New York, Kings County, with the limits of monetary jurisdiction of the Civil Court to apply.

NOTES

(1) The preceding case deals with removal down, *i.e.*, from the Supreme Court to a court of inferior jurisdiction. Removal down may be voluntary, CPLR 325(c), or may be against the plaintiff's wishes. In the latter case, the removal is authorized by CPLR 325(d). Authority to remove cases to an inferior court is also found in the Uniform Rules of the Supreme Court and County Courts, 22 NYCRR 202.13. The rule allows removal from the Supreme Court in the City of New York to the New York City Civil Court; from the Supreme Court in the Second, Third and Fourth Departments to the County and City Courts in those departments. The Supreme Court in Nassau and Suffolk Counties may also remove actions to the District Courts. Actions removed under these provisions are not subject to the monetary limitations of the transferee court.

Whether or not an implementing rule has been adopted, removal down may be made involuntarily pursuant to Article VI, § 19(a) of the New York Constitution, relied on in the principal case. Why does it matter whether the court invokes CPLR 325(d) or Article VI, § 19(a) in ordering removal?

The Uniform Rules were amended in 1998 to prohibit removal to the New York City Civil Court at a pretrial conference unless the case will be reached for trial in the transferee court within 30 days of the removal. If the case is not removed because it cannot be reached for trial within 30 days, then it must retain its original place on the Supreme Court docket. 22 NYCRR 202.26(g)(2). The amendment was made because backlogged dockets in the New York City Civil Court sometimes caused substantial delay in the trial of removed cases, contrary to the purposes of CPLR 325(d).

(2) Removal up or, indeed, laterally, is also permitted: If the plaintiff mistakenly commences the action in the wrong court, CPLR 325(a) provides that

rather than dismissing, the Supreme Court "upon motion, may remove the action to the proper court, upon such terms as may be just."

CPLR 325(b) overlaps paragraph (a) of CPLR 325, but is intended to meet a somewhat different problem. It provides that "a court having such jurisdiction may remove the action to itself" where "it appears that the court in which [the] action is pending does not have jurisdiction to grant the relief to which the parties are entitled." This situation typically arises when a plaintiff, believing the damages to be less than the jurisdictional maximum of the relevant inferior court, commences the action in an inferior court but later discovers that the injuries are more serious than first appeared, and that only in the Supreme Court may he obtain the proper recovery. The motion for removal "up" pursuant to CPLR 325(b) must be supported by a physician's affidavit clearly linking the new symptoms to the original tort, *Northern Ins. Co. of N.Y. v. Kregsman*, 26 A.D.2d 648, 272 N.Y.S.2d 427 (2d Dep't 1966), and should be made promptly after learning of the change in condition.

(3) In one unusual case, the Supreme Court, Kings County, transferred a breach of contract action from the New York City Civil Court to itself in order to amend the prayer for relief to an amount which exceeded the jurisdictional limit of the Civil Court. The Supreme Court then transferred the case back to the Civil Court pursuant to CPLR 325(d). In upholding the re-transfer to the Civil Court, the Appellate Division explained:

> It is not at all illogical that the Supreme Court might conclude that the plaintiff's damages will ultimately be more than the $25,000 originally sought but less than the $40,888.25 now sought in the increased ad damnum clause. Nor does it appear that the issues are so complex as to warrant a trial in the Supreme Court, with its attendant delays.

Mittman v. International Menswear, Ltd., 125 A.D.2d 377, 509 N.Y.S.2d 104 (2d Dep't 1986).

(4) In *Spinnell v. Sassower*, 155 Misc. 2d 147, 589 N.Y.S.2d 230 (N.Y.C. Civ. Ct. 1992), it was held that CPLR 325(d) does not permit the Supreme Court to transfer an action to an inferior court which lacks personal jurisdiction over the defendant, even if the transferor court itself had such jurisdiction. The court stated: "the Civil Court will not automatically have, or derivatively acquire, jurisdiction upon transfer simply because the Supreme Court had jurisdiction. . . . A plain reading of CPLR 325(d) reveals that the Legislature intended that the transferee lower court have both subject matter and personal jurisdiction." (Do you agree?) The Civil Court concluded that, since it lacked jurisdiction to hear the merits, it also lacked jurisdiction to transfer the case back to the Supreme Court. How could the plaintiff get to a tribunal that would hear the claims?

Incidentally, how could the lower court lack personal jurisdiction if the Supreme Court had it?

Chapter 4

VENUE: REFINING THE CHOICE
WITHIN NEW YORK

§ 4.01 GENERAL PRINCIPLES

Venue, like the concepts discussed in the preceding three chapters, restricts the plaintiff's choice of forum. State venue rules differ from those of personal jurisdiction and forum non conveniens in that they dictate the county within the state in which the action should be brought, rather than whether the action can be brought in the state at all.[1] Incorrect venue will not lead to dismissal but to transfer to the proper county. *See* CPLR 509; *Benson v. Eastern Building & Loan Ass'n.*, 174 N.Y. 83, 66 N.E. 627 (1903).

Experienced litigators know that the venue in which an action is tried can be important to the result. A New York Jury Reporter study of jury verdicts in New York City between 1984 and 1993 provides empirical support for this view. The study measured differences among the counties within New York City in the percentage of jury verdicts won by plaintiffs and defendants and the average amount of compensatory damages awarded to successful plaintiffs:

Personal Injury Verdicts by County 1984-93

County	Plaintiffs	Defendants	Avg. Verdict
New York	61%	39%	$1,266,000
Bronx	74%	26%	$1,342,000
Kings	65%	35%	$1,129,000
Queens	55%	45%	$1,935,000

Adams, *Venue Crucial to Tort Awards*, N.Y.L.J., April 4, 1994, at 2.

In subsequent years, reported verdicts continued to vary greatly by county. From 1995-99, the average of verdicts returned within New York City published by the New York Jury Verdict Reporter ranged from a high of $1,278,000 in Bronx County to a low of $176,000 in Richmond County. Other averages by county were: Kings County, $1,000,100; New York County, $724,000; Queens County, $449,000; and Westchester County, $112,000. *See* 17 New York Jury Verdict Reporter, Issue 30, p. 1 (2000). Averages for subsequent years were not

---

[1] As we saw in Chapter 3, there are special rules of in personam jurisdiction applicable in the inferior courts which may restrict the litigation to a particular place within the state. Such rules have no applicability in the Supreme Court, the Surrogate's Courts or the Family Courts.

available, but other interesting statistics show that during the period 1998-2003 the median plaintiff's verdict in actions against police was $357,000 in New York City and $100,394 in the rest of the state. 20 New York Jury Verdict Reporter, Issue 37, p. 1 (2003). The median plaintiff's verdict in motor-vehicle cases was $250,000 in Bronx County and $150,000 elsewhere in New York State. 20 New York Jury Verdict Reporter, Issue 41, p. 1 (2003).

Venue should not be confused with subject matter jurisdiction, because venue rules tell us not whether a particular court has the power to hear a case, but whether a court having such power should hear it. Though lack of subject matter jurisdiction can sometimes be cured under the removal provisions of CPLR 325 and the state Constitution, it, unlike improper venue, can sometimes result in dismissal.

As a general matter, a defect of venue, like one of personal jurisdiction but unlike one of subject matter jurisdiction, is waivable. CPLR 509. An exception to the waivability rule concerns actions based on consumer credit transactions and is discussed below.[2] Venue, it is often said, governs "the place of trial" and this terminology is used throughout CPLR article 5. *See, e.g.*, CPLR 509: "Notwithstanding any provision of this article, the place of trial of an action shall be in the county designated by the plaintiff. . . ." But the venue proper for trial is also proper (though not always exclusively so) for pre-trial proceedings such as motions, *see* CPLR 2212, and most depositions, *see* CPLR 3110.

How does venue differ from the doctrine of forum non conveniens? Re-read CPLR 327 and *Martin v. Mieth*, Chapter 2, *supra*.

§ 4.02 RULES GOVERNING VENUE[3]

[A] Designation by Plaintiff

The plaintiff designates the venue by stating it in the caption of the summons and complaint.[4] CPLR 305(a) further requires the summons to "specify the basis of the venue designated," *i.e.*, to state why the plaintiff believes the county indicated is the proper one. For an example, see the form of summons in § 5.04, *infra*.

---

[2] An additional exception to the general rule that defects of venue are waivable was announced in *Nolan v. Lungen*, 61 N.Y.2d 788, 473 N.Y.S.2d 388, 461 N.E.2d 874 (1984). The Court of Appeals there held non-waivable the requirement of CPLR 506(b) that proceedings against sitting judges of the Supreme and County Courts be brought in the Appellate Division.

[3] The remainder of this chapter has been adapted from Chapter 5 of Oscar G. Chase, CPLR Manual (Rev. ed.), 2005.

[4] CPLR 305(a); 2101(c).

[B] Rules Defining Proper County

[1] Transitory Actions; Residence of Parties

CPLR 503(a) sets forth the general rule governing venue of transitory actions.[5] With the exception of suits involving consumer credit transactions, to be discussed *infra*, CPLR 503(a) provides that venue in transitory actions may be placed in the county in which any one of the parties resides when the action is commenced. If the parties reside in different counties, the choice is made by the plaintiff.

It follows from the basic rule that if only one of the parties is a resident, proper venue is the county of residence of the resident party.[6] If none of the parties is a resident of the state, the statute expressly provides that any county that the plaintiff chooses to designate is the proper place of trial. CPLR 503(a).

Establishing the residence of an individual for venue purposes is not always easy. While the showing is not equivalent to that required to establish domicile[7] and a person may have more than one residence for venue purposes,[8] more is required than an occasional stay at a hotel.[9] The Court of Appeals has said that the residence of a party turns on whether he has a significant connection with some locality in New York as a result of living in the state for some length of time during the course of a year.[10] By its express terms, CPLR 503(a) gives way "where [venue is] otherwise prescribed by law." Special venue rules are other-

---

[5] For venue purposes, transitory actions are those not covered by CPLR 501 (agreements fixing venue), CPLR 507 (real property actions) or by CPLR 508 (actions to recover a chattel).

[6] *Petito v. Diesel*, 12 A.D.2d 792, 209 N.Y.S.2d 597 (2d Dep't 1961) (resident defendant).

[7] *Antone v. General Motors*, 64 N.Y.2d 20, 484 N.Y.S.2d 514, 473 N.E.2d 742 (1984) (domicile generally requires a physical presence in the state and an intention to make the state a permanent home). *See also Longwood Cent. Sch. Dist. v. Springs Union Free Sch. Dist.*, 1 N.Y.3d 385, 774 N.Y.S.2d 857, 806 N.E.2d 970 (2004) (domicile requires bodily presence in a place with an intent to make it a fixed and permanent home and an existing domicile is assumed to continue until a new one is acquired); *Hosley v. Curry*, 85 N.Y.2d 447, 626 N.Y.S.2d 32, 649 N.E.2d 1176 (1995) (for a change to a new domicile to be effected, there must be a union of residence in fact and an "absolute and fixed intention" to abandon the former and make the new locality a fixed and permanent home).

[8] *Katz v. Siroty*, 62 A.D.2d 1011, 403 N.Y.S.2d 770 (2d Dep't 1978); *Matter of Adoption of E.W.C.*, 89 Misc. 2d 64, 389 N.Y.S.2d 743 (Sur. Ct. 1976).

[9] *Katz v. Siroty*, 62 A.D.2d 1011, 403 N.Y.S.2d 770 (2d Dep't 1978):

> Although a person may have more than one residence for venue purposes (CPLR 503, subd [a]), to consider a place as such, he must stay there for some time and have the bona fide intent to retain the place as a residence for some length of time and with some degree of permanency. . . . Residence requires more stability than a brief sojourn for business, social or recreational activities. . . . The mere fact that plaintiff uses the Brooklyn home of his sister and brother-in-law as a stopover for convenience and to sleep there when in the area on business, does not establish a residence. . . .

[10] *Antone v. General Motors*, 64 N.Y.2d 20, 484 N.Y.S.2d 514, 473 N.E.2d 742 (1984) (while the case dealt with the interpretation of residence for the purposes of CPLR 202, the Court stated that the definition of residence for that section was the same as that used for venue purposes).

wise prescribed for specified types of parties by CPLR 504 and 505, for special proceedings by CPLR 506, for specified types of actions by CPLR 507 and 508, where venue is fixed by agreement by CPLR 501, and for consumer credit actions in CPLR 503(f). In addition, there are numerous more particular venue provisions elsewhere in the CPLR[11] and scattered throughout the substantive laws of the state, which take precedence over CPLR 503(a).[12] The general rule that the residence of the parties dictates venue is also qualified by CPLR 510(2), allowing a change of venue if an impartial trial cannot be had in the proper county, and by CPLR 510(3), allowing a change of venue for the convenience of material witnesses and the interests of justice. It is sometimes said that, because of the latter provision, and because most witnesses to an event will be found where the accident arose, that "other things being equal, a transitory action should be tried in the county where the cause of action arose."[13] This judge-made rule can be enforced by a motion to transfer venue or by a refusal to grant a change of venue from the county where the cause of action arose to a county in which a party resides.[14]

[2] Residence of Particular Types of Parties

The remainder of CPLR 503 contains special definitions of residence for particular types of parties.

[a] Certain Representative Parties

Subdivision (b) covers an executor, administrator, trustee, committee, conservator, general or testamentary guardian, or receiver. It provides that these representative parties have two residences for venue purposes — the county of appointment as well as the county of actual residence.

[b] Corporations

Pursuant to subdivision (c), a domestic corporation, or a foreign corporation authorized to transact business in the state, is deemed a resident of the county in which its principal office is located. A special provision regarding railroads

---

[11] *See, e.g.,* CPLR 7002(b) (habeas corpus); 7502(a) (arbitration).

[12] *See, e.g.,* Mental Hygiene Law § 78.03(b) (proceeding for declaration of incompetency must be brought in county of residence of alleged incompetent).

[13] *Risoli v. Long Island Lighting Co.,* 138 A.D.2d 316, 318, 526 N.Y.S.2d 449, 450 (1st Dep't 1988).

[14] *Varone v. Memoli,* 121 A.D.2d 213, 503 N.Y.S.2d 29 (1st Dep't 1986) (medical malpractice action, commenced in Bronx County where the treatment occurred, would not be transferred out of the Bronx even though no party resided there).

and other common carriers makes them residents of the county where the cause of action arose as well.

The county in which the principal office of a domestic corporation is located has been held to be the county designated in the certificate of incorporation as the place where the office of the corporation is to be located.[15]

A foreign corporation which has been authorized to transact business within the state is treated the same way as a domestic corporation; its "principal office" means, under § 102(10) of the Business Corporation Law, "the office the location of which is stated . . . in the application for authority of a foreign corporation or an amendment thereof." A foreign corporation which has not obtained authority to do business in the state is considered a nonresident in applying CPLR 503.[16]

[c]　Unincorporated Association, Partnership, or Individually Owned Business

A president or treasurer of an unincorporated association, suing or being sued on behalf of the association, is deemed a resident of any county in which the association has its principal office, as well as the county in which that person actually resides. Similarly, a partnership or an individually owned business is deemed a resident of any county in which it has its principal office, as well as the county in which the partner or individual owner suing or being sued actually resides.

[d]　Assignee

Subdivision (e) of CPLR 503 is designed to prevent circumvention of the venue rules by assigning a claim to a resident of the county in which venue is desired. Limited to "actions for a sum of money only" brought by an assignee, it provides that the assignee's residence shall be deemed the same as that of "the original assignor at the time of the original assignment." Reference to the "original" assignor's residence prevents circumvention of the provision by successive assignments. Actions by assignees for the benefit of creditors or holders in due course of a negotiable instrument are excepted from its coverage. The former are clearly bona fide assignees, and they are generally in no position to consider questions of venue in determining whether to accept the assignment; the sec-

---

[15] *Bryan v. Hagemann*, 31 A.D.2d 905, 298 N.Y.S.2d 101 (1st Dep't 1969). *But see Weiss v. Saks Fifth Avenue*, 157 A.D.2d 475, 549 N.Y.S.2d 400 (1st Dept. 1990) (the principal office for venue purposes could be the actual principal place of operations, even if different from the address designated in the corporate charter).

[16] *Reliable Displays Corp. v. Maro Industries, Inc.*, 67 Misc. 2d 747, 325 N.Y.S.2d 616 (Sup. Ct. 1971).

ond exclusion avoids interfering with the policy of free transferability of negotiable instruments.

[3] Real Property Actions

CPLR 507 provides that the place of trial of an action in which the judgment
demanded would affect the title to, or the possession, use or enjoyment of, real
property shall be in the county in which any part of the subject of the action is
situated.

The "real property action" is the classic "local" action, to be distinguished from
"transitory" actions. Trial in the county of the realty is favored "[i]n the interest of orderly procedure and for the sake of facility and certainty in title
records."[17] When local and transitory actions are consolidated, the courts will
normally apply the venue provisions of CPLR 507.[18] Difficulty sometimes arises
in determining what actions involving real property come within the scope of
this venue statute. It is often said that an action which affects title to real
property is local, while one which merely "involves" it is transitory,[19] but this
aphorism does not explain all the cases. In any event it seems clear that CPLR
507 embraces all those actions which were specifically enumerated in the predecessor provision — i.e., ejectment; partition; dower; foreclosure of a mortgage
upon real property, or upon a chattel real; compelling the determination of a
claim to real property; waste; nuisance; and procurement of a judgment directing a conveyance of real property. Other actions held to come within the statute
include those for trespass,[20] those on contracts for the sale of real property,[21]
and those, other than summary eviction proceedings,[22] which would affect a
leasehold interest.[23]

[4] Actions to Recover a Chattel

An action to recover a chattel pursuant to CPLR Article 71, often referred to
as replevin, can be treated for venue purposes as either local or transitory.

---

[17] *Reichenbach v. Corn Exch. Bank Trust Co.*, 249 A.D. 539, 541, 292 N.Y.S. 732, 734 (1st Dep't
1937). *See also Edward Joy Co. v. McGuire & Bennett, Inc.*, 199 A.D.2d 1015, 608 N.Y.S.2d 26 (4th
Dep't 1993) (because a mechanic's lien is an encumbrance on real property, an action to foreclose such
lien must be brought in the county in which the real property is located).

[18] *Town of Hempstead v. City of New York*, 88 Misc. 2d 366, 369, 388 N.Y.S.2d 78, 80 (Sup. Ct.
1976).

[19] *E.g., Winston v. Krinsky*, 30 A.D.2d 524, 290 N.Y.S.2d 247 (1st Dep't 1968).

[20] *Geidel v. Niagara Mohawk Power Corp.*, 46 Misc. 2d 990, 261 N.Y.S.2d 379 (Sup. Ct. 1965).

[21] *Merrill Realty Co. v. Harris*, 44 A.D.2d 629, 353 N.Y.S.2d 570 (3d Dep't 1974).

[22] These are governed by Article 7, Real Prop. Acts. & Proc. Law.

[23] *E.g., Moschera & Catalano, Inc., v. Advanced Structures Corp.*, 104 A.D.2d 306, 478 N.Y.S.2d
641 (1st Dep't 1984).

CPLR 508 provides that venue in such cases "may" be in the county in which any part of the subject property is located. By implication, the plaintiff has the option of relying on the residence provisions of CPLR 503(a).

[5] Consumer Credit Cases

CPLR 503(f) and its companion, CPLR 513, were enacted in 1973[24] to eliminate the harsh situation in which a consumer is sued in a county far from home and far from the county in which the sale took place. It provides that where a purchaser, borrower or debtor is a defendant in an action arising out of a consumer credit transaction, as defined in CPLR 105(f), the place of trial must be either in the county of the defendant's residence if that is in New York State, or in the county where the transaction took place, if it occurred within the state. Only if the defendant is a non-resident and the transaction occurred outside the state do the provisions of subdivision (a) of CPLR 503 apply. Because the right to proper venue is ordinarily waivable, CPLR 513 was enacted concurrently with CPLR 503(f) to effectuate it. Absent the enactment of CPLR 513, if venue had been misstated, a defendant would have been required to undergo the trouble and expense of making an appearance to contest venue. CPLR 513(a) requires a clerk in an action arising out of a consumer credit transaction to refuse to accept for filing a summons which on its face indicates that the proper venue is a county other than the county where such summons is offered for filing.

If there has been a failure to commence the action and file the summons in the proper county, the plaintiff need not go through the effort and expense of serving the defendant a second time with a summons citing the proper venue. Service of the original summons will be deemed complete ten days after the copy of the summons which was rejected for filing is filed in the proper county with proof of service upon the defendant of the summons together with other supporting papers specified in CPLR 513(c).

[6] Agreements Fixing Venue

A written agreement fixing the place of trial, made before an action is commenced, is enforceable by a motion for change of venue. CPLR 501. The court may refuse to enforce the agreement on the ground that an impartial trial may not be obtained in the specified county, CPLR 510(2), or because the enforcement of the provision would work extreme hardship.[25] A venue-fixing provision has also been nullified when the plaintiff attacked the validity of the entire contract.[26]

---

[24] Ch. 238, Laws of 1973, eff. Sept. 1, 1973.

[25] *Gardner & North Roofing & Siding Corp. v. Demko*, 82 Misc. 2d 922, 370 N.Y.S.2d 294 (Sup. Ct. 1974).

[26] *Colby v. Ben Constr. Corp.*, 57 Misc. 2d 850, 293 N.Y.S.2d 759 (Sup. Ct. 1968).

§ 4.03 CHANGE OF VENUE

[A] In General

CPLR 510 specifies the three grounds that authorize a change of venue from the county designated in the plaintiff's summons and complaint. It provides that:

> The court, upon motion, may change the place of trial of an action where:
>
> 1. The county designated for that purpose is not a proper county; or
>
> 2. there is reason to believe that an impartial trial cannot be had in the proper county; or
>
> 3. the convenience of material witnesses and the ends of justice will be promoted by the change.

Paragraph (1) applies when the county designated by the plaintiff is not a county authorized by the provisions of CPLR 503-508 or other more specific provisions of law governing venue or place of trial. In such cases, the "demand" procedure of CPLR 511, discussed in subsection [B] below, comes into play. If the plaintiff has designated a proper county, the defendant can obtain a change of venue by motion (not by demand) only by showing that paragraph (2) or (3) of CPLR 510 applies.

[B] Improper County

The defendant may have venue changed on the ground specified in CPLR 510(1), only if the county designated by the plaintiff is not a proper one.[27] But if the county designated by the plaintiff is improper, the defendant may have venue changed to a proper county as of right upon compliance with the procedure of CPLR 511(a) and (b). And when there is more than one proper county, the change must be to the one designated in the defendant's demand; by designating an improper county, the plaintiff has forfeited to the defendant the right to choose among them.[28] The plaintiff does have the right, on the other hand, to cross-move to retain venue in the "improper" county on grounds specified in CPLR 510(2) or (3).[29] The proper procedure for seeking a change on "improper county" grounds is set forth in CPLR 511, subdivisions (a) and (b). Instead of moving directly under CPLR 510(1), the defendant — with or before service of

---

[27] *Feldman v. No. Shore Univ. Hosp.*, 157 A.D.2d 831, 550 N.Y.S.2d 420 (2d Dept. 1990); *Schwartz v. Schwartz*, 274 App. Div. 1082, 85 N.Y.S.2d 616 (3d Dep't 1949).

[28] *E.g., Schenker v. Pepperidge Farm Inc.*, 42 Misc. 2d 380, 248 N.Y.S.2d 269 (Sup. Ct. 1964).

[29] *Dickman v. Stummer*, 20 A.D.2d 611, 245 N.Y.S.2d 519 (3d Dep't 1963).

the answer — serves upon the plaintiff a demand that venue be changed to a specified proper county. The plaintiff then has five days within which to serve a written consent to the change. If no such consent is served, the defendant may, within fifteen days from the time he served the demand, move to change the venue under CPLR 510(1) on the ground that the county specified by the plaintiff was improper.

By this procedure, the necessity for a motion is avoided in cases where the plaintiff does not dispute that the county originally designated is improper and that the one specified by the defendant is proper, or where for any other reason the plaintiff is willing to agree to the change. If the plaintiff does not agree, the parties' contentions as to the proper county are determined on the merits by the motion under CPLR 510(1).

An additional facet of the procedure concerns the place for making the motion. By virtue of the last sentence of section 511(b), the defendant whose timely demand has not been consented to, may make the motion to change venue returnable in the county he thinks is proper, unless the plaintiff, within five days after the defendant's demand, serves an affidavit, showing "either that the county specified by the defendant is not proper or that the county designated by him is proper." CPLR 511(b). If the plaintiff does serve such an affidavit, the defendant must make the motion to change venue in the county designated by the plaintiff or one of the alternatives permitted by CPLR 2212(a) for motions in an action pending in the county. The plaintiff's affidavit cannot simply assert in conclusory terms that the designated county is proper; it must set forth facts showing it to be proper or it will be treated as a nullity.[30]

[C] Impartial Trial

Paragraph 2 of CPLR 510 authorizes the court to change venue when there is reason to believe that an impartial trial cannot be had in the proper county. Either party may move to change venue on this ground, despite the fact that the plaintiff originally chose the venue. The plaintiff may not become aware of the bias until after commencing the action.[31] The statute itself expressly contemplates transfer from a "proper" county, and it is of no moment that the transfer results in placing venue in a county otherwise "improper."

The burden is on the moving party to show by facts and circumstances that there is a reasonable basis for his belief that an impartial trial cannot be had. This standard is not susceptible of precise application, but the prediction of partiality must be based on specifics; conjectural fears couched in conclusory language will not support a change. Venue transfers have been permitted when one

---

[30] *Payne v. Civil Service Employees Ass'n*, 15 A.D.2d 265, 222 N.Y.S.2d 725 (3d Dep't 1961).

[31] *See, e.g., Kenford Co. v. County of Erie*, 38 A.D.2d 781, 328 N.Y.S.2d 69 (4th Dep't 1972).

party has a personal relationship to the court which will try the action,[32] and when there is strong evidence of community partiality.[33]

[D] Convenience of Witnesses and Ends of Justice

The ground specified in paragraph 3 of CPLR 510 — that "the convenience of material witnesses and the ends of justice will be promoted by the change" — is the most common reason for changes of venue. The criteria for the motion under CPLR 510(3) are most directly pertinent to these objectives of the law of venue. In any event, upon motion by a party, they afford an important release from the sometimes arbitrary operation of the rules governing what is a "proper county."

The motion, which must be made within a "reasonable time after commencement of the action," CPLR 511(a), may be made by either party.[34] In the usual case it is made by the defendant when the county designated in the complaint is a proper one, and the action would therefore remain in that county, unless there are grounds for changing it to another under CPLR 510(2) or 510(3). As to the convenience of witnesses, the moving papers should include the following:

(a) [A]n affidavit of merits;

(b) the names, addresses and occupations of the witnesses demonstrating that the county where the trial is desired would serve their convenience . . . ;

(c) the party must show . . . what he expects to prove by these named witnesses, and has been advised by him that such witnesses are necessary and material on the trial, as he himself verily believes;

(d) the affidavits must disclose the substance of the testimony which the proposed witnesses will give at the trial and show how it is material.[35]

---

[32] *Cf. Burstein v. Greene*, 61 A.D.2d 827, 402 N.Y.S.2d 227 (2d Dep't 1978) (plaintiff's wife a sitting justice).

[33] *Althiser v. Richmondville Creamery Co.*, 27 Misc. 2d 456, 215 N.Y.S.2d 324 (Sup. Ct. 1960), *aff'd*, 13 A.D.2d 162, 215 N.Y.S.2d 122 (3d Dep't 1961) (plaintiffs, 126 dairy farmers, disputed milk prices; transfer ordered from their rural county of residence).

[34] *Lindsley v. Sheldon*, 43 Misc. 116, 88 N.Y.S. 192 (Sup. Ct. 1904). *But see Cosmos Forms, Ltd. v. Furst*, 172 A.D.2d 403, 568 N.Y.S.2d 783 (1st Dep't 1991) (a transfer of venue in the interests of justice could be granted on the court's own motion).

[35] *Searing v. Randall Cadillac Corp.*, 3 Misc. 2d 594, 596, 151 N.Y.S.2d 163, 165-66 (Sup. Ct. 1956), *aff'd after reargument*, 3 Misc. 2d 594, 158 N.Y.S.2d 358 (Sup. Ct. 1956); *see also Hurlbut v. Whalen*, 58 A.D.2d 311, 396 N.Y.S.2d 518 (4th Dep't 1977).

One disadvantage of moving to transfer venue on this ground should be apparent; it requires the movant to reveal not only the proposed means of proof, but also to openly assess the witnesses' importance.

Because most of the witnesses to an event giving rise to a transitory cause of action will usually live in the county where the cause of action arose, there is a rule of thumb under which that county is preferred.[36] As is illustrated by *Martin v. Mieth*, Chapter 2, *supra*, transfer to that county may be denied if it can be shown that the material witnesses do not reside there.

The respective calendar conditions in each of the counties under consideration are also sometimes considered on a motion to change venue.[37]

---

[36] *E.g., Risoli v. Long Island Lighting Co.*, 138 A.D.2d 316, 526 N.Y.S.2d 449, 450 (1st Dep't 1988); *Blackfriars Realty Corp. v. Ettlinger*, 56 A.D.2d 826, 393 N.Y.S.2d 30 (1st Dep't 1977).

[37] *E.g., Edwards v. Lamberta*, 42 A.D.2d 1003, 348 N.Y.S.2d 225 (3d Dep't 1973) (affirming denial of change of venue to a county with a backlogged calendar).

Chapter 5

COMMENCING THE ACTION AND SERVICE OF THE SUMMONS

§ 5.01 INTRODUCTORY NOTES

(1) A plaintiff who has considered the issues treated in Chapters 1-4 is ready to choose a forum and commence the action. In the Supreme Court and in the County Courts, an action is commenced by filing a summons with notice or summons and complaint with the clerk of the court in which the action is brought. CPLR 304. At the time of filing, the plaintiff must also pay the fee required for the issuance of an index number. CPLR 306-a. The fee is currently two-hundred ten dollars. CPLR 8018(a)(1), (3).

Prior to 1992, when the legislature enacted the "commencement by filing" system, actions were commenced throughout New York by the service of the summons or summons and complaint. Of course, even under the current system, jurisdiction over the defendant is not acquired merely by filing the summons with notice or summons and complaint and payment of the required fee. It is essential that these papers be served on the defendant. CPLR 306-b provides that service of the summons with notice, or summons and complaint, must be made within one-hundred-twenty days after the filing of those papers. In an action or proceeding governed by a statute of limitations of four months or less, however, service must be made "not later than fifteen days after the date on which the applicable statute of limitations expires." CPLR 306-b. These times may be extended by the court "upon good cause shown or in the interest of justice." CPLR 306-b.

Service of the summons is also required by the Due Process Clause. *E.g., Greene v. Lindsey*, 456 U.S. 444, 102 S. Ct. 1874, 72 L. Ed. 2d. 249 (1982). A judgment obtained in the absence of jurisdiction is void. *Peralta v. Heights Medical Center, Inc.*, 485 U.S. 80, 108 S. Ct. 896, 99 L. Ed. 2d 75 (1988). *See also Gager v. White*, 53 N.Y.2d 475, 487, 442 N.Y.S.2d 463, 468, 425 N.E.2d 851 (1981).

(2) *Conditions Precedent to Commencing an Action.* In some situations, there are legal steps which must be taken prior to commencing the action, on pain of dismissal. Such a requirement, called a "condition precedent," can be imposed by statute or by contract. Usually, the condition imposed is that a notice of claim, *i.e.*, a brief but formal description of the claim, be served on the potential defendant within a stated (and very short) time after the accrual of the cause of action. Unfortunately, there is no exhaustive compilation of all statutes imposing conditions precedent, so the attorney must ascertain in each case whether one is applicable. A helpful rule of thumb is that where damages are sought against a governmental entity, a condition precedent will be lurking about.

Frequently encountered are Gen. Mun. Law § 50-e and § 50-i, which apply to tort claims against any city, county, town, village, fire district, school district or their agents or employees. The plaintiff must serve a notice of claim within ninety days after the claim arose. § 50-e. Thereafter, the defendant has thirty days within which to settle the claim; no action may be commenced during that period, § 50-i. Moreover, the defendant has the right to demand an examination of the claimant by "oral questions" and by "physical examination." § 50-h(1). Commencement of the action is delayed by such a demand until the claimant complies. § 50-h(5).

The most troublesome feature of the typical condition precedent is the short period of time allowed for compliance. This aspect will be treated in Chapter 7, Statutes of Limitations.

§ 5.02 COMMENCEMENT BY FILING

HARRIS v. NIAGRA FALLS BOARD OF EDUCATION
New York Court of Appeals
6 N.Y.3d 155, 844 N.E.2d 753, 658 N.Y.S.2d 205 (2006)

GRAFFEO, J.

Plaintiff did not comply with the commencement-by-filing system when he commenced this personal injury action using an index number from a prior special proceeding. Because defendants timely objected to plaintiff's failure to purchase a new index number, the Appellate Division properly dismissed the complaint.

On May 2, 2002, plaintiff Qurrise Harris allegedly sustained injuries when a vehicle driven by defendant Carmen Granto, Jr. and owned by either defendant Niagara Falls Board of Education or defendant Niagara Falls City School District struck him while he was riding his bicycle. Since plaintiff did not serve a notice of claim on the school board or school district within 90 days of the accident (*see* General Municipal Law §§ 50-e, 50-i), plaintiff commenced a special proceeding in April 2003 requesting leave to serve a late notice of claim (*see* General Municipal Law § 50-e[5]). In connection with such application, plaintiff's counsel paid a filing fee to obtain an index number. In June 2003, Supreme Court granted plaintiff's application to the extent that plaintiff was permitted to file and serve a notice of claim on the City of Niagara Falls.

Plaintiff thereafter retained different counsel, who brought a second proceeding for leave to serve a late notice of claim against the school board and school district. Supreme Court granted plaintiff's application, which bore the same index number as the earlier application, and required plaintiff to serve the notice of claim and commence the personal injury action by July 30, 2003. Before this deadline, plaintiff filed and served the notice of claim. He then immediately initiated this action against the school board, the school district and the driver of the vehicle by filing a summons and complaint with the Niagara County Clerk's Office. Plaintiff, however, used the same index number as assigned to the previous late notice of claim applications.

Soon after, defendants moved to dismiss the complaint pursuant to CPLR 3211 as time-barred, claiming that plaintiff's failure to purchase a new index number resulted in the action not having been properly commenced prior to expiration of the statute of limitations. Plaintiff opposed the motion and alternatively sought leave to purchase a new index number. Relying on *Otero v New York City Hous. Auth.* (94 NY2d 800 [1999]), Supreme Court denied defendants' motion. The Appellate Division reversed and dismissed the complaint, holding that Supreme Court lacked subject matter jurisdiction because the action was not properly commenced in the absence of a new index number. We granted plaintiff leave to appeal and now affirm, but for a different reason.

Pursuant to the commencement-by-filing system, a party initiates an action or special proceeding by paying the necessary fee, obtaining an index number and filing the initiatory papers — a summons and complaint or a summons with notice in an action, or a petition in a special proceeding — with the clerk of the court (*see* CPLR 304, 306-a; *see also Matter of Mendon Ponds Neighborhood Assn. v Dehm*, 98 NY2d 745, 747 [2002]). Under the procedure mandated by the CPLR, "service of process without first paying the filing fee and filing the initiatory papers is a nullity, the action or proceeding never having been properly commenced" (*Matter of Gershel v Porr*, 89 NY2d 327, 330 [1996]).

In *Gershel*, the petitioner commenced a CPLR article 78 proceeding by paying the filing fee, securing an index number and filing the initiatory papers. In response to the respondent's motion to dismiss for improper service, the petitioner voluntarily withdrew the order to show cause and decided to begin anew. The petitioner then served the petition on respondent, together with a notice of petition, but did not file the new set of initiatory papers with the clerk or pay a filing fee for a new index number. We concluded that the respondent was entitled to dismissal of the proceeding because the petitioner was required to comply with each of the statutory filing requirements once he decided to bring a new proceeding. Thus, "the new proceeding was never properly commenced and the attempted service was a nullity" (*id.* at 332).

We made clear in *Matter of Fry v Village of Tarrytown* (89 NY2d 714 [1997]) that a defect in compliance with the commencement-by-filing system does not deprive a court of subject matter jurisdiction and, accordingly, is waived absent a timely objection by the responding party. In *Fry*, the petitioner did not fulfill the filing requirements when, after paying the filing fee, he filed an unexecuted order to show cause and petition with the clerk of the court. After examining the language and purpose of the filing provisions, we determined that the trial court had improperly dismissed the proceeding sua sponte because the respondents had waived any objection to the defective filing by appearing in the proceeding and litigating its merits without raising an objection. Significantly, we reaffirmed *Gershel*, stating that "[s]trict compliance with CPLR 304 and the filing system is mandatory, and the extremely serious result of noncompliance, so long as an objection is timely raised by an appearing party, is outright dismissal of the proceeding" (*id.* at 723).

Gershel and *Fry* strike a balance between the competing interests of opposing parties in the commencement process. As Professor Siegel has observed, "[p]laintiffs and petitioners are deterred from casualness by being put on notice that the technical requirements will be strictly construed, while defendants and respondents are warned that if they want to capitalize on technicalities they must mind their own procedures" (Siegel, NY Prac § 63, at 94 [4th ed]). A court should dismiss an action or proceeding only where the plaintiff or petitioner does not fulfill all the filing requirements *and* the defendant or respondent timely objects.

Here, after plaintiff successfully applied for leave to serve a late notice of claim in a separate special proceeding, he was required to comply with the filing requirements in commencing this personal injury action by paying a filing fee, obtaining a new index number, and filing the summons and complaint. Instead, plaintiff did not pay the fee and used the index number from the previously concluded special proceeding. Having failed to comply with the requirements of CPLR 304 and 306-a, plaintiff's action was subject to dismissal. Contrary to the Appellate Division's determination that Supreme Court lacked subject matter jurisdiction, plaintiff's failure to pay the filing fee is a commencement infirmity that is waivable. The Appellate Division, however, correctly dismissed the complaint inasmuch as defendants timely objected to plaintiff's defective filing in their pre-answer motion to dismiss (*see Fry*, 89 NY2d at 723).

Otero does not dictate a contrary result. In that case, the plaintiff similarly failed to comply with the filing requirements by commencing an action in 1994 using an index number from a prior late notice of claim application. We affirmed the denial of the motion to dismiss where, among other things, the defendant did not object to the plaintiff's filing deficiency until 1997, after the plaintiff had purchased a new index number at the County Clerk's request (94 NY2d at 801). Here, in contrast to *Otero*, defendants timely raised the proper objection.

Accordingly, the order of the Appellate Division should be affirmed, with costs.

NOTES

(1) In the principal case the Court states that the plaintiff's improper failure to obtain a new index number did not deprive the courts of subject matter jurisdiction over the new action. It further held, however, that the action was properly dismissed on motion because plaintiff's failure to obtain a new index number was a "commencement infirmity." Does the CPLR authorize dismissal of an action on this ground? See CPLR 3211(a), which lists the grounds on

which a defendant can move to dismiss an action. In a subsequent case dealing with the filing of an allegedly defective paper, *Ballard v. HSBC Bank USA*, 6 N.Y.3d 658, 664, 815 N.Y.S.2d 915, 919, 848 N.E.2d 1292 (2006), the Court opined that "[a]ny alleged technical defect as to the date on the notice of petition invokes a claim of improper commencement or personal jurisdiction, at best." Compare the Court's statement in *Gershel v. Porr*, quoted in the principal case to the effect that "service of process without first paying the filing fee and filing the initiatory papers is a nullity, the action or proceeding never having been properly commenced." What does it mean to say that service of process is "a nullity"?

(2) As *Harris* indicates, numerous problems of interpretation concerning CPLR 304, CPLR 306-a, and CPLR 306-b have arisen since the "commencement by filing" rules became effective in 1992. One issue concerns determining precisely when the key moment of filing occurs. The "safest way to assure satisfaction of the delivery requirement is to bring the papers to the clerk's office and manually hand them to the clerk (or the clerk's designee)." Alexander, N.Y.L.J., May 18, 2001, p. 3, col. 3. CPLR 304 also allows the mailing of process and fee to the clerk. If the papers are mailed, is the action deemed commenced on the day the papers and fee are mailed or the day the clerk receives them? In *Grant v. Senkowski*, 95 N.Y.2d 605, 721 N.Y.S.2d 597, 744 N.E.2d 132 (2001), the Court of Appeals held that it is the date of receipt.

In *Mendon Ponds Neighborhood Ass'n v. Dehm*, 98 N.Y.2d 745, 751 N.Y.S.2d 819, 781 N.E.2d 883 (2002), the Court of Appeals addressed the issue of papers filed with the wrong clerk. The Court affirmed the dismissal of appellants' CPLR article 78 proceeding on the grounds that, contrary to the requirement of CPLR 304, they had filed with the Supreme Court Clerk and not the County Clerk. The Court cited the New York State Constitution, as well as County Law § 525(1), in support of its conclusion that the "clerk of the court" referred to in CPLR 304 is the County Clerk, a "significantly different" position than Supreme Court Clerk. In justification of its apparent formalism, the Court wrote: "Adherence to this procedure ensures that the time of filing is authoritatively fixed when the County Clerk date-stamps the papers, and that the County Clerk, as custodian of public records, is properly informed of litigation that may affect local property."

(3) CPLR 306-b, which states the time within which the summons and complaint (or summons with notice) must be served, also provides that a court may grant an extension of the time to serve process for "good cause shown" or "in the interest of justice." The Court of Appeals, focusing on the disjunctive between the two grounds for extension, has held that they require separate analysis. *Leader v. Maroney, Ponzin & Spencer*, 97 N.Y.2d 95, 736 N.Y.S.2d 291, 761 N.E.2d 1018 (2001). While "good cause" requires some showing of reasonable diligence on the plaintiff's part, diligence is only one factor relevant to the "interest of justice" standard. Other factors listed by the Court were the expiration of the of the statute of limitations, the meritorious nature of the cause,

the length of the delay in service, the promptness of the request to extend the time, and the prejudice to the defendant.

Another court, noting that the legislative intent called for liberal construction, held that a 306-b extension can be granted to cure improper service as well as failure to serve. *Murphy v. Hoppenstein*, 279 A.D.2d 410, 720 N.Y.S.2d 62 (1st Dep't 2001). This issue was not raised in *Leader, supra.* Is the *Murphy* holding correct?

§ 5.03 SERVICE: CONSTITUTIONAL BACKGROUND

GREENE v. LINDSEY
United States Supreme Court
456 U.S. 444, 102 S. Ct. 1874, 72 L. Ed. 2d 249 (1982)

JUSTICE BRENNAN delivered the opinion of the Court.

A Kentucky statute provides that in forcible entry or detainer actions, service of process may be made under certain circumstances by posting a summons on the door of a tenant's apartment. The question presented is whether this statute, as applied to tenants in a public housing project, fails to afford those tenants the notice of proceedings initiated against them required by the Due Process Clause of the Fourteenth Amendment.

I

Appellees Linnie Lindsey, Barbara Hodgens, and Pamela Ray are tenants in a Louisville, Ky., housing project. Appellants are the Sheriff of Jefferson County, Ky., and certain unnamed Deputy Sheriffs charged with responsibility for serving process in forcible entry and detainer actions. In 1975, the Housing Authority of Louisville initiated detainer actions against each of appellees, seeking repossession of their apartments. Service of process was made pursuant to Ky. Rev. Stat. § 454.030 (1975), which states:

> If the officer directed to serve notice on the defendant in forcible entry or detainer proceedings cannot find the defendant on the premises mentioned in the writ, he may explain and leave a copy of the notice with any member of the defendant's family thereon over sixteen (16) years of age, and if no such person is found he may serve the notice by posting a copy thereof in a conspicuous place on the premises. The notice shall state the time and place of the meeting of the court.

In each instance, notice took the form of posting a copy of the writ of forcible entry and detainer on the door of the tenant's apartment. Appellees claim never to have seen these posted summonses; they state that they did not learn of the eviction proceedings until they were served with writs of possession, executed after default judgments had been entered against them, and after their opportunity for appeal had lapsed.

Thus without recourse in the state courts, appellees filed this suit as a class action in the United States District Court for the Western District of Kentucky, seeking declaratory and injunctive relief under 42 U.S.C. § 1983. They claimed that the notice procedure employed as a predicate to these eviction proceedings did not satisfy the minimum standards of constitutionally adequate notice described in *Mullane v. Central Hanover Bank & Trust Co.*, 339 U.S. 306 (1950), and that the Commonwealth of Kentucky had thus failed to afford them the due process of law guaranteed by the Fourteenth Amendment. . . .

II

A

"The fundamental requisite of due process of law is the opportunity to be heard." *Grannis v. Ordean*, 234 U.S. 385, 394 (1914). And the "right to be heard has little reality or worth unless one is informed that the matter is pending and can choose for himself whether to appear or default, acquiesce or contest," *Mullane, supra*, at 314. Personal service guarantees actual notice of the pendency of a legal action; it thus presents the ideal circumstance under which to commence legal proceedings against a person, and has traditionally been deemed necessary in actions styled in personam. *McDonald v. Mabee*, 243 U.S. 90, 92 (1917). Nevertheless, certain less rigorous notice procedures have enjoyed substantial acceptance throughout our legal history; in light of this history and the practical obstacles to providing personal service in every instance, we have allowed judicial proceedings to be prosecuted in some situations on the basis of procedures that do not carry with them the same certainty of actual notice that inheres in personal service. But we have also clearly recognized that the Due Process Clause does prescribe a constitutional minimum: "An elementary and fundamental requirement of due process in any proceeding which is to be accorded finality is *notice reasonably calculated, under all the circumstances, to apprise interested parties of the pendency of the action* and afford them an opportunity to present their objections." *Mullane*, 339 U.S., at 314 (emphasis added). It is against this standard that we evaluate the procedures employed in this case.

B

Appellants argue that because a forcible entry and detainer action is an action in rem, notice by posting is ipso facto constitutionally adequate. . . .

As in *Mullane*, we decline to resolve the constitutional question based upon the determination whether the particular action is more properly characterized as one in rem or in personam. 339 U.S., at 312. *See Shaffer v. Heitner, supra*, at 206. That is not to say that the nature of the action has no bearing on a constitutional assessment of the reasonableness of the procedures employed. The character of the action reflects the extent to which the court purports to extend it power, and this may roughly describe the scope of potential adverse consequences to the person claiming a right to more effective notice. But "[a]ll proceedings, like all rights, are really against persons." In this case, appellees have been deprived a significant interest in property: indeed, of the right to continued residence in their homes. In light of this deprivation, it will not suffice to recite that because the action is in rem, it is only necessary to serve notice "upon the thing itself." The sufficiency of notice must be tested with reference to its ability to inform people of the pendency of proceedings that affect their interests. In arriving at the constitutional assessment, we look to the realities of the case before us. . . .

It is, of course, reasonable to assume that a property owner will maintain superintendence of his property, and to presume that actions physically disturbing his holdings will come to his attention. *See Mullane, supra*, at 316. . . . Upon this understanding, a state may in turn conclude that in most cases, the secure posting of a notice on the property of a person is likely to offer that property owner sufficient warning of the pendency of proceedings possibly affecting his interests.

The empirical basis of the presumption that notice posted upon property is adequate to alert the owner or occupant of property of the pendency of legal proceedings would appear to make the presumption particularly well founded where notice is posted at a residence. With respect to claims affecting the continued possession of that residence, the application of this presumption seems particularly apt: If the tenant has a continuing interest in maintaining possession of the property for his use and occupancy, he might reasonably be expected to frequent the premises; if he no longer occupies the premises, then the injury that might result from his not having received actual notice as a consequence of the posted notice is reduced. Short of providing personal service, then, posting notice on the door of a person's home would, in many or perhaps most instances, constitute not only a constitutionally acceptable means of service, but indeed a singularly appropriate and effective way of ensuring that a person who cannot conveniently be served personally is actually apprised of proceedings against him.

But whatever the efficacy of posting in many cases, it is clear that, in the circumstances of this case, merely posting notice on an apartment door does not satisfy minimum standards of due process. In a significant number of instances, reliance on posting pursuant to the provisions of § 454.030 results in a failure to provide actual notice to the tenant concerned. Indeed, appellees claim to have suffered precisely such a failure of actual notice. As the process servers were well aware, notices posted on apartment doors in the area where these tenants lived were "not infrequently" removed by children or other tenants before they could have their intended effect. Under these conditions, notice by posting on the apartment door cannot be considered a "reliable means of acquainting interested parties of the fact that their rights are before the courts." *Mullane*, 339 U.S., at 315.

Of course, the reasonableness of the notice provided must be tested with reference to the existence of "feasible and customary" alternatives and supplements to the form of notice chosen. *Ibid.* In this connection, we reject appellants' characterization of the procedure contemplated by § 454.030 as one in which "posting" is used as a method of service "only as a last resort." Brief for Appellants 7. To be sure, the statute requires the officer serving notice to make a visit to the tenant's home and to attempt to serve the writ personally on the tenant or some member of his family. But if no one is at home at the time of that visit, as is apparently true in a "good percentage" of cases, posting follows forthwith. Neither the statute, nor the practice of the process servers, makes provision for even a second attempt at personal service, perhaps at some time of day when the tenant is more likely to be at home. The failure to effect personal service on the first visit hardly suggests that the tenant has abandoned his interest in the apartment such that mere pro forma notice might be held constitutionally adequate. *Cf. Mullane*, 339 U. S., at 317-318. As noted by the Court of Appeals, and as we noted in *Mullane*, the mails provide an "efficient and inexpensive means of communication," *id.*, at 319, upon which prudent men will ordinarily rely in the conduct of important affairs, *id.*, at 319-320. Notice by mail in the circumstances of this case would surely go a long way toward providing the constitutionally required assurance that the State has not allowed its power to be invoked against a person who has had no opportunity to present a defense despite a continuing interest in the resolution of the controversy. Particularly where the subject matter of the action also happens to be the mailing address of the defendant, and where personal service is ineffectual, notice by mail may reasonably be relied upon to provide interested persons with actual notice of judicial proceedings. We need not go so far as to insist that in order to "dispense with personal service the substitute that is most likely to reach the defendant is the least that ought to be required," *McDonald v. Mabee*, 243 U.S., at 92, in order to recognize that where an inexpensive and efficient mechanism such as mail service is available to enhance the reliability of an otherwise unreliable notice procedure, the State's continued exclusive reliance on an ineffective means of service is not notice "reasonably calculated to reach those who could easily be informed by other means at hand." *Mullane, supra*, at 319.

III

We conclude that in failing to afford appellees adequate notice of the proceedings against them before issuing final orders of eviction, the State has deprived them of property without the due process of law required by the Fourteenth Amendment.

JUSTICE O'CONNOR, with whom THE CHIEF JUSTICE and JUSTICE REHNQUIST join, dissenting.

Today, the Court holds that the Constitution prefers the use of the Postal Service to posted notice. The Court reaches this conclusion despite the total absence of any evidence in the record regarding the speed and reliability of the mails. The sole ground for the Court's result is the scant and conflicting testimony of a handful of process servers in Kentucky. On this flimsy basis, the Court confidently overturns the work of the Kentucky Legislature and, by implication, that of at least 10 other States. I must respectfully dissent.

. . . .

NOTES

(1) Does the principal case hold that actual notice of the commencement of an action is required by the Constitution? In *Mullane v. Central Hanover Bank & Trust Co.*, 339 U.S. 306, 314, 70 S. Ct. 652, 657, 94 L. Ed. 865 (1950), relied upon in *Greene v. Lindsey*, the Court held that notice by publication of a proceeding to settle trust accounts was acceptable, even though some named respondents (beneficiaries of the trust, whose whereabouts could not be ascertained even with due diligence), never actually saw the notice. Publication was held insufficient as to those beneficiaries whose addresses were known to the trustee. As to them, at least notice by mailing was required.

(2) Applying the *Mullane* standard, the Supreme Court also held inadequate the method of giving notice formerly permitted by New York law in condemnation proceedings — the property owner was served by publication in a local newspaper, and by posting on trees in the vicinity of (but not necessarily on) the property. "The general rule," said the Court, "is that notice by publication is not enough with respect to a person whose name and address are known or very easily ascertainable and whose legally protected interests are directly affected by the proceedings in question." *Schroeder v. City of New York*, 371 U.S. 208, 212-13, 83 S. Ct. 279, 282, 9 L. Ed. 2d 255 (1962). The Supreme Court returned to the problem of adequate notice in the context of a tax forfeiture proceeding in *Jones v. Flowers*, 547 U.S. 220, 126 S. Ct. 1708, 164 L. Ed. 2d 415 (2006). The Arkansas home owner had fallen behind in property tax payments, so his house was subject to sale by the state if the taxes were not paid. He was notified of the imminent forfeiture by a certified letters mailed to him at the subject house, but the notice was never received because he had moved, and the letters were returned to the sender. Framing the due process issue, the Court wrote: "It is true that this Court has deemed notice constitutionally sufficient if it was reasonably calculated to reach the intended recipient when sent. . . . But we have never addressed whether due process entails further responsibility when the government becomes aware prior to the taking that its attempt at notice has failed." In this case the state twice attempted to inform petitioner of the impending tax sale of his house via certified mail (which must be signed for), but the letters were returned unclaimed. Petitioner had moved and was renting out the house, but had not updated his record address. Rather than making a further effort to contact him, the state published notice in a local newspaper and then proceeded to take and sell his property. The Court held that due process required the state to "take additional reasonable steps to attempt to provide notice," if practicable, and maintained that the state could feasibly have used regular mail, mail addressed to "occupant," or notice posted on the front door.

(3) Unscrupulous process servers and attorneys have been known to obtain default judgments against persons by filing affidavits falsely stating that the defendant has been served with a summons and has failed to appear. Such conduct violates the defendant's constitutional right to notice and perpetrators are therefore subject to federal prosecution under 18 U.S.C. § 242 (a federal crimi-

nal statute). *See United States v. Wiseman*, 445 F.2d 792 (2d Cir.), *cert. denied*, 404 U.S. 967 (1971). On the continuing problem of such "sewer service," see Frank M. Tuerkheimer, *Service of Process in New York City: A Proposed End to Unregulated Criminality*, 72 Colum. L. Rev. 847 (1972). One method of deterring sewer service is by having rigorous requirements for proving the facts of service. *See* CPLR 306.

§ 5.04 FORM OF SUMMONS

[A] Generally

FORM

SUPREME COURT OF THE STATE OF NEW YORK
COUNTY OF NEW YORK

A. B., Plaintiff,

— against —

C.D., Defendant.

Summons with Notice
Index Number:
Date of Filing:

To the above-named defendant:

You are hereby summoned to appear in this action by serving a notice of appearance on plaintiff's attorney within twenty days after the service of this summons, exclusive of the day of service, or within thirty days after service is complete if this summons is not personally delivered to you within the State of New York.

Take notice that the object of this action and the relief sought is to recover damages for breach of contract, and that in case of your failure to appear judgment will be taken against you by default for the sum of twenty thousand dollars with interest from June 1, 1966, plus the costs and disbursements of this action.

The basis of the venue designated is [specify basis, as: the residence of plaintiff, which is (set forth address)].

Dated:

[Signature and printed name]

Attorney for Plaintiff
Address:
Telephone Number:

NOTES

(1) This is Form 3, "Summons Served Without Complaint With Notice of Judgment to be Taken in Case of Default," of the forms adopted by the Judicial Conference pursuant to CPLR 107 (with modifications to incorporate subsequent statutory amendments). If the complaint is served with the summons (which may be done at plaintiff's option), the summons form is similar but need not specify the object of the action or the relief sought. CPLR 305(b). Special requirements govern a summons in an action arising from a consumer credit transaction, CPLR 305(a), and in a medical malpractice action, CPLR 305(b).

(2) Since the summons is served on the defendant who is presumably not a lawyer, should it not be comprehensible to a lay person? Is it? Re-read the form. What is "personal delivery"? When is service "complete"?

The summons form required by the Uniform Civil Rules for the New York City Civil Court, 22 N.Y.C.R.R. 208.6, is quite different. It includes this instruction:

> NOTE: The law provides that:
>
> (a) If this summons is served by its delivery to you personally within the City of New York, you must appear and answer within TWENTY days after such service; or
>
> (b) If this summons is served by delivery to any person other than you personally, or is served outside the City of New York, or by publication, or by any means other than personal delivery to you within the City of New York, you are allowed THIRTY days after proof of service thereof is filed with the Clerk of this Court within which to appear and answer.

For actions arising out of consumer credit transactions, the Civil Court Rules go further still, graphically advising the defendant of the potential consequences of flouting a summons. Those rules also require that a Spanish translation accompany the English language version.

[B] Defects in Form; Amendments

TAMBURO v. P & C FOOD MARKETS, INC.
Appellate Division, Fourth Department
36 A.D.2d 1017, 321 N.Y.S.2d 487 (1971)

MEMORANDUM:

Plaintiff, who claimed to have been injured in defendant's place of business on April 29, 1966, delivered a summons to the Sheriff of Cayuga County on April 29, 1969, the last day on which an action for negligence could be commenced. (CPLR 214, subd. 5.) The summons failed to include in the caption the names of the court and county wherein the action was brought as required by CPLR

2101 (subd. [c]). It was served the same day by the Sheriff but defendant did not
enter a notice of appearance. A supplemental summons designating the
Supreme Court, Cayuga County was delivered to the Sheriff on June 19, 1969,
and served on defendant the following day. Defendant served a notice of appearance on July 3, 1969, and received a complaint on July 24, 1969. In its answer,
defendant raised the affirmative defense that the action was barred by the
Statute of Limitations, and subsequently it moved to dismiss the action pursuant to CPLR 3211 (subd. [a], par. 5). Special Term denied the motion and
granted plaintiff's cross motion to amend the caption of the summons to State
of New York, Supreme Court, County of Cayuga *nunc pro tunc* as of April 24,
1969. Defendant's motion should have been granted and the complaint dismissed, as plaintiff's action was barred by the Statute of Limitations. A summons which fails to name the court in which the action is brought is void (*Dix
v. Palmer and Schoolcraft*, 5 How. Prac. 233, 234;. . . .) and a void summons cannot be amended to cure the defect. (*Fischer v. Langbein*, 103 N. Y. 84;. . . .)
Defendant's failure to return the first summons did not waive the omission, since
it was a jurisdictional defect and not merely a defect in form. (CPLR 2101,
subd. [f].) The service on April 29, 1969, was a nullity and the Statute of Limitations had already run when the supplemental summons was delivered to
the Sheriff on June 19, 1969, and served on June 20, 1969. . . .

NOTES

(1) The principal case was decided prior to the 1992 change from the "commencement by service" regime to the current rule of CPLR 304 that an action
is commenced by filing the summons and complaint or other appropriate papers.
Suppose that under the present version of the CPLR, an action was purportedly
commenced by the filing of a summons similar to that described in *Tamburo* on
the last day permitted by the statute of limitations. Could the defendant successfully move to dismiss the action as was done in *Tamburo*? *See Harris v. Niagra Board of Education, supra*, this chapter.

Pursuant to CPLR 305(c), a court may allow a summons to be amended at any
time "if a substantial right of a party is not prejudiced." What rights were prejudiced by the summons defect treated in the principal case? *See also Scott v.
Uljanov*, 140 A.D.2d 830, 528 N.Y.S.2d 435 (3d Dep't 1988), *rev'd in part on other
grounds*, 74 N.Y.2d 673, 541 N.E.2d 398 (1998) (failure to include the name of
the court in the caption of the summons and complaint was a jurisdictional
defect; hence, for the purposes of the statute of limitations, the claim was not
interposed until an amended corrected complaint was served). *Compare Tobia
v. Town of Rockland*, 106 A.D.2d 827, 484 N.Y.S.2d 226 (3d Dep't 1984) (failure
to include the name of the court in the caption of the summons and complaint
was held a mere defect in form which could be disregarded because, before the
papers were actually served, the plaintiffs notified all the defendants and the
court that their papers were amended to read "Supreme Court" in the caption).

(2) CPLR 305(b) provides that if a summons is served without a complaint it must contain (or have "attached thereto") a "notice stating the nature of the action and the relief sought, and, except in an action for medical malpractice, the sum of money for which judgment may be taken in case of default." A failure to include this requisite "object notice" (as it is often called) is a jurisdictional defect which must result in a dismissal of the action on motion. *Parker v. Mack*, 61 N.Y.2d 114, 472 N.Y.S.2d 882, 460 N.E.2d 1316 (1984). In *Parker* the court did not address the question of how much detail the object notice must contain. On this score, see *Rowell v. Gould, Inc.*, 124 A.D.2d 995, 508 N.Y.S.2d 794 (4th Dep't 1986), holding that "The nature of the action is negligence" is sufficient. *Accord, Viscosi v. Merritt*, 125 A.D.2d 814, 510 N.Y.S.2d 30 (3d Dep't 1986) ("automobile negligence").

(3) What if the summons contains an error in the defendant's name? It will be held curable by amendment so long as, despite the error, the defendant was fairly apprised that the action was directed against her. *Stuyvesant v. Weil*, 167 N.Y. 421, 60 N.E. 738 (1901). In that case, the court found that Mary J. Stockton was fairly apprised by a summons referring to her as Emma J. Stockton. As the court said, "the object of the summons is to apprise the party defendant that the plaintiff therein seeks a judgment against him [sic] so that he may take such steps as may seem advisable to protect his interests. . . ." *Id.* at 425, 60 N.E. at 739.

The fair appraisal rule was also invoked in *Albilia v. Hillcrest General Hospital*, 124 A.D.2d 499, 508 N.Y.S.2d 10 (1st Dep't 1986), holding that jurisdiction was acquired over Dr. Nachman Rosenfeld personally even though the captions of the summons and complaint named Nachman Rosenfeld, M.D., P.C. The court said that it was obvious from the text of the complaint that the intent was to sue Dr. Rosenfeld personally. The captions were therefore deemed amended sua sponte.

(4) If the plaintiff does not know the name of the defendant, the attorney may rely on CPLR 1024 and refer to the defendant as either "John Doe" or "Mary Doe," designating so much as is known, *e.g.*, "an employee of the New York City Police Department."

(5) A "supplemental summons" should be distinguished from an amended summons in that the former is not used to correct a defect but to add a new party to the action. CPLR 305(a). A supplemental summons may be served only with court permission.

(6) The misnaming of a business entity presents peculiar problems in applying the fair appraisal test, as the case which follows illustrates.

PROVOSTY v. LYDIA E. HALL HOSPITAL
Appellate Division, Second Department
91 A.D.2d 659, 457 N.Y.S.2d 106 (1982),
aff'd, 59 N.Y.2d 812, 464 N.Y.S.2d 754, 451 N.E.2d 501 (1983)

On June 12, 1978 plaintiffs Leo and Mildred Provosty commenced a medical malpractice action (Action No. 1) against Lydia E. Hall Hospital and several doctors, in which they erroneously alleged in the "FIRST" paragraph of their complaint that "the defendant, Lydia E. Hall Hospital [is] a domestic corporation, licensed to do business and doing business in the State of New York". Subsequently, on September 18, 1978, the hospital, by its attorney, Morris Ehrlich, P.C., interposed an answer in which it specifically denied the allegations of the "FIRST" paragraph of the complaint, and alleged, inter alia, as an affirmative defense that the court lacked jurisdiction "over the person of the defendant Lydia E. Hall Hospital". In addition, the hospital interposed a cross claim for contribution and/or indemnification against the various individual doctors named in the complaint.

It is undisputed that Lydia E. Hall Hospital is not a corporation, and that it is a "trade name" employed by its sole owner, Dr. Carl H. Neuman. Moreover, it is further undisputed that a certificate of doing business under the assumed name "Lydia E. Hall Hospital" had been filed by Dr. Neuman in the Nassau County Clerk's office in the summer of 1974 (*see* General Business Law, § 130). In addition, it appears without contradiction that at an examination before trial conducted on July 19, 1979, *i.e.*, three months prior to the expiration of the applicable Statute of Limitations, the plaintiffs' attorney was apprised of the fact that the hospital in question was a proprietary institution owned exclusively by Dr. Neuman. Notwithstanding the foregoing actual and constructive notice, however, it is clear that no service was ever made upon Dr. Neuman in Action No. 1, and that it was not until after the expiration of the Statute of Limitations that he was served with process in the second (virtually identical) medical malpractice action commenced against the same individuals and "Carl [H.] Neuman d/b/a Lydia [E.] Hall Hospital". Dr. Neuman appeared in that action on or about August 19, 1981, and interposed an answer containing the Statute of Limitations as an affirmative defense. He thereafter moved to dismiss the complaint in Action No. 1 for lack of jurisdiction, whereupon the plaintiffs cross-moved, inter alia, to strike the Statute of Limitations as an affirmative defense in Action No. 2. As has already been indicated, Special Term ruled in favor of the plaintiffs on both of these motions and this appeal followed.

In arguing, inter alia, that the complaint in Action No. 1 must be dismissed, Dr. Neuman correctly maintains that a trade name, as such, has no separate jural existence, and that it can neither sue nor be sued independently of its owner, who in this case was concededly never served (*see Little Shoppe Around Corner v. Carl*, 80 Misc.2d 717, 363 N.Y.S.2d 784). Moreover, the fact of a separate corporate existence was specifically denied in the hospital's answer, and the jurisdictional objection was adequately preserved by the timely assertion of an appropriate affirmative defense (*see* CPLR 3211, subd. [e] . . .). Under these circumstances, the mere interposition of a related, protective cross claim in the hospital's answer cannot, without more, be held to constitute a waiver of the jurisdictional objection.

. . . .

Turning our attention to Action No. 2, we again believe that Special Term erred in concluding that Dr. Neuman should be equitably estopped from interposing the Statute of Limitations as an affirmative defense. . . .

. . . Assuming arguendo that the answer, when viewed as a whole, tended to mislead the plaintiffs into believing that the hospital was a separate legal entity or that it failed to disabuse them of their previous misconception in this regard (*see Marshall v. Acker*, NYLJ, July 14, 1981, p. 14, col. 4), the fact remains that the plaintiffs' attorney was specifically informed of the true facts regarding the hospital's ownership some three months prior to the expiration of the applicable Statute of Limitations, and that he nevertheless failed to cure the defect in service in Action No. 1. On these facts, there is simply no basis upon which to predicate an estoppel, as the conduct relied on ceased to be operational within a reasonable time prior to the expiration of the otherwise applicable period of limitations. . . .

NOTES

(1) The principal case illustrates the peril of suing a non-entity. How can such mistakes be avoided? *See* N.Y. Gen. Bus. Law §§ 130-131. The former requires that every person and corporation conducting business under a name other than its real name, file a certificate stating its true name and address with a designated public official. The information is available to the public through the county clerks. Gen. Bus. Law § 131 requires that any person or firm conducting a business must have the true name of the proprietor displayed in its window or on the exterior of the building.

(2) The "wrong entity" problem was solved for small claims court actions by the addition of § 1813 to the various Small Claims Court Acts (Article 18 of the New York City Civil Court Act and of each of the uniform court acts). It requires that any person or firm sued in a small claims court pay any judgment rendered against it in its true name or in any name under which it conducts business.

§ 5.05 SERVICE ON A NATURAL PERSON

[A] Generally

CPLR 308(1)-(4) authorize four distinct methods of serving the summons on a natural person, and subdivision (5) allows the court to fashion other methods where necessary. CPLR 312-a allows, as an alternative, service by first class mail to be made on natural persons or other entities. An additional alternative is available in certain tort cases pursuant to Vehicle and Traffic Law §§ 253-254. Further, as discussed in § 1.05, *supra*, the defendant may agree to be served in some other manner. *See also, e.g., Cohen v. Coleman*, 110 Misc. 2d 419, 442 N.Y.S.2d 834 (Sup. Ct. 1981) (service by first class mail held valid when defendant had previously agreed to accept such service in a phone conversation with plaintiff's attorney).

Some general rules govern all methods of service, whether on natural persons or institutions. The summons must be served by a person who is not a party to the action (unless served by mail under CPLR 312-a), and who has reached the age of eighteen. CPLR 2103(a). "Professional" process servers, *i.e.*, persons who derive income from serving summonses and who serve more than five per year, are regulated by General Business Law Article 8-A, which, among other things, requires them to keep records relating to each summons served.

A summons may not be served on a Sunday, Gen. Bus. Law § 11; nor may a Sabbatarian be served "maliciously" on a Saturday, *id.*, § 13. Service on infants, incompetents and conservatees is subject to the additional requirements of CPLR 309: Service must be made on the parent (or other guardian) of an infant and on a committee of an incompetent and on a conservator of a conservatee.

If a jurisdictional basis exists, service of the summons may generally be made outside the state in any manner in which it may be made in New York. CPLR 313. If the service is to be made in a foreign nation, however, some methods permitted in New York may not be acceptable and will not yield jurisdiction. *See* § 5.07, *infra*.

Recall that a non-resident voluntarily in the state to attend at litigation is immune from the service of process. *See* § 1.03, *supra*. A resident (or other person otherwise subject to jurisdiction) is not immune. Thus, it has been held that a person who is in court in order to testify in connection with a motion to dismiss an action on the grounds that prior service was invalid may properly be served with a new summons for the same action and that jurisdiction is thereby obtained. *Department of Housing Preservation & Development v. Koenigsberg*, 113 Misc. 2d 893, 509 N.Y.S.2d 270 (N.Y.C. Civ. Ct. 1986).

PROBLEM A

While working for a law firm during your summer "vacation," you are asked to serve a summons on each of the defendants in a Supreme Court action entitled Green v. Brown, Inc. and Robert Brown. (The individual defendant is the president of the corporate defendant.) Upon arriving at the corporate office in Mineola, N.Y., you are met by a receptionist who informs you that Mr. Brown is "not available," that she "takes all deliveries," and will be happy to accept the summons for Mr. Brown and the corporation. What do you do?

[B] Service by Mail

CPLR 312-a authorizes service of process by first class mail as an alternative to any other method of service. It allows service of the summons and complaint or summons with notice by mail on natural persons as well as on corporations, partnerships and governmental entities.

In addition to the summons or other paper served, the mailing must include two copies of a "statement of service by mail and acknowledgement of receipt" and a return envelope, postage prepaid, addressed to the sender. Forms for the statement and acknowledgement are set forth in CPLR 312-a(d).

CPLR 312-a(b) states that the defendant, defendant's attorney or one of their employees "must" complete the acknowledgment of receipt and mail or deliver a copy of it to the sender within thirty days of its receipt. The acknowledgement then constitutes proof of service. CPLR 312-a(b)(1). The only penalty imposed on a defendant who fails to complete and return the acknowledgment, however, is that the defendant will be taxed with the reasonable costs of the alternative service, as a disbursement, payable to the serving party "if such party is awarded costs in the action." CPLR 312-a(f). Only a prevailing party may be awarded costs. CPLR 8101.

Service of the summons is complete on the date the signed acknowledgment is mailed or delivered to the original sender. CPLR 312-a(b)(1). If a duly signed acknowledgment is not returned, the plaintiff must make service in another manner, *i.e.*, as authorized by CPLR 307, 308, 310, 311 or 312, depending on the type of entity served.

[C] Personal Delivery: CPLR 308(1)

MACCHIA v. RUSSO
Court of Appeals
67 N.Y.2d 592, 505 N.Y.S.2d 591, 496 N.E.2d 680 (1986)

PER CURIAM.

Delivery of a summons to defendant's son outside his house, after which the son goes into the house and gives the summons to his father, is not valid service on defendant pursuant to CPLR 308(1).

Plaintiff instituted this action for damages arising out of injuries incurred on February 27, 1975 while he was a passenger in defendant's car. Nearly three years later, on February 15, 1978, a process server — accompanied by plaintiff — went to the home of defendant, Salvatore Russo, to serve him with a summons. Upon arrival, the process server approached John Russo (Salvatore's son), who was outside the house washing a car. The process server said either "Mr. Russo?" or "Sal Russo?",* and handed John the summons. John Russo walked to the car in which plaintiff was seated, inquired of plaintiff's health, and asked what the papers were. The process server told him to read them and drove off with plaintiff. John then went into the house and handed the papers to his father.

Upon defendant's motion for summary judgment dismissing the complaint for inadequate service, Special Term ruled that service on defendant had been effected. . . . The Appellate Division reversed and dismissed the complaint. . . . We granted leave to appeal and now affirm.

None of the three grounds tendered by plaintiff in support of service has merit.

First, plaintiff urges that delivery to defendant was sufficiently close in time and space to the initial delivery to his son to constitute valid service under CPLR 308(1). The Legislature in CPLR 308 has provided a plaintiff with a range of methods for effecting personal service upon a natural person (*see, Feinstein v. Bergner*, 48 N.Y.2d 234, 239-240, 422 N.Y.S.2d 356, 397 N.E.2d 1161). Where plaintiff chooses to make service by personal delivery to defendant the statutory requirements could not be plainer: service must be made "by delivering the summons within the state to the person to be served" (CPLR 308(1)). While the Appellate Division has in certain circumstances sustained service where delivery initially was made to the wrong person (*see, Daniels v. Eastman*, 87 A.D.2d 882, 449 N.Y.S.2d 538; *Conroy v. International Term. Operating Co.*, 87 A.D.2d 858, 449 N.Y.S.2d 294; *Green v. Morningside Hgts. Hous.*

---

* John testified that he was asked "Mr. Russo?", and answered "Yes", at which point he was handed a paper. The process server testified he said "Sal Russo?" and John made no answer. The courts below made no finding on this issue.

Corp., 13 Misc.2d 124, 177 N.Y.S.2d 760, *affd.* 7 A.D.2d 708, 180 N.Y.S.2d 104), in *Espy v. Giorlando*, 56 N.Y.2d 640, 450 N.Y.S.2d 786, 436 N.E.2d 193, this court refused to recognize delivery of process to another person as constituting personal delivery to defendant. As we stated: "We see no reason to extend the clear and unambiguous meaning of CPLR 308 (subd 1)." (*Id.*, 56 N.Y.2d at p. 642, 450 N.Y.S.2d 786, 436 N.E.2d 193.) Thus, plaintiff's first contention must fail.

Second, citing *McDonald v. Ames Supply Co.*, 22 N.Y.2d 111, 115, 291 N.Y.S.2d 328, 238 N.E.2d 726, *supra*, plaintiff argues that service should be validated because "the process server has acted reasonably." *McDonald* was decided before the enactment of CPLR 308(2), which permits service to be made upon an individual by leaving a copy of the summons with a person other than the named defendant. Given this alternative, "any consideration of whether due diligence was or was not used in an effort to make delivery to [defendant] in person is irrelevant." (*duPont, Glore Forgan & Co. v. Chen*, 41 N.Y.2d 794, 797, 396 N.Y.S.2d 343, 364 N.E.2d 1115.) Whether a narrow exception to the requirements of CPLR 308(1) may be made in situations where a process server acts reasonably in the face of misrepresentations regarding the identity or authority of the person served is a question we do not reach, particularly in view of plaintiff's presence at the time the summons was delivered to defendant's son (*see, Bossuk v. Steinberg*, 58 N.Y.2d 916, 460 N.Y.S.2d 509, 447 N.E.2d 56; *and Bradley v. Musacchio*, 94 A.D.2d 783, 463 N.Y.S.2d 28).

Finally, plaintiff's contention that defendant has not been prejudiced, and therefore service should be upheld, must also be rejected. In a challenge to service of process, the fact that a defendant has received prompt notice of the action is of no moment (*see, e.g., De Zego v. Donald F. Bruhn, M.D., P.C.*, 67 N.Y.2d 875, 501 N.Y.S.2d 801, 492 N.E.2d 1217). Notice received by means other than those authorized by statute does not bring a defendant within the jurisdiction of the court. . . .

. . . .

NOTES

(1) The personal delivery contemplated by CPLR 308(1) must be distinguished from other modes of personal service authorized by CPLR 308. The former can ordinarily be satisfied only by handing the summons to the defendant directly. In addition to the principal case. *See Espy v. Giorlando*, 85 A.D.2d 652, 445 N.Y.S.2d 230 (2d Dep't 1981), *aff'd*, 56 N.Y.2d 640, 450 N.Y.S.2d 786, 436 N.E.2d 193 (1982) (no jurisdiction acquired over defendant physician under CPLR 308(1) by serving his nurse even though she held herself out as his "authorized agent"). *Compare Ellenbogen & Goldstein v. Brandes*, 215 A.D.2d 226, 626 N.Y.S.2d 160 (1st Dep't 1995) (service under CPLR 308(1) was validly made

when the process server left the summons and complaint outside the defendant's apartment door while she was at home after she refused to open the door).

(2) Suppose, in *Espy v. Giorlando, supra,* the process server had feigned illness to get the defendant physician to see him and then handed the summons to him. Would the service be valid? Service by trickery was upheld in *Gumperz v. Hoffman,* 245 App. Div. 622, 283 N.Y.S.2d 823 (1st Dep't 1935), *aff'd,* 271 N.Y. 544, 2 N.E. 687 (1936), so long as the defendant was not lured into the jurisdiction. *Cf., Hammett v. Hammett,* in § 1.03, *supra.* Accordingly, one professional process server says "Legally, you're entitled to lie." *Process Server Makes a Living with Duplicity,* N.Y. Times, August 5, 1989, p. 27, col. 1. Should the law countenance trickery to facilitate summons service?

In any event, the summons itself should not be masked, for if the defendant was properly uncertain what was being served, jurisdiction may not be acquired. *Matter of Bonesteel,* 16 A.D.2d 324, 228 N.Y.S.2d 301 (3d Dep't 1962).

[D] Delivery to a Suitable Person: CPLR 308(2)

BOSSUK v. STEINBERG
Court of Appeals
58 N.Y.2d 916, 460 N.Y.S.2d 509, 447 N.E.2d 56 (1983)

MEMORANDUM.

CPLR 308 (subd. 2) provides for delivery to "a person of suitable age and discretion" (other than the person to be served), while subdivision 1 provides for delivery to "the person to be served." However, except for additional requirements not relevant here, the two subdivisions are identical. In particular, each subdivision provides for "delivering the summons." Absent any indication to the contrary, therefore, we may assume that, by retaining the same delivery requirements in both subdivisions while amending CPLR 308 in other respects, the Legislature anticipated that, in this regard, judicial construction of both also would be the same (*see* McKinney's Cons. Laws of N.Y., Book 1, Statutes, § 75, pp. 162-163).

We have had occasion to hold that, under CPLR 308 (subd. 1), delivery of a summons may be accomplished by leaving it in the "general vicinity" of a person to be served who "resists" service (*McDonald v. Ames Supply Co.,* 22 N.Y.2d 111, 115, 291 N.Y.S.2d 328, 238 N.E.2d 726). Thus, under that provision, if the person to be served interposes a door between himself and the process server, the latter may leave the summons outside the door, provided the person to be served is made aware that he is doing so (*Levine v. National Transp. Co.,* 204 Misc. 202, 203, 125 N.Y.S.2d 679, *affd.* 282 App.Div. 720, 122 N.Y.S.2d 901; *Chernick v. Rodriguez,* 2 Misc.2d 891, 892, 150 N.Y.S.2d 149). Concordantly, we hold that the delivery requirement of CPLR 308 (subd. 2) may also be satisfied, as here, by leaving a copy of the summons outside the door of the person to be served upon the refusal of "a person of suitable age and discretion" to open the door to accept it, provided the process server informs the person to whom delivery is being made that this is being done. We add that no question has been raised concerning the fact that the youngsters, one 14 and the other 15, were of "suitable age and discretion."

Moreover, we reject defendant's contention that service which accords with our interpretation of the statute, as it was here, offends due process. It is hornbook law that a constitutionally proper method of effecting substituted service need not guarantee that in all cases the defendant will in fact receive actual notice (*Dobkin v. Chapman*, 21 N.Y.2d 490, 502, 289 N.Y.S.2d 161, 236 N.E.2d 451). It suffices that the prescribed method is one "reasonably calculated, under all the circumstances, to apprise [the] interested part[y] of the pendency of the action" (*Mullane v. Central Hanover Trust Co.*, 339 U.S. 306, 314, 70 S.Ct. 652, 657, 94 L.Ed. 865). The statute, as we read it, easily meets this standard.

. . . .

NOTES

(1) Note the discussion of "delivery" of a summons in the principal case. Is it consistent with the spirit or holding of *Macchia v. Russo*, the preceding case?

(2) CPLR 308(2) permits personal service to be made by leaving the summons with "a person of suitable age and discretion at the actual place of business, dwelling place or usual place of abode" of the defendant so long as another copy of the summons is mailed to the defendant at his last known residence or "actual place of business." If the mailing is to the defendant's business address, the envelope may not indicate that it is from an attorney or concerns an action against the person served, but must bear the words "personal and confidential." The mailing and the delivery must take place within twenty days of each other.

(3) A doorman at the apartment building in which the defendant resides has been held a proper person to whom the summons may be delivered if the process server is barred from going to the apartment itself. *F.I. Du Pont, Glore Forgan & Co. v. Chen*, 41 N.Y.2d 794, 396 N.Y.S.2d 343, 364 N.E.2d 1115 (1977).

(4) Nothing requires an attempt at personal delivery or any other method of personal service before resorting to service under CPLR 308(2). In matrimonial actions, however, substituted service is available only by court order, as CPLR 308(2) itself so provides.

(5) Suppose more than one defendant is to be served by leaving a copy of the summons with the same person of "suitable age and discretion." How many copies of the summons must be delivered to that person? As many as there are defendants so served, holds *Raschel v. Rish*, 69 N.Y.2d 694, 512 N.Y.S.2d 22, 504 N.E.2d 389 (1986). The defendants there were a doctor and a hospital. One

copy of the summons was served on the hospital administrator. Although a copy was also mailed to the doctor at his home, no jurisdiction was acquired over him:

> Where only one copy of the summons and complaint was delivered to the hospital administrator . . . actual notice to the doctor depended upon several contingencies. The administrator had to know, for example, that service was being made on the doctor as well as the hospital, notify him, and furnish him with copies of the documents.

[E] Service on an Agent: CPLR 308(3)

EDWARD V. GREEN ENTERPRISES, INC. v. MANILOW
Supreme Court, Broome County
103 Misc. 2d 869, 427 N.Y.S.2d 199 (1980)

RICHARD F. KUHNEN, JUSTICE PRESIDING.

Defendant appears specially and moves to dismiss the complaint on the ground that the court has no jurisdiction of the person of defendant as he was never served with a copy of the summons.

The action arises out of contracts between the parties by which defendant Manilow undertook to perform in concert at Providence, Rhode Island Civic Center on designated dates. Service of the summons and complaint was made by personal service upon Miles J. Lourie who is admittedly defendant's "manager."

The affidavits in opposition to the motion maintain that Lourie "was duly authorized by defendant Manilow to accept service of process on behalf of defendant," which is denied. The only argument in support of that contention is that Lourie was defendant's manager, which is conceded, and was his "agent in connection with the transactions which were the subject matter of the instant lawsuit." Counsel points out also that within five days after service of the summons plaintiff's attorneys "received a telephone call from Sandor Frankel, Esq., attorney for *defendant*, concerning the subject matter of the instant action" and that this fact "serves to validate and ratify the agency between Miles Lourie and defendant Manilow with regard to service of process herein."

The provisions for service upon a natural person are governed by CPLR 308, and require personal service unless service is effected by the other methods described in subdivisions 2 through 5, which is not asserted here. Nor does plaintiff assert that Lourie was an agent designated to receive process, as provided by Rule 318. Nor is it asserted that the contracts upon which the action is based provided for service upon Lourie, or that any power of attorney so provided. (General Obligations Law, § 5-1502H-6;. . . .)

The decisions cited by plaintiff's counsel all have to do with service upon a "managing or general agent" of a corporate defendant rather than a natural person. . . .

Other than the fact that a corporation can act only through an agency, there would seem to be no valid reason why a "managing or general agent" of a corporation should be designated by law for service of process whereas such a managing or general agent of a natural person should not be so designated. A natural person may conduct the same type and extent of business as a corporation and require the same type of managing or general agent, but choose not to incorporate. Persons in the performing arts usually do business through a managing agent, as the defendant here does, and should logically be as amenable to process as the managing agent of a corporation. That however is a matter for legislative, not judicial consideration.

The motion to dismiss the complaint is therefore granted without costs.

NOTES

(1) Under the facts of the principal case, would jurisdiction have been acquired if, in addition to delivery on Manilow's manager, a copy of the summons was mailed to Manilow at his last known residence?

(2) Various methods by which an agent for the service of process may be appointed are mentioned in the principal case and in § 1.05, *supra*.

[F] "Nail and Mail" Service: CPLR 308(4)

FEINSTEIN v. BERGNER
Court of Appeals
48 N.Y.2d 234, 422 N.Y.S.2d 356, 397 N.E.2d 1161 (1979)

GABRIELLI, J.

Plaintiffs appeal from an order of the Appellate Division which dismissed their complaint for failure properly to serve the defendant with process. The outcome of their appeal depends upon the correct interpretation of CPLR 308 (subd 4), which permits substitute service by "affixing the summons to the door of either the actual place of business, dwelling place or usual place of abode . . . of the person to be served" and by "mailing the summons to such person at his last known residence."

The case arises out of an automobile accident which occurred on April 2, 1972. Plaintiff Pauline Wilensky and her husband, Martin Wilensky, who died on the day of the accident, were injured when they were struck by a car owned and operated by defendant Bergner. At the time of the accident, Bergner was residing with his parents at 76 Aster Court, Brooklyn, the address he gave at the accident scene.

Some 30 months after the accident, plaintiff Pauline Wilensky and the administrator of the deceased Martin Wilensky's estate attempted to commence an action against Bergner for conscious pain and suffering and wrongful death. Plaintiffs' process server made two visits to the Aster Court address before affixing the summons and complaint to the door on August 27, 1974 and mailing copies of the papers to the Aster Court address on August 29.

Unbeknown to plaintiffs, however, defendant Bergner had moved from his parents' home in February of 1973, having married and established a household of his own at 2729 West 33rd Street in Brooklyn. Although he returned to his parents' home for a brief period in February of 1975, when his mother died, Bergner did not regularly frequent the Aster Court address. Thus, at the time the summons and complaint were affixed to the door at 76 Aster Court, that address was not and could no longer be considered defendant's dwelling place.

Bergner ultimately received notice that a suit was pending against him when his father mailed copies of the summons and complaint to his home. He thereafter timely moved to have the action dismissed on the ground that the attempted service was ineffective. Special Term denied the motion, finding at the outset that plaintiff had exercised "due diligence" in attempting to effect personal service before resorting to the substitute "nail and mail" method of service authorized by CPLR 308 (subd 4). As to defendant's contention that plaintiff had failed to comply with the CPLR 308 (subd 4) requirement of affixing process to the door of the "dwelling place" or "usual place of abode," Special Term concluded that defendant should be estopped from raising such a defense since his father's actions in mailing the summons and complaint to his new address rather than returning them to plaintiffs through the mails "effectively concealed" from plaintiffs the fact that Bergner had moved. On appeal to the Appellate Division, however, this determination was reversed. Although the Appellate Division agreed that due diligence had been exercised in the plaintiffs' preliminary efforts to effect service by personal delivery, it found the purported substitute service defective and, concluding that there could be no estoppel in the absence of fraud or misrepresentation on the part of defendant, granted Bergner's motion to dismiss.

At the outset, we note that we leave undisturbed the lower courts' findings that "due diligence" was exercised in the first instance, as we are unprepared to say that the finding was erroneous as a matter of law. We accordingly assume that the use of substitute service under CPLR 308 (subd 4) was authorized in this case and we address only the question whether the purported service conformed to the requirements of the statute. We conclude that it did not.

The "nail and mail" provision of the CPLR permits a plaintiff to mail duplicate process to the defendant at his last known residence, but clearly requires that the "nailing" be done at the defendant's "actual place of business, dwelling place or usual place of abode." While there may be some question as to whether there is a distinction between "dwelling place" and "usual place of abode,"[3] there has never been any serious doubt that neither term may be equated with the "last known residence" of the defendant (*Chalk v Catholic Med. Center of Brooklyn & Queens*, 58 AD2d 822; *Polansky v Paugh*, 23 AD2d 643; *Entwistle v Stone*, 53 Misc 2d 227; McLaughlin, Practice Commentaries, McKinney's Cons Laws of NY, Book 7B, CPLR 308:4, p 208; *see* Siegel, New York Practice, § 72, p 78). Indeed there are cogent reasons for preserving the distinction, apart from the obvious principle that where the Legislature has used different words in a series, the words should not be construed as mere redundancies (*see* McKinney's Cons Laws of NY, Book 1, Statutes, § 231).

Under the original version of CPLR 308, service by any method other than personal delivery to the defendant was impermissible unless prior "diligent" efforts had been made to serve the defendant in person. Many commentators, however, criticized this requirement as overly stringent, contending that it was the primary cause of the disreputable practice known as "sewer service" (Sixteenth Ann Report of NY Judicial Conference, 1971, p A38; *see* McLaughlin, Practice Commentaries, McKinney's Cons Laws of NY, Book 7B, CPLR 308:2, p 206; 1 Weinstein-Korn-Miller, NY Civ Prac, par 308.13). Accordingly, when the statute was revised in 1970 (L 1970, ch 852), the Legislature attempted to strike a balance between the need to ensure that defendants receive actual notice of the pendency of litigation against them and the need to build into the statute sufficient flexibility to discourage cynical practices such as "sewer service." To accomplish this goal, the Legislature enacted an amendment which permitted plaintiffs to serve by delivering process to "a person of suitable age and discretion" at the defendant's dwelling place or usual place of abode and mailing copies of the papers to the defendant's "last known residence" without first having to attempt to effect service by personal delivery (CPLR 308, subd 2). The Legislature stopped short, however, of making any substantive changes in the "nail and mail" method of substitute service. Significantly, in both the "leave and mail" and "nail and mail" subdivisions, the Legislature retained both the requirement that the summons be delivered or affixed to the defendant's actual place of business, dwelling place or usual place of abode and the

---

[3] Plaintiffs contend that, even if the summons and complaint were not affixed at defendant's "dwelling place," service should nonetheless be deemed proper because the papers were "nailed" to the door of Bergner's "usual place of abode," his parent's home. While we agree in principle that there may be a distinction between "dwelling place" and "usual place of abode" (*see Rich Prods. Corp. v Diamond*, 51 Misc 2d 675; McLaughlin, Practice Commentaries, McKinney's Cons Laws of NY, Book 7B, CPLR 308:2, p 207; 1 Weinstein-Korn-Miller, NY Civ Prac, par 308.13), we need not decide that question here, since plaintiffs' allegations are not sufficient to support the conclusion that defendant had a "usual place of abode" at the Aster Court address separate from his "dwelling place" at the West 33rd Street address. Plaintiffs have alleged only that Bergner voted from the Aster Court address in 1974 and returned there for a brief period in 1975. Such facts, however, are not sufficient to establish the degree of permanence and stability that is necessarily implied by the term "usual place of abode" (*see Smithtown Gen. Hosp. v Quinlivan*, 88 Misc 2d 1031; 1 Weinstein-Korn-Miller, NY Civ Prac, par 308.13). [Some footnotes have been omitted. — Eds.]

additional requirement that the summons be mailed to the defendant's last known residence. Presumably, the Legislature left these aspects of CPLR 308 intact in the belief that a further liberalization of the requirements for service would jeopardize the primary statutory purpose of ensuring that defendants receive actual notice of the pendency of litigation against them. In light of the Legislature's continued adherence to these dual requirements, we cannot and should not blur the distinction between "dwelling place" and "last known residence," since to do so would be to diminish the likelihood that actual notice will be received by potential defendants. While a rule which permits both the "nailing" and "mailing" steps to be completed at a defendant's last known residence would make it infinitely easier to serve the "hard-to-find" defendant, such a rule would not ensure that a readily accessible defendant is given adequate notice. Hence, we find the construction of CPLR 308 (subd 4) proposed by the plaintiffs to be unacceptable (*see Mullane v Central Hanover Trust Co.*, 339 US 306).

Nor do we find any "inherent inconsistency" in requiring the "affixing" to be done at the actual dwelling place or usual place of abode while permitting the "mailing" to be completed by mailing to the defendant's last known residence. Of course, we assume that plaintiffs will mail copies of the summons to the defendant's actual residence where that address is known (*see* Siegel, New York Practice, § 72, at pp 77-78). Indeed, in cases where the defendant's residence is known, the actual dwelling place and the last known residence would be the same location by definition. Nevertheless, we decline to view the "last known residence" clause as a mere redundancy or as evidence of inartful draftsmanship because we believe that the clause was inserted primarily to address those situations in which the defendant's residence is unknown, but his "actual place of business" is known to the plaintiff. In such cases, service would be literally impossible if the statute did not allow the second step of "mailing" to be completed by sending the papers to the defendant's last known residence. Thus, when the statute is read in its entirety, as it must be, it becomes clear that the Legislature deliberately used the term "last known residence" as a means of encompassing cases where only the actual place of business is known as well as cases where the defendant's current residence is known.[5]

Turning to the facts in this case, we find that the purported service was ineffective, since the plaintiff failed to comply with the specific mandates of CPLR 308 (subd 4). The summons here was affixed to the door of defendant's last known residence rather than his actual abode. That Bergner subsequently received actual notice of the suit does not cure this defect, since notice received by means other than those authorized by statute cannot serve to bring a defendant within the jurisdiction of the court (*see, e.g., McDonald v Ames Supply Co.*, 22 NY2d 111). Nor may Bergner be estopped from raising the defect in service

---

[5] We note that, in cases where neither the "actual place of business" nor the "dwelling place" or "usual place of abode" is known, the plaintiff may nonetheless serve the defendant, provided there is a jurisdictional basis, by obtaining a court order pursuant to CPLR 308 (subd 5) (*see Dobkin v Chapman*, 21 NY2d 490).

as a defense, since plaintiffs here have failed to demonstrate that Bergner engaged in conduct which was calculated to prevent them from learning of his new address (*see Cohen v Arista Truck Renting Corp.*, 70 Misc 2d 729). Since potential defendants ordinarily have no affirmative duty to keep those who might sue them abreast of their whereabouts (*cf. Dobkin v Chapman*, 21 NY2d 490, 504), we can find no basis for invoking the estoppel doctrine here.

The order of the Appellate Division should be affirmed, with costs.

FUCHSBERG, J. (dissenting).

As I read it, CPLR 308 (subd 4)'s use of diverse terms to specify the locations at which the two steps of "nailing" and "mailing" must take place renders the statute ambiguous. Therefore, until such time as the Legislature sees fit to revamp its confusing verbiage, I believe we should wield our well-recognized prerogative of construing procedural statutes so as not to foreshorten the legitimate claims and expectations of litigants (*see* CPLR 104; McKinney's Cons Laws Of NY, Book 1, Statutes, § 325). . . .

NOTES

(1) The accident which gave rise to the principal case occurred some seven years before the Court of Appeals made the decision here reproduced. The statute of limitations would therefore bar the plaintiff from attempting to recommence the action by proper service. Would that be so today? Or could the plaintiff in a similar situation (assuming proper commencement by filing) obtain an extension of time to serve the summons pursuant to 306-b?

Subsequent to the ruling in *Feinstein,* the Fourth Department held that a defendant was not estopped from challenging the correctness of service simply because service was made to the address on his driver's license. *New York State Higher Educ. Servs. Corp. v. Perchik*, 207 A.D.2d 1040, 617 N.Y.S.2d 610 (4th Dep't 1994). The court emphasized that the defendant made no attempt to conceal the correct address. But see *Benjamin v. Avis Rent-A-Car Sys.*, 208 A.D.2d 449, 617 N.Y.S.2d 719 (1st Dep't 1994), where the First Department held that a defendant was estopped from claiming the address given to both the Department of Motor Vehicles and the police at the accident was not proper for service.

(2) In 1987, CPLR 308(2) and (4) were amended to allow the mailing to be made to the defendant's business address as an alternative to the last known residence. Would this have helped the plaintiff in the principal case?

(3) What steps should plaintiff's attorney take to protect a client if the defendant seeks to dismiss the action on the ground of improper service and the statute of limitations will expire before the issue is decided?

(4) "Nail and mail" service may be resorted to only if the process server has first sought with "due diligence" to effect service as prescribed in CPLR 308(1)

or (2). The courts have been markedly demanding in defining the requisite diligence. *E.g., Barnes v. City of New York*, 70 A.D.2d 580, 416 N.Y.S.2d 52 (2d Dep't 1979), *aff'd*, 51 N.Y.2d 906, 434 N.Y.S.2d 991, 415 N.E.2d 979 (1980) (due diligence held lacking though process server tried to serve the individual defendants on four occasions at their home; since all attempts were made during normal business hours, the server should have realized that they were working people and should have returned after business hours or sought them at their place of business). *See also Smith v. Wilson*, 130 A.D.2d 821, 515 N.Y.S.2d 146 (3d Dep't 1987) (due diligence standard not met by three attempts to serve, outside working hours, since no attempts were made on weekends and the process server made no inquiries to determine defendant's whereabouts or place of employment).

(5) In eviction proceedings (which in New York City are brought in the Housing Part of the New York City Civil Court), nail and mail service is authorized by Real Prop. Ac. and Proc. Law § 735, if admittance to the premises cannot be made "upon reasonable application." Although this standard requires less effort than the "due diligence" requirement of CPLR 308(4), it has been held that a single visit by a process server during working hours does not meet this standard. *Eight Assocs. v. Hynes*, 102 A.D.2d 746, 476 N.Y.S.2d 881 (1st Dep't 1984), *aff'd*, 65 N.Y.2d 739, 492 N.Y.S.2d 15, 481 N.E.2d 555 (1985).

Why should there be a less exacting standard applied in eviction proceedings than in actions governed by CPLR 308(4)?

[G] Service Under V.T.L. § 253

As described in section 1.06[C], *supra*, § 253 of the New York Vehicle and Traffic Law subjects non-resident motorists to in personam jurisdiction for the purpose of claims arising out of accidents in New York. The same section authorizes a special method of serving the summons in such cases which is designed to ease the plaintiff's task. Service under VTL § 253 requires two steps:

(1) Service on the Secretary of State — by mailing a copy of the summons (and a fee of five dollars) to the Secretary's Albany office, or personally delivering it at one of the offices maintained by the Secretary throughout the State.

(2) Service on the defendant — by sending to defendant a notice of the service upon the Secretary of State and a copy of the summons and complaint by certified mail or registered mail with return receipt requested or by causing the papers to be delivered personally to defendant. If the certified or registered mail method is chosen, and the receipt is returned marked refused, VTL § 253 provides for a mailing to defendant by ordinary post mailing of a notice of the original mailing and refusal. If the original mailing is unclaimed, the statute provides for a second mailing, by ordinary post, of the summons.

Proof of service is required to be filed within 30 days after return of the registered mail receipt. Service is complete when proof of service is filed.

The utility of the elaborate § 253 lies in its avoidance of the need to personally serve the defendant in a remote jurisdiction, as might otherwise be required. The potential problem under § 253, that service on defendant might not be possible in the manner provided — *e.g.*, where defendant has moved before the mailing and left no forwarding address — may require resort to some other method of service. An example is found in the next case.

[H] Expedient Service Under CPLR 308(5)

DOBKIN v. CHAPMAN
Court of Appeals
21 N.Y.2d 490, 289 N.Y.S.2d 161, 236 N.E.2d 451 (1968)

CHIEF JUDGE FULD.

Each of these three cases stems from an automobile accident in New York in which the victim was either injured or killed. In two of the cases, the defendants were residents while, in the third, they had been domiciled in another state. Since the defendants' whereabouts were unknown, rendering normal prescribed methods of service of process upon them impossible, we are called upon to decide an important question of first impression, namely, whether the methods directed by the respective courts for such service were authorized by paragraph 4 [now paragraph 5]* of CPLR 308 and, if they were, whether they satisfied due process requirements. The Appellate Division, Second Department, upheld the method of service in each case, and the appeal is before us by permission of that court on a certified question.

The facts in the three cases may be briefly stated.

Dobkin v. Chapman

The plaintiff, a New York resident, sues to recover for personal injuries sustained in an accident in Kings County, in which he was struck by an automobile operated by one of the defendants and owned by the other. The car bore a Pennsylvania registration plate. The owner's registration certificate, produced at the time of the accident, indicated that he lived at an address in Aliquippa, Pennsylvania; this was also the address given by the owner to the Pennsylvania Bureau of Motor Vehicles. The driver's operator's license, also displayed, showed that the driver resided in the same town but at another address.

Numerous letters sent to these addresses by ordinary mail were not answered but were not returned. However, certified and registered mail sent to the same

---

* Subsequent references to the statute in the opinion have been changed to reflect current numbering. — Eds.

addresses were returned by the Post Office. The Sheriff of the county in which Aliquippa was located was unable to find the defendants to serve them with process sent him for that purpose. In his return, he stated that one of the addresses was that of the defendants' parents who told him that they had not heard from the defendants in four years. The plaintiff thereupon attempted to effect service pursuant to section 253 of the Vehicle and Traffic Law by serving the Secretary of State and mailing the summons and complaint to the defendants by registered mail. This attempt proved unsuccessful since the envelopes were returned, unopened, with the notation, "Moved. Left no address," and, thus, the required proof of the delivery or refusal of the registered mail was lacking.

On these facts, the Civil Court of the City of New York, Kings County, concluding that the defendants could not be served with process by any of the methods prescribed in paragraphs 1, 2 and 3 of CPLR 308, entered an ex parte order, pursuant to paragraph [5] of that section, permitting service by ordinary mail to the defendants at the Pennsylvania addresses. The Motor Vehicle Accident Indemnification Corporation (MVAIC), acting under article 17-A of the Insurance Law — having previously been notified of the claim and being satisfied, apparently, that the defendants were not insured — moved to vacate the service, presumably under CPLR 3211 (subd. [a], par. 8). . . .

Sellars v. Raye

An administratrix sues to recover for the wrongful death of her decedent, killed in an accident in Wantagh, Nassau County, while a passenger in an automobile owned and operated by the defendant. At the time of the accident, the defendant lived on Monroe Street in Brooklyn. The policy of insurance which covered his automobile had been cancelled 13 days before the accident.

The administratrix attempted to commence an action through personal service at the Brooklyn address but the defendant could not be found, and all correspondence directed to him at that address was returned. The plaintiff then sought an ex parte order under paragraph [5] of CPLR 308. In granting the application, the Supreme Court, Nassau County, in an order dated May 8, 1964, directed that service "upon the Secretary of State of the State of New York, in conformity with the provisions of section 254 of the Vehicle and Traffic Law, shall constitute due service" on the defendant. The plaintiff served the Secretary of State and sent two registered letters to the defendant at the Monroe Street address. Both letters were returned, one with a notation, "Unclaimed. Returned to Writer" and the other with a notation, "Moved. Left no address," thus failing to meet the requirements of the Vehicle and Traffic law. The plaintiff thereupon applied for and obtained another ex parte order, also under paragraph [5] of CPLR 308. In that order, dated August 6, 1964 — and it is the one with which we are concerned — the court directed that the steps already taken under the earlier order be deemed sufficient service, provided that a copy of the summons and of the order be published once in a designated Brooklyn newspaper. MVAIC, previously notified that the defendant was uninsured and acting on behalf of itself and of the defendant, moved, under CPLR 3211 (subd. [a], par. 8), to set aside the service and dismiss the complaint. . . .

Keller v. Rappoport

The plaintiff, a New York resident, sues to recover for injuries sustained when his automobile collided with the defendant's car in Baldwin, Nassau County. At the time, the defendant resided at an address in Long Beach in the same county. He moved from that place without leaving any forwarding address and the plaintiff was unable to serve him with process. Inquiry from persons residing in the neighborhood where the defendant had lived, from his last known employer and from the New York State Motor Vehicle Bureau, proved unavailing. Sometime later, the plaintiff was advised by the defendant's liability insurance carrier that the defendant had left New York and had moved to a specified address in California.

The plaintiff then attempted service pursuant to sections 253 and 254 of the Vehicle and Traffic Law. However, registered mail sent to the California address was returned with the notation, "Moved — Left no Address." Further attempts to locate the defendant were equally unsuccessful. The plaintiff then applied to the Supreme Court, Nassau County, for an ex parte order under paragraph [5] of CPLR 308. The court determined that service on the defendant under paragraphs 1, 2 and 3 of 308 was impracticable and, acting pursuant to paragraph [5], directed that service be made (1) by mailing a copy of the summons and complaint to the defendant's last known address in New York (in Long Beach) and (2) by delivering copies thereof to the insurance carrier.

Following such service, the defendant, by attorneys for the insurance carrier, moved, under CPLR 3211 (subd. [a], par. 8), to vacate the ex parte order directing the manner of service and to dismiss the action. The court at Special Term denied the motion and, noting that the insurance carrier had been able to tell plaintiff's counsel of the defendant's removal to California, held that "the most reasonable means of giving notice to defendant was notice to [such] insurance carrier." The Appellate Division unanimously affirmed that disposition.

As already indicated, the appellant in each case contends that the mode of service employed was unauthorized by the statute and that, if it was authorized, it violated the requirements of due process. Agreeing with the conclusion reached by the Appellate Division, we find no merit in either of these contentions.

Turning first to the issue of statutory construction, we direct our attention to CPLR 308. Entitled "Personal service upon a natural person," 308 provides how such service may be made. In its first three paragraphs, the statute specifies with some precision the manner of effecting such personal service and in paragraph [5] it recites that, "if service is impracticable" under the other paragraphs, then, service "shall be made . . . in such manner as the court, upon motion without notice, directs."

. . . .

Corp. (68 AD2d 756, 759, 760, *supra*) stands only for the proposition that where a receptionist has for years accepted service of process for the corporation without rebuke by her superiors, a strong inference arises that she was an "agent authorized by appointment" to receive service, which inference must be successfully rebutted by the corporation in order to avoid a finding that in personam jurisdiction over the corporation had been acquired (*see, also, Survey of New York Practice*, 54 St. John's L Rev 382, 389). In the prior appeal in this case involving service upon defendant Southern Railway Company, the process server left the summons with that defendant's office manager who was clothed with substantial managerial powers and to whom he had been directed as the proper person to receive process by other employees in that defendant's office (*Colbert v International Security Bur.*, 70 AD2d 945, *affd* 49 NY2d 988, *supra*). Suffice it to say that neither of those factors is present here (*see, also, Fashion Page v Zurich Ins. Co.*, 50 NY2d 265). The case of *Green v Morningside Hgts. Housing Corp.* (13 Misc 2d 124, 125, *affd* 7 AD2d 708), relied upon by plaintiffs, is simply authority for the limited proposition that where one of the enumerated persons entitled to receive service on behalf of a corporation is present in the office, is avoiding service, and the process server delivers the summons to a receptionist who immediately redelivers it to the proper person, service will be upheld because "the delivery [was] so close both in time and space that it can be classified as a part of the same act."

In summary on this point, we hold that service upon Mrs. Sobel, a receptionist employed by corporate defendant International Security, did not confer in personam jurisdiction on the corporation where she possessed no supervisory or administrative duties, she specifically told the process server that she was not authorized to accept service, and he was not directed to her by other employees as a proper person upon whom service could be made. While we are aware that the service provisions of the CPLR are to be liberally construed (CPLR 104; *Fashion Page v Zurich Ins. Co.*, *supra*, p 271), to uphold service upon International Security on these facts would be violating, rather than liberally construing, the mandate of the statute. . . .

NOTES

(1) In *Fashion Page, Ltd. v. Zurich Insur. Co.*, 50 N.Y.2d 265, 428 N.Y.S.2d 890, 406 N.E.2d 747 (1980), the Court of Appeals held service proper under these circumstances:

> [T]he process server testified that he went to the William Street address at approximately 12:45 on December 13, 1976. The building directory indicated that the defendant's offices were located on the third floor. When he arrived at the defendant's offices he went to the receptionist and stated: "I have a summons and complaint to serve on Zurich. Can you please tell me who I might see or who handles this." The receptionist told him to proceed down a certain corridor and "see the girl sitting

down there." He did as directed and found Ann Robertson sitting at a desk. He told her that he had a summons and complaint to serve on Zurich. She asked to see the papers and, after looking them over, said "Okay, leave it with me. . . . I'll take it." When he asked her if she was authorized "to accept this," she stated "I can take it."

It was conceded that the receptionist and Ann Robertson were employed by the defendant for many years at its New York office, where there were over 100 employees. The receptionist testified that she was responsible for directing visitors to the proper person within the office. Ann Robertson stated that she was the executive secretary for Joseph Scanlon, who was a member of the board of directors and the vice-president in charge of the New York office. Although she was the only executive secretary at that office and apparently had some independent authority over certain "files" and correspondence, she said that she was not an officer or managing agent of the corporation and had not been expressly authorized to accept service on its behalf.

She admitted, however, that she had received the summons and complaint in this case and that she had informed Mr. Scanlon of this when he returned from lunch. At his direction she had forwarded the papers to the company's legal department by interoffice mail. She also admitted that she had regularly done this without objection for at least five years, whenever Mr. Scanlon was not in his office. As a result, during that period about half of the summonses brought to his office had been accepted by her. Her testimony on these points was confirmed by Mr. Scanlon.

The Court held that the defendant had effectively if informally designated Ms. Robertson as its agent for the service of process and that the server had reasonably relied upon directions from the receptionist in delivering the summons to the former.

Note the Second Department's refusal to follow *Fashion Page* in *Colbert v. International Security Bureau, Inc., supra.* Can the cases be satisfactorily distinguished? Do they help you solve Problem A in § 5.05[A], *supra?*

(2) Service on domestic corporations and foreign corporations authorized to do business in New York should present no problem. N.Y. Bus. Corp. Law (B.C.L.) § 304, makes the Secretary of State the agent of every such corporation for the service of the summons. The method of service is prescribed in B.C.L. § 306:

§ 306. Service of process.

(a) Service of process on a registered agent may be made in the manner provided by law for service of a summons, as if the registered agent was a defendant.

(b) Service of process on the secretary of state as agent of a domestic or authorized foreign corporation shall be made by personally delivering to and leaving with him or his deputy, or with any person authorized by the secretary of state to receive such service, at the office of the department of state in the city of Albany, duplicate copies of such process together with the statutory fee, which fee shall be a taxable disbursement. Service of process on such corporation shall be complete when the secretary of state is so served. The secretary of state shall promptly send one of such copies by certified mail, return receipt requested, to such corporation, at the post office address, on file in the department of state, specified for the purpose. If a domestic or authorized foreign corporation has no such address on file in the department of state, the secretary of state shall so mail such copy, in the case of a domestic corporation, in care of any director named in its certificate of incorporation at his address stated therein or, in the case of an authorized foreign corporation, to such corporation at the address of its office within this state on file in the department.

(c) If an action or special proceeding is instituted in a court of limited jurisdiction, service of process may be made in the manner provided in this section if the office of the domestic or foreign corporation is within the territorial jurisdiction of the court and the process sets forth that the action or special proceeding is within the jurisdiction of the court.

(d) Nothing in this section shall affect the right to serve process in any other manner permitted by law.

(3) The B.C.L. also allows a special method for serving unauthorized foreign corporations:

§ 307. Service of process on unauthorized foreign corporation.

(a) In any case in which a non-domiciliary would be subject to the personal or other jurisdiction of the courts of this state under article three of the civil practice law and rules, a foreign corporation not authorized to do business in this state is subject to a like jurisdiction. In any such case, process against such foreign corporation may be served upon the secretary of state as its agent. Such process may issue in any court in this state having jurisdiction of the subject matter.

(b) Service of such process upon the secretary of state shall be made by personally delivering to and leaving with him or his deputy, or with any person authorized by the secretary of state to receive such service, at the office of the department of state in the city of Albany, a copy of such process together with the statutory fee, which fee shall be a taxable disbursement. Such service shall be sufficient if notice thereof and a copy of the process are:

(1) Delivered personally without this state to such foreign corporation by a person and in the manner authorized to serve process by law of the jurisdiction in which service is made, or

(2) Sent by or on behalf of the plaintiff to such foreign corporation by registered mail with return receipt requested, at the post office address specified for the purpose of mailing process, on file in the department of state, or with any official or body performing the equivalent function, in the jurisdiction of its incorporation, or if no such address is there specified, to its registered or other office there specified, or if no such office is there specified, to the last address of such foreign corporation known to the plaintiff.

(c)(1) Where service of a copy of process was effected by personal service, proof of service shall be by affidavit of compliance with this section filed, together with the process, within thirty days after such service, with the clerk of the court in which the action or special proceeding is pending. Service of process shall be complete ten days after such papers are filed with the clerk of the court.

(2) Where service of a copy of process was effected by mailing in accordance with this section, proof of service shall be by affidavit of compliance with this section filed, together with the process, within thirty days after receipt of the return receipt signed by the foreign corporation, or other official proof of delivery or of the original envelope mailed. If a copy of the process is mailed in accordance with this section, there shall be filed with the affidavit of compliance either the return receipt signed by such foreign corporation or other official proof of delivery or, if acceptance was refused by it, the original envelope with a notation by the postal authorities that acceptance was refused. If acceptance was refused, a copy of the notice and process together with notice of the mailing by registered mail and refusal to accept shall be promptly sent to such foreign corporation at the same address by ordinary mail and the affidavit of compliance shall so state. Service of process shall be complete ten days after such papers are filed with the clerk of the court. The refusal to accept delivery of the registered mail or to sign the return receipt shall not affect the validity of the service and such foreign corporation refusing to accept such registered mail shall be charged with knowledge of the contents thereof.

(4) Although the differences between sections 306 and 307 of the Business Corporation Law may at first glance seem trivial, the next case shows how important those differences are.

FLICK v. STEWART-WARNER CORP.
Court of Appeals
76 N.Y.2d 50, 556 N.Y.S.2d 510, 555 N.E.2d 907 (1990)

HANCOCK, J.

Defendant is a foreign corporation not authorized to do business in the State of New York. Plaintiff, mistakenly believing that defendant was authorized to do business in the State, commenced this action pursuant to Business Corporation Law § 306 instead of Business Corporation Law § 307 which governs service on unauthorized foreign corporations. Concededly, plaintiff effected personal service on the Secretary of State at her office in Albany and thereafter defendant received a copy of the process at its office in Chicago. The question is whether under these circumstances the court acquired personal jurisdiction over defendant although plaintiff did not send a copy of the process to defendant by registered mail as required by section 307(b)(2) or file the affidavit of compliance required by section 307(c)(2). The Appellate Division concurred with Supreme Court that jurisdiction had been acquired and affirmed its denial of defendant's motion to dismiss (CPLR 3211[a][8]). For reasons which follow, we disagree. Accordingly, there should be a reversal.

I

Plaintiff sustained injuries when a hose, allegedly manufactured by defendant, malfunctioned. Defendant is a Virginia corporation having a principal office in Chicago, lllinois. It had not designated the Secretary of State as its agent for service of process since July 21, 1952 when it surrendered its certificate of authority to do business in the State of New York. Apparently assuming that defendant's designation of the Secretary of State was still in effect, plaintiff served two copies of the summons with notice on the Secretary at her office in Albany pursuant to Business Corporation Law § 306. The Secretary of State's office, after signing a receipt for the process, found from its records that defendant's certificate of authority had been canceled in 1952. It nevertheless sent a copy of the process by certified mail, return receipt, to defendant at its designated address in Chicago in accordance with section 306 and thereafter got back the signed card signifying receipt of the process by defendant.

When defendant's time to answer expired, plaintiff moved for a default judgment. Defendant opposed the motion for default and filed a cross motion seeking a dismissal of the action upon the ground that the service was ineffective. It argued that the court had not acquired jurisdiction over it because plaintiff had not met the requirements of Business Corporation Law § 307 for service on an unauthorized foreign corporation in that: (1) a copy of the process was not sent "by or on behalf of the plaintiff to such foreign corporation by registered mail with return, receipt requested" as prescribed by section 307(b)(2) (instead a copy was sent by the Secretary of State by certified mail); and (2) plaintiff did not file with the clerk of the court proof of such service by registered mail in an affidavit of compliance as required by section 307(c)(2).

Although Supreme Court denied defendant's dismissal motion, it also denied plaintiff's motion for a default and ordered plaintiff to accept defendant's notice of appearance and to serve a complaint within 30 days. On defendant's appeal, the Appellate Division unanimously affirmed. That court rejected the argument that the failure to comply with section 307 was jurisdictional.

. . . .

II

The question is whether the procedures established in Business Corporation Law § 307 are requirements of a jurisdictional nature which must be strictly satisfied. Plaintiff's argument, adopted by the Appellate Division, is that the only jurisdictional requirement is personal service on the Secretary of State who by the terms of section 307(a) is appointed defendant's agent for service of process. Once service on the Secretary of State is complete, the argument goes, jurisdiction is acquired and subsequent deviations from required procedures (*i.e.*, mailing by certified rather than by registered mail and not filing the affidavit of compliance) may, in the absence of prejudice, be excused as "mere irregularities." We disagree. The argument overlooks both the critical differences in the legal bases for jurisdiction over a foreign corporation, which depend upon whether the corporation is or is not authorized to do business in the State, and the distinctions in the applicable statutes which reflect these differences.

The predicate for this State's jurisdiction over an unauthorized foreign corporation is the fact that it is doing business in the State and has thus created a constructive presence over which New York courts can exert general jurisdiction (CPLR 301; *see, Laufer v. Ostrow*, 55 N.Y.2d 305, 309-310; *see generally*, 1 Weinstein-Korn-Miller, N.Y. Civ. Prac. paras. 301.14, 301.16). Assuming that the predicate for general jurisdiction over an unauthorized foreign corporation exists, section 307 prescribes the method for effecting service of process.

Service may be commenced on an unauthorized foreign corporation by serving the process "upon the secretary of state as its agent" (§ 307[a]). Such process must be served personally at the office of the Secretary of State in Albany or on the deputy or an authorized agent for service (§ 307[b]). Thereafter, notice of the service and a copy of the process must either be delivered "personally without this state to such foreign corporation" in accordance with section 307(b)(1) or sent "by or on behalf of the plaintiff to such foreign corporation by registered mail with return receipt requested" in accordance with section 307(b)(2). Regardless of whether such service is effected personally (§ 307[b][1]) or by registered mail (§ 307[b][2]) an affidavit of compliance must be filed in accordance with section 307(c)(1) or section 307(c)(2) with the clerk of the court in which the action is pending within 30 days after such service. In either case service of process is not complete until "*ten days after [the affidavit of compliance containing proof of service is] filed* with the clerk of the court" (§ 307[c][1], [2] [emphasis added]).

In the case of an unauthorized foreign corporation — as contrasted with a domestic corporation or a foreign corporation authorized to do business in the

State — the designation of the Secretary of State as its agent for service is imputed, not actual. The designation is effected by statutory edict on the theory that by doing business in the State a foreign corporation has submitted itself to the jurisdiction of our courts (*see,* Revised Supp. to Fifth Interim Report to Joint Legislative Committee to Study Revision of Corporation Laws, 1961 N.Y. Legis. Doc. No. 12, at 23-24). Because the appointment of the Secretary of State as agent is a constructive rather than an actual designation, the statute contains procedures calculated to assure that the foreign corporation, in fact, receives a copy of the process. Section 307(b) specifies that service "*shall be sufficient if notice thereof and a copy of the process*" (emphasis added) are either delivered personally to the foreign corporation without the State (*see,* § 307[b][1]) or sent to it by registered mail (§ 307[b][2]). The proof called for in the affidavit of compliance is that the required actual notice has been given either by personal service or by registered mail (*see,* § 307[c][1], [2]). These are not mere procedural technicalities but measures designed to satisfy due process requirements of actual notice.

In contrast, service of process on a foreign corporation authorized to do business in the State is simple. There are no theoretical uncertainties concerning the basis for jurisdiction since the foreign corporation is concededly doing business in the State and, indeed, has applied for authority for the express purpose of doing so (*see,* Business Corporation Law § 1304[a]). As part of its application for authority to do business, the foreign corporation must file a signed and verified designation of the Secretary of State as its agent for service of process and it must set forth the address to which the copy of any process is to be mailed (*see* Business Corporation Law § 1304[a][6]). Because of this express designation of the Secretary of State, there can be no question that service on the Secretary of State as the foreign corporation's designated agent is the equivalent of actual service on the foreign corporation. Thus, Business Corporation Law § 306 — unlike section 307 — provides that "[s]ervice of process on such corporation *shall be complete when the secretary of state is so served*" (§ 306[b] [emphasis added]).

In sum, we hold that strict compliance with the procedures of Business Corporation Law § 307 is required to effect service on an unauthorized foreign corporation. . . . The case of *Marine Midland Realty Credit Corp. v. Welbilt Corp.* (145 A.D.2d 84), cited by the Appellate Division, presents the converse of the situation before us — a foreign corporation authorized to do business in the State being served with process under the more stringent procedures of section 307, rather than under section 306. The holding in *Marine Midland* — that personal delivery of process to the Secretary of State in Albany was sufficient for the completion of service and that the irregularities caused by proceeding under section 307 could be disregarded — highlights the crucial point. In *Marine Midland*, unlike the case at bar, the defendant was authorized to do business in the State and had filed an actual designation of the Secretary of State as agent for service of process (*see,* Business Corporation Law § 1304[a][6]).

NOTES

(1) The defendant was served by certified mail and returned a signed acknowledgment of receipt, yet the Court of Appeals holds that jurisdiction was not acquired. Is this holding defensible?

(2) The Franchise Sales Act, General Business Law §§ 680, *et seq.*, adopted in 1984, designates the secretary of state as the agent for the service of process on directors and officers (even if sued in their individual capacity) of any corporation that sells or offers to sell a franchise in New York. *Id.*, § 686. *See* discussion in *Retail Software Services, Inc. v. Lashlee*, 854 F.2d 18 (2d Cir. 1988).

(3) Service on partnerships is covered by CPLR 310, and CPLR 310-a, which have been discussed in that connection in § 1.03[B], *supra*.

(4) Service on limited liability companies and unincorporated associations has also been treated earlier. *See* § 1.03[B].

§ 5.07 SERVICE ABROAD

PROBLEM B

How would you serve a summons on Volkswagenwerk, A.G., described in the *DeLagi* case in § 1.03[C], *supra*? What about Hilton Hotels (U.K.) Ltd., also described in the *DeLagi* case? The Asahi Metal Industry Co., described in the *Lamarca* case in § 1.06[D]?

REYNOLDS v. KOH
Appellate Division, Third Department
109 A.D.2d 97, 490 N.Y.S.2d 295 (1985)

Main, Justice.

After plaintiff Sue M. Reynolds was severely injured in an August 23, 1983 auto accident in Tompkins County, she and her husband commenced this action against several defendants, including Nissan Motor Company, Ltd. (Nissan), which had manufactured the automobile that plaintiffs were driving. Nissan is a Japanese entity with its principal place of business in Tokyo, Japan, and is not authorized to transact business in this State. Plaintiffs served Nissan with an amended summons and complaint by registered mail, return receipt requested, and delivered a copy to the New York Secretary of State pursuant to Business Corporation Law § 307. Nissan does not dispute that it received the amended summons and complaint, but moved to dismiss for lack of personal jurisdiction due to improper service of process. Nissan contended that although service comported with the requirements of Business Corporation Law § 307, service was ineffective due to plaintiffs' failure to serve through the Japanese Minister for Foreign Affairs as required by an international treaty known as the Convention on the Service Abroad of Judicial and Extrajudicial Documents in Civil or Commercial Matters, commonly referred to as the Hague Convention (20 UST 361, TIAS 6638, reprinted in Fed.Rules Civ.Pro., rule 4 [28 U.S.C.A., pp. 87, 97, n. 12(3) (1985 supp.)]). Special Term granted Nissan's motion dismissing the complaint as against it and plaintiffs' appeal followed.

The Hague Convention is designed "to simplify service of process abroad so as to ensure that documents are brought to the notice of the addressee in sufficient time" (*Tamari v. Bache & Co. [Lebanon] S.A.L.*, 431 F.Supp. 1226, 1228, *affd.* 565 F.2d 1194, *cert. denied* 435 U.S. 905, 98 S.Ct. 1450, 55 L.Ed.2d 495). It allows signatory nations to ratify subject to conditions or objections (Hague Convention art. 21). The Hague Convention article 10 provides:

> Provided the State of destination does not object, the present Convention shall not interfere with —
>
> (a) the freedom to send judicial documents, by postal channels, directly to persons abroad,
>
> (b) the freedom of judicial officers, officials or other competent persons of the State of origin to effect service of judicial documents directly through the judicial officers, officials or other competent persons of the State of destination,
>
> (c) the freedom of any person interested in a judicial proceeding to effect service of judicial documents directly through the judicial officers, officials or other competent persons of the State of destination (reprinted in Fed.Rules Civ. Pro., rule 4 [28 U.S.C.A., pp. 88-89 (1985 supp.)]).

Japan objected "to the use of the methods of service referred to in subparagraphs (b) and (c) of article 10," but not to the provisions of article 10(a) (Hague Convention, reprinted in Fed.Rules Civ.Pro., rule 4 [28 U.S.C.A., p. 97, n. 12(4) (1985 supp.)]). Plaintiffs contend that they sent the amended summons and complaint by postal channels directly to Nissan and, therefore, pursuant to article 10(a), service was properly made. Nissan argues that service by postal channels cannot be accomplished under article 10(a). Plaintiffs' position is supported by *Chrysler Corp. v. General Motors Corp.*, 589 F.Supp. 1182 and *Shoei Kako Co. v. Superior Court*, 33 Cal.App.3d 808, 109 Cal.Rptr. 402, whereas Nissan's position is supported by *Ordmandy v. Lynn*, 122 Misc.2d 954, 472 N.Y.S.2d 274. Recognizing that these cases reach different results concerning the effect of article 10(a), we have reviewed these cases and considered the proper interpretation to be given to article 10(a). Our conclusion is that service by postal channels cannot be permitted under article 10(a).

In *Shoei*, upon which Chrysler relies, the court considered the Hague Convention as a whole and concluded that because it dealt with the service abroad of judicial documents, "[t]he reference to 'the freedom to send judicial documents by postal channels, directly to persons abroad' would be superfluous unless it was related to the sending of such documents for the purpose of service" (*Shoei Kako Co. v. Superior Court, supra*, p. 821, 109 Cal.Rptr. 402, p. 411). Thus, article 10(a) was found to allow effective service of a summons on a Japanese corporation by mailing the summons to the headquarters of the corporation in Japan. To the contrary, the court in *Ordmandy* construed "send" as used in article 10(a) not to include service of process in the legal sense because such a construction "would vitiate the fundamental intent of the parties [to the Hague Convention] to establish more formal modes of service" (*Ordmandy v. Lynn, supra*, p. 955, 472 N.Y.S.2d 274).

We are persuaded that the interpretation by the court in *Ordmandy* is correct. That article 10(a) refers to "send," whereas the Hague Convention repeatedly refers to "service" of documents, indicates to us that article 10(a) was meant to authorize something other than "service" in the legal sense, such as the mere transmittal of notices and legal documents which need not be "served" in the legal sense. To hold otherwise would relegate the role of the Japanese Minister for Foreign Affairs in a way that seems to us contrary to the import of the Hague Convention. Accordingly, we are of the view that the mere sending of the amended summons and complaint to Nissan in Japan did not satisfy the service requirements of the Hague Convention so as to gain jurisdiction over Nissan.

Also contrary to plaintiffs' argument, the Hague Convention article 5 fails to provide a basis for jurisdiction over Nissan. This article, in pertinent part, provides:

> The [Japanese Minister for Foreign Affairs] shall itself serve the document or shall arrange to have it served by an appropriate agency, either —

> (a) by a method prescribed by its internal law for the service of documents in domestic actions upon persons who are within its territory, or

> (b) by a particular method requested by the applicant, unless such a method is incompatible with the law of the State addressed.

> Subject to sub-paragraph (b) of the first paragraph of this article, the document may always be served by delivery to an addressee who accepts it voluntarily (reprinted in Fed.Rules Civ.Pro., rule 4 [28 U.S.C.A., p. 88 (1985 supp)]).

Plaintiffs never requested the Japanese Minister for Foreign Affairs to permit service in accordance with Business Corporation Law § 307. Furthermore, the law of Japan is apparently incompatible with the law of New York, which provides for direct service by one litigant upon another, because under Japanese law, service is the court's responsibility (*see* Minji sosho ho [Code of Civil Procedure], Law No. 29 of 1890 art 160 et seq. [Japan]). Thus, the voluntary acceptance by Nissan of the amended summons and complaint was not in accordance with article 5(b) and cannot be countenanced. For all the reasons expressed, we are unpersuaded by plaintiffs' reliance on *Tamari v. Bache & Co. (Lebanon) S.A.L.*, 431 F.Supp. 1226, *supra* for the proposition that methods of service other than those using the Japanese Minister for Foreign Affairs are permitted. We further note that *Tamari* relied on *Shoei*, which we have not followed.

In sum, we adopt the rule deduced in *Ordmandy*, for it appears to us most consistent with the intent and design of the Hague Convention. Accordingly, plaintiffs' reliance on Business Corporation Law § 307 for the method of service on Nissan was insufficient to gain personal jurisdiction over Nissan, thereby requiring affirmance of Special Term's order granting Nissan's motion to dismiss for lack of personal jurisdiction.

Order affirmed, without costs.

NOTES

(1) Although CPLR 313 authorizes service outside New York "in the same manner as service is made within the state," the principal case shows that matters are not so simple. The U.S. has ratified the Hague Convention on the Service Abroad of Judicial and Extrajudicial Documents (described in the principal case) and that treaty is therefore supreme over state law. U.S. Const. Art VI, § 2. Service which does not accord with the provisions of the treaty, including any reservations made by the nation in which service is to be made, is invalid.

(2) Whether service can be made by mail in Japan is a question which continues to divide the courts. An affirmative conclusion was reached in *Rissew v. Yamaha Motor Co. Ltd.*, 129 A.D.2d 94, 515 N.Y.S.2d 352 (4th Dep't 1987). Compare *Sardanis v. Sumitomo Corp.*, 279 A.D.2d 225, 718 N.Y.S.2d 66 (1st Dep't 2001), which agrees with the principal case that personal jurisdiction cannot be acquired by mailing process to a defendant in Japan.

(3) Although the Hague Convention governs the manner of service in a foreign nation, it is domestic law which determines where service must be effected. Thus, if under state law, service may properly be made within the United States on a foreign corporation, the Convention is not relevant. *See Volkswagenwerk AG v. Schlunk*, 486 U.S. 694, 108 S. Ct. 2104, 100 L. Ed. 2d 722 (1988) (Hague Convention does not apply because service was made on the defendant's domestic subsidiary, which was its agent for the service of process under relevant state law); *but see Stewart v. Volkswagen of America*, 81 N.Y.2d 203, 597 N.Y.S.2d 612, 613 N.E.2d 518 (1993). There, service purportedly under Business Corporation Law § 307 was held invalid because, after serving the Secretary of State, plaintiff mailed process to Volkswagen of America (VWOA) in New Jersey. The proper defendant was Volkswagen A.G. (VWAG) in Wolfsburg, Germany.

The fact VWOA was under VWAG's control, while perhaps relevant to the question of jurisdiction, is irrelevant to the § 307 mailing provisions.

(4) Service on a defendant in a nation that is not a signatory to the Hague Convention may, under New York law, be made pursuant to CPLR 313. Again, enforcement problems may ensue if service does not also comport with the law of the nation where service is made.

§ 5.08 PROOF OF SERVICE

Depending on the method used to serve the summons, the plaintiff may be required to file proof of service with the clerk of the court. Service under CPLR 308(2) (leave and mail) and CPLR 308(4) (nail and mail) for example, must be followed by proof of service within twenty days after service. Neither CPLR 308(2) nor CPLR 308(4) provide any sanction of failure to file proof of service, but both of those subdivisions provide that service is not "complete" until ten days after proof is filed. The time within which the defendant must appear does not begin to run until that time, CPLR 320. As we saw in *Flick v. Stewart-Warner Corp.*, in § 5.06, *supra*, proof of service is vital when service is made on an unauthorized foreign corporation under Bus. Corp. Law 307, and when made under other statutes there mentioned by the Court of Appeals.

Proof of service will in any case be required to secure a default judgment. CPLR 3215(e). It may also be needed if the defendant claims that service was not made and seeks dismissal of the action. *E.g., Denning v. Lettenty*, 48 Misc. 2d 185, 264 N.Y.S.2d 619 (Sup. Ct. 1965) (affidavit of deceased process server used as proof).

CPLR 306 provides that proof of service may be made in any of these ways: (1) by a certificate of service by a sheriff or other authorized public officer; or (2) by affidavit of the person who made the service or of a third person who has actual knowledge; or (3) by admission, in writing, of the service by the party served; or (4) by a signed acknowledgment of receipt of a summons or summons and complaint which has been served by mail pursuant to CPLR 312-a. An admission is the equivalent of an affidavit of service, but it is not a waiver of objection to the method of service. *Erickson v. Robison*, 282 A.D. 574, 125 N.Y.S.2d 736 (4th Dep't 1953). The affidavit or certificate of service should demonstrate that service was by an authorized person and in an authorized manner, and must specify the papers served, the person who was served and the date, place and manner of service.

If service has been made by delivery to an individual, the affidavit or certificate must, under CPLR 306(b), include a brief personal description, a requirement which is intended to reduce the likelihood that false affidavits would be used. And if service was by "nail and mail," which can only be done after other methods have been attempted with "due diligence," the proof must specify "the dates, addresses and the times" of other attempts to serve. CPLR 306(c).

Proof of service requirements are helpful in determining whether the server actually complied with the service requirements of CPLR 308. Also useful in regulating summons service is N.Y. Gen. Bus. Law § 89-b and § 89-c which together require all "process servers" (*i.e.*, persons other than attorneys who derive income from serving papers in lawsuits more than five times per year), to keep detailed records such as how, when and to whom each summons served by them was delivered.

Should defects in the form of proof of service be considered "jurisdictional" or should they be curable by amendment?

Chapter 6

DEFENDANT'S RESPONSE TO PLAINTIFF'S FORUM CHOICE: THE APPEARANCE

§ 6.01 INTRODUCTORY NOTE

Once the summons has been served, the next step in the litigation process will usually come from the defendant, for a failure to act will result in a default. CPLR 3215(a). It is at this stage that the defendant must decide whether to appear in the action and, if so, what kind of appearance to make. To put it another way, the defendant must either accept the plaintiff's assertion of jurisdiction (whether in personam or in rem), challenge it, or default with the expectation of attacking the judgment in another forum.

Students grappling with the appearance concept should be aware at the outset that it is complex because (1) there are several ways of making an appearance, including not only the three listed in CPLR 320(a), but also the amorphous "informal appearance," defined only by case law, and (2) the effect of an appearance depends in part on which of these forms it takes but also depends on whether the plaintiff has obtained jurisdiction in rem, quasi-in-rem, or in personam (and if the latter, whether or not it is "long arm" jurisdiction).

It will facilitate understanding to use different terminology for each type of appearance. As a term of art, the word "appearance" will be used in this chapter to refer only to the three types of formal appearance listed in CPLR 320(a). Related concepts, all defined below, are the informal appearance; the general (or jurisdiction-conferring) appearance; the restricted appearance and the limited appearance.

§ 6.02 HOW AN APPEARANCE IS MADE

The simplest kind of appearance is made by service of the Notice of Appearance.

FORM

SUPREME COURT OF THE STATE OF NEW YORK
COUNTY OF _____

_____
                          Plaintiff,   Notice of appearance
    vs. _____   and demand
                   Defendant.   Index No._____

PLEASE TAKE NOTICE, that the defendant (or the defendants, _____
_____
and _____) appears in this action and we have been retained as attorneys
for the defendant in this action, and demand that a copy of the complaint and
all notices and other papers in this action be served on us at our office, .
_____
Street, _____ , New York.

    (Date)

                          Signature:

                          _____ & _____ ,
                          Attorneys for Defendant,
                          Office and P.O. Address,
                          _____ Street,
                          _____ , New York
                          Telephone No.

To: _____ , Esq.,
Attorney for Plaintiff,
_____ Street,
_____ , New York

NOTES

(1) The above form includes a demand for a complaint. This is the common practice when the summons has been served without the complaint. Even if the demand is omitted, service of the notice of appearance alone requires the plain-

tiff to serve a complaint. CPLR 3012(b); *Bal v. Court Employment Project, Inc.*, 73 A.D.2d 69, 424 N.Y.S.2d 715 (1st Dep't 1980).

Alternatively, a demand for the complaint may be served without the notice of appearance. CPLR 3012(b). This procedure has the advantage of allowing the defendant to delay the appearance until the complaint is served. This may be especially advisable when the defendant is a non-resident with no assets in New York, who may wish to challenge New York's assertion of jurisdiction in another forum. An appearance in New York could prevent this. *See* CPLR 320(b); *Everitt v. Everitt*, discussed in the notes following *Matter of Einstoss* in § 6.04, *infra*. What other advantage would this practice give to a defendant, whether or not a non-resident?

(2) A defendant served with a complaint (either with the summons or separately pursuant to demand) may appear by serving an answer. A form is found in § 13.03, *infra*. Note that service of an answer is an appearance even though the document itself never uses that word. The same is true of the other kind of appearance permitted after receipt of the complaint, the "motion which has the effect of extending the time to answer." CPLR 320(a).

(3) What motions meet the just-quoted description of CPLR 320(a)? There are only two which do so in specific terms: a motion to correct the complaint, *see* CPLR 3024(c), and a motion to dismiss the complaint, *see* CPLR 3211(a), (f). It is unclear whether other motions, such as a motion to extend the time to respond to a summons, would be an "informal appearance." This problem is discussed in § 6.05, *infra*.

(4) CPLR 312-a, which allows service by first class mail, may be read to create a problem for the defendant so served because subdivision (b)(2) of CPLR 312-a states that a defendant served with a summons and complaint or notice of petition and petition by mail "shall serve an answer within twenty days of the date the signed acknowledgment of receipt is mailed or delivered to the sender." This subdivision conflicts with the general requirement of CPLR 320 that the defendant served with a summons and complaint must appear in the action by serving an answer *or* making a motion having the effect of extending the time to answer (*i.e.*, a motion for a more definite statement under CPLR 3024 or a motion to dismiss under CPLR 3211(a)). It seems unlikely that the Legislature intended to deprive the defendant of the "motion" option simply because the plaintiff chose to use mail service, especially since no amendment was made to CPLR 320. Reading the latter section together with CPLR 312-a(b)(2), therefore, indicates that the "motion" option may be used even when the summons is served by mail and acknowledged.

(5) May a defendant who has been served with a summons but no complaint, move to dismiss the action under CPLR 3211(a) prior to demanding the complaint? The plain meaning of the first sentence of CPLR 3211(e) indicates a positive answer, and such a motion has been permitted to assert the defense that the summons was jurisdictionally defective. *Ciaschi v. Town of Enfield*, 86

A.D.2d 903, 448 N.Y.S.2d 267 (3d Dep't 1982). If, however, the defense is a lack of jurisdictional basis, it has been held that a motion to dismiss is premature if the complaint has not been served. *Fraley v. Desilu Productions, Inc.*, 23 A.D.2d 79, 258 N.Y.S.2d 294 (1st Dep't 1965). The court reasoned that in the absence of the complaint, one could not tell whether jurisdiction could be based on CPLR 302, as that section depends in part on the nature of the plaintiff's cause of action.

The CPLR does not explicitly chart a procedural path for a defendant who has unsuccessfully moved to dismiss an action after receipt of the summons only. To avoid a default, it is apparently necessary to demand a complaint within ten days after service on him of the order denying the motion. *Cf.*, CPLR 3211(f); *Fraley v. Desilu, supra*, 23 A.D.2d at 83, 258 N.Y.S.2d at 298.

§ 6.03 TIME LIMITS

PROBLEM A

Tom sued Acme, Inc. in the Supreme Court, Albany County, by causing a summons and complaint to be personally delivered to the President of Acme (in Pittsburgh, PA) on June 1, 2006.

(a) What is the last day on which Acme could appear without defaulting? Would it matter that July 1, 2006 was a Saturday?

(b) Suppose Tom had also joined Joe, the President of Acme, as an individual defendant, and had a summons properly served on him by "nail and mail" at Joe's home in Pittsburgh on June 1, 2006. What is the last day on which Joe could appear?

(c) Suppose that Tom had served Joe (as an individual defendant) by mailing the summons and complaint to him, pursuant to CPLR 312-a, at his home in Pittsburgh on June 1, 2006?

NOTES

(1) In computing the time within which to appear, keep in mind not only CPLR 320, 312-a and 3012, but also Gen. Constr. Law §§ 20 and 25-a:

§ 20. Day, computation

A number of days specified as a period from a certain day within which or after or before which an act is authorized or required to be done means such number of calendar days exclusive of the calendar day from which the reckoning is made. If such period is a period of two days, Saturday, Sunday or a public holiday must be excluded from the reckoning if it is an intervening day between the day from which the reckoning is made and the last day of the period. In computing any specified period of time from a specified event, the day upon which the event happens is deemed the day from which the reckoning is made. The day from which any specified period of time is reckoned shall be excluded in making the reckoning.

§ 25-a. Public holiday, Saturday or Sunday in statutes; extension of time where performance of act is due on Saturday, Sunday or public holiday

1. When any period of time, computed from a certain day, within which or after which or before which an act is authorized or required to be done, ends on a Saturday, Sunday or a public holiday, such act may be done on the next succeeding business day and if the period ends at a specified hour, such act may be done at or before the same hour of such next succeeding business day, except that where a period of time specified by contract ends on a Saturday, Sunday or a public holiday, the extension of such period is governed by section twenty-five of this chapter.

. . . .

(2) A notice of appearance, demand for a complaint or answer may be served on the plaintiff's attorney by mail, in accordance with the rule of CPLR 2103 which allows papers to be served by mail, except where otherwise prohibited. The Court of Appeals has held that when papers are served by mail pursuant to CPLR 2103(b)(2), service is complete when mailed, not when received. Therefore, an affidavit by the addressee that the paper was not received does not create a question of fact as to whether service was made, so long as the sender has submitted a proper affidavit of service by mail. *Engel v. Lichterman*, 62 N.Y.2d 943, 479 N.Y.S.2d 188, 468 N.E.2d 26 (1984).

(3) A defendant who fails to appear within the time allowed is in default. This does not guarantee that the plaintiff will be victorious. Rather, the onus is then on the plaintiff to move for judgment by default. If the plaintiff fails to move within one year of the default, the action may be dismissed. CPLR 3215(c). If no judgment has been taken, the defendant can move for an extension of time to appear. CPLR 3012(d). If a default judgment has been taken, a motion for relief from the default may be made under CPLR 317 (if applicable) or CPLR 5015(a). The general policy of the CPLR is lenient treatment of pleading delays. See CPLR 2004, 2005, 3012(d). Relief from judgments taken by default is treated in § 16.05, *infra*.

(4) By serving the summons and complaint together, the plaintiff avoids some delay in moving the action to trial. CPLR 3012. The following diagram reflects this principle.

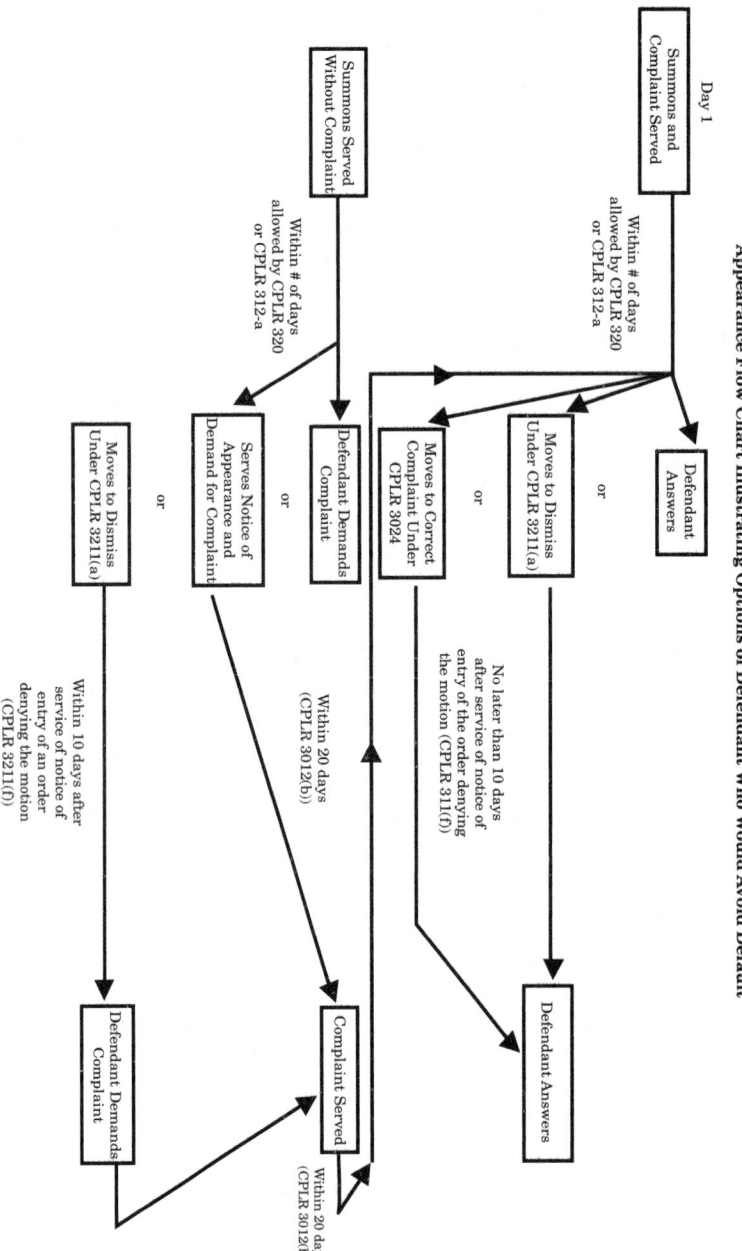

Appearance Flow Chart Illustrating Options of Defendant Who Would Avoid Default

(5) Note that defendant can delay the litigation by putting jurisdictional objections in a motion rather than in the answer. Is this a proper reason to do so? *See* Code of Professional Responsibility, Disciplinary Rules, 7-101, 7-102.*

DR 7-101. Representing a Client Zealously

(A) A lawyer shall not intentionally:

(1) Fail to seek the lawful objectives of his client through reasonably available means permitted by law and the Disciplinary Rules, except as provided by DR 7-101(B). A lawyer does not violate this Disciplinary Rule, however, by acceding to reasonable requests of opposing counsel which do not prejudice the rights of his client, by being punctual in fulfilling all professional commitments, by avoiding offensive tactics, or by treating with courtesy and consideration all persons involved in the legal process.

(2) Fail to carry out a contract of employment entered into with a client for professional services, but he may withdraw as permitted under DR 2-110, DR 5-102, and DR 5-105.

(3) Prejudice or damage his client during the course of the professional relationship, except as required under DR 7-102(B).

(B) In his representation of a client, a lawyer may:

(1) Where permissible, exercise his professional judgment to waive or fail to assert a right or position of his client.

(2) Refuse to aid or participate in conduct that he believes to be unlawful, even though there is some support for an argument that the conduct is legal.

DR 7-102. Representing a Client Within the Bounds of the Law

(A) In his representation of a client, a lawyer shall not:

(1) File a suit, assert a position, conduct a defense, delay a trial, or take other action on behalf of his client when he knows or when it is obvious that such action would serve merely to harass or maliciously injure another.

. . . .

§ 6.04 THE EFFECT OF AN APPEARANCE

An appearance has several effects: (1) It entitles the appearing party to a copy of every paper served in the action. CPLR 2103(c). (2) It avoids, for the moment, a default by the appearing defendant. CPLR 320. (Default is not permanently avoided because the appearance does not extinguish the defendant's obligation to serve an answer, respond to disclosure demands, or participate in the trial.) (3) It waives the defendant's objection to the court's assertion of personal jurisdiction unless the defendant subsequently takes the steps prescribed by CPLR 320 and CPLR 3211(e) (discussed in the next two cases) in order to preserve the objection, *i.e.*, unless the jurisdictional defense is asserted in a motion to dismiss under CPLR 3211 (if one is made), or in the answer, whichever is served first. Similarly, it waives defects in the manner of filing by which the action was commenced. *Harris v. Niagra Falls Board of Education*, 6 N.Y.3d 155, 844 N.E.2d 753, 658 N.Y.S.2d 205 (2006), § 5.02, *supra*. (4) It commits the appearing defendant to litigate any jurisdictional defenses in New York. This follows from the preceding point and from the generally accepted doctrine that a defendant who has unsuccessfully raised a jurisdictional point, may not collaterally attack an ensuing judgment on the same grounds. *See Vander v. Casperson*, 12 N.Y.2d 56, 236 N.Y.S.2d 33, 187 N.E.2d 109 (1962); *Ins. Corp. of Ireland, Ltd. v. Compagnie des Bauxites de Guinee*, 456 U.S. 694, 102 S. Ct. 2099 (1982).

IACOVANGELO v. SHEPHERD
Court of Appeals
5 N.Y.3d 184, 800 N.Y.S.2d 116, 833 N.E.2d 259 (2005)

R.S. SMITH, J.

We hold that a defendant who omits from an answer a defense based on lack of personal jurisdiction has not waived the defense if the defendant corrects the omission before the time to amend the answer without leave of court has expired.

Facts and Procedural History

Goldie Gilchrist, a New York resident, was walking on a highway in Georgia when she was hit by a truck owned by David Shepherd and driven by Thomas Rouse. Shepherd and Rouse are residents of Georgia. Gilchrist died several months later, and her administrator sued Shepherd and Rouse in New York, alleging that both of them negligently injured Gilchrist and caused her death, and also that Shepherd was vicariously liable for Rouse's negligence.

On November 8, 2002, defendants served an answer to the complaint that did not challenge the Court's jurisdiction over them. Plaintiff served an amended complaint dated November 14, 2002. On November 21, 2002, thirteen days after serving the original answer, defendants served a "Verified Amended Answer" alleging that "the Court lacks jurisdiction over the persons of the answering defendants."

Defendants moved to dismiss the action for lack of personal jurisdiction. Plaintiff, opposing the motion, argued that defendants had waived this defense by failing to assert it in their original answer. Supreme Court granted the motion, holding that "the defendants did not waive their jurisdictional defense." The Appellate Division affirmed, as do we.

Discussion

CPLR 3211(a)(8) permits a defendant to move to dismiss a complaint on the ground that "the court has not jurisdiction of the person of the defendant." CPLR 3211(e) provides in relevant part:

An objection based upon a ground specified in paragraphs eight or nine of subdivision (a) is waived if a party moves on any of the grounds set forth in subdivision (a) without raising such objection or if, having made no objection under subdivision (a), he does not raise such objection in the responsive pleading.

In *Addesso v Shemtob* (70 N.Y.2d 689, 512 N.E.2d 314, 518 N.Y.S.2d 793 [1987]), we applied CPLR 3211(e) in a case where defendants had moved to dismiss the complaint without raising a jurisdictional defense in the motion. We found "no reason to depart from the statute's plain language" (*id.* at 690), and held that the defense was waived. Here, we face an issue on which CPLR 3211(e) is not explicit: whether a waiver occurs when a party does not raise the defense in his or her first "responsive pleading", but does raise it in a pleading permitted by CPLR 3025(a), which says that "[a] party may amend his pleading once without leave of court within twenty days after its service. . . ."[1]

This issue was decided by Supreme Court in *Solarino v Noble* (55 Misc. 2d 429, 286 N.Y.S.2d 71 [Sup Ct NY Co 1967] [Spiegel, J.]), a case in which a defendant amended his answer two days after serving it to add a defense of lack of personal jurisdiction. The Court held the defense was not waived. Justice Spiegel referred to "'the general rule that an amendment relates back to the service of the original pleading'" (*id.* at 430, quoting *Blatz v Benschine*, 53 Misc. 2d 352, 354, 278 N.Y.S.2d 533 [Sup Ct Queens Co 1967]), to the absence of prejudice to the plaintiff, and to "the general principle that cases should be determined on the merits, rather than on the basis of the procedures followed" (*id.*). Several Appellate Division decisions also support the idea that a pleading amended as of right "relates back to and speaks as of the time of the filing of" the original pleading (*Abrams v Community Services, Inc.*, 76 A.D.2d 765, 766, 429 N.Y.S.2d 10 [1st Dept 1980]; *see also Naccarato v Kot*, 124 A.D.2d 365, 507 N.Y.S.2d 308 [3d Dept 1986] [Levine, J.] [distinguishing *Solarino* where the amendment is not "taken as of right" but is by leave of court]; *Boulay v Olympic Flame, Inc.*, 165 A.D.2d 191, 565 N.Y.S.2d 905 [3d Dept 1991] [same]).

In *DeFilippis v Perez* (148 A.D.2d 490, 539 N.Y.S.2d 22 [2d Dept 1989]), the Appellate Division referred to *Solarino* and similar decisions as "cases decided prior to the *Addesso* . . . decision" and reversed a ruling that it said "erroneously" relied on them. These comments were not necessary to the decision in *DeFilippis* — a case essentially identical to *Addesso* — and we think that, as Professor Siegel has suggested, the *DeFilippis* court erred in implying that *Solarino* and *Addesso* were inconsistent (*see*, Siegel, Practice Commentaries,

---

[1] Strictly speaking, the "Verified Amended Answer" in this case was not served pursuant to CPLR 3025(a), because plaintiff amended his complaint after the original answer was served; defendants were entitled to serve a new answer even without relying on CPLR 3025(a). No party argues, however, that this technical distinction is material. If, in the absence of an amendment to the complaint, defendants would have had a right to add a jurisdictional defense by amending their answer pursuant to CPLR 3025(a), it would obviously be unfair to hold that plaintiff deprived them of that right by amending his complaint.

McKinney's Cons Laws of NY, Book 7B, CPLR 3211:62). *Addesso* involved waiver by omission of a defense from a motion, not from an answer, and the two are not the same. There is no statutory right to amend a motion that is comparable to the right to amend an answer afforded by CPLR 3025(a).

We agree with the *Solarino* court that permitting a defendant to add a jurisdictional defense to an answer by an amendment as of right is consistent with CPLR 3211(e), and advances the purpose of CPLR 3025(a). CPLR 3025(a) gives a party 20 days after serving a pleading to correct it or improve upon it, and the addition of a jurisdictional defense is no less proper a correction or improvement than any other. We hold that a party who adds such a defense by an amendment as of right "raises such objection in the responsive pleading" within the meaning of CPLR 3211(e).

Accordingly, the order of the Appellate Division should be affirmed, with costs.

NOTES

(1) The defendant preserves the right to raise defenses to the assertion of personal jurisdiction by including them in a motion to dismiss or in the answer. CPLR 320(b). In *Addesso v. Shemtob*, 70 N.Y.2d 689, 518 N.Y.S.2d 793, 512 N.E.2d 314 (1987), cited in the principal case, the Court applied CPLR 3211(e) in accordance with its plain meaning and held that a defendant waives a personal jurisdiction defense by failing to include it in a pre-answer motion. In contrast, a jurisdictional defense based on improper service is waived even if it is asserted in the answer unless the defendant moves to dismiss within 60 days after service of the answer or the court extends the time because of "undue hardship." CPLR 3211(e).

(2) Recall that in *Harris v. Niagra Falls Board of Education*, § 5.02, *supra*, the Court of Appeals held that a defect in the manner or form in which an action or proceeding is filed is waived if the defendant fails to raise the issue in an answer or motion.

(3) Does removal to federal court waive the defense of lack of personal jurisdiction? In *Lamaglio Assocs. v. LBK Mktg. Corp.*, 876 F. Supp. 41 (S.D.N.Y. 1995), the court asserted jurisdiction on the basis that "removal constituted an appearance" by the defendant. *Compare Capitol Resource Funding v. Tri-County Bank*, 1997 U.S. Dist. LEXIS 13055 (N.D.N.Y. 1997) (removal does not waive any defenses available under Fed. R. Civ. Proc. 12(b)). A defendant who attempted to remove, but whose case was subsequently remanded back to state court by the federal district court, was held to have waived the right to move to dismiss the action for a lack of personal jurisdiction in state court. *Quinn v. Booth Mem. Hosp.*, 239 A.D.2d 266, 657 N.Y.S.2d 680 (1st Dep't 1997).

Under 28 U.S.C. § 1446(b), a defendant who wishes to remove an action to federal court must file a notice of removal within thirty days of receipt of the initial pleading. How can a defendant in an action brought in the New York Supreme Court preserve jurisdictional defenses and still file the notice of removal within the federal time limit?

GAGER v. WHITE
Court of Appeals
53 N.Y.2d 475, 442 N.Y.S.2d 463, 425 N.E.2d 851 (1981)

FUCHSBERG, J.

These five appeals are part of the aftermath of the Supreme Court's recent decision in *Rush v. Savchuk*, (444 U.S. 320), the effect of which was to vitiate the predicate for quasi in rem jurisdiction pioneered in 1966 by *Seider v. Roth* (17 N.Y.2d 111). In essence, *Seider* held that a liability insurance contract issued by a carrier authorized to do business in this State, contingent as its obligations may be, partakes of the character of a "debt" which by its attachment may be made to serve as the foundation for jurisdiction over its nonresident insured defendants. After this holding had survived 14 years of doctrinal dispute, *Rush* was to declare it violative of due process. The issue now is whether this ruling is to be applied prospectively alone or retrospectively as well.

The cases on which we are to act present typical *Seider* fact patterns. In each, a New York domiciliary seeks damages for injuries or death sustained in an automobile accident outside the State as a result of the alleged negligence of a nonresident operator or owner of a motor vehicle. Save for the plaintiff's residence, in all, for all practical purposes, the sole connection with this State was the policy's availability for attachment.

Because in every instance the cases before us were *pendente lite* when the Supreme Court administered its *coup de grace* they all became the subject of motions to dismiss. These initially were all denied, *nisi prius* declining to apply *Rush* to ongoing cases whose plaintiffs, in choosing this forum and foregoing others, had, as these courts saw it, placed justifiable reliance on New York's previously consistent, if vigorously contested, course of decisional support for *Seider*'s jurisdictional analysis (*see Baden v. Staples*, 45 N.Y.2d 889; *Donawitz v. Danek*, 42 N.Y.2d 138; *Neuman v. Dunham*, 398 N.Y.2d 999; *Simpson v. Loehmann*, 21 N.Y.2d 305, *mot. rearg. den.* 21 N.Y.2d 990; *see, also, O'Connor v. Lee-Hy Paving Corp.*, 579 F.2d 194, *cert. den.* 439 U.S. 1034; *Minichiello v. Rosenberg*, 410 F.2d 106, *aff'd. en banc*, 410 F.2d 117, *cert. den.* 396 U.S. 949).

The story in the intermediate appellate courts, however, was different. In Cachat v. Guertin Co., there was an affirmance, but only because no jurisdictional defense had been interposed. On the other hand, because some type of jurisdictional objection had been raised in the other four, each brought a reversal and dismissal. For the reasons that follow, we now hold that *Rush* must be applied only when a specific objection to the assertion of jurisdiction founded on the attachment of the out-of-State defendant's liability insurance policy was preserved by appropriate motion or affirmative defense (CPLR 3211, subd. [e]).

. . . .

Especially since almost every party touches on the matter, our discussion may well start with the reminder that, consonant with the common law's policy-laden assumptions, a change in decisional law usually will be applied retrospectively to all cases still in the normal litigating process (*People v. Pepper*, 53 N.Y.2d 213, *citing People v. Morales*, 37 N.Y.2d 262, 267-268; *Kelly v. Long Island Light Co.*, 31 N.Y.2d 25, 29 n 3). By way of departure from this generality, however, where there has been such a sharp break in the continuity of law that its impact will "wreak more havoc in society than society's interest in stability will tolerate," (Fairchild, *Limitation of New Judge-Made Law to Prospective Effect Only: "Prospective Overruling" or "Sunbursting,"* 51 Marq. L.Rev. 254), it is now recognized that, when adherence to the traditional course is strongly contraindicated by powerful factors, including strong elements of reliance on law superseded by the new pronouncement, a court may direct that it operate prospectively alone (*Chevron Oil Co. v. Huson*, 404 U.S. 97; *Great Northern Ry. v. Sunburst Co.*, 287 U.S. 358).

All the plaintiffs, stressing that the Statute of Limitations now may have foreclosed an action in a forum where jurisdiction would be constitutionally unassailable, argue that theirs are precisely the kind of cases in which retroactive application should be eschewed. But this is by no means a one-sided argument. As the defendants contend, that *Seider* might turn out to have not been the only possible "true rule" was not without forewarning (*see, e.g.*, Siegel, New York Practice [1978], § 105, p. 127; Stein, *Jurisdiction by Attachment of Liability Insurance*, 43 N.Y.U. L.Rev. 1075; Reese, *Expanding Scope of Jurisdiction Over Non-Residents — New York Goes Wild*, Ins. Counsel J. 118). Moreover, even if the balance on the issue of prejudice had to be struck in favor of those who preferred to rely on the authoritative pronouncements of the New York courts rather than those of its now clairvoyant critics, the fundamental nature of the jurisdictional determinations in *Rush* renders conventional criteria for fixing an appropriate line of demarcation for overruling academic. For a constitutional due process limitation on the power of a State's exercise of its jurisdiction under our Federal system of government, as distinguished, for instance, from one founded in due process considerations bearing on less fundamental substantive and procedural concerns, is an absolute abnegation of the offending State's ability to continue to act beyond the boundaries the determination defines.

. . . .

That, however, is not the end of the matter. Unlike subject matter jurisdiction, which limits the power of a particular court rather than the judicial jurisdiction of the State en gros, a defect in basis jurisdiction is waivable (CPLR 3211, subd. [e]). Under the CPLR, the objection may be raised either by a preanswer motion or by pleading it as an affirmative defense, whichever comes first (*see* Siegel, New York Practice, § 111, p. 137; 4 Weinstein-Korn-Miller; N.Y. Civ. Prac., pars. 3211.03-3211.05).[1] Absent the pursuit of either course, a defendant's voluntary participation in litigation in which the point can be raised, in and of itself, constitutes a submission to the jurisdiction of the courts of our State and, as such, acts as a predicate for basis jurisdiction (*see* Restatement, Conflict of Laws 2d, § 33; Siegel, *op cit.*, § 111, p 139; *cf. York v. Texas*, 137 U.S. 15; *Henderson v. Henderson*, 247 N.Y. 428).[2]

Examining the cases before us to determine whether quasi in rem jurisdiction has been appropriately controverted, we note that specific objections on that score were made in the answers filed in Gager v. White and Hill v. Elliott. In these cases, the Appellate Division's dismissal of the complaints being mandatory, there should be an affirmance.

In contrast, no jurisdictional protest having been lodged in Cachat v. Guertin Co., the Appellate Division also was correct when it there found that dismissal was not in order (CPLR 3211, subd. [e]).[3] Lastly, in Mei Yuet Chin v. Cray and Carbone v. Ericson, the answers raised objection to in personam jurisdiction only.[4] In Carbone, by way of its "Second Defense," the answer pleaded that "this Court does not have jurisdiction over the person of the defendant" and, as a "Third Defense," by way of a limited appearance, pleads that "any judgment . . . may be satisfied only out of the res allegedly attached." Since, as explained earlier, a defect in the categorically distinct concept of quasi in rem jurisdiction requires a sufficiently particularized pleading to apprise the plaintiff of its nature with sufficient clarity to avoid prejudice by inducing quiescence (*compare* CPLR 3211, subd[a], par. 8, *with* par. 9; *see* 4 Weinstein-Korn-Miller, N.Y. Civ. Prac., par. 3211.22, p. 32-66), it follows that the in rem issue must be deemed waived and the Appellate Division orders, which held to the contrary, reversed.

---

[1] Of course, if a defendant has not appeared at all, there is nothing to preclude essaying a collateral attack on jurisdiction (Restatement, Judgements, § 11; *see, generally,* Chief Judge Desmond's opn. in *Vander v. Casperson*, 12 N.Y.2d 56, 59, *supra*). [Some footnotes omitted; others renumbered. — Eds.]

[2] Historically, where the initial jurisdiction was in rem or quasi in rem, an appearance, followed by a defense upon the merits, automatically transformed the jurisdictional basis to one that was in personam (*see* Homburger & Laufer, *Appearance and Jurisdictional Motions in New York*, 14 Buf. L. Rev. 374, 386-388, 406-408; Frummer, *Jurisdiction and Limited Appearance in New York: Dilemma of the Non-Resident Defendant*, 14 Ford. L. Rev. 73; *cf.* Restatement, Judgments, §§ 38-40). Later, this practice was replaced by CPLR 320 (subd. [c]), which provides that when jurisdiction is quasi in rem, the appearance remains a limited one. Under these circumstances, the defendant is now permitted to defend without submitting to in personam jurisdiction (Siegel, *op cit*, § 113, p. 140).

[3] The nearest thing to a jurisdictional defense in Cachat was a much different claim, that of defective service.

[4] In Chin, in his "Sixth Separate and Complete Affirmative Defense," the answer pleaded that "the court lacks jurisdiction over the person of the defendant."

In sum, the orders in Gager v. White, Cachat v. Guertin Co., and Hill v. Elliott should be affirmed, while those in Chin v. Cray, and Carbone v. Ericson should be reversed, and the orders at Special Term in these cases should be reinstated.

NOTES

(1) By failing to raise their jurisdictional defenses in a timely manner, the defendants allowed their appearance to take on a new importance. It became what is often called a "general" appearance, but could more descriptively be called a "jurisdiction conferring" appearance.

(2) Will the plaintiffs in those actions decided with *Gager v. White*, in which the defendants waived their objections to jurisdiction, be able to recover the full amount of their damages to the extent they exceed the value of the attached insurance policies? Clearly not, for by virtue of CPLR 320(c)(1), the defendant's appearances were "limited" in their jurisdiction-conferring effect to the value of property attached. *See* footnote 2 in the case itself.

(3) In *Manufacturer's Hanover Trust Co. v. Farber*, 99 Misc. 2d 1001, 417 N.Y.S.2d 406 (Sup. Ct. 1979), the concept of the limited appearance was itself limited in an interpleader action which arose from a "cinema noir" scenario. Claimant Bessie Farber had the bank issue some official checks payable to the order of co-claimant Stan Farrar. The latter took the checks to Las Vegas and, as the court coyly put it, "returned without them." Grand Resorts, Inc., a competing claimant, was an endorsee. Farber and Farrar claimed that they were entitled to the proceeds because Grand Resorts had "imprisoned" Farrar and converted the checks. Manufacturer's, the plaintiff in interpleader, sought a determination from the court of the rightful owner of the proceeds. After Grand Resorts entered a claim for the proceeds, Farber and Farrar cross-claimed against Grand Resorts for damages and punitive damages. Held: Since Grand Resorts was not before the court pursuant to an order of attachment, and since Grand Resorts did not make a motion to dismiss under CPLR 3211(a)(8) or (9), it was "dubious" that its appearance was limited under CPLR 320. Grand Resorts was, however, protected by the rule of *Matter of Einstoss, infra*.

(4) If a plaintiff asserts jurisdiction in rem or jurisdiction over a marital "res," the defendant is not protected by CPLR 320(c)(1) but is covered by subsection (c)(2). The jurisdiction conferring appearance will not be "limited" and will confer full in personam jurisdiction on the court. The history of this complexity in the law is described in the Recommendation of the Law Revision Commission to the 1978 Legislature.*

(5) What policy justifications are there for the waiver scheme of CPLR 320 and CPLR 3211(e)? Why should a defense which implicates constitutional considerations be lost by misstep early in the litigation?

---

* *See* 1978 McKinney's Session Laws at 1654-1656.

In 1965, the Judicial Conference amended CPLR 320 so as to clarify the defendant's obligation to include jurisdictional defenses in his pre-answer motion if one was made. Its report offered the following justification for this policy:

> [The pre-amendment] language of subdivision (b) appears to contravene the traditional policy of favoring the disposition of jurisdictional defenses before defenses going to the merits. The consequences may be highly undesirable. The court may be required to determine issues going to the merits, possibly in favor of the plaintiff, even in a case where later jurisdictional objection by the defendant would necessitate dismissal.
>
> If such later jurisdictional objection were sustained after a ruling on a defense on the merits adverse to the defendant, a serious problem of res judicata would be involved in a second action with the same parties based on the same cause. It is far from clear whether or not a re-litigation of the same defense on the merits would be permitted on the ground that the determination thereof in the first action is void because rendered by a court not having jurisdiction.

1965 McKinney's Session Laws at 1979. *See also* Adolf Homburger & Joseph Laufer, *Appearance and Jurisdictional Motions in New York*, 14 Buff. L. Rev. 374 (1965).

Note that the jurisdictional waiver provisions of CPLR 320 are similar in broad outline to those of Rule 12(h) of the Federal Rules of Civil Procedure.

(6) Even a defendant who preserves jurisdictional objections runs a risk of waiving them by subsequent inconsistent conduct, as the next case indicates.

TEXTILE TECHNOLOGY EXCHANGE, INC. v. DAVIS
Court of Appeals
81 N.Y.2d 56, 595 N.Y.S.2d 729, 611 N.E.2d 769 (1993)

SMITH, J.

Plaintiff is a North Carolina corporation which buys and sells new and used textile mill equipment. Defendant is a New York rigger who handles the removal, transporting, repair and resale of such equipment. Plaintiff commenced this action for breach of a February 1986 oral partnership agreement in which defendant was to sell equipment owned by the plaintiff and divide the profits equally. It was alleged that the defendant did not account for the proceeds of the sale of various equipment. Defendant denied the allegations, asserted the affirmative defense of lack of personal jurisdiction (improper service), and asserted a counterclaim based upon "an agreement heretofore entered into between the parties to this action, wherein and whereby the plaintiff agreed to compensate the defendant for certain goods and services provided by the defendant, within six (6) years last past" for sums due and owing.

At the conclusion of the trial, defendant moved to dismiss the complaint for lack of jurisdiction. The trial court denied the motion, holding that the jurisdictional defense had been waived by the assertion of a counterclaim that was unrelated to the plaintiff's claim. This was based upon the finding that the complaint was based upon a contract "entered into in February 1986" but the counterclaim involved "several transactions which arose prior to February, 1986." On the merits, the trial court ruled that plaintiff's proof established a breach by the defendant, awarded damages and dismissed the counterclaim because the defendant had failed "to establish his cause of action."

By a 3-2 majority, the Appellate Division agreed that the jurisdictional defense had been waived because the counterclaim was unrelated to the plaintiff's claim. The majority found that the parties began a business relationship in 1985 when plaintiff, acting as the liquidator of equipment at the Industrial Knitted Fabrics (IKF) plant, referred business to defendant. In February 1986, the relationship changed when plaintiff purchased the majority of the IKF equipment and entered into the oral partnership agreement with defendant. The majority concluded: "Because it is solely this latter agreement which is the subject of plaintiff's complaint, defendant's assertion of a counterclaim involving various transactions predating that agreement amounted to the assertion of an unrelated counterclaim, thereby resulting in a waiver of his jurisdictional objection. . . ." The majority also found that the record supported the award of damages to plaintiff and the dismissal of the counterclaim.

The dissenters essentially concluded that there was an ongoing relationship between the parties involving a series of transactions concerning the sale of the contents of the IKF plant that began in 1985 and was basically unaltered by the February 1986 oral partnership agreement. Since the complaint and the counterclaim were based upon transactions during the course of that relationship, it was reasoned that they were sufficiently related to allow the jurisdictional objection to remain.

Defendant appeals as of right because of the two justice dissent (*see*, CPLR 5601(a)).

The issue before us is whether the defendant waived his jurisdictional defense by bringing an "unrelated" counterclaim. The Appellate Divisions have developed a rule that interposing a counterclaim related to plaintiff's claims will not waive the defense of lack of personal jurisdiction, but that asserting an unrelated counterclaim does waive such defense because defendant is taking affirmative advantage of the court's jurisdiction (*see*, *Prezioso v. Demchuk*, 127 A.D.2d 576, *lv dismis*sed 70 N.Y.2d 1002; *Liebling v. Yankwitt*, 109 A.D.2d 780, 781).

We agree with the underlying rationale of such rule and now adopt it. We clarify, however, that a counterclaim will only be "related" for these purposes when such counterclaim could potentially be barred under principles of collateral estoppel — where the parties or their privies are the same and where the issues in the plaintiffs' claims are potentially identical and decisive of issues raised in the counterclaims (*see, Gramatan Home Investors Corp. v. Lopez*, 46 N.Y.2d 481, 486). While all counterclaims are "permissive" (CPLR 3019), the specter of collateral estoppel often requires a defendant to bring certain counterclaims in order to avoid the risk of later preclusion (*see, e.g.*, Siegel, N.Y. Prac § 224, at 328 and § 452, at 684-685 [2d ed]). Where a defendant in effect must bring such counterclaims, it would be unfair to deem those counterclaims to waive a jurisdictional defense.

Applying these principles to this case, we conclude that defendant's counterclaims were not related to plaintiff's complaint. Defendant's counterclaims — involving a series of transactions prior to February 1986 — did not involve the same issues to be raised and determined in plaintiff's claim, which revolved around defendant's alleged breach of the February 1986 agreement. Defendant, thus, stood no risk of preclusion if he did not bring his counterclaims, and we see no unfairness in the conclusion that by bringing them anyway, he affirmatively sought relief from the court and waived his jurisdictional defense.

Accordingly, the order of the Appellate Division should be affirmed, with costs.

. . . .

PROBLEM B

Rhoan, Loads, Inc., a brokerage firm, arranged a sale of pork belly futures from Agribus, Inc. to Mantua, a European investor. When the latter reneged, Agribus sued him and Rhoan, Loads in New York, serving Mantua personally while he was in New York City attending an investment symposium. After Mantua served an answer which contained no jurisdictional defenses, Rhoan, Loads served a cross-claim on him seeking: (a) $50,000 as a brokerage fee; and (b) indemnification for any amount in which Rhoan, Loads was found liable to Agribus.

What result if Mantua moves to dismiss the cross-claim for want of jurisdiction over the person?

NOTE

In thinking about the preceding problem, consider, in addition to the following two cases, CPLR 302(c). The latter introduces another discrete concept, the "restricted" appearance. This results when a defendant makes a jurisdiction-conferring appearance in an action in which jurisdiction has been asserted under CPLR 302(a) or (b). The effect of the defendant's appearance is restricted by CPLR 302(c). Thus, the defendant could waive objection to causes of action he considered properly long-arm based, while contesting the court's jurisdiction over other causes of action in the same complaint. Moreover, it prevents the appearance of the long-arm defendant from justifying the subsequent addition of other, non-long arm causes of action by amendments to the complaint. Does it help here?

Are there non-statutory restrictions on the effect of an appearance which may be relevant? Consider the following case.

MATTER OF EINSTOSS
Court of Appeals
26 N.Y.2d 181, 309 N.Y.S.2d 184, 257 N.E.2d 637 (1970)

CHIEF JUDGE FULD.

The petitioner, the administrator of the estate of Sigmund Einstoss, brought this proceeding to disallow a claim against the estate by the State and Territory of Alaska. Mr. Einstoss had died in 1954, and Alaska's claim was based on a judgment rendered against him by the United States District Court for the Territory of Alaska in 1957, three years after his death. The New York administrator was never substituted as a party to the Alaskan proceeding, and the question posed on this appeal — here by our leave — is whether that judgment is entitled to full faith and credit and is enforceable against the decedent's assets here.

In 1951, Einstoss purchased land in Alaska, then a Territory, upon which he operated a salmon cannery. The property was subject to a mortgage of $25,000 and, in 1954, following Einstoss' default on his mortgage payments, the mortgagee instituted a foreclosure proceeding against him in the Territorial court. The Territory had filed a lien on the property for unpaid franchise taxes on the operation of the cannery, and it was named as a party defendant in the foreclosure proceeding. At the time, Einstoss was in Seattle, Washington, and was, therefore, not subject to the in personam jurisdiction of the Alaskan court. Nevertheless, upon the express representation of the mortgagee that she would satisfy any judgment solely out of the mortgaged property, Einstoss entered an "appearance" and admitted his liability for the amount outstanding on the mortgage note — $11,000 plus interest.

Two days after Einstoss' appearance, the Territory filed a cross-complaint against him seeking a judgment for the unpaid franchise taxes and foreclosure of its lien. It procured an order from the court . . . authorizing it to serve the cross-complaint "wherever the defendant . . . may be found." In accordance with that order, the cross complaint was personally served upon Einstoss in Seattle. . . .

On May 17, 1954, the day before he was required to answer the cross-complaint, Einstoss died. The Territory, however, apparently unaware of his death, procured an "entry of default" from the clerk of the court precluding him from defending against the cross claim (*see* Fed. Rules Civ. Pro., rule 55, subd. [a]). Despite this order, the decedent's ancillary administrator in Alaska attempted to appear in the action and file an answer but, in view of the default, her answer was, in the claimant's words, "properly treated by the court as a nullity." The mortgagee and the Territory then proceeded to litigate the priority of their respective liens and the Territory eventually prevailed. (*See Schlothan v. Territory of Alaska*, 276 F.2d 806, *cert. den.* 362 U.S. 990.) A final judgment was eventually entered against the decedent for his unpaid taxes — in an amount in excess of $95,000 — and, in 1961, Alaska, at that time a State, sold his property for about one third of that sum. Finally, in March of 1965, 11 years after Einstoss' death, his domiciliary administrator in New York was notified of the Alaskan judgment in a letter asserting a claim against the estate for the deficiency.

. . . .

. . . The judgment upon which Alaska's claim is grounded is not entitled to . . . recognition not only because the New York administrator was never made a party to the proceeding but also because the Alaskan court never acquired in personam jurisdiction for the tax claim during Einstoss' lifetime.

Relying on the doctrine of continuing jurisdiction, the claimant asserts that, once Einstoss had appeared in response to the initial claim by the mortgagee, the court retained jurisdiction over him for all further proceedings in the action, including its cross claim for taxes. Although this is the general rule, the doctrine has its limits and, where a party appears but takes no further action in a case, a court's jurisdiction does not go beyond the general subject matter of the suit in which he appeared. (*See Reynolds v. Stockton*, 140 U.S. 254, 264-265; *see, also*, Leflar, American Conflicts Law, § 28, p. 51.) Thus, in the present case, Einstoss' appearance in an action to foreclose a mortgage, did not, in itself, render him subject to the Territory's unrelated cross claim for taxes.

. . . .

. . . The action in which Einstoss appeared was a proceeding to foreclose a mortgage, involving a maximum liability, on his part, of little more than $11,000 (considerably less than the value of the property over which the court already had in rem jurisdiction) but the judgment which eventually resulted was based on an entirely different obligation, his liability to the Territory for taxes, and amounted to nearly $100,000. The mere fact that the Federal Rules permitted this claim to be asserted in a cross complaint does not alter the requirement that the court must obtain jurisdiction over the defendant anew before it may entertain a new and entirely unrelated claim against him. (*See United States v. Krasnov*, 109 F. Supp. 143, 147.) As one authoritative commentator has put it, (Leflar, American Conflicts Law, § 28, p. 51), a party may not "under the guise of continuing jurisdiction be subjected to what is essentially a new suit."

When the Territory sought and obtained an order, under section 1655 of title 28 of the United States Code, authorizing personal service upon a defendant outside the Territory, it, in effect, acknowledged that Einstoss was not yet subject to the court's jurisdiction for the purposes of its cross claim. Section 1655 expressly recites that it is available only against an absent defendant who "does not voluntarily appear," and service under that provision is neither necessary nor proper where jurisdiction has already been attained. Once the section was invoked the court could, of course, have proceeded to enter a judgment on the cross claim but, as section 1655 declares, it could only affect "the property which [was] the subject of the action" and could not subject the defendant to personal liability. In other words . . . although the claims were consolidated in a single action, the mortgagee's suit on the mortgage note and the Territory's claim for taxes were, for jurisdictional purposes, entirely separate causes of action. Einstoss may have personally appeared with respect to the former but the court's jurisdiction to render a judgment on the tax claim derived solely from the service pursuant to section 1655 and was limited, under that provision, to the foreclosure of the lien.

In any event, though, even if the court had obtained personal jurisdiction over Einstoss during his lifetime, this does not mean that the resulting judgment, which was not entered until three years after his death, would be binding upon his New York administrator and enforceable against his assets located in this State. . . . [The court held that the failure to substitute and serve process on the administrator was also a defect in the judgment.]

NOTES

(1) In accord with the main case is *Manufacturer's Hanover Trust Co. v. Farber*, 99 Misc. 2d 1001, 417 N.Y.S.2d 406 (Sup. Ct. 1979). *See, supra*, note 3 following *Gager v. White*. The court held that Farber and Farrar could not use Grand Resort's appearance as a jurisdictional basis for their damage claims, so long as Grand Resorts was not otherwise subject to jurisdiction.

(2) A variant of the problem of the plaintiff's right to rely on the appearance of a non-resident defendant is found in *Everitt v. Everitt*, 4 N.Y.2d 13, 171 N.Y.S.2d 836, 148 N.E.2d 891 (1958). Though the case was decided prior to the adoption of the CPLR, the point discussed remains of interest. The plaintiff had commenced an action by the service of a summons and notice upon the defendant while she was temporarily within this state. The defendant served a notice of appearance and demand for the complaint. When the complaint was served, the defendant was surprised to see that, instead of being confined to a contract cause of action for $46,900, as the notice served with the summons had indicated, it was combined with two other causes of action not disclosed by the notice, one for $1,500 on another contract, and the other for $350,000 for libel. The defendant had left this state when the complaint was served on her attorney and subsequently moved to dismiss the new causes of action. The Court upheld the denial of her motion, with the following explanation:

It may well be that if an action has been commenced against a non-resident by the service of a summons and complaint, the complaint cannot be amended by adding new causes of action after the defendant has left the State. Moreover, if defendant-appellant had defaulted in appearing in this action after the service of the summons with notice, judgment could not have been entered against her by default on any other cause of action or for more than the amount specified in the notice served with the summons.

Nevertheless, the law has long been established in this State that such a notice is effectual only in case of default, that its object is to enable judgment by default to be entered by the clerk without application to the court (Civ. Prac. Act, §§ 486-487) [now CPLR 305(b)], and that "if the defendant appears, the notice at once is rendered of no importance. No judgment can be taken against the defendant then until a complaint has been served upon him, and his liability and the rights of the plaintiff are measured entirely by the allegations of the complaint." (citation omitted.) This conclusion is supported by the language of rule 46 [now CPLR 305(b)] which limits the function of such a notice served with the summons to "stating the sum of money for which judgment will be taken *in case of default*." Except in case of default, the notice is not equivalent to "a short . . . complaint" . . . and loses its vitality when the defendant fails to default by appearing in the action. Defendant-appellant could have demanded a copy of the complaint. If, after receiving a copy of the complaint, defendant-appellant had chosen to contest the jurisdiction of the court over her person or the subject matter with respect to some but not all of the causes of action, she could have done.

To what extent has the defendant's dilemma in *Everitt* been obviated by CPLR 320? Note that it remains the rule that the amount demanded in the summons does not limit the amount which may be demanded in a later served complaint. *Silverman v. Scharf*, 74 A.D.2d 822, 425 N.Y.S.2d 352 (2d Dep't 1980).

§ 6.05 THE INFORMAL APPEARANCE

Two questions are relevant here. How does one make an informal appearance? In what ways do the effects of an informal appearance differ from those of an appearance?

PROBLEM C

Refer again to Problem A, *supra*. Assume that July 3, 2006, was the last date on which Acme could make a timely appearance. By July 10, 2006, Acme had done nothing except move (by notice of motion served on June 15, 2006) under CPLR 327 to dismiss the action on the ground that New York was an inconvenient forum. What result if:

(1) Tom moves for a default judgment on July 10, 2006?

(2) If no motion is made for a default judgment, and if the court on September 3, 2006, denies Acme's motion for relief on forum non conveniens grounds, may Acme subsequently move to dismiss the action because the court lacks in personam jurisdiction, or has that defense been waived?

RUBINO v. CITY OF NEW YORK
Appellate Division, First Department
145 A.D.2d 285, 538 N.Y.S.2d 547 (1989)

Asch, J.

Plaintiff Joan Rubino was injured on April 21, 1980, in a school yard controlled by the defendant Board of Education. Timely notice of claim was served. However, although a summons and complaint was served on the City of New York on April 7, 1981, listing both the City and the Board of Education as defendants, no process was ever served upon the Board of Education. The Corporation Counsel answered on behalf of the City only, in July 1981. Thereafter, however, the Corporation Counsel conducted itself as representing both the City and the Board of Education. The Corporation Counsel served a notice to take depositions, in March 1982, as attorney for "defendants." An examination before trial was held in June 1982, at which the City acted on behalf of both defendants. Trial, on the issue of liability only, commenced in March 1984, at which the City represented both defendants. After the plaintiffs' case was completed, the trial court dismissed the complaint. Upon appeal, in September 1985, we affirmed the dismissal as against the City, but held, as to the Board of Education, that the complaint should be reinstated, and directed a new trial against it (114 AD2d 243). Following this remand, the Corporation Counsel waited until October 9, 1987, again acting as attorney for "defendants," to move to dismiss the complaint on the ground jurisdiction was never obtained over the Board of Education. The IAS court granted the motion pursuant to CPLR 3211(a)(8).

The finding of the court at nisi prius that the Corporation Counsel had never acted as attorney for the Board of Education was clearly erroneous. Numerous papers served in this proceeding list the Corporation Counsel as attorney for "defendants." Indeed, the judgment entered after trial recites "on motion of . . . [the] Corporation Counsel, attorney for the City of New York and The Board of Education of the City of New York." On the appeal to this court, the Corporation Counsel represented itself as attorney for the "defendants." No issue was raised in either court questioning jurisdiction over the Board of Education.

When a defendant participates in a lawsuit on the merits, he indicates his intention to submit to the court's jurisdiction over the action. By appearing "informally" in this manner, he confers in personam jurisdiction on the court. . . .

While defendant Board contends there could be no informal appearance because it did not have knowledge of the lawsuit, this argument was not raised below nor was any evidence submitted to the IAS court showing that the Board was unaware of the action. Since there was a trial on liability, it appears likely the Corporation Counsel had some contact with employees of the Board of Education in preparing this case relating to an incident which took place on Board property. In any event, the absence of any evidence in the record herein to the contrary precludes a determination that the Board of Education was without knowledge of the action.

The Corporation Counsel also contends that any appearance by it was unauthorized by the Board. Once more, there is no evidence in the record showing that such is the case. Moreover, the Corporation Counsel, by statute, is authorized to appear for the Board of Education and is, in fact, the only counsel who can appear for the Board. Here, the purportedly unauthorized appearance is by the Corporation Counsel, who is both lawfully and by common knowledge the only person who could appear for the defendant. Under these circumstances, there appears to be no unfairness in holding that the Board is bound by such appearance.

The defendant also contends that any conduct by the Corporation Counsel which could be construed as an informal appearance did not occur until after the expiration of the applicable statute of limitations, *i.e.*, pursuant to General Municipal Law § 50-i, in July 1981, one year and 90 days after the occurrence of the injury. The Corporation Counsel asserts that any acts by it which would constitute an informal appearance occurred after the expiration of that period and cites *Guilford v Brody* (237 App Div 726 [an appearance after the statute of limitations has expired is invalid and cannot be construed to confer personal jurisdiction]). We agree with our prior holding in *Guilford*, but the defenses of personal jurisdiction and the statute of limitations, available to a defendant who appears informally, must be timely asserted, just as in a formal appearance, or they are otherwise waived.

Here, both the defenses of lack of jurisdiction and the statute of limitations were not timely raised or preserved. The egregious delay in raising the defenses has clearly been prejudicial to the plaintiffs. This matter was not only tried on liability, but was modified on appeal and remanded for a new trial before any motion was made attacking the jurisdiction of the court or raising the defense of the statute of limitations.

While defendant correctly asserts that estoppel will not generally lie against a public agency (*Morley v Arricale*, 66 NY2d 665, 667), this doctrine is not inflexible.

. . . .

Defendant here proceeded to trial and appeal, represented by the Corporation Counsel, without ever raising the defense of personal jurisdiction or statute of limitations. Such a participation on the merits of the action constituted an informal appearance conferring jurisdiction upon the court and, under the circumstances of this case, a waiver of these personal defenses. Defendant did not show that it was without knowledge of the lawsuit and, given the extent of the defendant's participation in this action, it cannot now complain that the Corporation Counsel was not authorized to defend the action.

Accordingly, the order of the Supreme Court, which granted the motion by defendant Board of Education of the City of New York for an order dismissing the complaint for lack of personal jurisdiction pursuant to CPLR 3211(a)(8), should be reversed, on the law, and the motion denied. . . .

NOTES

(1) The CPLR does not refer to the doctrine of the "informal appearance," but the principal case illustrates the continued vitality of the concept. Do you think the courts are correct to create this extra-statutory appearance? What could the plaintiff have done to avoid the need to rely on the informal appearance doctrine?

(2) We have seen that different types of appearances may have different effects. What is the effect of an informal appearance? Does it avoid default? In *McGowan v. Bellanger*, 32 A.D.2d 293, 301 N.Y.S.2d 712 (3d Dep't 1969), the court held, on facts somewhat similar to those in the principal case, that the defendant had made an informal appearance and thus had waived her jurisdictional defenses, but was nonetheless in default because she had not served an answer within the time allowed by law. (The court exercised its discretion to relieve her from her default.)

CITY OF NEW YORK v. JUEL REALTY ASSOCIATES
Supreme Court, Appellate Term, First Department
New York Law Journal, February 4, 1983, Page 6, Column 2

Plaintiff City of New York brought this action to recover civil penalties assessed against the defendant by the Environmental Control Board. A default judgment was entered in Nov. 1979. Defendant thereafter moved to vacate the default as excusable, seeking leave to interpose an answer (not annexed to the papers), no jurisdictional objection was raised at that time. The application was denied in the Civil Court, and the order of denial affirmed by this Court. . . . Subsequently, defendant moved at Special Term to renew its prior motion, this time alleging (for the first time) that it had been improperly served. Special Term correctly refused to grant the requested relief. Defendant, by seeking relief from the judgment without asserting any defect in service, affirmatively invoked the process of the court and appeared within the contemplation of CPLR 320 (*see* Weinstein Korn & Miller, New York Civil Practice, § 320.12; . . .). Where a party moves to vacate a default and seeks permission to answer the complaint and defend the action, thereby admitting the viability of the action, it would be procedurally anomalous to permit it to challenge jurisdiction at a later point in the litigation (*527 Madison Ave., Co. v. DeLoy Executive Service, Inc.*, 36 AD 2d 502). Defendant, by its conduct, waived its jurisdictional defense.

It is additionally noted that no acceptable reason is given as to why the jurisdictional objection was not made on the original motion.

PARROTTA v. WOLGIN
Appellate Division, Third Department
245 A.D.2d 872, 666 N.Y.S.2d 341 (1997)

YESAWICHH JR., J.

Plaintiff seeks to recover for personal injuries he allegedly sustained on June 16, 1991 while walking on the Sagamore Golf Course in the Town of Bolton, Warren County. Plaintiff commenced this action in March 1994 and sent defendants separate summonses and complaints along with acknowledgements of receipt by mail. Each of the acknowledgements was returned, unsigned, to plaintiff's counsel and service was not completed by any other method; accordingly, proofs of service were never filed. On June 3, 1996, defendants moved for summary judgment dismissing the complaint for failure to effect proper service and failure to timely file proof of same as required by CPLR 306-b. Supreme Court denied the motion, finding that defendants, having informally appeared in the action, were barred from raising these jurisdictional objections. Defendants appeal.

Prior to service of defendants' answer — in which they assert their jurisdictional defense — in March 1995, a claims representative from American International Adjustment Company, Inc., evidently acting on defendants' behalf, contacted plaintiff's counsel on several occasions, requesting extensions of time to answer (which were granted) and seeking discovery of medical reports, names of witnesses and the date of the incident. This conduct, as Supreme Court found, constituted an "informal appearance" sufficient to preclude entry of a default judgment against defendants

Nevertheless, defendants' motion should have been granted, for where, as here, "the substantial activity which constitutes the appearance occurs before the defendant's time to answer expires, it does not deprive him of the right to object to jurisdiction" (McLaughlin, Practice Commentaries, McKinney's Cons Laws of NY, Book 7B, CPLR C320:2, at 492; *see,* CPLR 320[b].) Hence, neither defendants' requests for additional time to answer nor their pursuit of discovery effected a relinquishment of their jurisdictional defense. Inasmuch as plaintiff essentially concedes that defendants were never properly served, the complaint should have been dismissed for this reason.

NOTES

(1) *See also Klein v. Mt. Sinai Hosp.*, 61 N.Y.2d 865, 474 N.Y.S.2d 462, 462 N.E.2d 1180 (1984). After service of a summons and complaint, defendant's attorney sent plaintiff's attorney a letter enclosing a proposed stipulation extending the time to file an answer or move to dismiss. The latter signed the stipulation and returned it after striking the provision for making a motion to dismiss and adding a provision admitting the propriety of service and jurisdiction. Defendant's lawyer then served an answer containing a jurisdictional defense. The defendant never signed the modified version of the stipulation. The Court of Appeals concluded that the stipulation was of no effect because it was not signed or made in open court as required by CPLR 2104. Therefore, the stipulation did not preclude the defense or extend defendant's time to answer. Although defendant's answer was untimely, the court notes that plaintiff never moved for a default judgment on this basis.

(2) The informal appearance problem can be avoided by a defendant who follows CPLR 320. How might it have been avoided by defendant in Problem C?

§ 6.06 NOTE ON CHALLENGING PLAINTIFF'S CHOICE OF FORUM

We have seen a number of ways in which the defendant can object to plaintiff's choice of forum. To recap, they are: move to change venue (CPLR 510-511); move to dismiss because the forum is inconvenient (CPLR 327); seek removal to a different court within the state system (CPLR 325); move to dismiss because the court lacks subject matter jurisdiction (CPLR 3211(a)(2)); and, as seen in this chapter, move to dismiss for lack of jurisdiction over his person or property (CPLR 3211(a)(8), (9)) or put the objection to personal, property or subject matter jurisdiction in the answer (CPLR 3211(e)) and later move for summary judgment (CPLR 3212). Too, the defendant could petition for removal to a federal court, assuming federal subject matter jurisdiction would allow. *See* 28 U.S.C. § 1446.

As this chapter shows with special force, it is not enough to know which defenses are available. It is crucial that the lawyer know how and when to raise each objection. A useful method of review at this point is to assume a case in which you represent a defendant who has been served with a summons and complaint, and in which you believe you can properly raise each of the procedural objections listed above. How would you do so?

Part Two
TIMELINESS OF THE LITIGATION

Chapter 7

THE STATUTES OF LIMITATIONS AND RELATED CONCEPTS

§ 7.01 INTRODUCTORY NOTE

One of a lawyer's principal responsibilities is to be sure that the clients' legal claims are not inadvertently lost by a failure to commence litigation in timely fashion. Very early in the development of a strategy, therefore, the attorney must determine all relevant cut-off dates. This chapter describes the rules by which those dates are determined. Most often, the only responsibility is to interpose the claim within the time allowed by the appropriate statute of limitations. Sometimes, however, a statute or contract will impose an additional requirement, a "condition precedent" to suit. These two types of time limits are quite different and are treated separately in this chapter.

Article 2 of the CPLR contains the principal statutes of limitations in New York, though there are many others.[*]

In addition to listing the relevant time periods for many causes of action, it also includes some rules of general applicability, of which one of the most important is CPLR 203(a): "The time within which an action must be commenced, except as otherwise expressly prescribed, shall be computed from the time the cause of action accrued to the time the claim is interposed." To find the time limit in a particular case, one first decides which period set forth in CPLR 211-217 (or elsewhere) is relevant; second, determines when the claim accrued; and third, considers the effect of any tolls or extensions which are applicable.

CPLR 201 states: "No court shall extend the time limited by law for the commencement of an action." This does not mean that the lawyer's skills are irrelevant in influencing the question of timeliness, as the following cases show. Careful investigation may reveal a cause of action which is not time barred even if another one is. In some cases, careful pleading may make the difference between success and failure.

---

[*] Unfortunately, the many statutes of limitations have never been compiled into a central list. Two rules of practice can help you avoid problems in this area: (1) whenever your client has an unfamiliar claim, be sure to carefully research the possibility that a special limitation period exists outside the CPLR; (2) be especially alert if the defendant is the state, a local government or one of their offices, for in such cases a short statutes of limitations will probably be lurking about, *see, e.g.*, Gen. Municipal Law § 50-i(1) (one year and ninety day limit applicable to tort claims against municipalities), and you will also be confronted with an even shorter period in which to serve a notice of claim.

As you will see, New York's application of its statutes of limitations is often defendant-oriented. This may suggest that when a more hospitable forum is available elsewhere, the plaintiff should use it. Beware: The other jurisdiction may have a statute similar to CPLR 202. These "borrowing statutes" are designed to prevent such forum shopping and, if applicable, will frustrate the plaintiff's intent. *See* § 7.08, *infra*.

§ 7.02 FINDING THE APPLICABLE STATUTE OF LIMITATIONS AND DETERMINING WHEN IT BEGAN TO RUN

There are several sources of difficulty in determining the statute of limitations applicable to any claim. The classifications found in Article 2 of the CPLR are not mutually exclusive. Some, for example, are stated in terms of a theory of liability, *viz.*, an action on a "contractual obligation . . . express or implied," CPLR 213(2), while others are phrased in terms of the type of injury suffered, *viz.*, an action "to recover damages for a personal injury," CPLR 214(5). Cases, however, do not always fit neatly into one or another theory of liability, and litigants often strive to fit their claims within the theory which invokes the more favorable time period. Further, a given fact situation may give rise to more than one remedy, *e.g.*, tort and contract, and after one remedy is barred, litigants often seek another which is still timely.

A second problem is to determine when the statute began to run. (The rule says that it is "from the time the cause of action accrued." CPLR 203(a)). This is also complex because the time of accrual depends, in large part, on identifying the correct cause of action, a sometimes difficult task.

Rather than try to treat every type of action, we shall look at some of the most important and problematical areas. As you read the following cases, think about whether they concern the length of time to be applied, or the time of accrual, or both.

[A] Tort and Contract Claims

PROBLEM A

Betty, a tenant in a building owned by Fred Bucks, was injured on Oct. 30, 2003, when she slipped and fell on the floor of the building's laundry room. As luck would have it, Fred was also doing his laundry at the same time and, as he came over to aid Betty, he also slipped on the wet floor, suffering much chagrin and a traumatized back.

On Oct. 6, 2005, Betty commenced an action against Fred and a co-defendant, Urban & Dismal, the architectural firm which designed the building, and General Contractors, Inc., the construction company. The theory of Betty's action was that the floor of the laundry room was improperly designed so as to allow water to accumulate on walkways. On Oct. 23, 2005, Fred commenced his own action against Urban & Dismal and General Contractors seeking (a) damages for his own personal injury, (b) indemnification for any damages assessed against him in Betty's action, and (c) the cost of re-doing the floor so as to make it safer.

Assuming that Urban & Dismal and General Contractors completed its work and turned the building over to Fred on Nov. 1, 1985, is Betty's action against Fred timely? Against U&D? Against General Contractors? Are the causes of action asserted in Fred's complaint timely? *See* CPLR 213(2); 214(4)-(6).

What effect, if any, does CPLR 214-d have on the answer to Problem A?

CHASE SCIENTIFIC RESEARCH, INC. v. NIA GROUP, INC.
Court of Appeals
96 N.Y.2d 20, 725 N.Y.S.2d 592, 749 N.E.2d 161 (2001)

CHIEF JUDGE KAYE.

Under CPLR 214(6), a three-year statute of limitations is applicable in non-medical malpractice actions, regardless of whether the underlying theory is based in contract or tort. The appeals now before us raise the novel issue of what "malpractice" means in this statute. Put another way, given that malpractice is professional misfeasance toward one's client, who is a "professional" within the section? The question arises in the context of insurance agents and brokers.

I.

In the first case, *Chase Scientific Research, Inc. v The NIA Group, Inc.*, plaintiff Chase, a manufacturer of precision rotors, in May 1995 engaged defendants — insurance brokers — to procure property insurance for its business; on May 31, 1995, defendants procured such a policy for plaintiff. Some months later, on January 19, 1996, a severe storm damaged plaintiff's warehouse and inventory. In response to plaintiff's insurance claim, the carriers acknowledged the incident as a "covered occurrence" under the policy but offered only $50,000 despite plaintiff's demand for the policy limit of $550,000 on claimed losses exceeding $1 million. Plaintiff later settled a case against the carriers for $275,000.

On January 7, 1999, plaintiff filed suit against defendants, asserting one cause of action for negligence and one for breach of contract based on defendants' failure to secure coverage adequate to indemnify plaintiff against losses to its highly specialized inventory. Defendants moved to dismiss the entire action as time-barred under CPLR 214(6), contending that the claim was one for malpractice, that it accrued on the policy date, and that more than three years had elapsed before this action was commenced. Plaintiff countered that the action was governed by the six-year statute of limitations applicable to contract actions (CPLR 213[2]), and that, even applying the three-year statute of limitations (CPLR 214[6]), the claim was timely because it accrued on the date of loss. Supreme Court agreed with defendants and dismissed the complaint. The Appellate Division affirmed.

In the second case, *Gugliotta v Apollo Roland Brokerage Inc., et al.*, defendant Apollo through its insurance agent (defendant Thomas Loveter) in December 1994 procured insurance for plaintiff's commercial building from defendant New York Merchant Bankers Insurance Company. In February 1995, Herman Fermin slipped and fell in the building, and in December 1995 commenced an action against plaintiff for personal injuries. Only after the accident did plaintiff discover that he lacked general liability coverage. With the assistance of Loveter, plaintiff engaged attorneys Charles L. Emma and Harry Cardillo to defend the Fermin action. After counsel failed to appear, a default judgment was entered for $767,900. Claiming both negligence and breach of contract, on March 6, 1998 plaintiff commenced the present action for failure to procure adequate insurance coverage, which defendants Apollo and Loveter sought to dismiss as time-barred under CPLR 214(6). As in *Chase*, Supreme Court determined that CPLR 214(6) was the applicable statute of limitations, rendering plaintiff's claims untimely, and the Appellate Division affirmed. We now reverse in *Chase*, reinstating both causes of action, and modify in *Gugliotta*, reinstating the breach of contract claim.

II.

While a malpractice action may be grounded in negligence — subject generally to a three-year statute of limitations — it can theoretically also rest on breach of contract to obtain a particular bargained-for result (*see,* Kenneth R. Kirby, *The Six-Year Legal Malpractice Statute of Limitations: Judicial Usurpation of the Legislative Prerogative?*, 66 NY State Bar Journal, December 1994, at 14). Breach of contract actions are subject generally to a six-year statute of limitations. When the Legislature amended CPLR 214(6) to apply a three-year limitations period to all nonmedical malpractice actions, whether based on tort or contract (L 1996, ch 623), it ended one quandary but exposed another: who are the "professionals" whose misfeasance toward clients is subject to the shortened limitations period?

"Malpractice" has for more than a century appeared in our statutes of limitation, without definition of the term. . . .

In 1962, the Legislature replaced the two-year limitations period contained in Civil Practice Act 50(1) with CPLR 214(6), bringing the statute of limitations for malpractice actions in line with the limitations period for negligence generally. The revisers noted that the new statute "was added on the suggestion that malpractice involving property damage — e.g., against an accountant — may be based on a contract theory and would otherwise be governed by the six year provision unless specific reference was made" (6th Report, NY Legis Doc [1962], No 8, pp 92-93). And indeed, 214(6) was construed to apply to malpractice claims against attorneys and other nonmedical professionals (*see, Gilbert Properties v Millstein*, 33 N.Y.2d 857, 307 N.E.2d 257, 352 N.Y.S.2d 198 [attorney malpractice claim time-barred by 214(6)]). Leaving 214(6) in place, in 1975, in response to a perceived health care crisis affecting medical malpractice insurance, the Legislature shortened the statute of limitations for medical malpractice actions to two and one-half years (CPLR 214-a; *Bleiler v Bodnar*, 65 N.Y.2d 65, 68, 489 N.Y.S.2d 885, 479 N.E.2d 230). The passage of CPLR 214-a thus again created a disparity among professions as to their period of exposure to a malpractice suit.

When this Court subsequently confronted nonmedical malpractice claims based on a breach of contract theory, it applied the six-year contract statute of limitations (*see, Sears, Roebuck & Co v Enco Assocs*, 43 N.Y.2d 389, 401 N.Y.S.2d 767, 372 N.E.2d 555; *Video Corp of America v Frederick Flatto Assocs*, 58 N.Y.2d 1026, 462 N.Y.S.2d 439, 448 N.E.2d 1350; *National Life Ins Co v Frank B. Hall & Co*, 67 N.Y.2d 1021, 503 N.Y.S.2d 318, 494 N.E.2d 449; *Santulli v Englert, Reilly & McHugh, PC*, 78 N.Y.2d 700, 579 N.Y.S.2d 324, 586 N.E.2d 1014). In all of these "contractual" malpractice cases, the Court's analysis centered on the nature of the claim asserted by plaintiffs — tort or contract — in determining the applicable statute of limitations. While the cases involved architects, lawyers and insurance brokers, no issue was raised — and none decided — as to whether those actors were capable of malpractice within the contemplation of CPLR 214(6).

Most recently, in response to *Sears* and its progeny, the Legislature amended 214(6) to clarify that the limitations period in nonmedical malpractice claims is three years, "whether the underlying theory is based in contract or tort" (CPLR 214[6], as amended by L 1996, ch 623). This change was intended not only to remediate the *Sears* line of cases but also to reduce potential liability of insurers and corresponding malpractice premiums, and to restore a reasonable symmetry to the period in which all professionals would remain exposed to a malpractice suit (Letter from NY State Ins Dept [July 16, 1996], Bill Jacket, L 1996, ch 623, at 9-10 ["The Courts have applied [a contract] theory to architect and legal malpractice"]; Legis Rep No 76-B of NY State Bar Assn, Bill Jacket, at 13-14 ["there is no rationale for subjecting professional malpractice by an architect, engineer, lawyer, or accountant to a statute of limitations over twice as long as that applied to doctors, dentists and podiatrists"]).

As a final link in the statute's litigation chain, barely five months ago, in *Brothers v Florence* and its companion cases (95 N.Y.2d 290, 739 N.E.2d 733, 716 N.Y.S.2d 367) — involving the alleged malpractice of attorneys and real estate appraisers — this Court concluded that the amended statute applied retroactively to bar certain claims accruing prior to the effective date of the statute.

Again, no one disputed that a real estate appraiser was capable of malpractice within the meaning of 214(6), and we resolved the appeal without reaching that question (*see, Brothers*, 95 N.Y.2d at 298, 306).

III.

Defining "professional" is a task engaging many courts, for many purposes (*see,* Michael J. Polelle, *Who's on First, and What's a Professional?*, 33 USF L Rev 205 [1999]). While the term has myriad applications in law — as, for example, in insurance policy exclusions, and peer negligence standards — we underscore that our definition is limited to the context presented: CPLR 214(6). Moreover, our objective, as always in matters of statutory interpretation, is to effectuate the will of the Legislature. Here, that task is complicated by the fact that, in CPLR 214(6), "malpractice" is undefined and "professional" unmentioned.

"Professional" is a term in wide usage, commonly understood to have several meanings. For example, it denotes a measure of quality, as in professional dry cleaners; a distinction from trade or businesspeople, and from amateur status, as in professional golfers; a lifework as opposed to pastime, as in professional musicians. Often there are study, licensure and continuing skills requirements, as for barbers, electricians and real estate brokers. Thus, neither common parlance nor licensure can determine the meaning of "professional," for surely the Legislature did not have such a vast, amorphous category of service providers in mind when it amended CPLR 214(6) (Alexander, Supplementary Practice Commentaries [1999] McKinney's Cons Laws of NY, Book 7B, CPLR C:214[6] 2001 Cumulative Pocket Part, at 214 ["The Legislature presumably sought to confer the protections of CPLR 214(6) on a relatively small group of defendants. Otherwise, it would have shortened the six-year breach of contract period to three years for all contracts for services."]).

Nor does the law defining "professional" for other purposes necessarily resolve the statute of limitations issue before us (*see, e.g., People v Kelly*, 255 N.Y. 396, 175 N.E. 108 [music a profession, not a trade, under zoning resolution]); *People ex rel. Tower v State Tax Commn*, 282 N.Y. 407, 26 N.E.2d 955 [customhouse broker not a professional for purposes of unincorporated business tax exclusion]; Business Corporation Law 1501; Education Law, Title VIII, art 130 et seq. ["The Professions"]). An abbreviated statute of limitations bars claims of allegedly injured parties, and should therefore reflect the Legislature's intent that the particular defendant groups receive such a benefit. In *Karasek v LaJoie* (92 N.Y.2d 171, 677 N.Y.S.2d 265, 699 N.E.2d 889), for example, we refused, absent legislative clarification, to include licensed psychologists within the category of "medical" services subject to the truncated limitations period of CPLR 214-a. . . .

The term "professional" is also commonly understood to refer to the learned professions, exemplified by law and medicine, which have particular relevance to the history of CPLR 214(6). The two- and three-year malpractice statutes of limitation, after all, began with doctors, enlarged soon after to encompass attorneys and accountants. In 1996, when CPLR 214(6) was before the Legislature for amendment, the report of the New York State Bar Association referred specifically to those categories in speaking of professional malpractice: "an architect, engineer, lawyer or accountant" (Legis Rep No 76-B of NY State Bar Assn, Bill Jacket, L 1996, ch 623, at 13-14).

The qualities shared by such groups guide us in defining the term "professional." In particular, those qualities include extensive formal learning and training, licensure and regulation indicating a qualification to practice, a code of conduct imposing standards beyond those accepted in the marketplace and a system of discipline for violation of those standards. Additionally, a professional relationship is one of trust and confidence, carrying with it a duty to counsel and advise clients.

This definition, we believe, implements the Legislature's intention to benefit a discrete group of persons affected by the concerns that motivated the shortened statute of limitations We are mindful as well that our definition ideally should establish a bright line, so that, absent legislative clarification, it can be fairly and uniformly applied. Moreover, with the rise of large numbers of skilled "semi-professions" (*see*, Polelle, *supra*, 33 USF L Rev at 205), any broader definition would, for the future, make it hard to draw meaningful distinctions and the groups covered by CPLR 214(6) would quickly proliferate.

Applying these criteria, we conclude that insurance agents and brokers are not within the ambit of CPLR 214(6). While agents and brokers must be licensed, they are not required to engage in extensive specialized education and training; rather, a person who has been regularly employed by an insurance company, agent or broker for at least one year during the three years preceding the date of license application may qualify to be a broker (Insurance Law 2104[c][1][B] and [C]). True, lawyers, engineers, architects and accountants also can circumvent the formal education criteria of their respective fields, but they must surmount far higher hurdles. Aspiring attorneys must complete at least one academic year as a matriculated student at an approved law school as well as an aggregate of four years in the supervised study of law in a New York State law office, with credit for law school attendance (22 NYCRR 520.4[a]); engineers, architects and accountants also face extensive work experience requirements (Education Law 7206[2] [engineers, 12 years]; Education Law 7304[2] [architects, 12 years]; Education Law 7404[2] [accountants, 15 years]).

Nor are insurance agents and brokers bound by a standard of conduct for which discipline might be imposed (*see, e.g.,* 22 NYCRR 603 [attorney discipline]; Education Law 6509, 6510, 6511 [professional misconduct, proceedings and discipline for accountants, architects, engineers and others, but not insurance agents or brokers]). Moreover, as this Court recently made clear, an insurance agent has a common-law duty to obtain requested coverage, but generally not a continuing duty to advise, guide or direct a client based on a special relationship of trust and confidence (*Murphy v Kuhn, supra,* 90 N.Y.2d at 273). To be sure, insurance agents and brokers are held to high standards of education and qualification (*see, e.g.,* Insurance Law 2103, 2104), but these criteria are simply not as rigorous as those embraced by what we conclude are the professionals within CPLR 214(6).

Thus, in both cases we conclude that the actions against defendant agents and brokers are governed not by CPLR 214(6), but by the limitations periods applicable to negligence actions (CPLR 214[4]) and breach of contract actions (CPLR 213[2]). In *Chase* (but not *Gugliotta*) plaintiff argues that — even applying CPLR 214(4) — its negligence cause of action should be reinstated, and we agree. Plaintiff's action was commenced on January 7, 1999, within three years of what both parties agree was the accrual date for the negligence claim, January 19, 1996. In both cases the "continuous treatment" doctrine is inapplicable. Finally, while plaintiffs' contract claims were indisputably brought within six years of accrual and thus must be reinstated, we note that the sole issue before us is the applicable statute of limitations. No challenge has been made to the viability of the breach of contract claims, and we do not pass on them.

Accordingly, in *Chase* the order of the Appellate Division should be reversed, with costs, and the complaint reinstated. In *Gugliotta*, the order of the Appellate Division, insofar as appealed from, should be modified, without costs, to reinstate the cause of action for breach of contract as against Apollo, and otherwise affirmed.

NOTES

(1) As the Court of Appeals notes in the principal case, there is a difference in the damages recoverable under tort, on one hand, and contract, on the other. For example, it has been said that lost profits may be awarded in tort actions but not usually in contract. *See, e.g., Sears, Roebuck & Co. v. Enco Assocs.,* 43 N.Y.2d 389, 401 N.Y.S.2d 767, 372 N.E.2d 555 (1977).

(2) In the principal case, the plaintiffs were apparently unaware of the defendants' mistakes until some time after they occurred. When did the breach of contract claims accrue? The Court of Appeals has held that a cause of action for breach of contract accrues at the time of the breach even if the plaintiff is unaware of the breach and even if the breach is committed in secret. *Ely-Cruikshank Co. v. Bank of Montreal,* 81 N.Y.2d 399, 599 N.Y.S.2d 501, 615 N.E.2d 985 (1993).

(3) In *Kliment v. McKinsey & Co.,* 3 N.Y.3d 538, 788 N.Y.S.2d 648, 821 N.E.2d 952 (2004), the Court held that a claim against an architect was governed by the three-year period of CPLR 214(6) rather than the six-year contract period, even though the plaintiff alleged a breach of an express contractual promises to perform the work according to code. The Court opined that when a claim is "essentially" one for malpractice despite the allegations of the complaint that the conduct violated the contract, it is subject to the shorter period.

(4) CPLR 213(2) excludes three types of contract actions from its six-year statute of limitations: (a) Rent overcharge cases are covered by CPLR 213-a, allowing a four-year period for suit; (b) Breach of warranty cases based on the sale of goods are covered by article 2 of the Uniform Commercial Code, which establishes a four-year period, and is discussed in § 7.02[B], *infra*; (c) Breach of warranty claims arising from the sale of new homes are covered by article 36-B of the General Business Law. This article, added in 1988, provides that actions brought to recover for the breach of an implied new home warranty must be commenced within the later of two periods — four years after the "warranty date" or one year after the expiration of applicable warranty period (this period depends on the type of defect at issue). New homes, for the purpose of this warranty, are defined as single family homes and units in buildings of five stories or less. *See* Gen. Bus. Law § 777.

(5) The three-year period of CPLR 214(4) and (5), applicable respectively to actions to recover for property damage and personal injury, *i.e.*, tort claims, does not apply when the defendant is a municipality. Gen. Mun. Law § 50-i imposes a one-year and ninety-day period on tort actions against local governments. As to actions against the state, see Court of Claims Act § 10(3), (6). In addition to short statutes of limitations, the person with a claim against a city will be faced with an even shorter period within which he must serve a notice of claim. Gen. Mun. Law § 50-3. *See* § 7.09, Conditions Precedent.

(6) Claims based on intentional torts, such as assault, are governed by the one year period of CPLR 215.

CUBITO v. KREISBERG
Appellate Division, Second Department
69 A.D.2d 738, 419 N.Y.S.2d 578 (1979),
aff'd, 51 N.Y.2d 900, 434 N.Y.S.2d 991, 415 N.E.2d 979 (1980)

HOPKINS, J.P.

The plaintiff, a tenant in an apartment house, fell in the laundry room on October 30, 1974. On October 6, 1977, she brought this action to recover damages for personal injuries based on the defendants' negligence. The complaint alleges that the defendant Gindele & Johnson was the architect which so negligently planned and designed the construction of the laundry room that water collected on the floor, causing the plaintiff's injuries.

Gindele & Johnson moved to dismiss the action on the ground that it was barred by the Statute of Limitations (CPLR 214, subd 6). The basis of its motion was that it had completed all its services on May 7, 1973, when the certificate of final inspection was sent to the owner, and that, consequently, more than four years had elapsed when the plaintiff's action was commenced.

Special Term denied the motion, holding that it would be unreasonable to apply the statute so as to extinguish a claim against the architect for its negligence prior to the time that the injury had been sustained or that an action could have been brought to recover damages for the injury (*Cubito v. Kreisberg*, 94 Misc 2d 56).

We affirm. The Statute of Limitations applicable to the liability of an architect for injuries suffered by third parties due to his negligence runs from the date of the injury.

I

. . . .

The architect contends that since [May 7, 1973] it has had no involvement with the project. It stresses, in particular, that it has had nothing to do with the maintenance and repair of the laundry room or its facilities. Hence, it argues that the three-year limitation prescribed for malpractice actions generally (as distinguished from medical malpractice) applies to the plaintiff's action (CPLR 214, subd 6). It urges that the date of completion of its work marks the time when the statute begins to run, and the plaintiff's action was brought well beyond the three-year period and is therefore barred. . . .

II

Since the defendant architect largely rests its argument on the statute, we begin by an analysis of its provisions. The statute provides for time periods for the institution of suits linked to the character of the action. As malpractice essentially is a special form of negligent conduct, it is instructive to note that the statute deals severally with types of actions grounded on negligence.

CPLR 214 (subd 5) provides that an action to recover damages for personal injuries, including an action based on the negligence of the defendant must be commenced within three years. CPLR 214 (subd 6) provides that an action to recover damages for malpractice, other than medical malpractice, similarly must be brought within three years. CPLR 214-a provides that an action for medical malpractice must be commenced within two years and six months. Thus, the statute formally treats malpractice actions differently from other actions based on negligence in limiting the time in which the action must be instituted. Even so, for our purposes in this appeal it is to be noted that the statute in dealing with an architect's malpractice makes no material difference from the conventional negligence action, since it prescribes the same three-year limitation.

Nevertheless, it is useful to recognize as an aid in analysis that malpractice, in its strict sense, means the negligence of a member of a profession in his relations with his client or patient. In this case the plaintiff is not, and never has been, in a professional relation with the architect. . . . On the other hand, the wrongful conduct of the professional in rendering services to his client resulting in injury to a party outside the relationship is simple negligence.

The importance of this distinction becomes evident in considering the measurement of time which the statute provides. CPLR 203 (subd a) states that the time within which an action must be commenced shall be computed from the time the cause of action accrued to the time the claim is interposed. The fulcrum of the statute is thus the meaning to be attached to the term of "accrual of a cause of action" — a meaning which has been supplied by judicial gloss.

III

Since the statute affords no definition, we must presume that the content of the meaning of an accrual of a cause of action has been left by the Legislature to judicial determination. . . .

. . . .

. . . Hence, the general rule that a cause of action for damages due to negligence accrues when the invasion of the plaintiff's personal rights occurred, *i.e.*, when she fell as a result of the defendants' claimed negligence, should apply, as Special Term held (*cf. Durant v Grange Silo Co.*, 12 AD2d 694; *Gile v Sears, Roebuck & Co.*, 281 App Div 95), unless we are required by reasons of compelling public policy to find that the cause of action accrued when the architect prepared the plans and found the building to have been completed according to the plans.

IV

As grounds for reversal, the appellant's argument is that it is unfair to an architect to hold him liable for errors in design when injuries are sustained many years after the rendition of his services and he is no longer associated with the project. It emphasizes that the building where the plaintiff fell is no longer within the appellant's supervision or control, that in the meantime the building may have been transferred from owner to owner, and that the conditions, if dangerous, could have been remedied by the owner. Doubtless, the interpretation of a Statute of Limitations produces hardships in many instances, and in this instance the general rule may place a hardship on an architect. . . .

. . . .

If a departure from the general rule governing the accrual of a cause of action for tort liability based on negligence is to be made on behalf of an architect sued by a person outside a professional relation with the architect, we think that it should be accomplished by the Legislature, just as the Legislature has acted on behalf of the medical profession (*see, e.g.*, CPLR 214-a; *see, generally*, Comment, *Medical Malpractice in New York*, 27 Syracuse L Rev 657). The general rule has been effective for some time, and the Legislature must be presumed to know its extent. The Statute of Limitations has been changed from time to time in New York in response to current needs and expectations in society and has been peculiarly a subject of legislative solicitude (Note, *Developments in the Law: Statutes of Limitations*, 63 Harv L Rev 1177, 1192-1193, n 157).

In weighing the force of the appellant's contention that liability may hang over its head for many years after its work has been finished, we must also put in the balance the fact, as Special Term observed, that an injured party may be barred from recovery because of the lapse of the statutory period even before his injury was sustained. There are detriments which will be experienced by either the injured party or the architect, depending on the character of the rule adopted. Weighing the relative detriments, we are not persuaded that we should depart from the general rule — a rule, which we note, is applied in other jurisdictions (*Chrischilles v Griswold*, 260 Iowa 453; *Abramovski v Kilps Sons Realty*, 80 Wis 2d 468; *Society of Mt. Carmel v Fox*, 31 Ill App 3d 1060; *cf. Hendrickson v Sears*, 365 Mass 83).

V

Kreisberg and Sprain have urged on this appeal that their cross-complaint against the architect should be preserved in the event we were to reverse Special Term. They assert that their right to indemnity or contribution as owners remains unaffected by the running of the Statute of Limitations against the plaintiff in favor of the architect.

A cause of action for indemnity and contribution does not accrue until payment of the underlying liability has been made by the suing party (*Klinger v Dudley*, 41 NY2d 362, 369; *Musco v Conte*, 22 AD2d 121, 125-126). Hence, even if we were disposed to hold that the plaintiff is out of court on her claim against the architect because the Statute of Limitations has run against her, the architect would still be obliged to defend against a claim of negligence alleged in the cross complaint by the owner. This consideration strengthens the conclusion that we should not, for the reasons of policy advanced by the architect, disregard the traditional and accepted rule.

. . . .

NOTES

(1) The foregoing opinion was affirmed "for reasons stated in the opinion by Mr. Justice James D. Hopkins at the Appellate Division. . . ." 51 N.Y.2d 900, 434 N.Y.S.2d 991, 415 N.E.2d 979 (1980).

(2) The principal case is helpful in answering at least part of Problem A. Does it (or *Chase Scientific Research, Inc. v. NIA Group, Inc., supra*) help you decide the timeliness of Fred's action against U & D for his personal injuries and property damage?

(3) CPLR 214-d, which was enacted and took effect in 1997, requires service of a notice of claim at least ninety days prior to the commencement of a malpractice action against an architect or engineer if the claim is asserted more than ten years after the alleged malpractice occurred. *Dorst v. Eggers Pshp.*, 265 A.D.2d 294, 696 N.Y.S.2d 478 (2nd Dep't 1999), holds that failure to serve the

requisite notice of claim necessitates dismissal of the action. Could the losing plaintiff cure the problem by subsequently serving a notice of claim and then commencing a new action, relying on CPLR 205? The *Dorst* court was not called upon to address that issue, but in *Kretschmann v. Board of Educ.*, 294 A.D.2d 39, 744 N.Y.S.2d 106 (4th Dep't 2002), it was held that the six-month extension afforded by CPLR 205(a) applied even though the plaintiff's first action was dismissed for a failure to serve the CPLR 214-d notice.

(4) What about Fred's claims for indemnification and contribution? See Section V of the principal case and CPLR 214-d.

Unlike claims for contribution and indemnification, a claim to subrogation begins to run from the date of the wrong. This is because the subrogee's right arises through subrogation of the subrogor's right, not independently of it. *See Allstate Ins. Co. v. Stein*, 1 N.Y.3d 416, 775 N.Y.S.2d 219, 807 N.E.2d 268 (2004) (an action for subrogation accrued on the date of the accident, rather than when the insurer paid its insured, the subrogor).

[B] Products Liability

PROBLEM B

After Joe was stricken by a bone disease, a metal pin was surgically inserted into his hip during an operation performed by Dr. Doolittle at Mount Hope Hospital on January 4, 2001. The pin had been manufactured in March, 2000, by Health Co., Inc., which sold it to the hospital on January 2, 2001. Later in 2001, Joe began to experience pains in his hip which grew progressively worse. When, in March, 2004, he brought the pains to the attention of Dr. Doolittle, an x-ray revealed that the pin had broken. The doctor thinks the break occurred a few days before the onset of pain. If Joe's action against Health Co., Inc., was commenced on January 3, 2006, and alleged negligence, breach of warranty, and strict products liability, was it timely in whole or in part? *See* CPLR 214-c; U.C.C. § 2-725, below.

NOTES

(1) Actions for breach of a contract for the sale of goods are not governed by the CPLR but by U.C.C. § 2-725, which provides:

> (1) An action for breach of any contract for sale must be commenced within four years after the cause of action has accrued. By the original agreement the parties may reduce the period of limitation to not less than one year but may not extend it.

(2) A cause of action accrues when the breach occurs, regardless of the aggrieved party's lack of knowledge of the breach. A breach of warranty occurs when tender of delivery is made, except that where a warranty explicitly extends to future performance of the goods and discovery of the breach must await the time of such performance the cause of action accrues when the breach is or should have been discovered.

(2) Many problems were presented by this statute, the most important of which was whether it barred an action in strict products liability against a manufacturer by a remote user (*i.e.*, a person not in privity with the seller) of the product. That question was answered in the next case. Some of the remaining issues are raised in the materials which follow the case.

VICTORSON v. BOCK LAUNDRY MACHINE CO.
Court of Appeals
37 N.Y.2d 395, 373 N.Y.S.2d 39, 335 N.E.2d 275 (1975)

JONES, J.

These three cases arise out of claims asserted against the manufacturer of allegedly defective products by remote users; the theory of liability is that which we have called strict products liability (*Codling v Paglia*, 32 NY2d 330). We now hold that the period of limitation with respect to these claims begins to run at the date of injury and that the duration of such period is that found in CPLR 214 (subds 4, 5) under which there is a limitation of three years in actions for personal injury and property damage. (*See* 1 Weinstein-Korn-Miller, NY Civ Prac, pars 214.13, 214.14, 214.15.) Accordingly, our court's holding to the contrary in *Mendel v Pittsburgh Plate Glass Co.* (25 NY2d 340) must be overruled.[1]

Defendant Bock Laundry Machine Company manufactured and marketed a centrifuge extractor for use in apartment house laundry rooms and commercial laundromats to spin water out of laundry after washing and preparatory to its being placed in a dryer. In *Victorson* the extractor was sold in 1948 and the injury occurred in 1969; in *Rivera* the sale was in 1959, the injury in 1967; and in *Brown* the sale was in 1955 and the injury in 1965. The Appellate Divisions have properly unraveled the procedural complexities, presenting for our determination, on motions addressed to the pleadings, the questions as to when the Statute of Limitations began to run and for what period it continued.

Preliminarily we observe as a matter of analysis that, while one seeking to recover from a manufacturer for injuries sustained in consequence of an alleged defect in its product may be said to have but a single claim, that claim may be

---

[1] For criticism of *Mendel see, e.g., Symposium on* Mendel v Pittsburgh Plate Glass Co. (45 St John's L Rev 62).

grounded in one or more of four causes of action or theories of liability. Depending on the factual context in which the claim arises, the injured plaintiff, and those asserting derivative claims, may state a cause of action in contract, express or implied, on the ground of negligence, or, as here, on the theory of strict products liability. In these cases now before us we are concerned only with claims based on the last theory. What we say here, therefore, should not be understood as in any way referring to the liability of a manufacturer of a defective product under familiar but different doctrines of the law of contracts for injuries sustained by a customer or other person with whom or for whose benefit the manufacturer previously has made a warranty or other agreement, express or implied. As indicated, it may be open to a particular plaintiff to base his case on contract liability or negligence or strict products liability, or on some combination thereof.

Some consideration of the theory of strict products liability is of assistance in the selection of the applicable Statute of Limitations. We acknowledge that for some years there has been a lively discussion as to whether this form of liability sounds in tort or in contract.

Initially we recognize the general distinction between these two areas of the law. "The fundamental difference between tort and contract lies in the nature of the interests protected. Tort actions are created to protect the interest in freedom from various kinds of harm. The duties of conduct which give rise to them are imposed by the law, and are based primarily upon social policy, and not necessarily upon the will or intention of the parties." (Prosser, Torts [4th ed], § 92, p 613.)

The development of what we now call the doctrine of strict products liability has been both tortuous and spasmodic (*Codling v Paglia, supra*; *Goldberg v Kollsman Instrument Corp.*, 12 NY2d 432; *see* discussion in *Mendel v Pittsburgh Plate Glass Co., supra*, dissenting opn, p 346 *et seq.*). In reaching and articulating our decision in *Codling*, we neither created nor discovered a new cause of action. On the contrary, in extending the remedy to plaintiffs who were neither buyers nor users of the product, we recognized in its modern guise a pre-existing theory of liability which had been evolving and maturing over the years, sometimes having been described by use of the phrase "breach of implied warranty."

In a simplistic sense it is obvious that this liability does not arise out of contract concepts if such concepts be thought of as the means for analyzing the jural relationship between two parties who have entered into a contractual relationship prior to the date on which injury is sustained. Here none of these plaintiffs had any association with the manufacturer of the centrifuge extractors prior to being injured. Nor are these claims grounded in any contention that the liability of the manufacturer stems from its nonperformance of an obligation to plaintiffs arising out of an agreement, express or implied. Rather than arising out of the "will or intention of the parties," the liability imposed on the manufacturer under strict products liability, whether it be to purchaser, user, or innocent bystander, is predicated largely on considerations of sound social policy (*Codling v Paglia*, *supra,* pp 340-341).

That in the emerging growth and development of the law of liability in these matters, in the best traditions of the common law, it has from time to time been found useful in justification or exposition to use terminology familiar to the law of contracts rather than of torts should be neither surprising nor diverting. As we have recognized, depending on the factual context in which the issue arises or the alternative theory pursued by the litigant, the liability of the product-manufacturer could indeed have been grounded in contract rather than tort theory, or indeed sometimes in both. Historically it even appears that these two fields have not been so categorically discrete as we are sometimes inclined to suppose. As in other instances in the law, analysis and enlightenment are not always advanced when heavy reliance is placed on labels; indeed understanding may even be obscured.

Whatever may have been earlier doubt and confusion, the authorities are now in general agreement that strict products liability sounds in tort rather than in contract.

Some further analysis is reassuring before jumping, knee-jerk-like, to the conclusion that if liability is grounded in tort, tort Statute of Limitations must automatically be applied. "[I]n applying the Statute of Limitations we look for the reality, and the essence of the action and not its mere name." (*Brick v Cohn-Hall-Marx Co.*, 276 NY 259, 264.)

Restrictions of time on claim assertion involve two aspects — how long shall the period be within which the claim may be asserted, and as of what date shall that period begin to run?

On principle, there having been no prior relationship between the parties in strict products liability cases, the cause of action if any there be, should accrue at the time the injury is sustained. To hold that it somehow came into being prior thereto would defy both logic and experience. "[It] is all but unthinkable that a person should be time-barred from prosecuting a cause of action before he ever had one" (*Mendel v Pittsburgh Plate Glass Co., supra*, p 346). In this perspective the analogy in principle is to "tort" claims, that is claims for injury to person or property, as to most of which, although not all, the statute runs from the date of injury. (*Schmidt v Merchants Desp. Transp. Co.*, 270 NY 287, 299-301; *Flanagan v Mount Eden Gen. Hosp.*, 24 NY2d 427; Restatement, Torts, § 899, comment c, p 525; *cf.* 14 CJS, Case, Action on, §§ 1, 2.) By contrast, in contract actions the statute runs from the date of the breach of performance of the contractual obligation, in the present context, the date of sale of the defective product. (CPLR 213, subd 2; Uniform Commercial Code, § 2-725, subd [2].)

Then over how long a period thereafter should the injured party be allowed to assert his claim? As in other instances in which periods of limitation must be fixed, the answer depends on a nice balancing of policy considerations. "Any Statute of Limitations reflects a policy that there must come a time after which fairness demands that a defendant should not be harried; the duration of the period is chosen with a balancing sense of fairness to the claimant that he unreasonably be deprived of his right to assert his claim" (*Caffaro v Trayna*, 35 NY2d 245, 250). We identify no material factors which suggest that the period of limitation should be different where it is sought to impose liability on the manufacturer on the theory of strict products liability rather than on the theory of negligence. Substantially similar considerations are equally cogent and persuasive.

One argument of policy is pressed on us by appellants in these cases. Is it fair or reasonable, they ask, to hold a manufacturer liable for a defect in production many years after the product has left the manufacturer's plant? The predicament of the manufacturer is not then significantly different whether its liability in tort be grounded in theories of negligence or of strict products liability. One can observe that while passage of time may work a deterioration of the manufacturer's capability to defend, by similar token it can be expected to complicate the plaintiff's problem of proving, as he must, that the alleged defect existed at the time the product left the manufacturer's plant. (*See* discussion in *Mendel v Pittsburgh Plate Glass Co.*, 25 NY2d 340, dissenting opn, p 351, *supra*.) In any event this consideration, of varying weight from case to case, cannot be accorded such significance as to dictate the outcome. . . .

Again the authorities are now in general agreement that Statutes of Limitations governing injuries to person or property are those properly applicable to strict products liabilities claims.[3]

. . . .

Accordingly each of the several orders of the Appellate Division should be affirmed.

. . . .

NOTES

(1) Plaintiffs in the principal case urged that the court should apply CPLR 214(5), a three-year statute, while defendants argued that U.C.C. § 2-725, a four-year statute was applicable. How do you explain this apparent anomaly?

(2) What if the injured remote user brings an action more than three years from the date of the injury, but within four years of the date of purchasing the product? Is the plaintiff free to disregard CPLR 214(5) and invoke U.C.C. § 2-725? As a matter of substantive law, an injured remote user has a cause of action based on breach of warranty as well as on strict products liability. U.C.C.

---

[3] We observe in passing that the Uniform Commercial Code, in treating of the liability of a manufacturer of a defective product, applies only where such liability is predicated on a contractual obligation, express or implied. As such its provisions are not pertinent when liability is based on the tort doctrine of strict products liability. . . .

§ 2-318, amended eff. September 1, 1975, provides: "A seller's warranty whether express or implied extends to any natural person if it is reasonable to expect that such person may use, consume or be affected by the goods and who is injured in person by the breach of the warranty." The four-year period of U.C.C. § 2-725 would apply to such claims, but does the four years within which to sue the manufacturer run from the date of sale from the manufacturer to the retailer or from the date of sale by the retailer to the consumer?

The Court of Appeals addressed the problem in *Heller v. U.S. Suzuki Motor Corp.*, 64 N.Y.2d 407, 488 N.Y.S.2d 132, 477 N.E.2d 434 (1985): "When the Legislature amended section 2-318, it did not amend the limitations period provided in section 2-725 of the Code, however, and notwithstanding the elimination of the requirement of privity, it remains the law that a cause of action against a manufacturer or distributor accrues on the date the party charged tenders delivery of the product, not on the date some third party sells it to plaintiff."

In *Heller*, the Court of Appeals also said: "A consumer who acts within three years of the date of the accident or four years from the date of the sale, as the pertinent statutes provide, may now maintain causes of action in New York to recover against both immediate and remote parties based on express or implied warranty, negligence or strict products liability. . . ."

Of course, a person injured by a product should ideally commence the action prior to the expiration of both the time limiting the strict products liability action and the breach of warranty action. As a matter of substantive law, the claim may be stronger under one of these theories as opposed to the other. *See Denny v. Ford Motor Co.*, 87 N.Y.2d 248, 639 N.Y.S.2d 250, 662 N.E.2d 730 (1995).

(3) Claims for property damage must be distinguished from personal injury claims. A purchaser in privity with the manufacturer is entitled to rely on the four-year-from-tender-of-delivery period of U.C.C. § 2-725 but may not sue in strict products liability and get three years from the date of property damage. *De Crosta v. A. Reynolds Constr. & Supply Corp.*, 49 A.D.2d 476, 375 N.Y.S.2d 655 (3d Dep't 1975), *aff'd*, 41 N.Y.2d 1100, 396 N.Y.S.2d 357, 364 N.E.2d 1129 (1977). Moreover, a person who sustains economic loss only and who is not in privity with the defendant may not recover on the basis of a breach of implied warranty. *Arthur Jaffee Assocs v. Bilsco Auto Serv.*, 58 N.Y.2d 993, 461 N.Y.S.2d 1007, 448 N.E.2d 792 (1983).

(4) In most cases in which a person is injured by a defective product, the date of injury is obvious. In some cases, the injury does not manifest itself until years after the plaintiff was exposed to the product. CPLR 214-c, adopted in 1986, was a legislative reversal of New York's long-standing general rule that a cause of action in tort accrued on the date of injury, not on the date the plaintiff discovered the injury. As the next case shows, slow-developing injuries continue to create problems when issues of timeliness arise.

BLANCO v. AMERICAN TELEPHONE & TELEGRAPH CO.
Court of Appeals
90 N.Y.2d 757, 666 N.Y.S.2d 536, 689 N.E.2d 506 (1997)

WESLEY, J.

Progress begets promise and problems. Computer technology has ushered in the "information age" and helped to create a global workplace that is accessible from one's home or office. These cases present us with a difficult question arising from the widespread use of computers in the workplace: when does a cause of action accrue against a keyboard manufacturer for repetitive stress injury (RSI) suffered by a keyboard user? We conclude that, in such cases, the cause of action accrues upon the onset of symptoms, or the last use of the keyboard, whichever is earlier.

I.

This appeal involves over 90 separate plaintiffs suing various keyboard manufacturers in a number of separate lawsuits. By order entered January 22, 1993, Administrative Judge Stanley Ostrau, in apparent recognition of the large number of RSI cases which were making their way through Supreme Court, New York County, assigned all cases involving RSIs to Justice Stephen Crane for pretrial purposes. Soon thereafter, Justice Crane established procedures for the joint briefing of various legal issues. Defendants' motions raising Statute of Limitations issues were treated as dismissal motions made pursuant to CPLR 3211(a)(5).

Most of the pleadings in the cases before us on this appeal contain common allegations with respect to the onset and manifestation of plaintiffs' RSIs. Each plaintiff outlines his or her history of keyboard use, including, to the extent known, the particular keyboards used. The pleadings then go on to state that plaintiffs' injuries were "insidious in their onset," such that "it is not possible to identify [either] the precise date of the onset of symptoms," or to say "that any initial symptoms experienced constituted the full manifestation or even partial manifestation" of the injury. Nevertheless, the plaintiffs do identify dates upon which they began experiencing some symptoms, such as numbness, tingling, pain and/or sensory motor impairments of the upper extremities, neck and torso. Plaintiffs further state the dates upon which they were diagnosed with various RSIs. Finally, the pleadings generally allege that the nature of each plaintiff's injury is "such that there is no precise moment of injury," but rather a "cumulative and prolonged process by which [each] plaintiff sustained injury [and] aggravated [an] existing injury."

RSI is one of several essentially synonymous terms, all of which "connote injury to the musculo-skeletal tissues from repeated motions and exertions" (Russ, Freeman and McQuade, 5 Attorney's Medical Advisor 66:4, at 66-8). RSIs can be caused by activities as divergent as playing video games or working a jackhammer. Carpal tunnel syndrome, probably the most prevalent keyboard-related injury, is a subcategory of RSI involving compression of the median nerve as it passes through the wrist between the flexor tendons and the transverse carpal tunnel ligament (the area known as the carpal tunnel) (Ausman and Snyder, 3 Medical Library Lawyer's Edition 4:18, at 53 [1989 ed]). While carpal tunnel syndrome can have a number of causes, ranging from arthritis or benign tumors to blunt trauma, the condition is seen with increasing frequency as a result of workplace use of keyboards. Indeed, according to various surveys, the occurrence of RSIs among workers rose roughly 1,000% between 1982 and 1991, to the point that today they account for 61% of all workplace illnesses (*see, Comment, Cumulative Trauma Disorders: A Hidden Downside to Technological Advancement,* 11 J Contemp Health L & Pol'y 479; Juge, Stokes and Pine, *Cumulative Trauma Disorders — "The Disease of the 90's": An Interdisciplinary Analysis,* 55 La L Rev 895).

In deciding what accrual rule to apply to these claims, the trial court felt compelled to follow *Wallen v American Tel. & Tel. Co.,* [which] ruled that accrual in RSI cases is measured from the onset of the plaintiff's symptoms without requiring a diagnosis of their cause. The Appellate Division disagreed. Finding this Court's exposure line of cases controlling, the Appellate Division held that a cause of action for RSI accrues upon first use of a keyboard. The Court recognized that there are some differences between the two types of claims, but held that RSIs in general "are not distinguishable from the cases where repeated, prolonged exposure to, e.g., asbestos, is necessary before the damages will develop and manifest themselves" (*Blanco v American Tel. & Tel. Co.,* 223 AD2d 156, 164).

While the Appellate Division found our toxic torts cases to be controlling, it also held that CPLR 214-c (providing a discovery rule in toxic torts cases) was inapplicable. The Court recognized the harshness of the rule it had pronounced, but held that the remedy, if there was to be one, lay with the Legislature rather than the courts.

II.

At the outset, we agree with the Appellate Division that CPLR 214-c is inapplicable in this case. CPLR 214-c was enacted in 1986 as part of a larger "tort reform" package (L 1986, ch 682), and provides that "the three year period within which an action to recover damages for personal injury or injury to property caused by the latent effects of exposure to any substance or combination of substances . . . must be commenced shall be computed from the date of discovery of the injury by the plaintiff or from the date when through the exercise of reasonable diligence such injury should have been discovered by the plaintiff, whichever is earlier." (CPLR 214-c [2].) CPLR 214-c was enacted to abrogate the exposure rule which this Court had formulated and adhered to in a line of cases stretching from *Schmidt v Merchants Desp. Transp. Co.* (270 NY 287) to *Consorti v Owens-Corning Fiberglas Corp.* (86 NY2d 449).

While CPLR 214-c is a remedial statute and as such, should be interpreted broadly, this maxim does not allow us to stretch the statute beyond its intended coverage. "[E]ven a remedial statute must be given a meaning consistent with the words chosen by the Legislature" (*Enright v Lilly & Co.*, 77 NY2d 377, 385, n 1). Plaintiffs argue that these cases fall within the plain language of CPLR 214-c, since they allege that their injuries occurred from contact with a substance — to wit, a keyboard. While CPLR 214-c does nominally cover situations where a plaintiff is injured due to "contact" with a "substance," it is plain from reading the statute as a whole that the types of substances intended to be covered are toxic substances. To the extent that confirmation of this point is necessary, it can be found in abundance in the legislative history. Virtually every memorandum in support of the bill, including that of the Senate sponsor, the Governor and the Attorney-General, refers to the law enacting section 214-c as the "toxic torts" bill. Obviously, a keyboard is not a toxic substance and therefore, CPLR 214-c is inapplicable to plaintiffs' claims. Thus, it is CPLR 214, rather than section 214-c, that controls the disposition of this case.

III.

CPLR 214 provides that an action for damages for personal injuries "must be commenced within three years." A cause of action accrues for purposes of CPLR 214 "when all of the facts necessary to the cause of action have occurred so that the party would be entitled to obtain relief in court" (*Aetna Life & Cas. Co. v Nelson*, 67 NY2d 169, 175). Prior to the enactment of CPLR 214-c, this Court had held that, in the case of latent injuries arising out of exposure to toxic substances, the cause of action accrued upon plaintiff's initial exposure (*see, Consorti v Owens-Corning Fiberglas Corp.*, *supra; Schwartz v Heyden Newport Chem. Corp.*, *supra; Schmidt v Merchants Desp. Transp. Co.*, *supra*). Both parties assume that this case is analogous to our exposure rule cases. We agree that there are similarities between the two types of cases, but there are significant differences as well.

In *Martin v Edwards Labs* (60 NY2d 417), this Court identified three separate categories of latent injury cases. The first, typified by *Schmidt v Merchants Desp. Transp. Co. (supra)* and *Schwartz v Heyden Newport Chem. Corp. (supra)*, were characterized as injuries arising from the inhalation, ingestion or injection of harmful substances which are assimilated into the body. As indicated above, in toxic tort exposure cases, we had long applied a first exposure rule, under which the time to sue for resultant injuries ran from plaintiff's first exposure to the substance, rather than from the discovery of the injury. This rule will be discussed in greater detail later.

The second line of cases is typified by *Flanagan v Mount Eden Gen. Hosp.* (24 NY2d 427). *Flanagan* involved a medical malpractice claim against a doctor for leaving surgical clamps in the plaintiff's abdomen following gall bladder surgery. The surgery was performed in 1958, and it was not until the spring of 1966 that the plaintiff actually experienced problems resulting from the unremoved clamps. She consulted a doctor at that time, and in June of 1966, X-rays revealed the clamps. After surgery to remove the clamps, plaintiff commenced an action in October 1966. This Court applied a discovery rule and held that the claim was timely.

Martin characterized the type of claim at issue in *Flanagan* as one based upon objects being implanted, but not assimilated, into the body. We reasoned that a discovery rule was justified in such cases based upon a balancing of typical Statute of Limitations policies. Specifically, we noted that there was little danger of feigned claims since the objects retained their identity within the body; that for the same reason the defendant was not unduly handicapped in defending such claims; that there was little or no possible causal break between the negligence and the injury; and that the claim did not rest to a significant degree on questions of credibility or professional diagnostic judgment (*Martin v Edwards Labs.*, *supra*, 60 NY2d, at 425).

The third line of cases identified in *Martin* is typified by *Victorson v Bock Laundry Mach. Co.* (37 NY2d 395). Victorson involved three product liability claims against manufacturers of defective products by remote users who were injured when the product defect manifested itself several years after manufacture. Because plaintiff suffered no actual injury until the defect manifested itself, we held that the cause of action did not accrue until the defect actually caused injury.

Martin itself involved claims against the manufacturer of a defective heart valve, and a defective Dalkon Shield. Even though these products were intended to be inserted into the body, and thus would seem to have fit into the second line of cases, we held that the third line of cases was controlling (*Martin v Edwards Labs.*, *supra*, 60 NY2d, at 428). Thus, the claims accrued upon causation of injury, which we noted in most cases would be correlated with the date the product malfunctioned. In the case of an artificial heart valve, the injury was the release of teflon particles into the blood stream; in the case of an IUD, the injury was the unintended introduction of infectious bacteria into the uterus.

Our conclusion that the implantation cases in *Martin* fell within the third category was reached after a careful evaluation of the various policy considerations underlying Statutes of Limitation. The Court noted that a discovery rule was not necessary in implantation cases, since "the implantation or insertion is with the recipient's knowledge and consent, knowledge which he or she can pass on to a physician seeking to diagnose the cause of later developing bodily problems" (*Martin v Edwards Labs.*, *supra,* 60 NY2d, at 427). The *Martin* Court also reasoned that an exposure rule was inappropriate, because, unlike the case where a toxic substance is ingested, and "the forces of harm are inexorably set in motion when the substance enters and is assimilated into the body," implants are intended to perform a continuing function, and "cause[d] no injury until the product malfunctions" (*id.,* at 427). Up until that time, the plaintiff has no reason to complain.

Martin also noted that the age of the claim would not present a great problem, because unlike assimilated substances, "[i]f through malfunction the product is thought to have caused harm, it can in most cases be removed and examined to ascertain whether in fact it malfunctioned and, if so, whether that was the cause of the harm" (*Martin v Edwards Labs.*, *supra*, 60 NY2d, at 427). Thus, credibility determinations would not play a major role in defining when the cause of action accrued. Because the product could be made available upon malfunction, there was not a great danger of feigned or frivolous claims. Finally, the Court noted that, while "complicated medical questions may be involved and professional diagnostic judgment implicated," these would concern primarily recent, rather than remote, events, and thus there was no significant staleness problem (*id.,* at 427).

A computer keyboard is not a toxic substance which is ingested into the body, nor is it an object implanted, but not assimilated, into the body. However, unlike a typical case involving products remaining outside of the body, there is no one readily discernible first date of injury in RSI cases. Thus, these claims would not appear to fit neatly within any of the three categories identified in *Martin*. It follows that this case requires us to strike a new balance with respect to the competing policy interests at stake in order to correctly determine the accrual question. However, given the analogies which may be drawn between this type of case and an exposure case, as identified by both the parties and the Court below, any principled balancing necessarily must take into consideration our holdings in the exposure cases.

IV.

The "first exposure" rule has its roots in *Schmidt v Merchants Desp. Transp. Co.* (270 NY 287, *supra*). The plaintiff in *Schmidt* sued his employer when he developed pneumoconiosis as a result of exposure to toxic silicone dust in the workplace. This Court pointed out that "'in actions of negligence damage is of the very gist and essence of the plaintiff's cause'" (*Schmidt v Merchants Desp. Transp. Co.*, *supra*, 270 NY, at 300, *quoting Comstock v Wilson*, 257 NY 231, 235). However, in answering the question of what constitutes injury, the Court pointed not to the physical manifestation of a disease such that it became identifiable to plaintiff, but instead held that "[t]he injury occurs when there is a wrongful invasion of personal or property rights . . . [w]hen substantial damage may result from any wrong affecting the person or property of another, a cause of action for such wrong immediately accrues." (*Schmidt v Merchants Desp. Transp. Co.*, *supra*, 270 NY, at 300-301.) Applying this principle, the Court held that "[t]he injury to the plaintiff was complete when the alleged negligence of the defendant caused the plaintiff to inhale the deleterious dust . . . [t]he disease of the lungs was a consequence of that injury" (*id.,* at 301).

In *Schwartz v Heyden Newport Chem. Corp.* (12 NY2d 212, *supra*), a case arising from a plaintiff's exposure to a substance used to make the sinus cavity perceptible to X-rays, this Court applied *Schmidt* and held that the action accrued upon the plaintiff's exposure to the toxic substance. We stated that "the action accrues only when there is some actual deterioration of a plaintiff's bodily structure," but went on to hold that "we must assume that the dust immediately acted upon Schmidt's lung tissue," thus producing injury (*id.*, at 217). *Schwartz* also acknowledged certain practical policy justifications for the first exposure rule. Specifically, we noted that, notwithstanding the "insidious and 'inherently unknowable' nature of cancer. . . a potential defendant's equities are the same whether the plaintiff knows of his condition or not. Repose is as beneficial to society in the one case as in the other" (*Schwartz v Heyden Newport Chem. Corp.*, *supra*, 12 NY2d, at 218). *Schwartz* thus recognized that knowledge of injury was not solely determinative in defining the moment a cause of action for exposure to a toxic substance accrues. The seeds planted in *Schwartz* came to full fruition in *Consorti v Owens-Corning Fiberglas Corp.* (*supra*, 86 NY2d, at 451-452), in which we recognized that the original premise of the first exposure rule was tenuous, but held that continued adherence to the rule was justified based upon various policy considerations.

Admittedly, there are similarities between toxic tort and repetitive stress injuries which would militate in favor of applying the same accrual rule in both types of cases. In each case, the plaintiff's appreciable injury does not manifest itself until some time after (and in many cases significantly after) initial exposure to the product. Thus, in both types of cases there is a gap between the manufacturer's breach of duty and the resulting ultimate injury to the plaintiff. As we recognized in *Consorti v Owens-Corning Fiberglas Corp.* (*supra*), this injects a substantial degree of uncertainty into a manufacturer's risk assessment calculation, and may give rise to significant problems of proof. Thus, in *Consorti*, we made clear that our rejection of a fact-based date of manifestation of injury test "was made for practical and policy reasons articulated in the developing case law, that is, the need to provide manufacturers, employers and other economic actors who are potential defendants with a degree of certainty or predictability in assessing the risk of liability and to avoid stale claims which often turn on questions of credibility or disputed medical judgments. Therefore, a bright line, readily verifiable rule was adopted in which, as a matter of law, the tortious injury is deemed to have occurred upon the introduction of the toxic substance into the body." (*Id.*, at 451-452.)

These same policy considerations would appear to point to the adoption of a first exposure rule in this case. Like a toxic tort, RSI may not develop until years after a person first uses a keyboard; indeed, according to plaintiffs' expert, the condition may not develop at all, or not until after one keyboard is discarded and a person subsequently uses different keyboards.

This Court has refused to waver from the first exposure rule where the policy considerations articulated in *Consorti* have dictated its application. While recognizing that the rule may seem unjust, we have generally left ameliorative efforts to the Legislature. Indeed, where the Legislature has deemed it necessary, it has abrogated the exposure rule (*see, e.g.,* CPLR 214-b [agent orange exposure]; CPLR 214-c [toxic torts]). Thus, defendants argue, given that the Legislature has, in fact, modified our accrual jurisprudence where it has deemed fit, this Court should leave the exposure rule in place, and allow the Legislature to modify it further if it so chooses. We reject this argument as applied in this case.

The exposure rule is premised upon the proposition that, while injury is necessary for the accrual of a cause of action, injury in a toxic tort case accrues upon exposure to the toxic substance, because it is at that point that there has been "a wrongful invasion of personal or property rights" (*Schmidt v Merchants Desp. Transp. Co.*, *supra,* 270 NY, at 300). This was based upon the assumption that a toxic substance acts immediately upon the body to produce injury (*see, Schwartz v Heyden Newport Chem. Corp.*, 12 NY2d 212, *supra; cf., Consorti v Owens-Corning Fiberglas Corp.*, *supra,* 86 NY2d, at 451-452). A keyboard is obviously not an inherently toxic or dangerous substance, and exposure to a keyboard is not a "wrongful invasion" in the same sense as is exposure to a toxic substance. Indeed, if we were to apply a first exposure rule literally, then we would have to justify it on the legal fiction that an injury occurs the first moment a person presses a button on a keyboard. It would be absurd to argue that a person who simply touches a keyboard sustains the type of trauma that will eventually lead to RSI. As plaintiffs' doctor noted in his affidavit, this type of injury has "no single initiating event, but rather an accumulation of events." Thus, because a keyboard is not an inherently toxic or dangerous substance, and a person who initially touches one does not necessarily sustain an injury, the justifications that gave rise to the exposure rule do not apply here.

Defendants are correct that we have long given deference to the Legislature to recast the accrual methodology of toxic torts if it saw fit and as noted earlier, the Legislature has on several occasions done so. However, in cases such as this, where we are presented with new categories of tort claims and injuries, we have always done a careful and balanced analysis of the nature of the claim and its intricate interplay with the policy considerations at the heart of our Statute of Limitations jurisprudence (*Martin v Edwards Labs.*, *supra,* 60 NY2d, at 427-428). Our analysis here is not a rejection of our long line of cases from *Schmidt* to *Consorti*; it is a recognition that RSI cases present new and different challenges in defining the accrual dates for plaintiffs' causes of action. To accept defendants' argument that we should rely upon the analysis we found appropriate in toxic tort cases is to ignore the significantly different nature of both plaintiffs' injuries and the alleged causes. With this in mind, we turn to the task of evaluating the policy interests at stake in RSI cases.

V.

Statutes of Limitation were "designed to promote justice by preventing surprises through the revival of claims that have been allowed to slumber until evidence has been lost, memories have faded, and witnesses have disappeared" (*Telegraphers v Railway Express Agency*, 321 US 342, 348-349). Other considerations include "promot[ing] repose by giving security and stability to human affairs" (*Wood v Carpenter*, 101 US 135, 139 [1879]), judicial economy, discouraging courts from reaching dubious results, recognition of self-reformation by defendants, and the perceived unfairness to defendants of having to defend claims long past (*see,* Fischer, *The Limits of Statutes of Limitation,* 16 SW U L Rev 1, 1-2; *see also,* Harshaw, *Not Enough Time?: The Constitutionality of Short Statutes of Limitations for Civil Child Sexual Abuse Litigation,* 50 Ohio St LJ 753).

In examining the policies underlying Statutes of Limitation, this Court has emphasized both a defendant's interest in repose and "in defending a claim before his ability to do so has deteriorated through passage of time" (*Martin v Edwards Labs., supra,* 60 NY2d, at 425). We have also taken note of considerations of judicial economy and possible plaintiff fraud where excessive factual inquiries would be necessary (*supra,* 60 NY2d, at 425-426). Balanced against these considerations is the injured person's interest in having a reasonable opportunity to assert a claim.

Weighing these competing policy considerations, we conclude that the proper rule in RSI cases is that the cause of action accrues against a given manufacturer upon the onset of symptoms or the last use of the injury-producing device, whichever is earlier (*see, Piper v International Bus. Machs. Corp.,* 219 AD2d 56, 60-62). Clearly in this case fairness to the plaintiff militates against a rule based on first use. Plaintiffs suffering from RSI have no reason to complain of their condition until a symptom actually manifests itself, and cannot be faulted for failing to exercise their legal rights prior to that time.

We reject plaintiffs' argument that accrual should be measured not from the time they experienced RSI symptoms, but from the date they actually became aware of the nature of their injuries. A date of diagnosis test would give a plaintiff "the power to put off the running of the Statute of Limitations indefinitely" (*Snyder v Town Insulation,* 81 NY2d 429, 435). Moreover, this approach would only further ensnare trial courts in a fact-based application of the rule (*see, Consorti v Owens-Corning Fiberglas Corp., supra,* 86 NY2d, at 452-453).

Judicial economy and the possibility of feigned claims militate in favor of some type of first use rule. However, it is likely that a plaintiff will seek medical treatment when the injury manifests itself in the form of RSI or pre-RSI symptomatology. This significantly reduces the possibility of a plaintiff indefinitely postponing or feigning a claim, since in the majority of cases there will be objective evidence of the onset of symptoms in the form of medical or work records. Although plaintiffs contend they are not able to identify a date for the onset of RSI symptoms, they have alleged a date on which the signs/symptoms of RSI were manifest. Requiring a symptom-based benchmark does not impose an inappropriate or unfair burden on plaintiffs.

Moreover, while an accrual period which bears some relationship to the onset of symptoms will certainly involve lower courts in limited factual inquiries, this was also true of the rule we adopted in *Martin v Edwards Labs. (supra,* 60 NY2d, at 428-429). As in *Martin,* the products in these cases retain their identity. Thus, the evidence would not appear to be stale except in the case of remote products long since discarded. By tying the accrual date to the date of last use, as well as the onset of symptoms, the rule we formulate today strikes a proper balance between these competing considerations. In addition, the last use condition will serve as an additional filter for claims where the date of injury remains in doubt.

Finally, the possibility of causal breaks between the claimed negligence and the injury is also a legitimate concern. However, the last use or onset of symptoms rule solves the causal breakdown problem, which is most pronounced in the case of keyboards used years prior to the onset of symptoms. For example, in one of the cases before us, *Sharib, Heholt & DeForest v Zenith Data Sys.* (Sup Ct, NY County, Index No. 125155/93), plaintiff Heholt sues two different manufacturers of four different keyboards which she used from 1979 through 1992. She commenced her action on October 5, 1993, and identifies April 1992 as the date upon which she began to experience some symptoms of RSI. Nevertheless, by suing the manufacturer of every keyboard she ever used, plaintiff implicitly alleges that each use of the defendants' keyboards contributed to her condition. This includes the keyboard which she used from 1979 to 1984 with no symptomatology. Certainly there comes a point in time when the causal link between use and injury becomes too remote as a matter of law.

The rule we announce today will bar direct actions against such remote manufacturers. It strikes a proper balance between giving a plaintiff an opportunity to commence an action after becoming aware of a symptom of injury and providing certainty and predictability to manufacturers, employers and other economic actors in their risk assessment, while also avoiding stale claims.

In adopting this rule, we are also cognizant of the fact that problems of proof will be inherent in these cases whether we define accrual by reference to the first use of the device or by the onset of symptoms. Unless first use is defined as any touching of a keyboard whatsoever (which, as previously noted, bears no relationship to actual injury), then the problem in defining the moment of injury would become determining when a plaintiff began using a keyboard with any substantial regularity. In an increasingly technological world, exposure to computer keyboards and other devices with the potential to cause RSI has become commonplace. Given this reality, defining "first use" would pose equally serious, if not greater, difficulty. Having carefully considered the various competing concerns presented by this information age injury, we conclude that the balance is best struck by defining accrual of a cause of action for RSI as the earlier of the onset of symptoms or last use.

Accordingly, the order of the Appellate Division should be modified, without costs, the actions remitted for action in accordance with this opinion, and the certified question answered in the negative.

NOTES

(1) How would the holding of the principal case affect the resolution of Problem B? Note also that CPLR 214-c(1) was amended in 1992 to include the word "implantation."

(2) Are natural substances, such as blood, covered by CPLR 214-c(2)? *Prego v. City of New York*, 141 Misc. 2d 709, 534 N.Y.S.2d 95 (1988), *aff'd*, 147 A.D.2d 165, 541 N.Y.S.2d 995 (2d Dep't 1989), held that blood contaminated by the AIDS virus was a covered substance and that the discovery provisions of CPLR 214-c applied to claims based on the negligent exposure to it. In a more recent case, *Plaza v. Estate of Wisser*, 211 A.D.2d 111, 626 N.Y.S.2d 446 (1st Dep't 1995), the Appellate Division applied this rule to semen. In *Plaza*, the plaintiff alleged that he was infected with HIV through sexual intercourse with his partner between August 1986 and October 1990 and that his partner tortiously failed to disclose previous "high risk" sexual encounters during this period. The court held that the negligence claims brought in late 1993 were timely because the plaintiff didn't discover that he was infected until early 1993.

With respect to HIV infection, see also CPLR 214-e. In that section, added in 1997, the Legislature revived claims against proprietary manufacturers of blood products that resulted in HIV contraction through infusion. Claimants were given two years within which to commence previously barred actions.

(3) CPLR 214-c(6) makes the "date-of-discovery" rule applicable to "acts, omissions or failures occurring . . . on or after" July 1, 1986, but prohibits the use of CPLR 214-c if (a) the act, omission or failure occurred prior to July 1, 1986, (b) the injury was discovered or through the exercise of reasonable diligence should have been discovered prior to July 1, 1986, and (c) the action was or would have been barred because the applicable statute of limitations had expired prior to July 1, 1986. CPLR 214-c was interpreted expansively in *Rothstein v. Tennessee Gas Pipeline Co.*, 204 A.D.2d 39, 616 N.Y.S.2d 902 (2d Dep't 1994), *aff'd*, 87 N.Y.2d 90, 637 N.Y.S.2d 674, 661 N.E.2d 146 (1995), to protect a claim based on exposure to a toxic substance forty years before the action was commenced. The court relied upon the fact that the injury was not discovered, and could not have been discovered, until after July 1, 1986.

(4) Another important question raised implicitly by CPLR 214-c is: What constitutes "discovery"? Is it when the plaintiff learns that he or she is ill? Or when the cause of the illness is traced to the defendant's product? In *Matter of New York County DES Litigation (Wetherill v. Eli Lilly & Co.)*, 89 N.Y.2d 506, 678 N.E.2d 474, 655 N.Y.S.2d 862 (1997), the Court held that the statute of limitations runs from the "manifestations or symptoms of the latent disease" except as specifically provided in CPLR 214-c(4).

(5) When the Legislature enacted CPLR 214-c, it also enacted an uncodified section which revived previously barred causes of action. Ch. 682, § 4, Laws of 1986. The revival was limited to claims arising from exposure to any of five

listed substances: DES, tungsten-carbide, asbestos, chlordane and polyvinylchloride. Plaintiffs whose claims were revived were given only one year from July 30, 1986, in which to commence an action. The constitutionality of the revival provision was upheld in *Hymowitz v. Eli Lilly & Co.*, 73 N.Y.2d 487, 541 N.Y.S.2d 941, 539 N.E.2d 1069 (1989).

(6) The impact of the discovery and revival rules on a manufacturer's liability are significant. Who will pay for the increased damage payments? A different approach to balancing the interests of the public, the manufacturer and the injured party is made in the Model Uniform Product Liability Act, drafted by the U.S. Department of Commerce (44 Fed. Reg. 62, 714 (1979)), and discussed in Michael M. Martin, *A Statute of Repose for Product Liability Claims*, 50 Ford. L. Rev. 745 (1982), and Note, *Various Risk Allocation Schemes Under the Model Uniform Product Liability Act*, 48 Geo. Wash. Univ. L. Rev. 588 (1980). The model act contains this "statute of repose":

> [1] *Generally.* In claims that involve harm caused more than ten (10) years after time of delivery, a presumption arises that the harm was caused after the useful safe life had expired. This presumption may only be rebutted by clear and convincing evidence.

> [2] *Limitations on Statute of Repose.*

> [a] If a product seller expressly warrants that its product can be utilized safely for a period longer than ten (10) years, the period of repose, after which the presumption created in subsection [B][1] arises, shall be extended according to that warranty or promise.

> [b] The ten (10) year period of repose established in subsection [B][1] does not apply if the product seller intentionally misrepresents facts about its product, or fraudulently conceals information about it, and that conduct was a substantial cause of the claimant's harm.

> [c] Nothing contained in subsection [B] shall affect the right of any person found liable under this Act to seek and obtain contribution or indemnity from any other person who is responsible for harm under this Act.

> [d] The ten (10) year period of repose established in subsection [B][1] shall not apply if the harm was caused by prolonged exposure to a defective product, or if the injury-causing aspect of the product that existed at the time of delivery was not discoverable by an ordinary reasonably prudent person until more than ten (10) years after the time of delivery, or if the harm, caused within ten (10) years after the time of delivery, did not manifest itself until after that time.

Would the claims made in the principal case be timely under the model act? What about those adjudicated in *Victorson v. Bock Laundry, Co., supra?*

(7) A bill adopting a federal fifteen-year statute of repose for product liability claims was adopted by both houses of Congress in 1996. (1995 House Bill No.

956, 104th Cong.) President Clinton vetoed the bill on May 3, 1996. *See* Stephen J. Werber, *The Constitutional Dimension of a National Products Liability Statute of Repose*, 40 Vill. L. Rev. 985 (1995)

(8) CPLR 214-c is discussed in Note, *Discovering Justice in Toxic Tort Litigation: CPLR 214-c*, 61 St. John's L. Rev. 262 (1987), and in Note, *New York State's Toxic Tort Discovery Rule: Defining the Concept of Discovery*, 38 Syracuse L. Rev. 1021 (1987). For a more general approach using an economic analysis, see Note, *A Time-Dependent Model of Products Liability*, 53 U. Chi. L. Rev. 209 (1986).

(9) The Court of Appeals limited the scope of the discovery rule of CPLR 214-c(2) by holding that the rule did not apply where injuries were not "'caused by the latent effects of exposure' to a toxic substance." *Germantown Cent. Sch. Dist. v. Clark*, 100 N.Y.2d 202, 206, 761 N.Y.S.2d 141, 143, 791 N.E.2d 398, 400 (2003). The owner of a school building had hired the defendants thirteen years previously to remove asbestos from the building. During later renovations, asbestos was discovered, and the building owner sued to recover the money paid to defendants and the costs to remove the asbestos. Because there was "no allegation by the plaintiff that the asbestos migrated to a different location," the injury was deemed to have occurred at the time of the original installation of asbestos in the building. The Court applied a general statute of limitations for malpractice instead of the three-year discovery-based statute of limitations, and the suit was therefore untimely.

[C] Medical Malpractice

PROBLEM C

Refer again to Problem B, *supra*. Suppose that in his action commenced on January 3, 2006, Joe also named Dr. Doolittle as a defendant, alleging that his use of a defective pin was negligent and that he, too, is liable for Joe's damages. Considering CPLR 214-a and the following cases, is Joe's action timely against this defendant?

LABARBERA v. NEW YORK EYE AND EAR INFIRMARY
Court of Appeals
91 N.Y.2d 207, 668 N.Y.S.2d 546, 691 N.E.2d 617 (1998)

BELLACOSA, J.

This appeal arises from a medical malpractice action whose viability is dependent on the application and contours of CPLR 214-a. This Court is obliged to determine whether a plastic stent, placed in plaintiff's nose for postsurgery healing purposes, constitutes a "foreign object" that would avoid the bar of the statute of repose. We conclude that the device is not a foreign object within the meaning of the statute and its purpose and history, as shaped by and reflected in our governing precedents.

In May 1986, defendant Dr. Jack Martin Shapiro performed a nasal reconstruction on plaintiff at the New York Eye and Ear Infirmary. At the conclusion of the procedure, Dr. Shapiro packed the nasal cavity with Bacitracin gauze and inserted a shaped piece of plastic — a silastic stent. This device was to provide temporary support, promote healing and prevent scarring. The packing material and the stent were expected to be removed by Dr. Shapiro approximately 10 days after the surgery. At that time, the doctor removed only the packing material.

For the next six years, plaintiff suffered persistent nasal and respiratory problems. He consulted with Dr. Shapiro and other doctors. The last contact with Dr. Shapiro occurred in September 1988. No one detected the presence of the stent or diagnosed the cause of the plaintiff's complaints or condition. In 1992, a new doctor performed an endoscopic rhinoscopy, discovered the stent and removed it. Plaintiff's troublesome symptoms ceased. He then commenced this action in June 1993, within one year of the discovery and extraction of the stent.

The case presents another application of the governing statute in the light of our precedents. The "foreign object" exception to the Statute of Limitations emerged in *Flanagan v Mount Eden Gen. Hosp.* (24 NY2d 427). There, we concluded that "where a foreign object [a surgical clamp] has negligently been left in the patient's body, the Statute of Limitations will not begin to run until the patient could have reasonably discovered the malpractice" (*id.*, at 431). We noted that "foreign object" cases differ from those involving "negligent medical treatment" because the former do not create "the danger of belated, false or frivolous claims" — one of the paramount goals of Statutes of Limitation (*id.*, at 430-431).

Six years after *Flanagan*, in 1975, the Legislature codified the precedential "foreign object" exception in CPLR 214-a (*see,* Siegel, NY Prac 42, at 52 [2d ed]). The statute prescribes that an action for medical malpractice "must be commenced within two years and six months of the act, omission or failure complained of . . . provided, however, that where the action is based upon the discovery of a foreign object in the body of the patient, the action may be commenced within one year of the date of such discovery or of the date of discovery of facts which would reasonably lead to such discovery, whichever is earlier" (CPLR 214-a). Importantly, the statute expressly excludes "chemical compound[s], *fixation device[s]* [and] prosthetic aid[s] or device[s]" from the definition of the term "foreign object" (*id.* [emphasis added]).

After the statutory codification, this Court decided *Rodriguez v Manhattan Med. Group* (77 NY2d 217). There, the Court held that "a 'fixation device' [an I.U.D.] originally implanted in a patient's body for a specific treatment purpose is [not] transformed into a 'foreign object' within the meaning of [CPLR 214-a] when a physician retained to remove it negligently fails to do so" (*id.*, at 218-219). The Court noted that, unlike *Flanagan*, "there [was] no claim against the physician who actually inserted the I.U.D.; instead, plaintiffs [sought] recovery from a different treating physician" (*id.*, at 223). We observed that "the gist of plaintiff's claim, i.e., a negligent failure to detect the continued presence of a previously inserted device, is most logically classified as one involving misdiagnosis — a category for which the benefits of the 'foreign object' discovery rule have routinely been denied" (*id.*, at 223).

Additionally, the Court explained that "the codification of the judicially created 'foreign object' rule in CPLR 214-a precludes our adoption of a more flexible discovery rule for these cases even if 'considerations similar to those which motivated the court in *Flanagan* [c]ould be applied with like effect to the . . . different circumstances [presented here]'" (*id.*, at 223-224, quoting *Beary v City of Rye*, 44 NY2d 398, 414). In other words, the statutory codification limited the range of common-law development. The *Rodriguez* Court concluded that application of the "foreign object" exception there would have "represent[ed] a giant step toward precisely what the statute's drafters feared: 'bringing virtually all medical malpractice cases under the discovery rule'" (*id.*, at 224, quoting Bill Jacket, L 1975, ch 109, Governor's Program Bill Mem, at 4).

The next and most recent poststatute explication on the "foreign object exception" occurred in *Rockefeller v Moront* (81 NY2d 560). There, the Court determined that a suture which was misplaced during a hernia operation did not constitute a "foreign object;" rather, it, too, was a "fixation device" (*id.*, at 562). The Court stated that "[o]bjects such as surgical clamps, scalpels, and sponges are introduced into the patient's body to serve a temporary medical function for the duration of the surgery, but are normally intended to be removed after the procedure's completion" (*id.*, at 564). The Court explained that "no assessment of the medical professional's expert judgment or discretion in failing to remove them is necessary to establish negligence" (*id.*). Rather, "items which are placed in the patient with the intention that they will remain to serve some continuing treatment purpose constitute 'fixation devices'" (*id.*). Additionally, the Court reasoned that a claim based on such negligent implantation "is more readily characterized as one predicated on negligent medical treatment, which, like misdiagnosis, is a category of malpractice not covered by the 'foreign object' rule" (*id.*, at 565).

In *Rockefeller*, the Court observed that it was "not unmindful of the harsh consequences of ruling [against] plaintiff, who first discovered the misplaced suture that caused his sterility only after undergoing exploratory surgery performed 18 years after the injury-producing herniorrhaphy" (*id.*, at 566). Nonetheless, "our holding [remained] consistent with this Court's prior cautionary directive that the 'foreign object' exception must not be broadened beyond the narrow confines announced in *Flanagan*" and delineated by the statute (*id.*). CPLR 214-a, its legislative history and our pre- and poststatute precedents evolved to a statement of a narrow rule: "only in circumstances where a foreign object is negligently 'left' in the patient's body *without any intended continuing treatment purpose* will the discovery rule be available to delay the running of the Statute of Limitations" (*id.* [emphasis added]).

This case presents yet another variation among a myriad of medical protocols, devices and procedures. It is not about the failure to detect an "object," like an I.U.D. inserted into a patient for an indefinite period of time; nor does it concern a doctor's negligence in improperly attaching an "object" to the wrong organ. Claims predicated on misdiagnosis and negligent medical treatment more readily implicate the rationale and policy direction of our precedents which is to prevent untimely claims dependent upon the assessment of a doctor's professional judgment or discretion. The instant scenario, on the other hand, presents a more elusive classification question. Nevertheless, our analysis comfortably rests on the same dispositional criterion used in *Rockefeller* — intentional insertion of a therapeutic item for postsurgery continuing treatment purposes.

The rule that emerges from *Rockefeller* also offers a measure of definiteness. A "foreign object" is one that is "negligently 'left' in the patient's body without any intended continuing treatment purpose" (*Rockefeller v Moront, supra*, 81 NY2d, at 566; *see,* McLaughlin, Practice Commentaries, McKinney's Cons Laws of NY, Book 7B, CPLR C214-a:3, at 603 ["(i)t has become relatively clear that a foreign object is one that the doctor does not intend to leave inside the body"]). That test removes this stent from the "foreign object" category and designation. Unquestionably, it was implanted with an intentional continuing treatment objective. Even in the vernacular, it cannot be said to have been "left" in plaintiff's nose. Rather, it was put there only to be removed after it had served its postsurgery healing purposes. The time frame was to be relatively short and conditionally fixed, but the key feature is the uncontroverted protocol of insertion as part of a continuing treatment modality. Thus, it may be an "object," but it is not "foreign" and not "left behind," in any medical or legal senses.

In sum, therefore, we disagree with plaintiff's theory that the relatively short and ordinarily definite nature of the stent's time in the nose should allow it to be treated as a "foreign object." We are similarly unpersuaded by the analysis propounded by the dissent in the Court below concerning a "multistage procedure" exception (*i.e.,* that the surgical procedure continued until the packing was removed). These understandable explorations searching for individualized justice in the midst of well-settled definiteness of the governing principles are theoretically unsupportable and would engender unevenness of application. Also, they are contrary to the legislative intent to limit the scope of the "foreign object rule." These efforts to enlarge the exception would also undermine, if not contradict, the statute and the policy lines and precedents that have emerged to fix boundaries for this troublesome field.

We are satisfied that an affirmance here is mandated by the statute and by our consistent restraint against opening up the "foreign object" exception. It has been noted that the codification of the judicially created "foreign object" rule in

CPLR 214-a constricts judicial expansiveness towards a more plaintiff friendly discovery rule

Yet, in closing our resolution and discussion of this case, we reiterate that this area of medical malpractice has engendered expressions of possible "unfairness" suffered by the strict adherence to definitive rules and policies. We conclude, nonetheless, that the Legislature, having statutorily occupied the field, is more appropriately suited to effectuate any redefinition or expansion of the application of the exception, if that is warranted.

NOTE

Is the Court's distinction of *Flanagan v. Mt. Eden Gen. Hosp.*, 24 N.Y.2d 427, 301 N.Y.S.2d 23, 248 N.E.2d 871 (1969), sound? Are clamps left inside a patient different than stents that should be removed after ten days?

GOLDSMITH v. HOWMEDICA, INC.
Court of Appeals
67 N.Y.2d 120, 500 N.Y.S.2d 640, 491 N.E.2d 1097 (1986)

TITONE, J.

When a prosthetic device malfunctions, does a cause of action for medical malpractice accrue upon implantation of the prosthetic device or upon injury to the patient? That is the sole question before us. We conclude that the cause of action accrues upon implantation.

In 1973, plaintiff Robert Goldsmith received a total hip replacement in an operation performed by defendant Chitranjan S. Ranawat. The femoral component of the implant, manufactured by defendant Howmedica, Inc., broke in 1981. Goldsmith commenced this action in 1983 against the doctor for malpractice;[1] Special Term granted Dr. Ranawat's motion for summary judgment and dismissed the complaint as to him on the ground that the Statute of Limitations barred the malpractice action.[2] The Appellate Division affirmed, but granted leave to appeal. We affirm.

The general rule is that an action accrues and the Statute of Limitations begins to run at the time of the commission of the alleged malpractice. . . . We have, to date, recognized but two exceptions. First, in a case where the doctor continues to treat the plaintiff after the act of malpractice, the Statute of Lim-

---

[1] The actions against the manufacturer are not the subject of this appeal.

[2] Since the alleged malpractice occurred before July 1, 1975, the action is governed by a three-year Statute of Limitations (CPLR 214, 214-a; *McDermott v Torre*, 56 NY2d 399, 407; Farrell, *Civil Practice*, 28 Syracuse L Rev 379, 391).

itations is tolled until after the plaintiff's last treatment for the same injury or illness (*McDermott v Torre*, 56 NY2d 399, 407; *Borgia v City of New York*, 12 NY2d 151). Second, in circumstances in which the doctor leaves a "foreign object" in the plaintiff's body, the action does not accrue until after the object is discovered by the plaintiff. (*Flanagan v Mount Eden Gen. Hosp.*, 24 NY2d 427.)[3]

Plaintiffs argue that *Martin v Edwards Labs.* (60 NY2d 417) represented a third exception because we allowed the assertion of a claim against the manufacturers of prosthetic devices within three years of injury even though the devices had been implanted years earlier. We do not agree.

Martin involved a products liability action against the manufacturers of a prosthetic device and its component parts. Products liability actions are vastly different from medical malpractice actions in this context, because until the device malfunctions, there is no cause to complain against, or privity to, the manufacturer of a prosthetic device.

Moreover, in analyzing the proper distribution of risks between manufacturers of prosthetic aids and patients in *Martin*, we did not attempt to apportion the risks between physician and patient, an issue involving substantially different policy considerations (60 NY2d at p 428, n). In this regard, it is noteworthy that in response to the medical malpractice crisis, the Legislature has enacted CPLR 214-a, covering actions involving acts of medical malpractice committed on or after July 1, 1975, which expressly excludes chemical compounds, fixation devices and prosthetic aids from the embrace of the term "foreign object." Although this case is not governed by CPLR 214-a and plaintiffs do not urge that a prosthetic device is a foreign object, we cannot ignore the clearly expressed legislative intent that the present exception to the general time of commission accrual rule not be broadened beyond its existing confines

Plaintiffs also claim that to require the bringing of an action within three years of the commission of the malpractice effectively forecloses an action against the doctor before any injury has been suffered. The argument is not new. We have carefully considered it on numerous occasions. In each, we weighed the detriments of such a result against the effect of potentially open-ended claims upon the repose of defendants and society, and held that the Statute of Limitations must run from the time of the act until the Legislature decrees otherwise

---

[3] Although some courts and commentators have urged that the factors mandating a date of discovery rule in "foreign object" cases are no less persuasive in malpractice cases involving implantation devices . . . others have reasoned that the causal connection between the surgeon and the plaintiffs' injuries is weaker in a case concerning prosthetic aids than in the cases involving an object left in the body during surgery. . . . *Cooper v Edinbergh*, 75 AD2d 757 [1st Dept] [wire sutures not "foreign object"]). We think that the latter decisions are more consistent with the policies behind the statute of Limitations. In cases involving prosthetic devices, the plaintiffs' injuries might have been caused by negligence of the attending physician, by the plaintiffs' physiological condition or by defects in the prosthetic aids.

For these reasons, the action against Dr. Ranawat accrued in 1973 and, therefore, is barred by the three-year Statute of Limitations.

NOTES

(1) The interplay between the courts and the legislature with respect to medical malpractice prompts us to question why different causes of action are subject to different time limits. Statutes of limitations are traditionally said to represent a legislative judgment that the occasional hardship which occurs when a just claim is barred because it was not timely sued upon is outweighed by competing interests. These include the desirability of repose, *i.e.*, allowing people to plan lives and businesses, secure in the belief that "ancient" misdeeds will not be the source of judicial action against them. There is also an often unstated feeling that a long dormant claim is unlikely to be meritorious. The policy consideration most frequently articulated by courts is the effect the passage of time is likely to have on the availability and reliability of evidence and the consequent prejudice to an accurate determination of factual disputes.

Do these considerations justify the adoption of a statute of limitations which is shorter for medical malpractice than for other kinds of malpractice (CPLR 214(6))? Do they justify the limitation on the discovery rule imposed by CPLR 214-a? It is noteworthy that, as noted in the principal case, CPLR 214-a was enacted in 1975 as part of a legislative package intended to reduce the expense of medical malpractice insurance by making it more difficult for plaintiffs to recover. The legislature was prompted to act when physicians threatened to curtail services to the people of the state. Legislative Memorandum, 1975 Session Laws of New York 1599. *See also* Comment, *Medical Malpractice in New York*, 27 Syracuse L. Rev. 657 (1976).

(2) The different limitation periods applicable to medical malpractice actions, on the one hand, and ordinary negligence actions, on the other, resulted in the predictable problem: The courts have been called on to define the difference between the two causes of action. In *Bleiler v. Bodnar*, 65 N.Y.2d 65, 72-73, 489 N.Y.S.2d 885, 889-91, 479 N.E.2d 230, 234-35 (1985), the Court considered claims against a hospital and against a nurse:

> Obviously, not every negligent act of a nurse would be medical malpractice, but a negligent act or omission by a nurse that constitutes medical treatment or bears a substantial relationship to the rendition of medical treatment by a licensed physician constitutes malpractice. Such a conclusion is warranted here. Doctor Bodnar and Nurse Doe, who assisted him in the emergency room, are both charged with having failed to take a proper medical history — a crucial element of diagnosis and treatment. Bodnar's alleged failure to elicit all information pertinent to treatment could unquestionably constitute medical malpractice. . . .

We next consider Bleiler's claims against the hospital for improper or inadequate hiring practices and administrative procedures. . . .

A hospital in a general sense is always furnishing medical care to patients, but clearly not every act of negligence toward a patient would be medical malpractice. Where a claim for breach of duty to use due care in the selection of doctors and nurses, and to furnish competent medical personnel, has been recognized . . . the requisite elements have been markedly different from a malpractice cause of action. For example, plaintiff would have to establish that the hospital failed to use due care in selecting and furnishing personnel — that is, that it failed to make an "'appropriate investigation of the character and capacity of the agencies of service'" (*Lewis v. Columbus Hosp.*, 1 A.D.2d 444, 447) — and that such failure was a proximate cause of his injury. Such a claim of negligence would be governed by the three-year Statute of Limitations.

Similarly, a hospital's failure to adopt and prescribe proper procedures and regulations has given rise to a cause of action . . . the elements of which differ from medical malpractice. Here too — like a cause of action for negligent maintenance of a sidewalk . . . or failure to provide a functioning wheelchair to a patient . . . — the cause of action would be subject to a three-year Statute of Limitations. In both instances, the gravamen of the complaint is not negligence in furnishing medical treatment to a patient, but the hospital's failure in fulfilling a different duty.

The Court of Appeals returned to the problem of defining medical malpractice in *Karasek v. LaJoie*, 92 N.Y.2d 171, 677 N.Y.S.2d 265, 699 N.E.2d 889 (1998), in which it held that actions against psychologists and other non-physician mental health professionals are not covered by CPLR 214-a.

NYKORCHUCK v. HENRIQUES
Court of Appeals
78 N.Y.2d 255, 573 N.Y.S.2d 434, 577 N.E.2d 1026 (1991)

WACHTLER, C.J.

This action for medical malpractice arises out of the defendant doctor's alleged failure to properly diagnose and monitor a lump in plaintiff's right breast. Plaintiff was ultimately diagnosed as having breast cancer, which required surgery and chemotherapy.

The question presented on the appeal is whether this suit, which was commenced more than eight years after the lump was first brought to defendant's attention and more than four years after plaintiff's last appointment with defendant in connection with another medical condition, is barred by the 2½-year Statute of Limitations for medical malpractice (*see*, CPLR 214-a). In opposition to defendants' motion to dismiss the complaint as time barred, plaintiff claimed the benefit of the "continuous treatment doctrine," which, when applicable, tolls the running of the Statute of Limitations until the end of the course of treatment for the particular medical condition (*see, id.*; *McDermott v. Torre*, 56 N.Y.2d 399; *Borgia v. City of New York*, 12 N.Y.2d 151).

Supreme Court denied the motions to dismiss, perceiving questions of fact as to whether the continuous treatment doctrine was applicable. The Appellate Division held, however, that the doctrine was inapplicable because plaintiff's allegations did not establish that defendant doctor had undertaken any treatment for plaintiff's breast condition (153 A.D.2d 316).

Plaintiff first began seeing Dr. Henriques in 1974 for infertility problems, which were determined to be secondary to endometriosis. The doctor treated plaintiff for that condition over a period of years, culminating in surgery in April 1982. During an office visit in July 1979, plaintiff brought to the doctor's attention a lump in her right breast. After examining the breast, he allegedly told plaintiff that the lump was attributable to noncancerous fibrocystic disease and that "we will have to keep an eye on it." In addition, lumps in both breasts were noted during an examination of plaintiff conducted by an unspecified person upon plaintiff's admission to the hospital for the April 1982 surgery. No further evaluation was performed at that time.

After the surgery, plaintiff saw the doctor three times, the last time in September 1983, for postoperative care and adjustment of estrogen replacement medication. The doctor phoned in renewals of plaintiff's prescriptions in 1984 and in June 1985. In December 1985, plaintiff scheduled an appointment with the doctor because she had detected enlargement of the mass in her right breast. The doctor examined defendant in January 1986 and immediately referred her to an oncologist, who diagnosed breast cancer. This action was commenced in December 1987.

A medical malpractice claim generally accrues on the date of the alleged wrongful act or omission and is governed by a 2½-year Statute of Limitations (*Davis v. City of New York*, 38 N.Y.2d 257, 259; CPLR 214-a). Under the continuous treatment doctrine exception, however, the 2½-year period does not begin to run until the end of the course of treatment "when the course of treatment which includes the wrongful acts or omissions has run continuously and is related to the same original condition or complaint" (*McDermott v. Torre*, *supra*, at 405, *quoting Borgia v. City of New York*, *supra*, at 155). The purpose of the doctrine is to "maintain the physician-patient relationship in the belief that the most efficacious medical care will be obtained when the attending physician remains on a case from onset to cure" (*McDermott v. Torre*, *supra*, at 408). The doctrine rests on the premise that it is in the patient's best interest that an ongoing course of treatment be continued, rather than interrupted by a lawsuit, because "the doctor not only is in a position to identify and correct his or her malpractice, but is best placed to do so." (*Id.*)

Thus, essential to the application of the doctrine is that there has been a course of treatment established with respect to the condition that gives rise to the lawsuit. We have held that neither the mere "continuing relation between physician and patient" nor "the continuing nature of a diagnosis" is sufficient to satisfy the requirements of the doctrine (*id.*, at 405, 406). In the absence of continuing efforts by a doctor to treat a particular condition, none of the policy reasons underlying the continuous treatment doctrine justify the patient's delay in bringing suit.

Here, plaintiff has failed to allege facts which would support a finding that a course of treatment was established in connection with her breast condition. The only course of treatment alleged was related to a separate medical condition, endometriosis. Under the relevant statute and case law, this is not sufficient. CPLR 214-a explicitly requires that, for the toll to apply, the continuous treatment must be "for the same illness, injury or condition which gave rise to the . . . act, omission or failure" complained of (*see also, McDermott v. Torre, supra*, at 405; *Borgia v. City of New York, supra*, at 155 [the course of treatment must be "related to the same original condition or complaint"]). No connection between plaintiff's breast condition and the course of treatment for endometriosis has been alleged.

Nor do the isolated breast examinations, only one of which is alleged to have been performed by defendant doctor during the relevant period, establish a course of continuous treatment with respect to plaintiff's breast condition (*see, Davis v. City of New York*, 38 N.Y.2d 257, *supra*). In *Davis*, we held that two diagnostic examinations, conducted a year apart, were "discrete and complete" and did not constitute continuous treatment (38 NY2d, at 260). The examinations in this case were equally "discrete and complete" and were separated by an even greater period of time.

A holding that the continuous treatment doctrine is applicable to these facts would fundamentally extend and alter the doctrine. The gravamen of plaintiff's claim is not that the doctor performed certain negligent acts or omissions during a course of treatment for her breast condition, but rather that the doctor was negligent in failing to establish a course of treatment at all. While the failure to treat a condition may well be negligent, we cannot accept the self-contradictory proposition that the failure to establish a course of treatment is a course of treatment.

For these reasons, we conclude that the continuous treatment doctrine is inapplicable and that the action is time barred.

KAYE, J. (dissenting).

In my view, plaintiff has made a sufficient factual showing of continuous treatment by her gynecologist — who treated her throughout more than 12 years — to avoid dismissal of her complaint as a matter of law on Statute of Limitations grounds. I would reverse the Appellate Division order and reinstate

Supreme Court's holding that there is an issue of fact as to defendant doctor's continuous treatment of the plaintiff.

Plaintiff first consulted defendant in September 1974. When, during plaintiff's regularly scheduled visit in July 1979, defendant diagnosed fibrocystic disease in plaintiff's right breast, he told her that "we will have to keep an eye on it."

Defendant saw plaintiff regularly over the next several years, including consultation for a "bump" near her left breast and a hysterectomy which he performed in April 1982; examination at that time revealed a cyst on her right breast and masses in each breast. After defendant performed the hysterectomy, he prescribed hormone replacements, including estrogen, for plaintiff at least through June 1985, the date he last approved refills of her prescriptions. Then, in defendant's own words, "On January 13, 1986, the plaintiff came to my office for a gynecological check-up. Upon examining the plaintiff, I detected a mass in her right breast. In accordance with proper medical practices, I immediately consulted with Dr. Frederick Lane, an oncologist surgeon at Albany Medical Center Hospital. Dr. Lane saw the plaintiff that same day and performed a biopsy which showed the right breast to be cancerous. Dr. Lane subsequently performed a mastectomy on the plaintiff."

On these allegations, there is at least an issue of fact as to the timeliness of plaintiff's suit commenced in December 1987, less than two years after the diagnosis of breast cancer and well within the Statute of Limitations.

Plaintiff has alleged that her gynecologist diagnosed a breast disease that he apparently felt at the time could be treated by close monitoring (unlike his later reference to an oncologist surgeon). According to plaintiff, defendant assured her that he would "keep an eye on [her disease]," thus "lulling [her] into a false sense of security by an apparent lack of concern about her breast mass." Despite his awareness of breast lumps or masses in 1979, 1980 and 1982, he at no time recommended any further testing, evaluation or consultation during her periodic contacts with him. Clearly, these acts of alleged negligence, combined with wrongful omissions, may constitute a continuous course of treatment, separate and apart from any treatment for endometriosis (see, Borgia v. City of New York, 12 N.Y.2d 151, 155).

Indeed, the majority's pivotal assumption throughout its writing that plaintiff was being treated by her gynecologist solely for the separate condition of endometriosis ignores the evidence of additional gynecological treatment — for example, defendant's diagnosis of breast disease, his assertion that he would monitor the disease, the later consultation for a breast lump, and the hysterectomy (the hospital admission examination revealing "bilateral mobile masses in the upper quadrant of each breast").

"[W]here the physician and patient reasonably intend the patient's uninterrupted reliance upon the physician's observation, directions, concern, and responsibility for overseeing the patient's progress, the requirements of the continuous treatment doctrine are satisfied" (*Richardson v. Orentreich*, 64 N.Y.2d 896, 898).

On this record, I would not deny the plaintiff her day in court.

NOTES

(1) See also *Young v. New York City Health & Hosps. Corp.*, 91 N.Y.2d 291, 670 N.Y.S.2d 169, 693 N.E.196 (1998), in which the defendant had failed to inform the plaintiff that a mammogram indicated a cancerous condition. The Court held that the statute of limitations would not be tolled during the time between the mammogram and the date plaintiff learned that she needed surgery since the patient was unaware of the continued need for treatment. *Compare Richardson v. Ostereich*, 64 N.Y.2d 896, 487 N.Y.S.2d 731, 477 N.E.2d 210 (1985). There, plaintiff had received periodic treatment from the defendant physician between January, 1973, and October, 1974. On her last visit she was given an appointment for December 4, 1974, but she failed to keep it. The Court of Appeals nonetheless held that the patient was under continuous treatment until the date of the December appointment.

In *Plummer ex rel. Heron v. N.Y. City Health & Hosps. Corp.*, 98 N.Y.2d 263, 746 N.Y.S.2d 647, 774 N.E.2d 712 (2002), the Court refused to apply the continuous treatment rule to an otherwise time-barred case. The malpractice suit was based on an allegation of negligent pre- and postnatal care of an infant. Plaintiffs failed to keep numerous appointments for treatment of the infant's birth defects. It was understood that defendant's treatment of the infant would cease when plaintiffs moved to Florida. Except for one visit upon the infant's return from Florida for a problem unrelated to the birth defects, he was not examined again by defendant until 16 months later.

(2) In the absence of continuous treatment, what are the rights of a patient who has relied to his detriment on a physician's erroneous assurance that all was well? It may depend on the state of mind of the physician when she made the assuring statement. Consider the next case.

SIMCUSKI v. SAELI
Court of Appeals
44 N.Y.2d 442, 406 N.Y.S.2d 259, 377 N.E.2d 713 (1978)

JONES, J.

We hold that this complaint by a patient against her treating physician sets forth a cause of action based on intentional fraud as well as a cause of action in negligence for medical malpractice. We further conclude that, because of the physician's alleged subsequent intentional concealment of the malpractice and misrepresentation as to its cure, the time within which the action in negligence could be brought was not limited to the then applicable three-year statutory period of limitations and that on the present motion to dismiss the complaint it cannot be said that the action was not thereafter commenced within a reasonable time after discovery of the malpractice. Finally we hold that the Statute of Limitations applicable to the claim for damages based on the intentional fraud is the six-year statute. We note that different measures of damages will be applicable to the two causes of action.

On defendant's present motion to dismiss the complaint under CPLR 3211 (subd [a], par 5) on the ground that the plaintiff's claims are barred by the Statute of Limitations, we accept the allegations of the complaint and the admissible portions of plaintiff's supporting affidavits (CPLR 3211, subd [c]). On October 19, 1970 Dr. Saeli performed a surgical excision of a node from plaintiff's neck. Plaintiff alleges that during the operation on her neck the surgeon negligently injured a spinal-accessory nerve in her neck and also injured branches of her cervical plexus. Following the operation plaintiff told her surgeon that she was experiencing numbness in the right side of her face and neck and that it was difficult and painful for her to raise her right arm. It is alleged that the physician was aware of the negligent manner in which he had performed the surgery and aware, too, that as a result of his negligence plaintiff had suffered a potentially permanent injury. It is further alleged that the physician willfully, falsely and fraudulently told plaintiff that her postoperative problems, pain and difficulties were transient and that they would disappear if she would continue a regimen of physiotherapy which he had prescribed and which was then being given by Dr. Lane. Plaintiff continued with the physiotherapy prescribed by Dr. Saeli until October, 1974. In the meantime she had moved to Syracuse, New York, where she sought further medical advice. In January, 1974 she was first apprised by the Syracuse physician of the true nature of her injury and that it probably had been caused at the time of her surgery. This doctor's diagnosis was substantially confirmed in October, 1974 by a professor of medicine, specializing in neurology, at Upstate Medical Center in Syracuse, who also advised that reanastomosis of the sectioned nerve four years after the surgery would not be a physiologically successful procedure. It is further alleged that Dr. Saeli had intentionally withheld information from plaintiff as to the true nature and source of her injury, in consequence of which she was deprived of the opportunity for cure of her condition.

The present action against Dr. Saeli was commenced in April, 1976. . . .

In our view the complaint sufficiently sets forth two causes of action although not explicitly or separately denominated — one in negligence for medical malpractice on the part of Dr. Saeli in connection with the surgical excision of the node on October 19, 1970, the other for an intentional tort in knowingly and fraudulently misinforming plaintiff as to her physical condition and misrepresenting that physiotherapy would produce a cure. Our analysis begins with the consideration of the cause of action in negligence.

The complaint sufficiently sets forth a cause of action for medical malpractice; the critical issue is whether this cause of action was barred by the then applicable three-year Statute of Limitations (CPLR 214, subd 6). Normally the statute would have precluded institution in April, 1976 of a claim for damages for malpractice alleged to have occurred in October, 1970. This complaint, however, further alleges that defendant intentionally concealed the alleged malpractice from plaintiff and falsely assured her of effective treatment, as a result of which plaintiff did not discover the injury to the nerve until October, 1974. In this circumstance principles of equitable estoppel are applicable to relieve plaintiff from the proscriptions of the statute. As noted by Mr. Justice Earle C. Bastow in *Erbe v Lincoln Rochester Trust Co.* (13 AD2d 211, 213, *mot for rearg and mot for lv to app den* 14 AD2d 509, *app dsmd* 11 NY2d 754): "Fraudulent representations may play a dual role. They may be the basis for an independent action for fraud. They may also, in equity, be a basis for an equitable estoppel barring the defendants from invoking the Statute of Limitations as against a cause of action for breach of fiduciary relations."

It is the rule that a defendant may be estopped to plead the Statute of Limitations where plaintiff was induced by fraud, misrepresentations or deception to refrain from filing a timely action. (*General Stencils v Chiappa*, 18 NY2d 125; *Erbe v Lincoln Rochester Trust Co.*, . . . *supra; see* Fraud, Misrepresentation, or Deception as Estopping Reliance on Statute of Limitations, Ann., 43 ALR3d 429.) The allegations of her complaint bring this plaintiff within the shelter of this rule. The elements of reliance by plaintiff on the alleged misrepresentations as the cause of her failure sooner to institute the action for malpractice and of justification for such reliance, both necessarily to be established by her, are sufficiently pleaded within the fair intendment of the allegations of this complaint.

    . . . .

It is as important to determine the effect of the doctrine of equitable estoppel as it is to determine that it applies. If the conduct relied on (fraud, misrepresentation or other deception) has ceased to be operational within the otherwise applicable period of limitations (or perhaps within a reasonable time prior to the expiration of such period), many courts have denied application of the doctrine on the ground that the period during which the plaintiff was justifiably lulled into inactivity had expired prior to the termination of the statutory period, and that the plaintiff had thereafter had sufficient time to commence his action prior to the expiration of the period of limitations. (*E.g., 509 Sixth Ave. Corp. v New York City Tr. Auth.*, 24 AD2d 975; . . . .) That is not the present situation. Plaintiff has alleged that her discovery of the malpractice in this case (the point at which the conduct here relied on ceased to be operational) did not occur until October, 1974 (or possibly in January of that year if inference be drawn from the letter of her Syracuse doctor dated January 9, 1974 submitted in opposition to the motion). Whichever the month of discovery in 1974, the three-year Statute of Limitations had already expired in October, 1973.

Where, as here, the conduct relied on ceases to be operational after the expiration of the period of limitations, two approaches may be discerned in the cases. By one, further delay on the part of the plaintiff in commencing his action may be held to be subject to the counterdefense of laches to be pleaded and proved by the defendant. . . . The preferable analysis, however, holds that due diligence on the part of the plaintiff in bringing his action is an essential element for the applicability of the doctrine of equitable estoppel, to be demonstrated by the plaintiff when he seeks the shelter of the doctrine. . . . Under this approach, which we endorse, the burden is on the plaintiff to establish that the action was brought within a reasonable time after the facts giving rise to the estoppel have ceased to be operational. Whether in any particular instance the plaintiff will have discharged his responsibility of due diligence in this regard must necessarily depend on all the relevant circumstances. The length of the legislatively prescribed period of limitations is sometimes said to be relevant, and courts have held that in no event will the plaintiff be found to have exercised the required diligence if his action is deferred beyond the date which would be marked by the reapplication of the statutory period, *i.e.*, that the length of the statutory period itself sets an outside limit on what will be regarded as due diligence. . . . In the present case such an outside limit was not exceeded; the action was brought less than three years after discovery in 1974. It is not possible or appropriate, however, on the present motion addressed to the pleading, presenting us as it must with only a skeletal record, to determine whether this plaintiff met her obligation of due diligence when she instituted the present action in April, 1976. It suffices for disposition of the present appeal to note our conclusion that it cannot now be determined as a matter of law that the reasonable time for bringing the present action had expired prior to its institution in April, 1976.

In passing we observe that if it is established that plaintiff is not precluded from prosecuting the cause of action in negligence and she proves that cause on the merits, the measure of damages which she will be entitled to recover will be that normally associated with medical malpractice actions in situations such as the present.

We turn then to consideration of the other cause of action, noting that it asserts a claim in fraud as an intentional tort. The essential elements, here alleged or within the reasonable intendment of the complaint, are knowledge on the part of the physician of the fact of his malpractice and of his patient's injury in consequence thereof, coupled with a subsequent intentional, material misrepresentation by him to his patient known by him to be false at the time it was made, and on which the patient relied to his damage — in this case, defendant's intentionally concealing from his patient the fact of the malpractice and thereafter fraudulently misstating that the therapy prescribed would effect a cure. This is more than another aspect of the malpractice or even another act of alleged negligent malpractice on the part of the treating physician; the complaint alleges an intentional fraud — that Dr. Saeli, knowing it to be untrue yet expecting his patient to rely on his advice, advised her that physiotherapy

would produce a cure, in consequence of which fraudulent misrepresentation the patient was deprived of the opportunity for cure of the condition initially caused by the doctor's alleged malpractice. If these allegations are proved they will establish an intentional tort, separate from and subsequent to the malpractice claim. (*Calabrese v Bickley*, 1 AD2d 874.) Recovery of damages in such case is governed by the six-year Statute of Limitations under CPLR 213 (subd 8). The application of the three-year Statute of Limitations is not mandated by the circumstance that the fraud alleged arises as a sequel to an alleged malpractice.[4]

In reaching this determination, we recognize and approve, but distinguish, cases which hold that, without more, concealment by a physician or failure to disclose his own malpractice does not give rise to a cause of action in fraud or deceit separate and different from the customary malpractice action, thereby entitling the plaintiff to bring his action within the longer period limited for such claims. . . . Such nondisclosure or concealment may affect the damages recoverable, or, conceivably in a proper case in conjunction with other factors, provide a foundation for seeking to invoke the doctrine of equitable estoppel to extend the applicable period of limitations. Standing alone such nondisclosure or concealment will not, however, serve as the basis for a distinct cause of action in fraud.

We observe that, as in the instance of fraud claims generally, this plaintiff, too, will be required to prove her claim by clear and convincing evidence (*Rudman v Cowles Communications*, 30 NY2d 1, 10; *see* 24 NY Jur, Fraud and Deceit, § 284, p 371). If she succeeds in this respect, the available measure of her damages will be that applicable in fraud actions, *i.e.*, damages caused by the fraud, as distinguished in this case from damages occasioned by the alleged malpractice.

In 1975 our Legislature determined as a matter of policy to limit the extent of liability in medical malpractice claims when it adopted a more stringent Statute of Limitations (CPLR 214-a; L 1975, ch 109, § 6). Lest the implications of our present decision be misapprehended as subjecting physicians to a greater exposure to liability in consequence of errors of professional judgment at a time when there is legitimate concern both from the standpoint of the profession and the public as to the economic import of recently ballooning malpractice recoveries and thus to run counter to or to flout the general policy direction articulated by the Legislature, it is appropriate to stress certain aspects of the present case and the theories of liability on which we sustain this complaint.

At the outset we observe that the exposure to liability we here discuss is not based on errors of professional judgment; it is predicated on proof of the commission of an intentional tort, in this instance, fraud. As to that cause of action:

---

[4] We observe that the alleged tortious conduct in this instance occurred prior to the adoption of CPLR 214-a (L 1975, ch 109, § 6, eff July 1, 1975). There is thus no basis here for any assertion that by the enactment of that statute the Legislature intended to prescribe a statutory period of limitations with respect to all claims arising out of the physician-patient relationship no matter on what legal theory predicated.

First, it must be established that the physician knew (or demonstrably had reason to know) of the fact of his malpractice and of the injury suffered by his patient in consequence thereof.

Second, it must be established that, knowing it to be false at the time, the physician thereafter made material, factual misrepresentation to the patient with respect to the subject matter of the malpractice and the therapy appropriate to its cure, on which the patient justifiably relied.

Third, all elements of the intentional tort of fraud must be established by clear and convincing evidence. Recognizing, too, the hazards of proliferating litigation of baseless claims, attention is drawn to the requirements of CPLR 3016 (subd [b]). While, of course, motions to dismiss under CPLR 3211 are properly addressed to the allegations set forth in the complaint, on motions for summary judgment under CPLR 3212 evidentiary proof in admissible form must be tendered in support of all the elements of the alleged cause of action.

Fourth, if there is not an available, efficacious remedy or cure which the plaintiff is diverted from undertaking in consequence of the intentional, fraudulent misrepresentation — as in many instances of medical malpractice there may not be — there will normally be only minimal damages, if any. It will be necessary to demonstrate that the condition caused by the malpractice could have been corrected or alleviated. Thus, in the present case, if it can be shown that at the time of Dr. Saeli's alleged fraudulent misrepresentations it was already too late to undertake a reanastomosis of the severed nerve, this plaintiff will have sustained little or no damages in consequence of the alleged fraud. If only a partial cure were then possible, damages would be assessable on that basis. Recovery would be greatest, of course, if plaintiff were diverted from what could otherwise have been a complete cure.

Accordingly, it will be seen that the present decision is not to be expected to open the proverbial floodgates. On the other hand, in human terms it would be unthinkable today not to hold a professional person liable for knowingly and intentionally misleading his patient in consequence of which, to the physician's foreknowledge, the patient was deprived of an opportunity for escape from a medical predicament which the physician by his own negligence had initially inflicted on his patient. With respect to the application of the doctrine of equitable estoppel to a defense of Statute of Limitations pleaded in a malpractice action, again we are concerned with an intentional, not merely negligent, wrong — the purposeful concealment and misrepresentation of the fact and consequences of the malpractice. It would not be tolerable to permit a physician by whose fraud, misrepresentation or deception his patient has been induced to delay filing legal proceedings until after the time limited by statute to reap the benefits of his own misconduct.

For the reasons stated the order of the Appellate Division should be reversed, with costs to abide the event, and the order of Supreme Court denying defendant's motion to dismiss reinstated.

NOTES AND CARTOON

(1) As you read the principal case, does it limit the application of the equitable estoppel doctrine to situations in which the doctor intentionally misstated the patient's condition, or does it include grossly erroneous statements made in good faith? If only the former, how would you go about proving the doctor's intent? In *Zumpano v. Quinn*, 6 N.Y.3d 666, 816 N.Y.S.2d 703, 849 N.E.2d 926 (2006), plaintiffs' actions seeking damages against individual clerics and a diocese for alleged child abuse were held time-barred when brought long after the applicable period had run. The equitable estoppel doctrine did not save the plaintiffs' claims even if, as alleged, the defendants were aware of the abuse and remained silent about it — the doctrine requires actual misrepresentation that prevents the timely prosecution of the claims. The Court allowed that if a defendant owes a fiduciary duty to the plaintiff, the mere concealment of wrong-doing might trigger equitable estoppel even in the absence of affirmative misrepresentation. This rule did not help the *Zumpano* plaintiffs because they could not show that the defendants' alleged concealment prevented them from bringing a timely action. The Court of Appeals also refused to apply equitable estoppel in *Putter v. North Shore University Hosp.*, 7 N.Y.3d 548, 858 N.E.2d 1140 (2006) (plaintiff, who had contacted hepatitis C during surgery at the defendant hospital, had "timely awareness of the facts requiring him to make further inquiry before the statute of limitations expired").

(2) What is the relevance of CPLR 214-a and the related materials to this cartoon from the New Yorker, June 13, 1983, p. 53?*

NOTE ON OTHER PROFESSIONAL MALPRACTICE

CPLR 214(6) imposes a three-year limit on "an action to recover damages for malpractice, other than medical, dental, or podiatric malpractice." In *McCoy v. Feinman,* 99 N.Y.2d 295, 755 N.Y.S.2d 693, 785 N.E.2d 714 (2002), an attorney malpractice case, the Court of Appeals held that the three years ran from the date in 1988 when the attorney filed a negligently drafted stipulation of settlement in the underlying divorce action. The stipulation had failed to preserve plaintiff's right to death benefits under her ex-husband's employee benefit plan. The Court considered it irrelevant that plaintiff did not learn of the negligence until after her ex-husband died in 1994. In fact, the Court declared that it has "recognized no exception" to the rule that a legal malpractice claim accrues "when all the facts necessary to the cause of action have occurred and an injured party can obtain relief in court" (citation omitted). The Court also declined to apply *Greene v. Greene*, 56 N.Y.2d 86, 94, 451 N.Y.S.2d 46, 50, 436 N.E.2d 496, 500 (1982), which held that the statute of limitations is tolled during a continuous professional-client relationship on the grounds that "a person seeking professional assistance has a right to repose confidence in the professional's ability and good faith, and realistically cannot be expected to question and assess the techniques employed or the manner in which the services are rendered. . . ." Although the defendant in *McCoy* had subsequently represented the plaintiff in a separate Family Court support action against her ex-husband, the Court deemed that action independent of the divorce and therefore not indicative of continuous representation.

On the other hand, the Court of Appeals did apply the continuous representation toll to an action against an attorney who had allowed his clients' claim to languish until it was barred by the statute of limitations. *Shumsky v. Eisenstein*, 96 N.Y.2d 164, 726 N.Y.S.2d 365, 750 N.E.2d 69 (2001). Under the facts presented, the representation continued until the clients were put on notice of the lawyer's withdrawal as their attorney. According to the Court, the notice of the withdrawal was given "at the earliest" when the defendant failed to return their telephone calls.

[D] Fraud

Paragraph 8 of CPLR 213 prescribes a six-year period for actions "based upon fraud." Application of this paragraph is limited to claims involving actual fraud as opposed to those involving "constructive fraud," which are covered by paragraph 1 of the same section. Since actions for both types of fraud are governed by a six-year period running from the date of the fraud, the significance of the distinction is important only with late-discovered frauds. When the claim is based on an actual fraud, CPLR 213(8) allows six years from the "accrual" of the cause of action (*i.e.*, the commission of the fraudulent act) or two years from the time the plaintiff "discovered the fraud or could with reasonable diligence have discovered it." CPLR 213(8), as amended by Ch. 403, Laws of 2004. (The 2004 amendment eliminated a drafting glitch but did not change the substance of the law.) In contrast, a cause of action based upon constructive fraud accrues at the time of the wrongful act and is not extended by a belated discovery. *Quadrozzi Concrete Corp. v. Mastroianni*, 56 A.D.2d 353, 392 N.Y.S.2d 687 (2d Dep't 1977). A colorable allegation of fraudulent intent in the complaint is apparently sufficient to take the case into the actual fraud category for statute of limitation purposes. *See id.*

The bottom line is that the plaintiff gets six years from the commission of the fraud or two years from discovery (actual or imputed), whichever is longer. *See* 1 Weinstein, Korn & Miller, N.Y. Civil Practice, ¶ 203.35 and cases cited.

Seeking to take advantage of the discovery rule applicable to fraud, some plaintiffs whose claims are essentially for breach of contract have added allegations based on fraud. The perils of this approach are illustrated in *Brick v. Cohn-Hall-Marx Co.*, 276 N.Y. 259, 11 N.E.2d 902 (1937), in which plaintiff alleged defendant had defrauded him by keeping false books in order to pay lower royalties. In their contract, defendant had agreed to "keep accurate books and records," and the court therefore held that the claim sounded not in fraud but in breach of contract, as to which no discovery rule applies.

Note, however, that a defendant who has fraudulently concealed a breach of a legal obligation can be equitably estopped from pleading the statute of limitations as a defense. *General Stencils, Inc. v. Chiappa*, 18 N.Y.2d 125, 272 N.Y.S.2d 337, 219 N.E.2d 169 (1966); *Simcuski v. Saeli, supra.* In order to use equitable estoppel to prevent the dismissal of an action, however, the plaintiff must show that they were unable to bring a timely law suit because they relied on the defendant's fraud, misrepresentation, and deception to their detriment. Thus, in *Zumpano v. Quinn*, 6 N.Y.3d 666, 816 N.Y.S.2d 703, 849 N.E.2d 926 (2006), plaintiffs' actions alleging child abuse against individual clerics and a Catholic diocese were held time-barred when brought long after the applicable period had run. The plaintiffs were admittedly aware of the alleged wrongs within the time allowed for suit and could not establish that subsequent and specific actions by the defendant had prevented them from timely commencing their actions.

[E] Wrongful Death

If a person dies as a result of wrongfully inflicted injuries, the estate may have two causes of action against the tortfeasor. One is the so-called "survival" action. This is a claim for the decedent's pain, suffering and other damages, which the decedent could have prosecuted but for the death. (An action for these damages is preserved for the estate by Estate Powers and Trust Law § 11-3.1.) The second is the action for damages (such as lost earnings) suffered by the estate as a result of the decedent's death. This cause of action is provided for by Estate Powers and Trusts Law § 5-4.1:

(1) The personal representative, duly appointed in this state or any other jurisdiction, of a decedent who is survived by distributees may maintain an action to recover damages for a wrongful act, neglect or default which caused the decedent's death against a person who would have been liable to the decedent by reason of such wrongful conduct if death had not ensued. Such an action must be commenced within two years after the decedent's death. . . .

Each of the estate's two causes of action is subject to its own period of limitations. The survival action is subject to whatever provision would have governed it if the victim had not died, *e.g.*, the three years from the date of injury if based on negligence. CPLR 214(5). As set out above, the personal representative of the estate gets two years from the date of death to bring the wrongful death claim. But note that the wrongful death claim will be barred if the survival action was already barred when the victim died. *McDaniel v. Clarkstown Cent. Sch. Dist. No. 1*, 110 A.D.2d 349, 353, 494 N.Y.S.2d 885, 888 (2d Dep't 1985), and cases cited. This is because EPTL § 5-4.1 requires, as a pre-condition of a wrongful death action, that the defendant "would have been liable to the decedent by reason of such wrongful conduct if death had not ensued." To illustrate: if A is injured by B on January 2, 1991, and dies as a result on January 3, 1994 (without having commenced a tort action), no timely wrongful death action could be brought by A's estate.

An extension is created for the wrongful death claim if a criminal prosecution has been commenced against the defendant with respect to the event or occurrence from which the wrongful death claim arose. In such case, the personal representative gets at least one year from the termination of the criminal action, even if the time to sue for wrongful death would otherwise have expired. EPTL § 5-4.1(2).

[F] Defamation

CPLR 215(3) provides a one-year limitations period for actions to recover damages for libel and slander. The time runs from the publication of the statement. Under the "single publication" rule, the publication creates a single cause of action regardless of the number of copies sent out or the number of outlets if broadcast over the air. *Gregoire v. G.P. Putnam's Sons*, 298 N.Y. 119, 81 N.E.2d 45 (1948). A republication of the defamatory material, however, will restart the limitation period. For instance, if a book comes out in a second printing, a new cause of action would arise.

When the defamatory material is on a website, does republication occur each time the website is accessed? In *Firth v. State*, 98 N.Y.2d 365, 747 N.Y.S.2d 69, 775 N.E.2d 463 (2002), the Court of Appeals answered in the negative. If the website statement is supplemented or changed, there will be no republication if the new material is unrelated to the original alleged defamatory statement. In *Firth*, it was not related. The implication is that if there is a relationship between the original alleged defamation and the later supplemented website material, there will be a republication.

§ 7.03 ALTERING THE PERIOD OF LIMITATIONS BY AGREEMENT OR CONDUCT

JOHN J. KASSNER & CO. v. CITY OF NEW YORK
Court of Appeals
46 N.Y.2d 544, 415 N.Y.S.2d 785, 389 N.E.2d 99 (1979)

WACHTLER, J.

In an action by an engineering firm to recover money allegedly owed for work done on a municipal contract the city asserted the Statute of Limitations (CPLR 213, subd 2) as a defense. . . .

In 1967 the plaintiff John J. Kassner & Co., a professional engineering corporation, entered into a contract with the City of New York to arrange the relocation of all utility facilities at the site of the proposed new police headquarters in Manhattan. The contract, and a later supplemental agreement, provided for a lump sum payment of approximately $200,000 to be paid to the plaintiff in percentage installments as the work progressed "subject to audit and revision by the Comptroller" of the city. The agreement also provides that "No action shall be . . . maintained against the City upon any claim based upon this contract or arising out of this contract . . . unless such action shall be commenced within six (6) months after the date of filing in the office of the Comptroller of the City of the certificate for the final payment hereunder. . . . None of the provisions of Article 2 of the Civil Practice Laws and Rules shall apply to any action against the City arising out of this contract."

On December 13, 1967 plaintiff submitted an itemized statement indicating that it had completed its work and claiming that there was a balance due of $39,523.69. Upon audit, however, the comptroller disallowed $38,423.69 claimed for "technical services" and only authorized a final payment of $1,100. The record does not indicate the date the plaintiff was informed of the comptroller's decision. It is evident though that the plaintiff was aware of the results of the audit by July 1, 1968 when it sent a letter of protest demanding payment of the full amount.

For over six years the plaintiff did nothing further to collect any part of the final payment. Then, on September 19, 1974, the plaintiff submitted a requisition for final payment of the undisputed balance of $1,100. A voucher for this amount was certified by the Department of Public Works, on September 27, 1974, and was forwarded to the comptroller. On November 8, 1974, a check for $1,100 was sent to the plaintiff and, on that same date, a certificate of final payment was filed in the comptroller's office.

Plaintiff commenced this action on April 18, 1975 by service of a summons and complaint seeking $39,523.69 as final payment due on the contract. By stipulation this amount was later reduced to $38,423.69 after plaintiff accepted the city's check for $1,100 representing the undisputed balance. In its answer the city asserted the Statute of Limitations as a second affirmative defense. The plaintiff, relying on the limitations provision in the contract, moved to dismiss the defense and the city cross-moved for summary judgment on the defense.

The city relied upon CPLR article 2 which provides that a suit on a contract must be commenced within six years (CPLR 213, subd 2) after the cause of action accrued (CPLR 203, subd [a]). The city urged that the plaintiff's cause of action "accrued no later than July 1, 1968" because the "Plaintiff was fully aware of the amount and nature of its claim as of July 1, 1968, and was enabled to bring its action at any time thereafter." The city also argued that the provision in the contract requiring the plaintiff to commence its action within six months of the filing of the certificate of final payment was inapplicable because it was intended to shorten the statutory period and not to extend it and, in any event, could not have the effect of extending the statutory period since the city has "no power to waive . . . the statute of limitations" (General City Law, § 20, subd 5).

The plaintiff on the other hand urged that the contract was controlling; that under the agreement the cause of action did not accrue until the certificate of final payment had been filed and that the suit commenced within six months of that date was timely under the contract. The plaintiff also argued that the contractual limitations provision did not violate the General City Law (§ 20, subd 5) because the city "has not waived the statute [of limitations], but has . . . selected the agreed event or contingency on which the cause of action would accrue and the statute would start to run."

. . . .

Two questions are presented by the appeal: (1) when did the cause of action accrue within the meaning of the Statute of Limitations, and (2) can a contractual limitations clause, which begins to run at a later date than the time of accrual under the statute, effectively extend the Statute of Limitations in an action on the contract.

In contract cases, the cause of action accrues and the Statute of Limitations begins to run from the time of the breach. . . . And, as a general rule, when the right to final payment is subject to a condition, the obligation to pay arises and the cause of action accrues, only when the condition has been fulfilled (36 NY Jur, Limitations and Laches, § 61; *Nolan v Whitney*, 88 NY 649; Simpson, Contracts, § 112). In this case, however, the contract does not state that the plaintiff's right to final payment is conditioned upon the filing of a certificate of final payment. On the contrary, the contract provides that the plaintiff is entitled to final payment when it has completed its work to the satisfaction of the Department of Public Works, subject only to an audit by the comptroller. Thus the plaintiff's right to final payment and the city's obligation to pay were conditioned upon completion of the audit (*City of New York v State of New York*, 40 NY2d 659, 668). But once the audit was completed and the plaintiff was informed of the results, the cause of action accrued. . . . The breach, if any, occurred at this point because the comptroller — the only official responsible and specifically designated in the contract to authorize payment on behalf of the city — unequivocally refused to pay the full amount demanded and allegedly due on the contract. Therefore the cause of action for breach of contract accrued, within the meaning of the Statute of Limitations, no later than July 1, 1968.

The limitations provision contained in the contract cannot serve, in this case, to extend the statutory period. Although the Statute of Limitations is generally viewed as a personal defense "to afford protection to defendants against defending stale claims," it also expresses a societal interest or public policy "of giving repose to human affairs" (*Flanagan v Mt. Eden Gen. Hosp.*, 24 NY2d 427, 429; *Schwartz v Hayden Chem. Co.*, 12 NY2d 212; *see, also*, Weinstein-Korn-Miller, NY Civ Prac, par 201.01). Because of the combined private and public interests involved, individual parties are not entirely free to waive or modify the statutory defense.

The parties may cut back on the Statute of Limitations by agreeing that any suit must be commenced within a shorter period than is prescribed by law. Such an agreement does not conflict with public policy but, in fact, "more effectively secures the end sought to be attained by the statute of limitations" (*Ripley v Aetna Ins. Co.*, 30 NY 136, 163). Thus an agreement which modifies the Statute of Limitations by specifying a shorter, but reasonable, period within which to commence an action is enforceable (*Sapinkopf v Cunard S.S. Co.*, 254 NY 111) provided it is in writing (CPLR 201).

But the power of the parties to make enforceable agreements which would extend the Statute of Limitations is, of course, more restricted. "The public policy represented by the statute of limitations becomes pertinent where the contract not to plead the statute is in form or effect a contract to extend the period as provided by statute *or to postpone the time from which the period of limitation is to be computed.*" (1961 Report of NY Law Rev Comm, pp 97, 98, emphasis added.) The validity of this type of agreement depends initially on the time at which it was made.

If the agreement to "waive" or extend the Statute of Limitations is made at the inception of liability it is unenforceable because a party cannot "in advance, make a valid promise that a statute founded in public policy shall be inoperative" (*Shapley v Abbott*, 42 NY 443, 452; . . . .) Of course at that stage there is a greater likelihood that a "waiver" or extension of the defense, as part of the initial contract or obligation, was the result of ignorance, improvidence, an unequal bargaining position or was simply unintended.

But if the agreement is made after the cause of action has accrued the Legislature has provided that it may be enforceable under certain circumstances.

The controlling statute (General Obligations Law, § 17-103, subd 1) is applicable only to actions arising out of a contract and requires that the agreement or promise "to waive, to extend, or not to plead the statute of limitation" be in writing and signed by the promisor "after the accrual of the cause of action." If these requirements are met the agreement or promise has the effect of renewing the Statute of Limitations for the applicable period, unless a shorter period is specified. The statute, it should be noted, is exclusive (*see* General Obligations Law, § 17-103, subd 3). Thus extension agreements made prior to the accrual of the cause of action continue to have "no effect" (General Obligations Law, § 17-103, subd 3).

An agreement to extend the Statute of Limitations is not truly a waiver unless it is made after the statutory period has run. . . . Thus, as a general rule a party who has not raised the Statute of Limitations as a defense in the answer or by a motion to dismiss is held to have waived it (*see* Weinstein- Korn-Miller, NY Civ Prac, par 201.11). A city, as noted, lacks the power to waive the Statute of Limitations (General City Law, § 20, subd 5; *Matter of City of New York* [*Elm St.*], 239 NY 220) but is not otherwise precluded from granting an extension. In New York City, for instance, the comptroller is expressly authorized to agree to an extension, although under circumstances and terms generally more restrictive than would otherwise be permitted by section 17-103 of the General Obligations Law (*see* Administrative Code of City of New York, § 93d-3.1).

The contractual limitations provision in this case is apparently a standard clause which, undoubtedly, was included to shorten the Statute of Limitations. . . . To that extent, of course, it would be enforceable (CPLR 201). It is doubtful that the parties actually intended to postpone the accrual of the cause of action or anticipated that this provision would ever be employed to extend the expiration of the statutory period. In any event, since it was adopted at the inception of the contract and not after the cause of action had accrued, it may not serve to extend the Statute of Limitations (General Obligations Law, § 17-103, subds 1, 3).

Accordingly, the order of the Appellate Division should be reversed. . . .

. . . .

NOTES

(1) The principal case applies the general rule that the parties may not, prior to the accrual of a cause of action, extend the time within which an action may be brought. See Gen. Oblig. Law § 17-103(3). After the cause of action accrues, a signed written agreement to waive or extend the period is valid, and the limitations period runs anew from the date of the writing unless the parties provide otherwise. *Id.*, § 17-103(1). A signed acknowledgment of a debt has the same effect. Gen. Oblig. Law § 17-101. An acknowledgment or promise to pay may be inferred from a part payment of the underlying debt. *Roth v. Michelson,*

55 N.Y.2d 278, 449 N.Y.S.2d 159, 434 N.E.2d 228 (1982). This is true whether the part payment (or acknowledgment) is made before or after the expiration of the statutory period. *See Roth, supra. Compare Petito v. Piffath*, 85 N.Y.2d 1, 623 N.Y.S.2d 520, 647 N.E.2d 732 (1994) (an agreement to settle an action on a claimed debt is not an acknowledgement of the debt sufficient to extend the statute of limitations in the absence of an express acknowledgment of the indebtedness or an express promise to pay the debt).

(2) As the principal case also states, an agreement to reduce the statute of limitations is enforceable whenever made, unless it is unreasonably short. *See also* CPLR 201.

(3) Agreements to alter the statute of limitations in contracts for the sale of goods are governed by U.C.C. § 2-725(1), reproduced in § 7.02[B], *supra*, providing that "[b]y the original agreement the parties may reduce the period of limitations to not less than one year but may not extend it." The seller has the power to protect the buyer's future rights by making a warranty which "explicitly extends to future performance of the goods," for in such a case, the claim can accrue when the breach is or should have been discovered, rather than at the time of tender. U.C.C. § 2-725(2).

§ 7.04 APPLYING STATE LIMITATIONS PERIODS TO FEDERAL CLAIMS

Congress has created some federal causes of action without providing statutes of limitations for them. The general rule is that the most appropriate statute of limitations of the relevant state should be "borrowed" and applied, whether the action is brought in a state or federal court. The problem of finding the right statute of limitations for 42 U.S.C. § 1983, the general federal civil rights statute, is considered in the following case.*

OWENS v. OKURE
United States Supreme Court
488 U.S. 235, 109 S. Ct. 573, 102 L. Ed. 2d 594 (1989)

Justice Marshall delivered the opinion of the Court.

In *Wilson v. Garcia*, 471 U.S. 261 (1985), we held that courts entertaining claims brought under 42 U.S.C. § 1983 should borrow the state statute of limitations for personal injury actions. This case raises the question of what limi-

---

* Editor's Note: Section 1983 provides:

    Every person who, under color of any statute, ordinance, regulation, custom, or usage, of any State or Territory, subjects, or causes to be subjected, any citizen of the United States or other person within the jurisdiction thereof to the deprivation of any rights, privileges, or immunities secured by the Constitution and laws, shall be liable to the party injured in an action at law, suit in equity, or other proper proceeding for redress.

tations period should apply to a § 1983 action where a State has one or more statutes of limitations for certain enumerated intentional torts, and a residual statute for all other personal injury action. We hold that the residual or general personal injury statute of limitations applies.

I

On November 13, 1985, respondent Tom U.U. Okure brought suit in the District Court for the Northern District of New York, seeking damages under § 1983 from petitioners Javan Owens and Daniel G. Lessard, two State University of New York (SUNY) police officers. Okure alleged that, on January 27, 1984, the officers unlawfully arrested him on the SUNY campus in Albany and charged him with disorderly conduct. The complaint stated that Okure was "forcibly transported" to the police detention center, "battered and beaten by [the police officers] and forced to endure great emotional distress, physical harm, and embarrassment." App. 5-6. As a result of the arrest and beating, Okure claimed, he "sustained personal injuries, including broken teeth and a sprained finger, mental anguish, shame, humiliation, legal expenses and the deprivation of his constitutional rights." *Id.*, at 6.

The officers moved to dismiss the complaint, which had been filed 22 months after the alleged incident, as time-barred. They contended that § 1983 actions were governed by New York's 1-year statute of limitations covering eight intentional torts: "assault, battery, false imprisonment, malicious prosecution, libel, slander, false words causing special damages, [and] a violation of the right of privacy." N.Y. Civ. Prac. Law § 215(3) (McKinney 1972).

The District Court denied the motion to dismiss. [The District Court applied the three year period of CPLR 214(5)]. . . . The Court of Appeals for the Second Circuit . . . affirmed. 816 F.2d 45 (1987). It stated that Wilson's description of § 1983 claims as general personal injury actions required a statute of limitations "expansive enough to accommodate the diverse personal injury torts that section 1983 has come to embrace." *Id.*, at 48. . . .

The dissent argued that § 1983 actions are best analogized to intentional torts, *id.*, at 51, and that, because § 215(3) governs "almost every intentional injury to the person," *id.*, at 50, it is more appropriate for § 1983 claims than § 214(5), which it contended had been confined primarily to negligence claims. *Ibid.* . . .

II

A

In this case, we again confront the consequences of Congress' failure to provide a specific statute of limitations to govern § 1983 actions. Title 42 U.S.C. § 1988 endorses the borrowing of state-law limitations provisions where doing so is consistent with federal law; § 1988 does not, however, offer any guidance as to which state provision to borrow.[2] To fill this void, for years we urged courts to select the state statute of limitations "most analogous," *Board of Regents, Univ. of New York v. Tomanio*, 446 U.S. 478, 488 (1980), and "most appropriate," *Johnson v. Railway Express Agency, Inc.*, 421 U.S. 454, 462 (1975), to the particular § 1983 action, so long as the chosen limitations period was consistent with federal law and policy. *Occidental Life Ins. Co. of California v. EEOC*, 432 U.S. 355, 367 (1977). . . .

The practice of seeking state-law analogies for particular § 1983 claims bred confusion and inconsistency in the lower courts and generated time-consuming litigation. Some courts found analogies in common-law tort, others in contract law, and still others in statutory law. Often the result had less to do with the general nature of § 1983 relief than with counsel's artful pleading and ability to persuade the court that the facts and legal theories of a particular § 1983 claim resemble a particular common-law or statutory cause of action. Consequently, plaintiffs and defendants often had no idea whether a federal civil rights claim was barred until a court ruled on their case. Predictability, a primary goal of statutes of limitations, was thereby frustrated.

In *Wilson*, we sought to end this "conflict, confusion and uncertainty." 471 U.S., at 266. Recognizing the problems inherent in the case-by-case approach, we determined that 42 U.S.C. § 1988 requires courts to borrow and apply to all § 1983 claims the one most analogous state statute of limitations. *Ibid. See id.*, at 275 ("[F]ederal interests in uniformity, certainty, and the minimization of unnecessary litigation all support the conclusion that Congress favored this simple approach"); *see also id.*, at 272 ("[A] simple, broad characterization of all § 1983 claims best fits the statute's remedial purpose"). We concluded, based upon the legislative history of § 1983 and the wide array of claims now embraced by that provision, that § 1983 "confer[s] a general remedy for injuries to personal rights." *Id.*, at 278. Because "§ 1983 claims are best characterized as personal injury actions," we held that a State's personal injury statute of limitations should be applied to all § 1983 claims. *Id.*, at 280.

As the instant case indicates, *Wilson* has not completely eliminated the confusion over the appropriate limitation period for § 1983 claims. In States where

---

[2] In relevant part, § 1988 provides:

The jurisdiction in civil and criminal matters conferred on the district courts by the provisions of this Title, and of Title "CIVIL RIGHTS," and of Title "CRIMES," for the protection of all persons in the United States in their civil rights, and for their vindication, shall be exercised and enforced in conformity with the laws of the United States, so far as such laws are suitable to carry the same into effect; but in all cases where they are not adapted to the object, or are deficient in the provisions necessary to furnish suitable remedies and punish offenses against law, the common law, as modified and changed by the constitution and statutes of the State wherein the court having jurisdiction of such civil or criminal cause is held, so far as the same is not inconsistent with the Constitution and laws of the United States, shall be extended to and govern the said courts in the trial and disposition of the cause. . . .

42 U.S.C. § 1988.

one statute of limitations applies to all personal injury claims, *Wilson* supplies a clear answer. Courts considering § 1983 claims in States with multiple statutes of limitations for personal injury actions, however, have differed over how to determine which statute applies. Several courts of appeals have held that the appropriate period is that which the State assigns to certain enumerated intentional torts. These courts have reasoned that intentional torts are most closely analogous to the claims Congress envisioned being brought under the Civil Rights Act, and to the paradigmatic claims brought today under § 1983. Other courts of appeals, by contrast, have endorsed the use of the state residuary statute of limitations for § 1983 actions. These courts have observed that § 1983 embraces a broad array of actions for injury to personal rights, and that the intentional tort is therefore too narrow an analogy to a § 1983 claim. The Court of Appeals for the Second Circuit followed this second approach when it concluded that New York's statute of limitations for certain enumerated intentional torts did not reflect the diversity of § 1983 claims.

B

In choosing between the two alternatives endorsed by the courts of appeals — the intentional torts approach and the general or residual personal injury approach — we are mindful that ours is essentially a practical inquiry. . . . Our decision in *Wilson* that one "simple broad characterization" of all § 1983 actions was appropriate under § 1988 was, after all, grounded in the realization that the potential applicability of different state statutes of limitations had bred chaos and uncertainty. *Id.*, at 275; *see also Burnett v. Grattan*, 468 U.S. 42, 50 (1984) (courts selecting a state statute of limitations for § 1983 actions must "take[e] into account practicalities that are involved in litigating federal civil rights claims"); *accord Felder v. Casey*, 487 U.S. 131 (1988). Thus, our task today is to provide courts with a rule for determining the appropriate personal injury limitations statute that can be applied with ease and predictability in all 50 States.

A rule endorsing the choice of the state statute of limitations for intentional torts would be manifestly inappropriate. Every State has multiple intentional tort limitations provisions, carving up the universe of intentional torts into different configurations. In New York, for example, § 215(3), the intentional tort statute endorsed by petitioners, covers eight enumerated torts. But different provisions cover other specified intentional torts. Malpractice actions are governed by one provision; certain veterans' claims, by another. . . . Were we to call upon courts to apply the state statute of limitations governing intentional torts, we would succeed only in transferring the present confusion over the choice among multiple personal injury provisions to a choice among multiple intentional tort provisions.

In marked contrast to the multiplicity of state intentional tort statutes of limitations, every State has one general or residual statute of limitations governing personal injury actions. Some States have a general provision which applies to all personal injury actions with certain specific exceptions. Others have a residual provision which applies to all actions not specifically provided for, including personal injury actions. Whichever form they take, these provisions are easily identifiable by language or application. Indeed, the very idea of a general or residual statute suggests that each State would have no more than one. Potential § 1983 plaintiffs and defendants therefore can readily ascertain, with little risk of confusion or unpredictability, the applicable limitations period in advance of filing a § 1983 action.

Petitioners' argument that courts should borrow the intentional tort limitations periods because intentional torts are most analogous to § 1983 claims fails to recognize the enormous practical disadvantages of such a selection. Moreover, this analogy is too imprecise to justify such a result. In *Wilson*, we expressly rejected the practice of drawing narrow analogies between § 1983 claims and state causes of action. 471 U.S., at 272. We explained that the Civil Rights Acts provided:

> [a] unique remedy mak[ing] it appropriate to accord the statute "a sweep as broad as its language." Because the § 1983 remedy is one that can "override certain kinds of state laws," *Monroe v. Pape*, 365 U.S. 167, 173 (1961), and is, in all events, "supplementary to any remedy any State might have," *McNeese v. Board of Education*, 373 U.S. 668, 672 (1963), it can have no precise counterpart in state law. *Monroe v. Pape*, 365 U.S., at 196, n. 5 (Harlan, J., concurring). Therefore, it is "the purest coincidence," *ibid.*, when state statutes or the common law provide for equivalent remedies; any analogies to those causes of action are bound to be imperfect.

Ibid.

The intentional tort analogy is particularly inapposite in light of the wide spectrum of claims which § 1983 has come to span. In *Wilson*, we noted that claims brought under § 1983 include:

> discrimination in public employment on the basis of race or the exercise of First Amendment rights, discharge or demotion without procedural due process, mistreatment of school children, deliberate indifference to the medical needs of prison inmates, the seizure of chattels without advance notice or sufficient opportunity to be heard.

Id., at 273 (footnotes omitted). *See also id.*, at 273, n. 31; Blackmun, *Section 1983 and Federal Protection of Individual Rights — Will the Statute Remain Alive or Fade Away?*, 60 N.Y.U. L. Rev. 1, 19-20 (1985).

Many of these claims bear little if any resemblance to the common-law intentional tort. Even where intent is an element of a constitutional claim or defense, the necessary intent is often different from the intent requirement of a related common-law tort. . . . Given that so many claims brought under § 1983 have no precise state-law analog, applying the statute of limitations for the limited category of intentional torts would be inconsistent with § 1983's broad scope.[11]

. . . .

We accordingly hold that where state law provides multiple statutes of limitations for personal injury actions, courts considering § 1983 claims should borrow the general or residual statute for personal injury actions.

III

The Court of Appeals therefore correctly applied New York's 3-year statute of limitations governing general personal injury actions to respondent Okure's claim. Our decision in *Wilson* promised an end to the confusion over what statute of limitations to apply to § 1983 actions; with today's decision, we hope to fulfill *Wilson*'s promise. Accordingly, the judgment of the Court of Appeals is Affirmed.

NOTES

(1) See also *423 S. Salina St., Inc. v. City of Syracuse*, 68 N.Y.2d 474, 510 N.Y.S.2d 507, 503 N.E.2d 63 (1986), holding (prior to the decision in the main case) that the three year period of CPLR 214(5) applies to a § 1983 action against a municipality, not the one-year and ninety-day period of Gen. Mun. Law § 50-i, which is otherwise applicable to a claim against it. The cited case also held, however, that § 1983 actions were subject to the "notice of claim" provision of Gen. Mun. Law § 50-e, and its attendant requirement that a notice be served within ninety days of the accrual of the claim (*see* § 7.09, *infra*). In the latter respect, *423 South Salina Street* was overruled by *Felder v. Casey*, 487 U.S. 131, 108 S. Ct. 2302, 101 L. Ed. 2d 123 (1988).

(2) In 1990 Congress adopted a uniform federal statute of limitations — but it applies only to causes of action created *after* the date of its enactment. *See* 28 U.S.C. § 1658, *enacted as* § 313 of the Judicial Improvements Act of 1990, P.L. 101-650 (1990). This section states: "Except as otherwise provided by law, a civil action arising under an Act of Congress enacted after the enactment of this section may not be commenced later than 4 years after the cause of action accrues." The Supreme Court has held that the four-year period of 28 U.S.C. § 1658 applies to all causes of action created by Congress after 1990, even if the new cause of action was added to an existing act of Congress by an amendment.

---

[11] The analogy to intentional torts also reflects a profound misunderstanding of § 1983's history. Section 1983 was the product of congressional concern about the Ku Klux Klan-sponsored campaign of violence and deception in the South, which was "denying decent citizens their civil and political rights." *Wilson*, 471 U.S., at 276; . . . . Although these violent acts often resembled the torts of assault, battery, false imprisonment, and misrepresentation, § 1983 was not directed at the perpetrators of these deeds as much as at the state officials who tolerated and condoned them.

See Jones v. R.R. Donnelley & Sons Co., 541 U.S. 369, 124 S. Ct. 1836, 158 L. Ed. 2d 645 (2004).

(3) Of course, when a state-created right is adjudicated in federal court pursuant to diversity jurisdiction, the state statute of limitations must be applied. *Guaranty Trust Co. of N.Y. v. York*, 326 U.S. 99, 65 S. Ct. 1464, 89 L. Ed. 2079 (1945). 28 U.S.C. § 1367 provides that a federal court with original jurisdiction in a civil matter may exercise supplemental jurisdiction over state claims bound up in the same "case or controversy." If the federal court declines to assert supplementary jurisdiction, the state claims may be commenced only in state court. What if the state statute of limitations has run? Section 1367(d) provides for a toll for the period when the claims are pending in federal court, and for 30 days after dismissal. In *Jinks v. Richland County*, 538 U.S. 456, 123 S. Ct. 1667, 155 L. Ed. 2d 631 (2003), the Supreme Court rejected the argument that the tolling provision violated state sovereignty principles and held it constitutional.

(4) A complaint alleging a violation of New York's anti-discrimination law, Executive Law § 296, is subject to the three-year period of CPLR 214(2), unless the claimant exercises the option of first seeking the aid of the State Division of Human Rights, in which case the statute of limitations is one year from the alleged unlawful discriminatory act. Executive Law § 297(5) applies. *Murphy v. Am. Home Products Corp.*, 58 N.Y.2d 293, 461 N.Y.S.2d 232, 448 N.E.2d 86 (1983).

§ 7.05 LACHES: THE JUDGE-MADE LIMITATION OF TIME

SOLOMON R. GUGGENHEIM FOUNDATION v. LUBELL
Court of Appeals
77 N.Y.2d 311, 567 N.Y.S.2d 623, 569 N.E.2d 426 (1991)

WACHTLER, J.

The backdrop for this replevin action (*see*, CPLR art 71) is the New York City art market, where masterpieces command extraordinary prices at auction and illicit dealing in stolen merchandise is an industry all its own. The Solomon R. Guggenheim Foundation, which operates the Guggenheim Museum in New York City, is seeking to recover a Chagall gouache worth an estimated $200,000. The Guggenheim believes that the gouache was stolen from its premises by a mailroom employee sometime in the late 1960s. The appellant Rachel Lubell and her husband, now deceased, bought the painting from a well-known Madison Avenue gallery in 1967 and have displayed it in their home for more than 20 years. Mrs. Lubell claims that before the Guggenheim's demand for its return in 1986, she had no reason to believe that the painting had been stolen.

On this appeal, we must decide if the museum's failure to take certain steps to locate the gouache is relevant to the appellant's Statute of Limitations defense. In effect, the appellant argues that the museum had a duty to use reasonable diligence to recover the gouache, that it did not do so, and that its cause of action in replevin is consequently barred by the Statute of Limitations. The Appellate Division rejected the appellant's argument. We agree with the Appellate Division that the timing of the museum's demand for the gouache and the appellant's refusal to return it are the only relevant factors in assessing the merits of the Statute of Limitations defense. We see no justification for undermining the clarity and predictability of this rule by carving out an exception where the chattel to be returned is a valuable piece of art. Appellant's affirmative defense of laches remains viable, however, and her claims that the museum did not undertake a reasonably diligent search for the missing painting will enter into the trial court's evaluation of the merits of that defense. Accordingly, the order of the Appellate Division should be affirmed.

The gouache, known alternately as Menageries or Le Marchand de Bestiaux (The Cattle Dealer), was painted by Marc Chagall in 1912, in preparation for an oil painting also entitled Le Marchand de Bestiaux. It was donated to the museum in 1937 by Solomon R. Guggenheim.

The museum keeps track of its collection through the use of "accession cards," which indicate when individual pieces leave the museum on loan, when they are returned and when they are transferred between the museum and storage. The museum lent the painting to a number of other art museums over the years. The last such loan occurred in 1961-1962. The accession card for the painting indicates that it was seen in the museum on April 2, 1965. The next notation on the accession card is undated and indicates that the painting could not be located.

Precisely when the museum first learned that the gouache had been stolen is a matter of some dispute. The museum acknowledges that it discovered that the painting was not where it should be sometime in the late 1960s, but claims that it did not know that the painting had in fact been stolen until it undertook a complete inventory of the museum collection beginning in 1969 and ending in 1970. According to the museum, such an inventory was typically taken about once every 10 years. The appellant, on the other hand, argues that the museum knew as early as 1965 that the painting had been stolen. It is undisputed, however, that the Guggenheim did not inform other museums, galleries or artistic organizations of the theft, and additionally, did not notify the New York City Police, the FBI, Interpol or any other law enforcement authorities. The museum asserts that this was a tactical decision based upon its belief that to publicize the theft would succeed only in driving the gouache further underground and greatly diminishing the possibility that it would ever be recovered. In 1974, having concluded that all efforts to recover the gouache had been exhausted, the museum's Board of Trustees voted to "deaccession" the gouache, thereby removing it from the museum's records.

Mr. and Mrs. Lubell had purchased the painting from the Robert Elkon Gallery for $17,000 in May of 1967. The invoice and receipt indicated that the gouache had been in the collection of a named individual, who later turned out to be the museum mailroom employee suspected of the theft. They exhibited the painting twice, in 1967 and in 1981, both times at the Elkon Gallery. In 1985, a private art dealer brought a transparency of the painting to Sotheby's for an auction estimate. The person to whom the dealer showed the transparency had previously worked at the Guggenheim and recognized the gouache as a piece that was missing from the museum. She notified the museum, which traced the painting back to the defendant. On January 9, 1986, Thomas Messer, the museum's director, wrote a letter to the defendant demanding the return of the gouache. Mrs. Lubell refused to return the painting and the instant action for recovery of the painting, or, in the alternative, $200,000, was commenced on September 28, 1987.

In her answer, the appellant raised as affirmative defenses the Statute of Limitations, her status as a good-faith purchaser for value, adverse possession, laches, and the museum's culpable conduct. The museum moved to compel discovery and inspection of the gouache and the defendant cross-moved for summary judgment. In her summary judgment papers, the appellant argued that the replevin action to compel the return of the painting was barred by the three-year Statute of Limitations because the museum had done nothing to locate its property in the 20-year interval between the theft and the museum's fortuitous discovery that the painting was in Mrs. Lubell's possession. The trial court granted the appellant's cross motion for summary judgment, relying on *DeWeerth v Baldinger* (836 F2d 103), an opinion from the United States Court of Appeals for the Second Circuit. The trial court cited New York cases holding that a cause of action in replevin accrues when demand is made upon the possessor and the possessor refuses to return the chattel. The court reasoned, however, that in order to avoid prejudice to a good-faith purchaser, demand cannot be unreasonably delayed and that a property owner has an obligation to use reasonable efforts to locate its missing property to ensure that demand is not so delayed. Because the museum in this case had done nothing for 20 years but search its own premises, the court found that its conduct was unreasonable as a matter of law. Consequently, the court granted Mrs. Lubell's cross motion for summary judgment on the grounds that the museum's cause of action was time barred.

The Appellate Division modified, dismissing the Statute of Limitations defense and denying the appellant's cross motion for summary judgment. The Appellate Division held that the trial court had erred. . . . [The Appellate Division also granted leave to appeal to the Court of Appeals. — Eds.]

New York case law has long protected the right of the owner whose property has been stolen to recover that property, even if it is in the possession of a good-faith purchaser for value (*see, Saltus & Saltus v Everett*, 20 Wend 267, 282). There is a three-year Statute of Limitations for recovery of a chattel (CPLR 214[3]). The rule in this State is that a cause of action for replevin against the good-faith purchaser of a stolen chattel accrues when the true owner makes demand for return of the chattel and the person in possession of the chattel refuses to return it (*see, e.g., Goodwin v Wertheimer*, 99 NY 149, 153; *Cohen v Keizer, Inc.*, 246 App Div 277). Until demand is made and refused, possession of the stolen property by the good-faith purchaser for value is not considered wrongful. . . . Although seemingly anomalous, a different rule applies when the stolen object is in the possession of the thief. In that situation, the Statute of Limitations runs from the time of the theft (*see, Sporn v MCA Records*, 58 NY2d 482, 487-488), even if the property owner was unaware of the theft at the time that it occurred (*see, Varga v Credit Suisse*, 5 AD2d 289, 292-293, *affd* 5 NY2d 865).

In *DeWeerth v Baldinger (supra)*, which the trial court in this case relied upon in granting Mrs. Lubell's summary judgment motion, the Second Circuit took note of the fact that New York case law treats thieves and good-faith purchasers differently and looked to that difference as a basis for imposing a reasonable diligence requirement on the owners of stolen art. Although the court acknowledged that the question posed by the case was an open one, it declined to certify it to this Court (*see*, 22 NYCRR 500.17), stating that it did not think that it "[would] recur with sufficient frequency to warrant use of the certification procedure" (836 F2d, at 108, n 5). Actually, the issue has recurred several times in the three years since *DeWeerth* was decided (*see, e.g., Republic of Turkey v Metropolitan Museum of Art*, No. 87 Civ 3750 [VLB], slip opn [SD NY July 16, 1990]), including the case now before us. We have reexamined the relevant New York case law and we conclude that the Second Circuit should not have imposed a duty of reasonable diligence on the owners of stolen art work for purposes of the Statute of Limitations.

While the demand and refusal rule is not the only possible method of measuring the accrual of replevin claims, it does appear to be the rule that affords the most protection to the true owners of stolen property. Less protective measures would include running the three-year statutory period from the time of the theft even where a good-faith purchaser is in possession of the stolen chattel, or, alternatively, calculating the statutory period from the time that the good-faith purchaser obtains possession of the chattel (*see generally*, Weil, *Repose*, 8 IFAR [Intl Found for Art Research] Rep, at 6-7 [Aug.-Sept. 1987]). Other States that have considered this issue have applied a discovery rule to these cases, with the Statute of Limitations running from the time that the owner discovered or reasonably should have discovered the whereabouts of the work of art that had been stolen (*see, e.g., O'Keefe v Snyder*, 83 NJ 478, 416 A2d 862; Cal Civ Proc Code § 338[c]).

New York has already considered — and rejected — adoption of a discovery rule. In 1986, both houses of the New York State Legislature passed Assembly Bill 11462-A (Senate Bill 3274-B), which would have modified the demand and refusal rule and instituted a discovery rule in actions for recovery of art objects brought against certain not-for-profit institutions. This bill provided that the three-year Statute of Limitations would run from the time these institutions gave notice, in a manner specified by the statute, that they were in possession of a particular object. Governor Cuomo vetoed the measure, however, on advice of the United States Department of State, the United States Department of Justice and the United States Information Agency. In his veto message, the Governor expressed his concern that the statute "[did] not provide a reasonable opportunity for individuals or foreign governments to receive notice of a museum's acquisition and take action to recover it before their rights are extinguished." The Governor also stated that he had been advised by the State Department that the bill, if it went into effect, would have caused New York to become "a haven for cultural property stolen abroad since such objects [would] be immune from recovery under the limited time periods established by the bill."

The history of this bill and the concerns expressed by the Governor in vetoing it, when considered together with the abundant case law spelling out the demand and refusal rule, convince us that that rule remains the law in New York and that there is no reason to obscure its straightforward protection of true owners by creating a duty of reasonable diligence. Our case law already recognizes that the true owner, having discovered the location of its lost property, cannot unreasonably delay making demand upon the person in possession of that property (*see, e.g., Heide v Glidden Buick Corp.*, 188 Misc 198). Here, however, where the demand and refusal is a substantive and not a procedural element of the cause of action (*see, Guggenheim Found. v Lubell*, 153 AD2d, at 147; *Menzel v List*, 22 AD2d 647; *compare*, CPLR 206 [where a demand is necessary to entitle a person to commence an action, the time to commence that action is measured from when the right to make demand is complete]), it would not be prudent to extend that case law and impose the additional duty of diligence before the true owner has reason to know where its missing chattel is to be found.

Further, the facts of this case reveal how difficult it would be to specify the type of conduct that would be required for a showing of reasonable diligence. Here, the parties hotly contest whether publicizing the theft would have turned up the gouache. According to the museum, some members of the art community believe that publicizing a theft exposes gaps in security and can lead to more thefts; the museum also argues that publicity often pushes a missing painting further underground. In light of the fact that members of the art community have apparently not reached a consensus on the best way to retrieve stolen art (*see*, Burnham, Art Theft: Its Scope, Its Impact and Its Control), it would be particularly inappropriate for this Court to spell out arbitrary rules of conduct that all true owners of stolen art work would have to follow to the letter if they wanted to preserve their right to pursue a cause of action in replevin. All owners of stolen property should not be expected to behave in the same way and should not be held to a common standard. The value of the property stolen, the manner in which it was stolen, and the type of institution from which it was stolen will all necessarily affect the manner in which a true owner will search for missing property. We conclude that it would be difficult, if not impossible, to craft a reasonable diligence requirement that could take into account all of these variables and that would not unduly burden the true owner.

Further, our decision today is in part influenced by our recognition that New York enjoys a worldwide reputation as a preeminent cultural center. To place the burden of locating stolen artwork on the true owner and to foreclose the rights of that owner to recover its property if the burden is not met would, we believe, encourage illicit trafficking in stolen art. Three years after the theft, any purchaser, good faith or not, would be able to hold onto stolen art work unless the true owner was able to establish that it had undertaken a reasonable search for the missing art. This shifting of the burden onto the wronged owner is inappropriate. In our opinion, the better rule gives the owner relatively greater protection and places the burden of investigating the provenance of a work of art on the potential purchaser.

Despite our conclusion that the imposition of a reasonable diligence requirement on the museum would be inappropriate for purposes of the Statute of Limitations, our holding today should not be seen as either sanctioning the museum's conduct or suggesting that the museum's conduct is no longer an issue in this case. We agree with the Appellate Division that the arguments raised in the appellant's summary judgment papers are directed at the conscience of the court and its ability to bring equitable considerations to bear in the ultimate disposition of the painting. As noted above, although appellant's Statute of Limitations argument fails, her contention that the museum did not exercise reasonable diligence in locating the painting will be considered by the Trial Judge in the context of her laches defense. The conduct of both the appellant and the museum will be relevant to any consideration of this defense at the trial level, and as the Appellate Division noted, prejudice will also need to be shown (153 AD2d, at 149). On the limited record before us there is no indication that the equities favor either party. Mr. and Mrs. Lubell investigated the provenance of the gouache before the purchase by contacting the artist and his son-in-law directly.

The Lubells displayed the painting in their home for more than 20 years with no reason to suspect that it was not legally theirs. These facts will doubtless have some impact on the final decision regarding appellant's laches defense. Because it is impossible to conclude from the facts of this case that the museum's conduct was unreasonable as a matter of law, however, Mrs. Lubell's cross motion for summary judgment was properly denied.

We agree with the Appellate Division, for the reasons stated by that court, that the burden of proving that the painting was not stolen properly rests with the appellant Mrs. Lubell. We have considered her remaining arguments, and we find them to be without merit. Accordingly, the order of the Appellate Division should be affirmed, with costs, and the certified question answered in the affirmative.

NOTES

(1) Does the Court's invocation of the laches doctrine unduly undermine its holding on the statute of limitations issue? How would you predict the lower courts would decide the laches question on remand?

(2) The laches doctrine may also bar an action for contribution if the party seeking it "delays unduly" in interposing the claim so as to prejudice the defendant. *Blum v. Good Humor Corp.*, 57 A.D.2d 911, 394 N.Y.S.2d 894 (2d Dep't 1977). The court held that laches could bar the assertion of a claim for contribution against an alleged joint tortfeasor when the action was commenced five years after the accident and more than thirteen months after the settlement of the underlying personal injury action was settled. What statute of limitations applies to a claim for contribution? When does the claim accrue? *See Cubito v. Kreisberg, supra,* § 7.02[A].

(3) See also *Krieger v. Krieger*, 25 N.Y.2d 364, 306 N.Y.S.2d 441, 254 N.E.2d 750 (1969), in which laches was applied to bar an action for a judgment declaring void a Florida divorce when the action was commenced twelve years after the divorce and a few months after defendant had remarried.

(4) In *Saratoga County Chamber of Commerce v. Pataki*, 100 N.Y.2d 801, 766 N.Y.S.2d 654, 798 N.E.2d 1047 (2003), the Court of Appeals invalidated a 1993 compact between the state and the St. Regis Mohawk Tribe allowing gambling on the Akwesasne Reservation under the Federal Indian Gaming Regulatory Act. The Court held that the compact was invalid because the Governor violated the separation of powers doctrine in signing the compact without legislative authority. Rejecting the defense's assertion of laches, the Court defined laches "as an equitable bar, based on a lengthy neglect or omission to assert a right and the resulting prejudice to an adverse party," which applies even where the statute of limitations period is met. 100 N.Y.2d at 816, 766 N.Y.S.2d at 662, 798 N.E.2d at 1055. As there was no evidence of economic losses to the tribe, so the Court refused to apply the doctrine of laches. The Court stated that "the prejudice caused by a loss of expected profits based on a predictably vulnerable compact is not the sort of prejudice that supports the defense of laches. Were it otherwise, very few suits would proceed past laches analysis, and certainly no suits seeking to invalidate illegal contracts could ever proceed." 100 N.Y.2d at 818, 766 N.Y.S.2d at 664, 798 N.E.2d at 1057.

§ 7.06 INTERPOSING THE CLAIM: CPLR 203

CPLR 203 sets forth the different ways in which a claim can be "interposed" for the purpose of satisfying a statute of limitations. The ordinary method of interposition is by filing the summons with notice or summons and complaint with the clerk of the court. CPLR 203(c); 304. Such filing interposes all claims contained in the complaint, even if it is not served with the summons.

Problems in relation to interposition arise when a defendant is "united in interest" with a co-defendant, CPLR 203(b), and when a claim in an amended pleading relates back to the original pleading, CPLR 203(f).

[A] Claims in Amended Pleadings: CPLR 203(f)

CAFFARO v. TRAYNA
Court of Appeals
35 N.Y.2d 245, 360 N.Y.S.2d 847, 319 N.E.2d 174 (1974)

JONES, J.

Does the fact that an independent action for wrongful death would be time-barred necessarily foreclose amendment of the complaint in a pending action for conscious pain and suffering to include the action for wrongful death? We hold that it does not.

During the period from September, 1966 to May, 1967 defendant physician treated the decedent for throat ailments. The treatment was not successful and in December, 1968 the decedent brought the present action in malpractice. While this action was pending, on June 24, 1969 the decedent died of carcinoma of the larynx, the condition which defendant allegedly had negligently failed to diagnose. For reasons which do not appear in this record, the decedent's will was not probated until September 18, 1972 on which day letters testamentary issued to the present plaintiff who was promptly substituted in the surviving action for personal injuries. It was not until the following January 15, however, that the substituted plaintiff moved to amend the complaint in the personal injuries action to add the cause of action for wrongful death. The present appeal is focused on the Appellate Division's affirmance of the denial of that motion to amend.

We recognize that historically the cause of action for wrongful death has been considered separate and distinct from the related cause of action for conscious pain and suffering. We also acknowledge that an independent action for wrongful death in this instance would have been time-barred by January 15, 1973 under the applicable Statute of Limitations — two years from the date of death (EPTL 5-4.1). Thus, unless the wrongful death action can be saved by inclusion with the surviving action for the decedent's personal injuries, it has been lost

. . . .

EPTL 11-3.3 (subd. [b], par. [2]), however, provides as follows: "Where an action to recover damages for personal injury has been brought, and the injured person dies, as a result of the injury, before verdict, report or decision, his personal representative may enlarge the complaint in such action to include the cause of action for wrongful death under 5-4.1." By this provision the Legislature has given the personal representative the right, if an action has already been brought for conscious pain and suffering, to join the related cause of action for wrongful death. The question for our determination is whether, when so joined, the cause of action for wrongful death would nonetheless be barred by the two-year Statute of Limitations if application for the joinder is made more than two years after the decedent's death.

. . . .

. . . Although not a part of the substantive right, the two-year statute would still operate as a procedural bar to the remedy were it not for the provisions of CPLR 203 (subd. [e]). [Now CPLR 203(f) — Eds.] That section provides: "A claim asserted in an amended pleading is deemed to have been interposed at the time the claims in the original pleading were interposed, unless the original pleading does not give notice of the transactions, occurrences, or series of transactions or occurrences, to be proved pursuant to the amended pleading." Thus, as to the cause of action for wrongful death to be added by amendment of the complaint, this section, if applicable, takes over for purposes of determining from what date the period of limitation shall be computed. Under it that date is related back to the date the action for conscious pain and suffering was commenced. So, here, the wrongful death cause of action is not barred if CPLR 203 (subd. [e]) is available.[1]

We turn then to the question of the applicability of CPLR 203 (subd. [e]) in the circumstances disclosed in this record. CPLR 203 (subd. [e]) applies "unless the original pleading does not give notice of the transactions, occurrences, or series of transactions or occurrences" on which the cause of action for wrongful death is predicated. No contention is advanced here that the pleadings in the personal injury action did not give the required notice of the transactions on which the wrongful death cause of action is based, and the record affords no ground for any such contention. Indeed, it would seem that any amendment authorized by EPTL 11-3.3 (subd. [b], par. [2]) — under which death must have resulted from the same injury on which the action for personal injuries is based — will necessarily meet the notice prerequisite of CPLR 203 (subd. [e]).

Thus, we conclude that by reason of the application, in combination, of EPTL 11-3.3 (subd. [b], par. [2]) and CPLR 203 (subd. [e]) the executrix of this decedent's estate had the right to amend the complaint in the surviving action for personal injuries to include the cause of action for wrongful death notwithstanding that the motion for such amendment was made more than two years after the decedent's death.

---

[1] In passing we note the apparent incongruity in considering a wrongful death action to have been interposed prior to death. CPLR 203 creates a legally effective fiction as to the date of interposition. As with other fictions in the law it does not unduly dismay us that the statutorily created fiction does not conform to the facts. Indeed the fiction is laid down for the very purpose of commanding a legal result which, without the fiction, would not follow from the facts.

We observe that policy considerations support the result dictated by our analysis of the relevant interrelated statutory provisions. Any Statute of Limitations reflects a policy that there must come a time after which fairness demands that a defendant should not be harried; the duration of the period is chosen with a balancing sense of fairness to the claimant that he shall not unreasonably be deprived of his right to assert his claim. Objectively, too, an inference is available that a genuine claim might normally be expected to have been made within the period of time selected. The balancing of these considerations (and perhaps others in certain instances) leads to the legislative choice of a specific time period. The recognition of such broad principles in the application of the relevant statutes here calls for permission to amend this complaint to include the wrongful death action. While considerations of fairness to the claimant estate might not require an extension beyond the customary two-year period following the claimant's death, and one might normally expect that means would have been found to assert this claim within that period, it cannot be said on this record that to allow the claim would work unfairness to this defendant. If there is here a provable claim, only unfairness to defendant or inescapable statutory mandate should foreclose assertion of that claim.

This defendant in any event will be required under the original pleadings to undertake defense of the issue of liability raised in the original malpractice action. Inclusion of the cause for wrongful death will not significantly expand the scope of proof or the relevant legal considerations on the issue of liability. The amendment will, of course, introduce new aspects on the issue of damages, but defendant does not suggest how the failure to bring this cause within two years after the decedent's death has prejudiced him in the assembly or introduction of evidence in support of his defense as to such additional elements of damage. There are not here considerations of judicial repose or foreclosure of stale claims so persuasive as to compel the recognition of a time-bar.

It is suggested in the dissent that a defendant may be prejudiced with respect to proof on the issue of causation of death. This particular defendant does not press this difficulty on us. As to the future, each defendant in a personal injury action will be alerted, after the announcement of today's decision, to the possibility, if the plaintiff dies, that the pending action may be enlarged to include the wrongful death claim even after the expiration of two years following death. Preparations for a possible defense then cannot be abandoned with the passage of two calendar years.

Even if it be accepted, as the dissenters suggest, that in the circumstances of this case no serious twinges of a sensitive conscience would be aroused if this particular claim for wrongful death were barred, the individual characteristics of a specific instance cannot be permitted to weigh heavily in the resolution of issues of statutory construction, the consequences of which will extend well beyond the particular case.

On our analysis, in sum, the inclusion of the claim for wrongful death is not "supplemental" in the sense that it is based on "subsequent transactions." The participation of the defendant, on which his liability, if any, must be predicated, had drawn to full conclusion before service of the complaint in the action for conscious pain and suffering. And by service of the original pleadings he was put fully on notice as to what it was claimed he had done or omitted or both for which it was then and is now asserted that he is liable. The injured person's death is simply an additional consequence of defendant's conduct for which he may be held responsible as surely would be true in more familiar instances of additionally discovered elements of damages.

We hold that it was error as a matter of law to have denied the motion to amend the complaint as proposed. Accordingly, the order of the Appellate Division should be reversed and the motion to amend should be granted.

CHIEF JUDGE BREITEL (dissenting).

The majority opinion draws a fine distinction to overcome the requirement, mandated in EPTL 5-4.1, that the wrongful death claim be brought within two years of death. With the statutory construction and policy considerations on which its analysis rests, however, I cannot agree. Most troublesome perhaps is the use of CPLR 203 (subd. [e]) to merge unjustifiably two disparate causes of action.

. . . .

It is staleness of proof to which Statutes of Limitation are primarily addressed, not to bar valid claims, but to prevent the assertion of claims, dubious, or difficult to disprove because of the lapse of time and its adverse effect on the availability and reliability of evidence (see 1 Weinstein-Korn-Miller, New York Civ. Prac., par. 201.01). Since the proximate cause of the death of plaintiff's testator is a decisive issue in the wrongful death action, one of the principal reasons for the two-year limitation period is to allow the defendant a reasonable opportunity to assemble evidence with respect to the circumstances surrounding death. . . . And there will in many instances, be a substantial issue of fact whether the death of the injured party was caused by the original malpractice. Thus, a physician charged with malpractice, notably only diagnostic malpractice, leading to wrongful death will have a valid concern with receiving timely notice of the event and circumstances of death, in order promptly to investigate and obtain evidence of the proximate cause of death and the likelihood of supervening malpractice or negligence by others. The two-year Statute of Limitations recognizes this concern, but is undermined by the ruling in this case.

. . . .

NOTES

(1) In *Goldberg v. Camp Mikan-Recro*, 42 N.Y.2d 1029, 398 N.Y.S.2d 1009, 369 N.E.2d 8 (1977), a father brought an action to recover for the wrongful death of his son. After the two-year statute of limitations had run, he served an amended

complaint asserting the same claim but in his new capacity as decedent's personal representative. Affirming a dismissal of the action, the court distinguished the principal case, stating:

> In this case . . . the original suit was not brought by one with the capacity to sue for the infant's personal injuries, the infant then being deceased and no personal representative of his estate having been appointed. Accordingly, when the [amended summons and complaint were] served . . . there was no pre-existing action to which it could "relate back. . . ."

(2) The principal case deals with an amendment to a complaint which already asserts a claim against the target of the new claim. What about claims against persons not previously a target of the claimant?

DUFFY v. HORTON MEMORIAL HOSPITAL
Court of Appeals
66 N.Y.2d 473, 497 N.Y.S.2d 890, 488 N.E.2d 820 (1985)

TITONE, JUSTICE.

The question presented is whether a plaintiff's direct claim against a third-party defendant, which is asserted in an amended complaint, relates back to the date of service of the third-party complaint for purposes of the Statute of Limitations, pursuant to CPLR 203(e) [now CPLR 203(f) — Eds.], where the third-party complaint and the amended complaint are based on the same transaction or occurrence. We hold that it does.

Plaintiff and her husband commenced this medical malpractice action in August 1979, alleging that defendants had failed to recognize and diagnose an early stage of the husband's lung cancer. The husband's condition deteriorated and he died in May 1981. Special Term subsequently granted plaintiff's motion for substitution and for an amendment of the complaint to add a wrongful death claim.

In June 1981, defendants brought a timely third-party action against Dr. Isidore Greenberg, the family physician who had treated the husband before and after a 1978 hospital examination. A deposition of Dr. Greenberg was conducted in October 1982, after which plaintiff sought to amend her complaint to name him as a defendant. Plaintiff urged that the claim was not barred by the Statute of Limitations because of the provisions of CPLR 203(e): "A claim asserted in an amended pleading is deemed to have been interposed, at the time the claims in the original pleading were interposed, unless the original pleading does not give notice of the transactions, occurrences, or series of transactions or occurrences, to be proved pursuant to the amended pleading."

. . . .

The language of the governing statute, CPLR 203(e), is not particularly helpful, since it does not state whether or not it is applicable to an amended complaint served upon someone not named in the original complaint. Analysis should, therefore, turn on the policy considerations underlying Statutes of Limitations (*see*, Friedenthal, Kane, Miller, Civil Procedure § 5.27; Green, Basic Civil Procedure, at 134-135 [2d ed.]; James & Hazard, Civil Procedure § 4.16 [3d ed.]).

We have emphasized that the primary purpose of a limitations period is fairness to a defendant (*Flanagan v. Mount Eden Gen. Hosp.*, 24 N.Y.2d 427, 429, 301 N.Y.S.2d 23, 248 N.E.2d 871). A defendant should "be secure in his reasonable expectation that the slate has been wiped clean of ancient obligations, and he ought not to be called on to resist a claim where the 'evidence has been lost, memories have faded, and witnesses have disappeared'" (*id.*, quoting *Developments in the Law: Statutes of Limitations*, 63 Harv.L.Rev. 1177, 1185). There is also the need to protect the judicial system from the burden of adjudicating stale and groundless claims.

An amendment which merely adds a new theory of recovery or defense arising out of a transaction or occurrence already in litigation clearly does not conflict with these policies (. . . *e.g.*, *Caffaro v. Trayna*, 35 N.Y.2d 245, 360 N.Y.S.2d 847, 319 N.E.2d 174. . . .)

The situation is far more difficult, however, when an amendment is sought to add a new party defendant. It is one thing to permit an amendment to relate back as applied to parties before the court. It is quite another thing to permit an amendment to relate back when a new party is sought to be added by the amendment against whom the Statute of Limitations has run. . . .

Thus, if the new defendant has been a complete stranger to the suit up to the point of the requested amendment, the bar of the Statute of Limitations must be applied. . . . But where, within the statutory period, a potential defendant is fully aware that a claim is being made against him with respect to the transaction or occurrence involved in the suit, and is, in fact, a participant in the litigation, permitting an amendment to relate back would not necessarily be at odds with the policies underlying the Statute of Limitations. . . . In such cases, there is room for the exercise of a sound judicial discretion to determine whether, on the facts, there is any operative prejudice precluding a retroactive amendment. . . .

It is evident that when a third party has been served with the third-party complaint, and all prior pleadings in the action as required by CPLR 1007, the third-party defendant has actual notice of the plaintiff's potential claim at that time. The third-party defendant must gather evidence and vigorously prepare a defense. There is no temporal repose. Consequently, an amendment of the complaint may be permitted, in the court's discretion, and a direct claim asserted against the third-party defendant, which, for the purposes of computing the Statute of Limitations period, relates back to the date of service of the third-party complaint (*see*, McLaughlin, Practice Commentaries, McKinney's Cons. Laws of N.Y., Book 7B, C203:11, p. 124; Siegel, N.Y.Prac. § 49, at 17-18 [1985 Supp.]; 6 Wright and Miller, Federal Practice & Procedure § 1498).

In this case, both Special Term and the Appellate Division erred in denying the motion to amend solely upon the ground that the claim would be barred by the Statute of Limitations. Accordingly, we must remit the matter to the Appellate Division to give that court the opportunity to exercise its discretion in determining whether an amendment is warranted. . . .

NOTES

(1) The defendant named in the amended complaint in the principal case had been made a third-party defendant prior to the expiration of the statute of limitations. Suppose he had not been made a defendant in any respect before that time? In *Liverpool v. Arverne Houses, Inc.*, 67 N.Y.2d 878, 879, 501 N.Y.S.2d 802, 802-03, 492 N.E.2d 1218, 1218 (1986), the plaintiff sought to amend his complaint and add a new defendant, after the statute of limitations had run. The attempt was rejected by the Court of Appeals, which said:

> Inasmuch as the party sought to be added as a defendant . . . was a stranger to the litigation prior to the expiration of the applicable Statutes of Limitations, plaintiff's claim against that party was necessarily barred as untimely.

In a subsequent case, the Court held that a motion to add a new party tolls the statute of limitations as to the new party from the date the notice of motion is filed until the date it is decided. *Perez v. Paramount Commc'ns, Inc.*, 92 N.Y.2d 749, 686 N.Y.S.2d 342, 709 N.E.2d 433 (1999).

(2) Although an amended complaint which adds a claim against a new party cannot relate back for the purpose of measuring the timeliness of the claim against the new party, the plaintiff may nonetheless be protected if the second defendant is "united in interest" with the first. The following principal case deals with this issue.

(3) As to timeliness of counterclaims, see CPLR 203(d), (e). By the terms of CPLR 203(d), "It is axiomatic that claims and defenses that arise out of the same transaction as a claim asserted in the complaint are not barred by the Statute of Limitations, even though an independent action by defendant might have been time-barred at the time the action was commenced." *Bloomfield v. Bloomfield*, 97 N.Y.2d 188, 193, 738 N.Y.S.2d 650, 652, 764 N.E.2d 950, 952 (2001). Accordingly, in a divorce action, defendant wife was not barred from challenging the validity of a 30-year-old prenuptial agreement, since the agreement directly related to the plaintiff husband's claim that the agreement precluded equitable distribution.

[B] Service on a Co-Defendant "United in Interest": CPLR 203(b), (c)

BURAN v. COUPAL
Court of Appeals
87 N.Y.2d 173, 638 N.Y.S.2d 405, 661 N.E.2d 978 (1995)

CHIEF JUDGE KAYE:

This case calls upon us to address a doctrine which "continues to bedevil the courts" (McLaughlin, 1990 Supplementary Practice Commentaries, McKinney's Cons Laws of NY, Book 7B, CPLR 203, 1995 Supp Pamph, at 28). Under what circumstances does an amended complaint adding a new defendant, united in interest with the original defendant, relate back to the initial complaint for statute of limitations purposes? In particular, must the party seeking leave of court to add a new defendant show "excusable mistake" for the failure to have named the new party originally, or is a mistake alone enough?

Concluding that New York law requires merely mistake — not excusable mistake — on the part of the litigant seeking the benefit of the doctrine, we hold that plaintiffs' second complaint relates back to their original complaint and is therefore timely, thus defeating defendants' claim of adverse possession.

I

In 1962, plaintiffs Robert and Arlene Buran purchased a one-acre lot in Beekmantown, New York the deed to which conveys property rights extending north into the waters of Lake Champlain. Five years later, defendants John and Janet Coupal obtained property known locally as Dickson's Farm which abuts the Burans' lot at its northeast corner. Since — unlike the Burans' waterfront property — Lake Champlain is not otherwise accessible from Dickson's Farm, the Coupals in 1973 erected a concrete seawall jutting diagonally across the border of their own lot and over the Burans' property into the waters of the lake.

Unhappy with the seawall, the Burans in 1979 brought a lawsuit for trespass, naming only John Coupal as defendant. Though omitting any reference to his wife in his first two answers, in September 1982, John Coupal filed an "amended" answer, for the first time arguing that he owned the lot with his wife as a tenant in the entirety and that the Burans' complaint should be dismissed for failure to name Janet Coupal as a necessary party. Shortly after filing this answer, however, the Coupals transferred ownership of their lot to Ultimate Investment Services Incorporated, Ltd., a corporation they owned and controlled.

After the Burans served a summons on Ultimate Investment, the lot was in 1984 reconveyed to the Coupals. The Burans then filed a second complaint in 1989, this time against Janet Coupal as co-owner. Both complaints contained substantially the same allegations as to the nature of the Coupals' trespass, the only substantive difference being the addition of Janet Coupal as a party defendant. As an affirmative defense to the second lawsuit, Coupal asserted that she and her husband were by then the owners of the disputed property, having adversely possessed it for a period of ten years.

After consolidation of the two actions in 1992 and a jury trial, Supreme Court ordered removal of the seawall within 120 days and restoration of the land to the Burans, and the Appellate Division affirmed. Both lower courts rejected defendants' contention that Janet Coupal had become owner of the property under the doctrine of adverse possession. Focusing, as did the Appellate Division, on the legal question whether plaintiffs' 1989 complaint against Janet Coupal relates back to the allegations contained in the 1979 complaint against her husband,[1] we agree that defendants failed to meet their burden of proving the affirmative defense of adverse possession.

II

As codified in New York's Civil Practice Law and Rules, what is commonly referred to as the relation back doctrine allows a claim asserted against a defendant in an amended filing to relate back to claims previously asserted against a co-defendant for statute of limitations purposes where the two defendants are "united in interest" (CPLR 203[b]; *see also*, CPLR 203[e] [relation back of new claims against same party]). Aimed at liberalizing the strict, formalistic pleading requirements of the past century (*see, Shaw v. Cock*, 78 N.Y.194; *Harriss v. Tams*, 258 N.Y. 229) or the "sporting theory of justice" condemned by Roscoe Pound (*see, Schiavone v. Fortune*, 477 U.S. 21, 32-33), while at the same time respecting the important policies inherent in statutory repose (*see, Duffy v. Horton Mem. Hosp.*, 66 N.Y.2d 473, 476-477), the doctrine enables a plaintiff to correct a pleading error — by adding either a new claim or a new party — after the statutory limitations period has expired. The doctrine thus gives courts the "sound judicial discretion" (*Duffy*, 66 N.Y.2d at 477) to identify cases "that justify relaxation of limitations strictures * * * to facilitate decisions on the merits" if the correction will not cause undue prejudice to the plaintiff's adversary (Harold S. Lewis, *The Excessive History of Federal Rule 15(c) and Its Lessons for Civil Rules Revision*, 85 Mich. L. Rev. 1507, 1512 [1987]).

As we observed in *Duffy v. Horton Memorial Hospital* (66 N.Y.2d 473), however, allowing the relation back of amendments adding new defendants implicates more seriously these policy concerns than simply the relation back of new causes of action since, in the latter situation, the defendant is already before the court (*id.*, at 477). Recognizing this difference, in *Mondello v. New York Blood Ctr.* (80 N.Y.2d 219, 226), we recently adopted the three-part test enunciated in

---

[1] Given our conclusion that the relation back doctrine applies to the circumstances of this appeal, we need not reach the ground principally relied upon by the trial court in dismissing the Coupals' adverse possession defense — that the two-year interval during which Ultimate Investment held title to Dickson's Farm defeated any claim of adverse possession.

Brock v. Bua (83 A.D.2d 61) now prevailing in the Federal and State courts for determining when the doctrine would permit the addition of a new party to relate back to an earlier pleading.

Under this standard, the three conditions that must be satisfied in order for claims against one defendant to relate back to claims asserted against another are that:

> (1) both claims arose out of same conduct, transaction or occurrence, (2) the new party is "united in interest" with the original defendant, and by reason of that relationship can be charged with such notice of the institution of the action that he will not be prejudiced in maintaining an action on the merits and (3) the new party knew or should have known that, but for an excusable mistake by plaintiff as to the identity of the proper parties, the action would have been brought against him as well.

Mondello involved claims of negligence brought first against a hospital and later against a blood bank arising from plaintiffs' infection with the HIV virus after receiving a blood transfusion. In applying the *Brock* test to the facts of that case and rejecting the argument that the hospital and the blood bank were sufficiently united in interest to support application of the doctrine, we had no occasion to consider the scope of the requirement under the third prong, or whether the failure of plaintiff's counsel to name the blood bank originally was "excusable" (80 N.Y.2d at 230). Here, by contrast, since it is undisputed that the first and second prongs of the *Brock* test are satisfied,[2] we now address the issue explicitly left open in *Mondello* and decide that excusability of the mistake is not an absolute requirement under New York law (*see, Virelli v GoodsonTodman Enterprises Ltd.*, 142 A.D.2d 479, 482-484 [applying *Brock*'s third prong, but declining to accept excusability requirement]).

Though patterned largely after the Federal relation back rule (*Mondello*, 80 N.Y.2d at 226), the test articulated in *Brock* differs from its Federal counterpart in one crucial respect: it contains, as an additional requirement, that plaintiff's omission of the party in the original pleading be excusable. In marked contrast to *Brock*'s third prong, rule 15(c) of the Federal Rules of Civil Procedure merely requires that "the new party knew or should have known that, but for a mistake concerning the identity of the proper party, the action would have been brought against the party" (Fed R Civ P 15[c][3][B]). Thus, unlike *Brock*, "the Federal rule does not qualify the nature of the mistake" (*Virelli*, 142 A.D.2d at 483; *see also, B.S. Livingston Export Corp. v M/V Ogden Fraser*, 727 F. Supp. 144, 146 ["The only additional condition precedent to invoking the New York relation back doctrine is excusable neglect."]).

Underscoring the difference is the fact that, though omitted from the text of Rule 15(c), language similar to "excusable mistake" is used in other provisions

---

[2] As husband and wife and tenants by the entirety/co-owners of the Dickson Farm who are jointly and severally liable for each other's acts with respect to the property, it is plain that the Coupals are "united in interest" for purposes of the relation back doctrine. . . .

of the Federal Rules. Rule 6, for example, permits parties to make late filings "where the failure to act was the result of *excusable neglect*" (Fed. R. Civ. P. 6[b] [emphasis added]; *see also*, Fed. R. Civ. P. 13[f] [amended counterclaim may be filed upon showing of excusable neglect]). It is thus plain that, at least with respect to the Federal rule on which New York's own three-part test was premised, there is no requirement of "excusable" mistake (*see also, Schiavone v. Fortune*, 477 U.S. 21, 31).

In fact, the "excusable mistake" requirement appears to have originated as a judicial gloss imposed on rule 15(c) in a category of Federal decisions denying plaintiffs the benefit of the doctrine on grounds that they deliberately failed to identify the proper party who was known to them at the time (*see, e.g., Bruce v. Smith*, 581 F. Supp. 902; *Jacobs v. McCloskey & Co.*, 40 F.R.D. 486), or where the proposed new defendant had no notice of the pendency of the action such that the defendant could not reasonably have expected to have been sued (*see, e.g., Kilkenny v. Arco Marine Inc.*, 800 F.2d 853; *Keller v. Prince George's County*, 923 F.2d 30). In both situations, the courts properly rejected application of the doctrine on the ground either that there was no "mistake" — *i.e.*, that plaintiffs knew of the existence of the proper parties at the time of their initial filing, or that application of the doctrine would unduly prejudice the defendant's rights. As described in a passage from Moore's Federal Practice cited in *Brock* (83 A.D.2d at 69), these cases rest on the sound conclusion that:

> it is often plaintiff's own dilatory conduct that is most relevant in assessing whether the prospective party knew, or should have known, that plaintiff simply made a mistake in failing to name the prospective party as a defendant. Thus, plaintiff's own inexcusable neglect would appear to be a proper consideration in a Rule 15(c) determination (3 Moore, Federal Practice § 15.15[4], at 15-168 [2d ed. 1995]).

Despite the existence of this judicially-created exception to the doctrine for reasons of lack of notice or bad faith, it is apparent that apart from excusability of the mistake, the *Brock* test already provides an independent ground for denying application of the doctrine in these cases — absence of mistake under the first prong or operative prejudice to the defendant under the second. Adding the word "excusable" to the third prong effectively converts what are already valid considerations under the first and second prongs into an independent factor under the third (*see, Bruce v. Smith*, 581 F. Supp. 902, 906; Note, *Schiavone v. Fortune: A Clarification of the Relation Back Doctrine*, 36 Cath. U. L. Rev. 499, 511 [1987]).

Moreover, addition of the word "excusable" also improperly de-emphasizes what the United States Supreme Court has called the "linchpin" of the relation back doctrine — notice to the defendant within the applicable limitations period (*Schiavone v. Fortune*, 477 U.S. 21, 31). As explained in *Virelli*, *Brock*'s "excuse qualification * * * shifts the focus away from the primary question of whether the new party had actual notice of the claim" (142 A.D.2d at 483).

Indeed, requiring courts to determine in each case whether plaintiff's mistake was "excusable" unwisely focuses attention away from what *Brock* assumed to be the primary consideration in such cases — whether the defendant could have reasonably concluded that the failure to sue within the limitations period meant that there was no intent to sue that person at all "and that the matter has been laid to rest as far as he is concerned" (*Brock*, 83 A.D.2d at 70).

Even more troubling, however, is that the excusability test often punishes the plaintiff for even minor drafting errors — precisely the situation that warrants application of the doctrine. As *Virelli* observed in rejecting addition of the word "excusable" to the third prong, "[p]laintiff's only explanation for the misidentification is that the attorney who drafted the summons and complaint had never seen the descriptive announcement. [S]imilar excuses have been rejected outright in *Brock* and its progeny" (142 A.D.2d at 483). Indeed, the practical effect for New York litigants has been to render the relation back doctrine meaningless in all but rare circumstances (*see, e.g., Sandor v. Somerstown Plaza Assocs.*, 210 A.D.2d 212 [relying on third prong in dismissing plaintiff's claims]; . . . .) Surely, such a result is not in keeping with modern theories of notice pleading and the admonition that the Civil Practice Law and Rules "be liberally construed to secure the just, speedy and inexpensive determination of every judicial proceeding" (CPLR 104).

This is not to say, however, that removing the excusability requirement from the third prong would prevent a court from refusing to apply the doctrine in cases where the plaintiff omitted a defendant in order to obtain a tactical advantage in the litigation. When a plaintiff intentionally decides not to assert a claim against a party known to be potentially liable, there has been no mistake and the plaintiff should not be given a second opportunity to assert that claim after the limitations period has expired (*see*, Note, *The Relation Back Doctrine of Claims Against Third-Party Defendants*, 7 Cardozo L. Rev. 281, 304 [1985]). Similarly, a court would be justified in denying a plaintiff the benefit of the doctrine in order to prevent delay or disruption in the normal course of the lawsuit. Application of the doctrine in such circumstances would likely result in prejudice to the adversary and, as noted above, bar application of the doctrine under the second prong.

III

Applying these principles to the facts before us, we agree with the Appellate Division that the trial court acted within its discretion in permitting relation back of the 1989 complaint against Janet Coupal to the 1979 claims against her husband. In that it is undisputed that Janet Coupal had notice of the action against her husband, the question whether the Burans' mistake in failing to name her initially was "excusable" was immaterial. Adding her as a party resulted in no delay or prejudice. As co-owner of the property, Janet Coupal was at all times united in interest with her husband who was timely served and had a full opportunity to make an investigation within the limitations period.

In fact, any prejudice or bad faith in this case is attributable entirely to the acts of the defendants. At the very time that John Coupal was amending his answer to add the defense that his wife was a necessary party, he and his wife were transferring their property to Ultimate Investment in an obvious effort to delay resolution of the Burans' claims. Thus, given that Janet Coupal was aware that trespass allegations were being made against her with respect to the disputed seawall at least as early as 1982 when she actively participated in transferring (and later re-transferring) the property, the claims against her were properly permitted to proceed on their merits.

Accordingly, the order of the Appellate Division should be affirmed, with costs.

NOTES

(1) There is little difficulty in concluding that the defendant Janet Coupal was "united in interest" with her husband and co-owner of the property at issue (*see* footnote 2 of the Court's opinion). A more expansive treatment of this sometimes knotty issue was given in *Connell v. Hayden*, 83 A.D.2d 30, 443 N.Y.S.2d 383 (2d Dep't 1981). The court explained:

The classic attempt at formulating a criterion for assessing unity of interest is contained in *Prudential Ins. Co. v. Stone*, 270 N.Y. 154, 159, 200 N.E. 679 in which the Court of Appeals stated that "[i]f the interest of the parties in the subject-matter is such that they stand or fall together and that judgment against one will similarly affect the other then they are 'otherwise united in interest.'" While this formulation says much, it also leaves much unsaid.

. . . The rationale behind [the rule] is that where the two defendants are united in interest their defenses will be the same and they will either stand or fall together with respect to plaintiff's claim. Timely service upon one of two such defendants gives sufficient notice to enable him to investigate all the defenses which are available to both defendants within the period of limitations. From this the rule has evolved that where one defendant "may" have a defense which is not available to the other, they cannot be said to be united in interest. . . . The mere possibility that a defendant who was served late could have such a different defense is all that is required because, the Statute having run, it is now too late for him to conduct an investigation into the viability of that defense. To determine unity of interest, therefore, one looks not to whether the two defendants will assert different defenses but rather whether they could assert such different defenses.

The *Connell* court gave these examples of parties "united in interest": (1) two tortfeasors, but only when one is vicariously liable for the tort of the other; (2) partners liable under substantive law for torts committed within the scope of the partnership; (3) business corporations and employees who commit torts in the course of their employment. Joint tortfeasors are not united in interest in the absence of vicarious liability because each has a separate defense, and this is so even if they are co-employees of the same corporation, unless one is the supervisor of the other. Hence, two physicians employed by a professional corporation are not united in interest with each other.

(2) Suppose two parties are united in interest and the summons (timely filed) is served on only one of them but names both. Note that while 203(b) may protect the plaintiff against a time bar, it does not affect jurisdiction. Hence, the second defendant must at some point be served with a summons. CPLR 305.

§ 7.07 TOLLS AND EXTENSIONS

[A] The Absence Toll: CPLR 207

PROBLEM D

Paul had an unfortunate encounter with a cantankerous waffle iron manufactured by WIRCO, a foreign corporation not authorized to do business in New York. Suppose Paul, who bought the iron in Boston, was injured by it while still there, on April 5, 2002. Would a products liability action be timely if commenced against WIRCO in the Supreme Court, Albany County, on June 6, 2006, by filing a summons and complaint with the clerk of that court and attaching a bank account maintained by WIRCO in New York? Assume that WIRCO would not be subject to jurisdiction in New York but for the attachment. Before answering, read carefully the first paragraph of CPLR 207 as well as subdivision (3) of CPLR 207.

YARUSSO v. ARBOTOWICZ
Court of Appeals
41 N.Y.2d 516, 393 N.Y.S.2d 968, 362 N.E.2d 600 (1977)

JONES, J.

We hold that when statutory authorization exists for obtaining personal jurisdiction by some manner other than personal delivery of the summons within the State — here, sections 253 and 254 of the Vehicle and Traffic Law — the Statute of Limitations is not tolled under CPLR 207 by defendant's absence from the State, even though plaintiff may in fact be unsuccessful in obtaining jurisdiction by the manner so provided. Further, uncompleted service under the Vehicle and Traffic Law sections on the Secretary of State, successfully challenged by defendant for lack of personal jurisdiction, does not stop the running of the limitation period.

The present action stems from an automobile accident that occurred on November 24, 1968 in Nassau County. Although defendant was a resident of New York at the time of the accident, in November, 1970 he left the State on the vessel *Moonmist* and traveled to the State of Florida where he resided on the vessel, moored at a North Miami Beach marina, until February, 1971, when he moved to an apartment at 3586 North West 43rd Street, Miami, where he remained until the following February. Other than for a brief visit to New York in February, 1972, defendant never returned to this State until January, 1974, when he took up the residence he has since maintained with his father at Port Washington.

Plaintiff made several attempts to secure jurisdiction over defendant for a personal injury action. On September 29, 1971, pursuant to the provisions of sections 253 and 254 of the Vehicle and Traffic Law, he sent the summons and complaint to the New York Secretary of State and mailed copies by registered mail, return receipt requested, to defendant at the North Miami Beach marina. Because defendant had left the *Moonmist* seven months earlier, the envelope addressed to him was returned marked "Return to sender, Not here. Unknown." On November 22, 1971 plaintiff again sought to obtain jurisdiction by resort to the Vehicle and Traffic Law provisions, this time addressing copies of the papers mailed to the Secretary of State to defendant at "3586 North West 41st Street, Miami, Florida." This latter mailing was returned by the Postal Service marked "addressee unknown," for, as noted, defendant resided on 43rd Street, not 41st Street, in Miami.

When, on May 15, 1974, plaintiff moved for default judgment on the basis of defendant's failure to respond to the service purportedly made in compliance with the Vehicle and Traffic Law provisions in 1971, defendant successfully cross-moved for dismissal of the action for lack of personal jurisdiction on the ground that service on him was never completed. No appeal was ever taken from the dismissal of this first action for want of personal jurisdiction.

While these cross motions were pending, on July 9, 1974 a summons and complaint were personally served on defendant at his then New York residence. Defendant then moved for summary judgment dismissing the second action, predicated on the service within the State on July 9, 1974, on the ground that it was time-barred. The denial of that motion by Special Term was affirmed at the Appellate Division. . . .

CPLR 207, on which plaintiff relies for his claims of tolling of the three-year Statute of Limitations otherwise applicable here and of the timeliness of the present action, contains a provision by which the section — which tolls the Statute of Limitations during substantial absence of the defendant from the State — is made inapplicable "while jurisdiction over the person of the defendant can be obtained without personal delivery of the summons to him within the state" (subd 3). The present case comes squarely within this language, with the result that the benefit of the statutory toll is not available to plaintiff.

At least two methods of obtaining personal jurisdiction over this defendant, without personal delivery of process within the State, were available to plaintiff. Because the alleged negligence of defendant in the operation of a motor vehicle was a tortious act committed within the State, personal jurisdiction could have been acquired under CPLR 313 and 302 by service in Florida, after defendant had transferred his residence there, in any manner in which service can be made in this State. Alternatively, plaintiff could have elected — as he did — to pursue the method of service provided by the Vehicle and Traffic Law for claims arising from automobile accidents occurring in this State. The fact that plaintiff's investigation was not adequate to uncover defendant's correct addresses made means and methods of out-of-State service no less available to plaintiff for the purpose of CPLR 207 (subd 3).

It has been suggested that the words "jurisdiction over the person . . . can be obtained" in CPLR 207 (subd 3) should be read as contemplating effective service in fact (or at least a substantial practical expectation that service can be effected), rather than merely the availability of an authorized method of service by which personal jurisdiction could be obtained. We reject what appears to us to be the too narrow reading of the statutory language implicit in this suggestion. The only conclusive test, of course, as to whether jurisdiction could be obtained in the operational sense would be whether in fact it had been obtained in the particular instance. Had that been the legislative intent, subdivision 3 would have been purposeless; tolling of a Statute of Limitations in that sense always occurs when jurisdiction is obtained. The broader, literal interpretation requiring only the availability of an authorized method of service comports with the treatment accorded resident defendants and conforms to policy considerations. As a matter of principle, considering the availability and practicality of long-arm jurisdiction, we see no reason to differentiate among resident, non-resident and former resident defendants. In general it is not significantly more difficult (if indeed it is more difficult at all) to locate persons residing outside the State of New York than those within its borders.

Accordingly, we are in agreement to the extent indicated with the position taken in *Goodemote v. McClain* (40 AD2d 22), but rejected by Special Term and the Appellate Division in this case, that the availability of statutory methods of acquiring personal jurisdiction other than by personal delivery within the State makes inapplicable the tolling provisions of CPLR 207.

. . . .

Accordingly, the order of the Appellate Division should be reversed. . . .

NOTES

(1) At the time the principal case was decided, a claim was interposed by service of the summons, not by filing the summons with the clerk of the court.

What, if anything is the relevance of the case now that an action is commenced by filing?

(2) In *Chapin v. Posner*, 299 N.Y. 31, 85 N.E.2d 172 (1949), it was held that under the predecessor to CPLR 207, the statute of limitations was tolled, even though personal jurisdiction over the defendant was not required to maintain the action because the res was in the state. Is this rule still valid? The legislative history of CPLR 207 is inconclusive. *See* 1 Weinstein, Korn & Miller, New York Civil Practice ¶ 207.02. What impact might *Shaffer v. Heitner*, 433 U.S. 186, 97 S. Ct. 2569, 53 L. Ed. 2d 683 (1977), have on this question? Does the principal case offer any arguments on either side of the issue?

(3) Suppose X is assaulted in New York by Y, a non-resident, whose address is unknown to X. Does the toll apply under the holding of the principal case? *See also* CPLR 308(5).

(4) If the defendant never comes into the state, and there is neither personal nor property-based jurisdiction available, when does the statute of limitations begin to run?

(5) In *G.D. Searle & Co. v. Cohn*, 455 U.S. 404, 102 S. Ct. 1137, 71 L. Ed. 2d 250 (1982), the Supreme Court considered a constitutional challenge to New Jersey's absence toll. That statute tolls the period of limitations against foreign corporations not represented in New Jersey by a person upon whom service may be made, even if New Jersey jurisdiction may be acquired by serving the corporation outside the state. In the instant case, a products liability action, the plaintiff commenced her action eleven years after the claimed injury. The Court held that the statute did not offend the Equal Protection Clause. Applying the rational basis test, the Court stated that the toll was justified because of the difficulty in locating and serving a corporation which could not be served in the state. The Court remanded so that the lower courts could rule on the defendants' claim that the Commerce Clause was violated by the New Jersey statute. Subsequently, the statute was declared unconstitutional on Commerce Clause grounds. *Coons v. Am. Honda Motor Co.*, 94 N.J. 307, 463 A.2d 921 (1983), *cert. denied*, 469 U.S. 1123 (1985).

An Ohio statute which was similar to that of New Jersey was also declared invalid as violative of the Commerce Clause. *Bendix Autolite Corp. v. Midwesco Enters., Inc.*, 486 U.S. 888, 108 S. Ct. 2218, 100 L. Ed. 2d 896 (1988). The Court reasoned that the statute improperly discriminated against out of state entities by depriving them of the protection of the statute of limitations unless they appointed an agent for the service of process in Ohio. State interests which might have justified this discrimination for equal protection purposes were held insufficient under the Commerce Clause.

[B] The New Action Toll: CPLR 205

ANDREA v. ARNONE, HEDIN, CASKER, KENNEDY & DRAKE, ARCHITECTS & LANDSCAPE ARCHITECTS, P.C.
Court of Appeals
5 N.Y.3d 514, 806 N.Y.S.2d 453, 840 N.E.2d 565 (2005)

R.S. SMITH, J.

We hold that dismissal of an action for failure to comply with discovery orders is a dismissal "for neglect to prosecute the action" within the meaning of CPLR 205(a). Therefore, these actions, filed after the dismissal of previous actions by the same plaintiffs, are not saved by CPLR 205(a) from the bar of the statute of limitations.

Facts and Procedural History

The Jefferson Middle School in Jamestown was renovated in 1992. In 1994 and 1995, more than 60 plaintiffs brought four lawsuits against more than 20 defendants, alleging that employees and students at the school had been injured by toxic substances released in the course of the renovation.

The first of several scheduling orders in these cases was entered in July 1995. By 1996, plaintiffs were in default in responding to several of defendants' discovery demands. Supreme Court then imposed more deadlines for discovery, but the deadlines were not met, and defendants moved to dismiss. In a December 1998 opinion, Supreme Court wrote that "plaintiffs' counsel have demonstrated such a disregard for the case management order and scheduling order that one would not believe such orders existed," but nevertheless denied the motion, reluctant to penalize "innocent plaintiffs who may have [a] meritorious case" for their counsel's conduct. Instead, Supreme Court ordered a hearing on monetary sanctions and imposed a new set of deadlines which, though extended, were again not met. Defendants again moved to dismiss.

In a July 1999 opinion, Supreme Court found "that the actions of plaintiffs' counsel have been frivolous . . . in that they have been undertaken primarily to delay or prolong resolution of this litigation." Supreme Court said that "dismissal of the actions would not be unfounded," but it gave plaintiffs one more chance, permitting them to avoid dismissal if they paid attorneys' fees to defendants and complied with yet another set of deadlines. The attorneys' fees were paid but the deadlines were not met, and on May 19, 2000 Supreme Court dismissed the actions. Plaintiffs appealed, and the Appellate Division affirmed the dismissal on June 8, 2001 (*Andrea v E.I. Du Pont De Nemours & Co.*, 284 A.D.2d 921, 725 N.Y.S.2d 904 [4th Dept 2001]).

Meanwhile, on December 19, 2000, 34 of the same plaintiffs brought the present two actions, based on the same events as the four earlier ones, against 13 of the same defendants. Two defendants moved to dismiss the new actions on the ground that they were barred by the statute of limitations. Supreme Court denied the motions, relying on CPLR 205(a), which permits actions brought after dismissal of a prior action to have, under certain circumstances, the benefit of the earlier filing date. Supreme Court rejected the argument that CPLR 205(a) was inapplicable because the previous actions were dismissed for neglect to prosecute; Supreme Court said that "it was never this Court's intention to dismiss the prior actions for failure to prosecute." Later, the remaining defendants moved to dismiss, and Supreme Court denied their motions also.

The Appellate Division reversed in two separate decisions, from the first of which two Justices dissented, and ordered that these actions be dismissed. Plaintiffs appeal to this Court, and we now affirm.

Discussion

These actions, begun some eight years after the events on which they are based, are obviously time-barred unless they are rescued by CPLR 205(a), which provides:

> "If an action is timely commenced and is terminated in any other manner than by a voluntary discontinuance, a failure to obtain personal jurisdiction over the defendant, *a dismissal of the complaint for neglect to prosecute the action*, or a final judgment upon the merits, the plaintiff, or, if the plaintiff dies, and the cause of action survives, his or her executor or administrator, may commence a new action upon the same transaction or occurrence or series of transactions or occurrences within six months after the termination provided that the new action would have been timely commenced at the time of commencement of the prior action and that service upon defendant is effected within such six-month period." (Emphasis added.)

For purposes of this statute, "termination" of the prior action occurs when appeals as of right are exhausted (*Lehman Bros. v Hughes Hubbard & Reed, LLP*, 92 N.Y.2d 1014, 1016-1017, 707 N.E.2d 433, 684 N.Y.S.2d 478 [1998]). Here, termination occurred on June 8, 2001, when the Appellate Division affirmed the dismissal of the prior actions, and thus if CPLR 205(a) applies, the commencement of these actions in December 2000 was not too late. Because the prior actions were, however, dismissed "for neglect to prosecute," CPLR 205(a) is inapplicable.

Our decisions make clear that the "neglect to prosecute" exception in CPLR 205(a) applies not only where the dismissal of the prior action is for "want of prosecution pursuant to CPLR 3216, but whenever neglect to prosecute is in fact the basis for dismissal (*see Carven Assoc. v American Home Assur. Corp.*, 84 N.Y.2d 927, 644 N.E.2d 1368, 620 N.Y.S.2d 812 [1994]; *Laffey v City of New York*,

52 N.Y.2d 796, 417 N.E.2d 1248, 436 N.Y.S.2d 707 [1980]; *Keel v Parke, Davis & Co.*, 50 N.Y.2d 833, 407 N.E.2d 1347, 430 N.Y.S.2d 51 [1980]; *Flans v Federal Ins. Co.*, 43 N.Y.2d 881, 374 N.E.2d 365, 403 N.Y.S.2d 466 [1978]). In *Carven*, as in this case, the prior action "had been dismissed for [plaintiffs'] willful and repeated refusal to obey court-ordered disclosure" (84 N.Y.2d at 930). We held that dismissal to be within the "neglect to prosecute" exception.

Plaintiffs stress that our memorandum in *Carven* referred to "the singular circumstances presented by this appeal" (*id.*). They say that the more relevant precedent is *Schuman v Hertz Corp.* (17 N.Y.2d 604, 215 N.E.2d 683, 268 N.Y.S.2d 563 [1966]), in which we reversed an Appellate Division decision dismissing a second action as time-barred. We based our decision in *Schuman* on the ground that "the dismissal of the original suit was not intended by the Justice presiding to be a dismissal for neglect to prosecute." Plaintiffs claim that here, as in *Schuman*, the statement by Supreme Court that it did not intend to dismiss the action for neglect to prosecute should be dispositive.

However, *Schuman*, even more than *Carven*, turned on its unique facts. The dismissal of the prior action in *Schuman* came after a complicated, and apparently unrecorded, series of discussions with the Justice presiding in a Supreme Court trial part and his law secretary. The trial judge dismissed the case when "plaintiffs' counsel stated he was not ready to comply with the court's direction to pick a jury," but the judge also allegedly said that the dismissal "would not be the end of the lawsuit" because plaintiff could rely on the predecessor statute to CPLR 205(a). In a situation where the true basis of the dismissal was less than clear, we held it proper to defer to the holding of the Supreme Court Justice "that the original [complaint] had not been dismissed for neglect to prosecute" (*id.* at 605-606). But where, as here, the record does make clear the basis for the prior dismissal, the question of whether it was a dismissal for neglect to prosecute is a question of law on which we need not defer to Supreme Court's judgment.

"Neglect to prosecute" is a correct description of the basis for the dismissal of these plaintiffs' prior actions. A series of discovery defaults beginning in 1996 and never fully cured finally led a patient Supreme Court Justice, who had done his best to protect plaintiffs from the consequences of their counsel's inaction, to dismiss the cases in 2000. Supreme Court's dismissal order refers to plaintiffs' "failure . . . to comply with discovery deadlines," their "delays," their "disregard for the case management order and scheduling order," their lack of diligence, their "inactions" and their "ongoing laxity."

Where a case is dismissed for reasons like this, it is not acceptable to permit plaintiffs to start all over again, after the statute of limitations has expired. To countenance that result would be to convert the dismissal itself into just one more opportunity to try again — and plaintiffs have already had at least as many opportunities to try again as they could reasonably expect. The plain purpose of excluding actions dismissed for neglect to prosecute from those that can be, in substance, revived by a new filing under CPLR 205(a) was to assure that a dismissal for neglect to prosecute would be a serious sanction, not just a bump in the road.

Supreme Court was of course correct in thinking it undesirable to punish plaintiffs for the failures of their counsel. But what is undesirable is sometimes also necessary, and it is often necessary, as it is here, to hold parties responsible for their lawyers' failure to meet deadlines. Litigation cannot be conducted efficiently if deadlines are not taken seriously, and we make clear again, as we have several times before, that disregard of deadlines should not and will not be tolerated (*see Miceli v State Farm Auto. Ins. Co.*, 3 N.Y.3d 725, 819 N.E.2d 995, 786 N.Y.S.2d 379 [2004]; *Brill v City of New York*, 2 N.Y.3d 648, 814 N.E.2d 431, 781 N.Y.S.2d 261 [2004]; *Kihl v Pfeffer*, 94 N.Y.2d 118, 722 N.E.2d 55, 700 N.Y.S.2d 87 [1999]).

Accordingly, the order of the Appellate Division should be affirmed, with costs.

. . . .

NOTES

(1) CPLR 205(a) does not apply if the first action was terminated by a "final judgment on the merits." Thus, if the order dismissing the first action states that the dismissal is "with prejudice." then CPLR 205(a) will not save the new action. This is so even if the court that dismissed the first action did not in fact reach the substantive merits of the claim. *See Yonkers Construction Co. v. Port Auth. Trans-Hudson Corp.*, 93 N.Y.2d 375, 690 N.Y.S.2d 512, 712 N.E.2d 678 (1999) (alternate ground). The same case also holds that CPLR 205(a) does not apply when the first action was dismissed for failing to comply with a condition precedent to suit.

(2) CPLR 205 was invoked successfully in *George v. Mt. Sinai Hosp.*, 47 N.Y.2d 170, 417 N.Y.S.2d 231, 390 N.E.2d 1156 (1979), where the first action was dismissed because the person named as the plaintiff had died prior to its commencement and the new action was brought in the name of the representative of the estate. It is instructive to compare *George* with *Goldberg v. Camp Mikan-Recro* (discussed in note 1 following *Caffaro v.* Tryna in § 7.06[A], *supra*), in which the Court refused to allow an amended complaint brought by an estate representative to relate back (pursuant to CPLR 203(f)) to the date of interposition of an earlier claim brought improperly in the name of the deceased. Why should CPLR 205 be interpreted differently?

(3) In answering Problem E following these notes, consider *Parker v. Mack*, 61 N.Y.2d 114, 472 N.Y.S.2d 882, 460 N.E.2d 1316 (1984). When this case was decided — prior to the 1992 amendments to CPLR article 3, discussed in Chapter 5, *supra* — an action was commenced by service, not by filing. The Court of Appeals held: "No action is commenced by the service of a summons alone

which neither contains nor has attached to it a notice of the nature of the action and of the relief sought; accordingly, when such a summons is dismissed plaintiff may not avail himself of the six-month extension for commencement of a new action upon the same transaction or occurrence provided by CPLR 205 (subd[a]). . . ."

PROBLEM E

Recall the facts of *Harris v. Niagra Falls Board of Education*, in § 5.02, *supra*. In that case, the plaintiff's personal injury action was dismissed on motion because he had failed to purchase an index number prior to commencing it. Suppose that within six months of the dismissal of Harris' action, he properly commenced a new action, based on the same facts, against the same defendant by paying the filing fee, obtaining a new index number, and filing a summons and complaint. Would this action get the benefit of the extension allowed by CPLR 205(a)? Or would CPLR 205(a) be of no avail on the grounds that Harris' first action was terminated "by . . . a failure to obtain personal jurisdiction over the defendant[s]"? Note that the Court of Appeals described Harris' failure to pay the filing fee as "a commencement infirmity that is waivable." Alternatively, would CPLR 205(a) be of no avail on the grounds that Harris initially commenced no an action at all, under *Parker v. Mack, supra* note 3?

In *Meiselman v. McDonald's Restaurants*, 305 A.D.2d 382, 759 N.Y.S.2d 506 (2d Dep't 2003), the court held that CPLR 205 did not apply to a new action commenced after the first action was dismissed for a failure to pay the filing fee, because the first action was a "nullity." Correct?

DREGER v. NEW YORK STATE THRUWAY AUTHORITY
Court of Appeals
81 N.Y.2d 721, 593 N.Y.S.2d 758, 609 N.E.2d 111 (1992)

MEMORANDUM:

In each of these actions a claim against the State or the Thruway Authority was dismissed for failure to serve a copy of the claim on the Attorney General in the manner prescribed by Court of Claims Act § 11. In *Dreger*, the claimant served the Thruway Authority but neglected to serve the Attorney General. In *Charbonneau* and *Dalton*, copies of the claims were mailed to the Attorney General but were not sent by certified mail as the statute requires. Because of these failures, the actions were subsequently dismissed and are now time-barred. Pursuant to Court of Claims Act § 10(6) and CLPR 205(a), however, a party whose "timely commenced" action has been dismissed and is now time-barred may apply to the court for permission to recommence the action, provided the action was not dismissed for failure to prosecute or under other circumstances not relevant here. The question on appeal is whether these claimants failed to meet the statutory timely commencement requirement because of their failure to serve the Attorney General properly.

. . . Claimants rely on our decision in *Finnerty v. New York State Thruway Auth.* (75 N.Y.2d 721), where we held that the requirement of service on the Attorney General could not be waived by the State because it implicated subject matter jurisdiction. They contend that it has long been the rule that recommencement under CLPR 205(a) or its predecessor is possible when a lack of subject matter jurisdiction was the basis for the dismissal of the prior action (*George v. Mt. Sinai Hospital*, 47 N.Y.2d 170; *Gaines v. City of New York*, 215 N.Y. 533). Inasmuch as *Finnerty* stated that failure to serve the Attorney General resulted in a loss of subject matter jurisdiction, they contend they are entitled to seek recommencement of their actions.

Resolution of these cases does not turn on whether proper service on the Attorney General is characterized as a matter of subject matter jurisdiction, personal jurisdiction or a condition precedent. CLPR 205(a) allows recommencement only where the prior action was "timely commenced." Accordingly, we look not to the characterization of the grounds for dismissal, but to the narrow question of what constitutes timely commencement. We have consistently held that, for purposes of CLPR 205(a) actions prior to the 1992 CLPR amendments (*see*, L 1992, ch. 215, § 4), timely commencement requires literal compliance with the relevant statutes governing notice (*Parker v. Mack*, 61 N.Y.2d 114, 117; *Markoff v. South Nassau Community Hospital*, 61 N.Y.2d 283, 288; *see*, CLPR 304 et seq.).

Court of Claims Act, section 11 establishes a notice requirement in addition to that which may be applicable under other statutes: serving a copy of the claim or notice of intention on the Attorney General, either personally or by certified mail (*see, MacFarland-Breakell Bldg. Corp. v. New York State Thruway Authority* (123 Misc. 2d 307, *affd*, 104 A.D.2d 139 [governmental entity separate from State must be served in addition to attorney general]). Under section 11, both filing with the court and service on the Attorney General must occur within the applicable limitations period, and there is no basis for believing that the Legislature intended filing to independently constitute commencement. Because suits against the State are allowed only by the State's waiver of sovereign immunity and in derogation of the common law, statutory requirements conditioning suit must be strictly construed (*Lurie v. State*, 73 A.D.2d 1006, *affd*, 52 N.Y.2d 849). Accordingly, where, as here, claimants have not met the literal requirements of Court of Claims Act § 11, their actions are not timely commenced, and relief under CLPR 205(a) is not available.

KAYE, J. (dissenting):

As this court has long recognized, a CLPR 205(a) request to recommence a dismissed action must be liberally viewed: "the statute is designed to insure to the diligent suitor the right to a hearing in court till he reaches a judgment on the merits. Its broad and liberal purpose is not to be frittered away by any narrow construction" (*Gaines v. City of New York*, 215 N.Y. 533, 539 [Cardozo, J.]). Today's decision ignores that mandate.

CLPR 205(a) allows recommencement of "timely commenced" actions that are later dismissed. As an action brought under the CLPR prior to July 1, 1992 could only be "commenced . . . by service of a summons" (CLPR 304), a defect in service meant the action had never been commenced and therefore could not be recommenced under 205(a) (*see, e.g., Markoff v. South Nassau Community Hosp.*, 61 N.Y.2d 283). This result, compelled by the explicit language of CLPR 304, constitutes a limited exception to the broad sweep of CLPR 205(a). CLPR 205(a) does not, however, require "literal compliance with the relevant statutes governing notice" (maj mem, p. 3) but rather, only requires compliance with the statutes specifically governing commencement. To require anything more would abrogate the utility of CLPR 205(a) as a remedial savings statute.

. . . .

NOTES

(1) A critical analysis of the principal case may be found in Robert A. Barker, *New York Practice*, New York Law Journal, January 29, 1993, p. 3, col. 1.

(2) As noted in the principal case, if proper service is not made within the time allowed by the Court of Claims Act § 10, the action will be dismissed for a lack of subject matter jurisdiction, a defect that cannot be waived. As explained in *Lyles v. State*, 3 N.Y.3d 396, 787 N.Y.S.2d 216, 820 N.E.2d 860 (2004), subject matter jurisdiction is implicated because the state's waiver of its sovereign immunity in the Court of Claims Act is conditioned on the claimant's compliance with that statute. If the claimant fails to comply, the courts lack subject matter jurisdiction because the sovereign is immune from suit. In *Lyles*, the claim was dismissed because the claimant had failed to serve the Attorney General with the claim within the two year limit found in Court of Claims Act § 10(3), even though he had served a "notice of intention to file a claim" within the ninety days, as also required by that section.

[C] Tolls for Legal Disability — Infancy and Insanity: CPLR 208

CPLR 208 provides for a tolling of the statute of limitations in those cases in which the plaintiff was an infant or was insane at the time of accrual of the cause of action. Infancy is defined by CPLR 105(j). "Insanity" includes any mental disability which prevents persons from protecting their legal rights because of an overall inability to function in society. *McCarthy v. Volkswagen of Am., Inc.*, 55 N.Y.2d 543, 450 N.Y.S.2d 457, 435 N.E.2d 1072 (1982).

The length of the toll turns in part on the period of limitation applicable to plaintiff's claim. If it is three years or more and would expire during the existence of the disability, or less than three years after the disability ends or the disabled party dies, it is extended so as to permit the action to be commenced at any time up to three years after the disability ceases or the disabled person dies. If the time otherwise limited is less than three years, it is extended by the period of the disability.

In the case of insanity, these extensions are subject to the proviso that the time otherwise limited shall not be extended more than ten years after the cause of action accrues. The maximum period is measured from the date that the cause of action accrued. Thus, for example, if the applicable period is six years, the net allowable extension for a person disabled by insanity would be four years.

Infants' claims are also subject to a ten year outside limit when they sound in medical, dental or podiatric malpractice.

Some claims are exempted from the protection of CPLR 208. *See id.*, last sentence; CPLR 217.

The operation of CPLR 208 is best illustrated by considering sample cases. If a ten year old was negligently injured 1984, the claim would have been barred, absent an extension, in 1987. But since under CPLR 208, the time limited was extended until three years after the disability ceased — that is, until three years after the age of majority in 1992 — the action would not have been barred until 1995. This would be eleven years after the cause accrued, an extension of eight years. Suppose the injury had been caused by medical malpractice. Would this matter?

If the disability involved was insanity, and the plaintiff was thirty years old in 1984 when the cause accrued, and the disability ceased twelve years later in 1996, the action would nevertheless have been barred in 1994. In the case of insanity, the maximum limit of ten years from accrual of the cause of action would apply. *Schmertz v. Friedlander*, 36 A.D.2d 606, 318 N.Y.S.2d 772 (1st Dep't 1971).

In no case will CPLR 208 shorten the time within which to commence an action. If for example, a cause of action in contract accrues in favor of a seventeen year old, the claimant will not need the infancy toll and will have six years from the date of the breach to commence an action.

CPLR 208 applies if the claimant is under the disability "at the time the cause of action accrues," and a subsequently arising disability will not invoke the extension.

The next case shows the difficulty the courts have had in applying the disability toll in wrongful death actions in which the person entitled to bring the action cannot be an infant, but the recovery obtained in the action would be paid in whole or in part to an infant.

HENRY v. CITY of NEW YORK
Court of Appeals
94 N.Y.2d 275, 724 N.E.2d 372, 702 N.Y.S.2d 580 (1999)

WESLEY, J.

The issue before us is whether an infant's action against a municipality is time-barred when the infant through a parent or guardian timely files a notice of claim pursuant to General Municipal Law 50-e, but fails to commence the action within the one-year and 90-day limitation period of General Municipal Law 50-i. We hold that CPLR 208 tolls a Statute of Limitations for the period of infancy, and the toll is not terminated by the acts of a guardian or legal representative in taking steps to pursue the infant's claim. Therefore, the infant plaintiffs' suit against the City of New York in this case is not time-barred.

In February 1993, plaintiff Evon Carmen Henry discovered that her three-year-old son Devon had been exposed to lead paint. Five months later, Evon received medical confirmation that her other son, Eann (11 months old), had also been exposed to lead paint. Evon hired an attorney and timely filed a notice of claim for each child pursuant to General Municipal Law 50-e. Each claim alleged that the infant plaintiff ingested lead paint while living in a City-owned apartment and that the City was negligent in the ownership, maintenance and control of the apartment.

In January 1995, plaintiff commenced this action alleging that she had timely filed notices of claim for her sons, that the City had conducted a statutory hearing and that the City had not settled or adjusted the claims. The complaint alleged a claim for each child's injuries and two derivative claims by Evon for loss of services. Because the action was not commenced within the one-year and 90-day period set forth in General Municipal Law 50-i, the City moved to dismiss the complaint as time-barred.

Supreme Court dismissed the derivative causes of action, but denied the City's motion with regard to the causes of action asserted on behalf of infant plaintiffs, holding that the infancy toll under CPLR 208 did not terminate when their parent filed a notice of claim on their behalf. The court noted that the City sought, in effect, "'to turn the benefit it received by the filing of the notice of claim during infancy into a penalty against infant plaintiffs because the parent or guardian has failed to commence an action within one year and ninety days'" (*Henry v City of New York*, Sup Ct, Kings County, June 3, 1997, Bruno, J., index No. 2233/95, *citing Reid v Braithwaite*, NYLJ, Feb. 26, 1997, at 26, col 4).

The Appellate Division reversed (244 AD2d 93). Relying on this Court's decisions in *Hernandez v New York City Health & Hosps. Corp.* (78 NY2d 687) and *Baez v New York City Health & Hosps. Corp.* (80 NY2d 571), the Appellate Division determined that infant plaintiffs were not under a "disability because of infancy" within the meaning of CPLR 208 (244 AD2d, at 95). The Court also noted that as a result of a 1974 amendment, CPLR 208 no longer affords protection by reason of the age of a prospective plaintiff, but rather applies only when the plaintiff is under a "disability because of infancy" (*id.,* at 97). The Appellate Division concluded that Devon and Eann no longer suffered a "disability because of infancy" as their interests were protected by their mother and counsel. We disagree.

Analysis

CPLR 208 provides that where the "person entitled to commence an action is under a disability because of infancy . . . at the time the cause of action accrues," the Statute of Limitations is tolled for the period of disability. The City contends that although Devon and Eann were infants at the time their causes of action accrued, their "disability because of infancy" ceased when their mother, through counsel, filed timely notices of claim pursuant to General Municipal Law 50-e on their behalf. Thus, the City argues, CPLR 208 is inapplicable to toll the Statute of Limitations set forth in General Municipal Law 50-i. The City's position is not supported by CPLR 208 or the prevailing case law interpreting the provision.

This Court has consistently recognized the special status that is accorded an infant plaintiff by virtue of the infant's tender age; that status is not altered by the action or inaction of the infant's parent or guardian. In *Murphy v Village of Fort Edward (supra,* 213 NY 397), we noted that an infant's right of action "at its origination is and remains in the infant. . . . Infancy does not incapacitate the infant from bringing the action" (*id.,* at 401). When the infant sues by a guardian ad litem, although the guardian may manage the suit and protect the infant's interests, it is the infant who is the real party to the action (*id.*). Thus, it could not "be justly held . . . that rights accorded by the law to infants are forfeited because a parent did not perform for an infant where performance was excused because of the infancy" (*id.,* at 403). In *Russo v City of New York (supra,* 258 NY 344), we reaffirmed that "it is the age and capacity of the infant rather than the conduct of its parents and guardians which control" (*id.,* at 348).

Other courts have concluded that the tolling provisions of CPLR 208 apply notwithstanding service of a timely notice of claim on an infant's behalf. In *Abbatemarco v Town of Brookhaven* (26 AD2d 664), the Second Department held that the one-year and 90-day time period of General Municipal Law 50-i did not bar an infant's action against the municipality. The Court specifically noted that "because of the *disability of infancy*, the bar of the statute never became effective" (*id.,* at 664 [emphasis supplied]). In *Rosado v Langsam Prop. Serv. Corp. (supra,* 251 AD2d 258), the First Department held that although the infant plaintiff's guardian, represented by counsel, filed a timely notice of claim but then failed to commence the action within the Statute of Limitations, the action was not time-barred. The Court noted that "the initial prosecution of [the infant's] claim by his legal representatives did not preclude him from invoking the CPLR 208 disability toll to prevent the running of the statutory period" (*id.,* at 258).

The City argues that most of these cases are distinguishable because they were based on language no longer found in the statute. Prior to 1974, CPLR 208 provided that the infancy toll applied where "a person entitled to commence an action is, at the time the cause of action accrues, under the age of twenty-one years" (former CPLR 208). Thus, the City argues, the application of former CPLR 208 was defined by the plaintiff's age.

In 1974, the statute was amended; the statute's use of age to define infancy was dropped and the phrase "disability because of infancy" was added. The City views this as a substantive sea change. The infancy disability, in the City's view, is no longer measured by age and is overcome when a parent, legal guardian or attorney takes steps to protect an infant's rights by filing a notice of claim. Thus, according to the City, there is no longer a disability once someone acts on the infant's behalf. We are unpersuaded by this argument.

In 1971, the 26th Amendment to the United States Constitution became effective, reducing the voting age from 21 to 18 for the purpose of State as well as Federal elections (1974 Report of NY Law Rev Commn, reprinted in 1974 McKinney's Session Laws of NY, at 1882). The Legislature ratified the Amendment that same year and made the necessary adjustments to the Election Law. The ratification also raised a number of issues concerning the advisability of reducing the age at which legal "infancy" terminates. In response, the Law Revision Commission undertook a review of the Consolidated and Unconsolidated Laws to determine what statutes should be promptly amended, what statutes should remain as they were and what statutes needed additional study by the Commission (*id.*).

The 1974 amendment to CPLR 208 was submitted by the Law Revision Commission along with amendments to 52 other statutes (*id.*, at 1883). In conjunction with the amendment to CPLR 208, the Legislature added definitions to the CPLR for the terms "infant" and "infancy." An "infant" is "a person who has not attained the age of eighteen years;" "infancy" means "the state of being an infant" (CPLR 105[j], as added by L 1974, ch 924). While the Legislature did not include a definition for the term "disability" and did not use the phrase "under the age of eighteen" to delineate those claims to which the toll of CPLR 208 applies, the resulting phrase "disability because of infancy" appears to be nothing more than a stylistic drafting choice.

According to the Law Revision Commission, "amendatory language has been kept to a minimum in order to interfere as little as possible with existing language. New provisions have been adapted to the existing style of each chapter amended" (Recommendation of NY Law Rev Commn to Legislature, 1974 McKinney's Session Laws of NY, at 1889). There is no indication that the Legislature intended the amendment to change the application of the infancy toll (*see,* Alexander, Supp Practice Commentaries, McKinney's Cons Laws of NY, Book 7B, CPLR C208:4, 1999 Cum Ann Pocket Part, at 114; *see also,* Siegel, NY Prac 54, at 66 [2d ed]). Thus, the legislative history to the 1974 amendment fails to support the City's contention that the Legislature intended to depart from settled statutory interpretation that the toll is based on the age of the prospective plaintiff.

The City also argues that a 1975 amendment to CPLR 208 creating a 10-year cap on the commencement of an infant's medical malpractice action is further proof that the tolling protection is tied to a person's ability to commence an action, not age. The legislative history for the 1975 amendment indicates that it was part of a larger package of reforms in response to the diminished availability of health care services as a result of the lack of affordable medical malpractice insurance coverage (Governor's Mem, Bill Jacket, L 1975, ch 109). Moreover, the 10-year ceiling was designed to cut down the large reserves or "tail" required by insurance carriers for possible claims by infants (*id.*). The amendment to CPLR 208 reflects nothing more than an attempt to place a time cap on infant medical malpractice claims equal to that provided for persons under other legal disabilities. It has no relevance to the reach of the tolling statute at issue here.

The City also relies on *Hernandez v New York City Health & Hosps. Corp.* (78 NY2d 687, *supra*) and *Baez v New York City Health & Hosps. Corp.* (80 NY2d 571, *supra*). It contends that these cases established that, once an infant's interests are protected by a guardian or personal representative, the tolling provisions of CPLR 208 are no longer applicable as the infant is no longer under a disability. The City misconstrues *Hernandez* and *Baez*.

Neither *Hernandez* nor *Baez* holds that the CPLR 208 toll becomes inapplicable when the infant plaintiff retains an attorney or takes steps to pursue litigation. Both *Hernandez* and *Baez* involved wrongful death actions where the "person entitled to commence an action" is the decedent's personal representative and not a distributee — infant or adult (EPTL 5-4.1).

Hernandez concerned an "unusual situation" where there was no personal representative of the decedent's estate and the infant sole distributee was not eligible to receive letters of administration pursuant to SCPA 707(1)(a). No one could commence a wrongful death action until a guardian was appointed for the infant sole distributee. Thus, the infant's disability was directly linked to identifying a prospective plaintiff (an administrator) and only the appointment of a guardian or the infant's eighteenth birthday could resolve the dilemma. In that rare situation, CPLR 208 tolls the Statute of Limitations for the wrongful death action until the "earliest moment there is a personal representative or a potential personal representative who can bring the action, whether by appointment of a guardian or majority of the distributee, whichever occurs first" (*id.*, at 693). *Hernandez* does not alter the definitional limits of CPLR 208. It bridges a "unique" statutory gap in a limited circumstance (*id.*).

In *Baez,* decedent's will named plaintiff the executrix. Thus, plaintiff could have sought appointment as the personal representative for the estate and commenced the wrongful death action; the infancy toll was inapplicable because the infant distributees were not "entitled to commence the action."

Infant plaintiffs should not be penalized by a parent's compliance with General Municipal Law 50-e in an effort to protect a right to recovery. Infancy itself, the state of being "a person [under] the age of eighteen" (CPLR 105[j]), is the disability that determines the toll. An interpretation of the infancy toll which measures the time period of infancy based on the conduct of the infant's parent or guardian cuts against the strong public policy of protecting those who are disabled because of their age (*see, Valdimer v Mount Vernon Hebrew Camps*, 9 NY2d 21, 25; *see also,* CPLR art 12). Because plaintiffs here were under the age of 18 when their causes of action accrued, they are entitled to the benefit of the infancy toll, and their claims against the City are not time-barred.

NOTE

In *Baez v. N.Y. City Health & Hosp. Corp.*, 80 N.Y.2d 571, 592 N.Y.S.2d 640, 607 N.E.2d 787 (1992), the children's grandmother could have brought the action for their mother's death, having been named in the mother's will as executrix and guardian. Thus, the Court of Appeals held that CPLR § 208 could not be applied as a toll for the children. Does the Court adequately distinguish *Baez* from the principal case?

[D] The Effect of Death: CPLR 210

[1] Death of Claimant

During the period between the death of a claimant and the appointment of a representative, there is ordinarily no one with capacity to enforce the claim by suit. If the time limitation on the claim is scheduled to terminate soon after the death, there is an obvious need for extending the period until a representative can qualify and commence suit. CPLR 210(a) insures that the representative has at least one year from the date of death to interpose the claim. The provision only operates, of course, if the claim was not barred at the time of the claimant's death, and the cause of action must be one which survives his death, a matter of substantive law. *See generally* Est., Powers & Trusts Law §§ 11-3.1 to 11-3.3. Since a wrongful death claim accrues at, not before, death, its two-year statute of limitations (*see* E.P.T.L. § 5-4.1) is not extended by CPLR 210(a). *Brandt v. Hashinsky*, 16 Misc. 2d 664, 177 N.Y.S.2d 648 (Sup. Ct. 1958).

[2] Death of Person Liable

During the period between the death of a potential defendant and the appointment of a representative for the estate, the claimant is unable to sue; consequently, as in the case of the claimant's death, there is a need for extending any time limitation that is scheduled to terminate soon after the death.

CPLR 210(b) allows an eighteen-month extension for a suit against the executor or administrator. This extension runs from the death of the party, rather than from the granting of letters of administration. If there is any undue delay in the appointment of an executor or administrator for a decedent against whom a cause of action exists, the claimant may seek the appointment of a representative under section 1002 of the Surrogate's Court Procedure Act.

CPLR 210(b) applies only if the cause of action accrues before the death of the decedent. *Glamm v. Allen*, 57 N.Y.2d 87, 453 N.Y.S.2d 674, 439 N.E.2d 390 (1982).

§ 7.08 THE BORROWING STATUTE: CPLR 202

GLOBAL FINANCIAL CORP. v. TRIARC CORP.
Court of Appeals
93 N.Y.2d 525, 693 N.Y.S.2d 479, 715 N.E.2d 482 (1999)

KAYE, J.

This appeal places before us a long-simmering question: where does a nonresident's contract claim accrue for purposes of the Statute of Limitations? CPLR 202 requires our courts to "borrow" the Statute of Limitations of a foreign jurisdiction where a nonresident's cause of action accrued, if that limitations period is shorter than New York's. The primary issue presented by this appeal is whether, for purposes of CPLR 202, the nonresident plaintiff's contract and quantum meruit claims accrued in New York, where most of the relevant events occurred, or in plaintiff's State of residence, where it sustained the economic impact of the alleged breach.

According to the complaint, by contract dated February 1, 1988, defendant retained plaintiff to perform certain consulting services. In March 1989 plaintiff located an investment company that agreed to purchase all of defendant's outstanding shares, and between February 1988 and August 1989, plaintiff additionally advised defendant regarding corporate planning. On November 6, 1989, plaintiff demanded payment of over nine million dollars for services rendered, which defendant refused the following week.

On November 9, 1995, plaintiff commenced an action in the United States District Court for the Southern District of New York to recover its commissions and fees. Because both parties were Delaware corporations, however, on April 10, 1996 the court dismissed the complaint for lack of subject matter jurisdiction. Three months later, plaintiff brought a substantially similar suit across the street, in Supreme Court, New York County. The parties do not dispute that this action is timely if the Federal action was timely when commenced on November 9, 1995 (CPLR 205).

Relying on CPLR 202, defendant sought dismissal of plaintiff's claims for failure to comply with the Statute of Limitations of Delaware (where plaintiff is incorporated) or Pennsylvania (where, according to the Federal complaint, plaintiff had its principal place of business). Plaintiff's claims would be time-barred in both States (*see,* Del Code Annot, tit 10, 8106 [three-year limitations period for actions on a promise]; Del Code Annot, tit 10, 8111 [one year for actions for services]; 42 Pa Cons Stat Annot 5525 [four years for contract actions]). In opposing defendant's motion, plaintiff maintained that New York's six-year Statute of Limitations applied because most of the events relating to the contract took place in New York, and that the action was timely because the Federal action was commenced within six years after defendant refused plaintiff's demand for fees and commissions (*see,* CPLR 213[2]).

Supreme Court agreed with defendant and dismissed the complaint, holding that under the borrowing statute plaintiff's causes of action accrued where it suffered injury: its place of residence. The Appellate Division unanimously affirmed both Supreme Court orders (251 AD2d 17), and this Court granted plaintiff leave to appeal so much of the Appellate Division order as affirmed the dismissal of the complaint, in order to resolve the issue definitively and eliminate the need for courts to engage in "guesswork" when determining the place of accrual for contract actions under CPLR 202 (*see,* Siegel, NY Prac 57, at 70 [2d ed]). Because we agree that plaintiff's cause of action accrued where it sustained its alleged injury, we now affirm.

When a nonresident sues on a cause of action accruing outside New York, CPLR 202 requires the cause of action to be timely under the limitation periods of both New York and the jurisdiction where the cause of action accrued.[2] This prevents nonresidents from shopping in New York for a favorable Statute of Limitations (*see, Antone v General Motors Corp.,* 64 NY2d 20, 27-28).

Plaintiff argues that the New York Statute of Limitations applies because its claims accrued in New York, where the contract was negotiated, executed, substantially performed and breached. In essence, plaintiff urges that we apply a "grouping of contacts" or "center of gravity" approach — used in substantive choice-of-law questions in contract cases — to determine where contract and quantum meruit causes of action accrue for purposes of CPLR 202 (*see, Zurich Ins. Co. v Shearson Lehman Hutton,* 84 NY2d 309, 317; *Matter of Allstate Ins. Co. [Stolarz],* 81 NY2d 219, 226).

At the threshold, however, there is a significant difference between a choice-of-law question, which is a matter of common law, and this Statute of Limitations issue, which is governed by particular terms of the CPLR. In using the word "accrued" in CPLR 202 there is no indication that the Legislature intended

---

[2] CPLR 202 states: "An action based upon a cause of action accruing without the state cannot be commenced after the expiration of the time limited by the laws of either the state or the place without the state where the cause of action accrued, except that where the cause of action accrued in favor of a resident of the state the time limited by the laws of the state shall apply."

the term "to mean anything other than the generally accepted construction applied throughout CPLR Article 2 — the time when, and the place where, the plaintiff first had the right to bring the cause of action" (1 Weinstein-Korn-Miller, NY Civ Prac ¶ 202.04, at 2-61).

CPLR 202 has remained substantially unchanged since 1902 (*see, Antone v General Motors Corp., supra,* 64 NY2d, at 27). While its predecessor, section 13 of the Civil Practice Act, used the word "arise" instead of "accrue," the Legislature intended no change in meaning when it adopted the present provision, in 1962, as part of the CPLR. The legislative purpose was simply to ensure that the language of CPLR 202 conformed with other CPLR provisions (*see,* 1962 NY Legis Doc No. 8, at 69; *Insurance Co. v ABB Power Generation,* 91 NY2d 180, 186, n 2). Because earlier iterations of the borrowing statute predate the substantive choice-of-law "interest analysis" test used in tort cases (*see, Babcock v Jackson,* 12 NY2d 473 [1963]) and the "grouping of contacts" or "center of gravity" approach used in contract cases (*see, Auten v Auten,* 308 NY 155 [1954]), these choice-of-law analyses are inapplicable to the question of statutory construction presented by CPLR 202 (*see generally,* 1 Weinstein-Korn-Miller, NY Civ Prac ¶ 202.04, at 2-61).

Indeed, while this Court has not addressed the issue in the context of a contract case, we have consistently employed the traditional definition of accrual — a cause of action accrues at the time and in the place of the injury — in tort cases involving the interpretation of CPLR 202. *Martin v Dierck Equip. Co.* (43 NY2d 583) is illustrative. There, the plaintiff was injured while operating a forklift at his employer's warehouse in Virginia. The forklift manufacturer and distributor were located in New York, and the forklift was sold to plaintiff's employer in New York. Plaintiff sued the manufacturer and distributor in negligence and strict products liability. The Court held that for purposes of the borrowing statute, the negligence causes of action as well as the cause of action which plaintiff labeled "breach of warranty" accrued in Virginia: "[p]laintiff possessed no cause of action, in tort or in contract, anywhere in the world until he was injured in Virginia" (*id.,* at 588, 591).

When an alleged injury is purely economic, the place of injury usually is where the plaintiff resides and sustains the economic impact of the loss (*see, e.g., Matter of Smith Barney, Harris Upham & Co. v Luckie,* 85 NY2d 193, 207, *rearg denied* 85 NY2d 1033, *cert denied sub nom. Manhard v Merrill Lynch, Pierce, Fenner & Smith,* 516 US 811; *Gorlin v Bond Richman & Co.,* 706 F Supp 236, 240 [SD NY 1989] [internal citation omitted] ["For purposes of the New York borrowing statute, a cause of action accrues where the injury is sustained. In cases involving economic harm, that place is normally the state of plaintiff's residence."]; *cf., Lang v Paine, Webber, Jackson & Curtis,* 582 F Supp 1421 [SD NY 1984] [Canadian plaintiff intentionally maintained separate financial base in Massachusetts; under the circumstances, injury of losing Massachusetts funds was felt in Massachusetts, not Canada]). Here, plaintiff's causes of action are time-barred whether one looks to its State of incorporation or its principal place of business. Thus, we need not determine whether it was in Delaware or Pennsylvania that plaintiff more acutely sustained the impact of its loss.

Plaintiff relies on *Insurance Co. v ABB Power Generation* (91 NY2d 180, *supra*) for the proposition that the place where the relevant contacts are grouped, not the place of the injury, determines accrual for purposes of the borrowing statute. The question in *ABB Power* was whether plaintiff's cause of action could accrue in California, even though the parties in their contract chose the forum and law of New York. The Court answered in the affirmative, holding that a forum-selection clause, or inability to obtain personal jurisdiction over a defendant in a foreign jurisdiction, would not override CPLR 202. Once the Court decided that CPLR 202 applied, it was clear that California was the State of accrual, as California was the place of the injury as well as the place where "all of the operative facts" occurred (*id.,* at 183). Thus, the Court did not have to decide whether to use a choice-of-law analysis or place-of-injury rule in order to determine where plaintiff's causes of action accrued.

Finally, as we underscored in *ABB Power*, "CPLR 202 is designed to add clarity to the law and to provide the certainty of uniform application to litigants" (*id.,* at 187). This goal is better served by a rule requiring the single determination of a plaintiff's residence than by a rule dependent on a litany of events relevant to the "center of gravity" of a contract dispute.

Accordingly, the order of the Appellate Division should be affirmed, with costs.

NOTES

(1) CPLR 202 does not come into play unless the claim (1) accrued in favor of one who was a non-resident at the time of accrual, and (2) accrued "without the state." In *Besser v. E.R. Squibb & Sons, Inc.*, 75 N.Y.2d 847, 552 N.Y.S.2d 923 (1989), the borrowing statute was construed to require the application of Pennsylvania law to a claim brought by a DES victim who was born in that state, even though she was a New York resident when she commenced her action.

(2) Who is a "resident" of New York for the purposes of the borrowing statute? In *Antone v. General Motors*, 64 N.Y.2d 20, 28-30, 484 N.Y.S.2d 514, 517-19, 473 N.E.2d 742, 745-48 (1984), the plaintiff had lived in a Pennsylvania nursing home (were he was an employee) for several months when he was involved in an accident (in Pennsylvania) which gave rise to the action. He sought to avoid the two-year Pennsylvania tort statute of limitations by suing in New York and claiming that, as a New York domiciliary, the borrowing statute did not apply to him. Although the plaintiff had lived in New York for several years prior to taking the job at the nursing home, the Court of Appeals rejected his argument:

Establishment of a domicile in a State generally requires a physical presence in the State and an intention to make the State a permanent home. . . . The term residence, on the other hand, has been employed by Legislatures for a variety of purposes, often with a meaning which is different than that of domicile. New York has long recognized that "residence" and "domicile" are not interchangeable. . . . Additionally, the purpose behind CPLR 202 of discouraging forum shopping by plaintiffs who have no significant contacts with New York is better served by focusing on whether the plaintiff has a residence in New York rather than on whether he is domiciled in this State. . . .

We thus hold that "resident" as used in CPLR 202 does not have the same meaning as "domiciliary." Rather, the determination of whether a plaintiff is a New York resident, for purposes of CPLR 202, turns on whether he has a significant connection with some locality in the State as the result of living there for some length of time during the course of a year. . . .

A review of the record here shows that the trial court used the proper meaning of "resident" in determining whether Antone was a resident of New York at the time of his accident. This determination was one of fact and as it was affirmed by the Appellate Division, and is supported by evidence in the record, it will not be disturbed by this court. Antone's action must thus be timely under both the Pennsylvania and New York limitations periods.

(3) Most states have statutes similar to CPLR 202. For this reason, a New York resident whose claim accrued in New York will generally be unable to take advantage of a more liberal statute of limitations, even if one should exist in another state in which the defendant is subject to jurisdiction.

(4) The distinction between a statute of limitations and a statute of repose is discussed in § 7.02, *supra*. The difference is crucial when applying the borrowing statute. For example, when a Connecticut statute of repose bars product liability claims accruing more than 10 years from the time the defendant sold the product, a New York citizen injured by a machine while working in Connecticut beyond 10 years from the sale may not invoke New York's CPLR 202, since the statute of repose is a substantive rule and choice of law rules require application of the Connecticut provision. *Tanges v. Heidelberg N. Am., Inc.*, 93 N.Y.2d 48, 687 N.Y.S.2d 604, 710 N.E.2d 250 (1999).

§ 7.09 CONDITIONS PRECEDENT

Some limitations of time are not true statutes of limitations but are conditions precedent. They are so called because compliance with them is a condition which must be satisfied before a valid action can be commenced. Like statutes of limitations, conditions precedent require the plaintiff to do an act prior to the expiration of time — sometimes the act is the commencement of an action. Too, they can have their origin in statute or contract. Small wonder that it is sometimes difficult to tell one from another. The following case illustrates both the difficulty and the importance of making the distinction.

YONKERS CONTRACTING COMPANY, INC. v. PORT AUTHORITY TRANS-HUDSON CORP.
Court of Appeals
93 N.Y.2d 375, 690 N.Y.S.2d 512, 712 N.E.2d 678 (1999)

LEVINE, J.

Plaintiff appeals from an order of the Appellate Division affirming the dismissal of this action against defendant, a wholly-owned subsidiary of the Port Authority of New York and New Jersey (Port Authority) because the action was not filed within the time constraints for commencement of suits against the Port Authority (see, McKinney's Uncons Laws of NY 7107 [L 1950, ch 301, 7]). The sole issue is whether section 7107's requirement that actions be commenced within one year of accrual may be overcome pursuant to CPLR 205(a) because the action was commenced within six months of the final dismissal of a previous action involving the identical claim.

The parties agree that the instant action is based upon the same series of transactions and occurrences giving rise to a disputed claim for damages by plaintiff as general contractor on a construction project of defendant Port Authority, undertaken between 1988 and 1990 (see, Yonkers Contr. Co. v Port Auth. Trans-Hudson Corp., 208 AD2d 63, affd 87 NY2d 927). The previous action, commenced in 1990, was undisputably timely. It was dismissed because plaintiff failed to comply with a condition precedent in the construction contract's alternative dispute resolution provision requiring it to plead that it had submitted the disputed claim to the project's Chief Engineer for resolution before instituting litigation (208 AD2d, at 65). In response to the motion to dismiss, plaintiff asserted only that the alternative dispute resolution provision was void as against public policy. The Appellate Division rejected plaintiff's public policy contention, granted defendant's motion and dismissed the complaint "with prejudice" (id., at 66-68).

This second action was commenced on August 1, 1996, less than six months after our decision on February 8, 1996, affirming the dismissal of the first case, but more than one year after the cause of action accrued. This time, plaintiff complied with the requirement to allege submission of the controversy to the Chief Engineer, but plaintiff now challenges the Chief Engineer's decision as infected by fraud or bad faith. Defendant moved to dismiss the present action on the ground that it was commenced well beyond the one-year requirement of section 7107. Both Supreme Court and the Appellate Division (248 AD2d 463) held that the toll of CPLR 205(a), which may extend a Statute of Limitations, could not obviate the requirements of a statutory condition precedent to suit. We agree and also hold that this second action should be dismissed because the first one was dismissed "upon the merits" (CPLR 205[a]). Therefore, we affirm.

Case law distinguishes between a Statute of Limitations and a statutory time restriction on commencement of suit. The former merely suspends the remedy provided by a right of action, but the latter conditions the existence of a right of action, thereby creating a substantive limitation on the right (see, *Tanges v Heidelberg N. Am.*, 93 NY2d 48, 55; *Romano v Romano*, 19 NY2d 444, 447). Both CPLR 205(a) and its equivalent predecessor statutes have been held to be inapplicable when the statutory time bar to the commencement of the second action falls into the latter category, as a condition precedent

The requirement to bring an action within one year under Unconsolidated Laws 7107 is such a condition precedent to suit, which cannot be tolled under CPLR 205(a). At common law, plaintiff would not have had a cause of action because the Port Authority enjoyed sovereign immunity (*Trippe v Port of N.Y. Auth.*, 14 NY2d 119, 123). In a single enactment, the State not only consented to suits against Port Authority but also expressly incorporated within the act a requirement of timely suit as an integral part of its waiver of sovereign immunity (L 1950, ch 301 [McKinney's Uncons Laws of NY 7101-7112]). Where a statute both "creates a cause of action and attaches a time limit to its commencement, the time is an ingredient of the cause" (*Romano v Romano, supra,* 19 NY2d, at 447). In such situations, "the limitation of time is so incorporated with the remedy given as to make it an integral part of it, and the condition precedent to the maintenance of the action at all" (*Hill v Board of Supervisors, supra,* 119 NY, at 347).

The legislative intent to condition the waiver of sovereign immunity with respect to the Port Authority on timely suit could not be more clear. Unconsolidated Laws 7107 unambiguously allows an action against the Port Authority only "*upon the condition that* any suit, action or proceeding prosecuted or maintained under this act shall be commenced within one year" (McKinney's Uncons Laws of NY 7107 [emphasis supplied]). Thus, CPLR 205(a) is inapplicable because, here, the "right to seek relief is specifically conditioned upon compliance with a particular time requirement rather than, or in addition to, a Statute of Limitations" (*Matter of Morris Investors v Commissioner of Fin. of City of N.Y.*, 69 NY2d 933, 936).

Plaintiff's reliance upon *Fleming v Long Is. R.R.* (72 NY2d 998) and *Dreger v New York State Thruway Auth.* (81 NY2d 721) is misplaced. Those cases addressed only the issue of whether the dismissed, initial action was "timely commenced" for purposes of obtaining the benefit of the CPLR 205(a) toll for a later, otherwise untimely suit. In both *Fleming* and *Dreger,* the time bars governing the claims were concededly Statutes of Limitation, not conditions precedent, as here. Therefore, in those cases there was no impediment to the application of CPLR 205(a) to toll the Statutes of Limitation. Contrastingly here, the statutory time limit on bringing suit, as demonstrated, is itself a condition precedent to the existence of the right of action, not merely a Statute of Limitations. That distinction is fatal to plaintiff's invocation of CPLR 205(a).

Accordingly, the order of the Appellate Division should be affirmed, with costs.

NOTES

(1) As the principal case holds, the tolls and extensions that can save a plaintiff whose action would otherwise be dismissed because of the statute of limitations do not apply when the relevant time limit is imposed by a condition precedent. Thus, it has been held that the infancy toll is not available in an action against an airline for personal injury because such claims are subject to the "Warsaw Convention," a treaty that requires all actions to be commenced within two years of the date of the flight. The court held that this limit imposed a condition precedent, not a statute of limitations. *Kahn v. Trans World Airlines, Inc.*, 82 A.D.2d 696, 443 N.Y.S.2d 79 (2d Dep't 1981).

Another important difference between a statute of limitation and a condition precedent is that, in general, the plaintiff must plead and prove compliance with the latter, whereas the statute of limitation is an affirmative defense. (This rule has been modified somewhat by CPLR 3015(a), which puts on the defendant the burden of pleading non-compliance with a condition precedent which is contractual in origin.) Thus, the plaintiff's failure to comply with a statutorily required condition precedent to suit is a defense which is not waived as a result of omission from the answer, although it is waived if not raised at all before the court of original jurisdiction. *Flanagan v. Board of Educ.*, 47 N.Y.2d 613, 419 N.Y.S.2d 917, 393 N.E.2d 991 (1979).

(2) How do you know when a time limit governing the commencement of an action is a statute of limitation, or a condition precedent? For example, what is the nature of the one-year and ninety-day time limit found in General Municipal Law § 50-i (1)(c)? Section 50-i (1) reads as follows:

> 1. No action or special proceeding shall be prosecuted or maintained against a city . . . unless, (a) a notice of claim shall have been made and served upon the city . . . in compliance with section fifty-e of this chapter, (b) it shall appear by and as an allegation in the complaint or moving papers that at least thirty days have elapsed since the service of such notice and that adjustment or payment thereof has been neglected or refused, and (c) the action or special proceeding shall be commenced within one year and ninety days after the happening of the event upon which the claim is based. . . .

It is similar in some respects to Unconsolidated Law § 7107, which in the principal case was held to be a condition precedent. Nonetheless, in *Campbell v. City of New York*, 4 N.Y.3d 200, 791 N.Y.S.2d 880, 825 N.E.2d 121 (2005), the Court, adhering to long-standing precedent, held that the one-year and ninety-day period of General Municipal Law § 50-i was a statute of limitations and was subject to the tolling provisions of CPLR article 2. In distinguishing Unconsolidated Law § 7107, the Court noted:

> The express terms of section 50-i and its legislative background are distinctly different. Nowhere in section 50-i does the term "condition" appear. . . . Nor, in the case of actions against the City, was there a single enactment consenting to suit and incorporating a time limitation as an integral part of a waiver of sovereign immunity. . . . [W]hen the State of New York waived its sovereign immunity in 1929, its subdivisions, including the City, also lost their protection from suit. While the State placed time limitations on suits against itself, it did not likewise set forth time limitations for suits against municipalities, it was not until 1959 that the Legislature evinced its intent to make uniform the provisions for commencing actions against municipalities by enacting section 50-i. . . . Thus, there is no evidence that the Legislature intended the year-and-90-day provision of section 50-i as a condition precedent to suit.

Campbell v. City of New York, 4 N.Y.3d 204-05, 791 N.Y.S.2d 882-83, 825 N.E.2d 123-24.

(3) Sometimes the condition precedent is not the commencement of an action but the service of a notice of claim (*i.e.*, a kind of minicomplaint describing the claim). Where a condition precedent is imposed, it is often additional to a short statute of limitations.

The most commonly encountered situation in which the service of a notice of claim is a condition precedent to suit, which is then additionally subject to a statute of limitations, is that of an action against a city, county or other local government entity for personal injury, wrongful death or property damage arising from the entity's negligence. The notice of claim must be served "within ninety days after the claim arises," Gen. Mun. Law § 50-e(1)(a), and, as we have seen, the action must be commenced within one year and ninety days "after the happening of the event upon which the claim is based," *id.*, § 50-i(1). The interplay between Gen. Mun. Law § 50-e and § 50-i is discussed in *Cohen v. Pearl River Union Free School District* (discussed in note 1, following *Williams v. Nassau County Medical Center, infra*).[*]

What justification is there for singling out one kind of defendant for special protection by these unusually short periods? As discussed in one study:

> The primary purpose of notice of claim provisions as conditions precedent to the commencement of actions against public corporations, espe-

---

[*] In wrongful death actions, the plaintiff gets ninety days from the appointment as representative of the estate to serve the notice of claim and two years from the death to commence the action, *id.*, §§ 50-e(1)(a), 50-i(1).

cially municipal corporations, has been variously stated by our Court of Appeals through the years. In *Curry v. City of Buffalo*, an action to recover damages for personal injuries resulting from a fall on a sidewalk, Chief Judge Earl, writing for a unanimous Court, put it this way:

> . . . These actions against cities are numerous, and the legislature seems to have been solicitous to protect them so far as possible against unjust or excessive claims, and also against the improvident or collusive allowance of such claims by municipal officers.
>
> . . . .

In more recent years the emphasis has been placed upon the need for efficient investigation of the claim. For example, in *Winbush v. City of Mount Vernon*, an action for wrongful death and conscious pain and suffering, Judge (later Chief Judge) Desmond stated, with reference to section 50-e, that its primary purpose "is to give to a municipality prompt notice of such claims, so that investigation may be made before it is too late for investigation to be efficient. . . ."

Many jurisdictions have spoken in like vein, and some have ascribed still other purposes to their notice of claim statutes. For example, one federal court has said that the purpose of the Federal Tort Claims Act is to ease court congestion and avoid unnecessary litigation. The highest court of another state has said that the purpose of its statute is to facilitate the planning of municipal budgets and to enable public officers to remedy defects in far-flung municipal property before other persons are injured.

Whatever the purpose ascribed in the particular jurisdiction, all seem to have but one end: protection of the public purse. Is it, therefore, true that "[t]he problem of municipal tort liability [of which notice of claim statutes are so integral a part] resolves itself finally into a question of dollars and cents?" Dismal though an affirmative answer to that question may be to those who believe, as does the author, that basic to American jurisprudence is the principle that liability follows fault, that does seem to be the answer.

Graziano, *Special Study, Recommendations Relating to Section 50-e of the General Municipal Law and Related Statutes*, Twenty-first Annual Report of the Judicial Conference 358, 363-64 (1976) (footnotes omitted).[*]

Whatever their justifications, these provisions are apparently secure from constitutional attack in New York for the present. *See Stanton v. Village of Waverly*, 29 N.Y.2d 719, 325 N.Y.S.2d 755, 275 N.E.2d 337 (1971); *Paulsey v. Chaloner*, 54 A.D.2d 131, 388 N.Y.S.2d 35 (3d Dep't 1976), and cases cited.

---

[*] Reprinted permission of the Office of Court Administration and the author copyright © 1976.

Compare Reich v. State Highway Dep't, 386 Mich. 617, 194 N.W.2d 700 (1972) (holding a similar statute unconstitutional on equal protection grounds). *See generally* Graziano, *supra*, at 365-67.

Some of the harshness of Gen. Mun. Law §§ 50-e and 50-i was removed by the 1976 amendments, *see* L. 1976, ch. 745, eff. September 1, 1976, which among other changes, adopted § 50-e(5) in its present form:

> 5. *Application for Leave to Serve a Late Notice.*
>
> Upon application, the court, in its discretion, may extend the time to serve a notice of claim specified in paragraph (a) of subdivision one. The extension shall not exceed the time limited for the commencement of an action by the claimant against the public corporation. In determining whether to grant the extension, the court shall consider, in particular, whether the public corporation or its attorney or its insurance carrier acquired actual knowledge of the essential facts constituting the claim within the time specified in subdivision one or within a reasonable time thereafter. The court shall also consider all other relevant facts and circumstances, including: whether the claimant was an infant, or mentally or physically incapacitated, or died before the time limited for service of the notice of claim; whether the claimant failed to serve a timely notice of claim by reason of his justifiable reliance upon settlement representations made by an authorized representative of the public corporation or its insurance carrier; whether the claimant in serving a notice of claim made an excusable error concerning the identity of the public corporation against which the claim should be asserted; and whether the delay in serving the notice of claim substantially prejudiced the public corporation in maintaining its defense on the merits.
>
> An application for leave to serve a late notice shall not be denied on the ground that it was made after commencement of an action against the public corporation.

(4) Some municipal ordinances require notification of a sidewalk hazard or defect prior to injury as a condition precedent to suing subsequent to the injury. While the stated legislative purpose of the law is to shift the duty of care regarding sidewalks to the citizenry, it also seems a convenient way of saving municipal money by reducing so-called slip and fall litigation. *See, e.g., Amabile v. City of Buffalo*, 93 N.Y.2d 471, 693 N.Y.S.2d 77, 715 N.E.2d 104 (1999) (actual notice must be provided even if the municipality had "constructive" notice of the defect).

(5) A particularly short condition precedent applies to claims made for benefits claimed from insurers under New York's No-Fault law (Insurance Law § 5106[a]) by motor vehicle accident victims. Regulations promulgated by the Superintendent of Insurance provide a 30-day time limit for a filing a notice of claim. These regulations have been upheld by the Court of Appeals. *See Medical Soc'y of State v. Serio*, 100 N.Y.2d 854, 863, 768 N.Y.S.2d 423, 428, 800 N.E.2d 728, 733 (2003).

PROBLEM F

Marcia, an infant, was a passenger in a car driven by her mother, Alice, when a New York City police car driven by Sid collided with their car on Feb. 17, 1995. Although both Marcia and Alice were seriously injured, neither of them served a notice of claim on the City of New York until April 5, 2001. On the same date, each commenced an action against the city and moved for permission to file a late notice of claim. How should the court rule on their respective motions? (Marcia turned eighteen on Feb. 15, 2001.) Consider Gen. Mun. Law § 50-e(5) and the following cases.

WILLIAMS v. NASSAU COUNTY MEDICAL CENTER
Court of Appeals
6 N.Y.3d 531, 814 N.Y.S.2d 580, 847 N.E.2d 1154 (2006)

Rosenblatt, J.

In General Municipal Law § 50-e, the Legislature enacted a protocol for serving a notice of claim as a condition precedent to a suit against a public corporation. Section 50-e(1) requires that the notice be served within 90 days after the claim arises. The Legislature, however, gave courts discretion to extend the time and devised criteria for determining whether to grant extensions (*see Cohen v Pearl River Union Free School Dist.*, 51 N.Y.2d 256, 265-266, 414 N.E.2d 639, 434 N.Y.S.2d 138 [1980]).

Section 50-e(5), the late-notice statute, directs the court to consider, in particular, whether within 90 days or a reasonable time thereafter the public corporation (or its attorney or insurance carrier) acquired actual knowledge of the facts underlying the claim. In deciding whether to grant an extension, the court must also consider a host of factors, including infancy and whether allowing late filing would result in substantial prejudice to the public corporation. . . .

In the case before us, the infant plaintiff alleges that his epilepsy and developmental disabilities were the result of negligence on the part of Nassau County Medical Center and its employees in connection with his birth in September 1993. The medical employees in attendance gave his mother pitocin, a drug used to facilitate the birth. The delivery involved two attempts at vacuum extraction and, ultimately, the use of forceps. According to the hospital records, the mother's pelvis was adequate to accommodate the baby's head and the birth was without complication. The infant weighed eight pounds, three and one-half ounces. His Apgar score (an index to evaluate the condition of a newborn infant with ten being a perfect score) was within satisfactory range: eight at one minute after birth and nine at five minutes after birth. The records also reveal that there were marks on his forehead from the forceps and his clavicle was broken.

In support of his motion for late service of a notice of claim, plaintiff submitted an affidavit from a physician who interpreted the hospital records and alleged that the hospital knew or should have known that complications would and did occur. He averred that the size of the mother's pelvis and signs of fetal distress argued against the use of pitocin, and that after birth the baby was trembling and showed physical signs of trauma. The defendants argue that plaintiff's disability was not apparent until, at the age of one or two, he began to experience epileptic seizures and show delayed development.

The record reveals that in 1995 plaintiff had an electroencephalogram (EEG), a test to trace his brain waves. The results were normal, but EEGs in 1998 and 1999 showed signs of abnormality. On September 3, 2003, ten years after plaintiff's birth, his counsel sent the hospital a notice of claim alleging, in essence, that plaintiff suffered brain damage resulting from the hospital's malpractice during his delivery.

Exercising its discretion, Supreme Court granted leave to serve the late notice. The Appellate Division, however, reversed "on the law and as a matter of discretion" (13 A.D.3d 363, 786 N.Y.S.2d 207 [2d Dept 2004]). We affirm. We will treat the three relevant General Municipal Law § 50-e(5) criteria in their statutory order.

Actual Knowledge of the Essential Facts

Plaintiff argues that the Appellate Division erred by requiring that the defendants have actual knowledge of the "specific claim." In support, plaintiff emphasizes that section 50-e(5) contemplates "actual knowledge of the essential facts constituting the claim," not knowledge of a specific legal theory. We agree with plaintiff's point, but do not read the Appellate Division's decision as deviating from that principle. The hospital's records reveal that the delivery was difficult, but that when it was over there was scant reason to identify or predict any lasting harm to the child, let alone a developmental disorder or epilepsy. The infant's Apgar scores were satisfactory, and even two years later his EEG was normal. Under these circumstances defendants could well have concluded that when plaintiff left the hospital there was nothing wrong with him beyond a broken clavicle (cf. Medley v Cichon, 305 A.D.2d 643, 761 N.Y.S.2d 666 [2d Dept 2003] [where hospital records indicated, among other things, that infant plaintiff required resuscitation and had an Apgar score of zero, actual knowledge of injury was established]).

We do not agree with plaintiff's suggestion that because defendants have medical records, they necessarily have actual knowledge of the facts constituting the claim. Merely having or creating hospital records, without more, does not establish actual knowledge of a potential injury where the records do not evince that the medical staff, by its acts or omissions, inflicted any injury on plaintiff during the birth process.

The relevant inquiry is whether the hospital had actual knowledge of the facts — as opposed to the legal theory — underlying the claim. Where, as here, there is little to suggest injury attributable to malpractice during delivery, comprehending or recording the facts surrounding the delivery cannot equate to knowledge of facts underlying a claim.

Infancy

As to this factor, plaintiff claims that the Appellate Division improperly required that he show a "nexus" between his infancy and the delay in service, or, put differently, that the delay was a product of his infancy. The history of section 50-e(5) and the case law demonstrate that a nexus between infancy and delay, while not a requirement, remains a statutory factor that a court should take into account. The Appellate Division concluded that "the 10-year delay in moving, in effect, for leave to serve a late notice of claim was not the product of the plaintiff's infancy" (13 A.D.3d at 364). Its holding does not treat the absence of a nexus as fatal to a plaintiff's claim.

Before 1976, section 50-e(5) allowed late service, at the discretion of the court, "where the claimant is an infant, or is mentally or physically incapacitated, *and by reason of such disability* fails to serve a notice of claim within the time specified" (emphasis supplied). Even then, this causation requirement was not inflexible. Analyzing the previous version of the statute, we stated in *Matter of Murray v City of New York* (30 N.Y.2d 113, 282 N.E.2d 103, 331 N.Y.S.2d 9 [1972]) that "the impediment [to timely filing] may reasonably be presumed to attend infancy; there is no requirement that it be factually demonstrated" (*id.* at 120). Rather, the causative relationship between infancy and the delay was a matter committed to the court's discretion, in view of the circumstances in a given case (*id.* at 119; *see also Sherman v Metropolitan Transp. Auth.*, 36 N.Y.2d 776, 329 N.E.2d 673, 368 N.Y.S.2d 842 [1975]).

The Legislature deleted the causation language and added a list of considerations that should come into play, including the simple fact of infancy. This change, however, does not preclude a court from examining whether infancy caused the delay in serving the notice. In deciding whether to allow late service of a notice of claim the court must consider "all other relevant facts and circumstances" (General Municipal Law § 50-e[5]). A delay of service caused by infancy would make a more compelling argument to justify an extension. Conversely, the lack of a causative nexus may make the delay less excusable, but not fatally deficient. It all goes into the mix. The Appellate Division, we conclude, did not exceed its discretion by pointing out that, among other reasons for denying an extension, the delay was not the product of plaintiff's infancy.

Substantial Prejudice

Plaintiff also asks us to hold that the Appellate Division incorrectly burdened him with the responsibility of showing lack of substantial prejudice to the defendants as a result of late service of the notice of claim. Although the length of the delay is not alone dispositive, it is influential.[3] Here, there was a 10-year delay.

---

[3] In an analogous situation, commencing an action or special proceeding, late service is permissible under CPLR 306-b "upon good cause shown or in the interest of justice." We have noted, in that context, that lengthy delays in service can lead a court to infer substantial prejudice (*Leader v Maroni, Ponzini & Spencer*, 97 N.Y.2d 95, 107, 761 N.E.2d 1018, 736 N.Y.S.2d 291 [2001]).

Plaintiff argues that the defendants were not substantially prejudiced on the theory that the hospital knew or should have known of the essential facts constituting his claim. Like the length of the delay in service, proof that the defendant had actual knowledge is an important factor in determining whether the defendant is substantially prejudiced by such a delay. We have no cause to disturb the Appellate Division's determination that defendants did not have actual knowledge. Accordingly, that court's finding of substantial prejudice was within its discretion.

In summary, the 1976 amendments to § 50-e(5) de-emphasized the importance of a nexus between a plaintiff's infancy and the delay in service of a notice of claim. The statute now contains a non-exhaustive list of factors that the court should weigh, and compels consideration of all relevant facts and circumstances. This approach provides flexibility for the courts and requires them to exercise discretion. Under the pre-1976 version of the statute, we noted that "where satisfied that the court has acted within the perimeters of reason, we have consistently affirmed the exercise of discretion whether it has been invoked to sustain or deny grants of permission for late filing" (*Matter of Murray*, 30 N.Y.2d at 119). In line with that premise, we find no abuse of discretion by the Appellate Division.

Accordingly, the Appellate Division order should be affirmed, with costs.

NOTE

In *Cohen v. Pearl River Union Free Sch. Dist.*, 51 N.Y.2d 256, 434 N.Y.S.2d 138, 414 N.E.2d 639 (1980), the Court of Appeals considered "whether the period during which a court may grant an extension of time within which to serve notice of claim [pursuant to Gen. Mun. Law § 50-e(5)] is tolled during the infancy of the claimant in accordance with CPLR 208." The infant petitioner had injured his foot on September 30, 1975 by stepping on a "hidden object" protruding from the Pearl River High School grounds. However, he did not bring suit until December 5, 1977, when his father applied for judicial leave to serve a late notice of claim. The school district opposed the application, arguing that it had been prejudiced by the delayed notice and that, regardless, the application was time-barred. The Court held that, under the statute as amended in 1976, applications pursuant § 50-e(5) get the benefit of the tolling provisions for of CPLR 208 for infants, because § 50-e(5) provides that "[t]he extension shall not exceed the time limited for the commencement of an action by the claimant against the public corporation." The Court wrote: "[W]here the Legislature has itself chosen to measure the time for complying with the condition precedent by making direct reference to an external Statute of Limitations . . . there is no basis in law for withholding application of the tolls and extensions which ordinarily affect that Statute of Limitations. This is particularly so in a case such as this, where the Legislature has manifested a clear intention that the toll for disability be taken into account. . . ."

MATTER OF NEWSON v. CITY OF NEW YORK
Appellate Division, Second Department
87 A.D.2d 630, 448 N.Y.S.2d 224 (1982)

MEMORANDUM BY THE COURT.

In a proceeding for leave to serve a late notice of claim pursuant to section 50-e of the General Municipal Law, claimants appeal. . . .

Special Term, in refusing to grant claimants permission to serve a late notice of claim, erroneously noted that such application is to be granted only in exceptional cases, and concluded that at bar there were no exceptional circumstances warranting such relief. The 1976 amendment to subdivision 5 of section 50-e of the General Municipal Law liberalized the granting of such applications and provided greater judicial discretion in granting relief from the 90-day filing requirement by permitting consideration of various factors, including whether the public corporation or those acting for it acquired factual knowledge of the essential facts of the claim (*see Matter of Beary v. City of Rye*, 44 N.Y.2d 398, 406 N.Y.S.2d 9, 377 N.E.2d 453). At bar, hospital records were kept of all procedures performed upon the injured claimant and all treatments provided him over the course of his medical treatment by respondents. Moreover, the allegedly negligent acts were necessarily performed by agents of the hospital. Accordingly, it cannot be said that respondents did not have actual knowledge of the essential facts constituting the malpractice claim. As such, respondents were not substantially prejudiced in maintaining their defense by the approximately four and one-half month delay in serving the notice of claim.

NOTES

(1) Not all courts are as forgiving as the preceding opinion might imply. See, in addition to *Williams v. County of Nassau Medical Center, supra, Robertson v. City of New York*, 146 A.D.2d 456, 536 N.Y.S.2d 70 (1st Dep't), *aff'd*, 74 N.Y.2d 781, 545 N.Y.S.2d 102, 543 N.E.2d 745 (1989) (the adult plaintiff, who had suffered serious injuries in an auto accident, was denied permission to file a late notice of claim when his application was made fifteen months after the accident notwithstanding that the defendant had otherwise been given timely notice of the accident and that the plaintiff suffered from post-accident amnesia).

(2) Under the facts given in Problem F, would service of a notice of claim on the City of New York be a condition precedent to an action against Sid (the policeman) personally? According to Gen. Mun. Law § 50-e(b) the answer is yes, if Sid is entitled to indemnification by the city. As to that point, see *id.*, § 50-a (indemnification required if motor vehicle was driven in the course of duty). *See also Alifieris v. American Airlines, Inc.*, 63 N.Y.2d 370, 482 N.Y.S.2d 453, 472 N.E.2d 303 (1984).

(3) The one-year and ninety-day statute of limitations applicable to an action against a municipality is automatically tolled during the pendency of an application to file a late notice of claim. *Giblin v. Nassau County Med. Ctr.*, 61 N.Y.2d 67, 471 N.Y.S.2d 563, 459 N.E.2d 856 (1984).

(4) A condition precedent may be imposed by contract as well as by statute. Many liability insurance policies require that notice of an occurrence be given to the insurer "as soon as practicable," or as soon as the insured learns of the claim. Failure to do so forfeits the protection of the policy. *See, e.g., Argo Corp. v. Greater N.Y. Mut. Ins. Co.*, 4 N.Y.3d 332, 794 N.Y.S.2d 704, 827 N.E.2d 762 (2005). There, plaintiff Argo Corporation had notified its insurer of a liability claim against it 14 months after it was first served with a tenant's lawsuit, and six months after a default judgment was entered against it. The policy contained a provision requiring the insured to notify the insurer "as soon as practicable" after an occurrence. The Court of Appeals held that the notice was unreasonably late and that the insurer was entitled to disclaim coverage without showing prejudice. Compare *Rekemeyer v. State Farm Mutual Automobile Insurance Co.*, 4 N.Y.3d 468, 796 N.Y.S.2d 13, 828 N.E.2d 970 (2005), in which the injured claimant had failed to give her insurer notice "as soon as practicable" of her claim to payment under the supplementary uninsured/underinsured motorists provision of her insurance contract. The Court held that since the insurer had actual notice of her injuries and could not show any prejudice resulting from the tardy notice, it could not disclaim coverage.

(5) An action based on 42 U.S.C. § 1983, the general federal civil rights statute, cannot be dismissed for failure to comply with a state notice of claim requirement, even if the claim arises out of conduct (such as an assault by a police officer) to which such a notice of claim requirement would be applicable if the action sounded only in state law. *Felder v. Casey*, 487 U.S. 131, 108 S. Ct. 2302, 101 L. Ed. 2d 123 (1988). Notice of claim statutes, the Supreme Court there held, are incompatible with the remedial purposes of § 1983. An earlier New York decision to the contrary is thus no longer to be relied upon. *See 423 S. Salina St., Inc. v. City of Syracuse*, 68 N.Y.2d 474, 510 N.Y.S.2d 507, 503 N.E.2d 63 (1986), *cert. denied*, 481 U.S. 1008 (1987).

Compare *Mills v. County of Monroe*, 59 N.Y.2d 307, 464 N.Y.S.2d 709, 451 N.E.2d 456, *cert. denied,* 464 U.S. 1018 (1983), which held that the "notice of claim" provision of County Law § 52 applies even to actions alleging violations of federal and state civil rights laws. The court held that plaintiff's claim, even though it alleged employment discrimination on the basis of race and national origin in violation of 42 U.S.C. § 1981, was barred for failure to serve a notice. This case is of doubtful validity as a result of *Felder v. Casey, supra.* Although *Felder* involved 42 U.S.C. § 1983 rather than § 1981, the same principle of incompatibility would appear to apply.

Part Three
THE STRUCTURE OF THE LITIGATION

Chapter 8
JOINDER OF PARTIES

§ 8.01 INTRODUCTORY NOTE

In this chapter we examine the rules governing the joinder of parties to the action and the tactical considerations affecting the use of those rules. In substantial part, the party structure of a case is determined by the plaintiff upon deciding whether to join forces with any co-plaintiffs and whether to join more than one person as defendants. (These decisions should be made prior to commencing the action — prior, indeed, to deciding in what forum to commence it, for the identity of the defendants will naturally affect the problem of jurisdiction.) The plaintiff is given a good deal of latitude in deciding whom to include as parties, CPLR 1002 (*see also* CPLR 1006 permitting interpleader and CPLR article 9 allowing class actions), but there are some who must be included, CPLR 1001.

The party structure of the action is not left completely in the plaintiff's hands. The defendant may "claim over" against another by commencing a third-party action, and the third-party defendant in turn may add still others, CPLR 1007, 1011. Strangers to the action may intervene in it. CPLR 1012, 1013. In certain situations, as when a party dies, substitution of new parties is required. CPLR 1015; *see also* CPLR 1016-1020.

§ 8.02 PERMISSIVE JOINDER: CPLR 1002

BENDER v. UNDERWOOD
Appellate Division, First Department
93 A.D.2d 747, 461 N.Y.S.2d 301 (1983)

Memorandum Decision.

Order, Supreme Court, New York County, entered March 16, 1982, unanimously modified, on the law, the facts and in the exercise of discretion, without costs or disbursements, only to the extent of denying the motion to consolidate for joint trial those actions where appellant, Ricardo Crudo, is a defendant and otherwise affirmed. . . .

These six personal injury actions were brought to recover damages sustained as a result of each plaintiff having undergone a hair implantation process under the medical advice and direction of appellant Crudo. In addition to appellant, the named defendants include the manufacturer, suppliers and distributors of the process formula used to implant synthetic hair, by which hair fibers were sutured through the scalp. The actions as against appellant proceed on a theory of medical malpractice and lack of informed consent, with allegations, *inter alia*, that appellant failed to properly treat and examine plaintiffs; improperly supervised or performed the implantation process; misrepresented that the process was safe; and failed to obtain plaintiffs' informed consent.

On review of the record we find that although common questions of law and fact are present, insofar as concerns appellant Crudo, individual issues predominate, concerning particular circumstances applicable to each plaintiff so as to preclude the direction of a joint trial. Although it is claimed that each plaintiff underwent the same implantation process and was allegedly subjected to the same basic type of malpractice, clearly, each treatment was separate and distinct, involving different plaintiffs, each with individual medical histories. Other individual issues relate to such matters as informed consent, culpable conduct by each plaintiff and the extent of any breach of duty by appellant. Moreover, under the circumstances of this case, the resulting and cumulative prejudice to appellant by permitting the jury, in one trial, to determine the multiple claims of malpractice at issue here, far outweighs the benefit derived from the conduct of a joint trial (*Reid v. Haher*, 88 A.D.2d 873, 451 N.Y.S.2d 775; CPLR § 603; *cf. Harby Associates, Inc. v. Seaboyer*, 82 A.D.2d 992, 440 N.Y.S.2d 422). In addition to the potential for resulting prejudice, of further relevance on the issue is the possibility of confusion for the jury (*see Doll v. Castiglione*, 86 A.D.2d 711, 446 N.Y.S.2d 537).

NOTES

(1) In the principal case, the court refused to permit the consolidation of separate actions. CPLR 602, 603. Could the plaintiffs simply have commenced one joint action? See CPLR 1002 and consider *Akely v. Kinnicutt*, 238 N.Y. 466, 144 N.E. 682 (1924), in which the Court of Appeals held that nearly two hundred victims of an alleged stock manipulation scheme could properly join their claims against the defendants, even though the plaintiffs purchased the stock in discrete transactions from various brokers. Said the Court:

> . . . The common issues are basic, and would seem to be the ones around which must revolve the greatest struggle, and to which must be directed the greatest amount of evidence. These are in the ones in substance whether the defendants conspired to organize a corporation and float its stock at much more than its real value, and whether in pursuance of this conspiracy they fraudulently issued a prospectus showing the stock to be much more valuable than it really was, and whether they did this with the deliberate intent to cheat and defraud the public into buying the stock at an unconscionable value. These questions are common to every cause of action. The separate issues, which must be tried in each instance, will be in the main whether the plaintiff saw the

prospectus or learned of its representations, was influenced thereby, and at a certain date bought a certain amount of stock at a certain price in advance of its real value in reliance thereon. While these latter may equal in number the common ones, it seems from the face of the complaint by which we must decide the question, that the majority of them cannot involve much evidence or lengthy dispute, but that the trial of them will yield in contentious importance and difficulty to the questions which have been first suggested, and that, therefore, this is a case which comes well within the meaning of the statute so far as related to common questions.

Then it is urged by appellants that there is lacking that feature, essential to the collection in one complaint of all of these causes of action, that they should be "in respect of or arising out of the same transaction or series of transactions." We do not find any basis for this claim. Each cause of action is based upon a purchase of stock at a fictitious value in reliance upon representations, as alleged, of defendants in respect of the value of that stock, which were untrue and fraudulent, and made for the purpose of inducing the public including plaintiff to make such purchases. The transaction in respect of or out of which the cause of action arises is the purchase by plaintiff of his stock under such circumstances, and such purchases conducted by one plaintiff after another respectively plainly constitute a series of transactions within the meaning of the statute. The purchase by plaintiff of his stock is not robbed of its character as a "transaction" because, as appellants seem to suggest, the transaction was not a dual one occurring between the plaintiff and the defendants, and the many purchases by plaintiffs respectively do not lose their character as a series of transactions because they occurred at different places and times extending through many months.

238 N.Y. at 473-74, 144 N.E. at 684.

In cases typified by *Akely v. Kinnicutt*, what institutional interests does the judiciary have in permissive joinder? Are the tactical concerns of the parties the same?

(2) Consolidation of separately brought and pending actions achieves somewhat the same result as joinder of parties. CPLR 602 authorizes consolidation upon motion and in the court's discretion. Consolidation is a somewhat broader device than permissive joinder, as the only requirement is the existence of common questions of law or fact. There is no requirement of identity of parties in the actions sought to be consolidated. Consolidation is intended to further the same goals as joinder of parties, and much the same criteria will be applied in granting consolidation as in denying a severance. Those criteria include possible prejudice accruing to the party opposing the motion, trial convenience, the possibility of jury confusion or needlessly complicated actions, the extent of the common questions, risk of inconsistent results, and avoidance of delay and

expense. An alternative to consolidation is joint trial of common issues, also authorized by CPLR 602.

(3) It was established in *Tanbro Fabrics Corp. v. Beaunit Mills, Inc.*, 4 A.D.2d 519, 167 N.Y.S.2d 387 (1st Dep't 1957), that joinder of defendants alleged to be liable in the alternative was permissible so long as "the alternative liability arises out of a common transaction or occurrence involving common questions of fact and law." 4 A.D.2d at 524, 167 N.Y.S.2d at 392. The court added that "[t]he right of joinder . . . is always counterbalanced . . . by the power of the court to grant a severance . . . if prejudice or injustice appear." 4 A.D.2d at 525, 167 N.Y.S.2d at 393. In the latter vein, see *Gunning v. Buffalo Transit Co.*, 20 A.D.2d 966, 249 N.Y.S.2d 999 (4th Dep't 1964), in which plaintiff joined as co-defendants two alleged tortfeasors who injured him in separate auto accidents occurring fifteen months apart. Held: a severance should have been granted on defendant's motion. *Compare Dolce v. Jones*, 145 A.D.2d 594, 536 N.Y.S.2d 134 (2d Dep't 1988) (plaintiff, injured in three separate auto accidents over an eighteen-month period, properly joined her claims against three defendants in one action; severance held improper).

(4) Uniform Rule for the New York State Trial Courts 202.69, promulgated on Jan. 24, 2002, creates a formal procedure for coordinating different actions pending in different judicial districts. The rule allows for the joinder of two or more actions having a common question of law or fact solely for pre-trial purposes. The rule establishes a Litigation Coordinating Panel of four Supreme Court Justices to determine the appropriateness of coordination in any given case. There are three ways coordination can be raised: the justice or administrative judge presiding over at least one of the actions can apply to the Panel, the Panel can *sua sponte* require parties to show why coordination should not be directed, or a party in at least one of the actions can file a motion for coordination. The Panel considers a number of factors in determining appropriateness of coordination, including "the complexity of the actions: whether common questions of fact or law exist, and the importance of such questions to the determination of the issues; the risk that coordination may unreasonably delay the progress, increase the expense, or complicate the processing of any action or otherwise prejudice a party; the risk of duplicative or inconsistent rulings, orders or judgments; the convenience of the parties, witnesses and counsel; whether coordinated discovery would be advantageous; efficient utilization of judicial resources and the facilities and personnel of the court; the manageability of a coordinated litigation; whether issues of insurance, limits on assets and potential bankruptcy can be best addressed in coordinated proceedings; and the pendency of related matters in the federal courts and in the courts of other states." 22 N.Y.C.R.R. § 202.69. *See also* David Fleischer & Jodi Kleinick, *Litigation: Coordinating Multidistrict Cases in State Courts*, N.Y.L.J., December 1, 2003, at S6. The rule is similar to the federal multidistrict litigation statute, 28 U.S.C. § 1407, but it sets forth more factors and allows the coordinating justice to try cases if the parties consent. *See* Mark Herrmann & Geof-

frey J. Ritts, *New York Adopts Procedures for Statewide Coordination of Complex Litigation*, N.Y. St. B.J., October 2003.

(5) Joinder of multiple defendants is also useful in product liability cases when the plaintiff does not know which of several competing manufacturers made the product which caused the injury. The Court of Appeals addressed the knotty issues presented by the competing claims of the plaintiffs and defendants in this situation:

HYMOWITZ v. ELI LILLY & CO.
New York Court of Appeals
73 N.Y.2d 487, 541 N.Y.S.2d 941, 539 N.E.2d 1069 (1989)

WACHTLER, CH. J.:

Plaintiffs in these appeals allege that they were injured by the drug diethylstilbestrol (DES) ingested by their mothers during pregnancy. They seek relief against defendant DES manufacturers. While not class actions, these cases are representative of nearly 500 similar actions pending in the courts in this state; the rules articulated by the Court here, therefore, must do justice and be administratively feasible in the context of this mass litigation. With this in mind, we now resolve the issue twice expressly left open by this Court, and adopt a market share theory, using a national market, for determining liability and apportioning damages in DES cases in which identification of the manufacturer of the drug that injured the plaintiff is impossible (*see, Kaufman v Lilly & Co.*, 65 NY2d 449, 456; *Bichler v Lilly & Co.*, 55 NY2d 571, 580). . . .

I

. . . .

Although strong evidence links prenatal DES exposure to later development of serious medical problems, plaintiffs seeking relief in court for their injuries faced two formidable and fundamental barriers to recovery in this State; not only is identification of the manufacturer of the DES ingested in a particular case generally impossible, but, due to the latent nature of DES injuries, many claims were barred by the statute of limitations before the injury was discovered.

The identification problem has many causes. All DES was of identical chemical composition. Druggists usually filled prescriptions from whatever was on hand. Approximately 300 manufacturers produced the drug, with companies entering and leaving the market continuously during the 24 years that DES was sold for pregnancy use. The long latency period of a DES injury compounds the identification problem; memories fade, records are lost or destroyed, and witnesses die. Thus the pregnant women who took DES generally never knew who produced the drug they took, and there was no reason to attempt to discover this fact until many years after ingestion, at which time the information is not available.

. . . .

It is estimated that eventually 800 DES cases will be brought under the revival portion of this recent statute. Moreover, as indicated in *Bichler v Lilly & Co.* (*supra*), and as apparent from the record now before the Court, in the vast majority of these cases identification of the manufacturer of the DES that injured the plaintiff will be impossible. The Legislature, however, while reviving these time-barred actions, did not resolve the identification problem.

The present appeals are before the Court in the context of summary judgment motions. In all of the appeals defendants moved for summary judgment dismissing the complaints because plaintiffs could not identify the manufacturer of the drug that allegedly injured them. . . . The trial court denied all of these motions. . . . The Appellate Division affirmed in all respects and certified to this Court the questions of whether the orders of the trial court were properly made. We answer these questions in the affirmative.

II

In a products liability action, identification of the exact defendant whose product injured the plaintiff is, of course, generally required (*see, e.g., Morrissey v Conservative Gas Corp.*, 285 AD 825, *affd* 1 NY 2d 741; Prosser & Keeton, Torts § 103, at 713 [5th ed]). In DES cases in which such identification is possible, actions may proceed under established principles of products liability. . . . The record now before us, however, presents the question of whether a DES plaintiff may recover against a DES manufacturer when identification of the producer of the specific drug that caused the injury is impossible.

A.

As we noted in *Bichler v Lilly Co.* (*supra* at 580, n5), the accepted tort doctrines of alternative liability and concerted action are available in some personal injury cases to permit recovery where the precise identification of a wrongdoer is impossible. However, we agree with the near unanimous views of the high state courts that have considered the matter that these doctrines in their unaltered common law forms do not permit recovery in DES cases (*see, e.g., Sindell v Abbott Labs*, 26 Cal. 3d 588; *Collins v Lilly & Co.*, 116 Wis 2d 166; *Martin v Abbott Labs, supra; but see, Abel v Lilly & Co.*, 418 Mich 311 [held that there was a question of fact presented as to alternative liability and concerted action]).

The paradigm of alternative liability is found in the case of *Summers v Tice* (33 Cal2d 80). In *Summers* (*supra*), plaintiff and the two defendants were hunting, and defendants carried identical shotguns and ammunition. During the hunt, defendants shot simultaneously at the same bird, and plaintiff was struck by birdshot from one of the defendants' guns. The court held that where two defendants breach a duty to the plaintiff, but there is uncertainty regarding which one caused the injury, "the burden is upon such actor to prove that he has not caused the harm" (Restatement [Second] of Torts § 433B[3]; *Bichler v Lilly & Co.*, at 580, n5; *cf., Ravo v Rogatnick*, 70 NY2d 305 [successive tortfeasors may be held jointly and severally liable for an indivisible injury to the plaintiff]). The central rationale for shifting the burden of proof in such a situation is that without this device both defendants will be silent, and plaintiff will not recover; with alternative liability, however, defendants will be forced to speak, and reveal the culpable party, or else be held jointly and severally liable themselves. Consequently, use of the alternative liability doctrine generally requires that the defendants have better access to information than does the plaintiff, and that all possible tortfeasors be before the court (*see, Summers v Tice*, at 86; Restatement [Second] of Torts § 433B, comment h). It is also recognized that alternative liability rests on the notion that where there is a small number of possible wrongdoers, all of whom breached a duty to the plaintiff, the likelihood that any one of them injured the plaintiff is relatively high, so that forcing them to exonerate themselves, or be held liable, is not unfair (*Sindell v Abbott Labs*, at 139).

In DES cases, however, there is a great number of possible wrongdoers, who entered and left the market at different times, and some of whom no longer exist. Additionally, in DES cases many years elapse between the ingestion of the drug and injury. Consequently, DES defendants are not in any better position than are plaintiffs to identify the manufacturer of the DES ingested in any given case, nor is there any real prospect of having all the possible producers before the court. Finally, while it may be fair to employ alternative liability in cases involving only a small number of potential wrongdoers, that fairness disappears with the decreasing probability that any one of the defendants actually caused the injury. This is particularly true when applied to DES where the chance that a particular producer caused the injury is often very remote. . . . Alternative liability, therefore, provides DES plaintiffs no relief.

Nor does the theory of concerted action, in its pure form, supply a basis for recovery. This doctrine, seen in drag racing cases, provides for joint and several liability on the part of all defendants having an understanding, express or tacit, to participate in "a common plan or design to commit a tortious act" (Prosser & Keeton, Torts, § 46, at 323 [5th ed]. . . .) As we noted in *Bichler v Lilly & Co.*, and as the present record reflects, drug companies were engaged in extensive parallel conduct in developing and marketing DES. There is nothing in the record, however, beyond this similar conduct to show any agreement, tacit or otherwise, to market DES for pregnancy use without taking proper steps to ensure the drug's safety. Parallel activity, without more, is insufficient to establish the agreement element necessary to maintain a concerted action claim. . . . Thus this theory also fails in supporting an action by DES plaintiffs.

In short, extant common law doctrines, unmodified, provide no relief for the DES plaintiff unable to identify the manufacturer of the drug that injured her. This is not a novel conclusion; in the last decade a number of courts in other jurisdictions also have concluded that present theories do not support a cause of action in DES cases. Some courts, upon reaching this conclusion, have declined to find any judicial remedy for the DES plaintiffs who cannot identify the particular manufacturer of the DES ingested by their mothers (*see, Zafft v Lilly & Co.*, 67 SW2d 241 [Mo] [*en banc*]; *Mulcahy v Lilly & Co.*, 386 NW2d 67 [Iowa] [stating that any change in the law to allow for recovery in nonidentification DES cases should come from the legislature]). Other courts, however, have found that some modification of existing doctrine is appropriate to allow for relief for those injured by DES of unknown manufacture (*e.g., Sindell v Abbot Labs, Collins v Lilly & Co., Martin v Abbott Labs, supra*).

We conclude that the present circumstances call for recognition of a realistic avenue of relief for plaintiffs injured by DES. These appeals present many of the same considerations that have prompted this Court in the past to modify the rules of personal injury liability, in order "to achieve the ends of justice in a more modern context" (*see, People v Hobson*, 39 NY2d 479, 489; *Codling v Paglia*, 32 NY2d 330, 341), and we perceive that here judicial action is again required "to overcome the inordinately difficult problems of proof" caused by contemporary products and marketing techniques (*see, Bichler v Lilly & Co.*, at 579-580 [quoting *Caprara v Chrysler Corp.*, 52 NY2d 114, 123]).

Indeed, it would be inconsistent with the reasonable expectations of a modern society to say to these plaintiffs that because of the insidious nature of an injury that long remains dormant, and because so many manufacturers, each behind a curtain, contributed to the devastation, the cost of injury should be borne by the innocent and not the wrongdoers. This is particularly so where the legislature consciously created these expectations by reviving hundreds of DES cases. Consequently, the ever-evolving dictates of justice and fairness, which are the heart of our common-law system, require formation of a remedy for injuries caused by DES (*see, Woods v Lancet*, 303 NY 349, 355; *see, also*, Kaye, *The Human Dimension in Appellate Judging: A Brief Reflection on a Timeless Concern*, 73 Cornell L. Rev. 1004).

We stress, however, that the DES situation is a singular case, with manufacturers acting in a parallel manner to produce an identical, generically marketed product, which causes injury many years later, and which has evoked a legislative response reviving previously barred actions. Given this unusual scenario, it is more appropriate that the loss be borne by those that produced the drug for use during pregnancy, rather than by those who were injured by the use, even where the precise manufacturer of the drug cannot be identified in a particular action. We turn then to the question of how to fairly and equitably apportion the loss occasioned by DES, in a case where the exact manufacturer of the drug that caused the injury is unknown.

B.

The past decade of DES litigation has produced a number of alternative approaches to resolve this question. Thus, in a sense, we are now in an enviable position; the efforts of other courts provided examples for contending with this difficult issue, and enough time has passed so that the actual administration and real effects of these solutions now can be observed. With these useful guides in hand, a path may be struck for our own conclusion.

First, this Court's opinion in *Bichler v Lilly & Co.* must be considered. There the jury was instructed on a modified version of concerted action, which, in effect, substituted the fact of conscious parallel activity by manufacturers for the usual common law requirement that there be proof of an actual agreement between actors to jointly act tortiously (*id.* at 584). The defendant in *Bichler* did not object to this instruction, and the modified concerted action theory became the law applicable to that particular case (*id.* at 583-584).

Now given the opportunity to assess the merits of this theory, we decline to adopt it as the law of this State. Parallel behavior, the major justification for visiting liability caused by the product of one manufacturer upon the head of another under this analysis, is a common occurrence in industry generally. We believe, therefore, that inferring agreement from the fact of parallel activity alone improperly expands the concept of concerted action beyond a rational or fair limit; among other things, it potentially renders small manufacturers, in the case of DES and in countless other industries, jointly liable for all damages stemming from the defective products of an entire industry. . . .

A narrower basis for liability, tailored more closely to the varying culpableness of individual DES producers, is the market share concept. First judicially articulated by the California Supreme Court in *Sindell v Abbott Labs*, variations upon this theme have been adopted by other courts. . . . In *Sindell v Abbott Labs* (*supra*), the Court synthesized the market share concept by modifying the *Summers v Tice* alternative liability rationale in two ways. It first loosened the requirement that all possible wrongdoers be before the court, and instead made a "substantial share" sufficient. The court then held that each defendant who could not prove that it did not actually injure plaintiff would be liable according to that manufacturer's market share. The court's central justification for adopting this approach was its belief that limiting a defendant's liability to its market share will result, over the run of cases, in liability on the part of a defendant roughly equal to the injuries the defendant actually caused (*id.* at 612).

In the recent case of *Brown v Superior Court* (44 Cal 3d 1049), the California Supreme Court resolved some apparent ambiguity in *Sindell v Abbott Labs*, and held that a manufacturer's liability is several only, and, in cases in which all manufacturers in the market are not joined for any reason, liability will still be limited to market share, resulting in a less than 100% recovery for a plaintiff. Finally, it is noteworthy that determining market shares under *Sindell v Abbott Labs* proved difficult and engendered years of litigation. After attempts at using smaller geographical units, it was eventually determined that the national market provided the most feasible and fair solution, and this national market information was compiled. . . .

Four years after *Sindell v Abbott Labs*, the Wisconsin Supreme Court followed with *Collins v Lilly & Co.* (116 Wis 2d 166). Deciding the identification issue without the benefit of the extensive California litigation over market shares, the Wisconsin court held that it was prevented from following *Sindell* due to "the practical difficulty of defining and proving market share" (*id.* at 189). Instead of focusing on tying liability closely to the odds of actual causation, as the *Sindell* court attempted, the *Collins* court took a broader perspective, and held that each defendant is liable in proportion to the amount of risk it created that the plaintiff would be injured by DES. Under the *Collins* structure, the "risk" each defendant is liable for is a question of fact in each case, with market shares being relevant to this determination (*id.* at 191, 200). Defendants are allowed, however, to exculpate themselves by showing that their product could not have caused the injury to the particular plaintiff (*id.* at 198).

The Washington Supreme Court, writing soon after *Collins v Lilly & Co.*, took yet another approach (*see, Martin v Abbott Labs*, 102 Wash 2d 581). The *Martin* court first rejected the *Sindell* market share theory due to the belief (which later proved to be erroneous in *Brown v Superior Court* [*supra*]) that California's approach distorted liability by inflating market shares to ensure plaintiffs of full recovery (*id.* at 601). The *Martin* court instead adopted what it termed "market share alternative liability," justified, it concluded, because "[e]ach defendant contributed to the risk of injury to the public, and consequently, the risk to individual plaintiffs" (*id.* at 604).

Under the Washington scheme, defendants are first allowed to exculpate themselves by proving by the preponderance of the evidence that they were not the manufacturer of the DES that injured plaintiff. Unexculpated defendants are presumed to have equal market shares, totalling 100%. Each defendant then has the opportunity to rebut this presumption by showing that its actual market share was less than presumed. If any defendants succeed in rebutting this presumption, the liability shares of the remaining defendants who could not prove their actual market share are inflated, so that the plaintiff received a 100% recovery (*id.* at 605-606).[1]

---

[1] The actual operation of this theory proved more mathematically complex when the court was presented with the question of what to do about unavailable defendants. Recognizing that the possibility of abuse existed when defendant implead unavailable defendants, who would then be assumed to have had an equal share of the market, the court placed the burden upon appearing defendants to prove the market share of the absent ones (*George v Parke-Davis*, 107 Wash 2d 584). If this can be proved, the plaintiff simply cannot recover the amount attributable to the absent defendant, and thus recovery in the case is less than 100%. If the market share of the absent defendant cannot be shown, the remaining defendants who cannot prove their market shares have their shares inflated to provide plaintiff with full recovery. Finally, if all appearing defendants can prove their market shares, their shares are never inflated, regardless of whether the market share of a non-appearing defendant can be proved or not; thus, in this situation, the plaintiff again will not recover her full damages (*id.*). The market shares of defendants is a question of fact in each case, and the relevant market can be a particular pharmacy, or county, or state, or even the country, depending upon the circumstances the case presents (*George v Parke-Davis, supra*).

Turning to the structure to be adopted in New York, we heed both the lessons learned through experience in other jurisdictions and the realities of the mass litigation of DES claims in this State. Balancing these considerations, we are led to the conclusion that a market share theory, based upon a national market, provides the best solution. As California discovered, the reliable determination of any market smaller than the national one likely is not practicable. Moreover, even if it were possible, of the hundreds of cases in the New York courts, without a doubt there are many in which the DES that allegedly caused injury was ingested in another State. Among the thorny issues this could present, perhaps the most daunting is the specter that the particular case could require the establishment of a separate market share matrix. We feel that this is an unfair, and perhaps impossible burden to routinely place upon the litigants in individual cases.

Nor do we believe that the Wisconsin approach of assessing the "risk" each defendant caused a particular plaintiff, to be litigated anew as a question of fact in each case, is the best solution for this State. Applied on a limited scale this theory may be feasible, and certainly is the most refined approach by allowing a more thorough consideration of how each defendant's actions threatened the plaintiff. We are wary, however, of setting loose, for application in the hundreds of cases pending in this State, a theory which requires the factfinder's individualized and open-ended assessment of the relative liabilities of scores of defendants in every case. Instead, it is our perception that the injustices arising from delayed recoveries and inconsistent results which this theory may produce in this State outweigh arguments calling for its adoption.

Consequently, for essentially practical reasons, we adopt a market share theory using a national market. We are aware that the adoption of a national market will likely result in a disproportion between the liability of individual manufacturers and the actual injuries each manufacturer caused in this State. Thus our market share theory cannot be founded upon the belief that, over the run of cases, liability will approximate causation in this State (*see, Sindell v Abbott Labs*, at 612). Nor does the use of a national market provide a reasonable link between liability and the risk created by a defendant to a particular plaintiff. . . . Instead, we choose to apportion liability so as to correspond to the overall culpability of each defendant, measured by the amount of risk of injury each defendant created to the public at large. Use of a national market is a fair method, we believe, of apportioning defendants' liabilities according to their total culpability in marketing DES for use during pregnancy. Under the circumstances, this is an equitable way to provide plaintiffs with the relief they deserve, while also rationally distributing the responsibility for plaintiffs' injuries among defendants.

To be sure, a defendant cannot be held liable if it did not participate in the marketing of DES for pregnancy use; if a DES producer satisfies its burden of proof of showing that it was not a member of the market of DES sold for pregnancy use, disallowing exculpation would be unfair and unjust. Nevertheless, because liability here is based on the overall risk produced, and not causation in a single case, there should be no exculpation of a defendant who, although a member of the market producing DES for pregnancy use, appears not to have caused a particular plaintiff's injury. It is merely a windfall for a producer to escape liability solely because it manufactured a more identifiable pill, or sold only to certain drugstores. These fortuities in no way diminish the culpability of a defendant for marketing the product, which is the basis of liability here.[2]

Finally, we hold that the liability of DES producers is several only, and should not be inflated when all participants in the market are not before the court in a particular case. We understand that, as a practical matter, this will prevent some plaintiffs from recovering 100% of their damages. However, we eschewed exculpation to prevent the fortuitous avoidance of liability, and thus, equitably, we decline to unleash the same forces to increase a defendant's liability beyond its fair share of responsibility.[3]

We are confronted here with an unprecedented identification problem, and have provided a solution that rationally apportions liability. We have heeded the practical lessons learned by other jurisdictions, resulting in our adoption of a national market theory with full knowledge that it concedes the lack of a logical link between liability and causation in a single case. The dissent ignores these lessons, and, endeavoring to articulate a theory it perceives to be closer to traditional law, sets out a construct in which liability is based upon chance, not upon the fair assessment of the acts of defendants. Under the dissent's theory, a manufacturer with a large market share may avoid liability in many cases just because it manufactured a memorably shaped pill. Conversely, a small manufacturer can be held jointly liable for the full amount of every DES injury in this State simply because the shape of its product was not remarkable, even though the odds, realistically, are exceedingly long that the small manufacturer caused the injury in any one particular case.

Therefore, although the dissent's theory based upon a "shifting the burden of proof" and joint and several liability is facially reminiscent of prior law, in the case of DES it is nothing more than advocating that bare fortuity be the test for liability. When faced with the novel identification problem posed by DES cases,

---

[2] Various defendants argue here that although they produced DES, it was not sold for pregnancy use. If a defendant was not a member of the national market of DES marketed for pregnancy, it is not culpable, and should not be liable. Consequently, if a particular defendant sold DES in a form unsuitable for use during pregnancy, or if a defendant establishes that its product was not marketed for pregnancy use, there should be no liability. From the record before the Court here, however, the facts are not developed well enough to establish that any defendants were not in the national market of DES sold for pregnancy use. Thus summary judgment cannot at this time be granted on this issue as to any defendants.

[3] The dissenter misapprehends the basis for liability here. We have not by the backdoor adopted a theory of concerted action. We avoided extending this theory, because its concomitant requirement of joint and several liability expands the burden on small manufacturers beyond a rational or fair limit. This result is reached by the dissent, not by the majority, so that criticism on this front is misplaced.

it is preferable to adopt a new theory that apportions fault rationally, rather than to contort extant doctrines beyond the point at which they provide a sound premise for determining liability.

Accordingly, in each case the order of the Appellate Division should be affirmed, with costs, and the certified question answered in the affirmative.

Opinion by CHIEF JUDGE WACHTLER. JUDGES ALEXANDER, TITONE and HANCOCK concur. JUDGE MOLLEN concurs in part and dissents in part in a separate opinion and votes to modify the opinion. JUDGES SIMONS, KAYE and BELLACOSA took no part.

. . . .

MOLLEN, J. (concurring in part and dissenting in part . . .).

The issue presented to the Court in this appeal is to determine whether the revival statute for DES claims is constitutional and has properly "opened the window" to enable injured parties to recover for their injuries caused by DES and, if so, how to best enable such plaintiffs to overcome the practical impossibility of bearing their normal burden of proof of demonstrating that the defendants caused their injuries. The majority has selected one approach to meet this issue. However, I am compelled to concur in part and dissent in part because I am convinced that another more appropriate method of approaching this issue is fairer and more just and equitable to the plaintiffs and to those defendants who could not have caused the plaintiff's injuries, and which is consistent with established principles tort law. . . . I am in complete agreement with the majority's view that the market share theory of liability, based upon a national market, is an appropriate means by which to accord DES plaintiffs an opportunity to seek recovery for their injuries. However, I respectfully disagree with the majority's conclusion that there should be no exculpation of those defendants who produced and marketed DES for pregnancy purposes, but who can prove, by a preponderance of the evidence, that they did not produce or market the particular pill ingested by the plaintiff's mother. Moreover, in order to ensure that these plaintiffs receive full recovery of their damages, as they are properly entitled to by any fair standard, I would retain the principle of imposing joint and several liability upon those defendants which cannot exculpate themselves.

. . . .

I fully concur with the above stated position of the majority and thus, I cannot agree that the imposition of liability on drug companies, in this case DES manufacturers, solely upon their contribution, in some measure, to the risk of injury by producing and marketing a defective drug, without any consideration given to whether the defendant drug companies actually caused the plaintiff's injuries, is appropriate or warranted. Rather, I would adopt a market share theory of liability, based upon a national market, which would provide for the shifting of the burden of proof on the issue of causation to the defendants and would impose liability upon all of the defendants who produced and marketed

DES for pregnancy purposes, except those who were able to prove that their product could not have caused the injury. Under this approach, DES plaintiffs, who are unable to identify the actual manufacturer of the pill ingested by their mother, would only be required to establish, (1) that the plaintiff's mother ingested DES during pregnancy; (2) that the plaintiff's injuries were caused by DES; and (3) that the defendant or defendants produced and marketed DES for pregnancy purposes. Thereafter, the burden of proof would shift to the defendants to exculpate themselves by establishing, by a preponderance of the evidence, that the plaintiff's mother could not have ingested their particular pill. Of those defendants who are unable to exculpate themselves from liability, their respective share of the plaintiff's damages would be measured by their share of the national market of DES produced and marketed for pregnancy purposes during the period in question.

I would further note that while, on the one hand, the majority would not permit defendants who produced DES for pregnancy purposes to exculpate themselves, the majority at the same time deprives the plaintiffs of the opportunity to recover fully for their injuries by limiting the defendants' liability for the plaintiff's damages to several liability. In my view, the liability for the plaintiff's damages of those defendants who are unable to exculpate themselves should be joint and several thereby ensuring that the plaintiffs will receive full recovery of their damages.

NOTES

(1) Under the holding of the principal case, a defendant may be held liable for injuries that it can prove it did not cause. Do you share the concerns expressed by the dissent? Or do you agree with the way the majority "balanced the equities" to arrive at its decision? In doing so, did the majority usurp the function of the Legislature? See, arguing for a result similar to that reached in the principal case, David Rosenberg, *The Causal Connection in Mass Exposure Cases: A "Public Law" Vision of the Tort System*, 97 Harvard L. Rev. 851 (1984).

(2) Evaluation of the result in the principal case must take into account not only the approach to liability described in the portion reproduced in this chapter, but also the background fact that the claims were time-barred until the Legislature revived them, as discussed in § 7.02[B]. In a separate section (not reproduced) of the *Hymowitz* case, the Court of Appeals rejected a constitutional challenge to this revival. How will these legal developments affect corporate planning in the future? How will they affect product safety?

Such concerns may well have contributed to a marked reluctance by the New York courts to extend the "market share" theory to other product liability claims. Notably, in *Hamilton v. Beretta U.S.A. Corp.*, 96 N.Y.2d 222, 727 N.Y.S.2d 7, 750 N.E.2d 1055 (2001), the plaintiffs sought to impose market share liability on handgun manufacturers who allegedly distributed their products negligently so as to allow them to fall into criminal hands and thus cause foreseeable injuries to innocent victims. The Court of Appeals (after rejecting plaintiffs' substantive claims of liability for reasons not relevant here) held that market share liability could not be maintained. *Hymowitz* was distinguished on the grounds that, unlike DES, guns are not fungible products which are indistinguishable from each other. Moreover, noted the Court, the defendants' marketing techniques (the heart of the case against them) were not alleged to be uniform. The *Beretta* opinion, at 96 N.Y.2d 242, 727 N.Y.S.2d 20, 750 N.E.2d 1068, lists no less than six other instances in which New York courts have refused to extend *Hymowitz*.

(3) A proverb familiar to trial lawyers is, "When in doubt, sue everyone." Is this still valid after *Hymowitz*? *But see* CPLR 8303-a.

(4) The principal case deals with joinder of defendants and its effect on the outcome of the litigation. Can (or should) the injured victims of a product like DES join together as plaintiffs? *Compare Bender v. Underwood, supra*, this section. As to class actions, see § 8.04, *infra*. A thorough analysis of the various possibilities is provided in Roger H. Transgrud, *Joinder Alternatives in Mass Tort Litigation*, 70 Cornell L. Rev. 779 (1985).

§ 8.03 COMPULSORY JOINDER: CPLR 1001

PROBLEM A

Tom, a New Yorker, and Ibn, a Saudi, entered into a contract with XYZ, Inc. to jointly purchase real estate in New York from the corporation. The contract was negotiated and executed in Riyadh. A deposit of one million dollars was paid to the seller, to be held in escrow until the date of the closing. Prior to closing, however, Tom discovered a minor cloud on the seller's title, so he announced a refusal to go ahead with the deal and demanded that half of the deposit be returned to him. Ibn, on the other hand, cabled the seller that he was prepared to take title, that he personally provided the entire deposit, and that no part of it belonged to Tom. If Tom thereafter brought an action against XYZ, Inc. for $500,000, could the latter successfully move to dismiss because of the failure to join Ibn?

MECHTA v. SCARETTA
Supreme Court, Queens County
52 Misc. 2d 696, 276 N.Y.S.2d 652 (1967)

J. Irwin Shapiro, J.

The plaintiff and his wife, she not being a party to this action, as purchasers entered into a contract with the defendants Scaretta, as sellers, for the purchase of a one-family home. Since the making of the contract the plaintiff and his wife have separated.

The action is by the plaintiff to recover the down payment of $2,000 upon the ground that the sellers have failed to comply with the terms of the contract by not delivering to the purchasers "a written statement issued by the Federal Housing Commission setting forth the appraised value of the property for mortgage insurance purposes of not less than $27,500.00."

I do not deem it necessary to pass upon the questions of credibility posed by the record since I must sustain the defendants' contention that this action is not maintainable without a joinder of the plaintiff's wife, one of the parties to the contract, as a party to this action.

CPLR 1001 provides as follows:

> (a) *Parties who should be joined.* Persons who ought to be parties if complete relief is to be accorded between the persons who are parties to the action or who might be inequitably affected by a judgment in the action shall be made plaintiffs or defendants. When a person who should join as a plaintiff refuses to do so he may be made a defendant.
>
> (b) *When joinder excused.* When a person who should be joined under subdivision (a) has not been made a party and is subject to the jurisdiction of the court, the court shall order him summoned. If jurisdiction over him can be obtained only by his consent or appearance, the court, when justice requires, may allow the action to proceed without his being made a party. In determining whether to allow the action to proceed, the court shall consider:
>
> 1. whether the plaintiff has another effective remedy in case the action is dismissed on account of the nonjoinder;
>
> 2. the prejudice which may accrue from the nonjoinder to the defendant or to the person not joined;
>
> 3. whether and by whom prejudice might have been avoided or may in the future be avoided;
>
> 4. the feasibility of a protective provision by order of the court or in the judgment; and
>
> 5. whether an effective judgment may be rendered in the absence of the person who is not joined.

These provisions merely codify what the decisions held to be the law under sections 193 and 194 of the Civil Practice Act. Thus the decisions interpreting sections 193 and 194 of the Civil Practice Act are applicable to CPLR 1001 (McKinney's [Cons. Laws of N.Y., Book 7B, CPLR] reference to the intent in connection with the statutory change of language and the conclusion therein expressed that the present statutory language merely expresses the existing decisional law).

In *Trade Bank & Trust Co. v. Equitable Fire & Mar. Ins. Co.* (50 N.Y.S. 2d 892, 893) the court used an apt illustration to establish that persons who are united in interest must be joined in an action either as plaintiffs or defendants before a complete determination of rights can be made when it said: "It is elemental law, if two men own a horse, one of them cannot sue for the horse and recover it. His companion is a necessary party."

The plaintiff claims that the moneys deposited under the contract were his and his alone, but in the absence of his wife as a party to this action no determination in that regard can be made which would bind her and if the plaintiff were permitted a recovery here there would be no legal bar to his wife instituting an action against the sellers and contending that the money was hers in whole or in part. Under the circumstances she is a necessary party to this proceeding since prejudice "may accrue from the nonjoinder to the defendant or to the person not joined" (CPLR 1001, subd. [b], par. 2) and it is not feasible to provide "a protective provision by order of the court or in the judgment" (subd. 4), and an effective judgment may not "be rendered in the absence of the person who is not joined" (subd. 5). . . .

The plaintiff's complaint is dismissed, without costs, and without prejudice to the institution of a new action in which the plaintiff's wife shall be joined as a party, either as plaintiff, if she consents, or as a defendant if she does not.

NOTES

(1) Should the court have allowed the action to proceed and protected the absent wife by requiring the husband to account to her for her share of any judgment he recovered? This approach was taken in a similar situation in *Keene v. Chambers*, 271 N.Y. 326, 3 N.E.2d 443 (1936).

(2) *Saratoga County Chamber of Commerce, Inc. v. Pataki*, 275 A.D.2d 145, 712 N.Y.S.2d 687 (3d Dep't 2000), *aff'd*, 100 N.Y.2d 801, 766 N.Y.S.2d 654, 798 N.E.2d 1047 (2003), presented the unusual situation in which the party that arguably should have been added, the St. Regis Mohawk Tribe, was entitled to sovereign immunity and was not subject to the jurisdiction of any court without its consent. Although the action challenged the defendant Governor's authority to enter into a contract with the Tribe authorizing expansion of its gaming facilities, the court held that a balancing of the factors listed in CPLR 1001(b) militated "against the harsh and rarely used remedy of dismissing the complaint for nonjoinder of an indispensable party." *Id.*, 712 N.Y.S.2d 687 (3d Dep't 2000). The Appellate Division found that the Tribe's interests were adequately represented by the named defendants, that no "great prejudice" could result from nonjoinder, and that the plaintiffs were without any other adequate remedy.

In affirming, the Court of Appeals noted that the tribe was not deprived of an opportunity to be heard because it could have waived its immunity and participated in the litigation. Moreover, if the case were dismissed on indispensable party grounds, the other parties would be deprived of any opportunity to have their claims adjudicated. The Court of Appeals described two principal purposes of requiring dismissal due to the absence of an indispensable party: "First, mandatory joinder prevents multiple, inconsistent judgments relating to the same controversy. Second, joinder protects the otherwise absent parties who would be 'embarrassed by judgments purporting to bind their rights or interests where they have had no opportunity to be heard.'" 100 N.Y.2d at 820, 766 N.Y.S.2d at 665, 798 N.E.2d at 1058. Explaining that dismissal under the CLPR is a "last resort," 100 N.Y.2d at 821, 766 N.Y.S.2d at 666, 798 N.E.2d at 1059, the Court concluded that neither purpose applied in this case, since the tribe had an opportunity to appear as a party.

RED HOOK/GOWANUS CHAMBER OF COMMERCE v. NEW YORK CITY BOARD OF STANDARDS AND APPEALS
Court of Appeals
5 N.Y.3d 452, 805 N.Y.S.2d 525, 839 N.E.2d 878 (2005)

CHIEF JUDGE KAYE.

Petitioner is a nonprofit organization composed of 85 local business owners in the Red Hook and Gowanus neighborhoods of Brooklyn. In 2000, respondent 160 Imlay Street Real Estate LLC, through a predecessor entity, acquired a 220,000 square foot warehouse and manufacturing facility in Red Hook. Claiming that it could not find a sufficient number of commercial tenants, in September 2002 Imlay applied to the New York City Board of Standards and Appeals (BSA) for a variance to permit conversion of the building from industrial to residential use. Following four days of hearings between March and November 2003 — petitioner appeared and opposed the variance — on December 24, 2003 the BSA granted Imlay a hardship variance.

Under Administrative Code of the City of New York § 25-207(a), petitioner had 30 days in which to challenge the decision. On the thirtieth day — January 23, 2004 — petitioner filed its CPLR article 78 petition naming only the BSA and the City as respondents, omitting Imlay. On January 27, 2004, petitioner hand-delivered a courtesy copy of the papers to Imlay's attorney.

Three weeks later the City moved to dismiss the petition on the ground that petitioner had failed to name a necessary party within the statute of limitations period. Petitioner cross-moved to amend its petition to add Imlay as a respondent. Supreme Court denied the City's motion to dismiss and granted petitioner's motion to file an amended petition, adding Imlay as an additional party. The Appellate Division reversed "on the law" and dismissed the proceeding.... We now reverse.

Discussion

(1) Plainly, Imlay was a necessary party, and should have been joined in the proceeding at its inception. Having invested significant resources in pursuing

its plan to convert the commercial space to luxury apartments, the developer "might be inequitably affected by a judgment" overturning the variance that permitted residential conversion (CPLR 1001[a]).

Further, while both Imlay and the City had the same immediate purpose in opposing the article 78 petition — maintaining the status of the variance — that, in and of itself, does not create a unity of interest such that an action against Imlay relates back to the filing date of the petition (*see* CPLR 203[c]; *see also Matter of Emmett v Town of Edmeston*, 2 N.Y.3d 817 [2004]). The status of Imlay's property represented a potential loss of millions of dollars to the developer, while the City is necessarily concerned with regulatory and administrative consequences. Such divergent long-term interests cannot be guaranteed to protect Imlay from future prejudice in the case. The trial court therefore erred in treating Imlay as united in interest with the City.

While Supreme Court granted petitioner's request to amend its petition to name Imlay, the Appellate Division rested its decision on CPLR 1001, concluding that the action could not proceed without the necessary party. For the Appellate Division, the fact that petitioner had offered no adequate explanation for its failure to name Imlay prior to expiration of the statute of limitations was as a matter of law determinative. That was error.

Under CPLR 1001 (b), when a necessary party

"has not been made a party and is subject to the jurisdiction of the court, the court shall order him summoned. If jurisdiction over him can be obtained only by his consent or appearance, the court, when justice requires, may allow the action to proceed without his being made a party. In determining whether to allow the action to proceed, the court shall consider:

"1. whether the plaintiff has another effective remedy in case the action is dismissed on account of the nonjoinder;

"2. the prejudice which may accrue from the nonjoinder to the defendant or to the person not joined;

"3. whether and by whom prejudice might have been avoided or may in the future be avoided;

"4. the feasibility of a protective provision by order of the court or in the judgment; and

"5. whether an effective judgment may be rendered in the absence of the person who is not joined."

This provision has deep roots in New York statutory law, dating to the Field Code, which declared that "[w]hen a complete determination of the controversy cannot be had without the presence of other parties, the court may order them to be brought in, by an amendment of the complaint, or by a supplemental complaint, and a new summons" (former Code Pro § 102 [1848]). While the joinder provision was amended several times between 1848 and 1963, most recently as part of the adoption of the Civil Practice Law and Rules, the provision for joinder when complete determination of the case required the presence of an additional party remained unaltered (*see* Code Pro §§ 119, 122 [1851]; Civ Prac Act § 193 [1946]; CPLR 1001 [1963]; 1st Preliminary Report of Advisory Comm on Prac and Proc, at 233-256 [1957]). Indeed, bringing necessary parties into the litigation whenever possible has been the common thread of New York's joinder statutes.

Joinder rules serve an important policy interest in guaranteeing that absent parties at risk of prejudice will not be "embarrassed by judgments purporting to bind their rights or interests where they have had no opportunity to be heard" (*First Natl. Bank of Amsterdam v Shuler*, 153 NY 163, 170 [1897]). They also protect against multiple lawsuits and inconsistent judgments. . . . When enacted in 1963, the CPLR eliminated the Civil Practice Act's distinction between "indispensable" and "conditionally necessary" parties, affording the courts greater discretion in permitting cases to go forward after weighing the interests of the litigants, the absent party and the public (*see* David Siegel, *Introducing: A Biannual Survey of New York Practice*, 38 St John's L Rev 190, 417 [1964]). Indeed, in its present incarnation, the joinder provision is to be employed to avoid dismissal (3 Weinstein-Korn-Miller, NY Civ Prac ¶ 1001.08 [2d ed]).

While a court, then, must use every effort to join a necessary party, there are situations when such a party may be beyond the reach of the court. CPLR 1001 distinguishes between a necessary party "subject to the jurisdiction of the court" and one over whom jurisdiction can be obtained only by consent or appearance. The statute directs that a party subject to the court's jurisdiction *shall be summoned*, while continuance of the action without a necessary party beyond the court's jurisdiction lies within its discretion. Was Imlay, by virtue of the lapsed statute of limitations, subject to, or beyond, the "jurisdiction" of the court as the term is used in CPLR 1001? We do not answer that question in this case because that issue was not timely, or seriously, raised before us. Rather, both the petitioner and the landowner assumed that jurisdiction over Imlay could only have been obtained by consent or appearance. We will do the same.

(2) When a necessary party can be joined only by consent or appearance, a court must engage in the CPLR 1001(b) analysis to determine whether to allow the case to proceed without that party. Though CPLR 1001(b) protects the absent party who might be inequitably affected by a judgment in the action, it also treats dismissal for failure to join a necessary party as a last resort (*see* Siegel, NY Prac § 133, at 227 [4th ed]). Thus, under the statute a court has the discretion to allow a case to continue in the absence of a party, as justice requires. To assist in reaching this decision, the Legislature has set forth five factors a court must consider. Of those five factors, no single one is determinative; and while the court need not separately set forth its reasoning as to each factor, the statute directs it to consider all five. One of the factors a court must

consider — "whether and by whom prejudice might have been avoided" (CPLR 1001[b][3]) — obviously includes inquiry into why a litigant failed to name a necessary party prior to the expiration of the statute of limitations.

Though article 78 challenges generally must be brought within four months, that limitations period may be shortened by law (CPLR 217). In this case, New York City's Administrative Code shortened the limitations period to 30 days. Short limitations periods are not unusual in municipal zoning (*see e.g.* General City Law § 38; Town Law § 195). The City's legislative determination to impose a 30-day period by which to file a challenge to a zoning decision balances powerful competing interests — allowing for citizen challenges on the one hand, while recognizing the urgency of private interests involving substantial financial investment on the other.

. . . .

Forceful though the concerns underlying the statutory limitations period are, however, a court nonetheless must have the opportunity to exercise its discretion in weighing the statutory factors. Lack of an adequate explanation for failing to timely join a necessary party does not as a matter of law in every case divest a court of the statutory directive to consider the enumerated factors. . . . In this case, the trial court granted petitioner's motion to amend and join Imlay, therefore not reaching the CPLR 1001(b) question whether the action should proceed in Imlay's absence. Having not reached that question, the trial court had no occasion to address the discretionary factors, nor did it. The Appellate Division, similarly, gave no indication that it had considered the CPLR 1001(b) factors. The Court not only explicitly rested its decision on the law but also found "preclusive" petitioner's failure to timely include the landlord without adequate explanation. . . . We thus cannot conclude, as the dissent does, that the Appellate Division really did exercise its discretion, or that it did not abuse its discretion.

While the City and Imlay point to the factual strength of their position under the statute, it is not for this Court in the first instance to weigh the factors. Moreover, we are persuaded by the profusion of cases raising the same or an analogous issue . . . that, for now as well as for the future, it is prudent to reverse and remit this case to the trial court to review the existing record and do what the statute says. . . . Thus, while an unexplained expired statute of limitations is very strong indication that an action should be dismissed, it is a *factor* in, not *preclusion* of, the requisite analysis.

Accordingly, the order of the Appellate Division should be reversed, with costs, and the matter remitted to Supreme Court, for further proceedings in accordance with this opinion.

. . . .

NOTES

(1) *See also Town of Brookhaven v. Marian Chun Enterprises, Inc.*, 71 N.Y.2d 953, 528 N.Y.S.2d 822, 524 N.E.2d 143 (1988). The Suffolk County Department of Social Services had provided temporary emergency housing for homeless families in a motel operated in Brookhaven by the defendant corporation. The Town brought this action to permanently enjoin the motel from operating a "rooming house" without an appropriate certificate of occupancy. Reversing a judgment in favor of the plaintiff, the Court said:

> We granted . . . the motion of the Commissioner of Social Services of Suffolk County to appear *amicus curiae*, and authorized a submission by Westchester Legal Services. . . . The interests of neither the Commissioner . . . nor any representative of the homeless aid recipients occupying the Lakeville Lodge Motel have been heard below. As the action is presently framed, their interests might be inequitably affected by the outcome of the action (CPLR 1001(a)). . . . Accordingly, we reverse . . . and dismiss the complaint without prejudice pursuant to CPLR 1003.

Assuming the Town wanted to recommence the action, which of the homeless tenants should be named defendants? Are all of them necessary parties?

(2) P sues D in New York. D moves to dismiss the action because of the non-joinder of X, who is not subject to the jurisdiction of New York courts. If the court agrees that X should be joined, is it proper for the court to dismiss the action on the condition that D submit to the jurisdiction of X's home state in P's action? One court has held such conditional dismissal improper. *Cushing-Murray v. Adams*, 49 A.D.2d 874, 373 N.Y.S.2d 191 (2d Dep't 1975). This decision has been criticized as unduly restrictive of the discretion given courts by CPLR 1001(b). David Siegel, New York Practice § 133 at 229-30 n.9 (4th ed. 2005).

(3) The precedential effect one action may have on other similar actions is not enough to require joinder of additional parties. *N.Y. State School Bus Operator's Ass'n v. County of Nassau*, 79 Misc. 2d 352, 357 N.Y.S.2d 641 (Sup. Ct. 1974), *modified on other grounds*, 48 A.D.2d 671, 367 N.Y.S.2d 825 (2d Dep't 1975), *aff'd*, 39 N.Y.2d 638, 385 N.Y.S.2d 263, 350 N.E.2d 593 (1976).

(4) The impact of substantive law on questions of compulsory joinder of parties can be important. In *Denker v. Twentieth Century-Fox Film Corp.*, 10 N.Y.2d 339, 223 N.Y.S.2d 193, 179 N.E.2d 336 (1961), one of three co-owners of copy-righted material sought to rescind a contract in which the co-owners had granted exclusive motion picture rights to use the material. Even though the other co-owners were joined as defendants (being unwilling to join as plaintiffs), the Court of Appeals dismissed the rescission action, holding that, as a matter of substantive law, an action to rescind a contract may be maintained only when all obligees join as plaintiffs. The court did not consider whether one of the co-owners could sue the obligor for damages without joining the co-obligees.

(5) As amended in 1996, CPLR 305 and CPLR 1003 allow a party to be added to an action without the necessity of a court order. It can be done at any time by stipulation of all the parties to the action, and can be done once on the initiative of any party within twenty days after service of the original summons, or before the expiration of the time allowed to respond to that summons, or within twenty days of a pleading responding to it.

§ 8.04 CLASS ACTIONS: CPLR ARTICLE 9

[A] Introductory Note

By allowing "[o]ne or more members of a class" to "sue or be sued" as representatives of all the class members,[1] CPLR Article 9, like other class action devices, cuts against the general principles that each person is free to determine whether, when, and how to enforce their substantive rights and that each person has the right to their own day in court before a judgment may affect them. The class action is nonetheless an important modern procedural vehicle which can serve the interests of the class members, the party opposing the class, the courts, and society at large.

Plaintiffs who sue as a class gain economically by combining claims which individually are too small to warrant the expense of litigation, tactically in confronting the defendant with greater liability exposure, psychologically in not having to stand alone, and procedurally by controlling the litigation on behalf of the aggrieved so that coordinated tactics are possible. Mootness, which can frustrate litigation seeking a resolution of major issues if the plaintiff's claim is settled, is usually avoided. There are, of course, disadvantages to the plaintiff suing as a class representative. Most important is the energy and time to be expended in litigating the threshold questions of whether the case is suitable for class relief and, if so, what kind of notice to the class members will be required. The task of the class representative is further complicated by the greater control the court will exercise over the conduct of the case and by the limitations Article 9 imposes on the freedom to settle.

Members of the class find the class action helpful for many of the same reasons it is favored by the party suing in their behalf. Most important, they may never have decided to litigate on their own. Class members are not liable for any costs or fees except those deducted from the proceeds of a successful litigation, and their personal claims may not be time barred because the statute of limitations has stopped running.[2] On the negative side, the class members will

---

[1] CPLR 901(a).

[2] *Sutton Carpet Cleaners v. Fireman's Ins. Co.*, 68 N.Y.S.2d 218, 224 (Sup. Ct. 1947), *aff'd*, 273 App. Div. 944, 78 N.Y.S.2d 565 (1st Dep't 1948), *aff'd*, 299 N.Y. 646, 87 N.E.2d 53 (1949).

probably be bound by the results obtained by those who represent them even if their efforts end in failure.

Although the party opposing the class (normally, but not always, a defendant) will frequently resist the assertion of a class action, it should be remembered that even for the defendant this device can be advantageous, at least where there are many claims which are likely to be prosecuted in any event. In that situation, the class action avoids the expense of defending multiple law suits. Moreover, because a settlement of a properly certified class action can resolve the claims of all members of the class (except those who have opted out), *Matsushita Elec. Indus. Co. v. Epstein*, 516 U.S. 367, 116 S. Ct. 873, 134 L. Ed. 2d 6 (1996), class actions are sometimes commenced solely in contemplation of settlement. This has been done with the acquiescence — or even encouragement — of a defendant which otherwise might face unpredictable and possibly ruinous litigation brought by large numbers of claimants. *Klein v. Robert's American Gourmet Food, Inc.*, 28 A.D.3d 63, 808 N.Y.S.2d 766 (2d Dep't. 2006) (reproduced in subsection [D], *infra*) (a leading case on settlement class actions in New York). It is also noteworthy that the Supreme Court has not disapproved the "settlement class action" concept and further held that the fairness of the settlement could be a factor in deciding the certification issue. See *Amchem Products, Inc. v. Windsor*, 521 U.S. 591, 117 S. Ct. 2231, 138 L. Ed. 2d 689 (1997), a purported class action involving asbestos-related claims in which a proposed settlement was submitted to the court on the same day that the action was filed. The Supreme Court affirmed the Third Circuit's decision to decertify the class because the requirements of Rule 23 were not met by the class. The case is discussed in Susan P. Koniak, *Feasting While the Widow Weeps:* Georgine v. Amchem Products, Inc., 80 Cornell L. Rev. 1045 (1995). *See also* Jay H. Tidmarsh, Mass Tort Settlement Class Actions: Five Case Studies (Federal Judicial Center 1998).

The judiciary and the public it serves also benefit, most obviously when a single class action is used in place of many individual claims, although even partisans of the class action device must admit that it sometimes adds to the burden of the courts by making possible the maintenance of complex lawsuits which would otherwise never have been brought at all in any form. But the value of a rule of procedure is not always measurable in terms of judicial economy. Despite the inconvenience to the judicial system, class suits are frequently beneficial to the public by permitting the resolution of broadly held grievances and by deterring wrongdoing otherwise beyond the reach of private civil redress.

[B] The Requirements for Certification

PROBLEM B

Harry Traveler returned from his two-week vacation cruise in a less than idyllic mood. He had booked passage on the S.S. Transylvania (a famous cruise ship) after reading enticing newspaper ads and reviewing an even more enticing brochure, all of which promised a "luxury vacation in the grand old style" with roomy quarters, entertainment, and gourmet style food. According to Harry, the ship, though certainly old, was far from grand. The rooms were cramped and poorly ventilated, the entertainment virtually nil, and the food left him with a case of gastrointestinal distress. Harry decided to bring an action against the ship's owners in Supreme Court, New York County (alleging fraud and breach of contract) to recover the $1,100 price of his tour, $5,000 for personal injury and $500,000 in punitive damages. He also asked for an injunction against further fraudulent representations. He sued in his individual capacity and as a representative of a class consisting of all passengers who were on the same cruise. The defendant steamship line served an answer denying Harry's allegations of wrongdoing. What result on Harry's subsequent motion to certify the class action pursuant to CPLR 902?

SMALL v. LORILLARD TOBACCO CO.

Appellate Division, First Department
252 A.D.2d 1, 679 N.Y.S.2d 593 (1998),
aff'd, 94 N.Y.2d 43, 698 N.Y.S.2d 615, 720 N.E.2d 892 (1999)

Rosenberger, J.P.

These consolidated appeals arise out of five related class actions brought by cigarette consumers against the leading cigarette manufacturers, their parent organizations, the Council for Tobacco Research (CTR) and the Tobacco Institute (TI).

In one of the orders appealed from, plaintiffs moved to certify two proposed classes: a damages class composed of all New York State residents who became nicotine dependent on or after June 19, 1980, and an injunction class of smokers who purchased defendants' cigarettes in New York State. For each of the five class actions, the IAS Court certified a class defined as persons who purchased and smoked defendants' cigarettes, in order to eliminate the need for proof of each class member's addiction. So defined, the plaintiff class for each of the five lawsuits would exceed one million people. In the other order, the court denied the defendants' motions to dismiss the action for failure to state a cause of action, lack of subject matter jurisdiction and lack of personal jurisdiction over Brown & Williamson's corporate parents. Both orders should be reversed.

Plaintiffs do not seek damages for ill health caused by smoking. Rather, they cast this action as a consumer fraud case and seek only recovery of the money they spent on cigarettes since 1980, as well as an injunction preventing defendants from making further misrepresentations about nicotine and ordering them to notify the class members about the drug's true effect on smokers.

Plaintiffs claim that they were deceived into becoming smokers because defendants lied about nicotine's addictive properties while secretly manipulating the nicotine content of their products in order to addict consumers. They allege common-law fraud, violations of General Business Law secs. 349 and 350 (deceptive business practices) and civil conspiracy.

The extent of the defendants' allegedly deceptive practices was first revealed to the public in the spring of 1994 during the Congressional investigation into the tobacco industry. This investigation uncovered cigarette manufacturers' internal memoranda and studies, going back as far as the 1950's, which appeared to show that the manufacturers extensively researched nicotine addiction with the express intention of designing products so addictive that people would be unable to stop buying them. Meanwhile, the manufacturers' public statements consistently denied that nicotine was addictive.

Among these manufacturers were defendants Philip Morris, Brown & Williamson, R.J. Reynolds, American Tobacco Company and Lorillard.

Defendants contend, first, that class certification is inappropriate because individual questions of fact predominate, particularly as to reliance and damages; and second, that in whatever form this action is brought, plaintiffs' claims fail to establish the elements of fraud and deceptive business practices, and are preempted by the Federal Cigarette Labeling and Advertising Act, as interpreted by the Supreme Court in *Cipollone v Liggett Group* (505 US 504). We share plaintiffs' concern that unethical business dealings should not go unpunished simply because defendants harmed so many people that judicial resolution of their claims would be unmanageable. Nevertheless, as to those particular actions, the law is on defendants' side.

CLASS CERTIFICATION

CPLR 901 (a) provides that the court has discretion to grant class certification only if:

"(1) the class is so numerous that joinder of all members, whether otherwise required or permitted, is impracticable;

"(2) there are questions of law or fact common to the class which predominate over any questions affecting only individual members;

"(3) the claims or defenses of the representative parties are typical of the claims or defenses of the class;

"(4) the representative parties will fairly and adequately protect the interests of the class; and

"(5) a class action is superior to other available methods for fair and efficient adjudication of the controversy."

While the plaintiffs bear the burden of showing that certification is appropriate, the statute should be broadly construed, especially where the denial of certification "'would effectively terminate further litigation'" (*Brandon v Chefetz*, 106 AD2d 162, 169 [citation omitted]).

Defendants do not dispute the IAS Court's finding of numerousness, for the obvious reason that each of the five classes would contain at least a million members.

The heart of defendants' argument is that individual issues predominate. First, even though they seek compensation only for economic losses as consumers, not personal injury damages, plaintiffs have not eliminated the very individualized issue of whether each was nicotine dependent. Second, it cannot be presumed that each class member even knew of the alleged misrepresentations, let alone relied on them.

The IAS Court distinguished *Castano v American Tobacco Co.* (84 F3d 734 [5th Cir]), in which the Fifth Circuit decertified a class of allegedly nicotine-dependent persons because proof of actual addiction would involve too many subjective and individualized factors. Unlike *Castano*, the IAS Court reasoned, proof of addiction was not an issue here because plaintiffs' theory of liability was based on the fraudulent nature of the transaction, not its health effects. The court accordingly redefined the class as all persons who purchased and smoked defendants' cigarettes.

Yet, this strategic redefinition superficially strengthened one aspect of plaintiffs' case only by fatally weakening another aspect. If plaintiffs do not prove addiction, they cannot show that they were harmed by defendants' deceptive exploitation of the addictive properties of nicotine to maintain their customer base.

Proof of injury is essential to plaintiffs' General Business Law claims. While General Business Law sec. 349 "does not require proof of justifiable reliance, a plaintiff seeking compensatory damages must show that the defendant engaged in a material deceptive act or practice that caused actual, although not necessarily pecuniary, harm" *Oswego Laborers' Local 214 Pension Fund v Marine Midland Bank*, 85 NY2d 20, 26). Section 349(h), which was added to the original statute to give private parties a right of action, grants that right only to "any person who has been injured" by deceptive business practices. Neither the case law nor the statutory language supports plaintiffs' argument that the deception is the injury.

Various courts around the Nation have denied class certification in tobacco lawsuits similar to this case because individual issues of fact as to addiction and personal injury predominated (*e.g., Lyons v American Tobacco Co.*, 1997 US Dist LEXIS 18365 [SD Ala]).

In the one tobacco case where such a class was certified (*R.J. Reynolds Tobacco Co. v Engle*, 672 So 2d 39 [Fla Dist Ct App] [certifying class of Florida residents who suffered medical conditions caused by nicotine addiction]), the court rejected a nationwide class of one million members as totally unmanageable because of the need for individualized consideration of reliance and damages and certified a much smaller class. There was no analysis of why the common issues predominated over the individual issues. Further, the action was ultimately dismissed as preempted by the Federal Cigarette Labeling and Advertising Act. *Broin v Philip Morris Cos.* (641 So 2d 888 [Fla Dist Ct App]), also relied on by plaintiffs, is simply inapplicable because all of the approximately 60,000 class members were passive, involuntary inhalers of secondhand smoke, and, thus, reliance was not a factor.

Lyons (supra) is more analogous to the facts at hand. In that case, as here, plaintiffs (former members of the decertified *Castano* class) unsuccessfully sought to hold the major tobacco manufacturers liable for fraud and negligent misrepresentation, based on the latter's manipulation of nicotine levels and denial of nicotine's addictive nature.

As the IAS Court acknowledged in the instant case, "a claim which turns on proof of actual addiction would involve far too many subjective factors and present many of the same manageability concerns cited in *Castano (supra)* to warrant class action treatment." (175 Misc 2d 294, 300.) It makes no difference that nicotine addiction itself was the injury claimed by the *Lyons* plaintiffs, while the present plaintiffs claim economic injuries resulting from addiction-induced purchases. No matter how the class and its theories of liability are redefined, plaintiffs' General Business Law claims do indeed turn on proof of addiction. Their only grounds for seeking recovery of the money they spent on cigarettes would be that defendants' deception prevented plaintiffs from making free and informed choices as consumers. Otherwise, plaintiffs' subsequent regret about their purchasing decisions, while understandable, is simply not actionable.

Just as individualized proof of addiction is essential to the General Business Law sec. 349 cause of action, individualized proof of reliance is essential to the causes of action for false advertising under General Business Law sec. 350 and for common-law fraud, a circumstance that further supports denial of certification. Generally, class actions premised on fraud require proof of reliance by each class member (*Vermeer Owners v Guterman*, 169 AD2d 442, 444, *affd* 78 NY2d 1114).

Reliance on defendants' misrepresentations will not be presumed where plaintiffs had a reasonable opportunity to discover the facts about the transaction beforehand by using ordinary intelligence (*supra,* at 445), or where a variety of factors could have influenced a class member's decision to purchase. Only when defendants effectively controlled all the information about the transaction will the existence of misrepresentations give rise to an inference of reliance without need for further proof (*King v Club Med*, 76 AD2d 123, 127 [vacation brochure fraudulently stated that hotel had plumbing and electricity]).

In *King* the misrepresentation was made in a limited uniform document actually received by each plaintiff, under circumstances giving rise to the legitimate inference that they considered it when making their decision. Here, by contrast, plaintiffs do not point to any specific advertisement or public pronouncement by the tobacco companies, or any statement by CTR or TI, which was undoubtedly seen by all class members. "The complaint does not show any one misrepresentation, or group of misrepresentations, or common thread that may be applicable to substantially the entire group" (*Ross v Amrep Corp.*, 57 AD2d 99, 103, *appeal dismissed* 42 NY2d 910 [denying certification because individual issues predominated]). Instead, plaintiffs base their claims on defendants' general strategy of trying to hide the fact that nicotine was addictive, a fact which plaintiffs claim was previously unknown to them before the 1994 Congressional hearings.

Plaintiffs' claim of ignorance is implausible in light of years of pre-1994 press coverage of research on nicotine addiction, as well as the well-known difficulty of quitting smoking. Over the past two decades, the major New York newspapers have published literally hundreds of articles about nicotine addiction and reported numerous public statements by the Government and the public health industry to the effect that cigarettes contain a highly addictive drug. . . .

As far back as 1969, the press publicized Congress's suspicions that cigarette manufacturers were adjusting nicotine levels to ensure that customers would be unable to quit (New York Times Information Back Abstracts, May 8, 1969, at 31). Thus, this particular practice, while duplicitous, was not kept carefully hidden from the public before 1994. At the least, this widely available information about nicotine forecloses any presumption of reliance and requires individualized inquiry into whether particular class members were unaware of such information.

In fact, plaintiffs have conceded that individual issues of causation and reliance must be dealt with at some point during the proposed trial. However, they succeeded in convincing the IAS Court that this investigation could be postponed to a later phase of the trial, after liability has been established on the common issues (basically, defendants' alleged conspiracy to deceive the public). The Fifth Circuit rejected such bifurcation in *Castano,* stating that a trial court "cannot manufacture predominance" by "[s]evering the defendants' conduct from reliance" (*Castano v American Tobacco Co., supra,* 84 F3d, at 745, n 21).

Like the District Court in *Castano,* the IAS Court wrongly "assumed that because the common issues [of defendants' coordinated scheme to manipulate nicotine content and misrepresent its effects] would play a part in every trial, they must be significant" (*supra,* at 745). Such a relaxation of the predominance requirement would effectively nullify it: if any element of fraud were common to all the individual trials, CPLR 901(a)(2) would be deemed satisfied no matter how much individualized proof was needed for the other elements.

The named plaintiffs' claims are also not typical of the claims of the putative class members, now that the class is no longer defined by addiction. At their depositions, plaintiffs took the position that they were addicted to nicotine and therefore lacked the free will to quit smoking. These plaintiffs are not similarly situated to a putative class of people who allegedly would never have begun smoking, or would have ceased immediately, if they had been told that cigarettes were addictive.

In an action based on alleged misrepresentations, a named plaintiff's claims are atypical if he or she did not rely on, or even see, these misrepresentations. . . . Here, the representatives' own claims fail to establish the reliance and causation elements. Some, such as Phyllis Small and Anilda Ross, admitted that they noticed the warnings on the cigarette packages and in the press about serious health risks from smoking, but ignored them.

Named plaintiffs Sharlene Hoberman and Catherine Zito, among others, testified that they could not recall relying on any particular statements by the tobacco companies or their lobbying organizations. Denise Fubini testified at her deposition that she had long been aware of claims by the Government and scientists that cigarettes were addictive, but said she was confused by the tobacco industry's general position to the contrary (though she could not remember any specific statements). The late Edwin Hoskins similarly testified that he read newspapers and magazines regularly but ignored the pervasive warnings about the risks of smoking. Small and Ross testified that they never saw or heard any statements by the companies they are suing.

The manner in which the named plaintiffs limited their claims makes them inadequate to represent a putative class of all persons who purchased and smoked cigarettes in New York. In an attempt to eliminate the need for individualized proof of addiction and injury, such as was found unmanageable in *Castano* (*supra*), plaintiffs only seek recovery of the purchase price of cigarettes. Moreover, they limit their claims to losses incurred after 1980, even though defendants have allegedly been defrauding the public since the 1950's, for no other apparent reason than to make this a "negative value" suit where each member's damages are so small that only a class action would be worth the expense of litigation.

Under New York's transactional approach to res judicata, once a claim is brought to final conclusion, all other claims arising out of the same transactions are barred, even if based on a different theory or seeking a different remedy (*O'Brien v City of Syracuse*, 54 NY2d 353, 357). Should these plaintiffs prevail, they will preclude all New York smokers' chances of bringing potentially more lucrative damages claims for personal injury and emotional distress from nicotine addiction. Defendants are also put at risk of uncertainty as to whether this action has finally disposed of the claims of all class members, since a later court might find that some or all members were not adequately represented. The ability to opt out of the class is insufficient to protect the rights of putative class members who would want to seek remedies other than those chosen by the representatives (*Ross v Amrep Corp.*, *supra*, 57 AD2d, at 103).

We find persuasive the reasoning of the Southern District Court of New York in *Feinstein v Firestone Tire & Rubber Co.*, (535 F Supp 595, 606-607 [SD NY]). In *Feinstein*, the named plaintiffs sued only for economic losses from allegedly defective tires and argued that class members could pursue their personal injury claims individually in other courts. The court disagreed, finding that representatives who "tailored the class claims in an effort to improve the possibility of demonstrating commonality" obtained this "essentially cosmetic" benefit only by "presenting putative class members with significant risks of being told later that they had impermissibly split a single cause of action" (*supra,* at 606). For this reason, they were inadequate representatives.

As discussed above, this proposed class action would be unmanageable because of the individual issues of reliance, causation and damages with respect to each of the five million plaintiffs. Defendants have a due process right to cross-examine each member, a task that would take hundreds of years. Even if the trial were bifurcated as plaintiffs propose, at some point it would have to be split into millions of individual trials. If the named plaintiffs' depositions are any indication, many of these class members might have no valid claims, either because they did not see any statements by defendants or because they ignored other widespread information about the addictive nature of cigarettes. By contrast, it would be more efficient if persons whose personal injury and fraud claims had individual merit brought individual actions against defendants.

FEDERAL PREEMPTION AND LACK OF JURISDICTION

Defendants made separate motions to dismiss the amended complaints on the grounds of failure to state a cause of action, failure to plead fraud and deceit with particularity and lack of subject matter jurisdiction due to Federal preemption. B.A.T. moved to dismiss as against it on the additional ground of lack of personal jurisdiction. The IAS Court consolidated these motions for purposes of disposition and denied them. We reverse this order and dismiss the action.

Accordingly, the orders, Supreme Court, New York County (Charles Ramos, J.), entered on or about October 28, 1997 and October 31, 1997, respectively, one of which granted plaintiffs' motions for class certification, and the other of which denied defendants' motions to dismiss, should be reversed, on the law, without costs, plaintiffs' motions should be denied, defendants' motions should be granted, the five classes should be decertified, and the five complaints dismissed.

NOTES

(1) On appeal, the Court of Appeals affirmed on the ground that the Appellate Division had not abused its discretion as a matter of law. 94 N.Y.2d 43, 698 N.Y.S.2d 615, 720 N.E.2d 892 (1999).

Would the plaintiffs have had a better chance of obtaining class certification if they had not raised the fraud issue and simply claimed that the cigarettes were a defective product that caused them serious injury?

(2) Class actions are not the only way of achieving economies of scale in products liability actions. For example, although class certification was denied to women injured by the Dalkon Shield contraceptive device, *see Rosenfeld v. A. H. Robins Co.*, 63 A.D.2d 11, 407 N.Y.S.2d 196 (1978), numerous Dalkon Shield actions which were brought against the same defendant in various federal courts around the country were consolidated for pre-trial proceedings in the District of Kansas by order of the Judicial Panel on Multidistrict Litigation pursuant to 28 U.S.C.A. § 1407. *In re A. H. Robins Co., Inc. "Dalkon Shield" IUD Products Liability Litigation*, 406 F. Supp. 540 (Jud. Panel on Multidistr. Lit. 1975). The defendant favored the consolidation, arguing that "every action shares common factual issues relating to what it did or did not do . . . with respect to the . . . Dalkon Shield."

Further, "transfer . . . will eliminate the possibility of duplicative discovery and conflicting pretrial rulings." How do you explain the apparent inconsistency between defendant's position in the federal actions and its successful objection to class action certification?

The attorneys representing individual Dalkon Shield plaintiffs also managed to reduce costs by creating an association that coordinated the pretrial discovery and shared the expense of other fact-gathering. See the description of this elaborate arrangement in *Rosenfeld v. A H. Robins Co.*, 63 A.D.2d 11, n.3, 407 N.Y.S.2d 196 (1st Dep't 1978). The Dalkon Shield litigation subsequently led A.H. Robbins Co. into bankruptcy, as described in Richard B. Sobol, Bending the Law: The Story of the Dalkon Shield Bankruptcy (1991). Inasmuch as a bankruptcy proceeding requires all claims to be heard by the court in which the proceedings are pending, it has been seen as another technique for aggregating mass tort litigation. *See* Judith Resnik, *Aggregation, Settlement and Dismay*, 80 Cornell L. Rev. 918, 930 (1995).

(3) Uniform Rule for the New York State Trial Courts 202.69 (*see* note 4 following *City of New York* in § 8.03, *supra*) provides an alternative to the economies of scale of class action suits, by allowing for the pre-trial coordination of multiple actions pending in different district courts. The coordinating justice is then able to try the case if the parties consent. This rule was originally created for the efficient handling of mass tort cases, but it has important applications in a wide range of commercial litigation. Similar to class actions, coordination allows parties to effectively manage their cases, minimizes discovery costs,

distributes responsibility for particular tasks, and reduces the risk of inconsistent rulings. *See* David Fleischer and Jodi Kleinick, *Litigation: Coordinating Multidistrict Cases in State Courts*, N.Y.L.J., December 1, 2003, at S1.

WEINBERG v. HERTZ CORP.
Appellate Division, First Department
116 A.D.2d 1, 499 N.Y.S.2d 693 (1986),
aff'd, 69 N.Y.2d 979, 516 N.Y.S.2d 652 (1987)

FEIN, J.

This is an action seeking injunctive relief and damages against the Hertz Corporation (Hertz) for acts and practices in the automobile rental business, alleged to be unfair, deceptive and in breach of contract. The allegations before us relate to (1) defendant's service charges for refueling returned rental cars; (2) the daily charges for insurance coverage in the nature of collision damage waiver (CDW) and personal accident insurance (PAI); and (3) the hourly charges added when a vehicle is returned in New York State beyond the contractual return date.

These charges were variously alleged to be unfair and deceptive, in violation of General Business Law § 349; unconscionably excessive and in bad faith, in violation of UCC 2-302 and 1-201, 1-203; and in breach of the Hertz rental agreements.

Specifically, plaintiff alleged that defendant's gasoline "refueling service charges" were grossly excessive, resulting in charges in the neighborhood of $1.85 per gallon, which were determined by procedures violative of standards for retail sale of gasoline, established by Federal, State and city statutes and regulations.

The second area of complaint related to defendant's CDW charges. The insurance on a rented vehicle provided collision damage coverage with, in effect, a $1,000 deductible. The customer could obtain full coverage, and defendant would waive the deductible, for an additional charge which, at the commencement of this action, amounted to $6 per day. Extrapolating over an entire year, plaintiff alleged that $2,190 for $1,000 worth of collision damage insurance was an unconscionable premium.

A similar charge of unconscionability was made concerning the $2.25 daily charge for PAI coverage, which figured out to an annual premium of $821.25.

Finally, plaintiff alleged that the charges for returning a vehicle late were exorbitant, permitting defendant to make a full day's extra charge in the first three hours of overtime. Further, defendant's practice allegedly added a full day's CDW and PAI charges, rather than prorating them, for every vehicle returned more than one hour late.

Plaintiff brought this action on behalf of "all those who have rented automobiles from Hertz and were subject to, or had imposed upon them, the illegal charges described [above], within the State of New York." In March 1984, Special Term sustained 6 of the 10 causes of action covering these charges, permitted class action certification with respect to actual damages sought under General Business Law § 349, and permitted limited discovery on the question of the numerosity of the class. We affirmed unanimously, without opinion (105 AD2d 1169).

After discovery and the furnishing of certain documents and information by Hertz under a stipulation of confidentiality, plaintiff renewed his motion for class action certification. This appeal is from the denial of that motion.

A class action in this State must satisfy the prerequisites of numerosity, commonality, typicality, adequacy of representation and superiority (CPLR 901[a]). Special Term based its denial of class action certification on the fifth criterion, which specifies that the class action must be "superior to other available methods for the fair and efficient adjudication of the controversy." (CPLR 901[a][5].) Special Term ruled that "economic impracticability renders this proposed class action an inferior form of adjudication." In doing so, the court accepted defendant's argument that a class action would impose an undue economic burden on it by requiring a search of millions of noncomputerized rental agreements around the country for those with a New York connection, at an estimated cost of at least $30 million. It was asserted that this would more than overshadow the average claim of $31 for each member of a class whose size plaintiff estimated in the tens or hundreds of thousands.

General Business Law § 349(h) affords a private right of action and treble damages for deception practiced against a consumer. Since such a statutory remedy does exist, potential class members must be given an opportunity to opt out of the class to pursue their private claims. Thus, identifying the members of the class becomes a necessity. According to Special Term, $30 million would be an unduly burdensome amount to expect defendant to expend, simply to reach the threshold determination of who should receive notice of this action.

On this record there is plainly inadequate substantiation for defendant's assertion that defining the class would cost $30 million. It is inconceivable that a nationwide company such as defendant would not be able to obtain the necessary data from its offices around the country or from its central processing center in Oklahoma City without the expenditure of millions of dollars. The bald assertions that defendant does not have a system in place to provide the data is especially surprising in light of the May 1983 decision of the California Court of Appeal in *Lazar v Hertz Corp.* (143 Cal App 3d 128, 191 Cal Rptr 849), in which virtually the same challenges were made in a class action suit against this defendant. The California court ruled that the benefits to the courts and the public in aggregating monetarily insignificant claims (estimated at an average $6) into a single, time-saving lawsuit outweighed any legal, administrative or economic burden on defendant in defining the class.

As the California court noted, the burden of searching out putative class members upon whom notice must be served is unpersuasive. In rejecting Hertz' economic burden argument it was concluded that the small recovery should not preclude class certification, despite the claim that the potential class might amount to five million individuals.

In accepting defendant's estimate of the $31 average claim, Special Term did not give adequate weight to the very point that impelled a class action here, namely, the unlikelihood of small claims being filed for what, cumulatively, might amount to overcharges in the millions of dollars, as alleged. The public benefit of the class action remedy has been described as "a means of inducing socially and ethically responsible behavior on the part of large and wealthy institutions which will be deterred from carrying out policies or engaging in activities harmful to large numbers of individuals," people who "frequently are damaged in a small sum (often less than $100) since, realistically speaking, our legal system inhibits the bringing of suits based upon small claims" (*Friar v Vanguard Holding Corp.*, 78 AD2d 83, 94). Plainly, individual actions are not preferable to or the equivalent of class actions in such a context.

Indeed, the amount of the average claim for each member of the class is without real legal significance. Thus, for example, in *Sternberg v Citicorp Credit Servs.* (69 AD2d 352, *affd* 50 NY2d 856), an average claim as low as 50 cents did not negate a class action. As a practical matter, a class action is not only a superior method of adjudication, but the only method available for determining the issues raised, for "the damages that may have been sustained by any single [customer] will almost certainly be insufficient to justify the expenses inherent in any individual action, and the number of individuals involved is too large, and the possibility of effective communication between them too remote, to make practicable the traditional joinder of action." (*King v Club Med*, 76 AD2d 123, 128.)

In attacking the superiority of the class action vehicle, defendant points to a further difficulty presented by the fact that many potential members of the class are not New York residents, but were only nonresident customers returning Hertz automobiles to defendant's agencies in this State. Assuming the availability of defendant's centralized computer data center, and a central headquarters in New York State to which all records are forwarded from defendant's branches around the State, there is no basis for denying class action status on this ground. Defendant estimates that of the 30 million rental agreements nationwide during the period in question, 2.8 million rentals were negotiated in New York, amounting to 9 1/3% of its nationwide volume of business. Although no estimates are given as to the number of nonresidents included in that figure, to whom an "opt-out" procedure would be made available, we can reasonably assume that a substantial portion of those customers were New York residents (*cf. Phillips Petroleum Co. v Shutts*, 105 S Ct 2965). At this juncture, prior to discovery on the identity of the class, it is unnecessary to determine the procedure for obtaining jurisdiction over nonresidents (*Stellema v Vantage Press*, 109

AD2d 423, 427). Moreover, the constitutional issue has now been laid to rest (*Phillips Petroleum Co. v Shutts, supra*). At the very least, Special Term should have granted certification with respect to the obviously substantial number of New York residents in the class (*Brandon v Chefetz*, 106 AD2d 162, 171).

It is readily apparent that there is a prospective class of several hundred thousand, plainly meeting the numerosity requirement. To the extent that there may be variations among the members of the class because not all sustained the same type of alleged overcharge, the authorities are clear that the Trial Judge may, in appropriate circumstances, carve out subclasses without destroying the action as a class action (*Friar v Vanguard Holding Corp., supra*).

This rationale fits rather nicely into the predominance requirement that "questions of law or fact common to the class . . . predominate over any questions affecting only individual members" (CPLR 901[a][2]). The statute clearly envisions authorization of class actions even where there are subsidiary questions of law or fact not common to the class (*King v Club Med, supra*). It is undisputed that the various charges complained of were imposed by defendant. That individuals who are members of the class might have been subjected to less than all of the conduct complained of is not a ground for denying class action. Whatever differences there are do not override the common questions of law and fact. As noted, subclasses may be created to deal with the differences, if needed. The emphasis by defendant on the alleged rule that because fraud claims are made, questions of individual reliance defeat a determination of class certification, has been answered otherwise by this court (*Brandon v Chefetz, supra*; *Stellema v Vantage Press, supra*). As those cases and others suggest, once it has been determined that the representations alleged are material and actionable, thus warranting certification, the issue of reliance may be presumed, subject to such proof as is required on the trial. Moreover, this court's unanimous rejection of defendant's dismissal motion (105 AD2d 1169) constitutes a determination that actionable claims have been alleged. Thus, the question of the extent to which reliance and unconscionability need be demonstrated by each class member is to be determined under well-accepted standards by the Trial Justice.

Defendant's assertion that plaintiff Weinberg's course of conduct is not typical of the class that he purports to represent because (1) he does not have an individual contract claim, (2) he cannot show on an individual basis "reliance" as to General Business Law § 349 claims and resulting injury, and (3) as a "sophisticated attorney" he could not show a lack of meaningful choice, is no basis for denying class action status, even if true. The predominance of questions of fact or law over questions affecting only individual members is the test which must be met, not a nice inspection of the claims of each class member. . . .

Finally, it is notable that in determining whether a class action is superior to other viable methods, it is clear that most of the individuals having claims averaging less than $31 would have no realistic day in court if a class action were not available (*see, Phillips Petroleum Co. v Shutts, supra* [where the average claims were $100 per plaintiff]; *Sternberg v Citicorp Credit Servs., supra* [involving 50 cent claims]). The nature of the notice is a matter for the Trial Judge. A decision granting class action can be altered or modified, or the class decertified, if required by subsequent events (CPLR 907; *Friar v Vanguard Holding Corp.*, 78 AD2d, at p 100), and subclasses may be created (CPLR 906[2]).

Accordingly, the order of Supreme Court, New York County, denying class action certification as an inferior form of adjudication due to economic impracticality, should be reversed, on the law, the facts, and in the exercise of discretion, and the motion for class action certification should be granted, with costs.

NOTES

(1) Are the two preceding principal cases consistent? According to one commentator:

> The courts of New York continue to be responsive and, with the exception of mass torts and actions challenging governmental operations, are receptive to meritorious class-action litigation.

Thomas A. Dickerson, *Article 9 Class Actions — A Review of Decisions in 1988*, N.Y.L.J., January 26, 1989, p.1, col. 1.

Do you agree that mass tort actions are less appropriate candidates for class action treatment than other cases? An exception to the general rule disallowing class action treatment is found in *In re "Agent Orange" Product Liability Litigation*, 818 F.2d 145, 166 (2d Cir. 1987), *cert. denied*, 108 S. Ct. 2899 (1988), applying Fed. R. Civ. P. 23(b). And, as noted in *Small v. Lorillard Tobacco Co.*, *supra,* a class action involving tort actions against tobacco companies was certified in Florida. *R.J. Reynolds Tobacco Co. v. Engle*, 672 So. 2d 39 (Fla. Dist. Ct. App.), *rev. denied*, 682 So. 2d 39 (Fla. 1996).

Class action treatment for mass torts has been much commented on. *See e.g.*, Richard L. Marcus, *They Can't Do That, Can They? Tort Reform Via Rule 23*, 80 Cornell L. Rev. 858 (1995).

(2) Disgruntled travelers alleging fraud have achieved mixed results. *Compare King v. Club Med, Inc.*, 76 A.D.2d 123, 430 N.Y.S.2d 65 (1st Dep't 1980) (affirming certification of class action), *with Reis v. Club Med, Inc.*, 81 A.D.2d 793, 439 N.Y.S.2d 127 (1st Dep't 1981) (class action certification held improper).

(3) Creating a specialized and questionable rule, the Court of Appeals has held that class status should usually be denied whenever non-monetary relief is sought against a government agency. *See, e.g., Martin v. Lavine*, 39 N.Y.2d 72, 382 N.Y.S.2d 956, 346 N.E.2d 794 (1976) (class status denied in Article 78 petitions challenging state administration of the Medicaid program). This restrictive approach is criticized in Barker, *Class Actions Against Governmental*

Agencies, N.Y.L.J., April 18, 1994, p. 3, col. 3, and in Daan Braveman, *Class Certification in State Court Welfare Litigation: A Request for Procedural Justice*, 28 Buff. L. Rev. 57 (1979). This rule, however, is not followed invariably. *See Lamboy v. Gross*, 126 A.D.2d 265, 513 N.Y.S.2d 393 (1st Dep't 1987), in which the plaintiffs were homeless families who claimed that the governmental defendants had unlawfully failed to provide them with emergency housing. In upholding the certification of a class action, the Appellate Division said:

> . . . the questions presented here are of public importance . . . and are likely to recur and yet evade review. [Defendants] failed to provide emergency housing to many eligible homeless families even after the entry of orders requiring the provision of such housing. . . . Moreover, . . . to require recourse to individual judicial proceedings would be to ignore the realities of the conditions of the homeless, destitute families desperately seeking shelter. . . .

See also Bryant Avenue Tenants' Ass'n v. Koch, 71 N.Y.2d 856, 527 N.Y.S.2d 743, 522 N.E.2d 1041 (1988) (affirmed class action certification although government officials were co-defendants); *Varshavsky v. Perales*, 202 A.D.2d 155, 608 N.Y.S.2d 184 (1st Dep't 1994) (class status approved for disabled public assistance recipients challenging defendant's refusal to hold administrative hearings at the petitioners' homes).

(4) CPLR 901 mandates that the representative parties "fairly and adequately protect the interests of the class." Unless the representation is adequate, the absent members of the class cannot be bound by the result of the law suit. *Hansberry v. Lee*, 311 U.S. 32, 61 S. Ct. 115, 85 L. Ed. 22 (1940). It has been held that the plaintiff should not be certified as a representative if he does not have the resources to effectively pursue the litigation. *See, e.g., Gilman v. Merrill Lynch, Pierce, Fenner & Smith*, 93 Misc. 2d 941, 404 N.Y.S.2d 258 (Sup. Ct. 1978). One trial court judge wryly noted: "This court would uphold the principle that, whatever their rank or riches, all men are equal before the law, but recognizes that, in class actions, at least, men of means are more equal than other men." *Stern v. Carter*, 97 Misc. 2d 775, 779, 412 N.Y.S.2d 333, 336 (Sup. Ct. 1979), *modified*, 82 A.D.2d 321, 441 N.Y.S.2d 717 (2d Dep't 1981). Another trial court, however, has indicated that the "relevant question" is the financial capability of the representative, class counsel, or a third party sponsoring organization. *Cannon v. Equitable Life Assurance Soc.*, 106 Misc. 2d 1060, 1068-69, 433 N.Y.S.2d 378, 386 (Sup. Ct. 1980), *aff'd in part, rev'd in part*, 87 A.D.2d 403, 451 N.Y.S.2d 817 (2d Dep't 1982).

The representative party must be independent of the class counsel. In *Tanzer v. Turbodyne Corp.*, 68 A.D.2d 614, 619, 417 N.Y.S.2d 706, 708 (1st Dep't 1979), the court denied class status, in part because it found that "the real interest of these plaintiffs is that of their lawyers. . . ." In *Stern v. Carter, supra*, the court noted that "suspicions of champerty . . . haunt [class action] litigation." 97 Misc. 2d at 779, 412 N.Y.S.2d at 336.

(5) As the principal case notes, the issue whether a state court may constitutionally adjudicate the rights of non-resident class members of a plaintiff class has been answered affirmatively in *Phillips Petroleum Co. v. Shutts*, 472 U.S. 797, 808-10, 105 S. Ct. 2965, 2972-74, 86 L. Ed. 2d 628, 639-41 (1985). The Supreme Court held that a non-resident class member may be bound by the judgment even in the absence of "minimum contacts" with the jurisdiction:

The burdens placed by a State upon an absent class-action plaintiff are not of the same order or magnitude as those it places upon an absent defendant. An out-of-state defendant summoned by a plaintiff is faced with the full powers of the forum State to render judgment against it. The defendant must generally hire counsel and travel to the forum to defend itself from the plaintiff's claim, or suffer a default judgment. The defendant may be forced to participate in extended and often costly discovery, and will be forced to respond in damages or to comply with some other form of remedy imposed by the court should it lose the suit. The defendant may also face liability for court costs and attorney's fees. These burdens are substantial, and the minimum contacts requirement of the Due Process Clause prevents the forum State from unfairly imposing them upon the defendant.

A class-action plaintiff, however, is in quite a different posture. The Court noted this difference in *Hansberry v. Lee*, 311 U.S. 32, 40-41, 61 S. Ct. 115, 117-118, 85 L.Ed. 22 (1940), which explained that a "class" or "representative" suit was an exception to the rule that one could not be bound by judgment in personam unless one was made fully a party in the traditional sense. . . . The absent parties would be bound by the decree so long as the named parties adequately represented the absent class and the prosecution of the litigation was within the common interest. 311 U.S., at 41, 61 S. Ct., at 117.

In sharp contrast to the predicament of a defendant haled into an out-of-state forum, the plaintiffs in this suit were not haled anywhere to defend themselves upon pain of a default judgment. As commentators have noted, from the plaintiffs' point of view a class action resembles a "quasi-administrative proceeding, conducted by the judge." . . .

A plaintiff class in Kansas and numerous other jurisdictions cannot first be certified unless the judge, with the aid of the named plaintiffs and defendant, conducts an inquiry into the common nature of the named plaintiff's and the absent plaintiffs' claims, the adequacy of representation, the jurisdiction possessed over the class, and any other matters that will bear upon proper representation of the absent plaintiffs' interest. . . . Unlike a defendant in a civil suit, a class-action plaintiff is not required to fend for himself. The court and named plaintiffs protect his interests. Indeed, the class-action defendant itself has a great interest in ensuring that the absent plaintiff's claims are properly before the forum. In this case, for example, the defendant sought to avoid class certification by alleging that the absent plaintiffs would not be adequately represented and were not amenable to jurisdiction.

The concern of the typical class-action rules for the absent plaintiffs is manifested in other ways. Most jurisdictions, including Kansas, require that a class action, once certified, may not be dismissed or compromised without the approval of the court. . . .

Besides this continuing solicitude for their rights, absent plaintiff class members are not subject to other burdens imposed upon defendants. They need not hire counsel or appear. They are almost never subject to counterclaims or cross-claims, or liability for fees or costs. Absent plaintiff class members are not subject to coercive or punitive remedies. Nor will an adverse judgment typically bind an absent plaintiff for any damages, although a valid adverse judgment may extinguish any of the plaintiff's claim which was litigated.

Unlike a defendant in a normal civil suit, an absent class-action plaintiff is not required to do anything. He may sit back and allow the litigation to run its course, content in knowing that there are safe-guards provided for his protection.

The quoted case is discussed in Arthur R. Miller & David Crump, *Jurisdiction and Choice of Law in Multistate Class Actions After* Phillips Petroleum Co. v. Shutts, 96 Yale L.J. 1 (1986).

[C] Notice Requirements

BOULEVARD GARDENS TENANTS ACTION COMMITTEE, INC. v. BOULEVARD GARDENS HOUSING CORP.
Supreme Court, Queens County
88 Misc. 2d 98, 388 N.Y.S.2d 215 (1976)

EDWIN KASSOFF, J.

[The defendant, a state-regulated housing corporation, had obtained permission from the New York Housing and Community Renewal Executive Department to increase the amount charged tenants with air conditioning from $3.00 per unit per month to $6.50. Plaintiff brought a proceeding under Article 78 of the CPLR claiming that the increase was illegal because the agency had not held a public hearing before approving it. Plaintiff also moved for injunctive relief. An individual tenant was a co-petitioner in a "representative capacity for all other tenants similarly situated."]

. . . The petitioner association is an organization of the tenants of defendant corporation and over 90% of them are members. There are in total 950 tenants of the defendant corporation and approximately 486 have air conditioners. While those without air conditioners are not presently affected by the increase, their future choice to have one installed will be subject to the payment of the then prevailing rate. From all of the evidence presented, it appears that petitioner association has the requisite standing.

The individual petitioner suing in a representative capacity is clearly within the purview of the class action statute. While the requisite application under CPLR 902 has not been made, the court now has sufficient information before it to determine that issue. From the evidence presented and cognizant of the considerations set forth in CPLR 901 and CPLR 902, the court finds that the individual petitioner is representative of that class of persons who are tenants of the defendant corporation and have air conditioners subject to the additional charge. The fact that this is a special proceeding does not bar class action treatment. (CPLR 103[b]; . . . .) Further, the court finds that no notice to the class is required as petitioner is seeking in substance "declaratory relief" (CPLR 904[a]), to wit, that no approval of increased charges may be had without public hearings. The term "declaratory relief" cannot be restricted to an action for declaratory judgment. . . . Such is particularly clear when consideration is given to the fact that an action for declaratory judgment and a special proceeding must both result in judgments determinative of the rights of the parties. (*Compare* CPLR 3001 with CPLR 411.)

[The Court held that petitioners were not entitled to relief on the merits.]

NOTES

(1) Like Rule 23 of the Federal Rules of Civil Procedure, CPLR 904 does not require notice in cases brought primarily for injunctive or declaratory relief. The rules take different approaches to notice in actions in which monetary relief is the primary remedy. Fed. R. Civ. P. 23(c)(2) requires "the best notice practicable under the circumstances, including individual notice to all members who can be identified through reasonable effort," whereas CPLR 904(b) mandates that "reasonable notice of the commencement of a class action shall be given to the class in such manner as the Court directs."

The federal rule has been interpreted to require first-class mail notice even where the class was so large that the practical effect of the requirement was to force the abandonment of the action. *Eisen v. Carlisle & Jacquelin*, 417 U.S. 156, 94 S. Ct. 2140, 40 L. Ed. 2d 732 (1974). Further, the cost of obtaining the names and addresses of class members must in general be borne by the class representative. *Oppenheimer Fund, Inc. v. Sanders*, 437 U.S. 340, 98 S. Ct. 2380, 57 L. Ed. 2d 253 (1978).

CPLR 904(d) allows the court to make the class opponent bear the cost of notice initially. This is forbidden under the federal rule. *Eisen v. Carlisle & Jacquelin, supra*.

(2) When no notice is required, as in the *Boulevard Gardens* case, will members of the class be bound by the determination against them? Or could they challenge it in a separate proceeding? The Supreme Court has suggested that adequate representation of the class is sufficient to bind its members. See the quotation from *Phillips Petroleum Co. v. Shutts, supra, citing Hansberry v. Lee*, 311 U.S. 32, 61 S. Ct. 115, 85 L. Ed. 22 (1940). The issue is far from settled. *See generally* Comment, *The Importance of Being Adequate: Due Process Requirements in Class Actions Under Federal Rule 23*, 123 U. Pa. L. Rev. 1217 (1975).

(3) On the other hand, it is clear that some form of notice is constitutionally required when the class action seeks predominantly monetary relief. This point was also discussed in *Phillips Petroleum Co. v. Shutts, supra,* and in the next principal case.

[D] Settlement and the Rights of Class Members

WOODROW v. COLT INDUSTRIES, INC.
Court of Appeals
77 N.Y.2d 185, 565 N.Y.S.2d 755, 566 N.E.2d 1160 (1991)

WACHTLER, C.J.

In this case, we consider whether the respondent, a Missouri corporation with no ties to New York, has a due process constitutional right to opt out of a New York class action in which the relief sought in the complaint was largely equitable in nature. We hold today that when a class action complaint demands predominantly equitable relief that will necessarily benefit the class as a whole if granted, the Trial Judge is not required to give class members the opportunity to opt out of the class. We also hold, however, that under that governing principle as applied to the facts of this case, the Trial Judge erred in approving a settlement agreement insofar as it purported also to extinguish the respondent's right to pursue a cause of action in damages.

This class action stems from a 1988 corporate merger involving appellant Colt Industries Inc. (Colt), a Pennsylvania corporation with offices in New York City, and appellant Morgan Stanley Group Inc. (Morgan Stanley), a New York-based securities firm. Colt and its subsidiaries were in the business of manufacturing and selling firearms and machine and engine parts. At the time the merger was announced in March of 1988, Colt had 32 million shares of common stock outstanding and approximately 16,300 shareholders of record. Of those 32 million shares, 62,000 were owned by the respondent James S. Merritt Company (Merritt), a Missouri corporation with its principal place of business in Kansas City.

In 1986, two years before the merger, Colt underwent a major recapitalization. Each share of Colt common stock held by its public shareholders was exchanged for $85 in cash and one new share. More than 30 million shares were repurchased as a result and Colt incurred $1.5 billion in debt.

In January of 1988, Morgan Stanley advised Colt of its interest in acquiring the company. A special committee consisting of Colt's outside directors, with the assistance of Colt's financial advisor, the First Boston Corporation, engaged in negotiations with Morgan Stanley over the terms of a merger agreement. The agreement, which was reached in March of 1988, provided that Colt Holdings Inc., a Morgan Stanley affiliate that came into existence to effectuate the merger, would make a tender offer to purchase all outstanding shares of Colt common stock at $17 per share. This tender offer was to be followed by the merger, in which all remaining shareholders would be entitled to the same $17 consideration for their stock.

The proposed merger ignited 15 separate shareholder suits in State courts in New York and Pennsylvania. Counsel for these plaintiffs stipulated to an order that consolidated these suits in Supreme Court, New York County. Thereafter, class counsel filed a first amended consolidated class action complaint naming Colt and its officers and directors as defendants. In substance, they alleged that the defendants: (1) had breached their common-law fiduciary duties to the class by offering a price per share that was grossly inadequate; (2) had engaged in a course of conduct that lacked any valid business purpose and was designed solely to eliminate the class as Colt shareholders; (3) were not exercising independent business judgment and were in fact engaging in self-dealing to the detriment of the class; and (4) had failed to solicit other, possibly more beneficial, bids from potential buyers.

In their prayer for relief, the plaintiffs demanded a declaration that the action was a class action, preliminary and permanent injunctive relief blocking the merger, rescission in the event the merger did go forward, an order requiring the defendants to disgorge all benefits that they may have received as a result of the transaction, costs and disbursements, including attorneys' fees, and any damages as may have been sustained.

By an order on consent dated April 12, 1988, the trial court certified the class action for purposes of settlement and defined the class as consisting of Colt's common shareholders as of March 1, 1987. The court noted that the prerequisites for a class action under CPLR 901 had been satisfied in this case. The court ordered that all members of the class be given notice of the proceeding and enjoined all class members from filing any other lawsuit in any other jurisdiction based on the facts giving rise to the New York-based class action.

The parties to the action on April 29, 1988 prepared a stipulation and agreement of compromise and settlement, based on an earlier Memorandum of Understanding. In substance, the agreement provided: (1) that Colt Holdings Inc. agreed to reduce, from $12 million to $10 million, the amount that it would be entitled to receive as reimbursement if the merger agreement were terminated; (2) Colt Holdings Inc. agreed to waive certain conditions to the offer that permitted Colt Holdings to terminate the offer or refuse to make payment for tendered shares if any change occurred in the operations or condition of Colt or if any material representations made in the merger agreement were not true and correct; (3) defendants agreed not to oppose plaintiffs' application for attorneys' fees in the amount of $425,000; and (4) plaintiffs agreed to the dismissal, with prejudice, of the class action, and to the release of all claims that could be asserted by the class regarding the offer and the merger.

By order dated May 10, 1988, the trial court redefined the class to include all Colt common shareholders as of March 1, 1988, scheduled a hearing for June 15, 1988 to determine whether the proposed settlement was fair and reasonable, and approved a Notice of Pendency of Action, Class Action Determination, Proposed Settlement of Class Action and Settlement Hearing that had been prepared by the parties and appended to the stipulation of settlement. The court ordered that this notice be published in the national editions of the New York Times and Wall Street Journal on or before May 17, 1988.

Merritt learned of the pendency of the class action and of the proposed settlement by reading the notice contained in the May 17 edition of the Wall Street Journal. Merritt's attorneys sent a registered letter to the trial court, dated May 27, requesting exclusion from the class. On June 9, Merritt filed a separate action for damages against Colt and other defendants in the United States District Court for the Western District of Missouri. One day later, on June 10, Colt's shareholders approved the merger.

On June 15, 1988, the Trial Judge signed an order denying Merritt's application for exclusion from the class. After conducting the settlement hearing, the court approved the settlement and the request for attorneys' fees. In the judgment, the trial court dismissed the class complaint with prejudice and enjoined class members and their successors-in-interest from asserting any "class, derivative, or individual claim for violations of federal, state, or other law, or of the common law . . . which has been or might have been asserted in the actions in connection with, arising out of or in any way related to . . . the leveraged buyout of Colt, the Agreement and Plan of Merger . . . the Offer to Purchase all outstanding shares of Colt common stock . . . the merger of Colt Transition Inc. with and into Colt . . . the consideration received or to be received by any Colt shareholder pursuant to the Offer or the Merger and the disclosures made in connection with the Offer or the Merger." The judgment released all claims against "each individual defendant, Colt, [Colt] Holdings, Morgan Stanley Group, Inc., and The Morgan Stanley Leveraged Equity Fund II, L.P. and their respective agents, servants, attorneys, [and] investment advisors. . . ." Merritt appealed the assorted orders and judgments that denied its opt-out request, bound it to the settlement agreement and precluded it from asserting its own damage claims. The Missouri action, while currently pending, is in abeyance pending the outcome of this appeal.

The Appellate Division, First Department, ruled in Merritt's favor (155 AD2d 154). The court stated that the merger on June 10 mooted out the class' equitable claims and left remaining only the request for fees and expenses, which the court categorized as a claim for damages. Consequently, the court concluded that Merritt had a due process right to receive notification of the class action and to seek exclusion from the class, citing *Phillips Petroleum Co. v Shutts* (472 U.S. 797).

We agree with the Appellate Division that the Supreme Court's analysis in *Shutts* is relevant in determining whether Merritt had a right to opt out of the class. We believe, however, that the Appellate Division rested its reading of *Shutts*, and consequently its holding, upon a faulty premise — that the June 10 merger mooted the class' equitable claims and converted the entire action into one for damages. The only element of the complaint that became moot upon consummation of the merger was the request for an injunction preventing the merger from going forward. The class' request for rescission, also an equitable remedy (*see generally*, Dobbs, Remedies sec. 4.3, at 254-256), certainly remained viable and indeed only became tenable after the merger was completed. Had the trial court not given its approval to the settlement, it is at the very least possible that the class would have pursued its action against the defendants and ultimately obtained rescission of the merger. It is not our role at this juncture to consider the merits of such a claim or to pass upon the likelihood that rescission would have been granted under the facts of this case. We note only that the class requested in its complaint that the court rescind the merger if it went forward and that this prayer for relief survived the shareholder vote approving the merger. This alone, then, undermines the Appellate Division's conclusion that the merger converted the action into one for damages.

We note further that the request for fees and expenses contained in the consolidated class complaint was improperly characterized by the Appellate Division as a claim for damages. "[T]he foundation for the historic practice of granting reimbursement for the costs of litigation other than the conventional taxable costs is part of the original authority of the chancellor to do equity in a particular situation" (*Mills v Electric Auto-Lite*, 396 U.S. 375, 392-393, *quoting Sprague v Ticonic Natl. Bank*, 307 U.S. 161, 166).

Having determined that the Appellate Division erred as a matter of law in concluding that the relief sought by the class in this case lost its equitable character when the merger was consummated on June 10, we must now consider a question that the Appellate Division did not: whether a member of a class that is seeking predominantly equitable relief has a due process right to opt out of the class.  Issue

This question was expressly left open by the United States Supreme Court in *Phillips Petroleum Co. v Shutts* (*supra*). The Court held in that case that in a State court class action for money damages, an out-of-State class member with no ties to the forum State could nonetheless be bound by a judgment entered there, provided he was adequately represented (*see, Hansberry v Lee*, 311 U.S. 32, 42-43, 45) and had notice of the action "plus an opportunity to be heard and participate in the litigation, whether in person or through counsel." (472 U.S., at 812.) In addition, "due process requires at a minimum that an absent plaintiff be provided with an opportunity to remove himself from the class by executing and returning an 'opt out' or 'request for exclusion' form to the court." (*Id.*)

But in a footnote to the majority opinion, the Court stated explicitly that its holding was "limited to those class actions which seek to bind known plaintiffs concerning claims wholly or predominately for money judgments." (*Id.*, at 811, n 3.)
The Court "intimate[d] no view concerning other types of class actions, such as
those seeking equitable relief." (*Id.*)

"The class suit was an invention of equity to enable it to proceed to a decree
in suits where the number of those interested in the subject of the litigation is
so great that their joinder as parties in conformity to the usual rules of procedure is impracticable." (*Hansberry v Lee*, 311 U.S. 32, 41, *supra; see also, Stern
v Carter*, 82 AD2d 321, 325-327 [Titone, J.].) The Supreme Court's distinction in
Shutts between class actions seeking equitable and monetary relief is consistent
with the pattern in State class action statutes and in rule 23 of the Federal
Rules of Civil Procedure to accord varying degrees of procedural protection to
class members depending upon the relief sought by the class.

. . . .

New York's class action statute (CPLR 901-909) has much in common with
Federal rule 23 . . .

More importantly for our purposes here, however, the New York statute also
looks to the relief sought by the class in determining what process is due the
class members. Section 904(a) deals with class actions brought predominantly
for injunctive or declaratory relief and provides that in such an action "notice
of the pendency of the action need not be given to the class" unless the court
believes notice to be necessary and determines that the cost of notice will not
prevent the action from going forward. Subdivision (b) applies to all other class
actions and provides that "reasonable notice" must be given according to the
instructions of the court.

Unlike rule 23, the New York statute does not specifically mandate opt out for
cases of a certain type. The statute clearly contemplates, however, that a Judge
may choose to exercise discretion to permit a class member to opt out of a class
(*see*, CPLR 903 ["(w)hen appropriate the court may limit the class to those
members who do not request exclusion from the class within a specified time
after notice"]; CPLR 904[c][III] [in considering the type of notice to be given to
class members, the court should consider "the stake of each represented member of the class, and the likelihood that significant numbers of represented
members would desire to exclude themselves from the class or to appear individually"]).

The question left open by the Supreme Court's holding in *Shutts*, then, is
whether the jurisdictional and due process concerns addressed by that decision
effectively eliminate the mandatory class action as a matter of constitutional
law, despite the fact that both State and Federal governments have for years recognized the need for mandatory classes where certain types of relief are sought.
We conclude that the Trial Judge committed no error in refusing to give Merritt
the opportunity to exclude itself from the class when it was first certified

because there is no due process right to opt out of a class that seeks predominantly equitable relief.

In arriving at this decision, we look to the reasons for treating equitable
relief differently from damage relief in this context. When a class seeks to compel certain behavior on the part of an entity, whether it be a governmental
agency or a private corporation, certain considerations come into play that distinguish the situation from a private damage suit. First, because the class
seeks to enjoin actual conduct that it considers to be detrimental to the class,
there is an interest in consolidating the action in a single forum in order to avoid
the possibility of conflicting judgments from different jurisdictions which would
subject the defendants to varying and possibly inconsistent obligations (*see*,
e.g., Weber, *Preclusion and Procedural Due Process in Rule 23(b)(2) Class
Actions*, 21 U Mich J of L Reform 347, 366-367). So long as the Judge certifying
a class seeking predominantly equitable relief makes a finding that the prerequisites to bringing a class action — numerosity, predominance, typicality,
adequacy of representation and superiority — are satisfied (*see*, *Friar v Vanguard Holding Corp.*, *supra*), we believe that the due process rights of the class
members, whatever their ties to the forum State, are protected. With claims of
this kind, a judgment benefits the class as a whole, and any interest in promoting individual control of litigation is outweighed by the importance of
obtaining a single, binding determination.

Further, where a class action suit seeks to bind defendants to a certain course
of conduct, the resolution of that action, especially if the case is settled before
trial, will involve the careful fashioning of a remedy that accommodates both the
class' and the defendants' interests. That was certainly the case here, where the
parties worked out a settlement that accorded the class relief that was primarily equitable in nature but at the same time recognized the interests of the
defendants in having the merger proceed. To permit limitless collateral challenges under these circumstances would greatly diminish the possibility that
complicated class actions for equitable relief would ever settle before trial,
because it would be likely that compromises carefully arrived at would be
unraveled by subsequent litigation in other jurisdictions. The specter of later,
equally binding litigation in different jurisdictions around the country would
doubtless inject a note of uncertainty into class actions for equitable relief and
would upset expectations on both sides that a final judgment ordering specific
conduct could ever be truly final (*see*, Note, *Developments in the Law — Class
Actions*, 89 Harv L Rev 1318, 1400-1401).

Our review of the complaint convinces us that at the time this class action
was certified, the class was primarily seeking injunctive relief. As noted above,
the court was under no statutory duty to grant Merritt the opportunity to opt
out of the class. Because of the distinct concerns that come into play when a
class seeks primarily equitable relief, we conclude that there was similarly no
due process constitutional right to opt out of the class at the time the class was
certified.

It does not follow from the foregoing, however, that the court's approval of the final settlement was proper. "[O]ne of the strengths of CPLR article 9 is its flexibility. A decision granting class action status is not immutable and if later events indicate that the decision should be reversed, altered or amended, requisite relief is authorized." (*Friar v Vanguard Holding Corp., supra*, at 100.) Specifically, CPLR 902 authorizes the court to alter or amend the order granting certification, CPLR 906 permits the court to sever issues for class determination or to divide the class into subclasses, and CPLR 902 permits the court to make, alter, or amend any order dealing with procedural matters (*see, Friar v Vanguard Holding Corp., supra*, at 100).

This case would be much easier if the judgment purported simply to preclude the relitigation of the class members' equitable claims. In a case of that kind, the foregoing analysis would compel the conclusion that Merritt was not entitled to opt out of this action and that Merritt is precluded from bringing any individual action for injunctive relief in any other forum, despite the fact that it does not possess minimum contacts with New York State. That, however, is not this case, and Merritt's lack of contacts with New York troubles us enormously when we consider the fact that the settlement purports to extinguish its rights to pursue a damage remedy as well.

We are well aware of the fact that we can neither dictate nor predict the res judicata effect that the New York judgment will be given by the Federal court in Missouri (*see*, Restatement [Second] of Judgments § 86[2], comment e). What we can do, however, is to review the trial court's determination that this settlement was fair, reasonable, and adequate and decide whether its decision to approve the settlement was error in light of the circumstances present in this case.

We hold that the trial court did err as a matter of law by seeking to bind an absent plaintiff with no ties to New York State to a settlement that purported to extinguish its rights to bring an action in damages in another jurisdiction. We reach this conclusion based on our consideration of the terms of the settlement reflected in the judgment, on our reading of *Shutts*, and on our belief that the Supreme Court in that decision intended to afford substantial protections to out-of-State plaintiffs in State class action suits.

The settlement in this case gave class members relief that was essentially equitable in nature, but exacted as a price for that relief a concession that the class members could not pursue damage claims based on the merger. This aspect of the settlement poses special difficulties because while contained in an agreement granting largely equitable relief, it nonetheless impinges upon a distinct right — the right to pursue a claim in damages. Thus, to the extent that the terms in this settlement had an impact upon the entirely separate and distinct right of the class members to pursue damage claims, the Supreme Court's analysis in *Shutts* and the due process concerns discussed in the body of that opinion become relevant.

In *Shutts*, the Court acknowledged that a class member's cause of action was a constitutionally protected property interest (472 U.S., at 807). Although the Court held that an absent class member need not possess minimum contacts with the forum State to be bound by a judgment in damages obtained by the class, the Court also required that certain procedural prerequisites be satisfied before the class member could be bound, including an opportunity to be excluded from the class. In this case, the court denied Merritt the opportunity to exclude itself from a settlement that extinguished rights the Supreme Court has recognized are deserving of constitutional protection. That the settlement arose out of a class action seeking equitable relief does not change the fact that property rights entitled to due process protection were implicated by the settlement's terms. Thus, we believe that the Supreme Court's holding in *Shutts* controls our analysis of the damage aspects of this case and that the due process concerns that motivated the Court in that case also have a place in the disposition of this one.

Despite the fact that Merritt had notice of the action and could have chosen to appear to contest the settlement, we do not believe that this was sufficient to protect Merritt's property interest in its cause of action in damages against Colt and other parties involved in the merger. The interest in obtaining a single binding judgment and in satisfying the expectations of the parties that such a judgment precludes additional litigation is not sufficiently compelling for us to ignore the jurisdictional and procedural impediments to binding out-of-State class members to class settlements such as this one without giving them the opportunity to exclude themselves from the class. CPLR article 9 is remarkably flexible and provides for a wide range of procedural and administrative approaches in the handling of class action disputes. The Trial Judge, for example, could have created subclasses instead of seeking to bind all class members to a settlement of this kind (*see*, CPLR 906). To adhere to a rigid view of the efficacy of the class action device without considering the jurisdictional and due process implications of that position was error.

Our recognition that the class complaint here sought predominantly equitable relief in no way alters our conclusion that it was erroneous for the trial court to approve a settlement that purported to extinguish Merritt's damage claims. By precluding out-of-State class members from litigating damage claims without giving them a chance to opt out of the class, the settlement negated the long-standing practice of distinguishing between class actions for monetary and equitable relief and granting varying degrees of procedural protection depending upon the relief sought. If the class complaint had sought only monetary relief or both substantial monetary relief and equitable relief, *Shutts* would have required that Merritt be given an opportunity to opt out of the class once it was certified. The mere fact that the relief initially demanded was largely equitable should not permit the court to circumvent the Supreme Court's holding in *Shutts* and bind Merritt to a settlement that eliminates constitutionally protected property interests without due process. The degree of due process accorded plaintiffs and the binding effect consequently accorded settlements should not be made to depend wholly upon the way in which class counsel styles an action through the mechanism of the class complaint. Litigants should not be able to subvert substantial constitutional rights by sleight of hand and artful pleading.

In conclusion, the Trial Judge was not required to give Merritt an opportunity to opt out of the class at the time that the class was certified, because at that juncture, the relief sought was predominately equitable. Given the class complaint as filed, the court properly considered the value of consolidating the action in a single forum and reaching one binding determination. However, once the parties presented the court with a settlement that accorded equitable relief and in turn required the class members to give up all claims in damages, the nature of the adjudication changed dramatically. We conclude that the trial court erred when it approved a settlement of this kind without affording Merritt the due process protections outlined in *Shutts*.

We have considered the parties' remaining arguments and find them to be without merit. Accordingly, the order of the Appellate Division should be modified, with costs to respondent, by (1) vacating so much thereof as grants Merritt's request to be excluded from the class and directs that Merritt is not bound by the class action insofar as it seeks equitable relief, (2) denying Merritt's request to be excluded from the class, and (3) adjudging that Merritt is not bound by the class action settlement insofar as Merritt seeks to assert an action for damages. As so modified, the Appellate Division order should be affirmed.

NOTES

(1) As you read the *Woodrow* decision, who won? Also, did the Court of Appeals negate the possibility of a future settlement by its holding regarding the rights of Merritt, the Missouri corporation, with respect to its damage claims?

(2) The Supreme Court of the United States subsequently addressed the power of state courts to bind absent class members with damage claims. In *Matsushita Elec. Indus. Co. v. Epstein*, 516 U.S. 367, 116 S. Ct. 873, 134 L. Ed. 2d 6 (1996), the Court held that a settlement of a class action approved by the Delaware Chancery Court after notice to the class members was binding on all of those who had not opted out, regardless of their residency. The settlement extinguished not only their damage claims under Delaware law but their federal claims as well. In *Matsushita*, the plaintiffs' claims arose out of a corporate merger, and, as in *Woodrow,* the class consisted of all shareholders of the defendant corporation. *Matsushita* does not address the rights of shareholders who were not given an opportunity to opt out. Should the New York Court of Appeals depart from *Woodrow* if the issue arises again? Is it critical that Merritt (the party the settlement purported to bind) was not given an opportunity to opt out of the *Woodrow* class action? The inter-jurisdictional problems are explored in Marcel Kahan & Linda Silberman, Matsushita *and Beyond: The Role of State*

Courts in Class Actions Involving Exclusive Federal Claims, 1996 Sup. Ct. Rev. 219 (1997).

(3) Opportunities to use state courts to bring class actions alleging violations of federal securities law were reduced by the passage of the Securities Litigation Uniform Standards Act of 1998, Pub. L. 105-353. The Act gave the federal courts exclusive jurisdiction over many such actions. The availability of state courts as a site of future class actions (regardless of the nature of the claim) was further cabined by the Class Action Fairness Act of 2005 (CAFA). It expands the jurisdiction of federal courts over class actions in which there is diversity between the defendant and any class member and the aggregate amount in controversy exceeds $5 million. 28 U.S.C. § 1332(d). CAFA also allows a defendant to remove such class actions to a federal court. 28 U.S.C. § 1453.

KLEIN v. ROBERT'S AMERICAN GOURMET FOOD, INC.
Appellate Division, Second Department
28 A.D.3d 63, 808 N.Y.S.2d 766 (2006)

FISHER, J.

On this appeal, we are presented with a challenge to the certification of a nationwide, settlement-only class action involving, inter alia, claims of fraud and the violation of sections 349 and 350 of the General Business Law. The facts are largely undisputed.

The defendant Robert's American Gourmet Food, Inc. (hereinafter Robert), created and distributed snack food products under the brand names Pirate's Booty, Fruity Booty, and Veggie Booty (hereinafter the Products). The Products were manufactured by the defendant Keystone Food Products (hereinafter Keystone).

When it became known that the fat and caloric content of the Products was substantially higher than advertised, lawsuits alleging, inter alia, fraud, and deceptive trade practices were instituted in state courts in New York, California, Florida, and New Jersey. In April 2002, the plaintiffs in this case commenced such an action in the Supreme Court, Nassau County, on behalf of themselves and others similarly situated. They moved for class certification, and soon began settlement negotiations with the defendants and with counsel representing the plaintiffs in other actions pending across the country. Those negotiations resulted in a proposed "Stipulation And Agreement of Compromise and Settlement," dated November 1, 2002, and later amended (hereinafter the Settlement).

The Settlement, among other things, required Robert to issue and redeem a total of $3.5 million in discount coupons for the purchase of Robert's snack food products. The coupons were to be redeemed at the point of purchase, and each was to be in an amount equaling approximately 20% of the retail price of the product purchased. The coupons were to be distributed at a rate reasonably calculated to result in the redemption of approximately $780,000 per six-month period. In addition, the Products were to be tested for fat and caloric content at monthly, and later at quarterly, intervals, and the results were to be reported to class counsel for a period of four years. In exchange, all class members who did not exclude themselves from the class would be enjoined from bringing suit against the defendants on any of the claims asserted in the various pending cases, other than personal injury claims. Lastly, the Settlement authorized the payment of up to $790,000 in attorney's fees.

By order entered November 6, 2002, the Supreme Court, in effect, conditionally certified a class (hereinafter the Class) for settlement purposes only. The Class consisted of "all persons in the United States who, between January 1, 1999 and October 1, 2002 purchased at retail any of the following products distributed by Robert's American Gourmet Food, Inc.[:] Pirate's Booty, Fruity Booty, or Veggie Booty snack foods." The Supreme Court also approved the Notice of Pendency and Settlement of Class Action (hereinafter the Notice), and set January 10, 2003, as the date for a "Settlement Fairness Hearing" (hereinafter the fairness hearing). Additionally, the order established procedures and deadlines for Class members to opt out of the Class or to file objections to the proposed Settlement up to and including January 2, 2003.

The appellant was the plaintiff in an individual action commenced in the Supreme Court, New York County, asserting essentially the same claims against the same defendants. Because she was a retail purchaser of one or more of the Products, she became a member of the Class in this action as well. As such, she filed an objection to the Settlement, contending, among other things, that it provided insufficient value to Class members, that it contained no injunction against, or admission of liability by, the defendants, that the proposed notice was inadequate, and that the proposed attorney's fees were excessive. The appellant subsequently filed a supplemental objection raising substantially the same issues.

Apart from the appellant, only a handful of other members of the Class filed objections. One objector withdrew her objection prior to the fairness hearing in exchange for small changes to the Settlement's monitoring provisions and the payment of $33,000 in fees to her attorney out of the $790,000 fund previously requested by the plaintiffs' counsel. At the fairness hearing, another objector withdrew her objection in exchange for a commitment by the defendants, inter alia, to publish a summary notice of the Settlement (hereinafter the Summary Notice) in a national newspaper within 15 days of the Settlement's approval, and to pay her attorney $25,000 in fees out of the same $790,000 fund. As part of the agreement with that objector, the plaintiffs' attorney represented to the court that Class members would be given an additional 30 days from the publication of the Summary Notice to opt out "despite the fact that the Settlement [will have] been approved." The Summary Notice was published in the January 23, 2003, edition of USA Today, and gave Class members until February 26, 2003, to opt out of the Class.

. . . The Supreme Court, inter alia, (1) certified the action as a class action for settlement purposes, (2) approved the Settlement as fair, reasonable, adequate, and in the best interests of the Class members, (3) dismissed the complaint, (4) enjoined Class members from prosecuting as against the defendants any claims released under the terms of the Settlement, and (5) awarded $790,000 in attorney's fees to be paid to the plaintiffs' attorneys and distributed in accordance with the terms of the Settlement.

. . . .

Having determined that the appellant has standing to challenge the Settlement and to pursue her challenge in this Court, we turn to the merits of her objections. In doing so, we are guided by three familiar considerations.

First, in New York, a class action may be maintained only if: (1) the proposed class is so numerous that joinder of all members is impracticable; (2) common questions of law or fact predominate over any questions affecting only individual members; (3) the claims of the representative parties are typical of the class as a whole; (4) the representative parties will fairly and adequately protect the interests of the class; and (5) the class action is superior to other available methods for the fair and efficient adjudication of the controversy (*see* CPLR 901[a][1]-[5], 902 . . .). Where, as here, a class is certified for settlement purposes only, these prerequisites and particularly those designed to protect absentee class members must still be met and, indeed, "demand undiluted, even heightened, attention" (*Amchem Prods., Inc. v Windsor*, 521 U.S. 591, 620 . . .).

Second, because the disposition of a class action binds class members who do not directly participate in the action, the trial court must act as "the protector of the rights of the absent class members" . . . in deciding whether certification as a class action is appropriate and, if so, whether any proposed settlement "is fair, reasonable and adequate". . . .

And, third, although the question of whether a lawsuit should be resolved as a class action ordinarily rests within the sound discretion of the court applying the statutory criteria to the facts presented, "the Appellate Division, as a branch of [the] Supreme Court, is vested with the same discretionary power and may exercise that power, even when there has been no abuse of discretion as a matter of law by the nisi prius court" (*Small v Lorillard Tobacco Co.*, 94 N.Y.2d 43, 52-53, 720 N.E.2d 892, 698 N.Y.S.2d 615).

A review of the record here reveals that, apart from a brief statement by counsel indicating approval of the Settlement, there is no transcript of what transpired at the fairness hearing. The record contains no detailed findings of fact or conclusions of law, and therefore we do not have the benefit of the Supreme Court's reasoning or the basis for its order and judgment. We find, therefore, that the record does not provide information sufficient to allow us to determine whether the Supreme Court made an informed decision and providently exercised its discretion when it certified a nationwide settlement-only class, and when it approved the Settlement as fair, reasonable, adequate, and in the best interests of the Class members (*see Negrin v Norwest Mtge.*, 293 A.D.2d 726, 727, 741 N.Y.S.2d 287). Our own concerns, based on the limited record before us, lie in three areas: the appropriateness of certifying a class action with respect to the class as defined, the reasonableness of the Settlement, and the award of an attorney's fees. We address them seriatim.

A. *The Certification of a Class Action for the Class as Defined*

As a general proposition, in a class action, "the class must not be defined so broadly that it encompasses individuals who have little connection with the claim being litigated; rather, it must be restricted to individuals who are raising the same claims or defenses as the representative" (7AWright & Miller, Fed Prac & Proc 2d § 1760). In other words, the class cannot be so broad as to include individuals who have not been harmed by the defendants' allegedly wrongful conduct. . . .

Here, the defendants' alleged wrongful conduct was the misrepresentation of the fat and caloric content of the Products. Notably, with the exception of the cause of action asserted under General Business Law § 349, all of the theories of liability advanced by the plaintiffs require proof of reliance. The Class, however, consists of "*all persons* in the United States who, between January 1, 1999 and October 1, 2002 purchased at retail any of the following products distributed by Robert's American Gourmet Food, Inc.[:] Pirate's Booty, Fruity Booty, or Veggie Booty snack foods" (emphasis supplied). Of all the persons in the nation who purchased the Products over that nearly four-year period, there were certainly some, and perhaps many, who did so for reasons wholly unrelated to the Products' advertised fat and caloric content. Those individuals would not have suffered any injury as a result of the defendants' alleged misrepresentations, and therefore their inclusion in the Class suggests that the definition is too broad. The Supreme Court apparently did not consider or address that issue.

Moreover, the barren record does not provide the basis for the Supreme Court's conclusion that common issues of law and fact predominate over issues affecting only individual members of the Class as defined. The complaint, for instance, asserts causes of action sounding in common-law fraud, negligent misrepresentation, breach of express warranties, and false advertising under General Business Law § 350. Each requires, inter alia, proof of reliance. . . . It would seem, therefore, that there are questions here that are not common to the Class, such as whether individual Class members purchased the Products in reliance upon the allegedly misrepresented fat and caloric contents, as opposed to other considerations (*see Strauss v Long Is. Sports*, 60 A.D.2d 501, 507, 401 N.Y.S.2d 233).

. . . .

We do not mean in any way to suggest that consumer fraud or deceptive trade practices cases should not be adjudicated or settled as class actions (*see*

Weinberg v Hertz Corp., 116 A.D.2d 1, 499 N.Y.S.2d 693, *affd* 69 N.Y.2d 979, 509 N.E.2d 347, 516 N.Y.S.2d 652; *King v Club Med*, 76 A.D.2d 123, 430 N.Y.S.2d 65; *see generally* 6 Newberg on Class Actions § 21:30 [4th Ed]). The existence of individual issues is but one of several factors to be weighed by the court in determining whether class certification is appropriate under the circumstances. . . . The record here, however, does not demonstrate that the Supreme Court took that factor into account at all.

Therefore, the matter must be remitted to the Supreme Court for the development of a proper factual record and thereafter, a new determination as to whether class certification is appropriate pursuant to the factors listed in CPLR 901 and 902.

B. *The Reasonableness of the Settlement*

Assuming that this action may properly be maintained as a class action for settlement purposes, the Supreme Court must further address whether the proposed settlement is fair, adequate, reasonable, and in the best interest of class members. Where, as here, the action is primarily one for the recovery of money damages, determining the adequacy of a proposed settlement generally involves balancing the value of that settlement against the present value of the anticipated recovery following a trial on the merits, discounted for the inherent risks of litigation. The amount agreed to here was $3.5 million to be issued and redeemed by the defendants, over a period of years, in the form of discount coupons good toward future purchases of Robert's snack foods. Settlements that include fully assignable and transferable discount coupons that can be aggregated and are distributed directly to class members have been approved because such coupons have been found to provide "real and quantifiable value to the class members". . . . Here, however, there is no indication that the discount coupons have any intrinsic cash value, or that they may be assigned, aggregated, or transferred in any way.

Moreover, under the Settlement, the proposed discount coupons are not to be distributed directly to members of the Class, but instead will be made available to the public at large. "In a settlement context, when an aggregate class recovery cannot economically be distributed to individual class members the parties, subject to court approval, may agree that undistributed funds will be distributed or disposed of for the indirect benefit of the class" (4 Newberg on Class Actions § 11:20 [4th Ed]). Such indirect compensation arrangements have been known, interchangeably, as cy pres or fluid class recovery distributions. In cases where it is difficult to locate class members or to distribute funds directly to them, a cy pres distribution may prove a useful complement to more traditional distribution formulas. . . . There is nothing in the record here, however, to suggest that the Supreme Court considered or explored the possibility or appropriateness of a cy pres distribution, and that is particularly troubling inasmuch as the proposed distribution of discount coupons to the public at large, without more, is unlikely to confer any benefit, either direct or indirect, upon those members of the Class who have the most serious grievances.

Class members who purchased the Products largely because of their advertised low fat and caloric content are those most likely to have been injured by the alleged misrepresentation. Yet, having sought a low-fat, low-calorie snack food, they would be the least likely to purchase the Products again now that their higher fat and caloric content has been revealed. Thus, they would be the least likely to reap any benefit from the distribution of discount coupons.

. . . .

C. The Attorney's Fees

The Supreme Court awarded the plaintiffs' attorney's fees in the sum of $790,000. Pursuant to CPLR 909, if a judgment is rendered in favor of the class, "the court in its discretion may award attorneys' fees to the representatives of the class based on the reasonable value of legal services rendered." The record in this case is insufficient to support the award.

The amount awarded in attorney's fees must be based on the "reasonable value of legal services rendered" (CPLR 909). The burden of showing the reasonableness of the fee lies with the claimant (*see Matter of Karp*, 145 A.D.2d 208, 216, 537 N.Y.S.2d 510), and "the determination of what constitutes a reasonable fee involves extensive consideration of the nature and value of the services rendered by the plaintiffs' attorneys" (*Friar v Vanguard Holding Corp.*, 125 A.D.2d 444, 447, 509 N.Y.S.2d 374). Although the claimant is not required to tender contemporaneously-maintained time records, "the court will usually, and especially in a matter involving a large fee, be presented with an objective and detailed breakdown by the attorney of the time and labor expended, together with other factors he or she feels supports the fee requested" (*Matter of Karp, supra* at 216). Otherwise stated, "the valuation process requires definite information, not only as to the way in which the time was spent (discovery, oral argument, negotiation, etc.), but also as to the experience and standing of the various lawyers performing each task (senior partner, junior partner, associate, etc.)". . . .

Here, the law firms representing the plaintiffs submitted brief affirmations attaching firm resumes and disclosed, for each attorney who worked on the case, the name and standing of the individual, as well as the total number of hours worked. The affirmations, however, contained only brief and general descriptions of the work performed by the firm as a whole, and, other than total hours, included no information regarding the tasks performed by any of the individual attorneys. For example, over 481 hours of work performed by the firm serving as lead counsel for the plaintiffs was attributed only to "drafting of pleadings, review of discovery, drafting of memoranda of law, and participation in settlement negotiations." Another 106 hours of work performed by another law firm is described in exactly the same terms. Without more, such descriptions were insufficient to support an award of an attorney's fee.

We conclude that the record below is inadequate to allow us to determine whether the Supreme Court considered factors necessary to make an informed decision and to exercise its discretion providently when it certified a nationwide settlement-only class, approved the Settlement as fair, reasonable, adequate, and in the best interests of the Class members, and awarded attorney's fees. Moreover, because the record is insufficient to permit an independent review by this court, we must remit the case for further consideration and factual development relating to those issues.

Accordingly, the order and judgment entered January 14, 2003, should be reversed, the matter should be remitted to the Supreme Court, Nassau County, for further proceedings consistent herewith. . . .

§ 8.05 INTERPLEADER: CPLR 1006

PROBLEM C

Recall the facts in Problem A, involving Tom, Ibn and XYZ Corp. Suppose that following the commencement of Tom's action against XYZ Corp., the latter, instead of moving to dismiss the action, served an answer asserting that it was exposed to multiple liability, and moved for permission to deposit the disputed funds into court and to serve an interpleader complaint on Ibn in Saudi Arabia.

(a) Should the motion be granted? *See* CPLR 1006(g) and the following two cases.

(b) If the motion were granted and Ibn asserted a claim to the disputed funds, could XYZ Corp. properly move for and be granted a discharge? *See* CPLR 1006(f).

CORDNER v. METROPOLITAN LIFE INSURANCE CO.
United States District Court, Southern District of New York
234 F. Supp. 765 (1964)

PALMIERI, DISTRICT JUDGE.

Joseph F. Cordner, deceased, was, at the time of his death on October 2, 1962, an employee of defendant Socony Mobil Oil Company, Inc. (Socony). On May 1, 1956, he became insured under the terms of Group Policy of Insurance No. 103, in effect between Socony and Metropolitan, and received at that time Certificate No. 158460. In that certificate, it was provided that all benefits payable at his death should be made payable to his children, "Maureen Joan and Michael Joseph, 50% each." These children were the issue of the marriage of Joseph F. Cordner to Patricia Ann Cordner.

Patricia Ann Cordner subsequently obtained a divorce from the deceased, and remarried. Now, as a resident of Minneapolis, Minnesota, and under her new name, Patricia Ann Lundeen, she is one of the parties whom Metropolitan seeks to bring into the action. The others are the children, Maureen Joan Cordner and Michael Joseph Cordner, and Northwestern National Bank of Minneapolis (Northwestern).

The plaintiff in this action, France J. Cordner, is the widow of Joseph F. Cordner. It is her claim that, prior to his death, on or about May 11, 1961, Joseph F. Cornder had executed a change of beneficiaries, and that at the time of his death, the proceeds were payable one-fourth to plaintiff, and the remaining three-fourths to Northwestern, to be held in trust for the uses set forth in decedent's Last Will and Testament. Defendant Metropolitan denies having received notice of this purported change of beneficiaries, as required by the terms of the insurance policy.

On November 5, 1963, Patricia Ann Lundeen commenced an action against Metropolitan in the United States District Court for the District of Minnesota, to recover the proceeds of decedent's policy on behalf of her children. The trial of this case appears to be imminent. The action before this Court was commenced three weeks later, on November 26, 1963, by France J. Cordner against Metropolitan and Socony, to recover the proceeds of the policy under the terms of the asserted change of beneficiaries. Because of these conflicting claims to the proceeds of this policy, Metropolitan has brought the instant motion [to convert the various actions into one suit in interpleader] in an effort to have the conflict resolved by the determination of a single tribunal.

The Inapplicability of Rule 22, Fed.R.Civ.P.

It should be noted that Metropolitan is proceeding under paragraph (1) of Rule 22, and not under paragraph (2) of that rule, relating to statutory interpleader as provided for by 28 U.S.C. §§ 1335, 1397 and 2361. The reason given for this by Metropolitan is that an action for statutory interpleader must be brought in the district where one of the claimants resides — in this case either Minnesota or North Dakota.[2] And, if the statutory interpleader action were commenced either in Minnesota or North Dakota, service of process on France J. Cordner, as required by 28 U.S.C. § 2361, would not be possible, and she could not be interpleaded.

In her brief in opposition to Metropolitan's motion, Patricia Ann Lundeen claims that, under Rule 22(1), Fed.R.Civ.P., this Court lacks jurisdiction over her and the other parties sought to be interpleaded, because service of process on the parties in Minnesota was not proper. . . .

The Inapplicability of New York CPLR § 314

Metropolitan finally asserts that the court can obtain jurisdiction over Mrs. Lundeen and the other parties in Minnesota pursuant to Section 314 of the New

---

[2] All of the claimants are residents of Minnesota except France J. Cordner who, though living in Libya, claims to be a citizen of North Dakota. [Some footnotes have been omitted; others have been renumbered.]

York Civil Practice Law and Rules. That section permits service without the state:

. . . .

   2. where a judgment is demanded that the person to be served be excluded from a vested or contingent interest in or lien upon specific real or personal property within the state; or that such an interest or lien in favor of either party be enforced, regulated, defined or limited; or otherwise affecting the title to such property, including an action of interpleader or defensive interpleader. . . .

. . . .

To understand the applicability of Section 314 in the instant case, it is necessary also to consider Section 1006(g) of the CPLR, which provides that, upon deposit into court of the funds which are the subject of an interpleader action, such funds "shall be deemed specific property within the state within the meaning of paragraph two of section 314."

In a commentary on this section, it is stated that, after deposit of the funds into court, "[s]ervice by personal delivery outside the state can then be made under CPLR 314, or, if that is not possible, by publication under CPLR 315. *New York Life Ins. Co. v. Dunlevy*, 241 U.S. 518, [36 S. Ct. 613, 60 L.Ed. 1140] (1916), suggested that jurisdiction could not be so obtained,[5] but the Judicial Conference felt that subsequent decisions had limited the effectiveness of *Dunlevy*." 2 Weinstein, Korn & Miller, New York Civil Practice ¶ 1006.15.

The "subsequent cases" referred to above, *Mullane v. Central Hanover Bank & Trust Co. et al.*, 339 U.S. 306, 70 S. Ct. 652, 94 L.Ed. 865 (1950), and *Standard Oil Co. v. State of New Jersey*, 341 U.S. 428, 71 S. Ct. 822, 95 L.Ed. 1078 (1951), do not seem to limit the effectiveness of the *Dunlevy* case. While the *Standard Oil* case held that choses in action (unpaid dividends and stock certificates) could escheat to the state, even though there was an unascertainable owner

---

[5] In *Dunlevy*, the Supreme Court held that an action in interpleader to determine the validity of a claim to the proceeds of a life insurance policy:

   . . . was an attempt to bring about a final and conclusive adjudication of [Mrs. Dunlevy's] personal rights, not merely to discover property and apply it to debts. And unless in contemplation of law she was before the court, and required to respond to that issue, its orders and judgments in respect thereto were not binding on her.

(241 U.S. at 521, 36 S. Ct. at 614).

Having thus held that an action similar to that in the instant case was a personal action, the Court went on to say:

   The established general rule is that any personal judgment which a state court may render against one who did not voluntarily submit to its jurisdiction, and who is not a citizen of the state, nor served with process within its borders, no matter what the mode of service, is void, because the court had no jurisdiction over his person.

(241 U.S. at 522-523, 36 S. Ct. at 614).

thereof, that case differs considerably from the instant case. And the difference was made perfectly clear by the Supreme Court in the case of *Estin v. Estin*, 334 U.S. 541, 68 S. Ct. 1213, 92 L.Ed. 1561 (1948):

> ... Jurisdiction over a debtor is sufficient to give the State of his domicile some control over the debt which he owes. It can, for example, levy a tax on its transfer by will, ... appropriate it through garnishment or attachment, ... collect it and administer it for the benefit of creditors. ... But we are aware of no power which the State of domicile of the debtor has to determine the personal rights of the creditor in the intangible unless the creditor has been personally served or appears in the proceeding. The existence of any such power has been repeatedly denied. ...

It is thus eminently clear that jurisdiction over the Minnesota claimants cannot be obtained by service either through the mails or by publication. And, in light of the doctrine enunciated in the *Dunlevy* and *Estin* cases, it seems unlikely that personal service, effected anywhere save in New York State, would give this Court jurisdiction over them. This is in fact borne out by the very caption to Section 314: "Service without the state not giving personal jurisdiction in certain actions." And since this action has been held to require personal jurisdiction over claimants, *New York Life Ins. Co. v. Dunlevy, supra*, 241 U.S. at 521, 36 S. Ct. 613, Section 314 is not here applicable, its own language regarding actions of interpleader notwithstanding.

It follows, therefore, that the motion of Metropolitan must be denied in all respects. ...

NOTES

(1) Under what circumstances may CPLR 1006(g) be used to compel a non-resident to assert a claim in a New York interpleader action? Professor Siegel has suggested that it is available when "the particular interpleader situation involves substantial New York contacts — which it may ordinarily be expected to when the requirements of CPLR 1006(g) ... are met. ..." David Siegel, New York Practice § 153 at 262 (4th ed. 2005).

(2) In cases involving non-residents, a stakeholder wishing to commence an interpleader action is ordinarily better advised to proceed in a federal court. Federal statutory interpleader is available when any two claimants are of diverse citizenship and the stake has a value of at least $500. 28 U.S.C. § 1335. The action may be commenced in a district in which any claimant resides, 28 U.S.C. § 1397, and process may be served on claimants in whatever state they may be found, 28 U.S.C. § 2361.

Would statutory interpleader solve the jurisdictional issue raised by Problem C?

(3) For another approach to the problem of the non-resident claimant, see CPLR 216, discussed fully in Weinstein, Korn & Miller, 1 New York Civil Practice, ¶ 216.01-¶ 216.03 (2004).

MACQUEEN REALTY CO. v. EMMI v. OWEN, INTERPLEADED DEFENDANT
Supreme Court, Monroe County
58 Misc. 2d 54, 294 N.Y.S.2d 566 (1968)

CARROLLTON A. ROBERTS, JUSTICE.

This is a motion for discharge of an alleged stakeholder in a dispute over payment of a real estate broker's commission earned by reason of the execution of a lease. The defendant who for the sake of brevity will be referred to as "Emmi" entered into a commission agreement with MacQueen Realty on or about the 19th day of October, 1965. In consideration of the execution of a leasing agreement, Emmi agreed to pay a total commission to MacQueen Realty of $20,000.00, one-half payable in advance and the balance payable in two equal installments. A payment in the amount of $10,000.00 was made to MacQueen in September of 1966 and an additional payment of $5,000.00 was payable in September of 1967 but was withheld because the interpleaded defendant Owen made claim to the balance due on the commission. Owen was the director of the motel division of MacQueen Realty Co. Inc., at the time of the execution of the commission agreement on the 19th day of October, 1965. The defendants Emmi have therefore moved pursuant to CPLR 1006(f) for a discharge of stakeholder and for costs and disbursements including attorneys fees.

Emmi has adopted a neutral and disinterested posture in the pleadings before this Court and on argument insofar as it does not question that $10,000.00 remains payable on the commission but only raises the point that two adverse claims are made to the fund and that in order to avoid possible multiple liability, this Court must permit the payment into Court or otherwise direct payment of the fund.

MacQueen Realty on the return date of the motion for discharge of stakeholder cross-moved for summary judgment demanding payment of the $10,000.00 remaining on the commission and denial of defendants' motion for payment of the fund into Court. In support of its motion MacQueen Realty submitted the affidavit of Virginia MacQueen, the president of the company, which detailed the execution of the agreement and the partial payment of $10,000.00 and further stated that at the time services were rendered to the defendants Emmi by MacQueen Realty, interpleaded defendant Owen was employed only as a salesman and was not a licensed real estate broker. MacQueen argues from this point that Section 442-a of the Real Property Law prohibits a salesman from seeking a commission from any party other than a licensed real estate broker and that by reason of this fact Owen must proceed if at all, against MacQueen and is without recourse against Emmi. MacQueen concludes that the fund must be paid to it and Owen left to whatever remedy he may have against MacQueen.

Ordinarily a Court must afford a party moving for a discharge as a stakeholder pursuant to our interpleader practice the most liberal interpretation of the applicable statute. Section 1006(a) of the CPLR defines a stakeholder as a "person who is or may be exposed to multiple liability as the result of adverse claims." The liberal definition of the CPLR is to a certain extent based upon similar language in cases interpreting earlier statutory and common-law interpleader. Thus, in *Boden v. Arnstein*, 293 N.Y. 99, 103, 56 N.E.2d 65, 67 (1944), Judge Lehman commented that interpleader would be available unless "the adverse claim . . . is so patently without substance that the defendant can reject it without risk. . . ." Even a "colorable" adverse claim may be sufficient to permit payment into Court and the discharge of a stakeholder and "for the purpose of the motion for a discharge, we should assume the truth of the allegations in the respective pleadings." *See Nelson v. Cross & Brown Co.*, 9 A.D.2d 140, 144, 192 N.Y.S.2d 335, 339 (1st Dep't 1959). . . . But the question here is whether we have even a "colorable" claim for purposes of invoking the interpleader statute.

Certainly this Court recognizes that the remedy of interpleader has often been invoked in disputes between two brokers for a commission. . . . We do not, however, in the instant situation have a dispute between two brokers. The memorandum of the commission agreement submitted to this Court after argument fixes the date of the agreement as being on or about the 19th day of October, 1965, and interpleaded defendant Owen neither offers evidence in opposition to this date nor otherwise disputes its accuracy. In fact, interpleaded defendant Owen failed to make any opposition other than oral argument to the cross-motion for summary judgment made on behalf of MacQueen Realty. The Court has before it the answer of interpleaded defendant Owen to the interpleader complaint of Emmi but this answer, while verified, consists only of general and specific denials and alleges nothing affirmatively. In fact, interpleaded defendant Owen does not contest that he was at best only a licensed real estate salesman at the time of execution of the commission agreement. As such, Owen would have no legal recourse against the Emmi interests. . . .

The cases are quite clear that the failure to submit an affidavit on personal knowledge and to otherwise make an evidentiary showing in opposition to the motion for summary judgment may be fatal to a party disputing the motion solely on an oral argument. . . .

There is nothing before this Court on behalf of the interpleaded defendant Owen setting forth his version of the transaction which is the subject matter of the motion and cross-motion. Accordingly, the cross-motion for summary judgment brought on behalf of MacQueen Realty is granted and the defendants Emmi are hereby ordered to make the remaining payments on the commission to MacQueen Realty. The motion for a discharge of stakeholder and for leave to pay funds into Court by the defendants Emmi and the interpleaded defendant Owen is denied.

While a stakeholder ordinarily is entitled to reimbursement for expenses including reasonable attorneys fees (*see, for example, Ellicott Paint Co. v. Buffalo Evening News Inc.*, 33 Misc.2d 896, 225 N.Y.S.2d 270 (Sup.Ct. Erie, 1961), *mod. mem.*, 17 A.D.2d 911, 233 N.Y.S.2d 309 (4th Dep't 1962), . . . the authorities are clear that the granting of costs including attorneys fees rest in the sound discretion of the Court, and, of course, should not be granted where the relief requested is denied. Therefore, the application of the defendants Emmi for costs including attorneys fees is denied and further this motion shall be without costs to any of the contesting parties.

NOTES

(1) CPLR 1006(a) permits interpleader only when the stakeholder is exposed to "adverse claims," *i.e.*, claims which are mutually inconsistent. *See Royal Bank of Canada v. Weiss*, 172 A.D.2d 167, 567 N.Y.S.2d 707 (1st Dep't 1991) (interpleader action dismissed where bank not subject to inconsistent claims). What if there is a dispute about whether the claims are truly adverse? *Nelson v. Cross & Brown Co.*, 9 A.D.2d 140, 192 N.Y.S.2d 335 (1st Dep't 1959), illustrates this problem. In *Nelson*, the stakeholder was a real estate brokerage firm and the claimants were two of its salespersons, each of whom claimed the right to a commission on a particular sale. It was the stakeholder's theory that the claimants should divide the amount it admittedly owed as a sales commission. The claimants had a different view. One (Nelson) thought he was entitled to the entire sales commission, while the other thought he was entitled to a half share, regardless of the amount owed to Nelson. Thus, noted the court, it was conceivable that each could establish his right to the full amount he claimed at trial and the stakeholder's motion for a discharge was therefore denied. But the court did permit the case to go forward as an interpleader action, emphasizing the judicial economy gained by trying the related claims together. Is any party tactically disadvantaged by this resolution of the problem?

(2) Because some forms of interpleader originated in equity courts, doubt exists as to the right to trial by jury. *See, e.g., Clark v. Mosher*, 107 N.Y. 118, 14 N.E. 96 (1887); *Geddes v. Rosen*, 22 A.D.2d 394, 255 N.Y.S.2d 585 (1st Dep't 1965), *aff'd mem.*, 16 N.Y.2d 816, 263 N.Y.S.2d 10 (1965). In *Geddes*, the court granted a jury trial and stated: "Appellant's remedy is at law and is adequate. . . . Nor should the single fact of interpleader suffice to change this action at law into one in equity so as to deny the right to trial by jury." 22 A.D.2d at 399, 255 N.Y.S.2d at 590. The court in *Geddes* suggested that the judge should decide if interpleader lies, but the jury should decide issues between the claimants if those issues are normally decided by juries.

§ 8.06 INTERVENTION: CPLR 1012–1014

Intervention is the procedural remedy of a non-party who wants to participate in litigation which she fears will affect her interests. Although the CPLR distinguishes between intervention by right, CPLR 1012, and by permission, CPLR 1013, both types are subject to a good deal of judicial latitude, as the following cases show.

VILLAGE OF SPRING VALLEY v. VILLAGE OF SPRING VALLEY HOUSING AUTHORITY
Appellate Division, Second Department
33 A.D.2d 1037, 308 N.Y.S.2d 736 (1970)

In this proceeding pursuant to section 57 of the Public Housing Law by the Village of Spring Valley (Village) to dissolve the Village of Spring Valley Housing Authority (Authority), the appeal, as limited by appellants' brief, is from so much of an order of the Supreme Court, Rockland County, entered October 15, 1969, as denied their separate motions for leave to intervene as parties respondent in the proceeding and to serve proposed answers. [Intervenors were the Spring Valley Chapter of the NAACP and four individual residents of the Village.] Order reversed insofar as appealed from, on the facts and the law and in the exercise of this court's discretion, without costs, and motions granted. Appellants' proposed answers to the petition shall be served within 10 days after entry of the order hereon. The Authority was established, pursuant to a special statute enacted on April 9, 1962 (L. 1962, ch. 406), as a public agency to construct and maintain public housing in the Village of Spring Valley for the benefit of low-income residents of the village and to alleviate slum conditions in the village. It consented to the motions to intervene. The village opposed. Appellants contend that they are low-income persons residing in substandard housing in a ghetto slum area of the village and seek to intervene individually and as representatives of the other low-income persons residing in slum areas of the village. We are of the opinion that the motions to intervene should have been granted as a matter of discretion under CPLR 1013 as there are common questions of law and fact raised by the Authority's and appellants' proposed respective answers, to wit: (a) the Authority's statutory right to continue as a public housing agency; (b) the Authority's right to seek to improve housing facilities for low-income persons who reside in the village; (c) the implementation of the Authority's intention to create public housing facilities for such low-income persons; and (d) the constitutional rights of such low-income persons to obtain adequate housing through the agency of the Authority. In our opinion the intervention will not unduly delay the proceeding or prejudice the substantial rights of any party. Moreover, we find that under the circumstances of this case the motions to intervene should also have been granted under CPLR 1012. Appellant's interests in this matter may not be adequately represented by the Authority and their interests would or may be bound by the judgment which will be rendered in this proceeding. BRENNAN, ACTING P.J., RABIN, HOPKINS, BENJAMIN and MUNDER, JJ., concur.

NOTES

(1) Why did the NAACP wish to intervene? Why did one of the parties oppose intervention and the other not?

(2) How could the intervenors' interests be bound by the ultimate result of the preceding case if they were not adequately represented? The Fourteenth Amendment has been interpreted to bar precisely such a result. *Hansberry v. Lee*, 311 U.S. 32, 61 S. Ct. 115 (1940). Yet CPLR 1012(a)(2) allows intervention when the intervenor "is or may be" inadequately represented, if he "is or may be bound by the judgment." Judge Meyer, later of the Court of Appeals, but then a Justice of the New York Supreme Court, suggested:

> The answer appears to lie in the words "may be," which by requiring a less than conclusive determination of adequacy and binding effect give a litigant the option of avoiding multiplicity of action and possible inconsistent results by intervening in the earlier proceeding unless it is clear that he will not be bound in a later action by the earlier judgment. . . .

Unitarian Universalist Church of Central Nassau v. Shorten, 64 Misc. 2d 851, 853-54, 315 N.Y.S.2d 506, 510-11 (Sup. Ct.), *vacated on other grounds*, 64 Misc. 2d 1027, 316 N.Y.S.2d 837 (Sup. Ct. 1970).

(3) Compare CPLR 1012(a)(2) and (a)(3) with Fed. R. Civ. P. 24, which grants a right to intervene to one who

> [C]laims an interest relating to the property or transaction which is the subject of the action and the applicant is so situated that the disposition of the action may as a practical matter impair or impede the applicant's ability to protect that interest, unless the applicant's interest is adequately represented by existing parties.

(4) An alternative to intervention is a request for permission to file a brief as *amicus curiae* or "friend of the court." The propriety of *amicus curiae* participation is well recognized in New York both at the trial level, *see Colgate-Palmolive Co. v. Erie County*, 68 Misc. 2d 704, 327 N.Y.S.2d 488 (Sup. Ct. 1971), and at the appellate level, *see* Rules of the Court of Appeals, 22 N.Y.C.R.R. § 500.23.

Amicus participation is ordinarily limited to the submission of briefs (although oral argument is also occasionally permitted); the participant obtains none of the rights of a true party to the action. A successful intervenor, however, has all the rights of any other party to participate fully in the litigation, unless specifically limited by the court.

REURS v. CARLSON

Supreme Court, Westchester County
66 Misc. 2d 968, 323 N.Y.S.2d 370 (1971)

JOHN W. SWEENY, JUSTICE.

[Plaintiff, the first wife of the defendant, brought an action to increase the amount of support she was receiving from him pursuant to a separation agreement. Intervention was sought by defendant's current wife and their children because they feared the impact the action might have on plaintiff's ability to support them.]

No authority is cited in support of movant's position but reliance is placed on section 1012(a)(3) of the CPLR which grants intervention as of right when the action involves disposition of property and the person seeking to intervene may be affected adversely by a judgment against a party.

While liberal construction and application of the intervention sections are called for . . . intervention must be restricted where the outcome of the matter to be determined will be needlessly delayed, the rights of the perspective intervenors are already adequately represented, and there are substantial questions as to whether those seeking to intervene have any real present interest in the property which is the subject of the dispute. . . .

. . . .

It was noted in *Matter of Spangenberg*, 41 Misc. 2d 584, 245 N.Y.S.2d 501 that:

> Despite the seemingly mandatory character of the statutory provision for intervention, courts always exercise discretion. They deny leave to intervene if they doubt the motive of the proposed intervenor or if they deem further intervention unnecessary.

It is obvious that the arguments to be advanced on behalf of defendant will almost certainly overlap those made on behalf of his children by his second wife and as such intervention is unnecessary.

While it cannot be disputed that a decision against defendant will affect his children, and might lower their standard of living, the question remains as to whether they have sufficient interest in the "property" of their father to warrant intervention.

The Court thinks not. Any other decision would open the flood gates to infant intervention whenever a parent is sued, based solely upon the possibility that the prospective estate of the infant might be diminished if plaintiff prevailed. . . .

NOTES

(1) In contrast with the principal case, an intervenor was found to have a property interest necessary to invoke CPLR 1012(a)(3) in *Cavages, Inc. v. Ketter*, 56 A.D.2d 730, 392 N.Y.S.2d 755 (4th Dep't 1977). The plaintiff, a retail record store adjacent to the State University of New York at Buffalo, brought an action against the president of the university seeking a judgment directing the president to close a record cooperative store run on the grounds of the university; the action was grounded upon the alleged improper use of state property in allowing the cooperative to operate. The president of the student association was properly allowed to intervene, since he had an interest in the property, in that the cooperative was a member organization of the student association and was funded solely by mandatory student activity fees administered by the student association.

(2) In an unusual case, the Court of Appeals held that CPLR 1013 authorized an insurer to intervene in an infant's personal injury action when the trial court was entertaining an application by the parties to approve a settlement of the claim. *Teichman v. Community Hosp. of W. Suffolk*, 87 N.Y.2d 514, 640 N.Y.S.2d 472, 663 N.E.2d 628 (1996). The intervenor had covered the injured infant's medical costs under a health insurance policy, and sought recoupment of expenses it had incurred on the infant's behalf. The Court noted that the intervenor's claim for a refund could have been adversely affected if intervention were denied, that there were common questions of law and fact, and that no prejudice was shown. *Teichman* was distinguished in *Berry v. St. Peter's Hosp.*, 250 A.D.2d 63, 678 N.Y.S.2d 674 (3d Dep't 1998), in which the Court reversed a decision that had allowed health insurers to intervene in a medical malpractice action brought by their insured, on whose behalf they had already paid substantial sums. The intervenors were entitled to subrogation from any compensation for medical expenses the plaintiff obtained from the defendants. The Third Department held that the conflicting interests of the insurers and the plaintiff were such that intervention would unduly prejudice the plaintiff. This was so in part because the insurers' claims for subrogation were far greater than the amount the plaintiff could recover from the malpractice defendant (because of limits to the malpractice policy), and in part because the trial court had not only permitted intervention but had given the intervenors a veto over any proposed settlements. This would have allowed them to prevent the plaintiff from obtaining a good faith settlement that allocated the money received to damages other than medical expenses.

The issue of intervention in personal injury actions by insurers is discussed in Barker, *Intervention By Health Insurers to Recover Payments*, N.Y.L.J., Nov. 16, 1998, p.3, and in Hayes, *Subrogation Rights of Health Care Providers*, 78 N.Y. St. Bar Ass'n J. 9, at 32 (November/December 2006).

(3) Intervention is also permitted by CPLR 7802(d), which applies to proceedings against a body or officer and provides that the court "may allow other

interested persons to intervene." This is a more relaxed requirement than that found in CPLR 1013, which requires that there be a "common question of law or fact" between the claim or defense of the proposed intervenor and those at issue in the existing action. *See Greater N.Y. Health Care Facilities Ass'n v. DeBuono*, 91 N.Y.2d 716, 674 N.Y.S.2d 634, 697 N.E.2d 589 (1998).

§ 8.07 THIRD PARTY PRACTICE: CPLR 1007-1011

PROBLEM D

Betty, whom we first met in Problem A, Chapter 7, *supra*, was the tenant injured when she slipped and fell on the floor of the laundry room in a building owned by Fred. The floor was wet because water had not drained off it. In this problem, we will focus on the availability of third party practice in the resulting litigation.

Suppose Betty, alleging personal injuries, commenced an action against Fred for $15,000, and that Fred's answer denies liability. May Fred thereafter properly commence a third-party action against Urban & Dismal (the architects responsible for the construction of the building), claiming: (a) indemnification and/or contribution for Betty's claim; (b) the cost of repairing the drainage problem; (c) damages for his own injuries; (d) damages arising from their malpractice in designing another building also owned by him?

May U&D commence and maintain a fourth-party action against Acme, Inc., its malpractice insurer, if the latter disclaims liability for Fred's and Betty's claims?

GEORGE COHEN AGENCY, INC. v. DONALD S. PERLMAN AGENCY, INC.
Court of Appeals
51 N.Y.2d 358, 434 N.Y.S.2d 189, 414 N.E.2d 689 (1980)

JASEN, JUDGE.

The significant issues on this appeal are whether CPLR 1007 permits a third-party plaintiff to seek damages in excess of the amount demanded by plaintiff in the main action and whether a third-party claim is maintainable in the face of a simultaneous contention that the third-party plaintiff is completely free from liability to the plaintiff in the main action.

This matter arises out of the transfer of a "portfolio" of insurance business from one insurance agency to another. At issue are the relative rights and liabilities of the buyer, seller, insurance carrier (whose underwriting potential was the stuff transferred) and the attorney who arranged the sale. The instant procedural web was spun about these parties as follows: Plaintiff George Cohen Agency, Inc., the seller, agreed to transfer to defendant-respondents Donald S. Perlman Agency, Inc., and Donald S. Perlman, a specified "portfolio" of insurance business consisting of certain policies issued by Continental Casualty Company. The Perlman Agency and Perlman himself executed promissory notes in payment. These notes, however, were not honored when due. Perlman asserted that the Continental policies were no longer salable because they contravened certain New York Insurance Department regulations and that no payment need be made for the spoiled portfolio. Cohen then sued Perlman for $52,528 on the notes. This is the main action.

In the answer to this main action, and in a counterclaim against Cohen, it was asserted that Cohen, either individually or in concert with Continental and attorney-broker I. Edward Pogoda, attempted to defraud defendants by knowingly inducing them to purchase the worthless package of insurance business. The counterclaim sought rescission or reformation of the contract of sale or, in the alternative, compensatory damages in the amount of $545,000, punitive damages in the amount of $2,500,000, an unspecified amount of money allegedly paid to Cohen, and over $25,000 in attorney's fees.

The same elements of legal damages, as well as indemnity and contribution for any potential liability of Perlman to Cohen, were demanded in third-party actions brought by Perlman against Continental and attorney Pogoda. These third-party actions, brought pursuant to CPLR 1007, were grounded upon the third-party defendants' alleged complicity in a conspiracy to defraud Perlman and upon third-party defendant Pogoda's alleged malpractice and breach of duty as an attorney.

Continental moved to dismiss Perlman's third-party action, contending: (1) that CPLR 1007 does not permit a third-party plaintiff to demand damages in excess of those demanded in the main action; (2) that no third-party action is maintainable where the third-party plaintiff alleges facts which negate liability on the main action; and (3) that recognition of a third-party action would in the circumstances of this case, prejudice Continental by impeding its ability to "remove" the case to Federal court. Special Term denied Continental's motion to dismiss. The Appellate Division unanimously affirmed, 69 A.D.2d 725, 419 N.Y.S.2d 584, as do we.

The law has long recognized the need for a procedure whereby one whose responsibility for an alleged legal wrong is to be tested in a lawsuit may bring before the court another who is claimed by the defendant to have a share in that responsibility so that all claims can be resolved in the one forum. The first procedural device commonly used to achieve this end was the common-law method of preserving one's indemnity claim against a third party known as "vouching in" or "vouching to warranty." . . . This device, acknowledged to be the forerunner of modern third-party practice, allows a party to bind a potential indemnitor to the result reached in the main action by simply notifying him of the pendency of the action and offering him control of the litigation. No direct judgment is available against the third party when this device is used. However, the procedure at least insures that, under principles of *res judicata*, the issue of defendant's liability to plaintiff need not be relitigated in a subsequent suit against the third-party indemnitor. Although still available today, this device is little used, for a much more comprehensive device — impleader — has been created by the Legislature.

The first impleader statute appeared in New York in 1922 as section 193 of the former Civil Practice Act. (L. 1922, ch. 624.) The basic language of the impleader statute, with minor changes, has been carried forward to the present day and currently appears as CPLR 1007. Although the basic structure of the statute has changed little over the years, the interpretation of the statute and, thus, its scope has changed greatly.

Early on, the statute was construed narrowly, requiring that a defendant (third-party plaintiff in the jargon of the statute) demonstrate that his third-party claim was identical to the claim upon which he was being sued by plaintiff in the main action. (*See, e. g., Nichols v. Clark, MacMullen & Riley, Inc.*, 261 N.Y. 118, 184 N.E. 729.) This interpretation, as might be expected, severely limited the utility of the device. Indeed, it was not until 1946 when the statute was amended that the effect of this restrictive interpretation was alleviated.

The 1946 amendment (L. 1946, ch. 971) added the following language to the statute: "The claim against such person, hereinafter called the third-party defendant, must be related to the main action by a question of law or fact common to both controversies, but need not rest upon the same cause of action or the same ground as the claim asserted against the third-party plaintiff." (Former Civ. Prac. Act, § 193-a.) This change signaled the end of the so-called "identity" rule. Interestingly, when the impleader statute was transferred to its present place in CPLR 1007, the above sentence was once again deleted. This amendment, however, did not require a return to the old "identity" rule. Rather, the second operative clause of the above sentence was deleted because practice had so changed that it was now "unnecessary" and the first clause was deleted because, if read literally, it narrowed rather than expanded third-party practice — a result not intended by the revisors. (*See Sixth Report of Senate Finance Committee Relative to Revision of Civil Practice Act*, N.Y.Legis.Doc., 1962, No. 8, p. 159; *Norman Co. v. County of Nassau*, 63 Misc.2d 965, 314 N.Y.S.2d 44 [Meyer, J.].) Thus, a review of the history of third-party practice in this State seems to disclose a trend toward liberalization and expansion of the availability of impleader. Recognition of this general trend, however, serves only as a starting point for our inquiry, for the scope of the statute remains unclear.

Indeed, the precise questions raised by this appeal — whether a third-party complaint may seek damages in excess of those sought on the main claim and whether such a claim may be maintained where the third-party plaintiff alleges facts which negate liability — have not yet been addressed by this court. They have been addressed by the lower courts in a way which, while it may not be truly inconsistent, certainly evinces a certain difference of opinion on these issues.

On the issue of "excess" damages, many lower courts have limited third-party practice solely to indemnity claims which do not exceed the amount of the main claim. . . . Others have focused upon not only the amount, but also the nature of a third-party claim and the liberal language of the statute and have noted that a third-party claim, if it is to be limited to "all or part of the plaintiff's claim against [a third-party plaintiff]" must "rise from" or be conditioned upon or be otherwise based upon the liability to the plaintiff in the main action. (*Cleveland v. Farber*, 46 A.D.2d 733, 361 N.Y.S.2d 99; *Horn v. Ketchum*, 27 A.D.2d 759, 277 N.Y.S.2d 177.) This narrow view of the purpose of the statute would lead, of course, to the conclusion that no "excess" may be claimed.

On the other hand, there has been expressed in some lower courts a more liberal view of third-party practice generally. . . . Such holdings, while they do not speak directly to the issue of excess recovery, do appear to recognize that although third-party practice has its origins in strict indemnity, it has grown beyond its early limitations and should now be seen primarily as a tool for economical resolution of interrelated lawsuits. We agree with this broad view of the practice.

The current New York impleader statute, although it retains the familiar language limiting a third-party plaintiff to recovery against "a person not a party who is or may be liable to him for all or part of the plaintiff's claim against him," should not be read as allowing recovery solely for claims sounding in strict indemnity. While it is true that the doctrine of impleader has its roots in strict indemnity, the history and development of impleader and the language of the current statute indicate that the device is no longer wedded to this single theory of recovery. The language of CPLR 1007 serves only to identify the persons against whom a third-party claim may be brought. It places no limit upon the amount which may be recovered or upon the legal theories which may be asserted as a basis for the claim. Indeed, a narrower reading would subvert the purpose of the statute. It has long been clear that one of the main purposes of third-party practice is "'the avoidance of multiplicity and circuity of action, and the determination of the primary liability as well as the ultimate liability in one proceeding, whenever convenient.'" (*Krause v. American Guar. & Liab. Ins. Co.*, 22 N.Y.2d 147, 153, 292 N.Y.S.2d 67, 239 N.E.2d 175; . . . .) In our view, this salutary goal can best be achieved by allowing a third-party plaintiff to plead and prove his entitlement to excess recovery over and above his liability to plaintiff, subject to the trial court's discretionary power to sever any claim which, in the circumstances of a particular case, appears unduly burdensome. (CPLR 1010.)

The soundness of such a rule becomes apparent upon an examination of the case before us. In the instant case, Perlman claims that Continental's acts and omissions caused him to enter into a transaction which may result in a finding that Perlman is liable to Cohen. Inasmuch as Perlman claims that Continental is responsible in part for any potential liability to Cohen, Perlman may implead Continental, making the insurer a party to the suit. Having successfully brought the new third-party defendant into the lawsuit to answer for its alleged wrong-doing, it would seem absurd to limit recovery for such wrongdoing to the amount demanded by plaintiff in the main action, for to do so can only result in an incomplete resolution of the dispute between the parties. Surely, if Perlman is successful on his "indemnity" claim, he will want to recover all the damages caused by the wrongdoing which formed the basis of that claim, including those which exceed the amount demanded by Cohen. If CPLR 1007 is narrowly con-strued to encompass only strict indemnity, Perlman would be required to com-mence a separate lawsuit in order to do so. Such a lawsuit would involve precisely the same factual issues as were involved in the main claim and coun-terclaim and, if brought separately, perhaps out of fear of "splitting" the cause of action (see Siegel, New York Practice, § 220, p. 264), would cause an unnec-essary drain upon judicial resources and create a risk of inconsistent results.

It is possible, of course, that such a second separate action could be consoli-dated or tried jointly with the main action. (CPLR 602.) This could provide the same conservation of judicial resources as would a claim for excess damages in a third-party suit. The availability of another procedural remedy is, however, not a reason to narrowly construe the impleader statute. Indeed, it would seem contrary to the modern spirit of liberal pleading to forego one commonsense rule in favor of a needless procedural dance which will arrive at the same result. Thus, we conclude that CPLR 1007 should not be construed as precluding a third-party suit for damages in excess of those demanded in the main action.

Continental also contends that the instant third-party claims should be dis-missed because the facts pleaded in the third-party complaint negate any lia-bility of Perlman to Cohen. (See Scivetti v. Niagara Mohawk Power Corp., 33 A.D.2d 884, 307 N.Y.S.2d 563.) We disagree. As noted by the Appellate Division, the facts alleged do not necessarily preclude liability on Perlman's part. The pleadings, in fact, allege many claims in the alternative, including a claim for indemnity. This type of alternative pleading is clearly permissible and should not result in a dismissal of the third-party complaint.

Finally, Continental contends that Perlman's third-party complaint should be dismissed because it somehow impedes Continental's right, as a foreign corpo-ration, to "remove" the case to Federal court pursuant to subdivision (c) of sec-tion 1441 of title 28 of the United States Code. This contention is without merit. The doctrine of "removal" is uniquely a Federal power to be exercised by Federal courts, applying Federal law. We see no reason to alter the civil prac-tice of the State of New York to either encourage or discourage the exercise of that power. Thus, while a litigant may well believe that the exercise by the Federal court of its removal power would be beneficial in a particular case, his remedy is merely to seek such removal in Federal court, taking State procedure as he finds it.

. . . .

NOTES

(1) Impleader has been disallowed when its use would create injustice. Two examples concern the role of an insurer:

(a) In *Ross v. Pawtucket Mut. Ins. Co.*, 13 N.Y.2d 233, 246 N.Y.S.2d 213, 195 N.E.2d 892 (1963), plaintiff had sued his collision insurer because his auto had been damaged in an accident and defendant had refused to pay the full amount of the claimed loss. The insurer sought to implead X, the party who allegedly caused the accident, but plaintiff's objection to the impleader was upheld. As the Court of Appeals explained in a later case discussing *Ross*:

> Automobile collision cases are numerous and involve minor claims, and the very purpose of collision insurance is to permit the insured to collect his damages promptly and use the funds to repair his car. Consequently, as a matter of judicial discretion, impleader can properly be denied in such cases in order to reduce court congestion and to assure that the prime object of the collision policy is not frustrated by the judicial process.

Krause v. American Guar. & Liab. Ins. Co., 22 N.Y.2d 147, 156, 292 N.Y.S.2d 67, 74, 239 N.E.2d 175, 180 (1968).

In *Krause, supra*, the Court limited *Ross'* holding to its facts and refused to disallow a third party claim asserted by insurers who had been sued to collect on broker's bonds issued by them. The insurers were thus permitted to implead the wrong-doer claimed to have caused the plaintiffs' injuries and triggered the insurers' liability. Said the Court:

> The only significant difficulty arising from allowing impleader would be that the plaintiff might have to incur the expense of litigating the claim against the tort-feasor sooner than it might have wished or, if the insured is made whole by a recovery against the insurer, the insured would sustain an unnecessary expense. Countering this consideration is the fact that much of the cost of preparing the claim against the tort-feasor can be shared with the insurer.
>
> Moreover, whatever additional expense to the plaintiff there may be is more than balanced by the advantages of judicial efficiency and the extreme injustice to the subrogee or, in this case, the insurers, if they are required to await the disposition of the main claim before commencing a third-party action. The opportunity to gather evidence and prepare a claim may be irretrievably lost. Furthermore, the insurer's subrogation claim may become time-barred if the plaintiff does not commence suit against the tort-feasor. . . .

Krause, supra, 22 N.Y.2d at 154-55, 292 N.Y.S.2d at 72-73, 239 N.E.2d at 179.

Why, if impleader was permitted, would the plaintiff have to litigate his claim against the tortfeasor "sooner than it might have wished"?

(b) In *Kelly v. Yannotti*, 4 N.Y.2d 603, 176 N.Y.S.2d 637, 152 N.E.2d 69 (1958), the plaintiffs alleged that the defendant, a contractor, negligently caused an explosion which destroyed plaintiffs' house. The defendant impleaded his liability insurer, alleging that it was obligated to indemnify the defendant if the latter were found liable to the plaintiffs. After a demand was made for a jury, the third-party defendant moved for severance (*see* CPLR 603, 1010). The Court of Appeals held that the severance should have been granted, because, otherwise, the jury trying the prime claim would be aware of the contractor's claimed right to insurance, and this might influence the jury's determination of both the prime claim and, per force, of the third-party complaint.

The rule of *Kelly v. Yannotti, supra,* has been applied even when the defendant-third-party plaintiff is an automobile owner and the third-party defendant is the owner's liability insurer. *E.g., DeLuca v. Schlesinger*, 39 A.D.2d 566, 331 N.Y.S.2d 698 (2d Dep't 1972). Does this make sense?

(2) CPLR 1007 requires the defendant commencing a third-party action to file a third-party summons and complaint with the clerk of the court in which the main action is pending and to pay a separate index number fee. CPLR 1007 gives the plaintiff one-hundred-twenty days within which to serve the third-party summons and complaint (and all prior pleadings served in the action) upon the third-party defendant.

Chapter 9
CLAIMS FOR CONTRIBUTION AND INDEMNIFICATION

§ 9.01 INTRODUCTORY NOTE

This chapter deals with the rules of contribution and indemnification and related doctrine. The law of contribution is found primarily in Articles 14, 14-A, and 16 of the CPLR. Article 14, which codifies the rule of *Dole v. Dow Chemical Co.*, 30 N.Y.2d 143, 331 N.Y.S.2d 382, 282 N.E.2d 288 (1972), *infra*, provides that when two or more persons have caused an injury to another person, each of the wrongdoers is entitled to "contribution" from the others. The amount of contribution is dependent on the wrongdoers' respective equitable shares of the judgment recovered by the plaintiff, *i.e.*, their degree of culpability for the damages sustained. Under *Dole*, the injured party was entitled to collect the full amount of the damages, even if this meant that one of the joint wrongdoers had to pay the full amount and could not obtain a proportional share from the other person liable — perhaps because the latter was judgment proof.[1]

Article 16, which was adopted in 1986 as part of a "tort reform" package,[2] cut back on the right to contribution and on the right of the injured party to collect full damages. Under CPLR 1601, a party whose equitable share is fifty per cent or less of the total liability need not pay more than their equitable share of the plaintiff's "non-economic loss." The latter term is defined by CPLR 1600 to include pain and suffering, mental anguish and loss of consortium. Thus, despite Article 16, each wrongdoer is still fully liable for the economic loss of the plaintiff, such as medical expenses and loss of income due to the injury. Moreover, because of CPLR 1602, which establishes numerous exceptions from the general rule of CPLR 1601, there are many situations in which CPLR Article 14 furnishes the entire rule of contribution.

The operation of Article 14 is illustrated by a scenario in which it is in fact commonly used — an automobile accident case in which the negligent acts of two drivers are claimed to have caused injuries to a passenger. Note that the driver defendants would not ordinarily be protected by Article 16 because of the

---

[1] CPLR 1404(a) provides that "Nothing in this article shall impair the rights of any person entitled to damages under existing law." Since the *Dole* case did not affect plaintiff's common law right to collect full damages, even, if need be, from a single tortfeasor, CPLR 1404(a) effectively preserves the same rule. *See Dufur v. Lavin*, 65 N.Y.2d 830, 493 N.Y.S.2d 123, 482 N.E.2d 919 (1985); *Hecht v. City of New York*, 60 N.Y.2d 57, 467 N.Y.S.2d 187, 454 N.E.2d 527 (1983); 2A Weinstein, Korn & Miller, N.Y. Civil Practice ¶ 1401.04 (1996).

[2] Ch. 682, Laws of 1986, effective July 30, 1986 and applicable to actions commenced on or after that date.

exception found in CPLR 1602(6). Assume that the jury finds that driver *B* bore seventy percent of the responsibility for the accident. Though each driver is liable to passenger *P* for all of *P*'s damages, driver *A* has a right to recover from *B* any amount that *A* pays *P* in excess of thirty percent of *P*'s damages, and *B* can recover from *A* any payments *B* makes to *P* in excess of *B*'s seventy percent share. Or *A* and *B* may simply each pay *P* their proportional share as established at trial. To introduce Article 16, assume further that a third defendant is *T*, the town responsible for the maintenance of the road on which the accident occurred. If the jury found that *T*'s faulty maintenance was one-fourth of the cause of *P*'s injuries, *T* (which gets the benefit of CPLR 1601) would be subject to liability to *P* for all of *P*'s economic loss but only for one-fourth of *P*'s non-economic loss. *T*'s liability to the other tortfeasors for contribution would be limited similarly.

The right to contribution is subject to these additional exceptions: (1) An otherwise culpable party who has a right to be indemnified by another cannot be subjected to a contribution claim by the indemnitor.[3] (2) A wrongdoer who settles prior to judgment gives up the right to seek contribution but is protected against contribution claims by other wrongdoers.[4] (3) contribution is not available when the damages suffered by the plaintiff are purely economic and are due solely to breach of contract (other than products liability).[5] (4) The employer of an injured plaintiff is subject to a claim for contribution only if the employee has died or suffered a "grave injury" as defined in Workers' Compensation Law § 11, as amended by Ch. 635, Laws of 1996.

Article 14 also spells out the procedure for interposing a claim for contribution, which may be "in a separate action or by cross-claim, counterclaim or third-party claim in a pending action." CPLR 1403.

An important procedural point for the plaintiff is that the assertion of a claim for contribution by a defendant against a third party does not protect the plaintiff's rights against that third party. *Klinger v. Dudley*, 41 N.Y.2d 362, 393 N.Y.S.2d 323, 361 N.E.2d 974 (1977). If, therefore, the defendant turns out to be judgment proof, the plaintiff cannot collect from a third party whom plaintiff has not sued, even though a court has determined that the third party was in whole or in part responsible for the plaintiff's injury.

For an ingenious solution to this plaintiff's pickle, see *Feldman v. New York City Health & Hosp. Corp.*, 107 Misc. 2d 145, 437 N.Y.S.2d 491 (Sup. Ct.), *rev'd*, 84 A.D.2d 166, 445 N.Y.S.2d 555 (2d Dep't 1981), *rev'd*, 56 N.Y.2d 1011, 453 N.Y.S.2d 683, 439 N.E. 398 (1982).

---

[3] CPLR 1404(b); *see* discussion in *D'Ambrosio v. City of New York*, § 9.02, *infra*.

[4] Gen. Oblig. Law § 15-108, reproduced in § 9.03, *infra*.

[5] *Board of Education v. Sargent, Webster, Crenshaw & Foley*, 71 N.Y.2d 21, 523 N.Y.S.2d 475, 517 N.E.2d 1360 (1987).

§ 9.02 THE RULES OF CONTRIBUTION

DOLE v. DOW CHEMICAL CO.
Court of Appeals
30 N.Y.2d 143, 331 N.Y.S.2d 382, 282 N.E.2d 288 (1972)

BERGAN, J.

Appellant Dow Chemical Company is defendant in an action for negligently causing the death of plaintiff's husband, and it is third-party plaintiff in a claim over against the husband's employer George Urban Milling Company. . . .

Dow is the manufacturer of chemicals. It produced methyl bromide, a penetrating and poisonous fumigant used for control of storage insects and mites. This product is labeled by Dow as poisonous, dangerous and highly volatile. Urban used it to fumigate a grain storage bin and shortly after fumigation it directed plaintiff's husband, its employee, to enter the fumigated bin to clean it. In doing this he was exposed to the poison which resulted in his death.

The negligence charged to Dow by plaintiff is that the poison was not properly labeled to warn users of its dangers; in failing to warn and instruct users that entry without protection into an enclosed area where the poison had been employed would be dangerous; and in failing to warn that use in an enclosed structure should be followed by effective dissipation of vapors or the lapse of time enough to allow dissipation.

Dow's answer to the complaint is both a denial of its own negligence and an allegation of affirmative negligence by decedent. Its third-party complaint against George Urban Milling Company alleges that the methyl bromide used by Urban was properly labeled with full warning of its dangerous nature; that it had furnished Urban with printed material relating to its use in fumigation and that Urban had access to and was aware of this material.

From this it is alleged by Dow that if decedent's death was caused by negligence it was the result of the "active and primary negligence" of Urban and the negligence of Dow "if any" was "merely passive and secondary."

. . . If plaintiff recovers Dow asks judgment over against Urban "for the full amount of such judgment."

Urban moved at Special Term to dismiss the third-party complaint as to it. This motion was denied. On Urban's appeal, the Appellate Division unanimously reversed and dismissed that pleading on the ground liability over would not be allowed if the plaintiff established that Dow's negligence in mislabeling and insufficient warning contributed to the accident.

This would be, the court noted, "active negligence of a character which would bar Dow from recovery against the user of the product" even though the user also was negligent. That view is consistent with decisions of this court. . . .

The "active-passive" test to determine when indemnification will be allowed by one party held liable for negligence against another negligent party has in practice proven elusive and difficult of fair application. The terms "primary" and "secondary" negligence, also used in the Dow pleading, have been regarded as more accurate and technically appropriate.

But the policy problem involves more than terminology. If indemnification is allowed at all among joint tort-feasors, the important resulting question is how ultimate responsibility should be distributed. There are situations when the facts would in fairness warrant what Dow here seeks — passing on to Urban all responsibility that may be imposed on Dow for negligence, a traditional full indemnification. There are circumstances where the facts would not, by the same test of fairness, warrant passing on to a third party any of the liability imposed. There are circumstances which would justify apportionment of responsibility between third-party plaintiff and third-party defendant, in effect a partial indemnification.

The basic theoretical bar at common law to any apportionment among those who committed torts, either by indemnity or by contribution, was the unwillingness of the law as a matter of policy to make relative value judgments of degrees of culpability among wrongdoers. . . . The rule springs from the celebrated decision in *Merryweather v. Nixan* (8 Durn. & E. 186; 101 Eng. Rep. 1337 [K.B., 1799]). . . .

Consistently with this theory at common law, the wrongdoer selected by the injured party for suit must have succeeded in avoiding any part of responsibility; and otherwise he would have to assume all of it without redress. This doctrine no longer is applied rigorously. For one thing the statute has altered the basic policy against contribution by allowing one joint tort-feasor subjected to judgment, to compel equal contribution by another who is subjected to the same judgment (CPLR 1401).*

The effective application of this statute depends, however, on the adjudication of joint tort responsibility which, as a matter of practice, depends in turn largely on the willingness or ability of the injured party to sue more than one of those responsible for his damage (*see* discussion of this aspect of the problem in *Putvin v. Buffalo Elec. Co.*, 5 N.Y.2d, p. 453, *supra*).

The "active-passive" negligence concept as it has developed in New York is itself an abandonment of the rigorous common-law policy; since it allows full indemnity in favor of one found to be passively negligent against another found to be actively negligent who could be brought into the action by the passively negligent party and required to answer the claim over.

This process in practical application became a measure of degree of differential culpability, although the degree was a large one. The "passive" negligent

---

* CPLR 1401, as it then read, allowed a tortfeasor who had paid more than his "pro rata share" to recover the excess from other defendants held liable. — Eds.

act was treated by the court as less a wrong than the "active" negligent act. The result has been that there has in fact emerged from the statutory change and from the judicial decisions an actual apportionment among those who participate responsibly in actionable torts.

This change in concept and the persistent criticism of the active-passive basis of apportioning liability between defendants found responsible in negligence make it useful for the court to re-examine the basic fairness of the uncertain and largely unpredictable nature of the measure of redress that has been allowed by indemnity in favor of a party found negligent against another who played an effective role in causing the damage.

The conclusion reached is that where a third party is found to have been responsible for a part, but not all, of the negligence for which a defendant is cast in damages, the responsibility for that part is recoverable by the prime defendant against the third party. To reach that end there must necessarily be an apportionment of responsibility in negligence between those parties.

The adjudication is one of fact and may be sought in a separate action . . . or as a separate and distinguishable issue by bringing in the third party in the prime action pursuant to CPLR 1007.

. . . .

It is fair to say that the rather widespread dissatisfaction with the inequity of result, as well as the looseness of terminology, in the "active-passive" axis foreshadowed for the Bar an attempt at realignment of the rule. This is to be observed both in some of the judicial opinions that have articulated the struggle toward fairness, and in professional commentaries. . . .

. . . .

The problem of apportionment of responsibility for tort has engaged the attention of several New York State study authorities. In 1934, for example, the Commission on the Administration of Justice recommended the enactment of a comprehensive statute giving a right of contribution among joint tort-feasors similar to the rights of co-obligors under contracts (N.Y. Legis. Doc., 1934, No. 50[D]).

One of the first studies made by the New York Law Revision Commission was on this subject (1936 Report, pp. 703-747) followed almost 20 years later by a further study in depth of the problem, and of the direction of decisional law (1952 Report, pp. 21-63).

The earlier study noted the refusal to allow contribution among joint tort-feasors was "of doubtful validity even in the most extreme case" (p. 720). The 1952 study observed what seems manifest in the willingness of the court to ameliorate an injustice by the "passive-active" concept, that essentially what had happened is the recognition by the court of a discernible "difference in the degree of the wrong committed" (p. 54).

Forty years ago Robert A. Leflar, a distinguished student of tort law, addressed himself to the closely related problems of indemnity and contribution as they were then developing (*Contribution and Indemnity Between Tortfeasors*, 81 U. of Pa. L. Rev. 130).

Although he then accepted the limitations on indemnity observed in contemporary law Leflar argued for a much broader view of apportionment of responsibility among joint tort-feasors by contribution than the law at that time allowed. The reasons outlined apply fully to the question of apportionment between Dow and Urban now before the court. "This result [contribution] is admittedly inconsistent with the doctrine of contributory negligence and related rules; it causes the law to settle between litigants disputes arising out of their own misconduct. But the reasons given against adjudications of such disputes, at least as between joint tortfeasors, are of doubtful validity, and are completely offset by the social evils which accrue from refusal to adjudicate the disputes. The deciding factor, then, should be fairness as between the parties" (81 U. of Pa. L. Rev., p. 159, op. cit.). *See, also*, Report of New York Law Revision Commission (1952, pp. 21-63, op. cit.).

The problem of apportioning liability between third-party plaintiff and third-party defendant in the present case requires consideration of the fact plaintiff represents the estate of the third-party defendant's employee and so no recovery could be had in an action brought by her against the employer or, indeed, by "anyone otherwise entitled to recover damages . . . on account of such injury or death" (Workmen's Compensation Law, § 11).

But she here asserts no such cause of action and the cause pleaded by Dow against Urban for indemnity is a very different kind of action. The relative responsibility of the employer and the chemical company for the wrongful death of the employee would be determined only in the action by the chemical company in which the cause asserted is based on a separable legal entity of rights to be adjudicated from the action by the administratrix against it (*Schubert v. Schubert Wagon Co.*, 249 N.Y. 253).

The theoretical difficulties have been resolved for this court by *Westchester Light. Co. v. Westchester County Small Estates Corp.* (278 N.Y. 175, *supra*) which sustained the right of plaintiff, a utility which had been found negligent in an action for causing the death of defendant's employee, to sue the employer on indemnity for having directly and negligently caused the death which in turn had compelled plaintiff to pay damages in an action by the employee's estate.

The difference between the causes of action and the parties pursuing them was decisive. "Plaintiff does not sue for damages 'on account of' Haviland's death. Plaintiff asserts its own right of recovery for breach of an alleged independent duty or obligation owed to it by the defendant" (opn. by Loughran, J., p. 179).

That is a precise description of Dow's third-party claim here.

. . . .

Although, as in *Westchester Light. Co.* (278 N.Y. 175, *supra*), an apportionment of responsibility could be pursued in a separate action by the party cast in damages, there should be no major difficulty in keeping apart the separable issues of liability of the defendant to the plaintiff and of the third-party defendant to defendant-third-party plaintiff in the same trial.

Whether the causes are tried together or separately would rest in the court's discretion, according to the requirements of fairness in the judicial management of the case. One or both actions could, on stipulation of the parties, be tried by the court.

If tried together before a jury, the instruction would be to consider the third-party plaintiff's cause over only if that party were found negligent; and if that were found, the remedy would depend on the proportion of the blame found against third-party defendant. There might, of course, be a finding leading to no apportionment or to full indemnity.

Where, however, there has been an apportionment of liability based on indemnity between a third-party plaintiff and third-party defendant and the apportionment is not equal, there should not thereafter be a further contribution between them pursuant to CPLR 1401. In authorizing equally shared contribution among tort-feasors jointly found liable, this statute[*] did not contemplate an apportionment already made in the judgment, and the "joint" responsibility described was not one of indemnity.

Right to apportionment of liability or to full indemnity, then, as among parties involved together in causing damage by negligence, should rest on relative responsibility and to be determined on the facts.

The order of the Appellate Division should be reversed, with costs to abide the event, and the order at Special Term reinstated.

NOTES

(1) In *Dole*, the Court undid a well-settled if much criticized rule of law. Was this example of judicial activism compelled by grievous injustice? What were the Court's goals in deciding *Dole* as it did? As you read the remainder of this chapter, consider whether the case solved the problems it addressed. Ask yourself, too, whether it created problems not foreseen when *Dole* was decided.

(2) Articles discussing the principal case include Wilner & Farrell, Dole v. Dow Chemical Co.: *The Kaleidoscopic Impact of a Leading Case*, 42 Brooklyn L. Rev. 457 (1976); Ausubel, *The Impact of New York's Judicially Created Loss Appor-*

---

[*] The reference is to CPLR 1401, which, as it then read, allowed a tortfeasor who had paid more than his "pro rata share" to recover the excess from other defendants held liable. — Eds.

tionment Among Tortfeasors: Dole v. Dow Chemical Company, 38 Albany L. Rev. 155 (1974). For a general discussion of the contribution doctrine, employing an economic analysis, see Kornhauser & Revesz, *Sharing Damages Among Tortfeasors*, 98 Yale L.J. 831 (1989).

(3) *Dole* was criticized because (among other reasons) it allowed an employer to be subjected to contribution liability for damages suffered by its employee even though the employee's own remedies against the employer were limited to rights under the Workers' Compensation Law. The Legislature addressed this issue when, in 1996, section 11 of the Workers' Compensation law was amended to bar third parties from seeking indemnification or contribution from the injured person's employer. An exception to the bar was carved out, however, under which an employer would be liable to third parties for contribution arising out of claims based on "grave injuries" suffered by the employee. "Grave injuries" include "death, permanent and total loss of multiple toes, paraplegia or quadriplegia, total and permanent blindness, total and permanent deafness, loss of nose, loss of ear, permanent and severe facial disfigurement, loss of an index finger, or an acquired injury to the brain caused by an external physical force resulting in permanent total disability." The Court of Appeals has held that the definition of grave injuries must be strictly construed. *Castro v. United Container Machinery Group, Inc.*, 96 N.Y.2d 398, 736 N.Y.S.2d 287, 761 N.E.2d 1014 (2001) (loss of multiple finger tips does not constitute "grave injury").

Would Workers' Compensation Law § 11 affect the outcome in *Dole* itself if the same facts arose today?

D'AMBROSIO v. CITY OF NEW YORK
Court of Appeals
55 N.Y.2d 454, 450 N.Y.S.2d 149, 435 N.E.2d 366 (1982)

GABRIELLI, JUDGE.

The issue on this appeal is the effect of our decision in *Dole v. Dow Chem. Co.*, 30 N.Y.2d 143, 331 N.Y.S.2d 382, 282 N.E.2d 288, on the so-called "special benefit" rule. This rule allows a municipality, charged with the duty of maintaining its sidewalks in a reasonably safe condition, to shift liability to the abutting landowner, where the cause of plaintiff's injuries is the failure of the landowner to reasonably maintain a sidewalk installation constructed for the special use and benefit of his property. We hold today that the "special benefit" rule is no longer available to shift entirely such liability to the landowner; rather, the liability is to be apportioned between the municipality and the landowner, based upon their respective degrees of fault.

Plaintiff sustained injuries when she was caused to trip on a metal disk embedded in the sidewalk. The disk, raised about one inch above the sidewalk, covered the housing for a shut-off valve in the service pipe which brought water to the abutting premises from the water main running under the street. The curb valve was installed by a former owner of the abutting premises, presumably for the benefit of his property.

Plaintiff brought suit against the City of New York (City), alleging that it had breached its duty to maintain the public sidewalk on which she fell in a reasonably safe condition, by suffering a dangerous and defective condition to exist, of which it had knowledge and notice. Prior to trial, plaintiff entered into a settlement agreement with the abutting landowner, by which plaintiff settled all "past, present and future claims" against the landowner in return for the sum of $22,500.

Following service of the complaint against the City, the City served a third-party summons and complaint upon the landowner, Harriet S. Hopp. This complaint sought recovery over against Hopp for any amount that might be recovered by the plaintiff against the City, on the ground that it was Hopp's negligent maintenance of the water box, installed for the special use and benefit of Hopp's premises, that caused plaintiff's injuries.

The testimony at trial indicated that plaintiff tripped over the raised water disk, which she could not see, as she was attempting to avoid cracks in the sidewalk a short distance ahead. The sidewalk immediately surrounding the condition was described as cracked and sloping downward toward the disk. Expert testimony was adduced to the effect that the one-inch elevation of the metal disk was improper, and that curb valves should be maintained flush with the surrounding sidewalk. Plaintiff testified that, about one year before her accident, she had seen a woman fall in the same area, and that a policeman and ambulance arrived at the scene to assist the injured woman, who stated that she had tripped over the water cap.

The case was submitted to the jury in two stages. With respect to the liability determination, the jury found that both the City and Hopp were negligent in allowing the sidewalk condition to go unrepaired, resulting in plaintiff's injuries. The issues of the amount of plaintiff's damages and of the relative fault of the City were then submitted to the jury. Plaintiff was awarded $100,000 in damages; the City was found 65% responsible. The City's motion for judgment over against Hopp was denied without comment by the court. Judgment was entered for plaintiff against the City in the amount of $65,000 (reduced by the proportionate amount of Hopp's fault, by reason of plaintiff's having settled her claim against Hopp [*see* General Obligations Law, § 15-108]).

. . . .

Turning to the merits of the appeal, we are asked to determine the effect of the rule announced in *Dole v. Dow Chem. Co.*, 30 N.Y.2d 143, 331 N.Y.S.2d 382, 282 N.E.2d 288, *supra*, allowing joint, actively negligent tort-feasors to seek contribution among themselves in proportion to their respective degrees of fault, upon the "special benefit" rule, which allows a municipality to shift liability for damages to one harmed by a defective condition in the sidewalk to the owner of the abutting premises, under some circumstances.

It was once the rule in this State that contribution among joint tort-feasors could not be had. The reason for this common-law rule barring apportionment was the belief that the courts should not participate in adjusting the relative rights of wrongdoers (*Dole v. Dow Chem. Co.*, 30 N.Y.2d 143, 147, 331 N.Y.S.2d 382, 282 N.E.2d 288, *supra*). This rule was abrogated partially in 1928, with the addition of section 211-a to the Civil Practice Act. Under that statute, if judgment were recovered by a plaintiff against more than one joint tort-feasor, one tort-feasor who had been required to pay more than his pro rata share to the plaintiff could recover the excess from the other adjudicated tort-feasors. The paying tort-feasor was expressly given the right to proceed against the others in a separate action. The statute left the decision of which defendants could be adjudicated joint tort-feasors entirely in the hands of the plaintiff, however, and a named defendant could not bring others into the suit on the basis of his belief that they should contribute to any judgment awarded to plaintiff (*Fox v. Western N.Y. Motor Lines*, 257 N.Y. 305, 178 N.E. 289).

Notwithstanding the rigid rules regarding contribution rights among joint tort-feasors, a common-law right of indemnification existed, allowing one who was compelled to pay for the wrong of another to recover from the wrongdoer the damages paid to the injured party. . . . Thus, for example, where the master had been held liable for the tort of his servant, on a theory of respondeat superior, but the master was himself free from wrong, the master was entitled to indemnification from his servant. . . . In the classic indemnification case, the one entitled to indemnity from another had committed no wrong, but by virtue of some relationship with the tort-feasor or obligation imposed by law, was nevertheless held liable to the injured party.

Over the years, the doctrine of "implied indemnification" was extended in response to the potentially harsh results of the inflexible rules barring contribution among joint tort-feasors. Thus, one who was cast in damages for negligence could, if his negligence were merely "passive," nevertheless shift his liability to the tort-feasor whose negligence was considered "active." The "actively negligent tort-feasor is considered the primary or principal wrongdoer and is held responsible for his negligent act not only to the person directly injured thereby, but also to any other person indirectly harmed by being cast in damages by operation of law for the wrongful act" (*McFall v. Compagnie Maritime Belge* [*Lloyd Royal*] *S.A.*, 304 N.Y. 314, 328, 107 N.E.2d 463; . . . . One who was himself actively negligent could not, of course, receive the benefit of this doctrine; it was available only to shift full liability from the secondary to the primary wrongdoer, and its availability depended upon the level of culpability of the one seeking indemnity. . . . The inquiry became primarily a question of the degree of fault, or the "factual disparity between the delinquency" of the several tort-feasors (*McFall v. Compagnie Maritime Belge* [*Lloyd Royal*] *S.A.*, 304 N.Y. 314, 330, 107 N.E.2d 463, *supra*). Such efforts to ameliorate the effects of the bar to contribution were far from complete, however, since the "active-passive" terminology was not easily applied. Moreover, the result of its application was complete, not ratable, recovery by the less negligent tort-feasor against the one guilty of "active" negligence.

Against this background, *Dole v. Dow Chem. Co. (supra)*, was decided, drastically changing the law of this State regarding the apportionment rights of joint tort-feasors. *Dole* rejected the unpredictable result of attempting to shift entire liability based upon the theory of whose negligence was the greater, and adopted the more realistic approach of holding joint tort-feasors liable according to their respective degrees of fault. To this end, the named defendant could either bring in another tort-feasor by impleading him into the plaintiff's main action, or seek contribution by way of a separate action against one believed to also be at fault.

In later cases, we clarified the scope of our holding in *Dole*. In *Rogers v. Dorchester Assoc.*, 32 N.Y.2d 553, 347 N.Y.S.2d 22, 300 N.E.2d 403, we explained that the rule of apportionment enunciated in *Dole* did not abrogate basic principles of "common-law indemnification between vicariously liable tort-feasors and tort-feasors guilty of the acts or omissions causing the harm. In short, the apportionment rule applies to those who in fact share responsibility for causing the accident or harm, and does not extend further to those who are only vicariously liable, as the employer of a negligent employee, the owner of a motor vehicle operated by a negligent driver, or . . . the owner of a building who contracts with an independent contractor exclusively responsible for maintenance of the building or parts of it" (*id.*, at pp. 565-566, 347 N.Y.S.2d 22, 300 N.E.2d 403). Thus, where one is held liable solely on account of the negligence of another, indemnification, not contribution, principles apply to shift the entire liability to the one who was negligent (*see, also, Logan v. Esterly*, 34 N.Y.2d 648, 355 N.Y.S.2d 381, 311 N.E.2d 512).

The issue in the present case is the effect of *Dole* and subsequent developments on the "special benefit" rule. The municipality owes a duty to keep the public sidewalks in a reasonably safe condition. A failure to repair a defective condition, of which it has notice, either actual or constructive, will cast the municipality in liability for damages to a person injured thereby. Where the cause of the injury is the defective condition of a sidewalk appurtenance installed for the special use or benefit of the owner of the abutting premises, however, the rule has developed that the municipality may receive indemnity from the landowner. . . . The precise question posed, then, is whether this "special benefit" rule was a recognition of a common-law right to indemnification, in that the municipality is entitled to recovery because it has been cast in liability solely for the landowner's negligence, or whether the rule is but one application of the doctrine permitting the secondary wrongdoer, notwithstanding his own negligence, to shift his liability to a wrongdoer guilty of a greater degree of negligence. An examination of the approach taken in cases involving the special benefit rule persuades us that the nature of this claim falls within the latter category. . . .

When a sidewalk appurtenance negligently falls into disrepair, both the municipality and the landowner have breached their respective duties to members of the public,[*] and both may be made to respond in damages to those injured by the defective condition. If the municipality pays the damages, it is not being compelled to pay for the wrong of another; it is simply being held liable for its own failure to exercise reasonable care. The landowner's obligation to maintain the sidewalk appurtenance runs, not to the municipality, but to the pedestrians who might be harmed by his negligence. The landowner has not undertaken any obligation to repair for the benefit of the municipality (*cf. Rogers v. Dorchester Assoc.*, 32 N.Y.2d 553, 347 N.Y.S.2d 22, 300 N.E.2d 403, *supra*). Thus, we conclude that the shifting of the municipality's liability to the landowner was not the classic form of indemnity; rather, it was a recognition that the municipality's culpability was only secondary where the precise instrumentality causing the injury was installed for the landowner's special benefit.

Since *Dole* has eliminated the necessity for continuing such distinctions, we conclude that the special benefit rule is not applicable to impose an obligation of indemnification on the landowner; liability is to be apportioned on the basis of the respective violations of duty owed by the alleged joint tort-feasors to the plaintiff. The primary inquiry in any such case should be the extent to which each of the negligent parties has contributed to the defective condition. In a particular case, of course, the inquiry may result in a finding that only one of the parties was responsible for the defect; in that event, full liability should be incurred by that party alone (*cf. Dole v. Dow Chem. Co.*, 30 N.Y.2d 143, 153, 331 N.Y.S.2d 382, 282 N.E.2d 288, *supra*).

Inasmuch as the City has failed to present a basis on which the jury's determination of its respective degree of fault should be overturned, the order of the Appellate Division should be reversed, with costs, and the judgment of Civil Court should be reinstated. . . .

NOTES

(1) Re-read the Court's footnote. Would the result have been different if there had been no evidence of cracks in the sidewalk?

---

[*] We note that the dissent (at pp. 470-471, at pp. 157-158 of 450 N.Y.S.2d, at pp. 374-375 of 435 N.E.2d) chooses to give no effect to the evidence adduced at trial that plaintiff was attempting to avoid cracks in the sidewalk a few feet ahead of her (a condition for which the City is concededly responsible) or to evidence regarding the City's actual notice of the defect in the sidewalk appurtenance. This evidence regarding the City's breach of its duty of care was properly before the jury, and while it was not made the basis of a specific theory of recovery, neither was the defect in the sidewalk appurtenance made a specific theory of recovery. Rather, the jury was instructed in very general terms, that on the evidence before it, it was to determine whether the City and/or the landowner breached their respective duties of care. The court did not marshal the evidence on this issue, nor did it refer specifically to any part of it.

(2) In *City of New York v. Kalikow Realty Co.*, 71 N.Y.2d 957, 529 N.Y.S.2d 62, 524 N.E.2d 416 (1988), the Court distinguished the principal case and held that the City was entitled to indemnification, not contribution, from an abutting property owner for all of the damages the City had paid to a pedestrian injured on a city street. Prior to the accident, the City had notified the landowner of the injury-causing defect and had placed a violation on the premises. The owner wrote to the City stating that it would repair the street and asked the City not to do any work on it. Indemnification was proper, the Court said, because the landowner had unequivocally assumed responsibility for the condition of the street.

We return to the distinction between indemnification and contribution later in this chapter when we take up the problem of settlements by and among co-tortfeasors.

(3) Cases in which a *Dole* claim has been made present a special problem in ordering the trial. When should the relative culpability of the alleged tort-feasors be determined? Before, after, or together with the trial of plaintiff's claim against the prime defendant? How did the trial judge solve the problem in the principal case? In *Dole* itself, the Court of Appeals anticipated the trial management problem and left the solution to the trial courts on a case by case basis. It went on to suggest that in some cases the plaintiff's claim against a tort-feasor and the latter's claim against a third-party defendant could be tried together, suggesting that "the instruction [to the jury] would be to consider the third-party plaintiff's cause over only if that party were found negligent; and if that were found, the remedy would depend on the proportion of the blame found against third-party defendant." *Dole v. Dow Chemical Co.*, 34 N.Y.2d 143, 153, 331 N.Y.S.2d 382, 391, 282 N.E.2d 288 (1972).

(4) Attention must also be paid to the burden of pleading and burden of proof rules relevant to claims for contribution. A party asserting a contribution claim is free to do so "in a separate action or by cross-claim, counterclaim or third-party claim in a separate action." CPLR 1403. Under traditional rules of common law, the claimant bears the burden of proving its entitlement. But if the defendant wants to invoke article 16 to limit its liability for non-economic loss, it has the burden of proving "by a preponderance of the evidence its equitable share of the total liability." CPLR 1603. In effect, it is up to the defendant to show that its liability for the injured party's loss is fifty percent or less. It does not appear that the defendant must plead the limitation.

The protection offered to defendants by article 16 is limited by the exceptions enumerated in CPLR 1602. A plaintiff who would invoke one or more of the exceptions must "allege and prove by a preponderance of the evidence" that it applies. A failure to plead the exception is fatal. *Cole v. Mandell Food Stores, Inc.*, 93 N.Y.2d 34, 687 N.Y.S.2d 598, 710 N.E.2d 244 (1999) (the alleged exception could not be raised for the first time on appeal, but plaintiff could have sought leave to amend his pleading during the course of the action). *See gener-*

ally Alexander, *CPLR Article 16: Substance and Procedure*, N.Y.L.J., September 17, 2001, p. 3.

(5) One reform sometimes begets another. In 1975, a year after codifying *Dole*, and only three years after *Dole* was decided, the legislature added CPLR Article 14-A, which moved New York from contributory to comparative negligence. Do you see why the old rule allowing contributory negligence as a complete defense was philosophically incompatible with *Dole*?

As the broad language of CPLR 1411 implies, it was the drafters' intention that it apply not only to negligence cases but also to actions for breach of warranty and strict products liability. Report of the Judicial Conference on the CPLR, McKinney's 1975 Session Laws 1482, 1483-4.

Note that the culpable conduct of the plaintiff or decedent is an affirmative defense which must be pleaded and proved by the party asserting it. CPLR 1412. Notwithstanding Article 14-A, the negligence of a plaintiff can in unusual circumstances still bar recovery entirely. *See Boltax v. Joy Day Camp*, 67 N.Y.2d 617, 499 N.Y.S.2d 660, 490 N.E.2d 527 (1986) (plaintiff's reckless decision to dive from a life guard chair into the shallow end of a pool was an unforeseeable superseding event that absolved the defendant of liability, even assuming negligence by the defendant). *Compare Soto v. N.Y.C. Transit Authority*, 6 N.Y.3d 487, 813 N.Y.S.2d 701, 846 N.E.2d 1211 (2006) (plaintiff, who was injured by an elevated subway train when walking on a "cat walk" connecting two stations, was assigned 75% of the fault by the jury with the remainder assigned to the defendant; the award was upheld because the plaintiff's conduct was not so egregious that it was a superseding caused of the accident and lead to total denial of recovery). *See also Morgan v. State*, 90 N.Y.2d 401, 662 N.Y.S.2d 421, 685 N.E.2d 202 (1997) (plaintiff assumed the risk inherent in sports activity and was barred from any recovery).

In practice, the rules of contribution and comparative negligence must often be used together. Problem A, in part, tests your ability to apply them.

PROBLEM A

Let us bring Problem D in Chapter 8 along. Betty has sued Fred for her injuries. Fred served an answer denying liability and alleging that Betty's own negligence caused her to slip and fall. Fred also brought a third-party claim against U&D seeking (a) indemnification or contribution for Betty's claim, (b) the cost of repairing the floor, and (c) damages for his own personal injuries. Betty has amended her complaint to assert a claim against U&D. The latter denies liability and alleges that Fred and Betty are responsible for their own injuries. All claims were timely interposed, for the purpose of this problem.

Assume that Betty's claims against Fred and U&D, and Fred's claim for contribution and for his own injuries are tried together. The jury finds that Betty suffered $10,000 in damages, of which $4,000 were for "non-economic loss" (as defined by CPLR 1600). It also finds that Betty's accident was 10% attributable to her own negligence, 70% attributable to U&D's improper design, and 20% attributable to Fred's poor maintenance. How much may Betty collect from Fred? From U&D? What are the rights of Fred and U&D vis-a-vis each other with respect to any recovery Betty obtains against either of them?

The jury goes on to find that Fred suffered $5,000 in property damage (cost of re-doing the floor) and $5,000 in personal injuries (of which $2,000 were for "non-economic loss"). Fred's damages were found to be 25% his own fault, for failing to maintain the floor properly, and 75% U&D's fault. How much may Fred collect from U&D?

NOTES

(1) The allocation of liability for Betty's injuries is affected by CPLR articles 14, 14-A and 16. Under article 14-A, Betty's recovery must be reduced by her share of fault, as found by the jury. While she is entitled to recover 90% of her loss if all defendants are solvent, how much will she recover from Fred if U&D is insolvent?

(2) CPLR 1602(1) provides that the protection of CPLR 1601 applies to claims for indemnification as well as to claims for contribution, except as stated in CPLR 1602(1)(a) and (b). Therefore, despite the arguable preservation of the rights of indemnitees found in CPLR 1602(b)(2)(ii), an indemnitor whose culpability is 50% or less is protected by CPLR 1601, *i.e.*, its liability for plaintiff's non-economic damages is limited to its degree of culpability. *Frank v. Meadowlakes Dev. Corp.*, 6 N.Y.3d 687, 816 N.Y.S.2d 715, 849 N.E.2d 938 (2006).

(3) What if Betty had been found 40% responsible for her own injuries, Fred found 10% and U&D found 50% culpable? Would U&D be liable for more than 50% of Betty's non-economic damages? The answer is yes, if we compute its culpability as between the defendants only, disregarding Betty's fault. Is that the right approach? One court held that it is. *Robinson v. June*, 167 Misc. 2d 483, 637 N.Y.S.2d 1018 (Sup. Ct. 1996). *Compare* CPLR 1601.

(4) In *D'Ambrosio v. City of New York*, *supra*, as in *Dole* itself, different acts of negligence produced a single injury to the plaintiff. Cases in which there are two injuries present special problems of apportionment. Consider the next two cases and accompanying notes.

RAVO v. ROGATNICK
Court of Appeals
70 N.Y.2d 305, 520 N.Y.S.2d 533, 514 N.E.2d 1104 (1987)

ALEXANDER, J.

In this medical malpractice action, defendant, Dr. Irwin L. Harris, appeals from an order of the Appellate Division unanimously affirming an amended judgment of Supreme Court, entered on a jury verdict, finding him jointly and severally liable with Dr. Sol Rogatnick for injuries negligently inflicted upon plaintiff, Josephine Ravo, and resulting in brain damage that has rendered her severely and permanently retarded. The issue presented is whether joint and several liability was properly imposed upon defendant under the circumstances of this case where, notwithstanding that the defendants neither acted in concert nor concurrently, a single indivisible injury — brain damage — was negligently inflicted. For the reasons that follow, we affirm.

I

Uncontroverted expert medical evidence established that plaintiff, Josephine Ravo, who at the time of trial was 14 years of age, was severely and permanently retarded as a result of brain damage she suffered at birth. The evidence demonstrated that the child was born an unusually large baby whose mother suffered from gestational diabetes which contributed to difficulties during delivery. The evidence further established that Dr. Rogatnick, the obstetrician who had charge of the ante partum care of Josephine's mother and who delivered Josephine, failed to ascertain pertinent medical information about the mother, incorrectly estimated the size of the infant, and employed improper surgical procedures during the delivery. It was shown that Dr. Harris, the pediatrician under whose care Josephine came following birth, misdiagnosed and improperly treated the infant's condition after birth. Based upon this evidence, the jury concluded that Dr. Rogatnick committed eight separate acts of medical malpractice, and Dr. Harris committed three separate acts of medical malpractice.

Although Dr. Rogatnick's negligence contributed to Josephine's brain damage, the medical testimony demonstrated that Dr. Harris' negligence was also a substantial contributing cause of the injury. No testimony was adduced, however, from which the jury could delineate which aspects of the injury were caused by the respective negligence of the individual doctors. . . . Indeed, plaintiff's expert, Dr. Charash . . . concluded that neither he nor anybody else could say with certainty which of the factors caused the brain damage. . . . Nor, as the Appellate Division found, did Dr. Harris adduce any evidence that could support a jury finding that he caused an identifiable percentage of the infant plaintiff's brain damage. Indeed, Dr. Harris' entire defense appears to have been that he was not responsible for the plaintiff's injury to any degree.

. . . .

[T]he jury returned a verdict for plaintiff in the total amount of $2,750,000 attributing 80% of the "fault" to Dr. Rogatnick and 20% of the "fault" to Dr. Harris.

In a postverdict motion, Dr. Harris sought an order directing entry of judgment limiting the plaintiff's recovery against him to $450,000 (20% of the $2,250,000 base recovery — the court having setoff $500,000 received by plaintiff in settlement of claims against other defendants) based upon his contention that his liability was not joint and several, but rather was independent and successive. This motion was denied. The Appellate Division dismissed Harris' appeal from the order denying the postverdict motion and affirmed the amended judgment entered on the jury's verdict.

II

When two or more tort-feasors act concurrently or in concert to produce a single injury, they may be held jointly and severally liable. . . . This is so because such concerted wrongdoers are considered "joint tort-feasors" and in legal contemplation, there is a joint enterprise and a mutual agency, such that the act of one is the act of all and liability for all that is done is visited upon each. . . . On the other hand, where multiple tort-feasors "neither act in concert nor contribute concurrently to the same wrong, they are not joint tort-feasors; rather, their wrongs are independent and successive" (*Suria v Shiffman*, 67 NY2d 87, 98. . . .) Under successive and independent liability, of course, the initial tort-feasor may well be liable to the plaintiff for the entire damage proximately resulting from his own wrongful acts. . . . The successive tort-feasor, however, is liable only for the separate injury or the aggravation his conduct has caused. . . .

It is sometimes the case that tort-feasors who neither act in concert nor concurrently may nevertheless be considered jointly and severally liable. This may occur in the instance of certain injuries which, because of their nature, are incapable of any reasonable or practicable division or allocation among multiple tort-feasors. . . .

We had occasion to consider such a circumstance in *Slater v Mersereau* (64 NY 138, *supra*), where premises belonging to the plaintiff were damaged by rainwater as a result of the negligent workmanship by a general contractor and a subcontractor. We held that where two parties by their separate and independent acts of negligence, cause a single, inseparable injury, each party is responsible for the entire injury: "Although they acted independently of each other, they did act at the same time in causing the damages . . . each contributing towards it, and although the act of each, alone and of itself, might not have caused the entire injury, under the circumstances presented, there is no good reason why each should not be liable for the damages caused by the different acts of all. . . . The water with which each of the parties were instrumental in injuring the plaintiffs was one mass and inseparable, and no distinction can be made between the different sources from whence it flowed, so that it can be claimed that each caused a separate and distinct injury for which each one is separately responsible . . . [t]he contractor and subcontractors were separately negligent, and although such negligence was not concurrent, yet the negligence of both these parties contributed to produce the damages caused at one and the same time" (*Slater v Mersereau*, 64 NY 138, 146-47, *supra*).

Our affirmance in *Hawkes v Goll* (281 NY 808, *affg* 256 App Div 940, *supra*) demonstrates that simultaneous conduct is not necessary to a finding of joint and several liability when there is an indivisible injury. In that case, the decedent was struck by the vehicle driven by the defendant Farrell and was thrown across the roadway, where very shortly thereafter he was again struck, this time by the vehicle driven by the defendant Goll, and dragged some 40 to 50 feet along the highway. He was taken to the hospital where he expired within the hour. The Appellate Division stated (256 App Div 940): "As the result of his injuries the plaintiff's intestate died within an hour. There could be no evidence upon which the jury could base a finding of the nature of the injuries inflicted by the first car as distinguished from those inflicted by the second car. The case was submitted to the jury upon the theory that if both defendants were negligent they were jointly and severally liable. While the wrongful acts of the two defendants were not precisely concurrent in point of time, the defendants may nevertheless be joint tort feasors where, as here, their several acts of neglect concurred in producing the injury."

A similar result was reached in *Wiseman v 374 Realty Corp.* (54 AD2d 119, *supra*). There, the decedent had sustained injuries in a fall caused by the defective stairway and handrail in the defendant 374 Realty Corp.'s building which resulted in his hospitalization. While hospitalized, he was treated, until his death, with a drug "Decadron," allegedly known to cause stomach bleeding as a side effect, and requiring an adequate amount of antacid therapy on a daily basis to prevent and protect against such occurrence. In reinstating *Dole v Dow* cross claims by the manufacturer of the "Decadron" and the hospital against 374 Realty Corp., the court observed that notwithstanding that the acts of negligence occurred at separate times, the injuries sustained by the decedent resulted in his death, and that no distinction could be made between the injuries sustained through the negligence of the building owner and those resulting from the improper conduct of the manufacturer and the hospital (*Wiseman v 374 Realty Corp.*, 54 AD2d 119, 122, *supra*).

Similarly, here the jury was unable to determine from the evidence adduced at trial the degree to which the defendants' separate acts of negligence contributed to the brain damage sustained by Josephine at birth. Certainly, a subsequent tort-feasor is not to be held jointly and severally liable for the acts of the initial tort-feasor with whom he is not acting in concert in every case where it is difficult, because of the nature of the injury, to separate the harm done by each tort-feasor from the others. . . . Here, however, the evidence established that plaintiff's brain damage was a single indivisible injury, and defendant failed to submit any evidence upon which the jury could base an apportionment of damage.

Harris argues, however, that since the jury ascribed only 20% of the fault to him, this was in reality an apportionment of damage, demonstrating that the injury was divisible. This argument must fail. Clearly, the court's instruction, and the interrogatory submitted in amplification thereof, called upon the jury to determine the respective responsibility in negligence of the defendants so as to establish a basis for an apportionment between them, by way of contribution, for the total damages awarded to plaintiff (*see*, CPLR 1401; *Dole v Dow Chem. Co.*, 30 NY2d 143, *supra*). In that respect, the jury's apportionment of fault is unrelated to the nature of defendants' liability (*i.e.*, whether it was joint and several or independent and successive).

As we said in *Schauer v Joyce* (54 NY2d 1, 5): "CPLR 1401, which codified this court's decision in *Dole v Dow Chem Co.* (30 NY2d 143), provides that "two or more persons who are subject to liability for damages for the same personal injury, injury to property or wrongful death, may claim contribution among them whether or not an action has been brought or a judgment has been rendered against the person from whom contribution is sought." The section "applies not only to joint tortfeasors, but also to concurrent successive, independent, alternative, and even intentional tortfeasors. . . ." The focus and purpose of the *Dole v Dow* inquiry, therefore, is not whether, or to what degree, a defendant can be cast in damages to a plaintiff for a third party's negligence, as was the case in *Zillman v Meadowbrook Hosp. Co.* (45 AD2d 267, *supra*). Rather, it seeks to determine "whether each defendant owed a duty to plaintiff and whether, by breaching their respective duties, they contributed to plaintiff's ultimate injury" claimed to have been caused by each defendant. . . .

Here, the jury determined that the defendants breached duties owed to Josephine Ravo, and that these breaches contributed to her brain injury. The jury's apportionment of fault, however, does not alter the joint and several liability of defendants for the single indivisible injury. Rather, that aspect of the jury's determination of culpability merely defines the amount of contribution defendants may claim from each other, and does not impinge upon plaintiff's right to collect the entire judgment award from either defendant (CPLR 1402). As we stated in *Graphic Arts Mut. Ins. Co. v Bakers Mut. Ins. Co.* (45 NY2d 551, 557): "The right under the *Dole-Dow* doctrine to seek equitable apportionment based on relative culpability is not one intended for the benefit of the injured claimant. It is a right affecting the distributive responsibilities of tort-feasors inter sese. . . . It is elementary that injured claimants may still choose which joint tort-feasors to include as defendants in an action and, regardless of the concurrent negligence of others, recover the whole of their damages from any of the particular tort-feasors sued (*see Kelly v Long Is. Light. Co.*, 31 NY2d 25, 30)." This being so, in light of the evidence establishing the indivisibility of the brain injury and the contributing negligence of Dr. Harris, and of the manner in which the case was tried and submitted to the jury we conclude that joint and several liability was properly imposed.

NOTES

(1) The Court of Appeals returned to the multiple injury problem in *Nassau Roofing & Sheet Metal Co., Inc. v. Facilities Development Corporation*, 71 N.Y.2d 599, 528 N.Y.S.2d 516, 523 N.E.2d 803 (1988). When a newly installed roof sustained damages, allegedly due to the excessive expansion of the insulation supplied by Celotex, the building owner, Facilities, retained Consultants to advise it. Consultants recommended the replacement of the entire roof, which was done, at a cost of $1,500,000. In the ensuing litigation, Celotex claimed that Consultants' advice had been wrong in that the roofing could have been repaired without replacement. Celotex therefore sought contribution from Consultants. The Court held that the claim had no merit:

> It is this essential requirement — that the parties must have contributed to the same injury — which defeats Celotex's third-party claim here. The injury suffered by Facilities for which Celotex is being sued and for which it seeks contribution from Consultants is a bad roof which had to be replaced. But Consultants — which had nothing to do with the installation of the roof — did not cause or contribute to this injury. If Consultants caused any injury to Facilities, it was the financial damage Facilities sustained from being negligently advised to replace a good roof, not the loss Facilities incurred from having a bad roof. Needlessly replacing a sound roof is obviously not the same as having a defective roof; it is an entirely separate and distinct injury. For this reason, the claim for contribution must fall.

> . . . Celotex contends [alternatively] that it should be permitted to obtain contribution from Consultants as a successor tort-feasor, because, by negligently advising Facilities to install a new roof, it increased the damages which could be recovered against Celotex. This reasoning is flawed, however, because the claimed negligence of Consultants could not have augmented the damages for which Celotex may be held responsible. . . . To the extent that Facilities, because of this erroneous advice, needlessly incurred the cost of replacing a sound roof, Celotex would have done nothing wrong, would not be liable to the owner, and could have no basis for its claim over. If, on the other hand, Consultants is correct and the roof required replacement in whole or part, then Celotex could be held responsible for such cost. In that event, Consultants would have done nothing wrong and would not have augmented the damages for which Celotex could be held liable.

71 N.Y. 2d at 603, 604, 528 N.Y.S.2d at 518-19, 523 N.E.2d at 805-06.

(2) The next case is an example of "successive" liability.

SCHAUER v. JOYCE
Court of Appeals
54 N.Y.2d 1, 444 N.Y.S.2d 564, 429 N.E.2d 83 (1981)

COOKE, CHIEF JUDGE.

In this case, the court must decide whether appellant, a lawyer being sued by a former client for malpractice, properly brought a third-party claim for contribution against respondent, another attorney who subsequently represented the client in the same matter. It is held that appellant's third-party claim is sufficient to withstand a motion to dismiss.

Vivian G. Schauer retained lawyer Patrick J. Joyce, the appellant, in November, 1975 to represent her in a matrimonial action. Joyce, on behalf of Mrs. Schauer, obtained from Supreme Court in January, 1976 a divorce judgment by default that included an award of $200 per week in alimony, counsel fees and possession of the marital residence. No alimony, however, was ever received by Mrs. Schauer under this decree. In fact, Mr. Schauer, who had been living in Michigan at the time of the divorce judgment, moved to vacate those parts of the judgment concerning alimony, counsel fees, and possession of the marital residence on the ground that the affidavit of regularity submitted in support of the default judgment falsely stated that he had not appeared in the action. Supreme Court granted Mr. Schauer's motion in April, 1977, and transferred jurisdiction over these matters to the Delaware County Family Court. Soon thereafter, Mrs. Schauer discharged Joyce and retained Thomas W. Gent, Jr., to represent her in the matrimonial matter. Through Gent's efforts, she began receiving support payments from her former husband in November, 1977.

In January, 1978, Mrs. Schauer began a malpractice action against Joyce, retaining another attorney not associated with either Joyce or Gent. Mrs. Schauer alleged that Joyce caused her to lose alimony and counsel fees through a variety of actions and omissions, particularly the filing of a false affidavit of regularity with Supreme Court that caused the partial vacatur of the divorce judgment. As a result of Joyce's malpractice, Mrs. Schauer claimed, she lost $200 per week alimony from December, 1975 to November, 1977, and $75 per week thereafter.

Joyce then brought this third-party action against Gent, alleging that after Gent took over Mrs. Schauer's case in April, 1977, Gent negligently failed to seek reinstatement of the vacated alimony award or to make any other application to obtain alimony for the period prior to the vacatur. In addition, Joyce alleged, Gent failed to seek a prompt Family Court hearing to obtain prospective alimony payments.

. . . .

CPLR 1401, which codified this court's decision in *Dole v. Dow Chem. Co.* . . . provides that "two or more persons who are subject to liability for damages for the same personal injury, injury to property or wrongful death, may claim contribution among them whether or not an action has been brought or a judgment has been rendered against the person from whom contribution is sought." The section "applies not only to joint tortfeasors, but also to concurrent, successive, independent, alternative, and even intentional tortfeasors" (Siegel, New York Practice, § 172, p. 213; *see* McLaughlin, Practice Commentaries, McKinney's Cons. Laws of N.Y., Book 7B, CPLR 1401, pp. 362-363).

Respondent Gent maintains that he was not in contractual privity with appellant Joyce and that there is no other basis on which it can be said that he owed a duty to Joyce. This misses the point. The relevant question under CPLR 1401 and *Dole* is not whether Gent owed a duty to Joyce, but whether Gent and Joyce each owed a duty to Mrs. Schauer, and by breaching their respective duties contributed to her ultimate injuries. . . . There is no need to search "for the existence of an elusive "'legal relationship' between the wrongdoers" (Twentieth Ann. Report of N.Y. Judicial Conference, 1975, p. 216).

It is beyond dispute that Joyce and Gent were each retained by Mrs. Schauer, at different times, in connection with her claim for support. Mrs. Schauer's complaint against Joyce alleges that Joyce's malpractice cost her substantial sums of lost alimony and other damages. The question is whether the third-party complaint against Gent alleges negligence by Gent that could have contributed to this loss.

The Appellate Division held that there was nothing alleged that could make Gent even partially liable for Mrs. Schauer's loss of alimony. This conclusion is erroneous. The pleadings set forth an ample basis for holding that the alleged negligence of both attorneys was responsible for the same injury. The primary injury of which Mrs. Schauer complains is the loss of alimony. She seeks $200 per week to compensate her for the back alimony due under a December, 1975 temporary award and the January, 1976 final judgment but not recovered because of the partial vacatur of the final judgment in April, 1977. She also seeks $200 per week for the period from April, 1977 to November, 1977, after which Mrs. Schauer began receiving support. Finally, she seeks $75 per week for the period beginning November, 1977, which apparently reflects the difference between the vacated judgment and the level of the support she eventually received.

Mrs. Schauer had discharged Joyce in April, 1977. A substantial portion of the damages she claims to have suffered thus occurred after she had replaced Joyce as her attorney with Gent. It may be that the loss of alimony after April, 1977, stemmed from the partial vacatur of the original divorce judgment. But if Gent was negligent in not quickly obtaining a new hearing on alimony and support, as Joyce's third-party complaint alleges, Gent could be found at least partially responsible for this loss. Likewise, if Gent negligently failed to seek reinstatement of the vacated alimony judgment, as Joyce alleges, he may well be partially responsible for the loss of the alimony that had been due under that judgment prior to its vacatur. In effect, Joyce has raised a claim that Gent, as an independent, successive tort-feasor, has contributed to or aggravated Mrs.

Schauer's injuries. This is clearly the type of claim encompassed by CPLR 1401. That Joyce may raise the defense of Mrs. Schauer's failure to mitigate damages does not affect his ability to also assert a third-party claim for contribution against Gent for those injuries for which Joyce may be liable to Mrs. Schauer.

In conclusion, both Joyce and Gent may be liable to Mrs. Schauer, if their respective representations of her were negligent, for at least a portion of the same damages claimed by her. Joyce's third-party complaint for contribution therefore states a valid cause of action and should not have been dismissed.

. . . .

NOTES

(1) Another example of "successive" liability is found in *Suria v. Shiffman*, 67 N.Y.2d 87, 499 N.Y.S.2d 912, 490 N.E.2d 832 (1986), cited with approval in the principal case. *P* was injured when Dr. *A* operated unsuccessfully on him in 1974. Post-operative care continued until September, 1976, when Dr. *A* referred *P* to Dr. *B*, who negligently performed corrective surgery. The Court held that Dr. *B* was a successive, rather than joint or concurrent tortfeasor, and that he was therefore liable only for plaintiff's damages attributable to the aggravating effects of his own tortious act. Dr. *A*, as the first of the successive tortfeasors, was liable for all of *P*'s injuries, including those traceable to Dr. *B*. Are this case and *Schauer v. Joyce* reconcilable with *Ravo v. Ragotnick*, *supra*, and *Nassau Roofing & Sheet Metal Co., Inc.* (*see* note 1, following *Ravo v. Rogatnick*, *supra*)?

(2) What is the objection to saying that even in the *Suria* case all the tort-feasors ought to be jointly and severally liable? If it is that it would be unfair to charge *B* with the damage caused by *A*, then why is this not taken care of by the *Dole* procedure? *See* Barker, *New York Practice, Successive Tort-feasors*, N.Y.L.J., December 27, 1988, p. 3, col. 2.

(3) In *Schauer v. Joyce*, the Court says that the "relevant question" is not whether the tortfeasor from whom contribution is sought (Gent) owed a duty to the party seeking to claim over (Joyce), but whether each of them owed a duty to the injured party (Schauer). The Court's view of the matter has not been static, however, and it may be said that the relevant question can indeed be whether one tortfeasor owed a duty to another, not only whether each owed a duty to the victim.

The development of the law has progressed in part through cases in which a tortfeasor who has injured an infant seeks contribution from the infant's parent on the theory that the parent breached a duty to supervise the child adequately. The Court of Appeals held initially that a claim for contribution would not lie and offered this reasoning: Since (as a matter of substantive law) a child has no cause of action against his parent for negligent supervision, and since the parent owes the child no duty in this regard, a tortfeasor who has injured the child may not seek contribution from the parent on this ground. *Holodook v. Spencer*, 36 N.Y.2d 35, 364 N.Y.S.2d 859, 324 N.E.2d 338 (1974).

In a later case presenting different facts, the Court recognized that contribution could be obtained from a party who owed no duty to the injured person, so long as a duty was owed to the claimant co-tortfeasor. In *Nolecheck v. Gesuale*, 46 N.Y.2d 332, 413 N.Y.S.2d 340, 385 N.E.2d 1268 (1978), a father, whose infant son had been killed in a motorcycle accident, brought an action for wrongful death alleging that the defendant owner of the land on which the accident had taken place had caused it by negligently creating a dangerous condition. The Court allowed the landowner to seek contribution from the father because the father had negligently entrusted his son with a dangerous instrumentality, *i.e.*, the motorcycle. The absence of a duty running from father to son, it was held, did not prevent the landowner from asserting the claim because the father had breached his duty to the landowner to protect him from unreasonable risks of harm. This duty encompassed an obligation to prevent foreseeable exposure to liability for injury by the landowner to the child.

See also, allowing contribution from a tortfeasor who breached a duty to a co-tortfeasor but not to the injured plaintiff, *Garrett v. Holiday Inns, Inc.*, 58 N.Y.2d 253, 460 N.Y.S.2d 774, 447 N.E.2d 717 (1983).

§ 9.03 THE EFFECT OF SETTLEMENTS

N.Y. Gen. Oblig. Law § 15-108. Release or Covenant Not to Sue

(a) Effect of release of or covenant not to sue tortfeasors. When a release or a covenant not to sue or not to enforce a judgment is given to one of two or more persons liable or claimed to be liable in tort for the same injury, or the same wrongful death, it does not discharge any of the other tortfeasors from liability for the injury or wrongful death unless its terms expressly so provide, but it reduces the claim of the releasor against the other tortfeasors to the extent of any amount stipulated by the release or the covenant, or in the amount of the consideration paid for it, or in the amount of the released tortfeasor's equitable share of the damages under article fourteen of the civil practice law and rules, whichever is the greatest.

(b) Release of tortfeasor. A release given in good faith by the injured person to one tortfeasor as provided in subdivision (a) relieves him from liability to any other person for contribution as provided in article fourteen of the civil practice law and rules.

(c) Waiver of contribution. A tortfeasor who has obtained his own release from liability shall not be entitled to contribution from any other person.

PROBLEM B

Varying the facts of Problem A somewhat, suppose that prior to trial, Fred settles with Betty by agreeing to pay her $8,000. Assuming that the jury finds the same proportions of liability as indicated in Problem A, what are Betty's rights against Fred? Against U&D? Fred's rights against U&D? U&D's rights against Fred? If Fred and Betty had settled for $1,000, would any of your answers change?

ROSADO v. PROCTOR & SCHWARTZ, INC.
Court of Appeals
66 N.Y.2d 21, 494 N.Y.S.2d 851, 484 N.E.2d 1354 (1985)

TITONE, JUDGE.

In this products liability action, defendant and third-party plaintiff, Proctor & Schwartz, Inc. (Proctor), appeals from an order . . . granting a motion made by third-party defendant, Comet Fibers, Inc. (Comet), to dismiss a cause of action seeking indemnification. The issue is whether a manufacturer of a defective product may obtain indemnification from the purchaser where the sales contract contains a provision requiring the purchaser to install certain safety devices and the purchaser's employee, who is injured by the failure to properly install such devices, brings an action against the manufacturer predicated on the manufacturer's marketing of a machine that is not reasonably safe. We hold that indemnification may not be obtained in such circumstances.

Plaintiff Hector Rosado was employed by Comet as one of the three operators of a garnett, a machine used in the textile industry to convert clumped fibers into a form of matting. The machine contains a series of massive chains and pulleys that operate the gears and rollers which straighten the fiber in the correct direction.

Comet purchased the garnett from Proctor in 1970. The contract of sale required Comet to install all "necessary guards for the exposed moving parts of the machine in accordance with the laws of the district in which the machine is to be located" as well as to "supply disconnect switches as required."

When delivered, the machine had no safety devices. Comet installed a mesh fence around the gear and pulley area, but there was a gap of two to three feet between the gate and the machine, and the gate had several broad doors. When these doors were opened, all the pulleys, chains and gears were exposed. There was only a simple latch on the gate, without any interlock, or other machine cut-off at the gate area. The garnett thus would be fully operative with the gate open, and it appears that it was customary for the workers to operate it in that manner.

A few moments before closing time on September 9, 1976, the plaintiff was instructed to rake the droppings around the machine. To do so, he was required to kneel next to the machine and, using a rake, pull debris from underneath. The plaintiff suddenly heard what he described as a "terrible noise" and immediately tried to stand up. Moving away, he hit his back on the fence and was caused to rebound in such a fashion that his right hand came into contact with unprotected chain and gears, severing his thumb and fingers.

Plaintiff Rosado commenced a suit against Proctor which, in turn, brought a third-party action against Comet, seeking contribution and indemnity. The indemnification claim, the subject of this appeal, was dismissed by Trial Term on the eve of trial. Comet then consummated a settlement agreement with plaintiff, thus foreclosing Proctor's claim for contribution (*see*, General Obligations Law § 15-108).

Proctor thereafter settled with plaintiff subsequent to the commencement of trial but prior to verdict. Proctor then appealed from the dismissal of its claim for indemnification. The Appellate Division, First Department, affirmed, by a divided court. . . . We affirm.

To place the issue before us in focus, it is useful to restate the important substantive distinctions between contribution and indemnity. Basically, in contribution the loss is distributed among tort-feasors, by requiring joint tort-feasors to pay a proportionate share of the loss to one who has discharged their joint liability, while in indemnity the party held legally liable shifts the entire loss to another. . . . Contribution arises automatically when certain factors are present and does not require any kind of agreement between or among the wrongdoers (Siegel, N.Y. Prac. § 169). Indemnity, on the other hand, arises out of a contract which may be express or may be implied in law "to prevent a result which is regarded as unjust or unsatisfactory" (Prosser and Keeton, op. cit., at 341).

Implied indemnity is frequently employed in favor of one who is vicariously liable for the tort of another (*see, e.g., Rogers v. Dorchester Assoc.*, 32 N.Y.2d 553, 347 N.Y.S.2d 22, 300 N.E.2d 403), but the principle is not so limited and has been invoked in other contexts as well (*see, e.g., McDermott v. City of New York*, 50 N.Y.2d 211, 428 N.Y.S.2d 643, 406 N.E.2d 460, *supra*). Nonetheless, "an indemnity cause of action can be sustained only if the third-party plaintiff and the third-party defendant have breached a duty to plaintiff and also if some duty to indemnify exists between them" (*Garrett v. Holiday Inns*, *supra*, at p. 471, 450 N.Y.S.2d 619).

The distinctions between contribution and indemnity take on added importance in settlement negotiations. In order to remove a disincentive to settlement, the Legislature amended General Obligations Law § 15-108 (L.1974, ch. 742) to provide that a settling tortfeasor can neither obtain, nor be liable for, a contribution claim. Inasmuch as an entire shifting of the loss to another would not act as a disincentive to settlement or necessitate an examination of relative degrees of fault, indemnification claims are not barred. . . . A party who has settled and seeks what it characterizes as indemnification thus must show that it may not be held responsible in any degree. The statutory bar to contribution may not be circumvented by the simple expedient of calling the claim indemnification.

Proctor recognizes, as it must, that by virtue of the settlement agreements, any claim for contribution has been statutorily extinguished, and also seems to accept that no basis for contractual indemnity exists since Comet did not explicitly agree to indemnify or hold it harmless from product liability claims. Proctor argues, however, that the entire loss may be shifted to Comet on an implied indemnity theory. It contends that Comet was primarily responsible for plaintiff's injury because it failed to properly install the safety devices as it was contractually obligated to do. According to Proctor, strict products liability is a species of liability without fault, so that even if its duty to manufacture and market a reasonably safe product is nondelegable, it may still recover its entire loss from its delegate if the jury were to conclude that it was otherwise blameless. Alternatively, Proctor urges that Comet undertook a duty to install the appropriate safety devices under the sales contract, and that Comet's breach of duty caused the loss, so that the equities compel that it be made whole. Neither premise is sound.

A strict products liability action is not analogous to vicarious liability, resulting in the imposition of liability without regard to fault. A manufacturer is held accountable as a wrongdoer, and, while the proof that must be adduced by a plaintiff is not as exacting as it would be in a pure negligence action, a prima facie case is not established unless it is shown, among other things, that in relation to those who will use it, the product was defective when it left the hands of the manufacturer because it was not reasonably safe. Any analogy to vicarious liability under the Labor Law, respondeat superior, or the Vehicle and Traffic Law — instances in which liability is fixed upon another without regard to any volitional act — is clearly flawed.

. . . .

[W]e hold that where, as here, the manufacturer is in the best position to know the dangers inherent in its product, and the dangers do not vary depending on jobsite, it is also in the best position to determine what safety devices should be employed. Preventing injuries in the first place is the primary public policy underlying the doctrine of strict products liability. To allow a manufacturer like Proctor, which sells a product like a garnett with no safety devices, to shift the ultimate duty of care to others through boilerplate language in a sales contract, would erode the economic incentive manufacturers have to maintain safety and give sanction to the marketing of dangerous, stripped down, machines. This we decline to do.

McDermott v. City of New York, 50 N.Y.2d 211, 428 N.Y.S.2d 643, 406 N.E.2d 460, *supra*, offers no support for Proctor. In that case, the manufacturer breached a duty to the injured plaintiff by supplying defective equipment to his

484 CLAIMS FOR CONTRIBUTION AND INDEMNIFICATION CH. 9

employer, the City of New York. We held that the city was entitled to indemnification for the damages that it had to pay on account of the manufacturer's breach of duty. Our holding rested on the duty running from the manufacturer to the employee (*McDermott v. City of New York, supra*, at p. 219, 428 N.Y.S.2d 643, 406 N.E.2d 460).

Here, Proctor seeks the converse. Proctor breached its duty to Comet's employee and seeks to recover from Comet based upon the contract between them. Unlike the manufacturer in *McDermott*, whose malfeasance compelled the city to pay damages to its employee, the damages Proctor is compelled to pay stem from its own wrong and there is no unjust enrichment on Comet's part. As Justice Fein observed below, at best Comet's failure to supply the safety devices amounted to a separate breach of contract, and inasmuch as there can be no liability for contractual indemnification unless it is explicitly assumed (*Vey v. Port Auth.*, 54 N.Y.2d 221, 226-227, *supra*; *Margolin v. New York Life Ins. Co.*, 32 N.Y.2d 149, *supra*; *Levine v. Shell Oil Co.*, 28 N.Y.2d 205, *supra*), there should similarly be no basis for implied indemnity (*see, Jackson v. Long Is. Light. Co.*, 59 A.D.2d 523, 524).

NOTES

(1) Assume that *P* is tortiously injured by *X*, acting within the scope of his employment for *Y*. *P* sues *X* and *Y* for $100,000 but, prior to trial, settles with *X* for $10,000. Note that *Y* is vicariously liable for *X*'s torts and is therefore entitled to indemnification from *X*. Does Gen. Oblig. Law § 15-108 affect the rights of any of the parties? A negative answer is given in *Riviello v. Waldron*, 47 N.Y.2d 297, 418 N.Y.S.2d 300, 391 N.E.2d 1278 (1979).

(2) Under the principal case, how can one tell if a tortfeasor is entitled to indemnification or contribution from co-wrongdoers? Does the test adopted by the Court adequately distinguish the result in *McDermott v. City of New York* (cited and discussed in the principal case)? There, the City, which had settled a claim against it by an injured sanitation worker, was held entitled to indemnification from the manufacturer of the injury-causing truck.

(3) Should Gen. Oblig. Law § 15-108 be amended to apply to indemnity situations? Professor Siegel argues that the case law excluding indemnification from the application of Gen. Oblig. Law § 15-108 discourages settlement "in all cases in which indemnification instead of contribution might prove to be the relationship involved." David D. Siegel, New York Practice 304 (4th ed. 2005).

(4) Gen. Oblig. Law § 15-108 does not apply to a settlement made after judgment at the conclusion of the trial. *Rock v. Reed-Prentice Div. of Package Mach. Co.*, 39 N.Y.2d 34, 382 N.Y.S.2d 720, 346 N.E.2d 520 (1976).

(5) A plaintiff's rights against one of two or more wrongdoers will be affected, not only by settling, but also by obtaining a judgment or arbitration award against one of them, which is later fully satisfied. Such a plaintiff will be barred

from proceeding against any other party, under principles of res judicata. *Velazquez v. Water Taxi, Inc.*, 49 N.Y.2d 762, 426 N.Y.S.2d 467, 403 N.E.2d 172 (1980) (*P*, who recovered an arbitration award against *X* for $2,500, which *X* satisfied, was barred from pursuing a claim for $1,000,000 against *Y*, a co-tortfeasor).

(6) For an example of how a settlement with one wrongdoer affects the victim's rights against other wrongdoers in a true contribution case, see *D'Ambrosio v. City of New York*, in § 9.02, *supra*.

(7) "A maxim is now prevalent among the plaintiff's bar in multi-party litigation: Settle with every defendant or settle with no defendant." Green, *G.O.L. Section 15-108 — An Unsettling Law*, N.Y.L.J., Mar. 3, 1983, p. 1, col. 3. How do you account for the maxim?

(8) Tortfeasors may stipulate among themselves to settle with the plaintiff without waiving their rights to contribution or indemnification. Their agreement is not prohibited by Gen. Obligations Law § 15-108 and is enforceable notwithstanding that law. *Mitchell v. New York Hospital*, 61 N.Y.2d 208, 473 N.Y.S.2d 148, 461 N.E.2d 285 (1984).

In the Matter of NEW YORK CITY ASBESTOS LITIGATION (DIDNER v. KEENE CORP.)
Court of Appeals
82 N.Y.2d 342, 624 N.E.2d 979, 604 N.Y.S.2d 884 (1993)

HANCOCK, JUDGE.

We granted leave in this case together with two other cases . . . primarily to resolve a question which we have not addressed pertaining to General Obligations Law § 15-108(a) as applied in an action with multiple defendants where two or more of the defendants have settled with the plaintiff prior to submission of the case to the jury. This question, not answered by the plain language of the statute, is: Which method for computing the amount of the General Obligations Law § 15-108(a) offset to the jury award should be adopted: (1) the case-by-case method, under which each settling defendant is taken separately and, for that defendant, the amount of the settlement or the amount of the corresponding apportioned share, whichever is higher, is deducted from the verdict; or (2) the aggregate method, in which the settling tortfeasors are viewed collectively, the settlement amounts and the corresponding apportioned shares are totaled, and the offset is allowed for the greater of the two totals.

I

Plaintiff commenced this action against 18 defendants to recover damages for wrongful death, pain and suffering and loss of consortium by reason of the death of her husband due to asbestos exposure. The trial was conducted in two stages, with the jury considering damages first and questions of liability, including apportionment of fault, second. On June 27, 1990, the jury returned a damages verdict totaling $5,867,353, later reduced by the trial court to $3,917,353. The liability phase commenced the next day, June 28, 1990.

On July 5, prior to the submission of the case to the jury, plaintiff's counsel announced in open court that settlements had been reached with various defendants, including Manville. The record contains the following colloquy:

> "*the court*: The Plaintiffs in the Didner case, *have settled at this time* with Owens Corning, Fiberboard?

> "*the court: We are going to lose Mr. Taber?*

> "*mr. gordon: Fiberboard and Pittsburgh-Corning. Eagle Pitcher [sic]*, Manville Asbestos Disease Compensation Fund, *National Gypsum, U.S. Gypsum, GAF, and Armstrong*. We are still open against Keene, H.K. Porter and Westinghouse. We are ready to proceed.

> "*the court:* We are ready to proceed with Dr. Suzuki?

> "*mr. gordon:* Yes. *For the record, we have also resolved our differences with* H.K. Porter and Southern" (emphasis added).

When the case was submitted to the jury, Keene and Westinghouse Electric Corporation (Westinghouse) were the only nonsettling defendants. The jury was asked to apportion liability pursuant to General Obligations Law § 15-108(a) among all 18 defendants — *i.e.*, the 16 settling defendants, including Manville, which were no longer participants in the trial, in addition to Keene and Westinghouse, the only defendants still in the case. On July 10, in its liability verdict, the jury apportioned fault among 13 of the 18 defendants, finding Keene responsible for 15%, Manville for 60.167%, and all other defendants responsible for the remaining 24.833% of liability.[3]

On July 23, 1990, plaintiff's counsel presented to the trial court a proposed form of order for a consent judgment to be entered against Manville. In the letter accompanying the proposed order, plaintiff's counsel stated, "[i]*n accordance with our agreement with the Manville Asbestos Disease Compensation Fund* in the above-captioned case, we enclose a proposed order awarding judgment against the Fund in the amount of $800,000" (emphasis added). The trial court signed the order memorializing the consent judgment on August 6, 1990.

On February 5, 1991, a judgment against defendant Keene was filed in the total sum of $618,452, an amount equal to 15% of the reduced total verdict plus interest. The judgment did not reflect General Obligations Law § 15-108(a) offsets for the amounts paid in settlement or the apportioned shares of the recovery for any of the settling defendants. Thereafter, defendant Keene filed objections to the judgment, contending that the court had erred in not following

---

[3] Westinghouse was exonerated by the jury which answered that it had not contributed in any degree to plaintiff's decedent's condition.

General Obligations Law § 15-108(a) and in simply basing the judgment against Keene on its apportioned share (15%) of the recovery as reduced.

In letter submissions to the court, Keene argued that the judgment should have reflected General Obligations Law § 15-108(a) offsets computed for each of the settling defendants individually on a case-by-case basis. Under this approach, for each defendant, except for Manville, the amount to be deducted would have been the amount of the agreed upon settlement because, in each case, the settlement was greater than the corresponding apportioned share. The total of the settlements for the defendants, other than Manville, is $2,500,000. For Manville, however, its apportioned share (60.167%) of the reduced recovery ($3,917,353) is $2,356,953.80, a sum in excess of the agreed upon consent judgment of $800,000. Applying Keene's proposed case-by-case method, the total of the settlements ($2,500,000) for the settling defendants exclusive of Manville, and the apportioned share for Manville ($2,356,953.80) are added together to compute the total offsets under General Obligations Law § 15-108(a) ($4,856,953.80), an amount which, if deducted from the reduced recovery ($3,917,353) would more than offset plaintiff's judgment against Keene. Keene filed a motion seeking to vacate the February 5, 1991 judgment and requested the court to enter the form of judgment it proposed using its case-by-case approach. The trial court denied this motion and adhered to the original judgment, reasoning that the Manville agreement was not a settlement within General Obligations Law § 15-108(a) because a stay order had been issued and Manville might be precluded from paying the $800,000 consent judgment.

The Appellate Division affirmed, with one Justice dissenting. *Didner*, 188 A.D.2d 15, 593 N.Y.S.2d 238, *supra*. . . .

We granted defendant Keene's motion for leave to appeal and now modify.

II

We turn first to whether the agreement between plaintiff and Manville, announced as a settlement in open court on July 5 prior to the conclusion of the case, was a settlement for purposes of General Obligations Law § 15-108(a). There can be no question that prior to the verdict the parties and the court treated the agreement with Manville as a settlement within General Obligations Law § 15-108(a). The remainder of the trial was conducted against Keene as one of two nonsettling defendants and, at its conclusion, the jury was asked to apportion fault against Manville as a settling defendant along with the other defendants which had settled and left the proceedings. The argument that the agreement with Manville did not trigger General Obligations Law § 15-108(a) depends on a literal reading of the statute as applying only when the settling tortfeasor has actually received a release in exchange for payment of the stipulated settlement sum.

In support of this construction of the statute, plaintiff points to the language in General Obligations Law § 15-108(a) which provides for a reduction of the verdict "to the extent of any amount stipulated by the release or the covenant, or in the amount of the consideration paid for it, or in the amount of the *released tortfeasor's* equitable share of the damages . . . whichever is the greatest" (General Obligations Law § 15-108[a]; emphasis added). She contends that the plain wording of the statute compels this restrictive application. We disagree. Such a literal interpretation ignores the realities of trial practice: that settlements made in open court during trial, although fully binding (*see,* CPLR 2104; *Matter of Dolgin Eldert Corp.,* 31 N.Y.2d 1, 334 N.Y.S.2d 833, 286 N.E.2d 228), are seldom formally consummated by the actual payment of the agreed sum in exchange for a release until after the trial has ended. We should not ascribe to the Legislature the intent of imposing the unreasonable requirement that the trial court must hold up the proceedings until all of the settling defendants actually have releases in hand before any effect may be given to the settlements of the defendants under General Obligations Law § 15-108(a). A construction of a statute which leads to such unreasonable result should be avoided (*see, New York State Bankers Assn. v. Albright,* 38 N.Y.2d 430, 436-437, 381 N.Y.S.2d 17, 343 N.E.2d 735; McKinney's Cons. Laws of N.Y., Book 1, Statutes § 143, and § 111, at 226 [to the effect that "the literal meanings of words are not to be adhered to or suffered to defeat the general purpose and manifest policy intended to be promoted"]).

Just as in the case of a release not delivered until after completion of the trial, the fact that plaintiff and Manville formalized their open court settlement by entering a consent judgment after the trial verdict is of no moment. As stated by the dissenting Justice at the Appellate Division: "A judgment would, of course, effectively end any action. The date of this purported 'consent judgment', again emphasized by the majority opinion, is of no importance, since the written agreement simply memorialized what had been agreed upon by the plaintiff and defendant Manville on July 5, 1990 in open court, and the settlement was effective as of that date." *Didner, supra,* 188 A.D.2d at 29, and 593 N.Y.S.2d 238 [Asch, J., dissenting]. . . .

III

The question of which method of calculating offsets under General Obligations Law § 15-108(a) for the settlement amounts or corresponding apportioned shares of the settling tortfeasors has been addressed extensively in opinions at the Appellate Division (*see* particularly, *Matter of New York City Asbestos Litig., supra*; and *Didner, supra,* 188 A.D.2d at 23-26, 593 N.Y.S.2d 238) and in Federal court (*see, In re Eastern & S. Dists. Asbestos Litig., supra,* at 1393-1397). As stated, under the aggregate approach, the verdict is reduced either by the total of the dollar amounts to be paid by the settling defendants or the total dollar amounts of their corresponding shares of the verdict, allocated in accordance with their apportioned liability, whichever is greater. Under the case-by-case approach — sometimes referred to as the "pick-and-choose" method — each settling defendant is viewed individually and the amount of the settlement for that defendant or the amount of the corresponding apportioned share of the verdict, whichever is higher, is deducted.

We agree with the conclusion reached by the above-mentioned courts that the aggregate method is preferable. It promotes the general purpose of General Obligations Law § 15-108(a) of encouraging settlements and "assuring that a nonsettling defendant does not pay more than its equitable share" (*Williams*, 81 N.Y.2d, at 443, 599 N.Y.S.2d 519, 615 N.E.2d 1003, *supra*). At the same time, it avoids the potential injustice that the case-by-case method of computing offsets can produce — *i.e.*, that a nonsettling defendant will be permitted to take advantage of the settlements of the apportioned shares of the settling defendants so as to reduce the amount that it pays below its equitable share by cutting the compensation the jury has awarded to plaintiff.

This is precisely the consequence of adopting defendant Keene's argument and applying the case-by-case method here. Keene, found by the jury to be responsible for 15% of the reduced recovery of $3,917,353, pays nothing; plaintiff, although entitled to compensation in the amount of $3,917,353, gets nothing beyond the $3,300,000, the total of the settlements including the $800,000 to be paid by Manville. Thus, we agree with the majority at the Appellate Division that: "where the verdict is reduced by either the total dollar amount of all payments received by plaintiff in return for releases or the total dollar value of the percentages of fault allocated to the settling tortfeasors, whichever aggregation is greater — is the preferable method since under such calculation defendants would not be compelled to absorb more than their equitable share of liability and plaintiffs would not obtain any windfall benefit thereby serving the statute's primary goals of encouraging settlements and preserving *Dole*'s equitable fault-sharing principles. *In re Eastern & S. Dists. Asbestos Litig., supra*, at 1393." (*Didner, supra*, 188 A.D.2d at 25, 593 N.Y.S.2d 238.)

Defendant Keene maintains, nonetheless, that the wording of General Obligations Law § 15-108(a) requires the application of the case-by-case method. This is the only permissible construction, it is argued, because the statute speaks throughout in the singular and refers to the reduction of the injured party's claim for *one settlement* when "*a release or a covenant* not to sue or not to enforce a judgment is given to one of two or more persons liable or claimed to be liable in tort for the same injury, or the same wrongful death" (General Obligations Law § 15-108[a] [emphasis added]). We find no merit in the argument. Nothing in the statute specifies how it should be applied in a case where the plaintiff, before the case is concluded, settles with two or more of the defendants. The statute simply does not address this situation. As pointed out by the Appellate Division in *New York City Asbestos Litig.* (188 A.D.2d 214, 593 N.Y.S.2d 43, *affd.* 82 N.Y.2d 821, *supra* [decided herewith]) in rejecting the same argument: "In view of the statutory [failure to address the case of settlements with multiple defendants], the courts are left to fashion an interpretation which is consistent with the object of the statute (McKinney's Cons. Laws of N.Y., Book 1, Statutes § 96), while avoiding an absurd result (McKinney's Cons. Laws of N.Y., Book 1, Statutes § 145). The particular outcome which the cases have attempted to avoid is the reduction of a nonsettling defendant's liability to an amount which represents far less than his proportionate share of fault as determined by the trier of fact," in some cases "virtually exonerating the non-settling defendant" (*id.*, at 218, 593 N.Y.S.2d 43).

Accordingly, the aggregate method of computing offsets under General Obligations Law § 15-108(a) should be used. Manville's apportioned share (60.167%) of the reduced recovery ($2,356,953.80) when added to the total of the apportioned shares of the other settling defendants ($976,047.70) makes a total of $3,333,001.50 for the apportioned shares of all the settling defendants. This sum is greater than the total of the settlements, including Manville's, which is $3,300,000. Therefore, $3,333,001.50 should be deducted from the recovery of $3,917,353 leaving the sum of $584,351.50.

NOTES

(1) The Court of Appeals resolved a related issue in *Williams v. Niske*, 81 N.Y.2d 437, 599 N.Y.S.2d 519, 615 N.E.2d 1003 (1993): How to treat the settlement of a party whose culpable share was never determined by the jury, because the issue was somehow not submitted to it. The Court held that the amount received by the plaintiff from the settlor should be deducted from the amount of the verdict and the remaining defendants' proportional shares should be applied to the verdict after the deduction. The Court noted, however, that because of the numerous possibilities that can arise in multi-defendant litigation, it is impossible to formulate a single method for reducing verdicts to account for the various settlements. In each case, the court should use the method that best furthers the broad purposes of the statute, Gen. Oblig. Law § 15-108. While the statutory purpose is to encourage settlements, it is also concerned with assuring that non-settling defendants do not pay more than their equitable share. *Williams* expressly left open the question of which party bears the burden to plead and prove the equitable share of a defendant who settled before trial.

The Court returned to the pleading burden issue in *Whalen v. Kawasaki Motors Corp., U.S.A.*, 92 N.Y.2d 288, 680 N.Y.S.2d 435, 703 N.E.2d 246 (1998), in which it held that Gen. Oblig. Law § 15-108, as an affirmative defense, must be pleaded by the party seeking its protection. Given the liberal pleading amendment practice of the CPLR, permission to amend a pleading to add the defense could be granted even after verdict, in the absence of prejudice.

Whalen also resolved another nettlesome problem concerning the relationship between the settlement set-off and comparative fault: Should the plaintiff's recovery be reduced first by his degree of fault, and then by the value of the settlement, or the reverse? The Court held that "settlement-first," rather than "fault-first," was the rule more consistent with the overall statutory scheme because it leads to a more precise allocation of loss.

(2) In *Gonzales v. Armac Industries, Inc.*, 81 N.Y.2d 1, 595 N.Y.S.2d 360, 611 N.E.2d 261 (1993), the plaintiff was injured while using a machine manufac-

tured by defendant Armac in the course of his employment with GTC. After receiving workers' compensation benefits for his injuries, plaintiff commenced a products liability action against Armac. The latter brought a third party action against GTC, seeking contribution. Before trial, plaintiff settled with Armac, which conceded liability for 2% of any damages which plaintiff might obtain from a jury. Plaintiff agreed not to enforce any judgment against Armac in excess of 2%, "except as loan arrangements may be necessary to permit the plaintiff to collect any monies from the third-party defendant in the event that there is an apportionment of liability against the third-party defendant." GTC, the employer and third-party defendant, moved to dismiss the claim against it on the ground that Armac, having settled with the plaintiff, was barred by Gen. Oblig. Law § 15-108 from pursuing claims against other tortfeasors. The Court of Appeals agreed.

Chapter 10

"SPECIAL" PARTIES: INDIGENTS, INFANTS, INCOMPETENTS AND CONSERVATEES

§ 10.01 POOR PERSONS: CPLR ARTICLE 11

PROBLEM A

David (who is represented by a Legal Aid Society lawyer) has commenced a divorce action against Lisa, accusing her of adultery. In addition to a divorce decree, he seeks custody of their two-year-old twins, as he claims Lisa is unfit by reason of "mental illness and amoral life style." As neither spouse has been able to find work for the last six months, they are living on David's unemployment insurance payments. If Lisa applies to court for an order appointing counsel for her, to be compensated by public funds, should it be granted? If either party (or both) apply for an order appointing a mental health worker to serve as an expert witness, may it be made at public expense?

In re SMILEY
Court of Appeals
36 N.Y.2d 433, 369 N.Y.S.2d 87, 330 N.E.2d 53 (1975)

BREITEL, CHIEF JUDGE.

The issue on this appeal is whether an indigent plaintiff wife in a divorce action and an indigent defendant wife in a similar action are entitled, as a matter of constitutional right, to have the County of Tompkins provide them with counsel or compensate counsel retained by them.

. . . .

The mandatory direction to provide counsel to defendants in criminal cases derives from the Federal and State cases applying Federal and State constitutional provisions. These cases recognize that the right to counsel in criminal cases means more than the right to appear by counsel, but that in the event of inability by a defendant to provide his own counsel, particularly because of indigency, the State must provide counsel. . . . The underlying principle is that when the State or Government proceeds against the individual with risk of loss of liberty or grievous forfeiture, the right to counsel and due process of law carries with it the provision of counsel if the individual charged is unable to provide it for himself. . . .

No similar constitutional or statutory provision applies to private litigation.

Inherent in the courts and historically associated with the duty of the Bar to provide uncompensated services for the indigent has been the discretionary power of the courts to assign counsel in a proper case to represent private indigent litigants. Such counsel serve without compensation. Statutes codify the inherent power of the courts (CPLR 1102, subd. [a]; *People ex rel. Acritelli v. Grout*, 87 App.Div. 193, 195-196, 84 N.Y.S. 97, 98-99, *affd. on prevailing opn. below*, 177 N.Y. 587, 70 N.E. 1105). Contrary to the statement of the Appellate Division, however, there is no absolute right to assigned counsel; whether in a particular case counsel shall be assigned lies instead in the discretion of the court. The obligation of the Bar to respond is expressed in the Code of Professional Responsibility, Judiciary Law Appendix (Canon 2, EC 2-25).

With respect to criminal actions and related matters arising in a criminal context, early in the articulation of the constitutional right to assigned counsel for indigent defendants it was anticipated that the private Bar could not carry the burden of uncompensated representation for the large numbers of defendants involved. Consequently, legislation was enacted to provide systematic representation of defendants by assigned counsel and for their compensation (*see* County Law, Consol.Laws. c. 11, art. 18-B; *see, also*, Judiciary Law, Consol. Laws, c. 30, § 35). Long before that, of course, there had been statutory provision for assigned compensated counsel in this State, but evidently only in capital cases and certain prosecutions involving imposition of a life sentence (former Code Crim.Proc., § 308).

In the several situations which arise in Family Court there are provisions for publicly-compensated counsel. These involve a mix of State and private action in proceedings affecting the liberty of persons and child custody (Family Ct. Act, §§ 245, 248, 831, 1043).

There are no similar statutory provisions to cover public provision or compensation of counsel in private litigation. Nor under the State Constitution may the courts of this State arrogate the power to appropriate and provide funds. . . . In this connection it may be observed that the State courts, in enforcement of the Federal Constitution, bypass limitations in the State Constitution, but that is not the situation in this case.

As a practical matter, representation of private litigants, too poor to retain their own lawyers, has been accomplished through the discretionary assignment of uncompensated counsel by the courts, and in more populated areas by voluntary legal aid and charitable organizations (*see, e.g., Matter of Bartlett v. Kitchin*, 76 Misc.2d 1087, 1091, 352 N.Y.S.2d 110, 114). Then, too, there are the more recent Federally-funded legal services programs for the poor (*see, generally*, Samore, *Legal Services For the Poor*, 32 Albany L.Rev. 508, 509-512).

Petitioners, on the basis of *Boddie v. Connecticut*, 401 U.S. 371, 91 S.Ct. 780, 28 L.Ed.2d 113, seek to extrapolate a constitutional principle mandating the provision and compensation of counsel in matrimonial matters. Assuming momentarily that the *Boddie* case could be so used to mandate the provision or compensation of counsel, it and the cases establishing the right to assigned counsel in criminal matters could not be used to mandate compensation by public funding. Even in expanding the criminal right to assigned counsel the courts, Federal and State, never presumed to direct the appropriation and expenditure of public funds.

The appropriation and provision of authority for the expenditure of public funds is a legislative and not a judicial function, both in the Nation and in the State. It is correlated, of course, with the taxing power (*see* N.Y.Const., art. XVI, § 1; U.S.Const., art. I, § 8, cl. 1).

But in any event the *Boddie* case (*supra*) does not support, or by rationale imply, an obligation of the State to assign, let alone compensate, counsel as a matter of constitutional right. The *Boddie* case held narrowly that because the State's regulation of marriage and divorce, in the generic sense, is an assumption of governmental power, the State could not deny access to its courts in matrimonial actions by exacting a court fee from indigent matrimonial suitors. In *Deason v. Deason*, 32 N.Y.2d 93, 343 N.Y.S.2d 321, 296 N.E.2d 229, this court extended the *Boddie* rationale to apply to the State's requirement that in certain circumstances costly service by publication of process could not be imposed as a precondition to an indigent bringing a matrimonial action. It was thus held that, under the constitutional principles articulated in the *Boddie* case, the State or its subdivisions would be required to pay the cost of such access to the courts, if such costly service of process were the only alternative.

On no view of the matter is counsel required in a matrimonial action as a condition to access to the court. Of course, counsel is always desirable, and in complicated matrimonial litigation would be essential. But however desirable or necessary, representation by counsel is not a legal condition to access to the courts (*see, generally*, Note, *A First Amendment Right of Access to the Courts for Indigents*, 82 Yale L.J. 1055, 1066-1067). Access to the courts was the only problem to which the *Boddie* and *Deason* cases were addressed.

Of course, the indigent matrimonial litigant is not without practical recourse. The need of counsel for the indigent has been and is still being handled in large measure in populated communities by legal aid, Federally-funded legal services programs, and voluntary organizations. Thus in the City of New York the Legal Aid Society, and other legal services agencies, handle annually a large number of matrimonial cases. The slack and conflict-of-interest problems are taken up by the discretionary assignment of uncompensated counsel under CPLR 1102 (subd. [a]). Moreover, because of the court's power in matrimonial cases to allow counsel fees in favor of the wife against the husband, and the availability of conditional fee arrangements, matrimonial litigation to be "unprofitable" to fee-charging lawyers must generally involve both spouses being indigent.

There is still another aspect to the matter. As in so many things it is the existence of assets or income which creates complications, and so it does in matrimonial litigation. Hence, in the absence of disputes over money or the custody of children, matrimonial litigation is likely to be quite simple, and if a lawyer is required, his task quite simple.

None of this is to say that the need and burden of representing indigent matrimonial suitors will not currently overtax voluntary private resources and the voluntary services available from the Bar on a noncompensated basis. The need and burden may become even greater in the future, especially with liberalized divorce laws. All of this, however, is a problem to be addressed to the Legislature which has the power to appropriate the funds required for publicly-compensated counsel.

It merits added comment that among the many kinds of private litigation which may drastically affect indigent litigants, matrimonial litigation is but one. Eviction from homes, revocation of licenses affecting one's livelihood, mortgage foreclosures, repossession of important assets purchased on credit, and any litigation which may result in the garnishment of income may be significant and ruinous for an otherwise indigent litigant. In short, the problem is not peculiar to matrimonial litigation. The horizon does not stop at matrimonial or any other species of private litigation.

As exemplified in some areas in the State, the undue burden which may be placed on the private Bar by assignments under CPLR 1102, may also become intolerable and some might say rank as a violation of the constitutional rights of lawyers. . . .

Lastly, it would be injudicious, as some have suggested, to mandate in all matrimonial cases involving indigents the assignment of counsel without the possibility of provision for compensation. It might then be unfair to the Bar to impose such a burden on them. Inevitably too, the availability of mandated assigned counsel might very well increase the litigation in any one area, as it has indeed in the criminal area not only as to trials but as to appeals as well. All of this suggests questions of policy and fiscal impact which the courts should not venture to decide, even if they had the power, which they do not.

In the meantime, courts and litigants must make do with what exists and with what lies within the powers and capacity of the courts and the Bar. The courts have a broad discretionary power to assign counsel without compensation in a proper case (CPLR 1102, subd. [a]; *see also, People ex rel. Acritelli v. Grout*, 87 App.Div. 193, 195-196, 84 N.Y.S. 97, 98-99, *affd. on prevailing opn. below* 177 N.Y. 587, 70 N.E. 1105, *supra*). Voluntary organizations and Federally-funded programs play their role. As for the Bar they follow, as they are obliged to do, the canons of their profession in performing obligations to the indigent and duties imposed by assignment of the courts. If more is required, the relief must be provided by the Legislature. The fundamental is that the courts constitute but one branch of government. The absence of appropriated funds and legislation to raise taxes under our State constitutional system, as in the rest of the Union, is not a judicially-fillable gap.

. . . .

FUCHSBERG, JUDGE (dissenting).

Though I agree generally with the result urged by my fellow dissenting Judges,[*] I would offer certain specific suggestions that I think the courts should take into account in assigning counsel in these cases.

. . . .

II

Since the decision in *Gideon v. Wainwright*, 372 U.S. 335, 83 S.Ct. 792, 9 L.Ed.2d 799, holding that a person has a constitutional right to be supplied with counsel when his or her liberty is threatened in a felony proceeding, the law has been confronted with *Gideon*'s implications for proceedings denominated as "civil" in which fundamental interests no less important than freedom from incarceration are threatened. These varieties of civil litigation include several areas in which personal liberty is very much at stake: habeas corpus actions, child custody cases, parole revocation proceedings, juvenile hearings, civil commitment suits, and other matters in which "certain nominally civil causes can result in a severe deprivation of liberty." (Note, *The Right to Counsel in Civil Litigation*, 66 Col.L.Rev. 1322, 1332.)

Boddie v. Connecticut, 401 U.S. 371, 91 S.Ct. 780, 28 L.Ed.2d 113, confirmed the importance of the personal interests at stake in divorce proceedings and held that the opportunity to be heard in such cases is an essential safeguard to the personal liberty of the parties. The State, through its courts, lawfully monopolizes the right to dissolve marriages; without such dissolution of the marriage contract, citizens are locked into untenable marriages permanently, and "more fundamentally [are confronted with] the prohibition against remarriage" (p. 376, 91 S.Ct. p. 785). New York recognizes that where marriage relationships are threatened by serious incompatibility (Domestic Relations Law, Consol.Laws, c. 14, § 170, subd. [6]), or, even more seriously, by such factors as adultery or cruel and inhuman treatment (Domestic Relations Law, § 170, subds. [1], [4]), the courts should be available to release the parties from matrimony and to resolve ancillary disputes involving property, support, and custody.

In *Boddie*, only the question of filing fees was at issue. The court held that, because indigents have a constitutional right to access to the courts for divorce litigation, States must allow them to file such cases without payment of the fees. But the principle of *Boddie* goes far beyond filing fees; the case stands for the proposition that people may not be denied the right to obtain a divorce solely on the ground of indigency.

That *all* real economic barriers to court access in divorce cases must fall is made clear by our decision in *Deason v. Deason*, 32 N.Y.2d 93, 343 N.Y.S.2d 321, 296 N.E.2d 229, holding that the printing cost of service by publication could not stand as an obstacle to an indigent seeking a divorce. Though *Deason* involved

---

[*] Judges Jones and Wachtler also dissented. — Eds.

payment of expenses to a third party rather than to the court system itself, "The effect of indigency is . . . the same . . . denial of access to the courts" (p. 95, 343 N.Y.S.2d p. 322, 296 N.E.2d p. 230).

Is denial of the right to counsel a real barrier to access to court for litigants, either in civil cases generally or in divorce actions in particular? Unfortunately, in our complex society, it is. As Mr. Justice Sutherland said in *Powell v. Alabama*, "The right to be heard would be, in many cases, of little avail if it did not comprehend the right to be heard by counsel. Even the intelligent and educated layman has small and sometimes no skill in the science of law."[2] (287 U.S. 45, 68-69, 53 S.Ct. 55, 64, 77 L. Ed. 158.) . . .

With this in mind, courts have recently been applying the reasoning of *Gideon v. Wainwright*, 372 U.S. 335, 83 S.Ct. 792, 9 L.Ed.2d 799, *supra*, to some "civil" matters where important issues of liberty or property were at stake. For instance, in *Matter of Ella B.*, 30 N.Y.2d 352, 334 N.Y.S.2d 133, 285 N.E.2d 288, our court ruled that an indigent parent, threatened in a neglect proceeding with termination of the right to custody of a minor child, had the right to be provided with counsel. Similarly, it was held in *People ex rel. Rogers v. Stanley*, 17 N.Y.2d 256, 270 N.Y.S.2d 573, 217 N.E.2d 636, that indigent mental patients have a constitutional right to be given counsel to challenge by habeas corpus their commitment to an institution. And in *People ex rel. Menechino v. Warden*, 27 N.Y.2d 376, 318 N.Y.S.2d 449, 267 N.E.2d 238, we determined that the due process clause of the State Constitution requires that counsel be given to an indigent parolee at the final hearing on revocation of his parole, a principle recently affirmed in *People ex rel. Calloway v. Skinner*, 33 N.Y.2d 23, 347 N.Y.S.2d 178, 300 N.E.2d 716.

. . . .

Nor does the need or should the right of all citizens to counsel stop here. As Learned Hand put it, "If we are to keep our democracy, there must be one commandment: Thou shalt not ration justice." So I most respectfully take issue with my fellow dissenters when they suggest a clear distinction between the right of indigents to be represented by counsel in litigation seeking the dissolution of a marriage as opposed to other types of civil litigation. Rather on that matter I stand with the majority when it says "the problem is not peculiar to matrimonial litigation. The horizon does not stop at matrimonial or any other species of private litigation."

However, it is one thing to state that the denial of counsel is an obstruction to access to courts in the civil litigation of matters of consequence to people generally, and another to apply that principle to divorce actions in particular. Therefore, a closer examination of divorce litigation is necessary to determine whether lack of counsel is a genuine obstacle in such cases.

---

[2] While there is, of course, no precise correlation between a person's level of affluence and his level of education, on a statistical basis low income persons are likely to be those least prepared by their own educational background to litigate actions pro se.

In the State of New York, many divorce cases are extremely simple. In a very large percentage of divorces involving indigents, there exists no legal dispute whatsoever; the court performs an essentially ministerial function either because the parties have executed and complied with a one-year separation agreement under subdivision (6) of section 170 of the Domestic Relations Law, or because the parties have agreed to a dissolution on grounds of cruelty, and one party appears in court to give summary unchallenged testimony of abuse. In such divorces, it is probable that many uncounseled litigants would be able to process the litigation by themselves, perhaps with the assistance of Bar-approved manuals for the layman or of trained paraprofessionals, or with the aid of court clerks who, aware of the shortage of legal services for the poor, are usually extremely helpful in explaining procedures to unrepresented parties, and should be encouraged to assist them.

In addition, a substantial number of contested divorces involve no disagreement about the decision to end the marriage, but only difficulty in resolving issues of custody or support. Even where custody and support are initially contested, the Supreme Court may refer those ancillary services to the Family Court, whose mediation services may resolve the dispute without requiring counsel. (Family Ct. Act §§ 464, 652, 424, 425.)

But indigents are also parties to divorces where the dissolution of the marriage itself is contested, or where issues of custody and support are not capable of informal mediation. In such cases, if the spouses ultimately disagree about any of these three issues — ending the marriage, support of a spouse, or custody and child support — in my view, the assistance of counsel is essential, because lay persons are generally incapable of effectively meeting their legal burdens where such issues are disputed. . . .

LASSITER v. DEPARTMENT OF SOCIAL SERVICES
United States Supreme Court
452 U.S. 18, 101 S. Ct. 2153, 68 L. Ed. 2d 640 (1981)

JUSTICE STEWART delivered the opinion of the Court.

I

In the late Spring of 1975, after hearing evidence that the petitioner, Abby Gail Lassiter, had not provided her infant son William with proper medical care, the District Court of Durham County, N.C., adjudicated him a neglected child and transferred him to the custody of the Durham County Department of Social Services, the respondent here. A year later, Ms. Lassiter was charged with first-degree murder, was convicted of second-degree murder, and began a sentence of 25 to 40 years of imprisonment. In 1978 the Department petitioned the court to terminate Ms. Lassiter's parental rights because, the Department alleged, she "has not had any contact with the child since December of 1975" and "has willfully left the child in foster care for more than two consecutive years without showing that substantial progress has been made in correcting the conditions which led to the removal of the child, or without showing a positive response to the diligent efforts of the Department of Social Services to strengthen her relationship to the child, or to make and follow through with constructive planning for the future of the child."

Ms. Lassiter was served with the petition and with notice that a hearing on it would be held. Although her mother had retained counsel for her in connection with an effort to invalidate the murder conviction, Ms. Lassiter never mentioned the forthcoming hearing to him (or, for that matter, to any other person except, she said, to "someone" in the prison). At the behest of the Department of Social Services' attorney, she was brought from prison to the hearing, which was held August 31, 1978. The hearing opened, apparently at the judge's insistence, with a discussion of whether Ms. Lassiter should have more time in which to find legal assistance. Since the court concluded that she "has had ample opportunity to seek and obtain counsel prior to the hearing of this matter, and [that] her failure to do so is without just cause," the court did not postpone the proceedings. Ms. Lassiter did not aver that she was indigent, and the court did not appoint counsel for her.

A social worker from the respondent Department was the first witness. She testified that in 1975 the Department "received a complaint from Duke Pediatrics that William had not been followed in the pediatric clinic for medical problems and that they were having difficulty in locating Ms. Lassiter. . . ."

After the direct examination of the social worker, the judge said:

> I notice we made extensive findings in June of '75 that you were served with papers and called the social services and told them you weren't coming; and the serious lack of medical treatment. And, as I have said in my findings of the 16th day of June '75, the Court finds that the grandmother, Ms. Lucille Lassiter, mother of Abby Gail Lassiter, filed a complaint on the 8th day of May, 1975, alleging that the daughter often left the children, Candina, Felicia and William L. with her for days without providing money or food while she was gone.

Ms. Lassiter conducted a cross-examination of the social worker, who firmly reiterated her earlier testimony. The judge explained several times, with varying degrees of clarity, that Ms. Lassiter should only ask questions at this stage; many of her questions were disallowed because they were not really questions, but arguments.

Ms. Lassiter herself then testified, under the judge's questioning, that she had properly cared for William. Under cross-examination, she said that she had seen William more than five or six times after he had been taken from her custody and that, if William could not be with her, she wanted him to be with her mother since "He knows us. Children know they family. . . . They know they people, they know they family and that child knows us anywhere. . . . I got four more other children. Three girls and a boy and they know they little brother when they see him."

. . . .

The court found that Ms. Lassiter "has not contacted the Department of Social Services about her child since December 1975, has not expressed any concern for his care and welfare, and has made no efforts to plan for his future." Because Ms. Lassiter thus had "wilfully failed to maintain concern or responsibility for the welfare of the minor," and because it was "in the best interests of the minor," the court terminated Ms. Lassiter's status as William's parent.

On appeal, Ms. Lassiter argued only that, because she was indigent, the Due Process Clause of the Fourteenth Amendment entitled her to the assistance of counsel, and that the trial court had therefore erred in not requiring the State to provide counsel for her. . . .

II

For all its consequence, "due process" has never been, and perhaps can never be, precisely defined. "Unlike some legal rules," this Court has said, due process "is not a technical conception with a fixed content unrelated to time, place and circumstances." *Cafeteria Workers v. McElroy*, 367 U.S. 886, 895, 81 S.Ct. 1743, 1748, 6 L.Ed.2d 1230. Rather, the phrase expresses the requirement of "fundamental fairness," a requirement whose meaning can be as opaque as its importance is lofty. Applying the Due Process Clause is therefore an uncertain enterprise which must discover what "fundamental fairness" consists of in a particular situation by first considering any relevant precedents and then by assessing the several interests that are at stake.

A

The pre-eminent generalization that emerges from this Court's precedents on an indigent's right to appointed counsel is that such a right has been recognized to exist only where the litigant may lose his physical liberty if he loses the litigation. . . .

That it is the defendant's interest in personal freedom, and not simply the special Sixth and Fourteenth Amendments right to counsel in criminal cases, which triggers the right to appointed counsel is demonstrated by the Court's announcement in *In re Gault*, 387 U.S. 1, 87 S.Ct. 1428, 18 L.Ed.2d 527, that "the Due Process Clause of the Fourteenth Amendment requires that in respect of proceedings to determine delinquency *which may result in commitment to an institution in which the juvenile's freedom is curtailed*," the juvenile has a right to appointed counsel even though those proceedings may be styled "civil" and not "criminal." *Id.*, at 41, 87 S.Ct., at 1451 (emphasis added). Similarly, four of the five Justices who reached the merits in *Vitek v. Jones*, 445 U.S. 480, 100 S.Ct. 1254, 63 L.Ed.2d 552, concluded that an indigent prisoner is entitled to appointed counsel before being involuntarily transferred for treatment to a state mental hospital. The fifth Justice differed from the other four only in declining to exclude the "possibility that the required assistance may be rendered by a competent layman in some cases." *Id.*, at 500, 100 S.Ct., at 1267 (separate opinion of Powell, J.).

Significantly, as a litigant's interest in personal liberty diminishes, so does his right to appointed counsel. In *Gagnon v. Scarpelli*, 411 U.S. 778, 93 S.Ct. 1756, 36 L.Ed.2d 656, the Court gauged the due process rights of a previously sentenced probationer at a probation-revocation hearing. In *Morrissey v. Brewer*, 408 U.S. 471, 480, 92 S.Ct. 2593, 2599, 33 L.Ed.2d 484, which involved an analogous hearing to revoke parole, the Court had said: "Revocation deprives an individual, not of the absolute liberty to which every citizen is entitled, but only of the conditional liberty properly dependent on observance of special parole restrictions." Relying on that discussion, the Court in *Scarpelli* declined to hold that indigent probationers have, per se, a right to counsel at revocation hearings, and instead left the decision whether counsel should be appointed to be made on a case-by-case basis.

Finally, the Court has refused to extend the right to appointed counsel to include prosecutions which, though criminal, do not result in the defendant's loss of personal liberty. . . . *Scott v. Illinois*, 440 U.S. 367, 99 S.Ct. 1158, 59 L.Ed.2d 383. . . .

In sum, the Court's precedents speak with one voice about what "fundamental fairness" has meant when the Court has considered the right to appointed counsel, and we thus draw from them the presumption that an indigent litigant has a right to appointed counsel only when, if he loses, he may be deprived of his physical liberty. It is against this presumption that all the other elements in the due process decision must be measured.

B

The case of *Mathews v. Eldridge*, 424 U.S. 319, 335, 96 S.Ct. 893, 903, 47 L.Ed.2d 18, propounds three elements to be evaluated in deciding what due process requires, viz., the private interests at stake, the government's interest, and the risk that the procedures used will lead to erroneous decisions. We must balance these elements against each other, and then set their net weight in the scales against the presumption that there is a right to appointed counsel only where the indigent, if he is unsuccessful, may lose his personal freedom.

This Court's decisions have by now made plain beyond the need for multiple citation that a parent's desire for and right to "the companionship, care, custody and management of his or her children" is an important interest that "undeniably warrants deference and, absent a powerful countervailing interest, protection." *Stanley v. Illinois*, 405 U.S. 645, 651, 92 S.Ct. 1208, 1212, 31 L.Ed. 551. Here the State has sought not simply to infringe upon that interest but to end it. If the State prevails, it will have worked a unique kind of deprivation. *Cf. May v. Anderson*, 345 U.S. 528, 533, 73 S.Ct. 840, 843, 97 L.Ed. 1221; *Armstrong v. Manzo*, 380 U.S. 545, 85 S.Ct. 1187, 14 L.Ed.2d 62. A parent's interest in the accuracy and injustice of the decision to terminate his or her parental status is, therefore, a commanding one.[3]

---

[3] Some parents will have an additional interest to protect. Petitions to terminate parental rights are not uncommonly based on alleged criminal activity. Parents so accused may need legal counsel to guide them in understanding the problems such petitions may create.

Since the State has an urgent interest in the welfare of the child, it shares the parent's interest in an accurate and just decision. For this reason, the State may share the indigent parent's interest in the availability of appointed counsel. If, as our adversary system presupposes, accurate and just results are most likely to be obtained through the equal contest of opposed interests, the State's interest in the child's welfare may perhaps best be served by a hearing in which both the parent and the State acting for the child are represented by counsel, without whom the contest of interests may become unwholesomely unequal. North Carolina itself acknowledges as much by providing that where a parent files a written answer to a termination petition, the State must supply a lawyer to represent the child. N.C.G.S. § 7A-289.29.

The State's interests, however, clearly diverge from the parent's insofar as the State wishes the termination decision to be made as economically as possible and thus wants to avoid both the expense of appointed counsel and the cost of the lengthened proceedings his presence may cause. But though the State's pecuniary interest is legitimate, it is hardly significant enough to overcome private interests as important as those here, particularly in light of the concession in the respondent's brief that the "potential costs of appointed counsel in termination proceedings . . . is [sic] admittedly de minimis compared to the costs in all criminal actions."

Finally, consideration must be given to the risk that a parent will be erroneously deprived of his or her child because the parent is not represented by counsel. North Carolina law now seeks to assure accurate decisions by establishing the following procedures: A petition to terminate parental rights may be filed only by a parent seeking the termination of the other parent's rights, by a county department of social services or licensed child-placing agency with custody of the child, or by a person with whom the child has lived continuously for the two years preceding the petition. N.C.G.S. § 7A-289.24. A petition must describe facts sufficient to warrant a finding that one of the grounds for termination exists, N.S.G.S. § 7A-289.25(6), and the parent must be notified of the petition and given 30 days in which to file a written answer to it, N.S.G.S. § 7A-289.27. If that answer denies a material allegation, the court must, as has been noted, appoint a lawyer as the child's guardian ad litem and must conduct a special hearing to resolve the issues raised by the petition and the answer. N.C.G.S. § 7A-289.29. If the parent files no answer, "the court shall issue an order terminating all parental and custodial rights . . .; provided the court shall order a hearing on the petition and may examine the petitioner or others on the facts alleged in the petition." N.C.G.S. § 7A-289.28. Findings of fact are made by a court sitting without a jury and must "be based on clear, cogent, and convincing evidence." N.C.G.S. § 7A-289.30. Any party may appeal who gives notice of appeal within 10 days after the hearing. N.C.G.S. § 7A-289.34.

The respondent argues that the subject of a termination hearing — the parent's relationship with her child — far from being abstruse, technical, or unfamiliar, is one as to which the parent must be uniquely well informed and to which the parent must have given prolonged thought. The respondent also contends that a termination hearing is not likely to produce difficult points of evidentiary law, or even of substantive law, since the evidentiary problems peculiar to criminal trials are not present and since the standards for termination are not complicated. In fact, the respondent reports, the North Carolina Departments of Social Services are themselves sometimes represented at termination hearings by social workers instead of by lawyers.[5]

Yet the ultimate issues with which a termination hearing deals are not always simple, however commonplace they may be. Expert medical and psychiatric testimony, which few parents are equipped to understand and fewer still to confute, is sometimes presented. The parents are likely to be people with little education, who have had uncommon difficulty in dealing with life, and who are, at the hearing, thrust into a distressing and disorienting situation. That these factors may combine to overwhelm an uncounselled parent is evident from the findings some courts have made. *See, e.g. Davis v. Page*, 442 F.Supp. 258, 261 (D.C.Fla.); *Oregon v. Jamison*, 444 P.2d 15, 17 (Or.1968). Thus, courts have generally held that the State must appoint counsel for indigent parents at termination proceedings. *State ex rel. Heller v. Miller*, 61 Ohio St.2d 6, 399 N.E.2d 66 (1980); *Dept. of Public Welfare v. J.K.B.*, 393 N.E.2d 406 (Mass. 1979); *Matter of Chad S.*, 580 P.2d 983 (Okl. Sup.Ct.1978); *In re Myricks*, 85 Wash.P.2d 252, 533 P.2d 841 (1975); *Crist v. Division of Youth and Family Services*, 128 N.J.Super. 402, 320 A.2d 203 (N.J.Super.Ct. 1974); *Danforth v. Maine Dept. of Health and Welfare*, 303 A.2d 794 (Me.Sup.Ct. 1973); *In re Freisz*, 190 Neb. 347, 208 N.W.2d 259 (1973).[6] The respondent is able to point to no presently authoritative case, except for the North Carolina judgment now before us, holding that an indigent parent has no due process right to appointed counsel in termination proceedings.

C

The dispositive question, which must now be addressed, is whether the three *Eldridge* factors, when weighed against the presumption that there is no right to appointed counsel in the absence of at least a potential deprivation of physical liberty, suffice to rebut that presumption and thus to lead to the conclusion that the Due Process Clause requires the appointment of counsel when a State

---

[5] Both the respondent and the Columbia Journal of Law and Social Problems, 4 Colum.J.L. Soc.Prob. 230 (1968), have conducted surveys purporting to reveal whether the presence of counsel reduces the number of erroneous determinations in parental-termination proceedings. Unfortunately, neither survey goes beyond presenting statistics which, standing alone, are unilluminating. The Journal note does, however, report that it questioned the New York family-court judges who preside over parental-termination hearings and found that 72.2% of them agreed that when a parent is unrepresented, it becomes more difficult to conduct a fair hearing (11.1% of the judges disagreed); 66.7% thought it became difficult to develop the facts (22.2% disagreed).

[6] A number of courts have held that indigent parents have a right to appointed counsel in child dependency or neglect hearings as well. *E.g., Davis v. Page*, 640 F.2d 599 (5th Cir.) (en banc); *Cleaver v. Wilcox*, 499 F.2d 940 (9th Cir.) (right to be decided case by case); *Smith v. Edmisten*, 431 F.Supp. 941 (W.D. Tenn.1977).

seeks to terminate an indigent's parental status. To summarize the above discussion of the *Eldridge* factors: the parent's interest is an extremely important one (and may be supplemented by the dangers of criminal liability inherent in some termination proceedings); the State shares with the parent an interest in a correct decision, has a relatively weak pecuniary interest, and, in some but not all cases, has a possibly stronger interest in informal procedures; and the complexity of the proceeding and the incapacity of the uncounselled parent could be, but would not always be, great enough to make the risk of an erroneous deprivation of the parent's rights insupportably high.

If, in a given case, the parent's interests were at their strongest, the State's interests were at their weakest, and the risks of error were at their peak, it could not be said that the *Eldridge* factors did not overcome the presumption against the right to appointed counsel, and that due process did not therefore require the appointment of counsel. But since the *Eldridge* factors will not always be so distributed, and since "due process is not so rigid as to require that the significant interests in informality, flexibility and economy must always be sacrificed," *Gagnon v. Scarpelli, supra*, 411 U.S., at 788, 93 S.Ct., at 1762, neither can we say that the Constitution requires the appointment of counsel in every parental termination proceeding. We therefore adopt the standard found appropriate in *Gagnon v. Scarpelli*, and leave the decision whether due process calls for the appointment of counsel for indigent parents in termination proceedings to be answered in the first instance by the trial court, subject, of course, to appellate review. *See, e.g., Wood v. Georgia*, 450 U.S. 261, 101 S.Ct. 1097, 67 L.Ed.2d 220.

III

Here, as in *Scarpelli*, "[i]t is neither possible nor prudent to attempt to formulate a precise and detailed set of guidelines to be followed in determining when the providing of counsel is necessary to meet the applicable due process requirements," since here, as in that case, "[t]he facts and circumstances . . . are susceptible of almost infinite variation. . . ." *Supra*, 411 U.S., at 788, 93 S.Ct., at 1762. Nevertheless, because child-custody litigation must be concluded as rapidly as is consistent with fairness,[7] we decide today whether the trial judge denied Ms. Lassiter due process of law when he did not appoint counsel for her.

The respondent represents that the petition to terminate Ms. Lassiter's parental rights contained no allegations of neglect or abuse upon which criminal charges could be based, and hence Ms. Lassiter could not well have argued that she required counsel for that reason. The Department of Social Services was represented at the hearing by counsel, but no expert witnesses testified and the case presented no specially troublesome points of law, either procedural or substantive. While hearsay evidence was no doubt admitted, and while Ms.

---

[7] According to the respondent's brief, William Lassiter is now living "in a preadoptive home with foster parents committed for formal adoption to become his legal parents." He cannot be legally adopted, nor can his status otherwise be finally clarified, until this litigation ends.

Lassiter no doubt left incomplete her defense that the Department had not adequately assisted her in rekindling her interest in her son, the weight of the evidence that she had few sparks of such interest was sufficiently great that the presence of counsel for Ms. Lassiter could not have made a determinative difference. True, a lawyer might have done more with the argument that William should live with Ms. Lassiter's mother — but that argument was quite explicitly made by both Lassiters, and the evidence that the elder Ms. Lassiter had said she could not handle another child, that the social worker's investigation had led to a similar conclusion, and that the grandmother had displayed scant interest in the child once he had been removed from her daughter's custody was, though controverted, sufficiently substantial that the absence of counsel's guidance on this point did not render the proceedings fundamentally unfair. Finally, a court deciding whether due process requires the appointment of counsel need not ignore a parent's plain demonstration that she is not interested in attending a hearing. Here, the trial court had previously found that Ms. Lassiter had expressly declined to appear at the 1975 child custody hearing, Ms. Lassiter had not even bothered to speak to her retained lawyer after being notified of the termination hearing, and the court specifically found that Ms. Lassiter's failure to make an effort to contest the termination proceeding was without cause. In view of all these circumstances, we hold that the trial court did not err in failing to appoint counsel for Ms. Lassiter.

IV

In its Fourteenth Amendment, our Constitution imposes on the States the standards necessary to ensure that judicial proceedings are fundamentally fair. A wise public policy, however, may require that higher standards be adopted than those minimally tolerable under the Constitution. Informed opinion has clearly come to hold that an indigent parent is entitled to the assistance of appointed counsel not only in parental termination proceedings, but in dependency and neglect proceedings as well. IJI-ABA Juvenile Justice Standards Project, Standards Relating to Counsel for Private Parties, Standard 2.3(b) (1980); Uniform Juvenile Court Act, § 26(a) (Uniform Laws Ann.1979); National Council on Crime and Delinquency, Model Rules for Juvenile Courts, Rule 39 (1969); U.S. Dept. of HEW, Children's Bureau, Legislative Guide for Drafting Family and Juvenile Court Acts, § 25(b) (1969); U.S. Dept. of HEW, Children's Bureau, Legislative Guides for the Termination of Parental Rights and Responsibilities and the Adoption of Children, Pt. II, § 8 (1961); National Council on Crime and Delinquency, Standard Juvenile Court Act, § 19 (6th ed. 1959). Most significantly, 33 States and the District of Columbia provide statutorily for the appointment of counsel in termination cases. The Court's opinion today in no way implies that the standards increasingly urged by informed public opinion and now widely followed by the States are other than enlightened and wise.

For the reasons stated in this opinion, the judgment is affirmed.

NOTES

(1) Should the New York courts deny the appointment of counsel at state expense in matrimonial cases pursuant to *In re Smiley, supra,* after *Lassiter v. Department of Social Services? See Taylor v. Taylor,* N.Y.L.J., May 10, 1991, page 22 col. 2 (Sup. Ct.) (the defendant-husband in a divorce action was impecunious and asked for court appointment of counsel; although finding that such appointment could be compelled at state expense, the court declined to do so and instead appointed an attorney who had agreed to serve without compensation). *See also* Chase, *Assigned Counsel in Civil Cases,* N.Y.L.J., July 27, 1982, p. 1, col. 1 (argues that *Lassiter* requires a case-by-case evaluation of the need for counsel when custody of children is in dispute and requires appointment at public expense in certain cases).

How significant for constitutional analysis is it that Ms. Lassiter's parental rights were subject to absolute termination? Does this distinguish a custody dispute between divorcing parents?

The Court of Appeals has relied on *Lassiter* in a related context. *See In re St. Luke's Hosp. Center (Marie H.),* 89 N.Y.2d 889, 653 N.Y.S.2d 257, 675 N.E.2d 1209 (1996) (petitioner was entitled to counsel at government expense because her constitutionally protected liberty interests were at stake when a proceeding was brought to appoint a guardian for the purpose of transferring her to a nursing home and making major medical decisions without her consent) (alternate ground).

(2) Does the threat of homelessness following the eviction of a poor person require, as a Constitutional matter, the provision of free counsel for indigent tenants? *See* Scherer, Gideon's *Shelter — The Need to Recognize a Right to Counsel for Indigent Defendants in Eviction Proceedings,* 23 Harvard C.R.-C.L. L. Rev. 557 (1988). Suggesting a negative answer is *Ortwein v. Schwab,* 410 U.S. 656, 93 S. Ct. 1172, 35 L. Ed. 2d 572 (1973) (no right to counsel for an indigent person who sought court review of an agency determination to reduce welfare benefits).

(3) In New York, the right to counsel in some kinds of civil litigation has been enacted into statute. *See, e.g.,* Family Ct. Act § 262; Mental Hygiene Law § 81.10(f). Family Court Act § 262, which grants counsel in a wide variety of custody cases, was interpreted expansively in *Borkowski v. Borkowski,* 90 Misc. 2d 957, 396 N.Y.S.2d 962, 963-65 (1977). The court held that § 262 not only provided counsel in Family Court, but that it also should be read as providing counsel for divorce cases in which custody was at issue since "clearly [the] Supreme Court may exercise every power of the Family Court." *Borkowski,* 90 Misc. 2d at 958, 396 N.Y.S.2d at 963.

(4) The question of effective access to the courts for the poor has arisen in areas of concern other than availability of counsel. *See* Note, *In Forma Pauperis Litigants: Witness Fees and Expenses in Civil Actions,* 53 Fordham L. Rev. 1461

(1985). CPLR § 1102 addresses availability of stenographic transcripts and other costs and fees. Here, too, there is a Constitutional ingredient. In *Little v. Streater*, 452 U.S. 1, 101 S. Ct. 2202, 68 L. Ed. 2d 627 (1981), a paternity proceeding, the trial court granted the putative father's motion for blood grouping tests, but denied his request that they be furnished at state expense. Though the tests were never made because the defendant could not afford them, the trial court found him to be the legal father. After commenting on the extensive state involvement in the case, the Supreme Court reversed, noting:

> [T]he defendant in a Connecticut paternity action faces an unusual evidentiary obstacle. . . . If the plaintiff has been "constant" in her accusation of paternity, the defendant carries the burden of proof and faces severe penalties if he does not meet that burden. . . . Among the most probative additional evidence the defendant might offer are the results of blood grouping tests, but if he is indigent, the State essentially denies him the reliable scientific proof by requiring that he bear its cost. . . .

> Apart from the putative father's pecuniary interest in avoiding a substantial support obligation and liberty interest threatened by the possible sanctions for noncompliance, at issue is the creation of a parent-child relationship. . . . Just as termination of such bonds demands procedural fairness, *see Lassiter v. Department of Social Services*, 452 U.S. 18, 101 S.Ct. 2153 (1981), so too does their imposition. . . .

> Given the usual absence of witnesses, the self interest coloring the testimony of the litigants, and the State's onerous evidentiary rule and refusal to pay for blood grouping tests, the risk is not inconsiderable that an indigent defendant . . . will be erroneously adjudged the father of the child. . . . [T]he availability of scientific blood tests clearly would be a valuable procedural safeguard. . . .

> The State admittedly has a legitimate interest in the welfare of a child born out of wedlock who is receiving public assistance as well as in securing support for the child. . . . [T]he State also . . . wishes to have paternity actions . . . proceed as economically as possible. . . . We must conclude the State's monetary interest "is hardly significant enough to overcome private interests as important as those here." *Id.* at 28, 101 S.Ct. at 2160. . . .

> Without aid in obtaining blood test evidence in a paternity case, an indigent defendant, who faces the State as an adversary . . . [and] who must overcome the evidentiary burden Connecticut imposes, lacks "a meaningful opportunity to be heard." *Boddie v Connecticut*, [401 U.S. 371, 377 (1971)]. Therefore, "the requirement of fundamental fairness" expressed by the Due Process Clause was not satisfied here.

Little v. Streater, 452 U.S. at 10-16, 101 S. Ct. at 2207-22, 68 L. Ed. 2d at 635-39 (1981).

In another case involving family relations, the Supreme Court held that the state was required to provide a free transcript to a poor person who wished to appeal an order terminating her maternal rights. *M.L.B v. S.L.J.*, 519 U.S. 102, 117 S. Ct. 555, 136 L. Ed. 2d 473 (1996). Justice Ginsburg's Opinion for the Court noted that the denial of the appeal raised equal protection as well as due process concerns. Although, as the opinion notes, there is no general due process right to an appeal, a state that allows appeals may not condition their availability on the ability to afford it, at least when important constitutional rights are at stake.

(5) Who is a poor person for the purposes of Article 11 and related Constitutional rights? *See* CPLR 1101(a), which sets forth the facts and documentation necessary to allow the court to make the determination, but does not specify an absolute monetary standard. CPLR 1101(e) simplifies matters. It provides that fees and costs related to the filing and service of process are waived for a party represented by a legal aid or like organization, provided that the attorney files a certificate stating that the person is unable to pay the costs, fees and expenses necessary to prosecute the action. Moreover, CPLR 1101(d) allows an indigent plaintiff to obtain an index number without payment of the required fee by filing an affidavit attesting to his or her inability to pay. If other litigation assistance is sought, such as a stenographic transcript of the trial for the purposes of an appeal, the courts make individualized determinations. *See, e.g., Mina v. Mina*, 83 A.D.2d 776, 443 N.Y.S.2d 471 (4th Dep't 1981).

§ 10.02 INFANTS, INCOMPETENTS AND CONSERVATEES: CPLR ARTICLE 12

BARONE v. COX
Appellate Division, Fourth Department
51 A.D.2d 115, 379 N.Y.S.2d 881 (1976)

WITMER, JUSTICE.

On this appeal from an order denying a motion to vacate a default judgment we are again called upon to state the duty of a creditor upon suing and entering judgment against an alleged debtor who the creditor knows or has reason to believe is incapable of protecting her interests. The judgment, in the sum of $10,034, was entered on June 11, 1970 against Lillian B. Pierce, defendant, who died on December 26, 1972. The Public Administrator for Erie County, Kevin D. Cox, was appointed administrator c.t.a. of her estate, apparently in early 1975, and he promptly moved to vacate the judgment.

The motion was supported by affidavits by Kevin D. Cox and Edna Y. McCurdy, defendant's daughter. It appears that defendant's heirs are Mrs. McCurdy and a grandson and three granddaughters, and that the only asset left by the deceased defendant is a residence property at 49 Haviland Place in Hamburg, New York, occupied by Mrs. McCurdy and her husband.

Mrs. McCurdy avers that prior to 1965 the plaintiff had invested money in a business enterprise in which her husband was a principal; that the venture was unsuccessful; and that plaintiff exerted "strong pressure and duress" upon her to make good his loss. Mrs. McCurdy avers that in compliance with plaintiff's demand she executed a promissory note in the sum of $10,000, payable to plaintiff, dated June 11, 1965, and forged the name of her mother, the defendant, as a co-maker thereof and delivered it to plaintiff. Plaintiff denies knowing that defendant's name was forged. Mrs. McCurdy does not assert that he knew of it, but she claims that her mother, the defendant judgment debtor, did not know about the note and that the note does not represent any money loaned or advanced by plaintiff to her or to the defendant. Plaintiff does not deny these assertions.

It appears that in 1967 defendant's mind was deteriorating seriously and such deterioration continued progressively until her death. In 1969 she was having hallucinations and was senile and disoriented to such an extent that she needed institutional care 24 hours per day. In October of that year she was committed to E.J. Meyer Memorial Hospital for examination in the Psychiatric Clinic. The Clinic reported that she should not be in a mental institution but in one for the aged and infirm; and in February, 1970 she was admitted to the Erie County Home for the Aged at Wende, New York, where she remained until the month of her death. The affidavits and supporting documents present a clear prima facie showing that defendant was incapable of protecting her interests, at least from February, 1970 onward.

Mrs. McCurdy avers that plaintiff frequently spoke to her about paying the note, and that shortly after defendant's admittance to the Home for the Aged, she told plaintiff thereof and he replied, "My God, the county will take everything." Plaintiff denies making the latter statement, but does not deny that Mrs. McCurdy told him that her mother was in the County Home for the Aged.

Thereafter, on April 30, 1970, without notice to Mrs. McCurdy, plaintiff served a summons and complaint upon defendant in an action against her alone on said promissory note, and on June 11, 1970 he entered judgment against her upon her default in answering. Mrs. McCurdy states that she saw a notice in the newspaper of the entry of the judgment.

In opposition to the administrator's motion to vacate the judgment, plaintiff submitted his own affidavit and that of his attorney. He does not deny the circumstances giving rise to the note; but, in effect, he relies on alleged laches on the part of the defendant, since four or five years elapsed before effort was made to vacate the judgment. He urges that Mrs. McCurdy's statement that she forged the note is inadmissible, since her mother has died; and he also points to the facts that although it is contended that defendant's mind began to deteriorate in 1967, no committee was named for her and she was not committed to a mental institution, suggesting the inference that she was, therefore, not incompetent. Part of the attorney's affidavit is clearly based upon hearsay and to that extent lacks validity. It is interesting to note, however, that through his attorney the plaintiff claims that prior to April, 1970 he had conversations with Mrs. McCurdy in which she promised to pay the note. Nowhere does plaintiff allege that he ever contacted the defendant about making the note or paying it. In October, 1970, in August, 1972 and in September, 1973 plaintiff's attorney wrote to Mrs. McCurdy and her husband demanding payment of the note and threatening to sell the residence in which they lived, owned by decedent in her lifetime, unless the judgment was paid.

The record presented a strong prima facie showing not only that defendant was incapable of protecting her interests at the time when the action was begun and the default judgment was entered but that plaintiff knew or had reason to know thereof. The administrator made the motion herein promptly after his appointment. In these circumstances Special Term erred in denying the motion to vacate the judgment.

CPLR 1201 provides for the manner in which an incapable adult may appear in an action against him, to wit, "[a] person shall appear by his guardian ad litem . . . if he is an adult incapable of adequately prosecuting or defending his rights." CPLR 1203 provides that, "[n]o default judgment may be entered against an adult incapable of adequately protecting his rights for whom a guardian ad litem has been appointed unless twenty days have expired since the appointment." The legal effect of the quoted provisions is that an action at law against a person incapable of protecting his interests or who apparently is so incapable and who has no committee or guardian, may not proceed without notice to the court of the circumstances and inquiry therein by the court.

> Incompetent persons become the wards of the court, upon which a duty devolves of protection both as to their persons and property. This duty is not limited to cases only in which a committee has been appointed, but it extends to all cases where the fact of incompetency exists.

(*Wurster v. Armfield*, 175 N.Y. 256, 262, 67 N.E. 584, 585; *Prude v. County of Erie*, 47 A.D.2d 111, 113, 364 N.Y.S.2d 643, 646). . . .

When a creditor becomes aware that his alleged debtor is or apparently is incapable of protecting his own legal interests it is incumbent upon him to advise the court thereof so that the court may make suitable inquiry and in its discretion appoint a person to receive service of a copy of the summons and complaint in behalf of the defendant . . . and so the court may thereafter in its discretion appoint a guardian ad litem to protect the defendant's interests. . . .

At this point it is not necessary for the court to reach a determination of the precise capability of the defendant at the critical times nor as to the admissibility of Mrs. McCurdy's averment that the defendant did not sign or know of the note. The merits of the action on the note are not reached on this motion or this appeal.

In compliance with the court's duty to protect a person who was apparently incapable of handling her affairs at the times of the service of the summons and complaint and entry of default judgment, the order should be reversed and the motion to vacate the judgment should be granted, without prejudice to plaintiff proceeding in a manner consistent with this opinion.

Order unanimously reversed with costs and motion to vacate judgment granted.

NOTES

(1) The approach of the principal case typifies the concern shown by the judiciary for persons unable to protect their own interests. CPLR Article 12 is a statutory expression of the same concern. Basic to it is the concept of "representation" beyond that provided by an attorney. A lawyer whose client has become incompetent is obliged to seek the appointment of a guardian ad litem for that client. *Brewster v. John Hancock Mutual Life Ins. Co.*, 280 A.D.2d 300, 720 N.Y.S.2d 462 (1st Dep't 2001). The representative who must serve for an infant, adjudicated incompetent, conservatee, or other person incapable of protecting their rights is charged with protecting the interests of the person under the disability. If the litigant is an infant, the representative will ordinarily be a custodial parent. CPLR 1201. The same section provides that judicially declared incompetents shall be represented by a committee and that conservatees shall be represented by a conservator. Note, however, that the appointment of committees and conservators is no longer authorized.

A new system for protecting the rights of "persons with incapacities" was introduced into New York law in 1992 with the enactment of Mental Hygiene Law article 81. It gives the courts power to appoint a "guardian" of the person and/or property of someone who is "likely to suffer harm" because of an inability to provide for personal needs and/or property management, provided that the person "cannot adequately understand and appreciate the nature and consequences of such inability." Mental Hygiene Law § 81.02.

A special proceeding for the appointment of a guardian may be commenced by the incapacitated person, or by a person with an interest in the welfare of that person. Mental Hygiene Law § 81.06. When a special proceeding has been commenced for the appointment of a guardian, the court must early on appoint a "court evaluator," who serves an investigating and reporting function for the judge and as a kind of consultant for the incapacitated person. Mental Hygiene Law § 81.09.

The same legislation that created the new system for appointing guardians also repealed articles 77 and 78 of the Mental Hygiene Law, which had respectively authorized the appointment of conservators for conservatees and of committees for incompetents. The legislation provides that such appointments previously made, however, continue in effect until modified or abrogated pursuant to article 81. Laws of 1992, Ch. 698 § 4. Thus, persons previously appointed to serve as a committee or conservator can continue to so serve. *See Matter of Arnold O*, 226 A.D.2d 866, 640 N.Y.S.2d 355 (3d Dep't 1996), *appeal denied*, 88 N.Y.2d 810, 649 N.Y.S.2d 377, 672 N.E.2d 603 (1996).

Although the legislature failed to amend article 12 of the CPLR, which thus still deals with conservatees, incompetents and adults incapable of adequately protecting their rights, CPLR 1201, the incongruity between the CPLR and Mental Hygiene Law article 81 is softened by § 4(b) of Ch. 698, Laws of 1992, which provides: "Whenever a statute uses the terms conservators or committees, such statute shall be construed to include the term guardian notwithstanding the provisions of such article, unless the context otherwise requires."

(2) CPLR 1207-1208 require judicial approval of the settlement of an action brought by an infant, incompetent or conservatee and set forth procedures for obtaining the approval. (No such requirement applies to settlement of an action brought against them.)

If an infant, incompetent or conservatee has a claim against another party on which no action has been commenced, judicial approval is not required to settle it, but any such agreement may not be enforceable against the represented party should he or she choose to disavow it. In *Valdimer v. Mount Vernon Hebrew Camps*, 9 N.Y.2d 21, 210 N.Y.S.2d 520, 172 N.E.2d 283 (1961), for example, the child's father had settled the child's personal injury claim for $400. He then signed a "Parents-Guardian Release and Indemnity Agreement" in which he promised to indemnify the defendant against all further liability in any later suit brought by or on behalf of the infant. Later, the infant, with the parent acting as guardian, brought an action based on the same injury. When the defendant sought to invoke the indemnification agreement, it was disallowed because "the indemnitor and indemnitee have attempted to circumvent a procedure designed for the safety of the child, a procedure established on the theory that no one but a court can bind an infant to a claim for the negligent infliction of personal injuries." 9 N.Y.2d at 27, 210 N.Y.S.2d at 524, 172 N.E.2d at 286.

In view of the possible ineffectiveness of such unapproved settlements, it is in the defendant's interest to commence a special proceeding to seek judicial approval. Recognizing this need, CPLR § 1208(f) allows the defendant's attorney to prepare the papers. This device is useful where the settlement is small and hiring an attorney for the ward would substantially diminish the recovery.

(3) When the represented party has won a judgment or received a settlement, CPLR 1206 governs the disposition of the award. Once the estate is created, the court can order certain expenses deducted and distribute the remainder to the guardian of the ward's property, to the committee, or to the conservator, to be held for the use and benefit of the ward until, in the case of an infant, the age of majority. See CPLR 1206 for additional options. Withdrawals from an account established for the benefit of a represented party are supervised by the courts.

In *Manikas v. Misercordia Hospital*, 111 Misc. 2d 323, 443 N.Y.S.2d 978 (Sup. Ct. 1981), the court held that under CPLR 1211(a), there was a presumption against withdrawing from the child's estate. This presumption could be rebutted by clear detailed proof that the money was urgently needed and "helpful to the reduction of the consequences of the injury that occasioned the estate." 111 Misc. 2d at 324, 443 N.Y.S.2d at 979.

Part Four
DEVELOPING THE LITIGATION

Chapter 11
MOTION PRACTICE

§ 11.01 MAKING A MOTION

A motion, says CPLR 2211, is "an application for an order." Usually a motion will seek an order which is not dispositive of the entire action but which will help the movant in some incidental way, such as a motion to compel or avoid disclosure. Some motions, such as those for accelerated judgment, can terminate the action if granted.

This chapter will deal with formal motions, *i.e.*, those made in writing and resulting in a written order. The student should be aware that some motions made during the course of a trial, such as a motion for a continuance, are made orally and do not yield an order in the formal sense but only a ruling which, unlike the former, is not appealable. Formal motions may be made on notice to one's adversary or ex parte (without notice).

The knowledge of how and when to use each method is vital to every litigator. It will also help you understand and apply the material which makes up the balance of this book.

Important, too, is a sound appreciation of *whether* to make a motion. A former Chief Judge of the U.S. District Court for the Southern District of New York advises:

> Before making any particular motion counsel typically might consider various strategic factors: Is this particular motion the best means of persuading the court to grant the desired relief? Should the motion be made at this particular time? Is the benefit to the client worth the time and expense involved in the motion? Will this motion, even if granted by the court, have a negative impact on the litigation as a whole, for example, by disclosing too much to opposing counsel?

Edelstein, *The Ethics of Dilatory Motion Practice: Time for Change*, 44 Fordham L. Rev. 1069, 1071 (1976).[*]

Judge Edelstein also cautions that counsel must consider whether the motion meets relevant ethical standards. *See* New York Code of Professional Responsibility DR 7-102(A)(1) (prohibiting a lawyer from taking action on behalf of a client "when the lawyer knows or when it is obvious that such action would serve merely to harass or maliciously injure another.").

---

[*] Reprinted permission of the Fordham Law Review and the author, copyright © 1976.

Such conduct is not only unethical, it may also subject the offending attorney and the client to monetary penalties pursuant to Part 130 of the Rules of the Chief Administrator of the Courts. 22 NYCRR 130-1.1 to -2.4. This rule gives the courts power to impose financial sanctions and to award costs (including attorney fees) reasonably incurred as a result of "frivolous conduct" during civil litigation. The sanction imposed may not exceed $10,000 for "any single occurrence of frivolous conduct," 22 NYCRR 130-1.2, but the rule does not limit the amount of costs that may be awarded. *See* § 13.09, Sanctions for "Frivolous Pleadings.")

Conduct is defined as "frivolous" if:

(1) it is completely without merit in law and cannot be supported by a reasonable argument for an extension, modification or reversal of existing law;

(2) it is undertaken primarily to delay or prolong the resolution of the litigation, or to harass or maliciously injure another; or

(3) it asserts material factual statements that are false.

22 NYCRR 130-1.1(c).

Notice of Motion*

Form:
Motion to
Dismiss Complaint

SUPREME COURT OF THE STATE OF NEW YORK
County of New York

A. B., Plaintiff, — against — X.Y.Z., Defendant.	Notice of Motion to Dismiss Complaint Index No.. . . .. Hon._____ , J.S.C. Oral argument is requested

Upon the affidavit of Charles Diller, sworn to December 1, 2006, and the complaint, the defendant will move this court in Room _____ , County Court House, 60 Centre Street, New York, New York, on December 20, 2006, at 9:30 A.M., for an order pursuant to CPLR 3211.

The above-entitled action is for damages for personal injury.

1. Dismissing the complaint on the ground that the court does not have jurisdiction of the person of the defendant.

---

* Based on the official form of Notice of Motion prescribed by 22 NYCRR 202.7.

2. Dismissing the first cause of action on the ground that it fails to state a cause of action.

3. Dismissing the second cause of action on the ground that it may not be maintained because of the statute of limitations.

4. Dismissing the third cause of action on the ground that there is another action pending between the same parties for the same cause of action in the Superior Court of New Jersey.

5. Granting such other and further relief as to the court may seem just and proper, plus the costs of this motion.

This action is for damages caused by negligence.

Pursuant to CPLR 2214(b), answering affidavits, if any, are required to be served at least seven days before the return date of this motion.

Dated: December 1, 2006

Nov. 15, 06

[Print and Sign Name]
Attorney for Defendant
Address:
Telephone Number:

To: _____
(Attorney for the other party)
Address:
Telephone Number:

PROBLEM A

The notice of motion reproduced above makes the motion returnable on December 20, 2006.

(a) What is the last day on which the notice may be served on the attorney for the respondent? *See* CPLR 2214(b); CPLR 2103(b)(2), (5).

(b) What is the last day on which A.B., the respondent, could serve answering papers on the attorney for X.Y.Z.? Assume that A.B.'s attorney wanted to serve the answering papers by mail. What is the last day they could be mailed?

(c) What is the last date on which A.B. could serve a cross-motion and make it returnable on the same day as the initial motion?

(d) What is the last day on which X.Y.Z could serve reply papers? *See* CPLR 2214(b).

NOTES

(1) When papers are served by mail, service is effected when they are mailed, not when they are received. CPLR 2103(b)(2); *Engel v. Lichterman*, 62 N.Y.2d 943, 479 N.Y.S.2d 188, 468 N.E.2d 26 (1984). Note that all answering and reply affidavits and briefs must be filed with the court no later than the time of argument or submission of the motion. 22 NYCRR 202.8(c).

(2) If the movant gives less than the number of days notice required by CPLR 2214(b), the motion may be denied, *Thrasher v. U.S. Liability Ins. Co.*, 45 Misc. 2d 681, 257 N.Y.S.2d 360 (Sup. Ct. 1965) (denying the motion with leave to renew upon proper notice), unless the respondent waives the defect by appearing in court to address the merits, *Todd v. Gull Contracting Co.*, 22 A.D.2d 904, 255 N.Y.S.2d 452 (2d Dep't 1964). Some courts treat a minor variation from the requirement as a "procedural irregularity" and simply ignore it. *E.g., Rustine v. Patterson*, 82 A.D.2d 969, 440 N.Y.S.2d 360 (3d Dep't 1981). Answering papers which are untimely served may be disregarded by the court. *Dominski v. Firestone Tire & Rubber Co.*, 92 A.D.2d 704, 460 N.Y.S.2d 392 (3d Dep't 1983).

(3) CPLR 2214(b) requires that movant's return date be "at least" eight days from the time of service, that answering affidavits be served at least two days before the return date (seven days if the notice of motion is served at least 12 days before the return date), and that any reply affidavits be served at least one day before the return date. This one-day rule obviously allows for no sur-replies, but has been approved in *Hemingway v. Pelham Country Club*, 14 A.D.3d 536, 789 N.Y.S.2d 178 (2d Dep't 2005).

(4) CPLR 2103(b) allows motion papers (and other legal papers served in the course of an action) to be served by electronic transmission or by an overnight delivery service. As with all methods of service of papers covered by CPLR 2103(b), these methods may be used in a "pending action" and not for the service of a summons.

Service by electronic transmission is defined by CPLR 2103(f)(2) as "any method of transmission of information between two machines designed for the purpose of sending and receiving such transmissions, and which results in the fixation of the information transmitted in a tangible medium of expression." This definition is broad enough to include not only "fax" machines but also computer-to-computer transmissions.

Regardless of the precise form it takes, however, electronic transmission service may be used only if the telephone number "or other station" is designated by the attorney to be served for that purpose. Listing of the number in the address block on a paper served or filed in the course of an action constitutes consent, although the attorney may change or rescind a number (or address) by serving a notice on the other parties to the action. CPLR 2103(b)(5). It has been held that inclusion of a fax number on a lawyer's stationery, or on the cover sheet of a fax sent to an adversary, does not constitute consent to be served by fax because those are not litigation "papers" within the meaning of CPLR 2103(b)(5). *Levin v. Levin*, 160 Misc. 2d 388, 609 N.Y.S.2d 547 (Sup. Ct. 1994) (denying the motion because of improper service).

Service by electronic transmission is not complete unless and until (i) the sender receives from the attorney served an electronic transmission indicating that the transmission was received, and (ii) the sender mails a copy to the recipient. CPLR 2103(b)(5). Mailing is effective at the time of deposit in a mailbox or post office.

CPLR 2103(b)(2) provides that if service is by mail, five days shall be added to the prescribed period. CPLR 2103(b)(5) allows motion papers (and other legal papers served in the course of an action) to be served by facsimile or by overnight delivery service. As with all methods of service of papers covered by CPLR 2103(b), these methods may be used in a "pending action" and not for the service of summons.

When service is made by overnight delivery service, one business day is added to any period of time that is measured from the service of the paper. CPLR 2103(b)(6).

(5) When a motion relates to disclosure or to a bill of particulars, the motion papers must be accompanied by an affirmation that a good faith effort has been made to resolve the issue. 22 NYCRR 202.7.

(6) In 1986, the Uniform Civil Rules for the Supreme Court and the County Court were amended to provide for an Individual Assignment System, or IAS. This means that, as a general rule, every civil action is assigned to one judge for all purposes, through and including trial. *See* 22 NYCRR 202.3. In any action in which a judge has not yet been assigned by the time the first motion is made, the notice of motion, order to show cause or application for ex parte relief must be accompanied by a "written request for judicial intervention" on a form authorized by the Chief Administrator of the Courts, with proof of service of the request on other parties to the action. 22 NYCRR 202.6. The assigned judge will then decide the motion. 22 NYCRR 202.8(b).

(7) An alternative to a notice of motion is the order to show cause, which is illustrated by the following form and discussed in the related materials.

FORM

(Reprinted below are an order to show cause and an affidavit in support of the application for that order. The papers were supplied by Raun Rasmussen, Ed Josephson and John C. Gray, Esqs., of Brooklyn Legal Services Corporation "B", who use them as representatives of the tenant.)

CIVIL COURT OF THE CITY OF NEW YORK
COUNTY OF KINGS

A. B., Plaintiff, — against — X.Y.Z., Defendant.	Order to Show Cause Index No.. . . .. Hon._____ , J.S.C. Oral argument is requested

Upon the annexed affidavit of FLORENCE DOE, sworn to the 23rd day of August, 2006, and on all the proceedings had herein, Let the Petitioner or her attorney show cause before me or one of the other Judges of this Court, at a Motion Term, Part 19, to be held at the Courthouse thereof, located at 141 Livingston Street, Borough of Brooklyn, in the County of Kings, City and State of New York, on the 4th day of September, 2006, at 9:30 A.M., or as soon thereafter as counsel can be heard, why an order should not be made, staying the execution of the warrant of eviction, vacating the judgment herein and dismissing the petition for reasons fully set forth in the annexed affidavit, and why such other and further relief should not be granted as may be just.

Pending the hearing and determination of this motion and entry of an Order thereon, Let all proceedings on the part of the Petitioner, her attorney and agents and any Marshal or Sheriff of the City of New York for the enforcement of said judgment be stayed.

SUFFICIENT CAUSE THEREFORE APPEARING, LET PERSONAL service of a copy of this Order, together with a copy of the affidavit annexed thereto by the tenant on the Petitioner or her attorney and any Marshal of the City of New York, if a warrant has been issued, and the Clerk of this Court on or before August 30, 2006, be sufficient, and it is further

ORDERED that any answering papers by Petitioner must be served upon Respondent or her attorney no later than one day before the return date of this order.

DATED: August 24, 2006

Brooklyn, New York

Very Wise

_____

Judge of the Civil Court

CIVIL COURT OF THE CITY OF NEW YORK
COUNTY OF KINGS

IRIS ROE,
          Petitioner-Landlord,

— against —

FLORENCE DOE,
          Respondent-Tenant.

L&T Index No. _____ /01

Affidavit in Support
of Order to Show Cause

State of New York

County of Kings

ss.:

FLORENCE DOE being duly sworn, deposes and says:

FIRST: I am the tenant in the above-entitled proceeding, and make this affidavit in support of the motion for an order staying execution of the warrant of eviction, vacating the judgment, and dismissing the petition herein.

SECOND: This is a dispossess proceeding and your deponent is in possession of the premises at. . . . . , Brooklyn, New York, Apartment No. — .

THIRD: On information and belief, a default judgment has been entered in the above-entitled proceeding on August 15, 2006.

FOURTH: On information and belief, a warrant of eviction was issued and may be executed momentarily causing severe hardship to deponent.

FIFTH: I did not appear for trial herein out of disrespect to this court, but because I waited forty-five (45) minutes at the President Street station for a train on the morning of August 15, 2006. Several trains went by the station but did not stop. I arrived in court shortly after my case was called and was told by the Clerk that it would not be called again.

SIXTH: I have a meritorious defense to this action, to wit:

1) I am a rent-controlled tenant and the amount sued for is in excess of the legal rent set by the Office of Rent Control.

2) Breach of Warranty of Habitability, including, but not limited to, the following:

. . . .

SEVENTH: No previous application has been made for the relief requested herein.

EIGHTH: I have no one other than myself to effectuate service of this order to show cause and therefore I request permission to serve this order as tenant in person.

WHEREFORE, your deponent prays that the relief requested in the annexed Order To Show Cause be granted.

FLORENCE DOE

Sworn to before me this
23rd day of August, 2006

NOTARY PUBLIC

MALLORY v. MALLORY
Supreme Court, Nassau County
113 Misc. 2d 912, 450 N.Y.S.2d 272 (1982)

VINCENT R. BALLETTA, JR., JUSTICE.

[The motion is made in the Mallory divorce proceeding by Ethel Aikens, the female friend of Mr. Mallory. She seeks a show cause order "vacating the order that vacated the judgment of divorce," alleging that Mr. Mallory is mentally incapable of testifying and that he is "being held captive" by Mrs. Mallory.]

CPLR 2214(d) provides in part as follows:

> Order to show cause. The court in a proper case may grant an order to show cause, to be served in lieu of a notice of motion, at a time and in a manner specified therein.

Traditionally, an order to show cause has been considered an alternate means of bringing on a motion. Vol. 7B McKinney's, Siegel's Commentaries to the CPLR, C2214:24. The justice presiding at Special Term has the obligation to determine if he wishes to sign the order to show cause, except in those cases in which an order to show cause is the required method of instituting process. An order to show cause differs in some ways from a notice of motion. The time within which the order is returnable is fixed in the order and may differ sharply from the time limitations in normal motion practice; while a motion is returnable at a particular Part of the court, an order to show cause may be returnable in the usual Motion Part or perhaps even before the judge who signs the order; the judge may determine the mode of service in an order to show cause which differs from those methods specifically set forth in the CPLR; and most significantly, an order to show cause may include a temporary restraining order which may continue to the return date of the motion or to the disposition of the motion.

It should be noted that CPLR 2214(d) specifically indicates that such an order may be signed "in a proper case." There is no specific definition of a proper case, and it is obvious that the legislative intent was to leave that question entirely within the court's discretion. Vol. 7B McKinney's, Siegel's Commentaries to the CPLR, C2214:25. If a judge finds that there is no reason why an order to show cause is required, he may refuse to sign such an order. Although it is unusual for a judge to refuse to sign such an order, an order to show cause is truly a product of judicial discretion.

. . . .

A careful examination of the affidavits in support of the motion makes it clear that the relief requested could not ultimately be granted to the movant under any circumstances. In making its determination, the court is convinced that Ethel Aikens lacks standing to bring this application. She is not one of the parties to the marital action and in fact, she seeks to dissolve the parties' married state. The public policy of New York does not permit such interference in the marital state by a third party. The fact that the movant possesses a power of attorney is of no assistance to her.

. . . .

The movant's concern that the plaintiff has been kidnapped by his wife and that he is now incompetent and incapable of protecting his rights can adequately be protected by any one of a number of remedies, including reporting the alleged kidnapping to the local police, a writ of habeas corpus, or an application for the appointment of a guardian ad litem. It does not require, nor should this court participate in, the obtaining of a divorce by a donee of a power of attorney executed in very general and broad terms.

Accordingly, the application for an order to show cause is denied since there are no circumstances under which the motion by this movant could be granted.

NOTES

(1) As the court states in the principal case, an order to show cause is an alternate method of making a motion on notice. What motion was brought on by the illustrative order to show cause form, *supra*? How many days notice did the respondents get?

A point which is sometimes confusing to students is that to obtain an order to show cause one makes a motion, *i.e.*, one applies for the order to show cause. This first motion is not made on notice but ex parte. Think of it this way: The movant (tenant) in Roe v. Doe, *supra*, had to apply for the order which Judge Wise signed. Notice of this application (motion) need not necessarily have been given to the respondent (landlord). *Cf.* CPLR 6313(a). Because of this and because a motion may be presented ex parte to a judge "out of court" (*e.g.*, at home) when court is not in session, CPLR 2212(b), legal relief is potentially available in emergency situations.

(2) In deciding whether to grant an order to show cause, should the court consider the merits of the relief requested by the movant? Compare the discussion of this point in the principal case with the rule announced in *Allison v. New York State Dep't of Correctional Services*, 73 A.D.2d 824, 423 N.Y.S.2d 751 (4th Dep't 1979):

> An order to show cause is simply a substitute for a notice of motion as a device for bringing on a special proceeding. [*See* CPLR 403 — Eds.] The merits of the petition are not reached in granting or denying the order. . . .

If a Justice of the Supreme Court denies an application for an order to show cause the movant may not appeal, but may apply for the order from the Appellate Division. CPLR 5704(a).

(3) What are the advantages and disadvantages of bringing a motion by an order to show cause? Study of the above form and case should enable you to answer the question. *See also* CPLR 2201.

(4) Could the movant who used the notice of motion form reproduced earlier in this Chapter have proceeded instead by order to show cause? *Cf.* CPLR 2214(d).

(5) In actions brought in Supreme Court or the county courts, an application for an order to show cause seeking a temporary restraining order ("t.r.o.") must be supported by an affirmation demonstrating that there will be significant prejudice to the party seeking the restraining order if it is not granted. Alternatively, the movant must demonstrate that a good faith effort has been made to notify the opposing party of the time and place the application will be made, in a manner sufficient to permit that party to have an opportunity to respond to the application for the t.r.o.

SULLIVAN & DONOVAN, L.L.P. v. BOND
Supreme Court, Bronx County
175 Misc. 2d 386, 669 N.Y.S.2d 389 (1997)

George Friedman, Justice.

Defendant moves to change venue of this Westchester County action to New York County pursuant to CPLR 511(a), based on a convenience of material witnesses. Plaintiffs cross-move to retain venue in Westchester County. The motion papers are silent on one crucial point — why is this motion pending in Supreme Court, Bronx County?

The court surmises that Bronx County has been chosen as the forum for the present motion pursuant to CPLR 2212(a). That section provides, as is here pertinent, that a contested motion "shall be noticed to be heard in the judicial district where the action is triable or *in a county adjoining the county where the action is triable*." (Emphasis added.) The derivation of this somewhat startling provision is rule 63 of former Rules of Civil Practice. The procedure permitting motions to be heard in an "adjoining county" was ostensibly motivated by a desire that parties in rural counties not be deprived of a forum to hear motions when no Motion Part was in session in the county where the action was brought. (2A Weinstein-Korn-Miller, NY Civ Prac ¶ 2212.02.)

Efforts were at one time undertaken to revise the availability of an adjoining county for motion practice, in order to discourage Judge shopping, but these efforts were rebuffed by the Bar (2d Prelim Report of Advisory Comm on Prac and Pro, 1958 NY Legis Doc No. 13, at 181-182). Now, almost 40 years later, may be a suitable time for the Legislature to consider abrogating this anachronism. Those valid considerations for permitting this procedure in the past no longer apply, especially in view of the adoption of the Individual Assignment System (IAS). Indeed, even before the advent of IAS, the procedure was criticized as placing an inordinate burden on the court system in maintaining duplicate files, encouraging forum shopping, and placing an undue imposition on Justices with ample motion calendars (*Baker, Voorhis & Co. v. Heckman*, 28 A.D.2d 673 [1st Dept 1967]; *Cwick v. City of Rochester*, 54 A.D.2d 1078 [4th Dept 1976]; *Cordero v. Grant*, 95 Misc.2d 153).

The court is mindful that the submission of the present motion in Bronx County does not violate the procedure established by the Individual Assignment System. The CPLR grants the Chief Administrator of the Courts the authority to vary the procedures set forth in CPLR 2212(a) through (c) (CPLR 2212[d]). The Uniform Rules for Trial Courts (22 NYCRR 202.1[d]) provide, "The provisions of this Part shall be construed consistent with the Civil Practice Law and Rules (CPLR), and matters not covered by these provisions shall be governed by the CPLR." A case such as the present case where there had been no prior request for judicial intervention (R.J.I.) prior to the bringing of the instant motion is "unassigned." Such a motion will be accompanied by a request for judicial intervention (22 NYCRR 202.8[b]). Specifically, where the moving party chooses to bring the first motion in an "unassigned" action in an "adjoining county," the Uniform Rules for Trial Courts (22 NYCRR 202.8[b]) provide, "Motion papers noticed to be heard in a county other than the county where the venue of the action has been placed by the plaintiff shall be assigned to a judge in accordance with procedures established by the Chief Administrator." This court is unaware of the promulgation of any special procedures by the Chief Administrator which apply in this instance. Consequently, absent any contrary IAS rules, the practice set forth in the CPLR governs, and this motion is technically properly brought in Bronx County.

As Siegel wryly observes, this matter could have been assigned by the Clerk's Office to a Justice in Westchester County (Siegel, Practice Commentaries, McKinney's Cons Laws of NY, Book 7B, CPLR C2212:1, at 52 ["the justice assigned is likely to be one who serves in the county of the action's main venue regardless of the county chosen for the motion"]). This did not occur here. Indeed, under the IAS rules, all future motions would have to be referred to me as the "assigned judge." (22 NYCRR 202.8[a].)

To avoid the anomaly of this court being assigned further motions in this action, and to circumvent a procedure which should be avoided under most conceivable situations, this court declines to hear the instant motion and cross motion. The court finds that it retains authority to transfer the motions to the proper court (*see, Cwick v. City of Rochester, supra; see also,* CPLR 2217[c]). The motion and cross motion are denied without prejudice to renew in the County of Westchester, where the parties are directed to file a new R.J.I.

The court urges the Chief Administrator to promulgate rules to discourage parties from pursuing similar tactics, at least with respect to courts sitting in urban areas, making provision for those rare cases when, perhaps due to the inability to find an impartial forum, some valid reason is presented to bring an action in an "adjoining county."

NOTE

CPLR 2212 gives the movant a degree of discretion as to the venue of the motion. Nonetheless, in *Cordero v. Grant,* 95 Misc. 2d 153, 407 N.Y.S.2d 383 (Sup. Ct. 1978), cited in the principal case, it was held improper to make a motion in Supreme Court, New York County, when the underlying action is pending in another county. The court was concerned about forum shopping and about administrative burdens caused by the transfer.

§ 11.02 RESOLVING THE MOTION

A motion is not resolved until the court issues an order granting or denying it. A judge who has decided how to resolve a motion, however, need not necessarily sign an order immediately. The judge might instead issue a decision. In that case, an order reflecting the decision must be prepared and signed. If the movant had submitted a proposed order with the moving papers, the judge may adopt and sign it. Alternatively, the court may issue its decision and require the parties to draft and submit for signing an order reflecting the result. The direction to "settle" an order means that the successful party should submit a proposed order to the court and should give the opponent five days advance notice of the date of submission (ten days if service is by mail) together with a copy of the order proposed for adoption. 22 NYCRR 202.48. Counter-proposals must be served not less than two days before the settlement date (seven days if by mail). *Id.* Once signed, the court will file the order with the clerk of the court. The movant will be notified of this filing by the court. (In the First and Second Departments, notice of this and other court actions is given by publication in the New York Law Journal.)

If a party explicitly directed to submit or settle an order fails to do so within sixty days after the court signs and files the decision directing the settlement or submission of the order, the failure "shall be deemed an abandonment of the motion or action, unless for good cause shown." 22 NYCRR 202.48(b). *See Funk v. Barry*, 89 N.Y.2d 364, 365, 653 N.Y.S.2d 247, 248, 675 N.E.2d 1199, 1200 (1996) (the rule applies "only where the court explicitly directs that the proposed order or judgment be settled or submitted for signature").

When one of the proposed orders (or a variation) is signed, the parties will be notified. If the order signed is "incorrect" in the light of the decision, either party may move, on notice, for "resettlement." *See* discussion in *Foley v. Roche* (reprinted in § 11.03[A], *infra*). If there is a conflict between the court's order and the written decision, it is the latter that governs, and a motion to resettle the order to conform it to the decision should be granted. *Dunlevy v. Youth Travel Associates, Inc.*, 199 A.D.2d 1046, 608 N.Y.S.2d 30 (4th Dep't 1993).

It is the responsibility of the prevailing party to see that an order determining a motion is filed with the clerk of the court in which the action is triable (*i.e.*, "entered") and that a copy of the order is served on the other parties. It is important that the order be promptly entered and that a copy of it, together with notice of entry, be served on the losing party. Not only is this necessary to obtain compliance with its terms, but such service also triggers the thirty-day period within which an appeal may be taken. CPLR 5513(a). Even if the winning party does not enter and serve the order, however, the opponent's right to appeal is not frustrated, for any interested party may effect the entry and serve the order and notice of entry on the winner. *E.g., Muka v. Bryant*, 53 A.D.2d 773, 384 N.Y.S.2d 515 (3d Dep't 1976). The prevailing party is chargeable with knowledge of the order and must comply with its conditions even if it is never served. *Lyons v. Butler*, 134 A.D.2d 576, 521 N.Y.S.2d 477 (2d Dep't 1987).

A judge must determine a motion by an order; the court has no power to simply refuse to entertain a motion. Otherwise, the losing party would be unable to obtain appellate review, as there would be no order from which to appeal. *See Goldheart Int'l Ltd. v. Vulcan Constr. Corp.*, 124 A.D.2d 507, 508 N.Y.S.2d 182 (1st Dep't 1986), and cases cited. As amended in 1996, CPLR 2219(a) requires that, upon the request of any party, any order or ruling made by a judge must "be reduced to writing or otherwise recorded."

The formal requirements of an order are prescribed by CPLR 2219(a). An adaptation from an official form, Form 27, Order on Motion to Dismiss Complaint (Long Form) (*see* 1 Weinstein, Korn and Miller, New York Civil Practice ¶ 107.02 at 1-169) reproduced below, illustrates an order granting a motion.

Form

Order on Motion to Dismiss Complaint

SUPREME COURT OF THE STATE OF NEW YORK
County of New York

A. B., Plaintiff,

— against —

X.Y.Z., Defendant.

Order
Index No. _____

Upon defendant's notice of motion dated December 1, 2006, for a dismissal of the complaint and for dismissal of the first, second and third causes of action therein, and upon the complaint, the affidavit of C.D. sworn to December 1, 2006, and the affidavit of A.B., sworn to December 8, 2006, and [plaintiff having appeared in opposition] [or] [there being no appearance in opposition], it is ordered that:

1. The first cause of action is dismissed. The plaintiff may upon application to the court, within _ days from service of a copy of this order with notice of entry thereof, submit evidence to the court to justify the granting of leave to plead again.

2. The motion to dismiss the second cause of action is denied, with leave to assert the statute of limitations as a defense in defendant's answer.

3. All further proceedings on the third cause of action are stayed, except upon leave of this court, until the final determination of the action entitled A.B., Plaintiff against X.Y.Z., Inc., Defendant, presently pending in the Superior Court of New Jersey (Index No.__), on condition that defendant file a stipulation, within _ days from service of a copy of this order with notice of entry thereof, that all discovery proceedings in the action in the Superior Court of New Jersey shall be usable in this action with the same force and effect as though originally taken herein.

4. In all other respects the motion of the defendant is denied.

New York, New York,
February 10, 2007.

_____
[Print name to be signed or initialed]
Justice, Supreme Court
New York County

§ 11.03 ATTACKING THE ORDER

FOLEY v. ROCHE
Appellate Division, First Department
68 A.D.2d 558, 418 N.Y.S.2d 588 (1979)

FEIN, J.P.

. . . .

The action arises out of an accident which occurred on January 26, 1975 in Vermont, when plaintiff, a New York resident, allegedly sustained personal injuries when a vehicle owned by defendant Roche and operated by defendant Tyzbir, both New Jersey residents, collided with the vehicle owned and operated by plaintiff. This action was commenced [in Supreme Court, New York County — Eds.] after plaintiff had obtained an order on October 19, 1976, attaching Roche's automobile liability policy and the obligation to defend and indemnify thereunder (order, Oct. 19, 1976, Stecher, J.). Pursuant to that order, the Sheriff of Suffolk County attached the policy and service was thereafter effected upon both defendants in New Jersey. Defendants then moved to vacate the attachment (CPLR 6223) and to dismiss the complaint for lack of personal and subject matter jurisdiction (CPLR 3211, subd [a], pars 2, 8, 9). The motion was denied, Special Term finding the attachment properly obtained and no sufficient ground urged to warrant its vacatur (order, April 19, 1977, Kirschenbaum, J.).

In their answer defendants interposed affirmative defenses, alleging the impropriety of the attachment, lack of personal and subject matter jurisdiction and forum non conveniens. Thereafter, defendants served a demand to change the venue to Nassau County and an application to change the place of trial was granted without opposition (order, June 17, 1977, Niehoff, J.). A prior motion by plaintiff to strike the third and fourth affirmative defenses of lack of subject matter jurisdiction and lack of jurisdiction by reason of the attachment was denied by Mr. Justice Tierney, with leave to renew in Nassau County following disposition of the motion to change the venue (order, July 27, 1977, Tierney, J.). Plaintiff then moved before Mr. Justice Velsor in Nassau County to strike the defenses upon the ground that the issue had been determined by Justice Kirschenbaum. Defendants claimed that an application for the same relief had already been denied by Justice Kirschenbaum. Justice Velsor concluded that the prior determination of Justice Kirschenbaum decided only so much of the motion as sought to vacate the attachment, but did not pass upon the jurisdictional issues. However, Justice Velsor denied the motion without prejudice to an application by plaintiff to Justice Kirschenbaum to resettle the prior order of April 19, 1977.

Defendants thereupon moved by order to show cause to resettle the prior order of Justice Kirschenbaum, demanding dismissal of the action for lack of jurisdiction and vacatur of the attachment. Plaintiff cross-moved to strike the third and fourth affirmative defenses. Justice Kirschenbaum, granting the motion and denying the cross motion, held that attachment of the obligation to defend or pay under a liability policy pursuant to *Seider v Roth* (17 NY2d 111, *supra*) could no longer be had in view of the recent Supreme Court opinion in *Shaffer v Heitner* (433 US 186, *supra*). Although the court concluded that jurisdiction was lacking, outright dismissal was not directed, since dismissal would foreclose plaintiff from instituting action in New Jersey, the applicable Statute of Limitations having run. Accordingly, the court conditioned dismissal upon the commencement of a new action in New Jersey within 30 days, acceptance by defendants of service of process in that action and waiver of any Statute of Limitations defense, other than that which could have been asserted as a defense in this action.

Defendants have appealed from the order to the extent that it imposed conditions to the dismissal. They contend that the court had no authority to dismiss the action conditionally since there was a finding that jurisdiction was lacking, distinguishing that situation from one where dismissal is premised upon forum non conveniens. [The court, in dicta, agreed with defendant on this point but also went on to consider whether jurisdiction was in fact lacking. — Eds.]

We disagree with the conclusion reached by Special Term in holding the *Seider* attachment procedure unavailable in the light of *Shaffer v Heitner (supra)*. *Baden v Staples* (45 NY2d 889) is dispositive. The court there held the *Seider* doctrine to survive the constitutional principles expressed in *Shaffer*.

. . . .

It is appropriate to comment on the procedure employed by the parties.

Defendants' motion is designated as one to "resettle an order as to vacation of attachment and dismissal of action for lack of jurisdiction." It is asserted that the motion was made pursuant to leave granted by Justice Velsor after the venue in the action had been changed to Supreme Court, Nassau County. However, the leave granted by Justice Velsor to apply to Justice Kirschenbaum to resettle the prior order was granted to plaintiff. Nonetheless, defendants, not plaintiff, moved for resettlement of Justice Kirschenbaum's order, seeking vacatur of the attachment and dismissal of the action for lack of jurisdiction. The motion was premised upon a different ground than that relied upon on the initial application. Plaintiff, in opposition, cross-moved to dismiss the third and fourth affirmative defenses.

Defendants' motion was not properly one for resettlement. Resettlement of an order is a procedure designed solely to correct errors or omissions as to form, or for clarification. It may not be used to effect a substantive change in or to amplify the prior decision of the court (*Ruland v Tuthill*, 187 App Div 314, 315; *Kegerreis v Sirotkin*, 273 App Div 771). Nor in most cases is it at all necessary for an independent application to be made for resettlement of an order, either by notice of motion or by order to show cause. The applicable rules in effect in this Department contemplate an application for resettlement to be made in the same manner as settlement of the original order. Bronx and New York Counties Supreme Court Rules, NYCRR 660.12 provide, "Unless it shall be otherwise directed by the court, notice of settlement on resettlement shall not be less than two days." Clearly, the present motion did not seek to correct any error or omission as to form. Rather, the application was directed at the merits, seeking dismissal of the complaint and vacatur of the attachment, the very substantive relief initially denied by Justice Kirschenbaum.

At the time of this application and at the time of the prior application before Justice Velsor, venue in the action had been changed from New York to Nassau County. The place of trial having been so changed, any further application for substantive relief was required to be made in Nassau County, or at least in conformity with CPLR 2212 (subd [a]), which requires a motion on notice to be "noticed to be heard in the judicial district where the action is triable or in a county adjoining the county where the action is triable." The venue of the present motion, therefore, was improper under the statute. Once the place of trial was changed to Nassau County, no further application for relief could be made in New York County.

Nor may the propriety of the motion be sustained under CPLR 2221, even assuming that the present application was a motion affecting a prior order as to require referral to the Justice who signed the original order. Despite the clear salutary purpose of CPLR 2221 to prevent inconsistent decisions by Justices of co-ordinate jurisdiction, we must also give effect to the intention of the Legislature expressed in CPLR 2212 (subd [a]), so as to require that motions be made returnable where the action is triable or in a county adjoining the county where the action is triable. In the event of any conflict between the two provisions, the statutory provision contained in CPLR 2212 (subd [a]) would take precedence over CPLR 2221. (CPLR 102; Judiciary Law, § 229; *Cormerly v McGlynn*, 84 NY 284.)

Nor was defendants' motion properly one for reargument or renewal of the original order. A motion for reargument, addressed to the discretion of the court, is designed to afford a party an opportunity to establish that the court overlooked or misapprehended the relevant facts, or misapplied any controlling principle of law. Its purpose is not to serve as a vehicle to permit the unsuccessful party to argue once again the very questions previously decided (*Fosdick v. Town of Hempstead*, 126 NY 651; *American Trading Co. v Fish*, 87 Misc 2d 193). Nor does reargument serve to provide a party an opportunity to advance arguments different from those tendered on the original application. It may not be employed as a device for the unsuccessful party to assume a different position inconsistent with that taken on the original motion. As was observed by the Court of Appeals in *Simpson v Loehmann* (21 NY2d 990), "A motion for reargument is not an appropriate vehicle for raising new questions." Moreover, were we to consider the present motion as one for reargument, it was clearly untimely, since such a motion may not be made after the time to appeal from the original order has expired. . . . To hold otherwise would permit circumvention of the prohibition against extending the time to take an appeal from the original order (*see* 2A Weinstein-Korn-Miller, NY Civ Prac, par 2221.03).

Nor was the motion properly one to renew. An application for leave to renew must be based upon additional material facts which existed at the time the prior motion was made, but were not then known to the party seeking leave to renew, and, therefore, not made known to the court. Renewal should be denied where the party fails to offer a valid excuse for not submitting the additional facts upon the original application. . . . Nor should the remedy be available where a party has proceeded on one legal theory on the assumption that what has been submitted is sufficient, and thereafter sought to move again on a different legal argument merely because he was unsuccessful upon the original application. Here, no additional material facts are alleged. There is no claim of mistake, inadvertence, surprise or excusable neglect. Nor is the application supported by new facts or information which could not have been readily and with due diligence made part of the original motion. The new argument sought to be raised by defendants in support of the motion is an insufficient basis for a motion to renew.

Accordingly, the order, Supreme Court, New York County (Kirschenbaum, J.), entered June 21, 1978, granting defendants' motion for resettlement, dismissing the action for lack of jurisdiction and vacating the order of attachment, should be reversed, on the law, without costs or disbursements on the appeal, and defendants' motion to dismiss the complaint and vacate the order of attachment should be denied.

NOTES

(1) After *Rush v. Savchuk*, 444 U.S. 320, 100 S. Ct. 571, 62 L. Ed. 2d 516 (1980), held that *Seider*-type jurisdictional attachments were invalid, the defendant in the principal case (which was still pending) tried again, moving to dismiss it in Supreme Court, Nassau County. That court granted the motion and plaintiff appealed to the Appellate Division, Second Department. (Why not the First, which had decided the principal case?) The Second Department affirmed the dismissal, 86 A.D.2d 887, 447 N.Y.S.2d 528 (1982), apparently ending this litigation six years, seven motions and two appeals after it began. In its opinion, the Second Department dealt with some thorny issues of motion practice:

> Defendants' motion to dismiss for lack of jurisdiction was essentially one to reargue a prior order (*Foley v. Roche*, 68 A.D.2d 558, 418 N.Y.S.2d 588) denying dismissal on that ground because the basis for that order . . . had since been overruled by the Supreme Court of the United States in *Rush v. Savchuk*, 444 U.S. 320, 100 S.Ct. 571, 62 L.Ed.2d 516, and the Court of Appeals in *Gager v. White*, 53 N.Y.2d 475, 442 N.Y.S.2d 463, 425

N.E.2d 851. Reargument for such purpose is proper even if the period within which to appeal the prior order had expired. . . .

That this prior order had been made by the Appellate Division, First Department (prior to a change of venue to Nassau County), presents no difficulty here, despite the general law of the case principle that an Appellate Division ruling on a legal issue precludes subsequent reconsideration not only by Special Term . . . but also by the Appellate Division itself . . ., as well as by a different Appellate Division. . . . The doctrine of law of the case is "not an absolute mandate on the court," since it may be "ignored" in "extraordinary circumstances" vitiating its effectiveness as a rule fostering orderly convenience . . . such as a change in the law or a showing of new evidence affecting the prior determination. . . . The error sought to be corrected must, however, be so "plain . . . [that it] would require [the] court to grant a re-argument of a cause. . . ."

. . . .

We believe a similar extraordinary situation exists in the case at bar. The prior determination of the First Department is plainly in error when viewed — retrospectively — in light of *Rush v. Savchuk* . . . and *Gager v. White*. . . . Since the prior intermediate order had not been appealed to the Court of Appeals, the issue would be reviewable by that court on appeal from the final judgment in this case (CPLR 5501, subd. [a] . . .). Were this court to reverse Special Term for its bold practicality, we would be unnecessarily subjecting defendants to the expense of trial and further appeals to obtain a preordained outcome. The law cannot be so unyielding.

(2) Professor Farrell singled out the *Foley v. Roche* litigation as an example of serious deficiencies in New York civil practice. Writing after the First Department's decision, but prior to that of the Second Department, he said:

Ten supreme court justices had been involved in this case and the net result was — well, what was it? A monumental waste of the time of four supreme court justices! One justice, not five, should have handled this case at the trial level. . . . Once a lawsuit begins, it becomes a public enterprise invoking the considerable powers of the judicial branch, and ceases to be a private matter. The reported cases, however, manifest the bar's addiction to motion and appeal, heedless of the diseconomy of these dilatory practices, and show the bench's puzzling tolerance of a situation that litters the courts daily with enough paper to cork Vesuvius.

What is the solution to this problem?

I suggest that the solution lies with the bench. Immediately upon commencement of an action, the courts, the judges themselves, or their delegates, should take an early and active role in controlling the progress of *every* lawsuit toward settlement or trial.

Farrell, *Civil Practice, 1979 Survey of New York Law*, 31 Syracuse L. Rev. 15, 50-51 (1980).[*]

To what extent were the problems identified by Professor Farrell solved by the adoption in 1986 of the Individual Assignment System (described in note 6, following Problem A, this Chapter)? According to the Office of Court Administration, there was a significant increase in the rate of disposition of civil cases in New York City since the adoption of the IAS system. *See IAS Update: Sharp Cut in Civil Case Backlog*, N.Y.L.J., February 28, 1989, page 1 col. 3.

(3) CPLR 2221, which governs motions affecting prior orders, was amended in 1999 to set forth the grounds on which a motion for leave to reargue and a motion for leave to renew may be made. Are the standards there set forth the same as described by the First Department in *Foley v. Roche*?

As amended, CPLR 2221(d) provides that a motion for leave to reargue must be made "within thirty days after service of a copy of the order determining the prior motion and written notice of its entry." One post-amendment case, however, holds that the motion may be made after that time if a notice of appeal has been filed and the motion is brought prior to the time the appeal is decided. *Millson v. Arnot Realty*, 266 A.D.2d 918, 697 N.Y.S.2d 435 (4th Dep't 1999). The Court did not discuss the time limit in CPLR 2221(c). See also the quote from *Foley v. Roche* in Note 1, *supra*.

Motions for leave to renew are not subject to any limitation of time found in CPLR 2221, thus leaving the matter within the discretion of the court before which the motion is made. Why do you think an application for leave to renew should have a different time limit than an application for leave to reargue?

(4) Returning to the procedures for challenging a judicial order, note that if the order to be attacked was made on default, the defaulting party may invoke CPLR 2221(a)(1) and CPLR 5015(a). Subdivision (1) of CPLR 5015(a) allows the court to grant relief if the default was "excusable." *See also* CPLR 2005. If the court which granted the order lacked jurisdiction to do so, CPLR 5015(a)(4) provides a remedy. CPLR 5015 is also treated in Chapter 20.

§ 11.04 NOTE ON THE ROLE OF THE APPELLATE COURTS IN MOTION PRACTICE

[A] The Appellate Division

The Appellate Division plays a lively role in motion practice for two reasons: (a) it has mandatory jurisdiction over a broad range of final and interlocutory orders made in Supreme Court or a County Court; and (b) it has original jurisdiction to hear motions.

---

[*] Reprinted with permission of the Syracuse L. Rev. and the author, copyright © 1980.

(a) The CPLR is remarkable for its rule that an appeal may be taken as of right from almost all interlocutory orders which result from motions made on notice. CPLR 5701(a)(2) provides that any such order is appealable which "(iv) involves some part of the merits" or "(v) affects a substantial right." These provisions have been construed very liberally to include, for example, orders deciding disclosure motions. *See generally* Weinstein, Korn & Miller, New York Civil Practice § 5701.15-5701.18 (2000).

Although some orders are specifically not appealable as of right, *see* CPLR 5701(b), these may be appealed if permission is granted by the judge who made the order or by a justice of the Appellate Division, CPLR 5701(c). Two kinds of decisions are never appealable however: a denial of an application pursuant to CPLR 2221 to reargue a motion, CPLR 5701(a)(2)(viii); *Fleischmann v. Stern*, 90 N.Y. 110 (1882), and a ruling made during the course of trial — for example, an evidentiary ruling. (The latter may be reviewed on an appeal from the final judgment.)

Since in many cases, several pretrial motions are made, the wide availability of appellate review can lengthen the time it takes to get to trial. In the federal courts, where generally one may appeal only from the final judgment, costs of litigation may be less. *See* 28 U.S.C. § 1291.

An interlocutory order may also be reviewed by an appeal from an adverse final judgment if the order is one which "necessarily affects the final judgment." CPLR 5501(a)(1). This test is more exacting than that which determines whether an interlocutory appeal would lie; hence an order which might have been reviewed on a pretrial appeal may not be reviewable when an appeal is taken from a final judgment. How would this factor affect a litigant's decision whether to appeal a pretrial order?

A source of guidance on the technical aspects of appeals to the Appellate Division is the New York State Bar Association's Practitioner's Handbook for Appeals to the Appellate Divisions of the State of New York (2005). One key point to note is that an appeal must be taken within thirty days after service of "a copy of the judgment or order appealed from and written notice of its entry." CPLR 5513(a).[1] This is a time limit rigidly applied. Moreover, the making of a motion to renew or reargue a prior motion does not extend the time within which to appeal from the order deciding the prior motion. A party seeking reargument or renewal would be prudent to also take an appeal from the original order in case reargument or renewal is denied. *See also* CPLR 5517.

(b) Orders obtained without notice are not appealable, but they may nonetheless be reviewed by the Appellate Division using its authority under CPLR 5704(a). This section allows that court to vacate or modify any order granted ex parte and to grant any order which was sought ex parte but denied by the lower court. The party seeking relief is simply making a motion in the Appel-

---

[1] An appeal as of right is "taken" by serving and filing a notice of appeal. CPLR 5515.

late Division. Only for compelling reasons will the Appellate Division grant such relief. *See, e.g., King v. Gregorie*, 90 A.D.2d 922, 457 N.Y.S.2d 938 (3d Dep't 1982). Thus the movant denied ex parte relief is better advised to seek vacatur of the order by a motion made on notice in the Supreme Court and, if denied, take an ordinary appeal pursuant to CPLR 5701(a)(3).

[B] The Court of Appeals

Review of non-final orders in the Court of Appeals is greatly limited in comparison to that available in the Appellate Division. In general, only an order which "finally determines the action" may be appealed to the Court of Appeals as of right. CPLR 5601(a), (b). (A narrow exception is found in CPLR 5601(c).) Even the permissive appellate jurisdiction of the Court of Appeals is generally limited to final orders. CPLR 5602(a)(1); *but see* CPLR 5602(a)(2), (b)(1). Most often, therefore, when an interlocutory order is reviewed by the Court of Appeals, it is because the action has been finally determined and the order is one which necessarily affected that determination. CPLR 5601(d); 5602(a)(ii).

The power of the Court of Appeals is further limited in that, in general, it may review only questions of law. Review of facts is permitted only when the Appellate Division has itself "expressly or impliedly" found new facts. CPLR 5501(b). Similarly, the Court of Appeals will not review an exercise of discretion unless there has been an abuse of discretion. *Patron v. Patron*, 40 N.Y.2d 582, 388 N.Y.S.2d 890, 357 N.E.2d 361 (1976).

The standard text on the jurisdiction of the court is Karger, Powers of the New York Court of Appeals (3d ed. 2005). A guide to appellate practice before it is the Practitioner's Handbook for Appeals to the Court of Appeals of the State of New York (2d ed. 1991). The website of the Court of Appeals (www.courts.state.ny.us/ctapps) includes an annual report with statistics detailing the Court's workload.

Chapter 12
PROVISIONAL REMEDIES

§ 12.01 IN GENERAL

A dramatic stroke in the early stage of a lawsuit is the use of a provisional remedy. As with any powerful weapon, it must be used carefully.

Articles 60, 62, 63, 64, 65 and 71 provide for provisional remedies: attachment, injunction, receivership, notice of pendency, and seizure of a chattel (also available as a final remedy). These remedies may be granted before judgment (CPLR 6212[c]) and, in some cases, before an action is commenced (CPLR 304). All look to an eventual adjudication on the merits and the substitution of a permanent remedy.

The principal function of the provisional remedies is to secure to the successful plaintiff the fruits of the litigation lest intervening acts of the defendant or third parties result in a hollow victory. To effect this purpose, the law of provisional remedies takes the extraordinary step of allowing a court to alter private property rights or restrict the conduct of one private party at the request of another before the merits of the underlying controversy are tried. As part of their function of securing the final judgment, the provisional remedies may prevent the successful interposition of competing claims by third parties by giving the plaintiff priority over other creditors or transferees of the defendant. CPLR 6226.

Can you think of any other legal or tactical advantages the plaintiff gains by obtaining a provisional remedy?

Are there disadvantages for the plaintiff who obtains one? *See* CPLR 6212(b), (e); 8012(b).

PROBLEM A

Leslie, who holds down a full time job in addition to being a single parent of grade school children, purchased a washing machine from Wacky Walter's, Inc., pursuant to a retail installment contract. The agreement, by which the seller retained a security interest, warranted the product's performance for one year. After several months of possession, she ceased making her monthly payments, stating that the machine was not performing properly. The seller has decided to commence an action in order to recover the remaining balance (approximately four hundred dollars) and/or to repossess the machine. What provisional remedies, if any, are available under the CPLR?

§ 12.02 SEIZURE OF CHATTEL: CPLR ARTICLE 71

MORNING GLORY MEDIA, INC. v. ENRIGHT
Supreme Court, Monroe County
100 Misc. 2d 872, 420 N.Y.S.2d 176 (1979)

JOHN A. MASTRELLA, JUSTICE

This is a motion for an order confirming an order of seizure granted to the plaintiff, Morning Glory Media, Inc., under the recently revised CPLR article 71. In this case, which appears to be one of first impression, the defendants question the constitutionality of the procedure of granting an order of seizure without notice, and also question to what extent a defense may be interposed to defeat an application for replevin of chattels.

On November 9, 1978, the plaintiff corporation acquired a typesetting machine. The defendant, Gene Fausette, personally guaranteed a loan for the machine; and the defendants, Thomas Enright and Gladys Fausette, posted collateral as security for the said purchase. On that same date the plaintiff corporation, Thomas Enright, and Gladys Fausette entered into an agreement whereby each would possess a one-third interest in the typesetting machine and the plaintiff would have the sole and exclusive right to operate and administer the machine and to provide, supervise, and/or administer the operator of the machine. As consideration, plaintiff agreed to pay Thomas Enright and Gladys Fausette the sum of $25 a month each as long as their security for the loan was posted with Manufacturers Hanover Trust Company. The agreement further provided that Enright and Fausette give plaintiff the exclusive right to exchange the security given by them to the bank and that they would do nothing to prevent plaintiff from eventually owning complete interest in the typesetting machine.

On February 11, 1979, the board of directors of the plaintiff corporation, including all three defendants, by resolution modified the original agreement to provide that the typesetting machine would still be owned with equal interests by the corporation, Thomas Enright, and Gladys Fausette, and that each party would be liable for one third of the maintenance costs and expenses of the machine. The resolution also provided that Kenneth Browne, the president of the corporation, and the corporation would have the right to use the typesetting machine at an hourly rate, and that the administration of the machine would be in the joint control of the corporation, Thomas Enright, and Gladys Fausette.

Plaintiff, by its president, Kenneth Browne, thereafter commenced this replevin action, and on April 27, 1979 obtained an order of seizure without notice pursuant to CPLR 7102, which was served on the defendants by the Sheriff on April 30, 1979. Prior to its seizure, the machine was located at the place of business of the defendant, Gene Fausette. The machine was moved by the Sheriff to a third party's place of business, Migdol Printers, Inc., Rochester,

New York. However, this court has been informed that Kenneth Browne has recently moved the machine to his apartment, where it is under the Sheriff's seal.

Plaintiff is now bringing this motion to confirm the order of seizure pursuant to CPLR 7102 (subd [d], par 4). In response to plaintiff's application, defendants first claim that the granting of the order of seizure without notice is in violation of constitutional procedural due process requirements.

It is clear, however, that a strong presumption of constitutionality attaches to an act of the Legislature and this presumption can only be overcome by clear and convincing proof, persuasive beyond a reasonable doubt. . . .

The last major revision of article 71 was in 1971 when the Legislature acted in response to the decision in *Laprease v Raymours Furniture Co.* (315 F Supp 716) in which the court held unconstitutional the provisions of CPLR 7102 permitting the seizure of chattels by a public officer without a court order. The statute, as then amended, was vague. The application to the court and the order of seizure and/or forcible entry was required to contain only sufficient facts and terms to conform to the "due process of law requirements of the Fourteenth Amendment to the Constitution of the United States." However, effective January 1, 1979, much of CPLR article 71 was amended by the Legislature (L. 1978, ch 81), as recommended by the Judicial Conference of the Office of Court Administration; and the requirements for the procedures governing the issuance of an order of seizure were made more specific (Twenty-third Ann Report of NY Judicial Conference, 1978, pp 255-271).

CPLR 7102 (subds [c], [d], par 1), taken together, provide what plaintiff must set forth in his papers and what plaintiff must prove in order to obtain the order of seizure:

> (c) Affidavit. The *application for an order of seizure shall be supported by an affidavit which* shall clearly identify the chattel to be seized and shall state:
>
> 1. that the plaintiff is entitled to possession by virtue of facts set forth;
>
> 2. that the chattel is wrongfully held by the defendant named;
>
> 3. whether an action to recover the chattel has been commenced, the defendants served, whether they are in default, and, if they have appeared, where papers may be served upon them;
>
> 4. the value of each chattel or class of chattels claimed, or the aggregate value of all chattels claimed;
>
> 5. if the plaintiff seeks the inclusion in the order of seizure of a provision authorizing the sheriff to break open, enter and search for the chattel, *the place where the chattel is located and facts sufficient to*

establish probable cause to believe that the chattel is located at that place;

6. that no defense to the claim is known to the plaintiff; and

7. if the plaintiff seeks an order of seizure without notice, facts sufficient to establish that unless such order is granted without notice, it is probable the chattel will become unavailable for seizure by reason of being transferred, concealed, disposed of, or removed from the state, or will become substantially impaired in value.

(d) Order of seizure.

1. Upon presentation of the affidavit and undertaking and upon *finding that it is probable the plaintiff will succeed on the merits and the facts are as stated in the affidavit,* the court may grant an order directing the sheriff of any county where the chattel is found to seize the chattel described in the affidavit and including, if the court so directs, a provision that, if the chattel is not delivered to the sheriff, he may break open, enter and search for the chattel in the place *specified in the affidavit. The plaintiff shall have the burden of establishing the grounds for the order.* (Italicized material is new.)

CPLR 7102 (subd [d], par 2) was amended to provide that "[u]pon a motion for an order of seizure, the court, without notice to the defendant, may grant a temporary restraining order that the chattel shall not be removed from the state if it is a vehicle, aircraft or vessel or, otherwise, from its location, transferred, sold, pledged, assigned or otherwise disposed of or permitted to become subject to a security interest or lien until further order of the court." CPLR 7102 (subd [d], par 3), which is new, provides that an order of seizure "may be granted without notice only if, in addition to the other prerequisites for the granting of the order, the court finds that unless such order is granted without notice, it is probable the chattel will become unavailable for seizure by reason of being transferred, concealed, disposed of, or removed from the state, or will be substantially impaired in value." Paragraph 4 of the same subdivision, which also is new, provides that if an order of seizure is granted without notice, the plaintiff must move within five days after seizure or such order shall have no further effect and shall be vacated on motion, and any chattel under such order must be returned to the defendant forthwith. Furthermore, "[u]pon the motion to confirm, the plaintiff shall have the burden of establishing the grounds for confirmation." (CPLR 7102, subd [d], par 4.) Plaintiff must also provide an undertaking executed by sufficient surety acceptable to the court in an amount not less than twice the value of the chattel so set forth by the plaintiff in his affidavit (CPLR 7102, subd [e]). Finally, CPLR 7108 (subd [a]) was amended to provide that "[i]f an order of seizure granted without notice is not confirmed . . . the plaintiff, unless the court orders otherwise upon good cause shown, shall be liable to the defendant for all costs and damages, including reasonable attorney's fees, which may be sustained by reason of the granting of the order of seizure without notice, and the plaintiff's liability shall not be limited to the amount of the undertaking."

Between 1969 and 1975 the Supreme Court of the United States, in a tetralogy of decisions, has set forth guidelines for courts to gauge whether provisional remedies, of which replevin is one, comply with procedural due process requirements (*see* Donnelly, *Study of Attachment, Replevin, Receivership, Arrest*, Twenty-first Ann Report of NY Judicial Conference, 1976, pp. 453-457, 463-471). In *Sniadach v Family Fin. Corp.* (395 US 337), the Supreme Court held a Wisconsin statute unconstitutional which permitted a creditor to garnishee a defendant's wages before a trial and without notice or a hearing. In *Fuentes v Shevin* (407 US 67), the Supreme Court held Florida and Pennsylvania statutes unconstitutional which permitted summary seizures of chattels without notice or a prior hearing to challenge the seizure. The court stated that the purpose of the hearing is to prevent "seizures of goods where the party seeking the writ has little probability of succeeding on the merits of the dispute." (407 US 67, 97, n 33, *supra*.) In *Mitchell v Grant Co.* (416 US 600), the Supreme Court held constitutional the Louisiana procedures for an order of sequestration which is granted without notice or an opportunity to be heard, but only issues with a Judge's consent and on a verified affidavit. The court also stressed that immediately thereafter the debtor may seek dissolution of the sequestration order by filing a bond or by challenging the grounds for the order. The creditor must then prove the debt, amount owing and default; and upon failure of such proof, the court may order the property returned and award damages, including attorney's fees. Finally, in *North Georgia Finishing v Di-Chem* (419 US 601, 607), the Supreme Court held unconstitutional a Georgia garnishment statute because "[t]here is no provision for an early hearing at which the creditor would be required to demonstrate at least probable cause for the garnishment." The court also appeared to limit the *Sniadach* preseizure hearing requirement to wages (419 US 601, 605, *supra*). Furthermore, the Court of Appeals has recently held that under the United States Constitution (14th Amdt, § 1) and the New York Constitution (art I, § 6) "[f]undamental notions of procedural due process require that before the State may deprive a person of a significant property interest in aid of a creditor, that person be given notice and an opportunity to be heard prior to deprivation of that interest" (*Sharrock v Dell Buick-Cadillac*, 45 NY2d 152, 163; . . .) especially where State process or intervention "is executed without even a modicum of judicial intervention of supervision" (45 NY2d 152, 164, *supra*).

In applying these standards to CPLR article 71, as amended, it is clear that procedural due process requirements are met whether an order of seizure is granted after a hearing on notice or without notice with an immediate confirmation hearing on notice. The granting of an order of seizure is now discretionary with the court after the plaintiff has met his burden of establishing all the specific requirements for an order of seizure. An order confirming seizure without notice may be granted only upon a showing of exigent circumstances, and if later proven unwarranted, the plaintiff may be held liable for damages, including attorney's fees. Furthermore, the defendant still has the option of reclaiming a chattel according to the procedures set forth in CPLR 7103. Additionally, commentators agree that the revised statute meets constitutional process requirements and was enacted to improve the previous vague statute and to assure its constitutionality in light of the guidelines set forth in the four Supreme Court decisions. . . .

Defendants next claim that plaintiff has not met its statutory burden of proof and that defendants have set forth sufficient defenses to defeat plaintiff's application for an order of confirmation of seizure. Defendants state that Browne has had free access to and has used the typesetting machine prior and subsequent to the seizure. They state that the machine was well cared for and in the same condition as when acquired. They claim that they have no intention of moving or disposing of or otherwise altering or damaging the machine.

Defendants further claim that the contract was modified because the agreement had been breached in that no $25 monthly payments had been made to Thomas Enright and Gladys Fausette as provided in the original agreement, nor had regular monthly payments been made to the bank which financed the loan. Defendants state that they are prepared to convey title to the machine upon the bank's release of the collateral security for the loan, which will enable them to buy a similar machine for use in their business. Thus, they request this court to deny plaintiff's application, order the return of the machine to its original location, and also order that the status quo prior to seizure, when all parties had access to and use of the machine, be maintained pending the trial of this action.

Prior to the recent amendments to the replevin statute, a court was required to issue an order of seizure upon a plaintiff's submission of an affidavit and posting an undertaking as security for the chattel against possible damages (cf. Gale v Morgan & Brother Manhattan Stor. Co., 65 AD2d 529). While courts have never been remiss in scrutinizing the merits of a replevin application to determine whether a plaintiff has demonstrated a superior possessory interest in the chattel . . . conclusory assertions of the defense that plaintiff has breached the underlying contract would not defeat a replevin application and thus permit a defendant to avoid the requirements for reclaiming a chattel as set forth in CPLR 7103. . . . Only those defenses which clearly indicated that plaintiff lacked a superior possessory interest in the chattel would defeat a replevin application, such as, where a plaintiff's proper performance was made a condition of payment under the contract . . . where the contract was incomplete because both parties had not signed it as required, or where the defense of rescission was asserted in good faith based upon fraud in the inducement (Scutti Pontiac v Rund, 92 Misc 2d 881).

The replevin statute, as amended, has substantially changed the requirements for an order of seizure. A court is now vested with broader discretion to determine whether replevin relief is appropriate and also the proper status for the parties pending the final outcome of the action to prevent mistaken and unfair deprivation of property. . . . (Commercial Law, 30 Syracuse L Rev 257, 307). The burden is now on the plaintiff to prove that he has met all the more detailed requirements set forth in CPLR 7102, and a finding by the court, similar to an application for a preliminary injunction, that it is probable that plaintiff will succeed on the merits.

In applying this standard to the facts in the present case, it is apparent that plaintiff has not met its statutory burden. Furthermore, defendants have set forth defenses to this action, which if proven, may well defeat plaintiff's claim to a superior possessory interest in the chattel. Balancing other factors in the present case — that plaintiff is a closely held corporation, that one defendant personally guaranteed the loan for the purchase of the machine, that two defendants posted collateral as security for the said loan, that two of the defendants are directors of the corporation and claim that they acted to prevent the chattel from being foreclosed and to keep the security for the chattel intact (*cf.* Business Corporation Law, § 717), and that they are willing to transfer title to the machine upon release of their security — also must be considered in determining a denial of plaintiff's motion.

Accordingly, plaintiff's motion for an order confirming an order of seizure granted without notice is denied and the Sheriff is directed to return the chattel to its location prior to seizure. However, pending the final outcome of this action, plaintiff is entitled to a restraining order that the chattel shall not be removed from its location, transferred, sold, pledged, assigned or otherwise disposed of, or permitted to become subject to a security interest or lien until further order of this court (CPLR 7103, subd [c], par 2), or unless the defendants transfer their title and interest in the machine to the plaintiff.

CHRISTIE'S INC. v. DAVIS
United States District Court, Southern District of New York
247 F. Supp. 2d 414 (2002)

LYNCH, DISTRICT JUDGE.

This action arises out of the efforts of plaintiff Christie's Inc. ("plaintiff" or "Christie's") to collect on multiple loans made to defendants Jerome and Sharon Davis ("defendants" or "the Davises"). The loans are secured by hundreds of pieces of fine and decorative art and antique furniture, most of which the Davises keep in their house in Greenwich, Connecticut. After the Davises defaulted on the loans, Christie's filed this action, seeking repossession of the collateral, pursuant to the New York recovery of chattels statute, C.P.L.R. Article 71. Plaintiff now moves for summary judgment. For the reasons discussed below, the motion will be granted.

. . . .

IV. Order Pursuant to C.P.L.R. § 7109(b)

Because the pledged property is unique, Christie's seeks, in addition to a judgment that it has superior possessory rights in the chattel, an order pursuant to C.P.L.R. § 7109(b) directing the Davises to return the collateral to it. (Pl. Mem. at 13 n. 9.) Section 7109(b) provides that, "[w]here the chattel is unique, the court, in addition to granting a judgment under section 7108 [that plaintiff has superior possessory rights in the chattel], may direct that a party in possession deliver the chattel to the party entitled to possession." N.Y. C.P.L.R. § 7109(b) (McKinney 2002). While conceding that the paintings in their collection are unique, *see* Danae Art International Inc. v. Stallone, 163 A.D.2d 81, 557 N.Y.S.2d 338 (1st Dep't 1990), defendants argue that Christie's has not adequately established that the furnishings and decorative objects among the collateral are unique. (Defs. Mem. at 18.) Contrary to defendants' argument, the uniqueness requirement does not force plaintiffs to prove that each chattel is rare or irreplaceable, but simply that it is not a mass-produced item readily available on the market, such that a money judgment enabling purchase of a replacement would be an adequate remedy. John Paul Mitchell Systems v. Quality King Distrib., Inc., 106 F.Supp.2d 462, 477-78 (S.D.N.Y.2000) (discussing uniqueness requirement and holding that mass-produced items cannot be unique). All of the furnishings and decorative objects in the Davises' collection are works created in Europe and China during the seventeenth through nineteenth centuries. (Compl.Ex. D.) These are clearly unique, as they have historical and artistic value that makes them relatively rare, impossible to replace through manufacturing, and attractive to collectors and dealers.[9]

Morse v. Penzimer, 58 Misc.2d 156, 295 N.Y.S.2d 125, 127 (1968) (holding that items with historical value and heirlooms are unique, while Ford trucks are not).

Christie's is therefore entitled to an order pursuant to § 7109(b) directing that the Davises return the collateral items valued at twice the undisputed debt amount. *See* Kunstsammlungen Zu Weimar v. Elicofon, 536 F.Supp. 829, 859 (S.D.N.Y.1981) (holding that the court could use its equitable discretion under § 7109(b) to direct the return of the chattels).

NOTES

(1) The constitutional strictures described in the *Morning Glory* case apply to every provisional remedy. Keep them in mind as you read the balance of the chapter. Should analysis of the constitutional problems presented by the pre-hearing seizure authorized by Article 71 (or any other provisional remedy) change if the defendant were a non-commercial party, as in Problem A, or were indigent? *See* footnote 7 of *Sharrock v. Dell Buick-Cadillac, Inc.* (reprinted in § 12.04, *infra*).

---

[9] The uniqueness of the pledged works is immediately evident from an examination of the descriptions of the works in the lists of collateral. Clearly, works such as the seventeenth-century "rhinocerous horn libation cup" and the nineteenth-century "flambe-glazed lingzhi-shaped brush washer" (Compl.Ex. D) are unique art objects, rather than mass-produced, mainly functional, utensils.

(2) Does the three-year statute of limitations (CPLR 214(3)) in a replevin action run from the time plaintiff loses possession of the chattel, or from the time plaintiff makes a demand for its return? *See Solomon R. Guggenheim Foundation v. Lubell*, 77 N.Y.2d 311, 567 N.Y.S.2d 623, 569 N.E.2d 426 (1991), § 7.05, *supra*.

(3) Can a creditor acting under Article 71 seize and retain possession of personal or business goods no matter how important they are to the defendant? *See* CPLR 7103(c). Is the washing machine described in Problem A exempt from the enforcement of a judgment? *See* CPLR 5205(a).

(4) If the chattel is truly unique, recourse directly to equity has in the past been approved. In *Chabert v. Robert & Co.*, 273 A.D. 237, 76 N.Y.S.2d 400 (1st Dep't 1948), over defendant's argument that replevin provided the exclusive remedy, the court found the chattel so unique and irreplaceable that plaintiff should not have to settle for the alternative remedy of money value of the item. Here the property was "Absolio Jasmin" used in the manufacture of perfume which defendant had for safekeeping with an understanding it would be returned to plaintiff on demand. Replevin, a legal remedy, was not seen as adequate. But under CPLR 7109(b), as described in the *Christies Inc.* case, it would appear that the equitable remedy is built right in and is available under that provision.

§ 12.03 ATTACHMENT: CPLR ARTICLE 62

[A] Introductory Note

Consider . . . the situation of a businessman in financial trouble who fails to pay for goods purchased or consigned. If his creditor brings suit for payment, the debtor can rely on the fact that it will be months and — given the usual reluctance of the courts to grant summary judgment — perhaps years before he will be required to pay. In the meantime he is free to turn a profit on the goods and to spend or invest the creditor's money and hope for a better day. But if the creditor can obtain an attachment of the debtor's bank account, the debtor will no longer be able to use or control the creditor's money prior to judgment. The plaintiff, although not himself receiving payment, has taken away the advantage of time. In this way attachment often motivates a defendant to settle a claim which he might not otherwise be willing to settle — at least at that time. For the same reason, an order of attachment could provide a swift and effective remedy against fraud or conversion and may even serve to deter a defendant from such acts. The defendant's benefit from or use of the improperly obtained property would be immediately terminated by an order of attachment. A would-be defendant who knows that attachment is available upon a plaintiff's prima facie showing that his property was improperly obtained may well abstain from any contemplated wrongful acts.

Attachment not only restricts a defendant's use of property, it also can cause a devastating impact on a defendant. Since orders of attachment often are granted ex parte, a defendant does not have notice and cannot protect himself against the unexpected disruptions they bring. Attachment of a bank account may cause checks to bounce, enrage employees who cannot be paid, or otherwise disrupt ongoing business relations. Under most lending agreements the entry of an order of attachment against the borrower's property constitutes an act of default. Consequently, a defendant's obligations to his lenders may be accelerated. The disruption of business and acceleration of debts exert powerful pressure on the defendant to settle prior to any adjudication of the dispute.

On the other hand, to many a plaintiff who seeks the prompt return of property owed by a defendant, an early settlement may be the only solution. A court "victory" ordering the return of plaintiff's property after years or even months may be as bad as losing the battle. The pressure that a plaintiff can exert with an order of attachment is thus the countervailing force which can get him a prompt and meaningful remedy, through the courts.

Kheel, *New York's Amended Attachment Statute: A Prejudgment Remedy in Need of Further Revision*, 44 Bklyn. L. Rev. 199, 202 (1978).*

How do these tactical implications of attachment relate to a situation such as that in Problem A, *supra*?

[B] Attachment Procedure

SOCIETE GENERALE ALSACIENNE DE BANQUE, ZURICH v. FLEMINGDON DEVELOPMENT CORP.
Appellate Division, Second Department
118 A.D.2d 769, 500 N.Y.S.2d 278 (1986)

The instant action was instituted by Societe Generale Alsacienne De Banque, Zurich (hereinafter Societe) to recover the sum of $350,000 extended in the form of credit by it in reliance upon a check payable to its order, which was issued in March 1984 by Flemingdon, a New York corporation. The check was signed on behalf of Flemingdon by Lieb Waldman, its president, director and sole shareholder.

Societe is a Swiss banking corporation located in Zurich, Switzerland. Waldman had maintained banking relations with Societe for personal and business purposes for several years prior to the March 1984 incident. One of the accounts maintained by Waldman at Societe was identified as account No. 2985, which was in the name of Flemingdon. Several times during the two years prior to the March 1984 incident, account No. 2985 had been overdrawn, and on such occasions, Societe advised Flemingdon that payment of the account deficit was required before further credit would be extended. On those occasions, Waldman, on behalf of Flemingdon, appeared at Societe's Zurich offices and deposited funds to cover the deficits in that account.

In early March 1984, account No. 2985 was again overdrawn and Flemingdon was advised that Societe would not honor any further payment orders drawn on that account until the debit position had been covered. On March 8, 1984, Waldman appeared at Societe's Zurich offices with a check in the amount of $350,000 drawn on Flemingdon's account at Chemical Bank, and signed by Waldman. Waldman subsequently admitted that at the time he presented the check he knew that there were insufficient funds in Flemingdon's account at Chemical Bank to cover it. However, Waldman claimed that he had every reasonable expectation that sufficient funds would be on hand at the time the check was presented to Chemical Bank. . . .

Meanwhile, on March 9, 1984, Societe forwarded the $350,000 check to Morgan Guaranty Trust Company of New York (hereinafter MGT), its correspondent bank in New York, for collection. . . . On March 14, 1984, Chemical Bank returned the check to MGT, advising MGT that the account upon which the check was drawn contained insufficient funds and that the account, in fact, had been closed at Chemical Bank's request on or about March 14, 1984, because of Flemingdon's continued pattern and practice of maintaining the account in a debit position. As a result of Chemical Bank's refusal to honor the $350,000 check, MGT reversed its credit to Societe's account. According to Societe, by the time the credit to its account was reversed by MGT, it had already honored payment orders on [defendant's behalf] in the amount of $350,000.

On March 22 and 23, 1984, Societe contacted Waldman by telephone and advised him that the $350,000 check had been returned due to insufficient funds. On March 22, 1984, Waldman told Societe that the check bore an incorrect account number at Chemical Bank and that Societe should re-present the check to Chemical Bank for payment. The next day, March 23, 1984, Waldman told Societe that he would personally contact Chemical Bank to insure that the check would be properly paid out of the correct account. When Societe represented the check for collection, however, it was advised by Chemical Bank that all accounts held by Flemingdon at Chemical Bank had been closed nearly two weeks earlier, on March 14, 1984. Subsequent attempts by Societe to contact Waldman by telephone and mail were futile.

Thereafter, Societe commenced an action against Flemingdon and Waldman in the United States District Court, Southern District of New York, seeking to recover the sum of $350,000. Jurisdiction in that Federal action was based upon the alleged diversity of citizenship of the parties. In June 1984, Societe obtained from the Federal court an ex parte order of attachment against the property of Flemingdon and Waldman. At the time the Federal ex parte order of attachment was issued, Societe had discovered a bank account in The Bank of New York (hereinafter BNY) held in the name of Flemingdon. When the Federal order of attachment was served upon BNY, Flemingdon's account at that bank had just been credited with a deposit of approximately $300,000 from the National State Bank of Elizabeth, New Jersey (hereinafter NSB). Upon being advised of the order of attachment on said account, Waldman allegedly attempted to have the funds of $300,000 returned to NSB in New Jersey. These efforts were unsuccessful.

Following the issuance of the Federal ex parte order of attachment, Flemingdon and Waldman moved to dismiss the Federal action for lack of diversity jurisdiction. . . .

While the motion to dismiss the Federal action was pending, Societe instituted the instant action against Flemingdon, Waldman and his wife, Eva Waldman, seeking to recover damages in the amount of $350,000, *inter alia*, for conversion, unjust enrichment and fraud. Societe also sought a concurrent order of attachment against the defendants' property pursuant to CPLR 6201(1) and (3). Societe stated that a concurrent order of attachment was necessary since it intended to request a voluntary dismissal of its pending Federal action and to pursue its claim in the courts of this State. The Federal action was eventually discontinued.

CPLR 6201 provides, in pertinent part, as follows:

> An order of attachment may be granted in any action, except a matrimonial action, where the plaintiff has demanded and would be entitled, in whole or in part, or in the alternative, to a money judgment against one or more defendants, when:
>
> 1. the defendant is a nondomiciliary residing without the state, or is a foreign corporation not qualified to do business in the state; or . . .
>
> 3. the defendant, with intent to defraud his creditors or frustrate the enforcement of a judgment that might be rendered in plaintiff's favor, has assigned, disposed of, encumbered or secreted property, or removed it from the state or is about to do any of these acts.

. . . .

In order to prevail under CPLR 6201(3), the plaintiff must demonstrate: (1) that the defendant has, or is about to conceal his or her property in one of the enumerated ways, and (2) that defendant has acted or will act with the intent to defraud his or her creditors or to frustrate the enforcement of a judgment for the plaintiff. . . . "Fraud is not lightly inferred, and the moving papers must contain evidentiary facts — as opposed to conclusions — proving the fraud"

(McLaughlin, Practice Commentaries, McKinney's Cons Laws of NY, Book 7B, CPLR C6201:4, p 13 . . .). Affidavits containing allegations raising a mere suspicion of an intent to defraud are insufficient. "It must appear that such fraudulent intent really existed in the defendant's mind. . . ." In addition to proving fraudulent intent, the plaintiff must also show probable success on the merits of the underlying action in order to obtain an order of attachment (*see*, CPLR 6212[a] . . .).

Based upon a review of the record herein, we conclude that Societe has produced sufficient evidentiary facts to warrant the issuance of an order of attachment under CPLR 6201(3) against Flemingdon and Lieb Waldman. In the first instance, Waldman drew the check in issue on Flemingdon's behalf, admittedly with the knowledge that there were insufficient funds in Flemingdon's Chemical Bank account to satisfy payment. This conduct in and of itself constitutes actionable fraud. . . .

In addition, Waldman's conduct after passing the bad check demonstrated an intent to secrete Flemingdon's assets in order to frustrate Societe's collection on the check. Such conduct included Waldman's statement to Societe that the check bore an incorrect account number and should be re-presented to Chemical Bank for payment even though Waldman knew or should have known that all of Flemingdon's accounts at that bank had been closed. In addition, Waldman's refusal to respond to Societe's subsequent telephone and mail inquiries concerning its inability to collect on the check, as well as his alleged attempts to remove the funds in Flemingdon's account at BNY following the service of the Federal ex parte order of attachment, evidences an intent to defraud Societe. In view of these facts, an order of attachment should have been issued under CPLR 6201(3) against him and Flemingdon.

In view of the above, we do not pass on the merits of Special Term's denial of an order of attachment under CPLR 6201(1).

In conclusion, we note that the branch of Societe's motion seeking an order of attachment against assets held by Eva Waldman was properly denied. Although Societe alleges that Eva Waldman, a director of Flemingdon, a joint signatory of the corporation's bank accounts and owner of the premises claimed as Flemingdon's place of business, was, in some way, involved in the scheme to defraud Societe, there is a question as to the bank's probability of success on the merits against that defendant. Accordingly, an order of attachment against Eva Waldman's assets is not warranted. . . .

NOTE ON ATTACHMENT PROCEDURE

An order of attachment is obtained, like other orders, by motion. As further developed below, the motion may be made on notice to the defendant or ex parte. It may be made at any time prior to final judgment, although, if the attachment is sought for jurisdictional purposes, the order should be obtained and the levy made prior to serving the summons. *See* CPLR 314(3).

The motion must be supported by an affidavit which, together with any other written evidence (*e.g.*, a copy of a contract) the plaintiff cares to submit, must meet the three-part test of CPLR 6212(a); it must show: (1) that "there is a cause of action" and that the plaintiff will probably succeed on the merits; (2) that at least one of the grounds for attachment found in CPLR 6201 exists; and (3) that the amount demanded in the complaint exceeds any counterclaims of which plaintiff has knowledge. Since the order of attachment, if granted, must specify the amount to be secured pursuant to it, plaintiff's affidavit must, by implication, also establish the amount of probable recovery. Finally, the affidavit should state whether any other provisional remedy has been sought in the same action against the defendant. CPLR 6001.

Plaintiff's papers should not only meet all the technical requirements for obtaining the attachment order but must convince the court that the issuance of the order will be just, as the court has discretionary authority to decline the order in the interests of fairness and justice (as noted in another context in *Morning Glory Media v. Enright*, § 12.02, *supra*). Could the requirements of CPLR 6212 be met by the plaintiff in Problem A?

The order itself is not directed to the defendant but to an appropriate sheriff, CPLR 6211(a), whom it directs to levy upon defendant's property found within the sheriff's jurisdiction or upon a garnishee (a person indebted to defendant, CPLR 105(i)) servable within his jurisdiction. The order should specify the amount to be secured pursuant to it, which will reflect plaintiff's claim plus interest, costs, and the sheriff's fees and expenses. CPLR 6211(a).

CPLR 6211(a), amended in 1977 as part of the legislative effort to shore up the constitutionality of the attachment process, authorizes the plaintiff to move for an order of attachment either ex parte or on notice. It encourages the plaintiff to move on notice (thus obviating some constitutional objections) by permitting the court to grant a temporary restraining order (t.r.o.) directed to a garnishee which prohibits him from transferring the defendant's property in his possession. Since the t.r.o. itself may be granted without notice to the defendant, CPLR 6210, the plaintiff is to some degree protected against the possibility that the defendant will remove the property from the state or alienate it.

In most cases, the plaintiff should move on notice for the order of attachment and obtain the t.r.o. to protect his rights. While the order of attachment must be delivered by the plaintiff to the sheriff for service on the garnishee or defendant, a t.r.o. may be served by any person qualified to serve papers. Thus, plaintiff may gain the element of speed by using the t.r.o. Unlike the service of an order of attachment on the sheriff, the restraining order does not give the plaintiff a lien on defendant's property. *Compare* CPLR 6203; *see also* CPLR 6226. Thus, if a lien is needed quickly to obtain a priority over other creditors, it is better to move for the attachment ex parte and dispense with the t.r.o.[1]

---

[1] *New York Janitorial Service, Inc. v. Easthampton DeWitt Corp.*, 100 Misc. 2d 814, 420 N.Y.S.2d 100 (Sup. Ct. 1979).

If the plaintiff does seek, and is granted, an order of attachment without notice to the defendant, the order granting it imposes a burden on the plaintiff which safeguards the defendant's due process rights by insuring the defendant a prompt opportunity to challenge the validity of the attachment. The order must require the plaintiff to move, no later than five days[2] after the levy, for another order confirming the order of attachment. CPLR 6211(b). The motion to confirm must be "on such notice as the court shall direct to the defendant, the garnishee, if any, and the sheriff." *Id.* An order which is not confirmed within the time specified may be vacated on motion. CPLR 6211(b); *see Great White Whale Advertising, Inc. v. First Festival Productions*, 81 A.D.2d 704, 438 N.Y.S.2d 655 (3d Dep't 1981).

A court which grants an attachment order ex parte may further minimize the impact on the defendant by directing the sheriff to refrain from taking the property into custody. CPLR 6211(b). Such direction should be made unless the sheriff's custody is necessary to protect the plaintiff's interest in the property.[3]

When an order of attachment is secured before a summons is served upon the defendant, the length of time during which the order will remain effective is limited in order to prevent a plaintiff from tying up the defendant's property indefinitely by not going forward with the action. CPLR 6213 provides that the order of attachment will be invalid unless the plaintiff, within sixty days[4] after the order is granted, effects service of the summons.

The order of attachment, the papers on which it was based, and the summons and complaint must be filed with the clerk of the issuing court within ten days after the order is granted. A failure to comply with this provision, like that regarding service of summons, makes the order void.

In *Connecticut v. Doehr*, 501 U.S. 1, 111 S. Ct. 2105, 115 L. Ed. 2d 1 (1991), the Supreme Court held that a Connecticut statute, which allowed for attachment of real property without a hearing and without a showing of some exigent circumstance, violated the Due Process Clause, as applied in the *Doehr* case. Plaintiff in *Doehr*, before commencing a tort action against defendant, obtained an attachment of defendant's home. The court found a due process violation because of three factors, 1) the serious deprivation of property since defendant could not sell or lease the property with a clouded title, 2) the potential for wrongful attachment was enormous because plaintiff merely had to file a conclusory affidavit, and 3) the interests of plaintiff in securing payment of a pos-

---

[2] The motion to confirm may be made within ten days after levy if the ground for the attachment is that the defendant is a nondomiciliary residing without the state or is a foreign corporation not qualified to do business in the state. CPLR 6211(b).

[3] If the sheriff has not taken custody of the attached property, the order of attachment expires ninety days after the levy, unless extended by the court. CPLR 6214(e).

[4] This period may be extended by court order, but for no more than sixty additional days. The extension must be sought prior to the expiration of the original period. CPLR 6213. Failure to serve the summons within the time allowed is a ground to vacate the attachment. *Raphael v. Gibson*, 65 A.D.2d 553, 409 N.Y.S.2d 18 (2d Dep't 1978).

sible judgment was too minimal to burden defendant's property interests without a pre-attachment hearing. In an appendix to the opinion, New York was listed as a jurisdiction requiring a showing of exigent circumstances as a requirement for an order of attachment without a hearing. 501 U.S. at 25, 111 S. Ct. at 2120, 115 L. Ed. 2d at 22. This lends some assurance that CPLR 6211 is sound. *See* Professor Alexander's Supplementary Practice Commentaries, McKinney's CPLR § 6211, 2006 pocket part, p. 34.

[C] Attachable Assets

PROBLEM B

(a) Is the washing machine described in Problem A attachable? *See* CPLR 6202; CPLR 5201.

(b) "Hot Dog" Wilson, a star player of the Los Angeles Dodgers, had a falling out with Jim, his former business partner, who claims that Wilson has defaulted on a debt to him of $350,000. Wilson's team won the National League Pennant and with it the right to play the Red Sox (yes, the Red Sox) in the World Series. Thus, each player on the team will eventually be paid either a loser's share (over $200,000) or (more likely) a winner's share (over $200,000) by the Commissioner of Baseball upon completion of the Series. Since the Commissioner's office is in New York, Jim would like to attach Wilson's share as a provisional remedy in connection with an action he plans to bring against Wilson in New York.

Is either the winner's or loser's share attachable prior to the Series?

ABKCO INDUSTRIES, INC. v. APPLE FILMS, INC.
Court of Appeals
39 N.Y.2d 670, 385 N.Y.S.2d 511, 350 N.E.2d 899 (1976)

JUSTICE JONES, J.

We hold that the property interest of this absent debtor in its contract with a resident corporation was subject to levy by order of attachment and that jurisdiction of the New York courts quasi-in-rem may properly be predicated on that attachment.

ABKCO Industries (ABKCO) seeks repayment of a loan allegedly made to Apple Films, Ltd. (LTD), an English corporation. Unable to obtain personal jurisdiction over its English debtor, the creditor seeks by way of attachment to obtain jurisdiction quasi-in-rem in New York for the prosecution of its claim.

LTD entered into a licensing agreement (Licensing Agreement) with Apple Films, Inc., a New York corporation (INC), whereby LTD granted a general license to INC to promote a motion picture film owned by LTD, "Let It Be," featuring the "Beatles." Under the terms of this Licensing Agreement, INC agreed to pay to LTD 80% of the net profits received by INC from the promotion of the film. Exercising the authority granted it under the Licensing Agreement, INC contemporaneously entered into a distribution agreement (Distribution Agreement) with United Artists under which INC transferred its rights and control over distribution of the film to United Artists and United Artists agreed to pay INC 50% of the adjusted gross receipts from distribution of the film. The critical question is whether in these circumstances there was a debt or property of LTD in New York which could be attached by LTD's creditor, ABKCO. The lower courts have held that LTD had an attachable interest, and we agree.

In our analysis the Distribution Agreement between INC and United Artists is irrelevant to our present inquiry, however significant it unquestionably is from an economic point of view. Our attention must be focused on the Licensing Agreement between LTD and INC, for it is that contract and the rights and obligations of the parties under it which must furnish the predicate for the attachment if any is to be found.

By virtue of CPLR 6202, an attachment under CPLR 6214 (subd [b]) is effective only if there is within the jurisdiction of our courts a debt or property of the debtor, here LTD, within the meanings of subdivisions (a) or (b) of CPLR 5201, which provide:

> (a) Debt against which a money judgment may be enforced. A money judgment may be enforced against any debt, which is past due or which is yet to become due, certainly or upon demand of the judgment debtor, whether it was incurred within or without the state, to or from a resident or nonresident, unless it is exempt from application to the satisfaction of the judgment. A debt may consist of a cause of action which could be assigned or transferred accruing within or without the state.

> (b) Property against which a money judgment may be enforced. A money judgment may be enforced against any property which could be assigned or transferred, whether it consists of a present or future right or interest and whether or not it is vested, unless it is exempt from application to the satisfaction of the judgment. A money judgment entered upon a joint liability of two or more persons may be enforced against individual property of those persons summoned and joint property of such persons with any other persons against whom the judgment is entered.

Here the issue turns on the proper analysis and classification of LTD's rights under the Licensing Agreement with INC, the New York corporation.

Appellants argue that LTD's right can only be classified as a debt within the meaning of CPLR 5201 (subd [a]). If this be the case, the argument continues, it is not an attachable debt because it is neither "past due" nor "to become due, certainly or upon demand." At the time of the purported attachment nothing was past due. In consequence of INC's having advanced expenses as to which INC was entitled to reimbursement from LTD and the fact that, since the film was still in the early stages of promotion, INC had not yet received any substantial sums from United Artists to which the 80% payover provision might apply, the net balance between LTD and INC was in INC's favor; thus there was at the time no indebtedness owing from INC to LTD. Nor, appellants assert, can it be said that anything was to become due, certainly or upon demand, since it could not be known, or even reliably predicted, when if ever gross receipts from the film would reach the point of black balances in favor of LTD against INC. Thus, it is said, the alleged debt of INC to LTD was subject to such contingencies as to fall outside the scope of subdivision (a) under the decided cases.

We take a different view of the legal classification of LTD's interests under the Licensing Agreement. We conclude that those interests constituted property, composed of the bundle of all its rights under the Agreement, of which, of course, the obligation of INC to pay under the 80% clause was the principal feature of economic significance. That property was attachable because concededly it was assignable by LTD (CPLR 5201, subd [b]).

Reflection on our holding in *Glassman v Hyder* (23 NY2d 354) is instructive. In that case it was sought to reach the interest of an absent debtor-landlord in a lease of real estate situate in the State of New Mexico. Analyzed from the perspective of property the interest of a landlord would not be classified simply as an interest in a contract; rather it would be an aspect of the leasehold. That approach, however, would have been unavailing since under recognized principles the situs of a leasehold of real estate is at the location of the real estate. In *Glassman* the real estate was in New Mexico; thus the property of the landlord-debtor was beyond the reach of the New York courts. Resort then was had to the debt theory. On this approach the debtor-tenant could be reached in New York State, but as a debt the tenant's obligation to pay future rents did not meet the statutory requirements for an attachable debt. The obligation to pay rent was not a debt and not certain to become due (*Glassman v Hyder, supra*, at p 359).

By contrast, the attachment here does not attempt to reach a debt or a property interest in a leasehold of real estate; rather it seeks to reach intangible personal property belonging to LTD — its interest in the Licensing Agreement. The situs of that intangible property is in New York where there is to be found the other party to the Licensing Agreement, INC, upon whom rests the obligation of performance. Tangible personal property obviously has a unique location and can only be attached where it is. It is true that some intangibles are deemed to have become embodied in formal paper writings, *e.g.*, negotiable instruments, and in such instances attachment depends on the physical presence of the written instrument within the attaching jurisdiction (*e.g.*, CPLR 5201, subd [c], par 4; 6202). No fact of physical location or concept of embodiment applies, however, to intangible property in an ordinary contract, written or oral; if in writing, that writing is only the evidentiary manifestation of the contract between the parties; it is not the contract itself. The CPLR contains no provision as to the situs of such property for attachment purposes, which we perceive to be the location of the party of whom performance is required by the terms of the contract. So here the intangible property of LTD, found in New York, may be attached.

Since we classify the subject of this attachment as property it is irrelevant that, had a balance been struck at the moment the attachment was effected, it would have disclosed that LTD was indebted to INC rather than that INC was indebted to LTD. We know of no threshold requirement that the attaching creditor show the value of the attached property or indeed that it has any value. Correlatively we know of no theory on which the debtor or the garnishee is entitled to a vacatur of the attachment if it can be established that the property in question is valueless. While the fact of value or lack of it has no legal effect on the validity of the attachment, it obviously will have real economic significance. Even that aspect, however, may not come into sharp focus until execution on the judgment, if any, in the action for which the attachment provides jurisdiction.

Thus we conclude that the interest of LTD in the Licensing Agreement was property; it was assignable and hence attachable. Accordingly, the orders of the Appellate Division in these related cases should be affirmed.

. . . .

NOTES

(1) Of what importance is the principal case after *Shaffer v. Heitner*, § 1.07[A], *supra*?

(2) The problem of defining attachable assets was revisited in *Supreme Merchandise Co. v. Chemical Bank*, 70 N.Y.2d 344, 520 N.Y.S.2d 734, 514 N.E.2d 1358 (1987). At issue was whether a letter of credit issued by Chemical Bank with Kinzoku, a Japanese corporation, as the beneficiary, was subject to attachment by a third party with an unrelated claim against Kinzoku. The letter of credit provided that drafts drawn against it by Kinzoku could be negotiated by any bank and would be paid by Chemical upon presentation of necessary documentation. The Court, distinguishing *ABKCO*, held that the letter was neither a debt certain to become due nor property for the purposes of attachment.

The Court stated:

> A guiding principle in our analysis is that, while CPLR 5201 is obviously intended to have broad reach, still the Legislature expressly put beyond the grasp of the statute the general category of contingent debts, "to preclude a levy against contingent obligations not certain to ripen into something real." (Siegel, NY Prac § 323, at 389. . . .)

There is a different, and in a relevant sense even greater, contingency in the beneficiary's interest here than in *ABKCO*. A letter of credit "is an executory contract that conditions performance of the issuer's obligation (payment) upon performance by the beneficiary (delivery of specified documents)." . . . In the absence of compliance with the terms and conditions of a letter of credit, the issuing bank owes nothing to the beneficiary. Whereas the debtor's interest in *ABKCO* was contingent solely as to value, which depended on events beyond its own control, Kinzoku's interest is dependent upon its own future performance. Before payment would be due, Kinzoku would have to perform by timely shipment of the goods, compliance with the terms of the credit, and presentation of conforming documents. Given that a beneficiary of a letter of credit retains the option to defeat the interest and render it worthless, we are mindful that allowing attachment in this instance — unlike *ABKCO* — could serve as a disincentive to a beneficiary's performance of the underlying contract as well as the terms of the letter of credit. While this contingency is particularly pertinent in a situation where the beneficiary is a seller of goods thousands of miles from New York, we nevertheless agree with the court below that even claims that depend on further action by the debtor may constitute "property" and that this distinction from *ABKCO* is not alone dispositive. . . .

The more profound difference from *ABKCO*, however, lies in the fact that what is at issue here is Kinzoku's interest in a negotiable letter of credit, an instrument extensively used in domestic and international trade, which because of its unique character typically implicates others than the immediate parties to the underlying transaction. The transaction before us, for example, involves not only Kinzoku and its buyer, but also the issuing bank and two negotiating banks — none of whom had any part in the dispute between petitioner and Kinzoku, yet whose interests could be affected by permitting attachment of Kinzoku's interest in the letter of credit.

We are persuaded that, for policy reasons, the rationale of *ABKCO* does not extend this far, and that Kinzoku's interest for present purposes must be considered a contingent, nonattachable "debt" under CPLR 5201(a) rather than attachable "property" under CPLR 5201(b). Letters of credit have been recognized "as an essential lubricant that permits the wheels of international trade to turn" . . . [and] as "indispensable to international trade". . . . Their peculiar value lies in the fact that by superimposing the financial strength and integrity of one party (typically a bank) on that of another (typically a seller) they add the virtual certainty that upon presentation of conforming documents payment will be made. . . .

This peculiar utility derives from two of the fundamental principles pertaining to letters of credit. First, a letter of credit contract must be strictly construed and performed in accordance with its terms. This principle of strict construction may be illustrated by the oft-quoted statement from *Equitable Trust Co. v Dawson Partners* (27 Lloyd's List L Rep 49): "There is no room for documents which are almost the same, or which will do just as well." Second, the credit engagement is independent of the underlying contract. . . . Thus, adherence to the terms of the credit as set forth in the letter of credit carries with it the virtual certainty that payment will be made. . . .

If an issuer's payment is blocked by an attachment order of a plaintiff seeking to establish jurisdiction for its own unrelated dispute with the seller — thereby often embroiling the parties in a contest as to priority among creditors — it is at the cost of diminution of confidence in the certainty and integrity of letters of credit in this jurisdiction. We fully endorse the conclusion of the court below that if this attachment were upheld in the circumstances presented "it would follow in many situations that an order of attachment secured by a creditor in an effort to reach the debtor's contingent interest would (1) cause the debtor not to take action necessary to the maturing of the claim, (2) disrupt separate contractual obligations involving unrelated parties, and (3) impair the capacity of letters of credit to discharge their important and intended functions." (117 AD2d 424, 431, *supra*.)

Based on the nature of Kinzoku's interest coupled with the policy considerations involved in negotiable letters of credit concerned with international sales transactions, we conclude that for the purposes of attachment this interest is not "property" within the meaning of CPLR 5201(b).

70 N.Y.2d at 350-53, 520 N.Y.S.2d at 737-39, 514 N.E.2d at 1361-63.

(3) It is unclear whether income is attachable pursuant to Article 62 even though CPLR 5231 allows a judgment to be enforced by obtaining an income execution which requires ten percent of the debtor's salary to be paid to the creditor. A pre-CPLR case, *Morris Plain Indus. Bank v. Gunning*, 295 N.Y. 324, 67 N.E.2d 510 (1946), held wage income attachable, but *dicta* in *Glassman v. Hyder*, 23 N.Y.2d 354, 296 N.Y.S.2d 783, 244 N.E.2d 259 (1968), indicates that the question is still open.

In *Nat. Union Fire v. Adv. Employment Concepts*, 269 A.D.2d 101, 703 N.Y.S.2d 2 (1st Dep't 2000), it was held that a bank account in another state cannot be attached merely because a branch of the same bank is in New York.

[D]　Remedy for Wrongful Attachment

A & M EXPORTS, LTD. v. MERIDIEN INTERNATIONAL BANK, LTD.
Appellate Division, First Department
222 A.D.2d 378, 636 N.Y.S.2d 35 (1995)

MEMORANDUM DECISION.

Order of the Supreme Court, New York County (William J. Davis, J.), entered February 22, 1995, which awarded defendants judgment in the amount of plaintiff's undertaking and severed that portion of defendants' claim for attorney's fees for an assessment thereof, unanimously reversed, on the law, without costs, and the matter remanded to Supreme Court for a hearing to determine the extent of defendants' damages pursuant to CPLR 6315.

Plaintiff commenced this action against defendants for failure to honor certain letters of credit. In connection with its application for an order of attachment pursuant to CPLR 6201(1), plaintiff obtained a temporary restraining order (CPLR 6210) prohibiting the transfer of $1,394,000 in assets maintained by defendants in a New York bank. However, plaintiff's complaint was ultimately dismissed on forum non conveniens grounds and the temporary restraining order vacated, this Court affirming (*A & M Exports, Ltd. v. Meridien Intl. Bank, Ltd.*, 207 A.D.2d 741, 616 N.Y.S.2d 621), without any order of attachment ever being issued. The present dispute concerns the extent of damages recoverable by defendants as a consequence of the restraint on asset transfers.

The temporary restraining order provides for an undertaking in the amount of $89,067.25 and recites that "plaintiff, if it is finally determined that it was not entitled to a temporary restraining order, will pay to the defendant [Meridien International Bank, Ltd.] and/or [Meridien Biao Bank Liberia Ltd.], all damages and costs which may be sustained by reason thereof." The undertaking itself recites that plaintiff will pay damages "not exceeding" $89,067.25. While plaintiff contends that the order and the undertaking are inconsistent, in a case involving a similar order, it was held that, absent malice, the undertaking provides the sole basis for relief. The Appellate Division, Third Department reasoned that "there is no common-law cause of action for damages sustained by an improperly procured preliminary injunction, nor does CPLR 6315 create a statutory cause of action. The basis for damages is the undertaking itself which is a contract between the parties 'that the plaintiff, if it is finally determined that he was not entitled to an injunction, will pay to the defendant all damages and costs which may be sustained by reason of the injunction' (CPLR 6312[b])" (*Honeywell, Inc. v. Technical Bldg. Servs.*, 103 A.D.2d 433, 434, 480 N.Y.S.2d 627; *RS Paralegal Recovery Servs. v. Poughkeepsie Sav. Bank*, 190 A.D.2d 660, 593 N.Y.S.2d 283).

In this case, defendants moved for an order awarding damages, 1) in the amount of the undertaking pursuant to CPLR 6212(b) and, 2) in the amount of $124,208.52, "representing costs and attorney's fees incurred in the action," pursuant to CPLR 6212(e). In response to plaintiff's contention that the court lacked jurisdiction to entertain the application, the court deemed the motion to be brought pursuant to CPLR 6210. As requested by defendants, the court applied the measure of damages provided in CPLR 6212(e), which does not limit recovery to the amount of the undertaking.

It bears emphasis that no order of attachment was ever issued in this case, and there is no basis for an award of damages premised upon the improper procurement of such an order. The temporary restraining order provided for in CPLR 6210 is issued pursuant to CPLR 6313(c), and any damages sustained by reason of the operation of the order are ascertained in accordance with the provisions of CPLR 6315, not by reference to CPLR 6212(e) (*Salamanca Trust Co. v. McHugh*, 156 A.D.2d 1007, 550 N.Y.S.2d 764 [damages under CPLR 6212(e) not recoverable unless property actually attached]; *Provisional Protective Comm. v. Williams*, 121 A.D.2d 271, 503 N.Y.S.2d 47 [TRO issued pursuant to CPLR 6210 insufficient basis for award of attorney's fees pursuant to CPLR 6212(e)]; *Augsbury v. Adams*, 108 A.D.2d 978, 484 N.Y.S.2d 962 [CPLR 6212(e) damages not recoverable where application for attachment denied]).

The summary procedure of CPLR 6315 permits the court that imposed the restraint on the transfer of a defendant's assets, which is presumably well acquainted with the dispute, to fix damages resulting from that restraint (McLaughlin, Practice Commentaries, McKinney's Cons Laws of NY, Book 7B, CPLR C6315:1, at 391). "The amount of damages so ascertained is conclusive upon all persons who were served with notice of the motion and such amount may be recovered by the person entitled thereto in a separate action" (CPLR 6315). Such an award may include counsel fees incurred in connection with an "erroneously granted temporary restraining order," where supported by the record (*Kaplan v. Werlin*, 626 N.Y.S.2d 817, 818; *Watmet, Inc. v. Robinson*, 116 A.D.2d 998, 999, 498 N.Y.S.2d 619; *see also, Hanley v. Fox*, 90 A.D.2d 662, 456 N.Y.S.2d 251).

Supreme Court did not assess the extent of defendants' damages, however, but simply rendered an award for the full amount of the undertaking. While it may yet be determined that defendants' damages are in excess of the undertaking by a substantial margin, there is no statutory provision for an award of liquidated damages in the amount of the undertaking. The only evidence of record is a "billing memorandum" from counsel listing various "unbilled" fees and disbursements. In the absence of a hearing as to the propriety of counsel fees (*Morgan & Finnegan v. Howe Chemical Co.*, 210 A.D.2d 62, 63, 619 N.Y.S.2d 719) or any findings with respect to the nature and extent of the damages incurred by defendants, the record is insufficient to sustain the award.

. . . .

NOTES

(1) The damages recoverable for an improper preliminary injunction or temporary restraining order are set forth in CPLR 6315. Damages caused by an attachment are covered by CPLR 6212(e). The latter, it has been held, authorizes the court to award damages that include the interest lost by the defendant as a result of the attachment. *See Dean v. James McHugh Constr. Co.*, 56 A.D.2d 716, 392 N.Y.S.2d 946 (4th Dep't 1977). Any interest or dividends earned by attached funds during the period of the attachment should be offset against the legal rate of interest assessed upon the finding of a wrongful attachment. *Richman v. Richman*, 52 A.D.2d 393, 384 N.Y.S.2d 220 (1976).

In *Ford Motor Credit Co. v. Hickey Ford Sales, Inc.*, 62 N.Y.2d 291, 476 N.Y.S.2d 791, 465 N.E.2d 330 (1984), the Court held that the damages for a wrongful attachment may include those resulting from mental distress, if the victim can show actual malice.

(2) The perpetrator of a wrongful attachment is liable for attorney's fees "sustained by reason of the attachment if the defendant recovers judgment, or if it is finally decided that the plaintiff was not entitled to an attachment of the defendant's property." CPLR 6212(e). When, if ever, should the defendant be able to recover all attorney's fees incurred in defending the action? *See Thropp v. Erb*, 255 N.Y. 75, 174 N.E. 67 (1930).

§ 12.04 NON-JUDICIAL REMEDIES AVAILABLE IN PROPERTY DISPUTES

PROBLEM C

Under the facts of Problem A, could Wacky Walter's, Inc., have legally repossessed the washing machine without the use of any judicial process? Consider U.C.C. §§ 9-609, 9-610 and the constitutionality of those sections.

U.C.C. § 9-609. Secured Party's Right to Take Possession after Default.

(a) Possession . . . After default, a secured party:

(1) may take possession of the collateral;

. . . .

(b) Judicial and nonjudicial process. A secured party may proceed under subsection (a):

(1) pursuant to judicial process; or

(2) without judicial process, if it proceeds without breach of the peace.

U.C.C. § 9-610(a). Disposition after Default.

After default, a secured party may sell, lease, license, or otherwise dispose of any or all of the collateral. . . .

A "secured party" is "a person in whose favor a security interest is created or provided for under a security agreement." U.C.C. § 9-102(a)(72).

SHARROCK v. DELL BUICK-CADILLAC, INC.
Court of Appeals
45 N.Y.2d 152, 408 N.Y.S.2d 39, 379 N.E.2d 1169 (1978)

COOKE, JUDGE.

Challenged here as violative of the due process clauses of the State Constitution (N.Y. Const. art. I, § 6) and the Fourteenth Amendment of the Federal Constitution is the statutory authorization afforded a garageman to foreclose his possessory statutory lien for repair and storage charges (Lien Law, § 184), by means of a public sale of the vehicle in his possession. We hold that sections 200, 201, 202 and 204 of the Lien Law, insofar as they empower a garageman to conduct an ex parte sale of a bailed automobile, fail to comport with traditional notions of procedural due process embodied in the State Constitution, as they deprive the owner of the vehicle of a significant property interest without providing any opportunity to be heard.

On October 12, 1975, plaintiff's husband took her 1970 Cadillac to Dell Buick-Cadillac, Inc. (Dell), for installation of a replacement engine he had purchased elsewhere. . . . Unfortunately, the replacement engine proved to be defective and had to be removed. Delivery of a replacement engine was then arranged. When the new replacement engine arrived, Dell informed plaintiff's husband that it would not be installed until Dell was paid the $225 due for the installation of the original defective engine. Although he agreed to pay this sum, plaintiff's husband did not have that amount of money with him at the time and soon thereafter was hospitalized, rendering him incapable of continuing his business dealings with Dell.

On January 14, 1976 plaintiff received a "Notice of Lien and Sale" by certified mail, informing her that pursuant to section 184 of the Lien Law Dell had imposed a possessory lien against the Cadillac in the amount of $304.95. That notice further advised that if plaintiff did not tender this sum within 30 days, the automobile would be sold at public auction on March 15, 1976 (see Lien Law, § 200). Plaintiff was subsequently informed by one of the auctioneers listed on the notice of sale that, her belief to the contrary notwithstanding, included in the lien was the sum of $79.95, representing storage charges. However, the auctioneer did agree to contact Dell in order to ascertain whether they would "take off" the storage charge from the amount due.

Several days later, the auctioneer informed plaintiff that Dell refused to waive its storage charge and that the amount now due had been increased to $545. He also advised her that since the book value of the car was appreciably greater than $545, it would be to plaintiff's advantage to pay the charges since Dell "had her over a barrel" because her husband had taken the car there for repair. On the day of the auction, March 15, 1976, Dell again modified its claim and informed plaintiff that the amount due had been reduced to $502. Later that day, plaintiff's 1970 Cadillac, having an established resale value of between $1,200 and $1,400, was sold to Dell for the sum of $502.

Plaintiff then commenced the instant action for declaratory and injunctive relief, as well as damages, claiming that the sale provisions of the Lien Law are violative of her due process rights as they authorize public sale of her automobile without affording the opportunity for a hearing. . . .

The threshold question in any judicial inquiry into conduct claimed to be violative of the due process clause of the Fourteenth Amendment is whether the State has in some fashion involved itself in what, in another setting, would otherwise be deemed private activity. . . . That much is made plain by the express terms of the amendment which specifies that "nor shall *any State deprive* any person of life, liberty, or property without due process of law" (emphasis added). Purely private conduct, however egregious or unreasonable, does not rise to the level of constitutional significance absent a significant nexus between the State and the actors or the conduct (*see Civil Rights Cases*, 109 U.S. 3, 11, 3 S.Ct. 18, 27 L.Ed. 835). This nexus has been denominated "State action" and is an essential requisite to any action grounded on violation of equal protection of the laws or a deprivation of due process of law. Further, it is settled that where the impetus for the allegedly unconstitutional conduct is private, the State must have "significantly involved itself" in order for that action to fall within the ambit of the Fourteenth Amendment. . . .

Despite its outward simplicity as a concept, State action is in fact an elusive principle, one which cannot be easily discerned by resort to ritualistic incantations or precise formalisms (*see Burton v. Wilmington Parking Auth.*, 365 U.S. 715, 722, 81 S.Ct. 856, 6 L.Ed.2d 45). Instead, a number of factors must be considered in determining whether a State is significantly involved in statutorily authorized private conduct. These factors include: the source of authority for the private action; whether the State is so entwined with the regulation of the private conduct as to constitute State activity; whether there is meaningful State participation in the activity; and whether there has been a delegation of what has traditionally been a State function to a private person (*Melara v. Kennedy*, 9 Cir., 541 F.2d 802, 805). As the test is not simply State involvement, but rather significant State involvement, satisfaction of one of these criteria may not necessarily be determinative to a finding of State action.[1]

---

[1] In the series of cases in which the Supreme Court has imposed the requirements of procedural due process in situations in which a creditor sought to deprive a debtor of a significant property interest (*Sniadach v. Family Fin. Corp.*, 395 U.S. 337, 89 S.Ct. 849, 21 L.Ed.2d 771; *Fuentes v. Shevin*, 407 U.S. 67, 92 S.Ct. 1983, 32 L.Ed.2d 556; *Mitchell v. Grant Co.*, 416 U.S. 600, 94 S.Ct. 1895, 40 L.Ed.2d 406; *North Ga. Finishing v. Di-Chem*, 419 U.S. 601, 95 S.Ct. 719, 42 L.Ed.2d 751), State action was manifest since the seizure was effected by officers of the State or by judicial process. In contrast, here the involvement of the State is concededly less direct.

We need not address plaintiff's contention that the actions taken by Dell are attributable to the State of New York for purposes of the due process clause of the Fourteenth Amendment. Recently, in *Flagg Bros. v. Brooks* (436 U.S. 149, 98 S.Ct. 1729, 56 L.Ed.2d 185), the Supreme Court rejected the argument that a private sale of property subject to a warehouseman's possessory lien pursuant to section 7-210 of the Uniform Commercial Code constitutes State action. The similarities between section 7-210 and the statutes at issue here might preclude any contrary finding by this court.[2]

But the mere fact that an activity might not constitute State action for purposes of the Federal Constitution does not perforce necessitate that the same conclusion be reached when that conduct is claimed to be violative of the State Constitution. . . . Indeed, on innumerable occasions this court has given our State Constitution an independent construction, affording the rights and liberties of the citizens of this State even more protection than may be secured under the United States Constitution. . . . This independent construction finds its genesis specifically in the unique language of the due process clause of the New York Constitution as well as the long history of due process protections afforded the citizens of this State and, more generally, in fundamental principles of federalism. . . .

In contrast to the due process clause of the Fourteenth Amendment, which is phrased in terms of State deprivation of life, liberty or property, section 6 of article I of the New York Constitution guarantees that "[n]o person shall be deprived of life, liberty or property without due process of law." Conspicuously absent from the State Constitution is any language requiring State action before an individual may find refuge in its protections. That is not to say, of course, that the due process clause of the State Constitution eliminates the necessity of any State involvement in the objected to activity (*see Stuart v. Palmer*, 74 N.Y. 183, 188). Rather, the absence of any express State action language simply provides a basis to apply a more flexible State involvement requirement than is currently being imposed by the Supreme Court with respect to the Federal provision.

The historical differences between the Federal and State due process clauses make clear that they were adopted to combat entirely different evils (*see* Schwartz, The Bill of Rights: A Documentary History, pp. 161, 165, 387, 855-856). Prior to the Civil War, the Federal Constitution had as its major concern governmental structures and relationships. Indeed, prior to the enactment of

---

[2] There are, of course, substantial differences between the private sale of goods authorized by the warehouseman's lien law and the private sale authorized by sections 200, 201, 202 and 204 of the Lien Law. Critical to the determination in *Flagg Bros.* that the private sale did not constitute State action was the "total absence of overt official involvement" (436 U.S., at p. 157, 98 S.Ct. at p. 1734). Here, that overt governmental involvement absent in *Flagg Bros.* is present to some degree. . . .

the Fourteenth Amendment, the Bill of Rights delimited only the power of the National Government, imposing few restrictions on State authority and offering virtually no protections of individual liberties (*see Barron v. Mayor & City Council of Baltimore*, 7 Pet. [32 U.S.] 243, 8 L.Ed. 672). The Fourteenth Amendment was a watershed — an attempt to extend and catalogue a series of national privileges and immunities, thereby furnishing minimum standards designed to guarantee the individual protection against the potential abuses of a monolithic government, whether that government be national, State or local. . . . In contrast, State Constitutions in general, and the New York Constitution in particular, have long safeguarded any threat to individual liberties, irrespective of from what quarter that peril arose. Thus, as early as 1843, Justice Bronson, in speaking of the due process clause of our State Constitution, noted: "The meaning of the section then seems to be, that no member of the state shall be disfranchised, or deprived of any of his rights and privileges, unless the matter be adjudged against him upon trial and according to the course of the common law. It must be ascertained judicially that he has forfeited his privileges, or that some one else has a superior title to the property he possesses, before either of them can be taken from him" (*Taylor v. Porter*, 4 Hill 140, 146; . . .).

Examination of the indices of State participation in nonjudicial foreclosure pursuant to the provisions of the Lien Law at issue here compels the conclusion that New York has so entwined itself into the debtor-creditor relationship as to constitute sufficient and meaningful State participation which triggers the protections afforded by our Constitution.

The garageman's lien is a statutory declaration of the common-law artisan's lien. At common law, a workman who by his labor enhanced the value of a chattel, obtained a lien upon it for the reasonable value of the work performed. That lien endowed the artisan with the exclusive right to possession of the repaired article until his charges were satisfied. . . . The possessory nature of the garageman's lien is not in issue here, and in any event, does not constitute State action. . . . For State action purposes, there is a fundamental distinction between a statute which, in regulating previously lawful conduct, does nothing more than merely acknowledge its lawfulness . . . and one which authorizes otherwise impermissible or unconstitutional conduct. . . .

As noted, common law afforded the garageman only the right to possession; it was the State which authorized enforcement of the lien by means of ex parte sale of the vehicle without first affording its owner an opportunity to be heard. . . . Thus, New York has done more than simply furnish its statutory imprimatur to purely private action. Rather, it has entwined itself into the debtor-creditor relationship arising out of otherwise regular consumer transactions. The enactment of substantive provisions of law which authorize the creditor to bypass the courts to carry out the foreclosure sale encourages him to adopt this procedure rather than to rely on more cumbersome methods which might comport with constitutional due process guarantees. Indeed, not only does the State encourage adoption of this patently unfair procedure, it insulates the garageman from civil or criminal liability arising out of the sale and requires one of its agencies, the Department of Motor Vehicles, to recognize and record the transfer of title (*see* Vehicle and Traffic Law, § 401), thus enabling the garageman to transfer title to a vehicle he would not otherwise be deemed to own (*Adams v. Department of Motor Vehicles*, 11 Cal.3d 146, 150-151, 113 Cal.Rptr. 145, 520 P.2d 961; *cf. Caesar v. Kiser*, D.C., 387 F.Supp. 645; . . .).

Even more fundamentally, the underlying purpose of the sale provisions of the Lien Law — that of conflict resolution — has always been deemed one of the essential attributes of sovereignty. Absent consent of the debtor, the power to fashion the means to order legally binding surrenders of property has always been exclusively vested in the State. Implementation of dispute settlement, irrespective of the strength of the competing interests of the parties, is the function of the judiciary, and is not dependent "on custom or the will of strategically placed individuals, but on the common-law model" (*Boddie v. Connecticut*, 401 U.S. 371, 375, 91 S.Ct. 780, 784, 28 L.Ed.2d 113). But by permitting the possessory lienor to take those steps necessary to foreclose his lien in a nonjudicial setting where the power of sale is premised on possession alone, the State has permitted the garageman to arrogate to himself the exclusive power of the sovereign to resolve disputes. However strong the interest of the garageman in the vehicle may be, his power of foreclosure has no vitality until it is sanctioned by the State. It follows, then, that such a person vested by the State with the power to resolve unilaterally an otherwise judicially cognizable controversy, is nothing more than a delegate of an exclusively governmental function. . . . For this reason, the debtor must be provided with that measure of due process as would be afforded in a court of law.

. . . The instant sale was made under the provisions of the Lien Law, the absence of which would have required Dell to go into court to prove both the validity of its lien and the charges due thereunder. Instead, by permitting the garageman to hold the sale ex parte, "the state has delegated the traditional roles of judge, jury and sheriff to [Dell] without providing for any judicial supervision or other safeguards" (*Cox Bakeries of N.D. v. Timm Moving & Stor.*, 8 Cir., 554 F.2d 356, 358).

Having determined that enforcement of the garageman's lien constitutes meaningful State participation inasmuch as New York has delegated to private parties functions traditionally associated with sovereignty, we therefore reach the substantive constitutional question. Fundamental notions of procedural due process require that before the State may deprive a person of a significant property interest in aid of a creditor, that person be given notice and an opportunity to be heard prior to deprivation of that interest. . . . Tested by this requirement, the statutes do not pass muster in light of the due process standards articulated in analogous circumstances by the Supreme Court. *Sniadach v. Family Fin. Corp.* (395 U.S. 337, 89 S.Ct. 849, 21 L.Ed.2d 771, *supra*) and *Fuentes v. Shevin* (407 U.S. 67, 92 S.Ct. 1983, 32 L.Ed.2d 556, *supra*) teach that even a temporary deprivation of property is entitled to due process protection. Although the implications of these holdings were left somewhat in doubt after *Mitchell v. Grant Co.* (416 U.S. 600, 94 S.Ct. 1895, 40 L.Ed.2d 406), in *North Ga. Finishing v. Di-Chem* (419 U.S. 601, 95 S.Ct. 719, 42 L.Ed.2d 751, *supra*), the Supreme Court made clear that it was the peculiar features of the Louisiana sequestration statutes that insulated them from due process infirmity. Viewed in this context, enforcement of the garageman's lien is as objectionable as the remedies struck down in *Sniadach, Fuentes* and *North Ga. Finishing* because it is executed without even a modicum of judicial intervention or supervision.

Moreover, the statutes challenged here display none of the "saving characteristics" (*North Ga. Finishing v. Di-Chem, supra*, at p. 607, 95 S.Ct. 719) of the provisions sustained in *Mitchell*. Twenty-four days after notice of sale is served, the garageman may proceed with the sale without having even approached a court or consulted the debtor, without filing a bond or affidavit, and without affording the owner a hearing in which he may contest the amount due. Even more objectionable is the fact that the statutes at issue here result in a permanent deprivation of what is today a necessity of life, not a temporary deprivation as would be occasioned by attachment, sequestration or replevin.

While the owner of a vehicle ordinarily understands that a garageman expects payment upon completion of the work, the contested provisions of the Lien Law afford him little redress to the garageman's retention and ex parte sale if the charges demanded exceed the previous estimate or there is a dispute as to the quality of workmanship. Instead, pursuant to his statutory grant of authority, a garageman may sell any vehicle, no matter how valuable, to satisfy any lien, no matter how small (*Parks v. "Mr. Ford,"* 3 Cir., 556 F.2d 132, 143, *supra*). To be sure, it is a reasonable exercise of the State's police power to give the garageman a security interest in vehicles which he has enhanced in value. However, it is unreasonable and constitutionally impermissible to provide absolutely no safeguards against unauthorized or unnecessary repairs or storage charges which may underlie the whole transaction, especially where an ownership interest hangs in the balance. By permitting a creditor to hold and sell a debtor's property unless his demands are met, the State empowers the garageman to engage in conduct which is tantamount to blackmail. In these circumstances, it is essential that the debtor be provided a forum to air his defenses.

Notwithstanding these patent inequities, it is urged that the vehicle owner may still enjoin an impending sale (CPLR art. 63), maintain an action for a judgment declaring the charges imposed unreasonable (CPLR 3001) or initiate a replevin action to recover the vehicle (CPLR art. 71; *see Dininny v. Reavis*, 100 Misc. 316, 165 N.Y.S. 97, *affd.*, 178 App.Div. 922, 165 N.Y.S. 97). However, when viewed from the standpoint of the persons involved this suggestion borders on the ludicrous. . . . Not only does it ask us to adopt a holding specifically rejected by the Supreme Court (*Fuentes v. Shevin*, 407 U.S. 67, 83, and n. 13, 92 S.Ct.

1983, and n.13, *supra*), it fails to take into account the delays and uncertainties inherent in any judicial proceeding and the fact that one whose automobile is subject to an impending sale is frequently poor, unrepresented by an attorney and unschooled in legal niceties. Moreover, as replevin and injunction are extraordinary remedies, they lack the certainty necessary to insure a hearing prior to permanent deprivation (*see Caesar v. Kiser*, D.C., 387 F.Supp. 645, 649, *supra*). Even assuming that these procedures could be deemed effective, the creditor's duty to afford the debtor an opportunity to be heard prior to the deprivation of a significant property interest would not be abrogated. The point is that by requiring a hearing prior to sale there would be assurance that all will have the opportunity to assert their claims.

Nor may the summary sale here be justified on the ground that the initial retention of the vehicle arose out of a voluntary transaction. At most, voluntary delivery of the automobile created a bailor-bailee relationship, which relationship could not divest the bailor of his continuing interest and title, irrespective of whether the bailee has a possessory lien on the bailed chattel. . . . Since that possessory lien is merely a security interest, the State may not constitutionally permit a garageman to extinguish the owner's interest without adherence to minimum due process standards. To be rejected also is the assertion that the statutes here may be justified because of the extraordinary circumstances present.[6] The property of a debtor may be summarily seized or sold only in a truly unusual situation and only "to secure an important governmental or general public interest or where the need for prompt action is paramount" (*Blye v. Globe-Wernicke Realty Co.*, 33 N.Y.2d 15, 21, 347 N.Y.S.2d 170, 176, 300 N.E.2d 710, 714, *supra*). But, as the Supreme Court has noted, where "no more than private gain is directly at stake" (*Fuentes v. Shevin, supra*, at p. 92, 92 S.Ct. at p. 2000), the opportunity to be heard is an indispensable bulwark against an arbitrary, and final, deprivation of property.

It must be concluded, therefore, that the sale provisions of sections 200, 201, 202 and 204 of the Lien Law violate the due process clause of the New York Constitution inasmuch as they fail to provide the owner of a vehicle an opportunity to be heard prior to permanent deprivation of a significant property interest. The garageman's right to retain his possessory lien is unaffected by this decision, but he may not sell the vehicle to satisfy his claim unless and until a method is

---

[6] We are not unmindful of the stake that a garageman has in the prompt enforceability of his lien. However, this interest should not be deemed inconsistent with the vehicle owner's right to be afforded the opportunity for some sort of prior judicial determination of the existence and scope of the lien. In this regard, we do not pass on the form of the hearing which the due process clause requires (*see* Friendly, *Some Kind of Hearing*, 123 U. of Pa.L.Rev. 1267, 1275). As the Supreme Court has aptly noted, "we deal here only with the right to an opportunity to be heard. Since the issues and facts decisive of rights . . . may very often be quite simple, there is a likelihood that many defendants would forgo their opportunity, sensing the futility of the exercise in the particular case. And, of course, no hearing need be held unless the defendant, having received notice of his opportunity, takes advantage of it" (*Fuentes v. Shevin, supra* pp. 92-93, n. 29, 92 S.Ct. at p. 2000 n. 29).

devised, consistent with due process, of affording the owner some opportunity to be heard.[7]

NOTES

(1) Soon after the principal case, the Legislature amended the Lien Law to preserve the lienor's right to sell goods in his possession, L. 1980, ch. 715. Prior notice of the sale must be given to the owner of the goods who then has ten days in which to commence a special proceeding to prevent the sale. *See especially* Lien Law § 201-a.

(2) The dissenters in the principal case were troubled by the possibility that U.C.C. § 7-210 (which allows the private sale, without court order, of property subject to a warehouseman's lien) would be held unconstitutional in New York despite having previously passed muster in the U.S. Supreme Court under the federal Constitution in *Flagg Bros. v. Brooks* (cited and discussed in the principal case). Their fears were later realized. *See Svendsen v. Smith's Moving and Trucking Co.*, 54 N.Y.2d 865, 444 N.Y.S.2d 904, 429 N.E.2d 411 (1981), *cert. denied*, 455 U.S. 927, 102 S. Ct. 1292 (1982).

(3) In footnote 7 of the principal case, the majority holds out the possibility that the garageman could obtain a waiver by the auto owner of a right to a hearing in the event a lienor's sale becomes necessary. Under what circumstances would an owner be likely to make such a waiver? Are there constitutional limits on the creditor's power to extract a waiver? See *D.H. Overmeyer Co. v. Frick Co.*, 405 U.S. 174, 92 S. Ct. 775 (1972), upholding a merchant debtor's grant of authority to a lender to take judgment against it, without a hearing, in the event it defaulted on a note. "Even if . . . we assume that the standard for waiver in a corporate-property-right case of this kind is the same standard applicable to waiver in a criminal proceeding, that is, that it be voluntary, knowing, and intelligently made . . . that standard was fully satisfied here." 405 U.S. at 186, 92 S. Ct. at 782.

(4) An attack on the constitutionality of U.C.C. §§ 9-503 and 9-504 (the predecessors to U.C.C. §§ 9-609 and 9-610) based on the principal case, was rejected

---

[7] . . . This is not a case involving merchants where commercial considerations might necessitate a greater degree of deference to legislative judgment (*cf.* Uniform Commercial Code, § 2-104). Involved here are consumers, frequently poor and unrepresented by counsel, who cannot be deemed to have forfeited their constitutional rights simply because they have engaged the services of someone in the commercial sector. We hold only that a garageman with a possessory lien on a repaired motor vehicle must afford its owner an opportunity to be heard before his ownership interest may be extinguished. The dissenters' concerns notwithstanding, this court has yet to shirk its responsibility and deprive persons of their constitutional rights because of unwarranted fears of overburdened court calendars. Moreover, nothing prevents the garageman from securing the owner's knowing waiver of his opportunity for a hearing when possession is initially transferred as many artisans and merchants are wont to do. . . .

in *Crouse v. First Trust Union Bank*, 86 A.D.2d 978, 448 N.Y.S.2d 329 (4th Dep't 1982), the court stating in part:

> In *Sharrock* the Court of Appeals struck down the provision of the lien law that authorized a garageman to foreclose his garageman's lien by private sale without notice to the owner. The Court held that this procedure deprived the owner of due process of law in violation of the New York State Constitution. The due process clause applies only where there is significant state action or involvement and the Court found such action or involvement from the fact that the state, by statute, gave the garageman a right that he did not have at common law — the right upon default to sell without notice. At common law the lien was possessory only.
>
> Here the form of the transaction was equivalent to a chattel mortgage. At common law, a chattel mortgagee had the right, upon default, to take possession of the chattel and thenceforth treat it as his own and to sell it if he chose (Jones, Chattel Mortgages and Conditional Sales [Bowers ed.], § 1; *Blake v. Corbett*, 120 N.Y. 327, 330-331, 24 N.E. 477; *Briggs v. Oliver*, 68 N.Y. 336, 339). The statute involved here, unlike that in *Sharrock*, does nothing more than merely acknowledge previous lawful conduct . . . and hence its enactment did not constitute significant state action or involvement.

Id., 86 A.D.2d at 978, 448 N.Y.S.2d at 329-30.

§ 12.05   INJUNCTION: CPLR ARTICLE 63

PROBLEM D

X Corporation and its attorney learn on December 3, 2006, that Austin, an employee who has tendered his resignation effective December 7, 2006, has plans to begin working for *Y* Corporation (a hated, feared and evil competitor) on December 10, 2006. If Austin carries out this plan, he will be breaching a contractual obligation not to work for a competitor of *X*. Moreover, *X* fears revelation of vital trade secrets to Y.

What legal steps can *X* Corporation's attorney take to prevent this wrong from taking place?

CREDIT AGRICOLE INDOSUEZ v. ROSSIYSKIY KREDIT BANK
Court of Appeals
94 N.Y.2d 541, 708 N.Y.S.2d 26, 729 N.E.2d 683 (2000)

LEVINE, J.

[Plaintiffs are three foreign banking institutions suing on unsecured debts of Rossiyskiy Kredit Bank totaling $30 million. In the loan agreement, defendants agreed to submit to the jurisdiction of New York courts in the event of default. The complaint sets forth two causes of action on the debts. In a third, plaintiffs allege defendants to be insolvent; that defendants had breached their fiduciary duty to preserve assets for the benefit of creditors by transferring assets to another Russian bank and that plaintiffs are entitled to permanent injunctive relief to protect their expected money judgment.

[At the outset of the action, plaintiffs moved for an order of attachment and a temporary injunction against further transfer of assets. Both provisional remedies were granted by the IAS court. The Appellate Division affirmed, but granted leave to appeal, the sole question in the Court of Appeals being whether the injunction was properly granted.]

The provisional remedy of a preliminary injunction in New York civil actions is governed by CPLR 6301, which provides in pertinent part:

"A preliminary injunction may be granted in any action where it appears that the defendant threatens or is about to do, or is doing or procuring or suffering to be done, an act in violation of the plaintiff's rights respecting the subject of the action, and tending to render the judgment ineffectual, or in any action where the plaintiff has demanded and would be entitled to a judgment restraining the defendant from the commission or continuance of an act, which, if committed or continued during the pendency of the action, would produce injury to the plaintiff."

Plaintiffs are unsecured contract creditors, whose ultimate objective is attaining an enforceable money judgment. Their third cause of action for injunctive relief to prevent the threatened dissipation of Rossiyskiy's assets, making it judgment proof, is incidental to and in aid of the monetary relief they seek. In applying provisional equitable remedies under civil procedure codes, from as early as 1892 in *Campbell v. Ernest* (64 Hun 188), our courts have consistently refused to grant general creditors a preliminary injunction to restrain a debtor's asset transfers that allegedly would defeat satisfaction of any anticipated judgment.

In *Campbell v. Ernest*, just as here, plaintiff averred that the "'defendant herein will, during the pendency of this action, *dispose of his property* . . . with intent to defraud the plaintiff herein, and to *render nugatory any proceeding or effort by this plaintiff to obtain payment of his claim in this action'*" (*id.*, at 189 [emphasis supplied]). At the time, section 604(2) of the Code of Civil Procedure authorized a preliminary injunction where the "defendant, during the pendency of the action, threatens or is about to remove or dispose of his property, with intent to defraud the plaintiff." The *Campbell* court held that section 604(2) did not apply "to an action of this character, where a moneyed judgment only is sought" (*id.*, at 192). Rather, provisional injunctive relief was limited to equitable actions where the defendant threatened to violate the rights of the plaintiff "*respecting the subject of the action*, which would tend to render the judgment ineffectual" (*id.* [emphasis supplied]). *Campbell* explained that, in a pure contract money action, there is no right of the plaintiff in some specific subject of the action; hence, no prejudgment right to interfere in the use of the defendant's property; and no entitlement to injunctive relief pendente lite.

> "In no proper or legal sense can a defendant do or permit any act in violation of the plaintiff's rights respecting the subject of the action, in an action on contract for the recovery of money only. The plaintiff in such an action *has no rights as against the property of the defendant* until he obtains a judgment, and *until then he has no legal right to interfere with the defendant in the use and sale of the same*" (*id.* [emphasis supplied]).

. . . .

Our courts have uniformly followed the precept of *Campbell v. Ernest (supra),* both before and after enactment of the CPLR (*see, Eastern Rock Prods. v. Natanson*, 239 App. Div. 529; *Babho Realty Co. v. Feffer*, 230 App. Div. 866 [under former Civil Practice Act]; *First Natl. Bank v. Highland Hardwoods*, 98 A.D.2d 924; *Fair Sky v. International Cable Ride Corp.*, 23 A.D.2d 633 [post-CPLR]).

It cannot be argued that CPLR 6301 was intended to expand or liberalize the traditional equity principle against provisional injunctive relief in a general creditor's action on a debt, to prevent the dissipation of assets necessary to satisfy the anticipated money judgment. To the contrary, the evidence is that section 6301 was intended to embody the very same traditional principles of equity jurisdiction *Grupo Mexicano* found reflected in Federal Rules of Civil Procedure, rule 65 in an action on a debt.[1] As one practice commentator has pointed out, article 63 of the CPLR does not represent "any radical departure from prior practice with regard to the availability of the provisional remedy of injunction. . . . Accordingly, New York's provisional remedy of injunction under current law continues, as it did under prior law, to be substantially similar to the preliminary injunction . . . that is available under federal practice and embodied in

---

[1] Indeed, the legislative history suggests, if anything, a restrictive rather than expansive objective in the drafting of CPLR 6301 regarding prejudgment injunctions to prevent asset transfers. Thus, Civil Practice Act § 878(2) (the equivalent of former code Civil Procedure § 604(2) discussed in *Campbell v. Ernest*) was eliminated in favor of the remedy attachment (*see,* Third Prelim Report of Advisory Comm. on Practice and Procedure, 1959 NY Legis Doc No. 17, at 150).

rule 65 of the Federal Rules of Civil Procedure" (13 Weinstein-Korn-Miller, NY Civ Prac § 6301.01).

Each of the cases cited by the courts below or plaintiffs here in support of a contrary view (that a threatened denuding of defendant's assets justifies a preliminary injunction in a suit for money damages) is inapposite, either because the equitable relief in the case was granted under procedures independent of CPLR 6301, or because the suit involved claims of the plaintiff to a specific fund, rightly regarded by the court as "the subject of the action" (CPLR 6301), making a preliminary injunction appropriate under the express wording of that provision.

Plaintiffs attempt to avoid the thrust of *Campbell v. Ernest* (*supra*) and its progeny by relying on their third cause of action alleging not just the claim to recover the debt due, but also the insolvent defendants' breach of fiduciary duty and plaintiffs' request for a permanent injunction as part of the judgment. Plaintiffs contend that this cause of action brings them within the clause of section 6301 authorizing a preliminary injunction "where the plaintiff has demanded and would be entitled to a judgment restraining the defendant from the commission or continuance of an act, which, if committed or continued during the pendency of the action, would produce injury to the plaintiff." This argument fails for a number of reasons.

First, undeniably, plaintiffs' third cause of action is incidental to and purely for the purposes of enforcement of the primary relief sought here, a money judgment. Making an exception on the basis that permanent equitable relief is sought in support of a suit essentially for money only would be too facile a way to avoid and undermine the settled proscription against preliminary injunctions merely to preserve a fund for eventual execution of judgment in suits for money damages. As Professor Siegel has put it, the mere danger of asset-stripping is not a sufficient basis to make an exception to the general rule:

> "Although the inclusion of a money demand will not necessarily preclude an injunction if other relief, which would satisfy this provision of CPLR 6301, is also sought, the court will refuse the injunction if convinced that a money judgment is the true object of the action and that all else is incidental. (In a money action, P often fears that D will secrete property during the action's pendency and thus make a money judgment uncollectable. P's remedy there, if P can establish such conduct by D convincingly, is an order of attachment under CPLR 6201[3], not an injunction under Article 63.)" (Siegel, NY Prac § 327, at 498 [3d ed]; *see also,* McLaughlin, Practice Commentaries, McKinney's Cons Laws of NY, Book 7B, CPLR C6301:1, at 209.)

Second, plaintiff's argument overlooks the substantive rule of equity which, as has been shown here, has prevailed for over two centuries, from Chancellor Kent through *Campbell v. Ernest* . . ., that a general creditor has no legally recognized interest in or right to interfere with the use of the unencumbered property of a debtor prior to obtaining judgment. Therefore, during the pendency of the action on the debt, even if the anticipated judgment might include permanent injunctive relief, the acts of the debtor in disposing of assets will not have "produce[d] [cognizable] injury to the plaintiff" and thus will not support a temporary injunction (CPLR 6301).

. . . .

Third, the only apparent basis for the alleged fiduciary duty owed plaintiffs here arises out of the so-called "trust fund doctrine" by virtue of which the officers and directors of an insolvent corporation are said to hold the remaining corporate assets in trust for the benefit of its general creditors (*see, New York Credit Men's Adj. Bur. v. Weiss*, 305 N.Y. 1, 7; *see also, Ward v. City Trust Co.*, 192 N.Y. 61, 74; Beveridge, *Does a Corporation's Board of Directors Owe a Fiduciary Duty to its Creditors?*, 25 St. Mary's LJ 589, 592 [1994]; Varallo and Finkelstein, *Fiduciary Obligations of Directors of the Financially Troubled Company*, 48 Bus Law 239, 244 [1992]). Nevertheless, our courts have never deviated from the prevailing majority rule that the trust fund doctrine does not automatically create an actual lien or other equitable interest as such in corporate assets upon insolvency (*see, Hollins v. Brierfield Coal & Iron Co.*, 150 U.S. 371, 381, 383; *In re MortgageAmerica Corp.*, 714 F.2d 1266, 1269 [5th Cir]).

The application of the trust fund doctrine in New York customarily has been for the purpose of imposing liability on corporate directors or transferees for wrongful dissipation of assets of an insolvent corporation, in actions later brought by court-appointed receivers, trustees in bankruptcy or judgment creditors (*see, New York Credit Men's Adj. Bur. v. Weiss, supra; Buttles v. Smith*, 281 N.Y. 226; *Trotter v. Lisman*, 209 N.Y. 174). Most significantly with respect to the possible application of the trust fund doctrine in the context of this case, we have followed the general rule that a simple contract creditor may not invoke the doctrine to reach transferred assets before exhausting legal remedies by obtaining judgment on the debt and having execution returned unsatisfied (*see, Hollins v. Brierfield Coal & Iron Co., supra,* 150 U.S., at 380-381; *Buttles v. Smith, supra,* at 235-236; *Trotter v. Lisman, supra,* at 179). This militates heavily against the use of the trust fund doctrine by a general creditor, having no cognizable interest in the debtor's property, to get a preliminary injunction in aid of a money judgment not yet obtained.

Finally, plaintiffs argue that even if New York has not up to now authorized the issuance of a temporary injunction to protect a general creditor suing on an unsecured debt from the debtor's divestiture of the assets necessary to satisfy the anticipated judgment, we should now liberalize and expand the remedies available under CPLR 6301 to permit courts to grant that relief. Plaintiffs urge that this is necessary in response to the increased globalization of capital markets, New York's preeminent position in those markets and the advances in technology facilitating ever faster transfer of funds. Plaintiffs suggest we follow the example of the English courts that, since the 1975 decision by the Court of Appeal in *Mareva Compania Naviera v. International BulkCarriers* (2 Lloyd's

Rep 509), have provided protection to general creditors from the risk of a debtor's dissipation of assets to frustrate satisfaction of an anticipated money judgment.

Justice Scalia, in *Grupo Mexicano [v. Alliance Bond Fund]* (*supra,* 527 U.S., at 328-329), and others (*see, e.g.,* Sibley and Smith, *Taking a Lesson From English Courts on Restricting the Movement of Assets,* NYLJ, Nov. 16, 1998, at 1, col 1) have cogently described the profound effects that the availability of world-wide Mareva preliminary injunctions would have on world-wide commerce. That is, the widespread use of this remedy would drastically unbalance existing creditors' and debtors' rights under the present Federal and State statutory and decisional schemes, and substantially interfere with the sovereignty and debtor/creditor/bankruptcy laws of, and the rights of interested domiciliaries in, foreign countries. At the very least, the availability of such a powerful, discretionary provisional remedy, even when that discretion is exercised by courts with caution and restraint, would introduce uncertainty in results which the present *Campbell v. Ernest* bright-line rule — more readily permitting investors accurately to assess likely risks, and to adjust interest rates accordingly — avoids.

Finally, when asked to exercise inherent judicial powers to impose significant innovations in the field of provisional remedies, we have previously determined that the balancing of important competing interests and crafting of appropriate safeguards and standards to ensure that the balance is fairly administered in the individual case, are "task[s] best left to statutes and rules rather than ad hoc judicial decision-making" (*Uniformed Firefighters Assn. v. City of New York,* 79 N.Y.2d 236, 241). The same self-restraint and deference to a legislative solution applies here, where judicial innovation may have far-reaching impact on the existing balance between debtors' and creditors' rights (*see, Grupo Mexicano de Desarrollo v. Alliance Bond Fund, supra,* 527 U.S., at 322-323, 333).

Accordingly, the order of the Appellate Division, insofar as appealed from, should be reversed, with costs, plaintiffs' motion for a preliminary injunction denied and certified question answered in the negative.

NOTES

(1) CPLR 6301 describes two situations in which a preliminary injunction is available: (i) In an action in which it appears the defendant is doing or going to do "an act in violation of the plaintiff's rights respecting the subject of the action and tending to render the judgment ineffectual" or (ii) in an action in which "the plaintiff has demanded and would be entitled to a judgment restraining the defendant from the commission or continuance of an act, which, if committed or continued during the pendency of the action, would produce injury to the plaintiff." *See generally*, O. Chase, CPLR Manual § 28.17 (2006).

(2) In determining whether to grant a preliminary injunction, the courts in fact focus more on criteria additional to those spelled out in CPLR 6301:

To be entitled to a preliminary injunction, the moving party must demonstrate (1) a likelihood of success on the merits, (2) irreparable injury if provisional relief is not granted and (3) that the equities are in his favor

J.A. Preston Corp. v. Fabrication Enterprises, Inc., 68 N.Y.2d 397, 406, 509 N.Y.S.2d 520, 524, 502 N.E.2d 197, 201 (1986).

Subdivision (C) of CPLR 6312 provides that defendant's mere showing of an issue of fact is not sufficient to defeat the injunction request. The judge can hold a hearing if necessary when defendant's fact issue creates doubt.

Judge Posner of the 7th Circuit Court of Appeals has made a controversial attempt to recast the conventional requirements for a preliminary injunction into an algebraic formula. Under this approach the relief should be granted "if, but only if $P \times Hp > (1 - P) \times Hd$, or in other words, only if the harm to the plaintiff if the injunction is denied, multiplied by the probability that the denial would be an error (that the plaintiff, in other words, will win at trial), exceeds the harm to the defendant if the injunction is granted, multiplied by the probability that granting the injunction would be an error." P here equals the probability that denial would be an error. The probability that the grant of the injunction would be an error is simply 1 minus the probability that the plaintiff will succeed at trial, for if the plaintiff has a 40 percent chance of winning then the defendant must have a 60 percent chance of success ($1.00 - .40 = .60$). *See American Hospital Supply Corp. v. Hospital Products Ltd.*, 780 F.2d 589, 593 (7th Cir. 1986).

Does this formula help you answer Problem D? Is it substantively different from the approach taken by the New York Court of Appeals in *J.A. Preston Corp. v. Fabrication Enterprises, Inc., supra*, this note?

Some cases consider not only the equities of the parties, but also the interest of the public. *See, e.g., City of New York v. New York Yankees*, 117 Misc. 2d 332, 458 N.Y.S.2d 486 (Sup. Ct. 1983). A preliminary injunction was granted to prohibit the Yankees from having their "home" opening game in Denver, in violation of their lease agreement for Yankee Stadium. Although only three games were involved, said the court, "it is the symbolism of the act not the quantity that counts. . . . No money damages can measure this kind of harm."

A thoughtful analysis of various approaches to the problem in general is provided in Leubsdorf, *The Standard for Preliminary Injunctions*, 91 Harv. L. Rev. 525 (1978).

(3) A special need for preliminary injunctive relief arises in some commercial landlord-tenant disputes. (These are commonly referred to as "Yellowstone" injunctions, after a seminal case, *First National Stores v. Yellowstone Shopping Center*, 21 N.Y.2d 630, 290 N.Y.S.2d 721 (1968)). If a landlord alleges that the tenant is acting in violation of the lease (perhaps by illegally subletting the premises), the landlord must (pursuant to a clause found in the standard lease)

serve a notice to cure the violation within a stated time. In the absence of a cure, the landlord may bring an eviction proceeding in New York City Civil Court or other court with jurisdiction over eviction actions. If the tenant wins, it is of course, protected. If the tenant loses however, the period allowed by the lease in which to cure the violation will have run and the lease will have terminated. To prevent this potential loss of the right to cure, the tenant may bring an action in the Supreme Court for a declaratory judgment that it is not in breach of the lease and, at the same time, move for a temporary restraining order and preliminary injunction staying the expiration of the cure period until the determination of the declaratory judgment action. If the tenant loses on the merits, it may cure the violation. Because the Civil Court does not have the equity jurisdiction necessary to grant the interim relief, the Yellowstone injunction must be sought in the Supreme Court.

A Yellowstone injunction will be granted on a lesser showing than is ordinarily required for preliminary injunctive relief. Irreparable injury and a probability of success on the merits need not be demonstrated. *Post v. 120 East End Avenue Corp.*, 62 N.Y.2d 19, 25, 475 N.Y.S.2d 821 (1984). The tenant need only show that: (1) it holds a commercial lease; (2) it has received from the landlord a notice to cure or other threat of termination of the lease; (3) the application for the temporary restraining order was made before the termination of the lease: and (4) it has the desire and ability to cure the alleged default by some means other than vacating the premises. *Continental Towers Garage Corp. v. Contowers Associates Limited Partnership*, 141 A.D.2d 390, 529 N.Y.S.2d 322 (1st Dep't 1988).

The need for a Yellowstone injunction ordinarily does not arise in connection with residential leases because the New York City Civil Court has been granted authority to grant a losing residential tenant a ten-day period within which to cure the defect. Real Property Actions and Proceedings Law § 753(4). If the defect cannot be cured within ten days, however, a Yellowstone injunction will be appropriate even in a residential lease case. *Post v. 120 East End Avenue Corp.*, 62 N.Y.2d 19, 475 N.Y.S.2d 821, 464 N.E.2d 125 (1984).

(4) A preliminary injunction may not be granted unless an action is pending that seeks some final relief, be it injunctive or monetary. The courts have no power to grant provisional relief when it is sought solely as incidental to an ongoing administrative proceeding that has not yet ripened into an action. *Uniformed Firefighters Assoc. of Greater New York v. City of New York*, 79 N.Y.2d 236, 581 N.Y.S.2d 734, 590 N.E.2d 719 (1992).

(5) In *Cornell University v. Livingston*, 69 Misc. 2d 965, 332 N.Y.S.2d 843 (1972), the university applied for an order for protesting students occupying Carpenter Hall to show cause why they should not be enjoined from continuing to interfere with university operations. Personal service of the order was impractical, but the court held that the reading of the order through a bullhorn was sufficient notice to uphold the contempt citations of the students who ignored the notice.

(6) Authorization for a temporary restraining order (t.r.o.) is found in CPLR 6313(a). Note that by implication it may issue only when the requirements for a preliminary injunction have been met. What is the difference between the two?

(7) A t.r.o. may issue without prior notice to the defendant. CPLR 6313(a). (Must the motion for it be made without notice?) Is this constitutional? Consider that when a t.r.o. is granted, a hearing on the (necessarily) accompanying application for a preliminary injunction must be held "at the earliest possible time." CPLR 6313(a).

(8) A person who violates an injunction may be held in contempt even if he correctly believes it unconstitutionally interferes with his fundamental rights. *Walker v. City of Birmingham*, 388 U.S. 307, 87 S. Ct. 1824 (1967).

There can be no civil contempt, however, if the court did not have jurisdiction to issue the order violated. But criminal contempt will lie nevertheless. *Mt. Sinai Hospital, Inc. v. Davis*, 8 A.D.2d 361, 188 N.Y.S.2d 298 (1st Dep't 1959).

§ 12.06 RECEIVERSHIP: CPLR ARTICLE 64

Temporary receivership, authorized by Article 64, is a provisional remedy by which a court, through a receiver, conserves and manages property which is the subject of an action pending the outcome of litigation. Since the appointment of a receiver involves a drastic intrusion into a defendant's right to control the property, it is available only if compelling reasons are shown.

A temporary receiver can be appointed only over property that is the subject matter of litigation. CPLR 6401. As a result, a receivership ordinarily is available only in actions of an equitable nature, such as for an accounting or to prevent waste and mismanagement of business assets. The remedy is not available in an action for money damages only. Further, the movant must show that the property which is or will become the subject of an action may be "removed from the state, or lost, materially injured or destroyed." CPLR 6401(a). Suspicion that this will happen is not enough. The plaintiff must show facts supporting his allegations.

As with other provisional remedies, the grant of temporary receivership is discretionary and may be denied even if the statutory requirements are met. The court must consider whether the contemplated interference with the defendant's property rights is outweighed by the need to protect the plaintiff's interest in the property. The court can decide to use a less drastic remedy, if appropriate, such as an injunction against removing or dissipating the property.

Pursuant to CPLR 8004, a person serving as receiver may be awarded compensation by the court which is paid out of funds collected by him or by the party who moved for his appointment.

§ 12.07 NOTICE OF PENDENCY: CPLR ARTICLE 65

In any action affecting title, possession, use or enjoyment of real property, the plaintiff may file a notice of pendency,[1] with the clerk of the county in which the property is located. CPLR 6501. Court authorization is not required; this distinguishes notice of pendency from the other provisional remedies included in the CPLR. In an action to foreclose a mortgage, and a few other cases, filing is mandatory, but it is normally a privilege initially available whenever the statutory grounds exist. Filing may be made before the action is commenced, but the summons must be served within thirty days thereafter. CPLR 6512.

The purpose of filing the notice is to assure the plaintiff that the claim to the property will not be subordinated to that of a third party to whom the property might be conveyed during the course of the plaintiff's action.

The constitutionality of the procedure under which the notice of pendency is available in New York has been upheld by the only court to directly consider the question. See United States v. Rivieccio, 661 F. Supp. 281 (E.D.N.Y. 1987). A case can be made that it violates due process requirements in that the filing of the notice reduces the market value of the property as a practical matter even though it deprives the owner of no legal interest. Further, while the defendant can move to discharge the notice on a variety of grounds, the merits of plaintiff's case is not among them.[2] This defect has been held critical in cases involving provisional attachment and seizure of property, as discussed earlier in this chapter. In favor of its constitutionality, the Rivieccio court observed that the notice is simply a warning to would-be purchasers that there is a dispute over the right to own or use the property. Thus, no significant property right is affected. This was also a primary ground on which an attack on the constitutionality of New York Lien Law Article 2, allowing the filing of a mechanic's lien under procedures similar to that at issue here, was rejected.[3]

Meanwhile, however, the Court of Appeals has displayed sensitivity to the concerns raised by the notice of pendency by insisting on its narrow application. In 5303 Realty Corp. v. O & Y Equity Corp., 64 N.Y.2d 313, 2319-24, 486 N.Y.S.2d 877, 881-84, 476 N.E.2d 276, 280-83 (1984), it held that a notice of pendency could not be used when the underlying action sought to specifically enforce a contract to sell stock which carried with it the ownership of real property:

---

[1] The notice of pendency is sometimes referred to as a "lis pendens." The latter is actually a distinguishable, if related, common law concept under which a purchaser of property took subject to pending litigation involving that property. See 5303 Realty Corp. v. O & Y Equity Corp., 64 N.Y.2d 313, 486 N.Y.S.2d 877, 476 N.E.2d 276 (1984); 7A Weinstein, Korn & Miller, New York Civil Practice, ¶¶ 6501.01-6501.04.

[2] Cf. Will of Sabatino, 90 Misc. 2d 56, 393 N.Y.S.2d 671 (Surr. Ct. 1977) (defendant may attack the notice if the allegations of the complaint show that the action is not one in which CPLR 6501 permits the notice to be used).

[3] Carl A. Morse, Inc. v. Rentar Ind. Dev. Corp., 56 A.D.2d 30, 391 N.Y.S.2d 425 (2d Dep't 1977), aff'd, 43 N.Y.2d 952, 404 N.Y.S.2d 343, appeal dismissed, 439 U.S. 804, 99 S. Ct. 59 (1978).

Determining the substantive scope of the notice of pendency, as embodied in CPLR 6501, cannot be divorced from consideration of the relative procedural ease with which it can be imposed throughout the duration of a lawsuit. Basically, a plaintiff can cloud a defendant's title merely by serving a summons and filing a proper complaint and notice of pendency stating the names of the parties, the object of the action, and a description of the property (CPLR 6511, subds [a], [b]; *see Israelson v Bradley*, 308 NY 511). Indeed, the notice of pendency may even precede the service of summons (CPLR 6511, subd [a]; 6512). The notice is valid for three years and it may be extended by court order (CPLR 6513).

Critically, the statutory scheme permits a party to effectively retard the alienability of real property without any prior judicial review. To the extent that a motion to cancel the notice of pendency is available (CPLR 6514), the court's scope of review is circumscribed. One of the important factors in this regard is that the likelihood of success on the merits is irrelevant to determining the validity of the notice of pendency. . . .

Usually, there is little a court may do to provide relief to the property owner. If the procedures prescribed in article 65 have not been followed or if the action has not been commenced or prosecuted in good faith, the notice must be canceled in the first instance and it may be in the second (*see Israelson v Bradley, supra*; CPLR 6514, subds [a], [b]). If the notice of pendency is valid, the court may, in its discretion, cancel the notice, but the moving party will generally have to post an undertaking (CPLR 6515). To counterbalance the case with which a party may hinder another's right to transfer property, this court has required strict compliance with the statutory procedural requirements. . . .

The same considerations that require strict compliance with the procedural prerequisites also mandate a narrow interpretation in reviewing whether an action is one affecting "the title to, or the possession, use or enjoyment of, real property" (CPLR 6501). Thus, a court is not to investigate the underlying transaction in determining whether a complaint comes within the scope of CPLR 6501. Instead, in accordance with historical practice, the court's analysis is to be limited to the pleading's face.

. . . The courts have been frequently confronted by attempts to file a notice of pendency in controversies that more or less referred to real property, but which did not necessarily seek to directly affect title to or possession of the land. In the absence of this direct relationship, the remedy was denied. . . .

In the present action, plaintiff cannot have the advantage of a notice of pendency. Although the prayer for relief seeks a transfer of title, the court must examine the complaint in its entirety. It is apparent from the allegations that the true action is to enforce a contract to sell stock. It is well settled that the property interests of a shareholder and the corporation are distinct. . . . But this does not necessarily leave plaintiff, and others similarly situated, with no protective devices whatsoever. The property's conveyance may be blocked by, for example, attachment or injunction. In this way, a party may guard against conduct that will defeat the purpose of a lawsuit, but a court will have an opportunity to review the interference with alienability before it begins to operate.

The Court of Appeals again reviewed CPLR 6513 in *Matter of Sakow*, 97 N.Y.2d 436, 741 N.Y.S.2d 175, 767 N.E.2d 666 (2002), and ruled that in order for a notice of pendency to be extended beyond its normal three-year life, the extension must be requested prior to the expiration of that period. If this requirement is not met, and the notice of pendency has lapsed, it cannot be revived on the same cause of action or claim.

As with the other provisional remedies, a party who improperly files a notice of pendency risks liability for abuse of process, as the following case illustrates.

PARR MEADOWS RACING ASSOCIATION, INC. v. WHITE
Appellate Division, Second Department
76 A.D.2d 858, 428 N.Y.S.2d 509 (1980)

In our view, the complaint adequately states causes of action for abuse of process against all of the defendants. Plaintiff satisfactorily alleges (1) the issuance of process (notices of pendency) compelling the performance or forbearance of some prescribed act, (2) that the defendants were moved by a purpose to do harm without economic or social excuse or justification, and (3) that defendants were seeking some collateral advantage or corresponding detriment to the plaintiff which is outside the legitimate ends of the process (*see Board of Educ. v Farmingdale Classroom Teachers Assn.*, 38 NY2d 397, 403).

The fact that the complaint further alleges that the notices of pendency were filed without just cause in the first instance does not necessarily cast plaintiff's cause as malicious prosecution rather than abuse of process. "While the courts commonly refer to abuse of process as being the perversion of a 'regularly' issued process, such language is used for the purpose of calling attention to the fact that the action commonly lies notwithstanding the process may have been regularly issued, rather than that the action will not lie if the process was void or irregular. The gist of the action is the misuse of process, and the regularity or irregularity of its issuance is immaterial." (1 Am Jur 2d, Abuse of Process, § 5.) . . .

Lastly, we find that the complaint adequately alleges willful and malicious conduct on the part of defendants so as to permit plaintiff to pursue its claim for punitive damages. . . .

§ 12.08 PROVISIONAL REMEDIES IN FORFEITURE ACTIONS: CPLR ARTICLE 13-A

NOTES ON ARTICLE 13-A FORFEITURE ACTIONS

(1) Article 13-A, enacted in 1984, is intended to "take the profits out of crime." It allows certain law enforcement officials to bring an action to recover the proceeds of a crime, the instrumentality of a crime, or the equivalent monetary value. Article 13-A authorizes the use of provisional remedies to seize the defendant's property even before the civil or criminal trial. It allows the District Attorney (or other law enforcement official) to attach assets of a person before he is tried for a crime and, after that person is convicted, to retrieve the proceeds and return them to the victim. (A pre-conviction forfeiture can be pressed only with respect to drug related crimes. § 1310(6). The provisional remedy is not limited to attachment, but might take the form of an injunction, a receivership or a notice of pendency.

Attachment seems to be the preferred provisional remedy, but before attachment can be ordered, the court must find a substantial probability that there will be a conviction and that the need to preserve the availability of the property outweighs the hardship to any party who may be affected. § 1312(3). The debt or property attached need not be the proceeds of the crime in specie, but can be any property. § 1313. The New York Court of Appeals gave Article 13-A a clean bill of health in *Morganthau v. Citisource*, 68 N.Y.2d 211, 500 N.E.2d 850, 508 N.Y.S.2d 152 (1986). Over the argument that attachment deprived defendant of the resources to hire counsel for his defense in the criminal prosecution, the court pointed out that if such can be proved, defendant may seek vacatur, modification, or even an initial determination that attachment is not in order.

(2) When, as in the *Morganthau* case, the defendant is accused of a "post-conviction forfeiture crime," the forfeiture does not become effective until after a conviction. CPLR 1311(1)(a). If the accusation is of a "pre-conviction forfeiture crime," however, the forfeiture may be ordered by the court notwithstanding an acquittal. It is only necessary that the claiming authority prove the commission of such a crime by clear and convincing evidence. CPLR 1311(1)(b). "Pre-conviction forfeiture" crimes are limited to felony violations of the state narcotics laws. CPLR 1310(6).

(3) In a case arising out of a federal forfeiture statute, the Supreme Court of the United States has rejected the arguments based on the Sixth and Fourteenth Amendments that there can not be a pre-conviction seizure of the defendant's assets which deprives him of the financial means to hire a private attorney. *Caplin & Drysdale v. United States*, 491 U.S. 617, 109 S. Ct. 2646, 105 L. Ed. 2d 528 (1989). Regarding the Sixth Amendment (right to counsel) claim, the Court said:

The notion that the government has a legitimate interest in depriving criminals of economic power, even in so far as that power is used to retain counsel of choice, may be somewhat unsettling. . . . But when a defendant claims that he has suffered some substantial impairment of his Sixth Amendment rights by virtue of the seizure or forfeiture of assets in his possession, such a complaint is no more than the reflection of the "harsh reality that the quality of a criminal defendant's representation frequently may turn on his ability to retain the best counsel money can buy."

(4) The Supreme Court has also rejected a constitutional challenge to forfeiture statutes on double jeopardy grounds. The Court held in *United States v. Ursery*, 518 U.S. 267, 116 S. Ct. 2135, 135 L. Ed. 2d 549 (1996), that forfeiture laws provide a civil remedy and are therefore not punishment for the purposes of the proscription against double jeopardy.

In *County of Nassau v. Canavan*, 1 N.Y.3d 134, 802 N.E.2d 616 (2003), which concerned the seizure of a car following the driver's arrest for DWI, the Court of Appeals held that due process required a "prompt" post-seizure hearing to be provided to all defendants whose vehicles are seized and held for forfeiture. Under the practice struck down by the Court of Appeals, a civil action seeking forfeiture in Nassau County had to have been commenced within 120 days of the seizure of the driver's car. Such an action might take months or even years to conclude, during which time the car remained in the possession of the police. The Court of Appeals applied the balancing test set out in *Matthews v. Eldridge*, 424 U.S. 319, 96 S. Ct. 893, 47 L.Ed.2d 18 (1976), and found a significant private interest in avoiding a lengthy deprivation, that the risk of erroneous deprivation would be minimized by a prompt hearing, and that despite a strong government interest in preventing drunk driving, due process required the government to establish the necessity of retention after seizure. The Court of Appeals rejected the car owner's argument that due process mandates a hearing prior to an initial seizure, finding that immediate seizure of a defendant's car in a drunk driving arrest "helps to secure important public and governmental interests in ensuring both safety on the roads and the enforceability of any subsequent forfeiture order."

The New York Court of Appeals in *Nassau* relied in part on *Krimstock v. Kelly*, 306 F.3d 40 (2d Cir. 2002), in which the plaintiffs had challenged a section of the New York City Civil Administrative Code that allowed the seizure and retention of a vehicle in a drunk driving arrest until the resolution of the criminal case, without providing for a hearing to determine if probable cause existed for the arrest or the seizure. The Second Circuit noted Fourth Amendment concerns with a deprivation lasting months or years before civil forfeiture proceedings commenced. Applying the *Matthews v. Eldridge* balancing test, the court held that plaintiffs must be afforded a prompt post-seizure, prejudgment hearing to determine if the City is likely to succeed on the merits of a forfeiture action, and whether retention of the vehicle is merited in order to prevent destruction or sale during the forfeiture proceedings.

Chapter 13

PLEADINGS

§ 13.01 INTRODUCTORY NOTE

A pleading is a paper in which a party states claims or defenses. The purposes of pleadings are well summarized in M. Green, Basic Civil Procedure 108-09 (2d ed. 1979):[1]

(1) to narrow the issues to be tried . . .

(2) to give notice to the parties in order to avoid surprise at trial . . .

(3) to give notice to the court of the nature of the case . . .

(4) to serve as a permanent record and as a basis for res judicata . . . and

(5) to dispose of cases without trial where the pleadings revealed there were no real issues of fact to be tried. . . .

The importance of the listed factors underscores a basic point: drafting a pleading should be a creative exercise. While form books abound and can provide a useful starting point, each case involves a unique set of facts which therefore requires a pleading artfully tailored to them. To plead skillfully, one must know the rules with which each pleading must minimally comply. Sections 13.01 through 13.05 of this chapter deal with these rules for particular kinds of pleadings. As the rules imply, part of the pleader's task is to investigate the facts and research the law before actually drafting. How else, for example, can one know whether the complaint states a cause of action?

Meeting minimal requirements is, well, just the minimum. The superior attorney should be aware of the tactical possibilities available within the rules and should use them to advantage. Stating one cause of action protects a complaint against dismissal, but a better complaint states every cause of action available to the plaintiff. Beyond that, the drafter must often make tactical decisions such as choosing between vagueness of style which leaves the adversary guessing, and specificity, which may impress him with the strength of the case. Think about the advantages and disadvantages of these competing approaches as you read this chapter, particularly § 13.07, The Effect of Pleadings.

Rules of timeliness governing pleadings are found in CPLR 3012. The time within which the defendant must serve an answer has been discussed in relation to the appearance in Chapter 6. It may be helpful to you, therefore, to look

---

[1] Reprinted with permission of Foundation Press, Inc. Copyright © 1979.

again at the chart in § 6.03 and the related materials. Delays in pleading, while certainly to be avoided, are rarely fatal, especially if there is demonstrable merit to the cause of action or defense at issue. CPLR 2005, adopted in 1983, legislatively overruled the unforgiving approach to pleading delays which had been taken in *Barasch v. Micucci*, 49 N.Y.2d 594, 427 N.Y.S.2d 732, 404 N.E.2d 1275 (1980), and its progeny. Moreover, it has been held that the right to object to late service of a complaint is waived unless the defendant (not having previously moved to dismiss on that ground) rejects the complaint when it is finally served. *E.g.*, *Capoccia v. Brognano*, 132 A.D.2d 834, 517 N.Y.S.2d 622 (3d Dep't 1987).

The courts' discretionary authority to relieve a party from a default is also taken up in Chapter 20.

§ 13.02 THE COMPLAINT

Form

Verified Complaint

SUPREME COURT OF THE STATE OF NEW YORK
COUNTY OF NEW YORK

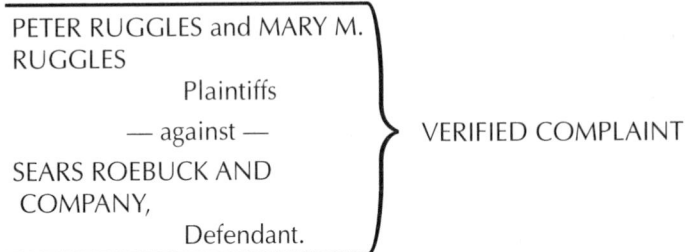

PETER RUGGLES and MARY M. RUGGLES

      Plaintiffs

— against —

SEARS ROEBUCK AND COMPANY,

      Defendant.

VERIFIED COMPLAINT

The plaintiffs, appearing by their attorneys, CROWE, McCOY, AGOGLIA, FOGARTY & ZWEIBEL, P. C., complain of the defendant and allege upon information and belief, as follows:

AS AND FOR A FIRST CAUSE OF ACTION ON BEHALF OF THE PLAINTIFF, PETER RUGGLES

FIRST: That at all times hereinafter mentioned, the defendant was a corporation duly licensed to conduct a retail department store business in the State of New York.

SECOND: That at all times hereinafter mentioned, the defendant, SEARS ROEBUCK AND COMPANY, hereinafter referred to as "SEARS", sold 5 ft. aluminum medium duty step ladders bearing serial number 42145.

THIRD: That prior to the 19th day of September, 2006, one Thomas A. Meade, purchased the aforesaid identified ladder.

FOURTH: That on the 19th day of September, 2006, this plaintiff, while using said ladder in the manner prescribed in the instructions contained on the side of the ladder, was caused to sustain serious personal injuries due solely to the negligence of the defendant in the manufacturing, selling, packaging, distributing and lack of inspection and testing of this ladder, all to the damage of this plaintiff in the sum of $850,000.00.

AS AND FOR A SECOND CAUSE OF ACTION ON BEHALF OF THE PLAINTIFF, PETER RUGGLES

FIFTH: This plaintiff repeats and reiterates all the foregoing allegations contained in paragraphs numbered "FIRST" through "FOURTH" inclusive, with the same force and effect as though fully set forth at length herein.

SIXTH: That by reason of the above stated facts, the defendant, its agents, servants and employees, are liable to this plaintiff in strict tort.

SEVENTH: That as a result of the aforesaid, this plaintiff has been damaged in the sum of $850,000.00.

AS AND FOR A THIRD CAUSE OF ACTION ON BEHALF OF THE PLAINTIFF, MARY M. RUGGLES

EIGHTH: This plaintiff, MARY M. RUGGLES, repeats, reiterates and realleges each and every allegation contained in paragraphs numbered "FIRST" through "SEVENTH" inclusive, with the same force and effect as though fully set forth at length herein.

NINTH: That at all times hereinafter mentioned, this plaintiff was the wife of the plaintiff, PETER RUGGLES, and resided with him.

TENTH: That by reason of the aforesaid, this plaintiff has been and will be deprived of the services, comfort, society and consortium of her said husband, PETER RUGGLES, all to her damage in the sum of $150,000.00.

WHEREFORE, the plaintiffs demand judgment against the defendant, as follows: (a) on behalf of the plaintiff, PETER RUGGLES, in the first cause of action, in the sum of $850,000.00; (b) on behalf of the plaintiff, PETER RUGGLES, in the second cause of action, in the sum of $850,000.00 and (c) on behalf of the plaintiff, MARY M. RUGGLES, in the third cause of action, in the sum of $150,000.00, together with the costs and disbursements of this action.

Attorneys for Plaintiffs
Office & P. O. Address

VERIFICATION

STATE OF NEW YORK, COUNTY OF NASSAU   ss.:
I, the undersigned, am an attorney admitted to practice in the courts of New York State, and
    ☐   certify that the annexed

Attorney's
Certification
          has been compared with me with the original and found to be true and complete
          copy thereof.

    ☒   say that: I am the attorney of record, or of counsel with the attorney(s) of record,
          for **Plaintiffs**

                     I have read the annexed   **Complaint,**

Attorney's
Verification

by Affirmation   know the contents thereof and the same are true to my knowledge, except those
          matters therein which are stated to be alleged   information and
          belief, and as to those matters I believe them to be true. My belief, as to those
          matters therein not stated upon knowledge, is based upon the following:
          Investigation, reports and records in file of deponent's office.
          The reason I make this affirmation instead of   **plaintiffs**   is   **because they**
          reside in a county other than that in which the attorney's office is located.

I affirm that the foregoing statements are true under penalties of perjury.
Dated: Mineola, N.Y.
        May 17, 2002

                                     (Signed)

                         . . . .
                         (Print signer's name below signature)

NOTE

The answer served by the defendant to the above complaint is in § 13.03, *infra*. These forms, adapted from an actual court file, are presented neither as a "how to" nor a "how not to" illustration but rather to stimulate discussion. As you read the accompanying material, think whether you would have drafted either pleading differently.

PROBLEM A

If the defendant in the action described in the above complaint moves to dismiss for failure to state a cause of action (CPLR 3211(a)(7)) or, in the alternative, for a more definite statement (CPLR 3024), how should the court decide the motion under the rules expressed in the following cases?

FOLEY v. D'AGOSTINO
Appellate Division, First Department
21 A.D.2d 60, 248 N.Y.S.2d 121 (1964)

EAGER, J.

This appeal is from an order which, upon motion pursuant to 3211 (subd. [a], par. 7) of the Civil Practice Law and Rules, dismissed plaintiffs' complaint and each of the three causes of action therein upon the ground that there was a failure to state any cause of action.

The action was brought by the plaintiffs as 50% shareholders in several related family close corporations engaged in conducting a chain of supermarkets in New York City with the prominent use of the family name "D'Agostino" in the names and businesses of the corporations. The first and second alleged causes, stated to be brought "on behalf of" plaintiffs "and in the right and for the benefit of the family corporations" are alleged to be maintained against the other 50% stockholder and certain directors, officers and employees of the corporations for an injunction and an accounting in connection with their alleged wrongful organization and threatened conduct of an independent and competing supermarket utilizing the family name. The first cause is claimed to be sustainable on the theory that the acts and threatened acts of the individual defendants are in violation of the fiduciary obligations owing by them as officers to the family corporations; and the second alleged cause is framed on the basis that such acts amount to unfair competition in violation of the rights of the family corporations. There is a third alleged cause of action which is set up on the alleged basis of the existence of a joint venture rather than on the theory of a derivative action.

Under the Civil Practice Law and Rules, the sufficiency of a pleading to state a cause of action or defense will generally depend upon whether or not there was substantial compliance with section 3013 providing that "Statements in a pleading shall be sufficiently particular to give the court and parties notice of the transactions, occurrences, or series of transactions or occurrences, intended to be proved and the material elements of each cause of action or defense." These provisions are declared to be "the heart of the pleading requirement and [represent] an attempt to set up a realistic requirement of pleading" (First Preliminary Report of Advisory Committee on Practice and Procedure [1957], p. 63). By virtue of the provisions, the emphasis with respect to pleading is placed, where it should be, upon the primary function of pleadings, namely, that of adequately advising the adverse party of the pleader's claim or defense. (*See* David D. Siegel, *A Biannual Survey of New York Practice*, 38 St. John's L. Rev., pp. 190, 199-200.) The "basic requirement . . . [now] is that the pleadings identify the transaction and indicate the theory of recovery with sufficient precision to enable the court to control the case and the opponent to prepare." (First Preliminary Report of Advisory Committee on Practice and Procedure [1957], p. 63.) So, generally speaking, "Pleadings should not be dismissed or ordered amended

unless the allegations therein are not sufficiently particular to apprise the
court and parties of the subject matter of the controversy." (3 Weinstein-Korn-
Miller, N.Y. Civ. Prac., par. 3013.03.)

The Civil Practice Law and Rules directive that a pleading shall contain
statements sufficiently particular to give "notice" to the court and the parties
replaced the provisions of former section 241 of the Civil Practice Act that
every pleading should contain a statement of the "material facts . . . on which
the party pleading relies." This shift in the statement of pleading requirements
is not without significance. By the elimination of the provision that pleadings
state "material facts" — a phrase that resulted in much needless motion practice under the Civil Practice Act — it was intended "that the considerable judicial effort formerly expended in distinguishing 'evidence' or 'conclusions' from
'facts' be directed to more useful purposes." (3 Weinstein-Korn-Miller, N.Y. Civ.
Prac., par. 3013.01.) But it is clear that, under the Civil Practice Law and Rules,
the statements in pleadings are still required to be factual, that is, the essential facts required to give "notice" must be stated. (*See* Wachtel, New York Practice, p. 102.) Nevertheless, a party may supplement or round out his pleading
by conclusory allegations or by "stating legal theories explicitly" if the facts
upon which the pleader relies are also stated. (*See* Notes, First Preliminary
Report of Advisory Committee on Practice and Procedure [1957], p. 63.)

In addition to the basic general requirements for pleading statements as set
out in 3013 of the Civil Practice Law and Rules aforesaid, there are special provisions for particularity to be followed in pleading (a) conditions precedent, (b)
corporate status, (c) judgment, decision or determination, and (d) special damages (CPLR 3015). There are also special provisions for the particularity
required for statements in specific actions, to wit, (a) libel or slander, (b) fraud
or mistake, (c) separation, (d) judgment, (e) law of foreign country and (f) sale
and delivery of goods or performing of labor or services. (CPLR 3016.) Of these
special provisions, only subdivision (b) of 3016 is relevant on the question of the
sufficiency of the complaint here. Therein, it is provided that in certain causes
of action, including causes based upon fraud or breach of trust, "the circumstances constituting the wrong shall be stated in detail." This follows a common-
law and code requirement of long standing, and was included in the Civil
Practice Law and Rules because it was thought that the provisions of 3013 of
the Civil Practice Law and Rules might not sufficiently indicate the rule in
this particular class of cases. (*See* First Preliminary Report of Advisory Committee on Practice and Procedure [1957], p. 68.) In any event, in view of the Civil
Practice Law and Rules objective for greater liberality in pleading matters (*see
post*) these special provisions should not be given the effect of requiring more
now by way of detail and specificity in pleadings in these actions than was formerly required under the Civil Practice Act. Furthermore, bearing in mind that
the sufficiency of a pleading statement primarily depends upon compliance
with 3013's (CPLR) basic requirements, these special provisions in subdivision
(b) of 3016 constitute no more than a directive that the "transactions and occur-

rences" constituting the "wrong" shall be pleaded in sufficient "detail" to give adequate notice thereof.

The basic pleading requirements hereinbefore referred to are supplemented also by 3014 setting forth guidelines in the matter of the form and arrangement of allegations, statements, causes of action and defenses. Therein, it is provided, *inter alia*, that every pleading shall "consist of plain and concise statements in consecutively numbered paragraphs." This provision applies to all pleadings and was designed to eliminate "loosely drawn, verbose, or poorly organized pleadings." (*See* 3 Weinstein-Korn Miller, par. 3014.01.) Where a pleading lacks such compliance with the plain and concise statement requirement as to be "so vague or ambiguous that a party cannot reasonably be required to frame a response he may move for a more definite statement." (CPLR 3024, subd. [a].)

Upon a 3211 (subd. [a], par. 7) motion to dismiss a cause of action, however, we look to the substance rather than to the form. Such a motion is solely directed to the inquiry of whether or not the pleading, considered as a whole, "fails to state a cause of action." Looseness, verbosity and excursiveness, must be overlooked on such a motion if any cause of action can be spelled out from the four corners of the pleading. (*See* Siegel, 38 St. John's L. Rev., p. 205.)

It was well settled and still is, of course, the rule that a pleading will not be dismissed for insufficiency merely because it is inartistically drawn. Where a pleading is attacked for alleged inadequacy in its statements, our inquiry should be limited to "whether it states in some recognizable form any cause of action known to our law" (*Dulberg v. Mock*, 1 N.Y.2d 54, 56). "However imperfectly, informally or even illogically the facts may be stated, a complaint, attacked for insufficiency, is deemed to allege 'whatever can be implied from its statements by fair and reasonable intendment' (*Kain v. Larkin*, 141 N.Y. 144, 151.) The question for us is whether the requisite allegations of any valid cause of action cognizable by the state courts 'can be fairly gathered from all the averments.'" (*Condon v. Associated Hosp. Serv.*, 287 N.Y. 411, 414.)

Finally, every pleading question should be approached in the light of the Civil Practice Law and Rules enactment that pleadings "shall be liberally construed. Defects shall be ignored if a substantial right of a party is not prejudiced."[2] (CPLR 3026.) The general provision for liberal construction was contained in the former Civil Practice Act but the last sentence quoted above was added new in the Civil Practice Law and Rules with the intent to put teeth in the mandate for liberal construction. Thereby, the burden is expressly placed upon one who attacks a pleading for deficiencies in its allegations to show that he is prejudiced. It was thus sought to discourage time- consuming pleading

[2] "This is a statement of a fundamental tenet of modern practice; the pleadings and other forms of procedures are only a means to the end of resolving the controversy between the parties. Even if a pleading be technically in violation of some rule of good pleading, what does it matter if substantial rights of other parties are in no way prejudiced." (Wachtel, New York Practice, p. 108.)

attacks which were unlikely to result in a final disposition of the action on the merits[3] . . . and which would have a tendency to defeat the over-all objective of the Civil Practice Law and Rules "to secure the just, speedy and inexpensive determination of every civil judicial proceeding." (*See* CPLR 104.)

The proper promotion of the general Civil Practice Law and Rules objective requires more than mere token observance of or lip service to its mandate for liberal construction of pleadings. To achieve such objective, we must literally apply the mandate as directed and thus make the test of prejudice one of primary importance. Thereby, we would invariably disregard pleading irregularities, defects or omissions which are not such as to reasonably mislead one as to the identity of the transactions or occurrences sought to be litigated or as to the nature and elements of the alleged cause or defense. If the irregularity, defect or omission represents an inherent deficiency, known by the adverse party to bar the pleader's right to recover or defend on the merits, rather than a mere pleading error, then the adverse party would be better advised to proceed under 3211 or 3212 upon affidavits or other proofs to secure an immediate determination on the merits. This would generally result in "the just, speedy and inexpensive determination" of the action without the waste of time involved in the motion to dismiss for mere insufficiency in statement.

On basis of the foregoing, we have no difficulty in arriving at the conclusion that the first and second causes in the complaint are sufficiently stated. The first cause "is sufficiently particular" as to facts and details to state a derivative cause of action to secure an injunction and an accounting with respect to acts and threatened acts of the defendants in breach of their fiduciary obligations as officers and directors of the family corporations.

"Directors and officers shall discharge the duties of their respective positions in good faith." (Business Corporation Law, § 717.) They may not assume and engage in the promotion of personal interests which are incompatible with the superior interests of their corporation. . . .

. . . So it follows that an officer or director who actively engages in a rival or competing business to the detriment of his corporation, must answer to the corporation for the injury it thereby sustains.

It is true that the first cause, as pointed out by the defendants, does not show with specificity the manner and extent of the competition between the existing family corporations and the new "D'Agostino" supermarket company organized by the individual defendants, nor does it show exactly how and to what extent the family corporations have been or will be damaged by the acts of the individual defendants. But the statements in the pleading, viewed with reason and liberality, are "sufficiently particular" to give the defendants notice

---

[3] "A study prepared for the Advisory Committee of cases involving pleading issues over a five-year period amply demonstrates the futility of motion practice addressed to the formal sufficiency of the pleadings." (3 Weinstein-Korn-Miller, N.Y. Civ. Prac., par. 3013.02.)

of the plaintiffs' claims in this connection and of the elements of plaintiffs' alleged cause of action; and furthermore, the defendants are and will not be prejudiced in any manner by the alleged deficiencies therein. Therefore, the pleading on this cause is immune from attack by motion under 3211 (subd. [a], par. 7) of the Civil Practice Law and Rules.

The second cause, also alleged in the right of the corporation, has been framed on the theory that the defendant directors, officers and employees are engaging and threaten to engage in unfair competition with the family corporations. The complaint alleges that the said defendants, through the new corporation, "have or are about to enter into direct competition with the family corporations and are about to siphon off and appropriate to themselves, the customers and potential customers of the family corporations . . . [that] several of the food stores and supermarkets owned and operated by the family corporations are located within a few blocks of the new corporation's stores premises"; that said defendants are using the name "D'Agostino" in the new store "thereby implying that the store is owned by the family corporations and the D'Agostino family"; that they threaten to palm off the new supermarket store as one owned and operated by the family corporations; that they have caused or will cause employees of the family corporations to devote time to the operation of the new store and that the new store has "used or will use the credit, funds, central purchasing and warehousing facilities of the family corporations."

Competing with one's employer represents a well-recognized instance of unlawful business injury. Where employees, during the period of their employment, and a corporation formed by them, engage in and carry out a conspiracy to compete with the employer in violation of the duties of loyalty owing by the employees, said conduct constitutes actionable unfair competition. (*See Jones Co. v. Burke*, 306 N.Y. 172; *Lamdin v. Broadway Surface Adv. Corp.*, 272 N.Y. 133; *Reis & Co. v. Volck*, 151 App. Div. 613; *Todd Protectograph Co. v. Hedman Mfg. Co.*, 254 F. 829.) Thus, the allegations of this second cause are "sufficiently particular" to give the defendants notice "of the transactions, occurrences, or series of transactions or occurrences" relied upon by plaintiffs as constituting the alleged unfair competition; and the allegations do set forth the "material elements" of such a cause of action. It is true, as pointed out by the defendants, that certain of the allegations are stated in the alternative and certain of them are conclusory in form, but where, as here, the pleading does state facts which are sufficient to give the defendants notice of the plaintiffs' claims, the pleading is not rendered insufficient by the presence of such allegations.

. . . .

NOTES

(1) The principal case, decided soon after the enactment of the CPLR, is now considered a classic statement of the liberal approach to pleadings taken by article 30.

(2) An important rule antedating the CPLR but still valid is that "conclusory allegations" do not meet acceptable pleading standards. "General allegations of misconduct will not do in the absence of statements of those facts upon which are based the pleader's conclusions that the acts of which complaint is made are wrongful. . . ." *Kalmanash v. Smith*, 291 N.Y. 142, 153, 51 N.E.2d 681, 686 (1943).

An early application of this rule is found in *Baby Show Exhibition Co. v. Crowell Publishing Co.*, 174 A.D. 368, 161 N.Y.S. 205 (1st Dep't 1916), where plaintiff alleged that he and defendant had entered into a contract to produce a show, that he had performed his side of the bargain, but that "defendant, contrary to and in violation thereof, neglected, omitted and refused to carry out the terms and conditions of said agreement. . . ." Granting a motion to strike the complaint, the court said:

> There is no allegation of *fact* with respect to any act or omission on the part of the defendant constituting a breach of contract. . . . It is well settled that in an action to recover damages for the breach of a contract *the facts constituting the breach* must be pleaded, and that it is insufficient to plead generally that the defendant failed to fulfill his obligations under the contract or that he has been guilty of a breach of the contract. . . .

174 A.D. at 369-70, 161 N.Y.S. at 207 (emphasis in original).

The same problem arises in negligence cases. In *Pagnillo v. Mack Paving & Construction Co.*, 142 A.D. 491, 492, 127 N.Y.S. 72, 73 (2d Dep't 1911), the court wrote of the complaint in a wrongful death action:

> It is not enough to allege that a dutiful servant was killed by the negligence of the master or his agent in charge respecting the work in which the servant was engaged. What was the omitted act that should have been done, or the culpable act that was done? Does it relate to place, appliance, tool, rule, instruction, or order? The complaint is silent.

An application of the same approach is found in *Travelers Insurance Co. v. Ferco, Inc.*, 122 A.D.2d 718, 511 N.Y.S.2d 594 (1st Dep't 1986). The plaintiff sought to recover for the cost of re-shooting a television commercial. The remake was necessary, plaintiff claimed, either because equipment rented by the defendant failed or because Kodak (a co-defendant) had supplied defective film. The complaint alleged that Kodak had breached warranties of fitness and merchantability. The court held that the cause of action against Kodak should have been dismissed under CPLR 3211(a)(7):

CPLR 3013's liberal pleading provision notwithstanding, a pleading must still be particular enough to provide the court and parties with notice of the transactions or occurrences intended to be proved. The subject pleadings aptly described by Special Term as "an either-or assemblage of bare allegations" do not give Kodak notice of any occurrence or transaction possibly constituting negligence or of any particular defect upon which the breach of warranty claim can be predicated.

(3) The illustrative form complaint promulgated by the Judicial Conference for a negligent driving case contains this allegation of the defendant's fault: "On June 1, 1966, in a public highway called Broadway in New York City, defendant C.D. negligently drove a motor vehicle against plaintiff who was then crossing the highway." Official Form 12.

Is this not a conclusory allegation? Why should a deviation from the normally required specificity be permitted in auto accident cases? *See* Clark, *Pleading Under the Federal Rules*, 12 Wyo. L. Rev. 177 (1958).

(4) Some cases hold that the facts underlying an assertion of long-arm jurisdiction must be pleaded in the complaint. *See, e.g., Teplin v. Manafort*, 81 A.D.2d 531, 438 N.Y.S. 2d 84 (1st Dep't 1981). Other courts have disagreed. *See, e.g., Fishman v. Pocono Ski Rental Inc.*, 82 A.D.2d 906, 440 N.Y.S.2d 700 (2d Dep't 1981). Which rule is preferable?

(5) Pleading requirements applicable to specific situations are found in CPLR 3015, 3016, and 3017. One most commonly encountered deals with no-fault pleading. Under New York's no-fault legislation (the Comprehensive Motor Veh. Ins. Reparations Act, Insurance Law art. 51), a victim of an auto accident may not maintain a lawsuit for personal injury without sustaining serious injury as defined in Insurance Law § 5102(d) (fracture, significant disfigurement, etc.) or unless economic loss exceeds $50,000, Insurance Law §§ 5102(a), 5104. CPLR § 3016(g), which governs the no-fault complaint, only requires that the plaintiff state injury or economic loss in excess of the statutory minimum, *i.e.*, in this situation conclusory pleading is permitted. The defendant who wants further detail about the injury may demand it in the bill of particulars under CPLR § 3043. *See generally Sanders v. Rickard*, 51 A.D.2d 260, 264, 380 N.Y.S.2d 811, 815 (3rd Dep't 1976).

(6) CPLR 3012-a, added in 1986, imposes an additional pleading requirement on the plaintiff in actions for medical, dental or podiatric malpractice. It requires that the complaint in such an action be accompanied by a certificate — which we might call a certificate of good faith investigation — signed by the attorney for the plaintiff. The certificate must state that the attorney has reviewed the facts of the case and has consulted with a practitioner of the discipline in which malpractice is alleged and that the attorney believes that there is a reasonable basis for the commencement of the action. (Under certain circumstances the attorney is excused from the consultation requirement. *See* CPLR 3012-a(2), (3).)

The Legislature did not provide a sanction for failing to comply with CPLR 3012-a. In *Kolb v. Strogli*, 158 A.D.2d 15, 558 N.Y.S.2d 549 (2d Dep't 1990), the court, in light of the determination in *Tewari v. Tsoutsouras*, 75 N.Y.2d 1, 550 N.Y.S.2d 572, 549 N.E.2d 1143 (1989), § 18.02, *infra*, which held that outright dismissal was inappropriate where plaintiff failed to file a notice of malpractice action under CPLR 3406(a), ruled that failure to comply with CPLR 3012-a could not result in dismissal. However, under the *Tewari* case, if plaintiff neglects to supply the necessary notice after being ordered to do so by the court, then the action may be dismissed.

P.T. BANK CENTRAL ASIA, NEW YORK BRANCH v. ABN AMRO BANK N.V.
Appellate Division, First Department
301 A.D.2d 373, 754 N.Y.S.2d 245 (2003)

CHARLES RAMOS, J.

[The defendant, ABN, was the agent for two loans, the Senior Loan and the Bridge Loan. The loans were to be made to Pioneer, a logging and timber company, and to Strategic Partners. The purposes of the loans were to permit Pioneer to restructure existing debt and to enable Strategic Partners to obtain title to Pioneer-owned assets. ABN was, through a public offering, to solicit funds from lending banks and disburse proceeds to the borrowers.

[Plaintiff, P.T. Bank, alleged that ABN represented that it was expert in structuring this kind of financing, and that there was no risk because the collateral had a value of $470 million, substantially in excess of the $305 total loan package. Plaintiff alleged further that, acting in reliance on ABN's representations, it purchased a $1 million interest in the Bridge Loan.

[Ultimately, the public offering was cancelled when it was discovered that the value of the collateral had been substantially overstated. The borrowers defaulted and plaintiff lost its $1 million investment. This action was commenced, the complaint, *inter alia*, alleging fraudulent misrepresentation, and fraudulent failure to disclose material information. ABN responded with a motion to dismiss which was granted by the IAS court. The Appellate Division reversed.]

The scope of a court's inquiry on a motion to dismiss under CPLR 3211 is narrowly circumscribed. The court must "accept the facts alleged as true . . . and determine simply whether the facts alleged fit within any cognizable legal theory" (*Morone v. Morone*, 50 NY2d 481, 484 [citation omitted]; *see also Guggenheimer v. Ginzburg*, 43 NY2d 268, 275). The complaint must be construed "liberally" (CPLR 3026; *see New York Trap Rock Corp. v. Town of Clarkstown*, 299 NY 77), and the court must accept as true not only "the complaint's material allegations" but also "whatever can be reasonably inferred therefrom" in favor of the pleader (*McGill v. Parker*, 179 AD2d 98, 105; *see also Cron v. Har-*

gro Fabrics, 91 NY2d 362, 366). In ruling on a motion to dismiss, the court is not authorized to assess the merits of the complaint or any of its factual allegations, but only to determine if, assuming the truth of the facts alleged, the complaint states the elements of a legally cognizable cause of action.

To state a legally cognizable claim of fraudulent misrepresentation, the complaint must allege that the defendant made a material misrepresentation of fact; that the misrepresentation was made intentionally in order to defraud or mislead the plaintiff; that the plaintiff reasonably relied on the misrepresentation; and that the plaintiff suffered damage as a result of its reliance on the defendant's misrepresentation (*see e.g. Swersky v. Dreyer & Traub*, 219 AD2d 321, 326). A cause of action for fraudulent concealment requires, in addition to the four foregoing elements, an allegation that the defendant had a duty to disclose material information and that it failed to do so (*Wiscovitch Assoc. v. Philip Morris Cos.*, 193 AD2d 542). In addition, in any action based upon fraud, "the circumstances constituting the wrong shall be stated in detail" (CPLR 3016[b]).

Supreme Court dismissed the fraudulent misrepresentation and concealment claims on the grounds that the complaint failed to include an allegation that defendant intended to deceive plaintiff or to conceal material information and that plaintiff, as a matter of law, was precluded by the terms of its agreement with ABN from asserting that it reasonably relied on any misrepresentations by ABN.

The complaint alleges, inter alia, that, at the time ABN solicited plaintiff's participation in the Bridge Loan, (1) ABN was a principal lender in the Senior and Bridge Loans, the syndication agent for the Senior Loan, the administrative agent for the Bridge Loan, and a self-described expert in timberland financing; (2) ABN, by virtue of its special position in the Pioneer timberland financing transactions, possessed specific knowledge and information, including "appraisals, financial statements, reports of consultants and other information," establishing that the value of the collateral for the Senior and Bridge Loans had been significantly overstated by the appraisal that was a prerequisite of the Bridge Loan; (3) despite this knowledge and information, ABN represented to plaintiff that the value of the loan collateral was in excess of the total amount of the loans; (4) ABN knew these representations were false; and (5) ABN misrepresented the value of the loan collateral, or failed to disclose that the value was not as stated in the appraisal, "in order to decrease its own financial exposure under Bridge Loan Agreement and in order to receive funds to disburse to itself as fees for acting as the Syndication Agent and Administrative Agent under the loan agreements."

Accepting the allegations of the complaint as true and construing the inferences that may be drawn from those allegations in plaintiff's favor, as we must, we believe the foregoing sufficiently allege that ABN intentionally misrepresented or failed to disclose material facts. Although Supreme Court found fault in plaintiff's failure to allege how or when ABN assertedly obtained information demonstrating that the appraised value was overstated, neither CPLR 3016(b) nor any other rule of law requires a plaintiff to allege details of the asserted fraud that it may not know or that may be peculiarly within the defendant's knowledge at the pleading stage. CPLR 3016(b) "requires only that the misconduct complained of be set forth in sufficient detail to clearly inform a defendant with respect to the incidents complained of and is not to be interpreted so strictly as to prevent an otherwise valid cause of action in situations where it may be 'impossible to state in detail the circumstances constituting a fraud'" (*Lanzi v. Brooks*, 43 NY2d 778, 780, *quoting Jered Contr. Corp. v. New York City Tr. Auth.*, 22 NY2d 187, 194). Nor, contrary to the suggestion of Supreme Court, must plaintiff produce evidence at this stage of the proceedings to support its contentions as to what ABN knew about the true value of the collateral when it solicited plaintiff's participation in the Bridge Loan.

. . . .

NOTES

(1) In *Lanzi v. Brooks*, 43 N.Y.2d 778, 402 N.Y.S.2d 384, 373 N.E.2d 278 (1977), cited in the principal case, the Court held a fraud complaint insufficient for failing to allege the necessary intent or any factual assertions from which intent could have been shown.

(2) In *Aetna Cas. & Sur. Co. v. Merchants Mut. Ins.*, 84 A.D.2d 736, 444 N.Y.S.2d 79 (1st Dep't 1981), an excess insurer sued a primary insurer for bad faith and breach of duty in handling lawsuits. The court dismissed the complaint on the following grounds:

> The complaint, a veritable novella, consisting of 42 pages and 104 paragraphs, one of which is eleven pages in length, includes quotations from testimony at the trial of the underlying action, examinations before trial and documents received in evidence, as well as the trial court's charge on contributory negligence. It is, in our view, a prime example of a loosely drawn, verbose and poorly organized pleading, and is totally at variance with the requirements of CPLR § 3014 that a "pleading shall consist of plain and concise statements in consecutively numbered paragraphs . . . separately stated and numbered. . . ."

84 A.D.2d at 736, 444 N.Y.S.2d at 79-80.

A complaint such as that described could as well be the subject of a motion for a more definite statement under CPLR 3024. This section has been relied upon when, for example, the vagueness is due to conclusory allegations. *Lence v. Sheldon*, 34 A.D.2d 966, 312 N.Y.S.2d 725 (2d Dep't 1970). It has also been used as a way of compelling separate statements and numbering within a complaint. *Weicker v. Weicker*, 26 A.D.2d 39, 270 N.Y.S.2d 640 (1st Dep't 1966).

(3) The opposition can also move to strike scandalous or prejudicial material not necessary to a pleading under CPLR § 3024(b). Scandalous was defined in *Hurley v. Hurley*, 266 A.D. 701, 40 N.Y.S.2d 671 (3d Dep't 1943), as allegations that are "immaterial" or "reproachful." This does not include allegations which are part of the dispute. If they are relevant to the case, they cannot be stricken because scandalous.

(4) The Court of Appeals wrote an instructive opinion regarding Court of Claims pleading where facts must be pleaded with more particularity than in Supreme Court under CPLR 3017. Under § 11(b) of the Court of Claims Act, the claim must state "(1) 'the nature of [the claim]'; (2) 'the time when' it arose; (3) the 'place where' it arose; (4) 'the items of damage or injuries claimed to have been sustained'; and (5) 'the total sum claimed.'" Claimants' argument that facts should be ascertained by the State from its personnel records, in an action seeking overtime compensation, was rejected by the Court as not being the State's burden to prove. Also, the Court held that the verification requirement in § 11(b) necessitates strict adherence to § 3022 of the CPLR (*see* § 13.06, *infra*). *Lepkowski v. State*, 1 N.Y.3d 201, 207, 770 N.Y.S.2d 696, 700, 802 N.E.2d 1094, 1098 (2003).

§ 13.03 THE ANSWER

Form

Verified Answer

SUPREME COURT OF THE STATE OF NEW YORK
COUNTY OF NEW YORK

PETER RUGGLES and MARY M. RUGGLES	
Plaintiffs	
— against —	VERIFIED ANSWER
SEARS ROEBUCK AND COMPANY,	
Defendant.	

Defendant, SEARS ROEBUCK AND COMPANY, by its attorneys, BOWER & GARDNER, as and for its verified answer to the complaint, respectfully shows to this Court and alleges, upon information and belief:

FIRST: The defendant denies each and every allegation contained in Paragraphs "FOURTH," "SIXTH," "SEVENTH" and "TENTH."

SECOND: Denies having knowledge or information sufficient to form a belief as to the allegations contained in Paragraph "NINTH."

THIRD: Denies having knowledge or information sufficient to form a belief as to the allegations contained in Paragraphs "SECOND" and "THIRD" and refers all questions of law to this Honorable Court.

FOURTH: Repeats each admission or denial heretofore made in response to Paragraphs "FIFTH" and "EIGHTH."

AS AND FOR A FIRST SEPARATE AND COMPLETE AFFIRMATIVE DEFENSE, THE DEFENDANT ALLEGES, UPON INFORMATION AND BELIEF:

FIFTH: That any amount of damages otherwise recoverable by the plaintiffs shall be diminished in the proportion which such culpable conduct of the plaintiffs bear to the total culpable conduct causing the injury.

AS AND FOR A SECOND SEPARATE AND COMPLETE AFFIRMATIVE DEFENSE, THE DEFENDANT ALLEGES UPON INFORMATION AND BELIEF:

SIXTH: That the Court lacks in personam jurisdiction over the answering defendant.

AS AND FOR A THIRD SEPARATE AND COMPLETE AFFIRMATIVE DEFENSE, THE DEFENDANT ALLEGES UPON INFORMATION AND BELIEF:

SEVENTH: That the action is barred by the applicable Statute of Limitations.

WHEREFORE, defendant demands judgment against the plaintiffs, dismissing the complaint herein, together with the costs and disbursements of this action.

_____
Attorneys for Defendant
Office & P.O. Address
415 Madison Avenue
New York, NY 10017
(212) 751-2900

[Attorney's verification omitted — Ed.]

NOTE

Compare the foregoing answer with the complaint to which it responds. Does it properly use the alternatives permitted by CPLR 3018? Can you think of another way defendants might have responded to paragraph fourth of the complaint? Paragraph second?

What response might you have made to this answer were you the plaintiff?

[A] Forms of Denial

BELLO v. TRANSIT AUTHORITY OF NEW YORK CITY
Appellate Division, Second Department
12 A.D.3d 58, 783 N.Y.S.2d 648 (2004)

FISHER, J.

. . . .

[The five-year-old plaintiff and her mother were passengers on a bus operated by defendant when the mother noticed a man acting strangely. When the man exited the bus, he left behind a large orange bag, the contents of which, according to the mother, were ticking. Other passengers became alarmed and general panic set in. The driver brought the bus to a sudden stop, opened the doors, and the passengers hurriedly exited and ran off. The mother then discovered that plaintiff had sustained an injury to her head, allegedly as a result of the sudden stop. This action was commenced, and defendant Transit Authority issued an answer denying negligence and asserting comparative negligence. The IAS court granted summary judgment to defendant. The issue on appeal was whether the answer should have contained the emergency doctrine as an affirmative defense.]

Negligence involves the failure to exercise the degree of care that a reasonably prudent person would exercise in the same situation (see Gray v. Gouz, Inc., 204 AD2d 390 [1994]; PJI3d 2:10 [2004]). It is not a fixed concept, but is shaped by "time, place and circumstance" (Sadowski v. Long Is. R.R. Co., 292 NY 448, 455 [1944]). The common-law emergency doctrine does not define an exception to those principles but rather fits neatly within their framework. The doctrine recognizes that, faced with an emergency, even a reasonable person might choose a course of action which, in hindsight, proves to have been mistaken or ill-advised.

Thus, the emergency doctrine holds that those faced with a sudden and unexpected circumstance, not of their own making, that leaves them with little or no time for reflection or reasonably causes them to be so disturbed that they are compelled to make a quick decision without weighing alternative courses of conduct, may not be negligent if their actions are reasonable and prudent in the context of the emergency (see Caristo v. Sanzone, 96 NY2d 172, 174 [2001]; Rivera v. New York City Tr. Auth., 77 NY2d 322, 327 [1991]). The essence of the emergency doctrine is that, where a sudden and unexpected circumstance leaves a person without time to contemplate or weigh alternative courses of action, that person cannot reasonably be held to the standard of care required of one who has had a full opportunity to reflect, and therefore should not be found negligent unless the course chosen was unreasonable or imprudent in light of the emergent circumstances (see Amaro v. City of New York, 40 NY2d 30, 36 [1976]).

Although the existence of an emergency and the reasonableness of a party's response to it will ordinarily present questions of fact (*see Morgan v. Ski Round-top*, 290 AD2d 618 [2002]), they may in appropriate circumstances be determined as a matter of law (*see Huggins v Figueroa*, 305 AD2d 460 [2003]). Here, invoking the emergency doctrine, the Transit Authority establishes prima facie entitlement to judgment as a matter of law by demonstrating that an emergency stop was made only after distressed and panicking passengers urgently told the driver that a man had left a bomb on the bus. In opposition, the plaintiff failed to raise a triable issue of fact as to the driver's negligence (*see Huggins v. Figueroa, supra*). Nevertheless, the plaintiff contends that, having failed to plead the emergency doctrine as an affirmative defense, the defendants are precluded from relying on it. We disagree.

CPLR 3018(b) provides that "[a] party shall plead all matters which if not pleaded would be likely to take the adverse party by surprise or would raise issues of fact not appearing on the face of a prior pleading." Applying that rule, the question whether the emergency doctrine must be pleaded as an affirmative defense necessarily turns on the particular circumstances of each case. Where the facts relating to the existence of an emergency are presumptively known only to the party seeking to invoke the doctrine, it must be pleaded as an affirmative defense lest the adverse party be taken by surprise. Thus, for example, where the driver of a vehicle involved in a collision claims to have been reacting to a sudden and unforeseen medical emergency, the emergency doctrine would have to be pleaded as an affirmative defense (*cf. Dalchand v. Missigman*, 288 AD2d 956 [2001]).

Conversely, where the facts relating to the existence of the emergency are known to the adverse party and would not raise new issues of fact not appearing on the face of the prior pleadings, the party seeking to rely on the emergency doctrine would not have to raise it as an affirmative defense (*see* CPLR 3018[b]).

Here, all of the facts leading to the stop of the bus were well within the plaintiff's knowledge. Thus, there was no unfair surprise arising from the defendants' failure to plead those facts in their answer. Moreover, inasmuch as the plaintiff was given ample opportunity in opposition to the defendants' summary judgment motion to challenge the application of the emergency doctrine, both procedurally and on the merits, the Supreme Court did not err in considering the doctrine (*see Rogoff v. San Juan Racing Assn.* 54 NY2d 883, 885 [1981]).

Accordingly, the order should be affirmed, with costs.

NOTES

(1) In *Rouse v. Champion Home Builders Co.*, 47 A.D.2d 584, 363 N.Y.S.2d 167 (1975), the complaint was verified and consisted of specific allegations. The answer contained only a general denial denying "each and every allegation in the complaint." An irritated court wrote: "We condemn the growing practice of

serving such an answer. . . . It is apparent that defendant knew at the time the answer was served, that certain of the allegations of the complaint were true. . . ."

(2) A general denial may encompass the entire complaint or one or more of its paragraphs. Were the general denials in paragraph first of the form answer appropriate?

(3) A plaintiff who uses CPLR 3016(f) in a proper case will discourage the general denial. In *Virginia Blue Ridge Railway v. Seeley*, 33 A.D.2d 871, 306 N.Y.S.2d 251 (3d Dep't 1969), plaintiff sued for payment of locomotive parts delivered to defendant. Plaintiff attached to the complaint an itemized list of the parts and their values as permitted by § 3016(f). Defendant admitted all the allegations on the action for the price of the parts, but generally denied the value of the parts. The court held this was insufficient to thwart summary judgment: "[T]he answer does not specify as required by CPLR § 3016, subd. (f), which items of value set forth on appellant's list are disputed. The answer is simply a general denial and as such does not put at issue the value of the goods sold. . . ." 33 A.D.2d at 872, 306 N.Y.S.2d at 252. The court granted summary judgment for plaintiff for the $4,773.75 it had specified since defendant had raised no other issues. *Compare Edwin F. Guth Co. v. Gurland*, 246 A.D. 67, 284 N.Y.S. 333 (1st Dep't 1935).

Other situations in which a general denial will not suffice are covered in CPLR 3015(a), (c); 3018(b).

[B] Affirmative Defenses

PROBLEM B

Consider the answer in the *Ruggles* case, *supra*. Could the defendant introduce evidence at trial, over plaintiff's objection, that an improper method of service of the summons was used? That there are insufficient contacts between the defendant and the State of New York to satisfy due process? That the plaintiff was injured because he did not use the ladder for the purpose for which it was intended?

MUNSON v. NEW YORK SEED IMPROVEMENT COOPERATIVE, INC.
Court of Appeals
64 N.Y.2d 985, 478 N.E.2d 180, 489 N.Y.S.2d 39 (1985)

Plaintiff is a bean farmer in Tompkins County. In July 1981 he contracted to purchase "foundation seed" from defendant for spring 1982, and tendered a $5,000 deposit with his order. In the spring of 1982 defendant informed plaintiff that it was unable to deliver the "foundation seed," and offered to sell "registered seed" at a reduced price of $14,500. Plaintiff agreed to the change and picked up the "registered seed." Shortly thereafter, he allegedly discovered that the "registered seed" was defective and attempted unsuccessfully to return it.

Plaintiff commenced this action against defendant alleging a breach of the agreement for "foundation seed" and seeking recovery for the diminution in customer goodwill resulting from the breach. Defendant counterclaimed for $9,500, the balance due on the agreement for "registered seed." In response, plaintiff interposed a reply containing a general denial.

At trial, following the opening statements, the plaintiff made an offer of proof concerning the inferior quality of the "registered seed" and his attempt to reject it. Neither claim was raised in the amended complaint or the reply. The court then dismissed the amended complaint and directed a verdict in favor of defendant on its counterclaim for the balance due for the "registered seed." It also denied plaintiff's motion to amend his pleadings.

The Appellate Division modified, on the law, by reversing the Supreme Court order insofar as it directed a verdict for defendant on the counterclaim, and otherwise affirmed as to the dismissal of the complaint. . . . Defendant contends that plaintiff failed to plead the affirmative defense of breach of warranty in his amended complaint or reply and is thereby precluded from offering such proof as a defense to the counterclaim.

The general rule stated in CPLR 3018(b) is that "[a] party shall plead all matters which if not pleaded would be likely to take the adverse party by surprise or would raise issues of fact not appearing on the face of a prior pleading." Defendant cannot claim surprise because the protestations as to the quality of the registered seed were communicated to it. However, the allegations concerning inferior quality and the attempted rejection raise factual issues which do not appear in the plaintiff's pleadings. The failure to plead these matters results in a waiver (*see, Surlak v Surlak*, 95 AD2d 371, *appeal dismissed*, 6 NY 2d 906) which entitles defendant to summary judgment on its counterclaim. Plaintiff's general denial is insufficient to raise the claims because a general denial puts in issue only matters which defendant is bound to prove on its counterclaim (*see generally, Hoffstaedter v Carlton Auto Supplies Co.*, 203 App Div 494, 496).

[The order of the Appellate Division was reversed.]

NOTES

(1) How did the plaintiff waive the defense to the counterclaim that the "registered" seed was defective? If, as the Court says, the defense did not surprise the defendant, was it an affirmative defense? *See* CPLR 3018(b).

(2) An affirmative defense, when one is pleaded, must meet the particularity standard of CPLR 3013. Remember that that is not a difficult standard to meet. The Court of Appeals held, in *Immediate v. St. Johns's Queens Hospital*, 48 N.Y.2d 671, 421 N.Y.S.2d 875, 397 N.E.2d 385 (1979):

> It was sufficient under CPLR 3013 that [defendant] pleaded the statute of limitations as a defense; it was not required to identify the statutory section relied on or to specify the applicable period of limitations.

(3) As the following case shows, more difficulty is encountered in pleading jurisdictional defenses.

GAGER v. WHITE
Court of Appeals
53 N.Y.2d 475, 442 N.Y.S.2d 463, 425 N.E.2d 851 (1981)

[The facts are found in the excerpt of this case in § 6.04, *supra*. Among other issues, the court had to decide whether the various defendants had properly preserved their objections to the assertion of jurisdiction by attachment of their insurance policies — Eds.]

. . . Unlike subject matter jurisdiction, which limits the power of a particular court rather than the judicial jurisdiction of the State *en gros*, a defect in basis jurisdiction is waivable (CPLR 3211, subd [e]). Under the CPLR, the objection may be raised either by a preanswer motion or by pleading it as an affirmative defense, whichever comes first. . . . Absent the pursuit of either course, a defendant's voluntary participation in litigation in which the point can be raised, in and of itself, constitutes a submission to the jurisdiction of the courts of our State and, as such, acts as a predicate for basis jurisdiction. . . .

Examining the cases before us to determine whether *quasi in rem* jurisdiction has been appropriately controverted, we note that specific objections on that score were made in the answers filed in *Gager v White* and *Hill v Elliott*. In these cases, the Appellate Division's dismissal of the complaints being mandatory, there should be an affirmance.

In contrast, no jurisdictional protest having been lodged in *Cachat v Guertin Co.*, the Appellate Division also was correct when it there found that dismissal was not in order (CPLR 3211, subd [e]).[11]

Lastly, in *Mei Yuet Chin v Cray* and *Carbone v Ericson*, the answers raised objection to in personam jurisdiction only.[12] Since, as explained earlier, a defect

---

[11] The nearest thing to a jurisdictional defense in *Cachat* was a much different claim, that of defective service.

[12] In *Chin*, in his "Sixth Separate and Complete Affirmative Defense," the answer pleaded that "the court lacks jurisdiction over the person of the defendant."

In *Carbone*, by way of its "Second Defense," the answer pleaded that "this Court does not have jurisdiction over the person of the defendant" and, as a "Third Defense," by way of a limited appearance, pleads that "any judgment . . . may be satisfied only out of the res allegedly attached."

in the categorically distinct concept of *quasi in rem* jurisdiction requires a sufficiently particularized pleading to apprise the plaintiff of its nature with sufficient clarity to avoid prejudice by inducing quiescence (*compare* CPLR 3211, subd [a], par 8, with par 9; *see* 4 Weinstein-Korn-Miller, NY Civ Prac, par 3211.15, p 32-66), it follows that the in rem issue must be deemed waived and the Appellate Division orders, which held to the contrary, reversed.

. . . .

NOTES

(1) In *Hatch v. Tran*, 170 A.D.2d 649, 567 N.Y.S.2d 72 (2d Dept. 1991), the affirmative defense was raised that "the Complaint was not properly served and hence, the Court lacks jurisdiction over the said defendants herein." The defense of lack of a basis for jurisdiction (on which the defendant had intended to rely but which was not pleaded) was held waived by the careless wording in the answer.

CPLR 3211(e) was amended in 1997 to require every defendant who asserts an improper service of process defense in an answer to move within 60 days for judgment dismissing the complaint. There are two exceptions to this rule: 1) when there is undue hardship the court may extend the time; 2) in proceedings under § 711(1) or (2) of the Real Property Actions and Proceedings Law the rule will not apply.

(2) For another case in which a defense going to quasi-in-rem jurisdiction was held inadequately pleaded, see *Walden v. Thagard*, 67 A.D.2d 973, 413 N.Y.S.2d 451 (2d Dep't 1979). The answer in that case alleged "That this Court lacks jurisdiction of the defendant . . . by reason of failure to serve summons on [her] in accordance with the provisions of statute." After the statute of limitations had run, the defendant moved to dismiss the complaint under CPLR 3211(a)(8) and (9) on the ground that the summons was served prior to the signing of the order of attachment (not after as required by CPLR 314(d)). Citing CPLR 3211(e) and CPLR 3018(b), the court held the defenses waived.

Walden v. Thagard, supra, was, however, distinguished by *Rich v. Lefkovits*, 56 N.Y.2d 276, 452 N.Y.S.2d 1, 437 N.E.2d 260 (1982), in which the answer pleaded that "The court does not have jurisdiction of the person of defendant because defendant was not personally served with a copy of the summons and complaint." This allegation was held sufficient to allow defendant to prove that service on him was defective in that while it was purportedly made pursuant to CPLR 308(4), "nail and mail," and while a copy of the summons was affixed to his office door, the second copy was not mailed to his last known residence as the statute requires but rather to his office. In holding that the arguable lack of particularity of the answer did not prejudice plaintiff, the court reasoned in part:

> [P]laintiff was not without the means of ascertaining what the claimed defect in service was: by a motion under CPLR 3024 (subd. [a]) for a

more definite statement of the defense; by demand for defendant's present address pursuant to CPLR 3118 . . .; by service of appropriate interrogatories (CPLR 3131); by deposition (CPLR 3106); or by motion to dismiss the defense for lack of merit or insufficiency (CPLR 3211, subd. [b]).

Rich v. Levkovits, supra, 56 N.Y.2d at 281, 452 N.Y.S.2d at 4.

(3) The burden of proving a matter is usually borne by the party who must plead it, but this is not always so. Although, for example, the defendant must plead the court's lack of jurisdiction over his person or property, the plaintiff has the burden of proving that it has been acquired. *E.g., Bernardo v. Barret*, 87 A.D.2d 832, 449 N.Y.S.2d 272 (2d Dep't 1982).

(4) What are the risks in pleading an affirmative defense in too much detail? One is suggested by *Linton v. Unexcelled Fireworks Co.*, 124 N.Y. 533, 27 N.E. 406 (1891), in which plaintiff had sued for wrongful discharge from employment. The defense was justification, and the answer alleged several examples of plaintiff's malperformance. At trial, when defendant tried to show still more examples, he was prevented from doing so because the plaintiff was entitled to believe that the list in the answer was exhaustive. How could defendant have avoided this dilemma?

§ 13.04 THE COUNTERCLAIM

[A] When Permitted

BROWN v. STONE
United States District Court, Eastern District of New York
66 F. Supp. 2d 412 (1999)

BLOCK, DISTRICT JUDGE.

Under New York statutory law, the State of New York ("State") is obliged to provide free care and treatment at its psychiatric hospitals for mentally ill indigents. Accordingly, it will not bill or sue a patient for services rendered unless or until the patient has the ability to pay. If, however, an indigent patient, or an indigent ex-patient, sues the State in the Court of Claims to recover damages for injuries arising out of his or her psychiatric treatment, the State, in the personage of the defendant James Stone, in his official capacity as Commissioner of the New York State Office of Mental Health ("Commissioner" or "AOMH"), has adopted a policy and practice of then assessing full care and treatment charges, and interposing a counterclaim in that lawsuit for payment. The counterclaim is restricted, however, to any sum which the plaintiff may recover.

. . . OMH has acknowledged that it has assessed such charges in respect to plaintiffs Limoni Brown ("Brown"), as Administrator of the Estate of Evelyn

Hasson ("Hasson"), and Jed Rothstein ("Rothstein"), indigent parties who have sued OMH employees in the State Supreme Court.

The Court concludes that the constitutionality of OMH's counterclaim policy and the interrelated assessment of charges in respect thereto, is not properly before the Court, since the counterclaim would be contingent on the success of an indigent plaintiff's litigation in the Court of Claims and, as a matter of State law, contingent counterclaims are prohibited. . . .

[Brown brings this suit for declaratory relief on the ground that OMH's policy has an unconstitutional chilling effect on the bringing of civil suits for injuries arising out of psychiatric treatment.]

B. Counterclaim Issue

 . . . .

Although the parties ask the Court to pass upon the constitutionality of OMH's counterclaim policy, it is a general practice that federal courts

> will not pass upon a constitutional question although properly presented by the record, if there is also present some other ground upon which the case may be disposed of. . . . Thus, if a case can be decided on either of two grounds, one involving a constitutional question, the other a question of statutory construction or general law, the Court will decide only the latter. . . .

1. Prohibition Against Contingent Counterclaims Under State Law

Under State law, "a counterclaim may be any cause of action in favor of one or more defendants." New York Civil Practice Law and Rules ("CPLR") § 3019(a). The test is "whether the counterclaim is itself sufficient to support an independent cause of action against plaintiff in the same capacity in which plaintiff sues," *Geddes v. Rosen*, 22 A.D.2d 394, 397, 255 N.Y.S.2d 585, 588 (1st Dep't 1965), and it is therefore "judged under the same standard as a complaint." Weinstein, Korn, & Miller, New York Civil Practice § 3019.06 (citing cases at n. 46). Thus, "[a] counterclaim cannot be contingent, it must allege a viable cause of action." *Fehlhaber Corp. v. State*, 69 A.D.2d 362, 374, 419 N.Y.S.2d 773, 779 (3d Dep't 1979); *see Kane v. Kane*, 163 A.D.2d 568, 571, 558 N.Y.S.2d 627, 629 (2d Dep't 1990) ("A counterclaim is in essence a complaint against the plaintiff and alleges a present viable cause of action upon which the defendant seeks judgment." (quotation and citation omitted)).

OMH is simply incorrect, therefore, in contending that a counterclaim need not be predicated upon an existing cause of action. *See* Dft.S.J.Mem. at 5-8. Indeed, one of the cases it relies upon, *Atlantic Gulf & West Indies S.S. Lines v. City of New York*, 188 Misc. 279, 67 N.Y.S.2d 753 (N.Y.Sup.Ct., N.Y.County, 1946), *modified*, 271 A.D. 1008, 69 N.Y.S.2d 796 (1st Dep't), *appeal denied*, 272 A.D. 793, 71 N.Y.S.2d 705 (1st Dep't 1947), specifically supports the opposite conclusion. Although Special Term in that case cryptically concluded "that the repeal and reenactment of [s]ection 266, Civil Practice Act, in 1936 removed the requirement that the counterclaim be a cause of action in existence at the time it is interposed," 188 Misc. at 280, 67 N.Y.S.2d at 754, relying upon the contingent nature of third-party actions and cross-claims for indemnification and contribution under sections 193 and 264 of the Civil Practice Act, the modification by the Appellate Division expressly dismissed the counterclaim "inasmuch as it fail[ed] to allege a presently existing cause of action," and "[s]ection 266 of the Civil Practice Act d[id] not alter this requirement." 271 A.D. at 1008, 69 N.Y.S.2d at 796 (citations omitted).

The Court of Appeals in *James Talcott, Inc. v. Winco Sales Corp.*, 14 N.Y.2d 227, 250 N.Y.S.2d 416, 199 N.E.2d 499 (1964), also inappropriately relied upon by OMH, explained that the 1936 counterclaim amendments to the Civil Practice Act, which have been carried over into the CPLR, broadened the reach of counterclaims when it defined a counterclaim as "any cause of action in favor of the defendant against the plaintiff," *id.*, 14 N.Y.2d at 232, 250 N.Y.S.2d at 419, 199 N.E.2d 499, whereas previously counterclaims were limited to recoupment ("a claim arising out of the same contract or transaction sued on in the complaint") and setoff ("a claim arising out of contract independent of the contract bottoming the complaint"). *Id.*, 14 N.Y.2d at 231, 250 N.Y.S.2d at 417, 199 N.E.2d 499 (citations omitted). However, prior to the amendments, a counterclaim in the nature of recoupment "was assertable in an action by an assignee even though said claim matured after the time of the assignments or after notice of the assignment," while a counterclaim in the nature of a setoff was not. *Id.*, 14 N.Y.2d at 231-32, 250 N.Y.S.2d at 419, 199 N.E.2d 499. The Court simply held in *Talcott* that the amendments did not affect this statutory distinction. There is nothing in *Talcott* that even remotely suggests that the 1936 amendments gave birth to contingent counterclaims.

The remaining cases cited by OMH to support its contention that State law sanctions contingent counterclaims are also of no avail. *See Delta Franchising, Inc. v. PCP Transmissions, Inc.*, 107 A.D.2d 734, 734, 484 N.Y.S.2d 94, 95 (2d Dep't 1985) (permitting counterclaims derived from existing rights which plaintiffs also claimed); *Rye Psychiatric Hospital Center v. Persky*, 54 A.D.2d 711, 711, 387 N.Y.S.2d 456, 456 (2d Dep't 1976) (permitting counterclaim for an existing cause of action by defendant to recover monies paid to plaintiff); *Paterno & Sons, Inc. v. Town of New Windsor*, 43 A.D.2d 863, 863-64, 351 N.Y.S.2d 445, 447-48 (2d Dep't 1974) (permitting liquidated damages counterclaim for delay in performance by plaintiff prior to breach of parties' contract based upon underlying facts in existence at time of counterclaim).

OMH does cite to one Special Term case that holds that a counterclaim for malicious prosecution contingent on the termination of the plaintiff's action in defendant's favor may be asserted in that lawsuit. *See Herendeen v. Ley Realty Co.*, 75 N.Y.S.2d 836, 837 (N.Y.Sup.Ct., N.Y.County, 1947). This is clearly a wrongly decided case since, consistent with the principle that contingent counterclaims are impermissible, the appellate courts have time after time expressly held that a counterclaim for malicious prosecution or abuse of process will not lie in the civil action that was allegedly wrongfully instituted for the very reason that it would be contingent upon the termination of that action in defendant's favor. [citations] . . . Thus, in accordance with the rule proscribing contingent counterclaims, it is impermissible to assert a counterclaim that is dependent on the outcome of a plaintiff's lawsuit. [citations]

NOTES

(1) In *Conant v. Schnall*, 33 A.D.2d 326, 307 N.Y.S.2d 902 (1970), plaintiff sued defendant as an individual for breach of a buy-out agreement. Defendant counterclaimed by way of a stockholder's derivative action for corporate mismanagement. The general rule is that a defendant may counterclaim only in the capacity in which he is sued. But the counterclaim was held proper since defendant was the sole shareholder of the corporation and thus his real interest was as an individual. The court also held that even if plaintiff's motion for summary judgment were granted, its entry should be stayed pending determination of the counterclaim.

(2) "Any cause of action in favor of one or more defendants . . . against one or more plaintiff[s]" is a counterclaim. CPLR 3019(a). Such claims can be raised regardless of whether they are related to the plaintiff's original claims. The counterclaim can seek an amount exceeding plaintiff's claim. Each claim must meet the specifications of CPLR 3013 and 3017. Claims needlessly complicating the original case can be severed. CPLR 603.

(3) The plaintiff must serve a reply when served with an answer containing a counterclaim "denominated as such." CPLR 3011.

[B] Compulsory Counterclaims?

There is no provision in the CPLR for compulsory counterclaims. Nonetheless, a defendant whose potential counterclaim is related to the plaintiff's claim must consider the potential res judicata effect of a plaintiff's judgment on the potential counterclaim. The next case is a good example.

CHISHOLM-RYDER CO. v. SOMMER & SOMMER
Appellate Division, Fourth Department
78 A.D.2d 143, 434 N.Y.S.2d 70 (1980)

SIMONS, JUSTICE.

This dispute between a client and its former attorneys is before us for the second time. In the prior appeal we granted the attorneys' motion for summary judgment, finding an account stated between the parties for legal services rendered during the eighteen years of the retainer. . . . The day before the argument of that appeal plaintiff commenced the present action charging the attorneys with malpractice in performing the same services. The attorneys moved to dismiss the complaint, asserting that the action was barred by the prior judgment. Special Term granted their motion and we affirm.

It is familiar law that the doctrine of res judicata or claim preclusion forecloses a party from relitigating a cause of action which was the subject matter of a former lawsuit or from raising issues or defenses that might have been litigated in the first suit (*see Gramatan Home Investors Corp. v. Lopez*, 46 N.Y.2d 481, 485, 414 N.Y.S.2d 308, 386 N.E.2d 1328). The related doctrine of collateral estoppel precludes a party from relitigating issues which were previously determined even though the prior suit involved a separate cause of action or a different adversary. By definition, collateral estoppel, or issue preclusion, does not bar the litigation of issues which were not previously raised. It will, however, foreclose issues which were necessarily decided in the first action, litigated or not (*Statter v. Statter*, 2 N.Y.2d 668, 672, 163 N.Y.S.2d 13, 143 N.E.2d 10 [in an action for separation, the validity of the marriage was "necessarily determined" and barred a subsequent action for annulment]; *and see, generally*, Siegel, N.Y. Prac., §§ 447, 464). The burden rests upon the litigant claiming the benefit of the former judgment to prove that the issue he now urges was involved in the prior action either by actual determination or necessary implication. In urging dismissal here, the attorneys rely upon settled New York law which holds that a favorable judgment for professional services is a bar to a subsequent action for malpractice (*see Blair v. Bartlett*, 75 N.Y. 150; . . .). They maintain that the issue of malpractice not only could have been presented in the prior action as a defense but that it was "necessarily determined" there that the attorneys' services were of value, else the client was not obliged to pay for them (*see Blair v. Bartlett, supra*, 154-155). The client contends that the issue is not precluded by the prior suit because that action was for an account stated, not an action in contract; that counterclaims are permissive in New York and that it was therefore not obliged to seek damages for malpractice in the prior action (*see* Siegel, N.Y. Prac., § 224, *but see* § 452); and that at the time of the prior motion it had insufficient knowledge upon which to predicate its claim of malpractice.

First the client asserts that an account stated is a cause of action separate and distinct from the underlying transaction. . . . But the account establishes only the amount of the debt; it does not create liability where none previously existed. . . . The creditor's claim may always be defeated because of the failure of consideration. . . . Thus, the prior action between these parties necessarily determined that services were performed by the attorneys for the client and that compensation was due them, and it is the nature of that claim, not its form, which controls here and estops the client from maintaining the present action (*see Matter of Reilly v. Reid*, 45 N.Y.2d 24, 29, 407 N.Y.S.2d 645, 379 N.E.2d 172). To hold otherwise would permit destruction of rights adjudicated in the first judgment by a different judgment in a subsequent action (*see Schuylkill Fuel Corp. v. Nieberg Realty Corp.*, 250 N.Y. 304, 306-307, 165 N.E. 456).

The procedural rules of permissive counterclaim do not help plaintiff either. True, enough, it was not required to plead malpractice as a counterclaim in the prior action but whether or not it did so is irrelevant. It could have raised the issue as a defense and it was required to do so or be precluded on it. . . . If it lacked information to tender the defense, it could have pleaded that fact in opposition to the motion for summary judgment (*see* CPLR 3212, subd. [f]).

. . . .

NOTES

(1) The currency of the principles underlying the main case is illustrated by *Henry Modell & Co., Inc. v. Minister, Elders and Deacons of the Reformed Protestant Dutch Church of the City of New York*, 68 N.Y.2d 456, 510 N.Y.S.2d 63, 502 N.E.2d 978 (1986). Plaintiff, the defendant's tenant, brought an action in the Supreme Court seeking declaratory and injunctive relief which would entitle it to remain in possession of the disputed premises. Plaintiff claimed that, for various reasons lying in the landlord-tenant relationship between the parties, it had become an assignee of the lease and was therefore entitled to remain in occupancy. In an earlier summary holdover proceeding brought in the New York City Civil Court, however, the landlord, as petitioner, had obtained an order of eviction against the tenant. In discussing the effect of the Civil Court judgment on the present case, the Court of Appeals held that:

> We have no occasion to consider the merits of plaintiff's claim, however, because we agree with the trial court that its assertion in the present action is barred under well-established principles of claim preclusion.
>
> It is elementary that, under the common-law doctrine of res judicata, a tenant who has been adjudged not entitled to possession in an action brought by the landlord cannot subsequently bring an action to recover possession on the basis of claims that could have been asserted in the first action. While New York does not have a compulsory counterclaim rule (*see*, CPLR 3011), a party is not free to remain silent in an action in which he is the defendant and then bring a second action seeking relief inconsistent with the judgment in the first action by asserting what is simply a new legal theory. . . . Underlying this rule is the recognition that "it is to the interest of the State that there should be an end to litigation" (*Israel v Wood Dolson Co.*, *supra*, p 118). Indeed, even a default judgment awarding possession to the landlord has been held to preclude litigation of subsidiary issues necessary to establish the tenant's subsequent claim for separate equitable relief, despite the fact that the equitable claim could not have been resolved in a counterclaim in the first action because of limitations on the court's jurisdiction (*Reich v Cochran*, 151 NY 122).

Plaintiff's present claim falls squarely within these principles. In the prior Civil Court holdover proceeding, the landlord sought to recover possession, and plaintiff defended, in part, by asserting a right of possession arising from the renewal clause in its sublease. Plaintiff's present claim, although technically based on the renewal clause in the prime lease, is really nothing more than a resuscitated assertion of a right to possession recast in terms of a new legal theory. As such, the claim, which could have been raised as a defense in the first action (*see*, RPAPL 743) and which now seeks to destroy or impair the "rights . . . established by the first [action]" . . . is barred.

. . . .

The absence of a compulsory counterclaim rule in New York (*see*, Siegel, NY Prac § 452, at 598-599) does not affect this analysis. Our permissive counterclaim rule may save from the bar of res judicata those claims for separate or different relief that could have been but were not interposed in the parties' prior action (*see*, *Batavia Kill Watershed Dist. v. Charles O. Desch, Inc.*, 83 AD2d 97, *affd* 57 NY2d 796). It does not, however, permit a party to remain silent in the first action and then bring a second one on the basis of a preexisting claim for relief that would impair the rights or interests established in the first action.

68 N.Y.2d at 461-62, 510 N.Y.S.2d at 65-66, 502 N.E.2d at 980-81.

(2) An unusual aspect of the *Henry Modell and Co.* case, *supra* note 1, was that the tenant sought to avoid the preclusive effect of the first case by invoking section 747(2) of the N.Y. Real Property Action and Proceedings Law, which is intended to mitigate otherwise applicable preclusion rules. The statute provides that a judgment in a summary proceeding to recover possession "shall not bar an action, proceeding or counterclaim, commenced within sixty days of entry of judgment, for affirmative equitable relief which was not sought by counterclaim in the proceeding because of the limited jurisdiction of the court."

Because the tenant failed to bring its action for declaratory and injunctive relief within the allowable sixty days, however, this provision was of no help to it.

BATAVIA KILL WATERSHED DISTRICT v. CHARLES O. DESCH, INC.

Appellate Division, Third Department
83 A.D.2d 97, 444 N.Y.S.2d 958 (1981),
aff'd, 57 N.Y.2d 796, 455 N.Y.S.2d 597, 441 N.E.2d 1115 (1982)

HERLIHY, JUSTICE.

In May of 1973, plaintiff entered into a contract with defendant Charles O. Desch, Inc. (Desch) for the construction of a dam by Desch. A performance bond was issued by defendant Travelers Indemnity Company (Travelers), guaranteeing Desch's performance.

In September of 1974, plaintiff terminated the contract for alleged unsatisfactory performance and thereafter Travelers refused the demand/offer of plaintiff that Travelers complete the contract. Desch instituted an action against
plaintiff to recover damages based on the contract and its termination. Plaintiff did not counterclaim for damages, but did assert the affirmative defense:

> That the plaintiff as contractor failed to prosecute the work with such
> diligence as would insure the completion within the time specified in the
> contract and as a result thereof, the defendant on the 6th day of Sep-
> tember, 1974 terminated said contract for said cause.

During the course of the trial in Desch's action, plaintiff agreed to pay certain
retained percentages and two requisitions, totalling $62,657.77. The remainder
of the Desch action was submitted to the jury with written interrogatories.
The jury found in part that Desch incurred certain additional costs and expenses
in the sum of $63,000 as the result of its reliance upon a representation by
plaintiff as to the manner in which certain debris would be disposed of. However,
the jury also unequivocally found that plaintiff was "justified in terminating the
contract" because of Desch's failure of timely performance.

Following the entry of judgment in the Desch action on April 17, 1978, plaintiff commenced this action against Desch and Travelers on April 12, 1979, seeking damages upon the ground that Desch failed to perform the contract and, in
particular, on the ground that it failed to diligently prosecute the work, causing
plaintiff to terminate the agreement and sustain certain damages in the completion of the contract. Defendants answered and, as joint affirmative defenses,
asserted estoppel, waiver, res judicata, election of remedies, and laches. As to
Travelers, defendants also asserted the defenses of accord and satisfaction,
exoneration and/or breach of the surety agreement by plaintiff's conduct which
precluded performance by Travelers and breach of Desch's contract and/or the
violation of certain statutes by plaintiff which allegedly exonerated Travelers.
Travelers also counterclaimed for damages against plaintiff.

Defendants moved for summary judgment on all of the grounds asserted as
affirmative defenses. Plaintiff crossmoved "for summary judgment . . . against
the defendant Desch on the issue of justification for the termination [of the con-
tract]. . . ."

Special Term granted defendants' motion upon a finding that plaintiff, having participated in the prior litigation with Desch and having failed to counterclaim for damages for Desch's failure to timely perform while relying upon
such failure as a defense, waived the counterclaim.

Special Term adopted the case of *Musco v. Lupi*, 6 Misc.2d 930, 164 N.Y.S.2d
84 as precedent. However, in the *Musco* case, the party seeking to recover damages in a second action, after having successfully used the claim as an affirmative defense in the original action, had been invited by the trial court in the first
action to amend his answer so as to counterclaim for damages. He had declined
to use the claim as anything other than a defense. Under these specific cir-

cumstances, Special Term found that this conduct "amount[ed] to an election and to a waiver and abandonment of his claim for damages" (*Musco v. Lupi, supra,* pp. 932-933, 164 N.Y.S.2d 84).

In the instant case, there was no such express invitation by the court followed by an election not to proceed with a counterclaim. At most, there was permission granted to the plaintiff in the first action to implead Travelers. There is, however, no showing of any express offer or refusal in regard to defendants' counterclaiming against Desch. (Travelers was not a party to the initial action.) We find that factually the case of *Musco* is not apposite and, since the decision in *Musco* was limited to the facts in that case, there is no need to approve or disapprove the result reached therein.

Special Term herein refers to the principles underlying estoppel by judgment as set forth in the opinion of Chief Judge Cooke in the case of *Gramatan Home Investors Corp. v. Lopez,* 46 N.Y.2d 481, 485, 414 N.Y.S.2d 308, 386 N.E.2d 1328. The problem is, however, that in this case, we do not have a party who is splitting his causes of action or who otherwise failed to litigate issues encompassed in a prior lawsuit. Accordingly, the *Gramatan* case is also distinguishable from the instant matter.

Permitting the present action to be maintained does not impair any rights or interests established in the prior action. . . . At the very most, the counterclaim would have been an offset against defendants' right to payment for the work performed prior to termination. Further, the question of judicial economy is not directly involved since the facts that Desch breached the contract as to timely performance and that plaintiff was justified in terminating the agreement were established in the prior action.

It is apparent that the CPLR does not require that a party plead counterclaims, and, with the possible exception of cases based on waiver such as *Musco v. Lupi (supra),* there is no requirement of compulsory pleading of counterclaims in this State (*see* Siegel, Practice Commentaries, McKinney's Cons. Laws of N.Y., Book 7B, CPLR 3019:2, pp. 216-217). While a compulsory rule would be more consistent with economical court administration, the lack thereof is not a significant factor in burdensome case loads. The use of summary judgment procedures effectively precludes relitigation of issues and, from a pragmatic view, proceeding to a jury with liability established is not likely except in extraordinary cases.

Defendants have failed to establish any basis for dismissal of the complaint based on the grounds of res judicata, collateral estoppel, or any theory of waiver and election. Plaintiff is entitled to summary judgment against Desch on the ground that Desch breached the contract by failure to timely perform its obligations.

The order and judgment should be reversed, on the law, with costs, and the motion by defendants for summary judgment denied. Cross motion by plaintiff for summary judgment granted to the extent of finding that there was a failure

to timely perform the obligations of the contract and that, therefore, plaintiff
was entitled to terminate the contract.

. . . .

NOTES

(1) Rule 13(a) of the Federal Rules of Civil Procedure provides:

> (a) *Compulsory Counterclaims.* A pleading shall state as a counter-
> claim any claim which at the time of serving the pleading the pleader
> has against any opposing party, if it arises out of the transaction or
> occurrence that is the subject matter of the opposing party's claim and
> does not require for its adjudication the presence of third parties of
> whom the court cannot acquire jurisdiction. But the pleader need not
> state a claim if (1) at the time the action was commenced the claim was
> the subject of another pending action, or (2) the opposing party brought
> suit upon the claim by attachment or other process by which the court
> did not acquire jurisdiction to render a personal judgment on that claim,
> and the pleader is not stating any counterclaim under this Rule 13.

Is it fair to say that the same rule applies to counterclaims in New York as in
the federal courts? To what extent do they differ? Should New York adopt a rule
similar to 13(a)?

(2) Refer to *Textile Technology Exchange, Inc. v. Davis*, 81 N.Y.2d 56, 595
N.Y.S.2d 729, 611 N.E.2d 768 (1993), reprinted in § 6.04, *supra*, where it was
held that the interposition of a related counterclaim will not waive a defense
based on lack of personal jurisdiction. The counterclaim will only be related
when it could potentially be barred under the rules of collateral estoppel. *Textile Technology Exchange* also illustrates the Court of Appeals' approach to
determining whether a particular counterclaim is related to the main claim
under that test.

§ 13.05 CROSS-CLAIMS

DEMATO v. COUNTY OF SUFFOLK
Supreme Court, Suffolk County
79 Misc. 2d 484, 360 N.Y.S.2d 570 (1974)

JOHN F. SCILEPPI, JUSTICE.

This is an action for personal injuries arising out of an automobile accident.
The plaintiffs' car collided with a vehicle driven by defendant Howard Widmaier and owned by the defendant Kathleen Widmaier, who was apparently not
a participant in the accident. The defendant Kathleen Widmaier, in her answer,
interposed a counterclaim against the plaintiffs for property damage to her

automobile. The plaintiffs, in their reply to the counterclaim, have asserted a "cross-claim" against the defendant Howard Widmaier only, the driver of the car, for indemnification under the rationale of *Dole v. Dow Chemical Co.*, 30 N.Y.2d 143, 331 N.Y.S.2d 382, 282 N.E.2d 288 (1972). The plaintiffs allege that the negligence of the defendant driver, Howard Widmaier, was at least part of the cause of the accident, so that they would be entitled to indemnification or contribution from Howard Widmaier for any recovery that may result from Kathleen Widmaier's counterclaim.

This motion is brought on by the defendants Widmaier for an order dismissing the plaintiffs' "cross-claim." They argue that, under CPLR § 3019, no cross-claim or counterclaim is permitted in a reply, citing *Habiby v. Habiby*, 23 A.D.2d 558, 256 N.Y.S.2d 634 (1st Dept. 1965); and *Chambland v. Brewer*, 51 Misc.2d 231, 272 N.Y.S.2d 903 (Sup.Ct. Queens Co. 1966). The moving parties are correct in their reliance on these authorities. *Chambland v. Brewer* is particularly in point in that the "cross complaint" asserted in the reply was for indemnification.

I also note that Article 14 of the CPLR, which dealt with indemnification, was repealed as of September 1, 1974 and replaced by a new article labeled "Contribution" — obviously in response to the impact of *Dole v. Dow Chemical Co.* § 1403 thereof states:

> A cause of action for contribution may be asserted in a separate action or by cross-claim, counterclaim or third-party claim in a pending action.

Thus, the new statute likewise does not provide for the type of pleading here sought to be asserted.

The one case cited by the plaintiffs in opposition to the motion is not squarely applicable in that, while a cause of action contained in a reply was considered by the court and decided on its merits, there was no challenge to the cause on procedural grounds and this was not in issue. However, the plaintiffs' arguments from logic are persuasive. They point out that the impact of *Dole v. Dow Chemical Co.* has substantially changed the case law in the procedural area. They also point out that, if this "cross-claim" is denied, the plaintiffs would still have a right to institute a separate action for indemnification against Howard Widmaier, should Kathleen Widmaier be successful on her counterclaim in this action. It was the rationale of the *Dole* case to have all such matters litigated at one time. The plaintiffs also observe that they could have moved for leave to amend the original complaint to assert another cause of action (*see* Weinstein-Korn-Miller, Para. 3019.05), except that the attorneys for the plaintiffs on their "cross-claim" and in defense of the counterclaim are not the same attorneys who represent the plaintiffs as main plaintiffs.

The question presented appears to be one of first impression, and it does not seem to have been discussed by any of the leading commentators on the CPLR. Although the authorities cited by the defendants are in point, they were cases decided before *Dole v. Dow Chemical Co.*, and the rationale of *Dole* and its progeny of lower court cases clearly favors the resolution of the indemnification questions and the negligence questions in the same law suit.

For the purpose of deciding this motion in accordance with the *Dole* philosophy, I might regard the plaintiffs' request herein as a request for leave to amend their complaint and to assert the cause of action for indemnity in that pleading. Considered as such, the plaintiffs' request might be granted, and this motion by the defendants denied. However, rather than employ such procedural legal fiction, I hold that the cross-claim asserted by the plaintiffs in their reply is permissible under *Dole v. Dow Chemical Co.*, and, accordingly, this motion by the defendants Widmaier is denied.

I call the question raised herein to the attention of the legislature and the scholarly commentators, so that it can be settled by the appropriate legislative authority.

NOTE

Cross-claims are claims for affirmative recovery by one defendant against another defendant. CPLR § 3019(b). Like the counterclaim, they can be asserted against non-parties as long as they assert a claim, at least in part, against a co-defendant. Also like the counterclaim, the cross-claim need not be related to the plaintiff's cause of action against the defendants. *A&R Construction Co. v. New York State Electric and Gas Corp.*, 27 A.D.2d 899, 278 N.Y.S.2d 165 (3d Dep't 1967).

No answer need be made to a cross-claim unless it contains a demand for an answer. CPLR 3011.

§ 13.06 VERIFICATION: CPLR 3020-3023

"A verification is a statement under oath that the pleading is true to the knowledge of the deponent. . . ." CPLR 3020(a). A complaint need not be verified unless a statute specifically imposes this requirement. An example is CPLR 7804(d), mandating a verified petition in an Article 78 proceeding. As to when other pleadings need to be verified, see CPLR 3020(a)-(c). Even if a pleading need not be verified, it must be signed by the attorney. Uniform Rules, Part 130-1.1-a, 22 NYCRR.

GIAMBRA v. COMMISSIONER OF MOTOR VEHICLES OF THE STATE OF NEW YORK

Court of Appeals

46 N.Y.2d 743, 413 N.Y.S.2d 643, 386 N.E.2d 251 (1978)

MEMORANDUM.

. . . .

A few words of clarification are in order, however, as to the problem perceived to exist by the Appellate Division with respect to the verification of the petition commencing this proceeding by petitioners' attorney rather than by petitioners themselves. Although not strictly necessary for the disposition of this appeal, it appears appropriate to alleviate some of the apparent confusion concerning this matter. Verification of a pleading by an attorney rather than a party is not normally permissible, and is usually not an advisable practice. Nonetheless, there are certain situations in which verification by someone other than a party is explicitly authorized by statute (CPLR 3020, subd [d]). One such instance is where the party "is not in the county where the attorney has his office" (CPLR 3020, subd [d], par 3). Since that is the situation which exists in the present proceeding, the attorney was in fact authorized to verify the petition.

We would note, however, that in such instances there must be careful compliance with the mandates of CPLR 3021. Thus, in the present instance, although the attorney properly explained in the petition the reasons why he rather than petitioners was verifying it, he failed to "set forth in the affidavit the grounds of his belief as to all matters not stated upon his knowledge" (CPLR 3021). Any objection to this defect, however, was waived by respondent's apparent failure to give notice with due diligence of respondent's intention to treat the pleading as a nullity on the basis of that defect (*see* CPLR 3022).

NOTES

(1) A typical verification of a complaint was used in the form in § 13.02, *supra*. Were the plaintiffs required by law to verify their complaint? If not, why did they do so? *See* CPLR 3020(a), (b).

(2) If a verification is not necessary, but a defective one has been supplied, the pleading may be treated as if unverified, and the responsive pleading need not be verified. CPLR 3022. If, however, the verification is mandatory, the party receiving the defective pleading may treat it as a nullity and refuse to respond or move for default. CPLR 3022. He must give notice of this intention to opposing counsel with "due diligence." In *State v. McMahon*, 78 Misc. 2d 388, 356 N.Y.S.2d 933 (Sup. Ct. 1974), "due diligence" was defined to mean notice within twenty-four hours. The notice must specify the inadequacies rather than generally state that there is some defect. *Westchester Life, Inc. v. Westchester Mag-*

azine Co., 85 N.Y.S.2d 34 (Sup. Ct. 1948). Treating a pleading as a nullity is risky, as a mistaken judgment may mean that the party who ignored his adversary's pleading will be held in default.

An alternative to ignoring a defectively verified pleading is to simply respond with an unverified pleading, and, if the opponent refuses to accept it, submit the matter for judicial resolution by a motion to compel acceptance. Where there is no prejudice, the defect should be ignored. *Kreiling v. Jayne Estates, Inc.*, 51 Misc. 2d 895, 274 N.Y.S.2d 291 (Sup. Ct. 1966).

(3) The utility of rules requiring or allowing verification is controversial to say the least. *See* discussion in Weinstein, Korn & Miller, 3 N.Y. Civil Practice — CPLR ¶ 3020.03 (2004). Objections center on the impracticality of punishing false verifications (although it should be noted that attorneys are sometimes disciplined for suborning such perjury, *id.* ¶ 3020.05); the recognition that since attorneys, not litigants, draft the pleadings, a verification by a party is often meaningless; and the tension between the rules of pleading which on the one hand allow alternative or hypothetical pleadings (CPLR 1002, 1007, 3014) and on the other hand allow, and in some cases require, a verification that such a pleading is true. Under the Federal Rules of Civil Procedure, verification is rarely authorized; instead Rule 11 requires the attorney to sign the pleading and provide that the signature certifies that there is "good ground to support" the pleading. Further, "[f]or a wilful violation of this rule an attorney may be subjected to appropriate disciplinary action."

§ 13.07 THE EFFECT OF PLEADINGS

Think for a moment about when and how pleadings are drafted. The complaint will ideally be written by the plaintiff's attorney only after she has carefully investigated the facts, researched the law, and thought about how, tactically, to best state her client's claims within the rules already treated in this chapter. The same should be true of the drafting of the answer and any other pleadings which will be required, although it should be noted that all pleadings after the complaint are usually prepared under time pressure not usually relevant to the complaint. (Why?)

But despite the most careful lawyering, the pleadings are drafted somewhat in the dark because neither party has had access to the other's proof, which comes only through the discovery process and is thus normally available only after issue is joined. Further, case law and statutes may change during the progress of the litigation, and the original pleadings may not have anticipated these developments. So even the best of pleadings may not accurately describe the parties' contentions by the time of the trial. Here is a dilemma, for it will be recalled that a pleading should give notice of the transactions to be proven. CPLR 3013. There is another aspect to this dilemma; not every lawyer always pleads perfectly (this no doubt surprises you) and sometimes allegations which should have been included are forgotten. One way out is through amendments, and that process will be considered in the next section. A preliminary question, to be addressed in this section, is whether (or when) to disregard variances from the pleadings even in the absence of amendment.

DIEMER v. DIEMER

Court of Appeals
8 N.Y.2d 206, 203 N.Y.S.2d 829, 168 N.E.2d 654 (1960)

FULD, J.

The question on this appeal is whether a wife's repudiation of the validity of her marriage and her refusal to have sexual relations with her husband unless he submits to a remarriage in a church of her religious faith entitle the husband to a decree of separation.

Mr. and Mrs. Diemer were married in 1947. He was a Protestant, 41 years of age, she a Roman Catholic, a year younger. Having anticipated problems in accommodating their religious differences, they discussed this issue and reached an agreement concerning it. Although other aspects of their agreement were in dispute at the trial, it seems clear that Mr. Diemer's doubts about the success of their marriage had been allayed by the assurance of his bride-to-be that her "main ambition" was to be with him "in all things, for all times" and by her agreement that his faith would be her faith and his church, her church. It was in fulfillment of their agreement that the Diemers were married in the Church of the Garden, a church of Protestant persuasion, and a year and a half later Mrs. Diemer was admitted as a member of her husband's church.

In 1950, after three years of marriage, a daughter was born to the Diemers. Although it would not be accurate to say that marital discord was born with the infant, the unfortunate fact is that her baptism and subsequent religious training proved sources of contention, at first latent, but soon overt and bitter. The religious conflict which revolved about the child reached a climax and took a new form in 1954, shortly after Mrs. Diemer suffered an accident which induced in her a fear of death. She consulted a priest and, following her talks with him, issued an ultimatum to her husband. She told him that in the eyes of her Church she was not considered married to him and that, since this was so, she would not have any further sexual relations with him unless he submitted to a second ceremony in the Roman Catholic Church. In the six or seven months which followed, Mr. Diemer continued to live with his wife and made constant attempts to change her mind, but she persisted in her refusal to have sexual relations with him.

In October, 1954, realizing that his wife's decision was final and unalterable, he left home and instituted this suit. Alleging, in substance, the facts as they are set out above, Mr. Diemer characterized his wife's conduct as "cruel and inhuman treatment," said that this conduct caused him suffering and seriously impaired his physical and mental well-being and sought relief in the form of a separation and custody of their child. Mrs. Diemer counterclaimed for separation, support and custody, but neither in her answer nor at the trial did she deny the essentials of her husband's story. In fact, on both occasions she reaffirmed that she did not consider herself married and unequivocally declared that she would not have any sexual relations with her husband until they were remarried before a Roman Catholic priest.

The trial court denied both husband and wife a separation and awarded custody of the child to the wife. On appeal by the husband — his wife sought no review — a divided Appellate Division affirmed the judgment. It was the view of both courts that the proof did not establish "cruel and inhuman treatment" on the part of the wife, apparently for two reasons: first, that the wife had not "willfully and deliberately intended to inflict mental or physical suffering" upon the husband and, second, that he had not actually suffered any damage to his health. Although we are of the opinion that the criteria thus applied were too restrictive and that the essentials of cruelty were made out in this case . . ., we prefer to place our decision of reversal and our award of a separation to the husband on the ground that the facts alleged and proved unquestionably establish the husband's right to a separation on the ground of abandonment. . . .

. . . .

. . . Obviously, not every denial of a marital right will be sufficient to support a charge of abandonment. The criterion is how fundamentally the denial strikes at the civil institution of marriage. Where primary rights and duties are involved, where the denial goes to one of the foundations of the marriage, it is the policy of our law to allow a separation from bed and board.

. . . Sexual relations between man and woman are given a socially and legally sanctioned status only when they take place in marriage and, in turn, marriage is itself distinguished from all other social relationships by the role sexual intercourse between the parties plays in it. This being so, it may not be doubted that a total and irrevocable negation of what is lawful in marriage and unlawful in every other relationship, of what unmistakably and uniquely characterizes marriage and no other relationship, constitutes abandonment in the eyes of the law. . . .

It is clear, therefore, that the plaintiff now before us is entitled to a separation on the ground of abandonment unless his wife had good legal cause to refuse to have sexual intercourse with him. And, as to that, it is equally clear that she had neither cause nor justification. Although it appears that she acted without malice and was activated by deep-felt and conscientious religious convictions, her motives were not sufficient in law to excuse the abandonment of her marital status. . . .

It is our conclusion, therefore, that on the evidence adduced the plaintiff is entitled to a separation on the ground of abandonment. However, the defendant contends — and the contention finds favor with our dissenting brethren — that the husband may not prevail on the ground of abandonment because in his complaint he characterized his wife's conduct as cruelty, without also calling it abandonment. The argument does not impress us for the complaint indisputably alleges, and, indeed, the defendant admitted both in her answer and in her testimony, all of the facts necessary to support a cause of action for separation based on abandonment. . . . The mere circumstance that the plaintiff did not in his complaint denominate his wife's conduct as "abandonment," as well as "cruel and inhuman treatment," does not change the legal force and effect of the factual allegations. The cause of action is for separation and such a cause is undeniably alleged no matter what the pleader called it. Surely, we have advanced far beyond that hypertechnical period when form was all-important and a pleader had to attach the correct label to his complaint, at the risk of having it dismissed. It is enough now that a pleader state the facts making out a cause of action, and it matters not whether he gives a name to the cause of action at all or even that he gives it a wrong name. If this be true of the cause of action itself, it is certainly true of the ground underlying it.

. . . .

The judgment appealed from should be modified by directing entry of a decree of separation in favor of the plaintiff and, except as so modified, affirmed, without costs.

CHIEF JUDGE DESMOND (dissenting).

The question stated in the opening paragraph of the majority opinion cannot be answered on this record unless we are to forget all about pleadings and issues. This separation action was brought, tried, dismissed and the dismissal affirmed in the Appellate Division on the sole ground of cruelty. Now our court is modifying the judgment below and directing entry of a judgment of separation (not even a retrial or a permission to replead) on the new ground of abandonment although abandonment was not pleaded, tried or in any manner passed upon in either court below.

The objection, we are told, is hypertechnical. Let us see. "Pleadings and a distinct issue are essential to every system of jurisprudence, and there can be no orderly administration of justice without them. If a party can allege one cause of action and then recover upon another, his complaint would serve no useful purpose" (*Cohen v. City Co. of New York*, 283 N.Y. 112, 117). "It is fundamental that in civil actions the plaintiff must recover upon the facts stated in his complaint, or not at all. In case a complaint proceeds on a definite, clear and certain theory, it will not support or permit another theory because it contains isolated or subsidiary statements consistent therewith. A party must recover not only according to his proofs but according to his pleadings" (*Walrath v. Hanover Fire Ins. Co.*, 216 N.Y. 220, 225). Where, when or why those settled rules disappeared from our system I do not know. For no reason at all we are making a precipitous retreat from the good old rule that the parties to a private lawsuit fix the theory of suit and that no appellate court can present the losing side with a new theory. I have not been backward in advocating modernized and speeded-up procedures but I can find no reason for this abrupt departure from the rules that courts and lawyers have always lived by.

It should not be necessary to demonstrate that in matrimonial law abandonment is a definite concept, different from cruelty, and that it must be pleaded and proved as such. Abandonment is "a voluntary separation of one party from the other without justification, with the intention of not returning" (*Williams v. Williams*, 130 N.Y. 193, 197; *Bohmert v. Bohmert*, 241 N.Y. 446, 451). Nothing like that was proven or decided in the present case. The entirely different charge of cruelty was urged on the courts below and that charge was dismissed. For our court to introduce and decide a new issue, whatever its merits, is unprecedented and unlawful (*see* Civ. Prac. Act, § 242; *Flagg v. Nichols*, 307 N.Y. 96, 99).

The judgment should be affirmed, with costs.

NOTE

The principal case was decided before the CPLR became effective. Is it consistent with the CPLR? *See* CPLR 3013, 3025(c), and 3026. The majority does not, in any case, bottom its holding on a statute but rather appeals to a kind of modernism when it announces, "Surely we have advanced far beyond that hypertechnical period when form was all important and a pleader had to attach the correct label to his complaint, at the risk of having it dismissed."

ROGOFF v. SAN JUAN RACING ASSOC., INC.
Court of Appeals
54 N.Y.2d 883, 444 N.Y.S.2d 911, 429 N.E.2d 416 (1981)

[Plaintiff sued to recover money due under a contract. After joinder of issue (*i.e.*, service of the complaint and answer), defendants moved for summary judgment on the ground that there was no writing which satisfied the Statute of Frauds. The Appellate Division, reversing the Supreme Court, held that the motion should have been granted.]

MEMORANDUM.

The order of the Appellate Division should be affirmed, with costs.

At the threshold it is appellant's contention that summary judgment on the ground that his claims were barred by the Statute of Frauds was improperly granted because that defense had not been pleaded in the answer. Examination of the papers on the motion discloses, however, that this defense was the principal ground relied on by defendants in support of their motion and that it was fully opposed by plaintiff (both on the procedural grounds of unavailability for failure to plead and of prematurity for failure to have completed disclosure procedures, and extensively on the merits — that there were "14 written documents which collectively met the requirements of the statute," that there had been full performance, and that the contract sued on was not subject to the statute). In this posture of the record we cannot say that it was error as a matter of law for the Appellate Division to have concluded, for the reasons stated by it, that failure expressly to have pleaded the defense in the answer did not mandate denial of defendant's motion for summary judgment based on the statute.

. . . .

NOTES

(1) Compare *Barber v. Dembroski*, 54 N.Y.2d 648, 442 N.Y.S.2d 768, 426 N.E.2d 175 (1981), in which defendant, a farmer, was sued because he failed to pay a state-imposed fee which was to be used to promote the sale of apples. After losing in the court below, he tried on appeal to raise the issues of deprivation of free speech, association, due process, equal protection and invalid delegation of state taxing authority. The Court of Appeals opinion in its entirety follows:

> The order of the Appellate Division . . . should be affirmed, with costs.

> Appellant's contentions that the statute and implementing order violates the First Amendment of the United States Constitution and section 7 of article VII of the New York Constitution were not raised in his answer and thus are not reviewable in this court. We find no merit to the appellant's other contentions.

54 N.Y.2d at 650, 442 N.Y.S.2d at 768.

(2) The next case also deals with the effect of the pleadings, but the question raised is not so much whether the parties could win with a theory not pleaded but whether they should be permitted to recover by proving facts not pleaded. Should the different types of variance be treated differently?

IANNONE v. CAYUGA CONSTRUCTION CORP.
Appellate Division, First Department
66 A.D.2d 745, 411 N.Y.S.2d 599 (1978)

MEMORANDUM DECISION.

Judgment, Supreme Court, New York County, entered April 26, 1977, after a jury trial before Justice Schwartz, which awarded each of the two plaintiffs $40,000 together with interest, reversed on the law, vacated, the second and fourth causes of action of the complaint dismissed and the matter remanded for a new trial with respect to the first and third causes of action, with $75 costs and disbursements of this appeal to abide the event.

This is an action to recover for property damage allegedly arising out of blasting operations performed by the defendants who entered into a contract with the City to construct a subway on Second Avenue between 110th Street and 120th Street. Construction work commenced in March, 1973 and blasting operations took place in October, 1974 until the end of 1975. The complaint contains four causes of action, two on behalf of plaintiff Di Giorgio, the owner of premises located at 2250 Second Avenue to recover damages to the building "as the result of blasting operations." The first cause of action (by the owner) is predicated on "absolute liability" and the second cause (by the owner) is predicated on negligence in that the defendants "failed to exercise reasonable care or to take necessary precautions *when they were blasting* and as such were negligent" (Emphasis supplied). The third cause of action brought by plaintiffs Carmine and Julia Iannone (tenants) who operate a store (meat market) at the premises to recover for loss of business, disturbance in their enjoyment of the leased space and for general physical and mental injuries and anguish, is predicated on "absolute liability." Similarly the fourth cause of action brought by these tenants is based on negligence in that the defendants "failed to exercise reasonable care or to take necessary precautions *when they were blasting* and as such were negligent" (Emphasis supplied). Defendants served a demand for particulars in which they specifically sought amplification of the complaint with respect to "[t]he cause of the alleged accident to plaintiff's property, including the immediate and proximate cause as well as remote cause." Plaintiffs responded in their bill of particulars to this request by merely reiterating certain allegations of the complaint. A fair reading of the complaint, thus unamplified, as to the acts claimed by plaintiffs to have caused them damage in consequence of defendants' negligence impels the conclusion that only negligence in blasting operations is claimed. In its charge to the jury, the trial court instructed that plaintiffs' claims against defendants were founded not only on the blasting operations, but also on negligence *before* blasting. Defendants voiced their strong objection to that part of the court's charge "as allows the jury to consider damages claimed to be caused by the [defendants] before blasting on the ground that a fair reading of the pleading . . . limits the negligence claim to damage while blasting or in the course of it." This objection is well taken.

CPLR 3013 required that "[s]tatements in a pleading shall be *sufficiently particular* to give the court and parties notice of the transactions, occurrences, or series of transactions or occurrences, intended to be proved and the material elements of each cause of action or defense" (Emphasis supplied). The primary function of the complaint herein was to adequately advise the defendants of the plaintiffs' claim or claims (*see Foley v. D'Agostino*, 21 A.D.2d 60, 62-63, 248 N.Y.S.2d 121, 124-125 [1st Dept. 1964]; . . .). Patently, the object of a complaint is to fully inform a defendant as to the extent of the claims being made against him and to achieve this goal, vagueness is to be avoided so that a defendant can intelligently plan and prepare to respond without risk of surprise. The complaint in this action, even interpreted fairly under the liberal approach adopted under the CPLR, failed to give any notice to defendants that the plaintiffs intended to rely on negligence before blasting.

Study of the record discloses no evidence of negligence on defendants' part in blasting. In addition to pleading a claim for damages sustained by virtue of defendants' negligence in blasting, plaintiffs . . . pleaded an alternative claim for absolute liability caused by defendants in blasting. In pleading a claim predicated on absolute liability, a plaintiff need not prove that the blaster was negligent, but must demonstrate causation, *i.e.*, that the blasting caused the damage. Of course, a claim based on absolute liability in blasting would, of necessity, be subsumed in a claim alleging negligence in blasting as long as the latter claim contained an adequate "notice of the transactions . . . intended to be proved and the material elements of [the] cause of action" (CPLR 3013). . . . It could well be argued, therefore, that the second and fourth causes of action pleading negligence in blasting are redundant in light of the first and third causes of action alleging absolute liability in blasting for the simple reason that plaintiffs' burden of proof would be the same under all the causes except that as to the first and third cause, plaintiffs need not show negligence. Therefore, on this record defendants are entitled to dismissal of the second and fourth causes of action based on negligence in blasting.

To reiterate, the trial court charged on absolute liability in blasting and on negligence before blasting, although the latter claim was not advanced in the complaint or during trial by the plaintiffs on their direct case. Indeed, it appears this claim was articulated for the first time by plaintiffs' counsel during motions at the end of the trial. The record demonstrates that defendants in light of the absolute liability claim made the central issue of causation the keystone of their defense and did not have an opportunity to prepare a defense for a claim of negligence before blasting. Accordingly, since the plaintiffs failed to prove a *prima facie* case of negligence in blasting operations, and since the case was sent to the jury on the issue of negligence prior to blasting operations which issue was not properly raised, as well as on the issue of absolute liability in blasting operations, a new trial is warranted on the causes of action pleading absolute liability in blasting. Inasmuch as it cannot be concluded that the general verdict of the jury in favor of the plaintiffs was not based on the ground of negligence prior to blasting operations, the verdict must be vacated and a new trial ordered (*Lebron v. New York City Transit Authority*, 44 N.Y.2d 782, 406 N.Y.S.2d 38, 377 N.E.2d 482 [1978]).

All concur except KUPFERMAN, J., who concurs in a separate memorandum.

FEIN and SULLIVAN, JJ., who dissent in part in a memorandum by SULLIVAN, J.

KUPFERMAN, JUSTICE (concurring).

I would remand for a new trial on damages only, with respect to the first and third causes of action, there being some elements thereof which are questionable in view of the requirement of proximate cause in a blasting case. *See*

Spano v. Perini Corp., 25 N.Y.2d 11, 302 N.Y.S.2d 527, 250 N.E.2d 31. However, there would be little advantage to be gained by eliminating the need to find the obvious absolute liability and, in order to resolve the problem, I join Judges Lupiano and Lane.

I would dismiss the second and fourth causes of action. As I see it, the so-called "negligence *before* blasting" is not a new factor but rather part of the configuration. There was sufficient evidence for the jury to determine liability, and, as the opinion with which I am concurring indicates, the negligence allegations are redundant in the light of the absolute liability conclusion warranted in this matter. . . .

SULLIVAN, JUSTICE (dissenting in part).

I agree with the majority that the judgment must be reversed because of prejudicial error in the charge which permitted the jury to consider negligence before blasting in an overly broad context so as to include "the opening of the cuts in the street, the pile-driving operations, heavy machinery, moving of utilities. . . ." Both the second and fourth causes of action charged defendants with negligence in that they "failed to exercise reasonable care or to take necessary precautions when they were blasting."

To place this case in proper perspective, it is important to recognize that the blasting complained of continued from October 1974 through the end of 1975, at the rate of four to seven blasts a day, every day of the work week. Furthermore, the complaint does allege a series of blasting operations. That being so, a fair interpretation of the allegation of negligence "when they were blasting" would include defendants' (1) failure to underpin properly the building which is claimed to have been damaged, (2) failure to brace the building when movement was observed, and (3) proceeding with dewatering operations without taking further precautions, as to all of which there was proof in this record sufficient to sustain the negligence causes of action.

Accordingly, I would reverse and remand all four causes of action, including those alleging negligence, for a new trial.

NOTES

(1) How could the complaint have been drafted to avoid the mess described in the principal case?

Aside from re-drafting the complaint, were there other steps plaintiff's lawyer could have taken to avoid the result?

(2) The case against allowing a variance between proof and pleading was put pungently by Judge Younger:

> If substantial disparities between pleading and proof are treated as mere trivia . . . why insist upon pleadings at all? Why not try the case

first and write the pleadings later? Why should the Bar inconvenience itself with the drafting of complaints and answers when a motion under CPLR 3025(c) will be granted routinely to relieve a party of the consequences of stupidity, inattentiveness, or prevarication? . . . Self-evidently, we need pleadings — so that litigants may know what claims or defenses they must prepare to meet, so that issues are defined for trial, so that parties will be discouraged from tempering their testimony to meet the needs of the occasion.

DuBose v. Velez, 63 Misc. 2d 956, 958, 313 N.Y.S.2d 881, 885 (Civ. Ct. 1970).

Do we need pleadings to serve those functions, or are they better performed by the tools of modern discovery? Consider the views of Professors James, Hazard and Leubsdorf:

Discovery and pre-trial hearings now have largely supplanted pleadings in performing these functions. But the concepts involved in pleading remain of importance, in three respects. First, many problems that arose in connection with pleadings have been carried over to discovery and pre-trial motions and orders. Second, the factual and legal issues formerly explained in pleadings now must be expressed in motions, requests concerning the terms of the pre-trial order (governing the matters to be determined at trial), and the parties' plan of proof and motions at trial. Third, dissatisfaction with the heavy costs that discovery entails has led to resurrection of pleading as a device for formulating issues, at least in certain types of cases.

F. James, G. Hazard & J. Leubsdorf, Civil Procedure 138-39 (4th ed. 1985).[*]

(3) In drafting factual allegations for a pleading, the attorney should bear in mind that a statement in a pleading is an admission which binds the party to that version of the facts unless relieved by the court. *Coffin v. President Grand Rapids Hydraulic Co.*, 136 N.Y. 655, 32 N.E. 1076 (1893). Such an admission is also admissible evidence against the pleader in another action. *See generally* Barker & Alexander, Evidence in New York State and Federal Courts § 8:13 (2001). *See also Cramer v. Kuhns*, 213 A.D.2d 131, 630 N.Y.S.2d 128 (3d Dep't 1995).

(4) A problem that may be created by an allowable variance is its impact on the right to a jury trial. See the next case.

---

[*] Reprinted permission of Little, Brown & Company. Copyright © 1985.

LANE v. MERCURY RECORD CORP.
Appellate Division, First Department
21 A.D.2d 602, 252 N.Y.S.2d 1011 (1964)

VALENTE, JUSTICE.

In this action, plaintiff seeks to compel defendant to account for royalties claimed to be due from the sale of phonograph records embodying the performance of a vocalist, plaintiff's intestate. A motion was made to dismiss the complaint for insufficiency on the ground that no cause of action for equitable relief was alleged. Plaintiff opposed the motion, insisting that the facts stated were sufficient to maintain an action for equitable relief, and Special Term upheld plaintiff's contention.

Under the Civil Practice Act, it was held that where a complaint was framed in equity and the demand for relief was equitable in nature, a motion to dismiss made before answer would be granted if the facts alleged merely entitled the plaintiff to some form of legal relief. (*Terner v. Glickstein & Terner, Inc.*, 283 N.Y. 299, 28 N.E.2d 846;. . . .) A royalty or percentage arrangement would not, in and of itself, establish a fiduciary relationship, and the fact that a statement of account was necessary to prove the claim would not require an equitable action. . . .

It is unnecessary to pass on Special Term's characterization of the complaint as sufficient to maintain an action for equitable relief since in our view the provisions of the CPLR have eliminated the distinctions which resulted in decisions such as *Terner v. Glickstein & Terner, Inc., supra*. In that case the Court said (283 N.Y. at p. 301, 28 N.E.2d at p. 846):

> We do not consider whether a good cause of action at law might be spelled out from the allegations of the complaint. The complaint here is framed in equity and equitable relief alone is demanded and if the action does not lie in equity for the reason urged by defendant, the complaint must be dismissed.

Section 8 of the then Civil Practice Act provided there was to be "only one form of civil action" and that "[t]he distinction between actions at law and suits in equity, and the forms of those actions and suits, have been abolished." In effect, that section reiterated a similar provision in the Code of Civil Procedure, adopted in 1848. (Sec. 62, Code of Civ. Proc.) But, despite the clear intent of those sections to bring about a fusion, or merger, of law and equity, the courts seemed reluctant to give full effect to that purpose. Decisions such as *Terner v. Glickstein & Terner, Inc., supra*; . . . insisted upon distinguishing equity and law actions at the pleading stage and to require that a complaint conform to a "theory of the pleadings." The results arrived at in those cases have been adversely criticized. (Kharas, *A Century of Law — Equity Merger in New York*, 1 Syr.L.Rev. 186; *Note — Law and Equity in New York — Still Unmerged*, 55 Yale L.J. 826;. . . .)

The adoption of the CPLR has, however, removed the main judicial stumbling blocks to the effective merger of law and equity actions envisaged since the passage of the Field Code in 1848. It is true that CPLR § 103(a) is identical with section 8 of the Civil Practice Act. Thus, CPLR § 103(a), by itself, could not accomplish any change which the Civil Practice Act failed to effect.

CPLR § 3013 provides that "[s]tatements in a pleading shall be sufficiently particular to give the court and parties notice of the transactions, occurrences, or series of transactions or occurrences, intended to be proved and the material elements of each cause of action or defense." As this Court pointed out in *Foley v. D'Agostino*, 21 A.D.2d 60, 248 N.Y.S.2d 121; CPLR § 3013 makes the primary function of a pleading "that of adequately advising the adverse party of the pleader's claim or defense" and that "pleadings should not be dismissed or ordered amended unless the allegations therein are not sufficiently particular to apprise the court and parties of the subject matter of the controversy" (3 Weinstein-Korn-Miller, N.Y.Civ.Prac. par. 3013.03). As was emphasized in *Foley*, particular stress must be given to CPLR § 3026 which provides that pleadings "shall be liberally construed" and that "[d]efects shall be ignored if a substantial right of a party is not prejudiced." . . .

Thus, there has been a shift from the requirement that a complaint conform to a "theory of the pleadings" to the necessity of giving notice of the transactions intended to be proved and the material elements of the cause of action. With the latter considerations in mind, the complaint in the instant case clearly gives notice of the transactions intended to be proved — a claim for royalties under a contract to make recordings for defendant — and contains the material elements of such a cause of action.

There remains the question as to whether the demand for equitable relief of an accounting is fatal to the complaint if plaintiff is eventually found to be entitled only to money damages for breach of contract. In construing the pleading liberally should we not ignore the defendant's objection if a substantial right of the defendant is not prejudiced? (CPLR § 3026.) One of the main impediments to giving full effect to the merger of law and equity, and which led to decisions such as *Terner v. Glickstein & Terner, Inc., supra*, was the fear that a complaint seeking equitable relief, only, would deprive a defendant of the right to a jury trial if it developed that the plaintiff was entitled only to money damages. The right to a jury trial was a most important one, and its curtailment would constitute substantial prejudice. Clearly a party should not be met at the trial — of what seemed to be an equitable action — with a judgment for legal relief without an opportunity to obtain a jury trial of the legal issues.

That element of possible prejudice has, however, been eliminated by CPLR § 4103 which provides in part:

> When it appears in the course of a trial by the court that the relief required, although not originally demanded by a party, entitles the adverse party to a trial by jury of certain issues of fact, the court shall

give the adverse party an opportunity to demand a jury trial of such issues. . . .

Hence, with the change effected by the CPLR in the essential requirements of a pleading and with the elimination of possible prejudice in the loss of a right to trial by jury, no substantial reason remains for perpetuating the technicalities of pleading rules found in the decisions spawned by *Jackson v. Strong* (222 N.Y. 149, *supra*).

The purpose of all pleading should be to facilitate a proper decision on the merits. It would be unfortunate if the liberalizing rules of the CPLR become encrusted by judicial decisions with the limiting concepts developed under the Code of Civil Procedure and Civil Practice Act. *Foley v. D'Agostino, supra*, demonstrated that this Court did not intend to revert to the ancient rules and would give full effect to the spirit of the new approach contained in the CPLR. In that spirit, the complaint herein must be held to be sufficient.

. . . .

NOTE

Ordinarily, a party who wishes a jury trial must, pursuant to CPLR 4102, demand one when he serves a note of issue (*see* the form in Chapter 18, *infra*), or within fifteen days after service of a note of issue by his opponent. As the court points out in the principal case, CPLR 4103 contains an exception to the normal rule. It protects a party who failed to demand a jury trial because his opponent's pleading misled him into thinking that neither party was entitled to one. Typically this happens when a complaint seeks equitable relief although the facts entitle him to legal relief.

How long can the defendant acquiesce in the plaintiff's mischaracterization before waiving his rights. Consider the principal case: when did it "appear" that the relief sought entitled the defendant to a jury trial? Could defendant have safely waited until mid-trial before making his demand?

§ 13.08 AMENDMENTS

Amendments to the pleadings are governed by CPLR 3025. Subdivision 3025(a) covers amendments as of right (without court permission), while CPLR 3025(b) and CPLR 3025(c) cover amendments made with the court's permission.

Those amendments permitted without leave of the court fall into three groups. Any party may make any type of amendment to any pleading, but he may do so only once. The amendment must be made either (1) within twenty days of the pleading's service or (2) before the period for responding to the pleading has expired (assuming a responsive pleading is required) or (3) within twenty days of receipt of a responsive pleading. The last situation is probably the most significant since it allows the pleader to cure those problems to which the adversary has called attention in his pleadings.

If the pleader needs to amend more than once, or if the time for amendment as of right has expired, he must resort to seeking the opponent's permission or a court order under CPLR §§ 3025(b) or 3025(c). These provisions give the court great discretion in granting leave to amend and even allow them to impose terms. The bounds within which that discretion must operate is the subject of the balance of this section.

IACOVANGELO v. SHEPHERD
Court of Appeals
5 N.Y.3d 184, 800 N.Y.S.2d 116, 833 N.E. 2d 259 (2005)
[Reprinted in § 6.04, *supra*]

NOTE

Reread the *Iacovangelo* case with a view toward the crucial role the amendment provision of CPLR 3025(a) has in rescuing plaintiff's defense of lack of personal jurisdiction.

HELLER v. PROVENZANO, INC.
Appellate Division, First Department
303 A.D.2d 20, 756 N.Y.S.2d 26 (2003)

SULLIVAN, J.

[Plaintiff fell and suffered injuries on defendant's freight elevator in January 1990. After trial in plaintiff's action, the jury returned a verdict for plaintiff for $2.25 million, reduced to $1.25 million by the trial judge. On appeal, the Appellate Division ordered a new trial because of the misconduct of plaintiff and his attorney. Plaintiff thereafter moved to amend the complaint to assert a claim for punitive damages alleging that the trial transcript revealed facts pointing to gross negligence on defendant's part. This amendment was sought six years after the filing of the original complaint. Defendant argued in opposition that the facts were known from the beginning, that the amendment was sought only to enhance plaintiff's bargaining position, and that its insurance did not cover punitive damage awards. The IAS judge granted plaintiff's motion to amend, and the Appellate Division here reverses.]

CPLR 3025 (b) provides that "[a] party may amend his pleading, or supplement it by setting forth additional or subsequent transactions or occurrences, at any time by leave of court or by stipulation of all parties. Leave shall be freely

given upon such terms as may be just including the granting of costs and con-
tinuances." Whether to grant the amendment is committed to the court's discretion (*Edenwald Contr. Co. v. City of New York*, 60 NY2d 957). It is also a
truism that "[m]ere lateness is not a barrier to the amendment. It must be
lateness coupled with significant prejudice to the other side, the very elements
of the laches doctrine" (*id.* at 959, *quoting* Siegel, Practice Commentaries, McK-
inney's Cons Laws of NY, Book 7B, CPLR C3025:5, at 477 [1974 ed]). We also
recognize that, in the absence of prejudice, a motion to amend an ad damnum
clause, whether made before or after trial, "should generally be granted" (*Loomis
v. Civetta Corinno Constr. Corp.*, 54 NY2d 18, 23).

Here, defendants are significantly prejudiced by the amendment. Contrary to
plaintiff's argument in support of affirmance, while he does not seek to assert
a new theory of liability, which, if that were the case, would be sufficient to warrant denial of the motion, given the six-year delay (*see Spence v. Bear Stearns
& Co.*, 264 AD2d 601; *Clayton Webster Corp. v. Bozell & Jacobs*, 167 AD2d 145),
no valid distinction can be drawn, either in law or in fact, between a new theory of liability and "an additional request for relief," particularly where, as
here, such an amendment to the ad damnum would involve different elements
and standards of proof and potentially subject defendants to a far greater and
different dimension of liability than would otherwise have been the case.

Unlike a claim for negligence, to establish a claim for punitive damages,
plaintiff must "demonstrate that the wrong to [him] rose to the level of 'such
wanton dishonesty as to imply a criminal indifference to civil obligations'"
(*Zimmerman v. Tarshis*, 289 AD2d 230, 231, *quoting Walker v. Sheldon*, 10
NY2d 401, 405). As a result of plaintiff's inexcusable and inordinate delay,
defendants have been deprived of the opportunity to conduct discovery and
establish a defense with respect to this belated damage claim. For example,
assuming, arguendo, that a punitive damage claim would have been appropriate if timely asserted, defendants would have been entitled, at the very least,
to conduct discovery or an investigation as to whether, at the time of the accident, a practice existed of allowing passengers to ride the freight elevators
and, if such practice existed, as claimed, whether it was dangerous. In that
regard, evidence of contemporaneous statistics involving garage elevator accidents would be relevant.

Furthermore, in light of the due process concerns implicated in the award of
punitive damages as postulated by the United States Supreme Court in *BMW
of N. Am., Inc. v. Gore* (517 US 559), discovery and investigation into the types
and scope of penalties and fines for comparable conduct and the ratio of such
sanctions to the actual harm or loss suffered would be appropriate. It is fairly
obvious that in allowing this belated amendment, Supreme Court failed to take
these relevant considerations into account.

The facts of the case can be likened to those in *Licameli v. Roberts* (277 AD2d
1057). In affirming the denial of a motion to amend the complaint to add a
claim for punitive damages, the Court noted the plaintiff's failure "to provide an

explanation for the lengthy delay in asserting the claim" and the "fact that discovery is complete and a note of issue has been filed." (*Id.*) Here, discovery has been completed and a note of issue filed more than four years ago. Nor does plaintiff offer any explanation for the lengthy delay in moving for the relief sought. . . .

Another factor warranting denial of the motion is the glaring absence from plaintiff's moving papers of any explanation for his inordinate six-year delay in asserting a punitive damage claim. "Where there has been an extended delay in moving to amend, the party seeking leave to amend must establish a reasonable excuse for the delay" (*Jablonski v. County of Erie*, 286 AD2d 927, 928; *see Reape v. City of New York*, 272 AD2d 533; *Schwab v. Russell*, 231 AD2d 820). In *Jablonski*, which involved a more than two-year delay in moving to amend, attributed to "inadvertent oversight," the Fourth Department affirmed the denial of the motion made on the eve of trial, stating, "In such case, there is a heavy burden on plaintiff to show extraordinary circumstances to justify amendment by submitting affidavits which set forth the recent change of circumstances justifying the amendment and otherwise giving an adequate explanation for the delay" (286 AD2d at 928, *quoting Hemmerick v. City of Rochester*, 63 AD2d 816, 816). As the record shows, this application to amend was made without explanation as to the delay, over 10 years after the accident, over six years after the commencement of the action, long after the completion of discovery and filing of the note of issue, over four years after the first trial of this action and over 1 1/2 years after the decision on the prior appeal.

NOTES

(1) What kinds of prejudice will justify the denial of an amendment adding a new defense or claim? See *Fahey v. County of Ontario*, 44 N.Y.2d 934, 408 N.Y.S.2d 314, 380 N.E.2d 146 (1978), in which defendant, after being served with the bill of particulars, moved to amend his answer to plead the statute of limitation. Reversing a refusal to grant an amendment, the Court of Appeals held that such motions should be granted unless the plaintiff shows surprise or other prejudice resulting from the delay. Compare *Shine v. Duncan Petroleum Transport, Inc.*, 60 N.Y.2d 22, 466 N.Y.S.2d 672, 453 N.E.2d 1089 (1983), in which the Court of Appeals held that a motion to stay a personal injury action so that the defense of the Worker's Compensation Law bar to a personal injury action could be decided by the Worker's Compensation Board, should not have been granted. The answer, the Court noted, did not raise the defense of the Board's "primary jurisdiction," and the movant had known of the defense for two years, yet the motion was not made until the eve of trial.

(2) How does a court's decision to grant an amendment to a pleading during or after trial differ from a decision to consider a new claim or defense without requiring an amendment (as in *Diemer v. Diemer*, § 13.07, *supra*)? Would different considerations be relevant to the two types of decisions?

(3) Of course, a party may seek leave of court to amend a pleading under CPLR 3025(b) after the time to do so by right has passed but well before the trial. According to the Appellate Division, First Department, the motion should not be granted if it seeks to add a new claim or defense which is not meritorious:

> The standard that a court must employ [in deciding the motion] is demonstrably different from the standards applied to either a CPLR 3211 motion to dismiss or a CPLR 3212 motion for summary judgment. . . . The analysis . . . begins with a two-pronged test. First, the proponent must allege legally sufficient facts to establish a *prima facie* claim or defense in the proposed amended pleading. If the facts alleged are incongruent with the legal theory relied on by the proponent, the proposed amendment must fail as a matter of law. . . . The next step is for the *nisi prius* court to test a pleading's merit. . . . The party opposing the motion to amend . . . must overcome a presumption of validity in favor of the moving party and demonstrate that the facts alleged and relied upon in the moving papers are obviously not reliable or are insufficient. . . .

Daniels v. Empire-Orr, Inc., 151 A.D.2d 370, 371, 542 N.Y.S.2d 614, 615 (1st Dep't. 1989).

(4) Recall that for purposes of the statute of limitations, a claim added in an amended pleading will relate back to the date the action was commenced if the requirements of CPLR 203(f) are met.

(5) A party may supplement a pleading (by stipulation or leave of court) "by setting forth additional or subsequent transactions or occurrences." CPLR 3025(b). The concept obviously overlaps the pleading amendment, but one difference between the two is that an amended pleading supersedes the original while a supplemental pleading does not. *See Stella v. Stella*, 92 A.D.2d 589, 459 N.Y.S.2d 478 (2d Dep't 1983). In that case, defendant had served an answer with counterclaim. Plaintiff thereafter served a supplemental complaint (wrongly labeled an amended complaint), and defendant again answered, this time without the counterclaim. The court held that the original counterclaim was still in effect, reasoning that since the original complaint was still effective (as supplemented), so, too, was the counterclaim.

(6) Where plaintiff failed to move for amendment of the complaint to add a cause of action which might have created an exception to the application of CPLR Art. 16 (which restricted her recovery), she could not seek the amendment for the first time on appeal. Once the County requested an apportionment charge, plaintiff should have moved to amend the complaint to include any possible article 16 exemptions. *Morales v. County of Nassau*, 94 N.Y.2d 218, 703 N.Y.S.2d 61, 724 N.E.2d 756 (1999).

(7) Prior to 2003, personal injury complaints would include an *ad damnum* clause setting forth the amount of damages sought. In *Loomis v. Civetta Corinno*

Construction Corp., 54 N.Y.2d 18, 444 N.Y.S.2d 571, 429 N.E.2d 90 (1981), the Court ruled that a plaintiff could move to increase the amount, whether before or after a verdict, so long as defendant would not be prejudiced. As examples of such prejudice, the court cited the instance where if the amount is increased beyond defendant's insurance coverage defendant, would have to retain separate counsel without having been put on notice of that prospect (one ground of prejudice found by the court in *Heller*); and also the instance where, if the original amount sought was not great, the defense might not be as thorough as it would have been had the increased amount originally been known. Also, prior to 2003, CPLR 3017(c) provided that in medical malpractice actions or in actions against a municipality, there should be no *ad damnum* clause.

In 2003, CPLR 3017(c) was amended to simply provide that in all personal injury and wrongful death actions, pleadings should contain a "prayer for general relief but shall not state the amount of damages to which the pleader deems himself entitled." Defendant has the option to "request a supplemental demand setting forth the total damages to which the pleader deems himself entitled." Were defendant to make such a request, it is presumed that the *Loomis* rationale would be applied in a personal injury or death action. *Loomis* involved property damage and so is unaffected by the CPLR 3017(c) amendment.

It has been observed that this amendment would not appear to cover the situation where a summons with notice is served pursuant to CPLR 305(b). *See* David D. Siegel, Supplementary Practice Commentary to CPLR 3017, 7B McKinney's Consolidated Laws of New York 85-86 (Supp. 2006).

§ 13.09 SANCTIONS FOR "FRIVOLOUS PLEADINGS"

PROBLEM C

Refer again to the complaint in § 13.02, in which Peter Ruggles alleges injuries caused by an allegedly defective ladder. Assume that, following disclosure (during which Sears, the defendant, made available for inspection another ladder of the same type as well as the design specifications of the particular ladder model involved in the accident), Sears moved for summary judgment on the ground that there was no evidence of negligence and no evidence of a design or manufacturing defect, nor of a breach of a duty to warn about the risks of use. Assume further that the motion for summary judgment is granted. On appeal, Ruggles argues that summary judgment should not have been granted because, although he could not produce any evidence of a defect, the New York law of products liability should be changed to allow recovery whenever a person is injured while using a product for the purpose for which it was intended. The appellate courts, adhering to well established law, rule against Ruggles and affirm the lower court.

Should the defendant move for an award of sanctions and attorney's fees? If the motion is made, should it be granted?

MATTER OF MINISTER, ELDERS AND DEACONS OF THE REFORMED PROTESTANT DUTCH CHURCH
Court of Appeals
76 N.Y.2d 411, 559 N.Y.S.2d 866, 559 N.E.2d 429 (1990)

Per Curiam.

Having unsuccessfully prosecuted two appeals and two prior motions in this court, respondent Henry Modell and Co. (Modell) has now moved for an order "recalling and amending the remittitur" of our 1983 decision upholding petitioner's right to possess the commercial premises that respondent formerly sublet. The motion is plainly untimely and, for that reason it should be dismissed (22 NYCRR 500.11[g][3]; see, e.g., Drzewinski v. Atlantic Scaffold & Ladder Co., 70 N.Y.2d 999, 526 N.Y.S.2d 434, 521 N.E.2d 441). Further, because the motion is utterly without legal support and was evidently made for the purpose of delaying enforcement of petitioner's seven-year-old judgment, we conclude that, as specifically requested by petitioner, a sanction in the amount of $2,500 should be imposed upon respondent Modell (see, 22 NYCRR 130-1.1-130-1.5).*

The present motion is the most recent of a lengthy series of efforts by respondent to overturn a 1982 Appellate Division decision awarding petitioner possession of certain commercial space located at 198 Broadway in Manhattan (88 A.D.2d 511, 450 N.Y.S.2d 4). The underlying dispute concerned respondent's right to renew its sublease in the face of the decision by the master tenant not to renew its master lease. Respondent took an appeal to this court pursuant to leave granted by the Appellate Division, and we affirmed the Appellate Division order (59 N.Y.2d 170, 464 N.Y.S.2d 406, 451 N.E.2d 164).

Respondent reacted to this decision, which was rendered in 1983, by initiating and pursuing what we later characterized as "a barrage of litigation" (Modell & Co. v. Minister, Elders & Deacon of Refm. Prot. Dutch Church, 68 N.Y.2d 456, 460, 510 N.Y.S.2d 63, 502 N.E.2d 978), including a declaratory judgment action based on a new legal theory, an unsuccessful appeal to this court from the Appellate Division order dismissing that action (see, id., affg. 114 A.D.2d 751, 494 N.Y.S.2d 594), two postappeal motions addressed to this court's disposition of that appeal (see, 69 N.Y.2d 741, 897, 512 N.Y.S.2d 369, 504 N.E.2d 696), and two separate motions to vacate the dispossess judgment that we upheld in 1983. Each of these motions to vacate was based on purported "newly discovered evidence" and relied upon yet another legal theory. Following the trial court's denial of the second motion to vacate — and respondent's unsuccessful attempts both to reargue and to appeal from this denial — respondent made the present motion, which seeks "clarification" of our 1983 ruling.

---

* Petitioner's express request for the imposition of sanctions pursuant to subpart 130-1 of the rules furnished respondent with adequate notice that such relief would be considered and rendered a formal hearing unnecessary (see, 22 NYCRR 130-1.1[d]).

The motion is "frivolous" within the meaning of rule 130-1.1(a) of the Uniform Rules for Trial Courts, since it is "completely without merit in law or fact" and "cannot be supported by a[ny] reasonable argument for an extension, modification or reversal of existing law" (22 NYCRR 130-1.1[c][1]). In addition to its having been made almost seven years after the time for making such motions expired (*see*, 22 NYCRR 500.11[g][3]), the motion is procedurally insupportable. Although it has denominated the present request a motion "to recall and amend the remittitur" to "clarify" a prior decision of this court, Modell is, in substance, asking the court to consider yet another "new" legal theory, ostensibly, supported by more "newly discovered evidence." Notably, much of the "newly discovered evidence" was either available or reasonably discoverable in the early stages of this litigation. Further, the newly coined legal theory is really nothing more than a recast version of Modell's prior arguments, all of which have already been rejected.

The present motion is also "frivolous" in that it was evidently "undertaken primarily to delay or prolong the resolution of the litigation" (McKinney's 1990 New York Rules of Court [22 NYCRR] § 130-1.1[c][ii]). In reaching this conclusion, we have considered, as part of "the circumstances under which the conduct took place" (22 NYCRR 130-1.1[c]), the extended history of this litigation and the numerous postjudgment efforts respondent has made to overturn the judgment. While some of the steps respondent took were legitimate and of at least colorable merit, many others, most notably respondent's two prior reargument motions addressed to this court, its second motion to vacate the judgment and its related efforts to reargue and/or appeal the denial of that motion, were so lacking in factual or legal merit as to demonstrate an intention to use the courts not as a means of resolving a genuine legal dispute but rather as a mechanism to delay respondent's inevitable eviction. We have also considered respondent's own status as a sophisticated corporate entity, the fact that respondent has been represented throughout the litigation by experienced counsel and respondent's obvious motive to postpone the surrender of valuable commercial premises for as long as possible.

Finally, in fixing the sanction at $2,500, we have taken into account the need to deter respondent from engaging in further frivolous motion practice in connection with this litigation, as well as the facts that petitioner has been unfairly deprived of the use of its property for a protracted period and that the time and attention of more than a dozen Judges of this State have been diverted unnecessarily. We have selected an amount within the lower range of permissible sanctions (*see*, 22 NYCRR 130-1.2), because this is the first time that sanctions have been imposed by our court and we deem it prudent to proceed cautiously in this area. While an additional sanction on the attorneys in this case is authorized by the rules, we elect not to impose one, in the absence of a specific request for such relief by Modell's adversary. Because of these circumstances, we leave for another day the questions of when, and in what situations, the parties' attorneys should be penalized for "frivolous conduct."

Accordingly, the motion to recall and amend remittitur should be dismissed, with costs; a sanction in the amount of $2,500 should be imposed upon respondent Henry Modell and Co.

NOTES

(1) In *Mitchell v. Herald Co.*, 137 A.D.2d 213, 529 N.Y.S.2d 602 (4th Dep't 1988), plaintiff had been criminally convicted of assault, yet sued defendant newspaper on the ground that its reporting of the incident was libelous. The news article was fully supported by the conviction, and plaintiff's suit was found frivolous. It was stated: "Plaintiff could recover . . . only if he proved that the newspaper account was false and that defendant was grossly irresponsible in printing it. From the outset of this action, it was or should have been apparent to plaintiff and his counsel that neither issue could be resolved in his favor." 137 A.D.2d at 219, 529 N.Y.S.2d at 606. The court held that the defendant was entitled to an award of costs and attorney's fees pursuant to CPLR 8303-a.

What differences do you see between 22 NYCRR Part 130 of the Uniform Rules for the Trial Courts (relied on in the principal case) and CPLR 8303-a? Note that, among other differences, CPLR 8303-a(c)(ii) requires that the court find "bad faith" in addition to a lack of reasonable basis before awarding attorney fees. How might bad faith be established?

Part 130 authorizes the court "in its discretion" to impose sanctions on, or award attorney's fees against, any party or attorney who engages in frivolous conduct. Conduct is defined as "frivolous" by 22 NYCRR § 130-1.1(c) if:

> (i) it is completely without merit in law or fact and cannot be supported by a reasonable argument for an extension, modification or reversal of existing law;

> (ii) it is undertaken primarily to delay or prolong the resolution of the action, or to harass or maliciously injure another; or

> (iii) it asserts material factual statements that are false.

The amount of sanctions awarded for any single occurrence of frivolous conduct may not exceed $10,000. 22 NYCRR § 130-1.2.

Part 130 was relied on to impose a $10,000 sanction on a pro se litigant characterized by the court as a "chronic abuser of the judicial system [who] moves from judge to judge and forum to forum in a pattern that enables him to avoid, or substantially delay his obligation to pay rent." *Winters v. Gould*, 143 Misc. 2d 44, 539 N.Y.S.2d 686 (Sup. Ct. 1989).

(4) "Vital changes have been wrought by those members of the bar who have dared to challenge the received wisdom, and a rule that penalized such innovation and industry would run counter to our notions of the common law itself." *Eastway Construction Corp. v. City of New York*, 762 F.2d 243 (2d Cir. 1985). Do

CPLR 8303-a and 22 NYCRR Part 130 threaten the industry and innovation of the bar? See, describing some negative aspects of the federal experience, Nelken, *Sanctions Under Amended Federal Rule 11 — Some "Chilling" Problems in the Struggle Between Compensation and Punishment*, 74 Geo. L.J. 1313 (1986). Are the arguments for and against sanction rules different in state court systems than in federal systems? Is it relevant that federal judges are appointed with life tenure whereas justices of the New York Sate Supreme Court are elected for 14 year terms? *See* Chase, *Sanctions in State Court — Proposed Rule Needs Changes*, N.Y.L.J., October 22, 1987, p. 1, col. 3 (arguing that sanctions in state court should be limited to litigation conduct which violates existing rules of process, such as the failure to respond to a disclosure demand).

(5) The New York Civil Rights Law, § 76-a(2) provides that a plaintiff in a "SLAPP" suit can recover damages only if it can be shown by clear and convincing evidence that the defendant acted with knowledge of falsity, or reckless disregard of its statements. "SLAPP" stands for "strategic lawsuit against public participation." The defendants in "SLAPP" suits are typically those who had objected for environmental or other reasons to the plaintiff's attempts to secure some right or privilege from a government agency. Disgruntled plaintiffs have attempted to "SLAPP" such defendants for this impertinence, and this legislation protects the defendants from such suits. In conjunction with the Civil Rights Law provisions, the Legislature in 1992 added subdivisions (g) and (h) respectively to CPLR 3211 and 3212, which provide the motions for pre-answer dismissal and summary judgment. These provisions cast the burden on plaintiff to establish that the action has a substantial basis, thus affording an early demise for these retribution suits. If defendants are successful in showing the baselessness of the "SLAPP" suit, the Civil Rights Law § 70-a provides for compensatory and punitive damages.

Chapter 14
THE BILL OF PARTICULARS

§ 14.01 THE NATURE OF THE BILL OF PARTICULARS

Form:

Demand for Bill of Particulars

SUPREME COURT OF THE STATE OF NEW YORK
COUNTY OF NEW YORK

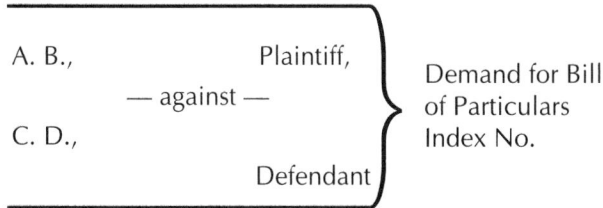

A. B.,   Plaintiff,

— against —   Demand for Bill
                               of Particulars
C. D.,   Index No.

                    Defendant

PLEASE TAKE NOTICE that defendant demands that you serve upon the undersigned within thirty days after service of this notice, a [verified] bill of particulars stating the following:

1. The date and approximate time of the occurrence.

2. The approximate location of the occurrence.

3. A general statement of the acts or omissions constituting the negligence claimed to have caused the plaintiff's injuries.

4. [Where notice of a condition is a prerequisite state whether actual or constructive notice is claimed.]

5. [If actual notice is claimed state when and to whom it was given.]

6. The injuries alleged to have been suffered by plaintiff and describe those which are claimed to be permanent.

7. [If the action is brought pursuant to Insurance Law § 5104 to recover for serious injury: state which injuries are alleged to come within the meaning of Insurance Law § 5102(d).]

8. [If the action is brought pursuant to Insurance Law § 5104 to recover economic loss greater than basic economic loss, set forth in which respects the economic loss is greater than basic economic loss as defined in Insurance Law § 5102(a).]

9. The length of time confined in bed and to house.

10. The length of time incapacitated from employment.

11. The total amounts claimed as special damages for: (a) physicians' services; (b) medical supplies; (c) loss of earnings with name and address of employer; (d) hospital expenses; (e) nurses' services.

[Print Name]

_____

Attorney for Defendant
Address:
Telephone Number:

TO: [Print Name]

_____

Attorney for Plaintiff
Address:

NOTES

(1) The above form is Proposed Official Form 26 in Automobile Accident Cases. *See* McKinney's CPLR forms § 4:623. The demand is authorized by CPLR 3041. *See also* CPLR 3043.

A defendant who wishes to demand a bill typically serves the demand at the same time as the answer is served. There is no outside time limit imposed by the CPLR on when the demand may be made. In general the party making a demand would want to serve it as early as possible. Why?

(2) The function of the bill has been well described by one court:

The question [addressed in the bill of particulars] . . . is not what may have been the actual facts, nor the knowledge of the opposite party concerning them, but rather what the aggrieved party claims them to be. . . . It is not the office of a bill of particulars to expose to his adversary the evidence of the party giving it. The purpose of such a bill is to amplify the pleadings and to indicate with more particularity than is ordinarily required in a formal plea the nature of the claim made in order that surprise upon the trial may be avoided and that the issues may be more intelligently met.

Dwyer v. Slattery, 118 App. Div. 345, 346, 103 N.Y.S. 433, 434-35 (1st Dep't 1907).

This description connotes both similarities and differences between the bill of particulars and the tools of disclosure. What are they? Keep this question in mind as you read both this chapter and Chapter 15 on disclosure itself. *See generally* O. Chase, CPLR Manual § 19.17[a] (2d ed. 2006).

(3) Is there any need for the bill of particulars in modern practice? Recall that the pleading itself is supposed to give "notice of the transactions [or] . . . occurrences, intended to be proved." CPLR 3013.

§ 14.02 LIMITS ON WHAT MAY BE DEMANDED

PROBLEM A

Recall the sample complaint in Chapter 13 concerning the allegedly defective ladder purchased at Sears Roebuck. Suppose after issue is joined, defendant serves a demand for a bill of particulars which includes the following:

As to the ladder alleged to be defective:

(a) Identify the part or parts of the ladder claimed to be defective;

(b) Specify the nature of each defect claimed;

(c) State the manner in which each defect contributed to the cause of the accident;

(d) Attach a copy of the receipt obtained when the product was purchased;

(e) Provide the serial number which appears on the product (on the bottom side of the top step).

Could the plaintiff successfully argue that this demand should be modified or vacated?

FELOCK v. ALBANY MEDICAL CENTER HOSPITAL
Appellate Division, Third Department
258 A.D.2d 772, 685 N.Y.S.2d 844 (1999)

CARDONA, P.J.

Appeal from an order of the Supreme Court (Malone, Jr., J.), entered July 17, 1998 in Albany County, which, inter alia, denied defendants' motion to strike certain portions of the verified bill of particulars.

Following her birth on June 29, 1987, plaintiff Elizabeth M. Felock (hereinafter the infant) was hospitalized at defendant Albany Medical Center Hospital (hereinafter defendant) until October 16, 1987. During her hospitalization, the infant allegedly suffered burns to certain areas of her skin where electrodes had been placed. In June 1997, the infant's mother commenced this medical malpractice action on behalf of the infant and herself against defendant and defendant Albany Medical College. Following joinder of issue, defendants served plaintiffs with a demand for a bill of particulars and plaintiffs, in turn, served defendants with a notice of discovery and inspection.

Thereafter, plaintiffs served the verified bill of particulars and defendants produced the documentation requested in the notice of discovery and inspection. Defendants objected to the verified bill of particulars arguing that the responses to certain questions were not sufficiently particular. Plaintiffs advised defendants that their ability to respond was severely hampered by defendants' failure to produce a complete set of hospital records which included copies of the nursing notes. In addition, plaintiffs objected to defendants' responses to the notice of discovery and inspection on the basis that the nursing notes were omitted. Plaintiffs subsequently served a notice to admit requesting confirmation that defendants were not in possession of the nursing notes. In their response, defendants represented that "[t]he hospital has a policy for maintaining records and, presumably, is in possession of the nursing notes for the 1987 hospitalization regarding [the infant]." Defendants further stated that "[t]he hospital does admit that, at this point in time, it has been unable to locate those records notwithstanding the fact that a search therefor has been made."

In January 1998, defendants moved pursuant to CPLR 3042 and 3126 to strike certain paragraphs of the verified bill of particulars on the ground that they were not sufficiently particular or were overly broad. Plaintiffs opposed the motion and cross-moved pursuant to CPLR 3124 and 3126 for sanctions against defendants based upon the failure to produce a complete set of medical records due to the absence of the nursing notes. Supreme Court denied defendants' motion and conditionally granted plaintiffs' cross motion by ordering that defendants produce the nursing notes within 90 days or be precluded from offering any evidence regarding the material contained therein. Defendants appeal.

We affirm. "'The purpose of a bill of particulars is to amplify the pleadings, limit the proof and prevent surprise at trial'" (*Hayes v. Kearney*, 237 A.D.2d 769, quoting *Twiddy v. Standard Mar. Transp. Servs.*, 162 A.D.2d 264, 265; *see, MacDormand v. Blumenberg*, 182 A.D.2d 991, 992). "'The responses to a demand for a bill must clearly detail the specific acts of negligence attributed to each defendant'" (*Hayes v. Kearney, supra*, at 769, quoting *Miccarelli v. Fleiss*, 219 A.D.2d 469, 470). They need not, however, provide evidentiary material or information to be gleaned from expert testimony (*see, Liddell v. Cree*, 233 A.D.2d 593, 594; *Heyward v. Ellenville Community Hosp.*, 215 A.D.2d 967). Notably, in a medical malpractice action, as in any action for personal injuries, the bill of particulars "requires only a '[g]eneral statement of the acts or omissions constituting the negligence claimed'" (*Rockefeller v. Hwang*, 106 A.D.2d 817, 818, quoting CPLR 3043[a][3]; *see, Coughlin v. Festin*, 53 A.D.2d 800).

Defendants objected to paragraphs 3(a), (b), (c), (d), (e), (f), (k), (n), (u) and (ee), and paragraphs 10, 11, 21, 26 and 27 of the verified bill of particulars. Paragraphs 3(a) through (f), (k), (n), (u) and (ee) of the demand requested plaintiffs to specify the acts and/or omissions constituting negligence and malpractice allegedly committed by defendants. The responses convey the general manner in which it is alleged that harm was caused to the infant. In particular, plaintiffs alleged, inter alia, that defendants failed to keep appropriate medical records and record physical findings properly. They further alleged that defendants did not possess the requisite medical knowledge involved in the treatment of the infant's skin nor properly supervise hospital employees to adequately monitor the infant. The foregoing allegations were sufficient and plaintiffs were not required to provide further evidentiary detail.

Paragraphs 10 and 11 of the demand requested plaintiffs to specify whether medications were improperly administered or whether defective equipment was used in the care and treatment of the infant. In their responses, plaintiffs stated that they did not have present knowledge of such facts but believe the information would be disclosed during further discovery. Given that the information requested in these paragraphs by defendants is likely contained in the nursing notes not yet produced, we find the responses adequate.

Paragraphs 21, 26 and 27 of the demand request plaintiffs to provide information concerning the infant's loss of earning capacity, special damages and medical expenses incurred as a result of the alleged injuries. Plaintiffs state that they do not presently have information in regard to these matters. Plaintiffs may provide this information at a latter time through a supplemental bill of particulars (*see, Miccarelli v. Fleiss, supra,* at 470) as long as it is done on a timely basis. Consequently, these paragraphs also need not be stricken.

In view of the foregoing, we conclude that Supreme Court properly denied defendant's motion to strike the above paragraphs of the verified bill of particulars. We further find that Supreme Court did not abuse its discretion in ordering defendants to produce the requested nursing notes or be precluded from offering evidence pertaining to information contained therein at trial. Notably, defendants have a legal duty to keep and maintain the infant's medical records (*see,* 10 NYCRR 405.10[a][3]) and have not provided plaintiffs with a conclusive answer as to whether the subject nursing notes are in their possession (*compare, Ashline v. Kestner Engrs.,* 219 A.D.2d 788). Under these particular circumstances, the issuance of the conditional order of preclusion was appropriate. Contrary to defendants' claim, we do not find the order unduly ambiguous and note that Supreme Court will determine the admissibility of particular evidence as it is offered at trial.

NOTES

(1) Whether to categorize information sought as "evidence," thereby making it unobtainable by a demand for a bill, is a much litigated question. (Why?) In addition to the principal case, see, *e.g., Bouton v. County of Suffolk,* 125 A.D.2d 620, 509 N.Y.S.2d 846 (2d Dep't 1986). There, plaintiff claimed that he was involved in a traffic accident because the defendant town failed to provide ade-

quate traffic controls and misplaced a stop sign at an intersection. The demand for a bill included requests to state where the stop sign should have been placed and what additional traffic controls should have been provided. These were held improper because they "sought matters which are evidentiary in nature requiring expert testimony and thus are outside the scope of a bill of particulars." In dissent, Justice Lazer argued that the demands should have been held proper in the interest of "meaningful preparation" of the case for trial.

See also *McKenzie v. St. Elizabeth Hospital*, 81 A.D.2d 1003, 440 N.Y.S.2d 109 (4th Dep't 1981), holding in a medical malpractice case that "those items which seek particularization of usual and accepted standards [of medical treatment] as well as those demanding what advice, diagnosis or treatment should have been made or given, call for expert testimony and are purely evidentiary . . . and must be vacated."

In these cases, did the defendants' demand seek "evidence" in the same sense in which you generally understand it?

"Evidence" unavailable by way of the demand for a bill may nonetheless usually be obtained through disclosure, or a supplemental bill, as the principal case notes. Why should it matter to the parties whether the material sought is revealed through a bill or through disclosure?

Despite the general "no evidence" rule, a few adventurous judges have allowed the bill of particulars to be used for evidence requests in smaller cases where full blown discovery is too costly. *See, e.g., Block v. Fairbairn*, 68 Misc. 2d 931, 328 N.Y.S.2d 497 (Sup. Ct. 1972).

§ 14.03 THE EFFECT OF THE BILL OF PARTICULARS

NORTHWAY ENGINEERING, INC. v. FELIX INDUSTRIES, INC.
Court of Appeals
77 N.Y.2d 332, 567 N.Y.S.2d 634, 569 N.E.2d 438 (1991)

[Defendants contracted to have plaintiff perform certain subcontractor work which eventually ended in a dispute concerning an $88,762 payment over which plaintiff brought suit. In its answer defendants asserted two counterclaims. Plaintiff sought a bill of particulars with respect to the counterclaims, but defendants failed to furnish any information, and they were ultimately dismissed under a preclusion order. Defendants nevertheless sought to use the facts underlying the counterclaims as defenses against plaintiff's claim. The Appellate Division held that since defendants were precluded from presenting proof as to the counterclaims, they were also precluded from using the same proof as defenses since all of it was "inextricably interwoven."]

WACHTLER, CHIEF JUDGE.

The question on this appeal is whether an order of preclusion, entered when the defendants failed to provide particulars relating to their counterclaims, also precludes the defendants from offering any defense to the complaint. The courts below held that it did and the defendants appeal.

In determining the scope of the preclusion order at issue in this case, it is important to emphasize that it relates to a demand for a bill of particulars and not to a disclosure notice or other discovery device. The distinction is important because these procedures serve different functions in the pretrial setting.

Under the broad discovery statutes now in effect in this State, any party may demand disclosure of evidence, or information leading to evidence, relevant to the case without regard to the burden of proof (CPLR 3101[a]; *Allen v. Crowell-Collier Publ. Co.*, 21 N.Y.2d 403, 406, 288 N.Y.S.2d 449, 235 N.E.2d 430; Siegel, N.Y.Prac. § 344, at 420-422). The sanctions for failure to comply with such a request are equally broad and include a preclusion order preventing the nondisclosing party from using the evidence in any manner during the course of the litigation (CPLR 3126[2]; *see also, e.g., Feingold v. Walworth Bros.*, 238 N.Y. 446, 144 N.E. 675).

A bill of particulars, on the other hand, is a more limited device, designed simply to amplify or supplement a pleading, and was first recognized at common law before the development of the modern discovery rules (*Dwight v. Germania Life Ins. Co.*, 84 N.Y. 489; *State of New York v. Horsemen's Benevolent & Protective Assn.*, 34 A.D.2d 769, 311 N.Y.S.2d 511). It was liberally employed by the courts at a time when it was virtually the only means by which a party could obtain any insight into the nature of the adversary's case (*Dwight v. Germania Life Ins. Co., supra; see also, e.g., Cunard v. Francklyn*, 111 N.Y. 511, 19 N.E. 92; *Elman v. Ziegfeld*, 200 App. Div. 494, 193 N.Y.S. 133). Over the years it has generated an extensive pretrial motion practice which the courts and the Legislature have sought to discourage by simplifying the procedure and discouraging motions relating to bills of particulars (*see, e.g.,* CPLR 3042[h] [denying costs]; 3043 [specifying content of bill in personal injury actions]). Some jurisdictions, including the Federal courts, have abolished the bill, concluding that broad disclosure statutes render it superfluous (Siegel, Practice Commentaries, McKinney's Cons.Laws of N.Y., Book 7B, CPLR C3041:1, at 477). The drafters of the CPLR also recommended its abolishment in conjunction with the expansion of the disclosure statutes now found in article 31 (*ibid.*). However, the Legislature retained the bill of particulars, not as a disclosure device (CPLR art. 31), but in its traditional and limited role as a means of amplifying a pleading (CPLR 3041 *et seq.*). The appropriate sanction for failure to provide a bill should also be limited to preventing the harm which would otherwise be caused by failure to furnish the particulars.

It is generally stated that a bill of particulars amplifies a pleading by setting forth in greater detail the nature of the allegations and what the party making them intends to prove (*Dwight v. Germania Life Ins. Co., supra, see also*, Siegel, N.Y.Prac., at 291-292). Thus it relates to the burden of proof and requires each party upon demand to provide particulars with respect to matters alleged in that party's pleading, whether it be a complaint, an answer, or any other type of pleading (3 Weinstein-Korn-Miller, N.Y. Civ. Prac. ¶ 3041.10; Siegel, Practice Commentaries, McKinney's Cons. Laws of N.Y., Book 7B, CPLR C3041:6, at 482). However, a party need not particularize general denials because these are matters on which the party making the allegations, and not the party denying them, has the burden of proof (*Silberfeld v. Swiss Bank Corp.*, 263 App. Div. 1017, 33 N.Y.S.2d 961; *Dommerich & Co. v. Diener & Dorskind*, 31 A.D.2d 516, 294 N.Y.S.2d 613; Siegel, N.Y. Prac. § 238, at 292).

If a party neglects or refuses to respond to a demand for a bill of particulars, the court may enter a preclusion order (CPLR 3042[c]). This bars the recalcitrant party from proving allegations it has failed to amplify and relieves the adversary from having to meet a claim which has not been clearly explained or defined. Typically preclusion orders are prospective and conditional, permitting the offending party to avoid preclusion by complying with the demand before the order goes into effect (CPLR 3042[e]), but the statute also permits the court to enter the order unconditionally without dispensation (CPLR 3042[c]). Unless a preclusion order is set aside, most courts hold that it may serve as a basis for summary judgment dismissing the complaint or counterclaim (*Vandoros v. Kovacevic*, 79 Misc.2d 238, 360 N.Y.S.2d 367 [App Term 1974]), and if the only defense to an action is an affirmative defense which has been precluded it would seem, on principle, that summary judgment should be awarded to the plaintiff. Thus a preclusion order is a strong sanction and as one authority observes: "the punishment here should fit the crime, precluding only as to that for which particulars have not been furnished." (Siegel, Practice Commentaries, *op. cit.*, C3042:5, at 530.)

In this case the plaintiff demanded particulars only with respect to the counterclaims. The plaintiff had no right to demand particulars concerning the general denials or the specific nature of the defenses they presented. When the defendants failed to comply with the demand, the court properly precluded the defendants from proceeding on the counterclaims, but there was no need to give the preclusion order the additional effect of stripping the defendants of their general denials. Although these defenses and the precluded counterclaims arise out of the same dispute, and thus may be factually interwoven, that is no reason to treat the demand for a bill as a demand for disclosure by giving the preclusion order a kind of collateral estoppel effect beyond the particular pleading or portion of the pleading the bill was intended to amplify. That is especially true when, as here, there was nothing in the motion papers or conditional preclusion order which would alert the defendants to this particular risk, and it is not the usual consequence of a preclusion order relating to a bill of particulars (*see, e.g., Vandoros v. Kovacevic, supra*, at 239, 360 N.Y.S.2d 367).

The purpose of a preclusion order is to make the demanding party whole. Whatever disadvantage the plaintiff suffered as a result of the defendants' failure to furnish particulars relating to the counterclaims was cured when the court effectively removed the counterclaims from the case by precluding the defendants from submitting evidence in support of them. To further preclude the defendants from asserting defenses which require only general denials, despite the existence of a genuine factual dispute, deprives the defendants of their day in court and gives the plaintiff more relief than is warranted by the defendants' failure to clarify counterclaims which the plaintiffs are no longer required to meet. It also blurs the distinction between the demand for a bill of particulars and a demand for disclosure, creating a sometimes redundant and misleading procedure, likely to revive the burdensome bill of particulars motion practice which the courts and the Legislature have long sought to avoid.

Accordingly, the order of the Appellate Division should be reversed, with costs, and the plaintiff's motion for summary judgment should be denied.

KAYE, JUDGE (dissenting).

I disagree with the majority's conclusion that interposition of a general denial insulated these defendants (a general contractor and its surety) from the effects of a preclusion order. In my view, the trial court and Appellate Division correctly awarded plaintiff subcontractor summary judgment for the balance due on its contract, which it has been litigating to collect for nearly five years.[*]

The majority's conclusion rests on an erroneous factual premise. Plaintiff's request for a bill of particulars was not addressed merely to defendants' counterclaims, as the majority persistently misportrays throughout its writing (majority opn., at 334, 335, 337, at 635, 636, 637 of 567 N.Y.S.2d, at 438, 439, 440 of 569 N.E.2d). Instead, plaintiff's request was directed to specific paragraphs of the answer which defendant itself had denominated "*counterclaim and defense*" (emphasis supplied).

No one disputes that a party need particularize only matters as to which it has the burden of proof (*see*, 3 Weinstein-Korn-Miller, N.Y. Civ. Prac. ¶ 3041.10). This includes a defendant's "counterclaims, cross-claims, and defenses in the answer." (Siegel, Practice Commentaries, McKinney's Cons. Laws of N.Y., Book 7B, CPLR C3041:6, at 482). Defendants, of course, had the opportunity to frame their own pleading, assuming a risk that the burden of proof might be shifted as to matters they chose — for whatever strategic advantage they perceived — to designate as defenses (*see*, Siegel, Practice Commentaries, McKinney's Cons. Law of N.Y., Book 7B, CPLR C3018:16, at 157).

This case comes down to a few simple points.

First, whatever historically interesting matters may have been true of bills of particulars (*see*, majority opn., at 335-336, at 636-637 of 567 N.Y.S.2d, at 439-

---

[*] After one full year of litigation, defendants conceded a portion of the claim, and allowed partial summary judgment to be entered against them.

440 of 569 N.E.2d), they are today an integral part of the CPLR, and they continue to serve what the Legislature obviously believes are important purposes. The CPLR specifies when and how a request for particulars should be made, amended and answered; when and how a request should be vacated and modified; and what sanctions are available for failure to comply with a request (CPLR 3042). In this very case, defendants requested — and plaintiff furnished — an extensive bill of particulars, including schedules of payments, names of witnesses and other exhibits.

Second, plaintiff complied with the CPLR when it sought particulars as to defendants' two counterclaims and defenses. Defendants, by contrast, ignored the CPLR; they in fact ignored all of plaintiff's discovery requests. While now complaining that the burden of proof was "unfairly" shifted to them, defendants had ample remedies to redress that complaint. Within 10 days, defendants could have moved to vacate or modify what they contend was an improper request for a bill of particulars (CPLR 3042[a]). Such a motion would have enabled the court, in an orderly fashion, to hear both sides and determine the propriety of plaintiff's request. Defendants also could have amended their answer to correct any mislabeling of their defenses (CPLR 3025[a], [b]).

Where a defendant fails to furnish a requested bill of particulars with respect to a defense, it may be precluded from introducing evidence relevant to that defense (*see*, Siegel, Practice Commentaries, McKinney's Cons. Laws of N.Y., Book 7B, CPLR C3042:5, at 530).

When defendant ignored plaintiff's request for particulars, plaintiff sought a preclusion order. When defendant ignored the motion for preclusion, the court— more than one year after plaintiff's request had been made — granted a conditional preclusion order. When defendant ignored the court's preclusion order for five months, plaintiff sought summary judgment, fully documenting its entitlement to relief. Only at that point did defendant claim the protection of its general denial, asserting that the request sought information as to which it did not have the burden of proof.

Third, defendants' calculated indifference to the CPLR — involving plaintiff and the court in costly, time-consuming motion practice — should not be rewarded by now reversing summary judgment. That is an improper result in this case, and a very poor example for other cases. Plaintiff should have the balance due on its contract rather than defendants' renewed foot-dragging, discovery runarounds, and litigation in the trial court — as well as a bill of costs from us.

SIMONS, ALEXANDER, HANCOCK and BELLACOSA, JJ., concur with WACHTLER, C.J.

KAYE, J., dissents and votes to affirm in a separate opinion in which TITONE, J., concurs.

Order reversed, etc.

Chapter 15

DISCLOSURE

§ 15.01 INTRODUCTORY NOTE

"Disclosure" as used in the CPLR refers to the methods found in article 31 for obtaining information from parties and, in certain cases, non-parties. In federal practice, the term "discovery" is used for the same concept. *See* Fed. R. Civ. Pro. 26.

With but few exceptions, the disclosure process is begun after the pleadings have been served, CPLR 3106, although the investigative process of which discovery is only a part will by then be well along. At least on the plaintiff's part, it will have begun before the action has been commenced. In studying the material in this chapter you should not lose sight of the availability of fact gathering methods which are not, strictly speaking, "disclosure." These include not only the state and federal Freedom of Information Acts, *see* § 15.04[G], *infra*, but also basic steps like interviewing witnesses, reviewing the client's files and, where appropriate, using public documents like corporate reports, business publications and litigation papers filed with a court in the course of other actions.

Even the best investigation cannot eliminate the need for disclosure in the effective handling of litigation. Not the least of the reasons is that an attorney may not communicate directly with an opposing party who is represented by counsel except with counsel's permission. Code of Professional Responsibility DR 7-104. *See Niesig v. Team I*, 76 N.Y.2d 363, 559 N.Y.S.2d 493, 558 N.E.2d 1030 (1990). Disclosure is thus the only route to information possessed exclusively by an opponent.

Disclosure serves ends which go beyond information gathering. It allows the preservation of evidence which can later be used at trial under certain circumstances. *See* CPLR 3117, 3131. And it helps make settlements more likely, because through it, each party learns a great deal about the strengths and weaknesses of his opponent's case. Disclosure can, at least theoretically, therefore, make the litigation process more efficient by reducing the number of trials.

Yet the "no free lunch" principle applies here as elsewhere, and in recent years, the costs of liberal disclosure rules have been increasingly a source of discomfort. Literature on the problem is extensive; the major issues have been astutely summarized by Justice Powell in a dissent from the Supreme Court's 1980 decision to approve only minor amendments to the federal discovery rules:

> When the Federal Rules first appeared in 1938, the discovery provisions properly were viewed as a constructive improvement. But expe-

rience under the discovery Rules demonstrates that "not infrequently [they have been] exploited to the disadvantage of justice." *Herbert v. Lando*, 441 U.S. 153, 179 (1979) (Powell, J., concurring). Properly limited and controlled discovery is necessary in most civil litigation. The present Rules, however, invite discovery of such scope and duration that district judges often cannot keep the practice within reasonable bounds. Even in a relatively simple case, discovery through depositions, interrogatories, and demands for documents may take weeks. In complex litigation, discovery can continue for years. One must doubt whether empirical evidence would demonstrate that untrammeled discovery actually contributes to the just resolution of disputes. If there is disagreement about that, there is none whatever about the effect of discovery practices upon the average citizen's ability to afford legal remedies.

Delay and excessive expense now characterize a large percentage of all civil litigation. The problems arise in significant part, as every judge and litigator knows, from abuse of the discovery procedures available under the Rules. Indeed, the National Conference on the Causes of Popular Dissatisfaction with the Administration of Justice, led by the Chief Justice, identified "abuse in the use of discovery [as] a major concern" within our legal system. Lawyers devote an enormous number of "chargeable hours" to the practice of discovery. We may assume that discovery usually is conducted in good faith. Yet all too often, discovery practices enable the party with greater financial resources to prevail by exhausting the resources of a weaker opponent. The mere threat of delay or unbearable expense denies justice to many actual or prospective litigants. Persons or businesses of comparatively limited means settle unjust claims and relinquish just claims simply because they cannot afford to litigate. Litigation costs have become intolerable, and they cast a lengthening shadow over the basic fairness of our legal system.

In New York, where discovery has traditionally been more restrictive than in the federal courts, the trend has been to expand its availability. In 1984, for example, CPLR 3101(a) was amended to make it easier to get discovery from non-parties and in 1985 discovery of expert testimony was broadened by the addition of CPLR 3101(d)(1). Again, in 1993, the Legislature made significant amendments to Article 31, some of which will be noted as they relate to topics covered in this chapter.

A good discussion of the advantages and drawbacks of disclosure from a litigator's viewpoint is in W. Barthold, Attorney's Guide to Effective Discovery Techniques 17-23 (1975). For a critical but fascinating description of the "dirty tricks" approach to disclosure, see Brazil, *The Adversary Character of Civil Discovery: A Critique and Proposals for Change*, 31 Vand. L. Rev. 1295 (1978).

The most thorough one volume treatment of discovery in New York is Durst, et al., Modern New York Discovery (1983, Supp. 2003).

This chapter examines four major problems which every practitioner must confront in using the disclosure rules:

(1) What information and material are subject to disclosure?

(2) Who is subject to disclosure?

(3) What are the available disclosure devices and how are they used?

(4) How is disclosure compelled or avoided?

§ 15.02 THE SCOPE OF DISCLOSURE: CPLR 3101

PROBLEM A

Review the complaint (§ 13.02, *supra*), answer (§ 13.03, *supra*) and demand for a bill of particulars (§ 14.01, *supra*) in the *Ruggles v. Sears* defective ladder case. Now suppose that the attorneys for the plaintiffs serve these interrogatories on Sears' counsel: (1) Describe each and every instance in which a ladder sold by Sears is reported to have malfunctioned, causing injury. (2) Describe each and every action brought against Sears which alleged injury caused by a defective ladder sold by Sears. Attach copies of all papers served by and on Sears in each such action. (3) Describe each and every report prepared by Sears evaluating the safety of any ladder sold by Sears. Will the court require them to be answered?

ANDON v. 302-304 MOTT STREET ASSOCIATES
Court of Appeals
94 N.Y.2d 740, 709 N.Y.S.2d 873, 731 N.E.2d 589 (2000)

CIPARICK, J.

[In a case where damages were sought for an infant who had ingested lead-based paint, defendant moved to compel plaintiff-mother to submit to an IQ test. The injuries allegedly sustained by the infant included "learning disabilities, developmental delays in speech and language skills, and behavioral problems." The purpose of the IQ test was to determine whether the infant's cognitive disabilities were, in fact, genetic. In support of the motion was an affidavit from Dr. Adesman who concluded that maternal IQ is relevant in assessing a child's cognitive development. The IAS court granted the motion, but the Appellate Division reversed, noting that the mother's mental condition was not in controversy. The Court of Appeals here affirms.]

Here, recognizing New York's policy favoring open disclosure, the Appellate Division considered defendants' need for the information against its possible relevance, the burden of subjecting plaintiff-mother to the test and the potential for unfettered litigation on the issue of maternal IQ (*Andon v. 302-304 Mott St. Assocs.*, *supra*, 257 A.D.2d, at 40-41). The Court noted specifically that "many variables" were involved and that permitting the IQ test in the instant case would "raise more questions than it will answer" (*id.*, at 40). Thus, the Court evaluated competing interests and concluded that, under the circumstances of this case, the potential for confusion and delay created by the information sought outweighed any benefit to the defense. Further, the Appellate Division's opinion stated that its reversal was "on the law and the facts." On this record, it cannot be said the Appellate Division categorically denied defendants' request as a matter of law.

Nor did the Appellate Division abuse its discretion as a matter of law. CPLR 3101(a) entitles parties to "full disclosure of all matter material and necessary in the prosecution or defense of an action, regardless of the burden of proof." What is "material and necessary" is left to the sound discretion of the lower courts and includes "any facts bearing on the controversy which will assist preparation for trial by sharpening the issues and reducing delay and prolixity. The test is one of usefulness and reason" (*Allen v. Crowell-Collier Publ. Co.*, 21 N.Y.2d 403, 406).

Here, the Appellate Division did not abuse its discretion in holding that Dr. Adesman's affidavit on which defendants' request was based was insufficient to justify compelling plaintiff-mother to take an IQ test. In his affidavit, Dr. Adesman stated that cognitive deficiencies are not unique to lead exposure, but may be attributed to other factors, including a child's genetic history. While Dr. Adesman indicated that he was familiar with scientific literature concerning the correlation between parental intelligence and a child's cognitive development, he failed to identify those studies or attach them to his affidavit. Thus, we are left with his conclusory statements that maternal IQ is "extremely relevant" without any indication of how he arrived at that conclusion. Certainly Dr. Adesman offered no evidence as to why maternal IQ was particularly relevant in the present case. Defendants' belated attempt to supplement Dr. Adesman's conclusions by attaching a compendium of scientific publications to their brief before this Court is impermissible. Defendants neither submitted these publications to Supreme Court, nor did they move to enlarge the record on appeal to include them. Consequently, these materials are not properly before this Court and cannot be considered (*see, Crawford v. Merrill Lynch, Pierce, Fenner & Smith*, 35 N.Y.2d 291, 298; *Johnson v. Equitable Life Assur. Socy.*, 16 N.Y.2d 1067, 1068-1069).

Upon reviewing the scientific basis for defendants' request, the Appellate Division was within its discretion in determining that the information sought was speculative and would delay the proceedings by "turning the fact-finding process into a series of mini-trials" regarding the factors contributing to the mother's IQ (*Andon v. 302-304 Mott St. Assocs., supra,* 257 A.D.2d, at 40-41). While open discovery is crucial to the search for truth, equally important is the need to avoid undue delay created by battling experts (*see, Allen v. Crowell-Collier Publ. Co., supra,* 21 N.Y.2d, at 406).

Finally, the Appellate Division was entitled to consider the burden imposed by an IQ examination and the personal nature of the information sought. Although New York's discovery provisions have been liberally construed to favor disclosure, "litigants are not without protection against [their] unnecessarily onerous application. 'Under our discovery statutes and case law, competing interests must always be balanced; the need for discovery must be weighed against any special burden to be borne by the opposing party'" (*Kavanagh v. Ogden Allied Maintenance Corp., supra,* 92 N.Y.2d, at 954, *quoting O'Neill v. Oakgrove Constr.,* 71 N.Y.2d 521, 529, *rearg denied* 72 N.Y.2d 910). Far from creating a blanket rule prohibiting discovery of maternal IQ, the Appellate Division evaluated defendants' request in the context of this case and in light of the evidence presented to it. The Appellate Division concluded that the burden of subjecting plaintiff-mother to an IQ test outweighed any relevance her IQ would bear on the issue of causation. The Court noted that the mother's mental condition is not in dispute and that IQ results, while not confidential, are private. Under these circumstances, we are satisfied that the Appellate Division did not abuse its discretion as a matter of law in denying defendants' discovery motion.

To the extent defendants rely on cases permitting discovery (*see, e.g., Anderson v. Seigel,* 255 A.D.2d 409; *Salkey v. Mott,* 237 A.D.2d 504), we emphasize that discovery determinations are discretionary; each request must be evaluated on a case-by-case basis with due regard for the strong policy supporting open disclosure (*see, Williams v. Roosevelt Hosp.,* 66 N.Y.2d 391, 397). Absent an abuse of discretion as a matter of law, this Court will not disturb such determinations.

Accordingly, the order of the Appellate Division should be affirmed, with costs, and the certified question answered in the affirmative.

NOTES

(1) The leading New York case on the scope of disclosure is *Allen v. Crowell-Collier Publishing Co.,* 21 N.Y.2d 403, 288 N.Y.S.2d 499, 235 N.E.2d 430 (1968), cited in the principal case. The Court of Appeals made it clear in *Allen* that disclosure in New York was far broader than one would gather from the precise language of CPLR 3101(a). It thus interpreted the word "necessary" in CPLR 3101 to mean "needful" and not indispensable. 21 N.Y.2d 407, 288 N.Y.S.2d 453. *Allen* held that plaintiffs, former employees of the defendant at its Springfield, Ohio plant, who were suing for severance pay and whose complaint alleged that defendant had a general policy of making such payments, were entitled to force the defendant to disclose information about its current and past practices

not only at its Springfield plant but elsewhere. Unlike the principal case, there was no claim by the objecting party in *Allen* that the discovery sought would be unduly burdensome.

(2) CPLR 3103(a) allows the court to grant protective orders "denying, limiting, conditioning or regulating the use of any disclosure device . . . to prevent unreasonable annoyance, expense, embarrassment, disadvantage, or other prejudice to any person or the court." When a disclosure request is objected to on one of these grounds, the courts generally evaluate the claimed burdensomeness in the light of the apparent usefulness to the propounder of the material sought, as was done in the principal case. *See, e.g., Morone v. Morone*, 85 A.D.2d 768, 445 N.Y.S.2d 605 (3d Dep't 1981) (tax returns held discoverable in palimony suit because they bore directly on the issue of whether parties had entered into an agreement exchanging domestic services for support).

(3) The burden can sometimes be moderated by tailoring the demand while still allowing effective discovery, as in *Mendelowitz v. Xerox Corp.*, 169 A.D.2d 300, 573 N.Y.S.2d 548 (1991). The case arose out of plaintiff's claim that exposure to asbestos from the defendant's copying machines caused him to become seriously ill. A major issue affecting liability concerned defendant's knowledge of the hazards of working around asbestos. Plaintiff served a notice of discovery demanding copies of any books, articles or other materials in defendant's library concerning that topic. The court held that the demand was too broad and required plaintiff to narrow it, or, in the alternative, to depose the librarian as to any pertinent materials in the library; or to serve a notice pursuant to CPLR 3120(a)(1)(ii) seeking inspection of the library for a reasonable period under appropriate safeguards. Also enforced by the court was a discovery demand for a list of employee health claims caused by asbestos in defendant's copying equipment and a demand for a list of other actions making similar claims.

The courts also set outside limits on the amount of disclosure burden any party can be made to bear. In *Cardona v. South Bend Lathe Co.*, 72 A.D.2d 758, 421 N.Y.S.2d 373 (2d Dep't 1979), for example, a set of interrogatories consisting of seventy questions "replete with sub parts" was held so obviously burdensome that the entire set was stricken with leave granted to the drafter to try again, but with less enthusiasm.

Note, too, that the court's broad authority to prevent abuse includes the power to shift the cost of compliance with a disclosure request to the party requesting it. *See, e.g., Ball v. State of New York*, 101 Misc. 2d 554, 421 N.Y.S.2d 328 (1982).

(4) Paragraph (i) was added to CPLR 3101 in 1993. It makes discoverable "any films, photographs, videotapes or audio tapes, including transcripts or memoranda thereof" of any party or agent of a party otherwise subject to disclosure. The Court of Appeals had previously held that surveillance tapes of a plaintiff in a personal injury action were protected by a conditional privilege and discoverable only on a showing of substantial need and hardship and also that plaintiff would not be entitled to the tapes until after he had been deposed.

DiMichel v. South Buffalo Ry. Co., 80 N.Y.2d 184, 590 N.Y.S.2d 1, 604 N.E.2d 63 (1992). Neither condition was included in paragraph (i), and the Court of Appeals ultimately ruled that this 1993 amendment governed, thus superseding the *DiMichel* holding. *Tran v. New Rochelle Hosp. Med. Ctr.*, 99 N.Y.2d 383, 756 N.Y.S.2d 509, 786 N.E.2d 444 (2003).

In *Zegarelli v. Hughes*, 3 N.Y.3d 64, 781 N.Y.S.2d 488, 814 N.E.2d 795 (2004), it was held that a copy of the tape would satisfy the disclosure demand as long as the original was available for inspection; and where the demanding party fails to seek inspection of the original he cannot complain at trial that the original has not been produced.

BERTOCCI v. FIAT MOTORS OF NORTH AMERICA, INC.
Appellate Division, First Department
76 A.D.2d 779, 429 N.Y.S.2d 1 (1980)

MEMORANDUM BY THE COURT.

. . . .

The action, predicated upon allegations of negligence and breach of warranty, seeks to recover damages resulting from the purchase by plaintiff of an alleged defective 1975 Fiat Model "128" vehicle. Following an inspection of Fiat's customer complaint files, plaintiff served his second set of interrogatories to elicit information as to the number of Fiat Model "128" vehicles sold in the United States for the model years 1974 through 1977, and the number of recommended replacement clutch cables, fuel pumps and timing belts for said models sold during that period of time. Special Term granted the motion for a protective order striking the interrogatories as irrelevant to the issues in dispute. We disagree. The inquiry, at least insofar as concerns the 1975 Fiat Model "128" vehicle, bears upon the central issue in dispute as to whether the vehicle and its component parts were defective. In products liability cases, disclosure has been permitted with respect to claims similar in nature to that asserted by plaintiff, whether such claims were made prior or subsequent to the claim advanced by plaintiff (*Johantgen v. Hobart Mfg. Co.*, 64 AD2d 858; *Carnibucci v. Marlin Firearms Co.*, 51 AD2d 1067; *Abrams v. Vaughan & Bushnell Mfg. Co.*, 37 AD2d 833; *Galieta v. Young Men's Christian Assn. of City of Schenectady*, 32 AD2d 711). Although these were personal injury actions, the principle is equally applicable to property damages cases. We conclude, however, from our review of the record that the interrogatories propounded are overly broad in seeking information pertaining to model years other than that purchased by plaintiff. There is neither allegation nor proof that the Fiat Model "128" vehicles for the model years 1974, 1976 and 1977 were identical or substantially similar to the 1975 model claimed to be defective, sufficient to sustain the expansive disclosure sought by plaintiff. Accordingly, we have limited the scope of the inquiry to the 1975 Fiat Model "128" vehicle (*see Savitsky v. General Motors Corp.*, 40 AD2d 1025).

NOTES

(1) In the *Savitsky* case, cited in the principal case, plaintiffs, whose suit concerned a 1965 vehicle, sought discovery of all documents relating to a different lawsuit concerning a 1961 vehicle settled in Federal court. The request was held to be too broad since nothing submitted showed any relevancy of the earlier litigation. Compare *Romain v. Schwartz*, 110 A.D.2d 694, 487 N.Y.S.2d 605 (2d Dep't 1985), holding that third-party defendant Chrysler Corporation, which manufactured the allegedly defective 1977 model Colt, was required to produce records relating to vehicles using fuel system construction similar to that of the subject vehicle for the years 1971-1977 (the years of manufacture for that model).

(2) Special rules regulate disclosure in particular types of cases:

(a) In shareholder derivative actions, a rule of case law protects individual defendants from depositions in the absence of special circumstances. *Condren v. Slater*, 85 A.D.2d 507, 508, 444 N.Y.S.2d 454, 455 (1st Dep't 1981). This is because of the "well-known potential for abuse and harassment in derivative actions, which are often brought by plaintiffs for reasons of their own and contrary to the best interests of the corporation they purport to represent." *Id.*

(b) Disclosure is also restricted in matrimonial actions, the general rule being that "examination with respect to the *grounds* upon which a divorce or separation is sought may not be permitted." *Billet v. Billet*, 53 A.D.2d 564, 384 N.Y.S.2d 826, 827 (1st Dep't 1976) (emphasis added). *See also Ginsberg v. Ginsberg*, 104 A.D.2d 482, 479 N.Y.S.2d 233 (2d Dep't 1984) (accord). The financial status of the parties is, contrariwise, broadly discoverable. *See* Domestic Relations Law § 236(B); 22 NYCRR 202.16.

(c) Journalists have an absolute privilege against disclosure of their news sources if they can show an express or implied agreement of confidentiality. N.Y. Civil Rights Law § 79-h(b); *Knight-Ridder Broadcasting v. Greenberg*, 70 N.Y.2d 151, 518 N.Y.S.2d 595, 511 N.E.2d 1116 (1987).

Moreover, a qualified privilege extends to non-confidential journalist's material by virtue of the state and federal constitutional guarantees of a free press. *O'Neill v. Oakgrove Construction, Inc.*, 71 N.Y.2d 521, 528 N.Y.S.2d 1, 523 N.E.2d 277 (1986). In the cited case, the plaintiff wanted copies of photos of an accident scene which had been taken by a non-party journalist but the newspaper refused to provide them and moved for a protective order. The Court, concerned about the burden on the press of repeated demands for resource materials, adopted a tripartite test to guide the decision of the lower court on remand:

. . . the [reporter's qualified] privilege bars coerced disclosure of resource materials, such as photographs, which are obtained or otherwise generated in the course of newsgathering or newspapering activities, unless the moving litigant satisfies a tripartite test which is more demanding than the requirements of CPLR 3101(a). Under the tripartite test, discovery may be ordered only if the litigant demonstrates, clearly and specifically, that the items sought are (1) highly material, (2) critical to the litigant's claim, and (3) not otherwise available.

In 1990, the Legislature enacted a measure which, in effect, codified the *O'Neill* case. N.Y. Civil Rights Law § 79-h(c).

HOLZMAN v. MANHATTAN AND BRONX SURFACE TRANSIT OPERATING AUTHORITY
Appellate Division, First Department
271 A.D.2d 346, 707 N.Y.S.2d 159 (2000)

Petitioner filed a timely notice of claim on June 15, 1999, alleging "negligence in the operation of a bus." He asserted that on May 20, 1999, between 8:30 and 8:35 A.M., as he was exiting from the rear doors of a southbound M15 bus, he "was caused to slip and violently fall resulting in personal injury." Notably, he did not give any more information as to the cause of his fall.

By order to show cause dated June 19, 1999, supported by counsel's affidavit and a copy of the notice of claim, petitioner moved pursuant to CPLR 3102(c) for pre-action discovery. Counsel's affidavit provided no further information as to the purported cause of the fall, merely reiterating that plaintiff "was caused to slip and violently fall, breaking his left ankle." The petition requested that petitioner be given an opportunity to inspect and photograph the bus before commencing the action, "in order to preserve any evidence of a defect which may have caused plaintiff's injuries." Respondents-appellants objected that petitioner had not even set forth a theory of liability, let alone a prima facie case, and was instead seeking pre-action discovery so as to tailor his complaint to fit whatever the inspection revealed. Nonetheless, the IAS Court granted the motion to the extent of directing respondents to identify the bus and produce it for inspection within 20 days after petitioner testified at the General Municipal Law 50-h hearing. We now reverse.

Under CPLR 3102(c), a plaintiff may petition the court to obtain discovery before service of a complaint. Pre-action discovery may be appropriate to preserve evidence or to identify potential defendants; however, it cannot be used by a prospective plaintiff to ascertain whether he has a cause of action at all (*Stump v. 209 E. 56th St. Corp.*, 212 A.D.2d 410). A petition for pre-action discovery should only be granted when the petitioner demonstrates that he has a meritorious cause of action and that the information sought is material and necessary to the actionable wrong (*Bliss v. Jaffin*, 176 A.D.2d 106, 108).

Petitioner has not met this burden, as he has failed to allege any facts supporting his bare claim that respondents were negligent and that this negligence caused his injury. A plaintiff cannot establish a prima facie case of negligence if he cannot explain what caused him to fall (*see, Lynn v. Lynn*, 216 A.D.2d 194). It also appears that petitioner has sufficient information to frame his complaint. He can identify the defendants, the bus route, and the time and place of the accident. Information concerning the extent of his injuries is presumably within his control. The notice of claim charged respondents with negligent operation of the bus. Inspection would reveal no facts relevant to this allegation. Under these circumstances, the only purpose of inspection would be to allow petitioner to determine whether the facts support alternate theories of liability, such as a defect in the bus. This is not an appropriate use of CPLR 3102(c) (*Matter of Manufacturers & Traders Trust Co. v. Bonner*, 84 A.D.2d 678, 679).

[A] Privileges — Attorney-Client Privilege; Attorney's Work Product; Material Prepared for Litigation

INTRODUCTORY NOTE

Subdivision (b) of CPLR 3101 provides that "Upon objection of a party privileged matter shall not be obtainable." The relevant evidentiary privileges (spousal, doctor-patient, etc.) are in CPLR article 45. But note that a plaintiff may not claim affirmative relief and at the same time refuse to disclose information bearing on the right to recover. *See Prink v. Rockefeller Center, Inc.*, 48 N.Y.2d 309, 422 N.Y.S.2d 911, 398 N.E.2d 517 (1979) (the plaintiff in a wrongful death action could not rely on the physician-patient or spousal privilege insofar as they would shield information indicating that decedent was a suicide). As to the waiver of privileges by a defendant, see *Dillenbeck v. Hess*, 73 N.Y.2d 278, 539 N.Y.S.2d 707, 536 N.E.2d 1126 (1989); § 15.04[F] *infra*.

PROBLEM B

(i) In the action described in Disclosure Problem A, Mr. Ruggles' attorney learns that Alice, defendant's general counsel, located a witness to the accident, interviewed the witness, and took verbatim notes of the interview. Suppose plaintiff wishes defendant to (1) disclose the name of witness; (2) provide a copy of the interview; and (3) reveal facts learned from the witness. Are any or all of these items protected from disclosure by CPLR 3101(b), (c) or (d)?

(ii) Suppose that, as soon as the accident was reported to defendant, Alice, following the corporate practice used whenever any such accident was reported, undertook an investigation and prepared a written report describing the facts as best as her investigation would allow. Is the report available to the Ruggles' attorney under CPLR 3101(g), or is it protected CPLR 3101(c), (d)(2) or by the attorney-client privilege?

SPECTRUM SYSTEMS v. CHEMICAL BANK
Court of Appeals
78 N.Y.2d 371, 575 N.Y.S.2d 809, 581 N.E.2d 1055 (1991)

KAYE, JUDGE.

In an action to recover fees for consulting services, Spectrum Systems International Corporation demanded that defendant, Chemical Bank, produce certain documents pertaining to the bank's internal investigation of possible fraud by employees and vendors, including Spectrum. Chemical responded by seeking a protective order, asserting that the documents were protected from disclosure by the attorney-client privilege, by the attorney work product doctrine, and as material prepared in anticipation of litigation. This appeal requires us to consider whether a report prepared by Chemical's specially retained outside counsel is privileged and therefore immune from discovery.

I

The facts are simply stated. Spectrum is a computer software consulting firm that provided services to Chemical Bank until the spring of 1987. According to the affidavit of a partner in the New York City law firm of Schulte Roth & Zabel, in June 1987 Chemical's general counsel retained the firm to perform an investigation and render legal advice to Chemical regarding possible fraud by its employees and outside vendors, and to counsel Chemical with respect to litigation options. According to the affidavits of Spectrum, Chemical's own investigation began even earlier. Over the next months, Schulte Roth conducted interviews of Chemical employees, of a former officer responsible for the bank's arrangements with Spectrum, and of representatives of Spectrum itself.

In a letter report dated August 20, 1987, signed by John S. Martin, Jr., then a partner, the law firm summarized the results of its investigation. After three pages of narrative regarding the central problem and the facts bearing on it, the final paragraph of the Spectrum section sets forth the law firm's opinion as to a possible claim against Spectrum, an estimate of Chemical's damages, a potential weakness if such a claim were to be asserted, and the firm's view that there was insufficient proof to establish particular matters described in the letter. The report was addressed to Chemical's vice-chairman — the company's senior legal officer — with copies to Chemical's general counsel and senior auditor.

Spectrum commenced the present action in October 1988, seeking $33,600 in fees, and Chemical counterclaimed for damages of at least $100,000 on the ground that Spectrum had falsified invoices and overcharged the bank.

After the close of pleadings, and before any other discovery, Spectrum demanded that Chemical turn over "[a] report and/or notes or written documents of investigation conducted by or on behalf of Chemical Bank of the business relationship between Chemical Bank and vendors." Spectrum's president had been told of the investigation by Chemical's former employee, and had himself been questioned in July 1987 by a Chemical investigator and again in August by the law firm, where he appeared with his counsel. Apparently, the Chemical investigator made a memorandum regarding his conversation with Spectrum's president, as did a Schulte Roth attorney of the later interview.

In response to Chemical's motion for a protective order, Supreme Court — without examining the documents — ordered them produced, holding that "an independent investigation cannot obtain privileged status merely because it may have been communicated to an attorney." The court subsequently denied Chemical's motion for reargument or for an in camera inspection of the documents in issue.

While agreeing that Chemical's motion for a protective order should be denied — the documents were not privileged, work product or material prepared in anticipation of litigation — the Appellate Division, having itself reviewed the documents, modified Supreme Court's orders and granted Chemical's alternative request for remittal for an in camera inspection to determine materiality and necessity (CPLR 3101[a]). The Appellate Division, further, granted leave to appeal to this Court, certifying the following question: "Was the order of this Court, which modified the orders of the Supreme Court, properly made?"

We now answer the certified question in the negative, concluding that the Appellate Division erred in denying Chemical's claim of privilege with respect to the Spectrum section of the Schulte Roth report — the only portion of the report in issue on this appeal.

II

The CPLR directs that there shall be "full disclosure of all evidence material and necessary in the prosecution or defense of an action." (CPLR 3101[a].) "The test is one of usefulness and reason." (*Allen v. Crowell-Collier Publ. Co.*, 21 N.Y.2d 403, 406, 288 N.Y.S.2d 449, 235 N.E.2d 430.) This statute embodies the policy determination that liberal discovery encourages fair and effective resolution of disputes on the merits, minimizing the possibility for ambush and unfair surprise (*see*, 3A Weinstein-Korn-Miller, N.Y. Civ. Prac. ¶¶ 3101.01-3101.03).

By the same token, the CPLR establishes three categories of protected materials, also supported by policy considerations: privileged matter, absolutely immune from discovery (CPLR 3101[b]); attorney's work product, also absolutely immune (CPLR 3101[c]); and trial preparation materials, which are subject to disclosure only on a showing of substantial need and undue hardship in obtaining the substantial equivalent of the materials by other means (CPLR 3101[d][2]).

Obvious tension exists between the policy favoring full disclosure and the policy permitting parties to withhold relevant evidence. Consequently, the burden of establishing any right to protection is on the party asserting it; the protection claimed must be narrowly construed; and its application must be consistent with the purposes underlying the immunity (*Matter of Priest v. Hennessy*, 51 N.Y.2d 62, 69, 431 N.Y.S.2d 511, 409 N.E.2d 983; *Matter of Jacqueline F.*, 47 N.Y.2d 215, 218-219, 417 N.Y.S.2d 884, 391 N.E.2d 967; *Koump v. Smith*, 25 N.Y.2d 287, 294, 303 N.Y.S.2d 858, 250 N.E.2d 857; *see generally*, Note, *The Attorney-Client Privilege and the Corporate Client: Where Do We Go After Upjohn?*, 81 Mich. L. Rev. 665 [1983]).

Against this backdrop, we consider Chemical's claims for a protective order.

III

The attorney-client privilege, the oldest among common-law evidentiary privileges (8 Wigmore, Evidence § 2290 [McNaughton rev. 1961]; *Upjohn Co. v. United States*, 449 U.S. 383, 389, 101 S.Ct. 677, 682, 66 L.Ed.2d 584), fosters the open dialogue between lawyer and client that is deemed essential to effective representation (*see, Matter of Vanderbilt [Rosner-Hickey]*, 57 N.Y.2d 66, 76, 453 N.Y.S.2d 662, 439 N.E.2d 378; *Matter of Priest v. Hennessy*, 51 N.Y.2d 62, 67-68, 431 N.Y.S.2d 511, 409 N.E.2d 983, *supra*).

A century ago this Court referred to the attorney-client privilege statute as a "mere re-enactment of the common-law rule" (*Hurlburt v. Hurlburt*, 128 N.Y. 420, 424, 28 N.E. 651); reliance on the common law continues to this day. CPLR 4503(a) states that a privilege exists for confidential communications made between attorney and client in the course of professional employment, and CPLR 3101(b) vests privileged matter with absolute immunity. For definition of what is encompassed by the privilege, courts still must look to the common law (*see*, Siegel, Practice Commentaries, McKinney's Cons. Laws of N.Y., Book 7B, CPLR C3101:25, at 37).

Although typically arising in the context of a client's communication to an attorney, the privilege extends as well to communications from attorney to client. The privilege is of course limited to communications — not underlying facts (*Upjohn Co. v. United States*, 449 U.S., at 395-396, 101 S.Ct., at 685-686, *supra*). In order for the privilege to apply, the communication from attorney to client must be made "for the purpose of facilitating the rendition of legal advice or services, in the course of a professional relationship." (*Rossi v. Blue Cross & Blue Shield*, 73 N.Y.2d 588, 593, 542 N.Y.S.2d 508, 540 N.E.2d 703.) The communication itself must be primarily or predominantly of a legal character (*id.*, at 594, 542 N.Y.S.2d 508, 540 N.E.2d 703).

As is plain from mere statement of the principles, whether a particular document is or is not protected is necessarily a fact-specific determination (*Rossi v. Blue Cross & Blue Shield*, 73 N.Y.2d, at 592-593, 542 N.Y.S.2d 508, 540 N.E.2d 703, *supra*), most often requiring in camera review.

Here, Spectrum does not challenge the confidential nature of the Schulte Roth report. Moreover, it is uncontested that the law firm was specially retained as outside counsel for the purpose of conducting an internal investigation into possible fraud on Chemical and rendering legal advice about that problem, including counseling about litigation options. Clearly the requisite professional relationship was established when Chemical retained the law firm to render legal assistance (*Radiant Burners v. American Gas Assn.*, 320 F.2d 314 (7th Cir.), *cert. denied*, 375 U.S. 929, 84 S.Ct. 330, 11 L.Ed.2d 262).

The report itself, after presenting facts, sets forth the firm's assessment regarding a possible legal claim, its approximate size and weaknesses. As a confidential report from lawyer to client transmitted in the course of professional employment and conveying the lawyer's assessment of the client's legal position, the document has the earmarks of a privileged communication.

The arguments against privilege in this case center on Schulte Roth's conceded investigative function, which led the Appellate Division to conclude that the report and other documents were not clearly communicated by counsel in the role of attorneys rendering legal advice. In the Appellate Division's view, the report was aimed at assisting Chemical in its business operations, as by suggesting measures to prevent future corruption and terminate or discipline implicated employees. We disagree.

That nonprivileged information is included in an otherwise privileged lawyer's communication to its client — while influencing whether the document would be protected in whole or only in part — does not destroy the immunity. In transmitting legal advice and furnishing legal services it will often be necessary for a lawyer to refer to nonprivileged matter (*see*, Code of Professional Responsibility EC 4-1 [lawyer should be fully informed of all facts]).

As we made clear in *Rossi*, the privilege is not narrowly confined to the repetition of confidences that were supplied to the lawyer by the client (*compare, Mead Data Cent. v. United States Dept. of Air Force*, 566 F.2d 242, 254 [D.C.Cir.]). That cramped view of the attorney-client privilege is at odds with the underlying policy of encouraging open communication; it poses inordinate practical difficulties in making surgical separations so as not to risk revealing client confidences; and it denies that an attorney can have any role in fact-gathering incident to the rendition of legal advice and services (*see, In re LTV Sec. Litig.*, 89 F.R.D. 595, 602 (Tex.); Wolfram, Modern Legal Ethics § 6.3.5 [Prac. ed.]). The memorandum in *Rossi* included the lawyer's conversations with plaintiff's counsel and with third parties as well as the lawyer's opinion and advice. Yet we determined, from reviewing the full content and context of the communication, that its purpose was to convey legal advice to the client, and we held the entire document exempt from discovery. We reach that same conclusion here.

Both Supreme Court and the Appellate Division were properly concerned that the attorney-client privilege not be used as a device to shield discoverable information. As they correctly observed, an investigative report does not become privileged merely because it was sent to an attorney. Nor is such a report privileged merely because an investigation was conducted by an attorney; a lawyer's communication is not cloaked with privilege when the lawyer is hired for business or personal advice, or to do the work of a nonlawyer (*People v. Belge*, 59 A.D.2d 307, 308-309, 399 N.Y.S.2d 539). Yet it is also the case that, while information received from third persons may not itself be privileged (*see, Kenford Co. v. County of Erie*, 55 A.D.2d 466, 390 N.Y.S.2d 715), a lawyer's communication to a client that includes such information in its legal analysis and advice may stand on different footing. The critical inquiry is whether, viewing the lawyer's communication in its full content and context, it was made in order to render legal advice or services to the client.

Here we conclude that facts were selected and presented in the Schulte Roth report as the foundation for the law firm's legal advice, and that the communication was primarily and predominantly of a legal character. We reach this conclusion both from our review of the document and from the undisputed facts in the record. While a court is not bound by the conclusory characterizations of client or counsel that the retention was for the purpose of rendering legal advice, here there is no reason to disregard the sworn statements describing the engagement as one for legal not business advice, which is evident in the report itself. The report offers no recommendations for desirable future business procedures or corruption prevention measures, or employee discipline — indeed, it reflects that the individuals involved in the challenged practices were no longer working for Chemical. Rather, the narration relates and integrates the facts with the law firm's assessment of the client's legal position, and evidences the lawyer's motivation to convey legal advice.

The Appellate Division, in rejecting Chemical's claim of privilege, additionally relied on the fact that the Schulte Roth report did not focus on any imminent litigation, that the report reflected no legal research, and that no conclusion was reached with regard to the parties' legal position. None of these factors changes the privileged character of the document.

The prospect of litigation may be relevant to the subject of work product and trial preparation materials, but the attorney-client privilege is not tied to the contemplation of litigation (*see, Root v. Wright*, 84 N.Y. 72, 76; *Bacon v. Frisbie*, 80 N.Y. 394, 400). Legal advice is often sought, and rendered, precisely to avoid litigation, or facilitate compliance with the law, or simply to guide a client's course of conduct. Proximity to litigation — as was the case in *Rossi* — may itself reveal that the motive in a lawyer's communication was to give legal advice, but the absence of pending or prospective litigation does not otherwise bear on the privilege analysis.

That the Schulte Roth report was inconclusive, looking toward future discussion, is also without significance. Legal advice often begins — and may end — with a preliminary evaluation and a range of options. More than that may not be possible upon an initial investigation (*see, State ex rel. Great Am. Ins. Co. v. Smith*, 574 S.W.2d 379, 385 [Mo.]). Similarly, the absence of legal research in an attorney's communication is not determinative of privilege, so long as the communication reflects the attorney's professional skills and judgments. Legal advice may be grounded in experience as well as research.

Finally, we have several times noted that the privilege may give way to strong public policy considerations (*see, Matter of Priest v. Hennessy*, 51 N.Y.2d, at 67-68, 431 N.Y.S.2d 511, 409 N.E.2d 983, *supra*). Surely this is not such an instance. Spectrum urges that disclosure would best serve the public interest, but Chemical underscores that it does not seek to deny disclosure of facts gathered during the Schulte Roth investigation, only of its attorney's expression of legal advice drawn on those facts. Spectrum has no right whatever to the production of this privileged communication, least of all on extraordinary public policy grounds.

Chemical argues, alternatively, that the Schulte Roth report is absolutely protected as attorney's work product, in that it reflects its lawyer's mental impressions and legal analysis (*see, e.g., Hoffman v. Ro-San Manor*, 73 A.D.2d 207, 211, 425 N.Y.S.2d 619). Whether or not privileged, a record may qualify in whole or in part as attorney work product, or even trial preparation materials. Our conclusion that the Schulte Roth report is privileged makes further inquiry along those lines unnecessary.

IV

The Appellate Division further held that the disputed documents are not protected as work product or trial preparation materials, conclusions Chemical challenges.

We note, however, that no document other than the Schulte Roth report has been put before the Court, or described with any particularity, or analyzed by the parties in their argument to us. Chemical's affidavits speak of memoranda of conversations with Spectrum's president, its briefs mention unspecified investigative records, and the Appellate Division refers to Chemical documents labeled "Attorney Work Product." A party's own labels are obviously not determinative of work product, and the generalized descriptions — lacking identification of persons, time periods and circumstances — do not convey the information and analysis necessary to decide whether a particular document should be immunized from disclosure under CPLR 3101(c) or (d). Chemical's offer to deliver the remaining documents for our in camera review obviously does not fill this gap.

Determining document immunity claims, and reviewing them, are largely fact-specific processes (*see, e.g., Rossi v. Blue Cross & Blue Shield*, 73 N.Y.2d 588, 542 N.Y.S.2d 508, 540 N.E.2d 703, *supra*; *Matter of Grand Jury Subpoena* [*Bekins Record Stor. Co.*], 62 N.Y.2d 324, 476 N.Y.S.2d 806, 465 N.E.2d 345). Indeed, we join in the observation of the Appellate Division that it would have been better practice for the trial court in this case, when first considering Chemical's motion, to have conducted an in camera review "to have allowed for a more informed determination as to whether the information was indeed protected from disclosure" on any of the grounds alleged. (157 A.D.2d 444, 447, 558 N.Y.S.2d 486.) The present record, similarly, leaves us with inadequate basis for determining whether the Appellate Division correctly concluded that Chemical's remaining documents were neither attorney's work product nor trial preparation materials. We therefore do not reach these issues, or the additional arguments propounded by the parties and *amici curiae* regarding CPLR 3101(c) and (d).

Accordingly, the order of the Appellate Division should be modified, with costs to defendant, in accordance with this opinion and, as so modified, affirmed. The certified question should be answered in the negative.

WACHTLER, C.J., and SIMONS, ALEXANDER, TITONE, HANCOCK and BELLACOSA, JJ., concur.

Order modified, etc.

. . . .

NOTES

(1) The problem in *Rossi v. Blue Cross and Blue Shield of Greater New York*, 73 N.Y.2d 588, 542 N.Y.S.2d 508, 540 N.E.2d 703 (1989), involved a memorandum from a corporate staff attorney to a corporate officer regarding a company form and its implication in an imminent defamation action. The contents of the memorandum were held to have involved legal advice, and the attorney-client privilege obtained even though the attorney was part of the client's staff.

(2) The ambit of the attorney-client privilege, as applied in the federal courts, was broadened substantially in *Upjohn Co. v. United States*, 449 U.S. 383, 101 S. Ct. 677 (1981), which held that the communication of any employee of a corporation to the attorney for the corporation could be protected by the privilege. The Supreme Court thus rejected the argument that only communications by members of the corporation's "control group" to corporate counsel would be protected. *See* Sexton, *A Post-*Upjohn *Consideration of Corporate Attorney-Client Privilege*, 57 N.Y.U. L. Rev. 443 (1982). In the principal case, were the communications at issue between the attorney and the control group of Blue Cross or does the Court of Appeals also implicitly reject the control group test?

In *D'Alessio v. Gilberg*, 205 A.D.2d 8, 617 N.Y.S.2d 484 (2d Dep't 1994), a prospective plaintiff claimed that attorney Gilberg had information as to the identity of the unknown driver of the hit and run car that had killed her father. She sought preaction disclosure pursuant to CPLR 3102(c), and the IAS court, over Gilbert's claim of attorney-client privilege, granted the motion. The Appellate Division reversed, seeing this as a situation where a client reported an already completed crime to the lawyer, a communication traditionally protected.

(3) The attorney-client privilege is not absolute in New York but may be pierced where strong public policy interests require disclosure. In *Matter of*

Jacqueline F., 47 N.Y.2d 215, 417 N.Y.S.2d 884, 391 N.E.2d 967 (1979), the Court directed disclosure by the attorney of the client's address. The client was the aunt of the subject infant and was hiding the child in violation of a judicial decree ordering return of the child to her natural parents.

(4) The privilege may be waived by the client, but it has been held, in a case rejecting the traditional view, that the waiver must be intentional to be effective. *Manufacturers and Traders Trust Co. v. Servotronics, Inc.*, 132 A.D.2d 392, 522 N.Y.S.2d 999 (4th Dep't 1987). The problem arose in the subject case because a paralegal inadvertently included six privileged documents in several box-loads of other papers turned over to the plaintiff.

(5) In *Niesig v. Team I*, 76 N.Y.2d 363, 559 N.Y.S.2d 493, 558 N.E.2d 1030 (1990), the Court interpreted Disciplinary Rule 7-104(A)(1) of the Code of Professional Responsibility to prohibit counsel from interviewing certain current employees of an adversary corporation in an accident case. These employees had the status of parties just as surely as did the corporation's officers. The "party" employee was defined as including those whose acts or omissions in the matter at issue are binding on the corporation, or imputed to the corporation for liability purposes, and also employees implementing the advice of counsel. All other employees could be informally interviewed.

HOFFMAN v. RO-SAN MANOR
Appellate Division, First Department
73 A.D.2d 207, 425 N.Y.S.2d 619 (1980)

SULLIVAN, JUSTICE.

[Plaintiff, an apartment house tenant, was assaulted and robbed in the building by a person who had obtained unauthorized access. She brought this action against the landlord, alleging that it had negligently failed to secure the premises. — Eds.]

The sole issue presented is whether a party in a negligence action is entitled to disclosure of the names and addresses of witnesses other than eyewitnesses to the accident. In keeping with the trend towards greater liberality of disclosure, we hold that the names and addresses of potential witnesses who can testify to notice and the condition of which plaintiff complains are also discoverable.

. . . .

Defendant served a notice to produce names and addresses of witnesses, calling for identification of witnesses to:

(a) The occurrence alleged in the complaint; or

(b) Any acts, omissions or conditions which allegedly caused the occurrence alleged in the complaint; or

(c) Any actual notice allegedly given to the defendants answering herein of any condition which allegedly caused the occurrence alleged in the complaint; or

(d) The nature and duration of any alleged condition which allegedly caused the occurrence alleged in the complaint.

Plaintiff responded by stating that she was unaware of the existence of any witnesses to the crimes or of any person who saw the doorman allow the unidentified third person into the premises, but that if her investigation revealed such a person defendants would be notified. Plaintiff refused to comply with the requests made in paragraphs (b), (c) and (d) on the ground that defendants were entitled to the names and addresses of witnesses to the actual incident, but not to the names and addresses of all witnesses who might ultimately testify at trial.

Subsequently, defendants moved for an order compelling plaintiff to make a proper response to the notice to produce. Special Term denied the motion and this appeal followed.

Prior to the enactment of the Civil Practice Law and Rules requests for disclosure of the names of possible witnesses, whether by discovery or examination before trial, had generally been denied. An exception was recognized if a witness was also an active participant, in which event his name and address were discoverable. The rationale for this exception was that the witness was "so closely related to the accident that his testimony [became] essential in establishing the happening of the accident." (*O'Dea v. City of Albany*, 27 A.D.2d 11, 12-13, 275 N.Y.S.2d 687, 689.)

The enactment in 1962 of the Civil Practice Law and Rules foreshadowed an even greater access to discovery of the names and addresses of witnesses:

There shall be full disclosure of all evidence material and necessary in the prosecution or defense of an action, regardless of the burden of proof. . . . (CPLR 3101[a].)

Such disclosure is subject to the protections afforded within CPLR 3101 to privileged matter (subd. [b]), attorney's work product (subd. [c]), and material prepared for litigation (subd. [d]). The trend since has been, however, toward a more expansive application. (*See* 3A Weinstein-Korn-Miller, New York Civil Practice, § 3101.11.)

In determining whether names of witnesses to an event were discoverable, this Court in *Rios v. Donovan*, 21 A.D.2d 409, 250 N.Y.S.2d 818 noted the trend toward greater disclosure and held that "the proper procedure would be to make inquiry as to the persons present at the time of the accident during the course of taking the oral depositions of the party or a witness pursuant to 3107 Civil Practice Law and Rules. . . ." (*Id.* at 414-15, 250 N.Y.S.2d at 823.) Eventually, this view was adopted by the Second Department, which decided that "the names of eyewitnesses to the occurrence, even if obtained by investigation made after the occurrence, are discoverable if they are material and necessary to the prosecution or defense of the action." (*Zellman v. Metropolitan Transp. Auth.*, 40 A.D.2d 248, 251, 339 N.Y.S.2d 255, 258.)

Inevitably, the courts were confronted with the discoverability of the identity of witnesses other than eyewitnesses to the accident. . . . To date the issue has not arisen in this Court.

Plaintiff challenges neither the materiality nor the necessity of production of the names sought. Instead she relies on the exemptions contained in the statute, claiming that the information is protected as either attorney's work product (CPLR 3101[c]) or material prepared for litigation (CPLR 3101[d]). Consequently, we must determine only whether the names are protected, for "if the information sought is in fact privileged, it is not subject to disclosure no matter how strong the showing of need or relevancy." (*Cirale v. 80 Pine St. Corp.*, 35 N.Y.2d 113, 117, 359 N.Y.S.2d 1, 4, 316 N.E.2d 301, 303, *citing* CPLR 3101, subd. [b]; . . . .) If materiality and necessity were also contested, we would, however, conclude that the names of witnesses are essential to a judicious resolution of this controversy.

Plaintiff apparently confuses work product with material prepared for litigation. Under CPLR 3101 they are not synonymous. The immunity which attaches to work product under subdivision (c) is absolute, while the immunity conferred on litigation material under subdivision (d) is conditional.

The discovery of witnesses, even though the result of the attorney's zeal and investigative efforts, does not qualify as an attorney's work product under subdivision (c).[2] Not every manifestation of a lawyer's labors enjoys the absolute immunity of work product. The exemption should be limited to those materials which are uniquely the product of a lawyer's learning and professional skills, such as materials which reflect his legal research, analysis, conclusions, legal theory or strategy. (*See* Richardson on Evidence, 10 Ed., § 422, *citing* Weinstein-Korn-Miller, New York Civil Practice, Vol. 3, §§ 3101.42-3101.55.)

Nor do we believe that the names and addresses of witnesses qualify as material prepared for litigation. Of the items exempted from disclosure by CPLR 3101[d] only "anything created by or for a party or his agent in preparation for litigation"* could arguably apply to the information sought here. The existence of a witness to an event, or to conditions bearing upon an event, is independent of and precedes any work done by an attorney. A witness and such incidentals as his address, as well as his knowledge, are not the creation of a party "in preparation for litigation," although the unearthing of the witness may well be the product of an attorney's labors. But the methods by which an attorney ascertains the witness' existence and whereabouts are neither the subject

---

[2] Precisely because the exemption of CPLR 3101[c] is absolute we do not view the revelation of witnesses' identities as an exception to the rule against discovery of work product. . . .

* CPLR 3101(d) was revised in 1985. Protection of material "prepared in anticipation of litigation or for trial" is now found in CPLR 3101(d)(2). — Eds.

of exemption as material prepared for litigation, nor, as already noted, an attorney's work product.

Fairness dictates that the identity of an individual who is to testify be discoverable by the opposing party. The search for truth is better served when the fullest possible range of disclosure is provided. Revealing the names of witnesses would not violate "the general policy against invading the privacy of an attorney's course of preparation." (*Hickman v. Taylor*, 329 U.S. 495, 512, 67 S.Ct. 385, 394, 91 L.Ed. 451.)

Accordingly, the order, Supreme Court, New York County, entered June 11, 1979, denying defendants' motion to direct plaintiff to respond to the demand for the names and addresses of witnesses, should be reversed, on the law, without costs or disbursements, and the motion granted. . . .

NOTES

(1) In *Kenford Co. v. County of Erie*, 55 A.D.2d 466, 390 N.Y.S.2d 715 (4th Dep't 1977), an officer of the defendant county refused to answer some of the questions put to him during a deposition on the ground that his exclusive knowledge of the facts came through his attorneys, who had learned them through investigative efforts. He argued that these facts were protected from disclosure both by the attorney-client privilege and as the work product of his attorneys. The court rejected both claims:

> It has long been settled that information received by the attorney from other persons and sources while acting on behalf of a client does not come within the attorney-client privilege. . . . Neither can the term "attorney's work product" serve as a talisman to bar all further inquiry respecting the factual underpinnings of the sometimes vague allegations in this counterclaim. In light of the narrow scope afforded section 3101(c), it is clear that information and material which would otherwise be discoverable under section 3101(a) cannot be shielded from discovery merely because the client has obtained his knowledge through his lawyer's investigative efforts.

> Because it affords an unqualified privilege, the commentators agree that the ambit of CPLR 3101(c) is to be construed narrowly to include only those materials prepared by an attorney which contain his analysis and trial strategy. . . . The Supreme Court has held that the phrase "work product" embraces such items as "interviews, statements, memoranda, correspondence, briefs, mental impressions, personal beliefs" conducted, prepared or held by the attorney (*Hickman v. Taylor*, 329 U.S. 495, 511, 67 S.Ct. 385, 91 L.Ed. 451). While not binding on them, New York Courts have accepted the definition of work product set forth in *Hickman* in determining the scope of subsection (c) (*see, e.g.*, 3A Weinstein-Korn-Miller, *supra* at para. 3101.-44,.47; . . .). Further, in

Hickman the Supreme Court commented that "A party clearly cannot refuse to answer interrogatories on the ground that the information sought is solely within the knowledge of his attorney."

55 A.D.2d at 469-70, 390 N.Y.S.2d at 718-19.

(2) Statements taken by an attorney from the employees of a corporate client have been held protected from disclosure by the work product rule of CPLR 3101(c). *Cornell Mfg. Co., Inc. v. Mushlin*, 85 A.D.2d 592, 444 N.Y.S.2d 709 (1981). Suppose statements are obtained by an investigator employed by a lawyer? Though the statements might be material prepared for litigation, CPLR 3101(d), they could not be an attorney's work product. *See Brunswick Corp. v. Aetna Cas. & Sur. Co.*, 27 A.D.2d 182, 278 N.Y.S.2d 459 (4th Dep't 1967). Might they be within the attorney-client privilege? *See* CPLR 4503.

(3) Where plaintiff, alleging injury at defendant's cardiac rehabilitation center, sought disclosure of other patients present at the time of the accident, the court, in ruling against plaintiff, held that this would reveal that the witnesses were present for cardiac treatment and thus breach their privacy and physician-patient privileges. *Gunn v. Sound Shore Medical Center*, 5 A.D.3d 435, 772 N.Y.S.2d 714 (2d Dep't 2004).

MIRANDA v. BLAIR TOOL & MACHINE CORP.
Appellate Division, Second Department
114 A.D.2d 941, 495 N.Y.S.2d 208 (1985)

Plaintiff, an employee of respondent Osrow Products, Inc. (hereinafter Osrow), seeks to recover damages for personal injuries allegedly sustained while operating a shredding machine owned by Osrow and manufactured by defendant Blair Tool & Machine Corp. She commenced this action against Blair and Blair commenced a third-party action against Osrow. The accident was witnessed by plaintiff's supervisor, who subsequently made an oral statement concerning the accident to a group consisting of the president of Osrow, the president of Blair and an unidentified lawyer who may have been employed by a private investigation firm. The statement was recorded and a written transcript was subsequently made. The supervisor was unable to read parts of the transcript because he had difficulty in reading English, and Osrow indicated in a letter to the investigator that it contained certain "discrepancies" due to the supervisor's alleged inability to understand all the questions. Plaintiff sought disclosure of this transcript as an accident report and Osrow moved for a protective order, contending that it was not discoverable because it was inaccurate and was in any event exempt because it was made in preparation for litigation. Special Term granted Osrow's motion for a protective order and denied as moot plaintiff's cross motion to compel disclosure. There must be a reversal.

CPLR 3101(g) provides for the disclosure of "any written report of an accident prepared in the regular course of business," other than a report in a criminal investigation. CPLR 3101(d) conditionally exempts from disclosure anything prepared for purposes of litigation. Taken together, the effect of the two subdivisions is to authorize disclosure of an accident report made in the regular course of business even if it is made solely for purposes of litigation (*Pataki v Kiseda*, 80 AD2d 100, *lv dismissed* 54 NY2d 831; *Matos v Akram & Jamal Meat Corp.*, 99 AD2d 527; *Viruet v City of New York*, 97 AD2d 435). It is only when an accident report has not been made in the regular course of business that it may be conditionally exempt if it is made solely for purposes of litigation (*see, e.g., Matter of Goldstein v New York Daily News*, 106 AD2d 323, 324). Moreover, the burden of proving that an accident report is exempt because it was not prepared in the regular course of business and that it was made solely for purposes of litigation is on the party seeking to prevent disclosure (*Motos v Akram & Jamal Meat Corp., supra*, at p 528; *Viruet v City of New York, supra*, at p 436).

In the instant case, the record contains no proof that the supervisor's oral statement, which was reduced to writing, was not made in the regular course of Osrow's business and was made solely for purposes of litigation. The conclusory statement to this effect contained in an attorney's affirmation was not based on personal knowledge and does not suffice to meet Osrow's burden of proof that the transcript is exempt from disclosure. . . .

Nor is the claim that the transcript may contain certain inaccuracies or inconsistencies sufficient reason to prevent disclosure. Disclosure is not limited to material which may be admissible as evidence-in-chief, and is thus not governed by normal evidentiary rules. . . . Here, although inaccuracies and inconsistencies may limit the usefulness of the transcript, it may reasonably be expected to aid counsel in investigating the accident and preparing for cross-examination of the supervisor. As such, it is discoverable.

NOTES

(1) The conflict between CPLR 3101(d)(2) and CPLR 3101(g) has led to frequent litigation over the availability of accident reports since the adoption of subdivision (g) in 1980. The (sparse) legislative history is discussed in *Pataki v. Kiseda*, 80 A.D.2d 100, 437 N.Y.S.2d (2d Dep't 1980). The principal case, applying the general rule, protects accident reports prepared solely for litigation if not made in the "regular course of business." When is an accident report not prepared in the regular course of business?

In *Goldstein v. New York Daily News*, 106 A.D.2d 323, 482 N.Y.S.2d 768 (1st Dep't 1984), the court held protected a report of an accident involving an employee of the defendant which had been prepared by the defendant's Manager of Safety and Loss Prevention upon instructions from its attorneys. The title page of the report stated that it was prepared in anticipation of litigation.

(2) Reports prepared by liability and casualty insurance companies are often sought through disclosure. When would such reports be prepared other than in

the regular course of business? *See Landmark Ins. Co. v. Beau Rivage Restaurant, Inc.*, 121 A.D.2d 98, 509 N.Y.S.2d 819 (2d Dep't 1986). Adopting the approach taken by the First and Fourth Departments, the court there held that only a report prepared by a casualty insurer after the insurer had made a firm decision to reject the claim in question would qualify for conditional immunity under CPLR 3101(d)(2).

The Second Department, however, also held, in *Vernet v. Gilbert*, 90 A.D.2d 846, 456 N.Y.S.2d 93 (2d Dep't 1982), that a report of an accident to a liability insurer is conditionally exempt from disclosure under subdivision (d) of CPLR 3101 (notwithstanding subdivision (g)) and is thus distinguishable from accident reports "which result from the regular internal operations of any enterprise. . . ." Do you see a distinction?

[B] Privileges — Experts

PROBLEM C

Alice learns that after the accident plaintiff's attorney, Phil, retained a safety expert to examine the ladder and write a report on whether mechanical failures contributed to the accident.

(a) May Alice obtain a copy of the report?

(b) May she require Phil to reveal the name of the expert?

(c) If she does learn the expert's name, may she retain him to write a similar report for the defendant?

(d) May she require Phil to state whether the expert will be called to testify at trial?

(e) May she require the expert to appear for a deposition?

SAAR v. BROWN AND ODABASHIAN, P.C.
Supreme Court, Rensselaer County
139 Misc. 2d 328, 527 N.Y.S.2d 685 (1988)

WILLIAM H. KENIRY, J.

[Plaintiff's decedent died of a heart attack. The plaintiff alleges that the death could have been prevented by by-pass surgery but that the surgery was delayed because of defendants' negligent handling of vital records. — Eds.]

In this medical malpractice action, the court is presented with a discovery issue with important ramifications arising out of the Legislature's amendments to CPLR 3101(d) which were part of the Medical Malpractice Insurance Comprehensive Reform Act enacted in 1985 (L 1985, ch 294, § 25). The plaintiff has served a notice for discovery and inspection upon the defendants Albany Medical Center and Harry C. Odabashian, Jr., which seeks, in pertinent part, the following information:

> Identify each person whom the defendant(s) expects to call as an expert witness at trial and with respect to each expert, disclose in reasonable detail the subject matter on which each expert is expected to testify, the substance of the facts and opinions on which each expert is expected to testify, the qualifications of each expert witness and a summary of the grounds for each expert's opinion.

In a supplemental response thereto, the defendant Albany Medical Center has stated as follows: "Defendant's expert is a graduate of Freien Berlin University, he is board certified in internal medicine and specializes in cardiovascular diseases. He will testify based on the medical record and the depositions that plaintiff had a clinically stable angina and that bypass surgery was an elective procedure. He will further testify that the patient did not require urgent or immediate surgery. He will further testify that all actions taken on behalf of the defendant Albany Medical Center Hospital were reasonable and that there was no malpractice on their part."

The defendant Odabashian responded to the plaintiff's demand that: "Defendant is unable to state, at this time, which expert witness it intends to call at trial, but will make such information available prior to the time of trial."

Plaintiff now moves for an order, pursuant to CPLR 3126, prohibiting the defendants Albany Medical Center and Dr. Odabashian from introducing any expert testimony or other expert proof at trial based upon their failure to meaningfully and properly respond to the plaintiff's demands for expert witness information. In addition, the plaintiff seeks a preclusion order against Dr. Odabashian based upon his failure to adequately respond to the plaintiff's demand for a bill of particulars seeking a specification of the acts of contributory negligence and culpable conduct on the part of the plaintiff's decedent, Elmer Hernits.

. . . .

Since its amendment, CPLR 3101(d)(1) has been scrutinized in a number of reported decisions (*Olden v Bolton*, 137 AD2d 878 [preclusion of testimony of expert witness upheld based upon failure to timely disclose]; *Travis v Wormer*, 136 AD2d 933 [plaintiff must disclose identity of medical expert to defendant drug manufacturer sued in strict products liability and breach of warranty notwithstanding other pending claim of medical malpractice against codefendants]; *Pizzi v Muccia*, 127 AD2d 338 [plaintiff failed to adequately demonstrate how disclosure of expert's qualifications would reveal his identity]; *Renucci v Mercy Hosp.*, 124 AD2d 796 [defendant's request for identity of medical experts was improper; its request for qualifications was excessively detailed and hospital was only entitled to "substance" of expert's testimony]; . . . *Dunn v Medina Mem. Hosp.*, 131 Misc 2d 971 [court cannot order party to retain expert at any particular stage of litigation particularly if discovery not completed]; *Salander v Central Gen. Hosp.*, 130 Misc 2d 311 [dilatory tactics in disclosing expert information will not be countenanced]).

No decision has addressed the specific issue that is raised in this motion. Plaintiff made a full and complete disclosure in compliance with CPLR 3101(d)(1) some 18 months ago. The defendants have had the benefit of such information throughout the discovery process. In return, the defendant hospital has given a somewhat terse and limited response, which in the court's opinion says no more than that the hospital was not negligent; that the plaintiff's condition was stable and that there was no need to expeditiously deliver the test results and records to Boston. Dr. Odabashian has simply stated that his compliance with CPLR 3101(d)(1) is premature since he has not yet designated an expert to testify on his behalf at trial. Plaintiff argues that her failure to receive an adequate response from the hospital and the delay of the defendant Odabashian in designating an expert will be prejudicial since her attorney will not have the benefit of such information in preparing for trial.

One of the reasons for the 1985 reform legislation was to expedite the resolution of malpractice claims in order to reduce litigation costs (mem of State Executive Dept, 1985 McKinney's Session Laws, at 3024). Such memorandum emphasized that: "Since the testimony of expert witnesses is often the single most important element of proof in medical malpractice and other personal injury actions, sharing information concerning these opinions encourages prompt settlement by providing both parties an accurate measure of the strength of their adversaries' case. In addition, both parties will be discouraged from asserting unsupportable claims or defenses, knowing that they will be required to disclose what, if any, expert evidence will support their allegations." (1985 McKinney's Session Laws, at 3025.)

It was hoped that such disclosure would weed out nonmeritorious claims or defenses. The statute itself and the legislative history provide no guidelines as to the timing of such discovery but the statute makes allowance for a last minute designation. A party may upon a showing of good cause retain an expert on the eve of trial and, with court permission, present such expert testimony without complying with CPLR 3101(d)(1) (*see*, 3A Weinstein-Korn-Miller, NY Civ Prac 3101.52[a]).

Although the court is empowered pursuant to 22 NYCRR 202.56(b) to set certain dates for the completion of pretrial discovery in IAS medical malpractice cases assigned to it, this court does not believe that such rule allows the court to interfere with an attorney's trial strategy which could indeed include whether an expert should be engaged to testify at trial and if so, when such a retention should be made. However, as the defendant Odabashian is well aware, this case is almost ready for the scheduling of a trial and the information- gathering process which sometimes is a necessary predicate for the selection and retention of a trial expert has been effectively completed. Though this court does not question the integrity of defendant Odabashian's counsel in tendering the present response, the court must emphasize that any litigant who attempts an 11th-hour response to an adversary's outstanding demand for expert witness information assumes the additional burden of explaining the late notice as well as establishing "good cause."

. . . .

It is conceivable that a showing of intentional noncompliance (*i.e.*, the eve-of-trial designation of a trial expert who was earlier retained as a consultant to assist in preparing the case) could result in the court's exclusion of such testimony. Other less egregious situations could be met with a monetary sanction or other penalty or ruling.

As in almost any case involving medical or technical issues, all parties have a legitimate interest in securing an adversary's expert witness information before trial. Such information may help in preparing an effective cross-examination or in making arrangements for rebuttal testimony. Although sympathetic to the plaintiff's concern about an eve-of-trial disclosure by defendant Odabashian, the court cannot compel a response where the statute provides no specific time for compliance. When and if compliance is attempted, the plaintiff will be able to object to such testimony. The plaintiff's motion with respect to defendant Odabashian is denied, without costs.

With respect to the response of the defendant Albany Medical Center, the court finds that it is inadequate and does not fulfill the minimal purpose for which CPLR 3101(d)(1) was intended. The information provided is so general and nonspecific that the plaintiff has not been enlightened to any appreciable degree about the content of this expert's anticipated testimony. Although the court cannot delineate the exact contents of a satisfactory disclosure, the court will state that any reply must represent a good-faith effort to comply with the statutory mandates. The plaintiff's motion with respect to defendant Albany Medical Center is granted, without costs, unless the defendant serves a second amended reply within 30 days of the service of a copy of the order to be entered herein with notice of entry.

. . . .

NOTES

(1) CPLR 3101(d)(1)(iii) allows disclosure of the expert's testimony additional to that required under subdivision (d)(1)(i) "only upon court order upon a showing of special circumstances." The latter term is discussed in *Rosario v. General Motors Corp.*, 148 A.D.2d 108, 543 N.Y.S.2d 974 (1st Dep't 1989), which adopted a per se rule that where material physical evidence (in this, case, an allegedly defective automobile) is inspected by an expert for one side, and then lost or destroyed before the adversary's expert has had a chance to examine it, special

circumstances exist warranting disclosure directly from the expert concerning the facts surrounding his inspection.

(2) A request under CPLR 3101(d)(1) is automatically deemed continuing, in the sense that the party receiving it is under a duty to supplement the response in the light of changes. *Pizzi v. Mucia*, 127 A.D.2d 338, 515 N.Y.S.2d 341 (3d Dep't 1987). *See also* CPLR 3101(h), added in 1993.

(3) What disclosure is available from or about an expert who has been retained or consulted but who is not expected to testify for the party who retained the expert originally? Is the report of such an expert obtainable under the standards set forth in CPLR 3101(d)(2)? What about the expert's name? Of what use is information from or about a non-testifying expert? The next case suggests some answers.

GILLY v. CITY OF NEW YORK
Court of Appeals
69 N.Y.2d 509, 508 N.E.2d 901, 516 N.Y.S.2d 166 (1987)

PER CURIAM.

The substance of a report prepared by a physician employed by defendant to examine plaintiff, and furnished to her, can be elicited by plaintiff as part of her direct case.

Plaintiff, Rose Gilly, was injured on November 7, 1978 when defendant's ferryboat, on which she was a passenger, struck a seawall. Plaintiff was thrown on her back and several passengers fell on top of her. She was admitted to the hospital complaining of shortness of breath and chest pains. Defendant's liability has already been established; only an assessment of damages and comparative fault are at issue in this action.

Prior to trial, defendant retained Dr. John Edson, a cardiologist, to examine plaintiff and report his findings. Dr. Edson's report, dated October 7, 1982, stated that plaintiff suffered from angina, that the condition was permanent, and that it would be impossible to refute that the condition had been caused or accelerated by the ferryboat accident. A copy of the report was sent to plaintiff's counsel pursuant to court rules (22 NYCRR 660.11; now 202.17). Plaintiff subpoenaed Dr. Edson to testify as to both his fact findings and his conclusions on the cause of her condition. Prior to the voir dire, it was reported that the doctor did not wish to get involved in the trial but would appear if subpoenaed; at the voir dire Dr. Edson indicated no opposition to relating his findings. On defendant's motion the trial court precluded his testimony in its entirety. Plaintiff, claiming that her injury resulted in heart disease, sought $500,000 in damages; she was awarded $15,000, and the Appellate Division affirmed the judgment. On appeal to this court, plaintiff contends that the trial court erred in precluding Dr. Edson's testimony. We agree that error was committed, but only to the extent that the court precluded the substance of Dr. Edson's report.

In *McDermott v Manhattan Eye, Ear & Throat Hosp.* (15 NY2d 20), we addressed the related issue of whether a physician-defendant could be called as an expert witness by the plaintiff in a medical malpractice case. We held that he could be, and refused to limit his testimony to "facts within his knowledge" and things he "actually saw and did." The more enlightened view, we concluded, was that plaintiff should be permitted to examine his doctor-opponent as fully and freely as other qualified witnesses, and that such testimony could include expert opinion (*id.*, at 26-29). We distinguished *People ex rel. Kraushaar Bros. & Co. v Thorpe* (296 NY 223) — in which we had held that a person may not be required to give an expert opinion involuntarily — noting that the defendant-physician was not an independent, disinterested witness forced to attend the trial merely because he is "accomplished in a particular science, art, or profession" who might be called upon in every case "in which any question in his department of knowledge is to be solved" (*id.*, at 29). Rather, he was already connected to the case. Thus, while the "unwilling witness who is in no way connected with the action" could not be compelled to testify as an expert for the plaintiff, we held in *McDermott* that the defendant-physician — by virtue of his existing association with the case — could be (*id.*).

. . . .

Here we conclude that a physician in the position of Dr. Edson, who has examined the plaintiff, formulated his findings and had them conveyed to both parties in litigation, should not be barred from relating the substance of his report when called as a witness by plaintiff. Permitting such evidence furthers truth- seeking objectives without engendering the concerns expressed in *McDermott* (*supra*) and *Kraushaar* (*supra*). First, disinterested persons need not fear being drawn into litigation on limitless occasions because of their distinctions and attainments. Dr. Edson voluntarily involved himself in the case when he undertook to — and did in fact — examine plaintiff and report his findings regarding her condition, and at trial expressed no objection to relating his findings. Second, the physician is not being compelled to express an opinion against his will, but only to relate conclusions already formulated and fully disclosed. . . . Finally, there is no danger that by giving this limited evidence the physician would be thrust into an ethical dilemma or pulled apart by competing loyalties (*see*, Meyer, *The Expert Witness: Some Prospects for Change*, 45 St John's L Rev 105, 114). Once a physician's report has been reduced to writing and served on the adversary, it ceases to be for the exclusive use of defendant. At that point both sides have access to this probative evidence and there is no basis for withholding it from the trier of fact.

In concluding that the evidence should not, as a general matter, be foreclosed, we of course do not negate the discretion that may be exercised by the lower courts in particular cases to protect against abuse, overreaching and undue prejudice to any party.

NOTES

(1) What are the ethical obligations of an expert who has been retained by one side and developed an opinion that is hostile to that party? In one case, a Supreme Court Justice stated:

> The testimony of a witness, particularly an expert, should be totally unaffected by the question of which party to the litigation retains that expert. An expert belongs to no one. With respect to his or her observations that expert should be subject to call (or subpoena) by any party. . . . With respect to the opinion of an expert, that opinion should be equally available to all parties willing to pay an appropriate fee for time consumed by travel and testimony, and for whom the expert is willing to testify as to that opinion. To conclude that the opinion will in any way, be based on which party pays for the examination (or tests or consultations) and on which party pays for the testimony, does gross disservice to the expert and to his or her integrity. The trier of fact is entitled to all available information so as to be in a position to make a reasoned, intelligent judgment. If, for example, two experts (retained by opposing parties) are in agreement, should this information be kept from the trier of facts because of a highly dubious concept of ethics?

> Indeed, this erroneous ethical view would enable one party to the litigation to deny access to outstanding experts in a particular field to its adversary by consulting and "retaining" those experts first.

Carrasquillo v. Rothschild, 110 Misc. 2d 758, 758-60, 443 N.Y.S.2d 113, 115 (Sup. Ct. 1981).

(2) In *Overeem v. Neuhoff*, 254 A.D.2d 398, 679 N.Y.S.2d 74 (2d Dep't 1998), it was held that where plaintiff's treating physician was to testify he need not be identified as an expert witness for purposes of CPLR 3101(d)(1). His report had been furnished to the defendant (although no opinion about causation was in the report), so defendant was on notice of his identity. *See also Rook v. 60 Key Centre, Inc.*, 239 A.D.2d 926, 660 N.Y.S.2d 238 (4th Dep't 1997).

(3) It is settled law that in medical malpractice suits, when a summary judgment motion has been made before discovery, the non-moving party need not furnish the identity of his or her expert witnesses to the moving party. However, in *Marano v. Mercy Hospital*, 241 A.D.2d 48, 670 N.Y.S.2d 570 (2d Dep't 1998), the court held that in a medical malpractice case, a party moving for summary judgment must disclose the identity of the expert witnesses to both the court and the non-moving party. The court justified this decision by distinguishing the posture of the movant from that of the non-movant.

The movant is on the offensive, and seeks summary judgment through proving that there are no questions of fact to be resolved. Without knowledge of the movant's expert witnesses, the court reviewing the summary judgment motion cannot decide whether there are questions of fact or not. This is because the disposition of the case relies, in part, on the credibility of the witnesses. The judge will not be able to ascertain the credibility of the witness without knowing the person's name, background and credentials.

(4) In *Roundpoint v. V.N.A., Inc.*, 207 A.D.2d 123, 621 N.Y.S.2d 161 (3d Dep't 1995), plaintiff fell on the wheelchair ramp exiting defendant's building. Plaintiff hired an architect to render an opinion that the ramp was in a dangerous condition at the time of the accident. The fact that the architect was the person hired by defendant to design the building, including the ramp, did not disqualify him from being retained by plaintiff. It was noted that the court has an inherent right to disqualify experts where retainer would cause a conflict of interest, but that here defendant's relationship with the architect was concluded before this accident happened.

§ 15.03 WHO IS SUBJECT TO DISCLOSURE: CPLR 3101(A)

DIOGUARDI v. ST. JOHN'S RIVERSIDE HOSPITAL
Appellate Division, Second Department
144 A.D.2d 333, 533 N.Y.S.2d 915 (1988)

In a medical malpractice action, the defendant appeals from an order of the Supreme Court, Westchester County (Marbach, J.), entered August 11, 1987, which (1) granted the plaintiff's motion to quash a subpoena and notice for deposition served upon nonparty witness Dr. John Tulenko, and (2) denied its cross motion to compel Dr. Tulenko to appear for a deposition.

The plaintiff suffered a cut on his left hand and left forearm and was treated at the defendant hospital's emergency room on December 12, 1982. Approximately two weeks later, on December 27, 1982, Dr. John Tulenko admitted the plaintiff into St. Clare's Hospital. Dr. Tulenko's notes indicate that the plaintiff's original injury, sustained on December 12, had been aggravated by an infection which developed during the course of the plaintiff's employment. The Supreme Court refused to direct a deposition of Dr. Tulenko as a nonparty. We affirm.

It is proper to direct disclosure against a nonparty witness only in the presence of adequate special circumstances (*see, Cirale v 80 Pine St. Corp.*, 35 NY2d 113, 116-117). This requirement survived the 1984 amendment to CPLR 3101(a)(4) (L 1984, ch 294; *see, New England Mut. Life Ins. Co. v Kelly*, 113 AD2d 285; *Slabakis v Drizin*, 107 AD2d 45, 48). The existence of such "special circumstances" may be shown by establishing that the information sought to be discovered cannot be obtained from other sources (*O'Neill v Oakgrove Constr.*, 71 NY2d 521, 526). The existence of "special circumstances" is not established, however, merely upon a showing that the information sought might be relevant (*Cirale v 80 Pine St. Corp., supra*).

Whether "special circumstances" have been shown to exist in a particular case is a question committed to the sound discretion of the court to which the application for discovery is made. . . . In the present case, the court did not abuse its discretion in denying disclosure. The defendant's claim that Dr. Tulenko advised the plaintiff to lie about the origin of his injury is manifestly without foundation. Otherwise, Dr. Tulenko's only connection with the case is as one of several physicians who treated the plaintiff for the injuries allegedly caused by the defendant's malpractice. We decline to hold that a defendant in a personal injury action may, as of right, depose any and all physicians who are shown to have treated the injuries claimed by the plaintiff. More than mere relevance and materiality is necessary to warrant disclosure from a nonparty (*see, Cirale v 80 Pine St. Corp., supra*). There has been no satisfactory showing that Dr. Tulenko's deposition might yield any information material to the issue of damages not already available from other sources, such as hospital records.

NOTES

(1) The language, if not the holding, of the principal case is controversial. In *Rosario v. General Motors Corp.*, 148 A.D.2d 108, 543 N.Y.S.2d 974 (1st Dep't 1989), the court said that disclosure was available "practically for the asking" even under the "special circumstances" requirement that applied to disclosure from non-parties under CPLR 3101(a)(4) prior to its 1984 amendment into its current format. As you read it, does that section require a showing of special circumstances? In contrast, the Second Department has steadfastly held to its "special circumstances" rule regarding non-parties, *Tannenbaum v. Tenenbaum*, 8 A.D.3d 360, 777 N.Y.S.2d 769 (2d Dep't 2004), and the Third Department has followed suit, *Cerasaro v. Cerasaro*, 9 A.D.3d 663, 781 N.Y.S.2d 375 (3d Dep't 2004). The First Department later expressly found itself in "conflict" with *Dioguardi. Schroeder v. Con. Ed.*, 249 A.D.2d 69, 670 N.Y.S.2d 856 (1st Dep't 1998).

(2) Only parties (and the officers, directors, members, agents and employees of parties, CPLR 3101(a)(1)) are subject to disclosure by interrogatories,[1] CPLR 3130; to physical or mental examinations, CPLR 3121(a); or to a notice to admit, CPLR 3123. Non-party witnesses are subject to disclosure only if covered by CPLR 3101(a)(2)-(4), and then only by deposition, CPLR 3107, and to discovery and inspection of documents on motion, CPLR 3120(b).

(3) To obtain the deposition of a non-party, one must serve a subpoena on the witness, CPLR 3106(b), and a notice on every other party, CPLR 3107. Deviation from the requirement of notice to the other parties in the action has met with severe condemnation. *Beiny v. Wynard*, 129 A.D.2d 126, 517 N.Y.S.2d 474 (1st Dep't 1987). There, the court disqualified the offending law firm from further representation of its client because it had improperly obtained privileged

---

[1] An exception to this rule is that non-parties may, by court order, be subject to interrogatories in matrimonial actions. CPLR 3130(2).

documents by serving a subpoena and notice of deposition on the non-party custodian without notice to the adverse party.

§ 15.04 DEVICES USED FOR DISCLOSURE

[A] In General

The disclosure methods are listed in CPLR 3102(a). Each is designed to serve a particular purpose. Though they often overlap in the sense that the same information may be obtained through more than one device, the decision as to which to use at a particular stage of the litigation is important from a tactical point of view. Oral questions at a deposition, for example, are obviously preferable to written interrogatories when spontaneity in questioning is desired. But the latter are usually more effective when basic information about structure or general methods of operation or the like is sought from a corporate or institutional defendant, as a clumsy progression of depositions from one corporate employee to another in the search for a full answer can be avoided. In some litigation, use of more than one device may be necessary. This is specifically authorized by CPLR 3102(a), and the courts have recognized the desirability of using one device to obtain information in anticipation that what is learned will help prepare further disclosure requests. *See Barouh Eton Allen Corp v. International Business Machines Corp.*, 76 A.D.2d 873, 429 N.Y.S.2d 33 (2d Dep't 1980); *A. Colish, Inc. v. Abramson*, 150 A.D.2d 210, 540 N.Y.S.2d 813 (1st Dep't 1989).

[B] The Deposition: CPLR 3106-3117

A deposition involves taking testimony under oath by asking questions directly of the witness. It is sometimes referred to as an examination before trial or "e.b.t." The mechanics of the deposition are governed by CPLR 3113-3116. See the discussion in O. Chase, CPLR Manual § 20.10 (2d ed. 2006). Some of the tactical aspects of the e.b.t. are found in the following excerpt from the Civil Trial Manual 2, R. McCullough & J. Underwood, 323-324 (Student Ed., 1981):[*]

6. QUESTIONING TECHNIQUE FOR DEPOSITIONS

The questioning technique used by counsel during a discovery deposition is different from that used by counsel at the trial or during the taking of a deposition for the purpose of preserving a witness's testimony for use in his absence. During the trial, attorneys often avoid asking certain questions because they fear that the answer might damage their side. Since one of the purposes of the discovery deposition is to learn the nature of the opposition testimony, this fear should usually not affect the questioner so strongly as it should during the trial. If, however, there is a strong possibility that the discovery deposition may also have to be used in place of live testimony at the trial, then counsel may have to use a questioning technique more suitable for trial.

a. *The Loquacious Deponent.* If the deponent is the opposing party or a key witness for that side and he is talkative, counsel should allow him to continue to talk, for it may lead to his discredit. If the witness rambles on in an answer, he usually should not be stopped. In the course of his rambling he might make some damaging statements.

b. *Atmosphere of Hearing.* A casual, relaxed atmosphere for taking the deposition of the opposing party should be created. In this atmosphere he may not weigh his words carefully and may blurt out a statement damaging to his side.

c. *Preparation.* Some lawyers who prepare assiduously for the trial itself put forth little or no effort to get ready for taking a deposition. Poor preparation for the deposition could result in ruining the case. Counsel should learn as much as possible about the deponent before the deposition by using interrogatories or other methods. If the witness is an expert, counsel should become familiar with the vocabulary of his specialty. It must be remembered that the quality of counsel's performance at the hearing may affect the chances of a good settlement as well as the type of information obtained.

The same authors also stress the importance of preparing one's own client when he will be deposed. *Id.* at 326-27:

e. Preparing the Client To Have His Deposition Taken by Opposing Counsel.

(1) *Reviewing Testimony of Client Shortly Before Deposition.* The client should be asked to meet with counsel prior to the time set for taking his deposition. During this time counsel should tell him the kind of questions to expect and review with him his knowledge of the incident under litigation. This makes it less likely that a poor memory will lead him to make inaccurate statements that can later be used to attack his credibility at the trial. The unethical practice of trying to make a witness think he remembers something that he does not actually remember should be avoided. If the description of the location of the incident is important, ask the client to revisit the scene shortly before the deposition to refresh his memory and check the distances between important landmarks.

If the case is a complicated one, such as an antitrust or patent infringement case, the period of time necessary for conducting this pre-deposition review may be far more lengthy than that for the simpler varieties of tort cases. The antitrust case may involve large numbers of corporate documents, such as sales records, market-share studies, and corporate or trade association minutes. These documents should be carefully reviewed with the witness prior to his deposition. Because of the complexity of discovery in antitrust and securities cases, a young, inexperienced attorney should consider associating with a specialist in these areas.

(2) *Advising the Client About the Technique of Answering.* The client should be warned not to give any more information than is strictly necessary to answer the question asked him. The more he elaborates, the greater the chance that he will blunder into a statement that can be used to discredit him at the trial. He should be advised not to answer a question that he does not understand, but rather he should ask to have the question repeated or rephrased.

(3) *Explaining the Importance of the Deposition.* Counsel should explain to the client the importance of the deposition. Because it is not the trial itself, the client may underestimate the significance of what he says or how he says it. The mechanics and purpose of depositions should be explained to avoid surprise, which could result in error by the client.

FORM:

Notice to Take Deposition Upon Oral Questions

SUPREME COURT OF THE STATE OF NEW YORK
NEW YORK COUNTY

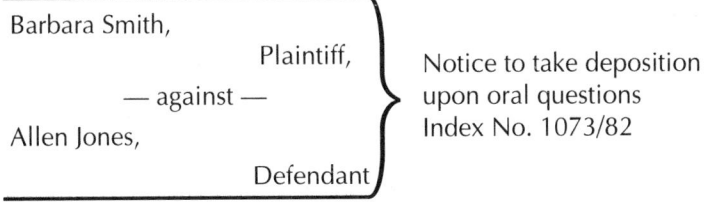

Barbara Smith,

               Plaintiff,

    — against —

Allen Jones,

             Defendant

Notice to take deposition upon oral questions
Index No. 1073/82

PLEASE TAKE NOTICE that, pursuant to Article 31 of the Civil Practice Law and Rules, the deposition upon oral questions of Barbara Smith, the above named party who resides at 80 Fifth Avenue, New York, New York, will be taken on the 20th day of May, 2006, at 10 o'clock in the forenoon of that day, at the office of Oscar G. Chase, Esq., at No. 40 Washington Square South, City of New York, County of New York, State of New York.

Said party is to be examined on all evidence material and necessary in the defense of this action and is required to produce upon the deposition all papers, books, and documents relevant to this action which are in her possession, custody or control.

May 1, 2006
TO: Robert A. Barker, Esq.
Attorney for Plaintiff

> OSCAR G. CHASE
> Attorney for Defendant
> 40 Washington Sq. South
> New York, New York 10012
> Telephone: 598-1212

NOTES

(1) The deponent may be required to produce "books, papers and other things in the possession, custody or control of the person to be examined," and these materials may be made exhibits to the deposition. CPLR 3111, 3116(c).

How narrowly must the document production request be drawn? That breadth of reach is great but not unlimited is illustrated by two decisions of the Appellate Division, Second Department, announced on the very same day. In *Weiss v. Rae*, 87 A.D.2d 629, 448 N.Y.S.2d 233 (2d Dep't 1982), an action to determine claims to real property, the court upheld a request that plaintiffs produce at their deposition "all papers, documents, deeds, letters of administration [and] correspondence relevant to plaintiffs' cause of action." Contrast *White Plains Coat & Apron Co. v. K.M. Lehmann*, 87 A.D.2d 629, 448 N.Y.S.2d 232 (2d Dep't 1982), a contract action seeking lost profits, in which the court held overly broad and impermissible a request which sought:

> [P]laintiff's books of account (including without limitation its general ledgers), financial statements, profit and loss statements, and federal and state tax returns for the entire period with respect to which damages measured by lost profits are claimed herein; and . . . [a]ll route cards, ledger cards, invoices, bills, statements, receipts, documents or business records of any kind and description relating to the linen supply services rendered by plaintiff to defendant K.M. Lehmann d/b/a Maxl's Restaurant, including without limitation all records relating to merchandise ordered by plaintiff especially for Maxl's Restaurant.

87 A.D.2d at 630, 448 N.Y.S.2d at 233.

Should the permissible breadth of a request to produce documents at a deposition differ from the breadth allowed in a notice of discovery and inspection under CPLR 3120?

(2) A deposition may also be taken by written questions. CPLR 3108. This does not mean that they are sent to the witness who answers them in writing.

The questions are instead provided to the "officer" (an attorney or notary) before whom the deposition is to be taken. They are read aloud to the witness who answers them orally for the record. CPLR 3113(b). The advantage of this method is that the attorney for the party taking the deposition need not be physically present. The chief disadvantage, which makes it unwise to proceed by written questions except perhaps when the witness is in a distant place, is that all spontaneity of questioning is lost.

An alternative available when the witness is to be deposed outside the state is the "commission" authorized by CPLR 3108. When the commission is "open" the witness is questioned orally by the person commissioned to do so, as at an ordinary in-state deposition. *See* discussion in *Stanzione v. Consumer Builders, Inc.*, 149 A.D.2d 682, 540 N.Y.S.2d 482 (2d Dep't 1989).

A letter rogatory, also provided for in CPLR 3108, is a request from a court in New York to a court in a foreign jurisdiction asking for that court's help in securing the deposition of a person in that jurisdiction. In *Cavaretta v. George*, 270 A.D.2d 862, 706 N.Y.S.2d 291 (4th Dep't 2000), there was no indication that any special circumstances need be shown.

GOBERMAN v. McNAMARA
Supreme Court, Nassau County
76 Misc. 2d 791, 352 N.Y.S.2d 369 (1979)

JOSEPH LIFF, JUSTICE.

During the examination before trial of plaintiff, counsel for the defendants posed three questions to plaintiff which were objected to by his attorney. Defendants sought to ascertain (1) whether plaintiff was ever convicted of a crime, (2) whether he was known by any other name or names within the last five years and (3) what were his addresses during the same period. Unable to settle their disagreement on the propriety of these matters counsel appeared before this Court in Special Term, Part II for a ruling. At the time the Court indicated that the questions should be answered. However, because of the request of plaintiff's counsel, the Court consented to take memorandums of law and make a formal ruling. That is not the preferred practice (*Cohen v. Heine & Co.*, 39 A.D.2d 563, 331 N.Y.S.2d 751) but since the Court heard the arguments and became familiar with the issues we thought time would be conserved by taking the submission.

In the first cause of action plaintiff seeks to recover damages for injuries he sustained as the result of an alleged assault by the defendants; the second cause of action alleges a scheme by defendants to defraud him of his money and property; and the third cause requests exemplary damages. The defendants respond to these allegations with denials and in their defenses they assert in essence that their actions "were justified by reason of the acts and threats of the plaintiff." (Item 12 in the verified answer.)

Counsel for defendants has not indicated the purpose for which he seeks this information or how it may be utilized at the trial. However, we may assume that it is sought in anticipation of a cross-examination of plaintiff during the trial and to reflect upon his credibility. "[T]he character of a party may not be shown in a civil case to raise an inference that he either did or did not do the act in question." (Richardson on Evidence [9th Ed.] § 163). Character evidence is admissible in a civil case where character is directly in issue, *i.e.* "(a) libel and slander; (b) malicious prosecution;" (Richardson on Evidence, *supra; see also* Fisch on New York Evidence § 172).

However, should plaintiff testify during the trial his credibility will be subject to impeachment in the same manner as any other witness (*see* Richardson on Evidence [9th Ed.] § 505; Fisch on New York Evidence, chapter 15) and he may be questioned as to whether he has been convicted of a crime (CPLR 4513). "There shall be full disclosure of all evidence material and necessary in the prosecution or defense of an action, regardless of the burden of proof" (CPLR 3101[a]) and as long as the "information is sought in good faith for possible use as evidence-in-chief or in rebuttal or for cross-examination, it should be considered 'evidence material . . . in the prosecution or defense . . .'" (*Allen v. Crowell-Collier Pub. Co.*, 21 N.Y.2d 403, 407, 288 N.Y.S.2d 449, 453, 235 N.E.2d 430, 432).

Accordingly, the plaintiff is directed to answer the questions asked.

We find ourselves in disagreement with the views expressed in *Counihan v. Knoebel* (N.Y.L.J., 11/21/73, p. 20, col. 7) which denied the request to compel answers to questions pertaining to credibility at an examination before trial. The comments of then Dean McLaughlin in his column "New York Trial Practice" in the New York Law Journal of December 14, 1973 at page 4, column 2, are more in keeping with the spirit of the CPLR 3101 *et seq.* and we are in agreement with his conclusion that such questions should be answered.

NOTES

(1) The principal case is a good illustration of the deposition's utility in trial preparation.

(2) "[I]n an examination before trial unless a question is clearly violative of the witness's constitutional rights, or of some privilege recognized in law, or is palpably irrelevant, questions should be freely permitted and answered, since all objections other than as to form are preserved for the trial and may be raised at that time." *Freedco Products, Inc. v. N.Y. Tel. Co.*, 47 A.D.2d 654, 655, 366 N.Y.S.2d 401, 402 (2d Dep't 1975).

Since it is only objections to "the form of the questions or answers," CPLR 3115(b), (c), which are waived by a failure to raise them at the deposition itself, why should the deponent's attorney object to any other question? See *White v.*

Martins, 100 A.D.2d 805, 474 N.Y.S.2d 733 (1st Dep't 1984): "But there is always the possibility of questions that infringe upon a privilege, or that are so improper that to answer them will substantially prejudice the parties; or questions that may be so palpably and grossly irrelevant that they should not be answered. . . . Thus, although the statute provides that the deposition shall proceed, it adds 'subject to the right of a person to apply for a protective order.'"

(3) When objection is made and the parties are unable to compromise their disagreement, resort to a judge for a "ruling" is common in some counties. Alternatively, the remainder of the deposition can be completed and the propriety of the disputed matters resolved by a motion to compel under CPLR 3124. *See Jarvis v. Jarvis*, 141 Misc. 2d 404, 533 N.Y.S.2d 207 (Sup. Ct. 1988) (suggests omnibus motion, at the conclusion of discovery, before the judge assigned to the case).

In October 2006, Uniform Rule Part 221 was added to the court rules. Entitled "Uniform Rules for the Conduct of Depositions," the new rules are designed to curb the conduct of lawyers who have increasingly instructed clients not to answer all sorts of questions at depositions thus thwarting what was originally intended to afford maximum disclosure with minimum supervision. The new rules, *inter alia*, require deponents to answer all questions at a deposition except those invading a right of privilege or confidentiality, those ignoring a limitation set forth in a court order, and those which would, if answered, cause significant prejudice to any person. *See* 22 NYCRR § 221, and a comprehensive review by Connors and Gleason in the New York Law Journal, Sept. 18, 2006, p. 3.

WOJTAS v. FIFTH AVENUE COACH CORP.
Appellate Division, Second Department
23 A.D.2d 685, 257 N.Y.S.2d. 404 (1965)

MEMORANDUM BY THE COURT.

In a negligence action by a wife and her husband to recover damages for personal injury, medical expenses and loss of services, brought against the defendants Fifth Avenue Coach Corporation and Charles Williams, the driver of one of its buses, in which the plaintiff wife was a passenger, the plaintiffs appeal from a judgment of the Supreme Court, Queens County, entered October 16, 1963 after trial upon a jury's verdict in favor of defendants, dismissing the complaint on the merits.

Judgment affirmed, without costs.

The plaintiffs' sole contention on this appeal is that the trial justice committed prejudicial error in permitting defendants' trial counsel to read into evidence the pretrial deposition of the defendant bus driver (taken by the plaintiff), although plaintiffs had not offered any part thereof at the trial (CPLR 3117, subd. [a], par. 2). It was in effect conceded by plaintiff's counsel that, at the time of the trial and as a consequence of a coronary thrombosis, Williams (the bus driver) was considered by his physician to be sick and unable to testify; and the trial justice so found.

In our opinion, the statute (CPLR 3117, subd. [a], par. 2) has made inapplicable those cases arising under the former Civil Practice Act which permitted a party to read in part or in whole his own pretrial deposition when the party at whose instance it was taken has refused to do so. We hold that, under the statute as it now reads, the party-deponent himself may not so use the deposition. Paragraph 2 of subdivision (a) of the rule (CPLR 3117) provides that the deposition of a party may be used only "by any adversely interested party" against the deponent. Under the CPLR, therefore, by legislative choice, only an adverse party may use a deposition in the first instance; and the deposition of a party-deponent may not be read in evidence by his own counsel without calling the deponent to the stand, unless the court finds that at least one of the conditions set out in the five subparagraphs of the third paragraph of subdivision (a) of the rule (CPLR 3117) exists at the time of trial (3 Weinstein, Korn & Miller, New York Civil Practice, par. 3117.04, pp. 31-167 to 31-168). The reference in paragraph 3 of subdivision (a) of the rule (CPLR 3117) that the deposition of "any person" may be used, as therein indicated, is to be construed as meaning any person — "whether or not a party" (3 Weinstein, Korn & Miller, par. 3117.06, p. 31-168).

Since at bar there was a finding by the trial justice that the illness of the defendant Williams precluded his attendance at the trial, the procedural requisite for reading his deposition by defendants' trial counsel was established (CPLR 3117, subd. [a], par. 3, subpar. [iii]).

NOTES

(1) A similar situation arose in *United Bank Limited v. Cambridge Sporting Goods Corp.*, 41 N.Y.2d 254, 392 N.Y.S.2d 265, 360 N.E.2d 943 (1976), where defendant served interrogatories on plaintiff banks. At trial the banks were allowed to use their answers as evidence-in-chief to show they were holders in due course. This was ruled error. A party cannot use discovery information as evidence-in-chief unless CPLR 3117 is in some respect satisfied. Here, the only reason plaintiffs could not produce testimony on the point in issue was that they saw to it that the key witness on the point was unavailable.

(2) The deposition of a medical witness may be used at trial by any party without a showing of special circumstances. CPLR 3117(a)(4). Why? *C.f.* CPLR 3101(a)(3).

[C] Interrogatories: CPLR 3130-3133

Interrogatories are written questions directed by one party to another. If served upon a corporation or other institutional party, they must be answered by an employee or official "having the information." The following excerpt may be helpful in understanding the use of this disclosure device.

1. STRENGTHS AND WEAKNESSES OF INTERROGATORIES AS A DISCOVERY DEVICE

Many new lawyers mistakenly believe that since interrogatories are inferior to oral depositions for some purposes, they are inferior for all purposes.

Interrogatories are generally considered ineffective for assessing the probable testimony of an opposing party or a witness expected to testify on basic issues of liability. Since interrogatories are conducted in writing, they afford no opportunity to assess the demeanor of a witness as he reacts to various questions. Since the answers are usually drafted by the opposing attorney, it is far more difficult to elicit a damaging admission from an adverse party.

. . . .

Because of the written nature of interrogatories, it is impossible to quickly follow up a new line of inquiry disclosed by an answer. By the time new interrogatories are drafted to pursue the new possibilities, the other side may have managed to fortify its position and make successful pursuit impossible.

Interrogatories, however, can be used for some purposes more effectively than depositions. Frequently the deposition of an opposing party cannot be taken profitably unless certain fundamental facts can be learned about that party and his case for use in preparation of the deposition. Included in information of this sort that interrogatories can be useful in obtaining are such items as a list of all persons known by the party to have information relevant to the incident under litigation, business statistics, lists of documents, and information concerning the structure of a corporation or other organization. Detailed technical information of an objective, noncontroversial variety sometimes can be most efficiently obtained by interrogatories. If information of this kind is sought by deposition, the witness may frequently have to reply, "I don't have the information now; I'll have to dig it out for you." Sometimes even advance notice to the deponent of the type of information that will be sought cannot prevent unproductive results. Interrogatories permit more time to gather the information needed. In a few cases, however, when the element of surprise is especially desirable in a deposition interrogatories prior to the deposition may ruin any hope of surprise.

. . . .

If the client is of modest means, the fact that interrogatories are frequently less expensive will be important in selecting among the various discovery devices. Interrogatories do not require expensive transcribing of notes by a court reporter. If the person having the information lives at a distant location, interrogatories can be mailed, and an expensive trip by counsel to attend a deposition hearing or the hiring of local counsel at the deposition site can be avoided.

Counsel is cautioned, however, that interrogatories will not always be less expensive. Each case should be studied individually. Sometimes so many different sets of interrogatories may be necessary to acquire the needed information that an oral deposition, with its more flexible on-the-spot rephrasing of questions, may be cheaper. Although interrogatories should be complete enough to obtain the needed information, counsel should realize that lengthy interrogatories expose him to a possible finding of harassment and a limiting order by the court restricting his use of interrogatories or directing that another discovery device be used instead.

R. McCullough & J. Underwood, Civil Trial Manual 2, 335-38 (Student Ed., 1981).[*]

NOTES

(1) A party cannot serve an extensive list of interrogatories and prior to the response date notice the other party for an examination before trial. While there is no order of priority as among discovery devices, the taking of depositions ought to await completion of interrogatories, especially in complex commercial litigation. *Barouh Eaton Allen Corp. v. International Business Machines Corp.*, 76 A.D.2d 873, 429 N.Y.S.2d 33 (2d Dep't 1980).

(2) Despite the desirability of using interrogatories in combination with depositions, counsel may not, without "leave of court," use both devices in "an action to recover damages for personal injury, injury to property or wrongful death predicated solely on a cause of action or causes of action for negligence." CPLR 3130(1). Thus, interrogatories may be used with depositions in an action based on negligence and another legal theory. *Niesig v. Team I*, 149 A.D.2d 94, 108-09, 545 N.Y.S.2d 153, 160-61 (2d Dep't 1989), *rev'd on other grounds*, 76 N.Y.2d 363, 559 N.Y.S.2d 493, 558 N.E.2d 1030 (1990).

(3) Under CPLR 3130, the use of interrogatories is flatly prohibited in any action (other than matrimonial actions) by a party who has demanded a bill of

---

particulars. Should a defendant in a products liability action forego the right to demand a bill in order to protect the right to serve interrogatories? How would this problem affect a defendant in a negligence action? The successful resolution of these tactical problems depends on understanding the differences, in scope and effect, between the superficially similar demand for a bill and interrogatories.

(4) The scope of a demand for a bill was treated in Chapter 14. You will recall that a demand for a bill may not seek evidentiary matters and that a bill may be demanded only with respect to items on which the party to whom it is directed bears the burden of proof. How does this compare with the scope of interrogatories? Is the effect of a statement in a bill the same as an answer to an interrogatory?

In *Medaris v. Vosburgh*, 93 A.D.2d 415, 461 N.Y.S.2d 415 (2d Dep't 1983), the court rejected an objection to interrogatories which sought opinions and amplifications of the allegations of medical malpractice:

> The "purpose of serving interrogatories is to secure evidence". . . . CPLR 3131 states that "[i]nterrogatories may relate to any matters embraced in the disclosure requirement of section 3101 and the answers may be used to the same extent as the depositions of a party." In this regard, we again take the opportunity to note that the purpose of interrogatories is distinct from that of a bill of particulars. While interrogatories seek evidentiary matter, the scope of a bill of particulars is merely "to amplify the pleadings, limit the proof and prevent surprise at the trial. . . ." Indeed, interrogatories 49 through 64 are virtually identical to those items which in the past have been stricken from demands for bills of particulars precisely because they sought evidentiary material and went beyond the limited scope of a bill of particulars. . . . Moreover, in several recent cases this court has upheld the propriety of interrogatories virtually identical to those at bar and has specifically rejected the argument . . . that the interrogatories improperly sought expert medical opinion rather than evidentiary material.

[D] Discovery and Inspection: CPLR 3120

A notice for discovery and inspection, authorized by CPLR 3120, is a means of obtaining access to documents or other things in the possession of another party in order to "inspect, copy, test or photograph" them. It is also available against non-parties provided that court permission is obtained. CPLR 3120(b).

MacKINNON v. MacKINNON
Appellate Division, Third Department
245 A.D.2d 690, 665 N.Y.S.2d 123 (1997)

SPAIN, J.

The parties were married in June 1951. Plaintiff commenced this divorce action in 1996 and made a demand pursuant to CPLR 3120 for the production of various financial documents and records concerning, inter alia, defendant's business holdings and personal finances covering a period from 1980 to the present, 1990 to the present or, in some instances, an unspecified time period. Defendant moved for a protective order to limit plaintiff's discovery demands on the ground that the demand was overly broad and burdensome. Supreme Court, inter alia, granted defendant's motion and limited discovery to a five-year period prior to the commencement of the divorce action and granted plaintiff leave to obtain further discovery of reasonable and identifiable documents and records following defendant's deposition. The court also required plaintiff to comply with the provisions of CPLR 3120(b) in obtaining information pertaining to businesses in which defendant possessed less than a controlling interest. This appeal by plaintiff ensued.

We affirm. It is well settled that, absent an unreasonable request, parties to a divorce action are entitled to full financial disclosure spanning the entire marriage (*see, Goldsmith v. Goldsmith*, 184 A.D.2d 619, 620; *Harley v. Harley*, 157 A.D.2d 916, 918; *see also*, Domestic Relations Law § 236[B]). Nevertheless, a court has broad discretion in limiting discovery "to prevent unreasonable annoyance, expense, embarrassment, disadvantage, or other prejudice" (CPLR 3103[a]), which includes the limitation of disclosure with respect to time (*see, Pomeranz v. Pomeranz*, 99 A.D.2d 407).

Here, plaintiff seeks disclosure of defendant's financial holdings as well as all financial transactions pertaining to numerous corporations with which defendant is connected. We agree with Supreme Court that plaintiff's use of "all" and "any and all" in most of the 42 paragraphs in the notice of disclosure, most requesting production of more than one item, constitutes an overly burdensome demand for discovery. Inasmuch as plaintiff admits that she is "in the dark regarding . . . defendant's finances," we find that plaintiff is using the notice of disclosure to conduct an impermissible fishing expedition (*see, e.g., Fascaldi v. Fascaldi*, 209 A.D.2d 578, 579). The "'proper procedure requires that the party seeking discovery and inspection pursuant to CPLR 3120 initially make use of the deposition and related procedures provided by the CPLR to ascertain the existence of such documents'" (*id.*, at 579, *quoting Haroian v. Nusbaum*, 84 A.D.2d 532, 533). Under these circumstances and taking into account that plaintiff has not yet deposed defendant to ascertain the existence of various financial information, we find no abuse of discretion in Supreme Court's decision limiting plaintiff's demand for discovery (*see, e.g., Hirschfeld v. Hirschfeld*, 69 N.Y.2d 842, 844; *Maillard v. Maillard*, 211 A.D.2d 963, 964). In addition, we find no error in Supreme Court directing that plaintiff comply with the provisions of CPLR 3120(b) in obtaining disclosure of any business, partnership or corporation information relating to defendant's noncontrolling interest in such companies.

NOTES

(1) The 1993 amendment to CPLR 3120(a)(2) provides that the discovery request shall set forth the material sought "by individual item or category, and shall describe each item and category with reasonable certainty." The term "reasonable certainty" was thought to broaden the specificity previously required, but it seems clear that "fishing expeditions" remain prohibited.

(2) CPLR 3120 contemplates the production of "things" as well as documents. *See, e.g., Great American Ins. Co. v. Giardino*, 71 A.D.2d 836, 419 N.Y.S.2d 367 (4th Dep't 1979) (defendant in breach of contract action compelled to provide a sample of his handwriting for analysis by plaintiff's expert).

(3) Note the overlap of CPLR 3120 with CPLR 3111 (production of documents and things at an examination before trial). How do they differ in scope? Compare also CPLR 3130 (documents, papers and photographs available through interrogatories).

(4) If the documents to be inspected are especially voluminous, the party seeking discovery may, by court order, be required to inspect them at the office in which they are kept. *Snyder v. Parke Davis & Co.*, 56 A.D.2d 536, 391 N.Y.S.2d 579 (1st Dep't 1977).

(5) Effective September 1, 2003, new CPLR 3122-a was added which, together with conforming amendments to CPLR 2305(b), 3120 and 3122, enables a requesting party to simply serve a subpoena for production of records from *non*parties. Formerly, a court order had to be obtained when information from nonparties was sought. Compliance requires respondent to sign a sworn certificate attesting that the documents are correct copies of documents prepared in accord with the business records requirements of CPLR 4518. Rather than moving to quash the subpoena, a reluctant respondent need only serve written objections.

LIPCO ELECTRICAL CORP. v. ASG CONSULTING CORPORATION

Supreme Court, Nassau County
4 Misc. 3d 1019(A), 798 N.Y.S.2d 345 (2004)

LEONARD B. AUSTIN, J.

[This dispute arose out of a failed joint venture formed for public works contract work. Material sought pursuant to the CPLR 3120 provisions include time records, tax returns and electronic computer data, *i.e.*, electronic files reproduced on disk or hard drive with identificaiton of the software needed to run the data. We are interested in this last category.]

. . . .

D. *Electronic Discovery*

. . . .

ASG was responsible for the bookkeeping for the Lipco/Action Projects. Lipco/Action has been provided with a hard copy print out of the records sought in Items 3, 4 and 5. Lipco/Action asserts that the only way that it can confirm that the hard copy data is true and accurate is by obtaining the raw data in computerized form.

Electronic discovery raises a series of issues that were never envisioned by the drafters of the CPLR. Neither the parties nor the Court have been able to find any cases decided by New York State Courts dealing with the issue of electronic discovery.

With traditional paper discovery, the issue is generally whether the demanded material exists and whether such material is subject to discovery; *i.e.*, whether the document is material and necessary to the prosecution or defense of the action and not subject to any legally recognized privileges. Once theses issues are resolved, the party in possession of the documents is required to produce the demanded material. Customarily, if the volume of documents demanded is small, the party upon whom the demand is made copies the documents and serves them upon the party demanding discovery. If the demanded documents are voluminous, the party responding to the demand advises the party demanding the documents that the documents are available for review, identification and copying at the demander's expense.

With electronic discovery, totally different issues arise. Some of the questions presented include: are the documents still on the hard drive or are they on some form of back-up; have the documents been deleted, what software was used to create and store the documents; and is that software commercially available or was the software created and/or licensed specifically for the user.

Whether the court is dealing with traditional paper discovery or electronic discovery, the first issue the court must determine is whether the material sought is subject to disclosure as "material and necessary" in the prosecution or defense of the action. In this case, the material sought in Items 3, 4 and 5 is "material and necessary." ASG does not contest that this material is discoverable. ASG asserts to the production of the material demanded in Items 3, 4 and 5 primarily on the grounds that ASG provided Lipco/Action with a print out or "hard" copy of this material and that extracting this information from its computer hard drive or back-up tapes would be extremely difficult, time consuming and expensive.

. . . .

CPLR 3103(a) permits the court either *sua sponte* or on motion of a party to issue protective orders ". . . denying limiting, conditioning or regulating the use of any disclosure device." A protective order ". . . shall be designed to prevent unreasonable annoyance, expense, embarrassment, disadvantage or other prejudice to any person or the court."

Raw computer data or electronic documents are discoverable. *See, Zubulake v. UBS Warburg LLC*, 217 F.R.D. 309 (S.D.N.Y. 2003); and *Playboy Enterprises, Inc., v. Welles*, 60 F.Supp.2d 1050 (S.D.Cal., 1999); and *Anti-Monopoly, Inc. v. Hasbro, Inc.*, 1995 U.S. Dist. LEXIS 16355 (S.D.N.Y.).

Once the court has determined that the electronic data is subject to discovery, the issue becomes who should bear the cost of discovery. The cost of providing computer records can be rather substantial.

With traditional paper records, the documents are generally stored in a usable and obtainable form, such as job folders. Furthermore, documents and records that are retained generally have a value since the company is willing to pay the cost involved in storing such documents. This is not true with computer or electronic documents. Records are kept not because they are necessary but because the cost of storage is nominal. Furthermore, electronic records are not stored for the purposes of being able to retrieve an individual document. Rather, they are retained for emergency uploading into a computer system to permit recovery from catastrophic computer failure. *See, Rowe Entertainment, Inc. v. The William Morris Agency, Inc.*, 205 F.R.D. 421 (S.D.N.Y. 2002); and *McPeek v. Ashcroft*, 202 F.R.D. 31 (D.D.C., 2001). Retrieving computer based records or data is not the equivalent of getting the file from a file cabinet or archives.

Further, computer discovery presents issues that are not faced in traditional paper discovery. Once a paper document has been destroyed, it cannot be produced. "Deleted" material is not expunged from a computer's hard drive. "Deleted" material can be retrieved by a person with sufficient computer savvy. *See, Antioch Co. v. Scrapbook Borders, Inc.*, 210 F.R.D. 645 (D.Minn., 2002); and *Simon Properties Group, L.P. v. mySIMON, Inc.*, 194 F.R.D. 639 (S.D.Ind., 2000); and *Playboy Enterprises, Inc. v. Welles, supra*, all of which hold that deleted e-mails are discoverable. Furthermore, computer experts can allegedly determine if data has been altered and reconstruct the originally entered data.

Having concluded that the material is discoverable, the Court must now determine the procedure for its production and who will bear the cost of the discovery.

The federal courts have developed and are developing procedures and analyses for determining who should bear the cost of electronic discovery. *See, Zubulake v. USB Warburg LLC, supra*; and *Rowe Entertainment, Inc v. The William Morris Agency, Inc., supra.* The party from who electronic discovery is sought should be required to produce material stored on a computer so long as the party being asked to produce the material is protected from undue burden and expense and privileged material is protected. *Playboy Enterprises, Inc. v. Welles, supra.*

The federal court's analysis of who should bear the cost of electronic discovery starts from presumption that, under the Federal Rules of Civil Procedure, the party responding to the discovery demand bears the cost of complying with discovery demands. *Oppenheimer Fund, Inc. v. Sanders*, 437 U.S. 340 (1978). *See also, Rowe Entertainment, Inc. v. The William Morris Agency, Inc., supra.* Thus, federal courts discuss factors to be considered in regard to cost shifting in connection with electronic discovery; to wit, what factors should the court consider when determining if the party seeking discovery of electronic records should bear all or some of the costs involved in the production of electronic records. *See, Zubalake v. UBS Warburg, LLC, supra* (applying a seven point analysis); and *Rowe Entertainment, Inc. v. The William Morris Agency, Inc., supra.*

However, cost shifting of electronic discovery is not an issue in New York since the courts have held that, under the CPLR, the party seeking discovery should incur the costs incurred in the production of discovery material. *Schroeder v. Centro Pariso Tropical*, 233 A.D.2d 314 (2nd Dept., 1996); and *Rubin v. Alamo Rent-a-Car*, 190 A.D.2d 661 (2nd Dept., 1993). CPLR 3103(a) specifically grants the court authority to issue a protective order to prevent a party from incurring unreasonable expenses in complying with discovery demands. Therefore, the analysis of whether electronic discovery should be permitted in New York is much simpler than it is in the federal courts. The court need only determine whether the material is discoverable and whether the party seeking the discovery is willing to bear the cost of production of the electronic material. This is especially true in this case where Lipco/Action has been provided with hard copies of the electronically stored data.

In this case, the cost factor for extracting the demanded information is unknown. ASG asserts that the cost of obtaining the information would be substantial. Lipco/Action asserts that the software program is available commercially and that extraction of the demanded information should be relatively simple.

. . . .

(c) Lipco/Action and Action's motion to compel production of the Items 3, 4 and 5 in its Discovery Demand is denied with leave to renew upon presentation of information regarding the actual cost for extracting this information and a statement that Lipco/Action and Action are willing to bear the initial cost involved for the extraction and production of such material subject to later apportionment on proper application. . . .

[E] The Notice to Admit: CPLR 3123

VILLA v. NEW YORK CITY HOUSING AUTHORITY
Appellate Division, First Department
107 A.D.2d 619, 484 N.Y.S.2d 4 (1985)

Plaintiff seeks damages for defendant's alleged negligence in failing to provide appropriate apartment window safeguards, resulting in the fatal fall by plaintiff's infant decedent.

The notice to admit (CPLR 3123) is not so much a traditional discovery device as it is a vehicle for resolving and eliminating from contention matters which, though factually relevant, are not really in dispute (*Falkowitz v Kings Highway Hosp.*, 43 AD2d 696). It is designed to remove from the case those uncontested matters which would merely present a time-consuming burden at trial. Unreasonable failure to admit such uncontestable facts may result in an order directing the intransigent party to bear the cost of such proofs. However, the notice to admit cannot be utilized to seek admissions of material issues or ultimate or conclusory facts (*Felice v St. Agnes Hosp.*, 65 AD2d 388, 395-396), interpretations of law, questions already admitted in responsive pleadings, or questions clearly irrelevant to the case. The notice was not designed to create an unreasonable burden on the party asked to admit.

The notice here is devoted to questions of defendant's ownership and control of the premises and its duty to install and maintain window guards for the safety of the tenants. Some of the questions were already answered in the affirmative in defendant's amended answer, which appears to have crossed in the mail with plaintiff's notice to admit. This is so with respect to questions as to the "registered ownership" of the premises (Nos. 3 and 4), status of the premises as a "multiple dwelling" (Nos. 6 and 7; *see* Multiple Dwelling Law, § 4, subd 7), timeliness of submission of the notice to claim (part of No. 16), and plaintiff's submission to defendant's oral examination (No. 18).

Paradoxically, defendant's amended answer denied "vested ownership" of the premises. There is no reason why defendant should not be called upon to admit such ownership (Nos. 1 and 2), or its responsibility for maintaining the premises in a safe condition (Nos. 8 and 12); likewise with regard to defendant's duty to install window safety guards (Nos. 9 and 10), and its knowledge of whether some windows remained without guards on the date in question (No. 15).

The status of plaintiff as tenant (No. 13) and whether defendant was aware thereof (No. 14) are proper areas of inquiry in a notice to admit where, as here, the answer equivocates on this issue.

While the notice to admit can be used to probe a party's understanding of his own duties under law (as in Nos. 9 and 10, *supra*), it is inappropriate as a vehicle for asking a party to interpret the law or someone else's compliance therewith. Consequently, it was improper to permit plaintiff to seek defendant's interpretation of section 131.15 of the New York City Health Code's general requirement as to when window guards are required (No. 11). Likewise, it was error to require defendant to admit or deny the propriety of plaintiff's notice of claim under section 50-e of the General Municipal Law (No. 16, *supra*), although there was nothing improper in asking defendant to confirm its written acknowledgement of the filing of that claim and its subsequent failure to indicate any defects in that notice (No. 17).

It was also error for Special Term to permit inquiry under a notice to admit with regard to an "ownership registration on file as a public record" (No. 5), inasmuch as plaintiff would have as much access to such information as does defendant.

We have ruled that it is not the task of the courts to prune interrogatories. . . . However, the notice here, consisting of only 18 questions, was not so lengthy or prolix as to render it unduly burdensome to answer. . . . Accordingly, we have modified to delete those questions which we deem improper.

. . . .

NOTES

(1) CPLR 3123(a) provides that if a respondent objects to compliance with the request, a sworn statement must be served setting forth reasons. Where, instead, respondent's attorney wrote a letter rejecting the notice to admit, apparently following provisions in CPLR 3122, "Objections to disclosure . . .," complications arose which could have been avoided with the proper CPLR 3123(a) response. *Webb v. Tire and Brake Distributors Inc.*, 13 A.D.3d 835, 786 N.Y.S.2d 636 (3d Dep't 2004). Since uncontested requests are "deemed admitted," it is possible that summary judgment could result upon respondent's default. *See Marine Midland Bank v. Bryce*, 70 A.D.2d 754, 417 N.Y.S.2d 23 (3d Dep't 1979).

(2) Some of the limits on the notice to admit are discussed in the principal case. These limits are sometimes tested in interesting ways. In *Rosario v. General Motors Corp.*, 148 A.D.2d 108, 543 N.Y.S.2d 974 (1st Dep't 1989), the defendant in a products liability action requested the plaintiff to admit that the only defect she relied upon is that in the "'left front wheel assembly' identified in her expert's report and reiterated in her answers to defendant's interrogatories." The

defendant argued that this request was proper to narrow the issues and prevent surprise at trial. The court rejected the argument: "Such a purpose, however, is served not by a notice to admit, which like the various other disclosure devices, serves the different purpose of obtaining evidence, but by a bill of particulars. . . ."

Would the request have been held proper if included in a demand for a bill of particulars?

(3) Why should a "formal" admission be sought pursuant to CPLR 3123 when the party could be asked to admit the same fact during an e.b.t. or by an interrogatory? One reason is suggested by CPLR 3123(c), Penalty for unreasonable denial. More important is the difference in the effect of the two sorts of admissions: A "formal" admission is binding against the party who made it unless a court relieves him from it. CPLR 3123(b).

[F] Physical and Mental Examinations: CPLR 3121

PROBLEM D

Irv sued Arnold and the Long Haul Truck Co., Inc. (Arnold's employer), for damages incurred when a truck driven by Arnold struck Irv's car in the rear while it was pulled onto the shoulder of the road. The complaint alleged that Arnold was negligent in failing to observe the parked car and avoid the collision; it also alleged that Long Haul was (i) vicariously liable and (ii) negligent because its driver had "inadequate vision or suffered from other mental or physical incapacity." Arnold has counterclaimed, seeking compensation for his own injuries. The counterclaim alleges that Irv's negligence was the cause of the accident.

A police report prepared by an officer on the scene stated that the weather was clear at the time of the accident, and that the emergency lights on Irv's car were functioning.

May Irv obtain:

(a) Arnold's medical records which are in the possession of his personal physician?

(b) Any medical records pertaining to Arnold in Long Haul's possession?

(c) An examination of Arnold by an opthamologist? A psychiatrist? A neurologist?

DILLENBECK v. HESS
Court of Appeals
73 N.Y.2d 278, 536 N.E.2d 1126, 539 N.Y.S.2d 707 (1989)

ALEXANDER, J.

In *Koump v Smith* (25 NY2d 287), we noted that a litigant does not waive the physician-patient privilege merely by defending a personal injury action in which his or her mental or physical condition is in controversy unless, in so defending, the litigant "affirmatively asserts the condition either by way of counterclaim or to excuse the conduct complained of by the plaintiff" (*id.*, at 294). Today, we hold that where a party defending a personal injury action validly asserts the privilege and has not affirmatively placed his or her medical condition in issue, the plaintiff may not effect a waiver of the privilege merely by introducing evidence demonstrating that the defendant's physical condition is genuinely "in controversy" within the meaning of the statute permitting discovery of medical records (CPLR 3121[a]).

I

[The action is based on death and serious injury arising out of a head-on collision with defendant's vehicle. The complaint alleged that defendant had been drinking at a tavern and was intoxicated at the time of the collision. Defendant also was seriously injured and a blood alcohol test was performed at the hospital for diagnostic purposes, but the test was not administered at the direction of the police or by court orders pursuant to Vehicle and Traffic Law § 1194.

[Defendant's answer simply denied the allegation of the complaint and asserted the affirmative defenses of comparative negligence and the failure of plaintiffs to wear seat belts.

[Plaintiffs moved pursuant to CPLR 3121(a) to compel defendant to disclose, *inter alia*, the result of the blood alcohol test (which showed a level of .27%). Papers in support of the motion included an attorney's affidavit, the police accident report, three affidavits of persons who claimed to have observed defendant's drinking in the hours preceding the accident, and the affidavit of the manager of the tavern. Defendant cross moved for an order of protection under CPLR 3122, asserting the physician-patient privilege. Plaintiff's motion was denied, the IAS court finding that defendant had not placed her physical condition in issue and thus she had the privilege. The Appellate Division affirmed. Here, the Court of Appeals also affirms after reviewing the nature and origin of the privilege.]

. . . .

III

In *Koump v Smith* (25 NY2d 287, *supra*), we examined the operation of the physician-patient privilege in the context of a personal injury action. In that case, the plaintiff was injured in an automobile accident and, as here, it was alleged that the driver of the offending vehicle was intoxicated at the time of the collision. The plaintiff served a discovery request pursuant to CPLR 3121(a), alleging that the defendant's physical condition was "in controversy" within the meaning of the statute and demanding production of the defendant's hospital records relating to the accident. The defendant refused to comply with the request and the plaintiff moved for a court order directing compliance. Citing the physician-patient privilege, the Appellate Division affirmed the trial court's denial of the motion. We affirmed, concluding that plaintiff had not demonstrated that defendant's physical condition was "in controversy" within the meaning of CPLR 3121(a) and that, in any event, the requested information was protected by the physician-patient privilege (CPLR 4504) which defendant had not waived by merely denying the allegations in the complaint.

We acknowledged in *Koump* that there is a strong presumption in favor of discovery and that "full disclosure of all evidence material and necessary in the prosecution or defense of an action" is ordinarily mandated by CPLR 3101. Consequently, where the mental or physical condition of a party is in controversy, a notice may be served pursuant to CPLR 3121(a) requiring that the party submit to a medical examination or make available for inspection relevant hospital and medical records. The initial burden of proving that a party's physical condition is "in controversy" is on the party seeking the information and it is only after such an evidentiary showing that discovery may proceed under the statute (*Koump v Smith*, 25 NY2d, at 300, *supra*).

Once this preliminary burden is satisfied, however, discovery still may be precluded if the requested information is privileged and thus exempted from disclosure (CPLR 3101[b]). The statutory scheme, by expressly providing an exception for privileged information, clearly contemplates that certain information, though otherwise material and relevant to a legal dispute, "shall not be obtainable" where it is shown to be privileged (CPLR 3101[b]). Physician-patient communications, privileged under CPLR 4504, may therefore be shielded from discovery and when it has been established that the requested information is subject to discovery under CPLR 3121(a), the burden shifts to the person claiming the privilege to assert it by seeking a protective order pursuant to CPLR 3122. . . . Once the privilege is validly asserted, it must be recognized and the sought-after information may not be disclosed unless it is demonstrated that the privilege has been waived. . . .

A litigant will be deemed to have waived the privilege when, in bringing or defending a personal injury action, that person has affirmatively placed his or her mental or physical condition in issue (*Koump v Smith*, 25 NY2d, at 294, *supra*). As we stated in *Koump*, this rule is necessary because, notwithstanding New York's strong policy in favor of the privilege, a party should not be permitted to affirmatively assert a medical condition in seeking damages or in defending against liability while simultaneously relying on the confidential physician-patient relationship as a sword to thwart the opposition in its efforts to uncover facts critical to disputing the party's claim (*id.; see*, 3A Weinstein-Korn-Miller, NY Civ Prac P3121.01). Nevertheless, a party does not waive the privilege whenever forced to defend an action in which his or her mental or physical condition is in controversy. In order to effect a waiver, the party must do more than simply deny the allegations in the complaint — he or she must affirmatively assert the condition "either by way of counterclaim or to excuse the conduct complained of by the plaintiff" (*Koump v Smith*, 25 NY2d, at 294, *supra*).

IV

Applying these principles to the facts of this case, we conclude that plaintiffs have satisfied their threshold burden of demonstrating that defendant's physical condition at the time of the accident is in controversy. The affidavits submitted in support of their discovery motion indicate that defendant had been drinking rather heavily over a seven-hour period leading up to the accident and there is at least some suggestion, albeit hearsay, that she may have been "shut off" by the bartender at Eddie's Conklin Inn because of her intoxicated condition. Moreover, it is a matter of public record, alluded to in the affidavit of plaintiffs' attorney, that defendant was convicted of criminally negligent homicide based on the events surrounding the accident. This evidence, we think, is plainly sufficient to demonstrate that defendant's physical condition at the time of the accident is "in controversy" within the meaning of CPLR 3121(a) and thus potentially subject to discovery.

The information sought by plaintiffs, however — hospital records relating to defendant's physical condition and blood alcohol content following the accident — indisputably falls within the scope of the physician-patient privilege as information acquired by a physician "in attending [defendant] in a professional capacity, and which was necessary to enable him to act in that capacity" (CPLR 4504). Defendant cannot be said to have waived the privilege simply by denying the allegations in the complaint or by testifying that she cannot remember any details of the incident where the fact of her memory loss is not being advanced to excuse her conduct (*Koump v Smith*, 25 NY2d, at 294, *supra*). Nor has she waived the privilege by asserting the defenses of comparative negligence and the failure of plaintiffs to wear seat belts since neither defense seeks to excuse the conduct complained of by asserting a mental or physical condition. Moreover, the mere fact that the privilege presents an obstacle to plaintiffs' discovery of legally pertinent information that would assist them in proving their claim is not, as the dissent seems to suggest, evidence that the privilege is not properly recognized in this case. Indeed, it is inherent in the very nature of an evidentiary privilege that it presents an obstacle to discovery and it is precisely in those situations where confidential information is sought in advancing a legal claim that such privilege is intended to operate. Were we to carve out an exception to the privilege whenever it inhibited the fact-finding process, it would quickly become eviscerated.

Plaintiff's contention that the privilege is somehow forfeited upon their submission of evidentiary facts demonstrating that defendant's physical condition is in controversy is without merit and confuses the amount of evidence required to justify discovery under CPLR 3121(a) with that required under CPLR 4504 to establish waiver. Plaintiffs may not effect a waiver of the privilege for the simple reason that the privilege is not theirs to waive but rather belongs to the patient. . . . Once it has been shown that the requested information is privileged under the statute, therefore, only the patient or an authorized representative may waive the privilege and permit disclosure. . . . That has not occurred in this case and thus plaintiffs' discovery motion was properly denied. We have examined plaintiffs' remaining contentions and find them to be without merit.

Accordingly, the order of the Appellate Division should be affirmed and the certified question answered in the negative.

BELLACOSA, J. (dissenting).

I respectfully disagree with the majority because in my view the rule in *Koump v Smith* (25 NY2d 287) is misapplied and then extended in a direction antithetical to that which was intended. Defendant is thus allowed to wield the physician-patient privilege against the truth-finding process in a case in which the remedial statutory protection (CPLR 4504[a]) and in which sound policy and interpretation compel the opposite result (*compare*, Vehicle and Traffic Law § 1194[a][a]; former § 1194-a[2][a]; § 1194[3][b][1]). I would grant disclosure of defendant's hospital record of a blood test showing an alcohol content of .27 — almost three times the legal limit (Vehicle and Traffic Law § 1192[2]). My vote is to reverse the denial in the lower courts of the plaintiffs' motion.

Tonia Dillenbeck was killed and her 10-year-old son, one of the plaintiffs here, was seriously injured when the vehicle in which they were riding was hit by one driven by defendant Hess. Hess was injured, hospitalized, and a blood alcohol test was administered. In a criminal action arising from this same incident, the defendant was convicted of criminally negligent homicide. Plaintiffs sue for wrongful death and personal injuries, and contend that Hess' intoxication caused the accident.

Hess pleaded in her answer by general denial that she was not intoxicated, and affirmatively asserted comparative negligence and plaintiffs' failure to wear seat belts. Also, during the examination before trial, she claimed to have no memory of the accident or its attendant details.

I disagree with what I perceive to be the majority's holding: (1) that the party enjoying the physician- patient privilege must personally waive it in the sense that a waiver cannot be effected by operation of law through a party's conduct, and (2) that it is defendant alone who subjectively determines whether her own physical condition is "in controversy" and who thus controls whether plaintiff may gain access to vital evidence. The practical consequence of the majority's holding is to deny drunk driving accident victims access to blood alcohol test results and to allow defendant to conceal key scientific evidence from plaintiffs and from the adjudication process.

The physician-patient privilege is a statutory shield overturning the common-law rule generally allowing disclosure of otherwise admissible communications to a physician, even those made in the strictest confidence. . . . The underlying rationale for this rule has more lately been questioned and criticized by commentators for conflicting with New York's modern, liberal disclosure scheme under CPLR 3101(a) and 3121, and for impeding the courts' primary truth-seeking function. . . . Misuse of the privilege prompted this observation: "Actually the privilege is utilized as a tactical maneuver, and is seldom invoked for any purpose other than to suppress facts that are injurious to the legal position of the person who seeks its protection. Rarely is it used to guard a secret" (Fisch, NY Evidence § 557 [2d ed]). For these reasons, the modern approach is to apply the privilege restrictively rather than expansively. . . .

The privilege and its underlying policy are also put in significant competition with statutory developments in the Vehicle and Traffic Law designed to address the great public concern and interest in dealing with drunk drivers. The law in this State now is that any person who operates a motor vehicle shall be deemed to have given consent to a chemical test where there are reasonable grounds to believe that the driver's ability was impaired by alcohol, provided the test is administered by or at the direction of a police officer (Vehicle and Traffic Law § 1194[2][a]). Furthermore, submission to a chemical test is compulsory when a person has been killed or seriously injured by a drunk driver (Vehicle and Traffic Law § 1194[3][b][1]). Holding that a person has a privilege of this kind in an area regarding information that the State explicitly elsewhere requires to be disclosed creates an unnecessary inconsistency in statutory application.

If a party comes forward with unequivocal proof of the other party's physical condition at the time of the accident, the condition should be deemed "in controversy" and evidence relating to it subject to discovery. When a party puts the other party's condition "in controversy" by such evidence and when a party is clearly not on a "fishing expedition," the interest of letting truth triumph outweighs the defendant's desire to cloak highly relevant scientific evidence in secrecy. This is consistent with the words of the statute, with the intent of the statutory protection, with a realistic interpretation of *Koump*, with sound construction of remedial statutes in derogation of the common law, and with present-day legislative attitudes reflected in related statutory developments. This should be especially so when that result and analysis also coincide with the general modern trend towards open and full reciprocal discovery and with fundamental fairness between the parties.

To allow defendant to sweep scientific evidence under the rug of a physician-patient privilege in this case is to allow her to hide the truth, without legal justification or good purpose.

JUDGES SIMONS, TITONE and HANCOCK, JR., concur with JUDGE ALEXANDER; JUDGE BELLACOSA dissents and votes to reverse in a separate opinion in which CHIEF JUDGE WACHTLER and JUDGE KAYE concur.

NOTES

(1) On the facts presented in the principal case, will it be difficult for the plaintiff to prove that the defendant was driving under the influence even in the absence of the medical records? Should this have been a factor in the court's discussion? How would the majority view the case if there was some indication of drunk driving but no criminal conviction and no proof other than the medical records?

(2) The Court of Appeals held that where plaintiff retains a nonphysician vocational rehabilitation expert who is prepared to testify as to plaintiff's lack of capacity to perform in the workforce, defendant is entitled to have plaintiff examined by a vocational rehabilitation expert retained by defendant. The liberal discovery provisions of Article 31 permit stretching CPLR 3121 to accommodate nonphysicians. *Kavanaugh v. Ogden Allied Maintenance Corp.*, 92 N.Y.2d 952, 682 N.Y.S.2d 156, 705 N.E.2d 1197 (1998).

(3) In *Robinson v. Meca*, 214 A.D.2d 246, 632 N.Y.S. 728 (3d Dep't 1995), it was held that defendant's eyesight was not in issue solely on plaintiff's claim that defendant should have seen her. Plaintiff was a pedestrian crossing the street, allegedly struck by defendant's car. However, plaintiff was entitled to defendant's optical records. Why? Because plaintiff claimed that they would show defendant to have lied in a deposition where she said she had not been prescribed corrective lenses. The records thus had potential impeachment value, and there was no privilege since defendant saw an optometrist and not a physician.

(4) Probably the most important consequence of placing one's mental or physical condition in controversy is that it entitles the adversary to require that party to submit to a physical, mental or blood examination. CPLR 3121(a). A copy of the report made by the examining physician must be provided to any other party who offers in exchange a copy of any report in his control made with respect to the condition in controversy. CPLR 3121(b). This "exchange" obligation is amplified by 22 NYCRR 202.17 of the Uniform Civil Rules for the Supreme Court and County Court, which became effective January 6, 1986. This rule applies to the exchange of medical reports in personal injury and wrongful death actions. It requires that not less than thirty nor more than sixty days notice be given of a physical examination scheduled pursuant to CPLR 3121. At least twenty days before the examination the party to be examined must give the other parties: (1) Copies of the medical reports of physicians who have previously treated or examined the party seeking recovery; and (2) Authorizations permitting all parties to obtain copies of all hospital and other relevant medical

records. Within forty-five days after the examination, the examining party must provide a copy of the report to every other party.

If, after the service of any of the reports referred to above, any party obtains evidence of additional or further injuries or conditions which they intend to offer at trial, such party must serve a supplemental report on the other parties and must specify a time within ten days thereafter that an additional medical exam may be held. The notice must be given within thirty days after the discovery of the new evidence and no less than thirty days before trial. Similarly, if any party intends to offer testimony at trial of additional treating or examining physicians, the medical reports of such physicians must be served no later than ten days before trial. 22 NYCRR 202.17(g).

(5) In an action in which the plaintiff alleges personal injuries, it is clear that plaintiff's physical condition is "in controversy" and that the defendant could demand that plaintiff submit to a physical examination under CPLR 3121 and 22 NYCRR 202.17. But suppose the defendant does not seek such an examination. May the defendant nonetheless obtain the reports of the physician who treated plaintiff? Such disclosure is not authorized by CPLR 3121. *Hoenig v. Westphal*, 52 N.Y.2d 605, 439 N.Y.S.2d 831, 422 N.E.2d 491 (1981), held, however, that CPLR 3121 does not provide the exclusive method of obtaining medical information and that the defendant could rely on the general disclosure provisions of CPLR 3101 to obtain the desired reports. What about the report of a physician who did not treat the plaintiff but examined him as an expert witness in preparation for litigation? *See* CPLR 3101(d) and the discussion of it earlier in this chapter. *See also Dorato v. Schilp*, 130 A.D.2d 348, 520 N.Y.S.2d 265 (3d Dep't 1987) (holding that such reports are protected from disclosure).

(6) Rule 35(a) of the Federal Rules of Civil Procedure provides that a physical or mental examination of a party whose condition is in controversy may be obtained only on court order, "for good cause shown." As to the "good cause" requirement, see *Schlagenhauf v. Holder*, 379 U.S. 104, 85 S. Ct. 234 (1964).

[G] Freedom of Information Law

The New York Freedom of Information Law (Pub. Off. L. §§ 84 *et seq.*) is not in any technical sense a disclosure device. But as a practical matter, it is a method of seeking information relevant to actual or potential litigation. This is true whether one's opponent is a governmental agency or a private party who has filed material with a state or local authority.

Pub. Off. L. § 87(2) requires that every governmental agency "make available for public inspection and copying all records . . ." subject to listed exceptions. The next case considers the relationship between the Freedom of Information Law and the CPLR disclosure provisions.

M. FARBMAN & SONS, INC. v. N.Y.C. HEALTH & HOSPITALS CORP.

Court of Appeals
62 N.Y.2d 75, 476 N.Y.S.2d 69, 464 N.E.2d 437 (1984)

KAYE, JUDGE.

Access to records of a government agency under the Freedom of Information Law (FOIL) (Public Officers Law, art. 6) is not affected by the fact that there is pending or potential litigation between the person making the request and the agency. Because the court below erroneously concluded that FOIL is unavailable to a litigant, and that CPLR article 31 is a blanket exemption from FOIL, we reverse the dismissal of the petition, with costs, and reinstate Special Term's order calling for an in camera inspection to test the agency's claimed exemptions.

In 1977, appellant, M. Farbman & Sons, Inc., contracted with the New York City Health and Hospitals Corporation (HHC), to perform plumbing work at Harlem Hospital. Although the work was to be finished by May, 1979, completion was delayed until November 12, 1980, evidently resulting in cost overruns. On April 13, 1981, Farbman made a FOIL request for 14 categories of records, encompassing most of the documents relating to the construction project. The HHC records access officer denied the request because its scope was "beyond the limits and objectives of the Freedom of Information Law." Pursuant to section 89 (subd. 4, par. [a]) of the Public Officers Law, Farbman appealed to respondent Stanley Brezenoff, HHC president, who affirmed the denial on the ground that the request was "so encompassing and unspecific that it is not in keeping with the spirit or the letter" of FOIL.

Farbman then commenced this article 78 proceeding to compel production in accordance with its request. HHC claimed in response that the petition should be dismissed because Farbman was using FOIL in an effort to gather material for litigation in circumvention of the CPLR, and because requested documents were exempt from disclosure under section 87 (subd. 2, par. [g]) of the Public Officers Law as interagency or intra-agency materials. Special Term held that HHC had not established an exemption from FOIL's disclosure requirements and ordered an in camera inspection of the documents as to which an exemption was claimed. Before any decision, however, Farbman filed a notice of claim and commenced a breach of contract action against HHC. In view of the litigation HHC moved to reargue and renew, but Special Term adhered to its determination. On appeal, the Appellate Division reversed and dismissed the petition, citing its "continually unanimous position against the use of FOIL to further in-progress litigation." (94 A.D.2d 576, p. 578. . . .)

FOIL implements the legislative declaration that "government is the public's business" (Public Officers Law, § 84), and imposes a broad standard of open disclosure upon agencies of the government. The statute "proceeds under the premise that the public is vested with an inherent right to know and that official secrecy is anathematic to our form of government." (*Matter of Fink v. Lefkowitz*, 47 N.Y.2d 567, 571, 419 N.Y.S.2d 467, 393 N.E.2d 463.) In furtherance of the legislative objective, all records of an agency are presumptively available for public inspection and copying, unless they fall within one of eight categories of exemptions.

To give the public maximum access to records of government, these statutory exemptions are narrowly interpreted, and the burden of demonstrating that requested material is exempt from disclosure rests on the agency. FOIL does not require that the party requesting records make any showing of need, good faith or legitimate purpose; while its purpose may be to shed light on government decision-making, its ambit is not confined to records actually used in the decision-making process. Full disclosure by public agencies, is, under FOIL, a public right and in the public interest, irrespective of the status or need of the person making the request.

CPLR article 31 proceeds under a different premise, and serves quite different concerns. While speaking also of "full disclosure," article 31 is plainly more restrictive than FOIL. Access to records under the CPLR depends on status and need. With the goals of promoting both the ascertainment of truth at trial and the prompt disposition of actions (*Allen v. Crowell-Collier Pub. Co.*, 21 N.Y.2d 403, 407, 288 N.Y.S.2d 449, 235 N.E.2d 430), discovery is at the outset limited to that which is "material and necessary in the prosecution or defense of an action." (CPLR 3101, subd. [a].) Broad, unparticularized document demands are improper. (*Compare* CPLR 3120 *and* Public Officers Law, § 89, subd. 3.) On its own initiative or on motion of any party or witness, a court may issue a protective order denying or regulating document production, to prevent unreasonable annoyance, expense, embarrassment, disadvantage or other prejudice to any person or the courts (CPLR 3103). Unlike the right of a member of the public to inspect and copy the files of government under FOIL, a litigant has no presumptive right under the CPLR to its adversary's files.

When, as here, a government agency is involved in litigation, is its adversary, for purposes of access to the agency's records, a litigant governed by article 31, or a member of the public under FOIL? Recognizing that compelling policy considerations support either position, we hold that FOIL's mandate of open disclosure requires that an agency's public records remain as available to its litigation adversary as to any other person. Contrary to the conclusion reached by the court below, and urged by respondents, we hold that CPLR article 31 is not a statute "specifically exempt[ing]" public records from disclosure under FOIL (Public Officers Law, § 87, subd. 2, par. [a]).

Given FOIL's purpose, its broad implementing language, and the narrowness of its exemptions, article 31 cannot be read as a blanket exception from its reach. While an express statement . . . is not necessary to establish an exemption from FOIL under a State statute, what is required is clear legislative intent to establish and preserve confidentiality. No such intention can be gleaned from the declaration of CPLR 3101 (subd [a]) that only evidence "material and necessary" to an action be produced. In the absence of indication from the Legislature, we refuse to read into FOIL the restriction that, once litigation commences, a party forfeits the rights available to all other members of the public and is confined to discovery in accordance with article 31. If the Legislature had intended to exempt agencies involved in litigation from FOIL, it certainly could have so provided. Nowhere in FOIL, enacted 11 years after the CPLR, is there specific reference to records already subject to production under article 31, and no provision of FOIL bars simultaneous use of both statutes. When FOIL was amended in 1977 (*see* L.1977, ch. 933, § 1), issues regarding the interplay between the two statutes already simmered in the courts, yet the Legislature made no reference to article 31 document production in FOIL, but only broadened public access to documents.

An article 31 exemption from FOIL, moreover, would be unique among FOIL exemptions in that it would depend not on the need to maintain individual privacy or the government's need for confidentiality of the records but on the status of the party making the request. Though denied to a litigant, these records would remain available to the public. As we have stated in *Matter of John P. v. Whalen*, 54 N.Y.2d 89, 99, 444 N.Y.S.2d 598, 429 N.E.2d 117, *supra*, "the standing of one who seeks access to records under the Freedom of Information Law is as a member of the public, and neither enhanced nor restricted because he is also a litigant or potential litigant." To be distinguished of course would be claimed exemptions from FOIL on the basis of privilege (CPLR 3101, subd. [b]), attorney's work product (CPLR 3101, subd. [c]), and material prepared for litigation (CPLR 3101, subd. [d]), none of them tied to the particular status of the party making the request. Since respondents have made no claim that any of its records are being withheld for these reasons, we have no occasion to consider whether these categories would be "specifically exempted" from disclosure by virtue of section 87 (subd. 2, par. [a]) of the Public Officers Law.

That FOIL may be used during litigation for improper purposes, such as harassment and delay, is a genuine concern. We note that the Appellate Divisions have addressed such problems as they have arisen in particular cases. In *Brady & Co. v. City of New York*, 84 A.D.2d 113, 445 N.Y.S.2d 724, for example, the court struck an action from the trial calendar where the plaintiff filed a note of issue and statement of readiness without having conducted discovery under the CPLR, and thereafter submitted a FOIL request. (*See, also, Moussa v. State of New York*, 91 A.D.2d 863, 458 N.Y.S.2d 377.) The potential for abuse through FOIL is in a sense a price of open government, and should not be invoked to undermine the statute.

Turning now to the request itself, the court below concluded that appellants' request was not sufficiently specific to meet the requirements of CPLR 3120, and this same test of specificity should apply to FOIL requests. While appellant's request may well have been insufficient under CPLR 3120, which demands that documents be "specifically designated," that standard is inapplicable under FOIL, which requires only that the records be "reasonably described" (Public Officers Law, § 89, subd. 3) so that the respondent agency may locate the records in question. While complaining that the request is so broad as to require thousands of records, respondents have not established that the descriptions were insufficient for purposes of locating and identifying the documents sought.

Respondents' final argument is that the five remaining items of appellant's FOIL request are exempt from production under section 87 (subd. 2, par. [g]), which protects inter-agency or intra-agency materials. Where an exemption is claimed, the burden lies with the agency "to articulate particularized and specific justification," and to establish that "the material requested falls squarely within the ambit of [the] statutory exemptions." (*Matter of Fink v. Lefkowitz*, 47 N.Y.2d 567, 571, 419 N.Y.S.2d 467, 393 N.E.2d 463, *supra*.) Respondents have not demonstrated as a matter of law that all of the records requested by appellant are in fact inter-agency or intra-agency materials or, even if so, that they are not statistical or factual tabulations, or instructions to staff that affect the public, or final agency policy or determinations. The proper procedure for reaching a determination is the in camera inspection ordered by Special Term. (*See Church of Scientology v. State of New York*, 46 N.Y.2d 906, 908, 414 N.Y.S.2d 900, 387 N.E.2d 1216.)

Accordingly, the order of the Appellate Division should be reversed, with costs, and the order of Special Term reinstated.

NOTES

(1) In *Matter of Newsday, Inc. v. State Department of Transportation*, 5 N.Y.3d 84, 800 N.Y.S.2d 67, 833 N.E.2d 210 (2005), petitioner, a news organization, was denied its FOIL request for the Department of Transportation's "priority list of hazardous intersections and locations" for the Long Island and New York City regions. The denial was based on 23 U.S.C. § 409, which provides that certain documents relating to traffic safety shall not be subject to discovery in traffic accident lawsuits. The court ruled that while this information might not be subject to pretrial discovery, it should be furnished pursuant to the FOIL. Judge R.S. Smith wrote, in part:

> The premise of FOIL is "that the public is vested with an inherent right to know and that official secrecy is anathematic to our form of government" (*Matter of Fink v. Lefkowitz*, 47 N.Y.2d 567, 571, 419 N.Y.S.2d 467, 393 N.E.2d 463 [1979]). This premise applies with full force to documents that show what the government is doing to make roads safer. The policy underlying section 409, to encourage states to collect information bearing on road safety, is important also, but Congress has not directed that the former policy give way entirely to the latter: section 409 does not say that lists of dangerous locations "shall be confidential," but only that they shall not be discoverable in certain litigations.

If the documents Newsday seeks here are disclosed to it, the protection offered by section 409 may be diminished, but it will not be eliminated. A tort plaintiff will not have access to the information except to the extent Newsday chooses to publish it. If the information is published, some tort plaintiffs may obtain the equivalent of discovery, but section 409 will continue to exclude the documents from evidence. Congress evidently did not think that the possibility that some plaintiffs would indirectly obtain information justified requiring nondisclosure of the documents for all purposes. If it had wanted to achieve that result, it could have said so.

This is not a case in which a tort plaintiff is using a FOIL request to avoid section 409's prohibition on discovery. No one disputes that Newsday's purpose in making its FOIL request was simply to gather news. Where a FOIL request for materials subject to section 409 is made by a tort plaintiff, or by someone acting on such a plaintiff's behalf, perhaps denial of the request will be justified (*cf. Ex parte Alabama Dept. of Transp.*, 757 So.2d 371 [Ala.1999]; *Seaton v. Johnson*, 898 S.W.2d 232 [Tenn.1995] [both relying on section 409 in rejecting attempts to invoke state of freedom of information statutes on behalf of injured plaintiffs]). We see no need to decide that question before it comes up.

(2) Requests for information under the FOIL have been denied in *Prisoners' Legal Services of New York v. New York State Department of Correctional Services*, 73 N.Y.2d 26, 538 N.Y.S.2d 190 (1988) (inmate grievance documents in the file of a particular correction officer held protected under the "personnel records" exemption), and in *Federation of New York State Rifle and Pistol Clubs, Inc. v. New York City Police Department*, 73 N.Y.2d 92, 538 N.Y.S.2d 226 (1989) (names and addresses of persons holding gun permits held protected from access by an organization which wanted them to engage in a membership drive; FOIL is not available to assist in fund-raising).

In *Matter of World Trade Center Bombing Litigation v. Port Authority*, 93 N.Y.2d 1, 686 N.Y.S.2d 743, 709 N.E.2d 452 (1999), involving alleged negligence in implementing security measures resulting in plaintiffs' injuries from the 1993 terrorist bombing of the World Trade Center, it was held that defendant was not required to disclose security-related plans and documents pending an in camera judicial assessment of whether the requested documents were protected by the public interest privilege. Such a privilege inheres in confidential communications between and to public officers in the performance of their duties.

(3) The federal Freedom of Information Act, 5 U.S.C. § 552 (1970), can also be useful in obtaining information which is relevant to litigation. *See, e.g., Kreindler v. Department of the Navy*, 363 F. Supp. 611 (S.D.N.Y. 1973) (attorney held entitled to obtain government reports on the cause of an air disaster; the documents were sought to determine whether to commence an action on behalf of his clients, the survivors of the crash). Some federal courts have in general

held that information is available pursuant to the Freedom of Information Act even if it would be protected from pre-trial discovery, so long as the party's need for it outweighs the government's interest in confidentiality. *See* Toran, *Information Disclosure in Civil Actions: The Freedom of Information Act and the Federal Discovery Rules*, 49 Geo. Wash. L. Rev. 843, 848-54 (1981). *C.f. F.T.C. v. Grolier, Inc.*, 462 U.S. 19, 103 S. Ct. 2209, 76 L. Ed. 2d 387 (1983) (attorney's work product rule applies to Federal FOIA requests).

(4) Left open by the principal case is the question whether material privileged under CPLR 3101 as attorney-client communications, attorney's work product or material prepared for litigation is also privileged under the FOIL. Should the answer necessarily be the same for all three categories?

§ 15.05 COMPELLING AND AVOIDING DISCLOSURE

PROBLEM E

(1) In a medical malpractice case, the plaintiff served a notice of deposition on the attorney for the defendant physician on June 6, 2006, scheduling the deposition for June 26, 2006. The defendant failed to appear on that date. Instead, the plaintiff's attorney was served with a motion for summary judgment on defendants' behalf. (A motion for summary judgment stays all disclosure until the motion is decided. CPLR 3214(b).) The plaintiff opposed the motion and cross moved for an order compelling the defendant to appear for a deposition. On November 12, 2006, the Supreme Court Justice to whom the case had been assigned denied the motion for summary judgment and granted the motion to compel. The defendant appealed, simultaneously moving for a stay of the deposition pending the appeal.

Should the stay be granted? *See* CPLR 3103(a), (b).

(2) Assume that the motion for a stay was granted by the IAS judge. The appeal, which was argued in February, 2006, resulted in an affirmance of both the motion and the cross-motion on June 19, 2006. The Appellate Division ordered the defendant to appear at a deposition on a date to be scheduled by the parties not later than twenty days from the date of service of its order on the defendant.

After conferring with counsel for the defendant, plaintiff re-noticed the deposition for July 7, 2006. On the day before that, defendant's attorney called plaintiff's lawyer to say that the defendant would not appear because he was "too busy with patients" and was not available to appear at a deposition until September 2006, because of the combination of his work and vacation schedules. Plaintiff then moved for an order striking defendant's answer pursuant to CPLR 3126(3). In response, the defendant argued that his failure to appear at a deposition was not willful and contumacious. The doctor submitted an affidavit stating that July 7, 2006, had been a very busy day and that he was now ready and able to appear at a deposition at such time as the court would order.

Should the motion be granted? What other relief should the court consider, if any?

SIEGMAN v. ROSEN
Appellate Division, First Department
270 A.D.2d 14, 704 N.Y.S.2d 40 (2000)

This consolidated action special proceeding seeks the payment of an unsatisfied money judgment that was entered against defendant Efraim Rosen in 1990. Plaintiff alleges that the formation of defendant Rosen Diamond Co., Inc. (RDC) by Efraim's wife Sarah, RDC's sole shareholder, the purchase of a house in Sarah's name only and subsequent improvements to the house allegedly valued at more than double its cost, and the dissolution of defendant Efraim Rosen Co., Inc., are all part of a series of fraudulent conveyances of Efraim's assets in order to frustrate collection of the judgment.

In June 1997, Justice Kapnick precluded plaintiff's discovery of all pre-March 2, 1986 transactions, but, on appeal, this Court removed that restriction as it pertained to plaintiff's claims for fraudulent conveyance (*Siegman v. Rosen*, 248 A.D.2d 180). As a result, Justice Kapnick, by order entered October 29, 1998, directed defendants to serve supplemental responses to the first set of interrogatories and document requests without regard to whether the documents sought pre-dated 1986.

Defendants, however, continually failed to produce any pre-1986 documents, despite several alleged promises to do so, and, as a result, plaintiff moved for sanctions in January 1999. At this juncture, defendants, for the first time, made the revelation that the documents in question could not be found. Thus, it was not until defendants contested the production of these documents, won the point at the trial court, saw the restriction removed on plaintiff's appeal, were subsequently ordered by the IAS Court to produce the documents, and had to answer a motion for sanctions after more delays and excuses, that they suddenly discovered that the documents simply could not be found. Further, what makes defendants' actions even more egregious is that they supply no indication whatsoever of the fate of the documents or what efforts were undertaken to locate them.

It is well settled that in order to impose the drastic remedy of preclusion, the court must determine that the offending party's failure to comply with discovery demands was willful, deliberate and contumacious (*see*, CPLR 3126[2]; *Dexter v. Horowitz Mgt.*, 267 A.D.2d 21; *Maillard v. Maillard*, 243 A.D.2d 448). Generally, willfulness can be inferred when a party repeatedly fails to respond to discovery demands and/or to comply with discovery orders, coupled with inadequate excuses for those defaults (*DiDomenico v. C & S Aeromatik Supplies*, 252 A.D.2d 41, 52; *Frias v. Fortini*, 240 A.D.2d 467).

In this matter, in view of the importance of the documents as they pertain to plaintiff's claims, the efforts expended by defendants to prevent their disclosure through judicial means and, when all legal maneuvering failed, their sudden, unexplained disappearance, the IAS Court should have concluded that defendants' actions were indeed willful and warranted the sanctions imposed herein (*see, Caruso v. Malang*, 234 A.D.2d 496; *Horowitz v. Camp Cedarhurst & Town & Country Day School*, 119 A.D.2d 548).

NOTE ON THE ENFORCEMENT PROCEDURES

CPLR 3122 to provides that if a party disputes the reasonableness of a discovery request, that party should so respond to the seeking party within 20 days of service of the discovery notice. If the parties are unable to resolve the dispute, the seeking party can move for an order under CPLR 3124 to compel disclosure. CPLR 3126 then provides the sanctions if a party refuses to obey an order of the court "or wilfully fails to disclose information which the court finds ought to have been disclosed pursuant to this article." The sanctions include resolving issues to which the disclosure requests relate in favor of the seeking party, an order precluding the "disobedient party" from producing evidence relevant to the subject issues, and an order striking pleadings or parts thereof. The court is given the discretion to allow another chance to comply.

CPLR 3124 and 3126 apply to all discovery requests contained in article 31, except for the notice to admit under CPLR 3123, which carries its own sanctions.

Some objections may not be waived when a party fails to respond to a discovery request. It has been held that where it can be shown that the material sought is privileged or is the attorney's work product under CPLR 3101(b)(d), it is *per se* unobtainable. *Coffey v. Orbach's*, 22 A.D.2d 317, 254 N.Y.S.2d 596 (1st Dep't 1964).

NOTES

(1) The standard applied to motions for preclusion under CPLR 3126 has been summarized in *Sawh v. Bridges*, 120 A.D.2d 74, 507 N.Y.S.2d 632 (2d Dep't 1986):

> We recognize that absent a showing that the noncomplying party's conduct was willful or contumacious, the harsh sanction of dismissal of a complaint will generally not be warranted. . . .

(2) In *Kihl v. Pfeffer*, 94 N.Y.2d 118, 700 N.Y.S.2d 87, 722 N.E.2d 55 (1999), plaintiff, injured in an auto accident, sued the Honda Motor Co. alleging negli-

gence and strict products liability. Honda immediately served 34 pages of interrogatories. A preliminary conference order directed discovery to be completed within six months, and Honda's interrogatories to be answered within 30 days. Instead of registering any objection pursuant to CPLR 3122 or seeking a protective order, plaintiff simply failed to respond. Five months after the due date, Honda moved to strike the complaint, or to compel responses within 10 days. Plaintiff's response was deemed inadequate, the IAS court dismissed the complaint, and the Court of Appeals affirmed. Chief Judge Kaye's Opinion for the Court stated: "If the credibility of court orders and the integrity of our judicial system are to be maintained, a litigant cannot ignore court orders with impunity." 94 N.Y.2d at 123, 700 N.Y.S.2d at 90, 722 N.E.2d at 58.

(3) It has been held that a plaintiff's failure to comply with disclosure obligations can be considered a failure to prosecute the action; hence the six-month extension of the statute of limitations authorized by CPLR 205 will not protect the plaintiff if a new action is commenced. *Ivory v. Ekstrom*, 98 A.D.2d 763, 469 N.Y.S.2d 478 (2d Dep't 1983).

(4) The threat of summary judgment is obviously effective only when the recalcitrance is by a party or someone under the control of a party. What about non-parties? Since disclosure from them is ordinarily pursuant to subpoena, CPLR 3106(b), disobedience is punishable as a contempt of court, CPLR 2308, 5104.

Part Five
RESOLVING THE LITIGATION

Chapter 16
ACCELERATED JUDGMENT

Scope of Chapter

The term "accelerated judgment" as used in CPLR article 32 embraces the various methods by which the normal progress of a lawsuit may be cut short and a final disposition made without a full trial. Primary among these devices are the subjects of this chapter: the pre-trial motion to dismiss a claim or defense, the motion for summary judgment and judgment by default. It is important that you understand the differences and similarities of these motions, their place in our litigation system, and when and how to use them. Note that while this chapter is for obvious reasons included in Part Five, Resolving the Litigation, some of the motions treated in this chapter may be made early in the litigation, *i.e.*, within the time allowed for an appearance. *See* CPLR 3211(e).

§ 16.01 MOTIONS TO DISMISS A CLAIM OR DEFENSE: CPLR 3211

Overview

The eleven paragraphs of CPLR 3211(a) list numerous grounds on which a claim can be dismissed on motion prior to serving a responsive pleading. The most problematic of these has been paragraph seven — dismissal for failure to state a cause of action, so it is treated (later in this chapter) in some detail. We will first note a few general points about CPLR 3211 motions and describe the other grounds on which a claim can be attacked under CPLR 3211(a).[*]

Considerable discretion is granted the court in hearing and disposing of a CPLR 3211 motion: The court may simply grant or deny the motion; it may order an immediate trial of any issues raised; it may — where essential facts are not then available to the opposing party — deny the motion with leave to raise the same objection in a responsive pleading, or order a continuance so that the party may obtain further affidavits or pursue disclosure proceedings, or make such other order as may be just; and finally, it may treat the motion as one for summary judgment, which brings into play several additional techniques of hearing and disposing of the motion.

---

[*] Parts of this description have appeared previously in O. Chase, CPLR Manual (2006).

A motion under either subdivision (a) or (b) extends the time to serve a responsive pleading until ten days after service of notice of entry of the order determining the motion. CPLR 3211(f). A motion under either subdivision also stays all disclosure until the motion is decided unless the court orders otherwise. CPLR 3214(b). Do these consequences of the motion suggest tactical considerations to be thought through when deciding whether to make a CPLR 3211 motion?

Some points on waiver: Under CPLR 3211(e), some of the grounds on which a cause of action may be dismissed on a pre-pleading motion under CPLR 3211(a) may be raised by a motion at any subsequent time in the action. Which are they? Why are they so treated? The motions described by CPLR 3211(a)(8) and (9), which go to jurisdiction over the defendant's person or property, are subject to the harsh waiver rules described in Chapter 6 on the appearance. The remaining grounds on which a cause of action can be dismissed are, according to CPLR 3211(e), waived if not raised by pre-pleading motion or in the responsive pleading. But remember that the waiver may be forgiven on a subsequent motion to include the defense in an amended pleading. *See* CPLR 3025 and Chapter 13.

Documentary Evidence

Paragraph 1 of CPLR 3211(a) allows a litigant to raise by motion any "defense . . . founded upon documentary evidence." Although the defenses listed in CPLR 3211(a)(5) are those which are normally founded upon documentary evidence, paragraph 1 was added "to cover all others that may arise, as for example, a written modification or any defense based on the terms of a written contract."[1] Affidavits are not, standing alone, documentary evidence for the purposes of this paragraph but can be used to supply connective links between the documents and the litigation and to assure the court of the genuineness of the documents.[2]

Lack of Subject Matter Jurisdiction

CPLR 3211(a)(2) allows a motion to dismiss for want of subject matter jurisdiction. The concept itself has been dealt with in Chapter 3.

---

[1] 1 N.Y. Adv. Comm. Rep. 85 (1957). *See also Heaney v. Purdy*, 29 N.Y.2d 157, 324 N.Y.S.2d 47, 272 N.E.2d 550 (1971) (judgment of a foreign court used as documentary evidence).

[2] *E.g., Rubin v. Rubin*, 72 A.D.2d 536, 421 N.Y.S.2d 68 (1st Dep't 1979) (judgment for defendant could not be predicated on copy of his income tax return because the motion did not include any affidavit that the copy submitted was correct and that the return accurately stated movant's income.)

Incapacity to Sue

Paragraph 3 provides for a motion to dismiss on the grounds that the claimant does not have legal capacity to sue.

The concept of incapacity to sue — which includes the obvious examples of infancy and mental incompetency — is otherwise somewhat vague. Often quoted is the language of the Court of Appeals in *Ward v. Petrie*:[3]

> There is a difference between capacity to sue, which is the right to come into court, and a cause of action, which is the right to relief in court. Incapacity to sue exists when there is some legal disability, such as infancy or lunacy or a want of title in the plaintiff to the character in which he sues.

That no comprehensive and precise definition of incapacity has been formulated is not surprising. Apart from the obvious examples mentioned, the question whether particular plaintiffs may maintain particular suits is often a matter of substantive law. CPLR 1004 reduces the dimensions of the problem by clearly expressing the right of various representative parties to sue in their own name.

Actions by foreign corporations that have not obtained proper certificates authorizing them to do business in New York[4] will be dismissed for "lack of capacity."[5]

Another Action Pending

Paragraph 4 of CPLR 3211(a) covers the objection that "there is another action pending between the same parties for the same cause of action. . . ." Dismissal of the second action is not required, as the paragraph adds the phrase "the court need not dismiss upon this ground but may make such other order as

---

[3] 157 N.Y. 301, 311 (1898) (a suit against a judgment debtor for fraudulent transfer of property could be brought only in the name of the judgment creditor; suit by another person would be dismissed for failure of a cause of action, not lack of capacity). *See* O. Chase, CPLR Manual ¶ 3211.17 (2006).

[4] Business Corp. Law § 1312(a). *See also Montco, Inc. v. Emergency Beacon Corp.*, 72 A.D.2d 765, 421 N.Y.S.2d 385 (2d Dep't 1979) (party for whom trustee in bankruptcy had been appointed lacked capacity to sue).

[5] *See United Environmental Techniques, Inc. v. State of New York Department of Health*, 88 N.Y.2d 824, 643 N.Y.S.2d 959, 666 N.E.2d 552 (1996) (because petitioner was a foreign corporation that had failed to file an amended certificate to do business in New York as required by B.C.L. § 1309, it lacked capacity to sue and its petition must be dismissed).

justice requires." This makes explicit the court's authority to stay, rather than dismiss, the second action,[6] or to consolidate the two.[7]

The objection under CPLR 3211(a)(4) will not be sustained unless the other action was instituted earlier in time and remained pending while the present one was commenced and the defense was asserted.[8]

It should be noted that while a dismissal on the ground of prior action pending cannot be granted unless the literal terms of paragraph 4 are met, the remedies of stay and consolidation exist independently and may therefore be available to reduce the inconvenience of multiple litigation even when paragraph 4 is inapplicable.[9]

Listed Defenses

Paragraph 5 of CPLR 3211(a) covers the defenses of arbitration and award, collateral estoppel, discharge in bankruptcy, infancy or other disability of the moving party, payment, release, res judicata, statute of limitations, and statute of frauds. The enumerated defenses are easily demonstrable bars to an action; they are generally difficult to fabricate and raise issues that are relatively easily resolved. Consequently, they pose a minimal danger of abuse for dilatory purposes, and that can save attorneys the considerable time and effort involved in preparing an answer in a complicated case. Since paragraph 5 does include nine different defenses, a motion based on it should specify the defense relied upon. The motion should be supported by affidavit, documentary evidence, or other appropriate proof (*e.g.*, a copy of an arbitration award). If issues of fact are in dispute, the court can order an immediate hearing, CPLR 3211(c), or reserve the issue for the trial.[10]

Counterclaim Improperly Interposed

The motion to dismiss a counterclaim under paragraph 6 of CPLR 3211(a), on the ground that "it may not properly be interposed in the action," is not to be

---

[6] *E.g, Hollendonner v. Kiem*, 138 A.D.2d 230, 525 N.Y.S.2d 43 (1st Dep't 1988); *Pierre Associates Inc. v. Citizens Casualty Co. of New York*, 32 A.D.2d 495, 304 N.Y.S.2d 158 (1st Dep't 1969); *see* Weinstein, Korn & Miller, N.Y. Civil Practice ¶ 3211.24.

[7] *See* CPLR 602. *Cf., Kent Development Co., Inc. v. Liccione*, 37 N.Y.2d 899, 378 N.Y.S.2d 377, 340 N.E.2d 740 (1975) (consolidation rejected because of inconvenience to other parties to the actions).

[8] *E.g, Merigone v. Seaboard Capital Corp.*, 85 Misc. 2d 965, 381 N.Y.S.2d 749 (Sup. Ct. 1976) (defendant was served after a traverse hearing in a prior action at which the prior action was dismissed due to defective service; it was held that there was no longer any prior action pending so as to allow dismissal of the second action).

[9] *See* CPLR 602 (consolidation); CPLR 2201 (stay).

[10] *Trepuk v. Frank*, 44 N.Y.2d 723, 405 N.Y.S.2d 452, 376 N.E.2d 924 (1978).

used as a substitute for the various other grounds on which a claim may be attacked under CPLR 3211(a), such as failure to state a cause of action. All of these are procedurally available against causes of action in a counterclaim as well as against claims in a complaint. *See* CPLR 3211(a). The motion under paragraph 6 is proper only when a counterclaim is asserted in violation of a restriction on the right to interpose it, *e.g.*, the rule which restricts counterclaims against a representative plaintiff to those that can be asserted against the plaintiff in the representative capacity in which the suit was brought.[11] and those of U.C.C. § 9-206 restricting some counterclaims against the assignee of a contract.

Under CPLR 3019(a), counterclaims need not be related to the main action, so there is no authority to dismiss on the ground of non-relatedness. As with any claim, the court has the authority to sever a counterclaim, or order separate trials to further convenience or avoid injustice. CPLR 603.

In Personam, In Rem, and Quasi In Rem Jurisdiction

Paragraph 8 of CPLR 3211(a) covers the objection that the court has no jurisdiction over defendant's person. This objection may be based on a defect in either the notice or the basis element of jurisdiction — *i.e.*, on the ground that either service of process is insufficient or that the person of the defendant or his property is not subject to the jurisdiction of the court. If the objection goes to lack of "long-arm" jurisdiction, however, the motion may not be made until the complaint has been served.[12] Thus, in such cases, the defendant will have to demand a complaint or serve a notice of appearance and await the service of the complaint.

Paragraph 9 is directed specifically to actions based on in rem or quasi in rem jurisdiction, discussed in Chapter 1. It is not always readily apparent whether paragraph 8 or paragraph 9 should be relied on in moving to dismiss, for, as we have seen in Chapter 1, the once clear boundaries between in rem and in personam jurisdiction have been blurred. If there is any doubt at all in the movant's mind about the type of jurisdiction plaintiff is asserting, the motion should be based on both paragraphs 8 and 9.

You will recall that under CPLR 320 and CPLR 3211(e), the defendant may assert a jurisdictional defense in the answer instead of moving to dismiss under CPLR 3211(a). A defendant who pleads the defense in the answer and then later wishes to seek dismissal on that ground by way of motion may do so. The proper vehicle then, however, is a motion for summary judgment under CPLR 3212.[13] If the defense pleaded is based on improper service, the defendant must

---

[11] *E.g., Grierson v. Wagner*, 78 Misc. 2d 479, 357 N.Y.S.2d 351 (Sup. Ct. 1974).

[12] *See Fraley v. Desilu Productions, Inc.*, 23 A.D.2d 79, 258 N.Y.S.2d 294 (1st Dep't 1965).

[13] *Rich v. Lefkovits*, 56 N.Y.2d 755, 452 N.Y.S.2d 1 (1982).

move for judgment on that ground within sixty days after serving the pleading, unless the court extends the time. CPLR 3211(e), as amended in 1996. The sixty-day period would not be renewed from the date of an amended answer. *Zucco v. Antin*, 257 A.D.2d 421, 682 N.Y.S.2d 354 (1st Dep't 1999).

Nonjoinder of Party

Paragraph 10 provides for a motion on the ground of nonjoinder of "a person who should be a party." It must be read together with the provisions of article 10 governing joinder of parties, and especially with CPLR 1003, which governs the consequences of nonjoinder. *See* Chapter 8.

It has been held that it is not necessary to first move that the absent party be joined,[14] as the court can, if it determines that the party should be joined, grant a motion for dismissal but make the dismissal conditional on a failure to add the party within a stated time.

The objection is not waived by failing to raise it by motion under CPLR 3211(a) or to assert it in the answer, CPLR 3211(e), but an unexplained delay in raising the point can affect the court's determination of the motion.[15]

Immunity of Directors of Charitable Organizations

Paragraph 11 allows a motion to dismiss on the ground that the movant is "immune from liability pursuant to section seven hundred-twenty-a of the not-for-profit corporation law." The latter section grants a qualified immunity from liability to directors, officers and trustees of certain charitable organizations. With a few listed exceptions, they are immune from liability to parties other than the corporation itself for conduct undertaken in the execution of their office unless they are grossly negligent or commit intentional harm.

The court is directed to dismiss an action pursuant to CPLR 3211(a)(11) if it finds that the defendant is entitled to the benefits of Not-for-Profit Law § 720-a and does not find that there is a "reasonable probability of gross negligence or intentional harm." Does this standard interfere with the plaintiff's right to a jury trial on the issue of intent or gross negligence?

---

[14] *Blumenthal v. Allen*, 46 Misc. 2d 688, 260 N.Y.S.2d 363 (Sup. Ct. 1965).

[15] *Aquavella v. Harvey*, 40 A.D.2d 940, 337 N.Y.S.2d 611 (4th Dep't 1972).

§ 16.02 FAILURE TO STATE A CAUSE OF ACTION: CPLR 3211(a)(7)

ROVELLO v. OROFINO REALTY CO., INC.
Court of Appeals
40 N.Y.2d 633, 389 N.Y.S.2d 314, 357 N.E.2d 970 (1976)

PER CURIAM.

Plaintiff purchaser seeks specific performance of an agreement under which defendant Nella Nicastro agreed to sell to plaintiff her late husband's insurance business and related real estate. Defendants, vendor and the sole corporation which holds some of the real estate, moved, pursuant to CPLR 3211 (subd [a], par 7), for judgment dismissing the complaint for failure to state a cause of action. Special Term denied the motion, a divided Appellate Division reversed, and plaintiff appeals.

The issue is whether a motion court may grant judgment under CPLR 3211 (subd [a], par 7), without treating the pleading motion as one for summary judgment, when the complaint is sufficient on its face, but the affidavits submitted indicate, not quite conclusively, that purchaser may have no cause of action. Determinative is the notice provision in the 1973 amendment to CPLR 3211 (subd [c]).

The order of the Appellate Division should be reversed, and the order of Special Term denying the motion reinstated. Under modern pleading theory, a complaint should not be dismissed on a pleading motion so long as, when the plaintiff is given the benefit of every possible favorable inference, a cause of action exists. Here, given the complaint and the affidavits, there is a reasonable chance, even if some think it small, that plaintiff purchaser will ultimately prevail on the merits. Although absent further evidence, the dispute may be finally resolved on the more embracive and exploratory motion for summary judgment, disposition by summary dismissal under CPLR 3211 (subd [a], par 7), is premature.

In October, 1970, after the death of her husband, defendant Nicastro entered into a written agreement with purchaser and one Edward Staib, now deceased, for the sale and purchase of properties relating to her husband's insurance business. The agreement involved three separate transfers: sales of (1) the insurance agency, (2) the building housing the agency and the parcel of land on which it was located, and (3) the outstanding stock in codefendant Orofino Realty Co., Inc., whose sole asset was a parcel of improved real estate adjoining the insurance agency. The first two transfers have long been fully executed. The present dispute involves only the transfer of stock in the real estate corporation.

In his complaint, the purchaser alleged defendant vendor's nonperformance of the third part of the agreement and his own continued willingness and readiness to perform. In support of their motion to dismiss defendants submitted affidavits averring that the purchaser never tendered the $5,700 down payment required under the agreement. The affidavit of plaintiff's attorney submitted in opposition to defendants' motion fails to meet this issue. None of the affidavits, separately or in combination, explain the extended delay in performance of this portion of the agreement. Plaintiff's appellate counsel now argues that at a trial of the issues of fact, plaintiff will be able to establish an excuse for this failure to tender the down payment at the time specified in the agreement.

Under CPLR 3211 a trial court may use affidavits in its consideration of a pleading motion to dismiss. . . . CPLR 3211 (subd [c]), by providing that "either party may submit any evidence that could properly be considered on a motion for summary judgment," leaves this question free from doubt. The real difficulty, however, particularly in view of the 1973 amendment to that section, lies in determining what effect shall be given the contents of affidavits submitted on a motion to dismiss when the motion has not been converted to a motion for summary judgment.

The mere fact that, judged on the complaint and affidavits alone, plaintiff could not withstand a motion for summary judgment under CPLR 3212, which requires disclosure of all the evidence on the disputed issues, cannot be controlling. Of course, CPLR 3211 allows plaintiff to submit affidavits, but it does not oblige him to do so on penalty of dismissal, as is the case under CPLR 3212 when defendant has made an evidentiary showing that refutes the pleaded cause of action. If plaintiff chooses to stand on his pleading alone, confident that its allegations are sufficient to state all the necessary elements of a cognizable cause of action, he is at liberty to do so and, unless the motion to dismiss is converted by the court to a motion for summary judgment, he will not be penalized because he has not made an evidentiary showing in support of his complaint. As amended in 1973, CPLR 3211 (subd [c]) explicitly requires that if the court decides to treat a CPLR 3211 (subd [a]) motion as one for summary judgment, it must first provide adequate notice to the parties, and thus give them an opportunity to make an appropriate record (*see* Nineteenth Ann Report of NY Judicial Conference, 1974, pp 62-63; *see, also, Mareno v. Kibbe*, 32 AD2d 825). Since no such precaution need be taken if the motion is not so treated, affidavits received on an unconverted motion to dismiss for failure to state a cause of action are not to be examined for the purpose of determining whether there is evidentiary support for the pleading.

On the other hand, affidavits may be used freely to preserve inartfully pleaded, but potentially meritorious, claims (*see, e.g., Kelly v. Bank of Buffalo*, 32 AD2d 875; *Raimondi v Fedeli*, 30 AD2d 802). Modern pleading rules are "designed to focus attention on whether the pleader has a cause of action rather than on whether he has properly stated one" (6 Carmody-Wait, 2d, NY Prac, § 38:19; *see Kelly v. Bank of Buffalo*, 32 AD2d 875, *supra*). In sum, in instances in which a motion to dismiss made under CPLR 3211 (subd [a], par 7) is not converted to a summary judgment motion, affidavits may be received for a limited purpose only, serving normally to remedy defects in the complaint, although there may be instances in which a submission by plaintiff will conclusively establish that he has no cause of action. It seems that after the amendment of 1973 affidavits submitted by the defendant will seldom if ever warrant the relief he seeks unless too the affidavits establish conclusively that plaintiff has no cause of action.

In this case, defendants' affidavits present a seemingly strong defense. If the trial court had chosen to treat defendants' motion as one for summary judgment under CPLR 3211 (subd [c]), and 3212, and had adequately notified the parties, plaintiff would have been forced to introduce further evidence to withstand the motion. In fact, such evidence might well exist. For instance, defendants might have waived the right to receive a down payment, or the delay in its tender, or otherwise acquiesced in the thus far unexplained nonperformance by the purchaser. In short, plaintiff may be able to shed more light than he has on the unexplained delay in performance of the disputed portion of the agreement.

For these reasons, Special Term properly denied defendants' motion to dismiss; the order of the Appellate Division should be reversed, with costs to abide the event, and the motion to dismiss denied.

WACHTLER, J. (dissenting).

The majority of this court has today ruled that on a motion to dismiss for failure to state a cause of action pursuant to CPLR 3211 (subd [a], par 7), the trial court may not dismiss as long as the complaint and the plaintiff's affidavit, if there be any, state all the elements of a cause of action, and that a defendant's affidavit, clearly showing the absence of one of these essential elements, is of no avail. In essence, the majority has abrogated the statute and has revitalized the common-law demurrer.

In October, 1970, the individual defendant entered into a written agreement with the plaintiff and one other calling for, *inter alia*, the sale by the defendant to the plaintiff of all the outstanding stock in codefendant Orofino Realty Co., Inc. The sole asset of the realty company was a parcel of improved real estate. The purchase price was $18,700; pursuant to the terms of the agreement, plaintiff was to make a down payment of $5,700 in cash or certified check within 16 months of December, 1970, with the balance payable in equal quarterly installments.

Plaintiff admittedly failed to make the down payment within the prescribed period; *i.e.*, prior to the end of April, 1972. Indeed, in the complaint in this action, plaintiff admits that he did not render any payment until April 21, 1975, some three years after the down payment was called for by the terms of the contract; and, the payment tendered was in the form of a personal check for $1,870, not the $5,700 called for by the agreement. Defendant rejected the tendered payment, and in May, 1975 plaintiff commenced this action for specific performance by the service of a summons and verified complaint.

While the plaintiff states in the complaint that "he stood ready, able and willing to complete the transaction" nowhere does he allege that he in fact had tendered the down payment.

Defendants, prior to the service of an answer, moved to dismiss the complaint for failure to state a cause of action. In support of their motion defendants submitted affidavits by their counsel and by the individual defendant pointing out the failure on the part of the plaintiff to make the required down payment. Plaintiff's counsel submitted an affidavit in opposition to the motion to dismiss, but the plaintiff himself did not submit an affidavit. In the affidavit in opposition plaintiff's counsel tacitly admits that there had been no tender of the requisite down payment; he claims, however, that any delays in the culmination of the transaction were either excusable by reason of the death of plaintiff's partner, or consented to, or the fault of, the individual defendant. The affidavit does not, however, place any fact in evidence or even present the offer of a scintilla of proof to support these conclusory claims.

Plaintiff's attorney claimed that the failure on the plaintiff's part to tender the down payment could be attributed to (1) the untimely death of his partner; (2) the absence of the individual defendant from the jurisdiction; and (3) the individual defendant's willingness to extend the closing time. In response to these allegations we need only note that (1) the plaintiff's partner died on June 30, 1974, some 26 months after the date the down payment was due; (2) plaintiff's attorney, in his affidavit, admits that the individual defendant was absent from the jurisdiction for only approximately 22.5% of the time since the date of the agreement in question; and (3) there has been no real evidence offered that the individual defendant consented to extend the time for closing.

A motion to dismiss for failure to state a cause of action is no longer, as it once was, limited to the face of the complaint (CPLR 3211, subd [c]). The question now is whether the plaintiff has a cause of action, not simply whether he has stated one. Thus, the court may consider affidavits and other extrinsic proof to determine whether a fact essential to the plaintiff's cause of action is lacking. . . .

Today, however, this court has held that these affidavits "are not to be examined for the purpose of determining whether there is evidentiary support for the pleading." Hence, the defendant can no longer move to dismiss under this section no matter how conclusively he can show that the plaintiff's cause of action, though properly pleaded, has no basis in fact. Thus, while CPLR 3211 (subd [c]) specifically provides that "either party may submit any evidence that could properly be considered on a motion for summary judgment" in connection with a motion to dismiss, the majority's decision makes it an empty exercise for the defendant to do so.

While the trial court should be more circumspect before using affidavits to cut short a plaintiff's "day in court" in connection with a CPLR 3211 (subd [a], par

7) motion which has not been treated as one for summary judgment, we cannot agree that this plaintiff should be allowed to defeat the motion to dismiss by means of a conclusory affidavit by his attorney asserting defenses of waiver and excuse of performance where, as here, it is clear that an essential element of the cause of action is admittedly absent. "Paragraph 7 . . . does not compel the movant to assume the truth of the allegations. If he can show that any material fact the pleader claims to be a fact is not a fact at all, and that no significant dispute can be said to exist regarding it, the motion lies and may be granted." (Siegel, Practice Commentaries, McKinney's Cons Laws of NY, Book 7B, CPLR 3211:25, p 31.) If this complaint and its concededly vacuous affidavit can survive, then it would be difficult to conceive of any complaint that would not.

. . . .

NOTES

(1) Both the majority and dissenters agree that the issue on a motion under CPLR 3211(a)(7) is not whether the complaint states a cause of action but whether the plaintiff has one. On what do they disagree, then?

The cost of the majority's position to the defendant and to society is clear — there will be at least another major motion with possible attendant appeals. What would be the cost of the dissenter's position if it were adopted?

As the majority says, the trial court could have converted the motion to dismiss to a motion for summary judgment, had it given the parties the notification required by CPLR 3211(c). The plaintiff could not then have rested on the complaint, but would have had to introduce "further evidence." The requirements of a summary judgment motion are treated in § 16.04, *infra*. On conversion of a CPLR 3211 motion to one for summary judgment, see *Mihlovan v. Grozavu*, 72 N.Y.2d 506, 534 N.Y.S.2d 656, 531 N.E.2d 288 (1988), § 16.04[C], *infra*.

(2) In *Held v. Kaufman*, 91 N.Y.2d 425, 671 N.Y.S.2d 429, 694 N.E.2d 430 (1998), the Court ruled that although CPLR 3211(e) permits but one motion to dismiss, the defendant-movant could add additional grounds for dismissal in a reply to plaintiff's answering affidavits. An interesting aspect of *Held* is its reaffirmation of *Rovello* that an unconverted CPLR 3211 motion to dismiss cannot be granted unless, giving plaintiff's complaint and other motion papers the benefit of every favorable inference, defendant's contentions are conclusively established. If plaintiff's papers contain admissions that establish that there is no cause of action, the motion to dismiss can be granted; otherwise, so long as plaintiff can keep a spark alive in the allegations of the complaint, fanned by supporting affidavits, the motion will not be granted as it might were the motion for summary judgment where defendant's affidavits could be considered.

(3) Rule 12(b)(6) of the Federal Rules of Civil Procedure allows a motion to dismiss for "failure to state a claim upon which relief can be granted." Does this imply a standard different from that contemplated by the phrase "cause of action" in CPLR 3211(a)(7)? *See Garcia v. Hilton Hotels Int'l, Inc.*, 97 F. Supp. 5, 7 (D.P.R. 1951):

> There is an obvious distinction between stating a cause of action and stating a claim upon which relief can be granted. . . . [T]here is no pleading requirement that the pleader state a cause of action upon peril of having his complaint dismissed.

The court refused to dismiss the action even though the complaint failed to allege a key element of the relevant cause of action.

Professor Siegel, in discussing the *Garcia* case, stated: "Although it is sometimes asserted that there is a difference between the two phrases . . . it is difficult at best to devise an explanation of what the difference is," and concluded that "[n]o significant difference at all is intended by the use of the one phrase rather than the other." Practice Commentary C3211.23, 7B McKinney's Consol. Laws of New York, p. 40 (2005).

(4) Will a complaint be dismissed under the CPLR if it fails to allege a key element of the cause of action?

LANZI v. BROOKS
Court of Appeals
43 N.Y.2d 778, 402 N.Y.S.2d 384, 373 N.E.2d 278 (1977)
[excerpted in § 13.02, *supra*]

NOTES

(1) What is the res judicata effect of a dismissal for failure to state a cause of action? Although a general discussion of res judicata is postponed until Chapter 23, you should note here the general rule that "[a] dismissal on such motion has preclusive effect only as to a new complaint for the same cause of action which fails to correct the defect or supply the omission determined to exist in an earlier complaint. . . ." *175 East 74th Corp v. Hartford Acc. Indem. Co.*, 51 N.Y.2d 585, 590, n.1, 435 N.Y.S.2d 584, 586, 416 N.E.2d 584 (1980). *See also* CPLR 5013.

(2) Prior to 2006, the party whose pleading was dismissed had to seek leave to replead and provide evidentiary support for that request. After January 1, 2006, that is no longer necessary, and the party may simply submit a new pleading without leave and without evidentiary support, although there is nothing that forbids such support. CPLR 3211(e).

(3) Alternatively, a plaintiff whose complaint has been attacked under CPLR 3211(a)(7) might serve an amended complaint as of right, *see* CPLR 3025(a), which purports to cure any defects in it. The effect of the new pleading on the motion is not entirely clear:

> A motion addressed to the sufficiency of an original complaint may not be circumvented by the service of an amended complaint (3 Weinstein-Korn-Miller, N.Y. Civ. Prac., par. 3025.07). The court may dismiss the original complaint if it finds the amended one sufficient or it can dismiss the motion addressed to the pleading that no longer exists (*ibid.*). Although Professor Siegel has expressed distaste for the latter approach (called "abatement" of the motion), he suggests that the court address the amended pleading. . . . This approach is especially appropriate where defendant has obliged with a second 3211(a)(7) motion attacking the amended complaint.

Taylor v. Eli Haddad Corp., 118 Misc. 2d 253, 256, 460 N.Y.S.2d 886, 890 (Sup. Ct. 1983).

(4) A pitfall for the unwary movant under CPLR (a)(7) is illustrated by *Quinn v. Cannabis Haircutters, Ltd.*, 72 A.D.2d 765, 766, 421 N.Y.S.2d 386, 387 (2d Dep't 1979): Defendant had successfully moved in the Supreme Court to dismiss all of plaintiff's nine causes of action. It soon came down off the resulting high because the Appellate Division, on appeal, held that the first cause of action was a proper one and then reinstated the remainder, because:

> Where individual causes of action are alleged by a plaintiff, but only one general motion to dismiss is made, which motion is addressed to the entire complaint in omnibus fashion, case law is clear that should any one cause of action be sustained as legally sufficient, then the entire complaint should be sustained and the motion to dismiss should be denied in its entirety.

What is the value, if any, of the quoted rule? How could movant have avoided this pitfall?

§ 16.03 THE MOTION TO DISMISS A DEFENSE: CPLR 3211(b)

PROBLEM A

As plaintiff's representative in this hypothetical action, you hired Jones, a licensed process server, to serve the summons and complaint on the non-resident defendant. Jones soon provided you with a proof of service affidavit comporting with CPLR 306. In due course you are served with an answer to the complaint which alleges that the court lacks jurisdiction over the defendant because there are insufficient contacts between the defendant and the forum state and because the summons was not served in a prescribed manner.

What is your next step?

RILAND v. FREDERICK S. TODMAN & CO.
Appellate Division, First Department
56 A.D.2d 350, 393 N.Y.S.2d 4 (1977)

BIRNS, JUSTICE:

In three causes of action, plaintiff-appellant charged members of an accounting firm with breach of fiduciary duty, fraud and deceit, and professional malpractice or negligence.

In essence, defendants' answer contains a general denial and various affirmative defenses. On this appeal we are concerned solely with plaintiff's challenge to the first affirmative defense contained in the answer, namely, that the complaint fails to state a cause of action. Special Term denied plaintiff's motion to strike the affirmative defense, holding, "Defendant may assert affirmative defenses addressed to the full spectrum of plaintiff's pleading and potential proof. . . ."

Relying upon *Sado v. Marlun Manufacturing Company, Inc.*, 96 N.Y.S.2d 32 (not officially reported), appellant urges simply that by electing to plead such defense defendants chose to test the sufficiency of the complaint; that Special term was required to examine the complaint and search the record in order to make a judicial declaration before trial as to whether the complaint was sufficient; and that the court should have stricken that defense inasmuch as the complaint in each of its branches sets forth a valid cause of action.

The Civil Practice Act was in effect when *Sado, supra*, was decided. Under the Civil Practice Act as well as its predecessor, the Code of Civil Procedure, the rule was that "[t]he defense that the complaint does not state facts sufficient to constitute a cause of action cannot be taken by answer." (*Falk v. MacMasters*, 197 App.Div. 357, 362, 188 N.Y.S. 795, 799;. . . .) Implicit in such ruling was the theory that the defense stated a mere conclusion of law . . . for which there was no statutory provision.

Cases and texts indicate that a different result should be reached under the provisions of the CPLR. In *Prompt Electrical Supply Co., Inc. v. W.E. Tatem, Inc.*, 43 Misc.2d 333, 250 N.Y.S.2d 906, where a similar challenge was made, the court noted that under the CPLR, unlike under the Civil Practice Act or Code of Civil Procedure, the defense of failure to state a cause of action is "one provided for by paragraph 7 of subdivision (a) of 3211. It is not waived by failure to move prior to answer or by failing to state it in the answer. Consequently, it is not required to be stated to be preserved." (*Prompt Electrical, supra*, at p. 335, 250 N.Y.S.2d at p. 908.) The court, thereupon, denied the motion to strike the defense "even though the pleading thereof is unnecessary," observing, "At best, it affords notice to the plaintiff that the defendant pleading it will assail the complaint as insufficient, a remedy that is not foreclosed to the defendant as the plaintiff already knows. At worst, it cannot prejudice the plaintiff."

Recently, the Appellate Division, Second Department, reached a conclusion contrary to *Prompt Electrical, supra*, holding as did *Sado, supra*, that a defense that a complaint failed to state a cause of action merely pleaded a conclusion of law and may not be asserted in an answer (*Glenesk v. Guidance Realty Corp.*, 36 A.D.2d 852, 853, 321 N.Y.S.2d 685, 687). However, *Glenesk, supra*, has been criticized (*see* 23 Syracuse L.Rev. 290-291).

. . . .

We agree with the rationale in *Prompt Electrical, supra*, that the defense of failure to state a cause of action may be inserted in an answer as an affirmative defense (CPLR 3211[a][7]). The pleading of that defense, is, however, surplusage, as it may be asserted at any time even if not pleaded (CPLR 3211[e]).

Nevertheless, inclusion of such defense in an answer is not prejudicial. It serves to give notice to the other side that the pleader may at some future time move to assert it. The choice whether or when to so move should remain with the pleader; the affirmative pleading of such defense is not a motion. "Since a defendant might not want to move under CPLR Rule 3211, preferring a later motion for summary judgment [CPLR 3212(a)], there is no reason why he should not be permitted to allege in his answer that a particular cause of action is substantively deficient, especially when it is recalled that this defect is unwaivable." (23 Syracuse L.Rev. 290; *see* CPLR 3211[e].)

The assertion of that defense in an answer should not be subject to a motion to strike or provide a basis to test the sufficiency of the complaint. This view is consistent with the modern procedural objective of reducing rather than extending at the pleading stage the opportunity for disputes which delay or prevent disposition on the merits.*

We cannot help but observe, however, that were we confronted with a motion challenging the sufficiency of the complaint on the ground that it failed to state a cause of action (CPLR 3211[a][7]), that motion would be denied.

Accordingly, the order of the Supreme Court, . . . should be affirmed, without costs.

. . . .

All concur.

---

* The Advisory Committee Report of October 1955 in alluding to this objective stated: "The intent and effect of the rules is . . . to discourage battles over mere form of statement and to sweep away needless controversies . . . that [serve] either to delay trial on the merits or, to prevent a party from having a trial. . . ." (2A Moore's Federal Practice ¶ 8.01[3], Advisory Committee Report of October, 1955.)

NOTES

(1) Why did the plaintiff move to dismiss the defense alleging that he had failed to state a cause of action? Wouldn't he prefer to "let sleeping dogs lie"? In any event, does the result reached in the principal case leave plaintiff with a "sword of Damocles" problem? How does his situation differ from that of the plaintiff in Problem A immediately preceding the case?

(2) Despite the rule that it is improper to move to dismiss the defense alleging a failure to plead a cause of action, it has been held that a motion to dismiss an affirmative defense "searches the record" and that the court should dismiss the movant's case if it finds that no cause of action has been stated. *Rand v. Hearst Corp.*, 31 A.D.2d 406, 298 N.Y.S.2d 405 (1st Dep't 1969), *aff'd*, 26 N.Y.2d 806, 309 N.Y.S.2d 348, 257 N.E.2d 895 (1970). Can this result be reconciled with the principal case?

(3) The Third Department has joined the First in adopting the rule of the principal case "that the pleaded defense of failure to state a cause of action is harmless surplusage and a motion to strike it should be denied as unnecessary." *Pump v. Anchor Motor Freight, Inc.*, 138 A.D.2d 849, 525 N.Y.S.2d 959 (3d Dep't 1988).

(4) Another limit on CPLR 3211(b) is that plaintiff cannot move to dismiss a denial; the proper way to attack a denial (aside from overcoming it at trial) is by motion for summary judgment. *Two Clinton Square Corp. v. Gorin Stores, Inc.*, 51 A.D.2d 643, 377 N.Y.S.2d 845 (4th Dep't 1976).

(5) Should defendant, rather than move for dismissal on the ground of failure of personal jurisdiction due to failure of proper service, include that ground as a defense in the answer? This is permissible, but the defense is waived if defendant does not move for dismissal within 60 days from service of the answer. CPLR 3211(e); *Wiebusch v. Bethany Memorial Reform Church*, 9 A.D.3d 315, 781 N.Y.S.2d 6 (1st Dep't 2004).

§ 16.04 THE MOTION FOR SUMMARY JUDGMENT: CPLR 3212

[A] When Granted

CPLR 3212 states that a motion for summary judgment "shall be granted if, upon all the papers and proof submitted, the cause of action or defense shall be established sufficiently to warrant the court as a matter of law in directing judgment in favor of any party. . . . [T]he motion shall be denied if any party shall show facts sufficient to require a trial of any issue of fact."

In reading the cases in this section, try to identify the issue or issues of fact that prevented the grant of summary judgment or, if it was granted, try to understand how the court concluded that there were no issues of fact. How do the courts distinguish between issues of fact and issues of law? Is the boundary always clear?

PROBLEM B

On March 10, 2006, Ms. Grey commenced an action in Supreme Court, New York County, by causing a summons and complaint to be served on Mr. Driver which stated, in its relevant paragraphs:

2. On March 1, 2005 plaintiff was injured when an automobile owned and operated by defendant smashed through a plate glass window of the Acme Drug Store at 1440 Nonesuch Parkway, N.Y., N.Y.

3. Said accident was caused by the reckless or negligent operation by defendant of his automobile.

4. As a result of the accident plaintiff sustained multiple lacerations, a broken bone in her left leg, and impaired use of her right arm due to a severed tendon. Wherefore, plaintiff demands judgment in the amount of $250,000 plus interest and costs.

In the only substantive portion of his Answer, Driver stated:

1. He denies the allegations of Paragraphs 3 and 4 of the Complaint.

At a deposition of plaintiff taken by defendant, she stated that she had been working as a counter waitress in the Acme Drug Store on March 1, 2005. She was stationed between the counter and a glass wall which formed the outer shell of the building and faced the street. Without warning, an automobile crashed through the glass wall into her.

At defendant's deposition, he testified that he had stopped his car in front of the Acme Drug Store, pulling into a parking place (parking was at right angles to the sidewalk) so that he could drop off a passenger. He testified that he did not turn off the engine but that he put the car into neutral and set the emergency brake. When his mother, who was in the right front seat, had difficulty opening her door, Driver got out, opened her door for her from the outside and helped her alight. As she did so, the car "suddenly began rolling into the drug store. I couldn't get back inside fast enough to stop it," said Driver.

On October 10, 2006, two months after signed copies of the depositions were exchanged, plaintiff moved for summary judgment on the issue of liability. Should her motion be granted? What should defendant include in his responsive papers which would improve his chances of defeating the motion?

UGARRIZA v. SCHMIEDER
Court of Appeals
46 N.Y.2d 471, 414 N.Y.S.2d 304, 386 N.E.2d 1324 (1979)

GABRIELLI, J.

The legal issue squarely presented is whether plaintiff in this automobile negligence action is entitled to summary judgment on the issue of liability, or whether there exist genuine and substantial triable issues of fact which serve to preclude summary judgment. Supreme Court, Suffolk County, granted plaintiff's motion to strike defendants' answer and set the case down for a hearing on the issue of damages only, stating that "there are no triable issues of fact." A majority of the Appellate Division reversed and denied plaintiff's motion, with one Justice dissenting. Plaintiff now appeals from that nonfinal order, pursuant to leave granted by that court. . . .

Although there once were significant limitations upon the type of action in which summary judgment was available (*see* Siegel, New York Practice, § 280), this is no longer true (*see* CPLR 3212). Indeed, as of January 1, 1979, the final prohibition was removed, and it is now possible for a plaintiff to obtain summary judgment even in a matrimonial action (L 1978, ch 532). That summary judgment is an available remedy in an appropriate negligence case has been accepted since 1959 (*see* 4 Weinstein-Korn-Miller, NY Civ Prac, par 3212.03). Summary judgment has been termed a drastic measure, however, since it deprives a party of his day in court and will normally have res judicata effects (*see* Siegel, New York Practice, § 287). Thus, it may be granted without a trial only if no genuine, triable issue of fact is presented (*Werfel v Zivnostenska Banka*, 287 NY 91; CPLR 3212, subds [b], [c]). Negligence cases by their very nature do not usually lend themselves to summary judgment, since often, even if all parties are in agreement as to the underlying facts, the very question of negligence is itself a question for jury determination. Only if it can be concluded as a matter of law that defendant was negligent, may summary judgment be granted in a negligence action. The matter before us is not such a case.

The parties are not in disagreement as to the pertinent underlying facts. Plaintiff, defendant Glenn Schmieder, and two other young people who had gathered at a local discotheque decided to travel to a diner several miles away in a car owned by defendant George Schmieder and operated by Glenn Schmieder. Plaintiff sat in the front passenger seat. It was then about 4 o'clock in the morning; the night was clear and traffic was light. Schmieder states that he was quite sober, having had only one drink during the course of the night, and plaintiff does not deny this. The driver had never been at the diner before, and was being given instructions by one of the other passengers. The diner was located on the south side of the highway, and to reach it Schmieder was required to make a left turn off the road. For some reason, not specified in the record, it was impossible to turn directly into the diner. Instead at another passenger's instructions, defendant made a left turn into the parking lot of a shopping center adjacent to and just past the diner. He then turned left once again, and began to drive across the parking lot towards the diner at a speed of between 20 and 25 miles per hour. There were no other vehicles in the unilluminated and blacktopped parking lot. Defendant states that he was alert and paying attention to his path, and plaintiff does not dispute this. Suddenly, all four persons in the car simultaneously saw something a few feet ahead, and each uttered an appropriate exclamation. Defendant applied the brakes, but was unable to stop before striking an unpainted, concrete divider separating two sections of the parking lot. The divider is variously described as being between 1 foot and 18 inches high, about 6 feet wide, and extending almost the length of the parking lot. As a result of the collision, both plaintiff and defendant were thrown into the windshield, and plaintiff allegedly sustained serious injuries.

Plaintiff now contends that on the basis of these facts, essentially concurred in by all parties, she is entitled to summary judgment on the issue of liability. In other words, plaintiff argues that the actions and omissions of defendant as described above constitute negligence as a matter of law. We disagree. Plaintiff places considerable reliance upon our latest statement in this area of the law, *Andre v Pomeroy* (35 NY2d 361). Her reliance is apparently based more on the specific result in that case, than on its rationale, and is hence sorely misplaced. There, as here, plaintiff was a passenger in defendant's car. That, however, is the only significant similarity between the cases. *Andre* involved an automobile accident in which defendant's car had run into the rear of the car in front of her. There, defendant admitted that although she was driving in heavy traffic and knew that the other car was in front of her, she nonetheless took her eyes off the road and looked down into her purse for her compact. When she looked back at the road, she found that she had driven too close to the other car, which had either stopped or slowed significantly, and she was unable to avoid striking it. We concluded in that case that in light of the conceded unusual facts it was proper to find as a matter of law that defendant was negligent, and thus to award plaintiff summary judgment.

Andre did not serve as a departure from prior law, nor was it intended as a signal that the prerequisites for a grant of summary judgment had been further modified. Rather, it indicates merely that if the admitted facts are such that no conclusion other than negligence can be drawn, summary judgment is not precluded in a negligence action. We cautioned, however, that even in those negligence cases in which "the facts are conceded there is often a question as to whether the defendant or the plaintiff acted reasonably under the circumstances. This can rarely be decided as a matter of law" (35 NY2d, at p 364). Accordingly, we declared that "when the suit is founded on a claim of negligence, the plaintiff will generally be entitled to summary judgment 'only in cases in which there is no conflict at all in the evidence, the defendant's conduct fell far below any permissible standard of due care, and the plaintiff's conduct either was not really involved (such as with a passenger) or was clearly of exemplary prudence in the circumstances'" (35 NY2d, at pp 364-365, quoting 4 Weinstein-Korn-Miller, NY Civ Prac, par 3212.03).*

In the instant case, unlike *Andre*, we cannot say as a matter of law that defendant's conduct fell far below any permissible standard of due care. Indeed, although not necessarily dispositive, we would note that here plaintiff has failed to suggest any affirmative act or even any articulable omission by defendant which could be characterized as negligent. She has merely made conclusory allegations of undefined negligence. It would appear that plaintiff seeks to have us conclude as a matter of law that there was negligence simply because there was an accident. Such would be contrary to both law and logic. In *Andre*, the accident was a result of defendant's conceded action in purposefully looking away from the road while driving in heavy traffic. We had no hesitation in denominating such conduct to be negligent as a matter of law. Here, however, defendant's negligence, if any, is not as evident. Thus, plaintiff is not entitled to summary judgment.

Accordingly, the order appealed from should be affirmed. . . .

NOTES

(1) In the principal case, the parties agreed on "the facts," *i.e.*, on the events that occurred. Why was summary judgment denied? Is the issue of negligence a question of fact or law? Can the answer be different in different cases? How does the principal case answer these questions?

(2) The issue of proximate cause, while ordinarily the province of the trier of the facts, can also sometimes be resolved on a motion for summary judgment. *See Howard v. Poseidon Pools, Inc.*, 72 N.Y.2d 972, 534 N.Y.S.2d 360, 530 N.E.2d 1280 (1988). Plaintiff, who was injured when he dove into a four foot deep pool, brought an action against the manufacturer, alleging a failure of the duty to warn of the dangers of diving. Summary judgment was granted against him because the only conclusion which could be drawn from the facts was that plaintiff's own reckless conduct was the proximate cause of the injury.

In *Eagan v. A.J. Construction Corp.*, 94 N.Y.2d 839, 702 N.Y.S.2d 574, 724 N.E.2d 366 (1999), plaintiff jumped six feet from a stalled elevator on a con-

---

* It should be noted that contributory negligence upon the part of plaintiff would have barred any recovery by plaintiff in *Andre*. This is no longer true, since with respect to any cause of action accruing on or after September 1, 1975, any "culpable conduct" by a plaintiff merely diminishes, without precluding, recovery (CPLR art 14-A). The accident in this case took place on November 1, 1975, and would thus appear to fall within the ambit of the statute. Interestingly, counsel for neither party mentioned this, nor did they discuss the possible significance or ramifications of the abolition of the contributory negligence bar upon the third element of the standard we enunciated in *Andre*. In light of our disposition of this appeal, and the absence of any argument by counsel on this issue, we find it neither appropriate nor necessary to reach it at this time.

struction site even though he was in no danger on the elevator and knew that a call had been made for help. He sued for his injuries and the Court of Appeals ruled that, as a matter of law, his jump "superseded defendants' conduct and terminated defendants' liability," thus permitting summary judgment in defendants' favor.

(3) A possible source of confusion on the availability of summary judgment in negligence cases is the role of the res ipsa loquitur doctrine. The following should be helpful:

> Ordinarily, res ipsa loquitur satisfies a plaintiff's duty of producing evidence sufficient to go to the jury. . . . That fact in and of itself does not normally warrant nor require the granting of summary judgment to a plaintiff. . . . However, the Court of Appeals noted that there may be cases where plaintiff's prima facie proof is so convincing that the inference of negligence arising therefrom is inescapable if not rebutted by other evidence. (*Foltis, Inc. v. City of New York*, 287 N.Y. 108, 121, 38 N.E.2d 455). Subsequently, the Courts have granted summary judgment in certain res ipsa situations where the particular defendant totally failed to rebut the inescapable inference of negligence.

Horowitz v. Kevah Konner, Inc., 67 A.D.2d 38, 41, 414 N.Y.S.2d 540, 543 (1st Dep't 1979). In *Morejon v. Rais Constr. Co.*, 7 N.Y.3d 203, 818 N.Y.S.2d 792, 851 N.E.2d 1143 (2006), the Court conducted a thorough review of the elements of res ipsa loquitur, noting that it could provide a basis for summary judgment only in the rarest of cases, and approving the denial of summary judgment in that case.

(4) When no-fault issues arise (Insurance Law § 5102(d)), defendants often move for summary judgment. The Court of Appeals in three cases decided together addressed the strength of plaintiff's showing needed to maintain a prima facie case and overcome defendant's motion. *Toure v. Avis Rent A Car Systems, Inc.*, 98 N.Y.2d 345, 746 N.Y.S.2d 865, 774 N.E.2d 1197 (2002). In one of the cases, the showing was held insufficient because plaintiff's chiropractor had no objective support for his opinion as to plaintiff's condition. In the other two cases, the showing was found adequate. The physicians based their opinions on MRI and CT procedures showing the extent of plaintiffs' disabilities. It appears from these cases that plaintiff must support the claim of serious injury by more than an objectively unsupported expert's opinion. See also *Parker v. Mobil Oil Corp.*, 7 N.Y.3d 434, ___ N.Y.S.2d ___, ___ N.E.2d ___ (2006), where defendant was entitled to summary judgment on a finding that there was an insufficient foundation for plaintiff's experts' opinion on causation.

(5) For a judicial discussion of the propriety of summary judgment on facts similar to those of Problem B, see *Di Sabato v. Soffes*, 9 A.D.2d 297, 193 N.Y.S.2d 184 (1st Dep't 1959).

(6) A different aspect of the law/fact distinction is addressed in the case that follows.

GONCALVES v. REGENT INT'L HOTELS, LTD.
Court of Appeals
58 N.Y.2d 206, 460 N.Y.S.2d 750, 447 N.E.2d 693 (1983)

[Plaintiffs, guests of the defendant hotel, had entrusted to it for safekeeping more than one million dollars in jewelry. Alas, the jewels were stolen, and the plaintiffs sued, claiming that the hotel had breached its duty to provide a "safe." Under § 200 of the General Business Law, the hotel's liability was limited to $500 (the limitation was increased to $1,500 in 1985) if it had made a safe available to its guests. At issue was whether the security device provided by defendant was a safe within the meaning of the law. The parties agreed that the available device was a safe-deposit box housed in a room built of plasterboard, entrance to which was controlled by two hollow-core wood doors. Defendant's summary judgment motion to limit its liability to $500 was granted and the order was affirmed by the Appellate Division. — Eds.]

COOKE, CHIEF JUDGE.

. . . Whether a "safe" was provided is a question of fact (*cf. Friedman v. Schindler's Prairie House*, 224 App.Div. 232, 236-237, 230 N.Y.S. 44, *affd. no opn.* 250 N.Y. 574, 166 N.E. 329 [whether establishment was "hotel" within scope of General Business Law a question of fact for jury]). This, of course, does not mean that the issue must always be submitted to the jury. As with any factual issue, a judge will make a determination on the evidence as a matter of law if there is no real controversy as to the facts. . . .

The dissent confuses the operations of construing statutes and of applying statutes. It is agreed that declaring the meaning of a statute is solely within the province of the court, as this constitutes part of its function to enunciate the law applicable in a case. The application of the statute, however, is a different matter. When there exists conflicting evidence, determination of the controversy is left to the fact finder. . . . The court today does no more than construe section 200 of the General Business Law by providing a standard where the Legislature has not, leaving application of that standard to the fact finder. Indeed, under the approach urged by the dissent, it would appear that all statutory rights would be removed from the fact finder's scrutiny

In the present case, it was improper to award summary judgment. Plaintiffs submitted an affidavit by an expert having 29 years' experience in the design, installation, and sale of safes and vaults. This witness expressed his opinion that defendants' facilities were inadequate, stating that safe-deposit boxes can be invaded in less than 30 seconds and that they should be housed in a vault, not a room of plasterboard and wooden doors. Defendants relied on the existence and operation of the safe-deposit boxes. Under the circumstances, there exists a material issue of fact as in whether defendants' safe-deposit boxes constituted a "safe" within the meaning of section 200.

. . . .

JASEN, JUDGE (dissenting).

The majority today holds that a jury and not a court must decide what constitutes a "safe" within the meaning of section 200 of the General Business Law. Since I believe that it is a well-established principle of law, based upon sound policy considerations, that it is for the court, rather than a jury, to construe the meaning of words contained in a statute, I am compelled to dissent from the majority holding.

What is involved here is simply a question of pure statutory construction. The issue presented is whether or not a bank of individually locked metal safe-deposit boxes enclosed in a separate sheetrock room constitutes a "safe," as that term is used in section 200 of the General Business Law.

. . . .

It is a fundamental principle of our system of administering justice that the jury decides questions of fact while the Judge decides questions of law. It is equally basic that the construction of a statute is a question of law to be resolved by the court. . . . It is too plain for argument that "[*t*]*hough the terms used in a statute are technical or unusual, or are ambiguous, the judge should not leave their meaning to the jury.*" (McKinney's Cons. Laws of N.Y., Book 1, Statutes, § 77 [emphasis supplied].) The cases adhering to this fundamental principle are legion.

Thus, it would seem to me that it is for the court to give each word or phrase of a statute its appropriate meaning. In doing so, the court must look primarily to the intent of the Legislature. (McKinney's Cons. Laws of N.Y., Book 1, Statutes, § 230.) . . . That the court, rather than a jury, should be the proper body to construe the meaning of words contained in a statute in accordance with the intent of the Legislature cannot be seriously disputed, for if the meaning of a word contained in a statute, such as the term "safe" as used in section 200 of the General Business Law, were to be decided on an ad hoc basis by a jury rather than the courts, the availability to hotels of the statutory limitation of liability would be subject to the vagaries of a body of lay individuals possessing no training or expertise in the task of discerning and applying legislative intent so as to effectuate the purposes and policies underlying the statute. The adoption of such a procedure will bring about widely divergent results which are in no way based on what the lawmakers intended to accomplish when they enacted the statute. Indeed, under the majority's view, a bank of safe-deposit boxes contained in a sheetrock room in a Buffalo hotel could be determined by a Buffalo jury to be a "safe" within the meaning of the statute, thus limiting the hotel's liability to $500, while the identical facility installed by an Albany hotel might be found by an Albany jury not to be a "safe" within the meaning of the statute, in which case the unfortunate Albany hotel would not be afforded the protection of the statute and would be subject to unlimited liability for losing a guest's valuables, the value of which was never disclosed.

... Consequently, recognizing that legislative intent is the keystone to statutory construction, I believe it imperative that the court, not a jury, construe the term "safe" in such a way as to give a meaning to the term "which serves rather than defeats the overall legislative goals." ... Until today, we have, almost without exception, zealously adhered to this rule. (*See Matter of Mobil Oil Corp. v. Finance Administrator of City of N.Y.*, 58 N.Y.2d 95, 459 N.Y.S.2d 566, 446 N.E.2d 130 ["maintenance" does not include cleaning services within the meaning of subdivision 6 of section L46-1.0 of the Administrative Code of the City of New York]; *Weinberg v. D-M Rest. Corp.*, 53 N.Y.2d 499, 506, 442 N.Y.S.2d 965, 426 N.E.2d 459 ["fee" as used in section 201 of the General Business Law does not include a tip]; *Zaldin v. Concord Hotel*, 48 N.Y.2d 107, 421 N.Y.S.2d 858, 397 N.E.2d 370 [hotel did not "provide" a safe within the meaning of section 200 of the General Business Law]; *Matter of Smith [Great Amer. Ins. Co.]*, 29 N.Y.2d 116, 324 N.Y.S.2d 15, 272 N.E.2d 528 [no "physical contact" between two vehicles within the meaning of section 617 of the Insurance Law]; *MVAIC v. Eisenberg*, 18 N.Y.2d 1, 271 N.Y.S.2d 641, 218 N.E.2d 524 [there was "physical contact" between two vehicles within the meaning of section 617 of the Insurance Law]; *Matter of Kelly v. Sugarman*, 12 N.Y.2d 298, 239 N.Y.S.2d 114, 189 N.E.2d 613, *supra* [31-year-old man with intelligence of a child was "crippled" within the meaning of subdivision 2 of section 16 of the Workers' Compensation Law].)

Certainly, in a common-law negligence action, the question of whether a person is crippled or whether there was physical contact between two vehicles or whether a hotel provided a safe could present factual questions calling for resolution by a jury. (*See Akins v. Glens Falls City School Dist.*, 53 N.Y.2d 325, 441 N.Y.S.2d 644, 424 N.E.2d 531.) A critical distinction, which the majority fails to perceive, must be drawn, however, where the Legislature has used such terms in a statute, in which case a purely legal question is presented, requiring the court, rather than a jury, to construe their meaning. ...

. . . .

Turning to the case before us, I would hold that the subject facility is a "safe" within the meaning of the statute. ...

While it would go too far to say that the Legislature cared nothing for the security of property belonging to the guests of a hotel, especially since the Legislature required that a safe be provided, it is imperative that the statute be construed in light of the fact that the primary concern of the lawmakers in enacting section 200 was to "protect the hotel from an undisclosed excessive liability". ...

In light of the conceded purpose of the statute, I believe that the facility provided by the defendant here clearly falls within the meaning of the term "safe" as it is used in section 200, since it was more than sufficient to safeguard $500 worth of property per guest. This conclusion finds support in both the plain meaning of the term and the decisions in other jurisdictions that have addressed the issue.

To assist a court in properly construing a term contained in a statute, resort may be had to definitions provided by lexicographers. . . . Black's Law Dictionary defines a safe as "[a] metal receptacle for the preservation of valuables." . . . The individually locked metal safety deposit boxes, enclosed in a sheetrock room which were provided by defendant, fall within all of these commonly accepted definitions of the term "safe."

In addition to the aforementioned definitions and the intent of the Legislature to protect hotels from excessive undisclosed liability, our holding finds further support in the decisions of at least two other States that have addressed the issue. . . .

. . . .

NOTES

(1) In your view, does the majority adequately respond to the arguments made by Judge Jasen in his dissent? How do you understand the majority's distinction between applying statutes and construing statutes? Note that in 1986 General Business Law § 200 was amended so that it covered "safe or safe deposit box."

(2) On policy grounds, is it better for a court or a jury to make the decisions required in the preceding two principal cases? To what extent is this a political issue? These are problems we will see again at the trial stage when we consider the right to a jury trial, as well as the motions for directed verdict and for judgment not withstanding the verdict. A useful discussion of these issues is found in *Markman v. Westview Instruments, Inc.*, 517 U.S. 370, 116 S. Ct. 1384, 1395-96 (1996), in which the Court held that the construction of disputed terminology in a patent "claim" (or description) was an issue for judicial determination, and should not be submitted to a jury.

(3) In *Access Capital, Inc. v. DeCicco*, 302 A.D.2d 48, 752 N.Y.S.2d 658 (1st Dep't 2002), a divided court ruled that plaintiff was entitled to summary judgment when defendant, because of a pending criminal proceeding, refused to answer any of plaintiff's allegations on Fifth Amendment grounds. The majority found defendant thus to be in default. The dissenter observed, *inter alia*, that while assertion of the Fifth Amendment can lead to adverse inferences in a civil action, it should not relieve plaintiff of the obligation to prove a case.

BRILL v. CITY OF NEW YORK
Court of Appeals
2 N.Y.3d 648, 781 N.Y.S.2d 261, 814 N.E.2d 431 (2004)

KAYE, CHIEF JUDGE

This appeal puts before us a recurring scenario regarding the timing of summary judgment motions that ignores statutory law, disrupts trial calendars, and undermines the goals of orderliness and efficiency in state court practice.

On June 4, 1998, plaintiffs Ona and Maurice Brill brought suit against the City of New York and others for injuries Ona Brill allegedly suffered on February 15, 1998 when she tripped and fell on a public sidewalk in Brooklyn. Following discovery, on June 28, 2001, plaintiffs filed their note of issue and certificate of readiness, and sought a preference due to Ona Brill's age.

On June 18, 2002, close to a year after the trial calendar papers were filed, the City moved for summary judgment. The City gave no explanation for filing the motion after the 120-day limit specified in CPLR 3212(a), simply arguing that it did not have prior written notice of the alleged defect at the accident site and that plaintiffs could not show an exception to the prior written notice requirement. Supreme Court determined that in the interests of judicial economy, and since Mrs. Brill did not manifest any prejudice from the delay, it would decide the summary judgment motion on the merits. The court granted the City's motion, finding plaintiffs did not prove that the City had notice of a defect at the accident site, and the Appellate Division affirmed.

We now reverse because, on these facts, Supreme Court should not have considered the merits of the City's motion for summary judgment.

Since New York established its summary judgment procedure in 1921, summary judgment has proven a valuable, practical tool for resolving cases that involve only questions of law (*see Merritt Hill Vineyards v. Windy Hgts. Vineyard*, 61 NY2d 106, 112 [1984]). Summary judgment permits a party to show, by affidavit or other evidence, that there is no material issue of fact to be tried, and that judgment may be directed as a matter of law, thereby avoiding needless litigation cost and delay. Where appropriate, summary judgment is a great benefit both to the parties and to the overburdened New York State trial courts (*see* Siegel, NY Prac §§ 278-279, at 438-440 [3d ed]; *see also* Weinstein-Korn-Miller, NY Civ Prac ¶ 3212.01, at 32-157).

In that a summary judgment motion may resolve the entire case, obviously the timing of the motion is significant. CPLR 3212(a) (as added by L 1962, ch 308) originally required only joinder of issue before a summary judgment motion could be made. In practice, however, the absence of an outside time limit for filing such motions became problematic, particularly when they were made on the eve of trial. Eleventh-hour summary judgment motions, sometimes used as a dilatory tactic, left inadequate time for reply or proper court consideration, and prejudiced litigants who had already devoted substantial resources to readying themselves for trial (*see Gonzalez v. 98 Mag Leasing Corp.*, 95 NY2d 124, 128 [2000]; *Auger v. State of New York*, 236 AD2d 177, 179 [3d Dept 1997]).

At the court system's request, in 1996 the Legislature stepped in to ameliorate the problem by amending CPLR 3212(a) to provide that:

> "the court may set a date after which no such motion may be made, such date being no earlier than thirty days after the filing of the note of issue. If no such date is set by the court, such motion shall be made no later than one hundred twenty days after the filing of the note of issue, except with leave of court on good cause shown."

By the amendment, the Legislature maintained the courts' considerable discretion to fix a deadline for filing summary judgment motions, after joinder of issue, but mandated that no such deadline could be set earlier than 30 days after filing the note of issue or (unless set by the court) later than 120 days after the filing of the note of issue, except with leave of court on good cause shown. Thus, the Legislature struck a balance, fixing an outside limit on the time for filing summary judgment motions, but allowing courts latitude to set an alternative limit or to consider untimely motions to accommodate genuine need.

Nonetheless, the practice of filing late summary judgment motions persisted, with the statutory "good cause" requirement a new litigation battleground. Some courts concluded that "good cause" required a satisfactory explanation for movant's delay, and refused to entertain the motion if no such showing was made [citations omitted]. Other courts read "good cause" to permit late filing where the motion had merit and there was no prejudice to the adversary [citations omitted].

We conclude that "good cause" in CPLR 3212(a) requires a showing of good cause for the delay in making the motion — a satisfactory explanation for the untimeliness — rather than simply permitting meritorious, nonprejudicial filings, however tardy. That reading is supported by the language of the statute — only the movant can *show* good cause — as well as by the purpose of the amendment, to end the practice of eleventh-hour summary judgment motions. No excuse at all, or a perfunctory excuse, cannot be "good cause."

Here, it is undisputed that the City did not file its motion within the requisite 120 days specified by the statute, and it did not submit any reason for the delay. Thus, there was no "leave of court on good cause shown," as required by CPLR 3212(a). The violation is clear. What to do is the more vexing issue.

In *Kihl v. Pfeffer* (94 NY2d 118, 123 [1999]), we affirmed the dismissal of a complaint for failure to respond to interrogatories within court-ordered time frames, observing that "[i]f the credibility of court orders and the integrity of our judicial system are to be maintained, a litigant cannot ignore court orders with impunity." The present scenario, another example of sloppy practice threatening the integrity of our judicial system, rests instead on the violation of legislative mandate.

If this practice is tolerated and condoned, the ameliorative statute is, for all intents and purposes, obliterated. If, on the other hand, the statute is applied as written and intended, an anomaly may result, in that a meritorious summary judgment motion may be denied, burdening the litigants and trial calendar with a case that in fact leaves nothing to try. Indeed, the statute should not "provide a safe haven for frivolous or meritless lawsuits" (*Rossi v. Arnot Ogden Med. Ctr.*, 252 AD2d 778, 779 [3d Dept 1998] [Graffeo, J.]), which is precisely why practitioners should move for summary judgment within the prescribed time period or offer a legitimate reason for the delay.

As Professor David Siegel — who has tracked this "controversial topic" — has promised, "we'd think better of judicial decisions that absolutely refuse to extend the time for meritorious summary judgment motions if they would tell us what is to happen in the case" (79 Siegel's Practice Review, *Time Limit on Summary Judgment*, at 2 [Jan. 1999]; *see also* 51 Siegel's Practice Review, *Strict Time Limit Placed on Motion for Summary Judgment*, at 1 [Nov. 1996]; Siegel, NY Prac § 279, at 440 [3d ed]).

What is to happen in this case is that summary judgment will be reversed and the case returned to the trial calendar, where a motion to dismiss after plaintiff rests or a request for a directed verdict may dispose of the case during trial. Hopefully, as a result of the courts' refusal to countenance the statutory violation, there will be fewer, if any, such situations in the future, both because it is now clear that "good cause" means good cause for the delay, and because movants will develop a habit of compliance with the statutory deadlines for summary judgment motions rather than delay until trial looms.

Accordingly, the order of the Appellate Division should be reversed, with costs, and the motion of the City of New York for summary judgment dismissing the complaint against it denied.

[Judge G.B. Smith's dissent omitted. — Eds.]

JUDGES CIPARICK, ROSENBLATT, GRAFFEO, READ and R.S. SMITH concur with CHIEF JUDGE KAYE; JUDGE G.B. SMITH dissents and votes to affirm in a separate opinion.

Order reversed, etc.

NOTES

(1) The tough stand taken in the principal case is also reflected in *Miceli v. State Farm Mut. Auto. Ins. Co.*, 3 N.Y.3d 725, 786 N.Y.S.2d 379, 819 N.E.2d 995 (2004), where again the Appellate Division's use of discretion was overruled. See the application of *Brill* and *Miceli* in *Perini Corp. v. City of New York*, 16 A.D.3d 37, 789 N.Y.S.2d 29 (1st Dep't 2005).

Professor Patrick Connors has thoroughly explored the *Brill* case in his arti-cle, *CPLR 3212(a)'s Timing Requirement for Summary Judgment Motions: Ona Brill's Stroll Through Brooklyn and the Dramatic Effect It Has Had on New York State's Civil Practice*, 71 Brook. L. Rev. 1529 (2006). The article prompted a post-script written by Chief Judge Kaye, *Brill's* author. While commending the "com-prehensive treatment" given the subject by Professor Connors, she took issue with his observation that some lawyers' attempts to avoid the time require-ments evidenced "the adventuresome nature of a healthy segment of the bar." Chief Judge Kaye stated: "I can't avoid offering some guidance of my own: just honor the deadlines, whether statutory or court-ordered. There's lots of other room for adventure in, and beyond, the law." 71 Brook. L. Rev. 1586.

(2) CPLR 3212(f) allows the court to deny, or stay decision of, a motion for summary judgment if "facts essential to justify opposition may exist but cannot then be stated." The opponent can then obtain disclosure or can conduct further investigation.

The general rule is that evidence submitted in support of or in opposition to the motion must be produced "in admissible form." *But see* CPLR 3212(f). What does "admissible form" mean when used in this context? Can it refer to the for-mal rules of evidence which prevail at trial? Apparently it does not, for a party's self-serving affidavits (which are not normally admissible at trial) have been accepted in support of a summary judgment motion held properly granted. *S.J. Capelin Associates, Inc. v. Globe Mfg. Corp.*, 34 N.Y.2d 338, 357 N.Y.S.2d 478, 313 N.E.2d 413 (1974). And CPLR 3212(b) specifically contemplates proof by affidavit. Would it make sense to say that the affidavits may be relied upon if the statements sworn to would be admissible if made at trial by the affiant? What then happens to cross-examination, "the greatest engine ever invented for the discovery of truth"? That not all of the rules of evidence are strictly appli-cable on a motion for summary judgment is demonstrated most forcefully by *Phillips v. Kantor & Co.*, 31 N.Y.2d 307, 338 N.Y.S.2d 882, 291 N.E.2d 129 (1972), which concerned CPLR 4519, often referred to as the "Dead Man's" statute. That statute makes testimony about certain kinds of statements by deceased persons inadmissible "[u]pon the trial of an action." Seizing on the quoted phrase, the court held that such statements were not excluded from judicial cognizance when a motion for summary judgment was under advise-ment because, among other reasons, the motion preceded the actual trial.

(3) If the facts are contested and the issue is one of credibility of the parties or their witnesses, summary judgment should be denied. *S.J. Capelin Associates, Inc. v. Globe Mfg. Corp.*, 34 N.Y.2d 338, 357 N.Y.S.2d 478, 313 N.E.2d 413 (1974). Why?

(4) As stated in *Ugarriza v. Schmieder, supra,* a grant of summary judgment "normally" has res judicata effect. Suppose defendant's answer had alleged a lack of jurisdiction over the person and property due to defective service, and later moved successfully for summary judgment on that ground. (Summary judgment motion would be the proper procedural vehicle. *See Rich v. Lefkovits*,

56 N.Y.2d 276, 452 N.Y.S.2d 1, 437 N.E.2d 260 (1982).) To what extent would the rules of res judicata require respect for the judgment? What is the effect of a denial of a motion for summary judgment?

(5) In *Grasso v. Angerami*, 79 N.Y.2d 814, 580 N.Y.S.2d 178, 588 N.E.2d 76 (1991), a personal injury action arising out of a motor vehicle accident, the defendant moved for summary judgment on the ground that the plaintiff had not sustained a "serious injury" as required by the New York No-Fault Law. *See* Insurance Law § 5102(d). In opposition to the motion, the plaintiff submitted an unsworn medical report, but the Court of Appeals held that it could not be considered because, being unsworn, it was not in admissible form. The Court noted that it was not deciding whether the report would have been admissible if the plaintiff had shown a valid excuse for his failure to submit evidence in proper form. The Third Department, in *Landisi v. Beacon Community Dev. Agency*, 180 A.D.2d 1000, 580 N.Y.S.2d 57 (3d Dept. 1992) (not a No-Fault case), had permitted hearsay evidence to defeat a summary judgment motion when a proper excuse for relying on it was shown. In *Pagano v. Kingsbury*, 182 A.D.2d 268, 587 N.Y.S.2d 692 (2d Dept. 1992), it was held that a sworn physician's report indicating serious injury was sufficient to create an issue of fact and thus require the denial of a summary judgment motion.

[B] Searching the Record

GLASS v. WEINER
Appellate Division, Second Department
92 A.D.2d 584, 459 N.Y.S.2d 471 (1983)

MEMORANDUM BY THE COURT.

In an action to recover damages for the forcible entry into an apartment, plaintiffs appeal from an order of the Supreme Court, Kings County, dated July 30, 1982, which denied their motion for summary judgment.

Order modified, on the law, by adding thereto a provision that the defendants are granted summary judgment dismissing the plaintiffs' complaint. As so modified, order affirmed, without costs or disbursements.

This action arises out of defendants' entry into the apartment of plaintiffs' deceased parents and the removal of the decedents' property. In their complaint, plaintiffs alleged that defendants forcibly entered into their parents' apartment and removed its contents, depriving plaintiffs of their rightful possessions and causing them mental anguish and emotional distress. Plaintiffs moved for summary judgment on the issue of liability and for an order directing an assessment of damages by a jury. That motion was properly denied by Special Term.

Despite the fact that the complaint alleged two causes of action based on forcible entry and wrongful removal of the decedents' property, plaintiffs did not establish their capacity to sue. The plaintiffs' suit was brought on their own behalf and as the sole heirs and distributees of their parents. However, a cause of action to recover damages for forcible entry sounds in tort and reposes only in the person who had possession of the property (RPAPL 853; *Novick v. Washington*, 110 Misc. 379, 176 N.Y.S. 387). Such an action could not be brought by parties who never had possession. . . . Based on the record, it is undisputed that the plaintiffs never had possession of the decedents' apartment. Inasmuch as the plaintiffs did not have capacity to sue under their causes of action, we are of the view that the defendants are entitled to summary judgment dismissing the complaint. Subdivision (b) of CPLR 3212 permits a court, on a summary judgment motion, to grant it instead to the movant's adversary, even though the latter did not request such relief. This relief is available even at the appellate level. . . .

The order appealed from is therefore modified so as to grant summary judgment to defendants dismissing plaintiffs' complaint. Such modification is made without prejudice to the institution of a subsequent action on behalf of the estate to recover damages for the conversion or destruction of the property.

NOTES

(1) The principal case illustrates the doctrine that a motion for summary judgment searches the record and can thus boomerang against the movant, not only in the trial court but even at the appellate stage. See, upholding the authority of the Appellate Division to grant summary judgment to a non-moving, non-appealing party, *Merritt Hill Vineyards, Inc. v. Windy Heights Vineyard, Inc.*, 61 N.Y.2d 106, 472 N.Y.S.2d 592, 460 N.E.2d 1077 (1984). Is the boomerang problem a reason to forego making the motion?

(2) The case also illustrates that a summary judgment motion can be the vehicle for presenting a defense (here, lack of capacity) which could have been the basis for a motion to dismiss under CPLR 3211(a).

(3) In *Dunham v. Hilco Construction Co., Inc.*, 89 N.Y.2d 425, 654 N.Y.S.2d 335, 676 N.E.2d 1178 (1996), the court placed a limit on the scope of the search. While the IAS court and the Appellate Division can search the record and award judgment to a nonmoving party under CPLR 3212(b), this is only with respect to a cause of action or issue which is the subject of the summary judgment motion. Where an employee of a subcontractor was injured in the workplace, he sued the owners, the general contractor, and a subcontractor. The subcontractor was the employer of the allegedly negligent co-worker. Plaintiff advanced two theories, one that there was an unsafe workplace, and the second that the co-worker was negligent. The Appellate Division granted summary judgment to all defendants. The Court of Appeals held this disposition exceeded its power to

search the record, since the co-worker's negligence was not implicated in the summary judgment motion which had been made by the owners and general contractor and was addressed only to the charge of unsafe conditions.

[C] Conversion to Summary Judgment: CPLR 3211(c)

MIHLOVAN v. GROZAVU
Court of Appeals
72 N.Y.2d 506, 531 N.E.2d 288, 534 N.Y.S.2d 656 (1988)

PER CURIAM.

In this defamation action, plaintiff alleged that defendants maliciously made false statements about him during the course of meetings on church elections. Defendants moved to dismiss the complaint asserting the defense of qualified privilege and Supreme Court granted the motion.

The Appellate Division incorrectly characterized Supreme Court's ruling on defendants' motion as a grant of summary judgment pursuant to CPLR 3212. Supreme Court's order, however, dismissed the complaint for failure to state a cause of action (CPLR 3211[a][7]), noting that defendants' preanswer motion sought dismissal "pursuant to CPLR 3211." Indeed, in their arguments to Supreme Court and the Appellate Division, both parties treated the motion solely as one for dismissal for failure to state a cause of action. Thus, the Appellate Division could not properly convert defendants' motion into a motion for summary judgment absent "adequate notice to the parties" (CPLR 3211[c]) which, in this case, should have been expressly given by the court. Neither party had otherwise received "adequate notice" by expressly seeking summary judgment or submitting facts and arguments clearly indicating that they were "deliberately charting a summary judgment course"* . . . Nor did the parties indicate that the case involved a purely legal question rather than any issues of fact. . . . Consequently, the court's sua sponte treatment of the motion as one for summary judgment deprived plaintiff of the "opportunity to make an appropriate record" and thus thwarted the very purpose of CPLR 3211(c) (*Rovello v Orofino Realty Co.*, 40 NY2d 633, 635).

Moreover, "given their most favorable intendment" (*Arrington v New York Times Co.*, 55 NY2d 433, 442), the allegations of plaintiff's complaint sufficiently state a cause of action for defamation. Notwithstanding defendants' assertion of a qualified privilege . . . plaintiff's allegations that the statements were maliciously made, if proven, would overcome that defense. . . .

---

* Contrary to the Second Department's holding in *Reed v. Shoratlantic Dev. Co.* (121 AD2d 525), we conclude that the unilateral actions of a party in seeking summary judgment on a CPLR 3211(a)(7) motion cannot constitute "adequate notice" to the other party in compliance with the requirement of CPLR 3211(c).

Accordingly, the order of the Appellate Division should be reversed, with costs, and the defendants' motion to dismiss the complaint denied.

NOTES

(1) CPLR 3211(c), though mandating "adequate" notice prior to converting a motion to dismiss a claim or defense to one for summary judgment, does not specify what form the notice must take. As you read the principal case, what constitutes adequate notice? Does the answer depend at all on the grounds on which summary judgment might be granted?

(2) Why is it important whether a motion under CPLR 3211(a)(7) is converted to one under CPLR 3212? Re-read *Rovello v. Orofino Realty Co.*, § 16.02, *supra*.

[D] The Effect of a Counterclaim

ROBERT STIGWOOD ORGANIZATION, INC. v. DEVON CO.
Court of Appeals
44 N.Y.2d 922, 408 N.Y.S.2d 5, 379 N.E.2d 1136 (1978)

MEMORANDUM.

The order of the Appellate Division, insofar as appealed from, should be reversed, with costs, and the stay of execution upon the partial summary judgment should be vacated.

The trial court, and thus the Appellate Division have wide discretion in imposing conditions upon the grant of partial summary judgment so as to avoid possible prejudice to the party against whom that judgment is granted (CPLR 3212, subd. [e]). The device used in this case, a stay of execution pending resolution of the remaining claims and counterclaims, is an appropriate method of effectuating that objective (*see* Siegel, Practice Commentaries, McKinney's Cons. Laws of N.Y., Book 7B, CPLR 3212:31, 3212:32). Such discretion, however, is not unlimited, and is to be exercised only if there exists some articulable reason for concluding that the failure to impose conditions might result in some prejudice, financial or otherwise, to the party against whom the partial summary judgment is granted should that party subsequently prevail on the unsettled claims (*see* Siegel, New York Practice, § 285). This is especially true where, as here, the counterclaims with respect to which partial summary judgment was granted are sufficiently independent of the plaintiff's claim as to have allowed defendant to bring a separate action upon them had it so chosen (*see Pease &*

Elliman v. 926 Park Ave. Corp., 23 A.D.2d 361, 260 N.Y.S.2d 693, *affd. without opn.* 17 N.Y.2d 890, 271 N.Y.S.2d 992, 218 N.E.2d 700).

The record in this case is completely bare of any indication that plaintiff would be in any way prejudiced if defendant is allowed to enforce its partial summary judgment. Under these circumstances, it was an abuse of discretion for the Appellate Division to impose a stay of execution upon that judgment.

NOTE

What are the sorts of prejudice which justify the denial or stay of summary judgment when counterclaims have been pleaded? The principal case mentions financial prejudice. Do you see how that could arise? In this connection, see also CPLR 5012.

Prejudice could also result from a grant of summary judgment when the unresolved counterclaim would, if valid, be a defense to the prime claim. *E.g.*, *Created Gemstones, Inc. v. Union Carbide Corp.*, 47 N.Y.2d 250, 417 N.Y.S.2d 905, 391 N.E.2d 987 (1979). The possible close connection between a counterclaim and a defense perhaps explains the otherwise puzzling point made in the principal case that the counterclaim there pleaded was "sufficiently independent of the plaintiff's claim as to have allowed defendant to bring a separate action on them had it so chosen. . . ." When, if ever, must a counterclaim be interposed in New York? *See* CPLR 3019 and § 13.04[B], *supra*.

[E] Commencing an Action by a Motion for Summary Judgment: CPLR 3213

WEISSMAN v. SINORM DELI, INC.
Court of Appeals
88 N.Y.2d 437, 646 N.Y.S.2d 308, 669 N.E.2d 242 (1996)

KAYE, CHIEF JUDGE

Two questions lie at the heart of this appeal. First, is the indemnification sued on an "instrument for the payment of money only" within CPLR 3213? Second, is the indemnification a guaranty by the individual defendants of the corporation's obligation? We answer both questions in the negative: the individual defendants' indemnification is neither "an instrument for the payment of money only" within CPLR 3213 nor a guaranty. The summary remedy is therefore not available to plaintiff and indeed summary judgment should be granted against him dismissing his action against the individual defendants.

Prior to March 5, 1992, plaintiff and the five individual defendants constituted all of the shareholders of Sinorm Deli, Inc., a New York corporation. To resolve irreconcilable differences among them, Sinorm agreed to buy out plaintiff's one-quarter interest in the corporation. The transaction was set out in a Stock Redemption Agreement dated March 5, 1992 with Sinorm as Buyer, plaintiff as Seller and the individual defendants as the Remaining Shareholders.

The purchase price was $250,000 to be paid by the corporation as follows: $50,000 at the closing in exchange for plaintiff's shares, and a $200,000 promissory note with interest of 7 percent per year to be paid in monthly installments. The installments were to be $1,667.07 per month for 36 consecutive months, then $2,500 per month until December 5, 2002, and a final payment of $1,696 on January 5, 2003.

The Stock Agreement further provided that the note was collateralized by an agreement which granted plaintiff a purchase money first security interest in Sinorm's assets; an assignment to plaintiff of Sinorm's lease; and a sublease between plaintiff as sublandlord and the corporation as subtenant. The lease and the assignment were to be deposited in escrow with plaintiff's attorneys under a written escrow receipt. Sinorm represented in the Stock Agreement that until full payment of the note was made it would not without plaintiff's written consent take any action which "will or might impair [its] obligations" under the Stock Agreement, including transferring, selling, assigning or encumbering any of its assets or properties.

The Stock Agreement also contained both default and indemnification provisions. Under the default provision, failure to make the monthly installment payment, after a ten-day cure period, allowed the holder of the note to call it due in its entirety. The indemnification provision (Article 10.1 of the Stock Agreement) stated:

> *Buyer's Indemnification.* Buyer and the Remaining Shareholders shall indemnify and hold Seller, his heirs, successors and assigns, harmless from and against all costs, losses, claims, taxes, liabilities, fines, penalties, damages and expenses (including any interest and court costs imposed in connection therewith and reasonable fees and disbursements of counsel) incurred by any of them in connection with any breach of any of the representations, warranties, covenants or agreements made by Buyer in this Agreement as well as all liabilities and obligations accruing from 7/23/91 and thereafter.

> *Seller's Indemnification.* Seller shall indemnify the Buyer and the Remaining Shareholders, their heirs, successors and assigns safe and harmless from and against any and all unpaid corporate taxes not reflected on Buyer's books and records up to and including July 31, 1991 to the extent of twenty-five (25 percent) percent of any assessment required to be paid by Buyer in excess of the taxes previously paid by the Buyer.

A separate Indemnification Agreement mirroring the indemnification language of the Buyer's Indemnification was also signed by the parties at closing.

During the closing, the last lines of the Buyer's Indemnification — reading "as well as all liabilities and obligations accruing from 7/23/91 and thereafter" — were handwritten into Article 10.1 and the Indemnification Agreement.

At the closing, the contract was executed, the corporation paid $50,000 and it delivered Sinorm's $200,000 note.

Promptly after Sinorm's default on the note installment due November 5, 1993, plaintiff moved under CPLR 3213 for summary judgment in lieu of complaint against the corporation and the individual defendants, seeking $189,984.31 plus interest. He based his motion on the note, the Indemnification Agreement and the Stock Agreement, asserting that the Indemnification Agreement represented a personal guaranty by the individual defendants of Sinorm's note.

The corporation did not oppose the motion. Two months after its default on the note, it had been evicted by its landlord in a non-payment proceeding. The individual defendants, however, cross-moved for summary judgment and submitted the affidavit of Burton Beal, the attorney who represented them in negotiating the various agreements. Apart from challenging the propriety of plaintiff's motion under CPLR 3213, the attorney contradicted plaintiff's assertion that the Indemnification Agreement was intended as a personal guaranty of the note, adding that when plaintiff at closing asked for individual guaranties, the request was adamantly refused. According to Beal, the parties agreed there would be no personal guaranty for the note. Rather, he asserted, the Indemnification Agreement was intended to protect plaintiff from any personal liability he might incur as a result of his status as a principal shareholder of the corporation. Plaintiff's reply affidavit denied the factual allegations of the Beal affidavit.

Supreme Court granted plaintiff's motion and denied the cross-motion, finding that plaintiff had established a *prima facie* case by proof of the promissory note, the Indemnification Agreement, and default in payment and indemnification. In granting summary judgment to the plaintiff, the court held

> the indemnification agreement, the latter portion of which was handwritten, clearly and unambiguously obligates the individual defendants to indemnify the plaintiff for losses he sustained arising from the corporate obligor's default on the promissory note.

The Appellate Division affirmed for the reasons stated by Supreme Court.

Before us defendants urge that the Indemnification Agreement does not qualify as an instrument for the payment of money only, as the agreement covers future, unstated, contingent liabilities to unknown third parties. Further, they contend that the Indemnification Agreement unambiguously does not constitute a guaranty of the corporation's promissory note, and consequently their cross-motion should have been granted. We consider each in turn.

Summary Judgment in Lieu of Complaint

Introduced more than three decades ago, CPLR 3213 was a procedural reform that, for the limited matters within its embrace, melded pleading and motion practice into one step, allowing a summary judgment motion to be made before issue was joined (*compare*, CPLR 3212). Its purpose was to provide quick relief on documentary claims so presumptively meritorious that "a formal complaint is superfluous and even the delay incident upon waiting for an answer and then moving for summary judgment is needless" (First Preliminary Report of Advisory Committee on Practice and Procedure, p 91, Legis. Doc. [1957] no. 6[b]). The statute provides:

> When an action is based upon an instrument for the payment of money only or upon any judgment, the plaintiff may serve with the summons a notice of motion for summary judgment and the supporting papers in lieu of a complaint.

CPLR 3213 begins with the seemingly straightforward — though stringent — requirement that the action be based on "an instrument for the payment of money only or a judgment."[1] The prototypical example of an instrument within the ambit of the statute is of course a negotiable instrument for the payment of money — an unconditional promise to pay a sum certain, signed by the maker and due on demand or at a definite time (*see* Weinstein-Korn-Miller, NY Civ Prac ¶ 3213.04, at 253). In fact, the remedy has proved an effective one, particularly for financial institutions recovering on promissory notes and unconditional guaranties (*see* Cozier, Summary Judgment, § 25.4 at 830, in 2 Commercial Litigation in New York State Courts [Haig ed.]).

Ironically, however, the threshold requirement has also generated a spate of litigation, leading one commentator to note that there have been "so many invocations of CPLR 3213 over the years in which the result was a dismissal of the application for want of a proper 'instrument'. . . [so as] to point up the illusory advantages of CPLR 3213 when used so carelessly" (Siegel, Practice Commentaries, McKinney's Cons. Laws of NY, Book 7B, CPLR 3213:1, at 497).

This Court last spoke to the threshold requirement in *Interman Industrial Products, Ltd. v. R.S.M. Electron Power, Inc.* (37 NY2d 151, 154-155), observing that cases within CPLR 3213 "have dealt primarily with some variety of commercial paper of which the party to be charged has formally and explicitly acknowledged an indebtedness." Where the instrument requires something in addition to defendant's explicit promise to pay a sum of money, CPLR 3213 is unavailable. Put another way, a document comes within CPLR 3213 "if a *prima facie* case would be made out by the instrument and a failure to make the payments called for by its terms" (*Interman*, 37 NY2d at 144 [*citing Seaman-Andwall Corp. v. Wright Mach, Corp.*, 31 AD2d 136, *affd* 29 NY2d 617]). The

---

[1] Proposals for legislative reform would broaden the statute's coverage to include several categories of common commercial transactions (*see* N.Y.S. 6775, N.Y.A. 9188, 219th Sess. [1966]).

instrument does not qualify if outside proof is needed, other than simple proof of nonpayment or a similar *de minimis* deviation from the face of the document (*see e.g., Bank Leumi Trust Company of New York v. Rattet & Liebman et al.*, 182 AD2d 541 [readily accessible interest rate]).

Plaintiff's action falls far short of satisfying the 3213 threshold requirement. There is no written instrument by which the individual shareholders explicitly obligated themselves to make a required payment of a sum certain (*Interman*, 37 NY2d at 156). The note at issue was signed only by Sinorm; the individual defendants never signed any commercial paper.

Critically here, the Indemnification Agreement does not qualify as an instrument for the payment of money only. The test "is not what the instrument may be reduced to by part performance or by elision of a portion of it . . . but rather how the instrument read in the first instance" (*Haug v. Metal City Findings Corp.*, 47 AD2d 837, 838).

The Indemnification Agreement contains no description of what constitutes the "liabilities and obligations arising from 7/23/91 and thereafter," and these unknown and unstated obligations cannot be proved from the instrument itself. The agreement also covers unknown future obligations and liabilities that will arise after March 5, 1992. Plaintiff faced contingent personal liabilities as a controlling shareholder of the corporation — for example, legal obligations for unpaid wages and salaries (*see* Business Corporation Law § 630) and unpaid taxes (*see* Tax Law § 1133), as well as potential liability from litigation involving the corporation — which were covered by the Indemnification Agreement. These liabilities and obligations, however, can only be ascertained by resorting to evidence outside the instrument.

Because the Indemnification Agreement fails to meet the threshold requirement of "an instrument for the payment of money only," we conclude that CPLR 3213 was improperly invoked.

Defendant's Cross-Motion for Dismissal

If, as in the present case, the plaintiff has mistaken his remedy and CPLR 3213 is in fact not available, the action typically should not be dismissed but simply converted to ordinary form as the statute provides. The statute, however, additionally authorizes the court to do "otherwise." Thus, if plaintiff's claim plainly fails on the merits, the court can grant summary judgment for defendant, denying the motion and dismissing the action (*see* Siegel, Practice Commentaries, McKinney's Cons. Laws of NY, Book 7B, CPLR 3213:11, at 509).

[The defendants' cross motion for summary judgment dismissing the action was granted. The court agreed with defendants' argument that the Indemnification Agreement did not constitute a guarantee of the corporation's promissory note.]

NOTES

(1) Note the last paragraph of the principal case. The fact that the plaintiff, if unsuccessful in convincing the court that the instrument qualifies under the stringent requirements of CPLR 3213, can simply proceed with the action anyway (unless thwarted as in the principal case by a successful cross-motion), suggests why this procedure is so often utilized. In *Schultz v. Barrows*, 94 N.Y.2d 624, 709 N.Y.S.2d 148, 730 N.E.2d 946 (2000), however, plaintiff was thwarted in his attempt to proceed under CPLR 3213 to enforce a Texas default judgment. Defendant, the judgment debtor, collaterally attacked the Texas judgment and the IAS court found that indeed it was void for lack of personal jurisdiction. The Appellate Division affirmed. Plaintiff argued that he ought to be allowed to proceed against defendant on the cause of action underlying the judgment, along with other causes of action, since the New York court had full jurisdiction. The Court of Appeals held that the IAS justice did not abuse his discretion in ordering "otherwise" and dismissing the proceedings altogether, since plaintiff had never sought such treatment of the case, had never argued that the cause of action underlying the default judgment should be tried on the merits if the judgment were found void, and had never pointed out that the statute of limitations would have run on his claim were the motion to be dismissed.

(2) Under the usual approach to CPLR 3213, an action on a bill for delivery of goods or provision of services is not one on an instrument for the payment of money only. Counsel for the plaintiff should, however, consider the benefits of pleading in accordance with CPLR 3016(f).

(3) As indicated in *Schulz v. Barrows,* above, CPLR 3212 is available when the action is upon a judgment unless, as in *Schulz*, the judgment is invalid. Foreign country judgments may likewise be attacked for invalidity. *See* CPLR 5303; § 22.06, *infra*. When the judgment to be enforced is of a court entitled to full faith and credit (*viz.*, a court in a sister state or of the United States), CPLR article 54 ordinarily makes resort to CPLR 3213 unnecessary, because it permits the judgment to become enforceable if plaintiff simply files the judgment in accordance with CPLR 5402.

(4) In an action to recover the balance on retail installment contracts allegedly cosigned by defendant, defendant's defense of forgery failed to block CPLR 3213 summary judgment. Defendant claimed her signature was forged, but her prelitigation conduct was not consistent with that defense, and the report from her handwriting expert was inadequate to raise a question of fact since, *inter alia*, there was no assertion that with reasonable professional certainty defendant's signature was not authentic. *Banco Popular N. Am. v. Victory Taxi Mgmt.*, 1 N.Y.3d 381, 774 N.Y.S.2d 480, 806 N.E.2d 488 (2004).

§ 16.05 JUDGMENT BY DEFAULT

A judgment may be obtained against a party who defaults on any of a number of obligations. CPLR 3215(a) is suitably open ended: "When a party has failed to appear, plead or proceed to trial of an action reached and called for trial, or when the court orders a dismissal for any other neglect to proceed, the plaintiff may seek a default judgment against him."

REYNOLDS SECURITIES, INC. v.
UNDERWRITERS BANK & TRUST CO.
Court of Appeals
44 N.Y.2d 568, 406 N.Y.S.2d 743, 378 N.E.2d 106 (1978)

FUCHSBERG, JUDGE.

The issue on this appeal, seemingly commonplace but a source of more controversy than one would expect, is whether, under the facts in this case, a default judgment, obtained as a result of a willful refusal to comply with discovery orders, was properly entered for the full amount of the ad damnum without the holding of an inquest to assess the damages.

On three separate occasions, the defendant, Andre Rostworowski, placed an order with the plaintiff, Reynolds Securities, Inc., a national brokerage firm, to sell shares of a particular stock for his account. Though notified that the sales had been executed, the specified settlement date came and went without Rostworowski's having delivered the certificates for transfer to the buyers. In fact, he never did so. Consequently, approximately two months after the initial sale, plaintiff proceeded to "buy-in" the required securities in the open market. In the intervening time, the securities appreciated considerably. This action was thereafter brought to recover $21,768.61, presumably the difference between the money it had expended, inclusive of the brokerage commissions, to purchase the covering stock and the amounts it had received for the stock ordered sold by the defendant.

After issue was joined and in personam jurisdiction unsuccessfully contested (51 A.D.2d 957, 381 N.Y.S.2d 1019), defendant willfully refused to comply with several discovery notices and four different court orders which directed him to appear for the taking of his deposition. As authorized by the last of these orders, upon a demonstration of defendant's failure to attend on the appointed date, plaintiff obtained an ex parte order striking the answer and directing the entry of judgment for the full amount demanded in the complaint. No proof of the actual loss sustained was submitted, either in testimonial or affidavit form, in support of the award.

. . . .

Defendant does not, and indeed cannot successfully, quarrel with the order to the extent that it struck the answer and directed the entry of a default judgment on liability, for the court was more than eminently justified in following that course (CPLR 3126; *cf. Laverne v. Meehan*, 18 N.Y.2d 635, 272 N.Y.S.2d 780, 219 N.E.2d 294, *app. dsmd.*, 386 U.S. 682, 87 S.Ct. 1324, 18 L.Ed.2d 403). Rather, he claims that the damages, not being liquidated, were not ascertainable without a hearing at which he could appear and offer evidence to contest the extent of plaintiff's claimed loss. In particular, he asserts that plaintiff unduly delayed its purchase of the covering securities and thus failed to "promptly cancel or otherwise liquidate the transaction" as mandated by Federal Reserve Board Regulation T (12 CFR 220.4, subd. (c), pars. (2), (5); *cf. Matter of Naftalin & Co. v. Merrill Lynch, Pierce, Fenner & Smith*, 8 Cir., 469 F.2d 1166).

The entry of a default judgment against a defendant, though it be for noncompliance with a discovery order, is governed by CPLR 3215 (4 Weinstein-Korn-Miller, N.Y. Civ. Prac., par. 3215.02). Where the damages sought are for a "sum certain or for a sum which can by computation be made certain," subdivision (a) of that section makes it permissible for the clerk, without notice to the defendant (subd. (f)) and upon proof by the affidavit of a party setting forth the facts constituting the claim, the default and the amount due, to enter judgment up to the amount demanded in the complaint. Otherwise, application to the court is required (CPLR 3215, subd. (b)), and a defendant who has appeared is entitled to five days' notice of the application (subd. (f)), as well as a full opportunity to cross-examine witnesses, give testimony and offer proof in mitigation of damages. . . .

The term "sum certain" in this context contemplates a situation in which, once liability has been established, there can be no dispute as to the amount due, as in actions on money judgments and negotiable instruments. Obviously, the clerk then functions in a purely ministerial capacity. . . .

In the present case, however, the damages sought cannot be determined without extrinsic proof, for the amount of plaintiff's damages is not readily ascertainable without consideration of the reasonableness of the time which plaintiff permitted to elapse before making the covering purchase . . . and the correctness of the calculation of the commissions. It follows that the entry by the clerk was unauthorized and an inquest should therefore have been ordered. . . .

On remittal for that purpose, it is not to be assumed that defendant's obligation to afford plaintiff the opportunity to pursue discovery terminated when the answer was stricken. Though as a result of his default, the defendant has now forfeited his right to take the plaintiff's deposition, it does not follow that plaintiff is to be handicapped in the proof of its damages by defendant's prior defiance of orders, notices, or subpoenas calling for his production of records or the taking of his deposition. . . .

Thus, to anticipate the eventuality that the defendant may elect to proceed with his avowed intention to contest the damage issue by opposing proof, plaintiff, if it chooses to do so, may press its right to discovery in advance of the inquest, whether for direct use as evidence in proving its damages or for the procurement of information that may lead to such evidence.

. . . .

Moreover, if the defendant's deposition or his response to subpoena is vital to plaintiff's proof and the defendant holds to his prior course by refusing to obey orders or subpoenas, the plaintiff's rights should not have to hang on the compulsion to comply which may follow the possible exercise of the trial court's powers of contempt against the defendant. Among other things, the defendant may then be precluded from offering any evidence at the inquest. . . .

Beyond that, if the plaintiff's ability to prove his affirmative case with a fair degree of precision is seriously hampered by the defendant's obstructiveness, the court, in order that a just result be achieved, is not without power, where necessary, to rely on lesser and more informal proofs. A defendant whose conduct has both caused injury to another and put obstacles in the path of the plaintiff's recovery is hardly in a position to complain when, as a consequence, the damages cannot be established with exactitude. . . .

Accordingly, the order of the Appellate Division should be modified by remitting the matter to the Supreme Court, New York County, for the purpose of conducting an assessment as to damages and for other proceedings consistent herewith, with costs to plaintiff to abide the event. And, pending the final disposition of this action, the judgment affected by this decision should continue to stand as security. . . .

NOTES

(1) Procedure for taking a default judgment is governed by CPLR 3215. As described in the principal case, the clerk of court, without judicial assistance, may enter judgment when the "plaintiff's claim is for a sum certain or for a sum which can by computation be made certain." CPLR 3215(a), (f). For other kinds of claims an assessment before a court is necessary. CPLR 3215(b). In either case, the party seeking the judgment must file proof of service properly commencing the action and "proof by affidavit made by the party of the facts constituting the claim, the default and amount due." CPLR 3215(e).

When the application for the judgment is made to the court, a defendant who has appeared in the action is entitled to five days notice of the time and place of the motion (a defendant who has not appeared is entitled to notice only if more than one year has elapsed since the default). CPLR 3215(f)(1). No notice to the defendant of the application for judgment is required when it is made to the clerk. *Id.*

(2) In *Matter of Brusco v. Braun*, 84 N.Y.2d 674, 621 N.Y.S.2d 291, 645 N.E.2d 724 (1994), the Court dealt with a default judgment in a New York City Civil

Court summary proceeding, and held that the procedure was governed by Real Prop. Actions & Proc. Law § 732(3), which directed that in case of a default in a proceeding brought by the landlord for rent the "judge shall render judgment in favor of the [landlord]." Under CPLR 3215, a judge presiding over an application for a default judgment in a general civil action may hold an inquest or assessment. But it was held that the two procedures were exclusive and that in a summary proceeding the "special" statute pertaining to such proceedings would take precedence over the general provisions of CPLR 3215. Since the direction in § 732(3) was peremptory, the Civil Court judge had no choice but to grant the judgment sought in the petition.

(3) Proof of the facts constituting the claim must be by an affidavit of a person having personal knowledge of them, or otherwise supported by documentary evidence. Thus, an application for a default judgment supported only by a complaint which had been verified by an attorney who had no personal knowledge of the underlying facts was rejected. *Joosten v. Gale*, 129 A.D.2d 531, 514 N.Y.S.2d 729 (1st Dep't 1987). The court explained:

> CPLR 3215 does not contemplate that default judgments are to be rubber-stamped once jurisdiction and a failure to appear have been shown. Some proof of liability is also required to satisfy the court as to the prima facie validity of the uncontested cause of action. . . . The standard of proof is not stringent, amounting only to some first-hand confirmation of the facts.

(4) Two other requirements must be noted. The federal Soldier's and Sailor's Relief Act, 50 U.S.C. § 520, which applies in state courts, mandates that an affidavit be filed by the movant stating that the defaulting defendant is not in military service. The purpose of the law is to protect persons who are unlikely to get notice of the action and will, in any event, be handicapped in defending against it in timely fashion. For a discussion of problems encountered in enforcing the law, see *New York City Housing Authority v. Smithson*, 119 Misc. 2d 721, 464 N.Y.S.2d 672 (N.Y.C. Civil Court 1983).

A second requirement is that plaintiff in an action against a natural person based on a contractual obligation must mail a copy of the summons to the defendant at least twenty days prior to the entry of a default judgment. CPLR 3215(f)(3).

(5) If the defendant defaults, plaintiff may not dawdle unduly. If the plaintiff fails to seek a judgment within one year, the action will be dismissed as abandoned. CPLR 3215(c).

Chapter 17
SETTLEMENTS AND STIPULATIONS

§ 17.01 INTRODUCTORY NOTE

Termination of the lawsuit by settlement serves important public and private goals. Not the least of the latter is the avoidance of the "all or nothing" risk of a trial. This in part explains why the great majority of cases started are ended by agreement rather than court ruling.

Much has been written — including much that is good — about the tactics of negotiation. *See, e.g.,* C. Craver, Effective Legal Negotiation and Settlement (4th ed. 2001); R. Fisher & W. Ury, Getting to Yes: Negotiating Agreements Without Giving In (2d ed. 1991); D. Gifford, Legal Negotiation, Theory and Applications (1989).

This chapter, however, is concerned not with how you get to a satisfactory agreement, but with what you do once that point is reached. It is about the "law" of settlement. This law is at the interstices of procedure and contract. Disputing parties are free, of course, to resolve their differences without commencing litigation. Subsequent disputes about the existence or meaning of their agreement are subject to the law of contracts.[*] When a lawsuit has been started before the agreement was reached, CPLR 2104 adds a refinement to contract law. Note that under it, the only binding agreements "relating to any matter in an action" are those which meet one of the three formal requirements there listed. Note too that it allows the attorney to bind the client.

CPLR 2104 applies to agreements which resolve issues affecting only part of the lawsuit, as well as those which terminate the entire matter. Common examples are the granting of extensions of time to plead or serve papers and the stipulation to issues not in dispute. Sometimes agreements on procedural points are reached by opposing counsel informally — even in a telephone conversation. What problems might you foresee with such informality?

There is truth to the frequently made assertion that the parties are free to "chart their . . . procedural course through the courts." *Stevensen v. News Syndicate Co.*, 302 N.Y. 81, 87, 96 N.E.2d 187, 190 (1950), and may therefore stipulate to virtually anything they choose. What limits are there on that freedom? At the least, one should occur to you.

---

[*] Prof. David H. Schwartz, referred aptly to the resolution of these conflicts as "settling the settlement." He believed, with justice, that an attorney whose settlement had to be settled had taken foolishly little care with the details of formality and drafting.

PROBLEM A

Robb's client is a landlord who has commenced an eviction proceeding for non-payment of rent against a tenant represented by Jim. On the morning the case is scheduled to be tried, Robb and Jim meet outside the courtroom to discuss it. Jim states that his client admits to owing the rent and will pay the rent if the eviction proceeding is terminated and if certain repairs to the premises are made. Robb believes that these terms are acceptable to his client and would like to enter into an enforceable agreement. Jim suggests that they shake hands on the deal and subsequently execute a written memorandum incorporating these terms. What should Robb do?

HALLOCK v. STATE
Court of Appeals
64 N.Y.2d 224, 485 N.Y.S.2d 510, 474 N.E.2d 1178 (1984)

KAYE, JUDGE.

A stipulation of settlement made by counsel in open court may bind his clients even where it exceeds his actual authority.

[Plaintiffs Hallock and Phillips commenced a declaratory judgment action challenging the state's right to take by eminent domain a full fee interest rather than just an easement on their land. On the trial date Hallock was ill and did not attend the pretrial conference, but Phillips and his lawyer were present. The state had previously made a settlement offer which was initially rejected. After discussion at the pretrial conference, plaintiff Hallock's counsel, Quartararo, agreed to the settlement offer and the agreement was dictated on the record. The trial judge had the attorneys affirm that they agreed to the settlement and the case was removed from the trial calendar. Phillips had not objected to the agreement and Hallock learned of the settlement later that day. Two months thereafter Hallock expressed dissatisfaction with the settlement and plaintiffs moved to vacate the stipulation. The trial court found that Phillips was bound by the stipulation because of his presence and that Quartararo had implicit authority to settle on behalf of Hallock. A divided Appellate Division reversed, finding that Quartararo had no such authority. The Court of Appeals restored the trial judge's determination.]

Stipulations of settlement are favored by the courts and not lightly cast aside. This is all the more so in the case of "open court" stipulations (*Matter of Dolgin Eldert Corp.*, 31 N.Y.2d 1, 10, 334 N.Y.S.2d 833, 286 N.E.2d 228) within CPLR 2104, where strict enforcement not only serves the interest of efficient dispute resolution but also is essential to the management of court calendars and integrity of the litigation process. Only where there is cause sufficient to invalidate a contract such as fraud, collusion, mistake or accident, will a party be relieved from the consequences of a stipulation made during litigation (*Matter of Frutiger*, 29 N.Y.2d 143, 149-150, 324 N.Y.S.2d 36, 272 N.E.2d 543). Neither court below found fraud, collusion, mistake or accident; nor can we conclude as a matter of law that such a showing was made. What plaintiffs must then demonstrate in order to sustain their position is that their agent, Quartararo, was without authority of any sort to enter into the settlement, and therefore no contract ever came into being.

From the nature of the attorney-client relationship itself, an attorney derives authority to manage the conduct of litigation on behalf of a client, including the authority to make certain procedural or tactical decisions (*see* Code of Professional Responsibility, EC 7-7; *Gorham v. Gale*, 7 Cow. 739, 744; *Gaillard v. Smart*, 6 Cow. 385, 388). But that authority is hardly unbounded. Equally rooted in the law is the principle that, without a grant of authority from the client, an attorney cannot compromise or settle a claim (*see Kellogg v. Gilbert*, 10 Johns. 220; *Jackson v. Bartlett*, 8 Johns. 361), and settlements negotiated by attorneys without authority from their clients have not been binding.

Quartararo unquestionably had authority from plaintiffs to conduct settlement negotiations with defendants as he had done with plaintiffs' knowledge and assent during the weeks prior to April 22, 1975. At most, on April 22 he exceeded the authority plaintiffs urge had been limited shortly before by their injunction to negotiate a better deal. The question raised by this appeal, then, is whether it should be plaintiffs, or defendants, who bear the responsibility for Quartararo's misfeasance in accepting the settlement they claim had been rejected. We conclude that plaintiffs must bear that responsibility, and are relegated to relief against their former attorney for any damages which his conduct may have caused them.

Phillips cannot be heard to challenge the settlement. He was in court during the entire pretrial conference. At no time during negotiation of the settlement or dictation of the agreement into the record — or indeed during the more than two months that followed — did Phillips voice an objection. Phillips acquiesced in, consented to, and is bound by the settlement.

Hallock also is bound by the settlement. Even if Quartararo lacked actual authority because, according to plaintiffs, Quartararo accepted the very settlement his clients had instructed him to reject, still Quartararo had apparent authority to bind Hallock.[4]

Essential to the creation of apparent authority are words or conduct of the principal, communicated to a third party, that give rise to the appearance and belief that the agent possesses authority to enter into a transaction. The agent cannot by his own acts imbue himself with apparent authority. "Rather, the existence of 'apparent authority' depends upon a factual showing that the third

---

[4] Since we conclude that Quartararo had apparent authority to bind Hallock, we do not reach the alleged evidentiary error in excluding testimony bearing on the issue of Quartararo's actual authority to bind Hallock, or the question whether the relationship between Hallock and Phillips was such that Phillips' conduct would itself bind Hallock.

party relied upon the misrepresentation of the agent because of some misleading conduct on the part of the principal — not the agent." (*Ford v. Unity Hosp.*, 32 N.Y.2d 464, 473, 346 N.Y. S.2d 238, 299 N.E.2d 659; *see, also*, Restatement, Agency 2d, § 27.) Moreover, a third party with whom the agent deals may rely on an appearance of authority only to the extent that such reliance is reasonable.

Here, as a matter of law, Hallock clothed Quartararo with apparent authority to enter into the settlement. Quartararo had represented plaintiffs through the litigation, engaged in prior settlement negotiations for them and, in furtherance of the authority which had been vested in him, appeared at the final pretrial conference, his presence there constituting an implied representation by Hallock to defendants that Quartararo had authority to bind him to the settlement (22 NYCRR 861.17 [now 22 NYCRR 202.26(e) — Eds.] . . .). The attendance of the coplaintiff, Phillips, further enforced that appearance. In the circumstances, it necessarily fell to Phillips or Quartararo himself to reveal any restrictions on the attorney's authority to settle, and absent such disclosure defendants' reliance on the appearance of authority was entirely reasonable.

Plaintiffs insist that apparent authority is an equitable doctrine, having its origins in the principle of estoppel (*see Rothschild v. Title Guar. & Trust Co.*, 204 N.Y. 458, 461, 97 N.E. 879), and that defendants must establish detrimental reliance before the settlement stipulation can be enforced. The discontinuance of lengthy litigation on the day of trial, in reliance on the adversary's settlement stipulation — even for defendants, who often may prefer that judgment be deferred — coupled with plaintiffs' silence for more than two months thereafter, is itself a change of position, if such a showing is indeed even required before the doctrine of apparent authority may be invoked. We need not inquire whether there was any actual loss of witnesses or evidence, for we recognize that, after five years, halting the machinery of litigation when a trial scheduled to begin that day is marked off the calendar constitutes detriment. Additionally, in the words of the dissenting Justice at the Appellate Division, to set aside this settlement stipulation "invites destruction of the process of open-court settlements, for every such settlement would be liable to subsequent rescission by the simple expedient of a litigant's self-serving assertion, joined in by his attorney and previously uncommunicated to either the court or others involved in the settlement, that the litigant had limited his attorney's authority" (98 A.D.2d 856, 858-859, 470 N.Y.S.2d 844).

NOTES

(1) Under the Uniform Rules for the New York State Trial Courts, any attorney who represents a party at a pretrial or preliminary conference must be authorized to make binding stipulations or be accompanied by a person who may do so. 22 NYCRR 202.26(e).

(2) CPLR 2104 provides:

> An agreement between parties or their attorneys relating to any matter in an action, other than one made between counsel in open court, is not binding upon a party unless it is in a writing subscribed by him or his attorney or reduced to the form of an order and entered.

In 2003, a second sentence was added to CPLR 2104 which states: "With respect to stipulations of settlement and notwithstanding the form of the stipulation of settlement, the terms of such stipulation shall be filed by the defendant with the county clerk." A $35 fee is required for this filing under CPLR 8020. Several questions have arisen because of this amendment, not the least of which is whether it covers stipulations of settlement in courts below the Supreme and County Court levels. Another issue raised concerns the filing of a voluntary discontinuance to include the "terms of such stipulation" without revealing the details of the settlement, which would jeopardize the confidentiality of the settlement and could remove the incentive to settle. *See* Alexander's 2003, C 2104:2 Practice Commentary, 7B McKinney's Consol. Laws of New York, Supp., p. 260.

CPLR 2104 may require an interpretation of the phrase "open court." In the leading case, *Matter of Dolgin Eldert Corp.*, 31 N.Y.2d 1, 334 N.Y.S.2d 833, 286 N.E.2d 228 (1972), the Court of Appeals said:

> Judicial proceedings in "open court," wherever held, including chambers of course, and informal conferences in chambers or robing rooms or even a courtroom are manifestly disparate. Even before full reporting in open court became universal in courts of record, the formality, publicity, and solemnity of an open court proceeding marked it as different from the preliminary atmosphere attached to informal conferences elsewhere. Moreover, the proceedings in open court would always have some formal entries, if only in the clerk's minutes, to memorialize the critical litigation events. In the latter days, it has also meant an available full transcript beyond dispute and the fallibility of memory. . . . To extend the exception of CPLR 2104 beyond its meaning to cover purported agreements reached elsewhere is to extend a limited exception derived from necessity (yet with significant safeguards) to an uncontrollable area.

31 N.Y.2d at 10, 334 N.Y.S.2d at 840, 286 N.E.2d at 233.

In the above case the Court of Appeals concluded that an oral agreement in chambers before a judge and a clerk unmemorialized in writing did not constitute compliance with the open court exception to CPLR 2104.

(3) Some cases have suggested that even a stipulation which did not comply with the formal requirements of CPLR 2104 would be enforceable on an estoppel theory if it could be shown that an agreement was reached and that the party seeking to enforce it relied upon it and would be prejudiced by non-

enforcement. *See* discussion in *Veith v. ABC Paving Co.*, 58 A.D.2d 257, 396 N.Y.S.2d 556 (4th Dep't 1977). The Court of Appeals, however, chose to construe the writing requirement strictly where defendant drew up the $3 million settlement papers and submitted them to the infant plaintiff. For some months, plaintiff's representative neither signed the papers nor sought the necessary court approval — and then the infant died. This event had an impact on the damage claim, and defendant withdrew its offer. On plaintiff's representative's motion to enforce the settlement, the Court ruled for defendant noting that although there had been a writing it never had been executed and plaintiff had not obtained the court approval, a stipulation in the writing. An estoppel argument raised by plaintiff was held insufficient given these facts. *Bonnette v. Long Island College Hosp.*, 3 N.Y.3d 281, 785 N.Y.S.2d 738, 819 N.E.2d 206 (2004).

(4) Formal judicial approval of a settlement agreement is neither required nor available in ordinary actions. *But see* CPLR 908 (class actions); CPLR 1207 (claims of infants, incompetents and conservatees); Estate, Powers and Trusts Law § 5-4.6 (wrongful death cases).

As the principal case notes, however, the courts have authority to set aside a settlement on a showing of fraud, mistake, collusion, accident or other grounds which could invalidate a contract. Examples include *Yuda v. Yuda*, 143 A.D.2d 657, 533 N.Y.S.2d 75 (2d Dep't 1988), setting aside a settlement of a divorce action as unconscionable, and *Pokora v. Albergo*, 130 A.D.2d 473, 525 N.Y.S.2d 56 (2d Dep't 1987), vacating a settlement of a personal injury action because of the plaintiff's belated discovery that the injuries were more severe than had appeared at the time of the settlement. Fraud, mistake or collusion perpetrated by the lawyer against the client, however, is not of the sort contemplated in this rule. Such would have to have been perpetrated between the parties. *Nash v. Y and T Distributors*, 207 A.D.2d 779, 616 N.Y.S.2d 402 (2d Dep't 1994) (where lawyer forged client's name to settlement agreement, the conduct would not abrogate the agreement — the inquiry remains whether in the contemplation of the other party the lawyer had apparent authority, and in this case it was held he did not).

(5) An offer to settle a case cannot be introduced at trial as an admission. CPLR 4547 provides that the offer itself shall be inadmissible as well as evidence of any conduct or statement made during the negotiations. These provisions do not immunize such evidence if independently discoverable or if relevant to some other purpose "such as proving bias or prejudice of a witness, negating a contention of undue delay of proof of an effort to obstruct a criminal investigation or prosecution." This is an adoption of Federal Rule of Evidence 408 and does away with the ancient rule of *White v. Old Dominion S.S. Co.*, 102 N.Y. 660, 6 N.E. 289 (1886), which held that any admissions of fact made during compromise negotiations, separate from the offer to compromise or the compromise itself, would be admissible. *See generally* Barker & Alexander, Evidence in New York State and Federal Courts § 408.1 (2001).

(6) How much independence of judgment may a lawyer exercise in deciding to settle a case or to resolve an issue in it by agreement? *See* E.C. 707 and DR 7-101(B)(1) of the Code of Professional Responsibility:

EC 7-7.

In certain areas of legal representation not affecting the merits of the cause or substantially prejudicing the rights of a client, a lawyer is entitled to make decisions. But otherwise the authority to make decisions is exclusively that of the client and, if made within the framework of the law, such decisions are binding on the lawyer. As typical examples in civil cases, it is for the client to decide whether to accept a settlement offer or whether he will waive his right to plead an affirmative defense. . . .

DR 7-101

. . . .

(B) In the representation of a client, a lawyer may:

(1) Where permissible, exercise professional judgment to waive or fail to assert a right or position of the client.

(7) CPLR 5003-a provides that the settlement amount must be paid within 21 days from the time the plaintiff serves a stipulation discontinuing the action and a release on the defendant. Defendant's failure to comply will result in the addition of costs and interests to the bill. If the decedent is the state or a municipality, longer time periods for the payment of interest are provided.

CROUSE-IRVING MEMORIAL HOSPITAL, INC. v. MOORE
Appellate Division, Fourth Department
84 A.D.2d 954, 446 N.Y.S.2d 705 (1981)

. . . Judgment unanimously reversed, without costs, and third-party complaint dismissed, in accordance with the following memorandum: Plaintiff Crouse-Irving Memorial Hospital sues to recover hospital and medical expenses due it by defendant third-party plaintiff Yvonne Moore, on behalf of her son, defendant third-party plaintiff, Ronald Bartell, who was injured in a motorcycle accident. Before the action was brought, Moore and Bartell sought medical assistance from the Onondaga County Department of Social Services (OCDSS), but assistance was denied because Mrs. Moore had resources available to her in the form of life insurance proceeds received after her husband's death. Inasmuch as the bills continued to accumulate, OCDSS agreed to pay the excess once Mrs. Moore used up these available assets. Declining to accept that determination, Mrs. Moore demanded a fair hearing on the question of eligibility. On the return date of the fair hearing, the attorney for OCDSS had in hand a statement from Crouse-Irving showing that some $8,985.63 of the Moore bill had been paid. Relying upon that statement, he stipulated that if Mrs. Moore would pay a hospital bill balance of $169.50 from her own resources, OCDSS would then pay the rest. Mrs. Moore agreed to do so and withdrew her request for a fair hearing without any ruling on her eligibility having been made. In fact, third-party plaintiffs have not paid anything on the bill (other than $169.50) and neither has anyone else and since the bill had not been paid, the hospital initiated this action. Mrs. Moore and her son impleaded OCDSS and the State agency, claiming that they were bound by the stipulation of settlement. Special Term granted summary judgment in favor of the hospital and judgment over in favor of defendants Moore and Bartell against the third-party defendants.

The Social Services Law establishes the State and local responsibility for medical assistance (*see* Social Services Law, § 365) and the eligibility standards which must be met for those seeking it (Social Services Law, § 366). Manifestly, in this case there has never been an administrative determination that Mrs. Moore and her son are eligible for assistance or that third-party defendants are responsible for their medical bills. On the contrary, the agency determined that the third-party plaintiffs were not eligible for assistance and that determination is still in effect. Nevertheless, third-party plaintiffs seek to impose liability on third-party defendants because of the stipulation of the OCDSS attorney at the fair hearing. They claim that counsel's statement is the equivalent of a settlement stipulation in a pending lawsuit (*see Yonkers Fur Dressing Co. v. Royal Ins. Co.*, 247 NY 435) and supersedes the determination of noneligibility. The rule that a stipulation of settlement in a pending dispute made by parties authorized to make it binds the parties is based upon the theory that the settlement terminates the existing litigation and gives rise to a new superseding agreement which is the measure of each party's obligation to the other. . . . It is questionable that any "agreement" was reached at this fair hearing, but even if it was, the rule binding the litigants presupposes attorneys competent to bind their principals, for an attorney cannot bind his client in relation to matters involved in litigation without his clients' consent. . . . Obviously, on a matter of eligibility defined by statute, counsel was without authority to bind the Department of Social Services or the State agency to advance medical payments to an ineligible recipient (*see Bush v O'Brien*, 164 NY 205; *Matter of Fischer v Bloomer*, 268 App Div 947; *Matter of Crenman v Brennan*, 265 App Div 1013). But even if it be held that the department's counsel had implied authority to settle the question of payment in this case, the department was entitled to be relieved of its commitment because the stipulation was made while counsel was operating under a mistake of fact. . . . The third-party judgment is reversed and the third-party complaint is dismissed, without prejudice to third-party plaintiffs' right to seek an independent determination of their eligibility for medical assistance.

. . . .

NOTES

(1) The principal case suggests that an attorney for a government agency cannot by stipulation bind the client to make a payment which the agency would not be compelled to make by a court after litigation. What problems would such a rule present for the administration of justice?

On this point, compare the principal case with *Salesian Society, Inc. v. Village of Ellenville*, 41 N.Y.2d 521, 525-26, 393 N.Y.S.2d 972, 976, 362 N.E.2d 604 (1977), in which the Court of Appeals held binding a stipulation in which the defendant had waived its right to assert as a defense the plaintiff's failure to serve a notice of claim. The Court said:

> Courts have long favored the fashioning of stipulations by opposing counsel as effective and enforceable means for expediting trials by permitting them to focus on the controverted issues. . . . Such a procedural path may be employed not only by attorneys who represent private litigants but those who represent public ones as well. . . .
>
> Of course, notwithstanding such considerations, if the waiver, though occurring in the course of litigation, were one tainted by collusion, fraud, overreaching or the like, of none of which is there any suggestion here, it might not be sustainable. Or, if, despite circumstances otherwise supporting a waiver in a litigation situation, it appeared that the underlying transaction to which the litigation was directed was illegal, the waiver might be disregarded.

Cases enforcing stipulations to pay damages entered into by public bodies include *Weiser v. City of New York*, 49 Misc. 2d 759, 268 N.Y.S.2d 457 (Sup. Ct.), *aff'd*, 268 N.Y.S.2d 460, 49 Misc. 2d 924 (App. T., 1st Dep't 1966), and *Radinsky v. City of New York*, 133 N.Y.S.2d 540 (Sup. Ct. 1954).

Note, however, that CPLR 2104 does not make binding oral stipulations agreed to before an administrative tribunal, "however similar to a courtroom proceeding the physical surroundings may be. . . ." *Silverman v. McGuire*, 51 N.Y.2d 228, 231, 433 N.Y.S.2d 1002, 1003, 414 N.E.2d 383 (1980).

(2) What was the "mistake of fact" which (in part) justified relief from the settlement in the principal case? It has been held that a mistake must be mutual, *i.e.*, be shared by both sides, in order to afford such relief. *Fox v. Wiener Laces, Inc.*, 105 Misc. 2d 672, 432 N.Y.S.2d 811 (Sup. Ct. 1980). Does *Veith v. ABC Paving Co., Inc.*, *supra*, note 3, following *Halleck*, apply a different rule?

§ 17.02 FORMAL OFFERS TO COMPROMISE

CPLR 3219, 3220 and 3221 are designed to encourage accelerated judgments by compromise and settlement before trial. With some differences in detail they each allow a defendant to formally offer a compromise payment to the claimant.

They encourage the latter to accept the offer by penalizing him if, after refusing the proffered settlement, he ultimately recovers a less favorable judgment. The penalty is a loss of costs (and under CPLR 3219, interest) to which he would otherwise be entitled after a litigated victory.

Provisions of this kind have had a long[1] but not glorious history in New York. They have been used infrequently and reluctantly. The potential saving of court costs, and even of interest, has apparently been of too little consequence to induce defendants to make a formal settlement offer at a time when informal settlement conferences between the parties are very likely taking place; and if defendant does make a statutory offer, the possibility of incurring costs has been too slight a penalty to deter plaintiff from taking his chances at trial. The constant attrition in real value of allowable costs, as contrasted with the actual cost of litigation, has made the procedures increasingly less attractive through the years. *See* CPLR article 82 for cost amounts.

The Advisory Committee, in order to provide greater incentive for the use of these three procedures, originally proposed to include reasonable attorney's fees, as well as costs, as the sanction for injudicious refusal of a sufficient tender or offer. The provisions for attorney's fees were later deleted.[2] This is not so regrettable in contract actions which lend themselves particularly well to other accelerating devices such as summary judgment; but a provision with teeth in it for making settlements attractive in the negligence field would have been welcome.

---

[1] The offer to liquidate damages and the offer of judgment first appeared as sections 385-387 of the Code of Civil Procedure (1848); tender after suit was introduced some twenty years earlier in the Revised Statutes of 1829. *See* 15 N.Y. Jud. Council Rep. 185, 193 (1949).

[2] *See* 1961 Sen. Fin. Comm. Rep. 507-08 (CPLR 3219 and 3220); 5 N.Y. Adv. Comm. Rep. A-482 (Advance Draft 1961) (CPLR 3221).

Chapter 18

PRE-TRIAL AND CALENDAR PRACTICE

§ 18.01 GETTING ON THE CALENDAR

In most counties of the state, there are far more cases ready to be tried than there are judges available to try them. The rules of calendar practice determine the order in which these cases are reached for trial. As a general matter, the rule is that the first case in line gets tried first. CPLR 3403(a). A case gets in line, again speaking generally, when a note of issue and statement of readiness are filed. *Id.*; *see also* 22 NYCRR § 202.21. (Examples of those forms are on the next page.)

Some cases are entitled to a preference which advances them ahead of other, older cases. CPLR 3403.

Under the Uniform Civil Rules for the Supreme Court and County Court, 22 NYCRR 202.1 *et seq.*, which became effective on January 6, 1986, an Individual Assignment System was adopted for the Supreme and County Courts throughout the state.

An integral part of the system is the grant of authority to each judge to control the calendaring of his or her own cases. 22 NYCRR 202.22. The calendars which the judge is authorized to establish by 22 NYCRR 202.22 may include the following:

(1) *Preliminary conference calendar.* A preliminary conference calendar is for the calendaring for conference of cases in which a note of issue and certificate of readiness have not yet been filed.

(2) *Motion calendar.* A motion calendar is for the hearing of motions.

(3) *General calendar.* A general calendar is for actions in which a note of issue and a certificate of readiness have been filed but which have not as yet been transferred to a pretrial conference calendar or a calendar containing cases that are ready for trial.

(4) *Pretrial conference calendar.* A pretrial conference calendar is for actions awaiting conference after the note of issue and certificate of readiness have been filed.

(5) *Reserve calendar.* A reserve calendar is for actions that have had a pretrial conference or where such conference was dispensed with by the court, but where the actions have not yet been transferred to a ready calendar.

(6) *Ready calendar.* A ready calendar is for actions in which a trial is imminent.

(7) *Military calendar.* A military calendar is for cases where a party to an action or a witness necessary upon the trial is in military service and is not presently available for trial, and a deposition cannot be taken, or, if taken, would not provide adequate evidence.

There are some calendar-related rules which the court must apply notwithstanding the Individual Assignment System. It must, of course, respect the preference rules of article 34 of the CPLR. Further, "[W]hen actions are advanced from one calendar to another they shall progress from the head of one calendar to the foot of the next calendar and otherwise progress in order insofar as practicable unless otherwise determined by the court." 22 NYCRR 202.22(b).

Specific rules govern the calendaring of medical and dental malpractice actions. *See* 22 NYCRR 202.56 and § 18.02, *infra.*

The Uniform Civil Rules for the Supreme and County Court retain the use of the Note of Issue and Certificate of Readiness. No action or special proceeding may be deemed ready for trial unless those documents are filed with the court with proof of service on the other parties. 22 NYCRR 202.21(a). The form in which the documents must be filed is prescribed in 22 NYCRR 202.21(b) and is set forth below.

Form
Note of Issue and Certificate of Readiness
NOTE OF ISSUE

For Use of Clerk

Calendar No._____
Index No._____
_____ Court, _____ County

NOTICE FOR TRIAL

Trial by jury demanded ☐
    ☐   Of all issues
    ☐   Of issues specified below or attached
        hereto
Trial without jury ☐
Filed by Attorney for _____
Date summons served _____
Date service completed _____
Date issue joined _____
        NATURE OF ACTION OR
        SPECIAL PROCEEDING
Tort:
    Motor Vehicle Negligence ☐
    Medical Malpractice   ☐
    Other Tort   ☐
Contract   ☐
Contested Matrimonial   ☐
Uncontested Matrimonial   ☐

Preference claimed	Tax Certiorari	☐
under _____	Condemnation	☐
on the ground that _____	Other (not itemized above)	☐

_____

Attorney(s) for Plaintiff(s)
Office and P.O. Address:

Phone No.:

Attorney(s) for Defendant(s)
Office and P.O. Address:
Phone No.:

(specify) _____
Indicate if this action is   ☐

brought as a class action

Amount Demanded $_____
Other Relief _____
Insurance Carrier(s), if known:

NOTE: The clerk will not accept this note of issue unless accompanied by a certificate of readiness.

CERTIFICATE OF READINESS FOR TRIAL

(Items 1-7 must be checked)

		Complete	Waived	Not required
1.	All pleadings served	_____	_____	_____
2.	Bill of particulars served	_____	_____	_____
3.	Physical examinations completed	_____	_____	_____
4.	Medical reports exchanged	_____	_____	_____
5.	Appraisal reports exchanged	_____	_____	_____
6.	Compliance with section 202.16 of the Rules of the Chief Administrator (22 NYCRR 202.16) in matrimonial actions	_____	_____	_____
7.	Discovery proceedings now known to be necessary completed	_____	_____	_____
8.	There are no outstanding requests for discovery	_____	_____	_____
9.	There has been a reasonable opportunity to complete the foregoing proceedings	_____	_____	_____

10. There has been compliance
    with any order issued
    ursuant to section 202.12
    of the Rules of the Chief
    Administrator
    (22 NYCRR 202.12)   _____ _____ _____

11. If a medical malpractice
    action, there has been
    compliance with any order
    issued pursuant to section
    202.56 of the Rules of the
    Chief Administrator
    (22 NYCRR 202.56)   _____ _____ _____

The case is ready for trial

Dated:
(Signature)
Attorney(s) for:
Office and P.O. address:

NOTES

(1) Study of the form (which is prescribed by 22 NYCRR § 202.21(b)) reveals why its service is required before a case can be put on the trial calendar. It also underscores the importance of the prompt completion of discovery proceedings.

(2) The note of issue can be served by either party, CPLR 3402(a), though it is usually only the plaintiff who would do so. Why? See CPLR 3216, which is the subject of *Baczkowski v. D.A. Collins Construction Co., Inc.*, § 18.03 *infra*.

§ 18.02 MEDICAL MALPRACTICE ACTIONS

You have already seen that medical, dental and podiatric malpractice actions are subject to occasional exceptions from otherwise applicable rules of procedure. *E.g.*, CPLR 214-a (statute of limitations); CPLR 3012-a (certificate of merit to accompany complaint); CPLR 3101(d)(1)(ii) (limits on disclosure of expert witnesses). Here we note the unusual hurdles which must be surmounted before a plaintiff can get such an action to trial.

CPLR 3406(a) requires the plaintiff to serve and file a "notice of dental, medical or podiatric malpractice" not more than sixty days after issue is joined. The prescribed form for the notice is at 22 NYCRR 202.56. It calls for a description of the parties and claim as well as a representation that disclosure requests that have been made by defendant have been met, if appropriate.

After the notice required by CPLR 3406(a) has been filed, the judge to whom the case has been assigned must "as soon as practicable" conduct a preliminary conference. 22 NYCRR 202.56(b). The purpose of the conference is to explore settlement, to secure compliance with pretrial disclosure and to generally expedite the handling of the action.

TEWARI v. TSOUTSOURAS
Court of Appeals
75 N.Y.2d. 1, 550 N.Y.S.2d 572, 49 N.E.2d 1143 (1989)

ALEXANDER, J.:

In 1985, as part of a comprehensive reform of medical malpractice, the Legislature enacted CPLR 3406(a) which requires plaintiffs to file a "notice of medical, dental or podiatric malpractice action" within 60 days of joinder of issue. As a sanction for her failure to timely file this notice, the Appellate Division dismissed the plaintiff's complaint. We now reverse. . . .

[Plaintiff commenced this medical malpractice action against defendant, a licensed physician, for negligently causing her daughter's death. Defendant answered and sought discovery of medical records of all other treating physicians and various hospital records and other material. Six months later, plaintiff not having responded in any way to the discovery requests, defendant moved to dismiss the action, noting that plaintiff, in addition to her other inaction, had failed to file a notice of medical malpractice action pursuant to CPLR 3406(a). The IAS court denied the motion, but the Appellate Division granted it and dismissed the action, calling noncompliance with the notice requirement a pleading default for which no excuse was offered. The Court also observed that plaintiff had made no demonstration of merit to the claim.]

II

Chapter 294 of the Laws of 1985 (hereinafter "the Medical Malpractice Reform Act") amended and added to various provisions of the public health law, the CPLR, the education law, the insurance law and the judiciary law as part of a comprehensive plan intended "to ensure the continued availability and affordability of quality health services" in this State by lowering malpractice insurance premiums and thereby lowering health care costs. . . . More specifically, the Medical Malpractice Reform Act was intended to reduce the cost of malpractice insurance premiums while assuring adequate and fair compensation to injured persons, to expedite the resolution of malpractice claims and thereby reduce the cost of malpractice litigation, and to reduce incidents of medical malpractice (L 1985 ch 294, Memorandum of State Executive Department, 1985 McKinney's Sess Laws at 3022-27). To expedite malpractice litigation, the Legislature provided for expanded discovery as to expert witnesses

(CPLR 3101[d][1]), the assessment of costs and attorneys fees against a party or attorney advancing frivolous claims (CPLR 8303-a), and a mandatory pre-calendar conference, presided over by the judge who would later try the case, in which the parties would explore settlement possibilities, simplify and limit issues and establish expedited discovery and trial schedules (CPLR 3406[b]). This pre-calendar conference is triggered by the plaintiff's filing of a "notice of medical, dental or podiatric malpractice action" pursuant to CPLR 3406(a). . . .

Neither the plain language of CPLR 3406(a) nor the structure of the newly enacted procedural scheme supports the conclusion that the Legislature intended dismissal to be a sanction for failure to timely file the notice. . . . CPLR 2004 provides that a court may grant an extension of time "upon such terms as may be just and upon good cause shown." By contrast, CPLR 3406(b), which directs the chief administrator of the courts to promulgate special calendar control rules providing for the pre-calendar conference and expedited discovery and trial schedules, expressly authorizes "dismissal of an action" as a sanction for "failure of a party or a party's attorney to comply with *these special calendar control rules* or any order of a court made thereunder" (emphasis added). . . . Thus the statute contemplates dismissal only as a sanction for noncompliance with the special calendar control rules promulgated under subdivision (b).

Consistent with the statute, the rules promulgated by the chief administrator do not authorize dismissal as a sanction for noncompliance with the notice requirement of CPLR 3406(a). Section 202.56 of the Uniform Rules provides in subdivision (a)(1) that a plaintiff must file a notice of medical malpractice action and in subdivision (b)(1) that upon the filing of such notice, the judge is to schedule the pre-calendar conference. Subdivision (a)(3) provides that the notice of dental, medical or podiatric malpractice action shall be filed after the expiration of 60 days only by leave of the court on motion and for good cause shown. The court shall impose such conditions as may be just, including assessment of costs. Thus while the rule tracks the requirement of CPLR 3406(a) and 2004 that an extension be granted only upon "good cause shown," the rule authorizes only the imposition of "conditions" upon the granting of the extension. Outright dismissal upon a denial of the motion to extend cannot be viewed as such a "condition" because it immediately terminates the action and thus is not conditional.

Furthermore, like the statute, the rule authorizes "dismissal of an action" as a sanction only for noncompliance with the provisions relating to the pre-calendar conference which are articulated in subdivision (b) of the rule. That subdivision expressly provides that a court may impose the sanction of dismissal for noncompliance with "a directive of the court authorized by the provisions of this subdivision" (22 NYCRR 202.56[b][3]).

. . . .

This construction of the Legislative scheme is consistent with the underlying purposes of the tort reforms enacted in 1985. Although the reforms were intended, in part, to expedite malpractice litigation, as has been noted by some trial courts, the CPLR 3406(a) notice has itself become the subject of extensive pretrial litigation. . . . To allow dismissal as a sanction for failure to timely file the 3406(a) notice would promote even more litigation on this collateral issue by encouraging defendants to litigate every instance of noncompliance. Indeed, defense counsel's obligation to zealously represent his or her client might well require that defense counsel seize the opportunity to attempt to obtain a dismissal on a mere showing of noncompliance with 3406(a) rather than risking a disposition on the merits (DR 7-101). Moreover, dismissal may completely nonsuit the plaintiff as defendants commonly wait until after the expiration of the relatively short statute of limitations in medical malpractice actions (*see* CPLR 214-a) to seek dismissal for noncompliance with CPLR 3406(a). . . . Thus we conclude that the Legislature never contemplated the imposition of such a draconian sanction for noncompliance with CPLR 3406(a), particularly where the practical effect of such a sanction would defeat the very purpose of the Medical Malpractice Reform Act.

We stress, however, that we do not condone the use of dilatory tactics by the plaintiffs' bar in failing to timely file these notices and note that our decision today does not leave defendants without a remedy for delays in litigation caused by such noncompliance with CPLR 3406(a). When a notice is not timely filed, a defendant truly seeking expeditious resolution of the underlying malpractice claim may move, even by order to show cause, to compel the filing of the notice. Once a defendant has obtained an order directing that the notice be filed, a plaintiff's disregard of such order may be deemed willful and construed as a deliberate effort to frustrate the calendar control rules promulgated under CPLR 3406(b). In that case, dismissal as authorized by that subdivision would be warranted. Disregard of a court order directing the filing of the notice and its attendant authorizations (*see* CPLR 3406[a]) may also be construed as a failure to comply with a court order directing discovery for which dismissal is an authorized sanction (CPLR 3126; *see Zletzz v Wetanson*, 67 NY2d 711, 713 [dismissal of complaint is within trial court's discretion where party deliberately disregarded court order to answer interrogatories]; *Reynolds Securities Inc v Underwriters Bank & Trust Co*, 44 NY2d 568 [willful failure to comply with court orders directing discovery warranted striking of answer and entry of default judgment]). Of course, plaintiffs who have delayed the litigation but nevertheless file the notice in response to such a court order or after having been granted an extension may be punished by the imposition of monetary sanctions such as costs and attorney's fees (22 NYCRR 202.56[a][3]). Alternatively, a defendant who does not seek to compel the filing of the notice may ultimately seek dismissal of the action pursuant to CPLR 3216 for plaintiff's failure to prosecute.

. . . .

III

We further conclude that the Appellate Division abused its discretion in analogizing the failure to timely file the CPLR 3406(a) notice to a pleading default and holding therefore that plaintiff's motion for an extension must be denied because she had not demonstrated both the meritorious nature of her claims and a "reasonable excuse" for the delay.

CPLR 2004 vests the trial court with discretion to extend the time to perform any act, including the filing of the 3406(a) notice, "upon such terms as may be just and upon good cause shown." In considering the motion, the court may properly consider factors such as the length of the delay, whether the opposing party has been prejudiced by the delay, the reason given for the delay, whether the moving party was in default before seeking the extension, and, if so, the presence or absence of an affidavit of merit. (*See generally* 2A Weinstein-Korn-Miller 2004.03.) In the case of pleading defaults, however, we have held that the absence of an affidavit of merit defeats the motion regardless of the weight of the other factors considered under CPLR 2004.

Contrary to the conclusion of the Appellate Division, failure to timely file the 3406(a) notice is not analogous to a pleading default. The notice requirement is a rule of calendar practice which functions to trigger the pre-calendar conference required by CPLR 3406(b). Unlike pleadings, the notice does not serve to apprise the adversary of a pending cause of action and imposes no obligation upon the adversary which may result in a default judgment against him or her. Accordingly, the stringent showing required to obtain an extension of time to file a pleading by a party already in default has no application here and plaintiff's motion does not fail simply because she did not submit an affidavit of the merit of her claims.

In seeking an extension after the time to file had passed, plaintiff averred that she "did not deliberately fail to comply with the directives of [CPLR 3406[a]], but was awaiting production of voluminous medical records to properly answer defendants [*sic*] demand for a Bill of Particulars, and serve defendant with appropriate authorizations." This excuse amounts to little more than law office failure, especially since defendant had repeatedly demanded the authorizations. Nevertheless, specifically rejecting our holdings to the contrary (*see Barasch v Micucci*, 49 NY2d 594; *Eaton v Equitable Life Assurance Soc of US*, 56 NY2d 900), the Legislature has held that upon a motion to extend the time to appear or plead (CPLR 3012) or to vacate a default (CPLR 5015[a]), the court may excuse a delay or default resulting from "law office failure" (CPLR 2005). We see no reason to impose a more stringent requirement for the showing of "good cause" under CPLR 2004, particularly where, as here, there is no evidence that defendant was at all prejudiced by plaintiff's delay while plaintiff will be severely prejudiced if the motion is denied.

. . . .

NOTE

The principal case is discussed in Barker, Tewari v. Tsoutsouras *Reversal*, N.Y.L.J., November 27, 1989, p. 3, col. 1.

§ 18.03 DISMISSAL FOR FAILURE TO PROSECUTE

BACZKOWSKI v. D.A. COLLINS CONSTRUCTION COMPANY, INC.
Court of Appeals
89 N.Y.2d 499, 655 N.Y.S.2d 848, 678 N.E.2d 460 (1997)

CIPARICK, J.

The Appellate Division dismissed plaintiff's complaint for neglect to prosecute pursuant to CPLR 3216. The question on appeal is whether plaintiff proffered a justifiable excuse for past delay and for failing to file a note of issue within 90 days after receiving a demand to do so from defendant. We hold that plaintiff failed to tender a justifiable excuse and, accordingly, the Appellate Division properly dismissed plaintiff's complaint.

This action stems from construction-site injuries sustained by plaintiff on November 18, 1986. Plaintiff was operating a truck owned by defendant D.A. Collins Construction Co. and had driven the vehicle atop a hill when the vehicle's brakes allegedly failed. As the truck started to roll down the hill, plaintiff jumped out and was injured when he hit the ground.

On November 2, 1989, plaintiff commenced this action in negligence and strict products liability by service of a summons and notice. Plaintiff thereafter served a complaint on defendant on December 26, 1989. On January 8, 1990, defendant answered plaintiff's complaint, and, on November 19, 1990, commenced a third-party action against plaintiff's employer, Kubricky Construction Corp. Very little activity occurred in the action during the next four years, aside from defendant taking plaintiff's deposition in February 1991 and September 1992.

On July 27, 1994, defendant served a demand on plaintiff to resume prosecution of the action and file a note of issue within 90 days (*see*, CPLR 3216[b][3]). Plaintiff did not file a note of issue within the 90-day period and took no other step to indicate an intention to proceed with the action. On December 13, 1994, 139 days after serving the 90-day demand, defendant moved to dismiss plaintiff's complaint pursuant to CPLR 3216. Plaintiff submitted no papers opposing the motion to dismiss. Instead, on January 20, 1995, 10 days before the return date of defendant's motion and 87 days after the expiration of the 90-day period, plaintiff filed a note of issue.

On April 13, 1995, Supreme Court preliminarily ruled on the motion by issuing a conditional order of dismissal, granting plaintiff an additional 30 days to
demonstrate a justifiable excuse for the delay and to submit an affidavit of
merit. In response, plaintiff submitted a two-page attorney's affidavit stating
that the delay was attributable to uncertainty over the status of third-party discovery requests, as evidenced by plaintiff's written inquiries directed to defendant in September and November 1993. Plaintiff's counsel also explained that
on December 21, 1994, his secretary attempted to file a note of issue, but,
because she was unfamiliar with recent amendments to the CPLR, her endeavors proved unsuccessful. In lieu of an affidavit of merit from plaintiff, his attorney submitted plaintiff's deposition transcript.

Supreme Court thereafter denied defendant's motion to dismiss, concluding
that plaintiff established a justifiable excuse and a meritorious cause of action.
The Appellate Division reversed, with two Justices dissenting. The Court held
that plaintiff did not demonstrate a justifiable excuse for failing to comply with
the 90-day requirement of CPLR 3216 and dismissed the action. Plaintiff
appealed to this Court as of right (*see,* CPLR 5601[a]), and we now affirm.

CPLR 3216 is the general statutory authority for neglect-to-prosecute dismissals. The provision has a checkered history, which this Court has recounted
on prior occasions (*see, e.g., Chase v. Scavuzzo,* 87 N.Y.2d 228, 231-233; *Cohn v.
Borchard Affiliations,* 25 N.Y.2d 237, 244-246; *see also,* Siegel, Practice Commentaries, McKinney's Cons Laws of NY, Book 7B, CPLR C3216:1-C3216:4 . . .).
As a result of a 1967 amendment to CPLR 3216, courts are prohibited from dismissing an action for neglect to prosecute unless the statutory preconditions to
dismissal are met (*see,* CPLR 3216[b]; *Cohn v. Borchard Affiliations, supra,* 25
N.Y.2d, at 246).

CPLR 3216, as it now reads, is extremely forgiving of litigation delay. A court
cannot dismiss an action for neglect to prosecute unless: at least one year has
elapsed since joinder of issue; defendant has served on plaintiff a written
demand to serve and file a note of issue within 90 days; and plaintiff has failed
to serve and file a note of issue within the 90-day period (CPLR 3216[b]). So long
as plaintiff serves and files a note of issue within the 90-day period, all past
delay is absolved and the court is then without authority to dismiss the action
(CPLR 3216[c]). However, if plaintiff fails to file a note of issue within the 90-
day period, "the court may take such initiative or grant such motion [to dismiss]
unless the [defaulting] party shows justifiable excuse for the delay and a good
and meritorious cause of action" (CPLR 3216[e]). Thus, even when all of the
statutory preconditions are met, including plaintiff's failure to comply with the
90-day requirement, plaintiff has yet another opportunity to salvage the action
simply by opposing the motion to dismiss with a justifiable excuse and an affidavit of merit. If plaintiff makes a sufficient showing, the court is prohibited
from dismissing the action.

In this case, the Appellate Division held that plaintiff failed to demonstrate
a justifiable excuse for not complying with the 90-day requirement. In view of

plaintiff's persistent neglect despite repeated opportunities to resume prosecution of the action and the absence of any timely proffered reasonable excuse for the extensive delay, we agree that dismissal was proper in this case (*see, Sortino v. Fisher*, 20 A.D.2d 25, 28-32; *see generally*, Siegel, Practice Commentaries, McKinney's Cons Laws of NY, Book 7B, CPLR C3216:29- C3216:31 . . . [discussing factors considered on CPLR 3216 motion]).

After commencement of the action in 1989, the action remained virtually dormant for nearly five years, with little indication by plaintiff that he was inclined to proceed. Even after defendant served the 90-day demand pursuant to CPLR 3216, plaintiff failed to file a note of issue or take any other step indicating an intention to resume prosecution of the action, such as moving to vacate the 90-day demand or seeking an extension of time within which to file a note of issue (*see*, 4 Weinstein-Korn-Miller, NY Civ Prac § 3216.10, at 32-378 to 32-380 [detailing options available to a plaintiff encountering difficulty in complying with 90-day demand]; Siegel, NY Prac § 375, at 559 [2d ed] [same]). When defendant thereafter moved to dismiss, 139 days after serving the 90-day demand, plaintiff chose to submit no papers in opposition.

Despite plaintiff's default on the motion to dismiss, Supreme Court provided plaintiff yet an additional 30 days to demonstrate a justifiable excuse and a meritorious claim. In response, plaintiff finally submitted a two-page attorney's affidavit, contending that uncertainty over pending third-party discovery excused the delay. This excuse was patently deficient because plaintiff's counsel admitted to having last inquired about the third-party discovery in November 1993, more than eight months before defendant served the 90-day demand. The alternative excuse that counsel's secretary had attempted to file a note of issue but was unsuccessful is inadequate: the attempted filing occurred on December 21, 1994, which was 57 days after the expiration of the 90-day period and, therefore, could excuse neither the past delay nor the failure to comply with the 90-day requirement. Of course, it is the professional obligation of counsel, not the secretary, to know and comply with the CPLR.

We note that under the plain language of CPLR 3216, a court retains some discretion to deny a motion to dismiss, even when plaintiff fails to comply with the 90-day requirement and proffers an inadequate excuse for the delay. Thus, the Appellate Division's statement that in "the absence of any justifiable excuse . . . Supreme Court lacked discretion to excuse plaintiff's default" (227 A.D.2d 789, 790) is unnecessarily rigid. If plaintiff fails to demonstrate a justifiable excuse, the statute says the court "may" dismiss the action — it does not say "must" (*see,* CPLR 3216[e]) — but this presupposes that plaintiff has tendered some excuse in response to the motion in an attempt to satisfy the statutory threshold.

Although a court may possess residual discretion to deny a motion to dismiss when plaintiff tenders even an unjustifiable excuse, this discretion should be exercised sparingly to honor the balance struck by the generous statutory protections already built into CPLR 3216. Even such exceptional exercises of discretion, moreover, would be reviewable within the Appellate Division's plenary discretionary authority. If plaintiff unjustifiably fails to comply with the 90-day requirement, knowing full well that the action can be saved simply by filing a note of issue but is subject to dismissal otherwise, the culpability for the resulting dismissal is squarely placed at the door of plaintiff or plaintiff's counsel. Were courts routinely to deny motions to dismiss even after plaintiff has ignored the 90-day period without an adequate excuse, the procedure established by CPLR 3216 would be rendered meaningless.

Thus, when a plaintiff's excuse, though inadequate, is timely interposed, a court in its discretion might dismiss the action or, in an appropriate case, deny the motion and impose a monetary sanction on plaintiff or plaintiff's counsel instead (*see, e.g., Lichter v. State of New York*, 198 A.D.2d 687, 688 [in tripling the sanction imposed by the lower court, court notes "the sanction imposed should be substantial enough to serve as a deterrent to dilatory behavior in the future"]; *Neyra y Alba v. Pelham Foods*, 46 A.D.2d 760; *see also,* 22 NYCRR 130-1.1[c][2] [sanctionable frivolous conduct includes conduct "undertaken primarily to delay or prolong the resolution of the litigation"]). As discussed above, plaintiff in this case failed to tender any reasonable excuse in timely response to defendant's dismissal motion. Therefore, dismissal was the appropriate result.

Accordingly, the order of the Appellate Division should be affirmed, with costs.

NOTES

(1) The principal case is interesting in part because of the historical perspective it brings to the intractable problem of delay in litigation. But then Hamlet listed the law's delay as one of his reasons for considering whether "to be or not to be." Nor was the problem new in Shakespeare's day, for in second century Rome, the poet Juvenal wrote:

> Term after term I wait till
> months be past
>
> And scarce obtain a hearing
> at the last
>
> Even when the hour is fixed,
> a thousand stays
>
> Retard my suit a thousand
> vague delays
>
> . . . wealth and patience
> worn away
>
> By the slow drag-chain of
> the law's delay.

Juvenalis, Satire XVI, lines 45-58, as quoted in Shetreet, *The Administration of Justice: Practical Problems, Value Conflict and Changing Concepts*, 13 British Col. L. Rev. 52, 54 (1979).*

In your view, would the approach to delay taken in CPLR 3216 and CPLR 2005 assuage these critical poets?

(2) The conflict between the courts and the legislature described in the principal case continues. CPLR 2005, which allows the courts to excuse a wide range of defaults even if they were the result of "law office failure" (*i.e.* neglect by an attorney), was passed after a "get tough" policy had been adopted by the Court of Appeals with respect to lawyer-caused delays in *Barasch v. Micucci*, 49 N.Y.2d 594, 427 N.Y.S.2d 732, 404 N.E.2d 1275 (1980), and its progeny. *See* discussion in Comment, *Law Office Failure: The Need for a Definition After Barasch and* Eaton, 47 Alb. L. Rev. 826 (1983).

The courts in general seem to prefer a tougher approach to delay than does the Legislature. In *Chase v. Scavuzzo*, 87 N.Y.2d 228, 638 N.Y.S.2d 587, 661 N.E.2d 1368 (1995), however, the Court adhered rigidly to the requirements of CPLR 3216 as a condition of dismissal. Plaintiff's earlier motion for summary judgment had been denied, and the IAS court had directed plaintiff to file a note of issue. A note of issue was ultimately received by defendants almost three years later. Defendants moved to strike the note of issue and dismiss the complaint. But defendants had never served a 90-day notice. The Appellate Division held that the judge's order requiring plaintiff to file a note of issue was, in effect, a substitute for a 90-day notice. The Court of Appeals disagreed and reversed, holding that the court order did not relieve defendants of the obligation to serve the 90-day notice.

(3) Once the plaintiff complies with the demand within the 90-day period, all prior delay is forgiven, CPLR 3216(d). The court can, however, grant a motion to dismiss for delay subsequent to filing a note of issue, and such a motion need not be preceded by the 90-day demand. *Travelers Indemnity Company v. Central Trust Company of Rochester*, 40 A.D.2d 1024, 374 N.Y.S.2d 483 (4th Dep't 1975) (note of issue filed 8 years after action commenced, followed by at least 5 adjournments of trial attributable to plaintiff). *See also* CPLR 3404, discussed at in § 18.04, *infra*.

(4) Subsection (e) of CPLR 3216 provides that a court may deny a motion to dismiss when "justifiable excuse for the delay" and a "good and meritorious cause of action" are shown. The courts enjoy a good deal of discretion in deciding these motions and have the power to deny the motion even if the delay was caused by law office failure. *Kurtin v. Cating Rope Works, Inc.*, 59 N.Y.2d 633, 463 N.Y.S.2d 196 (1983), *rev'g* 91 A.D.2d 677, 457 N.Y.S.2d 335 (2d Dep't 1982). On the other hand, the court may dismiss even a meritorious action if

---

* Reprinted permission of British Columbia Law Review, Copyright © 1979, and the author.

there is no adequate excuse for the delay. Such a dismissal may be "on the merits." *Jones v. Maphey*, 50 N.Y.2d 971, 431 N.Y.S.2d 466, 409 N.E.2d 939 (1980).

The courts normally weigh the extent of the delay in prosecution against the excuse for it and the merits of plaintiff's claim. *See generally Sortino v. Fisher*, 20 A.D.2d 25, 245 N.Y.S.2d 186 (1st Dep't 1963). Delay caused by law office failure is often unexcused. *Id.*, 20 A.D.2d at 29, 245 N.Y.S.2d at 192 and cases cited.

(5) Should the expiration of the statute of limitations during the pendency of the action be taken into account by a court entertaining a motion to dismiss under CPLR 3216? Note that the "new action" toll of CPLR 205 would not apply. *See* CPLR 205(a). The First and Second Departments are split on this question. *Compare Mound v. Bartos*, 60 A.D.2d 815, 401 N.Y.S.2d 83 (1st Dep't 1978) (mere fact that the statute had run was not sufficient to deny motion to dismiss when plaintiff did not have a sufficient excuse for filing note 10 months after defendant's demand), *with Moran v. Rynar*, 39 A.D.2d 718, 332 N.Y.S.2d 138 (2d Dep't 1972) (denied dismissal where action had merit, injury was serious, and statute had run), *and Terasaka v. Rehfield*, 28 A.D.2d 1011, 284 N.Y.S.2d 168 (2d Dep't 1967) (motion to dismiss was properly denied where defendant did not show that delay was excessive and statute had run).

(6) An alternative to dismissal of a meritorious case used by some courts is the imposition of costs on the tardy plaintiff's attorney. *See, e.g., Newell v. Lane*, 45 A.D.2d 704, 357 N.Y.S.2d 78 (1st Dep't 1974) ($350 plus $60 costs of appeal imposed; if not paid, action would be dismissed); *Cockfeld v. Apotheker*, 81 A.D.2d 651, 438 N.Y.S.2d 379 (2d Dep't 1981) ($2,500 costs imposed as alternative to dismissal for delay in pleading).

(7) A plaintiff might not be tardy but rather too alacritous: the note of issue might be served before the defendant is prepared for trial. Defendant's remedy for a prematurely filed note of issue is a motion to strike the case from the calendar. The motion must be made within twenty days after the note has been filed, or even later "for good cause shown." 22 NYCRR 202.21(e). If "unusual or unanticipated circumstances" arise requiring further disclosure, it may be allowed by the court without striking the case from the calendar. 22 NYCRR 202.21(d).

§ 18.04 ABANDONMENT OF CALENDARED CASES: CPLR 3404

CPLR 3404 allows a case to be dismissed as abandoned. Unlike dismissals under CPLR 3216, dismissal for abandonment can occur only if the case has been placed on, and then stricken from, the calendar and has not been restored to the calendar within a year. A case may be marked off a calendar so as to bring CPLR 3404 into play on the motion of a party because it was placed on the calendar prematurely by the plaintiff, 22 NYCRR § 202.21(e) (*see Arroyo v. New*

York City, 86 A.D.2d 521, 445 N.Y.S.2d 753 (1st Dep't 1982), in which the action was struck from the calendar because the certificate of readiness falsely stated that discovery was complete); or when the parties miss a scheduled court appearance, *Rodriguez v. Middle Atlantic Auto Leasing*, 122 A.D.2d 720, 511 N.Y.S.2d 595 (1st Dep't 1986) (plaintiff missed a pre-trial conference); or on consent of the parties, *Bergan v. Home for Incurables*, 124 A.D.2d 517, 508 N.Y.S.2d 434 (1st Dep't 1986).

CPLR 3404 states that a dismissal for abandonment is automatic. This allows the dismissal of the action to be made by the clerk in the absence of a motion. *See also Homowack Realty Corp. v. Gitlih*, 25 A.D.2d 703, 268 N.Y.S.2d 178 (3d Dep't. 1966). In another sense, however, the Court of Appeals has held that the language "deemed abandoned" in CPLR 3404 constitutes only a presumption, which can be rebutted by a party moving to restore the action to the calendar, who must show that there was in fact no abandonment. In *Marco v. Sachs*, 10 N.Y.2d 542, 226 N.Y.S.2d 353, 181 N.E.2d 392 (1962), the Court found that the activity of litigation indicated that neither party had intended to abandon the action.

If the action has been dismissed pursuant to CPLR 3404, the plaintiff can resurrect it by a motion to vacate the dismissal and restore the action to the calendar. The Second Department has held that a plaintiff whose case has been marked off the calendar may restore it by motion and that, so long as the motion is made before one year has passed, the plaintiff need not demonstrate a reasonable excuse, a meritorious action, lack of intent to abandon, or lack of prejudice to the defendant. *Basetti v. Nour*, 287 A.D.2d 126, 731 N.Y.S.2d 35 (2d Dep't 2001) (citing and criticizing cases holding that the plaintiff had to make such a showing as a condition of restoration even prior to the passage of a year). The court noted that if a plaintiff failed to appear or proceed when a case is called for trial, the presiding judge need not rely on CPLR 3404, but could dismiss the action pursuant to the Uniform Rules for Trial Courts, 22 NYCRR 202.27, where the 90-day rule does not apply. To restore the action after such a dismissal, the court said, the plaintiff would have to make a showing equivalent to that needed to vacate a default. As to motions to restore actions to the calendar after abandonment pursuant to CPLR 3404, see also *Bouvia v. Community General Hospital of Greater Syracuse*, 85 A.D.2d 909, 446 N.Y.S.2d 791 (4th Dept. 1981), where the vacatur of an order of dismissal was upheld because the plaintiff demonstrated a continuing personal interest in prosecuting the action even though his attorney had forgotten the case due to mental disability. Compare *Bergan v. Home for Incurables*, 124 A.D.2d 517, 508 N.Y.S.2d 434 (1st Dep't 1986), denying a motion to restore because the moving plaintiff failed to show merit to the action or a reasonable excuse for the delay.

In *Lopez v. Imperial Delivery Service, Inc.*, 282 A.D.2d 190, 725 N.Y.S.2d 57 (2d Dep't 2001), the court discusses all three dismissal provisions, CPLR 3216, 3404 and Uniform Rule 202.27. This is a helpful opinion and emphasizes that CPLR 3404 has no role when there has been no note of issue. See discussion in

Siegel's 2001 Practice Commentary, C3404:7, 7B McKinney's Consol. Laws of New York, supp., p. 17.

A defendant, by participating in the litigation after an action is deemed abandoned under CPLR 3404, waives the right to insist on the dismissal. *Marco v. Sachs*, *supra* (alternate ground).

§ 18.05 CALENDAR PREFERENCES: CPLR 3403

TINTNER v. MARANGI
Supreme Court, Rockland County
57 Misc. 2d 318, 292 N.Y.S.2d 779 (1968)

JOSEPH H. HAWKINS, JUSTICE.

There have been two prior motions for a special trial preference. The first — some two years ago — was denied since no showing, inter alia, had been made of "destitution." That denial, however, was with leave to renew. The subsequent application brought several months thereafter was again denied, it having been deemed that the submission did not satisfy "the stringent provisions of the rules of the Appellate Division. (*Brier v. Plaut*, 37 Misc.2d 476 [235 N.Y.S.2d 37])."

The rationale of the instant motion is a marked change in movant's circumstance resulting from his loss of part-time employment; he was superannuated. Such part-time employment yielded the modest sum of $28.73 per week, presumably the take-home pay, which, when combined with the plaintiff's and his spouse's social security stipend of $190.30, made a total of $305 per month. The plaintiff is seventy-two years of age and his spouse is one year younger.

It may well be that when weighed against plaintiffs' total budget, the loss of the part-time employment earnings does not constitute an appreciable sum. More important factors, however, must be considered: the dignity and self-respect which inure to a senior citizen who endeavors by partial employment to add to the austere stipend provided by social security. The loss of such part-time employment — here, completely involuntary and directly attributable to plaintiff's age — results in pecuniary, and more importantly, psychological deprivations.

Additionally, contributing to the plaintiffs' demeaning circumstances is their having to share a small bedroom in their son's home with their infant grandson and granddaughter. Surely, petitioners of advanced years merit more judicial solicitude than applying the criteria governing trial preferences with slide-rule rigidity; nor should courts be required to indulge in a near-morbid exercise of anticipating whether litigant or calendar will first expire. These, in our opinion, are considerations sufficient to justify the characterization "changed circumstances and in the interests of justice" employed in *Braman v. Auserehl & Son Contracting Corp.*, 22 A.D.2d 887, 255 N.Y.S.2d 313.

Lest there be any doubt, we add a new criterion to be considered in determining whether a special trial preference should be granted: if a litigant's resources are inadequate to permit living in dignity and self-respect — commensurate with age and prior milieu — it is both just and meet that we grant a special trial preference. Where a plaintiff manfully strains and struggles to avoid obtaining public assistance, such valiant efforts should be recognized rather than penalized.

Inquiry by the court revealed that the earliest possible date the action could be reached for trial in regular order is September of 1970. Under the circumstances, the plaintiffs' motion for a special trial preference is granted and the matter is set down for the first available date of the November 1968 Trial Term of this court, subject to prior preferred issues and the disposition of the Justice then presiding. The plaintiffs, further, are to comply with the Calendar Clerk's prerequisites.

NOTES

(1) CPLR 3403 was amended subsequent to the decision in the principal case. Subdivision (4) now mandates a special preference on the application of any party who is seventy years of age or more. Ch. 61, L. 1979. Nonetheless the case exemplifies the solicitude some courts show for the indigent in applying CPLR 3403(a)(3), which allows the courts to grant a preference in the interests of justice. *See also Sabater v. N.Y.C. Transit Authority*, 102 A.D.2d 804, 477 N.Y.S.2d (1st Dep't 1984). Compare *Morris Electronics of Syracuse, Inc. v. Stereo East Developments, Inc*, 71 A.D.2d 1061, 420 N.Y.S.2d 811 (4th Dep't. 1979), holding that the Supreme Court had abused its discretion by granting a special preference on plaintiff's claim that defendants would otherwise conceal their assets from the potential judgment.

(2) Other statutes granting special preferences (incorporated by reference in CPLR 3403(a)(2)) include Elec. L. § 16-116 (proceedings relating to elections); CPLR 7009(c) (habeas corpus proceedings); and CPLR 7804(h) (proceedings against bodies and officers).

(3) What if a plaintiff is entitled to a preference on more than one ground? It has been held that there is no right to "stack" them and automatically advance ahead of plaintiffs with only one preference. *Green v. Vogel*, 144 A.D.2d 66, 537 N.Y.S.2d 180 (2d Dep't 1989).

(4) A special preference may be denied if the action has been brought in an improper venue. 22 NYCRR § 202.24(b)(4).

§ 18.06 PRE-TRIAL CONFERENCES

The Uniform Rules for the Trial Courts contemplate two types of conferences with the judge prior to trial. A preliminary conference is held early in the litigation process. By contrast, a pretrial conference is held after the preparation for trial has been completed.

[A] The Preliminary Conference

Among the powers of the judge to whom a case is assigned is the scheduling of "a preliminary conference as soon as practicable after the action has been assigned." 22 NYCRR § 202.12. Whether to hold such a conference is discretionary with the assigned judge, except in medical, dental and podiatric malpractice actions (*see* § 18.02, *supra*). At the conference, the judge should attempt to settle the action or simplify the issues in dispute. The judge should also explore the need for the joinder of additional parties. If the action cannot be settled, the judge will establish a timetable for the completion of disclosure, with the general rule being that disclosure should be completed within twelve months after the action was assigned to the judge. 22 NYCRR § 202.12(c).

[B] Pretrial Conferences

The pretrial conference should be held after the filing of the note of issue and certificate of readiness. To the extent practicable, it should be held not less than fifteen nor more than forty-five days before trial is anticipated. 22 NYCRR § 202.26(b).

At the conference, the court will examine the marked pleadings, bills of particulars, medical proof (if any) and other litigation documents. If convinced that the amount recoverable is within the jurisdiction of an inferior court, the judge may remove the action to such court. 22 NYCRR § 202.26(g). If it does not remove the case, the court is to attempt to settle the case or at least simplify the actions to be tried. 22 NYCRR § 202.26(c).

How much leverage does the judge have in trying to encourage a settlement? The following case addresses the question.

WOLFF v. LAVERNE, INC.
Appellate Division, First Department
17 A.D.2d 213, 233 N.Y.S.2d 555 (1962)

PER CURIAM.

Defendant appeals from an order denying its motion to vacate the advancement of an action for work, labor and services to the head of the next term's General Jury Calendar by a justice sitting at a Pre-Trial Term of the Court.

Rule IX* of the New York County Supreme Court Trial Term Rules provides for a daily Pre-Trial Calendar where the justice presiding is to consider with counsel (1) the simplification and limitation of issues; (2) obtaining admissions of fact and of documents to avoid unnecessary proof; and (3) disposition of the action. The attendance of attorneys who are familiar with the case and are authorized to act is required, and the attendance of parties may also be directed. In the event of the failure of parties to appear or to be properly represented on the Pre-Trial call, the justice presiding has the same power with respect to dismissals or defaults as might be exercised when a case is reached for trial.

In addition to its other objectives, Pre-Trial affords — by informal discussion with the attorneys and the court — an opportunity for the exploration and consideration of the possibility of settlement. In fact, it is the duty of the justice to encourage talk of settlement at such pre-trial conferences and he can be of immeasurable help in acting as a catalyst in bringing the parties together to a fair settlement. Discussions of settlement can be facilitated through proper exertion of such influence that may naturally flow by virtue of his office. But this does not mean that in intervening to promote a fair settlement, undue pressure or coercive measures should be applied by the justice on either attorney.

The function of courts is to provide litigants with an opportunity to air their differences at an impartial trial according to law. While the existence of congested calendars calls for attempts to expedite the termination of suits in a minimum of time, these efforts must be consistent with the dictates of due process. Furthermore, they should not serve as a lever to exert undue pressure on litigants to oblige them to settle their controversies without their day in court. The objective should be a settlement voluntarily reached by mutual consent and not one forced on a party to his or his attorney's detriment.

Assuming the power to direct a preference . . . the circumstances under which it was used in the instant case did not warrant its exercise. To penalize the defendant for not succumbing to the pressure of the justice presiding at the Pre-Trial to settle the case by offering an additional one thousand dollars, by ordering a preference of the trial of this action constituted a gross abuse of discretion.

---

* Now 22 NYCRR § 202.26. — Eds.

What has been said above regarding the proper scope of a judge's participation in settlement discussions at Pre-Trial applies equally at other stages of an action where permissible efforts at settlement have proved unsuccessful and the parties insist upon their right to a trial. We view with disfavor all pressure tactics whether directly or obliquely, to coerce settlement by litigants and their counsel. Failure to concur in what the justice presiding may consider an adequate settlement should not result in an imposition upon a litigant or his counsel, who reject it, of any retributive sanctions not specifically authorized by law. Whether such sanctions assume the form of the direction of unwarranted preferences, of compelling attorneys and litigants unnecessarily to wait in the court room while their cases take a desultory course on the calendar, or the exhibition of evident signs of displeasure by the judge during or after the trial of the case, when reached, or whether such sanctions take any other devious or subtle forms, they merit and will meet with disapproval by this Court.

The order denying the motion to vacate the preference should be reversed on the law and the facts and in the exercise of discretion, and the motion granted, without costs, and the case should be restored to its original position on the calendar.

. . . .

NOTE

Where do the courts derive authority to grant a calendar preference to the plaintiff in order to punish a defendant who refuses to settle? *See* CPLR 3403(a)(3). Should they have such authority?

Chapter 19

TRIAL _ᴧ_

§ 19.01 OVERVIEW OF THE TRIAL PROCESS

This note will introduce you to the trial process. The balance of this Chapter then deals with some of the major problems encountered in applying the law regulating that process. The rules of evidence are properly the subject of another course, and are for that reason not treated here despite their central role in shaping the trial.

The trial may be before a jury, judge, or referee, depending on the nature of the case and the desires of the parties. Substantial procedural similarities exist regardless of which is used, although a greater degree of formality is observed in a jury trial because of the need to minimize jury confusion or bias. Trial before a jury also involves the use of procedures designed to prevent irrational or other improper decision making by the jurors. Examples are the voir dire, special interrogatories, and post-trial motions.

The issue of the proper trial forum will normally have been resolved when the action was placed on the calendar. Let us assume for the balance of this discussion that it is a jury trial. Once the action has reached its turn to be tried, the first step will be the selection of the jury. In New York, the civil jury consists of six persons. CPLR 4104. One or two alternate jurors may also be selected. CPLR 4106. The jurors must be selected from the "array" or "venire" of persons who are on jury duty at the time. Qualified people are chosen for the array at random in accordance with article 16 of the Judiciary Law. The qualifications are found in Jud. L. § 510. Members of the array are examined by the attorneys for the parties at the voir dire to ascertain whether there is any reason they should not serve in the particular case. In New York the judge need not be present during this questioning unless one of the parties requests it. CPLR 4107. It is reversible error for the judge to refuse to attend upon request. *Guarnier v. American Dredging Co.*, 145 A.D.2d 341, 535 N.Y.S.2d 705 (1st Dep't 1988). New York has been unusual in allowing attorneys to conduct the voir dire unsupervised by a judge. The practice has been criticized as leading to unnecessarily long and burdensome questioning of potential jurors. A full discussion of the practice and recommendations for change are presented in The Jury Project, A Report to the Chief Judge of the State of New York 50-55 (1994). Subsequent to this report, the new rules affecting the voir dire were promulgated. The trial judge is now required to preside at the commencement of the voir dire. 22 NYCRR 202.33(e).

Potential jurors can be eliminated for cause, relief only the judge can grant in the absence of stipulation. CPLR 4108. Cause includes a likelihood of bias,

voir dire [handwritten annotation in right margin]

cf., CPLR 4110(a), or personal relationship of a defined degree, CPLR 4110(b). Additionally, each party may exercise three peremptory challenges, plus one more for every two alternate jurors. CPLR 4109. No reason need be given for these challenges, and judicial approval is unnecessary.

Once selected, the jurors are subjected to opening statements by the attorneys in which the case to follow is explained. The party bearing the burden of proof has the right to make the first opening statement. (At the end of the trial, closing statements are made inversely from the order in which the parties opened. CPLR 4016.)

CPLR 4011 provides that "the court may determine the sequence in which the issues shall be tried," and may "otherwise regulate the conduct of the trial in order to achieve a speedy and unprejudiced disposition of the matters at issue in a setting of proper decorum." The power granted by CPLR 4011 to determine the sequence of trial is employed as a matter of discretion, and trial sequence reflects primarily convenience of the parties, the witnesses, and the court. Some general practices are prevalent: the plaintiff will ordinarily put on his or her entire case constructed in the order considered most effective. After the defendant's case, the plaintiff can offer rebuttal evidence. In personal injury actions the bifurcated trial is commonly used in some New York courts. Under this practice, issues of liability are tried first, and only if liability is established does the court proceed to try the damages. *See* 22 NYCRR 202.42.

During the course of a trial, the judge will make rulings on the admission or exclusion of testimony, the competency of witnesses, or other matters affecting the trial. An objection to any of these must be made known at the earliest opportunity, normally at the time that a ruling or order of the court is requested or made. CPLR 4017. In this way, the court can consider revising its ruling at the time it will do the most good.

The progress of the trial may be affected by one or more motions. We have already encountered the motion to amend a pleading made during the trial. CPLR 3025(b), (c). Under CPLR 4402, a court may grant a motion for a mistrial or, as it is also called, a motion for the withdrawal of a juror upon the request of either party. The motion is granted, with or without conditions in the discretion of the court, "when it appears that owing to some accident or surprise, defect of proof, unexpected and difficult questions of law, or like reason a trial cannot proceed without injustice to a party." *Matter of Taylor*, 271 App. Div. 947, 67 N.Y.S.2d 823, 825 (4th Dep't 1947). A continuance, *i.e.*, delay in the trial (also authorized by motion under CPLR 4402) is preferable to a new trial, since it avoids the necessity of repeating testimony as well as conducting a new voir dire and preparing new opening statements.

In addition to motions for an amendment, a mistrial, or a continuance, the CPLR allows any party to move during trial for judgment on the ground that the movant is entitled to judgment as a matter of law. CPLR 4401. The motion may be made at any time if based on admissions (a rare but theoretically possible occurrence) or if based on the pleadings. *See also* CPLR 3211(e). More commonly, the motion for judgment will be made at the close of the respondent's case and will urge that no prima facie case has been made out (if directed against the plaintiff) or that no legally sufficient defense has been proved (when directed against defendant). This is commonly called a motion for a directed verdict. The court may well deny the motion for directed verdict, or at least reserve decision on it, even if it believes the movant's position meritorious. This way the action can go to the jury after all evidence is in, and if the verdict is for the party believed entitled to it by the judge, it need not be disturbed. If the jury comes back the "wrong" way, the court can grant judgment notwithstanding the verdict on motion under CPLR 4404 (discussed below). Should the trial judge be reversed on appeal, there will be no need for a new trial. The jury's verdict can simply be reinstated.

The CPLR does not state the standard to be used in determining whether the movant is entitled to judgment. The Court of Appeals has stated that a direction of a verdict is supportable only when "by no rational process could the trier of the facts base a finding in favor of [the party opposing the motion] upon the evidence . . . presented." *Blum v. Fresh Grown Preserve Corp.*, 292 N.Y. 241, 255, 54 N.E.2d 809, 811 (1944). *See* § 19.04, *infra*.

Assuming that the trial is not cut short by a motion, the presentation of evidence will be concluded, and the attorneys will make their closing statements.

After the closing statements are made by counsel, the court will deliver a charge to the jury, instructing the jurors on how to proceed and on the law to be applied. The parties normally request the judge to make a particular charge. Under CPLR 4110-b, they are to file their requests, which are usually accompanied by memoranda of law, at the close of the evidence or earlier if the court so requests. Prior to the closing arguments to the jury, the court is to inform the parties of its proposed action (outside the jury's presence, of course). Objections to the charge are ordinarily made then, but objections are not waived unless not made prior to the time the jury retires to deliberate. If an erroneous charge is given and the error is so extreme as to be "fundamental," the waiver by failure to object will not stop the prejudiced party from attacking the charge on appeal. CPLR 4017, 4110-b; *Clark v. Interlaken Owners, Inc.*, 2 A.D.3d 338, 770 N.Y.S.2d 58 (1st Dep't 2003).

Guidance for the substance of the charge can be found in New York Pattern Jury Instructions. The charges provided there, while helpful, are not mandatory.

After hearing the charge, the jury retires to deliberate. Five of the six jurors must agree in order to render a verdict. CPLR 4113. If they cannot reach a verdict after a reasonable period, the court may discharge them and order a new trial before another jury. *Id.*

The jury's verdict may be of two types. A general verdict is a finding in favor of one or more parties. CPLR 4111(a). When such a verdict is given, all material fact questions are deemed determined in favor of the prevailing party. A special verdict is one in which the jury finds the facts only and the court determines which party is entitled to judgment on the basis of the findings. Thus, it is left to the court to ascertain the appropriate legal principles and to carry out the process of fact application. The special verdict to some extent obviates the need for charging the jury concerning legal principles and in general reduces the possibility of jury error in complex cases. In a case in which the court directs the jury to render a general verdict, it can require the jury to give special attention to particular questions by submitting written interrogatories to which the jury must give written answers in addition to the general verdict. CPLR 4111(c). These provide a means of evaluating the jury's application of the law to the facts; they also help the jury focus on the issues.

CPLR 4111(d), amended in 2003, provides for the itemization of damages in medical malpractice cases so as to coincide with the structured judgment provisions of CPLR articles 50-A and 50-B.

In actions for personal injury, property damage or wrongful death, if the jury returns a verdict awarding damages, it must specify the elements which make up the damages separating pain and suffering from out-of-pocket losses and further separating losses already incurred from those which will be suffered in the future. CPLR 4111(f).

After the verdict is received, the parties have the right to ask the clerk to poll the jury to make certain that the verdict is correct and represents the true intentions of each member of the jury. Any juror may dissent at this stage from a verdict to which he or she has previously agreed. *Labar v. Koplin*, 4 N.Y. 547 (1851). CPLR 4112 instructs the clerk how to enter the verdict and record certain information in his minutes. To be valid, the verdict must be duly recorded by the clerk.

At the conclusion of the trial (after the jury has delivered its verdict), the losing party may ask the court to grant a new trial and/or to grant judgment in her behalf, notwithstanding the verdict. CPLR 4404. Requests for both types of relief, if desired, must be joined in one motion, CPLR 4406, which must be made within fifteen days after the verdict is reached, CPLR 4405. A new trial may be ordered after verdict when the verdict is against the weight of the evidence or simply because it is in the interest of justice to do so (usually because of a prejudicial error which occurred during the trial). CPLR 4404(a).

A motion for judgment notwithstanding the verdict (or "judgment n.o.v.") raises the same questions of legal sufficiency of the evidence as the CPLR 4401 motion for judgment during trial: Was there evidence on which rational people could conclude that the winning party was entitled to the verdict? *See Cohen v. Hallmark Cards*, 45 N.Y.2d 493, 410 N.Y.S.2d 282, 382 N.E.2d 1145 (1978).

After resolving the post-trial motions, if any, the court will issue its judgment, the "determination of the rights of the parties." CPLR 5011.

The literature on trial advocacy rivals in volume, if not in depth, the literature on Shakespeare. Useful "beginners" manuals are T. Mauet, Trial Techniques (6th ed. 2002), R. McCullough & J. Underwood, Civil Trial Manual 2 (1980), and J. Kelner and F. McGovern, Successful Litigation Techniques: Student Edition (1981).

§ 19.02 SELECTING THE MODE OF TRIAL

[A] The Right to a Jury Trial

MATTER OF DES MARKET SHARE LITIGATION
Court of Appeals
79 N.Y.2d 299, 582 N.Y.S.2d 377, 591 N.E.2d 226 (1992)

WACHTLER, CHIEF JUDGE.

In *Hymowitz v. Lilly & Co.*, 73 N.Y.2d 487, 507, 541 N.Y.S.2d 941, 539 N.E.2d 1069, this Court, recognizing that "extant common-law doctrines, unmodified, provide no relief for the DES plaintiff unable to identify the manufacturer of the drug that injured her," adopted a market share theory to create a "realistic avenue of relief for plaintiffs injured by DES." Since our decision in that case three years ago, Supreme Court, Erie County, has issued an order severing the market share issue from every DES case pending in New York and consolidating these actions so that the market share issue can be resolved in a single proceeding. The question now before us is whether the DES plaintiffs are entitled to a jury trial on the issue of market share. We agree with the Appellate Division, 171 A.D.2d 352, 578 N.Y.S.2d 63, that plaintiffs have a constitutional right to a jury in the market share trial and consequently affirm.

. . . .

After *Hymowitz*, the market share issue remained to be litigated. By order filed April 4, 1990, the DES market share issue in the cases pending in the New York courts was severed, consolidated for the purpose of discovery and trial, and venued in Erie County. The trial court entered a case management order in August of 1990 in which it provided that certain motions could be filed within 45 days of entry, including a motion addressing whether any of the parties had a right to a jury trial. By notice of motion dated August 31, 1990, plaintiffs' liaison counsel requested an order granting a jury trial of the market share issue.

In a decision dated March 8, 1991, this motion was denied. Calling the market share theory a newly created remedy unknown at common law, the trial court concluded that the plaintiffs had neither a constitutional nor a statutory right to a jury trial. Further, the trial court held that the market share trial was not itself a cause of action, but was more in the nature of a pretrial proceeding.

Because causation and damages would be tried to a jury in the main action, the court determined that there was no right to a jury trial of the severed market share issue.

The Appellate Division reversed, with two Justices dissenting. The majority held that *Hymowitz* had not created a new equitable remedy, as the defendants urged; instead, it brought about the modification of a preexisting legal cause of action (171 A.D.2d 352, 354, 578 N.Y.S.2d 63). Because the essential nature of each DES case was a cause of action at law to recover money damages for personal injury, the plaintiffs were entitled to a jury trial under article I, § 2 of the New York Constitution. The dissenters by contrast termed the market share issue preliminary and collateral and reasoned that no right to a jury trial attached.

Article I, § 2 of the New York Constitution provides that "[t]rial by jury in all cases in which it has heretofore been guaranteed by constitutional provision shall remain inviolate forever." The express language of this provision exhorts us to consider as an historical matter the types of actions to which the right to a jury trial has traditionally attached (*see, Motor Vehicle Mfrs. Assn. v. State of New York*, 75 N.Y.2d 175, 180, 551 N.Y.S.2d 470, 550 N.E.2d 919). The first Constitution, that of 1777, guaranteed a right to trial by jury in all cases in which it had "heretofore been used" (N.Y. Const. of 1777, art. XLI). The effect of this language was to constitutionalize the right to a jury trial as it existed in the common law at that time (*see, Motor Vehicle Mfrs. Assn. v. State of New York, supra*, at 181, 551 N.Y.S.2d 470, 550 N.E.2d 919; *Matter of Luria*, 63 Misc.2d 675, 677, 313 N.Y.S.2d 12; *see also*, Siegel, N.Y. Prac. § 377). The Constitutions of 1821, 1846 and 1894 contained similar language guaranteeing the right to a jury trial in all cases as it had "heretofore been used"; the result of the continuation of this broad "heretofore" language was to accord constitutional significance to those cases in which the right to a jury trial had been guaranteed by statute between 1777 and 1894 (*see, Matter of Luria, supra*, at 677, 313 N.Y.S.2d 12). The 1938 Constitution narrowed the "heretofore" clause to grant the right to a jury trial only as it was "heretofore . . . guaranteed by *constitutional provision*" (emphasis added). This change in language thus guarantees a jury trial (1) in all those cases to which it would have traditionally been afforded under the common law before 1777, and (2) in all cases to which the Legislature by statute extended a right to a jury trial between 1777 and 1894 (*Motor Vehicle Mfrs. Assn. v. State of New York, supra*, 75 N.Y.2d at 181, 551 N.Y.S.2d 470, 550 N.E.2d 919; 4 Weinstein-Korn-Miller, N.Y. Civ. Prac. ¶ 4101.08). In addition, it has been held that the right to a jury trial is not strictly limited to those instances in which it was actually used in 1894, but also extends to new cases that are analogous to those traditionally tried by a jury (*Colon v. Lisk*, 153 N.Y. 188, 193, 47 N.E. 302; *Independent Church of Realization of Word of God v. Board of Assessors*, 72 A.D.2d 554, 420 N.Y.S.2d 765).

This right to a jury trial is additionally codified in CPLR 4101. CPLR 4101(1) provides that "issues of fact . . . [in] an action in which a party demands and sets forth facts which would permit a judgment for a sum of money only" are triable to a jury. This subdivision, which has its origins in a pre-1894 statute (Code Civ. Pro. § 968 [L.1876, ch. 448, § 968]), encompasses the largest group of actions triable to a jury at common law before 1777 and has been held to include actions in tort and contract (4 Weinstein-Korn-Miller, N.Y. Civ. Prac. ¶ 4101.11).

In the case now before us, the DES plaintiffs have the right to a jury trial on the merits of their personal injury claims because these causes of action are for money damages and would have been tried by a jury at common law. The question that remains is whether the severance and consolidation of the market share inquiry in one court converts an examination of the defendants' relative culpability into a wholly separate equitable proceeding to which no right to a jury trial attaches.

The defendants argue that in adopting a market share theory in *Hymowitz*, this Court created a new equitable remedy, unknown in the common law, that absolved DES plaintiffs from identifying the particular product that caused their injury and that apportioned liability in accordance with over-all culpability. In support of their argument, the defendants point to our use of the word "equitable" to describe our decision to use a market share theory in DES cases (*Hymowitz v. Lilly & Co.*, 73 N.Y.2d at 508, 541 N.Y.S.2d 941, 539 N.E.2d 1069 ["(w)e turn then to the question of how to fairly and *equitably* apportion the loss occasioned by DES" (emphasis added)], at 512, 541 N.Y.S.2d 941, 539 N.E.2d 1069 ["this is an *equitable* way to provide plaintiffs with the relief they deserve, while also rationally distributing the responsibility for plaintiffs' injuries among defendants" (emphasis added)]). They argue that this use of the word "equitable" signalled that litigation of the market share issue was akin to a traditional action in equity, and that consequently no right to a jury trial attached as a constitutional matter.

When we used the word "equitable" in *Hymowitz*, we were not categorizing the market share theory; rather, we were indicating the extent to which our decision was compelled by simple fairness. We adopted a market share theory because, as we noted at the time, "the ever-evolving dictates of justice and fairness, which are the heart of our common-law system, required[d] formation of a remedy for injuries caused by DES" (*id.*, at 507, 541 N.Y.S.2d 941, 539 N.E.2d 1069). . . .

We similarly reject the argument that the market share trial is a preliminary issue, relating to the parties' status, that does not trigger the plaintiffs' right to a jury trial (*see, e.g., Shippey v. Berkey*, 6 A.D.2d 473, 475, 179 N.Y.S.2d 366; *Bux v. Robinson*, 199 N.Y.S.2d 619, 621, *rev'd on other grounds* 216 N.Y.S.2d 2, *lv. denied* 13 A.D.2d 912, 217 N.Y.S.2d 1018). Identification of the exact defendant who produced the product that injured the plaintiff is normally required in a products liability action, as noted above (*Hymowitz v. Lilly & Co., supra*, 73 N.Y.2d at 504, 541 N.Y.S.2d 941, 539 N.E.2d 1069 [citing *Morrissey v. Conservative Gas Corp.*, 285 App. Div. 825, 136 N.Y.S.2d 844, *aff'd* 1 N.Y.2d 741, 152 N.Y.S.2d 289, 135 N.E.2d 45; Prosser and Keeton, Torts § 103, at 713 (5th ed.)]).

The plaintiffs no longer need to make this showing. They will, however, present evidence to establish the relevant market shares for each of the years that DES was marketed for pregnancy use. By all accounts, market share remains a hotly contested issue, with both sides planning to present a number of competing experts. The trier of fact will weigh the credibility of each expert and the validity of their models and statistics in its resolution of the market share issue. The market share percentages for each of the 24 years and the concomitant determination of each defendants' ultimate culpability will dictate the ability of all plaintiffs to recover damages in their main actions. It is therefore difficult to conceive how the market share issue can be denominated as either preliminary or collateral.

Thus, because we agree with the Appellate Division that market share is an issue in the plaintiffs' cause of action for money damages and not a separate cause of action, plaintiffs are entitled to a jury trial by virtue of article I, § 2 of the New York Constitution and CPLR 4101. Although the Trial Judge had the power to sever and consolidate the market share issue for the sake of judicial economy, he did not have the added power to defeat the plaintiffs' right to a jury trial.

Because of our holding that adoption of the market share theory did not create a new equitable remedy or cause of action, but instead modified an existing common-law remedy, we need not consider defendants' arguments that the market share theory is analogous to a long account, a bill of peace or equitable contribution. We would simply note that we do not accept the defendants' argument that the sheer complexity of the market share proceeding converts it into an equitable cause of action as a matter of law. This conclusion would have enormous ramifications in the area of complex litigation and is completely unwarranted under the facts of this case. Market share is a discrete legal issue that is an integral part of the plaintiffs' cause of action in tort for money damages. Since the issue is so clearly legal in nature, we decline to hold that the complexity of its resolution alone magically transforms it into an equitable matter that can defeat the plaintiffs' constitutional right to a trial by jury.

Accordingly, the order of the Appellate Division should be affirmed, with costs, and the certified question answered in the affirmative.

NOTES

(1) An interesting discussion of the jury trial right is found in *Matter of Luria*, 63 Misc. 2d 675, 313 N.Y.S.2d 12 (1970), where it was held that a widow who challenged the provisions in her husband's will was not entitled to a jury since she was seeking a constructive trust on certain estate assets, relief which was equitable in nature. Discussed in the opinion is the Court of Appeals' decision in *Matter of Garfield*, 14 N.Y.2d 251, 251 N.Y.S.2d 7, 200 N.E.2d 196 (1964), where it was held that while creditors who claim against the estate in Surro-

gate's Court waive their right to a jury trial, the executor defending the estate assets is entitled to a jury.

(2) Knotty problems still occasionally arise regarding a litigant's right to a jury trial. *See, e.g., Motor Vehicle Mfrs. Association of the United States, Inc. v. State of New York*, discussed in § 25.06, *infra*. Plaintiffs sought a declaratory judgment that the New Car Lemon Law, General Bus. Law § 198-a, unconstitutionally deprived auto makers of a jury trial in that it gave aggrieved consumers the option of submitting their claims to arbitration, regardless of the wishes of the seller. The court held that there was no right to a jury trial because the substantive remedies available under the law (replacement or refund of the purchase price) were equitable in nature. The court reasoned that even a claim for a refund was equitable because it was akin to an action for recision, which is concededly equitable.

(3) CPLR 4101(1) covers the very common situation in which the relief demanded is properly money damages. *See, e.g., Murphy v. American Home Products Corp.*, 136 A.D.2d 229, 527 N.Y.S.2d 1 (1st Dep't 1988) (plaintiff in an action for damages due to an alleged violation of the state age discrimination law held entitled to a jury trial).

CPLR 4101(2) encompasses a list of actions which might otherwise be troublesome. Various other statutes provide for trial by jury, such as Dom. Rel. L. § 173, dealing with divorce cases.

Problems do arise when legal and equitable claims are combined. See the following problem and related material.

PROBLEM A

Thad and Lucy are partners operating an art gallery in Soho. Lucy learns that Thad has sold, at below market prices, certain paintings which they agreed they would keep as a long-term investment. He has told her that he plans more such sales. Lucy thereupon commenced an action in Supreme Court, New York County, seeking (1) damages of $30,000, which she alleges were caused by the sale of the paintings; and (2) an injunction ordering Thad to refrain from further sales without her express permission. Thad's answer denies that any sales made or contemplated are in violation of their agreement. When the action comes to trial, may Lucy properly demand that a jury decide either or both of her claims? If she does not make such a demand, may Thad?

DI MENNA v. COOPER & EVANS CO.
Court of Appeals
220 N.Y. 391, 115 N.E. 993 (1917)

CARDOZO, J.

The action is brought to foreclose a mechanic's lien. The plaintiff, a sub-contractor, furnished labor and materials to the defendant Cooper & Evans Company, which had a contract with the city of New York for a public improvement. The complaint alleges that the defendant undertook to make advances to the plaintiff during the progress of the work; that it kept its promise for a time; but that in August, 1910, it refused to make further advances, discharged the plaintiff and terminated the contract. The value of the labor and material supplied at that time, in excess of payments already received, is placed at $3,650.43. Judgment is demanded that the plaintiff be declared to have a lien upon the moneys due to the contractor from the city of New York; that the lien be enforced, and "that the plaintiff have personal judgment against the defendant Cooper & Evans Company for the amount of his claim, together with interest and costs." . . .

[The question arose whether a jury trial was a matter of right.]

. . . .

We are unwilling to hold that the plaintiff's cause of action was triable by a jury as of right upon the plaintiff's demand. An action to foreclose a lien is one of equitable cognizance. . . . We do not doubt that a defendant by timely demand may preserve his right, in the event of failure of the lien, to trial by jury of the other issues. . . . The fact that the plaintiff has combined with a prayer for equitable relief an alternative claim for a money judgment, cannot deprive the defendant of the jury trial assured to him by the Constitution. But a different question is presented where it is the plaintiff who seeks a jury. The form of action in such a case is that of his own selection. The law does not require him to demand a personal judgment in the event of the failure of his lien. "It is intended to afford him a privilege — not to subject him to compulsion" (*Koeppel v. Macbeth*, 97 App. Div. 299, 301). If he takes advantage of that privilege, he elects that the whole controversy, in all its aspects, may be determined by the court. To hold otherwise would do violence to the plain purpose of the statute. One cannot be heard to urge as a breach of one's constitutional right the concession of a remedy which one has one's self demanded. The rule is fundamental that where a plaintiff seeks legal and equitable relief in respect of the same wrong, his right to trial by jury is lost. If any right remains, it is the right of the defendant. . . .

. . . .

NOTES

(1) There are two methods of handling the problem of joinder of legal and equitable claims with regard to the right to a jury trial. The first is the so-called issue approach, adopted by the federal and some state courts, under which the equitable issues are tried to the court after the legal issues are tried to the jury. *See* discussion in C. Wright, The Law of Federal Courts 611-14 (5th ed. 1994), and cases cited.

The second approach, historically predominant in New York, is to categorize the entire action as either "legal" or "equitable." If equitable, the party asserting the claim (but only that party) is said to have waived the right to jury trial on the legal issues. In addition to the principal case, see, *e.g., Sepinski v. Bergstol*, 81 A.D.2d 860, 438 N.Y.S.2d 870 (2d Dep't 1981). Note, however, that CPLR 4102(c) expressly instructs that the joinder of equitable and legal claims deriving from separate transactions does not waive the right to a jury trial on the legal claim.

(2) In *Hebranko v. Bioline Laboratories, Inc.*, 149 A.D.2d 567, 540 N.Y.S.2d 264 (2d Dep't 1989), the court, applying the general rule that the right to a jury trial is determined by the facts alleged in the complaint, not by the prayer for relief, held that a plaintiff who is entitled only to damages does not waive the right to a jury trial by including a demand for an equitable remedy in the demand for relief. Is this consistent with the principal case?

(3) In addition to the waiver of a jury trial by joining equitable and legal claims, a party may waive the right to a jury by failing to make a timely demand for a jury trial. The demand must be made with the note of issue when it is served or, if by the party upon whom the note is served, within fifteen days of such service. CPLR 4102. A court may permit a party to withdraw a waiver if no undue prejudice would result to the other party. *But see Fidler v. Sullivan*, 81 A.D.2d 733, 439 N.Y.S.2d 478 (3d Dep't 1981) (plaintiff's motion to amend the note of issue to provide for a jury trial was denied when it was made less than one month before the trial date and would have caused the case to move to the end of the calendar).

The court may also order a jury trial despite an earlier waiver when it appears during the trial that the relief required entitles the adverse party to a jury. CPLR 4103; *see Lane v. Mercury Record Corp.*, 21 A.D.2d 602, 252 N.Y.S.2d 1011 (1st Dep't 1964), § 13.07, *supra*.

A contractual waiver of the right to a jury trial in the event of litigation between the parties is enforceable so long as it is express and unequivocal, *see Barrow v. Bloomfield*, 30 A.D.2d 947, 293 N.Y.S.2d 1007 (1st Dep't 1968), and so long as not prohibited by statute, *see* Real Prop. L. § 259-c (waiver of jury in lease void with respect to actions between the landlord and tenant for personal injury or property damage).

(4) The main case states that a defendant may be entitled to a jury trial on all or part of plaintiff's claim even if plaintiff has waived the right to a jury. Of course, if only a single transaction is alleged in the complaint and the action is truly equitable, neither party has a right to a jury. But if the plaintiff seeks only equitable relief, the defendant may nevertheless demand a jury if the cause of action sounds essentially in law. See *City of Syracuse v. Hogan*, 234 N.Y. 457, 461, 138 N.E. 406 (1923), in which the court held the defendant entitled to a jury even though plaintiff's sole requested remedy was equitable because "the main issue to be tried" was the title to certain property, a legal issue. Implicitly, then, the courts must decide which issue predominates.

(5) How should the trial proceed if a case has both legal and equitable elements and the defendant has demanded a jury trial on the issues of law? To try some issues in a case before a jury and others before a court may be cumbersome, even if legally mandatory. A creative solution was offered in *Vinlis Construction Co. v. Roreck*, 23 A.D.2d 895, 896, 260 N.Y.S.2d 245, 247-48 (2d Dep't 1965), in which the complaint alleged legal and equitable claims based on separate transactions:

> Of course, when legal and equitable causes of action are thus united in one complaint, the court may sever the legal causes of action and direct that they be tried separately before a jury, leaving the equitable causes of action to be tried separately by the court. . . . But here a severance would be inadvisable and should not be directed. The legal and equitable actions are so intertwined and related that one trial of all the causes of action is both desirable and necessary. The justice presiding at the jury trial of the legal causes of action (the second and third) should at the same term try and determine without the jury the equitable cause of action (the first, for an accounting). Of course, in the proceedings before the trial justice it will be incumbent upon him to regulate and direct the sequence of the trial of the issues as he deems proper under all the circumstances then prevailing (CPLR 603).

The next case is also instructive.

MERCANTILE & GENERAL REINSURANCE CO. v. COLONIAL ASSURANCE CO.
Court of Appeals
82 N.Y.2d 248, 604 N.Y.S.2d 492, 624 N.E.2d 629 (1993)

SIMONS, JUDGE.

This appeal presents a question on the role of the jury, and the conclusiveness of its findings, in actions in which both legal and equitable claims are advanced by the parties.

The defendant Spanno Corporation was in the business of guaranteeing prospective purchasers of capital equipment that the equipment would have a stated residual value at a given future date. Since Spanno had to assure its customers that it would be able to make good on its guarantees, it obtained insurance for that purpose from the defendants Colonial Assurance Company and Union International Insurance Company. They, in turn, reinsured the risks with plaintiff.

Plaintiff instituted this action seeking to rescind the contracts of reinsurance with the insurers, claiming that Spanno had made material misrepresentations which had induced it to enter into the contracts. Rescission claims, of course, are equitable in nature and, thus, are to be tried by the court (*Motor Vehicle Mfrs. Assn. v. State of New York*, 75 N.Y.2d 175, 182-183, 551 N.Y.S.2d 470, 550 N.E.2d 919). Spanno, named as a defendant, asserted a legal counterclaim alleging that it was a third-party beneficiary to the reinsurance contracts with Colonial and Union, which were then in liquidation. It claimed that it had been injured because of nonpayments to its customers and its inability to obtain new customers and demanded damages for plaintiff's breach of the reinsurance contracts and its tortious interference with the insurance contracts with Colonial and Union.

At trial Supreme Court treated plaintiff's claim of material misrepresentation as an equitable defense and counterclaim to Spanno's contract action and ruled that the jury's verdict on equitable issues would be advisory (*see,* CPLR 4101, 4212; *see also, Phoenix Mut. Life Ins. Co. v. Conway*, 11 N.Y.2d 367, 229 N.Y.S.2d 740, 183 N.E.2d 754). It asked the jury to answer six interrogatories which addressed both the legal and equitable causes of action. In response, the jury concluded that Spanno was entitled to recover on the contract and that it made no material misrepresentations warranting rescission by plaintiff. It awarded damages of $14,708,779 on the breach of contract and tortious interference claims. Supreme Court set aside the verdict on Spanno's legal counterclaims. It treated the verdict on rescission as advisory and, contrary to the jury's determination, held that Spanno had made material misrepresentations entitling plaintiff to rescission of the reinsurance contract. On appeal, the Appellate Division reversed, holding that the Judge erred in setting aside the jury's verdict because there was a reasonable view of the evidence that could support it (*see, Cohen v. Hallmark Cards*, 45 N.Y.2d 493, 410 N.Y.S.2d 282, 382 N.E.2d 1145). It expressly held that the jury's finding of misrepresentation should have been treated as dispositive, not advisory (184 A.D.2d 177, 181, 591 N.Y.S.2d 1015).

The principal question presented is the legal effect of the jury's misrepresentation finding on the trial court's power to make a contrary factual finding. Defendant Spanno asserts that the jury's determination that there had been no material misrepresentations was a necessary part of its determination on the breach of contract action and not merely an advisory verdict on plaintiff's action for rescission. It concludes, therefore, that the jury's misrepresentation finding operated as a "type of collateral estoppel" and precluded the Judge from adjudicating the issue anew as part of plaintiff's action for rescission.

Spanno's argument fails because its original premise — that a determination on misrepresentation was necessary to resolve the breach of contract claim — is erroneous.

As the case was presented, plaintiff's action for rescission constituted an equitable defense and counterclaim to Spanno's breach of contract claim (*see, Tober v. Schenectady Sav. Bank*, 54 A.D.2d 1049, 1050, 389 N.Y.S.2d 38). Under the plain terms of CPLR 4101, when a legal claim is met with an equitable defense or counterclaim, "the issues of fact shall be tried by a jury . . . except that equitable defenses and equitable counterclaims shall be tried by the court" (*see also*, N.Y.Const. art. I, § 2). Following that direction, the jury could and did fully decide the disputed issues of fact necessary to the claim of contractual breach: the existence of a facially valid contract, breach and damages. At that point, the sole unresolved issue was whether the contract should be declared void from its inception because of material misrepresentation. All issues pertaining to that equitable defense and counterclaim, whether matters of fact or of law, were to be determined by the court under CPLR 4101 (*see, Grant v. Guidotti*, 67 A.D.2d 736, 737, 413 N.Y.S.2d 24). To find material misrepresentation, the court did not need to contradict any of the factual findings the jury made in deciding the factual issues pertinent to the legal claim for breach of contract because a finding of material misrepresentation is not inconsistent with a finding that the parties entered into a contract. To the contrary, the very essence of a rescission action is to set aside a contract that is otherwise valid and binding. The factual issues in the legal and equitable claims intersected only to the extent that the jury's finding of a facially valid contract necessitated that the court proceed to the rescission issue. That, however, is not the same as having a factual issue in common and, under CPLR 4101, the trial court was free to decide the rescission claim de novo (*cf., Skinner v. Total Petroleum*, 859 F.2d 1439, 1444; *see also,* 4 Weinstein-Korn-Miller, NY Civ Prac ¶ 4101.34, at 41-52; Siegel, NY Prac § 209, at 304 [2d ed]; *Beacon Theatres v. Westover*, 359 U.S. 500, 516, 79 S.Ct. 948, 960, 3 L.Ed.2d 988 [Stewart, J., dissenting]).

Because the jury verdict on misrepresentation was merely advisory, the trial court was not bound by it. It could disregard the advisory verdict, even if there was evidence to support it (*see, McClave v. Gibb*, 157 N.Y. 413, 52 N.E. 186; *Ruder v. Lincoln Rochester Trust Co.*, 18 A.D.2d 763, 235 N.Y.S.2d 191). The Judge's finding was the dispositive determination on that issue and, absent a contrary factual finding by the Appellate Division, is binding on this Court if there is evidence in the record to support it. The evidence here satisfies that standard and therefore the trial court's decision granting rescission of the contract should be sustained.

In view of this conclusion, the remaining issues raised on appeal need not be addressed.

Accordingly, the order of the Appellate Division should be reversed, with costs, and the judgment of Supreme Court reinstated.

NOTES

(1) The use of the declaratory judgment device should affect neither the plaintiff's nor the defendant's right to a jury trial, which should be determined by reference to "the basic nature of the lawsuit." *Douglas A. Edwards, Inc. v. Lax*, 85 A.D.2d 509, 444 N.Y.S.2d 103, 104 (1st Dep't 1981) (where underlying claim was to recover brokerage commissions, the factual issues should be resolved by a jury).

(2) If the parties are not entitled to a jury trial, but the court would like the assistance of a jury, it may empanel an advisory jury. CPLR 4212. As the term connotes, the verdict of an advisory jury is not binding on the court. *Ruder v. Lincoln Rochester Trust Co.*, 18 A.D.2d 763, 235 N.Y.S.2d 191 (4th Dep't 1962).

[B] The Jury Trial and Public Policy

The preceding cases illustrate part of the difficulty encountered in applying the jury trial right in modern civil litigation. Of course, even when there is no problem involved in deciding that a jury is necessary, the use of the jury itself imposes cost and delay on the civil justice system. Some scholars estimate that jury cases take an average of forty percent longer that judge-tried cases. Zeisel et al., Delay in the Court 71-81 (1959). Moreover, the amateur status of jurors as fact finders poses theoretical problems. Judge Jerome Frank thought them "hopelessly incompetent." *See* his Law and the Modern Mind 180-81 (1930). Further, jury duty imposes an often unwelcome burden on our citizens. Is abolition the answer? Some of the not so apparent reasons for retaining the civil jury are suggested in J. Dawson, A History of Lay Judges 287-93, *quoted in* P. Carrington & B. Babcock, Civil Procedure 171-72 (3d ed. 1983)*

> The most general reason would be that the process itself is so vital a part of community organization that the community itself has a right to share in the process. Translated into modern terms, deceptive as they may be, this is essentially a theory of political democracy applied to adjudication.
>
> Another possible reason for preserving lay participation is that the persons involved in disputes may accept the result more readily if they are judged by their own kind. This might be a general reason for enlisting a segment of the community, small or large, in the process of dispute settlement. . . . If acceptance of results is the object, this cannot mean in most cases that the parties involved, especially the losing parties, will express affirmative approval.
>
> More familiar to us is a phrasing that identifies this factor as a right of the individual — the right to be judged by one's "peers." . . . The

---

* Reprinted permission of Little, Brown & Company, copyright © 1977.

notion of "judgment by peers" moves into recorded history in the context of feudal relationships. It was first clearly phrased as the right of an individual vassal to be judged by his fellow vassals, especially in contests with his own feudal lord. In France it was well known as a special privilege of nobility and finally was reserved for a small and very exalted group, the Peers of France. In England the most famous provision of Magna Carta, c. 39, projected "judgment by peers" across the sky of history for all the world to see. Judicium parium was expressed as a privilege of all free men, not merely of the barons who extorted the Charter. The generality of the phrase, plus its close connection with the companion phrase, "the law of the land," enabled later generations to make the right to "judgment by one's peers" into a symbol of human freedom, especially against oppression by government. As originally used it was clearly not intended either as a generalized guaranty of jury trial or as a buttress for more ancient modes of community judging. But it was expressed as a restraint on royal action, and despite the narrow meanings that were originally intended, clause 39 of Magna Carta deserves an honorable place in the history of constitutionalism. It was not till much later that "peers" were connected with jury trial. It was only in the United States, later still, that the right to jury trial became more than protection against government and was riveted into all litigation conducted under the forms of the common law. Our American constitutions, state and federal, now confirm the right of all our citizens to this partial form of lay participation — provided the action is at "common law." We cannot stop now to review why this happened, for the career of the common law jury would take us far on a winding path. The jury has become, especially in the United States, a special form of "judgment by peers," contained by its own elaborate rules and invested with its own ethos. . . .

Apart from the individual's right to "judgment by peers" or the claims of the whole community to vote on such matters, there may be another, quite different reason for giving laymen a share in adjudication — the total performance of the legal system may be improved if it can draw on their resources. This kind of argument might have been used in various contexts. In the intermediate stage of the English Chancery's history — the sixteenth and early seventeenth centuries — the vagueness and variability of equity doctrines opened the way to court-sponsored arbitration, which helped to make results more sensible, as well as more acceptable. . . .

In highly developed systems of modern law, laymen have been installed in judicial offices deliberately and for similar reasons. In Germany, in other parts of central Europe, and in Scandinavia a pattern widely adopted is the mixed tribunal, in which laymen specially chosen for short terms of office form part of the bench, sitting with one or more professional judges. These modern Schoffen are not merely jurors, confined to the finding of facts under instructions from the professionals. They vote on the whole case and usually can outvote the professional judge if they will. Some of the arguments for using laymen in this way in commercial cases resemble arguments often made for commercial arbitration — that technical knowledge and specialized experience can be supplied by laymen and may be needed, not only to solve the immediate problem but to provide correctives where legal rules themselves are deficient. In criminal cases, where similar lay judges are also much used, the arguments must take a different form and are likely to approach the reason we sometimes give for using our juries — the conscripting of laymen, even in a limited role, provides a means for adjusting law to the purposes and convictions of the community at large. There may lie concealed in this argument an assumption that legal rules may be not only incomplete but positively wrong, when measured against the standards evolved through broader social experience. At the least there is an assumption that law is better administered if it draws on the good sense and practical wisdom of persons in whom these qualities have not been severely warped by excessive exposure to law.

[C] Trial Before Referees

CPLR 4001 authorizes courts to appoint referees to determine an issue, to report findings or to carry out some lesser administrative tasks. The difference between a reference to determine and a reference to report is critical because of the difference in power the two types of referees may exercise. A decision of a referee to determine replaces that of the trial court and is reviewable only on appeal. CPLR 4301; *Matter of the Voluntary Dissolution of Seamerlin Operating Co.*, 307 N.Y. 407, 121 N.E.2d 392 (1954). A reference to report, however, grants only an advisory power, and the referee's findings are subject to the confirmation or rejection of the court, usually but not necessarily, on motion by one of the parties. CPLR 4403. The reporting referee is given the greatest latitude in determining the credibility of witnesses because "His was the opportunity to observe. . . ." *Sakow v. Bossi*, 30 Misc. 2d 110, 116, 214 N.Y.S.2d 120, 126 (Sup.Ct. 1961). But see *Kardanis v. Velis*, 90 A.D.2d 727, 455 N.Y.S.2d 612 (1st Dep't 1982), where the court held that the testimony of a process server was "inherently more probable" than that of a physician who denied personal service and accordingly reversed as error the lower court's confirmation of the referee's report that the plaintiff had not proven personal service.

A reference to determine may be made by stipulation of the parties, generally without leave of the court. (*See* CPLR 4317(a) for some limited exceptions.) A reference to determine can also be ordered on a motion by one of the parties to the action or by the court itself, principally where the case will require an examination of a "long account." CPLR 4317(b). What constitutes a long account is unclear. *See, e.g., Starace v. Cimenti*, 75 Misc. 2d 668, 348 N.Y.S.2d 877 (N.Y.C.

Civ. Ct. 1973) (plaintiff's motion for reference of a long account was denied in an action for recovery of legal fees for submission of 35 motions in six actions). In general, the compulsory reference to determine is reserved for cases characterized by unusual complexity. *See Thibaudeau v. City of Niagra Falls*, 239 App. Div. 644, 268 N.Y.S. 397 (4th Dep't 1934).

The compulsory reference has been squared with the right to a jury trial by a recognition that the practice was permitted in the colonial era and that it is therefore constitutional when used in appropriate cases. *See, e.g. Glass v. Thompson*, 51 A.D.2d 69, 379 N.Y.S.2d 427 (2d Dep't 1976); *Longo v. Adirondack Drilling, Inc.*, 14 A.D.2d 476, 217 N.Y.S.2d 905 (3d Dep't 1961) (the substantial difficulty of a jury trial where the account is long and detailed is sufficient grounds to authorize a compulsory reference). A similar problem was discussed in the federal setting in *In re Japanese Electric Products Antitrust Litigation*, 478 F. Supp. 889 (E.D. Pa. 1979), *vacated*, 631 F.2d 1069 (3d Cir. 1980), an unusually complicated anti-trust case. The District Court denied defendants' motions to strike plaintiff's jury demands, holding that complexity alone is not a sufficient reason to deny the federal constitutional right to a jury trial. The Court of Appeals concluded instead that due process could be frustrated by compelling litigants to try their case before a jury which is unable to reasonably decide a highly complex issue. In this situation, held the court, the right to due process is more important than the right to a jury trial. The Ninth Circuit has upheld the jury trial right in the face of a similar argument. *In re U.S. Financial Securities Litigation*, 609 F.2d 411 (1979), *cert. denied sub nom. Gant v. Union Bank*, 446 U.S. 929, 100 S. Ct. 1866 (1980).

§ 19.03 SOME PROCEDURAL ASPECTS OF THE TRIAL

[A] Choosing the Jury

SIRIANO v. BETH ISRAEL HOSP.
Supreme Court, New York County
161 Misc. 2d 512, 614 N.Y.S.2d 700 (1994)

EDWARD H. LEHNER, JUSTICE:

During jury selection the six co-defendants have used their peremptory challenges to excuse all nine minority venirepersons (6 black and 3 Latino) who have to date been examined. Plaintiffs assert that this exclusion has been impermissibly based on race and request judicial relief.

Facts

The plaintiff Joseph Siriano, a white of Italian ancestry, asserts that he was injured in a construction accident and has instituted this action against the owner of premises where the accident occurred and five contractors and subcontractors.

Justice Helen Freedman granted each defendant three peremptory challenges and gave plaintiffs nine challenges. As of March 16, when an application was made to me, two jurors (both white) had been seated. Plaintiffs had exercised 5 challenges (four white and one black) while defendants jointly exercised 11 challenges (the nine referred to above as well as two whites). In addition the parties jointly excused approximately 180 prospective jurors, the vast majority of whom were apparently excused due to problems resulting from the stated length of the trial. No breakdown of the racial composition of these persons was available.

In the afternoon of March 16, plaintiffs' counsel complained of the actions of the defendants in excusing all of the minority jurors. After hearing argument, I determined that the statistics displayed a prima facie case of racial discrimination and directed defendants to offer race neutral explanations for their challenges. On the following two afternoons I heard defendants' explanations for the exercise of their challenges and examined, together with counsel, the three minority jurors (two black and one Latina) who were then available.

Discussion

In *Swain v. Alabama*, 380 U.S. 202, 85 S.Ct. 824, 13 L.Ed.2d 759 (1965), it was held that purposeful exclusion of blacks from juries violates the Equal Protection Clause, but proof was required that the prosecutor had followed such a pattern in cases other than the one before the court. This formulation was found unworkable and was therefore rejected in *Batson v. Kentucky*, 476 U.S. 79, 106 S.Ct. 1712, 90 L.Ed.2d 69 (1985), where it was held that "a defendant may establish a prima facie case of purposeful discrimination in selection of the petit jury solely on evidence concerning the prosecutor's exercise of peremptory challenges at the defendant's trial" (p. 96, 106 S.Ct. p. 1723). The court ruled that to "establish such a case, the defendant first must show that he is a member of a cognizable racial group, . . . and that the prosecutor has exercised peremptory challenges to remove from the venire members of the defendant's race . . . [and that the] facts and any other relevant circumstances raise an inference that the prosecutor used that practice to exclude the veniremen from the petit jury on account of their race" (p. 96, 106 S.Ct. p. 1723). As an example it was stated that a "'pattern' of strikes against black jurors included in a particular venire might give rise to an inference of discrimination," and that once there is a "prima facie showing, the burden shifts to the State to come forward with a neutral explanation for challenging black jurors, [and the] trial court then will have the duty to determine if the defendant has established purposeful discrimination" (pp. 97-98, 106 S.Ct. pp. 1723-24).

Although in 1993 the First Department in *People v. Doran*, 195 A.D.2d 364, 600 N.Y.S.2d 222, restated the foregoing requirements, including the necessity of showing that the prosecutor removed "members of [the] defendant's race from the panel" (at 365), it was held in *Powers v. Ohio*, 499 U.S. 400, 111 S.Ct. 1364, 113 L.Ed.2d 411 (1991), that a juror has a constitutional right not to be excluded from a jury on account of race and a defendant of a different race "can raise the third-party equal protection claims of jurors excluded by the prosecution because of their race" (p. 415, 111 S.Ct. p. 1373).

Two months after the decision in *Powers*, in *Edmonson v. Leesville Concrete Company, Inc.*, 500 U.S. 614, 111 S.Ct. 2077, 114 L.Ed.2d 660 (1991), it was announced that the harms recognized in *Powers* are not limited to the criminal sphere, and that courts must entertain a challenge to a private litigant's racially discriminatory use of peremptory challenges in a civil trial, concluding that it would be left to the trial courts in the first instance to develop evidentiary rules for implementing the decision.

. . . .

In deciding the present issue, I must observe that I am aware of a general perception of lawyers involved in the personal injury field of a preference of plaintiff's counsel for minority jurors and an opposite preference of defense counsel. These preferences are, of course, not true of all counsel, nor in all situations. But this general perception is reflected in the numerous venue motions wherein plaintiffs seek a trial in Bronx County (where there is more likely to be a minority jury), whereas defendants are likely to oppose such a trial location.

. . . .

Just as it is impermissible to eliminate blacks from a jury "on the assumption that they will be biased in a case simply because the defendant is black" (*Batson*, p. 97, 106 S.Ct. p. 1723), it is improper to exclude them from a jury because of a general perception that it is likely that they may be more sympathetic to an injured plaintiff.

In view of all of the evidence before me, I find that there has been a purposeful discrimination against the minority jurors excused and I therefore direct that to the extent that they are still available, the three examined jurors (Smith, Walker and Guzman) be seated together with the two jurors previously selected, and that jury selection continue. (*See People v. Frye*, 191 A.D.2d 581, 595 N.Y.S.2d 84 [2d Dept. 1993], where the court permitted the retention of jurors seated prior to the day the discriminatory pattern was revealed; and *People v. Mitchell*, 80 N.Y.2d 519, 530, 591 N.Y.S.2d 990, 606 N.E.2d 1381 [1992], where it was held that a *Batson* claim was sustained because "the exclusion of even a single juror on racial grounds is constitutionally forbidden").

. . . .

NOTES

(1) In *Edmonson v. Leesville Concrete Co., Inc.*, 500 U.S. 614, 111 S. Ct. 2077, 114 L. Ed. 2d 660 (1991), it was held that jury selection implicates "state action" so as to invoke the protection of the Equal Protection Clause of the Fourteenth Amendment. Thus, even in civil litigation between private parties, the *Batson*

constitutional considerations must be brought to bear and race-based peremptories may not be permitted. As in the principal case, plaintiff's complaint was that defendant had pointedly used its peremptory challenges to remove black prospective jury members. For a thorough discussion of this question, see Underwood, *Race Discrimination in Jury Selection: Whose Right Is It Anyway?*, 92 Columbia L. Rev. 725 (1992).

The constitutional supervision of peremptories was extended in *J.E.B. v. Alabama ex rel. T.B.*, 511 U.S. 127, 114 S. Ct. 1419, 128 L. Ed. 2d 89 (1994). The Court held that peremptories had to be exercised in a gender-neutral fashion. In the instant case, a proceeding to establish paternity and obtain child support, the judgment finding paternity was reversed because the petitioner (the state) had used peremptories to strike all males from the jury. Justice Blackmun's opinion for the Court noted that peremptories could still play an important role in jury selection:

> Parties still may remove jurors whom they feel might be less acceptable than others on the panel; gender simply may not serve as a proxy for bias. Parties may also exercise their peremptory challenges to remove form the venire any group or class of individuals normally subject to "rational basis" review. . . . Even strikes based on characteristics that are disproportionately associated with one gender could be appropriate, absent a showing of pretext.

114 S. Ct. at 1429.

(2) Generally, in New York civil litigation, attorneys are responsible for conducting voir dire examinations to ferret out unqualified or undesirable jurors. However CPLR 4107 makes mandatory the presence of a judge at an examination upon the request of either party. Such a request may arise from a party's attempt to prevent the opposing counsel from flirting excessively with jurors or from making preliminary opening statements. Additionally, a judge at a voir dire examination may exercise statutory power pursuant to CPLR 4011 to direct or supplement the examination to prevent delay or abuse. In any event, apart from the peremptory challenges discussed below, any challenge to a juror based on bias or relationship must be determined by the court. CPLR 4208; *see also* CPLR 4110; 22 NYCRR 202.33.

(3) CPLR 4109 had provided each party with three peremptory challenges plus an additional one for each two alternative jurors. The legislature in 1996 amended CPLR 4109 so as to limit the number of peremptories to three per side, regardless of how many parties are on a side. The amendment is said to end the "traditional inequality" faced by single plaintiffs who face an array of defendants.

(4) Because peremptory challenges are limited in number, attorneys use them sparingly, exhausting all other grounds for challenging a juror before resorting to a peremptory challenge. The use of other means to disqualify an undesirable juror with peremptory challenges afford the attorney optimum ability to exclude

the maximum number of jurors believed to be unfavorable to his case. Thus, an attorney may fail to challenge a juror for cause but later seek disqualification of that juror by peremptory challenge, provided that the challenge is made before the juror is sworn in. *Sorenson v. Hunter*, 208 App. Div. 1078, 52 N.Y.S.2d 872 (4th Dep't 1945).

CPLR 4110 allows an attorney to make challenges for cause to the favor or for relationships. These challenges are unlimited in number and are objections based upon the belief that the prospective juror cannot decide the case fairly. There are specific grounds set forth in CPLR 4110(a) for a challenge to a favor. Additionally, a prospective juror may be disqualified for any other reason that raises doubt about impartiality. *See Troiano v. Nardini*, 55 A.D.2d 732, 389 N.Y.S.2d 557 (3d Dep't 1976) (juror who had previously been a party to the litigation in which one of his adverse parties had been represented by plaintiff's counsel).

CPLR 4110(b) prevents persons related within the sixth degree "by consanguinity or affinity" to parties to a suit from serving as jurors. Consanguinity refers to a blood relation through a common ancestor, whereas affinity applies to relationships by marriage. A challenge based upon the consanguinity or affinity of parties raises the presumption that the juror will not try the case fairly. If such a relationship is admitted, the court should exclude the juror without further proof of bias. *Ballard v. Van Tuyl*, 142 App. Div. 278, 126 N.Y.S. 820 (4th Dep't 1911). *See also Maiello v. Johnson*, 24 A.D.2d 914, 264 N.Y.S.2d 595 (3d Dep't 1965).

[B] Compelling Proof at Trial

Form

Subpoena Duces Tecum*

SUPREME COURT OF THE STATE OF NEW YORK

COUNTY OF _____

(Caption)

Subpoena duces tecum

Index No.

THE PEOPLE OF THE STATE OF NEW YORK

TO _____ , GREETING:

WE COMMAND YOU, that all business and excuses being laid aside, you appear and attend before one of the Justices of our Supreme Court, at a _____ Term, Part _____ . , to be held at the County Court House, _____ , New York,

---

* Form 243, Bender's Forms for the CPLR (1982) at 383.

on the _____ day of _____ , 20 ____. , at _____ A. M., to testify and give evidence in a certain action now pending in the court between _____ , plaintiff, and. . . . . , defendant, on the part of the plaintiff, and that you bring with you, and produce at the time and place aforesaid, a certain _____ (set forth description of book, paper or other thing production of which is being required) now in your custody, and all othe _____ (describe) which you have in your custody or power.

Failure to attend will be deemed a contempt of court, and will make you liable to pay all losses and damages sustained thereby to the party aggrieved, and forfeit $50 in addition thereto.

WITNESS, Hon. _____ , one of the Justices of the Supreme Court of the State of New York, at the County Court House, in _____ , New York, on the _____ day of _____ , 20 ____.

_____
(Print name)
Attorney for Plaintiff
Address:
Telephone Number:

NOTES

(1) A subpoena is used to compel a person to attend and give testimony. CPLR 2301. The subpoena duces tecum differs only in that it requires, in addition, the production of documents or "other things." *Id.*

Either type of subpoena may be issued without court order by an attorney for a party in judicial proceedings, arbitrations, or administrative proceedings. CPLR 2302.

(2) A subpoena is served in the same manner as a summons. CPLR 2303. Authorized traveling expenses and one day's witness fee (*see* CPLR 8001(a)) must be tendered in advance of the date attendance is required. *Id.* Jud. L. § 2-b limits the service of subpoenas to persons "found in the state." Hence, the long-arm provisions of article 3 of the CPLR do not apply to subpoenas served on non-parties. *Wiseman v. American Motors Sales Corp.*, 103 A.D.2d 230, 479 N.Y.S.2d 528 (2d Dep't 1984); *Siemens & Halske v. Gres*, 37 A.D.2d 768, 324 N.Y.S.2d 639 (1st Dep't 1971). Testimony of non-party non-residents should be obtained by a deposition, which may be used to obtain testimony outside the state, CPLR 3108, 3113(a)(2), (3), and is admissible at trial, CPLR 3117(a)(3).

Judiciary Law § 2-b provides, *inter alia,* that a court of record has power "to issue a subpoena requiring the attendance of a person found in the state to testify in a cause pending in that court." CPLR 5224 (Article 52 covers enforcement of money judgments) provides for subpoenas requiring the respondent to produce books and records, and the information subpoena which requires only that answers to questions be sent by mail. Judiciary Law § 2-b, by its terms, applies to these subpoenas so that, by case law interpretation, they are ineffective if sought to be served outside New York. *Matter of Stephen*, 239 A.D.2d 963, 659 N.Y.S.2d 588 (4th Dep't 1997). In certain investigative proceedings, subpoenas may be served outside the state. *See, e.g., In re Grand Jury Subpoenas*, 70 N.Y.2d 700, 519 N.Y.S.2d 353, 513 N.E.2d 239 (1987) (Crim. Proc. Law § 640.10); *Application of American Dental Co-Op, Inc.*, 127 A.D.2d 274, 514 N.Y.S.2d 228 (1st Dep't 1987) (Gen. Bus. Law § 343).

(3) A form sometimes seen in New York practice, the "notice to produce" is directed to a party and, like a subpoena duces tecum, requires the production of documents. Unlike a subpoena, this notice is not judicially enforceable but, under a rule of evidence, failure to comply allows the issuing party to use secondary evidence to prove the contents of the writing, *See* Barker & Alexander, Evidence in New York State and Federal Courts § 10.8 (2001).

[C] Controlling the Trial — Motions Pursuant to CPLR 4402 for a Mistrial or Continuance

SANTANA v. NEW YORK CITY TRANSIT AUTHORITY
Supreme Court, New York County
132 Misc. 2d 777, 505 N.Y.S.2d 775 (1986)

DAVID B. SAXE, JUSTICE:

The outcome of a trial often rests upon the ability of a party or witness to express himself to a jury. Words often trigger powerful visual images and consequently, they act to persuade a court or jury. And, since words are the basic components of communication, the manner in which they are spoken and understood is basic to a fair trial. . . .

In this case, a Spanish speaking woman, sued for injuries she sustained as a result of a fall when a subway car in which she was a passenger stopped suddenly. At the plaintiff's request, a Spanish interpreter was provided.

The first problem at trial arose when the plaintiff's counsel asked the plaintiff to compare the velocity of the train's stop at the time when the plaintiff was injured to other stops that day. The answer communicated to the jury, as translated by the interpreter, was that the train stopped suddenly as if it had bumped into something. A juror who spoke Spanish and who said he was familiar with the dialect spoken by the plaintiff, believed that what the plaintiff meant was not that it felt as if the train bumped into something, but rather that the train "crashed" into something. The juror's view was made known to me during a recess in the trial when he passed a note to the court officer seeking permission to confer with me on this matter.

In chambers, the juror, with interpreter, court reporter, and counsel present brought his view to my attention. The juror explained that the verb "chocar" which translates into English as to bump, was used by the plaintiff to mean to crash. He grounded this view on the fact that in the dialect of Spanish spoken by the plaintiff, a Puerto Rican woman, the verb "bompiar" means to bump; and, had that been the verb with which she intended to describe the incident, it would have been used. The juror therefore claimed that the witness's answer was not correctly understood by the jury. The manner in which the train stopped was concededly important to a determination of liability.

The initial question before me concerned whether or not the passing of the note by the juror seeking to advise me on this matter prejudiced the jury panel because it placed the juror in the position of being a "witness" for the plaintiff. The appropriateness of declaring a mistrial was discussed.

According to CPLR 4011, the trial court has the authority to "regulate the conduct of the trial in order to achieve a speedy and unprejudiced disposition of the matters at issue." This statutory provision simply confirms the expansive common law powers of New York judges over conduct in their own courtrooms. A trial court is granted wide latitude in controlling the conduct of a trial (*Roma v. Blaustein*, 44 A.D.2d 576, 353 N.Y.S.2d 44 (2nd Dept.1974)). A mistrial however should not be ordered except to prevent a substantial possibility of injustice (*Halstead v. Sanky*, 48 Misc.2d 586, 265 N.Y.S.2d 426 (Sup.Ct. Kings Co., 1965)).

There are some instances where the conduct of jurors during the trial prevents the defendant from having a trial by a fair and impartial jury. (*People v. DeLucia*, 20 N.Y.2d 275, 282 N.Y.S.2d 526, 229 N.E.2d 211 (1967)). One such instance is when a juror visits the scene of the crime or accident and reenacts the purported criminal acts. (*People v. DeLucia, supra*). Such actions are inherently prejudicial to the defendant and will automatically warrant a new trial. Similarly, failure to answer a question correctly during voir dire warrants a new trial where it is demonstrated that the juror intentionally concealed facts, bias or prejudice that would render the prospective juror disqualified ab initio from service. . . .

In this case, I determined that the actions of the juror raised little possibility that either he had forfeited his impartiality or that the entire panel was prejudiced. I determined that the juror had not spoken to any other jurors concerning the matter nor did the jurors have any idea why this juror requested to speak with me. During the hearing, the juror was asked whether he would be able to cope with a situation in which his knowledge of Spanish would lead him to a different understanding of the partys'/witnesses' statement than that of the interpreter's. His response was that he would be able to deal with such a situation if it arose; however, if there was a large discrepancy, he would bring it to my attention. He reassured me that for the remainder of the trial he would be capable of and willing to rely solely on the interpreter's words rather than on his own knowledge of the language. Accordingly, I determined that no bias or prejudice existed (*People v. Rentz*, 105 A.D.2d 920, 481 N.Y.S.2d 1018) and that there would be no impediment to proceeding with the trial.

When the trial resumed, the plaintiff was re-called to the witness stand and questioned about the force of the crash. As it turned out, the plaintiff meant to convey, by her use of the word chocar, a crash and not a bump.

Perhaps more important than the trial practice issue raised here, is the extent to which an interpreter is obligated to interpret the dialect of the language spoken by party or a witness.

In New York County, Supreme Court, Civil Branch where there is a relatively large Spanish-speaking population, there are four Spanish interpreters employed on a full-time basis. A qualified interpreter must have a minimum of a high school diploma or equivalent. They are hired by the State only after passing a rigorous examination which tests skills in translating Spanish to English and vice versa. The test does not incorporate the usage of any form of Spanish dialect. So, any knowledge an interpreter may have of a particular Spanish dialect is through personal experience or study. . . .

The plaintiff here, it seems, spoke "Spanglish," which is the vocabulary derived from the practical everyday living and working in a two-language world where fluent command of those languages is rare. . . . The creation of the verb bompiar is such an example and reflects the activity of everyday life. . . .

Spanish speaking individuals who speak and understand New York City Spanish are frequent litigants in the Housing Court and other lower courts in the City. Fairness dictates that there is a need for assuring that interpreters of the Spanish language have an understanding and appreciation of the growth and scope of New York City Spanish. It is suggested that the Office of Court Administration develop guidelines for the hiring of interpreters which reflect the spirit of this decision.

NOTES

(1) CPLR 4402 allows the court to order a new trial at any time during the trial "in the interest of justice." Should the court have done that in the principal case? Suppose the bilingual juror continued to disagree with the interpreter's report of the plaintiff's testimony. Could the juror in fact disregard his own understanding of the plaintiff? Should he do so? More basically, should the juror's role be entirely passive? *See generally* Sand & Reiss, *A Report on Seven Experiments Conducted by the District Judges in the Second Circuit*, 60 N.Y.U. L. Rev. 423 (1985).

Misconduct of a juror can also be raised in a post-trial motion for a new trial. We return to this issue in note 3 following *Marine Midland Bank v. Russo*, in subsection [H], *infra*.

(2) The problems of conducting a fair trial in a multi-lingual society are illustrated by the principal case. Would it have been a wise tactic for either attorney in the main case to try to exclude jurors who either did or did not speak Span-

ish? How, as an attorney, can you deal with the hazards of interpretation which arise regardless of the language spoken?

(3) CPLR 4402 also allows the court to grant a continuance which would constitute a somewhat longer break in the trial than a mere recess. Where the court refused to grant a continuance over a Labor Day weekend in order that plaintiff's prime witness could testify and declared a mistrial instead, the Appellate Division, months later, declared this an abuse of discretion. Although the case could be retried, the trial, of course, would be before a different jury. *Balogh v. H.R.B. Caterers, Inc.*, 88 A.D.2d 136, 452 N.Y.S.2d 220 (1982). Compare *Fitzsimmons v. Wilder Mfg. Co.*, 53 A.D.2d 743, 384 N.Y.S.2d 523 (3d Dep't 1976), in which defendant's expert witness was scheduled to testify at 2:00 P.M. on a Friday and failed to appear and the trial judge adjourned the trial until 10:00 A.M. the following Monday. When defendant's expert did not appear at 10:00 A.M., an adjournment was granted until 11:00 A.M. and when the witness then failed to appear, defendant advised the court that the expert, who was then testifying in the Dutchess County Court, would "surely be available at noon." The witness did not appear at noon. At 12:04 P.M. the trial judge stated for the record that he had just received a telephone call from the Dutchess County Court Judge, before whom the witness was then testifying, who advised him that "the witness will not be available." It was held not to have been an abuse of discretion for the trial judge to have ordered a resumption of the trial under the circumstances.

(4) The following case deals with another motion which can be made before the trial is completed, the motion for judgment, authorized by CPLR 4401. It is often referred to as a motion for a directed verdict. This lawyers' shorthand is misleading; if the motion is granted, the jury plays no further role and there is in fact no verdict given.

[D] Judgment During Trial Under CPLR 4401

LICARI v. ELLIOT
Court of Appeals
57 N.Y.2d 230, 455 N.Y.S.2d 570, 441 N.E.2d 1088 (1982)

JASEN, JUDGE.

The issue raised on this appeal is whether the plaintiff in this negligence action brought to recover damages for personal injuries has established a prima facie case that he sustained a "serious injury" within the meaning of subdivision 4 of section 671 of the Insurance Law,[*] commonly referred to as the "No-Fault" Law.

---

[*] [Now Insurance Law § 5102. — Eds.]

[Plaintiff, a taxi driver, was injured in a motor vehicle accident. He was admitted to the hospital for tests which showed no problems except for "a very mild limitation" of movement in the back and neck areas. At trial, plaintiff testified that he had returned to work 24 days after the accident and that the only difficulty he experienced was helping passengers with their luggage. He stated also that he was unable to help his wife with some household chores and that he had occasional transitory headaches and dizzy spells.

[At the close of plaintiff's case, defendant moved to dismiss the complaint on the ground that plaintiff failed to establish that his injury amounted to a serious injury under Insurance Law § 671(4). The trial judge reserved decision and sent the case to the jury which returned a plaintiff's verdict. The court denied defendant's renewal of the motion to dismiss.

[The Appellate Division reversed and dismissed the complaint ruling that no serious injury was shown as a matter of law.

[The Court of Appeals affirmed. The policy underlying the no-fault legislation was reviewed — there should be no right to recovery for non-economic loss (pain and suffering) except where the injury was "serious," defined as "a personal injury which results in death; dismemberment; significant disfigurement; a fracture; permanent loss of use of a body organ, member, function or system; permanent consequential limitation of use of a body organ or member; significant limitation of use of a body function or system, or a medically determined injury or impairment of a non-permanent nature which prevents the injured person from performing [the person's usual activities] for not less than ninety days during the one hundred eighty days immediately following the occurrence of the injury or impairment."]

Tacit in this legislative enactment is that any injury not falling within the new definition of serious injury is minor and a trial by jury is not permitted under the no-fault system. We are required then to pass on the threshold question of whether the plaintiff in this case has established a prima facie case that he sustained a serious injury within the meaning of the statute.

Although the statute sets forth eight specific categories which constitute serious injury, we are only concerned on this appeal with construing two of them, to wit: whether the plaintiff suffered a serious injury which resulted in either (1) a "significant limitation of use of a body function or system;" or (2) "a medically determined injury or impairment of a non-permanent nature" which endured for 90 days or more and substantially limited the performance of his daily activities. . . .

There can be little doubt that the purpose of enacting an objective verbal definition of serious injury was to "significantly reduce the number of automobile personal injury accident cases litigated in the courts, and thereby help contain the no-fault premium." (Memorandum of State Executive Dept., 1977 McKinney's Session Laws of N.Y., p. 2448.) . . .

In No fault — serious injury not always jury Q

In light of this mandate, plaintiff's argument that the question of whether he suffered a serious injury is always a fact question for the jury is without merit. It is incumbent upon the court to decide in the first instance whether plaintiff has a cause of action to assert within the meaning of the statute. By enacting the No-Fault Law, the Legislature modified the common-law rights of persons injured in automobile accidents . . . to the extent that plaintiffs in automobile accident cases no longer have an unfettered right to sue for injuries sustained. Thus, to the extent that the Legislature has abrogated a cause of action, the issue is one for the court, in the first instance where it is properly raised, to determine whether the plaintiff has established a prima facie case of sustaining serious injury. Since the purpose of the No-Fault Law is to assure prompt and full compensation for economic loss by curtailing costly and time-consuming court trials . . . requiring that every case, regardless of the extent of the injuries, be decided by a jury would subvert the intent of the Legislature and destroy the effectiveness of the statute. The result of requiring a jury trial where the injury is clearly a minor one would perpetuate a system of unnecessary litigation. "[I]f the procedural system cannot find a way to keep cases that belong in no-fault out of the courthouse, the system is not going to work." (Schwartz, *No-Fault Insurance: Litigation of Threshold Questions under the New York Statute — The Neglected Procedural Dimension*, 41 Brooklyn L.Rev. 37, 53.) Thus, we believe the Legislature intended that the court should decide the threshold question of whether the evidence would warrant a jury finding that the injury falls within the class of injuries that, under no-fault, should be excluded from judicial remedy. If it can be said, as a matter of law, that plaintiff suffered no serious injury within the meaning of subdivision 4 of section 671 of the Insurance Law, then plaintiff has no claim to assert and there is nothing for the jury to decide. (*Montgomery v. Daniels, supra.*)

Turning to the case before us, plaintiff contends that his injuries were serious within the meaning of the statute in that he was prevented, for at least 90 days, from performing substantially all of the material acts which constituted his usual daily activities. (*See* Insurance Law, § 671, subd. 4.) It is undisputed, however, that plaintiff returned to work 24 days after the accident and that upon his return he immediately resumed his usual schedule of driving a taxi 12 hours per day, 6 days a week. Since plaintiff was able to maintain his daily routine for most of each day after returning to work, it should be abundantly clear that plaintiff was not prevented from performing substantially all of his daily activities during anything close to 90 days following the occurrence of the injury. Thus, the Appellate Division correctly held, as a matter of law, that plaintiff did not meet the statutory standard of serious injury. . . .

It requires little discussion that plaintiff's subjective complaints of occasional, transitory headaches hardly fulfill the definition of serious injury. Plaintiff offered no proof that his headaches in any way incapacitated him or interfered with his ability to work or engage in activities at home. In fact, plaintiff testified that such headaches occurred only once every two or three weeks and were relieved by aspirin. We do not believe the subjective quality of an ordinary headache falls within the objective verbal definition of serious injury as contemplated by the No-Fault Law. . . . To hold that this type of ailment constitutes a serious injury would render the statute meaningless and frustrate the legislative intent in enacting no-fault legislation.

As to plaintiff's contention that he suffered a "significant limitation of use of a body function or system" (see Insurance Law, § 671, subd. 4), taken in its most favorable light, the evidence at trial established only that plaintiff suffered a painful sprain which limited the movement of his neck and back. Plaintiff offered no evidence as to the extent of the limitation of movement. The only evidence of the extent of plaintiff's injury came from the hospital duty physician who examined plaintiff on February 15. This doctor testified that plaintiff had only a "very mild limitation" of movement in his neck and back. Plaintiff's family physician, who testified on plaintiff's behalf, did not offer any testimony to the contrary. The other injuries plaintiff complained of were a bruised chest and a concussion. No evidence was offered to show that any of these injuries caused a significant limitation of use of a body function or system. As to the occasional headaches and dizziness plaintiff complained of, no evidence was submitted to indicate that plaintiff suffered any significant limitation of any of his body functions or systems. No proof was offered to show that these ailments ever went beyond mere temporary discomfort, relieved by aspirin. The Legislature could not have intended headaches and dizziness of the type experienced by plaintiff to constitute a significant limitation of use of a body function or system.

After a careful examination of the record, we hold that there was no line of reasoning by which the jury could have concluded that plaintiff suffered a significant limitation of use of a body function or system, or that he was prevented from performing substantially all of his usual daily activities for 90 days. (See *Cohen v. Hallmark Cards*, 45 N.Y.2d 493, 410 N.Y.S.2d 282, 382 N.E.2d 1145.) While there is little doubt that plaintiff suffered discomfort as a result of the accident, the court has no choice but to enforce the legislative mandate and dismiss the complaint when a plaintiff fails to meet the burden of proving the threshold requirement of establishing a prima facie case that he sustained a serious injury within the meaning of the statute. (*Compare Ayala v. Reyes*, 66 A.D.2d 790, 411 N.Y.S.2d 40, *supra*; *Simone v. Streeben*, 56 A.D.2d 237, 392 N.Y.S.2d 500, *with* Liddy v. Frome, 85 A.D.2d 716, 445 N.Y.S.2d 841.)

Accordingly, the order of the Appellate Division should be affirmed. . . .

NOTES

(1) The trial court had allowed the jury to decide the no-fault issues in the principal case, and it had found that plaintiff met the serious injury test on both of his theories. Nonetheless, the Court of Appeals held that a judgment should have been directed in defendant's favor, in which case the jury would never

have heard the case. Why would such an approach not deprive plaintiff of the right to a jury trial? In an earlier case sustaining the use of the directed verdict procedure, the Court of Appeals explained the point:

> In 1842 the Court of Errors, then the court of final appeal in this State, formulated, in an opinion by the Chancellor, the rule then applied: "Although the jury is the constitutional tribunal to decide disputed facts, it does not follow that the court must submit every question of fact to their decision as a matter of course, although the party holding the affirmative has failed to introduce sufficient evidence in point of law to authorize the jury to give a verdict in his favor. Hence it is the duty of the court, if requested by the defendant to do so, to non suit the plaintiff, where the testimony is all on his side, and where it is wholly insufficient to sustain the suit. *And it is insufficient in point of law to sustain the suit where it would be the duty of the court to set aside the verdict and grant a new trial, if the jury find a verdict in favor of the complainant.* But where the testimony is sufficient to sustain a verdict in favor of the plaintiff, if the jury should find one in his favor, the questions of fact should be submitted to their decision; although the judge who tries the cause may think the evidence leaves the case in so much doubt that the jury would be fully justified in finding a verdict for the defendant." (Italics are ours.) . . .

> . . . Thus, the question whether a verdict of a jury is "unsupported by sufficient evidence" is always one of law for the Trial Judge. He *must* set aside such a verdict and in appropriate case he may then direct a contrary verdict. (*Getty v. Williams Silver Co.*, 221 N.Y. 34.) The court is justified in directing a verdict in such case "not because it would have authority to set aside an opposite one, but because there was an actual defect of proof, and, hence, as a matter of law, the party was not entitled to recover." (*McDonald v. Metropolitan St. Ry. Co.*, 167 N.Y. 66, 70.)

> . . . .

> This court has frequently pointed out that "insufficient evidence is, in the eye of the law, no evidence." In *Matter of Case* (*supra*, p. 204), opinion by Cardozo, J., it reiterated that rule and added: "In the words of Maule, J., in *Jewell v. Parr* (13 C.B. 916), 'When we say that there is no evidence to go to a jury, we do not mean that there is literally none, but that there is none that ought reasonably to satisfy a jury that the fact sought to be proved is established.'"

> The sufficiency of evidence "reasonably to satisfy a jury" cannot be mechanically measured. It is "incredible as matter of law" only where no reasonable man could accept it and base an inference upon it. That depends upon considerations which vary in accordance with the circumstances of the particular case. It would serve no purpose here to analyze the evidence produced by the defendant. When considered in its

setting of facts which are undisputed it lacks, we conclude, the substance which is required reasonably to support the finding of the jury.

Blum v. Fresh Grown Preserve Corp., 292 N.Y. 241, 244-45, 54 N.E.2d 809, 810 (1944).

Does the reasoning satisfy you?

(2) An interesting variation on the problem presented in *Licari v. Elliot* is found in *Smith v. Mouawad*, 91 A.D.2d 700, 457 N.Y.S.2d 608 (3d Dep't 1982):

> Plaintiff was injured when the vehicle in which he was a passenger and which was driven by defendant, Majid Mouawad, went out of control, left the road and struck a utility pole. Plaintiff sustained a head injury which required suturing. Plaintiff's injuries resulted in scarring largely obscured by his hairline. He sustained a 30 to 40% permanent hair loss in the area of the scarring and suffers from a sensitivity to hot and cold. After trial, the court directed a verdict in plaintiff's favor on the question of negligence and submitted a special question to the jury as to whether plaintiff had sustained a serious injury which resulted in significant disfigurement pursuant to subdivision 4 of section 671 of the Insurance Law. The jury found "no" on the special question and a verdict was entered for defendants. Plaintiff urges that the trial court erred in not directing a verdict for him on the issue of "significant disfigurement." In view of the nature of the injury sustained by plaintiff and the testimony relative thereto, the court properly permitted the issue of serious injury to be decided by the jury as a question of fact (*cf. Licari v Elliott*, 57 NY2d 230).

Suppose Mouawad moved at the close of the evidence for a defendant's directed verdict. Should it have been granted under the *Licari* standard?

(3) Could the defendant in *Licari v. Elliot* have presented the no-fault defense in advance of trial? Could the defendant have made a summary judgment motion under CPLR 3212? On what proof might it have been based? Would the standard applied in deciding it be different from that applied in *Licari* itself?

Alternatively, could the defendant have successfully moved to dismiss the complaint for a failure to state a cause of action under CPLR 3211(a)(7)?

(4) "A plaintiff in a wrongful death case is not held to as high a degree of proof as a plaintiff in a personal injury action and is entitled to benefit from every favorable inference which can reasonably be drawn from the evidence in determining whether a prima facie case has been made out. . . ." *Rivenburgh v. Viking Boat Co.*, 55 N.Y.2d 850, 447 N.Y.S.2d 707, 432 N.E.2d 600 (1982). Hence, the court reversed a grant of summary judgment for the defendant and remanded for a new trial.

What is the reason for the quoted rule?

(5) A party who fails to make a timely motion for directed verdict under CPLR 4401 waives the right to later seek a judgment notwithstanding the verdict under CPLR 4404, although the party may still move for a new trial if the verdict is against him. *See Miller v. Miller*, 68 N.Y.2d 871, 508 N.Y.S.2d 418, 501 N.E.2d 26 (1986) (plaintiff, who failed to move for a directed verdict on the question whether he had suffered a "serious injury" under the No-Fault Law, thereby conceded that the question was for the jury). In *Hurley v. Cavitolo*, 239 A.D.2d 559, 658 N.Y.S.2d 90 (2d Dep't 1997), the Appellate Division found the verdict for defendant against the weight of the evidence and remanded for a new trial, stating: "By failing to move for a directed verdict pursuant to CPLR 4401 on the issue of negligence at the close of evidence, the plaintiff implicitly conceded that the issue was for the trier of fact. . . ."

[E] The Summation

The summation affords counsel the opportunity to highlight the best aspects of their case for the jury. Much is permissible in the summation, and only in egregious circumstances does opposing counsel register any objection. "A wide latitude is allowed to counsel in his summation and we have no desire to curb a vigorous, robust summation. A witness may be characterized as untruthful, as a falsifier, as a liar, and even as a perjurer. That is a matter of propriety, of good taste and of judgment, with which a court will not interfere. But there is some line to be drawn." *Cohen v. Covelli*, 276 A.D. 375, 376, 94 N.Y.S.2d 782, 783-84 (1st Dep't 1950). Where do we find this line? In *Caraballo v. City of New York*, 86 A.D.2d 580, 446 N.Y.S.2d 318 (1st Dep't 1982), in which *Cohen* is cited, the Appellate Division ordered a new trial after defendant's counsel, in summation, called plaintiffs' attorney "tricky and deceptive," and charged that plaintiffs' witnesses had been paid to perjure themselves. *See also La Russo v. Pollack*, 88 A.D.2d 584, 449 N.Y.S.2d 794 (2d Dep't 1982) (new trial granted after defendant's counsel attacked the credibility of plaintiff's expert witnesses by speculating that plaintiff's attorney may have said to one such witness, "I paid the thousand, you voice my theories.").

In *Tate v. Colabello*, 58 N.Y.2d 84, 459 N.Y.S.2d 422, 445 N.E.2d 1101 (1983), it was stated in reference to plaintiff's counsel's rhetorical questions to the jury as to the value of pain over a protracted period of time: "This they would have us condemn as an impermissible resort to a so-called 'per diem' or 'unit of time' argument, under which small units of time of pain and suffering are given a specific monetary value and multiplied at their rate for the entire time for which it might be endured. . . . But review of the record discloses that counsel suggested no specific monetary value for units of time and, not having done so, perforce did not multiply them for the jury. So, while, concededly, the propriety of the unit of time approach is a subject on which the decisions of our sister States are in conflict . . . and we have not had the opportunity to pass on it, this case does not present the occasion to do so."

An earlier Appellate Division decision indicated that the per diem approach injected an element of "false simplicity" which cautionary instructions could not cure. *DeCicco v. Methodist Hosp. of Brooklyn*, 74 A.D.2d 593, 424 N.Y.S.2d 524 (2d Dep't 1980).

The *Tate* court also held that counsel was entitled to state the amount of damages being sought in the summation. On this point, an earlier case had held that when the amount is stated, the court must instruct the jury that the stated amount is not evidence which may be considered by the jury in fixing the amount of its verdict. *Terone v. Anderson*, 54 A.D.2d 562, 387 N.Y.S.2d 16 (2d Dep't 1976).

[F] The Charge

The court's charge to the jury serves principally to define the issues in contention and to instruct the jury how to go about resolving them; the charge serves secondarily to record the court's holding on the law for purposes of appellate review. Guidelines for the substance of the charge can be found in New York Pattern Jury Instructions. In summary, this guide suggests that a proper charge include an identification of the parties, a statement of their opposing contentions, a definition of the triable issues raised, instructions as to the process of decision and burden of proof, the proper measure of damages, and the required form of verdict.

CPLR 4110(b) allows parties to submit proposed jury instructions to the court. Objections to jury instruction must be made before the jury retires to consider the verdict, or are otherwise waived. One exception to the waiver provision occurs when a jury instruction is "fundamentally" erroneous. *See Di Grazia v. Castronova*, 48 A.D.2d 249, 368 N.Y.S.2d 898 (4th Dep't 1975) (charge that plaintiff had burden of proving freedom from contributory negligence was incorrect when contributory negligence in a vicious dog case is a defense and not an affirmative element of plaintiff's case; a new trial was therefore required in the interest of justice).

[G] The Verdict; Impeaching the Verdict

SCHABE v. HAMPTON BAYS UNION FREE SCHOOL DISTRICT
Appellate Division, Second Department
103 A.D.2d 418, 480 N.Y.S.2d 328 (1984)

LAZER, J.P.

Directly before us at last is the "identical five" issue — whether in a special verdict all answers approved by a five-sixths vote must have the concurrence of the identical five jurors. The appeal also presents the related question of whether a juror who has dissented from the answer to a special verdict question is bound by the answer as further questions are considered. Finally, we must decide whether it was error for the trial court to respond to the jury's inquiry during damage assessment by explaining how the award would be affected by their earlier apportionment of liability.

I

The action has its genesis in an injury suffered by Jennifer Schabe, a 12-year-old junior high school student who was struck by a school bus while running across the driveway of the Hampton Bays Jr.-Sr. High School. Although the ensuing lawsuit named the Hampton Bays Union Free School District, the Hampton Bays Jr.-Sr. High School, the East End Student Transportation Corp. and the bus driver as defendants, the plaintiffs subsequently settled their action against the bus company and the driver, leaving the school district and the school as the sole defendants. Despite the bus company's absence from the trial, its negligence remained at issue because section 15-108 of the General Obligations Law provides that the settling tort-feasor's settlement will serve to reduce the remaining tort-feasor's liability to the extent of the monetary settlement or the settling tort-feasor's proportion of fault, whichever is greater. The bus company's proportion of fault, if any, thus became a matter for resolution by the jury.

The trial revealed that upon dismissal of their classes on November 5, 1976, some of the junior high school students congregated at the front of the school in anticipation of boarding buses then parked in the school driveway. Although additional supervision of the departure process had been furnished on other days, on November 5 only one teacher was assigned to that task. Jennifer was standing near a small shuttle bus parked behind the other buses when yet another bus approached from the rear and was waved on by the shuttle bus driver. At that point, Jennifer ran into the driveway, slipped while trying to avoid the oncoming bus, and was pinned beneath its right front wheel.

The liability issues were submitted to the jury in the form of a special verdict containing seven written questions, the first six of which dealt separately with the issues of negligence and proximate causation relating to the conduct of the school district, the bus company and Jennifer. The seventh question asked the jury to apportion fault between these three named participants in the events at issue. In its charge, the trial court declared that at least five jurors would have to agree before any question could be answered but it was unnecessary that the same five agree on each answer. The jury was soon back with a request for guidance because different questions were drawing different dissenting jurors. After repeating its earlier instruction — that the law did not require that each answer be approved by the same five jurors — the court added that the dissenting juror "has to abide by the decision of the other five under our system," that the dissenter "has to go along with what the others do because five of the others are in accord" and that "once you decide one question on a five-sixths basis, the other dissenting juror must regard that as having been determined since five out of the six have spoken." This additional instruction drew a prompt exception from the defendants which argued that under the instruction a juror who disagreed as to the negligence of one of the participants in the events of November 5 would be unable to apportion liability between that participant and the others. The court denied the defendants' further request that the jury be told that in dealing with the separate questions of negligence and proximate causation as to any particular participant it was necessary that the same five jurors agree on both answers.

Upon return of the liability verdict, polling disclosed that on four questions answered by five-sixths vote, the majorities had not been comprised of the identical five jurors. In its answer to question 1, the jury unanimously found the school district negligent, but in answering question 2, juror number 2 abstained from his colleagues' finding that there was proximate causation. Responding to question 3, the jury found the bus company free from negligence, with juror number 4 dissenting; the next question relative to proximate causation was skipped because of this finding. By their fifth and sixth answers, the jury found Jennifer's conduct negligent and a proximate cause of the injury, but juror number 1 dissented. In their last answer, the jury apportioned 59% of the negligence to the school district and 41% to Jennifer, with juror number 2 dissenting.

After the trial proceeded through its damage phase, the jury was instructed to arrive at "a one hundred percent [dollar amount] and allow the Court to apply the necessary mathematics." Following brief deliberation, the jury inquired: "Is the dollar amount we agreed upon the exact amount Jennifer Schabe will be awarded or only a percentage?" Replying that the figure arrived at would be multiplied by 59%, the court reiterated its exhortation that the jurors find a "one hundred per cent valuation." The defendants then requested that the jury be instructed not to concern themselves with "any computations" in order to erase any feeling that the verdict should be adjusted to compensate for Jennifer's 41% responsibility for her injury. The request was denied. Still confused, the jury was soon back with its foreman informing the court that: "The concern of the jury was, sir, that the forty-one percent that's attributable to the Plaintiff in negligence would be subtracted from the fifty-nine percent." The court explained that Jennifer would receive 59% of the verdict and denied the defendant's request to charge that she would receive the entire amount awarded by the jury.

The jury subsequently returned a unanimous verdict of $750,000, from which the court deducted $225,000 (the value of the bus company's structured settlement), multiplied the remainder by 59%, and entered a judgment of $309,750 in favor of the infant plaintiff. Although the formula applied seems to be erroneous, it remains unchallenged on this appeal by the defendants, for they focus entirely on the significant issues we now discuss.

II

The Court of Appeals has never decided whether every nonunanimous answer in a special verdict must be approved by the identical five jurors. The Appellate Division, First Department, has held that any five jurors can answer questions in a general verdict accompanied by interrogatories (CPLR 4111, subd [c]), but even that issue was not before the Court of Appeals when it affirmed the judgment in that case (*see Bichler v Lilly & Co.*, 79 AD2d 317, *affd* 55 NY2d 571). The trial courts have divided on the question (*compare Aiello v Wenke*, 118 Misc 2d 1068; *Forde v Ames*, 93 Misc 2d 723; *Reed v Cook*, 103 NYS2d 539; . . . [any five], *with Cohen v. Levin*, 110 Misc 2d 464; *Murphy v Sherman Transfer Co.*, 62 Misc 2d 960 [the identical five]) as have jurisdictions across the country. . . .

Majority verdicts and special verdicts are hardly novel to the judicial process, but these days their joinder complicates a litigation scene in which the issues are complex enough without additional problems stemming from the identity of the majorities who voted in favor of certain answers (*see* Comment, *Vote Distribution in Non-Unanimous Jury Verdicts,* 27 Wash & Lee L Rev 360). Since the requirements for unanimity in civil cases was abandoned in this State in 1937 (*see* former Civ Prac Act § 463-a, added by L 1937, ch 120; NY Const, art I, § 2; Note, 37 Col L Rev 1235) and special verdicts have been with us since early common law, it is remarkable that the identity issue has never received final resolution in New York. CPLR 4113 (subd [a]) tells us that "[a] verdict may be rendered by not less than five-sixths of the jurors constituting a jury" and CPLR 4111 (subd [b]), authorizing special verdicts, also is barren of any hint that might help resolve the issue. It would seem apparent that the drafters of the two sections were oblivious to the problems that confront us now. In the absence of indications of intent in the statute relevant to the current issues, we are left to divine legislative purpose through the use of other construction devices.

One such device of universal acceptance is that rule that statutes be interpreted in light of the legislative reasons that brought about their enactment and that they be given meanings that serve rather than defeat those reasons. . . . The policy considerations underlying the abolition of the unanimity requirement are not difficult to discern. Nonunanimous verdicts decrease the number of mistrials and retrials and thus reduce court congestion, delay and the cost of maintaining the judicial system. They also reduce the number of unjust verdicts deriving from juror obstinacy or dishonesty and discourage compromise verdicts. . . .

The policy imperatives advanced by the abolition of the unanimity requirement are also furthered when special verdict questions can be answered by any five jurors rather than the same five that have approved all other answers. The "any five" principle reduces the number of mistrials and retrials while diminishing confusion for both court and jurors and it does not interfere with the operation of the jury or sacrifice fairness (*Juarez v Superior Ct.*, 31 Cal 3d 759, *supra*). There is no reason why a juror in an "any five" jurisdiction cannot decide a case just as conscientiously and well as a juror required to abide by an "identical five" mandate (*Ward v Weekes*, 107 NJ Super 351, *supra*). The identical five rule has been characterized as "mechanistic" and as not assuring additional fairness while substantially increasing the risk to hung juries and seriously undermining the usefulness and viability of laws that authorize majority and special verdicts (*see Tillman v Thomas*, 99 Idaho 569, 672, *supra*).

Although the arguments most often proffered to support the any five concept remain the strong public policy factors we have mentioned, there is yet another consideration that we all find compelling. The identical five concept tends to alter a fundamental premise of the jury system — that all members of a jury panel partake meaningfully in disposition of the case. Under the identical five principal, the casting of a dissenting vote on the question reduces the dissenter's influence to a state of practical impotence and creates a mandate for continued unanimity among the other jurors on the remaining questions if the verdict is to survive. The dissenter is then bereft of real voting power, for his vote on the remaining questions can no longer affect the verdict (*see Juarez v Superior Ct.*, 31 Cal 3d 759, *supra; Fields v Volkswagen of Amer.*, 555 P2d 48 [Okla]). With the dissenter stripped of the power to affect further answers, the six-person jury selected to decide the issues becomes for all practical purposes a jury of five because one member's opinion cannot be backed with a meaningful vote. . . .

Adherents of the identical five principle argue, however, that a verdict, whether general or special, is a nonfragmentable totality representing one ultimate finding, and jurors cannot be permitted to agree with only one part of the dispositions essential to the verdict. . . . They illustrate by noting that if two answers draw different dissenters, only four jurors have agreed on the ultimate conclusion (*see Dick v Heisler*, 184 Wis 77; Note, 3 Wis L Rev 51). Under this theory, a juror who dissents as to any of the answers cannot be counted in favor of the verdict and the fact that its form is that of a special verdict is immaterial (*see Plaster v Akron Union Passenger Depot Co.*, 101 Ohio App 27, *supra*).

Although application of the any five rule to verdicts that contain interrogatories is rooted in strong public policy considerations that transcend the origin of special verdicts, the historic basis for treating general and special verdicts differently still retains significance. Special verdicts were introduced to the judicial process early in common law by jurors fearful that their general verdicts might offend the authorities. By answering factual questions without deciding the case directly, these early jurors sought to avoid the charge of attainder for a false verdict — a matter triable before an attaint jury whose members were of higher rank than ordinary jurors (Morgan, *A Brief History of Special Verdicts and Special Interrogatories*, 32 Yale LJ 575, 576; Clementson, Special Verdicts & Special Findings by Juries, p 5). From the time of its creation, a special verdict was not merely a reflection of a general verdict split into parts, but was a device for returning the facts only — leaving the legal consequences to the Judge (Clementson, Special Verdicts & Special Findings by Juries, p 5; Sun-

(2) What are the advantages of special verdicts? In *Russo v. Rifkin*, 113 A.D.2d 570, 497 N.Y.S.2d 41 (2d Dep't 1985), a dental malpractice case, the Appellate Division held that the lower court's refusal to honor a party's request to use special verdicts on the issue of comparative fault and total damages was an abuse of discretion:

> General verdicts have been described as being "as inscrutable and essentially mysterious as the judgment which issued from the ancient oracle of Delphi". . . . Whatever the acceptability of such determinations in less complicated times, in this era of complex issues and comparative fault, the necessity that appellate bodies be provided with some illumination of the jury's rationale has been rendered quite acute. In providing that illumination, the special verdict has the advantage of offering a more precise definition of the jury's finding . . . and it is for that reason that the appellate judiciary and legal commentators have repeatedly suggested that special verdicts or general verdicts with interrogatories be utilized in comparative fault cases.

113 A.D.2d at 572, 497 N.Y.S.2d at 43.

(3) CPLR 4111(d) was amended in 2003, to provide for the itemization of damages in medical malpractice cases so as to coincide with the structured judgment provisions of CPLR articles 50-A and 50-B. *See* Gleason, 2003 Practice Commentary, 7B McKinney's Consol. Laws of New York, p. 114, supplement.

SHARROW v. DICK CORP.
Court of Appeals
86 N.Y.2d 54, 629 N.Y.S.2d 980, 653 N.E.2d 1150 (1995)

Simons, Judge.

The dispositive issue in this appeal is whether the trial court erred in refusing to conduct a limited inquiry to determine whether six jurors participated in the deliberations on all the issues submitted to the jury. Because one juror's responses during the poll of the jury suggested she may not have participated in all of the jury's deliberations, we conclude that the order of the Appellate Division must be reversed, the judgment vacated, and a new trial ordered.

Plaintiff Lyndon Sharrow, an iron worker employed by third-party defendant G & H Steel, was injured while using a Genie hoist to move a metal lockbox during construction of the Southport Correctional Facility. He brought this action against defendant Dick Corporation, the general contractor, and defendant Southern Steel Corporation, the subcontractor for the project, alleging common-law negligence and violations of sections 200, 240(1) and 241(6) of the Labor Law. Defendants in turn brought a third-party action for contribution and indemnification against G & H Steel, plaintiff's employer. Prior to trial, Dick and Southern successfully moved for summary judgment against G & H Steel for common-law and contractual indemnification. At trial, plaintiff withdrew all his claims except that for violation of Labor Law § 241(6) and the action proceeded on that claim alone.

At the conclusion of the jury's deliberations, the foreperson announced that five members of the jury had agreed to a verdict finding defendants' violation of the statute the proximate cause of plaintiff's injuries and awarding him damages in the amount of $430,000. Counsel for G & H Steel requested that the jury be polled. Departing from the usual procedure, the court clerk conducted the poll by reading each question on the verdict sheet and then asking each juror in turn his or her verdict on the question.[1] When the first question was asked — whether there was a violation of the Labor Law for which defendants were liable — juror No. 5 stated that her answer was "No." The clerk then read the second question — whether the Labor Law violation was a proximate cause of plaintiff's injuries — and again asked each juror "[w]hat is your verdict?" The transcript reflects juror No. 5's reply: "Juror number five: I had no" — "The clerk: Your verdict is no? the court: Well, she didn't make a determination because she didn't move on [sic]." When the poll on the third question — concerning the total amount of damages necessary to compensate plaintiff — reached juror No. 5, she apparently did not immediately answer. The transcript contains this exchange: "The clerk: Number 5? No response? Juror number five: No." To the remaining three questions, involving specific items of damages and of plaintiff's possible negligence, juror No. 5 replied "No response."

At the conclusion of the polling and before the jury was discharged, counsel for G & H Steel asked to approach the Bench and the court temporarily excused the jury. Counsel identified what he believed to be an inconsistency in the damage amounts stated by the foreperson. He also raised the separate question whether juror No. 5's answers indicated that she had not voted on any of the questions after the first and may not have participated in the deliberations on any issue other than that of liability. Contending that G & H may have been deprived of a trial by a full jury of six members, counsel requested that the trial court conduct a "very limited questioning of this juror" to determine the extent of her participation in the deliberations. After discussion with all counsel, the trial court denied the request, and judgment was subsequently entered for plaintiff.

The Appellate Division, with two Justices dissenting, modified, by ordering a new trial on the question of damages for pain and suffering, unless defendants stipulated to an additur increasing the amount of that component of the award from $13,000 to $150,000 (204 A.D.2d 966, 612 N.Y.S.2d 537). The majority of the court rejected the contention that defendants and third-party defendant G & H Steel had been deprived of the constitutional right to trial by six jurors, contending there was no evidence that juror No. 5 had refused to participate, or been prevented from participating, in the deliberations. . . .

---

[1] Customarily, the reported verdict is read to the jury and then each juror is asked: "Is that your verdict?", to which the juror responds yes or no (see, Supreme and County Court Operations Manual, State of New York, published by Office of Court Administration [Jan. 1991]).

We agree with the Appellate Division dissenters that the trial court erred in refusing to conduct a limited inquiry to determine whether juror No. 5 participated in the verdict process, an error that implicates the constitutional right to a trial by a six-member jury and mandates a new trial.

The common law required a jury of 12 members, and a unanimous verdict (*see, Patton v. United States*, 281 U.S. 276, 50 S.Ct. 253, 74 L.Ed. 854; *Cancemi v. People*, 18 N.Y. 128). In 1935, however, article I, § 2 of the New York Constitution was amended to authorize a legislative enactment permitting five-sixths jury verdicts in civil cases. The right to a jury trial was constitutionalized in its present form in 1938, and by then the Legislature had already enacted former Civil Practice Act 463-a (now CPLR 4113[a]), authorizing the five-sixths verdict (*see generally*, 4 Weinstein-Korn-Miller, N.Y. Civ. Prac. ¶ 4113.01 et seq.). When the Legislature subsequently provided, in 1972, that a civil jury "shall be composed of six persons" (*see*, CPLR 4104), the question arose whether a unanimous verdict rendered by five jurors was as valid as a verdict rendered by five-sixths of a six-member jury. The intermediate appellate courts addressing the question were uniformly of the view that, absent the express consent of the parties, CPLR 4104 did not diminish a party's right to a jury of six sworn to try the issues, and that all six jurors must participate in the deliberations leading to the verdict (*see, Schabe v. Hampton Bays Union Free School Dist.*, 103 A.D.2d 418, 480 N.Y.S.2d 328; *see also, Waldman v. Cohen*, 125 A.D.2d 116, 512 N.Y.S.2d 205; *Measeck v. Noble*, 9 A.D.2d 19, 189 N.Y.S.2d 748).

In *Arizmendi v. City of New York*, 56 N.Y.2d 753, 452 N.Y.S.2d 15, 437 N.E.2d 274 we suggested our agreement with the view that the constitutional right to a jury trial contemplates that all six jurors participate in the deliberative process.[2] Because we determined that the defendants had waived their objection to a juror's nonparticipation by failing to raise it before the trial court, we did not directly address the issue then, but today we confirm that view and hold that where the parties to a civil case have not agreed to a trial by fewer than six jurors, a valid verdict requires that all six jurors participate in the underlying deliberations. The parties are entitled to a process in which each juror deliberates on all issues and attempts to influence with his or her individual judgment and persuasion the reasoning of the other five (*see, Schabe v. Hampton Bays Union Free School Dist.*, 103 A.D.2d 418, 427-428, 480 N.Y.S.2d 328, *supra*). A juror, having disagreed with the remaining five on liability, must still participate in the deliberations. Otherwise, the jury becomes in essence one of five members only, less than the required number, and no valid verdict results from the deliberative process.

---

2 Although *Arizmendi*, like this case, involved a unitary trial, the Committee on Pattern Jury Instructions subsequently applied *Arizmendi* to the more complex bifurcated trial as well, commenting that "[i]f there is a 5-1 vote on liability after the first stage of a bifurcated trial, all jurors, including the liability dissenter, are requied to participate in the assessmenet of damages" (*see*, 1 N.Y. PJI 2d 32-33 [1995 supp]).

Plaintiff urges that there is no evidence here that juror No. 5 did not participate in all the deliberations in this case. That, however, is precisely the reason that the trial court should have conducted the limited inquiry requested, to resolve the doubts engendered by her answers during the poll. The court had the power to inquire into an "imperfect or incomplete" verdict before discharge of the jury (*see, Porret v. City of New York*, 252 N.Y. 208, 211, 169 N.E. 280) or if there was substantial confusion or ambiguity in the verdict (*see, Pogo Holding Corp. v. New York Prop. Ins. Underwriting Assn.*, 97 A.D.2d 503, 505, 467 N.Y.S.2d 872, *affd.* 62 N.Y.2d 969, 479 N.Y.S.2d 336, 468 N.E.2d 291) and it should have done so. A contemporaneous inquiry would have provided it with the opportunity to remediate the problem, or, if necessary, to order a new trial if no other permissible remedy was available (*see, Barry v. Manglass*, 55 N.Y.2d 803, 806, 447 N.Y.S.2d 423, 432 N.E.2d 125).

An inquiry to clarify a verdict before discharging a jury must be distinguished from an attempt to impeach a jury's verdict after discharge. In considering the propriety of any posttrial inquiry into the validity of a verdict or indictment, the majority of jurisdictions have adopted, either by statute or in case law, the rule embodied in rule 606(b) of the Federal Rules of Evidence. It directs that a juror may not testify "as to any matter or statement occurring during the course of the jury's deliberations" except in cases when an inquiry into external influences on the jury is necessary. The policy considerations underlying this rule were first expressed by the United States Supreme Court in *McDonald v. Pless*, 238 U.S. 264, 35 S.Ct. 783, 59 L.Ed. 1300 when it addressed the admissibility of juror evidence impeaching, posttrial, a quotient verdict. In rejecting the use of the evidence, the Court identified three important policies to be furthered: ensuring the finality of verdicts, preventing juror harassment by disappointed litigants or their attorneys, and encouraging "frankness and freedom of discussion and conference" among the jurors (*id.*, at 267-268, 35 S.Ct. at 784-785; *see also, Tanner v. United States*, 483 U.S. 107, 120, 107 S.Ct. 2739, 2747-48, 97 L.Ed.2d 90; *see generally*, Cammack, *The Jurisprudence of Jury Trials: The No Impeachment Rule and the Conditions for Legitimate Legal Decisionmaking*, 64 U. Colo. L. Rev. 57 [1993]). Although New York has not adopted a statute similar to rule 606(b), our case law is consonant with its underlying principles (*see, Kaufman v. Lilly & Co.*, 65 N.Y.2d 449, 460, 492 N.Y.S.2d 584, 482 N.E.2d 63; . . .). None of the policies enumerated in *McDonald* is compromised when the trial court itself, prior to discharge of the jury and entry of the verdict, undertakes a limited inquiry into an inconsistency or ambiguity in the jury's verdict that is apparent from the jurors' responses during polling.

The polling process here revealed such an ambiguity. Even if "no response" is considered the equivalent of "no award" in reply to the questions on damages, juror No. 5 also offered "no response" to the question whether plaintiff had been negligent. Her answers raised a legitimate question whether juror No. 5 had participated in the jury's discussion of issues other than liability, and defense counsel appropriately requested a limited inquiry to clarify that juror No. 5 had participated in the deliberative process.

In *People v. Pickett*, 61 N.Y.2d 773, 473 N.Y.S.2d 157, 461 N.E.2d 294, we concluded that it was error for a trial court to refuse to conduct such an inquiry, to the extent that it could be carried out without infringing upon the secrecy or integrity of the jury's deliberations. Here, a simple inquiry by the trial court into whether juror No. 5 had deliberated on all the questions before the jury would have been well within permissible bounds (*cf., State v. Drowne*, 602 A.2d 540 [RI] [adopting *Pickett* guidelines for conducting the inquiry, but ruling Trial Justice's inquiry into juror's "uncertain" verdict was improper where juror discussed the specific factors she considered in arriving at her verdict and defense counsel was permitted to question juror]).

Because a Trial Judge has wide discretion in determining whether to send the jury back for further deliberations, had juror No. 5 revealed that she had indeed failed to take part in the entirety of the jury's deliberations, the trial court could have directed her to do so in a new round of jury deliberations. However, in the absence of any inquiry, the possibility remains that defendants' constitutional right to trial by a full six-member jury was compromised. Accordingly, we see no remedy but to order a new trial. Moreover, because third-party defendant G & H Steel's liability is entirely derivative, a new trial must be ordered with respect to the nonappealing defendants as well in order to afford complete relief to the appealing third-party defendant (*see, Cover v. Cohen*, 61 N.Y.2d 261, 473 N.Y.S.2d 378, 461 N.E.2d 864).

Accordingly, the order of the Appellate Division should be reversed, with costs, the judgment vacated and a new trial ordered.

[H] General and Special Verdicts

The next case illustrates the use of a general verdict accompanied by special interrogatories to the jury.

MARINE MIDLAND BANK v. RUSSO
Court of Appeals
50 N.Y.2d 31, 427 N.Y.S.2d 961, 405 N.E.2d 205 (1980)

FUCHSBERG, J.

. . . .

The bank has accused the defendants of "check kiting," a practice in which checks are drawn against deposits which have not yet cleared through the bank collection process (*see* Black's Law Dictionary [5th ed], p 783). . . .

. . . .

This action for fraud and conversion followed. . . .

. . . .

The verdict's form also gave rise to controversy. Pursuant to CPLR 4111 (subd [c]), the jury had been directed not only to return a general verdict but also to supply written answers to 12 interrogatories, the first 10 of which were to specify whether each of . . . five . . . defendants were liable, first in fraud and then in conversion. The eleventh inquired in what amount, if any, the jury determined that Marine Midland had been injured, and the last whether the bank's claims had been satisfied by a demand note of Produce personally indorsed by John and Rita.

The answers to each of the first 10 interrogatories found the defendants free from liability, while the eleventh, in an answer the bank insists was inconsistent with the first 10, nevertheless fixed its loss at $309,800. The twelfth interrogatory went unanswered, and the clerk never inquired of the jury whether it had reached a general verdict.

When the jury announced these conclusions, and before it was discharged, the bank, in moving to set aside the verdict, in essence confined itself to arguing that the answers to the interrogatories were inconsistent with one another. It did not object to disbanding the jury. It was not until two days later, when Marine Midland tendered its formal postverdict motions under CPLR article 44, that it also contended that the jury should have been asked to clarify its answers and that the absence of a general verdict was a fatal defect. The Trial Judge denied the motions in their entirety.

We begin by observing that the trial court acted well within its power in posing the interrogatories it submitted to the jury. Doing so, it employed a technique especially well suited to cases with multiple parties and legal theories. . . .

Moreover, the options available to a Judge who has followed such a course, when confronted with apparent inconsistencies in a jury's determinations under this hybridization of general and special verdicts, are controlled by CPLR 4111 (subd [c]). The design of this section was alleviation of injustices not infrequently produced by the prior *ad hoc* approach to inconsistent verdicts. . . . In the main, it provides that, if a jury's answers to interrogatories are consistent with one another, but one or more is in conflict with the general verdict, the court has discretion to order a new trial or require the jury to reconsider or enter judgment according to the answers. But, if answers are inconsistent with one another and one or more conflicts with a general verdict, the court's alternatives are limited to ordering reconsideration or a new trial.

In terms of the case before us, while, of course, an explicit direction to the jury that it render its general verdict on the basis of its answers to the interrogatories might have been a wise precaution militating against inconsistency, Marine Midland's challenge to the result is ultimately defeated in any event on the threshold ground that the answers were in fact completely consistent. The jury unequivocally found no liability on the part of any defendant. And, its answer to question 11, while fixing the amount of the bank's loss, was by no means to be taken as an allocation of responsibility to the defendants, an assumption that would have been at odds with the definitive determinations that preceded it.

Nor was the jury's failure to report a general verdict fatal. Even if the bank had timely complained of its absence and a verdict adverse to the defendants had thereafter been pronounced, CPLR 4111 (subd [c]) would still have permitted the court to prefer the specific over the general by entering judgment in accordance with the answers the interrogatories had induced. Even more dispositively, we need not dwell on these hypotheses, for Marine Midland must be deemed to have waived its objections by failing to press them when it would have been possible to prevent or correct the "error." For, as indicated earlier, the bank neither pointed out the probably inadvertent failure to state a general verdict on the record nor requested that the jury be instructed to reconsider the case before it was discharged and beyond recall.

. . . .

NOTES

(1) The general verdict accompanied by interrogatories is something of a compromise between general and special verdicts. While a general verdict is rendered by the jury, the components of the jury verdict are also revealed. As described in the principal case, CPLR 4111(c) allows a trial judge to overlook inconsistencies between the interrogatory answers and the general verdict only where there are no inconsistencies within the answers themselves. Does this rule in effect allow a verdict when the jury really could not decide the case, or was confused about what was to be decided?

(2) If you had been the trial judge in *Marine Midland Bank v. Russo*, and if the bank had made its motion in a proper and timely fashion, how would you have ruled?

(3) In *Alford v. Sventek,* 53 N.Y.2d 743, 439 N.Y.S.2d 339, 421 N.E.2d 831 (1981), it was held that one juror's unauthorized visit to the accident scene did not poison the verdict for defendant since there was no actual prejudice. A poll of the jurors disclosed that the other five jurors had not been influenced, as they voted for defendant while the errant juror consistently voted for plaintiff. The court observed that plaintiff could not claim prejudice since this juror was favorable to him. In the opinion, the Court referred to, but found inapplicable, the exception to the general rule allowing impeachment of the verdict based on conduct not taking place in the jury room. In addition to unauthorized viewing, this had been held to include misstatements of a juror during *voir dire*. *People v. Leonti,* 262 N.Y. 256, 186 N.E. 693 (1933).

Some kinds of juror misconduct are ascertainable from the verdict itself in the context of the trial. See the discussion of the "compromise" verdict in *Figliomeni v. Board of Education,* 38 N.Y.2d 178, 379 N.Y.S.2d 45, 341 N.E.2d 557 (1975), § 19.04, *infra.*

(4) In a criminal case, *People v. Maragh,* 94 N.Y.2d 569, 708 N.Y.S.2d 44, 729 N.E.2d 701 (2000), the rule was observed that generally the verdict may not be impeached by probes into the jury's deliberative process; but in this case a nurse on the jury offered her professional opinion of the medical evidence to the other jurors and this was found prejudicial to the defendant. Can we suppose the same ruling would be applied in a civil case?

(5) Uniform Rule 220.10, 22 NYCRR, allows the judge to permit jurors to take notes. Guidelines for the use of the notes are set forth, *e.g.,* note-taking should not be a distraction; any notes are only for the purpose of memory refreshment.

§ 19.04 POST-TRIAL MOTIONS

COHEN v. HALLMARK CARDS, INC.
Court of Appeals
45 N.Y.2d 493, 410 N.Y.S.2d 282, 382 N.E.2d 1145 (1978)

GABRIELLI, J.

The question presented on this appeal is whether the Appellate Division was correct in concluding as a matter of law that the jury verdict awarding punitive damages to plaintiffs was based on insufficient evidence. For the reasons discussed below, we disagree with the conclusion reached by the Appellate Division, and thus the order appealed from must be reversed.

The plaintiffs in this action are a professional model and her daughter. In October, 1966, several pictures of the mother holding her then infant child were taken by one Ken Heyman, a professional photographer. On June 1, 1971, Heyman sold those pictures to defendant Hallmark Cards, Inc. (Hallmark), for publication in a collection of photographs entitled "Love Is Now" which was to be sold to the public by Hallmark for its profit. At that time, Heyman orally assured Hallmark that he had obtained written releases from plaintiffs. Additionally, Heyman represented in writing that use of the photographs by Hallmark would not infringe on the rights of others. Hallmark made no request for a copy of the written consents, and instead began printing the pictures and selling them in its publication.

In November, 1971, Heyman sent plaintiffs a letter advising them of the sale of their pictures, and asking them to sign written releases. He also sent them a copy of the Hallmark publication including their pictures. On December 8, 1971, plaintiffs' counsel informed Hallmark in writing that plaintiffs had never consented to the use of their pictures by Hallmark, and requested Hallmark to stop using the pictures. Hallmark made no reply to that letter. Instead, on December 21, 1971, Hallmark wrote to Heyman, asking if he had written releases from plaintiffs. On advice of his counsel, Heyman did not respond. Hallmark made no other attempts to learn if indeed there existed written consents to the use of plaintiffs' pictures. In late December, 1971, not having received any reply to their letter, plaintiffs commenced this action by service of a summons. On December 27, 1971, Hallmark ordered a new printing of the publication containing plaintiffs' pictures; and on February 10, 1972, without any further inquiry, Hallmark ordered yet another printing. Finally, on or about February 23, plaintiffs served a complaint, seeking injunctive relief as well as both compensatory and punitive damages. During the following few months, Hallmark ordered additional printings of the publication containing plaintiffs' pictures.

This action was commenced pursuant to section 51 of the Civil Rights Law, which provides for enforcement of New York's statutory right of privacy. In pertinent part, section 51 reads as follows: "Any person whose name, portrait or picture is used within this state for advertising purposes or for the purposes of trade without the written consent first obtained as above provided may maintain an equitable action in the supreme court of this state against the person, firm or corporation so using his name, portrait or picture, to prevent and restrain the use thereof; and may also sue and recover damages for any injuries sustained by reason of such use and if the defendant shall have knowingly used such person's name, portrait or picture in such manner as is forbidden or declared to be unlawful by the last section, the jury, in its discretion, may award exemplary damages."

Following a trial, the jury found in favor of plaintiffs, awarding them nominal compensatory damages as well as a total of $50,000 in punitive damages. Hallmark appealed solely from the award of punitive damages. It should be noted that Hallmark has not challenged the award of compensatory damages, nor does it contest the factual determination necessary to support such damages, namely, that it used plaintiffs' pictures "for advertising purposes or for the purposes of trade without the written consent" of plaintiffs. Rather, Hallmark contends that the factual conclusion that it acted knowingly, without which no award of punitive damages is available under the statute, was not founded on evidence sufficient to support such a conclusion. After reviewing the evidence presented at trial, the Appellate Division concluded that "there was insufficient evidence submitted to the jury to warrant a finding of knowing use of a photograph without written consent" (58 AD2d 770, 771). Accordingly, that court deleted the award of punitive damages as a matter of law. That decision cannot stand.

The Appellate Division decision did not turn on the factual question whether the jury determination was against the weight of the evidence. Rather, it was based on the legal issue whether there was sufficient evidence to support the factual finding that Hallmark acted knowingly. Although these two inquiries may appear somewhat related, they actually involve very different standards and

distinguish b/t

may well lead to disparate results. Whether a particular factual determination is against the weight of the evidence is itself a factual question. In reviewing a judgment of Supreme Court, the Appellate Division has the power to determine whether a particular factual question was correctly resolved by the trier of facts. If the original fact determination was made by a jury, as in this case, and the Appellate Division concludes that the jury has made erroneous factual findings, the court is required to order a new trial, since it does not have the power to make new findings of fact in a jury case. . . . The result is, of course, different in cases not involving the right to a jury trial, since then the Appellate Division does have the power to make new findings of fact. . . . In either situation, the determination that a factual finding was against the preponderance of the evidence is itself a factual determination based on the reviewing court's conclusion that the original trier of fact has incorrectly assessed the evidence. . . .

Here –
AD didn't look @ fact finders
determination, but whether TT met burden of proof.

In this case, however, the Appellate Division has not merely determined that the jury incorrectly decided the factual question whether Hallmark acted knowingly. In fact, the Appellate Division has not reviewed the factual conclusions reached by the jury. Rather, the Appellate Division has held that plaintiffs failed to present sufficient evidence to support the conclusion that Hallmark acted knowingly. In a jury case, the result of such an inquiry is of considerably greater significance than is a determination that a factual conclusion is against the weight of the evidence, for in the former case the result is a final judgment, while in the latter the result must be merely a new trial (. . . *see, also,* Siegel, New York Practice, §§ 405-406). Thus, the question whether a verdict is against the weight of the evidence involves what is in large part a discretionary balancing of many factors (*see Mann v Hunt*, 283 App Div 140). For a court to conclude as a matter of law that a jury verdict is not supported by sufficient evidence, however, requires a harsher and more basic assessment of the jury verdict. It is necessary to first conclude that there is simply no valid line of reasoning and permissible inferences which could possibly lead rational men to the conclusion reached by the jury on the basis of the evidence presented at trial.

(1)

Dir. verdict standard

The criteria to be applied in making this assessment are essentially those required of a Trial Judge asked to direct a verdict. It is a basic principle of our law that "it cannot be correctly said in any case where the right of trial by jury exists and the evidence presents an actual issue of fact, that the court may properly direct a verdict" (*McDonald v Metropolitan St. Ry.*, 167 NY 66, 69-70; . . .). Similarly, in any case in which it can be said that the evidence is such that it would not be utterly irrational for a jury to reach the result it has determined upon, and thus a valid question of fact does exist, the court may not conclude that the verdict is as a matter of law not supported by the evidence. . . .

If you lose dir. verdict, ct. can't say evidence can't support verdict as a matter of law

Applying these principles to the present case, we conclude that the Appellate Division erred in finding the evidence insufficient as a matter of law to support the factual conclusion that Hallmark acted knowingly. While there is, of course, no evidence that Hallmark knew prior to December, 1971 that it did not have written consent to use plaintiffs' pictures, the same cannot be said of the period subsequent to December 8, 1971, the date on which plaintiffs first notified Hall-

turn is end

[handwritten margin note at top: Not whether AD thought evidence was sufficient, but rather whether jury was irrational in their determination. There was a question of fact]

[handwritten margin note right: so, can't say — no [?] for IT as a matter of law]

mark that they had not given their consent to the commercial use of their pictures. Even assuming, arguendo, that this express notification itself did not suffice to inform Hallmark that the plaintiffs had not consented to the use of their pictures, it was not irrational for the jury to conclude on the basis of this plus the evidence that Hallmark continued to print the pictures even after Heyman had failed to reply to its query, that by the time the complaint in this action was served in February, 1972, Hallmark was acting either with actual knowledge, or at the very least with a reckless disregard for the truth of plaintiffs' assertions. . . . Since there did exist a question of fact which was properly submitted to the jury, it was error for the Appellate Division to conclude that there was insufficient evidence to sustain the factual determination of that jury.

[handwritten margin note: question of fact did exist]

This is not to say, however, that the factual determination at issue was correctly made. As was noted above, the Appellate Division has authority to review findings of fact made by the jury, and to decide whether such determinations are in accord with the weight of the evidence. Since the Appellate Division has not yet reviewed the facts in this case, we must remit to that court for exercise of its power to review the facts (CPLR 5613).[4] In light of the procedural posture of the case and our limited jurisdiction to review questions of fact (NY Const, art VI, § 3), we express no opinion as to whether the determination that Hallmark acted knowingly is in accord with the weight of the evidence. The question of imputation of knowledge is a question of fact which must be resolved in light of all the circumstances of the case. We would note, however, that in many instances the imputation of knowledge, and its concomitant responsibility, may not be avoided by the simple expedient of closing one's eyes, covering one's ears, and holding one's breath.

[handwritten margin note: AD should have)]

Accordingly, the order appealed from should be reversed, with costs, and the case remitted to the Appellate Division for further proceedings in accord with this opinion.

. . . .

NOTES

(1) According to the Appellate Division's opinion, reversed by the principal case:

> In the case at bar, Hallmark relied on the representations of the professional photographer that a written release was executed. When Hallmark received the letter from plaintiffs' counsel, it already had begun publication and incurred considerable expenditures of money. Hallmark had to weigh the written contract it had with a professional pho-

---

[4] Should the Appellate Division conclude that the factual determination that Hallmark acted knowingly was in accord with the weight of the evidence, it may then exercise its discretionary jurisdiction to review the amount of exemplary damages awarded by the jury (*see Nardelli v Stamberg*, 44 NY2d 500, 503-504).

tographer, and his representation to them that he had obtained written releases, against an attorney's letter notifying Hallmark of an alleged impermissible use of certain photographs. Under these circumstances, we find that there was insufficient evidence submitted to the jury to warrant a finding of knowing use of a photograph without written consent within the intendment of section 51 of the Civil Rights Law. . . .

58 A.D.2d at 771, 396 N.Y.S.2d at 398.

Does the Court of Appeals convince you that this reasoning was incorrect?

(2) Is it appropriate for the court to weigh the credibility of the evidence in deciding a motion for a directed verdict or for judgment n.o.v.?

It has been held that the rule that the credibility of a witness who is a party to the action must be submitted to the jury is not absolute and inflexible and that, where his evidence is not contradicted by direct evidence nor by any legitimate inferences from the evidence and is neither improbable nor suspicious in nature and in part corroborated by other evidence, it may be given conclusiveness on a motion for a directed verdict. . . .

Tirschwell v. Dolan, 21 A.D.2d 923, 924, 251 N.Y.S.2d 91, 94 (3d Dep't 1964).

(3) How would you predict the Appellate Division would decide the issues remanded to it in the principal case? *See Cohen v. Hallmark Cards, Inc.*, 70 A.D.2d 509, 415 N.Y.S.2d 657 (1st Dep't 1979).

NICASTRO v. PARK

Appellate Division, Second Department
113 A.D. 2d 129, 495 N.Y.S.2d 184 (1985)

LAZER, JUSTICE PRESIDING.

Resolution of these appeals involves the proper standard to be applied by a trial court in deciding a motion to set aside a jury verdict as contrary to the weight of the evidence. At specific issue is the correctness of the trial court's grant of a motion to set aside a jury's verdict in favor of appellants in a medical malpractice action in which it was claimed that the death of Alexander Nicastro was brought about by the negligence of Drs. Fred Eugene Park and Richard H. Mermelstein, plus certain others against whom the complaint was dismissed during the trial. Since Dr. Mermelstein died prior to the commencement of the action and Dr. Park died subsequent to its commencement but before the trial, none of the principal participants in the events underlying the action survived to testify at the trial. As a result, all parties relied heavily on relevant medical records and other documentary evidence as well as upon portions of an examination before trial of Dr. Park. There was also, of course, testimony by numerous medical experts.

At the conclusion of the lengthy trial, the jury rendered a special verdict in favor of appellants. The first question relating to each appellant in the special verdict form was whether the defendant was negligent, and, as to each, the jury's answer was "no." The jury was also instructed that if it answered the negligence question affirmatively with respect to any defendant, it was to determine whether the negligence of that defendant was a proximate cause of Nicastro's death. The jury found that neither defendant was negligent and the proximate cause questions were thus never reached.

Upon hearing the jury's verdict, plaintiff moved to set it aside and for a new trial pursuant to CPLR 4404(a). . . .

We conclude that the trial court did not abuse its discretion in finding that the verdict was against the weight of the evidence. . . .

In contending that the trial court abused its discretion by setting aside the verdict as against the weight of the evidence, appellants vigorously argue that the court improperly substituted its judgment for that of the jury. The plaintiff responds that the strength of her proof of negligence was such that this court should not interfere with the discretionary action of the Trial Judge who was in a better position to assess the testimony. The question, then, is whether the court properly exercised its discretion under the circumstances.

Judicial dissatisfaction with jury verdicts is hardly a new phenomenon, although at one time the consequences of judicial displeasure were potentially somewhat greater. Blackstone noted that English judges were once permitted to fine, imprison or otherwise punish juries that persisted in returning verdicts contrary to the court's instructions in criminal cases, although the practice had been abandoned by the time the Commentaries were written (4 Blackstone, Commentaries on the Laws of England, ch. 27, at p. 361 [5th ed., 1773]).

On the civil side, it was well settled by Blackstone's day that a jury verdict could be set aside and a new trial ordered if the verdict was contrary to the evidence or if for some other reason it appeared that substantial justice had not been done. This was deemed to be an intrinsic part of a viable judicial system, for it was believed that the acceptance of clearly erroneous verdicts would cause the courts to fall into disrepute (see, 3 Blackstone, Commentaries on the Laws of England, ch. 24, at pp. 387-393 [5th ed., 1773]). Thus the doctrine that permits judicial interference with jury verdicts had its origin in the idea that for a judicial system to function properly it must be perceived by the public as normally reaching the correct result. While this certainly remains true, current concepts may have shifted the focus to the desire to provide every litigant with substantial justice.

The power to set aside a jury verdict and order a new trial is an inherent one which is codified in New York in CPLR 4404(a). That statute provides that a court may order a new trial "[when] the verdict is contrary to the weight of the evidence, in the interest of justice or where the jury cannot agree." The power is a broad one intended to ensure that justice is done, but the proper standard for setting aside a jury verdict is elusive and has long defied precise definition. Nevertheless, a close examination of the precedents reveals several principles that may be of assistance in outlining the parameters of the judicial function on such a motion.

Initially, it must be reemphasized that whether a jury verdict is against the weight of the evidence is essentially a discretionary and factual determination which is to be distinguished from the question of whether a jury verdict, as a matter of law, is supported by sufficient evidence (*Cohen v. Hallmark Cards*, 45 N.Y.2d 493, 498-499, 410 N.Y.S.2d 282, 382 N.E.2d 1145). As the Court of Appeals has observed, "[a]lthough these two inquiries may appear somewhat related, they actually involve very different standards and may well lead to disparate results" (*Cohen v. Hallmark Cards*, *supra*, 45 N.Y.2d at p. 498, 410 N.Y.S.2d 282, 382 N.E.2d 1145). To sustain a determination that a jury verdict is not supported by sufficient evidence, as a matter of law, there must be "no valid line of reasoning and permissible inferences which could possibly lead rational men to the conclusion reached by the jury on the basis of the evidence presented at trial". . . .

The criteria for setting aside a jury verdict as against the weight of the evidence are necessarily less stringent, for such a determination results only in a new trial and does not deprive the parties of their right to ultimately have all disputed issues of fact resolved by a jury. Whether a jury verdict should be set aside as contrary to the weight of the evidence does not involve a question of law, but rather requires a discretionary balancing of many factors. The discretionary nature of this inquiry has been further highlighted by various determinations of the Court of Appeals declining to review motions to set aside verdicts on the ground that it "cannot re-examine the Appellate Division's exercise of discretion" in this area.

The fact that determination of a motion to set aside a verdict involves judicial discretion does not imply, however, that the trial court can freely interfere with any verdict that is unsatisfactory or with which it disagrees. A preeminent principle of jurisprudence in this area is that the discretionary power to set aside a jury verdict and order a new trial must be exercised with considerable caution, for in the absence of indications that substantial justice has not been done, a successful litigant is entitled to the benefits of a favorable jury verdict. Fact-finding is the province of the jury, not the trial court, and a court must act warily lest overzealous enforcement of its duty to oversee the proper administration of justice leads it to overstep its bounds and "unnecessarily interfere with the fact-finding function of the jury to a degree that amounts to an usurpation of the jury's duty" (*Ellis v. Hoelzel*, 57 A.D.2d 968, 969, 394 N.Y.S.2d 91). This is especially true if a verdict is contested solely on weight of the evidence grounds and interest of justice factors have not intervened to flavor the judicial response to the motion. Absent such complications, the challenge is directed squarely at the accuracy of the jury's fact-finding and must be viewed in that light.

Analysis of the cases reveals that particular deference has traditionally been accorded to jury verdicts in favor of defendants in tort cases because the clash of factual contentions is often sharper and simpler in those matters and the jury need not find that a defendant has prevailed by a preponderance of the evidence but rather may simply conclude that the plaintiff has failed to meet the burden of proof requisite of establishing the defendant's culpability.

Thus, it has often been stated that a jury verdict in favor of a defendant should not be set aside unless "the jury could not have reached the verdict on any fair interpretation of the evidence." A similar "fair interpretation" standard has since come to be applied as well to jury verdicts in favor of a plaintiff (see, Moffatt v. Moffatt, 86 A.D.2d 864, 447 N.Y.S.2d 313, affd. 62 N.Y.2d 875, 478 N.Y.S.2d 864, 467 N.E.2d 528, supra), especially in these days of comparative fault.

The history of the fair interpretation standard indicates that it was intended to accentuate the principle that when a jury, upon being presented with sharply conflicting evidence creating a factual dispute, resolved the controversy in favor of the defendant upon a fair interpretation of the evidence, that finding should be sustained in the absence of some other reason for disturbing it in the interest of justice.

Although at first glance the fair interpretation phraseology might seem to reduce the weight of the evidence question to one of law, this merely serves to illustrate the danger of relying upon set phrases rather than underlying principles. Catechistic use of the terminology cannot transform an intrinsically discretionary judicial function into the more constrained approach appropriate to the resolution of a question as a matter of law. It is well settled that a motion to set aside a verdict as contrary to the weight of the evidence invokes the court's discretion, and resolution of such a motion involves an application of that professional judgment gleaned from the Judge's background and experience as a student, practitioner and judge (see, Mann v. Hunt, supra, 283 App.Div. at p. 141, 126 N.Y.S.2d 823; Siegel, New York Prac. § 406; 4 Weinstein-Korn-Miller, N.Y.Civ. Prac., par. 4404.09). The significance of the fair interpretation standard is that it provides a strong cautionary note by stressing to the court that the overturning of the jury's resolution of a sharply disputed factual issue may be an abuse of discretion if there is any way to conclude that the verdict is a fair reflection of the evidence.

It is significant, however, that the mere fact that some testimony in the record has created a factual issue does not deprive the Trial Judge of the power to intervene in an appropriate case. To require the complete absence of factual issues as a condition precedent to setting aside a jury verdict would indeed transform the question into one of law and would ignore the distinction between setting aside a verdict because of insufficiency and doing so because it is against the weight of the evidence. In comparing the two standards in the context of a plaintiff's verdict, we stated in O'Boyle v. Avis Rent-A-System (supra, 78 A.D.2d at p. 439, 435 N.Y.S.2d 296) that "[r]ationality, then, is the touchstone for legal sufficiency, while fair interpretation is the criterion for weight of the evidence." Although the language of the two inquiries, viewed out of context and without regard for conceptual distinctions, is not dissimilar, there is a real difference between a finding that no rational jury could reach a particular resolution and a finding that a jury could not have reached its conclusions on any fair interpretation of the evidence (*see, Cohen v. Hallmark Cards*, 45 N.Y.2d 493, 498-499, 410 N.Y. S.2d 282, 382 N.E.2d 1145, *supra; O'Boyle v. Avis Rent-A-Car System, Inc., supra*, 78 A.D.2d at p. 103, 435 N.Y.S.2d 296). Were this not so and if an absence of bona fide factual issues were required, a court would never be justified in setting aside a defendant's verdict as being against the weight of the evidence and ordering a new trial, for in each such case the proper remedy would be entry of judgment notwithstanding the verdict. Indeed, it is the existence of a factual issue which justifies the granting of a new trial rather than a directed verdict.

It is, perhaps, the adjective "fair" which differentiates the two ideas most aptly although the concept is as elusive as the standard it is used to illuminate. Webster's Third New International Dictionary defines "fair" as "characterized by honesty and justice: free from fraud, injustice, prejudice or favoritism." In a further comment, the same lexicographers distinguish "fair" from synonyms such as "just," "equitable," "impartial," "unbiased" and others by describing "fair" as the most general of the terms and implying "a disposition in a person or group to achieve a fitting and right balance of claims . . . or a quality or result in an action befitting such a disposition." "Fair" is thus a broad and multifaceted concept that at various times may include definitions adopted by courts in other jurisdictions which have resorted to synonyms such as just, equitable, evenhanded, honest, impartial, reasonable, upright and free from suspicion of bias (*see*, Black's Law Dictionary [4th ed.]; 35 C.J.S., Fair, 597).

However the particular Judge faced with deciding the motion to set aside might view the word "fair" if that were the sole ingredient of the fair interpretation formula, the fact remains that this is not the only ingredient. That respect which is to be accorded the jury's determination must enter into the decision as well. Combining these two factors, the rubric that a defendant's verdict in a tort case can only be overturned if a jury could not have reached it "by any fair interpretation of the evidence" simply restates the guiding principle that in reviewing the whole trial to ascertain whether the conclusion was a fair reflection of the evidence, great deference must be given to the fact-finding function of the jury. While this approach clearly tilts the scales in favor of a verdict's survival, it leaves the court with a breadth of discretion which obviously varies with the facts and events in each case.

Clearly, that discretion is at its broadest when it appears that the unsuccessful litigant's evidentiary position was particularly strong compared to that of the victor. At that point, the question is whether the result the jury reached is so contrary to the conclusion that might fairly have been reached on the basis of the evidence that the court should exercise its power to overturn the jury's determination. Upon appellate review of the exercise of that power, the Judge's presence during the trial is a significant factor. Not only has the trial court heard and seen the witnesses testify, but it also has had the opportunity to observe courtroom events that might have influenced the jury's evaluation of the evidence while not at the same time achieving a magnitude that would warrant reversal under the interest of justice provision of CPLR 4404(a). What emerges, therefore, as a principle of appellate review, is that the trial court's decision to exercise its discretion and order a new trial must be accorded great respect (see, e.g., Micallef v. Miehle Co., supra; Mann v. Hunt, supra; Siegel, New York Prac. § 406; 4 Weinstein-Korn-Miller, N.Y.Civ. Prac., par. 4404.06). That respect compels the appellate tribunal to view with liberality the trial court's disposition of a motion to set aside on evidentiary considerations — not only because the trial court is in the best position to properly assess the evidence presented at trial, but also because judicial independence of mind in making that determination is an essential "ingredient to the sound health of the judicial process" (Mann v. Hunt, 283 App. Div. 140, 141, 126 N.Y.S.2d 823, supra.) What the appellate court reviews, after all, is the conclusion reached by the judicial participant in the trial who has attempted to balance the great deference to be accorded to the jury's conclusion against the court's own obligation to see that the jury's interpretation of the evidence was fair.

Applying these principles to the case at hand, we conclude that the record was so replete with evidence of negligence that the trial court did not abuse its discretion in setting aside the verdict and ordering a new trial. Alexander Nicastro died on July 10, 1977 as a result of a coronary thrombosis due to occlusive coronary arteriosclerosis. Nicastro, then a 35-year-old welder who owned a small welding company, had previously been hospitalized twice due to chest pains indicative of a coronary problem. On both occasions Dr. Park, his family physician, was his attending physician. During the first hospitalization, in May of 1976, Dr. Mermelstein was called in for consultation because Dr. Park's limited privileges at the hospital required him to obtain consultation for treatment of cardiac failure. Although the evidence at trial indicated that Nicastro was suffering from a developing myocardial infarction, which is a result of arteriosclerosis, Dr. Mermelstein misdiagnosed the problem as a virally induced pleurodynia on the basis of test results which even appellants' experts admitted were inconclusive at best and in the absence of numerous symptoms normally associated with virally induced pleurodynia. Moreover, after making this diagnosis, Dr. Mermelstein withdrew from the case and did not follow up on those test results which were inconsistent with his diagnosis.

As to Dr. Park, the record indicates no attempt to follow up electrocardiograms and other test reports which suggested a developing infarction both before and after Dr. Mermelstein's withdrawal. Moreover, the record indicates that Nicastro, a heavy smoker and coffee drinker whose work involved physical labor, was released to normal activity. There is no indication that he was given any treatment or even advised to change his lifestyle to avoid coronary risk factors, despite Park's belief, as indicated by his testimony at an examination before trial, that Nicastro was disabled and unable to work from May 1976 to the date of his death because he suffered from a coronary insufficiency.

Similarly, during the second hospitalization in February of 1977, Dr. Park failed to order appropriate tests and appears to have discharged Nicastro without adequate treatment. Indeed, in June of 1977, Dr. Park filled out a Social Services form in connection with Nicastro's application for disability, in which he stated that Nicastro, a welder, suffered only from a "coronary neurosis," could work full time without limitation, and was receiving no treatment.

Although appellants' experts testified that Park and Mermelstein had acted in accordance with accepted medical standards in the community, they also agreed that the test results were inconclusive at best, that further testing would have been helpful, and that the records were barren of any indication of treatment for a coronary problem. Weighing the persuasive and consistent testimony of plaintiff's experts and the stark proof of the documentary evidence against the pro forma declarations of appellants' experts and the deference to be given the jury's reaction to what it saw and heard, we conclude that the trial court did not abuse its discretion in setting aside the verdict as against the weight of the evidence.

. . . .

NOTES

(1) If, as the main case states, "the standard for setting aside a jury verdict is elusive and has long defied precise definition," why isn't the court's exercise of this power a violation of the right to a jury trial, if not to due process of law? Is it a satisfactory answer that the grant of the motion leads only to another trial before a new jury? Or that the power was apparently well established in the colonial era, *see* discussion in the principal case as well as in *Galloway v. United States*, 319 U.S. 372, 63 S. Ct. 1077 (1943), and therefore has an historic claim to constitutionality?

(2) Why, as a matter of policy, should a judge be able to set aside the jury's determination of the facts? An often quoted justification is found in *Mann v. Hunt*, 283 App. Div. 140, 126 N.Y.S.2d 823 (3d Dep't 1953):

> The point of interference is not fixed on the caprice of judicial individualism; it is rather arrived at by a synthesis of all the experience that the judge has had: in the beginning as a law student, in the later controversies of law practice, in the hearing of cases and the writing of decisions, in the sum of all that he has absorbed in the courtroom and in the library.

> In the end it is an informed professional judgment; and although lawyers might differ greatly about how the components of the judgment are arranged and added up, there would be a very considerable

agreement about the result to be reached in any case once the facts were thoroughly understood.

126 N.Y.S.2d at 824.

But why should one person's professional judgment be more important on an issue of fact than the lay judgment of five or more?

FIGLIOMENI v. BOARD OF EDUCATION OF THE CITY SCHOOL DISTRICT OF SYRACUSE
Court of Appeals
38 N.Y.2d 178, 379 N.Y.S.2d 45, 341 N.E.2d 557 (1975)

FUCHSBERG, J.

The question presented on this appeal is whether, on setting aside an $18,000 jury verdict for plaintiff, on the ground of inadequacy, in an action for damages arising out of personal injuries, the trial court properly exercised its discretion in ordering a new trial on the issue of damages alone rather than on the issues of both negligence and damages.

Defendants, contending that an entirely new trial was required, argued that the verdict represented an impermissible compromise as to liability as well as damages, but the Appellate Division, Fourth Department, rejected that contention and unanimously sustained the trial court (40 AD2d 954). Upon retrial of the damages issue, this time before a Judge sitting without a jury, plaintiff received an award of $125,000, which, on plaintiff's appeal, was modified by the Appellate Division, which increased it to $175,000. (44 AD2d 886). Our court having dismissed defendants' motion for leave to appeal to us from the affirmance of the order granting the second trial on grounds of nonfinality (32 NY2d 686), the judgment entered after the second trial, as modified by the Appellate Division, pursuant to CPLR 5501 (subd [a], par 1), brings up for review the original order granting the new trial.

The judgment should be affirmed for the reasons that follow.

The proof of liability which the original Trial Judge had before him appears to have been considerable. On May 20, 1966, Rocco Figliomeni, then 14 years of age, had already long been a severely handicapped child. Among other things, he had but one eye, his I.Q. was 73 and, as a result of a preexisting pathological condition, the shape of his head in general, and the location of his eye in particular, were in the words of his trial counsel "distorted," "depressed," "indented" and "protuberant." Because of his condition, he was enrolled at one of defendant Board of Education's schools, in a special class for children with severe problems.

The defendant Joseph Gangemi was a teacher assigned to care for and instruct these children. The physical and athletic activities the children were permitted to engage in consisted merely of skipping, jumping and playing with a small soft ball. Nevertheless, Gangemi, in the course of play with the class, threw a hard baseball to Rocco; the ball apparently struck him on the head. Gangemi had never taken the trouble to read Rocco's available health card, which would have alerted him to the danger of exposing this child to such a potential source of injury, a fact underlined by the testimony of the school nurse. He conceded that, had he known the contents of the card, he would not have thrown the ball.

Confirmatory testimony as to defendants' departure from appropriate safety standards also came from Lauren B. Sutherland, a highly-qualified health education expert, as well from the published safety recommendations of the State Education Department. Any serious contest on this issue was dissipated when Genevieve Doud, a teacher called as a witness in behalf of the defendant, testified that she would not have allowed Rocco to engage in a game with a hard baseball, and that it was the duty of teachers assigned to children like Rocco to protect them against themselves. Indeed, just about the only attempt at a liability defense was defendants' rather feeble reliance on Gangemi's assertion that, from approximately a hundred feet away, the distance that he had propelled the ball, he could only see that Rocco's glasses fell from his face and that the ball dropped to the ground from the direction of the boy's upraised gloved hand. Though Rocco's own testimony, understandably in the light of his handicaps, was somewhat confused, the only other eyewitness testified that the boy was indeed struck in the head.

At the time of the occurrence, Rocco's immediate complaints were minimal. After first attending a class, he went home. Because of the onset of drowsiness from which he could not be aroused, he was hospitalized. Among other things, tests performed at that time showed deformation of the arteries in the left frontal area of his brain. Surgical inspection by means of a craniotomy, performed by drilling burr holes through the skull, were reported to have disclosed a splintered, depressed fracture of the frontal bone. In the same area, though, the surgery also revealed fibromatosis, which the patient was known to have had long before the accident and which is characterized by bony and soft tissue tumors. About a month later, it was discovered that the surgical wound had been permitted to become infected. This required further surgery to remove infected bone and left an area through which a part of the brain could be seen pulsating under a covering of skin.

Well over two years later, Rocco experienced the first of a series of episodes which have since turned out to be recurrent epileptic seizures. Before the epilepsy, Rocco had apparently enjoyed a sufficient recovery to enable him even to have taken gainful employment as "a food server or dishwasher." However, during the later convulsive episodes, on a number of occasions he fell and struck his head, thus sustaining additional injuries. By the time of the second trial, seven years after the accident, his seizures were still unrelieved.

At common law, if a verdict was required to be set aside for inadequacy or excessiveness, a new trial on all issues was ordered. . . . In more modern practice, however, and in New York since 1951, it has come to be recognized that, where liability and damages are neither intertwined nor the result of a trade-off of a finding of liability in return for a compromise on damages, the court is empowered to limit the new trial to the issue of damages alone. (CPLR 4404; . . . .)

Here, if the entire catalogue of Rocco's medical conditions is regarded as causally connected to the incident of the hard ball striking him, it was certainly well within the discretion of the Trial Judge to set aside the $18,000 verdict for inadequacy (*Crellin v Van Duzer*, 269 App Div 806; Damages — Injury to Head or Neck, Ann., 11 ALR3d 370, 687), and it was for him to determine whether retrial should be on the damages issue alone. But it did not necessarily follow that, because the damages were inadequate, they were the result of an impermissible compromise or, if they were, that the compromise reached the liability issue. It is only when it can be demonstrated that an inadequate verdict could only have resulted from a compromise on the liability issue that the court must revert to the former rule requiring retrial on all issues. As we analyze the case before us, it presents a multiplicity of factors militating against any necessary conclusion that the damages' inadequacy infected the liability determination.

Parenthetically, it should be noted that this case is not like those where an amount due is fixed and certain, indeed liquidated, as in some contract actions, so that, if a party recovers at all, he must recover the full amount (*Friend v Morris D. Fishman, Inc.*, 302 NY 389). In such cases, a compromise on the question of the underlying breach becomes self-evident. In contrast, it is the rule rather than the exception that, in cases calling for the monetary evaluation of bodily and emotional injuries and the frequently subjective pain and suffering that may flow from them, that a wide and diverse range of opinion is to be expected among triers of the fact, whether Judges or jurors. . . .

Interestingly, wise Trial Judges can usually gauge the character of jurors selected for a particular case and are able, with a remarkably high degree of accuracy, to predict how they will vote on specific issues in the case. . . . The Trial Judge here had that opportunity and was in a position to sense whether the liability, which seems, on the record here, so clear, nevertheless appeared to present any difficulty for the jury as the proof of it unfolded in his presence, or whether it was only the damages proof to which the jury was reacting adversely. Such things are properly to be taken into account by a Trial Judge on a motion which calls as much for a judgmental determination as did this one.

Important as such general matters are, the Judge here did not have to limit himself to them. Thus, it could not have been lost on him that the medical picture here was not cleancut (*see De Luca v Wells*, 58 Misc 2d 878; *cf. Simmons v Fish*, 210 Mass 563), but beset by many practical and psychological uncertainties. . . . True, the law tells us, and the Trial Judge told the jury, that the liability

of an original tort-feasor also encompasses any supervening medical malpractice which may occur in the treatment of the injuries, but it is one thing for a
Judge to have so charged and another for him to consider whether damages have
been fixed too parsimoniously because the jury was unhappy with the law it
heard. All the more may it properly have concerned him in the framework of a
situation where the 12 citizen-taxpayers on the jury had to bring in the verdict
against their own local school board of education and a member of its teaching
staff.

Also open to serious question was the attribution of the epilepsy to the accident. . . .

. . . .

Under these circumstances, we cannot say as a matter of law that either the
Trial Judge, in deciding to set aside the verdict for inadequacy, or the Appellate
Division, in affirming that exercise of discretion, abused their discretion in
limiting the second trial to the issue of damages alone. The original verdict, as
the record reveals, was consistent with the rationale of a principled and deliberate, though inadequate, view on damages and certainly does not represent the
kind of relinquishment of a conscientious conviction by some jurors on the
issue of liability in return for relinquishment of such convictions by others on
the issue of damages that mandates a new trial of all the issues. . . .

It should be said that the afore-mentioned considerations are, of course,
directed towards this case as it was presented at the initial trial. In the second
trial, limited to damages, the parties waived a jury. On the basis of the new
record made there, the Appellate Division had the power to modify the judgment. (CPLR 5522.) We find no reason to disturb the modification.

Accordingly, the order appealed from should be affirmed in all respects.

COOKE, J. (dissenting).

I dissent and vote to reverse and order a new trial on the issues of both negligence and damages.

Carried to its logical conclusion, an affirmance here is indicative of the elimination of the concept of compromise verdicts in all cases, save those in which
liquidated damages and fixed sums which may be calculated are demanded.

Generally speaking, since a verdict must be the product of a deliberate exercise of the jurors' judgments (*Hamilton v Owego Water Works*, 22 App Div 573,
575, *affd* 163 NY 562), a verdict which is clearly the result of a compromise and
unwarranted by the evidence will not be permitted to stand. . . . Of course, in
those matters where the amount demanded is unliquidated or where the amount
to be recovered is not a fixed sum which may be derived by mathematical computation, a verdict should not be disturbed merely because of a reconciliation of
differences of opinion among the individual jurors on the question of the dam-

ages . . . but one which evolves from a compromise, not merely as to amount but as to liability as well, will be overturned. . . .

. . . .

There is presented here the classic example of a compromise verdict. The amount awarded the infant son, by a 10 to 2 vote, was less than that granted the father on the derivative cause of action, the son's award being approximately the amount of the medical specials. . . . If this plaintiff was entitled to recover at all, it was in an amount greatly in excess of that reported by the jury. In view of plaintiff's life expectancy, the nature and extent of the skull and brain injuries, the extraordinary surgical procedures performed, the tragic residuals and their permanency, the court's charge as to loss of earnings ($4,587.20) as being a part of the son's recovery and to which instruction no exception was taken, and the plaintiff's own right to recover for future, prospective and contingent expenses . . . one must arrive at the inescapable conclusion of a compromise, such as was suggested in *Wiegand v Fee Bros. Co.* (73 App Div 139), where it appeared that "the rights of the defendant were bargained away upon the main issue whether it was negligent or not, in consideration of an understanding that it should not be beaten in too large an amount" (p 142). Parenthetically, the award which respondent asks this court to affirm is approximately 10 times greater than that of the jury which determined negligence.

CHIEF JUDGE BREITEL and JUDGES GABRIELLI and WACHTLER concur with JUDGE FUCHSBERG; JUDGE COOKE dissents and votes to reverse in a separate opinion in which JUDGES JASEN and JONES concur.

Order affirmed, with costs.

NOTES

(1) The main case illustrates two of the remedies available to a court which concludes that a jury erred with respect to damages: it may grant an entire new trial or it may grant a new trial on the issue of damages only. Why is the difference between the two crucial to the parties? When, if ever, should an entire new trial be granted because of an improper damage award after the decision in the principal case?

(2) Yet another remedy which may be used to correct a damages award is the conditional grant of a new trial. For example, a court which believes the jury's award to have been excessive can order a new trial unless the plaintiff agrees to accept a lesser amount deemed proper by the court. *E.g., Gary v. Schwartz*, 43 A.D.2d 562, 349 N.Y.S.2d 322 (2d Dep't 1973) (new trial of damages issue ordered unless plaintiff consents to reduce the verdict from $98,000 to $50,000). This is often referred to as remittitur. The converse, sometimes called additur, requires a defendant to choose between an increased damage award or a new trial. *See O'Connor v. Papertsian*, 309 N.Y. 465, 131 N.E.2d 883 (1956).

The additur and remittitur powers, like those described in note (1), may be exercised by either the trial judge or the Appellate Division. *See Cohen v. Hall-mark Cards, Inc., supra*; Weinstein, Korn & Miller, 4 N.Y. Civil Practice § 4404.06 (1982). Neither court may, however, simply order that a verdict be entered which is different from that awarded by the jury.

In 1986 the Legislature enacted CPLR 5501(c), which imposed the "materially deviates" test for the "shocks-the-conscience" test, *i.e.*, a court reviewing the jury's award of damages must set it aside "if it deviates materially from what would be reasonable compensation." The United States Supreme Court in *Gasperini v. Center For Humanities, Inc.*, 518 U.S. 415, 116 S. Ct. 2211, 135 L. Ed. 2d 659 (1996), held that a federal court in a diversity case should apply CPLR 5501(c) rather than the federal rule ("shocks the conscience") since it is a rule of substantive law. Limitations on awards, said the majority, have always been considered substantive.

(3) The compromise verdict problem usually arises when the jury is unable to agree on liability but is convinced that the defendant was injured. One way of avoiding the problem, therefore, is to bifurcate the personal injury trial into two stages: liability and damages. When this is done, of course, the jury will not learn the extent of the damages until it has found the defendant liable. For a striking example of a court's desire to keep the two issues separate, see *Monteleone v. Gestetner Corp.*, 140 Misc. 2d 841, 531 N.Y.S.2d 857 (Sup. Ct. 1988). Plaintiff, who was ten years old at the time of the trial, was born without arms or hands and without normal legs. He claimed that these birth defects were caused by his parents' exposure to the defendant's products. After ordering a bifurcated trial, the court granted defendant's motion to exclude the plaintiff from the court room during the liability trial, noting the boy's inability to assist counsel and the prejudicial impact his presence would have on the jury.

(4) How can jurors determine the proper award of pain and suffering damages when they are given no guidelines by the court? It has been argued that jurors should be given information about the range of awards made by other juries for similar injuries. Oscar G. Chase, *Helping Jurors Determine Pain and Suffering Awards,* 23 Hofstra L. Rev. 763 (1995).

(5) Improper behavior of a jury can be grounds for an entire new trial, in the "interest of justice," although in this case, the majority found insufficient evidence of misbehavior. The term "interest of justice" is an obvious catch-all, designed to allow a new trial whenever error by the court, the jury, or counsel has so tainted the verdict that a new trial is required.

The interest of justice may also require a new trial when there is newly discovered evidence. *See, e.g., McCarthy v. Port of New York Auth.*, 21 A.D.2d 125, 248 N.Y.S.2d 713 (1st Dep't 1964) (new evidence revealed gross fraud upon the court). To some extent, then, this motion resembles that allowed by CPLR 5015 for relief from a judgment (considered in Chapter 20, *infra*), except that the latter may be made after the expiration of the fifteen days permitted for motions under CPLR 4404. *See* CPLR 4405.

(6) In addition to compensatory damages, courts sometimes award punitive damages against a defendant that has engaged in reprehensible conduct. The purpose is to punish the defendant and deter similar future conduct. In a series of cases beginning with *Pacific Mutual Life Insurance Co. v. Haslip*, 499 U.S. 1, 111 S. Ct. 1032, 113 L. Ed. 2d 1 (1991), the United States Supreme Court has developed a set of guidelines founded in the Due Process Clause that restrict the amount of punitive damages that may be awarded and the procedures used to determine tham. In *Haslip*, the punitive damage award came to more than 200 times plaintiff's out-of-pocket expenses (but only four times compensatory damages) and was far in excess of any fine that could have been levied under state law for defendant's misappropriation. The Court held that the defendant's rights were not violated because the judge's instructions to the jury regarding punitive damages were reasonably precise, because the judge conducted an adequate post-verdict hearing to review the punitive award, and because the state appellate court applied the correct standards in reviewing the award.

The Supreme Court considered another due process challenge to a punitive damage award in *TXO Production Corp. v. Alliance Resources Corp.*, 509 U.S. 443, 113 S. Ct. 2711 (1993), a case in which the punitive damages were over five hundred times the amount of the compensatory award. Nonetheless, the Court (three Justices dissenting) upheld the award on the grounds that the procedures followed were fair and the jury's determination was not necessarily "grossly excessive."

In *BMW of North America, Inc. v. Gore*, 517 U.S. 559, 116 S. Ct. 1589, 134 L. Ed. 2d 809 (1996), however, the Court held that an award of two million dollars in punitive damages violated the defendant BMW's due process rights because the amount was so disproportionate to the wrong. The defendant was found to have sold cars as new when they had in fact been damaged in shipping and repainted. Plaintiff was awarded compensatory damages of $4,000. A three-factor test for determining excessiveness was set forth: 1) the degree of reprehensibility of the defendant's conduct; 2) the ratio between the harm suffered by the plaintiff and the amount of punitive damages; and 3) the difference between the punitive damages awarded by the jury and the civil or criminal sanctions authorized or imposed for comparable misconduct. 517 U.S. at 574-75. While eschewing any hard-and-fast rule, the Supreme Court noted that a punitive damage award that did not exceed a single-digit multiplier of compensatory damages would ordinarily be reasonable. The Court applied the *Gore* test in *State Farm Mutual Automobile Insurance Co. v. Campbell*, 538 U.S. 408, 128 S. Ct. 1513, 155 L. Ed. 2d 585 (2003), and struck down an award of $145 million against an insurer that had engaged in a pattern of bad faith refusals to settle claims against its insureds. *See* Newman & Ahmuty, *Review of Punitive Damages*, N.Y.L.J., Oct. 4, 2006, p.3 (describing and analyzing this case law); Theodore Eisenberg et al., *Juries, Judges, and Punitive Damages: An Empirical Study*, 87 Cornell L. Rev. 743 (2002) (showing no substantial difference in the rate or amount of punitive damage awards made by juries and judges).

The Supreme Court further limited the availability of punitive damages in *Philip Morris USA v. Williams*, __ U.S. __, 127 S. Ct 1057 (2007), in which the Court remanded an Oregon decision awarding $79.5 million to the estate of a deceased smoker. The jury had found that smoking had caused the death and that the decedent had continued smoking because the defendant Philip Morris had deceived him into thinking it was safe to do so. The Supreme Court held that the lower court had erred in apparently allowing the jury to award punitive damages to punish the defendant for harm done to other smokers who were not parties to the action. The case is the first in which the Supreme Court made clear that the Due Process Clause prohibits the imposition of punitive damages for harm done to strangers to the litigation.

Part Six
THE EFFECTS OF THE LITIGATION

Chapter 20

JUDGMENTS AND RELIEF FROM JUDGMENTS

§ 20.01 THE JUDGMENT

CPLR 5011 defines a judgment as the determination of the rights of the parties in an action or a special proceeding. The actual judgment itself is prepared by the attorney for the victorious party, signed by the clerk and served on the losing party. It should include a clear statement of the relief to which the parties are entitled.

CPLR 5016 sets out the procedure for entering judgment, basically the signing and filing of the judgment by the clerk and the recording of it in a "judgment-book." *See also* CPLR 9702(1). It is the first in a series of steps that must be taken to perfect a judgment and to permit enforcement of it. Entry is also important because service of notice of entry of the judgment together with a copy of the judgment on a party, starts the thirty-day period which the party receiving notice has to take an appeal. CPLR 5513. CPLR 5017(a) provides that the judgment-roll shall be filed at the time judgment is entered, and CPLR 5017(b) defines the content of the judgment-roll. Prompt preparation and filing of the judgment-roll are important for a number of reasons. Under CPLR 5018(a), a judgment is not docketed until "immediately after filing the judgment-roll." Docketing, as described in CPLR 5018(c), is the recording of the judgment in a proper "docket book," a book kept by the clerk as a kind of judgment ledger. Docketing is one prerequisite to the securing of a judgment lien on the judgment debtor's real property under CPLR 5203(a) and to the issuance of an execution under CPLR 5230(b). Furthermore, pursuant to CPLR 5526, the record on appeal from a final judgment must include the judgment-roll. CPLR 5018 controls the mechanics of docketing of judgments.

§ 20.02 THE STRUCTURED JUDGMENT

In 1985 and 1986, the Legislature enacted CPLR Articles 50-A and 50-B respectively, which created the device applicable in personal injury cases known as the structured judgment, explained in the following case. The purpose behind the structured judgment was to lower malpractice and liability insurance premiums by the purchase of an annuity which would reduce the money actually paid out by the insurer. The annuity would apply when future damages were found to exceed $250,000. Prior to this legislation, future damages in any amount were payable in a lump sum, as were all other damages.

ROHRING v. CITY OF NIAGARA FALLS
Court of Appeals
84 N.Y.2d 60, 614 N.Y.S.2d 714, 638 N.E.2d 62 (1994)

SIMONS, JUDGE.

Plaintiff Eric Rohring suffered a serious foot injury while working on a construction site when his safety belt broke and he fell 20 feet to a concrete pavement. At the time, he was employed by third-party defendant Falls Steel Erectors, Inc. on a project for the defendant and third-party plaintiff, City of Niagara Falls. Rohring was granted summary judgment on the issue of liability and subsequently a trial was conducted which resulted in an award of $2,501,311 for past and future damages.[1] Thereafter, the trial court structured the award pursuant to CPLR article 50-B.

These cross appeals present two issues concerning the calculation of plaintiff's judgment. First, we are asked to review that part of the award for attorney's fees based on future damages. Second, the parties dispute the methodology employed by the courts below in calculating interest on future damages pursuant to CPLR 5002. For the reasons which follow, we agree with the computations of the Appellate Division and therefore affirm.

I

CPLR article 50-B was enacted in 1986 as part of the State's effort at tort reform (*see*, L.1986, ch. 682, § 9). In its essential features it closely parallels CPLR article 50-A, which had been enacted a year earlier in response to concerns about the increasing size of verdicts in medical and dental malpractice actions (*see generally*, Siegel, Practice Commentaries, McKinney's Cons. Laws of N.Y., Book 7B, CPLR art. 50-A, at 711, and CPLR art. 50-B, at 730-731). Though the statutory scheme of article 50-B is technical and complicated, its basic operation is easily stated. Past damages are paid in a lump sum (CPLR 5041[b]). Future damages, which are awarded by the jury without reduction to present value (CPLR 4111[f]), are bifurcated for purposes of article 50-B. The first $250,000 is paid as a lump sum (CPLR 5041[b]). The remainder, after the subtraction of attorney's fees and other adjustments, is to be paid in periodic installments (CPLR 5041[e]). To provide for these periodic payments, subdivision (e) further specifies that defendants are to purchase an annuity contract.

Addressing first the payment of attorney's fees based on the future damages award, CPLR 5041(c) states that such attorney's fees are payable in a lump sum "based on the present value of the annuity contract" called for in subdivision (e). Subdivision (e), in turn, says: "After making any adjustment [including that for attorney's fees], the court shall enter a judgment for the amount of the present value of an annuity contract that will provide for the payment of the remain-

---

[1] Eric Rohring's wife, Charlene, was awarded $20,000 on her derivative claim. That claim is not before us on this appeal.

ing amounts of future damages." The subdivision states further that this calculation is to be done by applying the discount rate to "the full amount of the remaining future damages, as calculated pursuant to this subdivision." Concededly, the two provisions, when read together, leave in doubt whether the attorney's fees are to be deducted before or after the reduction to present value.

Based on its interpretation of the statutory scheme, Supreme Court determined the present value of the attorney's fees and then subtracted that amount from the gross (undiscounted) value of subdivision (e) future damages before structuring the remaining amount into periodic payments. The Appellate Division disagreed and held that the present value of the attorney's fees should have been subtracted from the present value of future damages (192 A.D.2d 228, 232, 601 N.Y.S.2d 740). The Court reasoned that Supreme Court's methodology improperly inflated the value of the periodic payments that plaintiff would receive.

We agree with the Appellate Division's conclusion. All parties acknowledge that the present value of attorney's fees is the appropriate amount to use in the calculation. The sole question is whether that amount should be subtracted from the present value of subdivision (e) future damages or the gross value of those damages. The problem is that article 50-B, like article 50-A, fails to make clear the sequence of calculations to be followed by a trial court in applying subdivision (c) and subdivision (e) (*see*, Argentine, *From Verdict to Judgment: The Evolution, Confusion and Reformation of CPLR Articles 50-A and 50-B*, 40 Buff.L.Rev. 917, 939; *see also, Frey v. Smith & Sons*, 751 F.Supp. 1052, 1056-1057; *Ursini v. Sussman*, 143 Misc.2d 727, 731, 541 N.Y.S.2d 916). Read literally, the two provisions are in fact circular: To determine the amount of attorney's fees, a court must first know the amount of future damages to be structured (subd. [c]), but to determine the amount of future damages to be structured, the court must first know the amount of attorney's fees (subd. [e]). Thus, this appeal requires us to decide whether the amount to be structured is reduced to the present value and then reduced by the present value of attorney's fees, or whether the present value of attorney's fees is to be determined and then subtracted from the gross amount, with the remainder to be structured as required by subdivision (e).

Because the statute is patently ambiguous and is impossible to apply as written, we turn for guidance to the underlying intent of the statutory scheme. Articles 50-A and 50-B are technical administrative schemes intended to regulate and structure payment, and they should not be construed in such a way as to increase the underlying liability owed by defendants. Plaintiffs are entitled to be made whole, as determined by the trier of fact, but have no right to overcompensation. The method selected by the Appellate Division is consistent with those principles. Under the Appellate Division's approach, the full amount defendants have to pay — that is, the combined sum owed to plaintiff and plaintiff's legal counsel — is the amount awarded by the jury (absent other adjustments required by the statutory scheme and not relevant here). Under

Supreme Court's approach, on the other hand, defendants' combined payment to plaintiff and to plaintiff's counsel would actually exceed the amount awarded by the jury.[2] That result is inconsistent with the purposes of articles 50-A and 50-B. Thus, we conclude that the proper methodology is to determine the present value of subdivision (e) future damages before attorney's fees and then reduce that amount by the present value of attorney's fees.

II

Defendants challenge the trial court's calculation of interest on the future damages. The proceedings here were conducted in two parts. On March 9, 1989, plaintiff was granted summary judgment on liability pursuant to Labor Law § 240. Some two years later, the parties tried the damages portion of the claim. The jury announced its verdict on February 14, 1991. Defendants concede that as a general rule in this type of action interest is calculated from the date liability is established, even though the damage verdict is handed down later (*see*, CPLR 5001[a]; 5002; *Love v. State of New York*, 78 N.Y.2d 540, 542, 577 N.Y.S.2d 359, 583 N.E.2d 1296). Under the *Love* approach, courts are authorized to engage in the legal fiction that damages were known and became a fixed obligation at the moment liability was determined. In the instant case, Supreme Court and the Appellate Division calculated interest on both past damages and the present value of future damages from March 9, 1989 (the date of liability).

Defendants concede that they are liable for interest from the date of liability for all damages incurred prior to that date. They assign error only to the trial court's calculation of interest on future damages. First, they contend that no interest should accrue before plaintiff actually incurred a cost. Only then, they

---

[2] Consider, for example, a $1,000,000 award of future damages (irrespective of any required statutory adjustments) where the discount factor is 10% and the attorney is entitled to one third. The following results would be achieved under the two proposed methods:

Trial court

Gross award of future damages	1,000,000
Present Value of fees	− 300,000 (one third of Present Value of award, as required by statute)
	700,000
Present value of 700,000	= 630,000

Appellate Division

Gross award of future damages	1,000,000
Present Value of award	900,000
Present Value of fees	− 300,000 (one third of Present Value of award, as required by statute)
Remainder	600,000

The plaintiff is, of course, entitled to either $1,000,000 in gross damages or $900,000 in present value damages. Under the trial court's methodology, however, defendants owe $930,000 in present value ($300,000 to the attorney and $630,000 to the plaintiff). Under the Appellate Division's methodology, defendants owe the proper amount, $900,000 ($300,000 + $600,000).

assert, does plaintiff have a valid claim against defendants, and only then should late payment be subject to interest. Thus, as defendants see it, damages incurred after March 9, 1989 should not have been subject to interest until the date plaintiff was in fact deprived of the particular item of loss to be compensated. Second, defendants argue that where part of an award of future damages is subject to the periodic-payment scheme of article 50-A or 50-B, no interest should accrue on that part of the award until a periodic payment is overdue. Defendants' theory is that plaintiff has no entitlement to the money until the payment becomes due, and only when a payment deadline is missed can interest properly be charged.

Analysis begins with language of the statutory scheme. CPLR 5001, 5002 and 5003 set forth the interest requirements for three distinct periods: Interest prior to verdict (CPLR 5001), interest from verdict to judgment (CPLR 5002) and interest from judgment to payment (CPLR 5003). CPLR 5002 states that interest shall be recovered "upon the total sum awarded . . . from the date the verdict was rendered." Accordingly, defendants' argument is undercut by the plain language of the statute: The "total sum awarded" is subject to interest on the date of verdict — no matter whether the award is to compensate future damages, past damages or both.

Defendants nonetheless believe the plain language of the statute should not govern if it results in a "windfall" to plaintiffs, as they believe it does. They rely upon *Milbrandt v. Green Refractories Co.*, 79 N.Y.2d 26, 580 N.Y.S.2d 147, 588 N.E.2d 45, where in a wrongful death case we held that future damages should be discounted to the date of liability, which by statute is the date of death, before interest is calculated on them. To do otherwise, we held, would be to create an interest windfall by allowing interest on money not owed to plaintiff inasmuch as defendant had an obligation only for the present value of damages at the date of liability (at 34-35, 580 N.Y.S.2d 147, 588 N.E.2d 45). Though EPTL 5-4.3(a) literally states that interest is to be paid upon the principal sum from the date of death, our Court declined to interpret that language as allowing an interest windfall (at 35-36, 580 N.Y.S.2d 147, 588 N.E.2d 45).

The question here, however, is not the question of discounting posed in *Milbrandt*. Future damages here were discounted. Instead, defendants contend that they had no liability whatsoever for future damages on the date of liability. Thus, the essential premise in defendants' theory of an interest windfall is that they have no liability for future damages until either an actual loss is incurred or until a periodic payment is missed. It follows, then, that even if we were to accept defendants' contention that no interest windfalls should be allowed, their argument fails if future damages are properly deemed to be liabilities fully owed by defendants as of the date of the liability verdict.

We conclude that they are. The structured judgment schemes of articles 50-A and 50-B do not delay liability. They do not alter liability by making it incremental, nor were they designed to match the timing of periodic payments to the timing of plaintiff's actual accrual of damages. Instead, the articles merely made payment incremental. Put simply, the CPLR altered how the liability was to be settled; it did not delay liability or even spread it out over a period of time. A defendant's obligation to a personal injury plaintiff encompasses both past and future damages and becomes fixed as of the date of the liability verdict. That articles 50-A and 50-B did not change that established rule is shown by CPLR 5046 and 5036, which govern adjustments in the payment schedule. Those sections allow the courts, in certain hardship circumstances, to abandon the periodic-payment schedule and order a lump-sum judgment. A plaintiff's right to seek such an acceleration is necessarily premised on a preexisting liability on the part of the defendant for the full amount of future damages, for nothing about the plaintiff's unforeseen hardship could rightfully be a basis for imposing a new liability on the defendant.

Thus, we hold that the future damages here were properly treated as a debt owed entirely as of the date of the liability verdict, and interest was properly charged against the present value of future damages from that date under CPLR 5002. That result is consistent with *Love* and *Milbrandt* and, most importantly, with the plain language of the statute.

III

Defendants have also contended on this appeal that Supreme Court improperly allowed a double recovery to plaintiff by admitting evidence of inflation at trial and then imposing the 4% annual adjustment allowed under CPLR 5041(e). They objected to neither the introduction of inflation evidence nor to the court's subsequent 4% computation, however, and thus the issue is not preserved for our review. Defendants' remaining claims do not provide legal grounds for reversal.

NOTE

The Court of Appeals again dealt with "structured judgment" issues raised by Articles 50-A and 50-B in *Bryant v. New York City Health and Hospitals Corp.*, 93 N.Y.2d 592, 695 N.Y.S.2d 39, 716 N.E.2d 1084 (1999). The decision, which involved consolidated medical malpractice actions, addressed three questions. The first was whether the annual payments that a plaintiff receives for future damages pursuant to CPLR 5031(e) should be based on the present value of the plaintiff's damages or on the (considerably greater) future value. The Court held that it should be the future value, reasoning that this best met the Legislature's intention of assuring the plaintiff full recovery for his loss. The second question was whether a plaintiff's attorney's fees, which are based on the present value of the future damages, CPLR 5031(c), should be calculated by including in the future damages the four percent upward adjustment that must be made to the plaintiff's annual payments under CPLR 5031(e). The Court held that the four percent should be included, explaining that this approach was consistent with *Rohring v. City of Niagara Falls, supra,* and with the general rule that attorney's fees should be based on the plaintiff's damage award. Lastly, the

Court addressed the issue whether the collateral source rule of CPLR 4545 requires that the plaintiff's recovery be reduced by specified payments from third parties, such as Social Security survivor benefits. The Court held in the affirmative, noting that in an action (such as *Bryant*) by an infant to recover for the wrongful death of a parent, such benefits actually replace a particular category of loss, *i.e.*, lost financial support.

In *Desiderio v. Ochs*, 100 N.Y.2d 159, 761 N.Y.S.2d 576, 791 N.E.2d 941 (2003), the Court of Appeals struggled with the application of the structuring formula in Article 50-A and concluded by urging the Legislature "as we have done before," to revisit the statute and amend away its impenetrable provisions. Indeed, by L. 2003, C. 86, the Legislature revamped § 5031, prompting the observation that "if the old version was Novocain for the mind, the new is general anesthesia." Gleason, 7B McKinney's Consol. Laws of New York, 2003 Practice Commentary, p. 377, 2006 Supplement.

§ 20.03 RELIEF FROM JUDGMENTS

EUGENE DILORENZO, INC. v. A.C. DUTTON LUMBER CO., INC.
Court of Appeals
67 N.Y.2d 138, 501 N.Y.S.2d 9, 492 N.E.2d 116 (1986)

The issue on this appeal is whether the trial court abused its discretion as a matter of law in granting defendant Phil-Mar Lumber Corporation's motion to vacate a default judgment entered against it. We conclude that it did not, and remit the case to the Appellate Division for the exercise of discretion by that court.

Plaintiff brought a breach of contract action in Supreme Court against Phil-Mar Lumber Corporation (Phil-Mar) and A.C. Dutton Lumber Company, Inc. (Dutton). It served Phil-Mar, a New York corporation, by delivering two copies of the summons and complaint to the Secretary of State on June 29, 1983 (*see*, CPLR 311[1]; Business Corporation Law § 306). The Secretary of State promptly sent one of these copies by certified mail to the address listed by Phil-Mar with the Department of State for this purpose. This copy was returned to Secretary of State by the Post Office with the notation "Moved, Not Forwardable." Phil-Mar had apparently moved its place of business, but had not updated the address on file with the Department of State. When Phil-Mar failed to answer, plaintiff applied for a default judgment. Judgment was entered against Phil-Mar on Aug. 2, 1983 and the action against Dutton was severed. On Aug. 18, plaintiff sent a restraining notice to Phil-Mar's bank as garnishee.

By order to show cause dated Aug. 26, 1983, Phil-Mar moved to vacate the default judgment and set aside the restraining notice issued thereunder. Its motion papers alleged that it first received notice of the action on Aug. 23, when it learned of the restraint on its bank account. Phil-Mar also asserted that plaintiff knew the location of its place of business through the business dealings between them, yet never attempted to serve it personally at that office. The motion papers also proffered a defense to plaintiff's claim.

Plaintiff, in opposition to the motion, did not deny knowledge of Phil-Mar's place of business. It asserted, however, that Phil-Mar had deliberately failed to update its address with the Department of State in an attempt to defraud creditors, and that its default was therefore willful. Plaintiff submitted evidence showing that process sent by the Secretary of State in several other actions to Phil-Mar's address on file had been returned, and that in one of these other actions a default judgment had been entered on June 17, 1983. Phil-Mar, in reply, asserted that it had not realized that an improper address was on file until July 6, 1983.

Phil-Mar's order to show cause did not recite the statutory provision upon which it relied for vacating the default judgment. The attorney's affirmation in support of the motion asserted that the moving papers set forth entitlement to relief under CPLR 5015(a), and this provision was again referred to in the reply papers. CPLR 5015(a) provides that a party may be relieved from a judgment on the ground of, among others, "excusable default" (CPLR 5015[a][1]). A defendant seeking to vacate a default under this provision must demonstrate a reasonable excuse for its delay in appearing and answering the complaint and a meritorious defense to the action (*see, e.g., Gray v. B.R. Trucking Co.*, 59 N.Y.2d 649, 650; *Blake v. City of New York*, 90 A.D.2d 531).

A second provision for obtaining relief from a default judgment is found in section 317 of the CPLR. That section states, in part, that "[a] person served with a summons other than by personal delivery to him or to his agent for service under [CPLR] 318 . . . may be allowed to defend the action within one year after he obtains knowledge of entry of the judgment . . . upon a finding of the court that he did not personally receive notice of the summons in time to defend and has a meritorious defense." As has been emphasized in numerous cases, there is no necessity for a defendant moving pursuant to CPLR 317 to show a "reasonable excuse" for its delay (*see, e.g., Simon & Schuster, Inc. v. Howe Plastics & Chemicals Co.*, 105 A.D.2d 604, 605; *Zuppa v. Bison Drywall & Insulation Co.*, 93 A.D.2d 997). It is also well established that service on a corporation through delivery of process to the Secretary of State is not "personal delivery" to the corporation or to an agent designated under CPLR 318 (*see, e.g., Taieb v. Hilton Hotels Corp.*, 60 N.Y.2d 725; *Cecelia v. Colonial Sand & Stone Co.*, 85 A.D.2d 56, 57). Thus, corporate defendants served under section 306 of the Business Corporation Law have frequently obtained relief from default judgments where they had a wrong address on file with the Secretary of State, and consequently, did not receive actual notice of the action in time to defend (*see, e.g., Union Indemnity Insurance Co. v. 10-01 50th Avenue Realty Corp.*, 102 A.D.2d 727; *Meyer v. Chas. Fisher & Sons Dental Laboratory, Inc.*, 90 A.D.2d 889).

Special Term, although acknowledging that Phil-Mar had not cited to CPLR 317, granted relief pursuant to that section, finding that Phil-Mar had not personally received notice of the summons in time to defend the action and that the affidavits in support of the motion raised questions of fact supporting a meritorious defense. The court also concluded that Phil-Mar was entitled to relief under CPLR 5015(a). It found that plaintiff knew Phil-Mar's business address and had, in fact, served Dutton at that address, and held that under such circumstances the default was "excusable."

The Appellate Division, Third Department, reversed Special Term's order on the law and reinstated the default judgment against Phil-Mar. The court did not consider CPLR 317, and, with respect to CPLR 5015(a), held that a corporation's default is not "excusable" where its lack of actual notice was due to its own failure to keep a current address on file with the Secretary of State.

The court also noted the other default judgment which had been entered against Phil-Mar prior to the service here, though it did not make any findings as to when Phil-Mar received notice of that judgment.

The Third Department's failure to consider CPLR 317 was apparently based upon its prior holding that where a defendant cites to only CPLR 5015(a) in support of a motion to vacate a default judgment, the court may not grant such relief pursuant to section 317. . . . Other courts, however, have held that a defendant's specification of only CPLR 5015 does not preclude the court from considering CPLR 317 as a basis for vacating a default. . . . Particularly in view of the provision in CPLR 2001 for disregarding a "mistake, omission, defect or irregularity," we agree with the latter decisions that a court has the discretion to treat a CPLR 5015(a) motion as having been made as well pursuant to CPLR 317.

Accordingly, the decision by Special Term to consider section 317 was not an abuse of discretion, and reversal by the Appellate Division "on the law" was improper. Nor can we conclude, on the factual findings before us, that vacatur of the default under CPLR 317 was in any event an abuse of discretion. A defendant who meets the requirements of that section normally will be entitled to relief, although relief is not automatic, as the section states that a person meeting its requirements "*may* be allowed to defend the action" (emphasis added) (*see, also*, 1 Weinstein, Korn & Miller, New York Civil Practice ¶ 317.08). Thus, denial of relief under section 317 might be appropriate where, for example, a defendant's failure to personally receive notice of the summons was a result of a deliberate attempt to avoid such notice. . . .

We would also note that even under section 5015, there is no per se rule that a corporation served through the Secretary of State, and which failed to update its address on file there, cannot demonstrate an "excusable default." Rather, a court should consider, among other factors, the length of time for which the address had not been kept current.

Accordingly, the order of the Appellate Division should be reversed, and the matter remitted to that court for the exercise of discretion.

. . . .

NOTES

(1) Under the rule of the main case, a motion under CPLR 317 may be granted even if the movant cannot show a reasonable excuse for the default. Why should an excuse be required in situations covered by CPLR 5015(a)(1) and not in those covered by CPLR 317?

Relevant to the reasonableness of an excuse for a default is CPLR 2005, which allows the courts to grant relief even if the default was due to "law office failure." This judicial power remains discretionary, however. *See Hartwich v. Young*, 149 A.D.2d 769, 539 N.Y.S.2d 561 (3d Dep't 1989), *appeal denied*, 75 N.Y.2d 701, 551 N.Y.S.2d 905, 551 N.E.2d 106 (1989) (no abuse of discretion for trial judge to refuse to excuse a default which was part of a consistent pattern of neglect by the same attorney).

CPLR 5015 and CPLR 317 are not the sole source of judicial authority to affect default judgments. This is illustrated by a case in which the Second Department reduced the amount of damages assessed against a defaulting defendant, even though it agreed he did not have an acceptable excuse for his default. Said the court:

> It has long been held that courts have inherent power beyond that which is contained in the CPLR or its predecessor statutes to open defaults (*Ladd v. Stevenson*, 112 N.Y. 325, 332, 19 N.E. 842), and where the amount awarded on a default judgment has been perceived as excessive the courts have exercised their inherent power to modify or reduce the amount. . . .

Cervino v. Konsker, 91 A.D.2d 249, 253, 458 N.Y.S.2d 660, 662 (2d Dep't 1983).

(2) Although both CPLR 317 and CPLR 5015(a)(1) have outside time limits on their availability which should not be lightly disregarded, the courts have held that they retain inherent authority to grant relief from a judgment even after the expiration of these time limits. *E.g., Machnick Builders, Ltd. v. Grand Union Co.*, 52 A.D.2d 655, 381 N.Y.S.2d 551 (3d Dep't 1976).

(3) When a motion is made to vacate a judgment based on excusable neglect, should the court be any more or less forgiving of the neglect than if it were deciding whether to grant the preceding motion for the default judgment? *See A & J J Concrete Corp. v. Arker*, 54 N.Y.2d 870, 444 N.Y.S.2d 905, 429 N.E.2d 412 (1981).

(4) CPLR 5015(a)(4) permits relief from a default judgment for "lack of jurisdiction to render the judgment or order." This has been held applicable to per-

sonal jurisdiction, *see, e.g., Merit Oil Heating Corp. v. Bokal Realty Corp.*, 20 A.D.2d 550, 245 N.Y.S.2d 13 (2d Dep't 1963), and to subject matter jurisdiction, *see Friedman v. State*, 24 N.Y.2d 528, 301 N.Y.S.2d 484, 249 N.E.2d 369 (1969), *appeal dismissed*, 397 U.S. 317 (1970).

If there was no jurisdiction over the defendant to grant the judgment, then the motion to vacate it must be granted regardless of the passage of time or the merits of the movant's case. *Peralta v. Heights Medical Center, Inc.*, 485 U.S. 80, 108 S. Ct. 896 (1988). A party against whom a judgment or order has been granted on default may move to vacate it on the ground that the default was excusable, but must do so within a year of service of the order or judgment and notice of its entry. CPLR 5015(a)(1). No appeal lies from an order or judgment granted on default, CPLR 5511. But "[w]here a party appears and contests an application for entry of a default judgment, CPLR 5511 . . . is inapplicable and the judgment predicated upon the party's default is therefore appealable." *Achampong v. Weigelt*, 240 A.D.2d 247, 658 N.Y.S.2d 606 (1st Dep't 1997).

(5) CPLR 5015(c) allows the administrative judge of a court to move to vacate judgments procured on default through unconscionable means. This subdivision allows the courts to prevent misuse of process by the unscrupulous.

(6) Plaintiff obtained a four million dollar default judgment against defendant truck driver who had failed to appear. The IAS court granted defendant's motion to vacate on the basis of fraud because of inconsistencies in plaintiff's account of the accident. The Court of Appeals found this an abuse of discretion. Despite some inconsistencies, plaintiff was an eyewitness to the accident, the claim was clearly based on personal knowledge, she was consistent on the key issues, and nothing in the discrepancies that were shown could support a claim of fraud. *Woodson v. Mendon Leasing Corp.*, 100 N.Y.2d 62, 760 N.Y.S.2d 727, 790 N.E.2d 1156 (2003).

PROBLEM A

X, a New Yorker, has sued Y, a New Jerseyan, in the latter's home state alleging that Y caused an auto accident in which X was seriously injured. At trial, X testified that his legs were paralyzed because of the accident. The jury subsequently awarded him a substantial verdict. Two weeks after the judgment was paid, a private detective hired by Y's insurer took motion pictures of X playing tennis normally.

   a) May Y successfully bring a declaratory judgment action in New York seeking a decree that the New Jersey judgment is void?

   b) If the original judgment had been granted in New York, would Y be able to successfully move to vacate it under CPLR 5015(a)(2) or (3)?

TAMIMI v. TAMIMI

Appellate Division, Second Department
38 A.D.2d 197, 328 N.Y.S.2d 477 (1972)

SHAPIRO, JUSTICE.

In this action for a separation, for support and maintenance of the plaintiff and the children of the marriage, and for a declaratory judgment that a divorce obtained by the defendant in Thailand is null and void, the Special Term, after trial, dismissed the plaintiff's complaint, as a matter of law.

A statement of the facts, which are undisputed since the defendant, although represented by counsel at the trial, did not testify, is necessary to an understanding and determination of the question of law involved.

THE FACTS

The plaintiff wife, a citizen of Great Britain, and the defendant, an Iraqi national employed by the United Nations, were married in New York City in 1952. They have two children. In the course of his employment, the defendant took his family to Thailand in November of 1963. They leased their New Rochelle home before leaving.

After a few weeks in Thailand, the children became ill and the parents were advised by a physician to take them out of that climate. The defendant thereupon induced the plaintiff to take the children to visit her parents in England — she did that in May of 1964 — and he also told her he would join her some months later. In April of 1964, after the plaintiff had agreed to remove the children from Thailand, the husband instituted an action against her for divorce in the Bangkok Civil Court. The complaint alleged acts of misconduct by the plaintiff tantamount to cruel and inhuman behavior. The plaintiff was personally served with process in the Thailand action but she interposed no answer to the complaint.

Shortly thereafter, both her husband and his Thai attorney assured her that if she continued with the plan to take the children back to England and thereafter to America, the divorce action would be dropped. Despite that promise, and after she had left Thailand with the children, her husband proceeded with the action and obtained a decree of divorce by default on August 6, 1964, a copy of which was received by her through the mails. It is this decree which the plaintiff here seeks to have declared void.

DETERMINATION OF THE SPECIAL TERM

In dismissing the plaintiff's complaint, Judge Walsh, at a Special Term, held that the Bangkok court had acquired jurisdiction over the person of the plaintiff and that the acts complained of had occurred within that court's jurisdiction. Thus, said the court, as a matter of comity, the judgment should be recognized as valid in New York, since *Rosenstiel v. Rosenstiel* (16 N.Y.2d 64, 262 N.Y.S.2d

86, 209 N.E.2d 709) had erased any theretofore existing distinctions between the constitutional mandate of full faith and credit and the principle of comity.

With respect to the wife's contention that her husband's fraudulent misrepresentations induced her not to defend the divorce action in Thailand, Judge Walsh . . . held that, since the foreign court had acquired jurisdiction of the person of the plaintiff, it retained jurisdiction until the final decree was rendered and that therefore the decree must be regarded as valid and binding until set aside by the Thailand court. Judge Walsh also held that, while the purported fraud may have induced the Thailand court to commit error, the resulting judgment is susceptible to attack for such fraud in Thailand and not in New York (citing *Hunt v. Hunt*, 72 N.Y. 217).

THE LAW

I believe that the determination of the Special Term should be reversed and a new trial granted. The issue is not whether the Thai court had jurisdiction of the parties but whether the plaintiff was denied her day in court by the misrepresentation of her husband that he was not going to proceed with the action and whether that claim of fraud is litigable in this State.

In *United States v. Throckmorton*, 98 U.S. 61, 65, 25 L.Ed. 93 the court said:

> There are no maxims of the law more firmly established, or of more value in the administration of justice, than the two which are designed to prevent repeated litigation between the same parties in regard to the same subject of controversy; namely, *interest rei publicae, ut sit finis litium, and nemo debet bis vexari pro una et eadam causa.*

But it then added (pp. 65-66, 25 L.Ed. 93):

> But there is an admitted exception to this general rule in cases where, by reason of something done by the successful party to a suit, there was in fact no adversary trial or decision of the issue in this case. *Where the unsuccessful party has been prevented from exhibiting fully his case, by fraud or deception practised on him by his opponent, as by keeping him away from court, a false promise of a compromise;* or where the defendant never had knowledge of the suit, being kept in ignorance by the acts of the plaintiff; or where an attorney fraudulently or without authority assumes to represent a party and connives at his defeat; or where the attorney regularly employed corruptly sells out his client's interest to the other side, — *these, and similar cases which show that there has never been a real contest in the trial or hearing of the case, are reasons for which a new suit may be sustained to set aside and annul the former judgment or decree,* and open the case for a new and a fair hearing. . . .
>
> In all these cases, and many others which have been examined, relief has been granted, on the ground that, by some fraud practised directly upon the party seeking relief against the judgment or decree, that party

has been prevented from presenting all of his case to the court (emphasis supplied).

In consonance with the rule there laid down, the courts prior and subsequent thereto have clearly held:

It is a rule well settled, that every judgment may be impeached for fraud, and this applies as well to judgments of our own State, as to those of other States or foreign judgments; but what will constitute fraud sufficient to vitiate a judgment, and who can make the objection, and under what circumstances it can be interposed, are material questions.

The rule is that there must be facts which prove it to be against conscience to execute the judgment, and which the injured party could not make available in a court of law, or which he was prevented from presenting by fraud or accident, unmixed with any fraud or negligence in himself or his agents (*Kinnier v. Kinnier*, 45 N.Y. 535, 542-543).

. . . .

The text writers are in agreement with the cases. . . .

Professor Beale in his treatise The Conflict of Laws (vol. 2, § 440.4) states the law applicable here:

What Constitutes Fraud. — In general the rules as to what constitutes fraud in the procurement are the same both as to judgments of sister states and as to judgments of foreign countries. A distinction is made between extrinsic and intrinsic fraud. Intrinsic fraud is fraud which goes to the existence of a cause of action, and is held to be no defense. The American courts hold that a foreign judgment cannot be attacked on the ground that it was procured by false testimony. . . .

The fraud which will be available to a defendant in his attack upon a foreign judgment, in the main, is fraud which has deprived him of the opportunity to make a full and fair defense. There are many varieties of such fraud. *Thus, where the defendant failed to present his case because the plaintiff agreed to drop the suit or to compromise the case or notified the defendant that the proceeding had been dismissed, or by any other agreement or promise lulled the defendant into a false security, the judgment may be attacked by the defendant* (emphasis supplied).

. . . .

CONCLUSION

Upon the undisputed testimony in this case the plaintiff was "robbed" of her opportunity to make her defense in the Thai court by reason of the defendant's fraud and misrepresentation that he would discontinue the action which he had instituted against her. . . . Therefore, since she never had an opportunity to litigate the question determined in the Thai court, the judgment there obtained against her is not a bar to this action under the theory of those cases which prevent the relitigation in other states of issues already adjudicated. . . . Accordingly, the judgment appealed from should be reversed, on the law, and a new trial granted, with costs to appellant to abide the event. The questions of fact have not been considered.

. . . .

QUESTION

CPLR 5015 (a)(3) authorizes vacation of a judgment procured by fraud whether it was "extrinsic" or "intrinsic." Why, then, does the principal case consider the distinction important?

S.A.B. ENTERPRISES, INC. v. STEWART'S ICE CREAM COMPANY, INC.
Appellate Division, Third Department
242 A.D.2d 845, 662 N.Y.S.2d 614 (1997)

CASEY, J.

Plaintiff is a prior owner of certain real property located in the Village of Athens, Greene County. In 1974, defendant County of Greene conducted a tax foreclosure sale with respect to this property and ultimately sold it to defendant Stewart's Ice Cream Company, Inc. Plaintiff thereafter brought an action pursuant to RPAPL article 15 seeking to invalidate the tax sale. At the conclusion of the trial in 1990, a jury determined that the sale was properly conducted and a judgment was rendered in favor of defendants. We subsequently affirmed this judgment on appeal (187 AD2d 875, *lv denied* 81 NY2d 708). In June 1996, approximately six years after the trial, plaintiff moved to vacate the judgment pursuant to CPLR 5015(a)(2) and (3). Supreme Court denied the motion and plaintiff appeals.

Initially, plaintiff contends that the judgment should be vacated pursuant to CPLR 5015(a)(2) based upon newly discovered evidence. In particular, plaintiff claims that the tax notices sent to other property owners whose properties were foreclosed upon at the same time as plaintiff's property contain different type-print, thereby suggesting that the notice sent to plaintiff was fraudulently prepared after the sale. It is well settled that in order to vacate a judgment based upon newly discovered evidence, the movant must establish that the new evidence, if introduced at trial, would probably have produced a different result and that such evidence could not, despite due diligence, have been discovered in time to move for a new trial under CPLR 4404 (*see, Prote Contr. Co. v. Board of Educ.,* 230 AD2d 32, 39; *Gonzalez v. Chalpin,* 233 AD2d 367; *Travelers' Ins.*

Cos. v. Howard E. Conrad, Inc., 233 AD2d 890, 891-892; *see also,* CPLR 5015[a][2]). Such an application is addressed to the trial court's discretion (*see, Rubinow v. Harrington,* 194 AD2d 822) and, absent an abuse of that discretion, the court's ruling will not be disturbed (*see, Lehoczky v. New York State Elec. & Gas Corp.,* 180 AD2d 994, *appeal dismissed* 80 NY2d 924).

Based upon our review of the record, we find no abuse of discretion in Supreme Court's denial of plaintiff's motion pursuant to CPLR 5015(a)(2). Plaintiff has been in possession of the subject records since at least 1993, if not earlier, but has failed to set forth a legitimate excuse for its delay until 1996 in making its motion. In addition, because the subject records are of a public nature, they have been available to plaintiff since the date of the sale. Finally, the differences in typeprint appearing on the notices sent to other property owners do not, in our view, establish that the notice sent to plaintiff was fraudulently prepared, especially in view of the affidavit of the County Treasurer, which indicates that different persons using different typewriters prepared the notices which were sent to plaintiff and others during the time period in question. For this reason, we also find that plaintiff has failed to demonstrate fraud or misrepresentation warranting vacatur of the judgment under CPLR 5015(a)(3).

NOTES

(1) Note the criteria applied by the court to the motion for relief from the judgment on the grounds of newly discovered evidence. Are the same criteria relevant when the movant alleges fraud in addition to new evidence? *See Cohen v. Crimenti,* 24 A.D.2d 587, 262 N.Y.S.2d 364 (2d Dep't 1965) (in cases of clear evidence of gross fraud, it is required that the judgment be vacated), *compare McCarthy v. Port of New York Authority,* 21 A.D.2d 125, 128, 248 N.Y.S.2d 713, 716 (1st Dep't 1964) ("Thus, the court should weigh the likelihood and degree of the false testimony, the affront to the court, and the probability of changing the result against the degree of diligence exercised by the moving party and the time and manner in which the new trial is sought. . . .").

(2) Relief from a judgment may be obtained under CPLR 5015(a)(5) on the grounds of "reversal, modification or vacatur of a prior judgment or order upon which it is based." This has been held to apply only to the situation in which the earlier judgment had res judicata or collateral estoppel effect on the subsequent determination, not to that in which the earlier judgment had only stare decisis effect. *Jericho Union Free School District No. 15 v. Board of Assessors,* 131 A.D.2d 482, 516 N.Y.S.2d 247 (2d Dep't 1987). In the cited case, the court held that while CPLR 5015 did not apply, it had inherent authority to vacate or modify the judgment. Invoking this power, the court modified an earlier judgment in the case on the ground that an intervening Court of Appeals decision had destroyed the validity of the earlier judgment (which had not itself been appealed).

DeWEERTH v. BALDINGER
38 F.3d 1266 (2d Cir. 1994), *cert. denied*,
513 U.S. 1001, 115 S. Ct. 512, 130 L. Ed. 2d 419 (1994)

[Plaintiff, a well-to-do German woman, sent to the home of her sister Monet's *Impression: Sunrise, LeHavre* (1872) along with other treasures for safekeeping during the Second World War. The painting had been in the family since 1908 when it was purchased by her father. In 1945 plaintiff's sister noticed that the painting was missing and notified plaintiff who notified the German Federal Bureau of Investigation to no avail. Meanwhile, unbeknownst to plaintiff, the painting emerged in the international art market in 1956 and was purchased in 1957 by defendant for $30,900 and hung in her New York apartment. It remained there except for two occasions when it was loaned for exhibitions. Plaintiff finally learned of defendant's possession in 1981.

[A federal district judge in 1987 ruled that plaintiff's title was superior and that her efforts to locate the painting during the years were adequate, but the Second Circuit disagreed on the ground that she had not exercised due diligence in tracking it down and that defendant was a good faith purchaser. 836 F.2d 103 (1987). In early 1991, the New York Court of Appeals handed down a decision in *Guggenheim Foundation v. Lubell*, 77 N.Y.2d 311, 67 N.Y.S.2d 623, 569 N.E.2d 426, a case involving a Chagall watercolor stolen from defendant's museum 20 years before the action was brought, and held that the time within which to start the replevin action is three years from the demand and refusal — at least in cases where defendants are good faith purchasers. The proof in *Guggenheim* on defendant's motion for summary judgment was that the accepted practice is to do nothing to locate a stolen art object in hopes that it will surface sooner. The question of defendant's laches was thus determined to be a fact question.

[Plaintiff, on the strength of the holding in *Guggenheim* which was at odds with the Second Circuit's holding in her case, sought another chance to regain the Monet. In addition to the fact that this presents a classic *Erie* problem, Rule 60(b) of the Federal Rules of Civil Procedure provides that a party may be relieved from a final judgment because of mistake, newly discovered evidence, fraud, or "any other reason justifying relief from the operation of the judgment." The district court granted her relief, 804 F. Supp. 539 (S.D.N.Y. 1992), but the Second Circuit panel, in a 2-1 split, reversed and found that in the interests of finality, its earlier decision must stand.]

WALKER, CIRCUIT JUDGE:

Rule 60(b) provides that the district court may relieve a party or a party's legal representative from a final judgment, order, or proceeding in five enumerated circumstances and, according to the sixth subpart, for "any other reason justifying relief from the operation of the judgment." Fed. R. Civ. P. 60(b)(6). We have held that subpart (6) is "properly invoked where there are extraordinary circumstances or where the judgment may work an extreme and undue hardship." *Matarese*, 801 F.2d at 106 (internal quotations and citations omitted).

Judge Broderick determined that the Guggenheim decision, and its import for this case, constituted an "extraordinary circumstance" justifying relief under Rule 60(b)(6). Like *DeWeerth*, *Guggenheim* involved a suit by the owner of an allegedly stolen art object against the subsequent good faith purchaser for return of the stolen item. In the first appeal in *DeWeerth*, we held that New York's applicable statute of limitations required the previous owner to demonstrate that she had acted with reasonable diligence in attempting to locate the stolen object, and that absent such a showing, the owner's otherwise timely suit would be barred. 836 F.2d at 108. In *Guggenheim*, the New York Court of Appeals not only applied a contrary rule, but also expressly stated that the conception of New York law that we reached three years earlier in *DeWeerth* was wrong. In a unanimous decision, the Court of Appeals held that New York had a clearly established rule that the statute of limitations does not start to run until a bona fide purchaser refuses an owner's demand for return of a stolen art object, and that the Second Circuit should not have modified this rule by imposing a duty of reasonable diligence. 77 N.Y.2d at 318, 567 N.Y.S.2d 623, 569 N.E.2d 426. It reasoned that the Second Circuit's decision contravened New York's long-standing policy of favoring owners over bona fide purchasers so that New York would not become a haven for stolen art. *Id.* at 319, 567 N.Y.S.2d 623, 569 N.E.2d 426.

Based on the New York Court of Appeals' opinion, the district court determined that DeWeerth would have prevailed in this case had she originally brought her suit in the New York state courts. It then held that *Erie Railroad Co. v. Tompkins*, 304 U.S. 64, 58 S.Ct. 817, 82 L.Ed. 1188 (1938), and its progeny entitled plaintiff to a modification of the final judgment in this case to avoid this inconsistency. It determined that the countervailing interest of both the parties and the courts in the finality of litigation was outweighed by the need "to prevent the working of an extreme and undue hardship upon plaintiff, to accomplish substantial justice and to act with appropriate regard for the principles of federalism which underlie our dual judicial system." 804 F. Supp. at 550.

We have carefully considered the circumstances analyzed by the district court and conclude that they do not warrant relief under Rule 60(b)(6). While acknowledging that Judge Broderick engaged in a scholarly and thorough discussion of the issues, we think that his decision inappropriately disturbed a final judgment in a case that had been fully litigated and was long since closed. In our view, *Erie* simply does not stand for the proposition that a plaintiff is entitled to reopen a federal court case that has been closed for several years in order to gain the benefit of a newly-announced decision of a state court. The limited holding of *Erie* is that federal courts sitting in diversity are bound to follow state law on any matter of substantive law not "governed by the Federal Constitution or by Acts of Congress." 304 U.S. at 78, 58 S.Ct. at 822. However, the fact that federal courts must follow state law when deciding a diversity case does not mean that a subsequent change in the law of the state will provide grounds for relief under Rule 60(b)(6). *See Brown v. Clark Equip. Co.*, 96 F.R.D. 166, 173 (D.Me. 1982) ("mere change in decisional law does not constitute an 'extraordinary circumstance'" under Rule 60(b)(6), especially where "[p]laintiffs elected to proceed in the federal forum, thereby voluntarily depriving themselves of the opportunity to attempt to persuade the [state court]"); *Atwell v. Equifax, Inc.*, 86 F.R.D. 686, 688 (D.Md. 1980) (change in the state decisional law upon which appellate court based decision held "insufficient to warrant reopening a final judgment"). This principle also applies in federal cases where the Supreme Court has changed the applicable rule of law. *See Picco v. Global Marine Drilling Co.*, 900 F.2d 846, 851 (5th Cir. 1990); *Travelers Indem. Co. v. Sarkisian*, 794 F.2d 754, 757 (2d Cir.), cert. denied, 479 U.S. 885, 107 S.Ct. 277, 93 L.Ed.2d 253 (1986).

DeWeerth argues that this case is distinguishable because the state court did not announce a "change in the law," but rather clarified that New York law is — and always was — contrary to what the federal court held it to be. While we agree that *Guggenheim* did not involve a "change in the law" in the sense that it adopted a rule different from one that previously existed, we do not agree that *Guggenheim* stated, that the question decided by the *DeWeerth* panel had long been settled in New York. The *Guggenheim* court stated only that New York's demand and refusal rule was well established; it did not state that the question of whether a due diligence requirement should be added to this rule was clearly settled. In fact, no earlier New York case had addressed this issue. The earlier *DeWeerth* panel noted that this question was an open one; although it could have certified the question to the New York Court of Appeals, it chose to decide the issue itself since it did not think the issue would "recur with sufficient frequency to warrant use of the certification procedure." 836 F.2d at 108 n. 5.

When confronted with an unsettled issue of state law, a federal court sitting in diversity must make its best effort to predict how the state courts would decide the issue. *Stafford v. International Harvester Co.*, 668 F.2d 142, 148 (2d Cir. 1981). The comprehensive opinion by now Chief Judge Jon O. Newman in *DeWeerth* accordingly surveyed New York case law and determined that a New York court called upon to decide the issue would be likely to impose a requirement of due diligence. The decision was based in part on the fact that plaintiff's argument would create an incongruity in the treatment of bona fide purchasers and thieves. In New York, the three-year statute of limitations starts running against thieves once the owner discovers that the art object has been stolen, while under plaintiff's theory, it would not start running against a good faith purchaser until he refused the owner's request to return the art object. The court determined in *DeWeerth* that this rule conflicted with a policy inherent in certain New York cases of protecting bona fide purchasers of stolen objects from stale claims by alleged owners. 836 F.2d at 108-09. Based on this incongruity, New York's policy of discouraging stale claims in other settings, and the fact that in most other states the limitations period begins to run when a good faith purchaser acquires stolen property thereby prompting due diligence on the part of the previous owner, we determined that New York courts would adopt a due diligence requirement for owners attempting to locate stolen property.

It turned out that the *DeWeerth* panel's prediction was wrong. However, by bringing this suit, DeWeerth exposed herself to the possibility that her adversaries would argue for a change in the applicable rules of law. By filing her state law claim in a federal forum, she knew that any open question of state law would be decided by a federal as opposed to a New York state court. The subsequent outcome of the *Guggenheim* decision does not impugn the integrity of the *DeWeerth* decision or the fairness of the process that was accorded DeWeerth. The result in this case would be no different if DeWeerth had filed her claim in state court and Baldinger had removed the action to federal court. The very nature of diversity jurisdiction leaves open the possibility that a state court will subsequently disagree with a federal court's interpretation of state law. However, this aspect of our dual justice system does not mean that all diversity judgments are subject to revision once a state court later addresses the litigated issues. Such a rule would be tantamount to holding that the doctrine of finality does not apply to diversity judgments, a theory that has no basis in *Erie* or its progeny.

We believe that the prior *DeWeerth* panel made a reasonable ruling on the due diligence question given the information presented to it. In fact, a key reason for the *Guggenheim* court's contrary conclusion was not even presented to the *DeWeerth* panel as part of the parties' original briefing. In deciding not to adopt a due diligence requirement, the *Guggenheim* decision placed considerable weight on the fact that efforts to modify the demand and refusal rule by the New York State Legislature were unsuccessful. Specifically, in July 1986 Governor Mario Cuomo vetoed a bill passed by both houses of the State Legislature that would have caused the statute of limitations to start running from the time an art owner discovered or reasonably should have discovered the whereabouts of a work of art when bringing suit against certain not-for-profit institutions. As part of his veto message, Governor Cuomo stated that if the bill became law, it would have caused New York to become "a haven for cultural property stolen abroad." *See Guggenheim*, 77 N.Y.2d at 319, 567 N.Y.S.2d 623, 569 N.E.2d 426. The *Guggenheim* court concluded that "[t]he history of this bill and the concerns expressed by the Governor in vetoing it, when considered together with the abundant case law spelling out the demand and refusal rule, convince us that that rule remains the law in New York and that there is no reason to obscure its straight-forward protection of true owners by creating a duty of reasonable diligence." *Id.* The existence of this bill was not discussed in the *DeWeerth* opinion and was not brought to the attention of the court until *DeWeerth* filed a petition for rehearing. It is well established in this circuit that arguments raised for the first time on a petition for rehearing are deemed abandoned unless manifest injustice would otherwise result. *Anderson v. Branen*, 27 F.3d 29, 30 (2d Cir.1994). It is thus likely that the prior *DeWeerth* panel deemed DeWeerth to have waived a key component of the argument that was ultimately successful before the New York Court of Appeals.

We conclude that the prior *DeWeerth* panel conscientiously satisfied its duty to predict how New York courts would decide the due diligence question, and that *Erie* and its progeny require no more than this. The fact that the New York Court of Appeals subsequently reached a contrary conclusion in *Guggenheim* does not constitute an "extraordinary circumstance" that would justify reopening this case in order to achieve a similar result. There is nothing in *Erie* that suggests that consistency must be achieved at the expense of finality, or that federal cases finally disposed of must be revisited anytime an unrelated state case clarifies the applicable rules of law. Attempting to obtain such a result through Rule 60(b)(6) is simply an improvident course that would encourage countless attacks on federal judgments long since closed. While our conclusion relies in part on our belief that the prior *DeWeerth* decision fully comported with *Erie* and did not, as plaintiff suggests, mistakenly apply settled state law and reach a clearly wrong result, we note that even if those were the circumstances, the doctrine of finality would still pose a considerable hurdle to reopening the final judgment in this case. Whether, in such circumstances, the result would be different if the issue were raised within one year pursuant to Rule 60(b)(1) is an issue we need not decide.

The caselaw relied on by the district court as support for its decision is distinguishable from the present case. In *Pierce v. Cook & Co.*, 518 F.2d 720 (10th Cir.1975), *cert. denied*, 423 U.S. 1079, 96 S.Ct. 866, 47 L.Ed.2d 89 (1976), the Tenth Circuit granted Rule 60(b)(6) relief based on an Oklahoma Supreme Court decision that undermined the basis for the Tenth Circuit's three-year-old dismissal of plaintiff's action. However, a major factor in the *Pierce* decision was that the change in state law would have caused federal and state tort actions arising out of the same accident and involving the same parties to have opposite results. *See id.* at 723. Whatever the merits of this rationale, as to which we express no opinion, it cannot justify the district court's decision in this case since *DeWeerth* and *Guggenheim* do not arise out of the same facts.

In *American Iron & Steel Institute v. EPA*, 560 F.2d 589 (3d Cir. 1977), *cert. denied*, 435 U.S. 914, 98 S.Ct. 1467, 55 L.Ed.2d 505 (1978), the Third Circuit recalled its mandate because a subsequent Supreme Court case called into question the reasoning of the Third Circuit's decision issued one year and four months earlier. However, the court expressly stated that the mandate was recalled in part because the original panel decision placed on the defendant "continuing" obligations the validity of which was now suspect. *See id.* at 599. As discussed more fully below, the judgment in *DeWeerth* was finite in nature and did not have ongoing consequences for the parties involved. The other cases cited by the district court have fewer factual similarities to the instant case and provide even less persuasive authority for its holding.

We believe that the district court abused its discretion in ruling that the important interest in the finality of the judgment in this case, which was more than four years old at the time of that ruling, was outweighed by any injustice DeWeerth believes she has suffered by litigating her case in the federal as opposed to the state forum. Accordingly, we reverse the district court's decision granting her motion under Rule 60(b)(6). . . .

ALTIMARI, J. concurs, OWEN, J. dissents.

§ 20.04 CONFESSION OF JUDGMENT

FIORE v. OAKWOOD PLAZA SHOPPING CENTER
Court of Appeals
78 N.Y.2d 572, 578 N.Y.S.2d 115, 585 N.E.2d 364 (1991)

[Plaintiffs contracted to sell a 14.8 acre parcel of land in Pennsylvania to defendants' predecessor in interest. Defendants became bound under the contract which, as amended, contained terms including a $1.1 million purchase-money mortgage. The bond contained a provision whereby defendants confessed judgment in the amount of $1.1 million. Defendants failed to make the payments, and plaintiffs moved to enter judgments in the Pennsylvania Court of Common Pleas. Plaintiffs were unsuccessful in attempts to enforce the judgments and ultimately commenced this action in New York based on the Pennsylvania judgments which had become final after defendants' unsuccessful attempts to reopen and appeal. The Supreme Court granted plaintiffs' motion for summary judgment. The Appellate Division affirmed on the ground that the Pennsylvania cognovit judgments should be accorded full faith and credit. — Eds.]

KAYE, JUDGE.

I

. . . .

Judgments by confession, recognized both as "the loosest way of binding a man's property that ever was devised in any civilized country" (*Alderman v. Diament*, 7 N.J.L. 197, 198) and as devices that "serve a proper and useful purpose in the commercial world" (*Overmyer Co. v. Frick Co.*, 405 U.S. 174, 188, 92 S.Ct. 775, 783, 31 L.Ed.2d 124), in this State have been strictly limited by the Legislature (*see*, CPLR 3218). The present case calls upon us to determine whether a Pennsylvania cognovit judgment, obtained under that State's laws, should be given full faith and credit here (*see*, U.S. Const., art. IV, § 1; 28 U.S.C. § 1738). Given the procedures followed in Pennsylvania, we agree with the trial court and the Appellate Division that the Pennsylvania judgment may be enforced against defendant-appellants in New York. . . .

On this appeal, defendants again attempt to argue the merits of the Pennsylvania judgment. In addition, defendants argue that cognovit judgments as a matter of law are not entitled to full faith and credit in this State, citing this Court's decision in *Atlas Credit Corp. v. Ezrine*, 25 N.Y.2d 219, 303 N.Y.S.2d 382, 250 N.E.2d 474. Plaintiffs respond that United States Supreme Court decisions rendered after *Atlas* have made clear that cognovit judgments are not per se unconstitutional. Rather, plaintiffs assert, a case-by-case analysis is required to determine whether defendants voluntarily, knowingly and intelligently waived their rights to notice and an opportunity to be heard. The facts clearly demonstrate that such a valid waiver was effected, according to plaintiffs, and therefore the Pennsylvania judgment should be afforded full faith and credit. Agreeing with plaintiffs' arguments, we now affirm the Appellate Division order.

II

As a matter of full faith and credit, review by the courts of this State is limited to determining whether the rendering court had jurisdiction, an inquiry which includes due process considerations (*Parker v. Hoefer*, 2 N.Y.2d 612, 162 N.Y.S.2d 13, 142 N.E.2d 194, *cert. denied* 355 U.S. 833, 78 S.Ct. 51, 2 L.Ed.2d 45; *see also, Augusta Lbr. & Supply v. Sabbeth Corp.*, 101 A.D.2d 846, 475 N.Y.S.2d 878; 4 Weinstein-Korn-Miller, N.Y. Civ. Prac. ¶ 3213.04). Thus, inquiry into the merits of the underlying dispute is foreclosed; the facts have bearing only in the limited context of our jurisdictional review (*Parker v. Hoefer, supra*, 2 N.Y.2d at 616-617, 162 N.Y.S.2d 13, 142 N.E.2d 194). Moreover, although this is a confessed judgment, defendants have been offered, and have availed themselves of, a full and fair opportunity to argue the merits in the Pennsylvania courts.

The cognovit is a contractual provision, employed as a security device, whereby the obligor consents in advance to the creditor's obtaining a judgment without notice or hearing (*see, Overmyer Co. v. Frick Co.*, 405 U.S., at 176, 92 S.Ct., at 777-78, *supra*). In the present case, the cognovit contained a "warrant of attorney," a provision that empowers any attorney to enter the obligor's appearance in any court of record and to waive — on the obligor's behalf — process and consent to the entry of judgment (*Atlas Credit Corp. v. Ezrine*, 25 N.Y.2d, at 225, 303 N.Y.S.2d 382, 250 N.E.2d 474, *supra*).

In *Atlas*, this Court held that the Pennsylvania cognovit judgment in issue was not entitled to full faith and credit. First, we concluded that the cognovit "judgment" was a judgment in name only, having none of the "minimums of judicial process" usually associated with that term. For that reason alone, the cognovit judgment was not entitled to full faith and credit (25 N.Y.2d, at 229-230, 303 N.Y.S.2d 382, 250 N.E.2d 474, *supra*). Second, as recognition of the judgment was not constitutionally mandated, we determined that enforcing the cognovit judgment would be repugnant to New York policy (25 N.Y.2d, at 230, 303 N.Y.S.2d 382, 250 N.E.2d 474). Finally, we held that even assuming the cognovit could qualify as a judgment for full faith and credit purposes, the Pennsylvania judgment was not enforceable in this State because cognovit judgments that provide for entry of a judgment by confession anywhere in the world without notice are per se unconstitutional (25 N.Y.2d, at 231-232, 303 N.Y.S.2d 382, 250 N.E.2d 474).

In *Atlas*, this Court noted that United States Supreme Court precedent considering cognovit judgments stood only for the proposition that the terms of a warrant of attorney should be strictly construed (25 N.Y.2d, at 227, 303 N.Y.S.2d 382, 250 N.E.2d 474, *supra*). The Supreme Court had not yet spoken on the constitutionality of such judgments. Several years after *Atlas* — in the companion cases *Overmyer Co. v. Frick Co.*, 405 U.S. 174, 92 S.Ct. 775, *supra* and *Swarb v. Lennox*, 405 U.S. 191, 92 S.Ct. 767, 31 L.Ed.2d 138 — the United States Supreme Court did have the opportunity to consider whether cognovit judgments were per se unconstitutional.

In *Overmyer*, the Court ruled that Ohio's cognovit procedure was not per se unconstitutional (405 U.S., at 187, 92 S.Ct., at 783, *supra*). Instead, the Court directed attention to the effectiveness of the obligor's waiver of due process rights, a necessarily fact-specific inquiry, concluding from the facts that the obligor there had effectively waived those rights (*id.*). First, the Court assumed that the proper standard for determining the effectiveness of the waiver was the same as in criminal proceedings, that is, that it be voluntary, knowing, and intelligently made (405 U.S., at 185, 92 S.Ct., at 782). The Court emphasized that the obligors were sophisticated corporations, represented by counsel, involved in an arm's length commercial transaction. Furthermore, the cognovit clause was contained in a contract modification that had been effected after the obligor defaulted on its obligations and for which it received consideration. Thus, the Court concluded, the obligor in *Overmyer* had effectively waived its right to notice and a hearing.

Finally, the Court in *Overmyer* observed that the obligor was not — by execution of the cognovit clause — rendered defenseless (405 U.S., at 188, 92 S.Ct., at 783-84, *supra*). Rather, under Ohio law the obligor could seek to vacate the judgment — indeed, the obligor had in fact had a postjudgment hearing in an Ohio court. The concurrence emphasized the availability of postjudgment hearing as an avenue of relief for an obligor with a legitimate defense (405 U.S., at 189-190, 92 S.Ct., at 784-85 [Douglas, J., concurring]).[1]

In *Swarb*, the Supreme Court considered a constitutional challenge to the Pennsylvania cognovit judgment scheme, and rejected plaintiffs' argument that the procedure was invalid on its face. The Court, citing *Overmyer*, reiterated that "under appropriate circumstances, a cognovit debtor may be held effectively and legally to have waived those rights he would possess if the document he signed had contained no cognovit provision." (405 U.S., at 200, 92 S.Ct., at 772, *supra*.)

---

[1] Justice Douglas contrasted the Ohio postjudgment procedure with the Pennsylvania procedure involved in *Swarb v. Lennox* (405 U.S. 191), which he found imposed a stiffer — and "undue" — burden of persuasion on the debtor (405 U.S., at 190, n., *supra*). The Pennsylvania procedure was subsequently amended, and now places the same burden of persuasion on the debtor as was found in the Ohio scheme — sufficient evidence to raise a jury question (*see*, Pa. Rules Civ. Pro., rule 2959[e]).

We therefore consider the impact of *Overmyer* and *Swarb* on our earlier holding in *Atlas* that Pennsylvania cognovit judgments are not entitled to full faith and credit.

It is evident that the conclusion reached in *Atlas* concerning the per se unconstitutionality of the Pennsylvania cognovit scheme is itself no longer valid in light of the subsequent Supreme Court decisions (*see, Money Mgt. v. Vetere*, 107 Misc.2d 861, 863-864, 436 N.Y.S.2d 158; *In re PCH Assocs.*, 122 B.R. 181, 194-195 [S.D.N.Y.] [questioning the continued validity of the *Atlas* analysis in light of *Overmyer* and *Swarb*]; *see also*, Siegel, N.Y. Prac. § 300, at 430-431 [Prac.2d ed.] [same]). Cognovit judgments entered in other jurisdictions cannot automatically be denied full faith and credit; rather, enforceability must depend on the facts of each case. More particularly, it must be determined that the judgment debtor made a voluntary, knowing and intelligent waiver of the right to notice and an opportunity to be heard.

In that *Overmyer* and *Swarb* did not raise full faith and credit issues, it is arguable that the determination in *Atlas* that cognovit judgments are not judgments in the ordinary sense of the word would bar enforcement of such judgments in this State. Even assuming the continued validity of this line of reasoning, however, we note that the Pennsylvania cognovit judgment scheme has been amended in several areas relevant to the concerns expressed in *Atlas* (*see*, Pa. Rules Civ. Pro., rule 2951 et seq.). The main concern in *Atlas* was that the Pennsylvania cognovit procedure provided little in the way of judicial intervention, resembling more a "purely personal act." (25 N.Y.2d, at 230, 303 N.Y.S.2d 382, 250 N.E.2d 474, *supra*.) In addition to amending the procedure for opening the cognovit judgment to reduce the burden on the petitioning judgment debtor — thereby facilitating access to a judicial determination of the merits of the underlying claim — the Pennsylvania statute now provides that notice of entry be mailed by the court clerk rather than the plaintiff's attorney (Pa. Rules Civ. Pro., rule 236). Judgments rendered pursuant to this procedure are therefore judgments for full faith and credit purposes.

Defendants make one additional threshold argument concerning the validity of the Pennsylvania judgment, claiming that in the "predispute" context a hearing must be held to determine waiver prior to the entry of judgment in the forum State (*see, Isbell v. County of Sonoma*, 21 Cal.3d 61, 145 Cal.Rptr. 368, 577 P.2d 188, *cert. denied* 439 U.S. 996, 99 S.Ct. 597, 58 L.Ed.2d 669). The distinction, according to defendants, rests on the indicia of reliability present when the cognovit judgment is entered into following the development of a full-blown controversy. This argument is without merit.

Rather than an artificial dichotomy based on the timing of the "dispute" — one that finds no support whatever — the need for a hearing should be determined on a case-by-case basis. A hearing at some stage would clearly be warranted where the record is insufficient to support a waiver determination (*see, In re PCH Assocs.*, 122 B.R. at 193-194, *supra*). We cannot agree with defendants, however, that as a matter of law there must in every instance be a prejudgment hearing to determine whether the debtor waived its right to notice and a prejudgment hearing.[2]

Thus, there is no per se constitutional barrier to enforcement of Pennsylvania cognovit judgments.

III

We are left then with the Supreme Court's conclusion that "due process rights to notice and hearing prior to a civil judgment are subject to waiver." (*Overmyer Co. v. Frick Co.*, 405 U.S., at 185, 92 S.Ct., at 782, *supra*.) All that remains is to apply the waiver analysis in the present case to determine whether defendants voluntarily, knowingly and intelligently waived those rights. We conclude that they did waive those rights as a matter of law.

Defendants were sophisticated parties involved in an arm's length commercial transaction — the transfer of a parcel of land for development as a shopping mall (*see, In re FRG, Inc. v. Manley*, 919 F.2d 850, 857 [3d Cir.]). The purchase price of the land alone was well in excess of $1 million, indicating the magnitude of the project. Furthermore, the parties were represented by counsel in negotiating the terms of the agreement. Defendant Aronow claims not to have had counsel — a fact disputed by plaintiffs — but Aronow himself is an attorney.

Defendants also claim that they received no consideration for the cognovit provision, citing the Supreme Court's observation in *Overmyer* that the creditors in that case had made specific concessions in order to obtain the confession of judgment clause. In fact, the present case resembles *Overmyer* in this respect: defendants sought modification of the payment terms — from a lump sum due at closing to a two-year payment schedule — and in return for this modification executed the bond and warrant. Clearly, that security device was given in exchange for the extended payment schedule.

Finally, defendants argue that, unlike the obligors in *Overmyer*, they were unaware of the cognovit clause, which they claim was "buried" in the bond and warrant. In *Overmyer*, the Supreme Court noted that the obligor did not contend that it was unaware of the cognovit provision and that "[i]ndeed, it could not do so in the light of the facts." (405 U.S., at 186, 92 S.Ct., at 783, *supra*.) The facts before us likewise belie defendants' assertion that they were unaware of the cognovit provision. The bond and warrant is a three-page document, with the cognovit clause the only provision on the last page, several lines above defendants' signatures. The bald assertion that these sophisticated defendants, entering upon a significant transaction, did not read the document cannot excuse their

---

[2] The California Supreme Court in *Isbell* was concerned with an entirely different procedure. That court — in concluding that a hearing prior to entry of judgment was required — contrasted the California scheme to the Ohio scheme involved in *Overmyer* by emphasizing that California provided for no notice of entry of judgment and severely restricted the grounds for postjudgment attack (145 Cal. Rptr. 368, 375, 577 P.2d 188, 195). As noted, the Pennsylvania scheme is identical to the Ohio scheme in these respects.

legal obligation or overcome the substantial evidence of waiver (*see, Metzger v. Aetna Ins. Co.*, 227 N.Y. 411, 416, 125 N.E. 814).

As the Supreme Court noted, "where the contract is one of adhesion, where there is great disparity in bargaining power, and where the debtor receives nothing for the cognovit provision, other legal consequences may ensue." (*Overmyer Co. v. Frick Co.*, 405 U.S., at 188, 92 S.Ct. at 783, *supra*.) By contrast, the contract here was not one of adhesion, but rather represented a bargain struck between sophisticated commercial parties. It is clear that defendants made a voluntary, knowing and intelligent waiver of their right to notice and an opportunity to be heard, and should be held to the consequences of their conduct.

Accordingly, the order of the Appellate Division should be affirmed, with costs.

NOTE ON JUDGMENT ON SUBMITTED FACTS

CPLR 3222 provides that the parties can submit a case on an agreed statement of facts for a judgment by the court. Subdivision (b)(3) provides "if the submission is made to the supreme court, it shall be heard and determined either by the court, or by the appellate division, or, with his consent, by a specified judge or referee, as the parties may stipulate." The parties must show that there is a real controversy, and that it is submitted in good faith. Matrimonial actions are excepted. It has been held that the parties may switch to this procedure even after entering into the traditional litigation process. *Treichler v. Niagara Wheatfield Cent. School Dist.*, 184 A.D.2d 1, 590 N.Y.S.2d 954 (4th Dep't 1992).

§ 20.05 INTEREST, COSTS AND DISBURSEMENTS

LOVE v. STATE OF NEW YORK
Court of Appeals
78 N.Y.2d 540, 577 N.Y.S.2d 359, 583 N.E.2d 1296 (1991)

TITONE, JUDGE.

The question presented on this appeal is whether the claimant in this bifurcated personal injury action against the State was properly awarded prejudgment interest from the date of the decision establishing liability, rather than the date of the decision fixing damages, even though the State was not responsible for the extended delay in the assessment of damages. For the reasons that follow, we conclude that interest was correctly calculated from the date of the liability adjudication.

Claimant commenced this action in the Court of Claims to recover for personal injuries allegedly suffered as a result of the State's negligence. The trial which followed was bifurcated, with the issue of liability being decided in claimant's favor on November 4, 1988. The State did not appeal from the interlocutory judgment on liability that was subsequently entered. Nonetheless, a decision fixing claimant's damages was not rendered by the court until November 29, 1989 — more than 10 months after the trial on damages had concluded. The precise cause of the delay is unclear, but it is undisputed that neither party was responsible. When final judgment was thereafter entered it included prejudgment interest, pursuant to CPLR 5002, calculated from the date of the liability determination.

On appeal, the Appellate Division rejected the State's contention that its lack of blame for the delay in the trial court's assessment of claimant's damages relieved it of its obligation to pay interest from the date of the liability determination. The court concluded that, except in rare instances, prejudgment interest in bifurcated trials should be calculated from the date liability is adjudicated regardless of whose fault it is that the court's fixing of damages is delayed. 164 A.D.2d 155, 561 N.Y.S.2d 945. This Court subsequently granted the State leave to appeal. We now affirm.

A successful plaintiff's entitlement to interest on a civil damages award is, in general, governed by CPLR article 50. While the plaintiff in a personal injury action is not entitled to recover interest from the date the cause of action accrued (CPLR 5001[a]; *see*, 3d Preliminary Report of Advisory Comm. on Practice and Procedure, 1959 N.Y. Legis. Doc. No. 17, at 88), interest may be recovered "upon the total sum awarded" under CPLR 5002 "from the date the verdict was rendered . . . to the date of entry of final judgment."[1] While the application of this provision is straightforward in the usual case, it poses special difficulties in bifurcated trials, where the issues of liability and damages are tried seriatim (*see*, Siegel, Supp. Practice Commentaries, McKinney's Cons. Laws of N.Y., Book 7B, 1991 Supp. Pamph., CPLR 5002, at 529). Inasmuch as there are actually two verdicts in such trials — the first concerning liability and the second concerning damages, the proper application of CPLR 5002's rule computing interest from "the date the verdict was rendered" becomes somewhat problematic.

In *Trimboli v. Scarpaci Funeral Home*, 30 N.Y.2d 687, 332 N.Y.S.2d 637, 283 N.E.2d 614, *affg. on opn. below* 37 A.D.2d 386, 326 N.Y.S.2d 227, we answered one early question that arose in connection with the right of a defendant in a bifurcated trial to appeal from the interlocutory determination of liability[2] and to obtain a stay pending that appeal, thereby delaying the assessment of damages. We held that under such circumstances prejudgment interest under CPLR 5002 begins to accrue on the date of the verdict fixing liability, rather than the

---

[1] Interest from the date of entry of the final judgment until the date of payment is recoverable under CPLR 5002.

[2] *See Fortgang v. Chase Manhattan Bank* (29 A.D.2d 41).

date that the verdict assessing damages is rendered. In reaching that conclusion, we noted first that the intent of the statute authorizing prejudgment interest "is to indemnify the plaintiffs for the nonpayment of what is due to them" (*id.*, at 389, 326 N.Y.S.2d 227). Second, we observed that since the defendants had appealed from the interlocutory judgment on liability and had obtained a stay of the trial on damages pending that appeal, "the delay in the rendition of damages may properly be charged against the party causing it" (*id.*, at 389, 326 N.Y.S.2d 227).[3]

Our holding in *Trimboli* has been widely interpreted as establishing fault as the touchstone for determining in all cases whether interest should run from the date of the liability verdict or the date of the verdict on damages. . . . A number of courts, however, have expressed skepticism over whether a plaintiff's right to prejudgment interest should be made to turn on the issue of fault (*see, Brock v. State of New York, supra*, 77 A.D.2d at 671, 429 N.Y.S.2d 778; *Malkin v. Wright, supra*, 64 A.D.2d at 570-571, 407 N.Y.S.2d 36 [Fein, J., concurring]), and a few have even questioned whether *Trimboli* actually requires such a result (*Krause v. City of New York*, 149 Misc.2d 962, 567 N.Y.S.2d 1004; *see, Viscomi v. Kresge Co., supra*, 159 A.D.2d at 980, 552 N.Y.S.2d 761 ["fault for the delays *appears to have been* a prerequisite to the recovery of interest by plaintiffs" (emphasis supplied)]).

On this appeal, the State urges us to follow in the steps of those courts which have broadly read *Trimboli* as requiring a fault-based analysis whenever a plaintiff's right to prejudgment interest is at issue. To hold otherwise, argues the State, would be to penalize a defendant by requiring it to pay interest from the date of the liability determination even though it was not responsible for the delay in the assessment of plaintiff's damages. We find this argument to be unpersuasive.

Contrary to the State's contention, interest is not a penalty. Rather, it is simply the cost of having the use of another person's money for a specified period (*see*, Siegel, N.Y. Prac. § 411, at 623 [2d ed.]). It is intended to indemnify successful plaintiffs "for the nonpayment of what is due to them" (*Trimboli v. Scarpaci Funeral Home, supra*, 37 A.D.2d at 389, 326 N.Y.S.2d 227), and is not meant to punish defendants for delaying the final resolution of the litigation. It accordingly follows that responsibility for the delay should not be the controlling factor in deciding whether interest is to be computed from the date of the liability verdict or, instead, from the date of the verdict on damages.

Rather, what is dispositive on this point is when the plaintiff's right to be compensated for the damages he or she sustained becomes fixed in law. In a bifurcated trial, the plaintiff's right to be made whole becomes fixed when the verdict

---

[3] The *Trimboli* holding was reaffirmed and extended 15 years later in *Gunnarson v. State of New York* (70 N.Y.2d 923), where we concluded that it should be applied to the State when it has taken an interlocutory appeal and, as a result of the automatic stay provisions of CPLR 5519(a)(1), has delayed the assessment of damages.

holding the defendant liable is rendered. At that point, the defendant's obligation to pay the plaintiff is established, and the only remaining question is the precise amount that is due. The fact that damages are not yet liquidated is of no moment. As we explained in *Gunnarson v. State of New York*, 70 N.Y.2d 923, 924, 524 N.Y.S.2d 396, 519 N.E.2d 307, plaintiffs are entitled "to be compensated with interest for the delay in payment of the principal award certainly due them [even though] . . . the amount remain[s] uncertain." And, there is no logical objection to permitting the plaintiff to recover interest "retroactive[ly]" (*id.*, at 924, 524 N.Y.S.2d 396, 519 N.E.2d 307), after damages are computed. Indeed, as the concurrers in *Malkin v. Wright* (*supra*, 64 A.D.2d at 571, 407 N.Y.S.2d 36 [Fein, J., concurring]) observed, interest in breach of contract cases is always measured from the "earliest ascertainable date the cause of action existed" (CPLR 5001[b]), regardless of whether damages are liquidated or unliquidated. The need to compute damages in such cases has never been regarded as an obstacle to measuring the accrual of interest from a date well in advance of the rendition of the final damages verdict. There is no reason why it should be an obstacle here.

Accordingly, it follows that, if plaintiffs are to be fully compensated for their losses in bifurcated trials, prejudgment interest must be calculated from the date that liability is established regardless of which party is responsible for the delay, if any, in the assessment of the plaintiff's damages. Such a result undercuts the objection voiced by some that defendants in bifurcated trials should not be "penalized" for exercising a legitimate right ordinarily enjoyed by all litigants — *i.e.*, the taking of an interlocutory appeal (*see, Brock v. State of New York*, *supra*, 77 A.D.2d at 671, 429 N.Y.S.2d 778; *see also, Malkin v. Wright*, *supra*, 64 A.D.2d at 571, 407 N.Y.S.2d 36 [Fein, J., concurring]). As previously noted, the defendant is not being "penalized" by the assessment of interest during the pendency of the appeal; rather, the defendant is merely being directed to repay the plaintiff for the use of the plaintiff's money that the defendant enjoyed during that period.

In this regard, it is worthy of note that the defendant, who has actually had the use of the money, has presumably used the money to its benefit and, consequently, has realized some profit, tangible or otherwise, from having it in hand during the pendency of the litigation. There is thus nothing unfair about requiring the defendant to pay over this profit in the form of interest to the plaintiff, the party who was entitled to the funds from the date the defendant's liability was fixed. Indeed, inasmuch as the defendant was not entitled to the use of the money from the moment that liability was established, a rule that would permit the defendant to retain the cost of using the money (*i.e.*, interest) would provide the defendant with a windfall. Such a result is unacceptable irrespective of which party causes the delay. Regardless of who is responsible, the fact remains that the plaintiff has been deprived of the use of money to which he or she was entitled from the moment that liability was determined. That is a loss for which the plaintiff should be compensated.

In sum, we conclude that in a bifurcated personal injury action prejudgment interest under CPLR 5002 should be calculated from the date of the liability determination irrespective of whose fault it may be that the assessment of the plaintiff's damages is delayed. Accordingly, the order of the Appellate Division should be affirmed, with costs.

NOTES

(1) Interest in contract actions and actions involving interference with title, possession or enjoyment of property, runs from the accrual of the cause of action. CPLR 5001. The same is true for wrongful death actions. *See* note (2), below. In *Brushton-Moira Central School Dist. v. Fred H. Thomas Associates, P.C.*, 91 N.Y.2d 256, 669 N.Y.S.2d 520, 692 N.E.2d 551 (1998), a school district was entitled to prejudgment interest on the judgment in a breach of contract action based on the installation of defective insulated wall panels, computed from the date the claim accrued, *i.e.*, upon completion of the work and issuance of the certificate of occupancy. Preverdict interest is not provided for in personal injury cases under CPLR 5001, nor would such interest be imposed on an award of punitive damages. The personal injury exception is based on the idea that, as a policy matter, the jury's award includes compensation for future loss, and any addition of preverdict interest would be duplicatory. *DeLong v. Morrison-Knudson Co.*, 20 A.D.2d 104, 244 N.Y.S.2d 859 [1st Dept. 1963], *aff'd*, 14 N.Y.2d 346, 251 N.Y.S.2d 657, 200 N.E.2d 557 (1964). Since the award of punitive damages is designed, not to compensate plaintiff but to punish defendant, no interest is appropriate until the verdict is rendered. *See* Siegel's Commentaries to § 5001, C5001:2, McKinney's Consolidated Laws.

The concept of interest on the judgment is further complicated by the fact that there are three periods of time forming the bases for the calculation of interest. First, as we have seen, interest runs from the accrual of the cause of action under CPLR 5001 in contract and property cases. Under CPLR 5002, interest is calculated for the time between verdict and the entry of judgment "on the total sum awarded, including interest to verdict [in contract and property cases]." Thus, interest on personal injury and all other cases would run from the verdict. Then, under CPLR 5003, judgments will bear interest from entry. The practical significance of these three time periods is that a sort of compounding of interest takes place. The preverdict interest, if any, is included as part of the judgment upon which postverdict and post-judgment interest is calculated.

CPLR 5004 currently provides interest at the rate of nine percent. In *Rodriguez v. New York City Housing Auth.*, 91 N.Y.2d 76, 666 N.Y.S.2d 1009, 689 N.E.2d 903 (1997), it was held that nine percent was not a mandatory requirement in an action against the Authority brought under Public Housing Law § 157(5) and that the trial court had discretion to award a rate of interest lower than nine percent.

(2) In *Milbrandt v. Green Co.*, 79 N.Y.2d 26, 580 N.Y.S.2d 147, 588 N.E.2d 45 (1991), the court addressed the question of interest in wrongful death actions. EPTL 5-4.3 provides that damages should be the "fair and just compensation for the pecuniary injuries resulting from the decedent's death to the person for whose benefit the action is brought." That statute also provides that "interest upon the principal sum recovered by the plaintiff from the date of the decedent's death shall be added to and be a part of the total sum awarded." Thus, there is preverdict interest in wrongful death cases. But the Court held that since the award in the verdict (as in personal injury actions) contemplates an amount for future losses, it would be duplicative to add preverdict interest to the award for postverdict losses. Thus, the amount for future loss should be discounted, not back to the time of the award, but all the way back to the time of the death. Also, the court ruled that with regard to the calculation of preverdict interest, not all such interest shall be imposed from the time of death. There very well may be a series of losses accruing to the beneficiaries between death and verdict, and therefore interest should be computed from the time a particular loss occurs. Indeed, CPLR 5001(b) states that interest upon damages incurred after death shall be computed from the date incurred. Otherwise, the beneficiaries would collect interest from a date upon which they would not have yet incurred any loss.

(3) Where the contract cause of action involved unpaid monthly obligations, each such monthly obligation would be treated separately and interest would be due on each from the time the interest became due. The total interest due would be figured by simply adding up the separate figures. This total, said the Court, is simple interest, and is not arrived at by compounding. *Spode v. Park Property Dev.*, 96 N.Y.2d 577, 733 674, 759 N.E.2d 760 (2001).

(4) In *Pay v. State of New York*, 87 N.Y.2d 1011, 643 N.Y.S.2d 467, 666 N.E.2d 172 (1996), the Court was faced with the situation where there was a structured judgment in a personal injury case and the Court of Claims allowed interest on the entire award from the date of the liability finding. See the Appellate Division memorandum affirming this determination, 213 A.D.2d 991, 625 N.Y.S.2d 770 (4th Dep't 1995). The Court of Appeals reversed, finding that the interest on future damages should be discounted back to the time of the liability determination. After citing *Love, Milbrandt* and *Rohring v. City of Niagara Falls*, 84 N.Y.2d 60, 614 N.Y.S.2d 714, 638 N.E.2d 62 (1994), the court stated:

> . . . in *Rohring* . . . we noted that "the future damages here were properly treated as a debt owed entirely as of the date of the liability verdict, and interest was properly charged against the present value of future damages from that date under CPLR 5002. That result is consistent with *Love* and *Milbrandt* and, most importantly, with the plain language of the statute." Claimants misconstrue our holding in *Rohring*, which, following *Milbrandt*, held that interest was properly charged against the present value of future damages from the date of the determination of liability under CPLR 5002. Indeed, claimants have adduced

no reason why the avoidance of an interest windfall should not apply equally to personal injury actions and wrongful death actions.

(5) Costs are awarded to the victorious party under CPLR 8101. Under CPLR 8201, the party is entitled to $200 for proceedings before the note of issue; $200 for the proceedings between the note of issue and trial; and $300 for the trial phase. Thus, if a case goes through trial, the party would be entitled to $700.

Disbursements under CPLR 8301 are due the party to whom costs are awarded and, by way of example, consist of the items listed in that section, such as the legal fees of witnesses and referees, legal fees for publication and printing expenses. Disbursements do not include fees paid to expert witnesses.

Chapter 21

APPEALS

§ 21.01 INTRODUCTION

ANDON v. 302-304 MOTT STREET ASSOCIATES
Court of Appeals
94 N.Y.2d 740, 709 N.Y.S.2d 873, 731 N.E.2d 589 (2000)

CIPARICK, J.

We are called upon to decide whether, in this action for damages resulting from alleged lead-paint injuries to an infant plaintiff, the plaintiff-mother can be compelled to submit to an IQ examination in compliance with defendants' discovery demand under our civil action disclosure rules as a matter of law. We conclude, under the circumstances presented here, she cannot.

[The discovery aspects of this case appear in § 15.02, *supra*. Here is presented the brief discussion of the scope of the appeal in the appellate system.]

. . . .

Supreme Court granted defendants' motion and directed that an IQ test be administered by defendants' expert, Dr. Carlos Flores, in accordance with the procedures set forth in his affidavit. The court ordered that the results not be used for purposes other than this litigation, reserving for trial decision on the admissibility of the test results. On plaintiffs' appeal, the Appellate Division reversed. The Court concluded that the information sought was not discoverable under CPLR 3121(a), since the mother's mental condition was not "in controversy" (*Andon v. 302-304 Mott St. Assocs.*, 257 A.D.2d 37, 39 [internal quotations omitted]). It also concluded that the information was not discoverable under CPLR 3101, New York's general discovery provision. Although the Court acknowledged the statute's policy of "far-reaching" pretrial discovery, it concluded that the test result would "hardly aid in the resolution of the question of causality" (*id.*, at 40). The Court added that, if the test of the mother's IQ were compelled, it would unnecessarily broaden the scope of the litigation and invite extraneous inquiries into the factors contributing to her IQ (*id.*, at 40-41).

The Appellate Division granted defendants leave to appeal and certified the following question to us: "Was the order of this Court, which reversed the order of the Supreme Court, properly made?" We answer that question in the affirmative.

While discovery determinations rest within the sound discretion of the trial court, the Appellate Division is vested with a corresponding power to substitute its own discretion for that of the trial court, even in the absence of abuse (*Brady v. Ottaway Newspapers*, 63 N.Y.2d 1031, 1032; *Phoenix Mut. Life Ins. Co. v. Conway*, 11 N.Y.2d 367, 370). Where the Appellate Division has made such a discretionary determination, our review is limited to whether the Appellate Division abused its discretion as a matter of law (*Kavanagh v. Ogden Allied Maintenance Corp.*, 92 N.Y.2d 952, 954; *Brady v. Ottaway Newspapers*, *supra*, at 1032). Defendants acknowledge this standard of review but maintain that the Appellate Division's reversal here was not a discretionary determination, but rather was a "blanket prohibition" — as a matter of law — against discovery of maternal IQ in all lead-paint cases. We disagree.

Although the Appellate Division's certification order states that its decision was "made as a matter of law and not in the exercise of discretion," we are not bound by that characterization. Rather, we look to see whether the Appellate Division's decision, regardless of its characterization, nonetheless reflects a discretionary balancing of interests (*see, e.g., Small v. Lorillard Tobacco Co.*, 94 N.Y.2d 43, 53; *Brady v. Ottaway Newspapers*, *supra*, at 1032-1033; *Brown v. City of New York*, 60 N.Y.2d 893, 894). Here, recognizing New York's policy favoring open disclosure, the Appellate Division considered defendants' need for the information against its possible relevance, the burden of subjecting plaintiff-mother to the test and the potential for unfettered litigation on the issue of maternal IQ (*Andon v. 302-304 Mott St. Assocs.*, *supra*, 257 A.D.2d, at 40-41). The Court noted specifically that "many variables" were involved and that permitting the IQ test in the instant case would "raise more questions than it will answer" (*id.*, at 40). Thus, the Court evaluated competing interests and concluded that, under the circumstances of this case, the potential for confusion and delay created by the information sought outweighed any benefit to the defense. Further, the Appellate Division's opinion stated that its reversal was "on the law and the facts." On this record, it cannot be said the Appellate Division categorically denied defendants' request as a matter of law.

Nor did the Appellate Division abuse its discretion as a matter of law. CPLR 3101(a) entitles parties to "full disclosure of all matter material and necessary in the prosecution or defense of an action, regardless of the burden of proof." What is "material and necessary" is left to the sound discretion of the lower courts and includes "any facts bearing on the controversy which will assist preparation for trial by sharpening the issues and reducing delay and prolixity. The test is one of usefulness and reason" (*Allen v. Crowell-Collier Publ. Co.*, 21 N.Y.2d 403, 406).

Here, the Appellate Division did not abuse its discretion in holding that Dr. Adesman's affidavit — on which defendants' request was based — was insufficient to justify compelling plaintiff-mother to take an IQ test. . . .

NOTES

The *Andon* case presents a broad overview of the scope of review in New York's principal appellate courts. The following material will deal with the finer points of the powers of those courts, and also with the avenues for appeal in the lower courts.

The rules are laid out in CPLR article 55 (appeals in general), article 56 (appeals to the Court of Appeals), and article 57 (appeals to the Appellate Division).

Remember that there are intermediate appellate courts other than the Appellate Division. Appeals from City, Town and Village courts are taken to the County Court (UCCA § 1701; UJCA § 1701) except in New York City, where appeals from the New York City Civil and Criminal courts go to Appellate Term (NYCCCA § 1701), as do appeals from the District Courts of Nassau and Suffolk Counties (UDCA § 1701). In addition to appeals taken from Supreme Court (CPLR 5701), appeals from the Family Courts (FCA § 1111), the Surrogate's Courts (SCPA 2701, CPLR 5701), the County Courts and the Court of Claims go to the Appellate Division (Ct. Cl. Act § 24).

For help with the mechanics of appellate practice, see the handbooks published by the New York State Bar Association: The Practitioner's Handbook for Appeals to the Court of Appeals (2d ed. 1991), The Practitioner's Handbook for Appeals to the Appellate Division (2005), and Thomas R. Newman, New York Appellate Practice (1985 & Supp. 2006). The appellate courts maintain helpful websites that include court rules, official forms, and guidance for counsel. These can be accessed through www.courts.state.ny.us.

§ 21.02 APPELLATE DIVISION

[A] What Is Appealable?

BROWN v. MICHELETTI
Appellate Division, Second Department
97 A.D.2d 529, 468 N.Y.S.2d 160 (2d Dep't 1983)

MEMORANDUM

In an action to recover damages for personal injuries, etc., defendants third-party plaintiffs Henry Micheletti and Castagna & Son, Inc., and third-party defendants Castagna & Son, Inc. — Raisler Corp., a joint venture, and Raisler Corp. appeal from so much of a purported order of the Supreme Court, Kings County (Morton, J.), dated November 9, 1982, as, *inter alia*, granted plaintiffs' pretrial motion to dismiss defendants' affirmative defenses of workers' compensation and denied defendants' and third-party defendants' cross motion to dismiss the complaint pursuant to the Workers' Compensation Law. Appeal dismissed, with one bill of costs payable jointly by appellants appearing separately and filing separate briefs. The paper purportedly appealed from in this case is denominated an order of Trial Term and recites that plaintiffs had moved pursuant to CPLR 4401 (judgment during trial) to strike defendants' affirmative defenses of section 11 of the Workers' Compensation Law, and that defendants had cross-moved pursuant to CPLR 4401 as well as CPLR 3212 (summary judgment) to dismiss the complaint pursuant to those defenses. The paper further recites that an immediate "hearing" was held by the court pursuant to subdivision (c) of CPLR 3213 (meaning 3212). The decretal paragraphs of the paper granted plaintiffs' motion to strike defendants' affirmative defenses of workers' compensation, denied defendants' and third-party defendants' cross motion to dismiss the complaint, and stayed the "trial" of the action pending a determination of these appeals. The minutes of the "hearing" reveal that the purported order was entered, without objection, at the request of the defendants, for the purposes of taking this appeal.

On the eve of trial, plaintiff moved before Special Term to strike the defense of workers' compensation. The Justice presiding over that part denied the motion without prejudice to its renewal before Trial Term "in view of the triable issues to be resolved thereat." According to the minutes before Trial Term, after a jury had been selected and sworn, the parties unsuccessfully attempted to stipulate to sufficient facts so as to permit the court to rule on the defense of workers' compensation as a matter of law. It was determined that a "preliminary hearing" would be held before the court to adduce evidence respecting the facts not stipulated, and the jury was retired. The motion to dismiss the defenses and the cross motion to dismiss the complaint based on those defenses were argued after testimony was taken. Under these circumstances, the ruling that resulted, although reduced and entered as an "order," is not appealable.

As construed by the courts, CPLR 5701 (subd. [a], par. 2) authorizes appeals as of right to this court only from orders deciding motions made upon notice that, *inter alia*, affect a substantial right. Generally, decisions made by the court during the course of a trial of an action are deemed trial rulings, not orders, whether or not they are reduced to a writing in the form specified for orders in CPLR 2219 (subd. [a]) (*see Cotgreave v. Public Administrator of Imperial County* [Cal.], 91 A.D.2d 600;. . . .) This was the substance of subdivision 1 of section 583 of the former Civil Practice Act,* and the drafters of the CPLR intended no change by omitting this provision from the present statute (10 Carmody-Wait 2d, N.Y. Prac., § 70.37, p. 304). The discretion conferred by CPLR 2218, 3211 (subd. [c]) and 3212 (subd. [c]) to grant separate trials of issues of fact raised by pretrial motions is to be exercised prior to, and not during the course of the trial of the action, so that the resulting ruling, reduced to an

---

* "Review of rulings; *requirements as to exceptions*. 1. A ruling to which an exception is taken can be reviewed only upon an appeal from the judgment rendered after the trial, except in a case where it is expressly prescribed by law that a motion for a new trial may be made thereon."

order prior to trial of the action, is appealable. This conclusion follows from the fact that such pretrial motions authorize immediate trials of facts raised in the papers submitted only "when appropriate for the expeditious disposition of the controversy" (CPLR 3211, subd. [c]; 3212, subd. [d]). In other words, "[i]t is the case-ending prospect, though of course not the certainty, which governs judicial discretion as to whether to order immediate trial" (Siegel, N.Y. Prac., § 271, p. 329; § 284, p. 340; *see Barker v. Conley*, 267 N.Y. 43, 46; *Duboff v. Board of Higher Educ.*, 34 A.D.2d 824).

It may appear efficient in cases such as this one for Trial Term to resolve the narrow issues presented by pretrial motions at the commencement of the trial, in order to avoid the need to reintroduce at the trial evidence previously submitted with respect to pretrial motions. This commendable goal is what apparently motivated Trial Term and the parties in the case under review. Nevertheless, in the over-all administration of civil cases, efficiency dictates that issues raised by pretrial motions be tried separately and resolved by orders made prior to trial of the action (*see Korn v. Korn*, 56 A.D.2d 837; *Duboff v. Board of Higher Educ.*, *supra*; cf. *Matter of Parker Constr. Corp. v. Williams*, 35 A.D.2d 839). Separately trying issues raised by pretrial motions obviates the danger of back-handedly granting preferences for trial of the merits of the action (although in the case under review a general preference on account of disability had been granted). (*See* Siegel, 1973 Practice Commentaries, McKinney's Cons. Laws of N.Y., Book 7B, 1982-1983 Cumulative Annual Pocket Part, CPLR C3211:47, pp. 23-24; C3212:22, pp. 105-106.) In the case under review, the purported order resolving the pretrial motion and cross motion was a trial ruling made after the commencement of trial of the action in the course of one continuous proceeding before Trial Term (*see Matter of Parker Constr. Corp. v. Williams*, 35 A.D.2d 839, *supra*; *Hacker v. City of New York*, 25 A.D. 2d 35, 37). Accordingly, the purported order is not appealable.

Nevertheless, since the purported appeal was argued by the parties without reference to this determinative procedural point, we have examined the record and briefs in the interest of judicial economy and conclude that, had the merits been properly before us, we would affirm (*see Northern Operating Corp. v. Anopol*, 30 A.D.2d 690; *Tribolati v. Lippman*, 24 A.D.2d 769; *Bliss v. Londner*, 20 A.D.2d 640). . . .

NOTE

(1) CPLR 5701 is the basic provision governing appeal from the determinations of Supreme and County Courts to the Appellate Division. All judgments, whether interlocutory or final, are appealable as of right, subject only to an exception designed to prevent appeal as of right when all the issues in the case have already been decided by the Appellate Division on an earlier appeal. CPLR 5701(a).

(2) Generally, the taking of an appeal does not cause an automatic stay of the underlying litigation. One must navigate the somewhat labyrinthine provision of CPLR 5519(a) to discern those exceptions where a stay is automatic, otherwise a motion must be made to the court "from or to which an appeal is taken or the court of original instance" for a stay. Within 5519(a), paragraph 1 is the only provision that allows for an automatic stay based on the type of party; if the party is the state or any entity or official of the state, the stay will be automatic.

The problem that frequently arises from 5519(a) is determining the scope of the automatic stay. See the discussion of 5519(a)(1) in *Matter of Pokoik v. Department of Health Services*, 220 A.D.2d 13, 641 N.Y.S.2d 881 (2d Dep't 1996). The court said that where the order is "executory," it requires appellant to do something in consequence of the order and the doing of the act would be automatically stayed. But where the order is "self-executing," a motion must be made for a stay; service of a notice of appeal is not enough. An example of a "self-executing" order is one which denies a motion for summary judgment. The prevailing party should not automatically be stayed from proceeding with discovery, or advancing the litigation generally.

(3) Where a trial judge ordered a mistrial because an attorney was found "disrespectful" during trial, that order could not be appealed to the Appellate Division because it was not an order based on a motion on notice under CPLR 5701(a)(2). The proper procedure would have been to have moved to vacate the order and, if the motion was denied, then an appeal as of right could have been taken to the Appellate Division. *Sholes v. Meagher*, 100 N.Y.2d 333, 763 N.Y.S.2d 522, 794 N.E.2d 664 (2003). *Sholes* was invoked in a later case where, on a previous appeal (entertained prior to the *Sholes* decision), the Appellate Division had decided an issue arising from the trial judge's *sua sponte* determination. This decision could not be considered the law of the case since now, in light of *Sholes*, it turns out there was no right to appeal it. *Brown v. State*, 9 A.D.3d 23, 776 N.Y.S.2d 643 (3d Dep't 2004).

GASTEL v. BRIDGES
Appellate Division, Fourth Department
110 A.D.2d 146, 493 N.Y.S.2d 674 (4th Dep't 1985)

PER CURIAM.

This motion for leave to appeal from an order of the Monroe County Court, affirming an order of the City Court of Rochester, should be denied.

There is no inherent right to appeal. That right depends upon express constitutional or statutory authorization (*Friedman v. State of New York*, 24 N.Y.2d 528, 535, *mot. to amend remittitur granted*, 25 N.Y.2d 905, *lv. dismissed*, 397 U.S. 317); it may not be inferred by implication or construction (*Johnson v. International Harvester Co.*, 236 App. Div. 618). CPLR 5703(b) authorizes appeals to this court as of right from an order of a County Court which determines an appeal from a judgment of a lower court. No appeal lies as of right from an order of a County Court which determines an appeal from an order of a lower court (*Lincoln Rochester Trust Co. v. Howard*, 53 A.D.2d 1037, and cases cited therein). Nor do we have statutory authority to grant permission to take such an appeal.

The Appellate Division is authorized to grant permission to appeal only from orders in actions originating in Supreme and County Courts (CPLR 5701[c]), from orders of an Appellate Term (CPLR 5703[a]), and from judgments or orders of a court of original instance other than the Supreme or County Courts where the statute governing the practice in that court so provides (CPLR 5702; *see, e.g.*, Family Ct. Act § 1112). This action did not originate in Supreme or County Court; the appeal is not from an order of an Appellate Term; and the Uniform City Court Act, governing the practice in the court of original instance, does not provide for appeals to the Appellate Division.

We are aware of the cases to the contrary decided by the Appellate Division, Third Department, where the court granted leave to appeal *sua sponte* (*Matter of Cammarota v. Bella Vista Dev. Corp.*, 88 A.D.2d 703, *Matter of Swartz v. Wallace*, 87 A.D.2d 926, 927), and of cases decided by this court where we indicated that appeal might lie by permission (*Goldman v. Green*, 18 A.D.2d 1040, 1041; *Harding v. New York State Teamsters Council Welfare Trust Fund*, 60 A.D.2d 975, *lv. dismissed*, 44 N.Y.2d 697). Nevertheless, if we are to be empowered to grant permission to appeal from an order of a County Court determining an appeal from an order of a lower court, that power must come from the Legislature.

DILLON, P.J., HANCOCK, JR., CALLAHAN, DOERR and BOOMER, JJ., concur.

NOTES

(1) The Third Department in the *Cammarota* case cited above took an appeal from a decision of County Court affirming a Town Justice in a summary proceeding noting that ordinarily permission must be sought for such an appeal, but that in this case the court would take it *sua sponte*.

(2) In *Ellingsworth v. City of Watertown*, 113 A.D.2d 1013, 494 N.Y.S.2d 587 (4th Dep't 1985), we find this situation:

> Plaintiff's appeal to this court must be dismissed. Plaintiff's right to appeal is determined by CPLR 5703(b) which provides as follows: "An appeal may be taken to the appellate division as of right from an order of a county court or a special term of the supreme court which determines an appeal from a *judgment* of a lower court." (Emphasis added.)

> The right to appeal to this court is thus limited to review of County Court determinations on judgments of lower courts. In *Highlands Inc.*

Co. v. Maddena Constr. Co. (109 A.D.2d 1071), we reviewed a determination of County Court on an order of City Court because the City Court order there had dismissed a complaint for failure to prosecute after the Statute of Limitations had run. We took the approach that the order there was tantamount to a judgment because it was dispositive of the rights of the parties (CPLR 5011). We adopted the rationale that, in order to determine whether a paper is a judgment or an order, we should look to its effect, not its designation (*see, Matter of Mid-Island Hosp. v. Wyman*, 15 N.Y.2d 374, 379). Here, however, the City Court order was not finally dispositive but rather denied defendant's motion to dismiss and would have permitted the case to proceed to trial. It was, instead, the County Court order reversing the City Court order which granted defendant's motion and dismissed the complaint for lack of jurisdiction.

The statute thus creates an anomaly: If City Court had granted defendant's motion to dismiss and that order had been affirmed by County Court, the matter would be appealable as of right under the rationale we adopted in *Highlands* (*supra*); conversely, if City Court had granted defendant's motion and County Court had reversed and reinstated plaintiff's complaint defendant would have had an appeal as of right even though the County Court order would not have been finally determinative of the rights of the parties. This obvious logical inconsistency must, however, be rectified by the Legislature, not the judiciary.

113 A.D.2d at 1014, 494 N.Y.S.2d at 588.

[B] Scope of Review

HECHT v. CITY OF NEW YORK
Court of Appeals
60 N.Y.2d 57, 467 N.Y.S.2d 187, 454 N.E.2d 527 (1983)

CHIEF JUDGE COOKE.

This appeal presents a question respecting the limits of an appellate court's scope of review of a judgment rendered against multiple parties but appealed by only one. Generally, an appellate court cannot grant affirmative relief to a nonappealing party unless it is necessary to do so in order to accord full relief to a party who has appealed. Thus, it was error here for the Appellate Division to dismiss the action against a joint tort-feasor found liable at trial, but who took no appeal from the judgment.

Plaintiff commenced this negligence action against the City of New York and the Square Depew Garage Corporation for injuries sustained when she fell on a sidewalk located outside a garage operated by defendant corporation. After a jury trial, both defendants were found to be equally liable. Only the City of New York appealed the judgment.

The Appellate Division reversed on the law and dismissed the complaint, holding that there was no actionable defect in the sidewalk. The court added, however, that "[a]lthough only the city prosecuted an appeal, the whole of the judgment is before us . . . and our disposition necessarily effects a dismissal as to the garage defendant as well." This court now modifies the order of the Appellate Division by reinstating the judgment against Square Depew Garage Corporation.

The gravamen of plaintiff's complaint was that defendants failed to maintain the sidewalk in a condition reasonably safe for pedestrians, which failure proximately caused plaintiff's injuries. Plaintiff's proof established that there was a slight gap between two flagstone of the sidewalk. The gap may only be described as trivial. Consequently, it was not error for the Appellate Division to have found no actionable defect in the sidewalk and to have dismissed the complaint against the City of New York.

The other defendant, Square Depew Garage Corporation, however, took no appeal from the judgment. The Appellate Division, therefore, was without power to vacate the judgment against that defendant.

The power of an appellate court to review a judgment is subject to an appeal being timely taken (*see* CPLR 5513, 5515 . . .). And an appellate court's scope of review with respect to an appellant, once an appeal has been timely taken, is generally limited to those parts of the judgment that have been appealed and that aggrieve the appealing party (*see* CPLR 5501, subd. [a]; 5511 . . .). The corollary to this rule is that an appellate court's reversal or modification of a judgment as to an appealing party will not inure to the benefit of a nonappealing coparty . . . unless the judgment was rendered against parties having a united and inseverable interest in the judgment's subject matter, which itself permits no inconsistent applications among the parties. . . . (*See Matter of Winburn*, 270 N.Y. 196, 198; *United States Print. & Lithograph Co. v. Powers*, 233 N.Y. 143, 152-155).

It is, of course, axiomatic that, once an appeal is properly before it, a court may fashion complete relief to the appealing party. On rare occasions, the grant of full relief to the appealing party may necessarily entail granting relief to a nonappealing party (*cf. United States Print. & Lithograph Co. v. Powers*, 233 N.Y. 143, *supra*). At this time, there is no need to detail or enumerate the specific circumstances when such a judgment or order might be appropriate.

Having set forth the rule in general, the court turns to its application here. The appeal by the City of New York to the Appellate Division brought up for its review, with respect to the defendants, only so much of the judgment as imposed liability against the city. As full relief to the city can be achieved without granting relief to Square Depew, it was error to dismiss the complaint as to Square

Depew unless the city's interest could be said to be inseparable from that of Square Depew.

When multiple tort-feasors are found to be liable for damages, they may not be said to have an inseparable interest in the judgment, even though the factual basis for each party's liability is identical. Liability is said to be "joint and several," meaning that each party is individually liable to plaintiff for the whole of the damage (*see* Restatement, Torts 2d, § 875, and Comment [b]). A plaintiff may proceed against any or all defendants (*see Siskind v. Levy*, 13 A.D.2d 538; *Kapossky v. Berry*, 212 App. Div. 833). Moreover, a judgment for or against one tort-feasor does not operate as a merger or bar of a claim against other tort-feasors (*see* Restatement, Judgments 2d, § 49, and Comment [a]). Thus, Square Depew's interest was severable from that of its codefendant. Inasmuch as the judgment here was appealed only by the city, the Appellate Division's reversal was effective only as to that party.

Square Depew argues that the Appellate Division is vested with discretionary power to grant relief to a nonappealing party in the interest of justice, and that the Appellate Division has exercised that discretion in this case. In so arguing, Square Depew relies on CPLR 5522, which provides, in pertinent part, that "[a] court to which an appeal is taken may reverse, affirm, or modify, wholly or in part, any judgment or order before it, as to any party." It has been proposed that the clause "as to any party" vests the Appellate Division with discretionary power to grant relief to a nonappealing party who appears before the court as a respondent. The Appellate Division in the past has claimed this power and applied it on a number of occasions. . . . This court now holds that neither CPLR 5522 nor any other statutory or constitutional authority permits an appellate court to exercise any general discretionary power to grant relief to a nonappealing party.[*]

The common-law concept of a judgment rendered against multiple parties was that, if an error found on appeal required reversal as to one party, the judgment must be reversed as to all. . . . This result obtained even when theories of liability against the defendants differed or when there was error as to only one of the parties (*see Sheldon v. Quinlen*, 5 Hill 441, 442-443, *supra*). The rule was derived from the principle "that there can be only one final judgment in an action at law" (*Draper v. Interborough R.T. Co.*, 124 App. Div. 357, 359).

With the advent of statutory provisions permitting appellate courts to reverse, affirm, or modify a judgment, in whole or in part, with respect to any of the parties (*see* Code of Pro. [Field Code], § 330; Code Civ. Pro., § 1317; Div. Prac. Act, § 584), the common-law rule was effectively abrogated (*see Campbell v. Perkins*,

---

[*] To be distinguished is CPLR 5501 (subd. [a], par. 5), applicable when a trial court has granted additur or remittitur relief with respect to an excessive or insufficient verdict. When the beneficiary of that order appeals, the appellate court may, under this provision, grant affirmative relief to the nonappealing party by reinstating the verdict (*see* 7 Weinstein-Korn- Miller, N.Y. Civ. Prac., par. 5501.13).

8 N.Y. 430; *Van Slyck v. Snell*, 6 Lans 299; *Geraud v. Stagg*, 10 How. Prac. 369). Judgments are no longer necessarily viewed as indivisible entireties, reversal of which as to one of the parties necessarily effecting a reversal as to all parties against whom the judgment was rendered (*compare Sheldon v. Quinlen*, 5 Hill 441, *supra, with Goodsell v. Western Union Tel. Co.*,109 N.Y. 147). Rather, when multiple parties bring or defend an action or proceeding, and an appeal is taken from an adverse determination below, the appellate court can fashion relief to the various parties within the confines of the governing substantive law. That is the import of CPLR 5522. Moreover, nothing in the legislative history of this provision, its statutory antecedents, or its constitutional counterpart (*see* N.Y. Const., art. VI, § 5), nor any construction of these provisions by this court indicate that the "as to any party" language vests appellate courts with discretionary power to grant relief to a nonappealing party. The provisions were not meant to expand either the jurisdiction or the scope of review of an appellate court, but were merely intended to enumerate the forms of dispositions an appellate court may order. CPLR 5522, therefore, should be read in harmony with the statutory scheme which limits an appellate court's authority to the grant of relief to those who have appealed, except as discussed above.

Accordingly, the order of the Appellate Division should be modified, with costs to appellant, by reinstating the judgment in favor of plaintiff against Square Depew Garage Corporation and, as so modified, affirmed.

NOTES

(1) In *Sharrow v. G & H Steel Service*, 86 N.Y.2d 54, 629 N.Y.S.2d 980, 653 N.E.2d 1150 (1995), the court made an exception to the *Hecht* rule penalizing nonappealing parties where a derivatively liable party appealed, but the primary defendant did not appeal. P was injured at his work site and sued third parties who impleaded P's employer. The jury found the third parties liable and that the employer was liable over to the third parties. The employer successfully appealed, but the third parties did not appeal. The court stated: "Moreover, because third-party defendant G & H Steel's liability is entirely derivative, a new trial must be ordered with respect to the non-appealing defendants as well in order to afford complete relief to the appealing third-party defendant. . . ."

(2) CPLR 5501(c) reflects the long-settled law that the Appellate Division may review all questions of both law and fact on appeals before it. *Battaglia v. Schuler*, 60 A.D.2d 759, 400 N.Y.2d 951, 953 (4th Dep't 1977). The impact of the right to jury trial, however, produces a somewhat different scope of review of questions of fact in jury and non-jury cases.

In jury cases, the Appellate Division may, if it finds the verdict to be against the weight of the evidence, set it aside and order a new trial. *Cohen v. Hallmark Cards*, 45 N.Y.2d 493, 410 N.Y.S.2d 282, 382 N.E.2d 1145 (1978). It may direct a verdict for the other party only when the court can "conclude that there is simply no valid line of reasoning and permissible inferences which could possibly lead rational men to the conclusion reached by the jury on the basis of the evidence presented at trial. The criteria to be applied in making this assessment are essentially those required of a Trial Judge asked to direct a verdict." *Id.* at 45 N.Y.2d at 499, 410 N.Y.S.2d 285, 382 N.E.2d at 1148. The Appellate Division may also reverse the trial judge who grants judgment for the defendant notwithstanding the jury's verdict for the plaintiff and reinstate the verdict. *See McMorrow v. Trimpir*, 149 A.D.2d 971, 540 N.Y.S.2d 106 (4th Dep't 1989), *aff'd*, 74 N.Y.2d 830, 546 N.Y.S.2d 340, 545 N.E.2d 630 (1989).

The Appellate Division may condition the grant of a new trial on the losing party's acceptance of an increase or decrease in the damage award.

In a non-jury case, the Appellate Division may not only find the decision below erroneous, it may make new findings of fact. It is therefore freer to award a judgment for the party who lost below. *O'Connor v. Paperstein*, 309 N.Y. 465, 131 N.E.2d 883 (1956). Of course, the Appellate Division, recognizing that it is not always in as good a position as the trial judge to evaluate the evidence, attaches great importance to the views of the trial court. The latter can pass with greater safety upon "the memory, motive, mental capacity, accuracy of observation and statement, truthfulness and other tests of the reliability of witnesses." *Barnet v. Cannizero*, 3 A.D.2d 745, 747, 16 N.Y.S.2d 329, 333 (2d Dep't 1957).

Theoretically, there is no limitation on the Appellate Division's power — in contrast to that of the Court of Appeals — to review an exercise of discretion by the court below in granting or denying the relief sought. The Court of Appeals has said that the Appellate Division "is vested with the same power and discretion as the court at Special Term possessed, and it is not necessary, in order to justify the reversal, to demonstrate that Special Term abused its discretion." *Phoenix Mut. Life Ins. Co. v. Conway*, 11 N.Y.2d 367, 370, 229 N.Y.S.2d 740, 742, 183 N.E.2d 745 (1962).

Despite this plenary power to reverse if it simply disagrees with the lower court's exercise of discretion, the Appellate Division sometimes states that it will not reverse in the absence of compelling circumstances. *See, e.g., Linton v. Lehigh Valley R.R. Co.*, 32 A.D.2d 148, 300 N.Y.S.2d 468 (3d Dep't 1969).

(3) There are limits on the scope of review the court may exercise when a judgment is appealed to it. CPLR 5501. Thus, an appeal from the final judgment brings up for review only those non-final judgments or orders which necessarily affect the final judgment, CPLR 5501(a)(1), and certain other non-final matters listed in CPLR 5501(a)(2)-(5).

In *Madden v. Dake*, 30 A.D.3d 932, 935 n.2, 819 N.Y.S.2d 121 (3d Dep't 2006), it was stated:

> Contrary to plaintiff's claims, defendants' appeal from the final judgment brings up for review all interlocutory orders, including the order

denying defendants' summary judgment motion which has not previously been reviewed by this Court (*see Warnke v Warner-Lambert Co.*, 21 AD3d 654, 655 n 2 [2005]; *see also* CPLR 5501[a][1]). The fact that defendants previously had separately appealed from the order (denying their summary judgment motion), and then withdrew that appeal, does not alter its reviewability now on the appeal from the final judgment. Indeed, defendants' right to separately take a direct appeal from that intermediate order would have terminated upon entry of the final judgment upon the jury verdict (*see id.*).

Should an adverse determination on a motion for partial summary judgment await appeal until after determination of the other issues in the case, or should the appeal be immediately taken? Consider the *Andon* case, § 21.01, *supra*, and the following case.

[C] Appealability

BURKE v. CROSSON
Court of Appeals
85 N.Y.2d 10, 623 N.Y.S.2d 524, 647 N.E.2d 736 (1995)

TITONE, JUDGE.

[Certain County Court judges brought a proceeding against state officials claiming they were not receiving the same salary as certain other County Court judges. Plaintiffs alleged seventeen causes of action all based on the salary disparities. Sixteen were dismissed on a summary judgment motion, but the seventeenth, based on an equal protection claim, was sustained. Plaintiffs were awarded summary judgment on the merits on that cause of action and plaintiffs were awarded back pay and attorney's fees, the latter to be determined at a future hearing. Before that hearing, plaintiffs appealed the dismissal of the other sixteen claims, but defendants did not cross appeal their defeat on the seventeenth claim. The Appellate Division later held that determination to have been final, that it should have been promptly appealed, and that the appeal, not taken until the conclusion of the attorney's fee hearing, was untimely as the determination on the seventeenth cause of action had been severed. — Eds.]

. . . .

The critical threshold issue on this appeal by defendants from the final Supreme Court judgment awarding attorneys' fees is whether, in a prior appeal, the Appellate Division erred in declining to consider the merits of this determination on the ground that it was embodied in an earlier judgment that was final and therefore not reviewable under CPLR 5501(a)(1), 191 A.D.2d 997, 595 N.Y.S.2d 272. We now hold that the Appellate Division misapprehended the principles governing the finality of judgments and that, accordingly, its refusal to review the issue defendants proffered was error. . . .

Under CPLR 5501(a)(1), an appeal from a final judgment brings up for review "any non-final judgment or order which necessarily affects the final judgment . . . provided that such non-final judgment or order has not previously been reviewed by the court to which the appeal is taken." Since this provision authorizes review only of prior judgments and orders that are nonfinal, the classification of a particular judgment or order as final or nonfinal is critical to the statute's proper application. We note that, contrary to plaintiffs' argument here, the concept of finality as used in CPLR 5501(a)(1) is identical to the concept of finality that is routinely used to analyze appealability under article VI, § 3(b)(1), (2) and (6) of the State Constitution and the related statutory provisions (*see,* CPLR 5601, 5602).

The concept of finality is a complex one that cannot be exhaustively defined in a single phrase, sentence or writing (*see generally,* Cohen and Karger, Powers of the New York Court of Appeals § 9, at 39; Scheinkman, *The Civil Jurisdiction of the New York Court of Appeals: The Rule and Role of Finality,* 54 St. John's L. Rev. 443). Nonetheless, a fair working definition of the concept can be stated as follows: a "final" order or judgment is one that disposes of all of the causes of action between the parties in the action or proceeding and leaves nothing for further judicial action apart from mere ministerial matters (*see generally,* Cohen and Karger, op. cit., §§ 10, 11).[1] Under this definition, an order or judgment that disposes of some but not all of the substantive and monetary disputes between the same parties is, in most cases, nonfinal. Thus, a nonfinal order or judgment results when a court decides one or more but not all causes of action in the complaint against a particular defendant or where the court disposes of a counterclaim or affirmative defense but leaves other causes of action between the same parties for resolution in further judicial proceedings (*see, e.g., Marna Constr. Corp. v. Town of Huntington,* 31 N.Y.2d 854, 340 N.Y.S.2d 167, 292 N.E.2d 307).

An exception to these general principles exists in situations where the causes of action or counterclaims that have been resolved may be deemed to be "impliedly severed" from those that have been left pending. Where implied severance is available, the order resolving a cause of action or counterclaim is treated as a final one for purposes of determining its appealability or reviewability.

The "implied severance" doctrine has had a checkered history and our past articulations of the rule have been somewhat difficult to reconcile. . . . However, as may be discerned from a close review of our contemporary decisions on the

---

[1] Of course, this definition has no bearing on the entirely separate question of when a post-judgment order may be deemed final (*see, e.g.,* Coehn and Karger, op. cit., §§ 29, 36, 43, 44).

point, the "implied severance" doctrine has now evolved into a very limited exception to the general rule of nonfinality.[2]

Under this approach to implied severance, an order that disposes of some but not all of the causes of action asserted in a litigation between parties may be deemed final under the doctrine of implied severance only if the causes of action it resolves do not arise out of the same transaction or continuum of facts or out of the same legal relationship as the unresolved causes of action (*see, Heller v. State of New York*, 81 N.Y.2d 60, 62, n. 1, 595 N.Y.S.2d 731, 611 N.E.2d 770; *Lizza Indus. v. Long Is. Light. Co., supra*). Thus, for example, an order dismissing or granting relief on one or more causes of action arising out of a single contract or series of factually related contracts would not be impliedly severable and would not be deemed final where other claims or counterclaims derived from the same contract or contracts were left pending. Similarly, where a negligence cause of action has been dismissed but there remain other claims for relief based on the same transaction or transactions, the doctrine of implied severance is not available, even though the underlying legal theories may be very different.[3] Finally, implied severance is not applied where the court's order "decides some issues of relief but leaves pending between the same parties other such issues[, thereby] in effect divid[ing] a single cause of action" (*Sontag v. Sontag*, 66 N.Y.2d 554, 555, 498 N.Y.S.2d 133, 488 N.E.2d 1245).

Viewed against these principles, the November 15, 1991 order granting plaintiffs summary judgment on their first cause of action and dismissing the others cannot be deemed final. Although all of the substantive issues between the parties were resolved, the order was facially nonfinal, since it left pending the assessment of attorneys' fees — a matter that plainly required further judicial action of a nonministerial nature.

Moreover, implied severance was not available under these facts as a means of converting that facially nonfinal order to a theoretically final one. The resolved causes of action for declaratory and monetary relief were based on the same continuum of facts as the unresolved 42 U.S.C. § 1988 attorney-fee claim, *i.e.*, the enactment of a judicial salary scheme that, in plaintiffs' view, violated their right to equal protection of the laws. Without that legislative act and the surrounding circumstances that plaintiffs allege rendered the act unlawful, there was no predicate for either a substantive cause of action or a claim for the attorneys' fees incurred in vindicating plaintiffs' rights.

Indeed, plaintiffs' request for attorneys' fees was made in the form of a demand for "costs," which was included in the boilerplate portion of the com-

---

[2] The discussion that follows concerns only the doctrine of "implied severance." Cases where a cause of action or counterclaim has been expressly severed are analyzed under a different set of principles.

[3] To the extent that this Court's prior decisions, including *Sirlin Plumbing Co. v. Maple Hill Homes (supra), Orange & Rockland Utils. v. Howard Oil Co. (supra)* and *Ratka v. St. Francis Hosp. (supra)*, indicate the contrary, they should not be followed.

plaint seeking "[s]uch other, further and different relief which the Court may deem just and proper." As such, the request for attorneys' fees was an integral part of each of the asserted causes of action rather than a separate cause of action of its own. It has previously been said that a request for back pay and a request for attorneys' fees arising from the same wrong are "but a single cause of action" and that "one cannot divide a single cause of action" by "dividing the damage" in this manner (*Manko v. City of Buffalo*, 294 N.Y. 109, 111, 60 N.E.2d 828).[4] So too, in this case — where plaintiffs have asserted 17 causes of action based on the same legislative enactment and have requested attorneys' fees as an item of damages integral to each of those causes of action — the pending request for attorneys' fees could not have been divided from the otherwise resolved causes of action and implied severance was necessarily unavailable (*Sontag v. Sontag, supra*).[5]

Inasmuch as the November 15, 1991 order was not final and was not capable of being made final under the doctrine of implied severance, it should have been treated as a prior "non-final" order subject to review on plaintiffs' appeal from the final May 7, 1992 judgment pursuant to CPLR 5501(a)(1). Further, since the order presents a question of law and CPLR 5501(a)(1) also applies to the reviewability of prior orders in this Court, the correctness of the November 15, 1991 order is technically before us on this appeal. . . .

Accordingly, the judgment of Supreme Court appealed from and the order of the Appellate Division brought up for review should be reversed and the case remitted to the Appellate Division for further proceedings in accordance with this opinion.

NOTE

In *Sirlin Plumbing Co. v. Maple Hill Homes*, 20 N.Y.2d 401, 283 N.Y.S.2d 489, 230 N.E.2d 394 (1967), undercut in the main case, plaintiff brought an action to recover a certain balance said to be due from defendant for plumbing and heating work done by plaintiff. Defendant set up a counterclaim asserting overcharges related to the work alleged in the complaint as well as other work. Special Term denied plaintiff's motion to dismiss the counterclaim, but the Appellate Division reversed and granted the motion. Defendant appealed to

---

[4] In *Manko v. City of Buffalo, supra*, the Appellate Division had dismissed the claim for attorneys' fees, denominated a second "cause of action," without resolving the so-called "first cause of action" for back pay. Under modern jurisdictional principles, the resulting order would be deemed nonfinal and not subject to implied severance for the very reasons set forth in the *Manko* opinion, *i.e.*, that the dismissed claim and the pending claim were but a single, indivisible cause of action. Accordingly, an appeal presented in the precise posture of the *Manko* appeal would no longer be entertained in this Court.

[5] It is noteworthy that under these circumstances, any attempt expressly to sever the pending attorneys' fee claim from the resolved substantive claims (*see* n.2, *supra*) would be ineffectual, since items of relief within a single cause of action cannot be expressly or impliedly severed.

the Court of Appeals, and plaintiff argued that there was no final judgment being appealed. The Court of Appeals ruled that the judgment was final, and the motion to dismiss the appeal was denied. It was stated that the Appellate Division's order impliedly severed that part of the action from that which was still pending. An escape hatch was left by the Court when it was stated: "We need not decide whether the rationale of our earlier decisions [allowing inclusive appeals where the claims were related] may yet be apposite in some exceptional situations involving an extremely close interrelationship between the respective claims." 20 N.Y.2d at 403, 283 N.Y.S.2d at 490, 230 N.E.2d at 395.

This idea of the implied severance is as applicable in an appeal to the Appellate Division as it is in appeal from the Appellate Division to the Court of Appeals. The dictum regarding relatedness in *Sirlin*, however, has been liberally applied. In *In re Hillowitz*, 20 N.Y.2d 952, 286 N.Y.S.2d 677, 233 N.E.2d 719 (1967), it was stated: "The theory of implied severance on which cases such as *Sirlin Plumbing* . . . are predicated, is applicable only where there has been a final disposition 'as to a distinct cause of action or part thereof.' It has no relevance where, as here, the situation is 'merely that the Appellate Division has finally settled some of the issues involved in a single cause of action.'" 20 N.Y.2d at 954, 286 N.Y.S.2d at 679, 233 N.E.2d at 720. By the same token, the Appellate Division could entertain an appeal from a prior order which, although final, is interrelated with the rest of the case now being appealed. In the principal case, the Court of Appeals reduced the reach of the "implied severance" doctrine by holding that it does not apply when the issues separately determined by the lower court concerned the "same continuum of facts." Since the decision in *Burke v. Crosson*, this liberal exception to the old *Sirlin* rule has now become the rule. It would seem that the implied severance doctrine can only apply where the unappealed determination bears no factual relationship whatsoever to the other issues. Nevertheless, the cautious practitioner will file a prompt notice of appeal from determinations that have the earmarks of finality even though factual connections may be found to other unresolved issues in the case.

§ 21.03 THE COURT OF APPEALS

[A] Appealability

NOTES

(1) The finality aspect of appealability is dealt with in the *Burke* case and the notes following, *i.e.*, one must look to see whether the issue at hand arises out of the "same continuum of facts" as do the other issues.

(2) The jurisdiction of the Court of Appeals is controlled by Article VI, the Judiciary Article, of the State Constitution. CPLR 5601 and 5602 describe the determinations that are appealable to the Court of Appeals — the former, those

appealable as of right, and the latter, those requiring permission. The scope of review available in the Court of Appeals is covered by CPLR 5501(b). Several points are salient. In keeping with the court's role as final arbiter of the law in a state with two levels of appellate courts, (1) the appealable determination generally must be a final one, unless the Appellate Division certifies that it involves a question of law which the Court of Appeals ought to review (*but see* CPLR 5601(c) and 5602(a)(2)), (2) the court will generally hear only matters that have previously been passed upon by the Appellate Division (*but see* CPLR 5601(b)(2), direct appeal from lower court in certain constitutional cases).

CPLR 5601 specifies the cases in which an appeal may be taken as of right to the Court of Appeals. They are classified by subdivision into three major headings. All except subdivision (c) require a final determination in the courts below.

Subdivision (a) governs appeals as of right where there is a dissent by at least two justices of the Appellate Division on a question of law. Subdivision (b) provides, in two separate and noncongruent provisions, for appeal as of right from either the Appellate Division or the court of original instance based on the presence of a constitutional question. Subdivision (c) covers the only instance of appeal as of right from a non-final determination, authorizing appeal from an Appellate Division order granting or affirming the granting of a new trial upon appellant's stipulation that, if there is an affirmance, judgment absolute shall be entered against him. The Court of Appeals determination would have to be absolute in the sense that it would end the case. Thus, an appeal upon a stipulation for judgment absolute on liability only would not lie if damages remain to be tried. A Court of Appeals' decision affirming the Appellate Division's holding for plaintiff would not end the case, which would have to be sent back for the damage determination. *See Uesenskas v. Axelrod*, 81 N.Y.2d 300, 598 N.Y.S.2d 166, 614 N.E.2d 729 (1993).

Subdivision (d) provides that where a prior non-final order was not ripe for Court of Appeals' review and the case was sent back for further proceedings, appeal may be taken as of right from a final determination entered in the court of original instance from a final determination of an administrative agency, from a final arbitration award, or from an order of the Appellate Division "which finally determines an appeal from such a judgment or determination. . . ."

Despite the language of CPLR 5601, it is well to take the notion that these appeals are a matter of right with a grain of salt. The concepts on which the right turns, such as the substantiality of a constitutional question, are often a matter of judgment, and it is fair to say that the Court of Appeals exercises its judgment with more than an occasional eye to its calendar. One has an appeal as of right if — but only if — the Court says so.

CPLR 5602 outlines the situations in which appeals may be taken to the Court of Appeals only by permission. Subdivision (a) provides for permission to be obtained from either the Appellate Division or the Court of Appeals when the appeal is "from an order of the appellate division which finally determines the action and which is not appealable as of right." This includes not only cases (previously appealable as of right) where the Appellate Division reversed or modified the lower court or where just one justice dissented, but also cases in which there has been a simple affirmance.

When the reason why appeal does not lie as of right is either (1) that the determination is not final or (2) that the appeal to the Appellate Division was from an appellate determination of a lower appellate court, only the Appellate Division may grant permission. When neither (1) nor (2) is the case, both the Court of Appeals and the Appellate Division may grant permission. In one special situation, the Court of Appeals alone may grant permission — that is, from an Appellate Division order granting or affirming the grant of a new trial or hearing in a proceeding by or against a public officer, board, or agency. CPLR 5602(a)(2). Neither court has power to grant permission in a case which is appealable as of right, and a motion for leave to appeal in such a case will be dismissed or denied. *See, e.g., Unger v. Village of Falconer*, 2 N.Y.2d 731, 157 N.Y.S.2d 371, 138 N.E.2d 733 (1956); *cf. Sage v. Broderick*, 249 N.Y. 601, 16 N.E.2d 600 (1928). There is no danger that the time to take an appeal of right will expire before the motion for leave is dismissed, because the general extension of time provisions in CPLR 5514 covers such cases.

(3) In certain cases, the Court of Appeals may render an advisory opinion on a point of New York law. The request must come from the United States Supreme Court, a federal Court of Appeals, or the highest court in another state, and the questions submitted would have to be determinative of the action from which they originated. (This authority is granted under Article VI, § 3(b)(9) of the New York Constitution, and implemented in Rule 500.17 of the Court of Appeals Rules.) In *Kidney v. Kolmar*, a question involving the interpretation of New York's Social Services Law was submitted and decided by the New York Court of Appeals. 68 N.Y.2d 343, 509 N.Y.S.2d 491, 502 N.E.2d 168 (1986). In *Rufino v. United States*, 69 N.Y.S.2d 310, 514 N.Y.S.2d 200, 506 N.E.2d 910 (1987), on the other hand, the New York Court of Appeals refused a submission where the question involved was already in the New York State court system and should take its normal course, at least through the Appellate Division.

(4) Finally, note that § 500.4 of the Court of Appeals Rules allows the court summarily to deal with appeals, *i.e.*, the Court may select cases which have been appealed and decide them, without the submission of new briefs, on the papers already submitted at the Appellate Division. In *McMorrow v. Trimpir*, 74 N.Y.2d 830, 546 N.Y.S.2d 340, 545 N.E.2d 630 (1989), the Court utilized this procedure and affirmed in a case where the Appellate Division had reinstated the verdict of the jury for plaintiff in a negligence case (two justices dissenting), the trial judge having entered a judgment for defendant notwithstanding the verdict. 149 A.D.2d 971, 540 N.Y.S.2d 106 (4th Dep't 1989).

[B] Scope of Review

GLENBRIAR CO. v. LIPSMAN
Court of Appeals of New York
5 N.Y.3d 388, 804 N.Y.S.2d 719, 838 N.E.2d 635 (2005)

G.B. SMITH, J.

[Landlord sought to terminate tenants' rent controlled lease and brought a holdover proceeding in New York City Civil Court on the ground that the apartment was not being used as tenants' primary residence. The tenants spent half the year in Florida, but the facts were mixed as to whether New York or Florida was their primary residence. The Civil Court ruled in favor of the landlord. Appellate Term reversed. The Appellate Division reviewed the facts, affirmed the Appellate Term, and granted leave for the landlord to appeal to the Court of Appeals. Noting that the landlord did not claim that the evidence was insufficient to support the affirmed finding, the Court of Appeals affirmed.]

Our review of this case is circumscribed by the manner in which the appeal comes to us. The case was tried in the Civil Court of the City of New York. Subsequently, Appellate Term reversed the judgment and the Appellate Division affirmed. The Court of Appeals is a law court and ordinarily does not review facts except in a limited class of cases (NY Const, art VI, § 3). Where the Appellate Division reverses a trial court, this Court may review the facts to determine which court's determination more closely comports with the evidence. But where, as here, there are affirmed findings of fact supported by the record, even though the original Civil Court was reversed by Appellate Term, this Court cannot review those facts and substitute its own findings. This limitation on our jurisdiction is dispositive here, as the legal sufficiency of the evidence is not before us.

NOTES

(1) In an even more recent case, the Court put it this way:

Although 498 protests that it did not breach the lease, Supreme Court concluded otherwise and the Appellate Division affirmed. We may not revisit Supreme Court's affirmed factual findings underpinning the determination of breach, which are supported by the record (*see* Karger, Powers of the New York Court of Appeals § 13:10, at 489 [3d ed rev] ["[F]indings of fact made by the *nisi prius* court which have been expressly affirmed by the Appellate Division and have the requisite evidentiary support are . . . conclusive and binding on the Court"]). Moreover, in light of these factual findings 498 materially breached the lease. Thus, the only remaining issue for us to resolve — and the main point of contention between the parties — is whether the rent abatement clause is a proper remedy for this breach.

Bates Adv. USA v. 498 Seventh, 7 N.Y.3d 115, 120, 818 N.Y.S.2d 161, 850 N.E.2d 1137 (2006).

(2) As to reviewability, significant constitutional and statutory restrictions on the power of the Court of Appeals to review questions of fact reflect the prevailing conception of that court as primarily one of law. N.Y. Const., Art. 6, § 3(a); *see* the discussion in the *Andon* case at the beginning of this chapter. The constitutional restrictions are restated in CPLR 5501(b). In civil cases, the court is empowered to review the facts only when (1) the Appellate Division has reversed or modified (2) a final or interlocutory determination and (3) made new findings of fact, and (4) a final determination "pursuant thereto" has been entered. CPLR 5501(b). *See, generally*, Karger, Powers of the New York Court of Appeals (1997). Thus, there is no power to review the facts when the appeal is from a non-final determination or when the Appellate Division affirms the determination below, although the Court has sometimes reviewed them to the extent of ascertaining that the affirmed finding is supported by "some evidence." *E.g., Matter of Infant D.*, 34 N.Y.2d 806, 359 N.Y.S.2d 43, 316 N.E.2d 330 (1974). *Compare Rudman v. Cowler Communications, Inc.*, 30 N.Y.2d 1, 330 N.Y.S.2d 33, 280 N.E.2d 867 (1972) (findings of fact which have been affirmed by the Appellate Division are beyond the Court of Appeals' power to review).

A large complex of restrictions on review in the Court of Appeals is assumed in the statement that the court will not review an exercise of discretion. *E.g., Jacques v. Sears, Roebuck & Co.*, 30 N.Y.2d 466, 334 N.Y.S.2d 632, 285 N.E.2d 871 (1972).

But if the exercise has been abused, an issue of law is created, and the Court may review it. *E.g., Andon v. 302-304 Mott Street Associates*, 94 N.Y.2d 740, 709 N.Y.S.2d 873, 731 N.E.2d 589 (2000), § 21.01, *supra*.

§ 21.04 TAKING AND PERFECTING THE APPEAL

DOBESS REALTY v. CITY OF NEW YORK
Appellate Division, First Department
79 A.D.2d 348, 436 N.Y.S.2d 296 (1981)

PER CURIAM.

In 1973 defendant Warshaw Construction Company contracted with the New York City Transit Authority, as agent for the City of New York, to construct a new subway entrance at Broadway and 137th Street in Manhattan. The plan required exposing a 50-foot portion of a 36-inch diameter cast iron water main, which had been installed in 1903. As Warshaw was required to excavate 15 feet below the main to allow for placement of a new sewer line, the water main was suspended by cables which were supported by steel beams or 12-inch timbers placed across the beams. It remained this way without mishap for about seven months until 3:45 P.M. on September 23, 1974 when a piece of iron measuring approximately 12 to 15 inches long and 8 inches wide broke out near the bottom portion of the main, causing extensive flooding damage to plaintiffs.

Numerous lawsuits were filed against Warshaw, the Transit Authority and the city alleging negligence in the supervision and maintenance of the water main and charging the city with failing to act diligently to shut off the water after receiving notice of the break. Several of the actions were consolidated and a joint trial on the issue of liability only was held before Acting Supreme Court Judge Blangiardo and a jury. At the conclusion of the trial, but before submitting the case to the jury, the court dismissed the complaints and cross claims against the city, and the jury thereafter found in favor of the remaining defendants, Warshaw and the Transit Authority. Plaintiffs moved post trial pursuant to CPLR 4404 to set aside the verdict. The court granted the motion and directed the entry of judgment in favor of plaintiffs and against Warshaw and the Transit Authority. Warshaw and the Transit Authority appeal from the setting aside of the jury verdict, and plaintiffs appeal from the dismissal of the complaints and cross claims against the city.

We must first turn our attention to a procedural question regarding the timeliness of the appeals by plaintiffs Con Ed, Empire and New York Telephone from the trial court's dismissal of the complaints and cross claims against the City of New York. For reasons which follow, we find the appeals to be timely.

The attorneys for the plaintiffs in Action No. 4 (Daniel Brito, *et al.*) filed and served a judgment on April 11, 1979 which vacated the jury verdict in favor of Warshaw and the Transit Authority, directed that judgment be entered against these defendants, and ordered that the Transit Authority have judgment over on its cross claim against Warshaw. While the dismissal of the complaint and cross claims against the city was contained in the body or recital portion of the judgment, there was no ordering paragraph to that effect in the decretal portion of the judgment. The April 11, 1979 judgment was never served by the city upon any of the parties.

On August 20, 1980, Con Ed filed and served a final judgment decreeing that the complaint and cross claims against the city were dismissed and filed a notice of appeal from that judgment the same day. Empire filed a notice of appeal from that judgment on August 21. On September 2, 1980, New York Telephone Company filed a final judgment decreeing that New York Telephone's complaint against the city was dismissed, and filed a notice of appeal from that judgment the same day. Plaintiffs Brito *et al.* followed a similar procedure but they have withdrawn their appeal from the judgment entered by them on August 12, 1980.

Warshaw and the city now argue that any appeal by plaintiffs from the April 11, 1979 judgment would be time barred, and that the judgments entered by Con Ed, New York Telephone and Empire should be dismissed on the authority of

Halloran v. Virginia Chems. (41 N.Y.2d 386), wherein the Court of Appeals permitted an appeal to be taken from that portion of a judgment reciting the dismissal of a third-party complaint even though there was no ordering paragraph to that effect. We need not reach the issue whether the holding of *Halloran*, permitting an issue to be heard on appeal despite an omission in the judgment as a matter of form, should be extended to foreclose a party from entering and appealing from a separate judgment in a severed action. (*See Schuller v. Robison*, 139 App. Div. 97; *Tanzer v. Breen*, 131 App. Div. 654, 657; CPLR 5012).

We find that plaintiffs are not time barred from pursuing an appeal from the dismissal of their complaints and cross claims against the city because the city, the prevailing party on this issue, has never served plaintiffs with a judgment so providing. (*O'Brien v. City of New York*, 6 A.D.2d 63.) The rule that service of a judgment or order on the appellant by the prevailing party is necessary to start the 30-day limitation period running, dates back at least 123 years. *See Fry v. Bennett* (16 How. Prac. 402 [1858]) wherein it was stated at page 405 that the rule "enables the [losing] party to see and apprehend his precise condition in reference to the subject. And on the other hand, it leaves the prevailing party at full liberty to set the thirty days a running when he pleases, or to acquiesce in or allow an unlimited time within which to appeal, if he choose to do so."

In *Kilmer v. Hathorn* (78 N.Y. 228 [1879]) the Court of Appeals explicitly confirmed that rule, which today is apparently such a long-accepted part of New York's appellate practice as to require no case citations by one leading commentator. (Siegel, Practice Commentaries, McKinney's Cons. Laws of N.Y., Book 7B, CPLR, C5513:2, p. 138). When this court applied the rule in *O'Brien* (*supra*) Justice McNally stated in his opinion (6 A.D.2d at pp. 65-66): "In view of the fact that the City of New York in this case had the right to rely upon these previous decisions, no matter how well reasoned the argument for a contrary result might be, we cannot, in the circumstances, hold that its right to appeal is barred. If it should be deemed illogical to require, for appeal purposes, a notice of judgment to be served upon a party twice, merely because his appeal is against a co-defendant, then the matter should be one for correction by the Legislature rather than by this court. Until such action is taken by the Legislature or until the Court of Appeals rules differently, we feel constrained to enforce the statute as construed."

Since that time the Legislature has not revised the statute to provide that service upon appellant of the judgment with notice of entry by any party will start the 30-day period running, and the Court of Appeals, although not discussing the issue at length, has followed *O'Brien* since enactment of the CPLR, which states the time limitation in essentially the same language as was interpreted by our courts in the earlier cases discussed above. (*Farragher v. City of New York*, 19 N.Y.2d 831, *rearg. den.*, 19 N.Y.2d 1014, *decision on merits* 21 N.Y.2d 756, implicitly following *O'Brien v. City of New York.*) Accordingly, we find plaintiffs' appeals timely, but affirm the dismissal of the complaints and cross claims against the city. . . .

NOTES

(1) In *Masters, Inc. v. White House Discounts, Inc.*, 119 A.D.2d 639, 500 N.Y.S.2d 790 (2d Dep't 1986), it was stated:

> . . . CPLR 5513 requires service upon the appellant of a copy of the judgment or order appealed from together with notice of entry in order to commence the time to take an appeal. Although the section does not explicitly require service of a "true" copy or an "accurate" copy, we have consistently held that the requirements of statutes which regulate the right to appeal are to be strictly construed (*see, Kelly v. Sheehan*, 76 N.Y. 325; *Nagin v. Long Is. Sav. Bank*, 94 A.D.2d 710, 462 N.Y.S.2d 69; *O'Brien v. City of New York*, 6 A.D.2d 63, 174 N.Y.S.2d 819). The purported copy served here, containing as it does a substantial alteration of the original judgment, cannot satisfy the requirements of CPLR 5513, and its service was therefore ineffective to commence the running of the time within which to take an appeal (*see, Alesi v. City of New York*, 6 A.D.2d 779, 178 N.Y.S.2d 599). To the extent that any of our prior rulings in this case may be to the contrary, we decline to adhere to them, in the interest of justice (*see, Foley v. Roche*, 86 A.D.2d 887, 447 N.Y.S.2d 528, *lv. denied*, 56 N.Y.2d 507, 453 N.Y.S.2d 1025, 438 N.E.2d 1147).
>
> The appeal from the order entered February 21, 1984 must be dismissed. The motion was in actuality a motion to reargue (*see, Ginsberg v. Ginsberg*, 104 A.D.2d 482, 479 N.Y.S.2d 233), from the denial of which no appeal will lie (*Munz v. LaGuardia Hosp.*, 109 A.D.2d 731, 486 N.Y.S.2d 50).

119 A.D.2d at 640, 500 N.Y.S.2d at 791-92.

In *Reynolds v. Dustman*, 1 N.Y.3d 559, 772 N.Y.S.2d 247, 804 N.E.2d 411 (2003), it was held that the cover letter served upon petitioner along with an enclosed Supreme Court document dismissing his petition was insufficient as the notice of entry of a judgment or order required by CPLR 5513(a). The cover letter itself was not sufficient as a notice of entry. The enclosed document identified itself as a decision and order, but it was neither stamped with the date and place of entry nor signed by the clerk and thus did not qualify as a notice of entry.

(2) In *Rubeo v. National Grange Mut. Ins. Co.*, 93 N.Y.2d 750, 697 N.Y.S.2d 866, 710 N.E.2d 86 (1999), it was held that a party who lets lapse an appeal from an intermediate order will be barred from appealing the same issue if it arises in a subsequent judgment or order. This one bite at the issue rule finds a slight variation in *Montalvo v. Nel Taxi Corp.*, 114 A.D.2d 494, 494 N.Y.S.2d 406 (2d Dep't 1985), where it was written: "Where a party appeals from an intermediate order, thereafter abandons the appeal by failing to perfect, and the appeal is then dismissed by an appellate court, the party is estopped for reasons of judicial economy from seeking review of issues which could have been raised on the

appeal from the intermediate order (*Bray v. Cox*, 38 N.Y.2d 350; *Matter of Smith v. McManus & Sons*, 101 A.D.2d 890)."

(3) An appeal as of right must be taken 30 days from the service upon appellant of a copy of the judgment or order and written notice of its entry; or, if it is the appellant who serves a copy of the judgment or order and notice of entry, the 30 days run from such service. CPLR 5513(a). The cases noted above indicate the penalties in the offing for those who disregard these simple service rules. The appeal is actually taken by serving the adversary with a notice of appeal and "filing it in the office where the judgment or order of the court of original instance is entered. . . ." CPLR 5515(1). A 1999 amendment added subdivision (d) to CPLR 5513. It provides that the 30-day period may be augmented by the extra time provisions of CPLR 2103(b) allowing five extra days when service of the judgment or order appealed from is by mail, and one extra day when service is by overnight delivery. This provision applies "regardless of which party serves the judgment or order with notice of entry."

(4) When appeal is by permission, the appellant must serve the notice of motion for leave to appeal within thirty days after service of the judgment or order appealed from and notice of entry. CPLR 5513(b).

(5) Once an appeal has been taken, or permission to appeal has been granted, the appellant must perfect the appeal. Essentially, this involves serving and filing the record (or relevant portions of it) and a brief. The basic rules are set forth in CPLR 5525-CPLR 5530, but these are supplemented by more specific rules promulgated by each department of the Appellate Division and by the Court of Appeals which govern the practice in the respective court.

Thus, a rule of the Court of Appeals provides that within ten days of taking an appeal to that Court, the appellant must file a "jurisdictional statement." Rules of the First and Second Department require the appellant to file a "preargument statement" when the notice of appeal or order granting leave is filed. 22 NYCRR 600.17, 670.28.

The rules of all four departments of the Appellate Division provide that an appeal may be dismissed for want of prosecution if it is not perfected within periods ranging from six months to nine months after it was taken or permission to appeal was granted, unless an extension of time has been granted. *See* 22 NYCRR 600.11(a)(3), 670.8(e)(1), 800.12, 1000.12(b). The Court of Appeals rules require the appellant to file a "preliminary appeal statement" on a form prescribed by the Court within 10 days of the taking of the appeal, 22 NYCRR 500.9, whereupon the clerk will set in motion the procedures and schedule then to be followed, 22 NYCRR 500.10-500.12.

Chapter 22

ENFORCEMENT OF JUDGMENTS

§ 22.01 INTRODUCTION

The winning plaintiff is only part of the way home when the judgment is entered. Unless the defendant pays the judgment or has insurance fully covering the judgment debt, plaintiff, now the judgment creditor, must move against property owned by the judgment debtor, or debts owing to the debtor.

In this chapter we will examine what property and debts can be used to satisfy the judgment, the ways of locating those assets and protecting them from other creditors and the methods of seizing the assets. Non-money judgments and orders can be enforced by contempt proceedings, and this process will also be examined.

ALLIANCE BOND FUND, INC. v. GRUPO MEXICANO DE DESARROLLO, S.A.
United States Court of Appeals, Second Circuit
190 F.3d 16 (2d Cir. 1999)

JACOBS, CIRCUIT JUDGE:

[Holders of notes issued by the construction firm (GMD) hired by private concessionaires that built Mexico's intercity toll roads brought a breach of contract action in federal district court against GMD and others seeking a money judgment for principal and interest because of default in payment. Meanwhile, the Mexican government implemented a toll road "rescue program" by which it took control of the toll roads and promised to assume responsibility for the concessionaires' construction debt. The district court judge granted plaintiff note holders' motion for summary judgment in the amount of $82,444,259. Part of the judgment ordered the assignment or transfer to the noteholders an amount of toll road receivables or government notes as would satisfy the judgment. This is characterized as the "turnover order." In the opinion below, the Second Circuit panel found that the turnover order could not be achieved in this case, and reversed.]

. . . .

1. The C.P.L.R.

Under Federal Rule of Civil Procedure 69(a), "[p]rocess to enforce a judgment for the payment of money shall be a writ of execution," and "[t]he procedure on execution, in proceedings supplementary to and in aid of a judgment, and in proceedings on and in aid of execution *shall be in accordance with the practice and procedure of the state in which the district court is held*, existing at the time the remedy is sought" (emphasis added). The question is therefore whether the district court, in issuing the turnover order, acted in accordance with New York's procedures for the enforcement of judgments.

New York procedure for enforcement of judgments is set out in Article 52 of the Civil Practice Law and Rules ("C.P.L.R."). The first section of Article 52 describes the assets that New York law has made subject to enforcement, and thus available to judgment creditors. *See* C.P.L.R. § 5201; David D. Siegel, General Commentary on Article 52 at 49 (McKinney 1997) (hereinafter General Commentary); *see also Marshak v. Green*, 746 F.2d 927, 930 (2d Cir.1984) ("Those courts which have considered the issue have determined that state law also determines the type of property which can be subject to execution."). Different subsections control depending on whether the money judgment is to be enforced against a debt or against other property:

> (a) Debt against which a money judgment may be enforced. A money judgment may be enforced against *any debt, which is past due or which is yet to become due,* certainly or upon demand of the judgment debtor, whether it was incurred within or without the state, to or from a resident or non-resident, unless it is exempt from application to the satisfaction of the judgment. A debt may consist of a cause of action which could be assigned or transferred accruing within or without the state.

> (b) Property against which a money judgment may be enforced. A money judgment may be enforced against *any property which could be assigned or transferred,* whether it consists of a present or future right or interest and whether or not it is vested, unless it is exempt from application to the satisfaction of the judgment. . . .

C.P.L.R. § 5201 (emphasis added).

The remaining provisions of Article 52 "supply[ ] the devices whereby to reach" a particular asset. General Commentary, *supra,* at 49. In this appeal, the parties focus on C.P.L.R. §§ 5225 and 5227, which specify the devices for implementing what is known as a "delivery" or "turnover" order. Sections 5225 and 5227 provide a particular collection device for each of three categories of assets: (i) debts owed to the judgment debtor; (ii) property owned by and in the possession of the judgment debtor; and (iii) property owned by the judgment debtor but in the possession of someone other than the judgment debtor.

Under § 5227, a judgment creditor seeking to collect a debt that is owed to the judgment debtor must proceed against the person who owes the debt: the judgment debtor's debtor. *See* C.P.L.R. § 5227. In such a proceeding, "the court may require [the judgment debtor's debtor] to pay to the judgment creditor the debt upon maturity." *Id.*

Property, on the other hand, can be reached in one of two ways. Under § 5225(a), a judgment creditor pursuing property in the possession of the judgment debtor must seek a court order requiring the judgment debtor to turn it over. Under § 5225(b), a judgment creditor pursuing property in the possession of someone other than the judgment debtor must commence an action against the person in possession.

Although New York law draws a line between a debt owed to a judgment debtor and property owned by the judgment debtor but in the possession of another, that line can at times "become[ ] too fine to distinguish." David D. Siegel, Practice Commentaries § C5225:5 (McKinney 1997) (hereinafter Practice Commentaries). For that reason, the first and third categories are "close in both function and procedure." *Id.* In both instances, the third party against whom the judgment creditor must proceed is the "garnishee." David D. Siegel, New York Practice § 491, at 755 (2d ed. 1991) (hereinafter New York Practice).

In effect, §§ 5225 and 5227 require the judgment creditor to proceed against the party that can produce the asset that the judgment creditor seeks, whether that party is the judgment debtor itself, or some third party. This requirement allows for the possibility that there may be other claimants of the debt or the property, or other interests in it, assertable by the garnishee on its own behalf, or by fourth parties that are impleaded or who intervene. *See* § 5225(b) (stating that, in a proceeding commenced by the judgment creditor against a party in possession of the judgment debtor's money, "where it is shown that the judgment debtor is entitled to the possession of such property . . ., the court shall require such person to pay the money, or so much of it as is sufficient to satisfy the judgment, to the judgment creditor"); Practice Commentaries, *supra*, § C5225:5 ("[A]ny person claiming an interest in the property [that is the subject of the special proceeding against the garnishee] may intervene [in the proceeding]."); Practice Commentaries, *supra*, § C5227:1 ("If there is any possibility that the debt is owed to someone other than the judgment debtor, the garnishee (the respondent in the proceeding) must assure that the judgment debtor as well as any third person claimant is made a party. . . .").

A judgment creditor seeking a turnover order therefore must show: First, that the asset it seeks to collect has been made available to judgment creditors by § 5201; and second, that the party against which the creditor has chosen to proceed has the ability to produce the asset. For the reasons that follow we conclude that the noteholders so far have failed to make either showing.

[The toll road receivables were found not to be reachable even if characterized as debts because the Mexican government was not a party to the action and it had assumed the obligations. There was no showing that GMB could produce the money that Mexico had promised to pay in exchange for taking over the toll roads. The court found that it was unable to deal with the question of whether the receivables and notes constituted property since no evidence was taken by the district court concerning the nature of Mexico's promise to exchange government notes for toll road receivables or the financial characteristics of those government notes.]

2. The Effect of *ABKCO.*

The noteholders argue that the turnover order can be affirmed (at least) as to the assignment or transfer of the toll road receivables without a prior characterization of the receivables as either property or debt. The noteholders' argument runs as follows:

> As GMD's 1997 Annual Report discloses, there is no guarantee that the Mexican Government will ever make good on the promises it made when enacting the Toll Road Rescue Program.

> So even if the receivables are properly characterized as debt owed to GMD by the Mexican Government, that debt is neither "past due" nor "to become due, certainly or upon demand," and it therefore does not meet § 5201(a)'s definition of "[d]ebt against which a money judgment may be enforced."

> Since the toll road receivables are not "[d]*ebt* against which a money judgment may be enforced," they must be "[p]*roperty* against which a money judgment may be enforced." C.P.L.R. § 5201 (emphasis added).

In aid of that argument, the noteholders rely on *ABKCO Industries, Inc. v. Apple Films, Inc.,* 39 N.Y.2d 670, 385 N.Y.S.2d 511, 350 N.E.2d 899 (1976), in which the Court of Appeals concluded that a judgment creditor could attach the interest of an English debtor in the proceeds of its contract with a New York resident. The English debtor was a film producer that had licensed its film to a New York promoter in exchange for 80 percent of the net profits. *See id.* at 673, 385 N.Y.S.2d at 512, 350 N.E.2d 899. At the time of suit, however, no proceeds had materialized, and there was no guarantee that any ever would. *See id.* at 674, 385 N.Y.S.2d at 512-13, 350 N.E.2d 899. "The film might fail, for example, and produce no profits at all." Practice Commentaries, *supra,* § 5201:5. The debtor and the New York promoter — the putative garnishee — argued that the proceeds of the license were not subject to attachment because the obligation to pay was not yet "past due," nor was it "to become due, certainly or upon demand," and that therefore the obligation did not meet § 5201(a)'s definition of a "[d]ebt against which a money judgment may be enforced." *See ABKCO,* 39 N.Y.2d at 674, 385 N.Y.S.2d at 512-13, 350 N.E.2d 899.

The Court of Appeals held that the debtor's right under the licensing agreement was subject to attachment not as debt, but as "[p]roperty against which a money judgment may be enforced," and that, at least with respect to "[p]roperty against which a money judgment may be enforced," New York law contains "no threshold requirement that the attaching creditor show the value of the attached property or indeed that it has any value." *Id.* at 675, 385 N.Y.S.2d at 514, 350 N.E.2d 899.

. . . .

Citing *ABKCO*, the noteholders argue that in determining whether a particular asset has been made subject to enforcement by New York law, courts should eschew a technical analysis of whether the asset is debt or property, and should instead focus on whether the asset has economic potential:

> "Under [the Toll Road Rescue Program, GMD] ha[s] interests or rights in the Government Notes evidenced by [its] Toll Road Receivables. These interests or rights, while uncertain as to amount, are similar to the bundle of rights under the contract in *ABKCO*. *ABKCO*, therefore, permits Plaintiffs to treat these assets as property." Brief for Plaintiffs-Counter-Defendants-Appellees at 30.

The holding in *ABKCO* is potentially relevant to the noteholders' attempt to obtain cash in satisfaction of the judgment. *ABKCO* virtually erases the distinction in § 5201 between "debt" and "property" by re-characterizing — as "[p]roperty against which a money judgment may be enforced" — debts that otherwise are placed out of reach by § 5201(a)'s requirement that the debt being pursued be either past due or certain to become due upon demand. By so doing, *ABKCO* undertakes to elide "arbitrary distinctions": "If from the judgment creditor's point of view the asset is worth pursuing as a matter of economics, *ABKCO* authorizes the pursuit notwithstanding the contingent nature of the asset, and even though nothing may come of the chase." Practice Commentaries, *supra*, § 5201:5. Accordingly, if (as GMD's 1997 Annual Report seems to indicate) the toll road receivables do not meet § 5201(a)'s definition of "[d]ebt against which a money judgment may be enforced," then it may be that under *ABKCO*, those assets are nevertheless subject to enforcement as "[p]roperty against which a money judgment may be enforced" within the meaning of § 5201(b). *But see In re Supreme Merchandise Co., Inc. v. Chemical Bank*, 70 N.Y.2d 344, 350-51, 520 N.Y.S.2d 734, 736-37, 514 N.E.2d 1358 (1987).

But *ABKCO* does not allow us to affirm the turnover order, because it does not resolve the two issues that are essential to the resolution of this appeal: First, whether the toll road receivables have been made available to judgment creditors by § 5201; and second, whether GMD has the ability to produce what the noteholders seek — the money that Mexico has promised to pay in exchange for taking over the toll roads. . . .

. . . .

NOTES

(1) In *Glassman v. Hyder*, 23 N.Y.2d 354, 296 N.Y.S.2d 783, 244 N.E.2d 259 (1968), the New York plaintiff broker sued for real estate brokerage commissions. Defendants owned a building in New Mexico leased to a tenant who did business in New York. Plaintiff sought to obtain jurisdiction by attaching future rents payable by the tenant to defendant growing out of the New Mexico lease. Judge Breitel stated:

There are three kinds of things subject to execution. . . .

The first is a debt past due, or yet to become due, certainly, or upon demand, which is always an intangible (CPLR 5201, subd. [a]). The second is property, real or personal, tangible or intangible, which includes vested or unvested interests (CPLR 5201, subd. [b]). The third is income of various kinds, but subject to preconditions before it is available to levy by execution, and most often limited to garnishing of 10% (CPLR 5231, but compare 5226).

On any ordinary analysis, particularly an economic analysis, future rents might be treated either as a debt or as a form of income. . . . Where a duty to pay is conditioned on the creditor's future performance, or upon contractual consequences, there is no debt certain to become due. . . . An obligation to pay rent . . . is not a debt and is not certain to become due.

23 N.Y.2d at 358, 296 N.Y.S.2d at 785-86, 244 N.E.2d at 260-61.

The court had no reason to answer the question whether the rents could be attached as income since the elaborate garnishment provisions of CPLR 5231 had not been utilized. Judge Breitel did note that there is no problem with respect to getting at rents produced from property located within New York. The creditor "levies against the real property in this State simply by filing a notice of levy in the appropriate county clerk's office. . . . It then becomes a lien against the real property and the owner is effectively restrained from disposing of the property without first discharging the lien. If it is necessary to reach the accruing rents, a simple form of receivership is available after judgment (CPLR 5228, subd. [a]. . . .)"

Could the foreign lease in *Glassman* be considered "property" within the meaning of *ABKCO* and that whole "bundle of all its rights under the Agreement," including the rents, be deemed subject to execution? Does it affect the equation that the lessee is doing business in New York?

(2) CPLR 5205 sets forth the personal property exempt from application to the satisfaction of money judgments which includes a long list of household items and items used in trade to produce income. The statute provides other exemptions for certain kinds of income and trusts. CPLR 5206 provides for a $50,000 exemption to the judgment debtor when real property is sold to satisfy the judgment.

(3) In 1985, the Legislature enacted CPLR 5241 which provides for special income execution for family support. Under its detailed provisions, this statute allows the creditor to deduct sums up to 65% of the debtor's "disposable earnings." CPLR 5241(g)(1)(ii). CPLR 5242, also enacted in 1985, rather than providing for the execution and levy procedure found under CPLR 5241, sets forth the procedure for the obtaining of a direct court order for an income deduction. Subdivision (f) of CPLR 5242 states that a prior attempt at CPLR 5241 relief is

not required in order to seek the order under CPLR 5242. The order is discretionary with the court, however, and the court might be more disposed toward granting it were it shown that a prior execution and levy attempt was tried. *See* Siegel, Supplementary Practice Commentaries, McKinney's CPLR 5242 (1996).

Congress has been concerned with the special problems of enforcing family support awards. In 1994 it adopted 28 U.S.C. § 1738B, which requires the courts of each state to enforce child support orders made by the courts of another state, so long as the order to be enforced was made by a court that had personal and subject matter jurisdiction and had given the contestants reasonable notice and an opportunity to be heard. 28 U.S.C. § 1738(B)(a), (c). This provision should prevent parties from seeking to avoid the effect of a valid support order by moving to modify the order in a second state.

In a similar vein, 28 U.S.C. § 1738A, enacted as part of the Parental Kidnapping Prevention Act of 1980, requires each state to enforce child custody awards made by another state, so long as the issuing state had jurisdiction as defined by 28 U.S.C. § 1738A(c). New York law also requires the enforcement of child custody determinations made by the courts of other states, so long as they had jurisdiction over the child. *See* Domestic Relations Law § 77-b.

NOTE ON PROCEDURAL DUE PROCESS

In *Follette v. Vitanza*, 658 F. Supp. 492 (N.D.N.Y. 1987), the court addressed New York's wage garnishment procedures (CPLR 5230, 5231, 5240) in an action brought pursuant to 42 U.S.C. § 1983 on the contention that these provisions violated plaintiffs' due process rights. At the heart of the problem was that when compared to the federal Consumer Credit Protection Act, 15 U.S.C. § 1673(a) (1982), which provides an ample array of safeguards for the judgment debtor and a wage garnishment formula geared to the minimum wage, CPLR 5231(5) was found wanting. That provision simply allowed the judgment creditor to garnish 10% of the debtor's wages earned over a protected weekly minimum of $85. There were no provisions in the CPLR for advising the creditor of methods by which he could challenge the income execution, nor was there any requirement that the creditor be advised as to exemptions under the statutory scheme. The court found the CPLR provisions to be in violation of the due process rules laid down in the line of cases dealing with the fairness provisions of provisional remedies which include *Fuentes v. Shevin*, 407 U.S. 67, 92 S. Ct. 1983, 32 L. Ed. 2d 556 (1972), and *Sniadach v. Family Finance Corp.*, 395 U.S. 337, 89 S. Ct. 1820, 23 L. Ed. 2d 349 (1969). In an earlier case, another federal judge had found New York's judgment execution procedure (CPLR 5222) similarly defective. *Deary v. Guardian Loan Co.*, 534 F. Supp. 1178 (S.D.N.Y.), *modified*, 534 F. Supp. 642 (S.D.N.Y. 1982).

CPLR 5231, involving income execution procedures, was amended in 1987 to correct the deficiencies discussed in *Follette*. Among other changes is the abandonment of the $85 floor in favor of the federal formula. But the 10% maximum remains so that the yield, under an adaptation of the federal formula, cannot exceed 10% of gross wages. Likewise, the Legislature amended CPLR 5222, the judgment execution statute, so as to cure the defects found in the *Deary* case. The Second Circuit in *McCahey v. L.P. Investors*, 774 F.2d 542 (2d Cir. 1985), upheld the CPLR 5222 amendments, and put its seal of approval on New York's enforcement scheme.

§ 22.02 ENFORCEMENT DEVICES

[A] Disclosure

Unless the debtor's assets are prominent, the creditor will have to locate them. Since the debtor is unlikely to volunteer this information, it must be extracted by the familiar process of disclosure. Unlike pre-trial disclosure under CPLR Article 31, CPLR 5223 provides for initiation of the process by service of a subpoena "which shall specify all of the parties to the action, the date of the judgment, the court in which it was entered, the amount of the judgment and the amount then due thereon, and shall state that false swearing or failure to comply with the subpoena is punishable as a contempt of court." CPLR 5224 sets forth the kinds of subpoenas that may be served, including a call for the taking of a deposition, a subpoena duces tecum for the production of books and records, or an information subpoena. The latter is normally served on third parties, often potential garnishees. The deposition taking generally follows the procedures used in the pre-trial examination process.

Subdivision (f) of CPLR 5224 requires leave of court to compel the debtor to submit to the taking of a deposition or a production of books and records "within one year after the conclusion of a previous examination of him with respect to the same judgment." This is one of the rare times leave is required in the disclosure process. Third parties do not fall under this protection and may be re-subpoenaed at any time. They are entitled to fees under subdivision (b) of CPLR 5224, unlike the debtor and, like the debtor, may move for a protective order under CPLR 5240.

[B] Restraining Notice

Without court order, the creditor's attorney may serve a restraining notice on the debtor pursuant to CPLR 5222. The notice may be served on anyone whom the creditor believes holds the debtor's property or who owes the debtor (such as a bank in which the debtor has an account). The person served "is forbidden to make or suffer any sale, assignment, transfer or interference with any property," or to "pay over or otherwise dispose of any such debt, to any person other than the sheriff." CPLR 5222(b). The notice will apply also to after-acquired property and debts later to become due. The notice is to be served personally in the same manner as a summons, or by registered mail. Subdivision (d) requires that the notice provisions of subdivision (e) (advising the debtor of his rights as to exempt property) be sent to the debtor, if it had not already been provided within a year prior to service of the restraining notice. The effectiveness of the restraining notice is limited by the fact that it does not create a lien.

The restraining notice has a life of one year. Further notices can be made only by leave of court. While contempt charges face the debtor or garnishee who violates the order, they may make application for a protective order under CPLR 5240, and if the creditor specifies property not subject to restraint, he can be "liable to the owner of the property or the person to whom the debt is owed, if other than the judgment debtor, for any damages sustained by reason of the restraint." CPLR 5222(b).

NOTES

(1) CPLR 5222 is the section that received all the attention after the court in *Deary v. Guardian Loan Co.*, 534 F. Supp. 1178 (S.D.N.Y. 1982), held it and CPLR 5230 and 5232 unconstitutional because of the absence of any warnings as to the debtor's rights as to exempt property. Subdivisions (d) and (e) were then added to CPLR 5222.

(2) A restraining notice was served on the main office of the garnishee bank. The bank advised that it had no account of the judgment debtor and that it would circulate the order through the branch offices. Meanwhile, the judgment debtor closed out three accounts at a branch. *Held*: In order to reach a bank account, the judgment creditor must serve the office where the account is maintained. However, if the central office has high speed computers with central indexing capabilities (which this bank did not) then service on the central office will suffice. *Therm-X-Chemical and Oil Corp. v. Extebank*, 84 A.D.2d 787, 444 N.Y.S.2d 26 (2d Dep't 1981).

Subdivision (g) was added to § 5222 in 1994 and provides that the restraining notice in the form of a magnetic tape may be served upon a garnishee if the garnishee consents in writing. At the same time, the usual restraining notice in writing must be served on the judgment debtor. This provision will facilitate the processing by computer garnishees such as banks.

(3) A creditor, thwarted by a garnishee who disregards the restraining notice, is not confined to seeking a contempt citation; he may also seek damages in a separate plenary action. *Aspen Inds Inc. v. Marine Midland Bank*, 52 N.Y.2d 575, 439 N.Y.S.2d 316, 421 N.E.2d 808 (1981).

[C] Income Execution

The income execution is served on the sheriff in the county in which the debtor lives or works without any court order, but only after the debtor is given an opportunity to make the installment payments himself. If the debtor fails to pay over for a period of 20 days, the sheriff serves the execution on the garnishee. A somewhat complicated formula is invoked in CPLR 5231(b). Nothing shall be withheld toward payments "unless the disposable earnings of the judgment debtor for that week exceed thirty times the federal minimum hourly wage"; the amount withheld "shall not exceed twenty-five percent of the disposable earnings of the judgment debtor for that week [with a 10% limit on the debtor's gross earnings], or the amount by which the disposable earnings of the judgment debtor for that week exceed thirty times the federal minimum hourly wage"; and adjustments must be made where the debtor's earnings are also subject to deductions for alimony and support. Subdivision (c) defines earnings as "compensation paid or payable for personal services, whether denominated as wages, salary, commission, bonus, or otherwise, and includes periodic payments pursuant to a pension or retirement plan." Disposable earnings are described as those earnings left "after the deduction . . . of any amounts required by law to be withheld." Subdivision (g) mandates the inclusion of an elaborate statement in the execution informing the debtor of exempt earnings and how he can seek redress. Subdivision (j) states that if there are two or more outstanding income executions, priority will be determined by which creditor delivered the income execution to the sheriff first, not by which execution was first served by the sheriff.

[D] Installment Payment Orders

Suppose the debtor's income is not derived from an employer or any other readily identifiable source. The debtor may be self-employed. In such a case the creditor can obtain an installment payment order from the court under CPLR 5226. The judge will require the debtor to make periodic payments to the creditor, payments that will be reasonable given the debtor's other financial obligations. Notice of the motion for such an order will be served on the debtor "in the same manner as a summons or by registered or certified mail." Also, should the debtor be attempting to evade responsibility to the creditor "by rendering services without adequate compensation, the reasonable value of the services rendered" shall be taken into consideration. Refusal to abide by the order is punishable by contempt under CPLR 5251.

Should the creditor attempt to obtain an installment payment order to be served on a garnishee such as an employer, the question arises whether the amount to be held out for the creditor would be subject to the formula set forth under the income execution provisions of CPLR 5231. The cases are in conflict. *See* Weinstein, Korn & Miller ¶¶ 5226.03, 5226.13 and 5226.18.

[E] Executions

[1] Personal Property

Under CPLR 5230, the execution can be issued by the creditor's lawyer to the sheriff of the county in which the desired property is located. The sheriff then has 60 days in which to levy the execution; but this period can easily be extended under subdivision (c). The delivery of the execution to the sheriff establishes the lien. The lien is lost if within the 60 days, or an extended time ordered by the court, the levy is not made. The lien covers all property and debts in the county. *See* 6 Weinstein, Korn & Miller ¶ 5202.06.

The next step is the levy, the process by which the sheriff brings the property within his custody, either constructively, under CPLR 5232(a) where the asset held by the garnishee is frozen, or under CPLR 5232(b) where the sheriff can actually seize the property which is capable of delivery. The levy is then good for 90 days and will become void if the property or debt is not disposed of to satisfy the creditor. Again, this period can be extended on the creditor's motion (subdivision [a]). The creditor may also bring a special proceeding to compel delivery of the property or payment of the debt during the 90-day levy period if such is not otherwise forthcoming. (If the court does not have inherent power to entertain such a proceeding, the authority should be recognized under CPLR 5240 which gives the court omnibus powers to regulate the enforcement process. *See Carl B. Nusbaum, Inc. v. Calale*, 45 Misc. 2d 903, 258 N.Y.S.2d 8 (Sup. Ct. 1965).)

CPLR 5232(c) requires that the notice provisions of CPLR 5222(e) (advising the debtor of his rights as to exempt property) must be sent to the debtor by the sheriff if the execution does not recite that such notice has already been furnished.

[2] Real Property

The real property lien is established by the docketing of the judgment in the county in which the property is located. The lien operates against all such property in the county. The lien is good for 10 years. CPLR 5203(a) (But remember that the underlying judgment can be enforced for a period of 20 years under CPLR 211(b).)

CPLR 5236 sets forth the requirements for the sale of the real property which entail the posting of notice and actual notice to those people "who had of record any interest in or lien on such property forty-five days prior to the day fixed for the sale." The proceedings are triggered, after the docketing of the judgment, by the delivery of the execution to the sheriff who will make arrangements for the sale. CPLR 5235. If the 10-year lien period has run, CPLR 5235 allows the sheriff to file a notice of levy with the county clerk after which the sale arrangements may proceed.

NOTES

(1) When the sheriff levies on a bank account, the bank can be in a quandary when the account is jointly owned and the judgment lies against only one of the people whose names are on the account. By refusing to pay out on the levy, the bank will force a special proceeding which will afford notice to all with an interest and result in a court order which will solve the bank's dilemma. The proceeding will produce proof as to the degree of ownership in the joint account, and the judgment creditor can reach only so much of the account as truly belongs to the judgment debtor. Failure of a garnishee to respond to a levy does not constitute disobedience of a subpoena, restraining notice or court order under CPLR 5251 and so cannot prompt a contempt citation. *Household Finance v. Rochester Com. Sav.*, 143 Misc. 2d 436, 541 N.Y.S.2d 160 (Rochester City Ct. 1989).

(2) The CPLR 5206 $50,000 real property exemption applies when money judgments are sought to be satisfied. A mechanic's lien is not a money judgment. Thus, the exemption is not applicable upon foreclosure of a mechanic's lien. *Robert S. Moore, Inc. v. Whittaker*, 142 Misc. 2d 708, 538 N.Y.S.2d 415 (Schoharie Co. Ct. 1989).

(3) Often, if not always, the sale of real property to satisfy creditors will fetch far less than the market value of the property. Where injustices seemed to occur, some courts have invoked their authority under CPLR 5240 to undo the sale, or at least ameliorate the injustice to some extent. *See, e.g., Wandschneider v. Bekeny*, 75 Misc. 2d 32, 346 N.Y.S.2d 925 (Sup. Ct. Westchester Co., 1973). In *Guardian Loan Co. v. Early*, 47 N.Y.2d 515, 419 N.Y.S.2d 56, 392 N.E.2d 1240 (1979), however, the Court held that after the Sheriff's sale is complete and the deed delivered to the purchaser, the sale is not subject to reopening or adjustment under CPLR 5240. The sale may be set aside under CPLR 2003, said the Court, only if there is a defect in the notice, time or manner of the sale procedure resulting in substantial prejudice to the right of a party. While the courts have equitable powers to vacate a sale because of fraud or "exploitive overreaching," even a gross disparity between the sale price and the market value will not alone justify such action. The Court did note that CPLR 5240 may be relied upon in advance of the sale, in an appropriate case, to force the creditor to use a less invasive enforcement remedy if one is available.

(4) *The case of the stubborn judgment debtor:* The judgment was in the amount of $350. The debtor refused to pay it. The sheriff sold the debtor's apartment (market value $200,000) for $15,000 out of which the judgment creditor was paid the $350 and the balance of $11,500 was turned over to the judgment debtor. *House v. Lalor*, 119 Misc. 2d 193, 462 N.Y.S.2d 772 (Sup. Ct. N.Y. Co. 1983).

In *Matter of Mennella v. Lopez-Torres*, 91 N.Y.2d 474, 672 N.Y.S.2d 834, 695 N.E.2d 703 (1998), the Court held that a New York City Civil Court judge may not impose additional procedural hurdles on landlords who have obtained default judgments of eviction in summary proceedings. The initial service of notice of the petition and the petition afford sufficient due process to the tenant.

[F] Direct Payment of Money or Delivery of Property

CPLR 5225 affords the most direct method of satisfying the judgment by providing simply that the debt be paid to the creditor or the property turned over to him — this without any intervention by the sheriff. However, this approach requires a court order which might be just as time consuming. And here, unlike the situation when an execution is delivered to the sheriff, there is no lien to guard against disposition of the property while the creditor is in the process of procuring the order.

With respect to property in the hands of the debtor, a motion is made pursuant to CPLR 5225(a) on notice to the debtor, and the court can order payment of money and delivery of personal property where it is shown that the debtor is in possession of such. With respect to the debtor's property in the hands of a third party, a special proceeding must be brought under subdivision (b) with notice to the debtor. The debtor and anyone with an adverse interest may intervene. If the third party owes a debt to the debtor, then a proceeding must be brought pursuant to CPLR 5227. The notice and intervention rights are the same. Money payable by the third party under CPLR 5225(b) would be in that person's "possession or custody" and would not be the sort of regular debt contemplated under CPLR 5227. You will recall that this "turnover" order, as it is called, was the device at issue in the *Alliance Bond Fund* case that opened this chapter.

NOTES

(1) Observe that the creditor stands in the shoes of the debtor when the garnishee has a set-off against the debtor. In *Industrial Commissioner v. 5 Corners Tavern, Inc.*, 47 N.Y.2d 639, 419 N.Y.S.2d 931, 393 N.E.2d 1005 (1979), the bank loaned $1,800 to a depositor, 5 Corners. The bank was given as security a right of set-off upon the deposit. Plaintiff obtained a judgment against 5 Corners for overdue unemployment insurance taxes and levied against the account. The court ruled that the bank's set-off, protected under section 151 of the Debtor and Creditor Law, was not extinguished by plaintiff's levy. The creditor stood in the debtor's shoes with regard to the set-off.

(2) Where the debtor has transferred property to a third party, the creditor may bring a turnover proceeding against that transferee and need not resort to a plenary action. *Gelbard v. Esses*, 96 A.D.2d 573, 465 N.Y.S.2d 264 (2d Dep't 1983).

[G] Receivers

If the property subject to satisfaction of the judgment needs to be managed in some way (if, for instance it is an income producing business which it would be counterproductive to close), the court can appoint a receiver under CPLR 5228. The duties of the receiver would include administering, improving, leasing, repairing or selling the property or collecting rents during the enforcement process. The creditor must move for this relief, and the decision is wholly discretionary with the court.

§ 22.03 PRIORITIES

PROBLEM A

Abel, Baker and Charlie all enter money judgments against Zacharias within the same month. Abel is the first to do anything in pursuance of the judgment, and he serves an information subpoena and a restraining notice on Zacharias. Baker, a few days later, gets an execution to the sheriff. Charlie, a week later and before there is any levy on Baker's execution, procures an order that Zacharias turn over a tractor-trailer rig.

Has Abel by his diligence obtained a priority? As between Baker and Charlie, who has the priority on the tractor-trailer? If, considering Baker's execution alone, Zacharias ignores a subsequent levy, what is Baker's remedy? If Charlie's turnover order is ignored by Zacharias and he attempts to remove the rig from the state, what is Charlie's remedy?

[A] Personal Property

CPLR 5202(a) sets forth the rights of a creditor who has chosen to follow the execution and levy route and who has delivered an execution to the sheriff. A right is thus established against all the debtor's personal property in the county "superior to the extent of the amount of the execution to the rights of any transferee of the debt or property, except: 1. a transferee who acquired the debt or property for fair consideration before it was levied upon; or 2. a transferee who acquired a debt or personal property not capable of delivery for fair consideration after it was levied upon without knowledge of the levy." Subdivision (b) covers creditors who go after property having obtained a delivery order, an installment payment order or a receivership order. These orders create a right superior to others except those who are transferred the property for fair value and without notice of the order. Who has the priority as between an "execution" creditor and an "order" creditor? CPLR 5234(c) provides that the order is superior to an execution where there has been no levy. As to rights among order creditors, "where two or more such orders . . . are filed, the proceeds of the property or debt shall be applied in the order of filing." The priority of the order holds for 60 days from its filing, with the possibility of an order extending the time. As to rights among execution creditors, the same principle of first in time obtains (CPLR 5234[b]), and the execution is good for 60 days and can be extended (CPLR 5230[c]).

It will be remembered that the restraining notice affords no lien, certainly not with respect to transferees of the property, and also not with respect to another's subsequent delivery of an execution to the sheriff. It has been held, however, that a restraining notice gave the creditor a priority right in the debtor's property superior to that of an assignee for the benefit of creditors. The rationale is simply that assigning the property for the benefit of creditors was a transfer forbidden under CPLR 5222(b) in light of the outstanding restraining notice. *International Ribbon Mills, Ltd. v. Arjan Ribbons, Inc.*, 36 N.Y.2d 121, 365 N.Y.S.2d 808, 325 N.E.2d 137 (1975). As among creditors who have only restraining notices, the first in time rule would seem to apply.

For a discussion of the difference between a lien and a priority, see 6 Weinstein, Korn & Miller ¶ 5202.02.

[B] Real Property

Liens established by docketing have priority commensurate with the order of docketing. CPLR 5203(a). When the creditor-lienor delivers the execution to the sheriff pursuant to CPLR 3235, the sheriff will serve notice of the impending sale to all those with an interest in the property including prior judgment creditors-lienors (CPLR 5236(c)), who, if they fail to deliver their own executions to the sheriff, will lose their lien (CPLR 5236(e)). Otherwise, they would be eligible to share in the proceeds.

NOTES

(1) There may be, of course, competing creditors outside the realm of CPLR art. 52. For instance, in *Lerner v. United States*, 637 F. Supp. 679 (S.D.N.Y. 1986), it was held that where an execution had been delivered to the sheriff before the recording of a tax lien, the judgment debtor had priority. If there is an array of creditors, the priorities issue can be forced by a judgment creditor who can bring a proceeding pursuant to CPLR 5225 (property) or CPLR 5227 (debt). Adverse claimants may intervene and have their rights determined pursuant to CPLR 5239.

(2) CPLR 5241(h) and CPLR 5242(c) give a levy or an income deduction order for family support "priority over any other assignment, levy or process." CPLR 5241(h) also works out a pro rata division should the garnishee be served with more than one levy or order under these support provisions.

(3) In *City of New York v. Panzirer*, 23 A.D.2d 158, 162, 259 N.Y.S.2d 284, 288 (1st Dep't 1965), it was stated: "The result, then, is that in order for a judgment to attain status in the ranking of priorities there must either be a levy, an order directing delivery of property, or the appointment of a receiver. Any other measures taken by the judgment creditor, no matter how diligent, on an absolute or comparative basis, do not suffice to qualify for priority." In that case, a diligent creditor served an information subpoena and restraining notice; but this was of no avail against another judgment creditor who *subsequently* procured a levy pursuant to execution.

§ 22.04 JUDGMENTS NOT FOR MONEY

[A] Law Judgments

Most non-money judgments at law involve the awarding of possession of property. CPLR 5102 governs this process and provides that a judgment or order awarding real property or a chattel can be enforced by an execution, *i.e.*, the creditor will deliver an execution to the sheriff just as she would were she seeking to enforce a money judgment. In this respect the execution will conform to the provisions of CPLR 5230 (setting forth the form and issuance of executions) "except that it shall direct the sheriff to deliver possession of the property to the party designated." Where the landlord is suing to recover rented premises, the summary eviction proceedings of Article 7 of the RPAPL would provide the better remedy (*see* Siegel, Practice Commentaries, McKinney's C5102:1) as would the remedy under the replevin article which, if the chattel is unique, allows an order directed at defendant to give up the chattel. CPLR 7109(b). Otherwise the replevin article ties into CPLR 5012 so that the chattel's return depends on an execution being delivered to the sheriff. *See* Siegel, Practice Commentaries, McKinney's C5102:2.

[B] Equity Judgments

Non-money judgments will normally be equity judgments which mainly involve injunction and specific performance of contracts and which are enforceable by contempt provisions. CPLR 5104. Judiciary Law, section 753 sets forth the courts' contempt powers, and subdivision (A)(3) provides for contempt not only for non-payment of a sum of money ordered by the court to be paid but "for any other disobedience to a lawful mandate of the court." Remember also that contempt is available to enforce several of the money judgment enforcement procedures, *i.e.*, violation of a restraining notice, the delivery-turnover order and the installment payment order. CPLR 5251.

§ 22.05 CONTEMPT PROCEEDINGS

STATE OF NEW YORK v. UNIQUE IDEAS
Court of Appeals
44 N.Y.2d 345, 405 N.Y.S.2d 656, 376 N.E.2d 1301 (1978)

WACHTLER, J.

In this consumer fraud action initially brought by the Attorney-General under article 22-A of the General Business Law, a consent judgment was entered in December, 1974 against Unique Ideas, Inc., and its principal, Ernie Tucker. But the terms of that injunction were blatantly violated when the defendants waited less than one month before offering the same "get rich quick" scheme condemned in the consent judgment to some 2½ million potential new customers. Liability for restitution and for civil contempt has been clearly established by the Attorney-General acting on behalf of defrauded members of the public. The extent of that liability is alone at issue on this appeal.

Originally the defendants used the mails and magazine advertisements to promote sales of a $10 booklet containing Ernie Tucker's "proven easy money secret." Subscribers were supplied with instructions and mailing lists for home sales of the defendants' ornamental mink novelty items. The lists were usually stale, however, and actual home sales were apparently minimal.

Instead of achieving the promised 10% sales order response or even approaching Tucker's purported example of making "$35,000 in just one day at home in bed with the flu through the use of the plan," most subscribers in fact merely contributed to the defendants' wealth by initially paying $10 for the booklet and then advancing between $53 and $695 for mail order materials. Some of those customers sustained their losses in advance of the 1974 consent judgment, others as a result of the postjudgment mailings.

In December, 1975 Special Term granted the Attorney-General's motion to hold the defendants in contempt, finding that within five days from the entry of the consent judgment they had ordered four million envelopes for new bulk mailings of identically deceptive promotional materials. Proof was adduced from four commercial mailing companies that 2,438,648 individual solicitations were mailed to prospective customers. The number of actual subscribers and the extent of their losses, however, were not ascertained.

. . . Aside from restitution, the Attorney-General also sought to impose a civil fine of $250 for each and every one of the admitted 2½ million postjudgment mailings. The trial court found this to be theoretically within its powers since each fraudulent solicitation in its view "constituted a separate and wilful contempt in violation of the consent judgment, each being an independent misrepresentation which was completed upon the mailing of the false material after the entry of judgment."

Under this formula a fine of some $600 million could have been imposed above and beyond sums due in restitution. But Special Term found this "implausible" as well as "harsh and excessive" even under the outrageous circumstances of this case. The court therefore set a compromise figure by reducing the fine to $500,000 and further suspending all but $209,000 less reimbursement claims and expenses, but only on the condition that the defendants comply with the consent judgment in the future.

The Appellate Division affirmed the major factual findings of Special Term but concluded that the maximum fine available under section 773 of the Judiciary Law was $250 multiplied by the number of bulk mailings, which that court found to constitute the number of separate contempts for purposes of gauging the maximum amount of a civil fine. Finding but four bulk mailings, the court reduced the fine to $1,000. Writing for the court but speaking for himself alone, however, Mr. Justice Kupferman would have treated "each separate reply and the servicing thereof, of several thousand, to be a separate contempts." Given this difference of opinion the Appellate Division granted the Attorney-General permission to appeal and certified the question whether its modification was properly made.

Our reading of the statute governing the amount of the fine that may be imposed for civil contempt requires a negative response to the certified question. By its unambiguous terms the statute distinguishes between the amount of the fine assessable in two separate types of civil contempt cases, one where actual damage has resulted from the defendants' contemptuous acts and one where there may be prejudice to a complainant's rights but "it is not shown that such an actual loss or injury has been caused" (Judiciary Law, § 773, as amd by L 1977, ch 437, § 8). In the first type of case the fine must be "sufficient to indemnify the aggrieved party"; in the latter the fine may not exceed the amount of the complainant's costs and expenses plus $250 (§ 773; *see Moffat v. Herman*, 116 N.Y. 131).

In either case, unlike fines for criminal contempt where deterrence is the aim and the State is the aggrieved party entitled to the award (*e.g., Matter of Katz v. Murtagh*, 28 N.Y.2d 234; *cf. Nye v. United States*, 313 U.S. 33, 42-43), civil contempt fines must be remedial in nature and effect (*Gompers v. Bucks Stove & Range Co.*, 221 U.S. 418). The award should be formulated not to punish an offender, but solely to compensate or indemnify private complainants (*Geller v. Flamount Realty Corp.*, 260 N.Y. 346; *Socialistic Co-op. Pub. Assn. v. Kuhn*, 164 N.Y. 473), here represented but not displaced by the Attorney-General[1] (*see United States v. Mine Workers*, 330 U.S. 258).

---

[1] A fine imposed for civil contempt is payable to the "aggrieved party" (Judiciary Law, § 773). Here the Attorney-General is acting solely as a nominal party on behalf of defrauded subscribers who are the real parties in interest within the intendment of this statutory provision. It is their actual loss or injury which makes them "aggrieved" for purposes of the statutory fine, and it is that aggregate injury for which the statute affords indemnification.

In keeping with this compensatory policy, where there is actual loss or injury the statute does not provide for a general $250 fine, single or multiple. It calls instead for an assessment that will indemnify aggrieved parties, in this case the persons who sent money to the defendants in response to the deceptive post-judgment solicitations. Although it has yet to be established exactly how many persons suffered losses, the existence of a substantial injury itself is not disputed. And the extent of that injury could not possibly be less than the $209,000 balance traced to receipts from the contemptuous solicitations and found by Special Term to represent "but the residue of a larger amount of which consumers were defrauded."

Because these losses were shown to be actual and reasonably ascertainable though not yet fully ascertained, any civil fine based on separate acts of contempt multiplied by the statutory maximum for unprovable damages would be inappropriate in this case. Even if we were dealing with the case of mere prejudice rather than actual injury, that construction would be no less problematic, for it could be indiscriminately applied to achieve "extortion beyond the requirements of just compensation or indemnity, and to reward the omission of exact proof by multiplying the maximum award by the number of the offenders" or divisible offenses (*Socialistic Co-op. Pub. Assn. v. Kuhn*, 164 N.Y. 473, 476, *supra*). But we are in fact dealing with actual, provable losses and we therefore decline to adopt a construction which would substitute what would amount to exemplary damages for a reasonably certain compensatory fine.

In view of the statutory distinction based on the compensatory policy for imposing fines for civil contempt, we need not concern ourselves or speculate about the number of contempts, for we are dealing with a single enterprise. Although many deceptive solicitations were mailed and many people were injured, it is the extent of their compensable losses and not their potential strength in numbers which should define the appropriate limits of any civil fine imposed on their behalf. Only a fine properly related to the scope of the injury rather than the potential scope of the offense will serve the compensatory purposes of the civil contempt fine.

To that end and to avoid any enrichment of the defendants at the expense of their victims, the Attorney-General should exhaust all available means of implementing the claims procedure outlined by Special Term. Only after all reasonable avenues for locating and reimbursing claimants have been fully explored will the ultimate fine, including all related costs and expenses, be subject to confirmation upon further hearings. . . .

NOTES ON THE CONTEMPT PROCEDURE

The contempt prerogative may be exercised for either or both of the following purposes: (1) as a technique for vindicating the court's authority and dignity, and (2) as a method of enforcing a judgment or order rendered in favor of a private individual and, at the same time, avoiding further injury to him or his property. Exercise of the contempt power for the first purpose is termed "criminal contempt" whereas its use for the second is designated "civil contempt." *See Department of Environmental Protection of N.Y.C. v. Department of Environmental Conservation of N.Y.S.*, 70 N.Y.2d 233, 519 N.Y.S.2d 539, 513 N.E.2d 706 (1987). And, as noted in the *Unique Ideas* case, there are two kinds of civil contempt as respects the fine, "one where actual damage has resulted from the defendants' contemptuous acts and one where there may be prejudice to a complainant's rights but 'it is not shown that such an actual loss or injury has been caused' (Judiciary Law, § 773.... In the first type of case the fine must be 'sufficient to indemnify the aggrieved party'; in the latter the fine may not exceed the amount of the complainant's costs and expenses plus $250 (§ 773....)."

Section 750 of the Judiciary Law allows a civil court to punish for criminal contempt persons guilty of acts there listed — generally direct affronts to the court. Punishment for these contempts is provided in § 751 and is limited to $1000.00 fine or 30 days in jail, or both (with exceptions for specific kinds of cases). This is designed as punishment, not for redress to another litigant.

Section 753 gives the court power to punish for civil contempt. This is where a party refuses to carry out an injunction or is guilty of interference in some fashion with a court order. For instance, if a restraining order is violated, the judgment debtor may be held in contempt. CPLR 5251 provides for contempt in enforcement proceedings, and CPLR 5104 provides for contempt for refusal to obey any other judgment or order; but one looks to the Judiciary Law for the procedural scheme necessary to effect the contempt process. Fines, as noted above, are governed by § 773. Anomalously, the contemnor may be civilly imprisoned for up to six months and even longer if he still has it within his power to comply with the court's order. § 774. These penalties are invoked to induce the contemnor to comply.

Where the offense is committed in the immediate presence of the court, § 755 provides for summary punishment on the spot. This can be reviewed under article 78 procedures. In most instances of civil contempt, the affronted party will seek a show cause order or an order on notice and the return date will be no less than 10 days so that a defense can be prepared. § 756. The notice shall include in large type "WARNING: YOUR FAILURE TO APPEAR IN COURT MAY RESULT IN ARREST AND IMPRISONMENT FOR CONTEMPT OF COURT." § 756. Section 770 states that the party is entitled to assigned counsel if she cannot afford her own and she must be advised of her right to counsel. These safeguards are the result of the decision in *Vail v. Quinlan*, 406 F. Supp. 951 (S.D.N.Y. 1976), which gutted the contempt procedures then existing on due process grounds. Although this case was reversed by the Supreme Court on the abstention doctrine, 430 U.S. 327, 97 S. Ct. 1211 (1977), its criticism of New York's contempt procedures was taken to heart by the Legislature, which enacted amendments in 1977, including those providing for the warnings.

Note that there is an altogether different kind of contempt provided for in the Penal Law. Section 215.50 makes it a class A misdemeanor to make a disturbance tending to interfere with court proceedings, to be contumacious in other respects in connection with court proceedings or the intentional refusal to obey court orders, a provision overlapping Judiciary Law provisions. Section 215.51 makes it a class E felony when a witness improperly refuses to be sworn before a grand jury or when a protection order is violated. These contempts are prosecuted in the criminal courts in the usual way, *i.e.*, by information or indictment.

NOTE

In *Lu v. Betancourt*, 116 A.D.2d 492, 496 N.Y.S.2d 754 (1st Dep't 1986), a landlord was held in contempt both civilly and criminally, *i.e.*, she was fined $250, ordered imprisoned for 30 days, and also ordered imprisoned for civil contempt until she obeyed the court's order to provide heat and hot water to her tenants. The show cause order issued pursuant to Judiciary Law § 756 and was mailed. The Appellate Division ruled that mailing satisfied the requirements for civil contempt, but that the landlord should have been served personally in order for there to have been a proper criminal contempt proceeding. This result, even though the landlord appeared and contested the charge against her.

§ 22.06 FOREIGN JUDGMENTS

[A] Federal and Sister State Judgments

CPLR 5401 defines a "foreign judgment" as any judgment, state or federal, entitled to full faith and credit "except one obtained by default in appearance, or by confession of judgment." Under CPLR 5402, a foreign judgment need only be filed in any county clerk's office in the state and then enforced exactly like any domestic judgment. The filing must be made within 90 days of its authentication in the foreign jurisdiction and an affidavit must accompany the filing stating that the judgment was not a default or confession judgment and that it remains unsatisfied and has not been stayed.

While this would seem to provide the easiest method of applying New York assets to foreign judgments, CPLR 5406 states that the right of a creditor to move for summary judgment on the judgment in lieu of a complaint under CPLR 3213 is unimpaired. If this route were taken, the remedy of attachment would be available under CPLR 6201(4). Thus, if it is imperative that the New York asset be brought under the creditor's control with all haste and with the element of surprise, the creditor could start a new action in New York on the foreign judgment debt by attachment simultaneously with a motion for summary judgment.

A foreign judgment's full faith and credit effect may bar a New York action. Where plaintiff successfully prosecuted a divorce action in Vermont, she was barred from bringing a second action in New York for equitable distribution. The Vermont court could have distributed the marital property in the divorce proceeding, and since Vermont law prohibits a separate action for property distribution, the principles of res judicata and full faith and credit precluded the second action in New York. *O'Connell v. Corcoran*, 1 N.Y.3d 179, 770 N.Y.S.2d 673, 802 N.E.2d 1071 (2003).

A judgment which does not qualify under the CPLR 5401 definition because it is a default judgment or a judgment by confession can be sued on in New York as a debt. The summary judgment procedure under CPLR 3213 provides an expeditious approach. Note that a judgment reached by "consent" is not the same as a confession of judgment and does qualify under CPLR 5401 for CPLR 5402 treatment. *Mallan v. Samowich*, 94 A.D.2d 249, 464 N.Y.S.2d 122 (1st Dep't 1983).

If a disclosure subpoena is not obeyed, normally a contempt order can issue on motion. Judiciary Law § 756. However, where the judgment being enforced was rendered in another jurisdiction, a motion will not do. The contempt order must be sought by a special proceeding, since the court had no previous jurisdiction in the case. *Federal Deposit Insurance Corp. v. Richman*, 98 A.D.2d 790, 470 N.Y.S.2d 19 (2d Dep't 1983).

[B] Judgments of Foreign Countries

CPLR 5301(b) defines such a judgment as one "granting or denying a sum of money, other than a judgment for taxes, a fine or penalty, or a judgment for support in matrimonial or family matters." Unlike judgments entitled to full faith and credit, these cannot simply be filed and enforced. CPLR 5303 provides that a foreign country judgment "is enforceable by an action on the judgment, a motion for summary judgment in lieu of complaint [CPLR 3213], or in a pending action by counterclaim, cross-claim or affirmative defense." CPLR 6201(4) also makes attachment available.

Under CPLR 5304(a)(1), a foreign country judgment need not be recognized if it originated in a country which "does not provide impartial tribunals or procedures compatible with the requirements of due process of law." The English system clearly meets this standard, so an ex parte order freezing defendant's assets and directing discovery would be honored in New York. The English court had jurisdiction over defendant who appeared in the proceeding and, hence, the money judgment would be recognized in New York. *CIBC Mellon Trust Co. v. Mora Hotel Corp., N.V.*, 100 N.Y.3d 215, 762 N.Y.S.2d 5, 792 N.E.2d 155 (2003). CPLR 5304(b)(4) provides that a foreign judgment "repugnant to the public policy of this state" should not be enforced. A French court's default judgment awarding damages against a United States web site was deemed repugnant, since it violated our free speech requirements. *Sarl Louis Feraud International v. Viewfinder, Inc.*, 406 F. Supp. 2d 274 (S.D.N.Y. 2005).

But the judgment of a South Korean court based on a cause of action for economic loss resulting from a tortious act could be enforced here, even though damages for economic loss in tort cases is generally not recognized in New York. The fact a theory of recovery might not be recognized in New York does not make it necessarily repugnant. *Sung Hwan Co. v. Rite Aid Corp.*, 7 N.Y.3d 78, 817 N.Y.S.2d 600, 850 N.E.2d 647 (2006). Moreover, the South Korean judgment was enforceable notwithstanding that its exercise of personal jurisdiction was more expansive than that permitted by CPLR 302.

Chapter 23

RES JUDICATA

§ 23.01 INTRODUCTION

The rules which are intended to prevent parties from litigating the same grievance more than once are collectively referred to as the doctrine of res judicata. Unfortunately, this area of the law is plagued by a confusing use of different sets of terminology. It is therefore important to treat vocabulary before discussing doctrine. In the chapter headings and notes in this book we have followed the terminology used in the Restatement (Second) of Judgments (1982). Thus, the major branches of the law of res judicata are denominated "claim preclusion" and "issue preclusion." Restatement (Second) of Judgments, Ch. 1, p.2; §§ 23-29 Titles D-E, pp. 195-303.

Claim preclusion, which includes the doctrines of "merger" and "bar," is operative "when a judgment is rendered in an action and a second action is sought to be maintained on the same claim. Ordinarily, if the judgment was rendered for the plaintiff, the claim is held to be extinguished and merged in the judgment; if the judgment was rendered for the defendant, . . . the judgment is a bar to a second action on the same claim." *Id.*, § 23 Title D, p. 195.

The terminology of the Restatement has sometimes been used by the New York courts* but not consistently. Thus, res judicata is sometimes used to mean only claim preclusion, and "collateral estoppel" is used in place of issue preclusion. Keeping this dual vocabulary in mind will help avoid confusion.

Other terms sometimes encountered in this area are:

Direct estoppel: an aspect of issue preclusion which differs from collateral estoppel in that it refers to the situation in which the second action is on the same claim as the first, whereas the estoppel is "collateral" if the second case involves a different claim. Restatement § 27 comment b.

Splitting a cause of action: an aspect of merger, this doctrine provides that a plaintiff who brings an action for part of his claim is prevented from bringing a second action for the remaining part of it. *See, e.g., Stoner v. Culligan, Inc.*, 32 A.D.2d 170, 300 N.Y.S.2d 966 (3d Dep't 1969).

Law of the case: prevents the relitigation during the course of the same action of an issue already determined in it, *e.g.*, a court which had found, in deciding a pre-trial motion, that the action had been timely commenced could not enter-

---

* *See American Ins. Co. v. Messinger*, 43 N.Y.2d 184, 189, n.2, 401 N.Y.S.2d 36, 39, 371 N.E.2d 798, 802 (1977).

tain a defense based on lack of timeliness. This doctrine does not prevent review of a decision by an appellate court, nor does it prevent a re-examination of the issue by the trial court on the grounds authorized by CPLR 5015 or pursuant to a proper application to reargue or renew the motion under CPLR 2221.

Election of remedies: the doctrine of election of remedies was a product of the common law's intolerance of a litigant's taking inconsistent positions. In essence, it prevented a party who had chosen one of two mutually inconsistent remedies or legal theories, from later pursuing the other if the first foundered. For example, a party who had served a complaint seeking recovery for the goods on the theory of implied contract, could not later sue for conversion of the same goods because an essential, if fictional, aspect of the contract action was the assertion that the goods had been sold to the defendants. *Terry v. Munger*, 121 N.Y. 161, 124 N.E.2d 272 (1890). The CPLR tempers the election of remedies doctrine by expressly negating some of the rules in which it found expression. This is accomplished by the six subdivisions of CPLR 3002 and by CPLR 3003.

Even in situations in which CPLR 3002 or 3003 have no application, the courts will be slow to bar an action merely because plaintiff previously sought another remedy which was inconsistent, although such a plaintiff may well encounter res judicata problems. The election doctrine today properly survives only insofar as it serves to prevent the award, rather than the claim, of inconsistent remedies. In one representative modern case, the Appellate Division held that plaintiff could not recover damages for a claim of fraud under a contract and obtain rescission of the contract as well. "This is because an award of damages for fraud affirms the contract while penalizing the fraudulent party for his breach. Rescission vitiates the contract and places the parties in status quo prior to the transaction. . . ." *Vitale v. Coyne Realty, Inc.*, 66 A.D.2d 562, 568, 414 N.Y.S.2d 388, 393 (4th Dep't 1979) (Callahan, J., dissenting in part). Plainly, the court could not hold that there was, and was not, a contract in effect. In such situations, the modern plaintiff will have to "elect" one of the possible remedies at some point in the litigation, but not ordinarily until after trial, for only then is it clear what remedy is appropriate. *See Plant City Steel Corp. v. National Machinery Exchange, Inc.*, 23 N.Y.2d 472, 297 N.Y.S.2d 559, 245 N.E.2d 213 (1969).

Judicial estoppel: A party will be estopped from asserting a proposition of fact that differs from the position that party took respecting the same issue if the court previously adopted that party's position. *See, e.g., Kimco of New York v. Devon*, 163 A.D.2d 573, 558 N.Y.S.2d 630 (2d Dep't 1990) (when, in one action, a litigant had convinced a court to enforce an option agreement, that party was estopped from contesting the validity of the option in a subsequent action).

§ 23.02 CLAIM PRECLUSION

GOWAN v. TULLY
Court of Appeals
45 N.Y.2d 32, 407 N.Y.S.2d 650, 379 N.E.2d 177 (1978)

BREITEL, CHIEF JUDGE.

Petitioners are former part-time estate tax attorneys in the noncompetitive class of the civil service in the State Department of Taxation and Finance. They brought this proceeding under CPLR article 78 for reinstatement to the positions from which they had been removed by respondent commissioner. They appeal from an order of the Appellate Division which affirmed, one Justice dissenting, the dismissal of their petition on grounds of res judicata. An earlier petition seeking the same relief had resulted in a final judgment for respondent.

At issue is whether petitioners may escape the doctrine of res judicata by tendering an additional basis for finding their dismissals illegal, namely, that the dismissals were patronage dismissals made in bad faith in contravention of the Supreme Court's intervening decision in *Elrod v. Burns* (427 U.S. 347, 96 S.Ct. 2673, 49 L.Ed.2d 547).

The order of the Appellate Division should be affirmed. Once a cause of action has been finally adjudicated, tender of an additional legal issue not raised in the original action does not avoid the bar of res judicata merely because the Supreme Court of the United States had not fully articulated the additional issue until after the cause of action had been adjudicated.

Petitioners were among 44 part-time estate tax attorneys, all of whom resigned or were removed during 1975 and were replaced by members of a different political party. In July, 1975, before the removals had been completed, several of the attorneys brought a proceeding seeking reinstatement (*see Matter of Nolan v. Tully*, 52 A.D.2d 295, 383 N.Y.S.2d 655, *mot. for lv. to app. den.* 40 N.Y.2d 803, 387 N.Y.S.2d 1030, 356 N.E.2d 482, *mot. to dismiss app. granted* 40 N.Y.2d 844, 387 N.Y.S.2d 1034, 356 N.E.2d 492). That proceeding, the *Nolan* proceeding, was determined to be a class action on behalf of all estate tax attorneys who had been or might be discharged before final determination of the proceeding (CPLR 902). Petitioners in the present case were, therefore, members of the class, although they were not actually discharged until after the *Nolan* proceeding was brought.* Relief was sought primarily under section 75 of the Civil Service Law, but the petition, as amended, also alleged a violation of State and Federal constitutional rights.

---

* Not questioned by petitioners is the res judicata effect, generally, of class action judgments against members of the class who do not actually participate in the litigation. The issue has been extensively treated elsewhere (*see, e.g.*, Restatement, Judgments 2d [Tent. Draft No. 2, 1975], § 85, subd. [1], par. [e], comment e; . . .).

The instant proceeding was brought while the *Nolan* matter was still pending. In addition to the allegations made in the *Nolan* proceeding, the petition alleged that the terminations were not in good faith and that "the incumbents were removed . . . for the sole purpose of appointing successors with different political affiliations." By agreement of counsel, the instant proceeding was held in abeyance pending final adjudication of the *Nolan* proceeding.

At the Appellate Division in the *Nolan* proceeding, the *Nolan* petitioner argued that the dismissals were made in bad faith, and sought to have the court take judicial notice of allegations to that effect made in the petition in the instant proceeding. The Appellate Division, in affirming the dismissal of the *Nolan* petition, however, discussed only the issues arising under section 75 of the Civil Service Law. The court held that despite the fact that petitioners were in the noncompetitive class of the civil service, they were not entitled to tenure because they were independent officers under section 22 of the Civil Service Law. . . . Then, in *Elrod v. Burns* (427 U.S. 347, 96 S.Ct. 2673, 49 L.Ed.2d 547, *supra*), decided shortly after the Appellate Division's affirmance in *Nolan*, a three-Judge plurality of the Supreme Court concluded that patronage dismissals were unconstitutional under the First and Fourteenth Amendments of the United States Constitution (*id.*, at p. 373, 96 S.Ct. 2673). Leave to appeal the *Nolan* case to this court was nevertheless denied, and an appeal as of right was dismissed for lack of a substantial constitutional question. . . . A motion by petitioners in this case to intervene in this court was dismissed as academic.

Following final adjudication of the *Nolan* proceeding, the instant proceeding was dismissed on res judicata grounds, and the dismissal was affirmed at the Appellate Division, one Justice dissenting. At the outset, it should be evident that the gravamen in this proceeding is the same as that in the *Nolan* proceeding. In each case, petitioners challenged the patronage dismissals, and seek reinstatement. The foundation facts are the same, and so is the relief sought. Mere differences in legal theory do not create separate causes of action. . . .

The only question of even marginal substance involves the purported unavailability in the *Nolan* proceeding of a legal issue tendered in this proceeding. Petitioners contend that since the issue in *Elrod v. Burns* (427 U.S. 347, 96 S.Ct. 2673, 49 L.Ed.2d 547, *supra*) was not resolved in time to raise the unconstitutionality of patronage dismissals in the *Nolan* proceeding, they should not be barred from raising that issue now.

It is settled law, however that "[t]he conclusive effect of a final disposition is not to be disturbed by a subsequent change in decisional law" (*Slater v. American Min. Spirits Co.*, 33 N.Y.2d 443, 447, 354 N.Y.S.2d 620, 623, 310 N.E.2d 300, 302). . . . The principle applies even when the change heralds a new policy as important as the relative apportionment doctrine evolved in *Dole v. Dow Chem. Co.* (30 N.Y.2d 143, 331 N.Y.S.2d 382, 282 N.E.2d 288; *see Slater v. American Min. Spirits Co.*, 33 N.Y.2d 443, 447, 354 N.Y.S.2d 620, 623, 310 N.E.2d 300, 302, *supra*). That the change in legal doctrine is constitutional in nature does not, automatically, dictate a different result. It may be that where a final adjudication affects "important ongoing social or political relationships," a subsequent major change in constitutional doctrine should permit reconsideration of the original claim, at least as to its future effect (*see* Restatement, Judgments 2d (Tent. Draft No. 1, 1973), § 61.2, Comment E). That possibility need not be addressed, for the situation posited is not presented in this case.

Moreover, it is not clear that the *Elrod* case represents a major change in the law. First, the scope of the decision remains uncertain, since a majority of the Supreme Court was unwilling to hold all patronage dismissals constitutionally impermissible. . . . Second, as petitioners acknowledge, civil service employees in this State have long been protected from certain kinds of dismissals made in bad faith upon change in the appointing power. . . . Although this protection originates in the merit selection provisions of the State Constitution rather than in the Federal Constitution, and the extent of the protection may not be completely defined, the issue was there for petitioners to raise. Not having done so in the *Nolan* proceeding, they may not now be heard to complain. Accordingly, the order of the Appellate Division should be affirmed, with costs.

MATTER OF HODES v. AXELROD
Court of Appeals
70 N.Y.2d 364, 520 N.Y.S.2d 933, 515 N.E.2d 612 (1987)

KAYE, JUDGE.

[Petitioners Hodes and Herman, owners of a nursing home, were convicted of Medicaid fraud in April, 1979. The Department of Health pursuant to a hearing revoked their nursing home operating certificate; but it was determined on appeal that a provision in the Correction Law barring automatic license revocations based on convictions prevented the revocation. *Matter of Hodes v. Axelrod*, 56 N.Y.2d 930, 453 N.Y.S.2d 607, 439 N.E.2d 323, *rearg. denied*, 57 N.Y.2d 775, 454 N.Y.S.2d 1033, 440 N.E.2d 1343 (1982). The Public Health Law and the Correction Law were promptly amended by the Legislature to eliminate the conflict, whereupon the Department of Health commenced a second proceeding to revoke petitioners' certificate. The IAS court enjoined the proceeding on res judicata grounds and a divided Appellate Division affirmed, the majority finding that petitioners had a vested property right in the first determination.]

The question raised by this appeal is whether the doctrine of vested rights or res judicata bars a second administrative proceeding — where the first has failed — for automatic revocation of petitioners' nursing home operating certificate owing to their industry-related felony convictions. . . .

The Vested Rights Doctrine

Although a statute is not invalid merely because it reaches back to establish the legal significance of events occurring before its enactment, a traditional principle applied in determining the constitutionality of such legislation is that the Legislature is not free to impair vested or property rights (*United States Trust Co. v. New Jersey*, 431 U.S. 1, 97 S.Ct. 1505, 52 L.Ed.2d 92; 2 Rotunda, Nowak & Young, Constitutional Law § 15.9). The vested rights doctrine recognizes that a "judgment, after it becomes final, may not be affected by subsequent legislation." (McKinney's Cons. Laws of N.Y., Book 1, Statutes § 58.) Once all avenues of appeal have been exhausted, under this doctrine a judgment becomes an inviolable property right which thereafter may not constitutionally be abridged by subsequent legislation (*id.*).

Germania Sav. Bank v. Village of Suspension Bridge, 159 N.Y. 362, 54 N.E. 33 — decided in 1899 — is a representative application of the traditional principle of "vested rights." In that case, this court had initially denied a motion for leave to appeal in an action on coupon bonds because the statute then in effect did not allow such an appeal absent permission of the General Term when the complaint demanded less than $500; the statute was thereafter amended to remove the monetary limitation. In dismissing a second motion for leave, we held that applying the statute retrospectively in such circumstances would unconstitutionally deprive the defendant of a vested property right: "A judgment is a contract which is subject to interference by the courts so long as the right of appeal therefrom exists, but when the time within which an appeal may be brought has expired, it ripens into an unchangeable contract and becomes property, which can be disposed of or affected only by the act of the owner, or through the power of eminent domain. It is, then, beyond the reach of legislation affecting the remedy, because it has become an absolute right which cannot be impaired by statute." (*Id.*, at 368, 54 N.E. 33; *see also, Saltser & Weinsier v. McGoldrick*, 295 N.Y. 499, 68 N.E.2d 508; *Feiber Realty Corp. v. Abel*, 265 N.Y. 94, 191 N.E. 847; *Livingston v. Livingston*, 173 N.Y. 377, 383, 66 N.E. 123; *Matter of Greene*, 166 N.Y. 485, 492, 60 N.E. 183.)

Since *Germania Sav. Bank* (*supra*), however, the traditional principle has undergone more critical analysis. We have recognized that the vested rights doctrine is conclusory, and indeed a fiction that "hides many unmentioned considerations of fairness to the parties, reliance on pre-existing law, the extent of retroactivity and the nature of the public interest to be served by the law. (Hochman, *Retroactive Legislation*, 73 Harv. L. Rev. 692.)" (*Matter of Chrysler Props. v. Morris*, 23 N.Y.2d 515, 518, 297 N.Y.S.2d 723, 245 N.E.2d 395). While there is a persisting aversion to retroactive legislation generally (*see, e.g.*, 2 Rotunda, Nowak & Young, Constitutional Law § 15.9), we have noted that the modern cases reflect a less rigid view of the Legislature's right to pass such legislation and more candid consideration — on a case-by-case basis — of the various policy considerations upon which the constitutionality of retroactive legislation depends (*Matter of Chrysler Props. v. Morris*, 23 N.Y.2d 515, 521-522, 297 N.Y.S.2d 723, 245 N.E.2d 395, *supra*). "[T]his is an area where broad conclusions are to be studiously avoided for it is impossible to predict in advance how in each concrete case the various factors will line up." (*Id.*, at 519, 297 N.Y.S.2d 723, 245 N.E.2d 395.)

Balancing the various factors, we hold that the vested rights doctrine does not preclude application of the amended statute to these petitioners.

Examining first the nature of the right petitioners allegedly secured by the judgment, plainly there can be no vested right in their continued operating license; petitioners themselves acknowledge this. The amended legislation does not reopen petitioners' criminal prosecution. At most, the judgment could give them an advantage over their fellow facility operators whose certificates under the amended law are automatically revoked upon an industry-related felony conviction. It is, further, significant in the balance that petitioners' alleged right arises as the unfortunate result of an inadvertent gap or anomaly in the interrelationship of two laws, which the Legislature within weeks cured by the amended statute now sought to be enforced. Any reliance by petitioners on the judgment thus would have been the product of a legislatively unintended windfall which was, immediately upon identification, eliminated. (*See*, Hochman, *The Supreme Court and the Constitutionality of Retroactive Legislation*, 73 Harv. L. Rev. 692, 705-706.)

To be weighed with these considerations is the fact that petitioners continue to run a public health facility. Nursing homes care for the aged and infirm, and receive State funds for such care under the Medicaid program (*see*, Social Services Law § 363). There is a public interest in policing this industry and removing persons convicted of industry-related felonies from the operation of nursing homes. That this is a compelling interest is plain not only from the nature of the services offered but also from the publicized scandals that have plagued this industry. Automatic revocation in these circumstances in itself serves the public interest, so that upon conviction such operators may be removed expeditiously; nearly a decade has already elapsed since petitioners' convictions. The amended statute purports to reach "all existing operating certificates," thus affecting only those licensees continuing to offer health care to the public. The application of the law to all such persons is rationally related to a legitimate governmental purpose, and results in the equal treatment of licensed operators.

Thus, we conclude that there is a strong public interest to be served by permitting the law to be enforced as amended in 1983, and that in this case the public interest overrides petitioners' claimed constitutional objection.

Res Judicata

Finding no constitutional impediment in the application of the amended statute to petitioners, we next consider whether the cause of action for automatic revocation was somehow extinguished by the judgment in the prior proceeding, brought under the old law.

Simply stated, where there is a valid final judgment the doctrine of res judicata, or claim preclusion, bars future litigation between those parties on the same cause of action. The doctrine rests not on constitutional underpinnings but on sound public policy considerations. Putting an end to a matter for all time is fair to the party who has endured the cost and travail of a litigation, fair to the party whose claim has once been heard, and in the interest of the judicial system generally (*Matter of Reilly v. Reid*, 45 N.Y.2d 24, 28, 407 N.Y.S.2d 645, 379 N.E.2d 172; 5 Weinstein-Korn-Miller, N.Y. Civ. Prac. ¶ 5011.07; *see also,* Restatement [Second] of Judgments § 17 *et seq.*).

While simply stated, the doctrine often eludes ready application because of difficulty determining whether there is the requisite identity between an earlier cause of action and a later one. The fact that causes of action may be separately stated or statable, or invoke different legal theories, will not permit relitigation of claims (*Matter of Reilly v. Reid, supra,* at 29, 407 N.Y.S.2d 645, 379 N.E.2d 172; *see also, O'Brien v. City of Syracuse,* 54 N.Y.2d 353, 357, 445 N.Y.S.2d 687, 429 N.E.2d 1158; *Smith v. Russell Sage Coll.,* 54 N.Y.2d 185, 192, 445 N.Y.S.2d 68, 429 N.E.2d 746). In this State, we have adopted a "transaction" test for resolving such questions: a judgment extinguishes "all rights of the plaintiff to remedies against the defendant with respect to all or any part of the transaction, or series of connected transactions, out of which the action arose"; a "transaction" is determined pragmatically, depending on whether the facts form a convenient trial unit and whether their treatment as a unit conforms to the parties' expectations or business understanding or usage (Restatement [Second] of Judgments § 24; *Matter of Reilly v. Reid, supra,* 45 N.Y.2d at 29, 407 N.Y.S.2d 645, 379 N.E.2d 172; *see also,* Siegel, N.Y. Prac. § 442).

Twice recently this court has applied the transaction test where the only real difference between the first and second actions was an intervening change in law. In *Matter of John P. v. Whalen,* 54 N.Y.2d 89, 94, 444 N.Y.S.2d 598, 429 N.E.2d 117, we held that res judicata did not bar a second request for documents pursuant to an amended version of the Freedom of Information Law even though the original request was essentially the same and properly denied under preexisting law. The statutory amendment materially changed the parties' rights such that the new request was independent from the first and thus a wholly distinct transaction. In *Matter of Meegan S. v. Donald T.,* 64 N.Y.2d 751, 485 N.Y.S.2d 982, 475 N.E.2d 449, a paternity proceeding was initially dismissed as untimely under the then-applicable two-year Statute of Limitations. The Statute of Limitations was thereafter enlarged to five years and the proceeding was recommenced within the new limitations period. We held that the amended Statute of Limitations was to be applied retroactively and that the second petition was not subject to dismissal on the ground of res judicata: "The issue disposed of by the order of dismissal in the first proceeding, however, was only that petitioner's claim was untimely under the Statute of Limitations then applicable to paternity suits, and it did not reach the issue of timeliness under the amended law, which would permit petitioner's claim." (*Id.,* at 752, 485 N.Y.S.2d 982, 475 N.E.2d 449.)

Although both revocation proceedings instituted against petitioners are based on the same felony convictions, seeking the same remedy, it is equally true that petitioner in *John P.* twice made virtually the same FOIL requests and plaintiff in *Meegan S.* twice commenced the same paternity suit. The operative consideration in all three cases is that the statutory rights of the parties were altered between the first and second proceedings. This being so, the two proceedings against petitioners can be said to lack the requisite identity for application of res judicata (*see, State Farm Ins. Co. v. Duel*, 324 U.S. 154, 162, 65 S.Ct. 573, 89 L.Ed. 812).

We find this analysis particularly apt in the present situation because of the public importance of the issues involved (*see,* Restatement [Second] of Judgments § 28[2], comment c; § 26[1][d]). For compelling reasons in the public interest, the Legislature provided that all persons holding operating certificates at the time of the amended law should be equally subject to automatic forfeiture upon conviction of an industry-related felony. If the pending proceeding against petitioners under the amended statute were precluded by res judicata, petitioners would be left with a license to operate a public health facility despite their convictions and despite the fact that others operating comparable facilities automatically lose their licenses upon comparable convictions.

Petitioners' arguments in support of res judicata are in the end much the same as their plea for application of the vested rights doctrine — that permitting a second revocation proceeding to go forward against them unfairly impairs rights already adjudicated by this court in the first proceeding. Indeed, the doctrines of vested rights and res judicata — while resting on different foundations and implicating different values — do have certain common elements, most powerfully a central concern for fairness. In this respect, however, our "vested rights" analysis and conclusions are pertinent. A second revocation proceeding is not unfair to petitioners in any sense that is protected by law; this proceeding is, to the contrary, supported by supervening considerations of public interest that have been properly balanced by the Legislature.

Accordingly, the order of the Appellate Division should be reversed, with costs, and the petition dismissed.

DeWEERTH v. BALDINGER
38 F.3d 1266 (2d Cir. 1994)

[reprinted in § 20.03, *supra*]

NOTES

(1) The perils of the rules of claim preclusion are nowhere more dramatically illustrated than by *Hahl v. Sugo*, 169 N.Y. 109, 62 N.E. 135 (1901), which arose when defendant constructed a building, part of which encroached on plaintiffs' land. The latter obtained a judgment granting them recovery of their property, but they were unable to get it enforced because the sheriff reported it impracticable to do so. Plaintiffs then brought an action in equity to compel defendant to remove the wall from the property but here they foundered, the Court of

Appeals holding that despite the shift in remedy sought, they were attempting to sue on the same cause of action on which they had already recovered a judgment.

How could plaintiffs' lawyer have avoided this pitfall?

(2) Does the doctrine of claim preclusion underlie the "compulsory" counterclaim cases we explored in Chapter 13? Reconsider, in particular, *Henry Modell & Co., Inc. v. Minister, Elders and Deacons of the Reformed Protestant Dutch Church of the City of New York*, discussed in note 1, following *Chisholm-Ryder Co. v. Sommer & Sommer*, in § 13.04[B]. Under that case, a party may be claim precluded as a result of prior litigation in which it was the defendant, even if it asserted no counterclaims. The preclusion is avoided, however, if the defendant in the first action asserts the claim only as an affirmative defense. *See Batavia Kill Watershed District v. Charles O. Desch, Inc.*, § 13.04[B], *supra*. Is this consistent with the general rule of claim preclusion? Is it otherwise justifiable?

(3) May a party avoid the impact of claim preclusion by showing that in the first action he did not have a full and fair opportunity to be heard? In *Kremer v. Chemical Const. Corp.*, 456 U.S. 461, 102 S. Ct. 1883, 72 L. Ed. 2d 262 (1982), the Supreme Court said:

> While our previous expressions of the requirement of a full and fair opportunity to litigate have been in the context of collateral estoppel or issue preclusion, it is clear . . . that invocation of res judicata or claim preclusion is subject to the same limitation.

456 U.S. at 481, n.22, 102 S. Ct. at 1897, 72 L. Ed. 2d at 1897.

PROBLEM A

Refer again to *Iannone v. Cayuga Constr. Corp.*, *supra*, § 13.07. Assume that following the reported case, plaintiff Iannone commenced a new action against the same defendants, alleging that they injured his property by negligently driving piles and moving heavy equipment while performing their construction tasks on the new subway during the period March, 1973-December, 1975.

What result if the defendants move under CPLR 3211(a)(5) for a dismissal of the action on the grounds of claim preclusion?

O'BRIEN v. CITY OF SYRACUSE
Court of Appeals
54 N.Y.2d 353, 445 N.Y.S.2d 687, 429 N.E.2d 1158 (1981)

COOKE, CHIEF JUDGE.

A property owner who unsuccessfully asserts against a governmental entity a claim for *de facto* appropriation may not later bring another action for trespass in an attempt to recover damages for the same acts as those on which the first lawsuit was grounded.

Plaintiffs owned property in an area of Syracuse subject to urban rehabilitation. In 1973, plaintiffs commenced an article 78 proceeding against the same parties as are defendants in the present litigation. In this earlier suit, plaintiffs alleged that defendants had committed a number of acts that so seriously interfered with plaintiffs' property rights as to amount to a *de facto* appropriation by the city. In a nonjury trial, the 1973 suit was dismissed for failure to establish a *de facto* taking. The Appellate Division, Fourth Department, affirmed. . . .

In March, 1978, plaintiffs filed a new complaint, essentially restating the allegations of their previous petition, but with the added averment that the city had taken the property by tax deed on June 1, 1977. Defendants moved to dismiss the complaint on the ground of *res judicata*, which motion was granted with leave to amend. Plaintiffs then filed an amended complaint reiterating the original complaint's allegations and adding general statements that defendants "wrongfully, unlawfully and willfully" trespassed upon the property at various times during the period 1967 to 1978, and that the property was damaged during these numerous intrusions. Defendants again moved to dismiss on the grounds of *res judicata*, Statute of Limitations, and failure to serve timely a notice of claim.

Supreme Court denied the motion on all three points. As to the issue of *res judicata*, the Trial Judge concluded that no bar existed because there were involved materially different elements of proof for the two theories of recovery, citing *Smith v. Kirkpatrick*, 305 N.Y. 66, 111 N.E.2d 209. Specifically, the Judge indicated that an action for *de facto* appropriation required proof that the city owned the property, while an action for trespass required the plaintiffs to prove title in themselves. As to the two other grounds, the Judge calculated the time from June 1, 1977, when the tax deed was executed, and ruled that the action was not time-barred.

The Appellate Division, Fourth Department, reversed on the reasoning that the entire action was barred by the doctrine of *res judicata*. That court granted the motion and dismissed the complaint. The order should be affirmed, but on a different basis than that employed by the Appellate Division in viewing the general allegations of trespass in the instant action.

In analyzing the complaint, plaintiffs' allegations fall into two categories: (1) those concerning activities underlying the 1973 litigation; and (2) those asserting trespass generally. Only the claims encompassed by the first category are definitely barred by *res judicata*.

This State has adopted the transactional analysis approach in deciding *res judicata* issues (*Matter of Reilly v. Reid*, 45 N.Y.2d 24, 407 N.Y.S.2d 645, 379 N.E.2d 172). Under this address, once a claim is brought to a final conclusion, all other claims arising out of the same transaction or series of transactions are barred, even if based upon different theories or if seeking a different remedy (*id.*, at pp. 29-30, 407 N.Y.S.2d 645). Here, all of defendants' conduct falling in the first category was also raised during the 1973 suit as the basis for that litigation. That proceeding having been brought to a final conclusion, no other claim may be predicated upon the same incidents.

Plaintiffs, relying on *Smith v. Kirkpatrick*, 305 N.Y. 66, 111 N.E.2d 209, *supra*, urge that *de facto* appropriation and trespass are actions having different theoretical bases and requiring different evidentiary proof. This contention, however, erroneously characterizes the bases of the two causes. *De facto* appropriation does not involve a proof of title in the governmental defendant. Rather, *de facto* appropriation, in the context of physical invasion, is based on showing that the government has intruded onto the citizen's property and interfered with the owner's property rights to such a degree that the conduct amounts to a constitutional taking requiring the government to purchase the property from the owner; only at that point does title actually transfer. "[T]he taking occurs when interference with the owner's use has occurred to such an extent that an easement by prescription will rise by lapse of time" (Dunham, Griggs v. Allegheny County *in Perspective: Thirty Years of Supreme Court Expropriation Law*, 1962 S.Ct.Rev. 63, 87). In effect, *de facto* appropriation may be characterized as an aggravated form of trespass. The pertinent evidence in both actions is the same. The basic distinction lies in the egregiousness of the trespass and whether it is of such intensity as to amount to a taking.

In any event, even if it were assumed that the two actions involved materially different elements of proof, the second suit would be barred as to the claim predicated upon the first category allegations. When alternative theories are available to recover what is essentially the same relief for harm arising out of the same or related facts such as would constitute a single "factual grouping" (Restatement, Judgments 2d, § 61 [Tent Draft No. 5]), the circumstance that the theories involve materially different elements of proof will not justify presenting the claim by two different actions.[1] Consequently, plaintiffs' action is barred by the doctrine of *res judicata* insofar as the allegations in the first category are concerned.

Finally, the second category of allegations — the general trespass allegations — are not barred by *res judicata* to the extent that they describe acts

---

[1] To the extent *Smith v. Kirkpatrick*, 305 N.Y. 66, 111 N.E.2d 209, *supra* may be to the contrary, it is overruled.

occurring after the 1973 lawsuit. They are, however, barred by reason of plaintiffs' failure to serve timely a notice of claim.[2]

. . . .

NOTES

(1) Do not overlook footnote 1 of the preceding opinion, for it eliminates a previously well established exception to the general rule governing claim preclusion in New York. Under the now overruled case of *Smith v. Kirkpatrick*, 305 N.Y. 66, 72, 111 N.E.2d 209, 212 (1953), a second lawsuit arising from the same transaction as an earlier one would not be barred if the "requisite elements of proof and hence the evidence necessary to sustain recovery vary materially." Thus, the plaintiff in *Smith* was permitted to maintain an action in *quantum meruit* for the reasonable value of his services against a defendant who had defeated Smith's earlier action against him for breach of contract to pay sales commissions allegedly earned by Smith. The second suit was not barred, even though it involved the same work that was at issue in action number one; the proof necessary to sustain it "varied materially" in that there was no need to prove an agreement and the focus was instead on the work actually done.

(2) A case which has never been overruled is *Reilly v. Sicilian Asphalt Paving Co.*, 170 N.Y. 40, 62 N.E. 772 (1902), which held that one who suffered personal injury and property damage in a driving accident (he was driving a horse and buggy!) could maintain separate lawsuits for each type of injury because each gave rise to a different cause of action. In justification of its approach, the court pointed to some legal distinctions between the two claims:

> Different periods of limitation apply. The plaintiff's action for personal injuries is barred by the lapse of three years; that for injury to the property not till the lapse of six years. The plaintiff cannot assign his right of action for the injury to his person, and it would abate and be lost by his death before a recovery of a verdict, and if the defendant were a natural person also by his death before that time.

170 N.Y. at 44, 62 N.E. at 773.

Are all of these distinctions still valid today? Are other factors relevant, such as the likelihood that a plaintiff has different insurers for his person and his property? Interestingly, the Court of Appeals has embraced the *Reilly* doctrine in modern dicta. *See Velazquez v. Water Taxi, Inc.*, 49 N.Y.2d 762, 764 n.*, 426 N.Y.S.2d 467, 468, 403 N.E.2d 172 (1980).

---

[2] The notice refers to the taking by tax deed in 1977. This is a transaction independent from the others and occurring after the termination of the first suit. Thus, it is not barred by the doctrine of *res judicata*. . . .

New York is in a distinct minority in allowing two actions in this situation. For a thorough discussion of the issue, see F. James, G. Hazard & J. Leubsdorf, Civil Procedure § 11.10, pp. 688-92 (5th ed. 2001).

XIAO YANG CHEN v. FISCHER
Court of Appeals
6 N.Y.3d 94, 810 N.Y.S.2d 96, 843 N.E.2d 723 (2005)

CIPARICK, J.

[Plaintiff Chen married Ian Fischer on March 22, 2001. Shortly thereafter Fischer commenced a divorce action on the ground of cruel and inhuman treatment. Chen counterclaimed on the same grounds, alleging specifically Fischer's acts of cruelty causing injury. She also included a fraudulent inducement cause of action. Prior to trial of the divorce action, the parties stipulated to withdraw all fault allegations save one and ultimately a dual judgment of divorce was granted on May 8, 2002, on the one fault ground and the fraudulent inducement ground. The equitable distribution issue was also determined. Chen commenced this personal injury action on January 18, 2002, while the matrimonial action was still pending. The IAS court granted Fischer's CPLR 3211(a)(5) motion to dismiss on grounds of res judicata.]

The Appellate Division affirmed, agreeing that the action was barred because the tort claim could have been litigated with the divorce action and Chen did not expressly reserve the right to bring that claim when she withdrew her fault allegations for purposes of the stipulation. The Court extended the rule we set forth in *Boronow v. Boronow* (71 NY2d 284, 290 [1988]) — that issues relating to marital property be decided with the matrimonial action — to interspousal tort actions. Specifically, the Court found that "[s]ocietal needs, logic, and the desirability of bringing spousal litigation to finality now compel us to . . . hold that an interspousal tort action seeking to recover damages for personal injuries commenced subsequent to, and separate from, an action for divorce is . . . barred by claim preclusion" (12 AD3d 43, 47 [2004]). We granted Chen leave to appeal and now reverse.

Typically, principles of res judicata require that "once a claim is brought to a final conclusion, all other claims arising out of the same transaction or series of transactions are barred, even if based upon different theories or if seeking a different remedy" (*O'Brien v. City of Syracuse*, 54 NY2d 353, 357 [1981]). In the context of a matrimonial action, this Court has recognized that a final judgment of divorce settles the parties' rights pertaining not only to those issues that were actually litigated, but also to those that could have been litigated (*Rainbow v. Swisher*, 72 NY2d 106, 110 [1988]; *see also O'Connell v. Corcoran*, 1 N.Y.3d 179, 184-185 [2003]). The primary purposes of res judicata are grounded in public policy concerns and are intended to ensure finality, prevent vexatious litigation and promote judicial economy (*see Matter of Hodes v. Axelrod*, 70 NY2d

364, 372 [1987]; *Matter of Reilly v. Reid*, 45 NY2d 24, 28 [1978]). However, unfairness may result if the doctrine is applied too harshly; thus "[i]n properly seeking to deny a litigant two 'days in court,' courts must be careful not to deprive [the litigant] of one" (*Reilly*, 45 NY2d at 28).

It is not always clear whether particular claims are part of the same transaction for res judicata purposes. A "pragmatic" test has been applied to make this determination — analyzing "whether the facts are related in time, space, origin, or motivation, whether they form a convenient trial unit, and whether their treatment as a unit conforms to the parties' expectations or business understanding or usage" (Restatement [Second] of Judgments § 24[2]; *see Smith v. Russell Sage Coll.*, 54 NY2d 185, 192-193 [1981]; *Reilly*, 45 NY2d at 29).

Applying these principles, it is apparent that personal injury tort actions and divorce actions do not constitute a convenient trial unit. The purposes behind the two are quite different. They seek different types of relief and require different types of proof. Moreover, a personal injury action is usually tried by a jury, in contrast to a matrimonial action, which is typically decided by a judge when the issue of fault is not contested. Further, personal injury attorneys are compensated by contingency fee, whereas matrimonial attorneys are prohibited from entering into fee arrangements that are contingent upon the granting of a divorce or a particular property settlement or distributive award (*see* Code of Professional Responsibility DR 2-106[c][2][i] [22 NYCRR 1200.11(c)(2)(i)]).

This case is distinguishable from the situation presented by *Boronow*. There, we noted that title issues are "intertwined" with the dissolution of the marriage relationship and could usually "be fairly and efficiently resolved" along with the matrimonial action (*see Boronow*, 71 NY2d at 290). Typically, however, a personal injury action is not sufficiently intertwined with the dissolution of the marriage relationship as to allow for its efficient resolution. Thus, the interspousal tort action does not form a convenient trial unit with the divorce proceeding, and it would not be within the parties' reasonable expectations that the two would be tried together.

Significant policy considerations also support this conclusion. To require joinder of interspousal personal injury claims with the matrimonial action would complicate and prolong the divorce proceeding. This would be contrary to the goal of expediting these proceedings and minimizing the emotional damage to the parties and their families. Delaying resolution of vital matters such as child support and custody or the distribution of assets to await the outcome of a personal injury action could result in extreme hardship and injustice to the families involved, especially for victims of domestic violence. In addition, parties should be encouraged to stipulate to, rather than litigate, the issue of fault (*see Blickstein v. Blickstein*, 99 AD2d 287, 293- 294 [2d Dept 1984]; *see also O'Brien v. O'Brien*, 66 NY2d 576, 589, 590 [1985] [noting that fault should only be considered "in egregious cases" for purposes of equitable distribution, in part, "because fault will usually be difficult to assign and because introduction of the issue may involve the courts in time-consuming procedural maneuvers relating to collateral issues"]).

Unlike the Appellate Division, we decline to adopt the reasoning of the New Jersey Supreme Court in *Tevis v. Tevis* (79 NJ 422, 400 A2d 1189 [1979]). In *Tevis*, the court held that under that State's "single controversy" rule, the interspousal personal injury claim should have been brought with the matrimonial action so that the issues between the parties could be decided in one proceeding in order to prevent protracted litigation (*see Tevis*, 79 NJ at 434, 400 A2d at 1196). However, that view is decidedly the minority view and the New Jersey Supreme Court has recently acknowledged the potential drawbacks to litigating an interspousal tort claim prior to the divorce proceeding — noting that it "may have a negative psychological impact on parties by prolonging the uncertainty of their marital status" (*Brennan v. Orban*, 145 NJ 282, 303, 678 A2d 667, 678 [1996]). Indeed, other states to address the issue have reached the conclusion we reach today, emphasizing the fundamental differences between the two types of actions and noting the complications that could result from the rigid application of res judicata principles (*see Delahunty v. Massachusetts Mut. Life Ins. Co.*, 236 Conn 582, 590-594, 674 A2d 1290, 1295-1296 [1996]; *Henriksen v. Cameron*, 622 A2d 1135, 1141-1142 [Me 1993]; *Heacock v. Heacock*, 402 Mass 21, 23-24, 520 NE2d 151, 153 [1988]).

Here, although the personal injury claim could have been litigated with the matrimonial action — as the facts arose from the same transaction or series of events — it was not, as all of Chen's fault allegations, save one, were withdrawn by stipulation for the salutary purpose of expediting the matrimonial action. She is therefore not precluded from litigating that claim in a separate action.

Parties are free, of course, to join their interspousal tort claims with the matrimonial action (*see* CPLR 601[a]) and the trial court retains discretion to sever the claims in the interest of convenience, if necessary (*see* CPLR 603). If a separate interspousal tort action is contemplated, however, or has been commenced, the better practice would be to include a reservation of rights in the judgment of divorce. Finally, if fault allegations are actually litigated in a matrimonial action, res judicata or some form of issue preclusion would bar a subsequent action in tort based on the same allegations.

Accordingly, the order of the Appellate Division should be reversed, with costs, and the case remitted to Supreme Court for further proceedings in accordance with this opinion.

CHIEF JUDGE KAYE and JUDGES G.B. SMITH, ROSENBLATT, GRAFFEO, READ and R.S. SMITH concur.

Order reversed, etc.

NOTES

(1) In *O'Connell v. Corcoran*, 1 N.Y.3d 179, 802 N.E.2d 1071 (2003), plaintiff commenced an action in New York seeking equitable distribution of marital property one year after being granted a divorce by a Vermont court. Plaintiff had made no attempt to seek property distribution in the Vermont divorce action, although the Vermont court would have had jurisdiction over the claim. The doctrine of res judicata would have barred the litigation of plaintiff's later property distribution claim in Vermont because it could have been litigated in the initial divorce action. The Court of Appeals found that the divorce action had the same conclusive effect in New York, holding that where a divorce decree in another state would serve as a bar to later action for equitable distribution in the courts of that state, the decree had the same effect in New York.

In a later case, the Court held claim preclusion applicable where the beneficiary of a testamentary trust sought to contest the trustee's management of the trust, a claim which could have been raised in a prior Surrogate's proceeding involving a companion trust. *Matter of Hunter*, 4 N.Y.3d 260, 794 N.Y.S.2d 286, 827 N.E.2d 269 (2005).

(2) Another exception to the general rule of claim preclusion states that there is no preclusive effect if the forum in which the initial action is brought did not have the power to grant the full relief sought in the second action. *Davidson v. Capuano*, 792 F.2d 275 (2d Cir. 1986), illustrates the point. Applying the law of preclusion of New York, the court held that a plaintiff could bring a federal damage action arising out of a violation of his constitutional rights by state officers even though he had previously brought a successful article 78 proceeding for mandamus relief. Even though the two actions were based on the "same cause of action," there was no preclusion because the state court had lacked authority to award the damages sought in the context of the article 78 proceeding.

(3) It has long been the rule in New York that the first adjudication be "on the merits" to have res judicata effect. *See Rudd v. Cornell*, 171 N.Y. 114, 63 N.E. 823 (1902). Nonetheless, in *Smith v. Russell Sage College*, 54 N.Y.2d 185, 445 N.Y.S.2d 68, 429 N.E.2d 746 (1981), the Court held that a second action was precluded when an earlier suit on the same cause of action was dismissed on statute of limitations grounds. This, the Court said, was "sufficiently close" to the merits. In a later case, *Matter of Meegan S. v. Donald T.*, 64 N.Y.2d 751, 485 N.Y.S.2d 982, 475 N.E.2d 449 (1985), the Court held that the dismissal of a paternity suit as untimely did not bar the prosecution of a second suit for the same relief commenced after the applicable statute of limitations had been increased by the Legislature. The Court said:

> Ordinarily, a dismissal based on the Statute of Limitations is considered to be "on the merits" (*see Smith v. Russell Sage College . . .*), precluding relitigation of that issue in a subsequent action. . . . "The earlier decision may be a conclusive adjudication of the petitioner's rights, existing then; it cannot be an adjudication of rights thereafter conferred by law,

or bar a new proceeding to vindicate new rights." ... 64 N.Y.2d at 752, 485 N.Y.S.2d at 983, 475 N.E.2d at 450.

Does the "on the merits" requirement survive? Which of the following adjudications would be entitled to res judicata effect: A dismissal of a complaint because of a failure to obtain in personam jurisdiction; a dismissal of a complaint for failing to state a cause of action, leave to replead having been denied (*see* CPLR 3211(e)); a grant of summary judgment for plaintiff? *See also* CPLR 5013.

(4) In *Marinelli Associates v. Helmsley-Noyes Co.*, 265 A.D.2d 1, 705 N.Y.S.2d 571 (1st Dep't 2000), it was held that the joint venturer's breach of contract claims against the venture's managing agent could have been considered during arbitration of fraud claims against the co-venturers arising from the same transactions, and under the doctrine of transactional analysis those breach claims were deemed barred.

(5) In the context of a criminal case, *People v. Evans*, 94 N.Y.2d 499, 706 N.Y.S.2d 678, 727 N.E.2d 1232 (2000), the Court had occasion to discuss the distinction between claim preclusion and law of the case, the latter sometimes described as a sort of "intra-action res judicata," which is not to be rigidly enforced in a retrial of the defendant. Here the court held that the judge on retrial was not bound by an evidentiary ruling made at the original trial. In effect, the evidentiary rulings at the first trial are not binding at the second.

§ 23.03 ISSUE PRECLUSION

[A] The Doctrine in General

Issue preclusion (or collateral estoppel) is a branch of the law of res judicata. It differs from claim preclusion in that (1) it is not limited to situations in which there are successive suits involving the same cause of action, and (2) it does not affect issues which might have been, but were not, resolved in the first action; only those actually decided in it.

Issues of law are less subject to preclusion than those of fact. The Restatement (Second) of Judgments takes the position that decisions on issues of law should not be accorded preclusive effect where the two actions involve substantially unrelated claims, or where a new determination is warranted in order to take account of an intervening change in the applicable legal context, or otherwise to avoid inequitable administration of the laws. It has been held in New York that "unmixed" issues of law are not subject to preclusion. *McGrath v. Gold*, 36 N.Y.2d 406, 369 N.Y.S.2d 62, 330 N.E.2d 35 (1975); *Department of Personnel of the City of New York v. City Civil Service Commission*, 94 A.D.2d 5, 462 N.Y.S.2d 878 (1st Dep't 1983). How does New York treat the preclusion of issues in which law and fact are mixed? Consider this question as you read the material in this section.

In *Schwartz v. Public Administrator of Bronx County*, 24 N.Y.2d 65, 71, 298 N.Y.S.2d 955, 960, 246 N.E.2d 725, 729 (1969), discussed in note 1, in subsection [C], *infra*, the Court of Appeals neatly summarized the requisites of issue preclusion:

> New York law has now reached the point where there are but two necessary requirements for the invocation of the doctrine of collateral estoppel. There must be an identity of issue which has necessarily been decided in the prior action and is decisive of the present action, and, second, there must have been a full and fair opportunity to contest the decision now said to be controlling.

The questions and cases which follow show the complexity of these requirements.

PROBLEM B

Bob and Tim were each driving their respective cars when they collided at an intersection. As Bob was wearing a seat belt, his injuries were minor and did not exceed the No-Fault threshold, but his recently purchased luxury car cost $12,000 to repair. Bob commenced an action for that amount in New York City Civil Court. Tim defended solely on the ground that he was not negligent. After a non-jury trial (neither party having demanded a jury), Bob obtained a judgment for the amount claimed, the court finding that Tim's negligence caused the accident.

In a subsequent action, brought in the Supreme Court, Gerry, who was a passenger in Tim's car at the time of the collision, sought to recover personal injury damages amounting to $400,000 from Bob and Tim. Gerry's complaint alleges that each of them were in whole or in part the cause of the accident. In his answer to Gerry's complaint, Tim denies that he was negligent and alleges that the accident was caused by (1) Bob's negligence; or (2) the negligence of the impleaded City of New York, which should have installed a traffic light at the intersection where the crash occurred. Tim also asserts a claim for contribution and or indemnification from the City and from Bob.

In separate motions for summary judgment, Gerry seeks dismissal of Tim's defenses, and Bob and the City seek dismissal of Tim's claims against them. All of the summary judgment motions rest on the preclusive effect of the judgment in Bob's action against Tim. Among other things, Bob, Gerry and the City argue that Tim's defenses have been necessarily determined in the earlier action by Bob against Tim. Tim argues, to the contrary, that his failure to raise an issue cannot be given preclusive effect, citing *Kaufman v. Eli Lilly and Co.*, *infra*.

What result on each of the motions?

KAUFMAN v. ELI LILLY AND CO.
Court of Appeals
65 N.Y.2d 449, 492 N.Y.S.2d 584, 482 N.E.2d 63 (1985)

SIMONS, JUDGE.

This is one of 15 similar actions pending in the First Department seeking to recover from pharmaceutical companies for injuries allegedly sustained by the plaintiff daughters as a result of their mothers' ingestion of the drug diethylstilbestrol (DES) while pregnant. In 1977 the Assistant Administrative Justice designated the actions as "complex litigation cases" and assigned them to Justice Arnold Fraiman, directing him to handle all matters relating to them. The first of the 15 actions chosen to be tried was *Bichler v. Lilly & Co.*, 55 N.Y.2d 571, 450 N.Y.S.2d 776, 436 N.E.2d 182 and the rest were held pending its disposition. The principal issue in this appeal is the collateral estoppel effect to be given to certain jury findings in that action.

After we sustained a jury verdict against Lilly in *Bichler*, plaintiff moved for partial summary judgment precluding Lilly from relitigating six issues decided by the *Bichler* jury, a severance of the action against Lilly and an immediate trial on the issues of DES ingestion, causation and damages. Lilly cross-moved to depose two of the jurors in the *Bichler* case to establish that their verdict was a compromise. The remaining defendants cross-moved for a severance in the event the court granted plaintiff's motion for collateral estoppel against Lilly. Special Term granted plaintiff's motion for partial summary judgment, denied Lilly's cross-motion and granted the codefendants' motions for a severance. 116 Misc.2d 351, 455 N.Y.S.2d 329. A divided Appellate Division affirmed and granted Lilly leave to appeal to this court on a certified question. 99 A.D.2d 695, 471 N.Y.S.2d 830. We now modify the order of the Appellate Division and hold that Lilly may not be collaterally estopped from relitigating the jury's finding that it acted in concert with other drug manufacturers in testing and marketing DES for use in treating accidents of pregnancy. Our modification is required because the concerted action liability found in *Bichler* was based on an unresolved question of law which should not be given preclusive effect in this litigation.

I

In early 1954, plaintiff's mother, then pregnant with her, was prescribed DES to prevent a miscarriage. In July 1973, when plaintiff was 18 years old, it was discovered that plaintiff had cancer of the cervix. A radical hysterectomy was performed and, as a result, plaintiff will be unable to bear children. She instituted this action in 1976 alleging in her amended complaint that her mother's ingestion of DES while pregnant was the proximate cause of the injuries she sustained. Because she was unable to clearly identify the manufacturer of the DES her mother took, plaintiff joined as defendants nine of the approximately 147 pharmaceutical companies manufacturing and marketing DES for the prevention of miscarriages in pregnant women in 1954. She alleged that the defendants were liable to her, *inter alia*, on a concerted action theory of liability because they had "combined and conspired to obtain the approval for DES" without adequate testing.

The *Bichler* action involved a young woman who developed cervical and vaginal cancer at the age of 17. She brought suit against Eli Lilly & Company and others, alleging that her mother's ingestion of DES in 1953 while she was pregnant with her caused her injuries. Plaintiff's theory was that DES had been marketed without adequate testing to determine its safety. After the plaintiff was unsuccessful in attempting to prove that Lilly manufactured the DES prescribed for her mother, she submitted her case to the jury on a concerted action theory of liability. In addition to returning a general verdict for plaintiff, the Bichler jury answered seven special interrogatories in her favor as a basis for imposing liability on Lilly.[1] On appeal the Appellate Division and this court affirmed. The courts below gave collateral estoppel effect in this action to six of the *Bichler* jury's findings.[2]

Lilly raises three grounds for reversal of the order granting that relief. First, it contends that the decision in *Bichler* should not be given collateral estoppel effect because (1) the cases do not raise identical issues, (2) there are indications that the *Bichler* verdict was based on jury compromise, (3) there are adjudications inconsistent with *Bichler* on each of the issues involved and (4) the *Bichler* decision is based on an unresolved and novel application of the law of

---

[1] The interrogatories and the jury's answers to them were as follows:

(1) Was DES reasonably safe in the treatment of accidents of pregnancy when it was ingested by plaintiff's mother in 1953? (No)

(2) Was DES a proximate cause of plaintiff's cancer? (Yes)

(3) In 1953 when plaintiff's mother ingested DES, should the defendant, as a reasonably prudent drug manufacturer, have foreseen that DES might cause cancer in the offspring of pregnant women who took it? (Yes)

(4) Foreseeing that DES might cause cancer in the offspring of pregnant women who took it, would a reasonably prudent drug manufacturer test it on pregnant mice before marketing it? (Yes)

(5) If DES had been tested on pregnant mice, would the tests have shown that DES causes cancer in their offspring? (Yes)

(6) Would a reasonably prudent drug manufacturer have marketed DES for use in treating accidents of pregnancy at the time it was ingested by the plaintiff's mother if it had known that DES causes cancer in the offspring of pregnant mice? (No)

(7) Did defendant and the other drug manufacturers act in concert with each other in the testing and marketing of DES for use in treating accidents of pregnancy? (Yes).

(*See Bichler v. Lilly & Co.*, 55 N.Y.2d 571, 587, n. 10, 450 N.Y.S.2d 776, 436 N.E.2d 182, *supra*.)

[2] In her motion for summary judgment, plaintiff deleted the second *Bichler* interrogatory dealing with proximate cause. There is one other difference between the *Bichler* interrogatories and the issues on which plaintiff seeks partial summary judgment in this case. In the first, third and sixth *Bichler* interrogatories, the relevant time period was changed from 1953 (when Mrs. Bichler ingested DES) to 1953-1954 (when plaintiff's mother ingested the drug). Contrary to Lilly's claim, these variations in the years do not destroy the identity of issues. That plaintiff's mother took the drug in 1954 could not mitigate the failure to test found wanting in 1953 or lessen the basis of knowledge upon which a duty to warn cause of action rests.

concerted action not expressly adopted in New York. Second, Lilly asserts that if we find its proof of jury compromise in *Bichler* insufficient as it now exists to defeat the application of collateral estoppel, it should be allowed to depose two named jurors from the *Bichler* jury to demonstrate further its contention. Finally, Lilly urges that the lower court erred in severing plaintiff's action against it from actions against the remaining defendants.

II

The doctrine of collateral estoppel precludes a party from relitigating "an issue which has previously been decided against him in a proceeding in which he had a fair opportunity to fully litigate the point" (*Gilberg v. Barbieri*, 53 N.Y.2d 285, 291, 441 N.Y.S.2d 49, 423 N.E.2d 807; *see, Schwartz v. Public Administrator*, 24 N.Y.2d 65, 69, 298 N.Y.S.2d 955, 246 N.E.2d 725). It is a doctrine intended to reduce litigation and conserve the resources of the court and litigants and it is based upon the general notion that it is not fair to permit a party to relitigate an issue that has already been decided against it. There are now but two requirements which must be satisfied before the doctrine is invoked. First, the identical issue necessarily must have been decided in the prior action and be decisive of the present action, and second, the party to be precluded from relitigating the issue must have had a full and fair opportunity to contest the prior determination. The party seeking the benefit of collateral estoppel has the burden of demonstrating the identity of the issues in the present litigation and the prior determination, whereas the party attempting to defeat its application has the burden of establishing the absence of a full and fair opportunity to litigate the issue in the prior action (*see, Ryan v. New York Tel. Co., supra*, at p. 501, 478 N.Y.S.2d 823, 467 N.E.2d 487; *Schwartz v. Public Administrator, supra*, 24 N.Y.2d at p. 73, 298 N.Y.S.2d 955, 246 N.E.2d 725). Applying these rules, we hold that collateral estoppel effect should be denied for the *Bichler* jury's finding on concerted action but that Lilly should be precluded from relitigating the five remaining issues relevant to this action and decided adversely to it in that trial (*see*, n. 2, at p. 455, at p. 587 of 492 N.Y.S.2d, at p. 66 of 482 N.E.2d, *supra*).

A

When *Bichler* was before this court Lilly challenged the concerted action theory of liability on two grounds. It claimed that it was not an appropriate theory of liability in DES litigation when the identity of the manufacturer is not established and that the court's charge on the theory was erroneous. Although both of these issues could have been raised by appropriate objection in the trial court, they were not, and because they were not, we did not pass on them. We held only that the evidence was legally sufficient to support the jury's findings of concerted action and foreseeability based on the charge given and that the trial court did not err in refusing Lilly's request to charge on its duty to warn (*see, Bichler v. Lilly & Co.*, 55 N.Y.2d 571, 584-587, 450 N.Y.S.2d 776, 436 N.E.2d 182, *supra*). We noted in a footnote that there were several theories upon which similar DES cases were proceeding or it had been suggested they might proceed but we expressed no view in *Bichler* and, express none now, on which of the proposed theories — concerted action, alternative liability, enterprise liability or market share liability — if any, should be adopted in this or similar DES cases (*see, Bichler v. Lilly & Co., supra*, at p. 580, n. 5, 450 N.Y.S.2d 776, 436 N.E.2d 182). The question is still an open one in New York. [The Court later settled on the market share theory. *See Hymowitz v. Eli Lilly & Co.*, 73 N.Y.2d 487, 541 N.Y.S.2d 941, 539 N.E.2d 1069 (1989), found in § 8.02, *supra*. — Eds.]

The point is significant because collateral estoppel effect will only be given to matters "actually litigated and determined" in a prior action (*see*, Restatement [Second] of Judgments § 27, *quoted in Koch v. Consolidated Edison Co.*, 62 N.Y.2d 548, 554, n. 2, 479 N.Y.S.2d 163, 468 N.E.2d 1; *see also, Ryan v. New York Tel. Co.*, 62 N.Y.2d 494, 478 N.Y.S.2d 823, 467 N.E.2d 487, *supra*). If the issue has not been litigated, there is no identity of issues between the present action and the prior determination. An issue is not actually litigated if, for example, there has been a default, a confession of liability, a failure to place a matter in issue by proper pleading or even because of a stipulation (*see*, Restatement [Second] of Judgments § 27 comments d, e, at 255-257; *see also, Gilberg v. Barbieri*, 53 N.Y.2d 285, 441 N.Y. S.2d 49, 423 N.E.2d 807, *supra*). Because Lilly did not challenge the appropriateness of the concerted action theory in *Bichler*, it was not actually litigated and there is no identity between that issue in *Bichler* and here. Although it may seem a paradox that we should permit defendant to benefit in this litigation because of its failure to challenge concerted action in the prior litigation, the policy reasons for refusing to do so outweigh the reasons for limiting litigation on the issue. It is of paramount importance that the courts establish and develop the law in this emerging area of mass tort liability, rather than permit it to be fixed, even in this limited number of DES actions, on the basis of the law of the case. The need for uniformity and certainty mandates that in such cases collateral estoppel should be rejected (*see, Schwartz v. Public Administrator*, 24 N.Y.2d 65, 72, 298 N.Y.S.2d 955, 246 N.E.2d 725, *supra*; Restatement [Second] of Judgments § 28 comment b, at 275-276; *see, id.* § 29[7] and comment i, at 292, 297). This is particularly so when the other defendants will be free to claim, against this same plaintiff, that concerted action is not an appropriate theory of liability and thereby cause inconsistent results.

B

The fact that no exception was taken to the charge on concerted action, however, has no bearing on the factual issues resolved by the jury when it answered the remaining interrogatories and Lilly should be precluded from relitigating them. Identity of issues does exist as to them because the legal theory in both actions is the same and because there are no significant factual differences between them. The plaintiff in *Bichler*, the first of the 15 related cases chosen to be tried, sought to establish Lilly's negligence in testing and marketing DES. The issues Lilly will be precluded from relitigating in this case relate solely to the facts underlying its negligence in testing, questions found against it by the

Bichler jury and questions which are also involved in this case. Moreover, both plaintiffs' mothers ingested DES in the same time period (1953-1954), both plaintiffs were born in 1954 within seven months of each other and both developed cancer of the cervix and/or vagina at approximately the same age. The issue of proximate cause has been specifically deleted from the *Bichler* interrogatories by plaintiff's motion and Lilly will have the opportunity to demonstrate that plaintiff's injuries were not caused by her mother's ingestion of DES due to minor differences between the plaintiffs or the circumstances surrounding their mothers' ingestion of DES. Thus, the appeal fits the example described by Professors James and Hazard of an instance in which there are several similar cases and the first tried is "roughly typical" of the rest. In that situation, the professors noted, it is not unfair to preclude the defendant from retrying the issues previously litigated and decided adversely to it (James & Hazard, Civil Procedure § 11.24, at 581 [2d ed].) [Now 3d ed. at p. 635 — Eds.]

Similarly unpersuasive is Lilly's assertion that the *Bichler* verdict is not entitled to collateral estoppel effect because there are indications it was the result of jury compromise. Although indications of jury compromise is one factor properly to be considered in determining whether a party against whom collateral estoppel is sought had a full and fair opportunity to litigate the issues in the prior determination (*see, Koch v. Consolidated Edison Co.*, 62 N.Y.2d 548, 555, n. 4, 479 N.Y.S.2d 163, 468 N.E.2d 1, *supra, quoting Schwartz v. Public Administrator*, 24 N.Y.2d 65, 72, 298 N.Y.S.2d 955, 246 N.E.2d 725, *supra*), the evidence offered to defeat application of the doctrine in this case is insufficient. Lilly relies only on inadmissible hearsay allegations contained in an affidavit of its former attorney in which he alleges that he interviewed three *Bichler* jurors immediately after the verdict and that one of them told him there had been a compromise and on Lilly's speculation that a compromise resulted because the jury returned its verdict after five days of apparently hopeless deadlock. As we recently emphasized in *Koch*, evidence of this nature is not sufficient to defeat a motion for partial summary judgment on collateral estoppel grounds (*see, Koch v. Consolidated Edison Co., supra,* 62 N.Y.2d at p. 557, 479 N.Y.S.2d 163, 468 N.E.2d 1)

Finally, although adjudications on the same issue inconsistent with the one to be given preclusive effect are relevant evidence that the party contesting estoppel did not have a fair opportunity to litigate the prior determination and may be a factor in refusing to apply the doctrine of collateral estoppel (*see, id.*, at p. 555, and n. 4, 479 N.Y.S.2d 163, 468 N.E.2d 1, *quoting* Restatement [Second] of Judgments § 29[4]), the cases relied on by Lilly do not support that result here. Those cited include generally cases in which the jury returned a verdict for Lilly on a failure to warn theory[3] and others in which the court granted

---

[3] *See, Mink v. University of Chicago*, No. 77-C-1432 (N.D.Ill Mar. 24, 1983); *Keil v. Lilly & Co.*, No. 75-70997 (E.D.Mich.1981); *Sardell v. Lilly & Co.*, No. 18268/77 (N.Y.Sup.Ct., Kings County, Nov. 24, 1982); *see also, Miller v. Lilly & Co.*, No. CV 80 0047107 S (Conn.Super.Ct., Feb. 20, 1985 [jury finding of no ingestion or causation]).

Lilly judgment either because concerted action was an inappropriate legal theory for DES litigation or because the evidence was insufficient to raise a factual issue on concerted action.[4] Those in the first group are not inconsistent with the *Bichler* jury's responses to the interrogatories finding Lilly negligent on a theory of inadequate testing. The second group, cases involving summary judgment and directed verdicts in Lilly's favor, support Lilly's contention that it should not be estopped from contesting liability on the theory of concerted action but we have found in its favor on that issue on other grounds. Thus, contrary to its contentions, those cases provide no basis for permitting Lilly to relitigate the remaining issues involving Lilly's negligence. In only one case cited by Lilly did a jury return a verdict inconsistent with *Bichler* on the issue of inadequate testing (*see, Barros v. Squibb & Sons*, Civ Act No. 75-1226 [E.D. Pa.1976]). Lilly relies on that decision and claims the benefit of that jury determination although it was not a party to the litigation. We find no basis to nullify the jury findings in *Bichler*, the first case tried of the several pending before Justice Fraiman and a case in which Lilly participated fully, on the basis of the *Squibb* verdict, a case in which it did not participate at all. Lilly can hardly claim that the *Squibb* determination provides any indication that it lacked a full and fair opportunity to defend against the issues decided adversely to it in *Bichler*.

III

Two other matters remain for our consideration. Notwithstanding the insufficiency of its evidence to support a finding of a compromise verdict in *Bichler*, Lilly contends that it should be allowed to depose two *Bichler* jurors in order to further substantiate its claim. It asserts that our firm rule against impeaching a verdict in the action in which it was rendered is inapplicable here when its attack is not for the purpose of impairing the *Bichler* verdict but for the purpose of preventing collateral estoppel effect to be given it. The policy reasons behind the rule are to prevent "the posttrial harassing of jurors for statements which might render their verdicts questionable" and to avoid the chaos that a contrary rule would create (*People v. De Lucia*, 20 N.Y.2d 275, 278, 282 N.Y.S.2d 526, 229 N.E.2d 211; *see, McDonald v. Pless*, 238 U.S. 264, 267-268, 35 S.Ct. 783, 784-785, 59 L.Ed. 1300; *King v. United States*, 576 F.2d 432, 438 [2d Cir]). They are equally applicable to this case. Moreover, it is not insignificant that the desire

---

4 . . . Nor is *McElhaney v. Lilly & Co.*, 575 F.Supp. 228 [D.S.D.1983], *affd.*, 739 F.2d 340 [8th Cir.] persuasive on this point. In *McElhaney*, Lilly won a directed verdict when the plaintiff conceded that she could offer no proof that Lilly knew or should have known of the dangerous condition of DES. This admission was fatal to her strict products liability action under section 402A of the Restatement (Second) of Torts. When no similar concession was made in *Bichler*, the jury found that Lilly should have foreseen that the use of DES in pregnant women would be dangerous. Thus, there is nothing to indicate that a jury in the *McElhaney* case would have reached an opposite conclusion absent the plaintiff's concession there. Similarly, the directed verdict for Lilly in *McMahon v. Lilly & Co.*, No. 82 C 2822 [N.D.Ill.1984] is not inconsistent with *Bichler* because it was based solely on the plaintiff's failure to make a prima facie showing that Lilly manufactured the DES that her mother ingested or that Lilly knew or should have known of the risk of preterm labor or prematurity among pregnant DES daughters, a risk not even at issue in either *Bichler* or this case.

to depose the jurors is intended to impair the effect of factual findings made in the first of several related cases selected for trial.

Finally, we cannot find that the trial court abused its discretion as a matter of law in severing plaintiff's action against Lilly from her action against the other defendants, particularly in light of the obvious prejudice the other defendants would suffer if they were forced to litigate the action with Lilly despite our conclusion that it is precluded from relitigating the findings of negligence as made in *Bichler*.

. . . .

[B] Identity of Issue

In addition to providing a graphic example of the reach of the doctrine of issue preclusion (or collateral estoppel) in New York, *Kaufman v. Eli Lilly and Co.* also provides an enlightening "tour" of the elements of the doctrine. Consider the treatment of the requirement that the issue sought to be precluded in the second action be identical to the issue determined in the first. The concept is complex. The Court tells us that Eli Lilly is precluded from relitigating those issues, such as whether DES was reasonably safe, that were determined against it in the earlier case of *Bichler v. Eli Lilly & Co.*, because "the legal theory in both actions is the same and because there are no significant factual differences between them." When is a factual difference significant? The next case addresses the problem.

O'CONNOR v. STATE OF NEW YORK
Court of Appeals
70 N.Y.2d 914, 524 N.Y.S.2d 391, 519 N.E.2d 302 (1987)

MEMORANDUM.

The order of the Appellate Division should be affirmed, with costs.

Claimant's decedent was crossing a street on the State Office Building Campus in Albany in a marked pedestrian crosswalk when he was struck and killed by a bicyclist involved in a time trial. Claimant sued the cyclist and others involved in the time trial in Supreme Court, where damages were assessed at $980,000 and comparative negligence was found to be 60%. The claimant then commenced this action against the State in the Court of Claims, where the court found that the decedent and the State were each 50% at fault and assessed damages at $680,870. The Appellate Division affirmed the Court of Claims order, from which the State now appeals.

We agree with the Appellate Division that the State, like other landowners, owed a duty of care to the plaintiff to maintain its property, held open to the public, in a reasonably safe condition and that it breached that duty. . . .

The State's position that collateral estoppel is a bar to relitigating the issue of decedent's comparative negligence in the Court of Claims is similarly unpersuasive. Although the decedent's comparative negligence was at issue both in the Supreme Court and in the Court of Claims actions, there has been no showing by the State that the Supreme Court addressed relative culpability as between the decedent and the State, which was an issue squarely before the Court of Claims (*see, O'Connor v G & R Packing Co.*, 53 NY2d 278, 280 . . .).

Further, the State was not and could not have been a party to the first action in Supreme Court (Court of Claims Act §§ 8, 9 . . .). Collateral estoppel is, therefore, inapplicable (1) because the issues of decedent's comparative negligence with respect to the defendants in the Supreme Court action and with respect to the later proceeding against the State in the Court of Claims are discrete, not identical; and (2) because, in any event, claimant never had a full and fair opportunity to litigate decedent's comparative negligence in relationship to the State (*see, Schwartz v Public Adm'r.*[, 24 N.Y.2d 65, 298 N.Y.S.2d 955, 246 N.E.2d 725], *supra*).

NOTES

(1) The logistics of the principal case are interesting. In the Supreme Court action, there were other defendants in addition to the errant cyclist. They settled for $225,000. The jury assessed fault 60% to the decedent, 34% to the cyclist, and 6% to the settling defendants. The cyclist's insurance coverage was limited to $25,000, and therefore the anticipated recovery in Supreme Court was a total of $250,000. In the Court of Claims, the Attorney General stipulated with claimant's counsel that the recoveries in the Supreme Court action would constitute a credit of $250,000 against any award in the Court of Claims. The Court of Claims award of $680,870 was reduced by decedent's 50% fault to $340,435. This was then further reduced by the $250,000 from the recovery in Supreme Court resulting in a Court of Claims award of $182,968 including interest. Thus, decedent's estate recovered a grand total of $432,968, about half of the Supreme Court jury verdict. In the end, then, decedent's estate recovered roughly what it should have considering the two damage figures and the two estimates of decedent's comparative negligence.

(2) A finding in one action that a product is defective would ordinarily be preclusive against the manufacturer defendant in a second suit brought by another injured user. *See Kaufman v. Eli Lilly and Co.*, *supra*. But beware of the significant difference test. In *Vincent v. Thompson*, 50 A.D.2d 211, 377 N.Y.S.2d 118 (2d Dep't 1975), the court refused to preclude Parke Davis & Co. from litigating whether the vaccine "Quadrigen" was defective even though, in an earlier action, a jury had so found. The court noted in *Vincent* that the symptoms of the plaintiff there were very different from those of the first plaintiff and were consistent with a different theory of the cause of her injuries. Thus, it held, the issues of the defect were not identical in the two cases.

Claimants commenced parallel actions in state and federal courts alleging that their detention by police following the commission of a crime was based on their status as African-Americans rather than for reasonable cause. The state claim was for damages in the Court of Claims, and the New York Court of Appeals held they had a cause of action under the New York Constitution. In federal court, the action was premised on denial of equal protection. Ultimately the Second Circuit dismissed the claim, holding that plaintiffs were legitimately stopped and questioned on the basis of the physical description given by the victim of the crime, and hence there was no violation of any federal constitutional rights. Did that determination bind the New York courts which were now determining various motions in the Court of Claims case? The Appellate Division held that although the equal protection clauses in both constitutions "afford the same breadth of coverage," there was no collateral estoppel here since the federal courts had never entertained the state constitutional question. The parties had stipulated in the federal proceedings to the dismissal of all state law claims. Thus, "an adverse federal court decision on an equal protection claim under the US Constitution does not preclude litigation for the first time of a state equal protection claim in state courts." *Brown v. State of New York*, 9 A.D.3d 23, 27, 776 N.Y.S.2d 643 (3d Dep't 2004).

(3) Even if there is no significant difference between the issues in two actions, the identity of issue test is not necessarily satisfied, according to *Kaufman v. Eli Lilly and Co.* This is because "if the issue has not been litigated, there is no identity of issues between the present action and the prior determination. An issue is not actually litigated if, for example, there has been a default, a confession of liability, a failure to place a matter in issue by proper pleading or even because of a stipulation. . . ." 65 N.Y.2d at 456-57, 492 N.Y.S.2d at 589, 482 N.E.2d at 68. Thus, *Kaufman* seems to lay to rest the oft-criticized New York rule that a party could be estopped from litigating an issue which had been "necessarily determined" against it, even if that issue had not been actually litigated and had been resolved by default. *See Reich v. Cochran*, 151 N.Y. 122, 45 N.E. 367 (1896).

In *Reich*, the plaintiff, "P," sued to cancel a rental agreement, alleging that it was in fact a disguised usurious mortgage. The Court held him estopped from litigating the issue because in earlier litigation between the parties, the present defendant, claiming to be P's landlord, had won an eviction proceeding against P when P defaulted. In its opinion, the Court of Appeals said that the prior judgment for eviction necessarily implied that the contract was a lease and not a mortgage: "The general rule is well settled that the estoppel of a former judgment extends . . . also to those matters which, although not expressly determined, are comprehended and involved in the thing expressly stated and decided, whether or not they were or were not actually litigated or considered." 151 N.Y.2d at 127, 45 N.E.2d at 368. See the critical discussion of the case in Rosenberg, *Collateral Estoppel in New York*, 44 St. John's L. Rev. 165, 174-77 (1969).

While *Reich v. Cochran* appears to have been undercut by *Kaufman v. Ely Lilly & Co.*, the Court of Appeals has, in another context, recently upheld an estoppel on the grounds that the issue had necessarily been decided against the party estopped, albeit not actually litigated. *See Henry Modell & Co., Inc. v. Minister, Elders and Deacons of the Reformed Protestant Dutch Church of the City of New York*, discussed in note 1, following *Chisholm-Ryder Co. v. Sommer & Sommer*, in § 13.04[B], *supra*. In that case, the estoppel was justified, the Court held, by claim preclusion.

These cases could be reconciled if *Reich* could be considered a claim preclusion case rather than an issue preclusion case. In claim preclusion cases, all issues are merged in the judgment whether litigated or not; and *Reich* involved the same parties in both actions.

(4) Suppose the parties actually litigate several issues. Does the court's determination in favor of one party entitle that party to preclude relitigation of some, none or all of the issues so litigated? See the next case.

O'CONNOR v. G & R PACKING CO.
Court of Appeals
53 N.Y.2d 278, 440 N.Y.S.2d 920, 423 N.E.2d 397 (1981)

MEYER, J.

Issue preclusion is available to protect a defendant who was not a party to an earlier lawsuit from the relitigation of an issue considered alternatively in the prior trial only when it is clear that the prior determination squarely addressed and specifically decided the issue. On the record before us it cannot be said that contributory negligence, which would bar plaintiffs' recovery in the instant action,[1] was so determined in plaintiff's prior action against other defendants. Defendant's motion for summary judgment was, therefore, correctly denied.

Plaintiff, Anthony O'Connor, then 16 years of age, was injured on February 11, 1967 in a Brooklyn railroad yard, when, having climbed a ladder on a freight car, he attempted to throw a snowball at his companions and his hand touched an overhead wire carrying 11,000 volts. An action brought by Anthony and his father against the railroads using the yard was dismissed at the end of the plaintiffs' case, the Trial Judge ruling (1) that as a trespasser Anthony was owed only the duty of refraining from inflicting a willful or wanton injury; (2) that Anthony had violated Penal Law and Railroad Law provisions by going upon defendants' tracks and cars; (3) that many cases, a number of which he cited, hold that in those circumstances the railroad is not liable, even though some of the plaintiffs involved in those cases were younger than Anthony; and (4) that plaintiffs had not substantiated a last clear chance theory because Anthony was not in a position from which he could not extricate himself, and the

---

[1] The incident out of which the action arises predates enactment of CPLR 1411 (L 1975, ch 69).

evidence did not establish that any of defendants' employees had knowledge of Anthony's situation in time to avoid the accident or failed to exercise care to do so. As part of his oral decision, the Trial Judge, just prior to his reference to the cases supporting his conclusion that defendants were not liable, stated: "The infant plaintiff not only disobeyed these statutes which were enacted for the benefit of the public but also deliberately and needlessly exposed himself to a known danger by climbing to the top of a freight car and moving about in a close proximity to live high tension wires." No appeal was taken from the dismissal of the action against the railroads.

In this action Anthony and his father seek to recover from G & R Packing Co. whose yard adjoined the railroad yard and through whose yard Anthony gained access to the railroad yard. Contending that dismissal of the prior action was grounded on both absence of a breach of duty by the railroads and presence of contributory negligence, G & R Packing moved under CPLR 3211 and 3212 to dismiss. Its motion was granted by Special Term, but that ruling was reversed in an exhaustive opinion by the Appellate Division.

We write essentially to place this matter in context with our decision in *Malloy v Trombley* (50 NY2d 46). . . . *Malloy* concerned the preclusive effect to be given a finding by the Court of Claims in negligence actions against the State, jointly tried, that both plaintiffs had been guilty of contributory negligence. In those actions both Malloy and Trombley contended that a State trooper had been negligent in stopping his vehicle on the southbound side of the roadway and leaving its headlights on while he went to inquire why Malloy's vehicle was parked without lights at 10:30 P.M. partially on the northbound side of an unlighted rural highway. Trombley's vehicle collided with the Malloy vehicle as Trombley proceeded northbound on the roadway. After a Bench trial, the Court of Claims Judge, aware of the pendency of the Supreme Court actions, held that each claimant had failed to prove negligence on the part of the State, and "[a]lthough unnecessary to a decision herein" (at p 50) that each was barred from recovery by his own contributory negligence. We held the contributory negligence finding preclusive in the later actions, noting that the thorough and careful deliberation of the Court of Claims Judge and the substantial operational purpose of his determination in relation to the judicial process made it evident that, though an alternative finding, the determination was neither "casual [n]or of any lesser quality than had the outcome of the trial depended solely on this issue" (50 NY2d, at p 52).

The contrast between the two situations is clear. *Malloy* dealt with findings of fact, made by the trier of fact, after a full trial, in an opinion which made evident that the Judge had firmly in mind the possible preclusive effect of his factual findings on the then pending other actions and which, since it spoke directly of "contributory negligence," left no doubt that the precluded litigant had been given his day in court on that issue. In the present action, we deal with a Trial Judge's ruling at the end of the plaintiff's case which involves no findings of fact. Rather it constitutes a holding that as a matter of law the evidence adduced was insufficient to present a question of fact for the jury.

Because the statement of that holding was phrased in terms of Anthony's status as a trespasser,[2] and the cases cited in support of the holding all concerned the duty of a landowner to a trespasser, there can be no question that the essence of the ruling was that no breach of duty had been proved. The same cannot be said with respect to the sentence quoted above in which the Judge before whom the railroad actions were tried arguably touched on plaintiff's duty of care for his own safety. The ambivalence of the words used, and of the holding in relation to that issue, arises from a number of factors: the words "contributory negligence" were not used; the Trial Judge could not have had in mind the effect of his holding on the present action which was not begun until several months after his dismissal of the action against the railroads; none of the cases cited concerned contributory negligence, nor does the language used indicate that consideration had been given to Anthony's age, experience, intelligence, and degree of development (*see* PJI 2:48), to "the well-known propensities of children to climb about and play" which a jury would be entitled to consider . . . or to the rule that contributory negligence "is a jury question in all but the clearest cases". . . . Litigation of the contributory negligence issue is not precluded by such a nonspecific nonfactual determination (*cf. Bell v Merrifield*, 109 NY 202, 211; *City Bank Farmers Trust Co. v Macfadden*, 13 AD2d 395, 404, *aff* 12 NY2d 1035; Restatement, Judgments 2d [Tent Draft No. 2], § 88, Comment g).

. . . .

Because the less than explicit holding in the prior action should not be given preclusive effect and we cannot say on the evidence before us that Anthony was guilty of contributory negligence as a matter of law, the order of the Appellate Division should be affirmed, with costs, and the certified question answered in the affirmative.

WEISS v. MANFREDI
Court of Appeals
83 N.Y.2d 974, 616 N.Y.S.2d 325, 639 N.E.2d 1122 (1994)

MEMORANDUM.

The order of the Appellate Division should be modified, without costs, in accordance with the memorandum herein, and, as modified, affirmed.

William Weiss died on June 14, 1979 as a result of injuries sustained in a fall from a ladder while waterproofing the roof of an apartment building in Manhattan. On September 14, 1979, decedent's widow, plaintiff Lynn Weiss, retained defendant Manfredi & Bondi who, on her behalf, commenced in Supreme Court,

---

[2] Not until 1976 was the status distinction excised from premises liability law (*Basso v Miller*, 40 NY2d 233 . . .).

Nassau County, an action for wrongful death against the premises owner, who impleaded decedent's employer. The law firm also represented plaintiff in obtaining general letters of administration and, on April 29, 1981, settled the wrongful death action, with court approval, for $300,000. Plaintiff received her share of the settlement proceeds, less a one-third contingency fee, on June 8, 1981. Through at least November 21, 1985, defendant Manfredi continued to represent plaintiff in connection with her workers' compensation claim.

After retaining new counsel, in July 1987 plaintiff moved to vacate the Nassau County settlement for inadequacy and failure to comply with the EPTL, alleging that the trial court should have awarded limited (not general) letters of administration in recognition of the interests of decedent's three minor children, which would have precluded plaintiff from settling on behalf of the children. Supreme Court denied the motion, concluding that the court, misled by plaintiff's petition declaring that she was the sole interested party, had found the settlement adequate in light of the facts known at the time. The Appellate Division affirmed Supreme Court's order (150 A.D.2d 678, 543 N.Y.S.2d 272).

On April 28, 1987, plaintiff commenced this action against defendant attorneys in Supreme Court, New York County, seeking damages for legal malpractice and fraud in connection with the Nassau County settlement. Supreme Court dismissed the complaint, concluding that plaintiff was collaterally estopped from challenging the adequacy of the settlement on the ground that the settlement had been found adequate in the Nassau County action, precluding a finding of legal malpractice against plaintiff's attorneys. The Appellate Division affirmed,* and this Court granted leave to appeal.

At issue is application of the settled doctrine of collateral estoppel, which bars a party from relitigating in a subsequent proceeding an issue clearly raised in a prior proceeding and decided against that party where the party to be precluded had a full and fair opportunity to contest the prior determination (see, D'Arata v. New York Cent. Mut. Fire Ins. Co., 76 N.Y.2d 659, 664, 563 N.Y.S.2d 24, 564 N.E.2d 634; Ryan v. New York Tel. Co., 62 N.Y.2d 494, 500-501, 478 N.Y.S.2d 823, 467 N.E.2d 487). "What is controlling is the identity of the issue which has necessarily been decided in the prior action or proceeding" (Ryan v. New York Tel. Co., 62 N.Y.2d, at 500, 478 N.Y.S.2d 823, 467 N.E.2d 487, supra). That doctrine was erroneously applied here.

In the prior action to vacate the settlement, the sole issue necessarily decided was that — as between plaintiff and the settling defendants (the premises owner and decedent's employer) — there was no fraud, collusion, mistake or accident to vitiate the settlement (see, Hallock v. State of New York, 64 N.Y.2d 224, 230, 485 N.Y.S.2d 510, 474 N.E.2d 1178). At issue in the current action for legal malpractice, by contrast, is whether defendant attorneys were negligent in their representation of plaintiff. Because there is no identity of issue, plain-

---

* No appeal was taken from Supreme Court's dismissal of the complaint as against the premises owner, decedent's employer and their insurers, originally named defendants.

tiff is not collaterally estopped in this action. Moreover, as neither the adequacy of the settlement nor plaintiff's role in prosecuting the action was in issue in the first action, the findings that the previous court was "satisfied with the amount of the settlement" and that "[p]laintiff, herself, created the situation which caused the misunderstanding in relation to her ability to settle the action for her children" are not entitled to preclusive effect. . . .

[C] A Full and Fair Opportunity to Be Heard

NOTES

(1) In *Schwartz v. Public Administrator of Bronx County*, 24 N.Y.2d 65, 298 N.Y.S.2d 955, 246 N.E.2d 725 (1969), the Court held that where two drivers were sued by the passenger of one of them, the findings of negligence on their part barred a second suit between the two. The court articulated the "full and fair opportunity" test, *i.e.*, did the party against whom the prior judgment was sought to be used have a full and fair opportunity to contest the same issues in the prior action. This would, said the court, require an inquiry into various elements such as the size of the claim, the forum in which the prior litigation was conducted, the use of counsels' initiative, the extent of the litigation and the competence and experience of counsel. This test was brought to bear in *Gilberg v. Barbieri*, the next case.

Schwartz was decided prior to the revision of CPLR Article 14 caused by *Dole v. Dow Chemical Co.*, 30 N.Y.2d 143, 331 N.Y.S.2d 382, 282 N.E.2d 288 (1972), and perforce prior to the adoption of New York's comparative negligence rule (CPLR Article 14-A). How would the rule of the *Schwartz* case be applied in the light of these developments? Assume that P, a passenger in a car driven by D-1, is injured when that car collides with a car driven by D-2, and that P recovers a judgment against both drivers. If D-1 is found 20% the cause of P's damages and D-2 80%, what result if D-1 later sues D-2 to recover the full amount of his own injuries? Before answering, refer again to *O'Connor v. State of New York*. See also discussion in D. Siegel, New York Practice § 468(L) at 792 (4th ed. 2005).

(2) Is it relevant in applying the full and fair opportunity test whether the preclusion will be used offensively (*i.e.* to impose liability) or defensively (to avoid liability)? The next two cases are instructive.

GILBERG v. BARBIERI
Court of Appeals
53 N.Y.2d 285, 441 N.Y.S.2d 49, 423 N.E.2d 807 (1981)

WACHTLER, JUDGE.

The question on this appeal is whether a conviction for the petty offense of harassment can later be used to preclude the defendant from disputing the merits of a civil suit for assault, involving the same incident and seeking a quarter of a million dollars in damages. The Trial Court held that collateral estoppel precluded the defendant from contesting the merits of the civil complaint and that the plaintiff was therefore entitled to summary judgment on the liability issue. The Appellate Division affirmed with one dissent and granted the defendant leave to appeal to this court on a certified question concerning the correctness of its order.

Plaintiff is a lawyer who for many years had been representing defendant's former wife in various matrimonial proceedings involving the defendant. In February, 1976 he called the defendant to appear for an examination before trial in connection with a claimed breach of a separation agreement. Defendant arrived at plaintiff's office without an attorney and repeatedly refused to answer questions until he had retained a lawyer. After several minutes of unproductive questioning plaintiff granted defendant an adjournment and shouted at him to get out of his office. Defendant then came around the desk toward the plaintiff and the two men scuffled until pulled apart by the plaintiff's sons. The plaintiff recovered the defendant's glasses and threw them at him. As he left, the defendant reciprocated by throwing plaintiff's glasses at him.

Plaintiff filed an information accusing defendant of harassment, a petty offense designated a violation by the Penal Law.* A nonjury trial was held in the City Court of Mount Vernon on the afternoon of July 27, 1976. The plaintiff testified that after he told the defendant to leave the defendant stood up, came around to where the plaintiff was seated behind his desk and repeatedly "pummelled" him. The defendant stated that he had merely shoved the plaintiff in self-defense when the plaintiff shouted at him to get out and reached, in a threatening manner, toward a hard object on his desk. The stenographer, called by the People, testified that both men rose from their chairs and grappled after a heated exchange. She claimed, however, that the defendant struck the first blow.

During the brief trial the court informed defense counsel that a felony hearing was scheduled to begin when this trial concluded. At the close of argu-

---

* Defendant was charged with violating subdivision 1 of section 240.25 of the Penal Law, which states "A person is guilty of harassment when, with intent to harass, annoy or alarm another person: 1. He strikes, shoves, kicks or otherwise subjects him to physical contact, or attempts or threatens to do the same. . . . Harassment is a violation." [Section 240.25 was amended in 1994 to expand the scope of harassment in ways not relevant here. — Eds.]

ments for both sides the court immediately found the defendant guilty of harassment for "using physical force against" the plaintiff. The court noted, however, "You're not found guilty of a crime, it's a violation. It's merely a pushing or shoving of somebody, it's not assault third degree." The court also immediately sentenced the defendant to a one-year conditional discharge, the condition being that "you are not to have any encounters with the law firm of Gilberg and Gilberg whether you like it or not." The court strongly suggested that the defendant retain a lawyer to act as his spokesman in future dealings with his former wife's attorneys.

The plaintiff then commenced this civil action for assault. The summons was issued the day following the defendant's conviction for harassment. The complaint, subsequently served, alleges that the defendant "assaulted and beat" the plaintiff "by striking him repeatedly." A quarter of a million dollars in damages are sought for injuries which allegedly include emotional distress, "injuries to head, face, arm and chest, causing discomfort, massive sweating, diarrhea, nausea" and aggravation of a preexisting heart condition.

After the case had been placed on the jury calendar plaintiff moved for summary judgment noting that the defendant had previously been convicted of harassment as a result of this incident and contending that therefore there was no "issue as to the assault for determination by a court or jury." The trial court agreed that at the prior City Court proceeding defendant "was afforded a full and fair opportunity to litigate the very issue raised upon this motion . . . *viz*, did defendant lay violent hands upon plaintiff" and, noting the City Court Judge's finding that defendant used "physical force against" the plaintiff, concluded that defendant's liability is "no longer disputable." Accordingly the court granted the motion for summary judgment against the defendant on the issue of liability and ordered the matter to proceed on the issue of damages alone.

The Appellate Division, 74 A.D.2d 913, 426 N.Y.S.2d 72 affirmed. . . .

The doctrine of collateral estoppel is based on the notion that it is not fair to permit a party to relitigate an issue which has previously been decided against him in a proceeding in which he had a fair opportunity to fully litigate the point (*see, e.g., Schwartz v. Public Administrator of County of Bronx*, 24 N.Y.2d 65, 69, 298 N.Y.S.2d 955, 246 N.E.2d 725; . . .). Properly utilized it also serves to conserve the resources of courts and litigants. Because the doctrine is based on general notions of fairness there are few immutable rules.

Due process, of course, would not permit a litigant to be bound by an adverse determination made in a prior proceeding to which he was not a party or in privity with a party (*Postal Tel. Cable Co. v. Newport*, 247 U.S. 464, 38 S.Ct. 566, 62 L.Ed. 1215; *Provident Bank v. Patterson*, 390 U.S. 102, 88 S.Ct. 733, 19 L.Ed.2d 936). Until recently the prior determination generally could not even be used against a party to the prior suit unless his current opponent had also been a party who would have been mutually bound by the determination had it been unfavorable to him (*see* Siegel, New York Practice, § 460). In 1967, however, we held that mutuality of estoppel "is a dead letter" in this State. . . . The rejection of the mutuality principle in civil actions also undermined the rule, which had long prevailed in this State, that a conviction in a criminal case could not be given conclusive effect in a subsequent civil suit. . . . That rule was abandoned in 1973 (*S.T. Grand, Inc. v. City of New York*, 32 N.Y.2d 300, 344 N.Y.S.2d 938, 298 N.E.2d 105).

These developments were not merely a remodeling of a rigid mechanism with fewer parts. In the *Schwartz* case and subsequent decisions it was emphasized that historically and necessarily collateral estoppel is a flexible doctrine which can never be rigidly or mechanically applied. . . . The question as to whether a party has had a full and fair opportunity to contest a prior determination cannot be reduced to a formula. It cannot, for instance, be resolved by a finding that the party against whom the determination is asserted was accorded due process in the prior proceeding (*People v. Plevy*, 52 N.Y.2d 58, 65, 436 N.Y.S.2d 224, 417 N.E.2d 518, *supra*). The point of the inquiry, of course, is not to decide whether the prior determination should be vacated but to decide whether it should be given conclusive effect beyond the case in which it was made (*see, e. g.*, Restatement, Judgments 2d [Tent. Draft No. 3], § 88, Comment i).

. . . .

The City Court action was a relatively minor one. Although nominally a criminal trial, the defendant was not actually charged with committing a crime, which by definition includes only felonies and misdemeanors (Penal Law, § 10.00, subd. 6). As the drafters of the Penal Law noted, petty infractions below the grade of a misdemeanor are, like traffic violations, more accurately described as "noncriminal offenses" (*see* Gilbert's Criminal Law and Procedure, [1970 ed], Commission Staff Notes on Proposed Penal Law, § 15.00, p. 2-190). By statute collateral estoppel effect is denied to traffic convictions (Vehicle and Traffic Law, § 155) and determinations in small claims actions (*see* section 1808 of the Uniform City Court Act, Uniform Justice Court Act and New York City Civil Court Act). Even in the absence of statute, however, these minor suits are illustrative of the type of determination which, under accepted common-law principles, should not be held conclusive in later cases (*see, e.g.*, Restatement, Judgments 2d [Tent. Draft No. 4], § 68.1, subd [c], and Comment d).

Because of the relative insignificance of the charge, the defendant had no constitutional or statutory right to a jury trial, as he would have in a true criminal prosecution . . . or even in the subsequently initiated civil action for damages (CPLR 4101, subd. 1; *see, also,* N.Y.Const. art. I, § 2). Nor could he reasonably expect or be expected to defend with the same vigor. The brisk, often informal, way in which these matters must be tried, as well as the relative insignificance of the outcome, afford the party neither opportunity nor incentive to litigate thoroughly or as thoroughly as he might if more were at stake.

Of course the defendant did not choose to litigate the matter first in the City Court. It was the plaintiff who had the initiative. Nor is there any suggestion that the defendant or the City Court Judge were aware of the possibility that a conviction on the petty criminal charge might later be used to conclusively establish liability in a quarter million dollar damage suit. As noted that action was not initiated until the day following the conviction. Consistent with the apparent minor nature of the charge, and the general practice in the local criminal courts, the nonjury trial was brief, consuming but part of an afternoon, followed immediately by verdict, allocution and sentence. In short the defendant was not afforded the same opportunity to litigate his liability in the City Court as he would in the Supreme Court. Thus it is not unfair to permit him one opportunity to fully defend the civil complaint on the merits in a manner consistent with the potential magnitude of the suit.

A contrary ruling, granting collateral estoppel effect to convictions in this type of case would not reduce the amount of litigation in the long run. It would, of course, provide an incentive to potential plaintiffs to file a minor criminal charge before commencing a civil action. If the defendant is convicted the prosecution will have also won the plaintiff's civil action, without the expense of a civil trial and, more important, without the plaintiff having to convince a jury of the merits of his action. If, on the other hand, the defendant is acquitted, the plaintiff's civil action would not be jeopardized because he could not be bound by the acquittal for the reason, among others, that he was not a party to the criminal trial. Of course a defendant alerted to the potential impact in future cases would be compelled to defend the violation charge with a vigor out of all proportion to its otherwise petty nature, and at variance with the proper function of the local criminal courts, to provide expeditious disposition of minor cases. As one commentator has noted in a similar context: "In the end this could frustrate the very purpose of res judicata to reduce contention and dispute. Instead of more litigation later, there will be more litigation now" (Rosenberg, *Collateral Estoppel in New York*, 44 St John's L.Rev. 165, 177).

Accordingly, the order of the Appellate Division should be reversed. . . .

MEYER, JUDGE (dissenting).

Respectfully, I dissent. I would affirm because (1) the issues in this action and the prior criminal proceeding are identical; (2) defendant was represented in the criminal proceeding by the same attorney who represents him in this action and had a full and fair opportunity in the criminal proceeding to litigate the question whether he struck plaintiff; (3) the absence of a right to jury trial in the criminal proceeding raises neither a constitutional nor a statutory bar to the application of the rules of collateral estoppel; and (4) the fact that harassment is a violation, rather than a misdemeanor or felony is, by itself, an insufficient basis for denying collateral estoppel effect to the criminal court's finding.

. . . .

The transcript of the City Court trial is part of the record on this appeal. It is 100 pages in length and shows that before trial began defendant's attorney moved to dismiss for failure to accord defendant a speedy trial and in the interest of justice, that the witnesses for the prosecution were plaintiff, the court reporter who had taken the record of the examination before trial during which the altercation between plaintiff and defendant occurred, and one of plaintiff's sons, who had been called into the examination room by the reporter when the altercation began, all of whom were cross-examined at considerable length by defendant's attorney, that at the end of the People's case defendant's attorney moved to dismiss and when that motion was denied presented defendant as a witness in his own behalf, after which he acknowledged that he had no other witnesses to present. The City Court Judge then heard closing arguments from each side before rendering his decision and, after hearing defendant in his own behalf, imposed sentence. Since the sentence imposed was a one-year conditional discharge (the condition being not to harass the Gilberg firm) and the factual issue to be determined was essentially one of credibility relating to whether defendant struck plaintiff, there simply was no reason why decision and sentence should not have followed immediately after the close of trial. To characterize the procedure as brisk and informal and speak of a vigorous defense as out of proportion with the function of the court is utterly inconsistent with the record in this case, which shows beyond peradventure that the trial was conducted and completed with as much formality, dignity and decorum as any Supreme Court trial. Nor apart from the record in this case am I prepared to accept the majority's conception of the operations of a local criminal court as a basis for denying preclusion to the determination of such a court, except when concrete objective factors indicate that in a particular case there has not been full and fair opportunity to litigate the issue. . . . To equate the City Court's trial of a violation which carries with it the possibility of a sentence of imprisonment for 15 days (Penal Law, § 70.15, subd. 4) with the determinations made in small claims, mostly without lawyers or court reporters, is unrealistic and inconsistent with New York's statutory scheme. . . .

. . . .

NOTES

(1) The Court notes that under some circumstances a determination in a criminal case will have preclusive effect in a subsequent civil action. What should be the effect on a civil action of a prior acquittal of criminal charges?

The courts are wary of the use of issue preclusion against a defendant in a criminal proceeding regardless of the forum in which the issue was first tried. Why? *See People v. Plevy*, 52 N.Y.2d 58, 436 N.Y.S.2d 224, 417 N.E.2d 518 (1980). In criminal cases, a withdrawn guilty plea cannot be used by the prosecution even as an informal admission against defendant. *People v. Spitaleri*, 9 N.Y.2d 168, 212 N.Y.S.2d 53, 173 N.E.2d 35 (1961). The Court of Appeals recently held, however, that a withdrawn guilty plea may be used in a related personal injury suit. *Cohens v. Hess*, 92 N.Y.2d 511, 683 N.Y.S.2d 161, 705 N.E.2d 1202 (1998). A guilty plea to a traffic offense was involved. *Spitaleri* is not controlling, since in criminal cases, different considerations obtain. Of course this is only an evidentiary matter and not issue preclusion; and since the admission is informal, it is not binding and defendant can try to explain it away.

(2) Like criminal proceedings, arbitration awards can have a preclusive effect if the tests for issue preclusion are otherwise met. *Clemens v. Apple*, 65 N.Y.2d 746, 492 N.Y.S.2d 20, 481 N.E.2d 560 (1985); *American Ins. Co. v. Messinger*, 43 N.Y.2d 184, 401 N.Y.S.2d 36, 371 N.E.2d 798 (1977). In the *American Ins. Co.* case, the Court described a limit on the applicability of the "full and fair opportunity" test; the test would not restrict the preclusive effect of a first judgment when the second was between the very same parties who were in fact adversaries in the prior action. Under this approach, if A obtained a judgment for property damage against B, a negligent driver, A could then use that judgment in a subsequent action for personal injury even if B could somehow show that the first litigation did not offer him a full and fair opportunity to be heard.

NOTE ON ADMINISTRATIVE PROCEEDINGS

Administrative proceedings which take the form of "quasi-judicial" determinations are also entitled to preclusive impact if preclusion is otherwise appropriate. *See Allied Chemical v. Niagara Mohawk Power Corp.*, 72 N.Y.2d 271, 532 N.Y.S.2d 230, 528 N.E.2d 153 (1988) (determination of the Public Service Commission given preclusive effect in subsequent litigation). In *Ryan v. New York Telephone Co.*, 62 N.Y.2d 494, 478 N.Y.S.2d 823, 467 N.E.2d 487 (1984), the plaintiff in a wrongful discharge action was estopped from establishing that he was fired without cause because the issue had been determined against him in an earlier proceeding in which he had been denied unemployment insurance benefits. The *Ryan* decision was much criticized, *see, e.g.*, Carlisle, *Getting a Full Bite of the Apple: When Should the Doctrine of Issue Preclusion Make an Administrative or Arbitral Decision Binding in a Court of Law?* 55 Fordham L. Rev. 63 (1986), and was legislatively overruled insofar as unemployment insurance decisions are concerned, *see* Ch. 258, Laws of 1987, amending New York Labor Law § 623. It remains the rule that other quasi-judicial decisions can be preclusive. *See Allied Chemical v. Niagara Mohawk Power Corp., supra.*

In *David v. Biondo*, 92 N.Y.2d 318, 680 N.Y.S.2d 450, 703 N.E.2d 261 (1998), the Court held that a disciplinary board's finding that a dentist had not committed malpractice could not be used by the dentist as an issue preclusion defense to the malpractice action for damages brought by the complaining patient. The patient had not been a party to the disciplinary proceeding and had never had a full and fair opportunity to litigate the facts. Even where the party against whom the administrative determination is sought to be used is the same, collateral estoppel may not apply. Where defendant physician was found in an administrative decision to have engaged in sexual misconduct with a patient, that finding was held not conclusive in the patient's civil action. The administrative panel was split in their decision, and in a criminal proceeding the physician's conviction was reversed on appeal, and he was acquitted after retrial. *Jeffreys v. Griffin*, 1 N.Y.3d 34, 769 N.Y.S.2d 184, 801 N.E.2d 404 (2003). Contrariwise, in *Parker v. Blauvelt Volunteer Fire Co., Inc.*, 93 N.Y.2d 343, 690 N.Y.S.2d 478, 712 N.E.2d 647 (1999), it was held that defendant Fire Company could use an administrative finding upholding its action in discharging plaintiff as a defense to plaintiff's 42 U.S.C. § 1983 civil rights action for damages arising out of the same underlying facts. The difference here is that the party against whom the prior determination was used had a full and fair opportunity to litigate in the administrative proceeding. The Court reaffirmed the underlying soundness of *Ryan v. New York Tel. Co.*, by citing it as precedent.

But in *Matter of Balcerak v. Nassau County,* 94 N.Y.2d 253, 701 N.Y.S.2d 700, 723 N.E.2d 555 (1999), a corrections officer who sought an award under Gen. Mun. Law § 207-c for injuries incurred in the course of employment, attempted to use a Workers' Compensation Board award as collateral estoppel. The Court of Appeals refused to allow this, finding that the Workers' Compensation process involves a more lenient and more inclusive universe of activity, while the General Municipal Law applies a stricter standard. The same "protocols" are not involved and so one administrative finding should not be binding on the other.

Given the principal case, under what circumstances will the result of a non-jury administrative determination be given preclusive effect in a subsequent case in which the parties have a right to a jury trial? The Supreme Court of the United States has held that the Seventh Amendment right to a jury trial (which applies only to federal actions) does not prohibit giving preclusive effect to an issue determined without a jury in a subsequent action in which there is a right to a jury trial. *Parklane Hosiery Co. v. Shore*, 439 U.S. 322, 99 S. Ct. 645, 58 L. Ed. 2d 552 (1979).

Nonetheless, in the same case, the Supreme Court presented a strong case against the use of offensive issue preclusion in the federal courts in cases sounding in federal law. The Court said:

> First, offensive use of collateral estoppel does not promote judicial economy in the same manner as defensive use does. . . . Thus defensive collateral estoppel gives a plaintiff a strong incentive to join all potential defendants in the first action if possible. Offensive use of collateral estoppel, on the other hand, creates precisely the opposite incentive. Since a plaintiff will be able to rely on a previous judgment against a defendant but will not be bound by that judgment if the defendant wins, the plaintiff has every incentive to adopt a "wait and see" attitude, in the hope that the first action by another plaintiff will result in a favorable judgment. . . . Thus offensive use of collateral estoppel will likely increase rather than decrease the total amount of litigation, since potential plaintiffs will have everything to gain and nothing to lose by not intervening in the first action.

A second argument against offensive use of collateral estoppel is that it may be unfair to a defendant. If a defendant in the first action is sued for small or nominal damages, he may have little incentive to defend vigorously, particularly if future suits are not foreseeable . . . *cf. Berner v. British Commonwealth Pac. Airlines*, 346 F.2d 532 (CA2) (application of offensive collateral estoppel denied where defendant did not appeal an adverse judgment awarding damages of $35,000 and defendant was later sued for over $7 million). Allowing offensive collateral estoppel may also be unfair to a defendant if the judgment relied upon as a basis for the estoppel is itself inconsistent with one or more previous judgments in favor of the defendant. Still another situation where it might be unfair to apply offensive estoppel is where the second action affords the defendant procedural opportunities unavailable in the first action that could readily cause a different result. . . .

We have concluded that the preferable approach for dealing with these problems in the federal courts is not to preclude the use of offensive collateral estoppel, but to grant trial courts broad discretion to determine when it should be applied. . . . The general rule should be that in cases where a plaintiff could easily have joined in the earlier action or where, either for the reasons discussed above or for other reasons, the application of offensive estoppel would be unfair to a defendant, a trial judge should not allow the use of offensive collateral estoppel.

439 U.S. at 329-31, 99 S. Ct. at 650-52, 58 L. Ed. 2d at 552.

KOCH v. CONSOLIDATED EDISON CO. OF N.Y.
Court of Appeals
62 N.Y.2d 548, 479 N.Y.S.2d 163, 468 N.E.2d 541 (1984),
cert. denied, 469 U.S. 1210, 105 S. Ct. 1177 (1985)

JONES, J.

On July 13, 1977 at approximately 9:36 P.M. there was a complete failure of electrical service in the City of New York except for an area in the Borough of Queens which was supplied by the Long Island Lighting Company. The blackout lasted for approximately 25 hours with power not being completely restored until approximately 10:40 P.M. on July 14.

The present action was instituted on September 7, 1978 by the City of New York and 14 public benefit corporations to recover damages allegedly sustained as a result of Con Edison's gross negligence and reckless and willful conduct with respect to the blackout. Plaintiffs moved for partial summary judgment with respect to Con Edison's liability for gross negligence "on the ground that, under the doctrine of collateral estoppel, a prior determination in another lawsuit (*Food Pageant, Inc. v. Consolidated Edison Co., Inc.*, Supreme Court, Bronx

County, Index No. 16971/77)[1] that the July 13-14, 1977 electric power failure . . .
resulted from the gross negligence of the defendant Consolidated Edison, is
conclusive and binding on the defendant Consolidated Edison in this action". . . .

. . . .

We agree with both courts below that on the issue of Con Edison's liability for
gross negligence in connection with the blackout, Con Edison is precluded by the
adverse determination of the issue in *Food Pageant v. Consolidated Edison
Co.* (54 N.Y.2d 167). The applicable principle in this case is that of third-party
issue preclusion.

It is plaintiffs who seek to invoke the principle of third-party issue preclusion
to bar Con Edison from relitigating its liability for gross negligence. It is not disputed that this issue was actually litigated and determined by a valid and final
judgment in *Food Pageant* and that the determination of that issue was essential to the judgment in that case. Plaintiffs contend, therefore, that the determination in *Food Pageant* is binding and conclusive in this case. Con Edison,
having the burden to demonstrate that the circumstances of the prior determination justify affording it an opportunity to relitigate the issue of liability,
advances several arguments in support of its contention that the determination
in *Food Pageant* is not to be given preclusive effect.[4] These arguments, taken

---

[1] When this case reached our court we upheld the jury verdict which found Con Edison to have
been grossly negligent in causing the 1977 blackout and which awarded plaintiff grocery store
chain damages in the sum of $40,500 for food spoilage and loss of business. (*Food Pageant v. Con-
solidated Edison Co.*, 54 N.Y.2d 167).

[4] The relevant factors to be considered are set out in section 29 of the Restatement of Judgments,
Second, and in Schwartz. Section 29 provides in full as follows:

§ 29. Issue Preclusion in Subsequent Litigation with Others

A party precluded from relitigating an issue with an opposing party, in accordance with
§§ 27 and 28, is also precluded from doing so with another person unless the fact that he
lacked full and fair opportunity to litigate the issue in the first action or other circumstances justify affording him an opportunity to relitigate the issue. The circumstances to
which considerations should be given include those enumerated in § 28 and also whether:

(1) Treating the issue as conclusively determined would be incompatible with an applicable scheme of administering the remedies in the actions involved;

(2) The forum in the second action affords the party against whom preclusion is
asserted procedural opportunities in the presentation and determination of the
issue that were not available in the first action and could likely result in the issue
being differently determined;

(3) The person seeking to invoke favorable preclusion, or to avoid unfavorable preclusion, could have effected joinder in the first action between himself and his present
adversary;

(4) The determination relied on as preclusive was itself inconsistent with another
determination of the same issue;

(5) The prior determination may have been affected by relationships among the parties to the first action that are not present in the subsequent action, or apparently
was based on a compromise verdict or finding;

(6) Treating the issue as conclusively determined may complicate determination of
issues in the subsequent action or prejudice the interests of another party thereto;

singularly or in combination, do not warrant the result for which Con Edison contends, and Con Edison has not tendered sufficient proof in admissible form to require trial of any issue of fact or reversal of the exercise of judgment by the courts below.

It is first contended that third-party issue preclusion should not apply because there are other judicial determinations concluding that Con Edison was not guilty of gross negligence in connection with the blackout. Whatever might be said of the effect properly to be given to inconsistent determinations of like judicial stature, in this instance it suffices to dismiss Con Edison's contention to observe that the inconsistent determinations on which it would rely are those in cases tried in the Small Claims Part of the Civil Court of New York City as to which informal and simplified procedures are applicable and which by express statutory provision are not to be deemed an adjudication of any fact at issue (other than the amount involved) with respect to any other action.[7]

Con Edison next argues that there is now available exculpatory evidence which in fairness requires that it be permitted to relitigate the issue of liability. Reference is made to investigative reports, in particular to the so-called Clapp Report. These reports were available and offered but rejected in the *Food Pageant* trial. Nothing suggests that the exclusion of this hearsay evidence was error (and any contention that it was could have been subjected to appellate review on the appeal in that case), and no persuasive argument is now advanced to support admissibility in this case.

Con Edison next makes an oblique plea that we should reintroduce the former requirement of mutuality which we declared "a dead letter" in *B.R. DeWitt, Inc. v. Hall* (19 N.Y.2d 141, 147). To grant this plea would, of course, be entirely to eliminate third-party issue preclusion. It is understandable that Con Edison should express concern, in the light of the multiplicity of claims arising out of

---

(7) The issue is one of law and treating it as conclusively determined would inappropriately foreclose opportunity for obtaining reconsideration of the legal rule upon which it was based;

(8) Other compelling circumstances make it appropriate that the party be permitted to relitigate the issue.

The articulation in Schwartz appears at page 72, as follows:

A decision whether or not the plaintiff drivers had a full and fair opportunity to establish their nonnegligence in the prior action requires an exploration of the various elements which make up the realities of litigation. A comprehensive list of the various factors which should enter into a determination whether a party has had his day in court would include such considerations as the size of the claim, the forum of the prior litigation, the use of initiative, the extent of the litigation, the competence and experience of counsel, the availability of new evidence, indications of a compromise verdict, differences in the applicable law and foreseeability of future litigation.

[7] CCA 1808 provides:

A judgment obtained under this article may be pleaded as res judicata only as to the amount involved in the particular action and shall not otherwise be deemed an adjudication of any fact at issue or found therein in any other action or court.

the blackout, that the issue of its gross negligence will have been established in each case. Nevertheless, no sufficient justification is advanced to turn the clock back with respect to so fundamental a legal development as the elimination of the requirement of mutuality. We have been committed since *DeWitt*, and indeed even before (*Israel v. Wood Dolson Co.*, 1 N.Y.2d 116), to the proposition that efficient utilization of the judicial system is served by preclusion of relitigation of issues as to which a litigant has had a full and fair opportunity for resolution, irrespective of the identity of his particular opponent. Nor does Con Edison advance any intermediate position warranting a different application of the principles of third-party issue preclusion with respect to a multiplicity of claims arising out of a community-wide disaster such as the blackout in this case.

It is then argued that the determination in *Food Pageant* should not be given preclusive effect because of indications that it was the result of compromise in the jury room. No tender has been made, however, of proof in admissible form sufficient to require trial of this factual issue. The arguments of Con Edison are grounded only in speculation, and it cannot be said as a matter of law that the *Food Pageant* verdict was the result of impermissible compromise.

The circumstance, to which Con Edison next points, that the claim in *Food Pageant* and the amount of the jury's verdict ($40,500) may be said to be "small in absolute terms and particularly so when compared to the aggregate of over $200 million in claims against Con Edison arising out of the 1977 blackout," provides no basis to deny application of third-party issue preclusion. In *Food Pageant*, Con Edison had a full and fair opportunity to litigate the issue of gross negligence, the forum and applicable procedures were the same, the burden of persuasion was the same, and Con Edison, explicitly then recognizing the potential preclusive effects of an adverse determination in that case, had every incentive to defend that action fully and vigorously.

Nor does the adoption of a rule of comparative negligence in New York (CPLR art 14-A) foreclose application of third-party issue preclusion in the circumstances of this case. No contention whatsoever is put forth by Con Edison that any action or omission to act on the part of any of plaintiffs contributed to cause the blackout. There simply is no issue of comparative negligence involved in the question of Con Edison's responsibility for the blackout. It may be, however, that principles of mitigation will require consideration of certain action or inaction on the part of plaintiffs in the determination of damages.

Finally with respect to the preclusion issue, we reject as wholly without merit Con Edison's assertion that to apply third-party issue preclusion would be to deprive it of the due process to which it is constitutionally entitled. The characterization of this appeal as "presenting a question of fundamental fairness" neither concludes nor advances the argument. Con Edison cites no authority, and we know of none, which now regards the application of third-party issue preclusion as posing a question of constitutional dimension where in the prior action a full and fair opportunity to litigate has been afforded.

For the reasons stated we conclude that the prior determination in *Food Pageant* with respect to Con Edison's liability for gross negligence in connection with the 1977 blackout is binding and conclusive on Con Edison in this action.

§ 23.04 THE PRIVITY PROBLEM

The implication of the cases we have seen in this chapter is that neither claim nor issue preclusion can be used against one who was not a party to litigation thought to be the source of the preclusive effect. A major exception to this rule turns on the concept of privity.

BUECHEL v. BAIN
Court of Appeals
97 N.Y.2d 295, 740 N.Y.S.2d 252, 766 N.E.2d 914 (2001)

SMITH, J.

[This is an action to determine defendant attorneys' rights to receive proceeds from a trust set up under an agreement to pay them for legal services rendered to plaintiffs in connection with a patent application for a medical prosthetic device. In a prior lawsuit brought by one Rhodes, a former law partner of defendants Bain and Gilfillan, it was determined that the fee agreement was improper and limited Rhodes' recovery to a quantum meruit amount. The issue in the present action likewise concerns the right of the attorneys to contract payments under the identical agreement. Defendants in the present action argue that they were simply nominal parties in the prior action and did not participate actively in it.]

. . . .

The equitable doctrine of collateral estoppel is grounded in the facts and realities of a particular litigation, rather than rigid rules. Collateral estoppel precludes a party from relitigating in a subsequent action or proceeding an issue raised in a prior action or proceeding and decided against that party or those in privity (*Ryan v New York Tel. Co.*, 62 NY2d 494, 500 [1984]). The policies underlying its application are avoiding relitigation of a decided issue and the possibility of an inconsistent result (*D'Arata v New York Cent. Mut. Fire Ins. Co.*, 76 NY2d 659, 664 [1990]).

Two requirements must be met before collateral estoppel can be invoked. There must be an identity of issue which has necessarily been decided in the prior action and is decisive of the present action, and there must have been a full and fair opportunity to contest the decision now said to be controlling (*see, Gilberg v Barbieri*, 53 NY2d 285, 291 [1981]). The litigant seeking the benefit of collateral estoppel must demonstrate that the decisive issue was necessarily decided in the prior action against a party, or one in privity with a party (*see, id.*).

The party to be precluded from relitigating the issue bears the burden of demonstrating the absence of a full and fair opportunity to contest the prior determination.

The doctrine, however, is a flexible one, and the enumeration of these elements is intended merely as a framework, not a substitute, for case-by-case analysis of the facts and realities. "In the end, the fundamental inquiry is whether relitigation should be permitted in a particular case in light of . . . fairness to the parties, conservation of the resources of the court and the litigants, and the societal interests in consistent and accurate results. No rigid rules are possible, because even these factors may vary in relative importance depending on the nature of the proceedings . . ." (*see, Staatsburg Water Co. v Staatsburg Fire Dist.,* 72 NY2d 147, 153 [1988] [citations omitted]).

Applying these principles, we conclude that defendants are barred from now once again litigating the validity of a trust agreement that was — after extensive pretrial and trial proceedings involving them — found to be invalid.

In determining whether collateral estoppel applies here, the initial question is whether defendants — parties in the *Rhodes* action who were not named in the plaintiffs' counterclaim — should, nevertheless, be bound by the determination rescinding the trust. Because for purposes of collateral estoppel, defendants were in privity with their former law partner Rhodes as to the validity of the fee arrangements, we conclude they should be bound.

In the context of collateral estoppel, privity does not have a single well-defined meaning (*Matter of Juan C. v Cortines,* 89 NY2d 659, 667 [1997]). Rather, privity is "'an amorphous concept not easy of application' . . . and 'includes those who are successors to a property interest, those who control an action although not formal parties to it, those whose interests are represented by a party to the action, and [those who are] coparties to a prior action'" (*id.,* at 667-668 [citations omitted]). In addressing privity, courts must carefully analyze whether the party sought to be bound and the party against whom the litigated issue was decided have a relationship that would justify preclusion, and whether preclusion, with its severe consequences, would be fair under the particular circumstances. Doubts should be resolved against imposing preclusion to ensure that the party to be bound can be considered to have had a full and fair opportunity to litigate.

For present purposes, Bain and Gilfillan were in privity with their former law partner, Rhodes, as he was a co-signatory to the fee agreement and co-beneficiary to the trust proceeds arising from the fee agreement. Considering the facts and realities of the matters before us, we agree with the Appellate Division that defendants should be deemed to be in privity with Rhodes for purposes of litigating the validity of their fee arrangements as embodied in the trust. Defendants' rights to receive payments were coextensive with Rhodes' and derived from the identical arrangement entered into when the three were law partners. As the Appellate Division concluded, "[a]s partners in the law firm that entered into the fee agreement with plaintiffs, [Bain and Gilfillan's] right to receive trust income stands or falls with the contract." (*Supra*, 275 AD2d, at 74.) Indeed, defendants themselves recognized that adjudication of Rhodes' conduct as a partner or agent of the law firm would have consequences for them. Defendants' interests were aligned with Rhodes' with respect to the lawfulness of the fee arrangements where millions of dollars were at issue. Thus, it is appropriate to bind them by the judgment in *Rhodes* under the doctrine of collateral estoppel.

Defendant trustees — parties to the *Rhodes* action with notice of the issues to be decided in that case — acknowledged that they were themselves "unclear as to how the wording of portions of the counterclaim [could] be so narrowly construed" to exclude them. Given these facts, as a policy matter we agree with the Appellate Division that a "party to a lawsuit cannot sit by idly while a contract, to which he is also a party, is judicially construed without being precluded by the result" (*id.*).

Knowing that the validity of the trust was being vigorously contested in *Rhodes,* and knowing the potential serious adverse consequences of the litigation, in this particular case it is appropriate to deem defendants' interests represented by Rhodes. Defendants cannot be rewarded for their conscious, tactical decision not to take a more active role in that litigation by now allowing the very same issues and facts to be relitigated. A contrary determination would undermine a policy interest that is at the heart of collateral estoppel — discouraging relitigation of issues and the potential for inconsistent outcomes.

We turn next to whether the two basic requirements for collateral estoppel have been met.

A comparison of the issue raised in the present action with the issue raised in the *Rhodes* action reveals that the identical issue was already litigated and decided. In the *Rhodes* action, Supreme Court determined, after extensive pretrial and trial proceedings, that the original fee agreement was unlawful as it was procured in violation of the canons of ethics. Supreme Court further concluded "that with regard to fees, the Trust Agreement merely recodified the prior fee arrangements entered into" and that because "[plaintiffs] did not have the benefit of truly independent counsel and were never instructed to seek [independent legal] advice . . . the trust agreements are rescinded." This is the very issue that defendants seek to relitigate in the present action hoping that the second time around a court will reach a contrary determination.

Defendants, moreover, have failed to establish the lack of a full and fair opportunity to litigate the validity of the fee agreement in the *Rhodes* action. Because defendants were in privity with Rhodes, the critical question is whether Rhodes had a full and fair opportunity to litigate the issue (*see, D'Arata v New York Cent. Mut. Fire Ins. Co., supra*, 76 NY2d, at 666). We conclude that he did. In extensive proceedings, Rhodes vigorously defended the validity of the trust. Moreover, as noted by the Appellate Division, defendants were not just nominal parties but, as trust beneficiaries, were essential parties whose rights were affected by the outcome of the *Rhodes* action. The record reflects that defendants produced documents for the litigation, received copies of select documents used in the trial (including deposition transcripts), and agreed to testify as witnesses on behalf of Rhodes before changing their minds at the last minute.

Defendants make much of the fact that Supreme Court denied plaintiffs' motion to amend their counterclaims to assert claims against defendants. While true, this fact does not undermine the holding of *Rhodes* which disposed of the essential claim in the instant action in holding the fee agreement was unenforceable. All that denial of the motion to amend guaranteed was that defendants would not be subject to a monetary judgment in the *Rhodes* action. Additionally, it was defendants who beseeched the trial court to stay this action pending a determination in *Rhodes,* fully intending to invoke the benefits of the judgment if the outcome was favorable to them. Although, as the dissenting opinion points out, abolition of the mutuality of estoppel doctrine authorizes such use of issue preclusion, nothing in our case law correspondingly prohibits taking this fact into account in analyzing whether defendants — parties in the *Rhodes* action who had notice of all the proceedings — should be bound by a determination against one with whom they are united in interest as to the particular issue.* Moreover, it was defendants who vigorously opposed the expansion of the *Rhodes* case to include specific claims by Buechel and Pappas against Bain and Gilfillan. Defendants based their opposition on the prospect of additional delay in the *Rhodes* litigation.

. . . .

[The dissenter wished to restrict the use of privity to the three traditional New York concepts: where the party's rights are derivative of the rights of the party to the previous litigation; where the nonparty controlled or substantially participated in control of the prior litigation; or where the nonparty had its interests represented by the losing party in the prior litigation. 97 N.Y.2d at 317, 740 N.Y.S.2d at 261, 766 N.E.2d at 923.]

NOTES

(1) In *Gramatan Home Investors Corp. v. Lopez*, 46 N.Y.2d 481, 414 N.Y.S.2d 308, 386 N.E.2d 1328 (1979), it was argued that a consumer fraud action, prosecuted successfully by the State Attorney-General against plaintiff's assignor

---

* Further addressing the dissent, no one factor is determinative in our conclusion that defendants here were in privity with Rhodes. It is, rather, a confluence of factors that persuades us to affirm, including defendants' relationship with Rhodes vis-à-vis the fee arrangements, their involvement in the action, their awareness of issues that would be decided, and their acknowledged tactical decisions regarding the *Rhodes* litigation. Additionally, because we hold that collateral estoppel bars relitigation of the validity of the trust, defendants' conclusory affidavits (dissenting opn, at 312-313) are irrelevant in this action.

based on a vinyl siding scam perpetrated by the assignor against homeowners, collaterally estopped assignee plaintiff from suing the homeowners on the same home improvement contract. But the Attorney-General's action did not occur until almost two years after the assignment was made. The Court held that while an assignee could be in privity with the assignor as to matters occurring prior to the assignment, the assignor could not be bound by matters occurring after the assignment.

(2) "Generally, to establish privity the connection between the parties must be such that the interests of the nonparty can be said to have been represented in the prior proceeding. . . . Thus, there can be privity to make a legal determination in a declaratory judgment action brought by a union binding in a subsequent action by a member . . .; to cause a judgment against an insured to have binding effect in a subsequent action against his liability insurer . . .; to make a judgment in an action brought by a trustee in bankruptcy a bar in a subsequent action by a creditor . . .; or to make a dismissal on the merits of a shareholders' derivative action binding on other shareholders as members of a represented class so as to preclude them from bringing a similar action. . . ." *Green v. Santa Fe Industries, Inc.*, 70 N.Y.2d 244, 253, 519 N.Y.S.2d 793, 796, 514 N.E.2d 105, 108 (1987).

In *Green*, the Court held that one shareholder is not necessarily in privity with other holders of stock in the same company. Therefore, a judgment against one group of shareholders would not have preclusive effect on a second action brought by others if the first was not in the form of a derivative action. Res judicata bars a stockholder's derivative action when a similar action, brought by another stockholder, was dismissed on the merits, provided that the second stockholder was not excluded from the first action, that both actions arose out of the same underlying transaction or related transactions and that the first action was not collusive or fraudulent. *Parkoff v. General Telephone & Elec. Corp.*, 53 N.Y.2d 412, 442 N.Y.S.2d 432, 425 N.E.2d 820 (1981).

(3) Allen, the driver of a car involved in a two car accident, sued Charles, the other driver (who was driving a car owned by Betty) and recovered a judgment against Charles based on a finding of Charles' negligence. If Tim, a passenger in Allen's car later sues Betty, will she be precluded from litigating the issue of Charles' negligence? Note that as a matter of substantive law, Vehicle and Traffic Law § 388 provides that the negligence of a person driving a car with the owner's permission is imputed to the latter when she is sued by an accident victim.

(4) When can privity be found between a class representative and a member of the class? *See Gowan v. Tully*, § 23.02, *supra. Compare Hansberry v. Lee*, 311 U.S. 32, 61 S. Ct. 115, 85 L. Ed. 2d 22 (1940); Weinstein, *Revision of Procedure, Some Problems in Class Actions*, 9 Buff. L. Rev. 433 (1960); Restatement (Second) of Judgments § 28 comment h, p. 282 and § 41, p. 393 (1982).

(5) Where plaintiff sued the City for injuries to her daughter allegedly caused by a City vehicle driven by a City employee, and obtained a default judgment

against the employee in a separate action, that judgment could not be used against the City. Collateral estoppel does not operate where the City was not a party to the action against the employee, and the City and employee are not in the sort of privity that would invoke that doctrine. *Chambers v. City of New York*, 309 A.D.2d 81, 764 N.Y.S.2d 708 (2d Dep't 2003).

Part Seven
SPECIAL LITIGATION PROBLEMS

Chapter 24

CONFRONTING UNLAWFUL GOVERNMENT ACTIVITY: ARTICLE 78 AND RELATED REMEDIES — A PROCEDURAL BRAMBLE BUSH

§ 24.01 INTRODUCTION

To protect one's client, and thus the public, from the unlawful exercise of governmental power is a lawyer's most valuable contribution to the life of democracy. In New York, affirmative litigation of this kind requires the successful negotiation of complex procedures. This chapter is intended to introduce you to the relevant issues.

To begin with, counsel must decide whether to use one or more of several possible vehicles, each of which leads to a different remedy. Not all of them are available in every situation. Some of these may be combined, but others may not. Here is a brief review of the principal possibilities.

The Action for Damages

Although for the most part similar to a damage action against a private entity, some special rules are confronted when a damage action is brought against the state or a local government. Depending on the nature of the wrong alleged, the commencement of the action may be subject to a condition precedent, usually the service of a notice of claim. *See* § 7.09 *supra*. There will probably also be a short statute of limitations to contend with. *See* CPLR 217, § 24.04, *infra*.

If the state is the defendant, the action must be brought in the Court of Claims. Court of Claims Act §§ 8, 9; *c.f. Koerner v. State*, 62 N.Y.2d 442, 478 N.Y.S.2d 584, 467 N.E.2d 232 (1984). The Court of Claims may not award equitable relief, however, except as incidental to monetary relief. *See* Court of Claims Act § 9; *Koerner v. State, supra*. This creates difficulties for a person with claims for injunctive and monetary relief against the state. One alternative would be to seek relief in the Supreme Court, which has the power to grant coercive relief, such as mandamus or prohibition, against the state, *see* CPLR 7803(3); *Klostermann v. Cuomo*, 61 N.Y.2d 525, 475 N.Y.S.2d 247, 463 N.E.2d 588 (1984), and the power to grant such monetary damages as are "incidental to the primary relief sought by the petitioner. . . ." CPLR 7806. Whether damages are "incidental" for this purpose depends on the facts of the particular case. *See Gross v. Perales*, 72 N.Y.2d 231, 532 N.Y.S.2d 68, 527 N.E.2d 1205 (1988) (order directing the state to pay $20,000,000 to the petitioner New York County Department of Social Services held "incidental" to a determination that the state had made an arbitrary and capricious decision that had caused the withholding of these funds). *See also Pauk v. Board of Trustees of the City of New York*, 68 N.Y.2d 702, 506 N.Y.S.2d 308, 497 N.E.2d 675 (1986) (if the petitioner, a former teacher who claimed that he had been denied tenure illegally, prevailed on the merits, salary lost as a result would be incidental damages). *Compare Davidson v. Capuano*, 792 F.2d 275 (2d Cir. 1986) (prisoner's claim for compensatory and punitive damages from prison officials based on claim of unconstitutional deprivation of his property was not incidental to a former article 78 proceeding based on the same wrong).

If the damages are not incidental to the primary claim, the claimant seeking injunctive and monetary relief from the state will ordinarily have to bring two separate proceedings. *C.f., Davidson v. Capuano, supra.* Remember that the federal courts are not a proper forum for damage actions against the state because of the bar of the Eleventh Amendment.

There is one type of case in which the Supreme Court has the power to grant both coercive relief and damages (even if not "incidental" under the test described above) against the state: an action based on a violation of the state Human Rights Law (Executive Law § 296). In *Koerner v. State*, 62 N.Y.2d 442, 478 N.Y.S.2d 584, 467 N.E.2d 232 (1984), it was held that the state has waived its immunity from suit for damages in the Supreme Court in such cases.

The Suit for Injunction

The action for an injunction is an appropriate vehicle for obtaining coercive relief when there is no adequate remedy at law. As you will recall from your reading of § 12.05, *supra*, preliminary injunctions and temporary restraining orders are useful for getting a judicial decree quickly. Such preliminary relief is available against governmental officials. *See McCain v. Koch*, 70 N.Y.2d 109, 517 N.Y.S.2d 918, 511 N.E.2d 62 (1987) (upholding the power of the Supreme Court to provide adequate emergency housing to persons in need).

Since the Supreme Court may grant coercive remedies against government officers and bodies through article 78 proceedings, and since article 78 orders are legal (not equitable) remedies, the availability of article 78 relief can lead to a denial of injunctive relief. *State Division of Human Rights v. New York State Department of Correctional Services*, 90 A.D.2d 51, 70, n.9, 456 N.Y.S.2d 63, 76 (2d Dep't 1982), and cases cited. There is thus some danger that counsel will use the wrong vehicle in seeking coercive relief. The penalty, if any, for a mistaken choice in remedy is treated later in this chapter.

It has been held that the Supreme Court has jurisdiction to grant equitable relief against the state and its subdivisions. *Koerner v. State*, 62 N.Y.2d 442, 478 N.Y.S.2d 584, 467 N.E.2d 232 (1984); *Cavaioli v. Board of Trustees of State University of New York*, 116 A.D.2d 689, 498 N.Y.S.2d 7 (2d Dep't 1986).

The Declaratory Judgment

CPLR 3001 authorizes the declaratory judgment action in New York. It allows the court to declare "the rights and other legal relations of the parties to a justiciable controversy." This device has proven useful in resolving many types of legal problems, such as establishing the invalidity of a foreign divorce decree[1] or determining whether an insurance policy obligates the insurer to defend a particular claim against the insured.[2] (A comprehensive survey of the situations in which declaratory judgments have been used is found in 5 Weinstein, Korn & Miller, N.Y. Civil Practice ¶ 3001.06a *et seq.*). For present purposes, it is important that the declaratory judgment action can and has been used to attack unconstitutional or otherwise illegal governmental acts.[3]

It is not necessary that coercive relief be available in order to obtain a declaration that a particular governmental policy is illegal.[4] Moreover, the courts have broader power to grant declaratory judgments than to grant the coercive remedies available under article 78.[5]

An important limit on the availability of declaratory judgment actions is that they may not be used to obtain an advisory opinion.[6]

The Article 78 Proceeding

Article 78 of the CPLR, "Proceeding Against Body or Officer," allows a litigant to seek review of agency decisions and to challenge the actions of any of a variety of entities including government agencies and their officers and employees, *see* CPLR 7802(a), by a specially tailored special proceeding, CPLR 7804. As with any special proceeding, *see* CPLR article 4, swift resolution is contemplated. The proceeding is commenced by service of a notice of petition (or order to show cause) and a petition. CPLR 304, 403, 7804(c). These documents take the place of a summons and complaint. Unlike a summons, however, the notice of petition requires the opponent to respond in court on a date certain in order to be heard on the merits. Disclosure is kept to a minimum by virtue of CPLR 408, which

---

[1] *Sorrentino v. Mierzwa*, 25 N.Y.2d 59, 302 N.Y.S.2d 565, 250 N.E.2d 58 (1969).

[2] *Aetna Casualty and Surety Co. v. Lauria*, 54 A.D.2d 183, 388 N.Y.S.2d 432 (4th Dep't 1976).

[3] *E.g., Klostermann v. Cuomo*, 61 N.Y.2d 525, 475 N.Y.S.2d 247, 463 N.E.2d 588 (1984) (reprinted in § 24.03[A], *infra*); *Morgenthau v. Erlbaum*, 59 N.Y.2d 143, 464 N.Y.S.2d 392, 451 N.E.2d 150 (1983) (declaratory relief held available to test judge's policy of granting jury trials to persons accused of prostitution).

[4] *Klostermann v. Cuomo*, 61 N.Y.2d 525, 475 N.Y.S.2d 247, 463 N.E.2d 588 (1984) (reprinted in § 24.03[A], *infra*).

[5] *Morgenthau v. Erlbaum*, 59 N.Y.2d 143, 464 N.Y.S.2d 392, 451 N.E.2d 150 (1983) (declaratory judgment was available to challenge the propriety of an interlocutory order in a criminal proceeding even though a writ of prohibition pursuant to CPLR 7803 was not).

[6] *Cuomo v. Long Island Lighting Co.*, 71 N.Y.2d 349, 525 N.Y.S.2d 828, 520 N.E.2d 546 (1988) (a suit for the declaration of the legality of LILCO's emergency evacuation plan was dismissed because the plan had not been approved by the federal Nuclear Regulatory Commission, and until approved, questions arising under state law called for advisory opinions only).

allows it only by court order. If a trial of the facts is needed, it is to be held "forthwith." CPLR 7804(h). Interim relief, such as a stay of an administrative determination, can be granted pursuant to CPLR 7805. If successful, the petitioner may be granted a broad range of relief, including an order to do or refrain from doing an unlawful act, CPLR 7806, but "restitution or damages granted to the petitioner must be incidental to the primary relief sought by the petitioner," *id. See* the discussion of damages above.

The advantages of the article 78 proceeding to the petitioner should be obvious. There are drawbacks as well. One is the extremely short applicable statute of limitations. CPLR 217. Another is the difficulty of obtaining disclosure, which in some cases might be vital to success on the merits. Yet another is the difficulty encountered in deciding whether article 78 relief is available and, if so, which sort; CPLR 7803 offers a list of grounds on which the petition may be based and each is appropriate to a specific type of grievance.

Combining Different Types of Suit

CPLR 601 provides that "The plaintiff in a complaint . . . may join as many claims as he may have against an adverse party." Thus, except in the already noted special situation of the suit against the state, there is a broad grant of authority to seek in one action at least three of the remedies discussed above — damages, an injunction and a declaratory judgment. But combining these forms of relief with an article 78 proceeding is another matter. Since the procedures to be followed under it are so different from those used to prosecute an ordinary action, it is cumbersome to combine the two. Moreover, CPLR 7803 lists "[t]he *only* questions that may be raised under . . . this article . . ." (emphasis supplied). CPLR 7806 restricts the relief a court may award if the petitioner is successful, and the Court of Appeals has held that some kinds of relief available by injunction cannot be obtained in an article 78 proceeding, making it necessary to "convert" one into the other when the wrong one is used. On the other hand, it has been said that "where claims within a single pleading are partly in the nature of an article 78 proceeding and partly in the nature of a plenary action, the respective claims may be separately treated in light of the procedural and substantive provisions applicable to each." *Ashley v. Curtis*, 96 Misc. 2d 45, 48, n.3, 408 N.Y.S.2d 858, 861 (Sup. Ct. 1978), *modified on other grounds*, 67 A.D.2d 828, 413 N.Y.S.2d 528 (4th Dep't 1979). A request for declaratory relief has been successfully combined with an article 78 proceeding in the nature of mandamus. *Klostermann v. Cuomo*, 61 N.Y.2d 525, 475 N.Y.S.2d 247, 463 N.E.2d 588 (1984).

The award of damages in connection with an article 78 proceeding is authorized to a very limited extent by CPLR 7806, as discussed under "The Action for Damages," above. In cases outside the scope of that section, one may be well advised to bring two suits — one under article 78 and the other an ordinary plenary action. *E.g., Adams v. New York State Civil Service Commission*, 51 A.D.2d 668, 378 N.Y.S.2d 171 (4th Dep't 1976). See also *Corbeau Construction Corp.* and the notes following it in the next section. (Do you begin to see the origins of the sub-title of this chapter?)

Attorney's Fees

A successful litigant may be able to recover attorney's fees from a governmental opponent. The Civil Rights Attorney's Fees Awards Act of 1976, 42 U.S.C. § 1988(b), provides for attorney's fee awards to a prevailing party who has succeeded on any of a variety of federal Constitutional or civil rights claims. This law applies to litigation in the state as well as the federal courts. *Johnson v. Blum*, 58 N.Y.2d 454, 461 N.Y.S.2d 782 (1983). Moreover, New York's Equal Access to Justice Act (adopted in 1989 as Article 86 of the CPLR) allows for the recovery of attorney's fees and other reasonable expenses in actions against the state, its agencies and its officers, if the position of the State which was successfully challenged in the litigation was not "substantially justified." The ramifications of article 86 are discussed in Fried, *Attorney's Fees Against the State: The Equal Access to Justice Act,* N.Y.L.J., April 2, 1990, p. 1, col. 1.

§ 24.02 CHOOSING THE PROPER FORM OF SUIT

PROBLEM A

Taylor, an Associate Professor of Economics at a college which is part of the City University of New York, was also an aggressive member of the faculty union. In November 2000, she was notified by the president of the college that her application for tenure was rejected. As an automatic consequence of this, her employment was terminated at the end of the Spring 2001 semester. She believes that the decision was not based on her scholarly record, but rather on an unwritten but real policy prohibiting tenure award to union activists. Taylor believes that the alleged policy violates the First Amendment to the U.S. Constitution and the New York Constitution. She also claims that in applying the policy to her, the college violated its contract with her in that it had agreed to "fairly evaluate her for promotion and tenure."

Assume that in July, 2001, Taylor wishes to seek a judicial decree: (i) declaring that the alleged anti- union policy is a violation of the First Amendment; (ii) reinstating her to her job; (iii) awarding her tenure (or at least a re-hearing on the issue); (iv) restoring wages lost since her dismissal; and (v) awarding her damages for injury to her reputation.

What type of action or proceeding is appropriate in the state courts, and what procedural problems do you think will be encountered?

CORBEAU CONSTRUCTION CORP. v. BOARD OF EDUCATION, UNION FREE SCHOOL DISTRICT, NO. 9, TOWN OF GREENBURGH

Appellate Division, Second Department

32 A.D.2d 958, 302 N.Y.S.2d 940 (1969)

[Supreme Court dismissed petitioners' article 78 proceeding to compel respondents to pay money allegedly due on a construction contract, and petitioners appeal.] The petitioners are general contractors who are seeking to recover moneys, certified by the respondent board's architect as due and owing, with respect to additional work performed on a school improvement, pursuant to a contract between the parties. As long ago as April 6, 1967, the petitioners-appellants were informed in the decision on their first CPLR article 78 proceeding that that remedy was unavailable and inappropriate. They have persisted in this second CPLR article 78 proceeding. Mandamus relief, pursuant to CPLR article 78, may not be used when there are other available remedies at law as, for example, an action to recover damages for breach of contract (*Matter of Lyon Co. v. Morris*, 261 N Y 497;. . . .) Moreover, the respondent Board is not being charged with the violation of a statutory duty (*see Matter of Phalen v. Theatrical Protective Union No. 1*, 27 A D 2d 909, *revd.* 22 N Y 2d 34). In *Phalen* the Court of Appeals agreed that the extraordinary remedy of mandamus pursuant to CPLR article 78 was unavailable in that case, which involved a union's unfair and discriminatory practices; nevertheless, the Court of Appeals reversed the order that had dismissed the proceeding. In the portion of the majority opinion, pertinent herein, the Court of Appeals said: "Our determination that petitioners have prosecuted their action in an improper form and requested relief to which they are not entitled does not, however, serve to put them out of court. The improper form in which their action has been brought and their failure to request the appropriate relief is not a bar to their receiving whatever relief they may be entitled to. CPLR 103 (subd. [c]) provides that once a court has obtained jurisdiction over the parties in a "civil judicial proceeding" the proceeding "shall not be dismissed solely because it is not brought in the proper form," but the court shall make whatever order is required for its proper prosecution and CPLR 105 (subd. [d]), which defines "civil judicial proceeding," is clearly broad enough to include the instant proceeding, defining a "civil judicial proceeding" as a "prosecution, other than a criminal action, of an independent application to a court for relief." Similarly, CPLR 3017 (subd. [a]) provides, in part, that a court "may grant any type of relief within its jurisdiction appropriate to the proof whether or not demanded." Accordingly, the order appealed from should be reversed and the case remanded to Special Term so that an order may be entered allowing its proper prosecution. Upon the proceedings had following remand we believe it would be best if the parties would develop the fullest possible record, and this would undoubtedly be aided if petitioners were to plead over or otherwise expand upon the allegations contained in the present petition and supporting affidavits. A fully developed record will be of inestimable value to Special Term in moulding whatever remedy or remedies it should deem necessary and to any reviewing court, should there be occasion for another appeal. Special Term is fully competent to devise an adequate and proportionate remedy for petitioners should their charges of discrimination be sustained (*cf. State Comm. for Human Rights v. Farrell*, 43 Misc 2d 958) and for this reason we refrain from suggesting at this point what specific remedies ought to be afforded petitioners, preferring instead to leave these matters for determination in the first instance to Special Term (pp. 41-42). In the case at bar, a contract dispute is the problem and, until the contract is interpreted and construed with a resultant judgment, there are no obligations enjoined on or charged against the board other than contractual ones. Contractual rights may not be resolved in CPLR article 78 proceedings seeking mandamus relief. Our remand of this case, in accordance with *Phalen* (*supra*), will permit Special Term to prescribe, in a proper order pursuant to CPLR 103 (subd. [c]), the further prosecution of this action, as amplified and delineated by new pleadings and whatever other steps are considered appropriate. For this reason we pass on no other questions arising out of this dispute. . . .

. . . .

NOTES

(1) The principal case applies the general rule that an action or proceeding should not be dismissed because it was brought in the wrong form, but should be converted instead. That the rule is not invariable, however, is illustrated by *Maas v. Cornell University*, 94 N.Y.2d 87, 699 N.Y.S.2d 87, 721 N.E.2d 966 (1999), in which the plaintiff had brought a plenary breach of contract action to challenge his dismissal from the Cornell faculty. Defendant moved in the trial court to convert the action into an article 78 proceeding, but the plaintiff opposed conversion and the motion was denied. On an appeal from a later decision dismissing his action on the merits, Maas changed tactics and sought to convert the action to an article 78 proceeding. Affirming the Appellate Division's dismissal of the plenary action and denial of the conversion motion, the Court of Appeals held that review of the petitioner's dismissal would have been available only under article 78 and that plaintiff's application to convert the action came too late.

(2) Petitioner in the principal case apparently complained of some kind of discriminatory treatment in addition to seeking money due for construction work, yet the court is clear that "a contract dispute is the problem." How would this apply to Problem A?

(3) If the state is a defendant, a claim for money under a contract must, ordinarily, be brought in Court of Claims. *See* Court of Claims Act § 9(2). The action must be preceded by service of a notice of claim. *Id.*, § 10(4). This gives added importance to the question of whether the grievance is remedial by way of arti-

cle 78 (in which case it would be brought in the Supreme Court). The boundary between article 78 proceedings in the nature of mandamus and the contract action was discussed in *Finley v. Giacobbe*, 79 F.3d 1285 (2d Cir. 1996). The medical director of a county hospital resigned her employment and brought an action in federal court against the County Commissioner of Hospitals, the County Executive and the hospital for damages asserting a breach of her employment contract and tortious interference with her employment. She also included a § 1983 claim asserting that she was deprived of procedural due process when she was advised that her probationary term of employment would not result in appointment to a permanent staff status. One of the questions was whether the proper remedy was under article 78 in the state court. The Second Circuit, affirming the district court's decision that article 78 was the proper remedy, stated:

> The district court held that *Austin v. Board of Higher Education*, 5 N.Y.2d 430, 440, 186 N.Y.S.2d 1, 9, 158 N.E.2d 681, 686-87 (1959) "clearly established that a public employee seeking damages for his or her termination must first bring an article 78 proceeding to establish the wrongfulness of the termination," and therefore that Dr. Finley's breach of contract claim should have been presented first by way of an article 78 proceeding. *Finley II*, 848 F.Supp. at 1150. The district court explained that the "very purpose for requiring the article 78 proceeding articulated in *Austin* is to apply the shorter statute of limitations in order to prevent public employees from delaying in bringing damage actions." *Id.* Since Dr. Finley failed to bring her claim within the four-month statutory period, the court concluded that, "even if a federal court had the power to preside over an article 78 proceeding, we cannot do so here," and granted summary judgment to the defendants on the contract claim.[1] *Id.*

> Dr. Finley advances two arguments to challenge the district court's determination that she should first have brought her claim in an article 78 proceeding; first, that a public employee's claim seeking damages as the principal form of relief — rather than reinstatement or back pay — is akin to a contract claim, an action at law that need not first be brought in an article 78 proceeding; second, that article 78 is inapplicable to her case, since, as a matter of law, the Rockland County Commissioner of Hospitals lacks authority to terminate the Medical Director. We address each argument separately.

---

[1] The district court refused to dismiss the tortious interference claim on the same ground, however, because it was brought against defendants Giacobbe and Grant in their *individual* capacities, and because under New York law "damages against an officer in his or her individual capacity cannot be recovered in an article 78 proceeding." *Finley II*, 848 F.Supp. at 1151 (citation omitted). Dr. Finley's tortious interference claim against the officers thus survived the defendants' attack under article 78.

Article 78: Applicability to Contract Claims.

The New York courts have held that article 78 is inapplicable to contract actions against the state government that seek damages as the principal remedy. . . . It is just as clear, however, that a successful article 78 proceeding for reinstatement is a prerequisite to a claim for damages by a discharged public employee. *Austin v. Board of Higher Education*, 5 N.Y.2d 430, 440, 186 N.Y.S.2d at 9, 158 N.E.2d at 686-87. Even non-tenured or probationary employees must invoke article 78 to review dismissals that are allegedly arbitrary, capricious, or prohibited by statute or the constitution. . . .

This seeming contradiction is reconciled by New York's view that public employment claims were historically based on *property* rather than *contract* principles. . . . New York is heir to ancient common law principles that analyze public employment cases, including salary claims, as matter of property rather than contract law: An officer holds title to his office, and a tenured employee holds title to his position; therefore removal or dismissal in violation of law is analyzed in terms of ouster rather than defeasance of title or breach of contract, thus permitting recourse to proceedings under . . . article 78 to obtain a reinstatement to the office or position and all its emoluments. *State Div. of Human Rights on Complaint of Geraci v. New York State Dep't of Correctional Servs.*, 90 A.D.2d 51, 456 N.Y.S.2d 63 (2d Dep't 1982) (citations omitted).

Dr. Finley concedes that article 78 proceedings are proper where, as in *Austin*, a public employee contests an official agency decision to terminate her. But she casts her claim as one for breach of the "fundamental terms of her employment relationship" rather than as a challenge to an administrative decision to terminate her, and she points for support to *Gerber v. New York City Hous. Auth.*, 42 N.Y.2d 162, 397 N.Y.S.2d 608, 366 N.E.2d 268 (1977), and *Hussey v. Town of Oyster Bay*, 24 A.D.2d 570, 262 N.Y.S.2d 396 (2d Dep't 1965), among other cases. *Gerber* and *Hussey* permitted permanent employees under suspension to maintain actions at law for back salary withheld in contravention of their rights under the New York Civil Service Law. However, these cases are distinguishable from *Austin* (and from Dr. Finley's claim) because they involve suspension rather than termination.

The primacy of article 78 proceedings conserves public money by forcing a quick and efficient resolution of claims against state agencies. *Austin*, 5 N.Y.2d at 441, 186 N.Y.S.2d at 9-10, 158 N.E.2d at 686-87. Presumably to serve that end, the statute of limitations under article 78 is foreshortened to four months. N.Y. Civ. Prac. L. & R. § 217; *see also Meyers*, 208 A.D.2d at 264-65, 622 N.Y.S.2d at 534 (dismissing breach of employment claim as time barred under article 78). Reinstatement is, of course, not at issue in back pay claims for wrongful suspension (such as in *Gerber* and *Hussey*); moreover, agencies can limit the cost of a wrongful suspension claim simply by modulating the length of the suspension. This distinction is also significant under *Geraci*, historically which views illegal "removal or dismissal" in terms of "ouster rather than defeasance," and therefore in terms of property rather than contract. *Geraci*, 90 A.D.2d at 68 n. 8, 456 N.Y.S.2d at 75 n. 8. Wrongful suspension denies the employee salary during the period of employment and may therefore be viewed in terms of a contract right. Assuming, however, that Dr. Finely was ousted (disregarding for this purpose her resignation), all claims on appeal (including her back pay claim) depend on a right to reinstatement, an issue that, as *Austin* requires and the district court held, must be first addressed in an article 78 proceeding. The need for wrongful discharge claims to be corrected promptly by reinstatement, so that the accrual of damages can be arrested, is illustrated by this case: if Dr. Finley had prevailed in an article 78 proceeding, the case on appeal would not entail potential damages for the years of back pay claimed to be accruing since May 18, 1992; and if Dr. Finley had lost her article 78 proceeding, the present proceedings — lasting years — would have been obviated.

(4) On the question of the proper form of proceeding, see also *Maas v. Cornell University*, 94 N.Y.2d 87, 699 N.Y.S.2d 87, 721 N.E.2d 966 (1999), described in note (1), *supra*, in which the Court held that article 78 provides the proper vehicle for challenging termination decisions of colleges and universities, even if the aggrieved party alleges a breach of contract.

(5) One of the most difficult problems has been locating the boundary between article 78 proceedings and declaratory judgment actions. In *Solnick v. Whalen*, 49 N.Y.2d 224, 425 N.Y.S.2d 68, 401 N.E.2d 190 (1980), a nursing home operator challenged his Medicaid reimbursement rate, by bringing a declaratory judgment action. Because such a challenge would have had to have been brought within four months of the disputed determination by the Commissioner of Health, his complaint was dismissed. Had the action been timely it could have been converted to an article 78 proceeding. The Court remarked that declaratory judgment would be proper to challenge an administrative act of a legislative nature such as rate making, citing *Matter of Lakeland Water Dist. v. Onondaga County Water Auth.*, 24 N.Y.2d 400, 301 N.Y.S.2d 1, 248 N.E.2d 855 (1969).

In *Allen v. Blum*, 58 N.Y.2d 954, 460 N.Y.S.2d 520, 447 N.E.2d 68 (1983), where the Social Services Department discontinued certain home relief payments, declaratory judgment was proclaimed the correct remedy, since what was being challenged was a policy determination that applied to many recipients across the board. The action was brought beyond four months of the challenged determination. The waters were further muddied by the decision in *Press v. County of Monroe*, 50 N.Y.2d 695, 431 N.Y.S.2d 394, 409 N.E.2d 870 (1980), which held that the determination of a tax assessment rate, which might appear to be *quasi* legislative in nature, could only be challenged through an article 78 proceeding, chiefly because time was of the essence in such matters if government was to function smoothly. In the following case, the court attempted to straighten out all of this.

NEW YORK CITY HEALTH AND HOSPITALS CORP. v. McBARNETTE
Court of Appeals
84 N.Y.2d 194, 616 N.Y.S.2d 1, 639 N.E.2d 740 (1994)

TITONE, JUDGE.

This appeal raises the question we left open in *New York State Assn. of Counties v. Axelrod*, 78 N.Y.2d 158, 166, 573 N.Y.S.2d 25, 577 N.E.2d 16 ("*NYSAC*"): what Statute of Limitations should be applied to declaratory judgment actions brought to challenge promulgated Medicaid reimbursement rates on the ground that they are irrational or affected with error of law. Reaffirming the principles that were articulated in such cases as *Solnick v. Whalen*, 49 N.Y.2d 224, 425 N.Y.S.2d 68, 401 N.E.2d 190, we hold that in the circumstances presented here the four-month Statute of Limitations for proceedings against a body or officer is applicable (*see*, CPLR 217).

Plaintiff, which operates both hospitals and residential care facilities, commenced this declaratory judgment action to challenge two separate aspects of its Medicaid reimbursement rate. The first part of plaintiff's challenge sought relief from defendants' effort to use a "recalibration adjustment" that was promulgated in December 1991 to calculate its residential-care facility rates for the rate years between 1989 and 1991 (10 NYCRR 86-2.31[a]). The proper resolution of this issue is governed by *Matter of Jewish Home & Infirmary v. Commissioner of N.Y. State Dept. of Health*, 84 N.Y.2d 252, 616 N.Y.S.2d 458, 640 N.E.2d 125 [decided herewith], in which we hold that Public Health Law § 2807(7)(a) prohibits such retroactive rate-making.

The second part of plaintiff's challenge involves a disputed change in the manner in which hospitals are reimbursed for services provided to certain of their patients. Effective January 1, 1988, defendants replaced their existing per-diem method of computing reimbursement with a new per-case approach. Services for patients whose hospital stays "straddled" the period before and after the new system's effective date were initially to be reimbursed under the former per-diem computation method. However, by letter dated July 3, 1989, the Commissioner of Social Services, after consultation with the Department of Health (DOH) and the Division of the Budget, advised hospitals providing service to Medicaid recipients that only those "straddle" patients categorized as needing "acute" care would be subject to the apparently more favorable per-diem rate. Services to "alternative level of care" patients, *i.e.*, those who could be cared for in residential nursing facilities, would be reimbursed on the newer per-case basis. Reimbursement amounts in excess of the allowable rates that had already been paid were to be recouped through reductions in current payments.

The July 3, 1989 rate decision was challenged in a timely CPLR article 78 proceeding brought by the Hospital Association of New York State (*Matter of Hospital Assn. v. Axelrod*, 165 A.D.2d 152, 565 N.Y.S.2d 884 [1991], *lv. denied* 78 N.Y.2d 853, 573 N.Y.S.2d 467, 577 N.E.2d 1059) ("*HANYS*"). Although it was aware of the *HANYS* litigation, plaintiff, which is not a member of the Hospital Association, decided not to intervene or commence a separate suit, choosing instead to rely on that organization's efforts to obtain relief.

The Appellate Division held in *HANYS* that the statute governing reimbursement for "straddle patients" did not leave room for distinguishing between "acute care" patients and "alternative level of care" patients. Accordingly, the policy was deemed arbitrary and unlawful (165 A.D.2d, at 154-155, 565 N.Y.S.2d 884). As a result of that decision, defendants, who represent agencies responsible for administering the Medicaid program, were ordered to repay to the Hospital Association and its members any funds that had been withheld or recouped pursuant to the invalidated decision.

In October of 1991, plaintiff applied for a refund of moneys that defendants had recouped pursuant to the rule invalidated in *HANYS*. After it was advised that defendants did not intend to grant such a refund, plaintiff promptly brought the present proceeding in February 1992 to challenge both the July 3, 1989 rule and the more recent refusal of its refund request.

On cross motions for summary judgment, the Supreme Court ordered defendants to recalculate plaintiff's nursing home reimbursement rate without regard to the "recalibration adjustment." With respect to the claims that were based upon the invalidated "straddle patient" rate determination, Supreme Court concluded that the four-month Statute of Limitations for CPLR article 78 proceedings was applicable and that, accordingly, those claims were time-barred.

On plaintiff's appeal, the Appellate Division affirmed the first aspect of Supreme Court's ruling, but reversed on the latter point, 195 A.D.2d 391, 600 N.Y.S.2d 245. Holding that the action was, in reality, one for reimbursement under title XIX of the Social Security Act (42 USC § 1396 et seq.), the Appellate Division cited the Second Circuit's decision in *Hollander v. Brezenoff*, 787 F.2d 834, applied the three-year limitations period for actions to recover on a liability imposed by statute (CPLR 214[2]) and ruled the action timely. Inasmuch as the merits had previously been resolved in *HANYS* (*supra*), the Court granted plaintiff summary judgment on its claim for a refund. This appeal, taken by permission of this Court, ensued.

Initially, we note that the Appellate Division's reliance on *Hollander v. Brezenoff* (*supra*) was misplaced. The only issue in *Hollander* was whether a proceeding to enforce a social service agency's obligation to pay a Medicaid provider was governed by the six-year limitations period for actions on a contractual obligation (CPLR 213[2]) or was instead governed by the three-year period for actions on a liability imposed by statute (CPLR 214[2]). The court was not called upon to consider whether the shorter four-month limitations for proceedings against a body or officer (CPLR 217) was applicable. Consequently, its holding has no persuasive significance here.

The proper starting point for determining which Statute of Limitations should be applied in a proceeding or action against a State or municipal governmental entity is this Court's 1980 decision in *Solnick v. Whalen, supra*, 49 N.Y.2d 224, 425 N.Y.S.2d 68, 401 N.E.2d 190. In that case, the Court held that when the proceeding has been commenced in the form of a declaratory judgment action, for which no specific Statute of Limitations is prescribed, "it is necessary to examine the substance of that action to identify the relationship out of which the claim arises and the relief sought" in order to resolve which Statute of Limitations is applicable (49 N.Y.2d, at 229, 425 N.Y.S.2d 68, 401 N.E.2d 190; *cf., Koerner v. State of New York*, 62 N.Y.2d 442, 447, 478 N.Y.S.2d 584, 467 N.E.2d 232 [*Solnick* rule does not govern when "a specific limitations period is clearly applicable to a given action, [and] there is no need to ascertain whether another form of proceeding is available"]). Only if there is no other "form of proceeding for which a specific limitation period is statutorily provided" may the six-year catch-all limitations period provided in CPLR 213(1) be invoked (49 N.Y.2d, at 229-230, 425 N.Y.S.2d 68, 401 N.E.2d 190). In other words, if the claim could have been made in a form other than an action for a declaratory judgment and the limitations period for an action in that form has already expired, the time for asserting the claim cannot be extended through the simple expedient of denominating the action one for declaratory relief (49 N.Y.2d, at 230, 425 N.Y.S.2d 68, 401 N.E.2d 190; *accord, Press v. County of Monroe*, 50 N.Y.2d 695, 701, 431 N.Y.S.2d 394, 409 N.E.2d 870). Of course, when the claim is one against a governmental body or officer, the form of action that immediately springs to mind is a proceeding brought under CPLR article 78, a traditional, and surely the most common, vehicle for challenging a governmental decision or action.

Plaintiff contends that an article 78 proceeding is inapplicable here because the challenged agency decision is legislative in nature in that it applies across the board to all hospitals providing care to "straddle patients." In support of this position, plaintiff cites a line of cases holding that article 78 does not lie to challenge a legislative act (*e.g., Bryant Ave. Tenants' Assn. v. Koch*, 71 N.Y.2d 856, 527 N.Y.S.2d 743, 522 N.E.2d 1041; *Matter of DuBois v. Town Bd.*, 35 N.Y.2d 617, 364 N.Y.S.2d 506, 324 N.E.2d 153; *Matter of Kovarsky v. Housing & Dev. Admin.*, 31 N.Y.2d 184, 335 N.Y.S.2d 383, 286 N.E.2d 882; *Matter of Overhill Bldg. Co. v. Delany*, 28 N.Y.2d 449, 322 N.Y.S.2d 696, 271 N.E.2d 537). However, despite the unquestionable validity of this line of cases, we conclude that further analysis is necessary because there remains some confusion as to what constitutes a "legislative act" (*compare, Press v. County of Monroe, supra*, 50 N.Y.2d, at 703-704, 431 N.Y.S.2d 394, 409 N.E.2d 870, *with id.*, at 704-706, 431 N.Y.S.2d 394, 409 N.E.2d 870 [Jasen, J., dissenting], *and Solnick v. Whalen, supra*, 49 N.Y.2d, at 231, 425 N.Y.S.2d 68, 401 N.E.2d 190; *see*, 8 Weinstein-Korn-Miller,

NY Civ Prac ¶ 7801.02, at 78-11), and, consequently, the formula on which plaintiff relies is insufficient to resolve the issue presented by plaintiff's case.

Among the apparent sources of the confusion is *Matter of Lakeland Water Dist. v. Onondaga County Water Auth.*, 24 N.Y.2d 400, 301 N.Y.S.2d 1, 248 N.E.2d 855, in which the Court held that article 78 was unavailable to challenge a rate decision made by a public benefit corporation charged with the responsibility of regulating the price of water to private customers and water districts. Drawing on the principle that an article 78 proceeding may not be used to review legislative action, the *Lakeland* Court reasoned that "an order of an administrative agency fixing rates is deemed a legislative act, at least where no provision has been made for notice and a hearing" (*id.*, at 407, 301 N.Y.S.2d 1, 248 N.E.2d 855). Inasmuch as the rate determination at issue was not subject to any notice and hearing requirements, the Court concluded, it was legislative in nature and not subject to article 78 review (24 N.Y.2d, at 409, 301 N.Y.S.2d 1, 248 N.E.2d 855).

Lakeland was followed by *Solnick v. Whalen, supra*, 49 N.Y.2d, at 231-232, and n. 3, 425 N.Y.S.2d 68, 401 N.E.2d 190, in which this Court, in an effort to explain that decision, suggested that an agency rate-setting determination may be "legislative" or "administrative" depending upon whether it is an "across-the-board" ruling or is instead determinative only of an "individualized rate[ ] established for a particular litigant." However, in *Press v. County of Monroe (supra)*, a case involving a generally applicable rate schedule, the Court simply relegated the analysis in *Lakeland* to a "cf." citation and did not follow, or even discuss, the *Solnick* distinction. Instead, it referred to an entirely different principle, *i.e.*, that article 78 is not the proper vehicle for challenging the constitutionality of a legislative enactment (*see, e.g., Matter of Ames Volkswagen v. State Tax Commn.*, 47 N.Y.2d 345, 348, 418 N.Y.S.2d 324, 391 N.E.2d 1302; *New York Pub. Interest Research Group v. Steingut*, 40 N.Y.2d 250, 254, 386 N.Y.S.2d 646, 353 N.E.2d 558; *Matter of Merced v. Fisher*, 38 N.Y.2d 557, 559, 381 N.Y.S.2d 817, 345 N.E.2d 288) and then went on to hold that the rate-setting decision at issue was not "legislative" because it lacked a number of traits that ordinarily characterize enactments of a legislative body (50 N.Y.2d, at 701-704, 431 N.Y.S.2d 394, 409 N.E.2d 870). Despite *Press*, subsequent cases involving rate setting and other types of governmental determinations have relied on the *Solnick* distinction between generalized and individualized decision-making (*see, e.g., Matter of Klein v. Axelrod*, 54 N.Y.2d 818, 443 N.Y.S.2d 653, 427 N.E.2d 950, *affg.* 81 A.D.2d 935, 439 N.Y.S.2d 510; *cf., Eve v. Power Auth.*, 123 A.D.2d 532, 506 N.Y.S.2d 700 [relying on *Lakeland* distinction premised on notice and hearing requirements]; *but cf., Lenihan v. City of New York*, 85 A.D.2d 562, 445 N.Y.S.2d 708, *affd.* 58 N.Y.2d 679, 458 N.Y.S.2d 528, 444 N.E.2d 992).

Viewed in the proper light, the difficulty in this field seems to lie not in the rationales or results of the salient cases, but rather in the ambiguity of the terminology and the absence of a cohesive analytical structure to lend perspective to the existing case law. The case law often does not distinguish between true legislative acts and those administrative acts that are deemed "quasi-legislative," and there has been little reasoned discussion as to why the latter class of acts should necessarily be treated in the same way as the former.[1] Moreover, while it may be helpful to consider the distinctions drawn in *Lakeland* and *Solnick* between generalized and individualized decision-making and the existence or nonexistence of a notice-and-hearing requirement, these categories cannot adequately be understood in the legal and historical vacuum in which they are often discussed.[2]

The maxim that article 78 does not lie to challenge legislative acts is derived from the separation-of-powers doctrine which made the use of the judiciary's "prerogative writ" unavailable as a vehicle for challenging an act of a legislative body (*e.g., Matter of Neddo v. Schrade*, 270 N.Y. 97, 200 N.E. 657; *Matter of Long Is. R.R. Co. v. Hylan*, 240 N.Y. 199, 148 N.E. 189; *People ex rel. Trustees of Vil. of Jamaica v. Board of Supervisors*, 131 N.Y. 468, 30 N.E. 488; *see*, McLaughlin, Practice Commentaries, McKinney's Cons Laws of NY, Book 7B, CPLR C7801:1, at 25 [1981]).[3] That same principle, however, has no application to the quasi-leg-

---

[1] Indeed, it is the failure to recognize the critical distinction between true "legislative" acts of legislative bodies and the quasi-legislative acts of administrative bodies that renders the Court's syllogism in *Matter of Lakeland Water Dist. v. Onondaga County Water Auth.*, 24 N.Y.2d 400, 409, 301 N.Y.S.2d 1, 248 N.E.2d 855, *supra* fundamentally flawed.

[2] The *Solnick* distinction between individualized and across-the-board administrative rate determinations may be viewed as consistent with, or at least overlapping, the *Lakeland* distinction premised on the presence or absence of a provision for advance notice and a hearing, since notice and hearing requirements are often associated with decision-making aimed at individual rights. In the article 78 context, however, it is important to recognize that there are different types of hearings with different legal consequences. Evidentiary hearings that are constitutionally required and have some of the characteristics of adversary trials, including cross-examination, result in "quasi-judicial" determinations that are subject to article 78 review in the nature of certiorari, where the "substantial evidence" inquiry is applicable (*see, e.g., Matter of Older v. Board of Educ.*, 27 N.Y.2d 333, 318 N.Y.S.2d 129, 266 N.E.2d 812; *see generally*, McLaughlin, Practice Commentaries, McKinney's Cons Laws of NY, Book 7B, CPLR C7801:2, at 26-27 [1981]). Hearings that are not required as a matter of due process, in contrast, result in what have been termed "administrative" determinations, which are subject to review only by mandamus and are governed by the "arbitrary and capricious" standard (McLaughlin, op. cit., at 28-29). This class of hearings, which may result in either individualized or across-the-board determinations, can, in turn, be divided into at least two separate categories: (1) those in which an agency or body will give notice to either the public at large or the affected segments of the public and will thereafter hold a nonevidentiary public hearing and (2) those in which an agency will give notice to the individual regulated concerns and afford them an opportunity to be heard, again in a nonevidentiary forum. In both of these instances, the resulting determination is usually deemed "quasi-legislative" and is reviewable, if at all, by mandamus to review. Because of this variety in the types of notice and hearings that may be held, *Lakeland*'s reference to "notice and hearing" as a means of distinguishing reviewable administrative acts from those that are immune from article 78 review is, at best, misleading. Indeed, as noted, in most cases where "provision has been made for notice and a hearing" (24 N.Y.2d, at 407, 301 N.Y.S.2d 1, 248 N.E.2d 855, *supra*), the resulting determination is quasi-judicial and the availability of mandamus to review is irrelevant.

[3] Of course, in a proper case, other means may exist to challenge true legislative enactments on the grounds that they are unconstitutional, ultra vires or adopted in violation of lawful procedure (*see, e.g., Matter of Save the Pine Bush v. City of Albany*, 70 N.Y.2d 193, 202, 518 N.Y.S.2d 943, 512 N.E.2d 526; *Matter of Ames Volkswagen v. State Tax Commn.*, 47 N.Y.2d 345, 418 N.Y.S.2d 324, 391 N.E.2d 1302, *supra*).

islative acts of administrative agencies. With respect to those acts, there is no reason why article 78 review in the nature of "mandamus to review" should not be available to the extent that the challenge fits within the language and accompanying gloss of CPLR 7801 and 7803(3).**4**

CPLR 7801 provides that the relief historically available by the former writs of certiorari to review, mandamus and prohibition are all available now through proceedings brought under article 78. CPLR 7803 supplements that provision by setting forth "[t]he only questions that may be raised in a proceeding under . . . article [78]." Taken together, these statutes and the body of common law they incorporate are necessarily the prime reference points for determining whether a particular claim against a public body or officer may be brought in the form of an article 78 proceeding. Thus, where a quasi-legislative act by an administrative agency such as a rate determination is challenged on the ground that it "was made in violation of lawful procedure, was affected by an error of law or was arbitrary and capricious or an abuse of discretion" (CPLR 7803[3]), a proceeding in the form prescribed by article 78 can be maintained and, as a corollary matter, the four-month Statute of Limitations that ordinarily governs such proceedings is applicable.

To be sure, in most situations, agencies' generally applicable decisions do not lend themselves to consideration on their merits under the provisions for mandamus to review, because they concern rational choices among competing policy considerations and are thus not amenable to analysis under the "arbitrary and capricious" standard.**5** Nonetheless, there are certainly cases in which even a nonindividualized, generally applicable quasi-legislative act such as a regulation or an across-the-board rate-computation ruling can be challenged as being "affected by error of law," "arbitrary and capricious" or lacking a rational basis (CPLR 7803[3]). The claim raised by plaintiff here presents precisely such a case.

As did the petitioners in *HANYS*, plaintiff here is claiming that defendants' decision concerning the proper method for computing the reimbursement rate for "straddle patients" was unlawful and arbitrary and capricious in that it had no foundation in the relevant statutes (*see, HANYS*, 165 A.D.2d, at 154-156, 565 N.Y.S.2d 884, *supra*). The nature of plaintiff's claim requires it to convince the court that defendants promulgated a rule affecting hospital rates that represented an irrational construction of the governing statutes. Such a claim is plainly encompassed within the grounds for mandamus to review set forth in CPLR 7803(3), which include "whether a determination . . . was affected by an

---

4 The questions set forth in CPLR 7803(1) and (2) are generally applicable only to proceedings in the nature of mandamus to compel and prohibition, respectively (*see*, McLaughlin, op. cit., CPLR C7803:1, at 331 [1981]). The question set forth in CPLR 7803(4) pertains only to certiorari proceedings to review quasi-judicial determinations (McLaughlin, op. cit.; *see*, n 2, *supra*).

5 This circumstance may well have been what the *Solnick* Court had in mind when it distinguished between across-the-board determinations and those that affected only identified individuals (49 N.Y.2d, at 231, 425 N.Y.S.2d 68, 401 N.E.2d 190, *supra*).

error of law or was arbitrary and capricious" (*see also*, *NYSAC*, *supra* [claim that rate adjustment regulation was arbitrary because it was not based on empirical facts]). Additionally, since the claim concerns a quasi-legislative act of an administrative agency rather than a true legislative enactment, there is no sound basis for invoking the historical bar precluding use of the prerogative writ as a vehicle for reviewing true legislative acts, even though the regulation in question is indisputably one of general applicability. Accordingly, plaintiff's challenge could have been brought in the form of an article 78 proceeding, and the present action, brought more than 2½ years after the July 3, 1989 letter advising of defendants' policy was sent, was untimely.

We note that our holding with regard to the Statute of Limitations question presented here is in accord with the public policies identified in *Solnick v. Whalen*, *supra*, 49 N.Y.2d, at 232, 425 N.Y.S.2d 68, 401 N.E.2d 190 and reiterated in *Press v. County of Monroe*, *supra*, 50 N.Y.2d, at 704, 431 N.Y.S.2d 394, 409 N.E.2d 870. A rule that requires those subject to regulatory decisions such as Medicaid rate-making to bring their challenges promptly facilitates rational planning by all concerned parties and ensures "'that the operation of government [will] not be trammeled by stale litigation and stale determinations'" (*Solnick v. Whalen*, *supra*, 49 N.Y.2d, at 232, 425 N.Y.S.2d 68, 401 N.E.2d 190, *quoting Mundy v. Nassau County Civ. Serv. Commn.*, 44 N.Y.2d 352, 359, 405 N.Y.S.2d 660, 376 N.E.2d 1305 [Breitel, Ch. J., dissenting]).

We are not persuaded by plaintiff's opposing contention that the policies represented by the decision in *Matter of Jones v. Berman*, 37 N.Y.2d 42, 371 N.Y.S.2d 422, 332 N.E.2d 303 militate against such a rule because it compels all potentially aggrieved litigants to bring duplicative suits rather than waiting to see what the outcome will be in a pending test case. In *Jones*, the Court held only that a class action is generally an inappropriate vehicle for asserting a claim against a governmental entity, since "where governmental operations are involved" similarly situated parties other than the individual litigant "will be adequately protected under the principles of stare decisis" (37 N.Y.2d, at 57, 371 N.Y.S.2d 422, 332 N.E.2d 303; *accord, Matter of Rivera v. Trimarco*, 36 N.Y.2d 747, 749, 368 N.Y.S.2d 826, 329 N.E.2d 661). By its terms, that holding concerns itself only with the inefficiency of using the class action form when the prospective rights of interested nonlitigants can be safeguarded by other means. Nothing in the *Jones* decision suggests that the same policies justify either the use of a long limitations period or the creation of a toll solely to enable aggrieved parties to sit on their existing rights pending the outcome of an early challenge brought by others (*cf., American Pipe & Constr. Co. v. Utah*, 414 U.S. 538, 554, 94 S.Ct. 756, 766, 38 L.Ed.2d 713). . . .

Accordingly, the order of the Appellate Division should be modified, without costs, by reinstating the judgment of the Supreme Court and, as modified, affirmed.

NOTES

(1) In addition to sorting out the problems theretofore plaguing the quest for relief against government action, the *McBarnette* decision makes it clear that if a party wants the benefit of a court determination correcting that action, it had better become a participant in the proceeding.

(2) In *Matter of Save the Pine Bush v. City of Albany*, 70 N.Y.S.2d 193, 518 N.Y.S.2d 943, 512 N.E.2d 526 (1987), cited in footnote 3 of the principal case, the Court held that article 78 relief is not available to challenge a municipal ordinance on the ground that it is unconstitutionally vague. Thus, the four month statute of limitations does not apply to such a claim. If the challenge is based on a defect in the process by which the ordinance was enacted (such as a failure to follow state environmental review requirements), however, article 78 is available and CPLR 217 applies. And while the validity of legislation may not be tested pursuant to article 78, the officer against whom the proceeding is brought may defend on the ground that the legislation sought to be enforced is invalid. Thus in a proceeding brought against the Mayor to enforce New York City's Equal Benefits Law, the Mayor could assert the law's invalidity. *NY City Council v. Bloomberg*, 6 N.Y.3d 380, 813 N.Y.S.2d 3, 846 N.E.2d 433 (2006).

(3) Note that the time at which a cause of action for relief under article 78 accrues depends on the kind of administrative action (or inaction) that is challenged. *See* CPLR 217(1).

(4) New York State Administrative Procedure Act § 205 expressly authorizes review of rules promulgated by administrative agencies. To what extent does it prescribe the proper form of proceeding?

§ 205. Right to judicial review of rules

Unless an exclusive procedure or remedy is provided by law, judicial review of rules may be had upon petition presented under article seventy-eight of the civil practice law and rules, or in an action for a declaratory judgment where applicable and proper. . . .

§ 24.03 THE VARIETIES OF ARTICLE 78 PROCEEDINGS

[A] Mandamus to Compel: CPLR 7803(1)

HAMPTONS HOSPITAL & MEDICAL CENTER, INC. v. MOORE
Court of Appeals
52 N.Y.2d 88, 436 N.Y.S.2d 239, 417 N.E.2d 533 (1981)

JASEN, J.

We hold that the Public Health Council had power to re-evaluate an initial determination of public need for establishment of a hospital where its initial determination had not received final approval and that the Public Health Council was not estopped from re-evaluating that determination of public need.

In 1972, the Public Health Council passed a resolution whereby it proposed to approve petitioner's application to establish a 220-bed hospital in Suffolk County subject to certain financing conditions. For the following four years, petitioner encountered difficulty in securing proper financing in compliance with the conditions set forth in the initial determination of public need. Meanwhile, in the summer of 1976, the Bureau of Facility and Service Review of the Department of Health began a review of the public need for all pending hospital projects, including petitioner's, using a substantially different methodology than had been employed in 1972 when the initial determination of public need was made. A preliminary staff report finding no need for petitioner's project was submitted to the Public Health Council on December 16, 1976. Subsequently, the petitioner was invited to and did attend a meeting with a subcommittee of the New York State Hospital Review and Planning Council relative to the public need for the proposed hospital. On February 3, 1977, the subcommittee, concluding that the construction of the facility would result in a surplus of hospital beds in the area, recommended the disapproval of petitioner's application because there was no public need for the project.

The Public Health Council, on April 22, 1977, adopted a resolution that it was "considering disapproving" petitioner's application for establishment and informed petitioner that its disapproval would become final unless a hearing was requested within 20 days. A scheduled public hearing was held in abeyance after petitioner commenced a CPLR article 78 proceeding seeking judgment enjoining respondents from reconsidering the question of public need.

Special Term dismissed the petition, holding that the Public Health Council had the power to reconsider its initial determination of public need. . . .

The Appellate Division, Second Department, converted the proceeding into an action for an injunction pursuant to section 2801-c of the Public Health Law, concluding that such an action was the proper procedural vehicle by which to test the Public Health Council's power to reconsider its prior determination. . . .

. . . .

When the final disposition of the application for approval is made that disposition and the methodologies of the underlying determination of public need will, of course, be subject to the limited judicial examination which can be obtained in a proceeding under CPLR article 78. But the freedom to make such a final determination cannot be permitted to be constrained by prior, nonfinal, conditional determinations or other actions of the State agencies. . . .

. . . .

Having determined that the Public Health Council had authority and responsibility to reconsider its initial tentative finding of public need, and that it was not estopped to do so, we conclude that petitioner is not entitled to an injunction preventing the council from exercising its authority and discharging its responsibility pursuant to law.

We note also that we differ with the proposition advanced by the dissent that it was error as a matter of law on the part of the Appellate Division to have converted this proceeding from one under CPLR article 78 to a proceeding for an injunction under section 2801-c of the Public Health Law. The relief sought by petitioner is an injunction against reconsideration by the Public Health Council of its prior determination of public need for petitioner's establishment and an order directing the council to make a prompt determination approving petitioner's application for establishment. Because there had been no final determination by the council with respect to that application, an article 78 proceeding by way of certiorari or of mandamus to review does not lie. The absence of such a final determination, a prerequisite for relief in those categories, would not of itself, however, necessarily require dismissal of the article 78 proceeding; finality of action on the part of the administrative agency is not the prerequisite to all proceedings under article 78.

An article 78 proceeding may lie in the absence of a final determination where the relief sought is by way of prohibition[2] or by way of mandamus to compel performance by an administrative agency of a duty enjoined by law. Mandamus for such purpose, however, lies only where the right to relief is "clear" and the duty sought to be enjoined is performance of an act commanded to be performed by law and involving no exercise of discretion. (Weinstein-Korn-Miller, CPLR Manual [rev ed], par 32.02, subd [b].) The unavailability of an article 78 proceeding in the present instance inheres in the character of the action petitioner seeks to compel — proscription of any reconsideration of the determination of public need for petitioner's establishment. . . . The relief sought — in essence authorization for additional hospital facilities — involves the exercise

---

[2] No one asserts that the present proceeding was one in the nature of prohibition; there is no contention that the Public Health Council intends or threatens to act in excess of its jurisdiction.

of the ultimate judgmental responsibility vested by the Legislature in the Public Health Council.[3] The innately discretionary character of this determination is not altered by petitioner's vigorous assertion that, because of its actions in the past, the council is now constrained to reach but one ultimate conclusion — approval of the application — or by any verbal characterization of the proceeding as one "in the nature of mandamus to compel a nondiscretionary administrative act." The Appellate Division, concluding that the hospital was entitled to the relief sought on the merits, recognized the procedural problem because of the unavailability of article 78 relief and properly converted the action under CPLR 103 (subd [c]). We entertain the proceeding as converted but reach the opposite conclusion on the merits. The availability under article 78 of mandamus to compel performance of a duty by an administrative agency depends not on the applicant's substantive entitlement to prevail, but on the nature of the duty sought to be commanded — *i.e.*, mandatory, nondiscretionary action.

Nor is it internally inconsistent, as the dissent suggests, to find that the controversy before us is "ripe" even though it may not be reviewed pursuant to CPLR article 78. The "ripeness" of a controversy does not turn solely upon the question of which procedural vehicle is appropriate to bring the controversy before the court. Hence, it is not at all inconsistent to state on the one hand that we agree with the dissent that the question in this case is "ripe" in the sense that it is appropriate for judicial examination at this time, but to hold, on the other, that the question should be examined through the procedural vehicle embodied in section 2801-c of the Public Health Law which empowers a court to enjoin "threatened violations" of the Public Health Law.

Nothing in the language of section 2801-c of the Public Health Law forecloses recourse to its provisions to enjoin asserted violations or threatened violations by the Public Health Council or the Department of Health of provisions of article 28 of the Public Health Law. Indeed, the availability of such a judicial remedy pending the issuance of a final determination by the public agencies may be a very useful procedural vehicle for applicants such as petitioner.

Accordingly, the order of the Appellate Division should be modified to the extent of denying the relief sought in the converted application for an injunction pursuant to section 2801-c of the Public Health Law, and, as so modified, affirmed.

GABRIELLI, J. (dissenting in part).

I am in complete agreement with the majority's conclusion that the determination of the council in this instance was subject to reconsideration at any

---

[3] *Matter of Utica Cheese v Barber* (49 NY2d 1028), cited by the dissent, is inapposite. That was a proceeding to compel the State agency to act on an application for the issuance of a milk dealer's license. The applicant there did not, as does the applicant here, seek a judicial direction that the administrative agency act in a particular manner substantively favorable to the applicant. What was complained of in *Utica Cheese* was failure to take any action on a license application, and the relief sought was the performance of a nondiscretionary duty enjoined by law, namely, some action on the license application — one way or the other.

time prior to the final approval of petitioner's application for permission to open a new hospital in eastern Suffolk County. I cannot agree with the majority's decision, however, insofar as it leaves intact that portion of the Appellate Division order which converted the instant litigation from a proceeding under CPLR article 78 to an action for injunctive relief under section 2801-c of the Public Health Law (*see* CPLR 103).

. . . .

The majority's unexamined assumption that petitioner sought to compel the performance of a discretionary act in this mandamus proceeding rests upon a fundamental misunderstanding of the nature of the three basic remedies available under article 78. Historically, the remedy of certiorari was used only as a vehicle for obtaining judicial review of agency determinations made on the basis of evidentiary hearings. . . . The familiar "substantial evidence" test was and continues to be the appropriate standard of judicial review where the remedy of certiorari is sought (CPLR 7803, subd 4; . . .). The second remedy now subsumed under article 78 may be traced to the "ancient and just" writ of prohibition, which was used, in general terms, to enjoin a public officer acting in a judicial or quasi-judicial capacity from taking steps in excess of his jurisdiction. . . . Article 78 petitions seeking relief under either of these two remedies are ordinarily fairly easy to distinguish, since the underlying official or agency conduct associated with each remedy is readily identified and classified.

In contrast, the remedy of mandamus, the third broad category of relief now subsumed under the modern procedural vehicle of the article 78 proceeding, has led to some confusion, because it "most often straddled the line between the two old writs" of certiorari and prohibition (Siegel, New York Practice, § 558, at p 778). Indeed, the concept of mandamus really encompasses two distinct types of relief, both of which may be associated for purposes of the present analysis with one of the two ancient remedies discussed above. "[M]andamus to review," which is analogous to certiorari, was developed as a vehicle to permit judicial review of final agency determinations that did not require evidentiary hearings (Siegel, New York Practice, § 561). Such determinations characteristically rest within the sound discretion of the administrative agency and cannot be overturned unless they are shown to be "arbitrary and capricious" (§ 561). On the other hand, "mandamus to compel," which is really only the converse of the remedy of prohibition, by definition cannot apply to agency decisions involving the exercise of discretion, since it entails compelling a public officer to perform an act which he is obligated by law to perform.

Although the distinction between the two different types of mandamus is ordinarily unimportant in modern article 78 proceedings since that statute has eliminated the rigidities of the former writs . . . the distinction remains of crucial significance in cases such as this, where the courts must decide whether the finality requirement embodied in CPLR 7801 (subd 1) is applicable. As noted above, the former provisions of the Civil Practice Act required finality only where certiorari or the related relief of "mandamus to review" was sought; no similar requirement was imposed where the petitioner sought judicial relief in the form of prohibition or "mandamus to compel" (Civ Prac Act, § 1284). It thus becomes apparent that unless the petitioner seeks "mandamus to review," the equivalent of certiorari for situations not requiring a hearing, the agency decision in question may be challenged under article 78 even though the decision may be characterized as interlocutory.

In this case, petitioner commenced the article 78 proceeding to compel the administrative agency to abide by its prior determination concerning the public need for the proposed medical facility. Such a proceeding obviously does not involve certiorari, since the agency's decision to reopen its determination was not preceded by a hearing and there is no claim that the decision is unsupported by "substantial evidence." Similarly, the proceeding cannot logically involve "mandamus to review," since it is based not upon a claim that the agency abused its discretion in making a determination that was within its power to make, but rather upon the assertion that the agency had a legal duty to act under the doctrine of equitable estoppel. In fact, it was petitioner's position that the agency no longer had any discretion in the matter because it had already made a determination on the issue and had induced petitioner to act in reliance upon its conditional approval. Clearly, a petition framed in these terms states a claim for relief in the nature of "mandamus to compel" a nondiscretionary administrative act.[1] Accordingly, the finality requirement established in CPLR 7801 (subd 1) is not applicable, and there is no logical impediment to the maintenance of petitioner's claim under article 78 (*see Matter of Utica Cheese v Barber*, 49 NY2d 1028).[2]

The majority's decision to approve the conversion of this litigation from an article 78 proceeding to an action for injunctive relief under section 2801-c of the Public Health Law is particularly objectionable in this situation, because it establishes for the first time that section 2801-c may be used by a health services provider as a vehicle for suing the Public Health Department and the various agencies which operate under its supervision. . . .

In this connection, it is worthwhile to stress that the finality requirement contained in CPLR 7801 (subd 1) is not a mere "technicality," but rather is the statu-

---

[1] That petitioner may not, in fact, have had a clear legal right to compel the agency to act as a matter of substantive law does not alter the conclusion that its petition stated a claim for article 78 relief in the nature of "mandamus to compel."

[2] I do not take issue with the majority's assertion that the Public Health Council's ultimate determination is essentially discretionary (at pp 96-97) but I would question the pertinence of this observation in the context of the instant dispute. Contrary to the majority's assertions, petitioner did not commence the proceeding to compel the agency to make its ultimate decision in its favor, although a favorable decision is, no doubt, petitioner's underlying aspiration. Instead, as the majority correctly notes earlier in its opinion, petitioner commenced the proceeding in order to challenge the interlocutory decision of the agency to reopen its prior finding of public need. Inasmuch as this discrete decision is itself subject to challenge in a proceeding brought pursuant to article 78 (*cf. Matter of Utica Cheese v Barber*, 49 NY2d 1028, *supra*), the discretionary character of any "ultimate" decision that the agency might make on petitioner's entire application can only be regarded as irrelevant.

tory embodiment of the substantive "exhaustion of remedies" doctrine, which is designed to ensure that the courts will abstain from intervening in administrative disputes until the agency has completed its deliberations and the controversy has become "ripe" (*see* Siegel, New York Practice, § 558, at p 778). Under the doctrine and the applicable provisions of the statute, an applicant must exhaust all administrative avenues and await a final agency determination before coming to court and seeking judicial relief in the form of certiorari or "mandamus to review," although no similar requirement is imposed when the official decision in question is one of those that may be remedied through prohibition or "mandamus to compel." In this case, although the majority has concluded that the agency decision at issue is nonfinal and has further concluded that the decision is among those that must be final in order to be subject to judicial review under article 78, it apparently sees no difficulty in holding that petitioner may nonetheless seek judicial review immediately through an action for injunctive relief. In my view, however, this position is inherently illogical and, more seriously, represents a misuse of the "conversion" device authorized by CPLR 103 to enable a litigant to avoid the substantive "exhaustion of remedies" rule contained in CPLR 7801 (subd 1).

The central difficulty in the majority's analysis lies in its internal inconsistency. If, as the majority contends, the agency decision under review is one subject to the finality requirement of article 78, the observation that the decision does not meet that requirement leads inexorably to the conclusion that the decision ought not be reviewed in the courts at all, at least at this stage of the proceeding. Thus, under the majority's own analysis of the facts, the petition in this case should not have been "converted," but rather should have been dismissed without a full consideration of its merits upon the theory that, since petitioner failed to exhaust its administrative remedies as required, the matter is not yet ripe for judicial review. On the other hand, if, as I have proposed, the decision in question is not among those made subject to the finality rule embodied in CPLR 7801 (subd 1) because it is reviewable through the vehicle of "mandamus to compel," the "exhaustion of remedies" doctrine would present no logical barrier to a judicial review of the merits and the matter may properly be considered in a proceeding brought pursuant to article 78. In short, whether we regard the claim for relief as one sounding in "mandamus to review," as the majority apparently has done, or we regard the claim as one sounding in "mandamus to compel," as I contend we must, the unavoidable conclusion is that the "conversion" below of the proceeding to an action for injunctive relief was wholly inappropriate.

Accordingly, I cast my vote to reconvert the action to an article 78 proceeding and reverse the order of the Appellate Division in its entirety.

JUDGES JONES, WACHTLER and FUCHSBERG concur with JUDGE JASEN; JUDGE GABRIELLI dissents in part and votes to reverse in a separate opinion in which CHIEF JUDGE COOKE and JUDGE MEYER concur.

. . . .

NOTES

(1) CPLR 7803, which prescribes the types of questions one can raise in an article 78 proceeding, says nothing about the common law writs of mandamus, prohibition and certiorari, but CPLR 7801 incorporates them into article 78 and, as the principal case shows, the courts continue to use the traditional terminology.

(2) The general scope of mandamus to compel is described in *State Division of Human Rights v. New York State Dep't of Correctional Services*, 90 A.D.2d 51, 65-68, 456 N.Y.S.2d 63, 72-73 (2d Dep't 1982) (footnotes omitted):

> As a legal remedy controlled by equitable principles . . ., mandamus is essentially a judicial command to perform a ministerial act specifically required of a public or corporate officer or body by law . . . in one of two senses: (1) a common-law, statutory or other rule of general application so enjoining the officer or board as invoked by a petitioner coming within its express terms . . . or (2) a rule of limited application laid down in the form of a legislative, judicial or administrative determination or a corporate charter or contract with a public dimension fixing petitioner's right to such performance.

(3) The principal case applies the well settled rule that mandamus to compel (not to be confused with mandamus to review) is not available unless the petitioner's right to relief is absolute. It sounds as if the availability of the procedural vehicle is coterminous with the validity of the case on the merits. (Would the majority disagree with this way of putting it?) While this is true to some extent, note that it is possible that the petitioner may have a right to some form of relief (if not mandamus) even if the respondent did have some discretion. The majority seems to recognize that an injunction might be obtainable in some cases, even if mandamus to compel was not. Under what circumstances might this be so?

(4) In *Garrison v. Office of the Comptroller of the City of New York*, 92 N.Y.2d 732, 685 N.Y.S.2d 921, 708 N.E.2d 994 (1999), the petitioner brought an article 78 proceeding to compel the respondent Comptroller to register petitioner's contract with the City. Under the New York City Charter, petitioner was required to obtain such registration as a condition of payment. The Court held that mandamus to compel was not the proper remedy because the Comptroller had some discretionary authority whether to register contracts. The petitioner could, instead, obtain review of the decision on the grounds that it was arbitrary and capricious, so the Court remanded the proceeding to the trial court.

(5) A successful proceeding for mandamus to compel may not provide the basis for a subsequent federal civil rights suit for damages (42 U.S.C.A. § 1983), *i.e.*, the finding that a municipality was arbitrary and capricious in denying building permits will not without "significantly more," support the damage

claim for delays occasioned by the denials. *Bower Associates v. Town of Pleasant Valley*, 2 N.Y.3d 617, 781 N.Y.S.2d 240, 814 N.E.2d 410 (2004).

(6) The following case upholds the use of mandamus to compel. Arguably, it also stretches the boundaries of that doctrine.

KLOSTERMANN v. CUOMO
Court of Appeals
61 N.Y.2d 525, 475 N.Y.S.2d 247, 463 N.E.2d 588 (1984)

COOKE, CHIEF JUDGE.

The mentally ill, whether in a State institution or previously institutionalized and now homeless in New York City, are entitled to a declaration of their rights as against the State. Their claims do not present a nonjusticiable controversy merely because the activity contemplated on the State's part may be complex and rife with the exercise of discretion. Rather, the judiciary is empowered to declare the individual rights in all such cases, even if the ultimate determination is that the individual has no rights. Moreover, if a statutory directive is mandatory, not precatory, it is within the courts' competence to ascertain whether an administrative agency has satisfied the duty that has been imposed on it by the Legislature and, if it has not, to direct that the agency proceed forthwith to do so.

These two actions, each seeking declaratory relief and mandamus, were initiated by persons treated for mental illness in State institutions, claiming that their constitutional and statutory rights have been violated by the various defendants. The essence of their demands is that they are entitled to be released into the community under a program that will ensure continued treatment and adequate housing. The courts below unanimously dismissed each complaint on the ground that the controversies presented were nonjusticiable because their resolution would involve an excessive entanglement of the courts with the executive and legislative branches. This court now reverses. The background details of each action are briefly outlined, the facts being taken from the allegations in the complaints which, in reviewing these motions to dismiss, are taken as true.

Klostermann v. Cuomo

Plaintiffs are nine persons suing individually and on behalf of all others similarly situated. Each was treated in a State psychiatric hospital and discharged as part of the State's policy to release patients to less restrictive, community-based residences. Each plaintiff became one of the homeless wandering the streets of New York City. Efforts to receive assistance from State and municipal agencies were unavailing or, at best, resulted in only minimal, periodic assistance.

. . . .

The crux of plaintiffs' complaint is an asserted right under State law to receive residential placement, supervision, and care upon release from a State institution. Their claims are grounded in the provisions of subdivisions (f) through (h) of section 29.15 of the Mental Hygiene Law, which prescribe certain acts that must be undertaken when a patient in a State psychiatric institution is to be discharged or conditionally released into the community. Summarized, the statute requires that a "written service plan" be prepared for each patient before his or her release. At a minimum, the plan must set forth what will be required by the patient upon discharge or conditional release, specifically recommend the type of residence in which the client should live, and list the services available at that residence as well as organizations and facilities in the area which are available to provide services in accordance with the identified needs of the patient. Lastly, the director of any department facility must create, implement, and monitor a program to ensure that a patient is living in an adequate facility and is receiving the services he or she needs.

Plaintiffs' prayer for relief sought class certification and certain substantive remedies. They asked for a declaration that defendants have violated Federal and State law by their failure to comply with section 29.15 and by failing to provide treatment under the least restrictive conditions suitable to plaintiffs' needs. Plaintiffs also asked for an order directing defendants "to develop and implement a plan with all due speed which will provide sufficient community-based residential facilities for plaintiffs and members of the class they represent." Plaintiffs also requested damages.

Defendants did not answer but, instead, moved to dismiss on the grounds that the court lacked subject matter jurisdiction and the complaint failed to state a cause of action (CPLR 3211, subd. [a], pars. 2, 7). Their jurisdictional argument was founded on the position that treating the mentally ill essentially involves questions of allocating resources, matters that are within the competence of the executive and legislative branches and that should be guarded from judicial intervention.

Special Term granted the motion, holding that the controversy was nonjusticiable. . . . [T]he court declined to consider the request for declaratory judgment because such relief would be futile in light of the unavailability of any further remedies to enforce any rights declared. The court summarily dismissed plaintiffs' constitutional and Federal claims on the same ground of nonjusticiability.

On appeal, the Appellate Division . . . affirmed.

Joanne S. v. Carey

Plaintiffs in this action seek essentially the same relief as those in *Klostermann*, albeit from a different starting point. Suing individually and on behalf of all others similarly situated, plaintiffs are 11 patients hospitalized at Manhattan Psychiatric Hospital who have each been found ready to return to the community but have not been discharged or released because of the lack of adequate residential placements. At the time the complaint was drafted in

August, 1982, the individual plaintiffs had been in this predicament for as long as a year.

. . . .

II

On this appeal, the court is asked to consider whether the complaints present claims that lie within the judiciary's power to review, *i.e.*, whether the controversy is a justiciable one. It is concluded that the courts below erred in holding that they could not properly consider the issues raised by plaintiffs. It should be emphasized that, in reaching this conclusion, this court does not express any opinion as to the merits of plaintiffs' causes of action. Their ultimate success on the substantive questions must await further proceedings.

Plaintiffs seek two remedies — declaratory judgment and mandamus. Defendants contend that no relief can be afforded to plaintiffs because fashioning any judgment would necessarily involve the allocation of resources and entangle the courts in the decision-making function of the executive and legislative branches. In making their argument, defendants fail to distinguish between a court's imposition of its own policy determination upon its governmental partners and its mere declaration and enforcement of the individual's rights that have already been conferred by the other branches of government.

The difficulty in determining what is "justiciable" arises in part from the nebulous quality of that concept. It is a far-reaching term that incorporates, among other things, political questions and mootness (*see Jones v. Beame*, 45 N.Y.2d 402, 408, 408 N.Y.S.2d 449, 380 N.E.2d 277). "Even within a particular category of justiciability, as with political questions, the line separating the justiciable from the nonjusticiable has been subtle, and with the passage of time, it might be said, has even moved (*see, e.g., Baker v. Carr*, 369 U.S. 186, 208-237 [82 S. Ct. 691, 705-720, 7 L. Ed. 2d 663])" (*id.*).

The paramount concern is that the judiciary not undertake tasks that the other branches are better suited to perform. Acquiring data and applying expert advice to formulate broad programs cannot be economically done by the courts. This restraint is particularly important when the creation of a program entails selecting among competing and equally meritorious approaches so as to allocate scarce resources. Generally, the manner by which the State addresses complex societal and governmental issues is a subject left to the discretion of the legislative and executive branches of our tripartite system (*see Matter of Abrams v. New York City Tr. Auth.*, 39 N.Y.2d 990, 992, 387 N.Y.S.2d 235, 355 N.E.2d 289).

This approach was exemplified in the companion cases of *Jones v. Beame* and *Bowen v. State Bd. of Social Welfare,* 45 N.Y.2d 402, 408 N.Y.S.2d 449, 380 N.E.2d 277, *supra. Bowen* involved a challenge by the City of Long Beach to the State's policy of deinstitutionalizing the care of the mentally ill, the same program that is now at issue in the present appeals. This court ruled that the matter was not one properly presentable in a judicial forum, in part because the plaintiffs there sought to litigate the wisdom of the State's policy, which involved the conflicting views of experts as to what constituted the better course of treatment — institutions or private settings in the community. . . . In rejecting the suits, the court was careful to note that it was refusing only to become ensnarled in an attempt to weigh and select policies, but not to review the implementation of those policies on a case-by-case basis: "In short, resolution of the ultimate issues rests on policy, and *reference to violations of applicable statutes is irrelevant except in recognized separately litigable matters brought to enforce them*" (*id.*, at p. 409, 408 N.Y.S.2d 449, 380 N.E.2d 277 [emphasis added]).

The instant cases raise the precise situation that was contemplated in *Bowen*. Plaintiffs are individuals who claim that they hold certain rights under the pertinent statutes and are seeking to enforce those rights.[2] In effect, they assert that the Legislature has mandated certain programs and that the executive branch has failed to deliver the services. The appropriate forum to determine the respective rights and obligations of the parties is in the judicial branch.

Defendants contend that the controversy is nonjusticiable because any adjudication in support of plaintiffs will necessarily require the expenditure of funds and a concomitant allocation of resources. Defendants have set forth in affidavits all of their efforts to care for the psychiatric patients released from State hospitals, and argue that there simply is not enough money to provide the services that plaintiffs assert are due them. Although defendants' attempts are commendable, they are irrelevant. "[T]he '[c]ontinuing failure to provide suitable and adequate treatment cannot be justified by lack of staff or facilities'". . . . This defense is particularly unconvincing when uttered in response to a claim that existing conditions violate an individual's constitutional rights (*see* Frug, *Judicial Power of the Purse*, 126 U. of Pa.L.Rev. 715, 725, and n 71).

In sum, there is nothing inherent in plaintiffs' attempts to seek a declaration and enforcement of their rights that renders the controversy nonjusticiable. They do not wish to controvert the wisdom of any program. Instead, they ask only that the program be effected in the manner that it was legislated.

III

As noted, plaintiffs have sought declaratory judgment and mandamus. Defendants contend that, even if the controversy is justiciable, these remedies are not available. The crux of defendants' argument is that the courts cannot draft any

---

[2] Plaintiffs are also attempting to pursue their claims as class actions. This, conceivably, may create a situation similar to that in *Bowen*, requiring the court to consider broad policy matters rather than their application to individuals. Whether this difficulty will arise cannot now be determined as no class has been described and certified. Accordingly, this court expresses no opinion on the suitability of the present litigation to be pursued as a class action.

Similarly, inasmuch as none of the lower courts ruled on defendants' motions insofar as they seek dismissals on other grounds, this court does not express any opinion on those issues.

coercive order or judgment to enforce plaintiffs' rights, if any, so that mandamus is inappropriate and declaratory relief is meaningless because it could never be followed by an executory decree. This misapprehends the scope of mandamus and the nature of declaratory judgments.

Mandamus, of course, is an extraordinary remedy that, by definition, is available only in limited circumstances. Declaratory relief, on the other hand, "'is a remedy sui generis and escapes both the substantive objections and procedural limitations of special writs and extraordinary remedies' (Borchard, *Declaratory Judgments,* 1939, 9 Bklyn.L.Rev. at p. 14)" (*Matter of Morgenthau v. Erlbaum,* 59 N.Y.2d 143, 147, 464 N.Y.S.2d 392, 451 N.E.2d 150, *cert. den.* — U.S. —, 104 S.Ct. 486, 78 L.Ed.2d 682).[3]

One aspect of the distinctive nature of an action for declaratory judgment is that not only is the ultimate decree noncoercive, but the rights declared need not be amenable to enforcement by an executory decree in a subsequent action. The belief that an executory order is required arises from the misconception that the judicial power is necessarily a coercive one.

> The coercion or compulsion exerted by a judgment, while essential to its effectiveness, is not due to a coercive order to act or refrain, but to the very existence of the judgment, as a determination of legal rights. Many judgments are incapable of, and do not require, physical execution. They irrevocably, however, fix a legal relation or status placed in issue, and that is all that the judgment is expected to do. It is this determination which makes it res judicata.

(Borchard, *Declaratory Judgments* [2d ed], p. 12.)

> While ordinarily a case or judicial controversy results in a judgment requiring award of process of execution to carry it into effect, such relief is not an indispensable adjunct to the exercise of the judicial function.

(*Fidelity Nat. Bank v. Swope,* 274 U.S. 123, 132, 47 S.Ct. 511, 514, 71 L.Ed. 959.)

> [I]t is not necessary, in order to constitute a judicial judgment that there should be both a determination of the rights of the litigants and also power to issue formal execution to carry the judgment into effect, in the way that judgments for money or for the possession of land usually are enforced. A judgment is sometimes regarded as properly enforceable through the executive departments instead of through an award of execution by this Court, where the effect of the judgment is to establish the duty of the department to enforce it.

---

[3] This court has recently reviewed the distinction between extraordinary writs and declaratory judgments in the context of requesting prohibition to review an interlocutory order in a criminal trial (*Matter of Morgenthau v. Erlbaum,* 59 N.Y.2d 143, 147-149, 464 N.Y.S.2d 392, 451 N.E.2d 150). Suffice it here to say that the discussion in *Erlbaum* is equally applicable to the present case.

(*Old Colony Trust Co. v. Commissioner of Internal Revenue*, 279 U.S. 716, 725, 49 S.Ct. 499, 502, 73 L.Ed. 918).

The primary purpose of declaratory judgments is to adjudicate the parties' rights before a "wrong" actually occurs in the hope that later litigation will be unnecessary (*see Matter of Morgenthau v. Erlbaum*; 59 N.Y.2d 143, 148, 464 N.Y.S.2d 392, 451 N.E.2d 150, *supra*, and authorities cited there). The action, therefore, contemplates that the parties will voluntarily comply with the court's order. It is anomalous to contend that such an action should not be permitted because it may be necessary at some future date to coerce one party who has refused to act in accordance with the judicial determination. Indeed, defendants' argument in this regard is especially offensive in its implication that they will deem themselves free to disregard their judicially declared obligations should a court rule in favor of plaintiffs.

Thus, the ultimate availability of a coercive order to enforce adjudicated rights is not a prerequisite to a court's entertaining an action for declaratory judgment. In any event, this objection is without merit because, in the present cases, if plaintiffs' claims are borne out, a coercive order may be drafted by the courts.

Traditionally, "[m]andamus lies to compel the performance of a purely ministerial act where there is a clear legal right to the relief sought" (*Matter of Legal Aid Soc. v. Scheinman*, 53 N.Y.2d 12, 16, 439 N.Y.S.2d 882, 422 N.E.2d 542). The long-established law is that "'[w]hile a mandamus is an appropriate remedy to enforce the performance of a ministerial duty, it is well settled that it will not be awarded to compel an act in respect to which the officer may exercise judgment or discretion'" (*Matter of Gimprich v. Board of Educ.*, 306 N.Y. 401, 406, 118 N.E.2d 578, *quoting People ex rel. Hammond v. Leonard*, 74 N.Y. 443, 445; *but cf. Scheinman, supra*, 53 N.Y.2d at p. 16, n. 1, 439 N.Y.S.2d 882, 422 N.E.2d 542).

Defendants argue that preparing written service plans and creating followup programs are activities replete with decisions involving the exercise of judgment or discretion. This is inarguably true. What must be distinguished, however, are those acts the exercise of which is discretionary from those acts which are mandatory but are executed through means that are discretionary. For example, the decision to prosecute a suit is a matter left to the public officer's judgment and, therefore, cannot be compelled (*see People ex rel. Hammond v. Leonard*, 74 N.Y. 443, *supra*). In contrast, when a town council is directed by statute to designate up to four newspapers having the largest circulation for the purpose of receiving city advertising, the court can compel the council to execute its statutory duty, but it may not direct the particular papers to be named (*see People ex rel. Francis v. Common Council*, 78 N.Y. 33). What has been somewhat lost from view is this function of mandamus to compel acts that officials are duty-bound to perform, regardless of whether they may exercise their discretion in doing so.

[T]he writ of mandamus . . . may also be addressed to subordinate judicial tribunals, to compel them to exercise their functions, but never to require them to decide in a particular manner. . . . This principle applies to every case where the duty, performance of which is sought to be compelled, is in its nature judicial, or involves the exercise of judicial power or discretion, irrespective of the general character of the officer or body to which the writ is addressed. *A subordinate body can be directed to act, but not how to act, in a manner as to which it has the right to exercise its judgment.* The character of the duty, and not that of the body or officer, determines how far performance of the duty may be enforced by mandamus. Where a subordinate body is vested with power to determine a question of fact, the duty is judicial, and though it can be compelled by mandamus to determine the fact, it cannot be directed to decide in a particular way, however clearly it be made to appear what the decision ought to be.

(*People ex rel. Francis v. Common Council, supra,* at p. 39 [emphasis added].)

"The general principle [is] that mandamus will lie against an administrative officer only to compel him to perform a legal duty, and not to direct how he shall perform that duty". . . . This rule was recently given effect in *Matter of Gonkjur Assoc. v. Abrams,* 57 N.Y.2d 853, 455 N.Y.S.2d 761, 442 N.E.2d 58, *affg. on opn. below* 82 A.D.2d 683, 688, 443 N.Y.S.2d 69, when this court held that the Attorney-General could be directed to issue a letter stating that a co-operative apartment prospectus had been filed or was deficient, although the order could not direct the Attorney-General to approve the plan (*accord Matter of Utica Cheese v. Barber,* 49 N.Y.2d 1028, 429 N.Y.S.2d 405, 406 N.E.2d 1342 [Commissioner of Agriculture directed to hold hearing and render determination on milk dealer's license application within 90 days]; *Matter of Stuart & Stuart v. State Liq. Auth.,* 29 A.D.2d 176, 286 N.Y.S.2d 861 [agency can be compelled to decide license applications but not to grant the licenses]; *see Matter of Thomas v. Wells,* 288 N.Y. 155, 157, 42 N.E.2d 465; *Southern Leasing Co. v. Ludwig,* 217 N.Y. 100, 105, 111 N.E. 470).

In conclusion, plaintiffs have properly petitioned the courts for a declaration of their rights, whether derived from the Federal or State Constitutions, statutes, or regulations. Moreover, to the extent that plaintiffs can establish that defendants are not satisfying nondiscretionary obligations to perform certain functions, they are entitled to orders directing defendants to discharge those duties. The activity that the courts must be careful to avoid is the fashioning of orders or judgments that go beyond any mandatory directives of existing statutes and regulations and intrude upon the policy-making and discretionary decisions that are reserved to the legislative and executive branches.

[B]　Prohibition: CPLR 7803(2)

LA ROCCA v. LANE
Court of Appeals
37 N.Y.2d 575, 376 N.Y.S.2d 93, 338 N.E.2d 606 (1975),
cert. denied, 424 U.S. 968 (1976)

BREITEL, CHIEF JUDGE

This is a proceeding brought to prohibit respondent, a Judge in the Criminal Court, from requiring petitioner, a Roman Catholic priest, to change his clerical garb before appearing as defense counsel in a criminal jury trial. . . .

The preliminary question is whether prohibition under CPLR article 78 lies. If it does, the issue becomes whether the court's direction violated petitioner's right to free exercise of religion.

. . . .

Prohibition is available to restrain an inferior court or Judge from exceeding its or his powers in a proceeding over which the court has jurisdiction. While a court has authority to regulate the conduct and appearance of counsel in proceedings before it, that authority is not unlimited. In exercising the power to regulate conduct and appearance, a court may not violate the constitutional right of counsel to free exercise of religion. Petitioner has presented a substantial claim that the Judge in the Criminal Court has exceeded his powers. Thus, petitioner should be able, in the first instance, to seek redress by prohibition.

The free exercise of religion is a highly protected interest but is not absolute. The incidental burden on petitioner's freedom to exercise his religion must be balanced against the State's paramount duty to insure a fair trial in a criminal action for both defendant and the People. In striking the balance it is concluded that the performance of the State's paramount duty to insure a fair trial may not be substantially jeopardized because of petitioner's right, however significant, to free exercise of his religion.

. . . .

Petitioner has been an ordained Roman Catholic priest for 25 years. Admitted to the Bar in 1973, petitioner is a lawyer employed for his second year by the Legal Aid Society. He was assigned by the society to represent an indigent defendant in a criminal jury trial in the case of the People against Cecilia Daniels in the Criminal Court of the City of New York.

. . . .

After considerable colloquy, the court directed that, unless petitioner were to remove his clerical collar, he would not be permitted to continue as defense counsel. The court's directive was grounded in its expressed concern that members of the jury might be prejudiced by the appearance of petitioner in his clerical costume, and therefore a fair trial could not be assured. Petitioner refused to remove his clerical collar and instituted the present proceeding. The trial in the criminal action, although not stayed, has never taken place. In his petition, petitioner contended only that the judicial direction to remove his clerical collar denied him his constitutional right to free exercise of religion.

. . . .

The "ancient and just" writ of prohibition is rooted deep in the common law. Originally used by the English king to curb the powers of ecclesiastical courts, prohibition has evolved into a basic protection for the individual in his relations with the State. . . .

It is well settled, and has been restated many times, that prohibition is available both to restrain an unwarranted assumption of jurisdiction and to prevent a court from exceeding its authorized powers in a proceeding over which it has jurisdiction (*see, e.g.,* CPLR 7803, subd. 2; . . .). The extraordinary remedy of prohibition is never available merely to correct or prevent trial errors of substantive law or procedure, however grievous. . . . The orderly administration of justice requires that correction of litigation errors merely be left to the ordinary channels of appeal or review. Otherwise one would erect an additional avenue of judicial scrutiny in a collateral proceeding and thus frustrate the statutory or even constitutional limits on review. . . .

If, however, a court acts without jurisdiction, or acts or threatens to act in excess of its powers, other principles are applicable. Prohibition is not mandatory, but may issue in the sound discretion of the court. . . . In exercising this discretion, a number of factors should be considered.

The gravity of the harm which would be caused by an excess of power is an important factor to be weighed. . . . Also important, but not controlling, is whether the excess of power can be adequately corrected on appeal or by other ordinary proceedings at law or in equity. . . .

If an adequate remedy is available, the burdening of judicial process with collateral proceedings, interruptive of the orderly administration of justice, would be unjustified. If, however, appeal or other proceedings would be inadequate to prevent the harm, and prohibition would furnish a more complete and efficacious remedy, it may be used even though other methods of redress are technically available. . . . For example, to force a person, faced with a court acting or threatening to act without jurisdiction, or in excess of its powers, to proceed in contempt, and to remain confined until "ultimate justice" is obtained upon appeal in habeas corpus proceedings, would be to undermine the very reason for the remedy. . . .

. . . .

True, there is no sharp line between a court acting in error under substantive or procedural law and a court acting in excess of its powers, if only because every act without jurisdiction or in excess of its powers in a proceeding over which it has jurisdiction of necessity involves an "error of law." But the absence of bright lines of demarcation in the law is not unusual; man's language and capacity to conceptualize is not perfect. The fact is that in extreme enough cases the distinction is easily apparent. At one extreme, a trivial error in excess of jurisdiction may be just that, trivial, and hardly worthy of treatment as an excess of power. On the other hand, at the other extreme, a gross abuse of power on its face and in effect may be in reality so serious an excess of power incontrovertibly justifying and requiring summary correction. A good example of the last was the gross, unprecedented, and even suspect as to motivation, direction to disclose an entire transcript of a Grand Jury investigation in a case involving limited issues (*see Matter of Proskin v. County Ct. of Albany County*, 30 N.Y.2d 15, 18-19, 330 N.Y.S.2d 44, 45-46, 280 N.E.2d 875, 876, *supra*). The law generally and the extraordinary remedy of prohibition has not developed as a linguistic exercise but as a response in language and concept to the recognized needs and accommodations in a society governed by the rule of law. There is a larger logic than that delineated by etymology. To eliminate or minimize the concept of an excess of power, on presumed verbalistic grounds, would undermine a common-law principle of ancient standing and the continuous statutory statement of that principle. . . .

Petitioner does not, as he could not, dispute the power of the court to regulate generally counsel's conduct and appearance. . . . Instead, petitioner argues that the trial court exceeded its powers in directing removal of his clerical garb, a direction allegedly violative of petitioner's right to free exercise of religion. He offers a "substantial" argument in support of his contentions. True, upon reaching the merits, the court may decide the issue adversely to petitioner. But this would not foreclose the remedy. When a petitioner, whether party or not, but especially where one is not a party, presents an arguable, substantial, and novel claim that a court has exceeded its powers because of a collision of unquestioned constitutional principles, he may, in the first instance, seek redress by prohibition.

Thus, petitioner seeks to vindicate his right to free exercise of religion, certainly a preferred right included among the great human rights in a free and open society. . . . With respect to such a preferred right, and its safeguarding, prohibition is a "more complete and efficacious remedy" to redress the alleged excess of power, if that it were. Petitioner should not be compelled to test the alleged excess of power in such a significant area of constitutional right by proceeding in contempt of court and habeas corpus proceedings. Nor is appeal in the criminal action an adequate remedy since his client, the defendant, might be acquitted or a conviction reversed on another ground, or she might refuse to take an appeal. Moreover, on a conviction there would be an additional obstacle to establish, namely, that the "error" was material, a condition difficult to surmount in the particular criminal action since as an indigent with assigned counsel she had a right to counsel but lacked the right to stipulate who that counsel should be. . . . Thus, prohibition should be available in the discretion of the court to test whether petitioner is entitled to restraint of an inferior court from directing removal of petitioner's clerical garb.

Having determined that the remedy of prohibition is appropriate, the merits of the application may be addressed. . . .

The trial court in directing change of petitioner's garb if he persisted in trying the case before a jury, acted to preserve the right of both the defendant and the People to a fair trial. In so doing, the court of necessity limited defense counsel's right to free exercise of religion in that he was compelled to remove the symbol of his religious calling, a requirement of his calling which is not unconditional or beyond dispensation. The risk that a fair trial could not be had outweighed this incidental limitation.

. . . .

NOTES

(1) Do you see why Judge Gabrielli, in his dissent in *Hamptons Hospital & Medical Center, Inc. v. Moore*, § 24.03[A], *supra*, referred to mandamus to compel as the "converse of the remedy of prohibition"? Note, however, that the principal case holds that while petitioner was entitled to invoke the remedy of prohibition, it ruled against him on the merits.

(2) The principal case should be compared with *Morgenthau v. Erlbaum*, 59 N.Y.2d 143, 464 N.Y.S.2d 392, 451 N.E.2d 150 (1983), which held that prohibition was not available in a proceeding brought by a district attorney to challenge the policy of a criminal court judge under which jury trials were granted to all persons accused of prostitution. The Court held, however, that a declaratory judgment action would lie.

(3) The remedy of prohibition is not available unless the respondent is exercising judicial or quasi-judicial functions. *See, e.g., McGinley v. Hynes*, 51 N.Y.2d 116, 432 N.Y.S.2d 689, 412 N.E.2d 376 (1980), *cert. denied*, 450 U.S. 918 (1981) (prohibition would not lie against a special prosecutor insofar as the proceeding was directed to his executive functions).

[C] Review of Administrative Determinations; Mandamus to Review and Certiorari: CPLR 7803(3) and (4)

125 BAR CORP. v. STATE LIQUOR AUTHORITY
Court of Appeals
24 N.Y.2d 174, 299 N.Y.S.2d 194, 247 N.E.2d 157 (1969)

BREITEL, JUDGE.

Petitioner, owner of a bar on 125th Street in Manhattan, was denied a renewal of its restaurant liquor license after an interview pursuant to the regulations of the State Liquor Authority. It sought to overturn the determination of the Authority in this article 78 proceeding on the ground that the action of the Authority had been arbitrary and capricious. The Appellate Division confirmed the determination.

While the adverse determination, after an interview of a renewal application need not be supported by substantial evidence, or, for that matter, competent common-law evidence, to sustain the determination, there must be a rational basis for the administrative agency's action (*Matter of Fink v. Cole*, 1 N.Y.2d 48, 53, 150 N.Y.S.2d 175, 178, 133 N.E.2d 691, 693). Because, in this case, the data before the Authority does not rationally support the determination, the judgment of the Appellate Division should be reversed, the determination of the Authority annulled, and the matter remanded to the Authority for appropriate proceedings.

Petitioner has held a license for the premises in question since April 28, 1966, having succeeded a prior licensee. During the two years 1966 and 1967 it received four warning letters from the Authority concerning alleged incidents of threatened or actual illegal conduct occurring on the premises. There was an additional incident which had not been the subject of a warning letter. These warnings and the additional incident were reasons given by the Authority in requesting a nonrenewal interview.

At the interview hearing three of the notices were supported by police or Authority investigation reports of the alleged incidents; one was unsupported at the interview but is now covered by a police report attached to the Authority's answer in this proceeding, and the additional incident was supported by testimony taken at a revocation hearing determined in favor of the licensee.

The first warning of June 16, 1966 related to the employment of felons by the licensee's predecessor and another unrelated licensee in the neighborhood. It is irrelevant to this licensee's application for renewal. The second warning of August 17, 1966 related to the employment of a convicted gambler. Apart from the fact that the licensee denies ever having employed the named person, it is conceded that no gambling incidents were ever reported to have occurred in the licensed premises. This notice, therefore, is hardly relevant to the renewal application.

Of the remaining notices, one, dated January 18, 1967, warned the licensee to tighten its supervision of the premises, citing a solicitation by a prostitute which occurred on the premises on May 25, 1966, another on September 26, 1966, and a surreptitious narcotics sale on July 22, 1966. The last notice, of July 7, 1967, cited a prostitution solicitation on April 9, 1967. The additional specification, not covered by the notices, related to a prostitution solicitation on August 3, 1967, the same matter in which, after a full hearing in revocation proceedings, the licensee was found blameless.

The gist of the matter then is that, giving full credit to the hearsay reports which resulted in the notices, as well as to the testimony concerning the last solicitation, in the year 1966 there were but two prostitution solicitations and one narcotics sale in the premises, and in the year 1967 there were two prostitution solicitations. With respect to none of these was it claimed that the licensee knew or suffered the conditions to arise, and with respect to all but two of them the police testimony or report expressly observed that the offending conduct was surreptitious and not within the sight or hearing of the employees in the premises.

The premises are located on Harlem's main business street between avenues through which pass the Penn-Central Railroad and the Lexington Avenue subway. It is a hub area of the district with heavy transient and local pedestrian traffic.

It is well established that in renewal proceedings, in which a hearing is not mandated by law, the Authority is not as circumscribed as in revocation or cancellation proceedings, nor are the substantive standards the same. . . . The review of a determination in such renewal proceedings is not in the nature of certiorari but mandamus, on which the standard is not substantiality of the evidence but the rationality of the administrative act. . . . Nevertheless, the determination must have a reasonable or rational basis, a test that is often indistinguishable from that of substantiality of the evidence, except that competent common-law evidence is not required (*Matter of Sled Hill Cafe v. Hostetter, supra*, 22 N.Y.2d p. 612, 294 N.Y.S.2d p. 500, 241 N.E.2d p. 716, and cases cited; . . .).

Hence, the Authority was entitled to rely on the investigation reports of the police and its own investigators. But if their contents were on their face insufficient, inapplicable, or irrelevant, they would not provide rational support for the determination. That was the situation here.

Two of the notices, as already observed, were either inapplicable to this licensee or irrelevant to what later was alleged to have occurred. The remaining incidents were very few in number: three in one year, and two in the other. None was shown to have occurred with the actual or constructive knowledge of the licensee. Indeed, some were described as surreptitious and without the knowledge or possibility of knowledge of the licensee. Moreover, they occurred in premises in a busy quarter, an area of hubbub and transient traffic, a factor of some significance. . . . Had the number of incidents been very large, even if all were not established to be within the awareness of the licensee, the permissible inference would be different. . . . Hence the facts revealed in this case, even after complete acceptance of the hearsay evidence, fail to provide a rational basis for the failure to renew the license.

. . . .

Since this article 78 proceeding was a review of an administrative determination not resting on a hearing mandated by law, Special Term should have determined the matter. However, once transferred to the Appellate Division, that court was required to determine all the issues (CPLR 7804, subd. [g]; . . .). This it did, and therefore, there is no occasion for remanding the proceedings to Special Term.

Accordingly, the judgment of the Appellate Division, denominated an order, should be reversed, the determination of the Authority annulled, and the matter remanded to the Authority for appropriate proceedings.

. . . .

NOTES

(1) The overlap between CPLR 7803(3) "mandamus to review" and (4) "certiorari" is obvious. Each permits review of a "determination." In order to invoke subdivision (4), the determination must have been "made as a result of a hearing held, and at which evidence was taken, pursuant to direction by law. . . ." Not every "hearing" meets this definition, only quasi-judicial or evidentiary hearings mandated by statute or Constitution. *See Sanford v. Rockefeller*, 35 N.Y.2d 547, 364 N.Y.S.2d 450, 324 N.E.2d 113 (1974), *cert. denied*, 421 U.S. 973; *Rochester Colony, Inc. v. Hostetter*, 19 A.D.2d 250, 241 N.Y.S.2d 210 (4th Dep't 1963).

(2) What consequences follow when the case is slotted into either subdivision (3) or (4) of CPLR 7803? Procedurally, it clearly makes a difference, for if the proceeding is in the nature of certiorari (subdivision 4), it must be heard by the Appellate Division. *See* CPLR 7804(g). Otherwise the proceeding should be heard in the Supreme Court. As a matter of substance, there appears to be little difference between review under the two sections, at least when petitioner claims that the decision challenged was wrong because of legal or factual error:

> The arbitrary or capricious test [of CPLR 7803(3)] chiefly "relates to whether a particular action should have been taken or is justified . . . and whether the administrative action is without foundation in fact." (1 N.Y. Jur., Administrative Law § 184, p. 609). Arbitrary action is without sound basis in reason and is generally taken without regard to the facts. In *Matter of Colton v. Berman* . . . this court (per Breitel, J.) said,

"the proper test is whether there is a rational basis for the administrative orders, *the review not being of determinations made after quasi-judicial hearings required by statute or law*." (Emphasis supplied.) Where, however, a hearing is held, the determination must be supported by substantial evidence (CPLR 7803, subd 4); and where a determination is made and the person acting has not acted in excess of his jurisdiction, in violation of lawful procedure, arbitrarily, or in abuse of his discretionary power, including discretion as to the penalty imposed, the courts have no alternative but to confirm his determination (CPLR 7803, subd. 3). Rationality is what is reviewed under both the substantial evidence rule and the arbitrary and capricious standard.

Pell v. Board of Education, 34 N.Y.2d 222, 231, 356 N.Y.S.2d 833, 839, 313 N.E.2d 321 (1974). *See generally*, Gabrielli & Nonna, *Judicial Review of Administrative Action in New York: An Overview and Survey*, 52 St. John's L. Rev. 361 (1978).

(3) *In Matter of Kelly v. Safir*, 96 N.Y.2d 32, 724 N.Y.S.2d 680, 747 N.E.2d 1280 (2001), the Court said that judicial review of an administrative penalty is limited to whether it constitutes an abuse of discretion as a matter of law. After transfer from the IAS court, the Appellate Division decided that the penalty of dismissal from his job was too severe for a police sergeant and remanded to the Police Commissioner for reconsideration. Although confirming the finding of the sergeant's misconduct, the court felt that his service record should have been given more consideration. The Court of Appeals reversed. Not only was the Appellate Division limited by the facts in the administrative record, which did not include the service record, but it also should have adhered to the substantial evidence rule and not substituted its evaluation in the absence of any administrative abuse of discretion which would "shock one's sense of fairness."

§ 24.04 CPLR 217, TIME LIMITATION

BEST PAYPHONES, INC. v. DEPARTMENT OF INFORMATION TECHNOLOGY AND TELECOMMUNICATION
Court of Appeals
5 N.Y.3d 30, 799 N.Y.S.2d 182, 832 N.E.2d 38 (2005)

CHIEF JUDGE KAYE.

At issue before us is the date when an administrative determination became "final and binding upon the petitioner," so as to trigger the four-month limitations period for CPLR article 78 review (CPLR 217[1]).

Petitioner, Best Payphones, Inc., owned and operated sidewalk payphones in New York City. Respondent, the New York City Department of Information Technology and Telecommunications (DOITT), regulates pay telephone operations on city streets. On August 11, 1999, the City approved petitioner's payphone franchise, subject to certain conditions, including the execution and delivery of a Franchise Agreement.

On January 13, 2000, DOITT notified petitioner that, because it did not submit executed copies of the Franchise Agreement and other required closing documents, it "failed to meet an essential condition of [City] approval, and the [City] can therefore be deemed to have determined not to approve a franchise for Best." The letter went on to state that Best had 60 days to enter into an agreement to sell its payphones to an entity that had been awarded a public pay telephone franchise by the City, or to remove its public pay telephones from the City's property, or to submit executed copies of the Franchise Agreement and all required closing documents. If petitioner failed within 60 days to pursue one of those courses, the letter continued, its phones would be subject to removal from city property and Best would be considered for all purposes a nonholder of a city franchise.

Best took none of the three options within the 60-day period. Thus, in early May 2000, the City issued notices of violation for illegal maintenance of such phones and began removing petitioner's phones from city property. On May 10, 2000, petitioner executed and delivered the Franchise Agreement to DOITT. On June 19, 2000, the City notified petitioner that it was unlawfully maintaining public telephones on city property.

On July 11, 2000, Best filed this article 78 petition seeking to compel DOITT to accept the executed Franchise Agreement, compel DOITT to allow it to sell its assets to another entity and, if necessary, to compel DOITT to allow petitioner to reapply for a franchise. Petitioner alleged that DOITT selectively imposed unlawful and discriminatory procedures and arbitrary deadlines on it, which resulted in the denial of a franchise. DOITT sought an order dismissing the petition pursuant to CPLR 217 and 306-b on the grounds that all but one of Best's claims were barred by the statute of limitations and that service of process was untimely as to all claims.

Supreme Court dismissed the petition on the ground of improper service. Although stating that it need not even reach the statute of limitations issue, the court found petitioner's claims barred by the four-month statute of limitations, reasoning that petitioner's claims accrued at the latest on January 13, 2000.[*] The Appellate Division affirmed on the statute of limitations ground alone, agreeing that the agency determination became final and binding on January 13, and the petition was therefore untimely. We agree.

---

[*] The City did not challenge, as time-barred, petitioner's claim that the City improperly removed its payphones in May 2000. The trial court, however, correctly found that claim untenable based on the lack of timeliness of the other claims.

An article 78 proceeding must be brought "within four months after the determination to be reviewed becomes final and binding upon the petitioner" (CPLR 217[1]). A strong public policy underlies the abbreviated statutory time frame: the operation of government agencies should not be unnecessarily clouded by potential litigation (*see Solnick v Whalen*, 49 NY2d 224, 232 [1980]).

This Court has identified two requirements for fixing the time when agency action is "final and binding upon the petitioner." First, the agency must have reached a definitive position on the issue that inflicts actual, concrete injury and second, the injury inflicted may not be prevented or significantly ameliorated by further administrative action or by steps available to the complaining party (*see e.g. Stop-The-Barge v Cahill*, 1 N.Y.3d 218, 223 [2003]; *Matter of Essex County v Zagata*, 91 NY2d 447, 453 [1998]; *see also Church of St. Paul & St. Andrew v Barwick*, 67 NY2d 510, 519, 521 [1986], *cert denied* 479 US 985 [1986] [ripeness for review]).

In *Essex*, for example, we found agency action final when petitioner was notified that it was required to file a new application for its landfill proposal with the Adirondack Park Agency (APA) (91 NY2d at 451). At that point, the agency "left no doubt that there would be no further administrative action and that the expenditure of additional litigation expense and effort before the APA would do nothing to change the agency's position or alleviate appellants' injury" (*id.* at 454). Here, similarly, DOITT's January 13, 2000 letter left no doubt that the agency had reached a definitive position regarding petitioner's payphones that inflicted actual, concrete injury on Best. DOITT notified petitioner that it had to execute the agreement as proposed, sell the business to an approved entity or remove the phones. The 60-day grace period offered petitioner no opportunity to ameliorate the injury, or to avoid it, except by agreeing to the agency's demands. The January 13 letter held out no hope of further administrative action, or change in the agency's position, but left petitioner only with the choice of accepting DOITT's position or initiating suit. Thus, DOITT's action was final and binding upon petitioner on January 13, and its article 78 petition filed in July was untimely.

Accordingly, the order of the Appellate Division should be affirmed, with costs.

NOTES

(1) Despite the wording in the petition in the principal case which sought to "compel" DOITT to accept the Franchise Agreement, what was really involved was a review pursuant to CPLR 7803(4) of DOITT's January 13th notification letter. If a proceeding is brought under CPLR 7803(1) to compel an official to perform a non-discretionary duty, there is no decision after hearing to be reviewed and thus no "final and binding decision" that would constitute the accrual date. Instead, the claim accrues "after the respondent's refusal, upon the

demand of the petitioner or the person whom he represents, to perform its duty." CPLR 217(1). This rule was determinative in *Matter of Bottom v. New York State Department of Correctional Services*, 96 N.Y.2d 870, 730 N.Y.S.2d 767, 756 N.E.2d 55 (2001), in which the petitioner-prisoner sought an order compelling the respondent to recalculate his "jail time credit" so as to accelerate his release date. The respondent's original calculation had been made in 1977 when petitioner began serving his sentence. In December, 1998, petitioner asked for a recalculation that would take into account time served awaiting trial in 1975-76. The respondent failed to reply to the request, and, in February, 1999, the petitioner commenced the proceeding. Rejecting a challenge to its timeliness, the Court held that since mandamus to compel was the proper procedural vehicle (because the respondent's duty was non-discretionary), the four-month limitation period of CPLR 217 ran from the respondent's refusal to recalculate. The Court did not have to deal with the issue of when respondent's failure to reply to the letter would amount to a "refusal" for the purposes of CPLR 217(1) because the petitioner brought the proceeding within four months of his own demand. What should be the rule in such situations?

In *Matter of Heck v. Keane*, 6 A.D.3d 95, 774 N.Y.S.2d 214 (4th Dep't 2004), the City terminated petitioner's disability benefits. Petitioner brought an Article 78 proceeding seeking reinstatement of the benefits more than four months after the City's letter of termination, but within four months of the City's refusal to comply with her demand for reinstatement or for a hearing in the matter. If this were mandamus to review, the proceeding would be late as measured from the date of the City's letter of termination. But it was held that this was a proceeding to compel and was timely as measured from the date of the City's refusal to afford a hearing to which petitioner was entitled.

(2) Since the limitations period applicable to article 78 proceedings is so short, there is more than occasional litigation over whether article 78 is the correct procedural vehicle. See the discussion in *New York City Health and Hospitals Corp. v. McBarnette, supra*, § 24.02. See also *Walton v. New York State Department of Correctional Services*, ___ N.Y.3d ___, ___ N.Y.S. 2d ___, ___ N.E.2d ___ (Feb. 2007), where prison inmates challenged an agreement which allowed the imposition of allegedly excessive charges for collect telephone calls from prison. This was not a declaratory judgment action calling for the six-year period under CPLR 213(1), since the proceeding was in the nature of mandamus to review the decision by the Correction Department approving such charges by the telephone company and thus was governed by CPLR 217. Even under this interpretation, the proceeding was timely. The four month period was found to have started running at the point the Public Service Commission approved the rates, after which the rates could no longer have been affected by the Department's action.

Chapter 25
ARBITRATION: AN ALTERNATIVE TO LITIGATION

§ 25.01 INTRODUCTORY NOTE

A trial in a court of record is one way of resolving disputes. It is neither cheap nor speedy and society has long sought for alternative ways to resolve disputes that do not really require full blown trials. Arbitration and administrative adjudication are familiar mechanisms . . . other alternatives include mediation, conciliation, fact-finding and negotiation.

A.B.A., Report of Pound Conference Follow-Up Task Force 9 (1976).[*]

This Chapter deals primarily with arbitration, which is but one of several alternatives to litigation. Note that the broad issues raised by the arbitration materials must be confronted whenever the use of any of the alternatives is considered: To what extent should the state permit, encourage or require alternate modes of dispute resolution? Should agreements to use them be enforced? If so, under what circumstances? Should the participating parties be bound by the results reached if the loser seeks to challenge it in litigation? Should these alternatives be regulated to insure minimal standards of fairness and accuracy, or are these matters not the state's concern?

Arbitration is distinguished from litigation principally in that the decision maker is not a judge (and need not even be an attorney). Further, the arbitrator need not apply the substantive legal rules which would govern a court, "submissions are for determinations based on the ad hoc application of broad principles of justice and fairness in the particular instance. . . . Predictability is not an objective and awards do not have, nor is it intended that they should have, the precedential value that we attach to judicial determinations." *SCM Corp. v. Fisher Park Lane Co.*, 40 N.Y.2d 788, 793, 390 N.Y.S.2d 398, 403, 358 N.E.2d 1024 (1976).

Arbitration is also distinguished by its reduced emphasis on procedural niceties. There are no formal pleadings, and, ordinarily, no discovery, no motion practice and no application of the rules of evidence at the hearing. The minimal standards which must be met are set forth in CPLR 7506. These are, basically, that the arbitrator be sworn to decide the controversy fairly and that the par-

---

[*] Excerpted from the American Bar Association Report of Pound Conference Follow-Up Task Force, copyright © 1976 by the American Bar Association. All rights reserved. Reprinted with permission.

ties have notice, an opportunity to present evidence, cross-examine witnesses and be represented by an attorney. *See generally* Jones, *Arbitration from the Viewpoint of the Practicing Attorney: An Analysis of Arbitration Cases Decided by the New York State Court of Appeals from January, 1973 to September, 1985,* 14 Fordham Urb. L.J. 523 (1986).

Arbitration will be compelled when the parties have made a "written agreement" to submit to it. CPLR 7501. Such agreements are quite common between commercial parties in some industries.

In a few situations, arbitration is compulsory even in the absence of agreement. Most notable is the rule applicable in some courts of inferior jurisdiction that claims for money only not exceeding six thousand dollars (ten thousand dollars in the New York City Civil Court) must be arbitrated, subject to the right of the parties to demand a jury trial de novo after the arbitrator has made an award. *See* CPLR 3405; 22 NYCRR § 28. The issues raised by compulsory arbitration statutes which do not provide for de novo review are treated in § 25.06.

A special article of the CPLR, article 75-A, governs the procedure for "health care arbitrations." It applies when the parties have agreed to arbitrate claims for damages arising from health care or treatment. CPLR 7551. *See generally* O. Chase, CPLR Manual § 31.01-b at 31-37 (Rev. ed 2006).

Article 75 of the CPLR is the principal source of state law governing arbitration in New York, but the reader should be alert to the increasing federalization of arbitration law. In a series of decisions applying the Federal Arbitration Act (9 U.S.C. § 1 et seq.), the Supreme Court of the United States has held various state limitations on arbitration agreements to be unenforceable. This is because the federal law, which is supreme, applies to any contract "evidencing a contract involving interstate commerce," 9 U.S.C. § 2, and makes arbitration agreements in such contracts enforceable. The issue is discussed in § 25.05, *infra*.

§ 25.02 THE ARBITRATION AGREEMENT

PROBLEM A

When the law firm of Able & Willing decided to move from the Wall Street area to the newly trendy Times Square area, it hired Six Sisters, Inc., to handle the move. After reaching agreement on the phone as to the price and date, Able & Willing sent Six Sisters a part payment and a contract. The contract provided that Six Sisters, Inc., would perform the move for the stated fee ($80,000). The contract also contained this clause:

Arbitration

Any dispute between the parties relating to the performance of this contract shall be subject to arbitration in accordance with the rules of the American Arbitration Association. The arbitrator shall be selected by Able & Willing from among any present or former officers of the New York County Lawyer's Association.

Six Sisters did not sign the contract, but it deposited the check. A few days later, Able & Willing notified Six Sisters they had decided not to move and demanded the return of the deposit. The movers refused, however, and instead commenced an action for the contract price and punitive damages. The defendant law firm timely moved to stay the action on the ground that arbitration was the exclusive remedy under the contract.

Should the plaintiffs oppose the motion? If they do, should the motion be granted?

GOD'S BATTALION OF PRAYER PENTECOSTAL CHURCH, INC. v. MIELE ASSOCIATES, LLP
Court of Appeals
6 N.Y.3d 371, 812 N.Y.S.2d 435, 845 N.E.2d 1265 (2006)

ROSENBLATT, J.

On this appeal, we reiterate our long-standing rule that an arbitration clause in a written agreement is enforceable, even if the agreement is not signed, when it is evident that the parties intended to be bound by the contract. We conclude that the lower courts properly directed the matter to arbitration.

Plaintiff-appellant God's Battalion of Prayer Pentecostal Church, Inc. operates a church and school on Linden Boulevard in Brooklyn. In May 1995, the Church hired defendant Miele Associates, LLP, a firm of architects, to expand and renovate the Church's facilities. Miele prepared an agreement between the parties, dated May 1995 (on a "Standard Form of Agreement Between Owner and Architect" published by the American Institute of Architects), and forwarded it to the Church, which retained it, unsigned. The agreement contained an arbitration clause providing that "[a]ll claims, disputes and other matters in question arising out of, or relating to, this Agreement or the breach thereof shall be decided by arbitration."

In its complaint, the Church alleges that at Miele's behest it hired Ropal Construction Corp. as general contractor. When Ropal did not perform to the Church's satisfaction, it sued Miele in Supreme Court, asserting breach of contract and architectural malpractice. The contract on which the Church relies contains the very arbitration clause at issue.* Indeed, the Church's complaint

---

* The record contains two written agreements pertaining to the work: the unsigned agreement between the Church and Miele, dated May 1995, and a signed agreement, between the Church and Ropal, dated August 29, 1996. Miele was not a party to the latter agreement. The Court therefore takes the Church's complaint to rest on the May 1995 agreement, insofar as it asserts that *Miele* "failed to perform the terms, covenants and conditions of the agreement" and on the August 29, 1996 agreement insofar as it asserts that *Ropal* "failed to comply with the terms, covenants and condi-

expressly claims that Miele "failed to perform the terms, covenants and conditions of the agreement."

Miele moved for an order permanently staying the action and compelling the parties to proceed to arbitration. The Church countered that neither party executed the agreement and that there had been no meeting of minds regarding arbitration. Supreme Court, upon reargument, directed the matter to arbitration. The Appellate Division affirmed, as do we.

Although CPLR 7501 confers jurisdiction on courts to enforce written arbitration agreements, "[t]here is no requirement that the writing be signed so long as there is other proof that the parties actually agreed on it" (*Crawford v. Merrill Lynch, Pierce, Fenner & Smith,* 35 N.Y.2d 291, 299, 361 N.Y.S.2d 140, 319 N.E.2d 408 [1974] [internal quotation marks deleted]; *see also Flores v. Lower E. Side Serv. Ctr., Inc.,* 4 N.Y.3d 363, 370, 795 N.Y.S.2d 491, 828 N.E.2d 593 [2005]). A party to an agreement may not be compelled to arbitrate its dispute with another unless the evidence establishes the parties' "clear, explicit and unequivocal" agreement to arbitrate (*Matter of Waldron [Goddess],* 61 N.Y.2d 181, 183, 473 N.Y.S.2d 136, 461 N.E.2d 273 [1984]), but our case law makes it clear that a signature is not required.

Although the Church did not sign the Miele agreement, it is evident that it intended to be bound by it. The Church has not successfully refuted Miele's claim that, after Miele forwarded the contract, both parties operated under its terms. Most tellingly, the Church's complaint alleges that Miele breached their agreement, thereby acknowledging and relying on the very agreement that contains the arbitration clause it seeks to disclaim. Moreover, the Church does not assert that the arbitration clause would be unenforceable even if the agreement were signed. That being so, it may not pick and choose which provisions suit its purposes, disclaiming part of a contract while alleging breach of the rest. A contract "should be read to give effect to all its provisions" (*Mastrobuono v. Shearson Lehman Hutton, Inc.,* 514 U.S. 52, 63, 115 S.Ct. 1212, 131 L.Ed.2d 76 [1995]; *see also Muzak Corp. v. Hotel Taft Corp.,* 1 N.Y.2d 42, 46, 150 N.Y.S.2d 171, 133 N.E.2d 688 [1956]). The lower courts therefore correctly ruled that the case go to arbitration.

We have considered appellant's remaining contentions and find them without merit. Accordingly, the order of the Appellate Division should be affirmed, with costs.

CHIEF JUDGE KAYE and JUDGES G.B. SMITH, CIPARICK, GRAFFEO, READ and R.S. SMITH concur.

Order affirmed, with costs.

---

tions of its agreement." While the Church now argues that there was a controlling parallel oral agreement, the lower courts correctly concluded that the parties intended to be bound by the terms of the written contracts.

NOTES

(1) In *Schubtex, Inc. v. Allen Snyder, Inc.*, 49 N.Y.2d 1, 424 N.Y.S.2d 133, 399 N.E.2d 1154 (1979), the court found no agreement to arbitrate where textile orders were taken orally. There were followup confirmation forms on the back of which were boilerplate arbitration agreements. The lower courts found that the agreement was essentially oral, but because the parties had engaged in previous agreements (oral, followed by confirmation writings containing the arbitration agreements) the agreement to arbitrate could be inferred. The Court of Appeals disagreed, stating that while prior dealings can be relevant, the repeated use of the same "ineffective" form could not be determinative that the parties here expressly agreed to arbitrate.

(2) In *Marlene Industries Corp. v. Carnac*, 45 N.Y.2d 327, 408 N.Y.S.2d 410, 380 N.E.2d 239 (1980), the court found no agreement to arbitrate, stating:

> It has long been the rule in this State that the parties to a commercial transaction "will not be held to have chosen arbitration as the forum for the resolution of their disputes in the absence of an express, unequivocal agreement to that effect; absent such an explicit commitment neither party may be compelled to arbitrate. . . ." The reason for this requirement, quite simply, is that by agreeing to arbitrate a party waives in large part many of his normal rights under the procedural and substantive law of the State, and it would be unfair to infer such a significant waiver on the basis of anything less than a clear indication of intent. . . .

Id., 45 N.Y.2d at 332-34, 408 N.Y.S.2d at 412-13 (footnotes omitted).

(3) *Marlene Industries* was distinguished in *Ernest J. Michel & Co. v. Anabasis Trade, Inc.*, 50 N.Y.2d 951, 431 N.Y.S.2d 459, 409 N.E.2d 933 (1980). The parties had entered into a series of oral purchase agreements which were confirmed by written forms. The buyer signed and returned one of the seven forms, each of which contained a clause requiring arbitration, but did not sign any others. The Court of Appeals upheld a decision that the buyer could be compelled to arbitrate disputes arising out of any of the agreements:

> An agreement to arbitrate was manifested by . . . signing the first confirmation of order form with admitted knowledge that an arbitration clause was contained therein and, thereafter, by receiving and retaining six additional confirmations of orders on the same contract form without objection except for a request for one change as to credit terms, which change was made by the respondent seller.

Id., 50 N.Y.2d 952, 431 N.Y.S.2d 460.

(4) When a dispute involves a transaction in interstate commerce, the Federal Arbitration Act will apply and will displace the CPLR to the extent it differs. *See* § 25.05, *infra*. It has been held that the rule of *Marlene Industries* requiring "an

express, unequivocal agreement" to arbitrate does not apply to cases covered by the FAA, as the latter requires only the same level of agreement needed under the ordinary law of contracts. *Aceros Prefabricados, S.A. v. TradeArbed, Inc.*, 282 F.3d 92 (2d Cir. 2002) (rejecting *Marlene Industries* and compelling arbitration).

MATARASSO v. CONTINENTAL CASUALTY CO.
Court of Appeals
56 N.Y.2d 264, 451 N.Y.S.2d 703, 436 N.E.2d 1305 (1982)

GABRIELLI, J.

The question presented on this appeal is whether a motion to stay arbitration may ever properly be entertained outside the 20-day period specified in CPLR 7503 (subd [c]). We hold today that such a motion may be entertained when, as here, its basis is that the parties never agreed to arbitrate, as distinct from situations in which there is an arbitration agreement which is nevertheless claimed to be invalid or unenforceable because its conditions have not been complied with.

Claimants were injured in an automobile accident involving an uninsured motor vehicle. They recovered the maximum benefits allowable under the uninsured motorist indorsement contained in their primary automobile liability insurance policy. Claimants then sought to recover their excess damages under a "Commercial Umbrella Liability Policy" issued by respondent. This policy provides coverage to Daniel Matarasso (one of the claimants) and A. Matarasso & Co., Inc., for general liability, automobile liability and employer liability over and above the limits of similar coverage contained in several underlying policies issued by other insurers. One such underlying policy is the automobile liability policy under which claimants had already recovered uninsured motorist benefits.

A demand for arbitration was served upon the respondent insurer on August 21, 1980, asserting a claim for uninsured motorist damages under the umbrella policy. Approximately two months later, respondent moved to stay arbitration on the ground that it was not a party to any agreement providing uninsured motorist protection or requiring arbitration of such claims. Claimants asserted, in opposition to the motion, the bar of CPLR 7503 (subd [c]), contending that respondent's failure to move for a stay of arbitration within the 20-day period set forth in the statute precluded the granting of a stay.

Special Term granted respondent's motion to stay arbitration. The Appellate Division unanimously affirmed (82 A.D.2d 861). We granted claimants' application for leave to appeal to this court, and we now affirm.

CPLR 7503 (subd [c]) provides that a party upon whom a proper notice of intention to arbitrate has been served must apply to stay arbitration within 20 days of service of the notice. If a party fails to make a timely application, "he shall thereafter be precluded from objecting that a valid agreement was not made or has not been complied with." It is undisputed that, in the present case, respondent was served with a proper notice of intention to arbitrate, but failed to move to stay arbitration until approximately 60 days had passed. Claimants argue that the failure to make the motion within the statutory 20-day period absolutely bars respondent from obtaining a stay. We disagree and hold that where the application for a stay is made on the ground that no agreement to arbitrate exists, it may be entertained notwithstanding the fact that the stay was sought after the 20-day period had elapsed.

Generally, where the parties have entered into an agreement to arbitrate their disputes, and the party desiring arbitration has served a proper notice of intention to arbitrate, the party seeking to avoid arbitration on the ground that the agreement is invalid or has not been complied with, must, under the statute's clear language, seek a stay of arbitration within 20 days of service. The courts have no discretion to extend this time period to permit consideration of an untimely application (*Aetna Life & Cas. Co. v. Stekardis*, 34 N.Y.2d 182). However, this rule barring judicial intrusion into the arbitral process operates only when an agreement to arbitrate exists. Support for this view can be found in the wording of the statute itself. CPLR 7503 (subd [c]) speaks in terms of "parties" (e.g., "A *party* may serve upon another *party*" [emphasis supplied]), the natural connotation being that the statute is directed toward parties to an agreement to arbitrate (*Glasser v. Price*, 35 A.D.2d 98). Given the ease with which a broader class of persons could have been included within the statute's ambit, we cannot impute to the Legislature an intent to bind persons to the arbitral process by their mere inaction for 20 days where no agreement to arbitrate has ever been made.

Thus, if there is no agreement to arbitrate between claimants and respondent, the motion to stay arbitration was properly granted. In this connection, we note that the umbrella policy itself contains no provision for arbitration of disputes. Further, the incorporation of the underlying automobile liability policy did not extend to the provisions for uninsured motorist coverage (and arbitration of claims arising thereunder), as the umbrella policy covers only liability of the insureds for damages owing third parties.

Claimants argue, however, that the uninsured motorist indorsement is included in the policy by virtue of subdivision 2-a of section 167 of the Insurance Law. That statute applies to any automobile liability policy issued upon a motor vehicle principally garaged or used in this State, and requires the inclusion of uninsured motorist coverage in every such policy. The umbrella policy involved herein, however, is not an automobile liability policy; rather, it is an excess liability policy providing additional coverage for claims arising under three separate policies of varying types of insurance. Therefore, the mandatory uninsured motorist indorsement of section 167 has no application to this policy.

As claimants have failed to establish that any agreement to arbitrate has been entered into by themselves and respondent, the motion for a stay of arbitration was properly granted.

NOTES

(1) The *Matarasso* holding should be narrowly construed as evidenced by the later decision in *Matter of State Farm Insurance Co.* (*Steck*), 89 N.Y.2d 1082, 643 N.Y.S.2d 961, 681 N.E.2d 1285 (1996), where the Court rejected an argument that a post-20-day petition for a stay of arbitration ought to be entertained. The issue was not whether there was an agreement to arbitrate, but whether certain conditions of the contract had been complied with — a question for the arbitrator. A generalization that can be drawn is that if there is or was an arbitration provision in the governing document, the question as to its coverage, or even whether it lapsed, is for the arbitrator, and the *Matarasso* rule will not apply.

(2) The party desiring arbitration need not serve the demand or notice but may simply "apply for an order compelling arbitration." CPLR 7503(a). This is the preferable course when an opponent has commenced litigation in violation of an agreement to arbitrate. The application is then by way of motion in the court in which the action is pending, which will entertain any threshold objections. If the application is granted, the court will also stay the action until the arbitration is resolved. CPLR 7503(a).

If arbitration is ordered but the objecting party fails to appear, the arbitrator may proceed to hear and determine the controversy. CPLR 7506(c).

(3) Where A served a notice to arbitrate under CPLR 7503(c) and B brought a proceeding to stay the arbitration which was dismissed, it was held that B must file and pay for a new index number for a new proceeding at the end of the arbitration process if he desired court review of an adverse decision under CPLR 7511. The court did not retain jurisdiction after the initial proceeding was dismissed. *Matter of Solkav v. Besicorp Group, Inc.*, 91 N.Y.2d 482, 672 N.Y.S.2d 838, 695 N.E.2d 707 (1998). The Legislature was invited to amend CPLR 7502(a) were it preferred that all court applications in the arbitration process be treated in one comprehensive proceeding. Such an amendment became effective in 2000 (*see* CPLR 7502(a)(iii)), thus nullifying the *Solkav* holding.

WEINROTT v. CARP
Court of Appeals
32 N.Y.2d 190, 344 N.Y.S.2d 848, 298 N.E.2d 42 (1973)

WACHTLER, J.

This is the second time this case has been before this court in a long and tortuous journey which started over five years ago. It first appeared in 1967, when appellants sought to stay arbitration proceedings on the ground that the contract containing the arbitration clause was induced by fraud. In affirming the denial of a stay we impliedly adhered to the 1957 decision of *Matter of Wrap-Vertiser Corp. (Plotnick)* (3 N Y 2d 17) which held that fraud in the inducement of a contract was an issue for the court and not the arbitrators. The reason for our denial of the stay was that the evidence did not raise a substantial question of fact as to the existence of such fraud (*Matter of Carp* [*Weinrott*], 20 N Y 2d 934).

Following our decision, the parties proceeded to arbitration. Protracted hearings resulted in an award directing appellants to pay respondents $30,713.47, and that award has been upheld by both the Supreme Court and the Appellate Division. On this appeal we have decided to consider, among other things, whether our determination in *Matter of Wrap-Vertiser Corp. (Plotnick)* (3 N Y 2d 17, *supra*) has retained its vitality in the light of subsequent experience and contemporary attitudes concerning the role of arbitration in the settlement of commercial disputes and to decide whether in the future, fraud in the inducement of a contract containing a broad arbitration clause should be an issue for the arbitrators.

The substantive disagreement in this case arises from a licensing and joint-venture agreement pursuant to which the appellants were licensed to use a process developed for the construction of single- and double-story buildings. . . . Assertions of fraud in the inducement consist of alleged misrepresentations regarding the capabilities of the process, respondents' experience in using it, its approval by governmental agencies, ownership of the process, and its actual use in the construction of model homes.

. . . .

We turn now to review the decision which gave birth to this protracted litigation (*Matter of Wrap-Vertiser Corp.* [*Plotnick*], 3 N Y 2d 17, *supra*). Read strictly, *Wrap-Vertiser* concerned itself solely with the contractual language employed by the parties in an arbitration provision, giving that language a narrow interpretation. Some courts have interpreted it accordingly. . . . Read broadly, however, *Wrap-Vertiser* asserts the legal proposition that fraud in the inducement, coupled with a claim for rescission, is always a matter for judicial determination prior to arbitration. Either reading, we now believe, frustrates rather than promotes both the intention of the parties and the salutary function of arbitration agreements.

There is no doubt that parties can contract to submit the issue of fraud in the inducement to arbitration. . . . The problem lies in discerning exactly what issues the parties have committed to the jurisdiction of the arbitrators. Courts construing differently worded but nonetheless similarly broad arbitration agreements have come to different conclusions as to whether the parties intended to submit the issue of fraud in the inducement to the arbitrators. . . .

. . . In the case now before us the arbitration clause reads: "All disputes, controversies or claims arising hereunder, the interpretation of any of the provisions or the performance called for thereunder shall be settled by arbitration in New York, in accordance with the rules then obtaining of the American Arbitration Association and any decision arising therefrom may be entered as a judgment in any court of competent jurisdiction."

This provision is clearly a "broad" provision, and whether or not it will be given effect depends more on policy than on the wording of the provision itself.

In the case of *Atcas v. Credit Clearing Corp. of Amer.* (292 Minn. 334, 338, *supra*), the Supreme Court of Minnesota held that fraud in the inducement was to be decided by the courts under an arbitration provision which mandated that "Any controversy whatsoever relating to this Agreement shall be settled by arbitration." The court stated that "the contract contains no reference to fraud in the inducement or how that issue should be resolved if it is raised" (*id.*, at p. 341) and, therefore, since it was not a specified issue, it could not be submitted to arbitration. Such a demand for specificity as to which particular issues should be submitted to the arbitrators would make the drafting of arbitration agreements burdensome, confusing and often impossible.

The alternative to making parties specifically name fraud in the inducement as an issue they wish to go to arbitration would be to give full effect to a broad arbitration clause. A broad arbitration agreement reflects a general desire by the parties to have all issues decided speedily and finally by the arbitrators. If, in the case at bar, we hold that the arbitration agreement did not contemplate the submission of fraud in the inducement to the arbitrators we would be opting for the "specifically enumerated" approach since it is difficult to construct any generic wording which would have a broader sweep than the provision used in this case.

The theoretical underpinning of the *Wrap-Vertiser* approach can be found in the assertion that one fraud is fraud to all. There is a long line of New York cases holding that an arbitration agreement was generally not separable from the principal contract . . . and, therefore, if the substantive provisions of the contract were to fall, the entire contract including an arbitration clause would also fall.

The *Wrap-Vertiser* case continued the nonseparability approach. It was the first case where this court directly confronted the separability issue as applied to fraud in the inducement and it did so by dictum which asserted that the nonseparability doctrine applies to fraud in the inducement. "If he were seeking rescission, none of the items in his arbitration demand could be arbitrated until the issue of rescission had been determined in the courts." (3 N Y 2d 17, 19, *supra*.)

A contrary view was taken by the seminal case of *Lawrence Co. v. Devonshire Fabrics* (271 F.2d 402 [2d Cir.], *supra*), which held that an arbitration clause is separable from the balance of the contract. . . . The cases holding that the arbitration clause is separable assert that the fraud must go to the arbitration provision itself in order to avoid submission to arbitration. . . . Of course, if the alleged fraud was part of a grand scheme that permeated the entire contract, including the arbitration provision, the arbitration provision should fall with the rest of the contract. (*See Mosley v. Electronics Facilities*, 374 U. S. 167; *Housekeeper v. Lourie*, 39 A D 2d 280, *supra*.)

The technical argument about separability or nonseparability has often obscured the main goal of the court's inquiry which is to discern the parties' intent. (*See generally*, 43 St. John's L. Rev. 1.) When the parties to a contract have reposed in arbitrators all questions concerning the "validity, interpretation or enforcement" of their agreement, they have selected their tribunal and no doubt they intend it to determine the contract's "validity" should the necessity arise. Judicial intervention, based upon a nonseparability contract theory in arbitration matters prolongs litigation, and defeats, as this case conclusively demonstrates, two of arbitration's primary virtues, speed and finality. . . .

There is nothing in our statutory law which prohibits our conclusion. CPLR 7503 (subd. [a]) states: "A party aggrieved by the failure of another to arbitrate may apply for an order compelling arbitration. When there is no substantial question whether a *valid agreement* was made or complied with . . . the court shall direct the parties to arbitrate." (emphasis added).

The "valid agreement" referred to concerns a valid agreement to arbitrate. . . . Since we now hold that an arbitration provision of a contract is separable, the agreement to arbitrate would be "valid" even if the substantive portions of the contract were induced by fraud.

The result we suggest in this case is consistent with the policy adopted by the Federal courts, and is significant since the Federal arbitration statute is almost identical to, and is derived from, our own arbitration statute. (*See Prima Paint v. Flood & Conklin*, 388 U.S. 395, *supra*; *Lawrence Co. v. Devonshire Fabrics*, 271 F.2d 402 [2d Cir.], *supra*.)

The policy arguments for overruling the *Wrap-Vertiser* approach to fraud in the inducement are as compelling as the legal arguments.

The case at bar demonstrates the problem inherent in allowing parties to claim that fraud in the inducement, even under a broad arbitration clause, should be an issue triable by the courts. As often happens in this type of case, appellants moved to stay the arbitration on the ground that there was fraud in the inducement of the contract. Although appellants' contention was "not supported by the record and is refuted by documentary evidence" (*Matter of Carp* [*Weinrott*], 28 A D 2d 671-672), the arbitration continued to be stayed while that preliminary issue laboriously worked its way through the New York court system. Finally, after the issue fell exhausted at the Court of Appeals, the arbitration hearings commenced.

The CPLR arbitration provisions (CPLR 7501 *et seq.*) evidence a legislative intent to encourage arbitration. Certainly the avoidance of court litigation to save the time and resources of both the courts and the parties involved make this a worthwhile goal. One way to encourage the use of the arbitration forum would be to prevent parties to such agreements from using the courts as a vehicle to protract litigation. This conduct has the effect of frustrating both the initial intent of the parties as well as legislative policy. In the case at bar, there were 21 hearings and 2,750 pages of testimony. If not for the arbitration, that entire burden would have been placed on our court system. Indeed, had the case been tried in the formality of the courtroom, it would have taken longer to dispose of than it did before the arbitrators. A broad arbitration clause should be given the full effect of its wording in order to implement the intention of the parties. Of course, where a form contract is involved or an arbitration provision seems to be less than broad, a court should give the provision and the circumstances surrounding its inclusion in the contract great scrutiny. As a general rule, however, under a broad arbitration provision the claim of fraud in the inducement should be determined by arbitrators.[2]

In this case it is unnecessary to order arbitration of the fraud issue. Appellants had a full chance to present that issue to the courts. There is no need to give appellants another bite of an apple that has already been chewed to the core. . . .

NOTES

(1) Is the principal case reconcilable with the spirit of *Schubtex v. Allen Snyder, Inc.*, and *Marlene Industries v. Carnac* (discussed in the notes following *God's Battallion of Prayer Pentecostal Church, supra*)? Recall that those cases preserved a party's right to use the judicial process absent an express, unequivocal commitment. A rule of thumb is that the courts may be careful about finding an agreement to arbitrate, but that once they do, they tend to allow the arbitrators to decide the entire dispute.

It has been held that in order to preserve an issue for judicial determination, the arbitration clause of the agreement must specifically enumerate the matters which are beyond the arbitrator's reach. *Silverman v. Benmor Coats*, 61 N.Y.2d 299, 473 N.Y.S.2d 774, 461 N.E.2d 1261 (1984). See, for example, *Schlaifer v. Sedlow*, 51 N.Y.2d 181, 433 N.Y.S.2d 67, 412 N.E.2d 1294 (1980), which arose from a dispute among the parties to an employment contract which included an arbitration clause. Upon receiving a $5,000 severance payment, the employee executed a general release to the corporation from all claims against it. Thereafter he sought additional compensation and, when the corporation demurred, demanded arbitration under the contract. Upholding his right to arbitration, the court indicated that it was for the arbitrator to determine the effect of the release. Only an express cancellation of a contract containing a

---

[2] An additional, and desirable, result of this decision is to bring New York State law in accord with Federal law relating to fraud in the inducement.

broad arbitration clause, not a mere release, would be effective in eliminating a pre-existing obligation to arbitrate, said the court.

In *Matter of Meisels v. Uhr*, 79 N.Y.2d 526, 583 N.Y.S.2d 951, 593 N.E.2d 1359 (1992), the Court reversed a holding that a real property dispute was not arbitrable because part of the arbitration award was equitable, a power said by the lower courts not to have been in the agreements. The Court of Appeals held the award sustainable since the agreements generally covered real property and thus, "whether or not the panel was specifically granted [equitable] authority, the arbitration agreements were broad enough to encompass disputes concerning title to the properties. . . ." It was added that it was never required that arbitration agreements specifically identify areas of possible dispute.

Where the question is whether by its own terms a contract has terminated, that question is for the arbitrator despite the argument that the arbitration clause within the contract would also have expired. *Schenkers International Forwarders, Inc. v. Meyer*, 164 A.D.2d 541, 564 N.Y.S.2d 323 (1991). On the other hand, where the termination of the contract is beyond dispute, the arbitration clause has no effect. *Matter of Waldron (Goddess)*, 61 N.Y.2d 181, 473 N.Y.S.2d 136, 461 N.E.2d 273 (1984). Where, however, the agreement is dissolved but the parties treated it as if it were still in effect, the arbitration clause may be resorted to. *Matter of Van (Kreindler, Relkin & Goldberg)*, 54 N.Y.2d 936, 445 N.Y.S.2d 139, 429 N.E.2d 817 (1981).

(2) Under the principal case, could arbitration be avoided by a party who claimed that the agreement was void in toto? See *Candid Productions, Inc. v. SFM Media Service Corp.*, 51 A.D.2d 943, 381 N.Y.S.2d 280 (1st Dep't 1976), holding that the arbitrator, not the courts, should decide the merits of an argument that the entire contract was void because entered into under economic duress.

Where a former wife brought a proceeding under CPLR 7503 to stay a securities arbitration brought by the former husband seeking damages against the wife, a securities broker, and her employer, the stay was properly granted. The joint brokerage account at the heart of the husband's claim was dealt with in the couple's judgment of divorce. Thus, when a court's judgment is at issue, the effect of that judgment should be left to the court. *Merrill Lynch v. Benjamin*, 1 A.D.2d 39, 766 N.Y.S.2d 1 (1st Dep't 2003). Where an arbitration agreement between an attorney and the New York law firm for which he worked broadly covered any disputes, the firm was entitled to have enjoined the attorney's suit brought in Mexico where the firm had a branch office and where statutes facilitated the claims. The lawyer, although a Mexican native, resided in New York where he was a member of the bar. The firm's New York office was the only office where he worked. The matters in dispute arose in New York and thus there was no reason to circumvent the strong policy favoring agreements to arbitrate. *Curtis v. Garza-Morales*, 308 A.D.2d 261, 762 N.Y.S.2d 607 (1st Dep't 2003).

§ 25.03 THE PROCEEDING

SIEGEL v. LEWIS
Court of Appeals
40 N.Y.2d 687, 389 N.Y.S.2d 800, 358 N.E.2d 484 (1976)

FUCHSBERG, J.

This proceeding was brought by petitioner Murray Siegel to vacate Samuel Kooper's and Eugene Birnbaum's designation as arbitrators in advance of the commencement of an arbitration under a stock purchase agreement. The question is whether the two arbitrators' prior relationships as attorney and accountant, respectively, for respondent Henry Lewis as well as their personal knowledge of facts bearing both on the making of the agreement and on the subsequent dispute between the parties were sufficient to disqualify them at that early juncture. Special Term held that it was and entered judgment accordingly. By a divided court, the Appellate Division affirmed. For the reasons which follow, we believe its order should be reversed.

A resume of the facts will be helpful.

By the terms of the stock purchase agreement, Lewis, then owner of all the stock of Henry Lewis Lamp Shade Corporation, sold one half of his interest to Siegel. The consideration for the sale was $55,000, of which $10,000 was to be paid in cash and the balance at the rate of $1,000 per month. Lewis also retained an option to rescind the sale anytime before final payment by returning to Siegel all moneys paid by him along with an amount equal to one half of any increase in the "net worth" of the corporation.

The agreement named Kooper, who then had been Lewis' and the corporation's lawyer for about 15 years, and Birnbaum, who had served as their accountant for an equally long period, as sole arbitrators. Kooper represented Lewis in the making of the agreement; Birnbaum was named the escrowee. Both were familiar with the negotiations between the principals preceding the sale. Siegel was represented by his own counsel. Kooper and Birnbaum were continued as the corporation's attorney and accountant after Siegel became its half owner.

All these relationships remained unchanged for about three more years. At that time Lewis accused Siegel of having converted funds of the business. In rapid-fire order, there then followed an attempt by Lewis to exercise his option, an attempt by Siegel to extinguish the option by tendering $7,200, the amount of the balance then still due, and a demand for the arbitration of both these claims, which, if the exercise of the option were upheld, would also require the arbitrators to determine the method of arriving at "net worth" and the amount of any increase in it. These events were preceded by a meeting among Lewis, Siegel, Kooper and Birnbaum; it did not succeed in resolving the differences.

With these facts in mind, we note, at the very outset, that commercial arbitration is a creature of contract. Parties, by agreement, may substitute a different method for the adjudication of their disputes than those which would otherwise be available to them in public courts of law. . . . When they do so, they in effect select their own forum. Their quest is usually for a nonjudicial tribunal that will arrive at a private and practical determination with maximum dispatch and at minimum expense. . . . It has long been the policy of the law to interfere as little as possible with the freedom of consenting parties to achieve that objective.

Central to that freedom is the recognized right of the parties, subject to limited exceptions (*e.g.*, NY Const, art VI, § 20, subd b, par [4]; Labor Law, § 702, subd 8), to name those who are to be the arbitrators, or, if the parties prefer not to name them directly, to choose the way in which they are to be selected. In fealty to that principle, we have made clear that " '[t]he spirit of the arbitration law being the fuller effectuation of contractual rights, the method for selecting arbitrators and the composition of the arbitral tribunal have been left to the contract of the parties.' (*Matter of Lipschutz [Gutwirth]*, 304 N Y 58, 61- 62. . . .)" (*Matter of Astoria Med. Group [Health Ins. Plan of Greater N.Y.]*, 11 NY2d 128, 133.)

Significantly, our statutes, which provide specifically for the enforcement of private arbitration agreements and for the vacatur or modification of awards improperly made, are completely silent on any power to disqualify arbitrators in advance of arbitration proceedings (CPLR art 75). It is only when an arbitrator cannot act for reasons of health or unavailability or other circumstances tantamount to the occurrence of a vacancy that there is statutory authorization for a court to appoint a replacement (CPLR 7504).

Arbitrators, though their office is not one established by law, are expected to "faithfully and fairly" hear and decide the respective claims of the parties by whose consent they are chosen (CPLR 7506, subd [a]), but their qualifications are not measured by the standards prescribed for Judges (Sturges, *Arbitration — What Is It?*, 35 NYU L Rev 1030, 1045-1046). The parties' reasons for the selection of particular arbitrators may in fact be the very ones which would have disqualified Judges or jurors. . . . For example, a particular expertise in the general area of factual knowledge involved in the arbitration may be an especially desirable qualification to the parties (8 Weinstein-Korn-Miller, NY Civ Prac, par 7506.18). Also, "[i]f the parties so agree, the relationship of an arbitrator to the party selecting him or to the matters in dispute will not disqualify him" (Eager, Arbitration Contract and Proceedings, § 96, subd 1, p 272; *see, also*, Arbitrators — Disqualification, Ann., 65 ALR2d 755, esp § 5, p 764). Indeed, our court long ago held that parties may be bound by a determination by an arbitrator selected to decide the issues before him on the basis of his knowledge alone. . . .

Therefore, strange as it may seem to those steeped in the proscriptions of legal and judicial ethics, a fully known relationship between an arbitrator and a party, including one as close as employer and employee . . . or attorney and client . . . will not in and of itself disqualify the designee. Of course, if there has been a failure to disclose such an existing or past financial, business, family or social relationship between the arbitrator and a party as is likely to affect the arbitrator's impartiality, the situation would be different. The consensual basis for the choice then would be lacking. However, assent by a party to the choice of an arbitrator in the face of that party's knowledge of a relationship between the other side and the arbitrator is a waiver of his right to object. And, "[s]ince waiver is a matter of intention . . . the touchstone . . . is the knowledge, actual or constructive, in the complaining party of the tainted relationship or interest of the arbitrator" (*Matter of Milliken Woolens* [*Weber Knit Sportswear*], 11 AD2d 166, 168-169, *affd* 9 NY2d 878; *see, also*, Domke, Commercial Arbitration, § 21.04).*

With these principles in mind, we note that the parties here agree that the relationship between each of the arbitrators and Lewis was well known to Siegel when their contract was entered into. Siegel had by then been a managerial employee of the business for a year and a half, having embarked on that employment in preparation for his anticipated acquisition of an ownership interest. He himself stresses the fact that to his own knowledge Kooper was not only Lewis' attorney but the chief draftsman of the stock purchase agreement. Birnbaum, whose familiarity with the corporation's books and net worth were also known to Siegel, was actually named as escrowee.

True it is that Lewis in the course of negotiating the agreement had suggested, and perhaps insisted, on the naming of Kooper and Birnbaum, who had for so long enjoyed his confidence. He also had insisted on retaining the option to repurchase. These he indisputably had a right to do, as he would have had a right to insist, had he desired to do so, that, in the event of the exercise of the option, there be no payment for any increase in net worth but only a return of the cash consideration. Or he could have insisted, as he did not, on a larger purchase price or perhaps a much larger cash payment. On the other hand, Siegel, for his part, could have refused to assent to any or all of these terms; in fact, he could have rejected the arbitration clause altogether.

In short, the agreement, inclusive of the naming of Kooper and Birnbaum was one concededly arrived at freely by both parties. Siegel does not make the slightest claim that its terms were the product of any fraud, duress, overreaching or even grossly unequal bargaining power. As Justice Martuscello cogently observed in his dissenting memorandum below, "In the absence of a real possibility that injustice will result, the courts of this State will not rewrite the contract for the parties (*see Matter of Lipschutz* [*Gutwirth*], 304 NY 58, 64)" (50 AD2d 858, 859). Needless to say, if the arbitrators, in the actual execution of their office, prove to have been unfair or unfaithful to their obligations,

---

* While the adoption of judicial standards for arbitrators is currently receiving important encouragement (*see* Preliminary Exposure Draft, Sept. 1, 1976, Code of Ethics for Arbitrators in Commercial Disputes sponsored by American Arbitration Association and American Bar Association), it is recognized that they remain subject to the volition of the parties.

their award is not impervious to judicial action (CPLR 7506, subd [a]; 7511, subd [b]; *see Matter of American Eagle Ins. Co. v. New Jersey*, 240 NY 398, 405). We therefore conclude that there was no basis for advance disqualification of the arbitrators.

Accordingly, the order appealed from must be reversed and the proceeding dismissed.

CHIEF JUDGE BREITEL (concurring).

I agree that there should be a reversal but prefer not to go beyond the reasons which are necessary to the conclusion. . . .

It is true that CPLR makes no provision for disqualification of arbitrators (CPLR art 75, esp 7503). But I have no doubt that a selection which would be a nullity for whatever reason, as, for example, mental incompetence, identity with a party, or the like, would leave the matter without an agreed arbitrator and the selection, on application, would devolve on the court (CPLR 7504).

Once it is held that the designation of the arbitrators is lawful it is inappropriate to lecture them or hector them on ethical alternatives and options. However diplomatically stated, these fulminations become a menace of a kind, perhaps intentionally, which may deprive the arbitrators of the fortitude and independence which they, like Judges, are supposed to possess. It is enough to say that an award, if rendered, may be set aside for demonstrated partiality, excess of power, or improper conduct (CPLR 7511).

Accordingly, I concur and vote to reverse and dismiss the petition, without costs.

. . . .

NOTE

As the principal case suggests, the courts are disinclined to interfere with agreements as to how the arbitration should be conducted. CPLR 7506 provides only an outline of procedures that must be followed. Even these few requirements may be waived. CPLR 7506(f); *but see* CPLR 7506(d) (no waiver permitted of the right to representation by an attorney).

Parties to an arbitration agreement often wisely chart the procedural course in advance of any dispute by providing in the original agreement that any arbitration shall be conducted in accordance with a stated set of rules, often the Commercial Arbitration Rules of the American Arbitration Association. Given the broad authority enjoyed by an arbitrator, how far should the freedom of contract respected in the principal case be taken? Consider Problem A in this light. Suppose the plaintiffs had not objected to the arbitrator, but only to the list from which one has to be chosen. Should the court invalidate that portion of the agreement and use its power under CPLR 7504 to impose an alternative means of choosing an arbitrator? Or is the court's power to review the results of the arbitration under CPLR 7511(b)(1) sufficient to insure fairness? The principal case suggests, if it does not hold, that a court has no power to disqualify an arbitrator selected by the parties and can take the matter up only on a review of the award. Is this sound public policy?

It has been held that a party who proceeds to arbitration without objecting to the arbitrator when there was reason to do so will have waived the objection. *Milliken Woolens, Inc. v. Weber Knit Sportswear, Inc.*, 11 A.D.2d 166, 202 N.Y.S.2d 431 (1st Dep't 1960), *aff'd*, 9 N.Y.2d 878, 216 N.Y.S.2d 696, 175 N.E.2d 826 (1961). "Actual partiality, however, may not be deemed waived." 11 A.D.2d at 434. *See also J.P. Stevens & Co. v. Rytex Corp.*, 34 N.Y.2d 123, 356 N.Y.S.2d 278, 312 N.E.2d 466 (1974).

In any event, it is quite common when a three person arbitration panel is used that each of the two parties will appoint an arbitrator who will see that their side is represented. Neutrality is neither expected nor required as a condition of service, *Astoria Medical Group v. Health Ins. Plan*, 11 N.Y.2d 128, 227 N.Y.S.2d 401, 182 N.E.2d 85 (1962), but the arbitrator is nonetheless under a competing obligation to act fairly. *See* discussion at note 2 following *Hackett v. Milbank, Tweed, Hadley & McCloy, infra.*

§ 25.04 THE AWARD AND ATTACKS ON IT

PROBLEM B

Suppose that the arbitration contemplated in Problem A was held before a single arbitrator, Jones, who is a partner in the firm of Able and Willing and a former officer of the New York County Lawyers' Association. After hearing the evidence, his decision was that Six Sisters, Inc. should receive no damages and that it is liable for his fee in the amount of $2500, and the arbitration fee of $500. No supporting opinion was written. Will Six Sisters be able to successfully attack the decision under CPLR 7511(b)(1)?

HACKETT v. MILBANK, TWEED, HADLEY & McCLOY
Court of Appeals
86 N.Y.2d 146, 630 N.Y.S.2d 274, 654 N.E.2d 95 (1995)

SIMONS, JUDGE.

[Petitioner left respondent's law firm to become a partner in another law firm. Respondent's Articles of Partnership provide for certain payments to withdrawing partners. The dispute concerned what if any of these payments were due petitioner under the circumstances. The matter was submitted to an arbitrator as required by the partnership agreement. The arbitrator ruled in respondent's favor. Petitioner successfully challenged the arbitrator's determination, the courts below holding that the interpretation of the Articles of Partnership violated public policy in unduly restricting the practice of law.]

. . . .

I

The focus of this litigation is section 15.4 of the 30th Amendment to the Milbank, Tweed Articles of Partnership.

In order to avoid the dissolution and subsequent accounting which would ordinarily follow a partner's departure, many law firms, respondent among them, include in their articles of partnership an agreement under which a withdrawing partner waives his or her right to an accounting in exchange for certain payments specified in the articles.

[Petitioner claimed he was owed $641,339 in "supplemental" payment under section 15.4 of the partnership agreement, an amendment to which reduced the supplemental payment when the withdrawing partner's annual earned income from any source, including earnings from a competing law firm, exceeded $100,000. This was deemed by the arbitrator not to be primarily a noncompetitive provision that might be against public policy, but rather as a safety net to the partner who departs for a less lucrative position. The provision was found not to restrict the practice of law. Rather, it was "competition neutral," because the reduction in supplemental payments was made without regard to the source of the annual earned income.]

In moving to vacate the award, petitioner alleged that the arbitrator's factual findings and conclusions were irrational and that he had exceeded his powers and rendered an award in violation of public policy. Supreme Court rejected the arbitrator's conclusions, and found "contrary to the finding of the arbitrator" that the withdrawal payment "constitute[s] an approximation of the withdrawing partner's share of undistributed earned income," and that section 15.4 is an unenforceable forfeiture and a restriction on the practice of law. [The Appellate Division affirmed.]

II

Preliminarily, we note that the matter before us is governed by New York law. Respondent contends that the partnership agreement comes within the scope of the Commerce Clause, because it applies to partners in the firm's offices located in various States and countries, and that it is accordingly governed by the Federal Arbitration Act (see, Allied-Bruce Terminix Cos. v. Dobson, 513 U.S. 265, 115 S.Ct. 834, 130 L.Ed.2d 753). The overriding policy of the Act, however, is the enforcement of arbitration agreements according to their terms, including the parties' choice of governing law (see Volt Information Sciences v. Leland Stanford Jr. Univ., 489 U.S. 468, 109 S.Ct. 1248, 103 L.Ed.2d 488; Matter of Salvano v. Merrill Lynch, Pierce, Fenner & Smith, 85 N.Y.2d 173, 623 N.Y.S.2d 790, 647 N.E.2d 1298). The parties' agreement here not only provided for binding arbitration of their dispute, it explicitly provided that New York law would govern that arbitration, and that the only grounds for vacating the arbitrator's award are those encompassed by CPLR 7509 and CPLR 7511. Such an explicit and unambiguous choice of law in an arbitration agreement must be given effect (*see, Volt Information Sciences supra; cf., Mastrobuono v. Shearson Lehman Hutton*, 514 U.S. 52, 115 S.Ct. 1212, 131 L.Ed.2d 76).

Under CPLR 7511, an award may be vacated only if (1) the rights of a party were prejudiced by corruption, fraud or misconduct in procuring the award, or by the partiality of the arbitrator; (2) the arbitrator exceeded his or her power or failed to make a final and definite award; or (3) the arbitration suffered from an unwaived procedural defect. Even where the arbitrator makes a mistake of fact or law, or disregards the plain words of the parties' agreement, the award is not subject to vacatur "unless the court concludes that it is totally irrational or violative of a strong public policy" and thus in excess of the arbitrator's powers. . . .

Supreme Court erred in substituting its own characterization of the supplemental payments as "an approximation of the withdrawing partner's share of undistributed earned income" for the contrary finding of the arbitrator. Although the court noted correctly that "mere labels" or a party's statement of contrary intent will not insulate a forfeiture clause from invalidation, an arbitrator's factual or legal determination is an evaluation of the competing labels and claims offered by the parties, and as such is not subject to judicial second-guessing, but only to a review to determine whether the award is on its face prohibited by public policy considerations (*see, Matter of Sprinzen* [*Nomberg*], 46 N.Y.2d 623, 631, 415 N.Y.S.2d 974, 389 N.E.2d 456, *supra; see also, Maross Constr. v. Central N.Y. Regional Transp. Auth.*, 66 N.Y.2d 341, 346, 497 N.Y.S.2d 321, 488 N.E.2d 67, *supra; Matter of Port Wash. Union Free School Dist. v. Port Wash. Teachers Assn.*, 45 N.Y.2d 411, 417, 422, 408 N.Y.S.2d 453, 380 N.E.2d 280). Accordingly, the only question before us is whether the courts below correctly concluded that the arbitrator's award violated public policy.

In *Denburg v. Parker Chapin Flattau & Klimpl*, 82 N.Y.2d 375, 604 N.Y.S.2d 900, 624 N.E.2d 995, we considered the validity of a provision in the Parker Chapin partnership agreement that bears some similarities to respondent's agreement. The Parker Chapin agreement required withdrawing partners to make certain payments to the firm upon demand: if the withdrawing partner practiced law in the private sector prior to July 1988, he or she was to pay the firm either (1) 12.5% of the firm's profits allocated to that partner over the two previous years or (2) 12.5% of any billings to former Parker Chapin clients by the partner's new firm during the ensuing two years, whichever amount was greater. An exception was provided for withdrawing partners whose previous year's profit share was less than $85,000, providing that the partner's new firm did no work for Parker Chapin clients during the two-year period following withdrawal.

Assessing this agreement in the light of *Cohen v. Lord, Day & Lord (supra)*, we concluded that the provision violated the public policy against anticompetition clauses. This was so, we said, because the provision, by its terms, applied only to withdrawing partners who went into private practice, and hence into potential competition with Parker Chapin; it required the payment of the higher of two possible amounts, one of which was "directly proportional to the success of a departing partner's competitive efforts"; and the exemption for a low-paid partner applied only if no Parker Chapin clients were served (82 N.Y.2d at 381, 604 N.Y.S.2d 900, 624 N.E.2d 995). Recognizing Parker Chapin's argument that no noncompetitive effect was intended, we nevertheless determined that the agreement was unenforceable because the effect of the clause was to improperly deter competition.

Unlike the clauses disapproved in *Cohen* and in *Denburg*, the Milbank, Tweed supplemental payment provision is not inevitably anticompetitive on its face. Where the Parker Chapin clause clearly discriminated between partners departing for private practice and those, for example, entering academia or government service, section 15.4 makes no such distinction: the reduction in supplemental payments applies to the withdrawing partner's earned income from any source. Where the Parker Chapin clause exempting lower-paid partners from the agreement was applicable only to those lower-paid partners who did not subsequently do work for former Parker Chapin clients, the Milbank, Tweed $100,000 cutoff applies to all withdrawing partners and no financial disincentive specifically devolves on partners withdrawing to compete with Milbank, Tweed in contrast to all other withdrawing partners.

We noted in *Cohen* that a contested provision must be assessed within its own particular litigation context (*see,* 75 N.Y.2d at 102, 551 N.Y.S.2d 157, 550 N.E.2d 410), and the arbitrator's determination here that section 15.4 is "competition neutral" does not on its face contravene the public policy concerns underlying our rulings in *Cohen* and in *Denburg*.

Further support for the conclusion that the anticompetition policy may yield to other public policy concerns may be found in *Denburg*. Although the Parker Chapin partnership agreement was unenforceable as against public policy, we nevertheless remitted the matter for the determination of certain factual issues concerning a purported settlement agreement under which Parker Chapin contended the plaintiff had agreed to settle any obligation to the firm by yielding the balance in his capital account. Because of the strong policy considerations favoring the routine enforcement of voluntary settlements, we concluded that "an agreement to settle a dispute involving a forfeiture-for-competition provision may be enforced even though the clause itself is unenforceable," and that "public policy is best served by permitting parties to amicably resolve disputes arising under such provisions rather than forcing each such controversy to be decided by the judiciary" (82 N.Y.2d at 385, 604 N.Y.S.2d 900, 624 N.E.2d 995).

Similar concerns underlie our strong public policy favoring arbitration. Where the parties have agreed to submit their dispute to binding arbitration, an award that is not clearly in violation of public policy should be given effect (*see, West-inghouse Elec. Corp. v. New York City Tr. Auth.*, 82 N.Y.2d 47, 53, 603 N.Y.S.2d 404, 623 N.E.2d 531; *Matter of Siegel*, 40 N.Y.2d 687, 689, 389 N.Y.S.2d 800, 358 N.E.2d 484). The arbitrator's award here both factually and legally answers the public policy challenge raised by petitioner. Whether or not we agree with his findings and conclusions, the award does not on its face clearly violate public policy, and should not have been vacated on that basis.

Accordingly, the order of the Appellate Division should be reversed, with costs, and the matter remitted to Supreme Court for further proceedings in accordance with this opinion.

NOTES

(1) The grounds on which an arbitrator's award may be challenged are specified in CPLR 7511(b). Note that only a party who neither participated in the arbitration nor received a notice of it may raise the threshold issues in an attack on the award. CPLR 7511(b)(2). Other parties must look to the grounds listed in (a)(1) of section 7511.

(2) In *Sprinzen v. Nomberg*, 46 N.Y.2d 623, 415 N.Y.S.2d 974, 389 N.E.2d 456 (1979), the Court set the boundaries for review of an arbitration award as follows:

> In furtherance of the laudable purposes served by permitting consenting parties to submit controversies to arbitration, the law has adopted a policy of noninterference, with few exceptions, in this mode of dispute resolution. Quite simply, it can be said that the arbitrator is not bound to abide by, absent a contrary provision in the arbitration agreement, those principles of substantive law or rules of procedure which govern the traditional litigation process. . . . An arbitrator's paramount responsibility is to reach an equitable result, and the courts will not assume the role of overseers to mold the award to conform to their sense of justice. Thus, an arbitrator's award will not be vacated for errors of law and fact committed by the arbitrator . . . and "[e]ven where the arbitrator states an intention to apply a law, and then misapplies it, the award will not be set aside (*Matter of Schine Enterprises [Real Estate Portfolio of N.Y.]*, 26 NY2d 799, 801)." (*Matter of Associated Teachers of Huntington v Board of Educ.*, 33 NY2d 229, 235, *supra*.)

> Despite this policy of according an arbitrator seemingly unfettered discretion in matters submitted to him by the consent of the parties, it is the established law in this State that an award which is violative of public policy will not be permitted to stand (*Garrity v Lyle Stuart, Inc.*, 40 NY2d 354, 357, *supra*.) The courts, however, must exercise due restraint in this regard, for the preservation of the arbitration process and the policy of allowing parties to choose a nonjudicial forum, embed-

ded in freedom to contract principles, must not be disturbed by courts, acting under the guise of public policy, wishing to decide the dispute on its merits, for arguably every controversy has at its core some issue requiring the application, or weighing, of policy considerations. Thus, there are now but a few matters of concern which have been recognized as so intertwined with overriding public policy considerations as to either place them beyond the bounds of the arbitration process itself or mandate the vacatur of awards which do violence to the principles upon which such matters rest. (*See Matter of Port Jefferson Sta. Teachers Assn. v Brookhaven-Comsewogue Union Free School Dist.*, 45 NY2d 898, 899.)

Some examples would be instructive. It has been held that an arbitrator is without power to award punitive damages, a sanction reserved solely to the State (*Garrity v Lyle Stuart, Inc.*, 40 NY2d 354, *supra*; . . .), and that an agreement to arbitrate, when sought to be enforced by a lender, cannot divest the courts of their responsibility to determine whether a purported sales agreement is in fact a usurious loan, and thus illegal. (*Compare Durst v Abrash*, 22 AD2d 39, 44, affd 17 N.Y.S.2d 445, *with Rosenblum v Steiner*, 43 NY2d 896, 898.) Matters involving the enforcement of our State's antitrust laws, recognized as representing "public policy of the first magnitude," cannot be left to commercial arbitration (*Matter of Aimcee Wholesale Corp.* [*Tomar Prods.*], 21 NY2d 621, 625), and claims concerning the liquidation of insolvent insurance companies have been held to be beyond the reach of an arbitrator's discretion where a State statute bestows upon the Supreme Court exclusive jurisdiction over these proceedings. (*Matter of Knickerbocker Agency* [*Holz*], 4 NY2d 245.)

In public school matters, it has been held that agreements which purportedly reflect a bargain by a board of education not to inspect teacher personnel files cannot be enforced through arbitration insofar as such right is supported by statute and public policy. (*Board of Educ. v Areman*, 41 NY2d 527.) Nor can a board of education surrender its authority to discharge a nontenured teacher at the end of his probationary period to the arbitration process pursuant to a collective bargaining agreement, and an award the terms of which would bestow upon a probationary teacher tenure, as distinguished from procedural guarantees, will be struck down as violative of public policy. (*Compare Matter of Cohoes City School Dist. v Cohoes Teachers Assn.*, 40 NY2d 774, *with Matter of Candor Cent. School Dist.* [*Candor Teachers Assn.*], 42 NY2d 266.)

46 N.Y.2d at 629-31, 415 N.Y.S.2d at 976-78, 389 N.E.2d at 458-59.

(3) In *Correctional Assn. v. State*, 94 N.Y.2d 321, 704 N.Y.S.2d 910, 726 N.E.2d 462 (1999), the Court held that an award reinstating a correctional officer, suspended for displaying a Nazi flag outside his home, should not be vacated on the

ground it violates public policy of the state. The public policy ground for disturbing an arbitration award is only invoked if the award intrudes into areas reserved to others to resolve (here it was conceded that the dispute was a proper one for arbitration); because the award violates an explicit law of the state; or if the arbitration agreement itself violates public policy. In *NYC Tr. Auth. v. Workers' Union*, 6 N.Y.3d 332, 812 N.Y.S.2d 413, 845 N.E.2d 1243 (2005), the Court stated that an arbitrator exceeds his power only where the award violates strong public policy, or is irrational or clearly exceeds a specific limitation in the agreement, none of which occurred there, where the arbitrator found termination of an employee unjustified and reduced the penalty to suspension and reinstatement to his job. And in *United Federation of Teachers v. Bd. of Educ.*, 1 N.Y.3d 72, 769 N.Y.S.2d 451, 801 N.E.2d 827 (2003), it was found that the arbitrator did not exceed her powers when she overruled the Board of Education's decision not to select a teacher for a certain position. Even though the arbitrator's decision was "debatable," the Court would not substitute its judgment.

(4) Partiality of an arbitrator "appointed as a neutral" is another ground on which the award may be vacated. CPLR 7511(b)(1)(ii). See, generally, *J.P. Stevens & Co. v. Rytex Corp.*, 34 N.Y.2d 123, 356 N.Y.S.2d 278, 312 N.E.2d 466 (1974), where an award was vacated because an arbitrator appointed as a neutral was an employee of a firm which did millions of dollars of business each year with the successful party. This relationship should have been disclosed in advance of the arbitration, the Court held.

What of an arbitrator not appointed as a neutral? CPLR 7511(b)(1)(ii) implicitly accepts his partiality, but CPLR 7506(a) requires the arbitrator to take an oath to "decide the controversy faithfully and fairly," and CPLR 7511(b)(1)(i) makes the award vulnerable if any arbitrator is guilty of fraud or corruption.

(5) A challenge to an award may be made by an application under CPLR 7511; any of the grounds which would justify vacating an award may also be raised as a defense to an application to confirm the award. CPLR 7510.

CPLR 7510 authorizes a party to seek confirmation of an arbitration award within one year after it has been delivered to him. Since a confirmed award allows an enforceable judgment to be entered reflecting the award, CPLR 7514, a prompt application to confirm is the indicated course for a victor in arbitration. The confirmation application will ordinarily be brought in the form of a special proceeding as provided in CPLR 7502. An award which is not confirmed within a year is for all practical purposes unenforceable, because CPLR 215(5) time bars any subsequent action to enforce it.

An incongruity appears if the time limits of CPLR 7510 and 7511 are read together. An application to confirm may be made within one year after delivery of the award, whereas an application to vacate or modify must be made within ninety days after delivery. Nonetheless, the defenses to a confirmation proceeding may apparently be asserted whenever it is brought, even after the expiration of the ninety-day period for an application to vacate the award.

§ 25.05 THE ROLE OF FEDERAL LAW

MASTROBUONO v. SHEARSON LEHMAN HUTTON, INC.
United States Supreme Court
514 U.S. 52, 115 S. Ct. 1212, 131 L. Ed. 2d 76 (1995)

JUSTICE STEVENS delivered the opinion of the Court.

New York law allows courts, but not arbitrators, to award punitive damages. In a dispute arising out of a standard-form contract that expressly provides that it "shall be governed by the laws of the State of New York," a panel of arbitrators awarded punitive damages. The District Court and Court of Appeals disallowed that award. The question presented is whether the arbitrators' award is consistent with the central purpose of the Federal Arbitration Act to ensure "that private agreements to arbitrate are enforced according to their terms." *Volt Information Sciences, Inc. v. Board of Trustees of Leland Stanford Junior Univ.,* 489 U.S. 468, 479, 109 S.Ct. 1248, 1256, 103 L.Ed.2d 488 (1989).

I

In 1985 petitioners, Antonio Mastrobuono, then an assistant professor of medieval literature, and his wife Diana Mastrobuono, an artist, opened a securities trading account with respondent Shearson Lehman Hutton, Inc. (Shearson), by executing Shearson's standard-form Client's Agreement. Respondent Nick DiMinico, a vice president of Shearson, managed the Mastrobuonos' account until they closed it in 1987. In 1989, petitioners filed this action in the United States District Court for the Northern District of Illinois, alleging that respondents had mishandled their account and claiming damages on a variety of state and federal law theories.

Paragraph 13 of the parties' agreement contains an arbitration provision and a choice-of-law provision. Relying on the arbitration provision and on §§ 3 and 4 of the Federal Arbitration Act (FAA), 9 U.S.C. §§ 3, 4, respondents filed a motion to stay the court proceedings and to compel arbitration pursuant to the rules of the National Association of Securities Dealers. The District Court granted that motion, and a panel of three arbitrators was convened. After conducting hearings in Illinois, the panel ruled in favor of petitioners.

In the arbitration proceedings, respondents argued that the arbitrators had no authority to award punitive damages. Nevertheless, the panel's award included punitive damages of $400,000, in addition to compensatory damages of $159,327. Respondents paid the compensatory portion of the award but filed a motion in the District Court to vacate the award of punitive damages. The District Court granted the motion, 812 F.Supp. 845 (ND Ill.1993), and the Court of Appeals for the Seventh Circuit affirmed. 20 F.3d 713 (1994). Both courts relied on the choice-of-law provision in Paragraph 13 of the parties' agreement, which specifies that the contract shall be governed by New York law. Because the

New York Court of Appeals has decided that in New York the power to award punitive damages is limited to judicial tribunals and may not be exercised by arbitrators, *Garrity v. Lyle Stuart, Inc.*, 40 N.Y.2d 354, 386 N.Y.S.2d 831, 353 N.E.2d 793 (1976), the District Court and the Seventh Circuit held that the panel of arbitrators had no power to award punitive damages in this case.

We granted certiorari, 513 U.S. 921, 115 S.Ct. 305, 130 L.Ed.2d 218 (1994), because the Courts of Appeals have expressed differing views on whether a contractual choice-of-law provision may preclude an arbitral award of punitive damages that otherwise would be proper. . . .

II

Earlier this Term, we upheld the enforceability of a predispute arbitration agreement governed by Alabama law, even though an Alabama statute provides that arbitration agreements are unenforceable. *Allied-Bruce Terminix Cos. v. Dobson*, 513 U.S. 265, 115 S.Ct. 834, 130 L.Ed.2d 753 (1995). Writing for the Court, Justice Breyer observed that Congress passed the FAA "to overcome courts' refusals to enforce agreements to arbitrate. . . ." After determining that the FAA applied to the parties' arbitration agreement, we readily concluded that the federal statute pre-empted Alabama's statutory prohibition. *Allied-Bruce*, 513 U.S., at 272-273, 281-282, 115 S.Ct. at 839, 843.

Petitioners seek a similar disposition of the case before us today. Here, the Seventh Circuit interpreted the contract to incorporate New York law, including the *Garrity* rule that arbitrators may not award punitive damages. Petitioners ask us to hold that the FAA pre-empts New York's prohibition against arbitral awards of punitive damages because this state law is a vestige of the "ancient" judicial hostility to arbitration. *See Allied-Bruce*, 513 U.S., at — , 115 S.Ct. at 838, *quoting Bernhardt v. Polygraphic Co. of America, Inc.*, 350 U.S. 198, 211, n. 5, 76 S.Ct. 273, 281, n. 5, 100 L.Ed. 199 (1956) (Frankfurter, J., concurring). Petitioners rely on *Southland Corp. v. Keating*, 465 U.S. 1, 104 S.Ct. 852, 79 L.Ed.2d 1 (1984), and *Perry v. Thomas*, 482 U.S. 483, 107 S.Ct. 2520, 96 L.Ed.2d 426 (1987), in which we held that the FAA pre-empted two California statutes that purported to require judicial resolution of certain disputes. In *Southland*, we explained that the FAA not only "declared a national policy favoring arbitration," but actually "withdrew the power of the states to require a judicial forum for the resolution of claims which the contracting parties agreed to resolve by arbitration." 465 U.S., at 10, 104 S.Ct. at 858.

Respondents answer that the choice-of-law provision in their contract evidences the parties' express agreement that punitive damages should not be awarded in the arbitration of any dispute arising under their contract. Thus, they claim, this case is distinguishable from *Southland* and *Perry*, in which the parties presumably desired unlimited arbitration but state law stood in their way. Regardless of whether the FAA pre-empts the *Garrity* decision in contracts not expressly incorporating New York law, respondents argue that the parties may themselves agree to be bound by *Garrity*, just as they may agree to forgo arbitration altogether. In other words, if the contract says "no punitive damages," that is the end of the matter, for courts are bound to interpret contracts in accordance with the expressed intentions of the parties — even if the effect of those intentions is to limit arbitration.

We have previously held that the FAA's pro-arbitration policy does not operate without regard to the wishes of the contracting parties. In *Volt Information Sciences, Inc. v. Board of Trustees of Leland Stanford Junior Univ.*, 489 U.S. 468, 109 S.Ct., 1248, 103 L.Ed.2d 488 (1989), the California Court of Appeal had construed a contractual provision to mean that the parties intended the California rules of arbitration, rather than the FAA's rules, to govern the resolution of their dispute. *Id.*, at 472, 109 S.Ct., at 1252. Noting that the California rules were "manifestly designed to encourage resort to the arbitral process," *id.*, at 476, 109 S.Ct., at 1254, and that they "generally foster[ed] the federal policy favoring arbitration," *id.*, at 476, n. 5, 109 S.Ct., at 1254 n. 5, we concluded that such an interpretation was entirely consistent with the federal policy "to ensure the enforceability, according to their terms, of private agreements to arbitrate." *Id.*, at 476, 109 S.Ct., at 1254. After referring to the holdings in *Southland* and *Perry*, which struck down state laws limiting agreed-upon arbitrability, we added: "But it does not follow that the FAA prevents the enforcement of agreements to arbitrate under different rules than those set forth in the Act itself. Indeed, such a result would be quite inimical to the FAA's primary purpose of ensuring that private agreements to arbitrate are enforced according to their terms. Arbitration under the Act is a matter of consent, not coercion, and parties are generally free to structure their arbitration agreements as they see fit. Just as they may limit by contract the issues which they will arbitrate, *see Mitsubishi v. Soler Chrysler-Plymouth*, 473 U.S. 614, 628, 105 S.Ct. 3346, 3354-55, 87 L.Ed.2d 444 (1985), so too may they specify by contract the rules under which that arbitration will be conducted." *Volt*, 489 U.S., at 479, 109 S.Ct., at 1256.

Relying on our reasoning in *Volt*, respondents thus argue that the parties to a contract may lawfully agree to limit the issues to be arbitrated by waiving any claim for punitive damages. On the other hand, we think our decisions in *Allied-Bruce*, *Southland*, and *Perry* make clear that if contracting parties agree to include claims for punitive damages within the issues to be arbitrated, the FAA ensures that their agreement will be enforced according to its terms even if a rule of state law would otherwise exclude such claims from arbitration. Thus, the case before us comes down to what the contract has to say about the arbitrability of petitioners' claim for punitive damages.

III

Shearson's standard-form "Client Agreement," which petitioners executed, contains 18 paragraphs. The two relevant provisions of the agreement are found in Paragraph 13. The first sentence of that paragraph provides, in part, that the entire agreement "shall be governed by the laws of the State of New York." App. to Pet. for Cert. 44. The second sentence provides that "any controversy" arising out of the transactions between the parties "shall be settled by arbitration" in accordance with the rules of the National Association of Securities Dealers (NASD), or the Boards of Directors of the New York Stock Exchange and/or the American Stock Exchange. *Ibid.* The agreement contains no express reference to claims for punitive damages. To ascertain whether Paragraph 13 expresses an intent to include or exclude such claims, we first address the impact of each of the two relevant provisions, considered separately. We then move on to the more important inquiry: the meaning of the two provisions taken together. *See* Restatement (Second) of Contracts § 202(2) (1979) ("A writing is interpreted as a whole").

The choice-of-law provision, when viewed in isolation, may reasonably be read as merely a substitute for the conflict-of-laws analysis that otherwise would determine what law to apply to disputes arising out of the contractual relationship. Thus, if a similar contract, without a choice-of-law provision, had been signed in New York and was to be performed in New York, presumably "the laws of the State of New York" would apply, even though the contract did not expressly so state. In such event, there would be nothing in the contract that could possibly constitute evidence of an intent to exclude punitive damages claims. Accordingly, punitive damages would be allowed because, in the absence of contractual intent to the contrary, the FAA would pre-empt the *Garrity* rule.

Even if the reference to "the laws of the State of New York" is more than a substitute for ordinary conflict-of-laws analysis and, as respondents urge, includes the caveat, "detached from otherwise-applicable federal law," the provision might not preclude the award of punitive damages because New York allows its courts, though not its arbitrators, to enter such awards. *See Garrity*, 40 N.Y.2d, at 358, 386 N.Y.S.2d at 834, 353 N.E.2d, at 796. In other words, the provision might include only New York's substantive rights and obligations, and not the State's allocation of power between alternative tribunals. Respondents' argument is persuasive only if "New York law" means "New York decisional law, including that State's allocation of power between courts and arbitrators, notwithstanding otherwise-applicable federal law." But, as we have demonstrated, the provision need not be read so broadly. It is not, in itself, an unequivocal exclusion of punitive damages claims.

The arbitration provision (the second sentence of Paragraph 13) does not improve respondents' argument. On the contrary, when read separately this clause strongly implies that an arbitral award of punitive damages is appropriate. It explicitly authorizes arbitration in accordance with NASD rules; the panel of arbitrators in fact proceeded under that set of rules. The NASD's Code of Arbitration Procedure indicates that arbitrators may award "damages and other relief." NASD Code of Arbitration Procedure ¶ 3741(e) (1993). While not a clear authorization of punitive damages, this provision appears broad enough at least to contemplate such a remedy. Moreover, as the Seventh Circuit noted, a manual provided to NASD arbitrators contains this provision:

B. *Punitive Damages* "The issue of punitive damages may arise with great frequency in arbitrations. Parties to arbitration are informed that arbitrators can consider punitive damages as a remedy."

20 F.3d, at 717. Thus, the text of the arbitration clause itself surely does not support — indeed, it contradicts — the conclusion that the parties agreed to foreclose claims for punitive damages.

Although neither the choice-of-law clause nor the arbitration clause, separately considered, expresses an intent to preclude an award of punitive damages, respondents argue that a fair reading of the entire Paragraph 13 leads to that conclusion. On this theory, even if "New York law" is ambiguous, and even if "arbitration in accordance with NASD rules" indicates that punitive damages are permissible, the juxtaposition of the two clauses suggests that the contract incorporates "New York law relating to arbitration." We disagree. At most, the choice-of-law clause introduces an ambiguity into an arbitration agreement that would otherwise allow punitive damages awards. As we pointed out in *Volt*, when a court interprets such provisions in an agreement covered by the FAA, "due regard must be given to the federal policy favoring arbitration, and ambiguities as to the scope of the arbitration clause itself resolved in favor of arbitration." 489 U.S., at 476, 109 S.Ct., at 1254. *See also Moses H. Cone Memorial Hospital v. Mercury Constr. Corp.*, 460 U.S. 1, 24-25, 103 S.Ct. 927, 941-42, 74 L.Ed.2d 765 (1983).

Moreover, respondents cannot overcome the common-law rule of contract interpretation that a court should construe ambiguous language against the interest of the party that drafted it. . . . Respondents drafted an ambiguous document, and they cannot now claim the benefit of the doubt. The reason for this rule is to protect the party who did not choose the language from an unintended or unfair result. That rationale is well-suited to the facts of this case. As a practical matter, it seems unlikely that petitioners were actually aware of New York's bifurcated approach to punitive damages, or that they had any idea that by signing a standard-form agreement to arbitrate disputes they might be giving up an important substantive right. In the face of such doubt, we are unwilling to impute this intent to petitioners.

Finally the respondents' reading of the two clauses violates another cardinal principle of contract construction: that a document should be read to give effect to all its provisions and to render them consistent with each other. *See, e.g., In re Halas*, 104 Ill.2d 83, 92, 83 Ill.Dec. 540, 546, 470 N.E.2d 960, 964 (1984); *Crimmins Contracting Co. v. City of New York*, 74 N.Y.2d 166, 172-173, 544 N.Y.S.2d 580, 583-84, 542 N.E.2d 1097, 1100 (1989); *Trump-Equitable Fifth Avenue Co. v. H.R.H. Constr. Corp.*, 106 App. Div.2d 242, 244, 485 N.Y.S.2d 65, 67 (1985); Restatement (Second) of Contracts § 203(a) and Comment b (1979); *id.* § 202(5). We think the best way to harmonize the choice-of-law provision with the arbitration provision is to read "the laws of the State of New York" to encompass substantive principles that New York courts would apply, but not to include special rules limiting the authority of arbitrators. Thus, the choice-of-law provision covers the rights and duties of the parties, while the arbitration clause covers arbitration; neither sentence intrudes upon the other. In contrast, respondents' reading sets up the two clauses in conflict with one another: one foreclosing punitive damages, the other allowing them. This interpretation is untenable.

We hold that the Court of Appeals misinterpreted the parties' agreement. The arbitral award should have been enforced as within the scope of the contract. The judgment of the Court of Appeals is, therefore, reversed.

It is so ordered. . . .

[Justice Thomas, dissenting alone, was unable to distinguish this case from the *Volt* case, discussed by Justice Stevens, where the state rule was applied.]

NOTES

(1) In sweeping aside the longstanding New York rule that public policy would not permit an arbitrator to award punitive damages, the principal case illustrates the powerful role federal law now plays in the arbitration area. The reach of the FAA is further demonstrated by *Allied-Bruce Terminix Cos. v. Dobson*, 513 U.S. 265, 115 S. Ct. 834, 130 L. Ed. 2d 753 (1995). There, the Court held that an Alabama statute making pre-dispute arbitration agreements unenforceable could not apply to an arbitration agreement covered by the FAA. Moreover, the Court held that the FAA applied to what seemed a local dispute — a homeowner's claim that a termite protection company had failed to eliminate the termites. The Court noted that the FAA in terms applies to "a written provision in any maritime transaction or a contract evidencing a transaction involving commerce." 9 U.S.C. § 2. It held that this language should be construed to include the full breadth of the Commerce Clause of the Constitution and that the FAA therefore applied even though the parties to the particular transaction did not contemplate interstate commerce activities. It was enough that the Allied-Bruce firm was engaged in interstate commerce.

(2) The contract at issue in the principal case contained a choice-of-law clause adopting New York law. Can such a clause be relied on to give New York courts personal jurisdiction over proceedings to compel or stay arbitration? If the choice of law provision does not of itself create personal jurisdiction, how can jurisdiction be laid in New York when there are no contacts? It cannot, said the Appellate Division in *Merrill Lynch, Pierce, Fenner & Smith, Inc. v. McLeod*, 208 A.D.2d 81, 622 N.Y.S.2d 954 (1st Dep't 1995). There, a Florida investor invested $200,000 with the broker at its Florida office. Several years later, claiming certain misrepresentations, she demanded arbitration in accordance with her customer agreement. An arbitration was commenced in Florida, but the broker sought a judicial stay of arbitration in a proceeding brought in New York. The customer agreement provided that arbitration should be conducted under either the rules of the New York Stock Exchange, or the Code of the National Associ-

ation of Securities Dealers. Holding that there was no New York jurisdiction, the court stated: "Some minimal New York nexus is required in order to commence a special proceeding in our courts to stay arbitration. . . . In determining such a nexus, the focus must be on respondent's [investor's] purposeful activity within this State, not petitioners' [brokers']." 208 A.D.2d at 84, 622 N.Y.S.2d at 955-56.

(3) Just prior to the rendition of the *Mastrobuono* case, the New York Court of Appeals handed down *Smith Barney Harris Upham & Co., Inc. v. Luckie*, 85 N.Y.2d 193, 623 N.Y.S.2d 800, 647 N.E.2d 1308 (1995), which held that, where the arbitration agreement in a customer contract provided for the application of New York law, the question whether the time period had run on arbitrating the dispute was for the court under CPLR Art. 75, and not for the arbitrator as it would be under the Federal Arbitration Act (FAA) or under the rules of the National Association of Securities Dealers (NASD). The applicable time period was the six-year provision for contract causes of action. CPLR 213(2). The continuing viability of *Luckie* was at least implied in a case decided by the Court of Appeals after *Mastrobuono*, in which it was held that the applicable statute of limitations was for the arbitrator. *Matter of Smith Barney Shearson v. Sacharow*, 91 N.Y.2d 39, 666 N.Y.S.2d 990, 689 N.E.2d 884 (1997). In *Sacharow*, the time period was designated in the contract itself and was not statutory and for this reason was an arbitrable issue. It was reiterated that where the applicable time period is governed by state law as in *Luckie*, there is a substantive issue which, under the *Mastrobuono* reasoning, would be a threshold issue for the court. It was also noted that in *Luckie,* unlike *Sacharow,* the contract provided for the applicable New York law not only for contract interpretation, but also for its enforcement, and the NASD rules, incorporated in the *Sacharow* contract, committed all issues, including issues or arbitrability and timeliness, to the arbitrators.

(4) In *Wien v. Helmsley-Spear*, 300 A.D.2d 32, 751 N.Y.S.2d 21 (1st Dep't 2002), the court held that New York law applied when New York entities were involved, and the arbitrable dispute did not have a substantial effect on interstate commerce, and upheld the award under the liberal New York standard. Subsequently the United States Supreme Court handed down the decision in *Citizens Bank v. Alafabco, Inc.*, 539 U.S. 52, 123 S. Ct. 2037, 156 L. Ed. 2d 46 (2003), which held that the FAA applies to any transaction "affecting commerce" whether or not there is any substantial effect on interstate commerce. The Supreme Court reversed the *Wien* decision and directed the Appellate Division to reappraise the case in light of *Alafabco*. 540 U.S. 801, 124 S. Ct. 222, 157 L. Ed. 2d 12 (2003). Doing so, the Appellate Division vacated the arbitration award, applied the stricter FAA standard, and found that the arbitration panel had disregarded contract law. 12 A.D.3d 65, 783 N.Y.S.2d 339 (1st Dep't 2004). On appeal, the Court of Appeals disagreed, finding that even under FAA standards, the award should be upheld. 6 N.Y.3d 471, 813 N.Y.S.2d 691, 846 N.E.2d 1201 (2006).

The Court of Appeals applied the *Alafabco* doctrine in *Diamond Sys. v. 55 Liberty*, 4 N.Y.3d 247, 793 N.Y.S.2d 831, 826 N.E.2d 802 (2005), which affected two important issues. First, although the parties may agree as to what law should apply, such choice of law provision should specifically designate New York law if that is what is intended. If the clause, as in *Diamond Systems*, merely says that the contract shall be governed by the "law of the place where the project is located," that is insufficient to trigger New York law even though the project was located in New York. This led to resolution of the second major issue: Since the FAA governed, there being no New York designation, the question of timeliness of the demand for arbitration would be left to the arbitrator. Under New York law, the timeliness question would have been for the court.

In *Aceros Prefabricados, S.A. v. Tradearbed, Inc.*, 282 F.3d 92 (2d Cir. 2002), a case decided under the FAA, the court stated: "The parties' briefs assume that New York substantive law governs the issues of contract formation here, and such 'implied consent . . . is sufficient to establish choice of law.' [citation]." 282 F.3d at 97, n.4.

New York courts have applied the "manifest disregard" standard of review to arbitration awards governed by the FAA. In *Roffler v. Spear, Leeds & Kellogg*, 13 A.D.3d 308, 788 N.Y.S.2d 326 (2004), the Appellate Division reversed the trial court's judgment vacating an amended arbitration award and reinstated the award. The Appellate Division found that the award was not made with manifest disregard for the law and held that an award should be enforced "as long as there is a barely colorable basis for the decision," which it found to exist in this case. In another case, *Sawtelle v. Wadell & Reed, Inc.*, 304 A.D.2d 2d 103, 754 N.Y.S.2d 264 (1st Dep't 2003), where plaintiffs were awarded $25 million in punitive damages in an employment termination arbitration, the Appellate Division vacated the award, finding that the arbitrators had manifestly disregarded the law in determining the amount, and that the award was grossly excessive. The Appellate Division rejected the argument that the award also violated public policy.

§ 25.06 COMPULSORY ARBITRATION

Where a statute provides that if one party to a dispute opts for arbitration, the other party must submit to that remedy, that party, in effect, has no say in the matter and is compelled to submit. Such provisions are found in the Public Employees' Fair Employment Act (Civ. Serv. L. Art. 14 (§ 209)); in Labor Law § 716, governing disputes affecting non-profit hospitals; and in Insurance Law § 5106, affecting No-Fault insurance disputes. Disputes between a lawyer and client over a legal fee must be resolved by arbitration if the client so chooses and if the amount involved is more than $1,000 and less than $50,000. Rules of the Chief Administrator of the Courts, 22 NYCRR Part 136, as amended effective June 1, 2001.

The Court of Appeals has resolved the legitimacy of compulsory arbitration. The case arose out of New York's "Lemon Law," which provides recourse to consumers who claim that automobiles they purchased were defective. General Business Law § 198-a(K) gives the consumer the option of arbitration rather than legal proceedings and compels the manufacturer to participate. In the declaratory judgment action brought to declare the statute invalid, the manufacturers' trade associations argued that the act worked a deprivation of the right to a jury, was an unconstitutional delegation of Supreme Court jurisdiction and a violation of New York's Administrative Procedure Act. The court held that since the remedies provided under the "Lemon Law" are essentially equitable, there would be no right to a jury in any event; the Supreme Court is not unduly ousted of jurisdiction since the consumer always has the choice of going to court; and if arbitration is chosen, the court has the supervisory powers afforded by CPLR Article 75. Finally, New York's Administrative Procedure Act, which would require findings of fact, conclusions of law, or stated reasons for an administrative determination, simply does not apply to the alternative arbitration procedure. *Motor Vehicle Manufacturers Association of the United States, Inc. v. State of New York*, 75 N.Y.2d 175, 551 N.Y.S.2d 470, 550 N.E.2d 919 (1990). One could speculate that, were the arbitrator empowered to award money damages as the basic remedy, the right to jury question might not be handled so easily.

§ 25.07 AN ALTERNATIVE TO ARBITRATION: SIMPLIFIED PROCEDURE FOR JUDICIAL DETERMINATION OF DISPUTES[*]

The Simplified Procedure for Court Determination of Disputes set forth in CPLR 3031 through CPLR 3037 gives litigants the opportunity to obtain the advantages of speed and simplicity inherent in arbitration without giving up the right to a judicial decision on the merits of the dispute. The goal is "a procedure that is as simple and informal as circumstances will admit." CPLR 3035. Any justiciable controversy, regardless of subject matter, may be submitted to the court under the Simplified Procedure, but only if both sides agree. Agreement can be reached in advance of the dispute and reflected in a contract. CPLR 3033.

CPLR 3033 enables parties to enter into a contract to submit any existing or future controversy to the court for determination under the New York Simplified Procedure for Court Determination of Disputes. CPLR 3033, which permits submission of existing and future disputes pursuant to contract, complements CPLR 3031, which provides for the submission of disputes without a preexisting contract. The procedure to be followed in both cases is the same. While the making of the contract necessarily waives the right to a jury trial, a jury trial

---

[*] This note adapted from O. Chase, CPLR Manual § 31.16 (Rev. ed. 2006).

may be demanded under CPLR 3033, if a substantial issue of fact is "raised as to the making of the contract or submission, or the failure to comply therewith." Ordinarily, such an issue would come up when one party, believing a contract to exist, sought to compel the other to comply pursuant to the procedure prescribed by CPLR 3034, discussed below.

CPLR 3034 elaborates upon the motion procedure to be followed when there has been a failure to perform a contract that provides for the submission of a controversy for determination under the Simplified Procedure. A motion under CPLR 3034 is available for two purposes. If the parties are unable to agree on the contents of the statement, either or both may move for settlement of the terms by the court. Or, if one party refuses to perform a contract to submit the controversy or contests the validity or existence of a contract to submit, the aggrieved party may move for an order directing the determination of the controversy pursuant to the Simplified Procedure and, if necessary, settlement of the terms of the statement. The filing of a signed and acknowledged proposed statement by the moving party must precede or accompany the motion.

CPLR 3031 provides that to commence an action under the Simplified Procedure, all that is necessary is to present the court with a simple statement, signed by the parties or their attorneys, specifying the claims and defenses between the parties and the relief requested.

By commencing the action in this fashion, the parties consent to the application of the procedure set forth in CPLR 3034, CPLR 3035, and CPLR 3036 and waive their right to jury trial. Summons and pleadings are not necessary. The signing of the statement constitutes a certificate that the issues are genuine, and the filing of the statement and a note of issue acts as a joinder of issues.

According to CPLR 3032, the statement required by CPLR 3031 must contain the claims and defenses of each of the parties and the relief sought. The text of CPLR 3032 makes it clear that the statement must be plain and concise and the request for relief must include the amount of money demanded, if any. A statement under CPLR 3032 need not comply with the form or content prescribed for pleadings and none of the technical rules applicable to pleadings in ordinary actions have any relevance to actions under the Simplified Procedure.

CPLR 3036 gives the court great discretion in directing the course of the action in furtherance of the goal of simplicity. Thus, pretrial disclosure, including depositions, is available only by court order. CPLR 3036(5).

If the action is to be tried, the court should, in the interest of speed, waive local rules requiring steps preliminary to placing the case on the calendar and should direct a trial as soon as "may be practicable." CPLR 3036(6). The court may restrict the number of expert witnesses to be used, CPLR 3036(5), and may direct that the service of an impartial expert be obtained, CPLR 3036(2). The rules regulating admissibility of evidence are, with the exception of those protecting privileged communications, not to apply at the trial, unless the court directs otherwise. CPLR 3036(1).

An appeal may be taken from a judgment or from an order determining the making of the contract or submission or the failure to comply. In order to prevent the subversion of the economies in time and expense effected by the Simplified Procedure, CPLR 3037 eliminates the right of appeal from an intermediate order of the court, except with the permission of the court trying the action or the appellate court.

Also of importance to the goals of economy is the last sentence of CPLR 3037, which states that the decision of the trial judge is final if there is any "substantial evidence" to support it. This restriction of the scope of review should minimize the number of appeals taken. It is arguable, however, that though the appellate court must accord more than ordinary deference to the trial court's findings of fact, its power to review issues of law is the same as on any other appeal.

For an analysis of the Simplified Procedure, a discussion of relevant cases and an argument in favor of more expansive use of this device, see Carlisle, *Simplified Procedure for Court Determination of Disputes Under New York's Civil Practice Law and Rules,* 54 Brooklyn L. Rev. 95 (1988).

Table of Cases

References are to pages.

I

Table of Statutes

References are to pages or to pages and footnotes.

CRIMINAL PROCEDURE LAW

DIVISION PRACTICE ACT

DOMESTIC RELATIONS LAW

EDUCATION LAW

ELECTION LAW

PARENTAL KIDNAPPING PREVENTION ACT

PARTNERSHIP LAW

PENAL LAW

PUBLIC HEALTH LAW

PUBLIC HOUSING LAW

PUBLIC OFFICERS LAW

REAL PROPERTY ACTIONS AND PROCEEDINGS LAW

REAL PROPERTY LAW

REVISED LIMITED PARTNERSHIP ACT

SMALL CLAIMS COURT ACT

SOCIAL SERVICES LAW

INDEX

[References are to pages.]

I-1

[References are to pages.]

[References are to pages.]

[References are to pages.]

[References are to pages.]

[References are to pages.]

[References are to pages.]